Hispanic Writers

Hispanic Writers

A
Selection
of Sketches
from
**Contemporary
Authors**

*Contains more than four hundred entries on
twentieth-century Hispanic writers, all originally
written or updated for this volume.*

Bryan Ryan, Editor

 Gale Research Inc. · DETROIT · NEW YORK · LONDON

STAFF

Bryan Ryan, **Editor**

Marilyn K. Basel, Barbara Carlisle Bigelow, Christa Brelin, Carol Lynn DeKane, Janice E. Drane,
Kevin S. Hile, Thomas Kozikowski, Sharon Malinowski, Emily J. McMurray, Louise Mooney,
Michael E. Mueller, Kenneth R. Shepherd, Les Stone, Diane Telgen,
Polly A. Vedder, and Thomas Wiloch, **Associate Editors**

Marian Gonsior, Katherine Huebl, James F. Kamp, Margaret Mazurkiewicz,
Jani Prescott, and Neil R. Schlager, **Assistant Editors**

Arlene True and Curtis Skinner, **Contributing Sketchwriters**

Hal May and Linda Metzger, **Senior Editors,** *Contemporary Authors*

Mary Rose Bonk, **Research Supervisor, Biography Division**

Jane Cousins, Alysa I. Hunton, Andrew Guy Malonis, and Norma Sawaya, **Editorial Associates**

Mike Avolio, Reginald A. Carlton, Shirley Gates, Steve Germic, Sharon McGilvray,
Diane Linda Sevigny, and Tracey Head Turbett, **Editorial Assistants**

Mary Beth Trimper, **Production Manager**
Evi Seoud, **Assistant Production Manager**

Arthur Chartow, **Art Director**
Kathleen A. Mouzakis, **Graphic Designer**
C. J. Jonik, **Keyliner**

Laura Bryant, **Production Supervisor**
Louise Gagné, **Internal Production Associate**

The paper used in this publication meets the minimum requirements
of American National Standard for Information Sciences—Permanence
Paper for Printed Library Materials, ANSI Z39.48-1984. ∞™

Copyright © 1991
Gale Research Inc.
835 Penobscot Bldg.
Detroit, MI 48226-4094

Library of Congress Catalog Card Number: 90-83635
ISBN 0-8103-7688-1

Printed in the United States of America.

Published simultaneously in the United Kingdom
by Gale Research International Limited
(An affiliated company of Gale Research Inc.)

Contents

Introduction vii

Guide to Authors Included in This Volume ix

Author Listings 1

Nationality Index 511

Introduction

An Important Information Source on Hispanic Literature and Culture

Hispanic Writers provides students, teachers, researchers, and interested readers with comprehensive and accurate biographical and bibliographical information on more than 400 authors who are a part of twentieth-century Hispanic literature and culture in the Americas. Those covered include authors from the United States, Puerto Rico, Cuba, Mexico, the Spanish-speaking countries of Central and South America, as well as a limited number of authors from Spain who have influenced the literature of the New World. Most of the authors represented in *Hispanic Writers* are available in English translation, making this book an especially useful guide to American audiences interested in Hispanic culture.

Forty percent of the entries in *Hispanic Writers* were selected from Gale's acclaimed *Contemporary Authors* series and completely updated for the publication of this volume. The other sixty percent, over 250 sketches, were written especially for this collection to furnish the most comprehensive coverage possible. A number of these entries will appear in future volumes of *Contemporary Authors*.

Broad Coverage in a Single Source

Before preparing *Hispanic Writers*, the editors of *Contemporary Authors* conducted a telephone survey of librarians and mailed a print survey to more than four thousand libraries to help determine the kind of reference source libraries wanted. The list of authors compiled was then submitted for review to an advisory board of prominent members of the Hispanic community: Oscar Hijuelos, Pulitzer Prize-winning novelist; Nicolás Kanellos, founder and publisher of Arte Público Press in Houston; Luis Leal, director of the Center for Chicano Studies at the University of California, Santa Barbara; Doris Meyer, professor of Hispanic studies at Connecticut College; and David Unger, co-director of the Latin American Writers Institute in New York City.

Built upon these suggestions, *Hispanic Writers* provides single-source coverage of a diverse set of authors:

- *Major literary figures* such as Benito Pérez Galdós, Miguel de Unamuno, Federico García Lorca, Pablo Neruda, Gabriela Mistral, Rubén Darío, Jorge Luis Borges, Gabriel García Márquez, Carlos Fuentes, Camilo José Cela, and Isabel Allende.

- *Social and political figures*, including Mexican statesman and educator Jaime Torres Bodet, Marxist revolutionary "Ché" Guevara, Nicaraguan priest Ernesto Cardenal, and former Costa Rican president Oscar Arias Sánchez.

- *Scholars, historians, and journalists* such as Ricardo E. Alegría, Guillermo Díaz Plaja, Ramón Menédez Pidal, Eduardo Galeano, Elena Poniatowska, and Geraldo Rivera.

- *Lesser-known writers not well covered in other sources*, including exiled Salvadoran novelist Manlio Argueta, black Ecuadoran novelist Adalberto Ortiz, and women writers such as Mexican playwright Elena Garro and Argentine novelist Silvina Bullrich.

Easy Access to Information

Both the newly written and the completely updated entries in *Hispanic Writers* provide in-depth information in a format designed for ease of use. Individual paragraphs of each entry, labeled with descriptive rubrics, ensure that a reader seeking specific information can quickly focus on the pertinent portion of an entry.

A typical entry in *Hispanic Writers* contains the following, clearly labeled information sections:

- *PERSONAL:* dates and places of birth and death; parents' names and occupations; name of spouse(s), date(s) of marriage(s); names of children; colleges attended and degrees earned; political and religious affiliation.

- *ADDRESSES:* complete home, office, and agent's addresses.

- *CAREER:* name of employer, position, and dates for each career post; resumé of other vocational achievements; military service.

- *MEMBER:* memberships, and offices held, in professional and civic organizations.

- *AWARDS, HONORS:* literary and professional awards received and dates.

- *WRITINGS:* title-by-title chronological bibliography of books written and edited, listed by genre when known; list of other notable publications, such as plays, screenplays, and periodical contributions.

- *WORK IN PROGRESS:* description of projects in progress.

- *SIDELIGHTS:* a biographical portrait of the author's development; information about the critical reception of the author's works; revealing comments, often by the author, on personal interests, aspirations, motivations, and thoughts on writing.

- *BIOGRAPHICAL/CRITICAL SOURCES:* books, feature articles, and reviews in which the writer's work has been treated.

Nationality Index Reveals Country-by-Country Coverage

Authors represented in *Hispanic Writers* appear alphabetically in an index organized by country of birth and/or citizenship. More than 20 nations are represented, reflecting the international scope of this book.

Acknowledgments

The editor wishes to thank: Michael E. Mueller for his editorial assistance; Marian Gonsior, Neil R. Schlager, and Diane Telgen for their Spanish-language review; and James G. Lesniak and Susan M. Trosky, editors of the *Contemporary Authors* series, for their cooperation and assistance, and for that of their staffs.

Comments Are Appreciated

We hope that you find *Hispanic Writers* a useful reference tool and welcome your comments about this work. Suggestions of authors to include in future editions of *Hispanic Writers* are also welcome. Send comments and suggestions to: The Editors, *Hispanic Writers*, Gale Research Inc., 835 Penobscot Bldg., Detroit, MI 48226-4094. Or, call toll-free at 1-800-347-GALE.

Guide to Authors Included in This Volume

Oscar Zeta Acosta 1935(?)-
Acosta, who produced two volumes of autobiographical "gonzo" fiction, disappeared in the early 1970s.

Rodolfo F. Acuña 1932-
A professor of Chicano studies, Acuña has written historical works, including *Occupied America: The Chicano's Struggle Toward Liberation.*

Leonard Adame 1947-
Adame is a Chicano poet who writes moving accounts of family and places with an eye toward cultural and historical significance.

Jorge Enrique Adoum 1926-
Author of several nonfiction volumes and such verse collections as *Ecuador amargo* and the prize-winning *Dios trajo la sombra.*

Marjorie Agosín 1955-
A new voice in Chilean literature noted for such poetry volumes as *Brujas y algo más (Witches and Other Things)* and for her critical studies of Latin American writers.

Pancho Aguila 1945-
Ex-convict Aguila is a respected poet whose publications include *Hi-jacked, Dark Smoke,* and *Clash.*

Ricardo Aguilar Melantzon 1947-
A prominent poet and critic, Aguilar Melantzon is a professor of literature at the University of Texas at El Paso.

Demetrio Aguilera Malta 1909-1981
Aguilera Malta was an Ecuadorean novelist and playwright best known for depicting the plight of his country's *cholos,* or peasantry.

Delmira Agustini 1886-1914
Agustini, an esteemed poet who was murdered in 1914, produced only a few volumes, including the collection *Los cálices vacíos.*

Leopoldo Alas 1852-1901
Alas, who frequently wrote under the pseudonym Clarín, was an important Spanish novelist and literary critic.

Ciro Alegría 1909-1967
A Peruvian novelist who lived in exile much of his life, Alegría often wrote of the Indians of the Marañon River struggling in a modern world.

Claribel Alegría 1924-
Poet, novelist, and essayist Alegría writes of the political conflicts of her native Nicaragua in works such as *Luisa in Realityland.*

Fernando Alegría 1918-
Chilean critic and novelist living in exile in the U.S., Alegría served as cultural consultant for President Allende before the latter's assassination in 1973.

Ricardo E. Alegría 1921-
Noted Puerto Rican scholar, historian, and anthropologist, Alegría is a former director of the prominent Institute of Puerto Rican Culture.

Vicente Aleixandre 1898-1984
Spanish poet and winner of the Nobel Prize in Literature in 1977, Aleixandre's best loved work creates sympathetic portraits of everyday Spanish life.

Isabel Allende 1942-
Influenced by magic realism and the assassination of her uncle, Chilean President Salvador Allende, Allende combines politics and imaginative situations in novels such as *La casa de los espíritus (The House of Spirits)* and *Eva Luna.*

Dámaso Alonso 1898-1990
Alonso was considered Spain's foremost literary critic as well as one of its most important poets. Among his works are *Poesía española* and *Hijos de la ira.*

Alurista
See Urista, Alberto H.

Alejandro Rodríguez Alvarez 1903-1965
Known under the pseudonym Alejandro Casona, Alvarez fled Spain during the Civil War and gained popularity in Buenos Aires with plays that blend fantasy with reality.

Lynne Alvarez
American poet and playwright Alvarez is the author of the poetry collection *The Dreaming Man* and the play "El Guitarrón."

Héctor Alberto Alvarez Murena 1923-
Writing under the name H. A. Murena, Argentine author Alvarez Murena is known for works that explore the existential problems of twentieth-century life in Latin America.

Enrique Amorim 1900-1960
A novelist and story writer, Amorim wrote about the people and places of the pampas region of Argentina and Uruguay.

Rudolfo A. Anaya 1937-
Best known for his trilogy, *Bless Me, Ultima, Heart of Aztlán,* and *Tortuga,* Anaya offers a unique blend of American mythology and contemporary social concerns.

Enrique Anderson Imbert 1910-
Anderson Imbert is a prominent teacher of Hispanic American literature at Harvard University.

Rudy S. Apodaca 1939-
A Chicano lawyer and appellate judge, Apodaca is the author of a suspense novel titled *The Waxen Image.*

Germán Arciniegas 1900-
Arciniegas is a renowned scholar whose translated works include *Latin America: A Cultural History* and *America in Europe: A History of the New World in Reverse.*

Reinaldo Arenas 1943-
A renowned Cuban writer imprisoned by the Castro government, Arenas emigrated to the United States in 1980. His best-known works are the novels *Singing from the Well, Hallucinations,* and *Farewell to the Sea.*

Rafael Arévalo Martínez 1884-1975
Credited with bringing modernism to Guatemala, Arévalo Martínez is best-known for psycho-zoological tales such as *El hombre que parecía un caballo,* in which he compared his characters to animals.

José María Arguedas 1911-1969
Arguedas, a strong advocate of Peru's Quechua Indians, often wrote about the interrelationship of Indian and Hispanic culture.

Manlio Argueta 1936-
One of Central America's leading writers, this Salvadoran poet and novelist is known for two novels of social protest, *One Day of Life* and *Cuzcatlán: Where the Southern Sea Beats.*

Ron Arias 1941-
A journalist and short story writer influenced by Gabriel García Márquez and magic realism, Arias wrote *The Road to Tamazunchale,* which was nominated for a National Book Award.

Oscar Arias Sánchez 1941-
As president of Costa Rica, Arias Sánchez won the 1987 Nobel Peace Prize for his efforts to establish a treaty with Nicaragua, El Salvador, Honduras, and Guatemala.

Homero Aridjis 1940-
A respected Mexican poet and novelist, Aridjis's translated works include *Persephone* and *Exaltation of Light.*

Roberto Arlt 1900-1942
Argentine novelist, playwright, and journalist Arlt earned recognition for his novel *The Seven Madmen* and for weekly newspaper columns appearing in Buenos Aires' *El Mundo.*

Octavio Rafael Armand 1946-
A Cuban writer and editor, Armand immigrated to the United States and now teaches at Bennington College.

Marcelino Arozarena 1912-
A Cuban poet noted for his writings concerning Afro-Cuban folklore, Arozarena is the author of *Canción negra sin color.*

Juan José Arreola 1918-
Mexican writer Arreola's fiction, such as short pieces collected in *Confabulario and Other Inventions,* is admired for defying strict literary convention.

Antón B. Arrufat 1935-
Among the prolific Arrufat's many writings are the verse collections *En claro* and *Repasa final* and the drama compilation *Teatro.*

Jorge Artel 1909-
Former reporter and diplomat Artel has produced such works as the poetry collection *Tambores en la noche* and the novel *No es la muerte, es el morir.*

Miguel Angel Asturias 1899-1974
Guatemalan statesman and winner of the 1967 Nobel Prize for literature, Asturias sought to bring the world's attention to Latin American issues through such novels as *El señor presidente* and *Men of Maize.*

Juan Bautista de Avalle-Arce 1927-
Avalle-Arce is known for his studies of the works of Cervantes and other medieval and Renaissance Spanish-language literature.

Fausto Avendaño 1941-
Considered one of Chicano literature's foremost scholars, Avendaño is known for his short stories and his historical drama, *El corrido de California.*

Azorín
See Martínez Ruiz, José

Arturo Azuela 1938-
Winner of Mexico's Premio de Ciencias y Artes for literature, Azuela is noted for such politically informed novels as his acclaimed *Shadows of Silence.*

Mariano Azuela 1873-1952
A physician, revolutionary, and one of Mexico's foremost novelists, Azuela chronicled the Mexican Revolution in a number of works, including *The Under Dogs* and *Andrés Pérez, Maderista.*

María Teresa Babín 1910-
A highly esteemed literary critic and professor, Babín founded one of the first Puerto Rican Studies departments in the United States.

Jimmy Santiago Baca 1952-
A former prison inmate, Baca earned the American Book Award for poetry in 1988 for his collection *Martin and Meditations on the South Valley.*

Joan Baez 1941-
Baez became famous during the 1960s for her folk music and political activism. Her memoirs are contained in *Daybreak* and *And a Voice to Sing With.*

José Agustín Balseiro 1900-
Also a talented musician and composer, Balseiro has earned a reputation for novels and criticism that focus on connections between Hispanic and American culture.

Enrique J. Banchs 1888-1968
Argentine poet and journalist Banchs composed classic verse set in modernist style.

Barayón, Ramón Sender
See Sender Barayón, Ramón

Raymond Barrio 1921-
Barrio is a teacher, artist, and writer known for his 1969 *The Plum Plum Pickers,* an examination of Chicano migrant workers that has become an underground classic.

Eduardo Barrios 1884-1963
Chilean Eduardo Barrios authored critically acclaimed works such as the novella "El niño que enloqueció de amor" and the novel *Brother Asno.*

Pilar E. Barrios 1889-
A poet, editor, and activist, Barrios was instrumental in the development of black literature and politics in his native Uruguay.

Bastos, August Roa
See Roa Bastos, Augusto

Carlos Germán Belli 1927-
In his poetry, Peruvian Belli combines seventeenth-century Spanish diction and meter with modern technological terminology to express his political and philosophical beliefs.

Jacinto Benavente 1866-1954
Nobel Prize-winning playwright Benavente dominated the Spanish theatre during the early twentieth-century with plays translated as *The Bonds of Interest* and *The Passionflower.*

Mario Benedetti 1920-
One of Uruguay's best-known writers, Benedetti has penned the story collection *Marcel Proust y otros ensayos* and the novels *La tregua* and *Gracias por el fuego.*

Benedetto, Antonio di
See di Benedetto, Antonio

Walter Beneke 1923-
Beneke is a Salvadorian playwright who wrote *El paraíso de los imprudentes* and *Funeral Home.*

Fernando Benítez 1911-
Benítez writes fiction and nonfiction about Mexican history and society, including *In the Footsteps of Cortés* and *In the Magic Land of Peyote.*

Vicente J. Bernal 1888-1915
Bernal is known for *Las primicias,* a posthumously published volume (his only book) featuring poems and prose—some in Spanish, some in English.

Adolfo Bioy Casares 1914-
A popular novelist in his native Argentina, Bioy Casares is best-known in the U.S. for his collaborations with Jorge Luis Borges.

Rubén Blades 1948-
A Panamanian who revolutionized salsa music with his thoughtful lyrics and urban sound, Blades is also a noted actor and screenwriter.

Rufino Blanco Fombona 1874-1944
The Venezuelan politician and writer was best known for satiric novels such as *La mitra en la mano,* a portrait some critics have compared to *Elmer Gantry.*

Vicente Blasco Ibáñez 1867-1928
The most important works of this Spanish novelist paint vivid portraits of Valencia, his native region of Spain.

Bodet, Jaime Torres
See Torres Bodet, Jaime

María Luisa Bombal 1910-1980
A Chilean novelist whose style prefigured magic realism in Latin American literature, Bombal portrayed women who escape unhappy lives through fantasy in *The Final Mist* and *The Shrouded Woman.*

Jorge Luis Borges 1899-1986
World-acclaimed Argentine essayist, short story writer and poet, Borges is best-known for his short stories which emphasize metaphysical or intellectual content rather than the regionalism previously in vogue.

Miriam Bornstein-Somoza 1950-
Bornstein-Somoza, a Mexican native, has published numerous poems in anthologies such as *Siete poetas* and *Flor y Canto IV and V,* and in her collection *Bajo cubierta.*

Juan Bosch 1909-
Bosch, a former president of the Dominican Republic, is the author of numerous novels, short stories, and historical studies.

Aristeo Brito 1942-
Brito is a poet and fiction writer whose works include the novel *El diablo en Texas* and the collection *Cuentos y poemas de Aristeo Brito.*

Juan D. Bruce-Novoa 1944-
Bruce-Novoa is a Chicano poet and short story writer who addresses universal themes.

Enrique Buenaventura 1925-
A proponent of stylistically experimental, socially committed theater, Buenaventura denounced the repressive political heritage of his native Colombia.

Buendía, Manuel
See Girón, Manuel Buendía Téllez

Antonio Buero Vallejo 1916-
Despite the censorship of the Franco era in Spain, Buero Vallejo became a significant force in Spanish theater with such plays as "The Sleep of Reason."

Silvina Bullrich 1915-
A popular Argentine novelist who in works such as *Bodas de cristal* and *Reunión de directorio* explores the repression of women in a male-dominated society.

Luis Buñuel 1900-1983
One of the most acclaimed filmmakers in cinema history, Spanish-born Buñuel aimed to shock audiences with surrealistic movies that attacked conventional morality and organized religion.

José Antonio Burciaga 1940-
American artist and author, Burciaga published poems and drawings in *Restless Serpents* and *Drink cultura refrescante.*

Manuel Caballero 1931-
Venezuelan journalist and historian Caballero is best known for his books about communism in Latin America.

Eduardo Caballero Calderón 1910-
Author of fiction and nonfiction, Caballero Calderón has worked as a diplomat, statesman, and journalist. His novels include *El Cristo de espaldas,* considered a masterpiece.

Omar Cabezas 1951(?)-
Cabezas is the author of *Fire from the Mountain: The Making of a Sandinista,* about his early years as a member of the Sandinista National Liberation Front.

Lydia Cabrera 1900-
Cuban-born resident of Miami, Cabrera has spent her life studying the Afro-Cuban culture of her native land.

G. Cabrera Infante 1929-
With publication of the novel *Tres tristes tigres (Three Trapped Tigers),* Cabrera Infante established his reputation as a writer of innovative fiction.

Arthur L. Campa 1905-
Campa's writings reflect his interest in Spanish folklore and the hispanic culture.

Nellie Campobello 1912-
Many of Campobello's writings, including *Cartucho* and *My Mother's Hands,* concern the author's childhood experiences during the revolution in her native Mexico.

Cordelia Candelaria 1943-
A professor of English, Candelaria is known for her studies of Chicano literature.

Nash Candelaria 1928-
New Mexican author whose novel *Not By the Sword,* a look at the Mexican War of the mid-1800s, won the Before Columbus Book Award in 1983.

Emilio Carballido 1925-
Influential in the 1950s and '60s as part of a generation of playwrights who strove to revitalize Mexico's theater, Carballido often dealt with the psychological problems of the Mexican middle class.

Ernesto Cardenal 1925-
Nicaraguan poet and Minister of Culture, Catholic priest, and founder of the Christian commune Solentiname, Cardenal is an outspoken supporter of self-determination and justice for Central Americans.

Reyes Cardenas 1948-
Novelist, poet, and short story writer, Cardenas is the author of *Chicano Territory* and *I Was Never a Militant Chicano.*

Onelio Jorge Cardoso 1914-1986
A prolific writer who penned his first story at the age of twelve, Cardoso's fiction focused on the ordinary people of his native Cuba.

Luis Cardoza y Aragón 1904-
Guatemalan poet, art critic, and essayist best known for his lyric essay titled *Guatemala, las líneas de tu mano,* Cardoza y Aragón won the 1986 Premio Rubén Darío.

Inez Cardozo-Freeman 1928-
Cardozo-Freeman is an American educator at Ohio State University who wrote *The Joint: Language and Culture in a Maximum Security Prison.*

Alejo Carpentier 1904-1980
A respected figure throughout much of twentieth-century Cuba's literary development, Carpentier has written such works as *The Kingdom of This World* and *Explosion in a Cathedral.*

Jorge Carrera Andrade 1903-1978
Ecuadorean diplomat Carrera Andrade was the author of numerous essays as well as a poet who adapted the Japanese *haiku* form into Spanish.

Gabriel Casaccia Bibolini 1907-
Casaccia Bibolini is a Paraguayan fiction writer whose works include the novels *Hombres, mujeres y fantoches* and *Los herederos* and the short story collections *El guajhú* and *El pozo.*

Casares, Adolfo Bioy
See Bioy Casares, Adolfo

Casona, Alejandro
See Alvarez, Alejandro Rodríguez

Carlos Castaneda 1931(?)-
The enigmatic Carlos Castaneda achieved fame with his "anthropological" accounts of his apprenticeship with the Yaqui Indian sorcerer, Don Juan.

Rosario Castellanos 1925-1974
Mexican writer and one of that nation's leading feminists, Castellanos wrote about the plight of women and the Indians of southern Mexico.

Ana Castillo 1953-
An American poet and novelist, Castillo is best known for her epistolary novel *The Mixquiahuala Letters.*

Américo Castro 1885-1972
Ford Emeritus Professor at Princeton University for nearly two decades, Brazillian-born Castro produced many books about Spanish history and culture.

Rafael Catalá 1942-
In his book, *Cienciapoesía,* Rafael Catalá introduced the concept of sciencepoetry—the process of unifying the humanities and science.

Camilo José Cela 1916-
Spanish novelist Cela won the 1989 Nobel Prize for his experimental prose, which includes the widely-translated narratives *The Family of Pasquale Duarte* and *The Hive.*

Luis Cernuda 1902-1963
A Spanish poet who looked to nineteenth-century English romanticism for inspiration, Cernuda is best known for *La realidad y el deseo, (1924-1962).*

Lorna Dee Cervantes 1954-
Editor in chief of *Mango,* Cervantes is a promising new Chicana poet who published her debut collection, *Emplumada,* in 1981.

Eusebio Chacón 1869-1948
New Mexican author who is believed to be the author of the first novels written in Spanish in the New Mexico-Colorado area.

Denise Chávez 1948-
Chávez is a poet and playwright whose works include the poetry volume *Life Is a Two-Way Street* and the award-winning short story collection *The Last of the Menu Girls.*

Chávez, Fray Angélico
See Chávez, Manuel

John R. Chávez 1949-
A scholar of Chicano history and literature, Chávez was nominated for a Pulitzer Prize for *The Lost Land: The Chicano Image of the Southwest.*

Manuel Chávez 1910-
Chávez, a former Franciscan monk and Roman Catholic priest, is best known by his name in religion, Fray Angélico Chávez.

José Santos Chocano 1875-1934
Publicly crowned national poet of Peru in 1922, Chocano is the author of numerous collections, including *Alma América* and *Spirit of the Andes.*

Alí Chumacero 1918-
Poet and critic Chumacero is perhaps the best known of the Mexican intellectual group Tierra Nueva. His works include *Páramo de sueños* and *El viaje de la tribú.*

Antonio Cisneros 1942-
Widely considered the foremost poet in Peru, Cisneros is acclaimed for his satirical poems collected in such volumes as *The Spider Hangs Too Far from the Ground,* and *At Night the Cats.*

Sandra Cisneros
Cisneros is an American writer whose works include *Bad Boys, The House on Mango Street, The Rodrigo Poems,* and *My Wicked, Wicked Ways.*

Clarín
See Alas, Leopoldo

Judith Ortiz Cofer 1952-
An acclaimed author of several books of poetry, including *Letters from a Caribbean Island,* Cofer also wrote the 1989 novel *The Line of the Sun.*

Jesus Colón 1901-
Colón is a Puerto Rican writer best known for his collection *A Puerto Rican in New York, and Other Sketches.*

Antonio J. Colorado 1903-
Colorado, a Puerto Rican government official, has written several books on his homeland of Puerto Rico and on Latin America.

Lucha Corpi 1945-
Mexican-born poet Corpi is the author of *Fireflight: Three Latin American Poets, Palabras de mediodía: Noon Words,* and a novel, *Delia's Song.*

Julio Cortázar 1914-1984
An Argentinian exile, Cortázar stretched the boundaries of fiction with his short stories and with such novels as *A Manual for Manuel* and *Hopscotch,* a revolutionary work.

Humberto Costantini 1924(?)-1987
Costantini, an Argentine political satirist who lived in Mexico from 1977 to 1983, was best known for his anti-oppression novels.

Arturo Cruz, Jr. 1954(?)-
Cruz recounts his experiences on both sides of the Nicaraguan conflict in *Memoirs of a Counter-revolutionary.*

Gilbert R. Cruz 1929-
A Chicano historian, Cruz specializes in the history of San Antonio, Texas, and Texas's Rio Grande Valley.

Victor Hernández Cruz 1949-
Cruz is a poet who writes in English but with a definite Spanish voice of the many differences between his native Puerto Rico and New York City.

Lidio Cruz Monclova 1899-
Lidio Cruz Monclova is the most prominent historian of nineteenth-century Puerto Rico.

Pablo Antonio Cuadra 1912-
Cuadra is a leading member of Nicaragua's *vanguardia* literary movement whose books of poetry include *The Jaguar and the Moon* and *The Birth of the Sun.*

Belkis Cuza Malé 1942-
Belkis Cuza Malé is a Cuban-born poet whose works include *El viento en la pared, Tiempos de sol,* and *Cartas a Ana Frank.*

Rubén Darío 1867-1916
A Nicaraguan journalist, diplomat, critic, poet, and fiction writer, Darío also founded the *modernista* literary movement.

Virgilia Dávila 1869-1943
Puerto Rican poet Dávila also worked as a teacher and politician. Most of his verse dates from the 1910s and 1920s.

Nephtalí De León 1945-
De León is a Chicano activist and prolific author of poems, plays, children's stories, and essays.

Abelardo B. Delgado 1931-
Often anthologized, Delgado's poems promote social justice for Mexican-Americans and other minority groups.

Miguel Delibes Setien 1920-
Novels by Spanish author Delibes Setien show the negative effects of technological progress and encourage modern man to return to his primitive roots.

Marco Denevi 1922-
An Argentine novelist and playwright, Denevi is the author of *Rosaura a las diez,* a detective novel translated as *Rosa at Ten O'Clock.*

Jorge Díaz 1930-
A former architect who became interested in plays while working on stage sets, Díaz's works are characterized by their humor and witty dialogue.

Carlos F. Díaz-Alejandro 1937-1985
A Cuban-born scholar specializing in Latin American economics, Díaz-Alejandro served on the Reagan administration's National Bipartisan Commission on Latin America.

Salvador Díaz Mirón 1858-1928
Díaz Mirón was a Mexican poet who aspired to a political career. His writings include *Poesías, Lascas, Poesías completas,* and *La giganta y otros poemas.*

Guillermo Díaz Plaja 1909-1984
One of Spain's most important literary historians, Díaz Plaja was also an essayist, poet and literary critic.

Emilio Díaz Valcárcel 1929-
Díaz Valcárcel has received several awards for short stories such as those in his collection translated into English, *Schemes in the Month of March.*

Antonio di Benedetto 1922-
A journalist and experimental novelist, di Benedetto has won a number of prizes for his writings, which include the novel *Zama,* and the short story collection *Grot.*

Gerardo Diego 1896-1987
Primarily known as a poetry anthologist, Diego's own poetry was considered to be competent, though not innovative.

Fabián Dobles 1918-
Fabián Dobles is an award-winning Costa Rican author whose novels, short stories, and poetry reflect his concern for social justice for the poor.

José Donoso 1924-
Because of works such as *The Obscene Bird of Night,* Chilean Donoso is considered one of the most talented novelists to emerge in twentieth-century Latin America.

Ariel Dorfman 1942-
Exiled from his adopted homeland after a 1973 coup, Dorfman's writing has protested the violence and intimidation perpetrated by Chilean dictator Augusto Pinochet.

Osvaldo Dragún 1929-
Considered one of the most talented young playwrights to emerge in Argentina during the 1950s and '60s, Dragún's works range from historical drama to the absurd.

Quince Duncan 1940-
Among Central America's best-known black writers, Duncan is acclaimed for his works concerning the plight of blacks in his native Costa Rica.

Roberto Durán 1953-
A poet who co-authored the collection *Triple Crown,* Durán is known for writings that deal with drug abuse, discrimination, and the justice system.

José Echegaray 1832-1916
Considered an important link between the romantic and modern periods in Spanish theater, Nobel Prize winner Echegaray's plays are often melodramatic and feature heroic figures.

Sergio D. Elizondo 1930-
Elizondo is a Mexican-American poet and fiction writer who also edits Chicano anthologies.

José Enamurado Cuesta 1892-
A member of the Puerto Rican Communist Party, Enamurado Cuesta has written several works of Puerto Rican history.

Aurelio M. Espinosa 1880-1958
Espinosa was a prominent folklorist and authority on Spanish grammar who was a professor at Stanford University for thirty-seven years.

Aurelio M. Espinosa, Jr. 1907-
Espinosa was a writer, editor, and professor of Romance languages at Stanford University for twenty-five years.

Nelson Estupiñán Bass 1915-
Ecuadorian Estupiñán Bass celebrates Afro-Hispanic life in his numerous poetry collections and novels, including *When the Guayacans Were in Bloom.*

Roberto G. Fernández 1949-
A Cuban-born author of short stories and novels, Fernández published in 1988 his first novel in English, *Raining Backwards.*

Eugenio Fernández Méndez 1924-
A professor of anthropology, Fernández Méndez has written and edited many books in his field.

Baldomero Fernández Moreno 1886-1950
An Argentine poet and literature teacher, Fernández Moreno practiced medicine until 1924, but then became a full-time poet.

César Fernández Moreno 1919-
Fernández Moreno is an Argentinian poet, literary critic, and editor whose writings include *Gallo ciego, Sentimientos,* and *Los aeropuertos.*

Roberto Fernández Retamar 1930-
Fernández Retamar is a Cuban editor and author of poetry and essays. His writings include *Elegía como un himno,* and *Ensayo de otro mundo.*

José Ferrater-Mora   1912-
Ferrater-Mora is noted for his philosophical studies.

Rosario Ferré   1942-
Recognized for her incisive and ironic depictions of Puerto Rican society, Ferré is one of that country's most respected feminist writers.

Loida Figueroa   1917-
Loida Figueroa is a Puerto Rican historian who wrote *History of Puerto Rico from the Beginning to 1892.*

Pablo Figueroa   1938-
Figueroa is best known for his plays, his study of Hispanic theater, and his work for children.

Angel Flores   1900-
A Puerto Rican-born college professor, Flores is noted for his modern literary criticism and his many translations of noted Hispanic writers.

Eugenio Florit   1903-
Florit is a lawyer and former Cuban diplomat who has written numerous books of poetry and has published a number of articles on literary criticism.

Maria Irene Fornes   1930-
Fornes is the foremost Hispanic playwright in the U.S. and occupies a prominent position in American theater with six Obie Awards to her credit.

Carlos Fuentes   1928-
An influential Mexican novelist, essayist, literary critic, playwright, and author of short stories, Fuentes typically explores Mexican themes through magic realism.

Juan Pablo Fusi   1945-
Director of Spain's National Library and a former professor of history, Fusi has written several historical works, including *Franco: A Biography.*

Ernesto Galarza   1905-1984
A Mexican-born American union leader and writer, Galarza's writings helped bring about the end of the hated "bracero" system that exploited Mexican agricultural laborers.

Galdós, Benito Pérez
See Pérez Galdós, Benito

Eduardo Galeano   1940-
A Uruguayan-born journalist and novelist, Galeano is best known for his 1989 American Book Award-winning trilogy "Memory of Fire."

Edward Gallardo
Gallardo has written such Off-Off-Broadway productions as "Bernie," "In Another Part of the City" and such Off-Broadway productions as "Women without Men."

Laura Gallego   1924-
Gallego is a noted Puerto Rican poet and professor of education. Her poetry is collected in *Celajes, 1951-1953* and *Laura Gallego: obra poetica.*

Rómulo Gallegos   1884-1969
Gallegos is remembered as one Venezuela's finest authors and as its first freely elected president. His translated novels include *Doña Bárbara* and *Canaima.*

Manuel Gálvez   1882-1962
One of the earliest professional novelists in Argentina, Gálvez was known for his simple style and socially significant themes.

Eduardo Gamarra   1957-
A political scientist at Florida International University, Gamarra is the coauthor of *Revolution and Reaction: Bolivia, 1964-1985.*

Griselda Gambaro   1928-
Considered one of the foremost playwrights to emerge from Latin America during the 1960s, Gambaro gained international renown for stark dramas such as *El campo (The Camp).*

Harry Gamboa, Jr.
Gamboa wrote "Jetter's Jinx," a play presented at the Los Angeles Theatre Centre in 1985.

Lionel G. García   1935-
Garcia, a veterinarian by vocation, has written several short stories and three novels dealing with the differences between Mexican and Anglo cultures.

Richard A. García   1941-
García is a poet and scholar of Chicano history; he has edited *The Chicanos in America, 1540-1974: A Chronology and Fact Book.*

Sam Garcia   1957-
A member of the Los Angeles Theater Center's Latino Workshop, Garcia is a promising playwright.

Federico García Lorca   1898-1936
One of the best known of all Spanish authors, García Lorca was a poet and dramatist renowned for his sonorous verse and his gripping portrayals of human emotion.

Gabriel García Márquez   1928-
1982 Nobel laureate García Márquez has gained international attention with novels such as *One Hundred Years of Solitude* which draw on factual events, but incorporate magic realism.

Juan García Ponce   1932-
Writer, literary critic, and editor García Ponce has written short stories, essays, novels, and art criticism.

Rina García Rocha   1954-
This Chicana poet has given numerous readings of her poetry in the Chicago metropolitan area.

Elena Garro   1920(?)-
A well-regarded Mexican playwright, Garro is best known in English-speaking circles for her novel *Recollections of Things to Come,* a forerunner of García Márquez's *One Hundred Years of Solitude.*

Roberto J. Garza   1934-
Chicano historian and educator, Garza is the editor of *Chicano Theatre: An Anthology.*

Gasset, José Ortega y
See Ortega y Gasset, José

Vincente Géigel Polanco 1904-1979
Géigel Polanco was a Puerto Rican statesman and writer who served as his island's attorney general under Governor Luis Muñoz Marín.

Juan Gelman 1930-
Gelman is a poet associated with the *El Pan Duro* and *La Rosa Blindada* literary groups in Argentina. His works include *Violín y otras cuestiones* and *Gotán*.

Alberto Gerchunoff 1883-1950
Argentine Jewish writer Gerchunoff was a prominent journalist affiliated for several decades with the Buenos Aires-based *La Nación*.

Martha Gil-Montero 1940-
Argentine-born American Martha Gil-Montero is a former Argentine government official who wrote about Latin American legend Carmen Miranda in *Brazilian Bombshell*.

Manuel Buendía Téllez Girón 1926(?)-1984
Best known for his controversial column appearing in Mexico City's *Excelsior*, Giron was assassinated in 1984.

Oliverio Girondo 1891-1967
An Argentine humorist and experimentalist, Girondo wrote the poetry volumes *Veinte poemas para ser leidos en el tranvia* and *En la masmédula*.

Alberto Girri 1919-
Alberto Girri is an award-winning Argentine poet noted for his exploration of philosophical issues in such volumes as *Examen de nuestra and Existenciales*.

Lucila Godoy Alcayaga 1889-1957
Writing under the pseudonym Gabriela Mistral, poet Godoy Alcayaga was the first Latin American writer to receive the Nobel Prize for literature.

Isaac Goldemberg 1945-
Born in Peru of Jewish parents, Goldemberg writes about "the Jewish experience in Peru."

Ramón Gómez de la Serna 1888-1963
A Spanish humorist who invented the *greguería*, a semi-aphoristic metaphoric way of looking at the world, Gómez de la Serna is considered a precursor of the surrealists.

Juan Gómez-Quiñones 1942-
A Mexican-born American author and educator, Gómez-Quiñones wrote numerous books on figures in Latin American history.

Alexis Gómez Rosa 1950-
A Dominican-born poet and teacher who lives in the United States, Gómez Rosa is also involved in social work with immigrants.

Sylvia Alicia Gonzáles 1943-
An educator and concerned supporter of women's and Hispanic concerns, Gonzáles's writing addresses the study of cultural differences in the world.

José Luis González 1926-
González is considered one of Puerto Rico's foremost writers and was awarded Mexico's prestigious Xavier Villaurrutia Prize for his novel *Ballad of Another Time*.

F. González-Crussi 1936-
González-Crussi is a Mexican pathologist whose essay collections, especially *Notes of an Anatomist*, have gained him recognition as a witty, insightful writer.

Enrique González Martínez 1871-1952
A noted Mexican physician and diplomat, González Martinez wrote poetry of a serious and reflective nature.

Manuel González Prada 1844-1918
This Peruvian essayist and poet dedicated his talents to political reforms in Peru and thus became the mentor of a generation of Latin American revolutionaries.

César A. González T. 1931-
González T., who teaches Chicano studies, is best known for poetry such as *Unwinding the Silence*, which expresses concern with transience, unity, and transcendence.

Celestino Gorostiza
Gorostiza is a playwright who has written for and about the Mexican theater.

José Gorostiza 1901-1973
Mexican diplomat and author Gorostiza wrote the poem translated as *Death Without End* and the collection *Canciones para cantar en la barcas*.

Juan Goytisolo 1931-
Widely considered the best Spanish novelist of his generation, Goytisolo spent many years in self-imposed exile from the ultraconservative regime of Francisco Franco.

Jorge J. Gracia 1942-
Cuban-born scholar Gracia is an author and editor of numerous works on philosophy, including *Philosophy and Literature in Latin America*.

Guevara, Ché
See Guevara, Ernesto

Ernesto Guevara 1928-1967
Argentine-born Marxist revolutionary "Ché" Guevara inspired a generation of radical youth during the 1960s.

Beatriz Guido 1924-1988
Guido was an esteemed Argentine fiction writer known for her leftist political and social commentary.

Jorge Guillén 1893-1984
Considered among the best of twentieth-century Spanish poets, Guillén was a member of the "Generation of 27" writers who used strong metaphor and pure aestheticism in their poetry.

Nicolás Guillén 1902-1989
Guillén, considered one of twentieth-century Cuba's greatest poets, helped popularize the "Afro-Cuban" style, intertwining various African elements in a single poem.

Ricardo Güiraldes 1886-1927
Güiraldes is the author of one of Argentina's most famous twentieth-century novels, *Don Segundo Sombra,* a classic of gaucho literature.

Gustavo Gutiérrez Merino 1928-
Gutiérrez Merino is a Peruvian priest and theologian whose works explore the Catholic church's role in resisting political oppression in Latin America.

Martín Luis Guzmán 1887-1976
Guzmán was a Mexican politician and writer whose experiences in the Mexican Revolution of 1913 are reflected in his novels *El águila y la serpiente* and *La sombra del caudillo.*

Oscar Hahn 1938-
Hahn is a Chilean-born American poet and professor of Spanish-American literature. Among his works are *Arte de morir,* translated as *The Art of Dying,* and *Texto sobre texto.*

Javier Héraud 1942-1963
Héraud was a promising Peruvian poet who was killed by his government for his leftist activities.

Luis Hernández Aquino 1907-?
Widely known for verse appearing in such collections as *Isla para anguista,* Puerto Rican Hernandez Aquino won the Institute of Puerto Rican Literature's 1964 Poetry Prize.

Juan Felipe Herrera 1948-
The works of American artist and writer Herrerra include *Rebozos of Love* and *Exiles of Desire.*

María Herrera-Sobek
Herrera-Sobek is the author of highly-recommended studies of *braceros* (Chicano folk musicians) and Chicana literature.

Julio Herrera y Reissig 1875-1910
One of the first modernist poets in the Spanish language, Uruguayan Herrera y Reissig was involved in the *ultraísmo* movement.

Oscar Hijuelos 1951-
Hijuelos, an American novelist of Cuban descent, is the author of *Our House in the Last World* and the Pulitzer Prize-winning *The Mambo Kings Play Songs of Love.*

Rolando Hinojosa 1929-
A Chicano novelist and scholar, Hinojosa is best known for his "Klail City Death Trip" novels portraying life in the Lower Rio Grande Valley.

Adolfo de Hostos 1887-
Hostos, a historian and archeologist living and writing in Puerto Rico, is the son of the author and political activist, Eugenio María de Hostos.

Eugenio María de Hostos 1839-1903
Hostos was a zealous political activist, educator, and author who sought Cuban and Puerto Rican independence.

Angela de Hoyos 1945-
A Chicana poet whose books include *Arise, Chicano! and Other Poems, Chicano Poems: For the Barrio,* and *Woman, Woman.*

Jorge A. Huerta 1942-
A professional director and leading authority on Chicano drama, Huerta launched America's first master's program in Chicano theater.

Huidobro, Vicente
See Huidobro Fernández, Vicente García

Vicente García Huidobro Fernández 1893-1948
Under the name Vicente Huidobro, this Chilean poet was among the founders of *creacionismo,* a literary school that promoted inventiveness and experimentation.

Juana de Ibarbourou 1895-1979
Ibarbourou was consecrated "Juana de América" by Uruguay's legislature for her simple poems of nature and love, including *Las lenguas de diamante* and *Ejemplario.*

Jorge Ibargüengoitia 1928-1983
A prize-winning novelist and playwright, Mexican writer Ibargüengoitia was known for his satiric treatment of Mexican social behavior, government, and the corruption of individuals.

Jorge Icaza 1906-1979
Icaza was one of Ecuador's most prominent playwrights until his plays were banned. He went on to become a novelist, detailing native American life in *Huasipungo* and *Huairapamushcas.*

Infante, G. Cabrera
See Cabrera Infante, G.

Arturo Islas 1938-
American novelist Islas wrote *The Rain God* and *Migrant Souls.*

Ricardo Jaimes Freyre 1868-1933
An Argentine historian and *modernista poet,* Jaimes Freyre is best known for his verse collection *Castalia bárbara* ("Primeval Fountain").

Francisco Jiménez 1943-
Mexican-born American scholar Jiménez is the author of *¡Viva la lengua! A Contemporary Reader* and *Mosaco de la vida: Prosa chicana, cubana y puertorriquena.*

Juan Ramón Jiménez 1881-1958
Winner of the Nobel Prize in 1956, Jiménez was one of Spain's most influential poets. He became the link between Spain's modernists and contemporary poets.

Roberto Juarroz 1925-
Juarroz, a prolific poet living in Argentina, writes about the continuity and infinity of the human experience.

Nicolás Kanellos 1945-
Kanellos founded the magazine *Revista Chicano-Riqueña* and the Arte Público Press, which promote the works of Hispanic-American writers.

Gary D. Keller 1943-
Keller is a leading educator whose work with the U.S. Hispanic Higher Education Coalition has promoted educational opportunities for minority students.

Enrique A. Laguerre 1906-
Regarded as one of Puerto Rico's most important novelists, Laguerre is noted for such socially informed works as *La llamarada* and *El laberinto*.

Luis Leal 1907-
Leal is a Mexican-born American scholar whose works include *México: Civilizaciones y culturas, Literatura chicana,* and studies of Mariano Azuela.

Miguel León-Portilla 1926-
León-Portilla's studies of Nahuatl literature and his examinations of the history and art of the Aztecs have won him an international reputation.

José Lezama Lima 1910(?)-1976
Called "the Proust of the Caribbean," Lezama Lima is best known for his encyclopedic novel *Paradiso*.

Enrique Lihn 1929-1988
One of modern Chile's most celebrated poets, Lihn drew upon his country's rich poetic tradition to fashion satiric poetry with a sense of anguish.

Joseph Lizardi 1941-
A Puerto Rican born playwright, Lizardi has written such Off-Off Broadway works as "El Macho," "Block Party," and "Blue Collars."

Washington Lloréns 1900-
Lloréns is a Puerto Rican pharmacist and author whose writings include *La magia de la palabra* and *Humor, Epigram, and Satire in Puerto Rican Literature*.

Llosa, Mario Vargas
See Vargas Llosa, Mario

Diana López 1948-
Lopez is the author of the first Chicana bildungsroman, *Victuum*.

José López Portillo 1920-
López Portillo was president of Mexico from 1976 to 1982 and wrote a best-selling autobiography, *Mis tiempos* ("My Times").

Violeta López Suria 1926-
Puerto Rican López Suria is a lyrical, intellectual poet whose writings include *Diluvio* and *Obesión de Heliotropo*—a collection of essays and short stories.

Gregorio López y Fuentes 1897(?)-1966
A Mexican journalist and author, López y Fuentes wrote several novels examining the Mexican Revolution of 1910 to 1920 and its aftermath.

Lorca, Federico García
See García Lorca, Federico

Leopoldo Lugones 1874-1938
Lugones, a *modernista* poet noted for such innovative verse collections as *Lunario sentimental,* is also credited with composing the first Argentine science fiction work.

Benito Lynch 1885-1951
An Argentinian novelist and short story writer, Lynch is especially noted for his frank and honest portrayal of the Argentinian gauchos.

Eduardo Machado 1953-
Machado is known for his off-beat plays of Cuban life. Among his many stage productions are "The Modern Ladies of Guanabacoa," "Fabiola," and "Broken Eggs."

Salvador de Madariaga 1886-1978
A highly respected Spanish historian and writer, Madariaga published many works of poetry, fiction, drama, and biography.

Manuel Maldonado-Denis 1933-
Maldonado-Denis is a noted Puerto Rican scholar and essayist and a recipient of a Casa de las Américas Prize.

Eduardo Mallea 1903-1982(?)
Mallea was a leading South American writer of philosophical essays, short stories, and novels, many of which center on solitary figures who strive to bring meaning to their lives.

Alberto Manguel 1948-
An Argentine-born Canadian editor, translator, and author, Manguel is noted for his anthologies *Black Water: The Book of Fantastic Literature* and *Other Fires*.

Leopoldo Marechal 1900-1970
After years of neglect, Marechal's visionary urban novel *Adán Buenosayres* has become recognized as a forerunner to the Latin American fiction "boom" that began in the 1960s.

René Marqués 1919-1979
Marqués won numerous awards for his fiction and plays, including "Palm Sunday" and "The Oxcart."

Márquez, Gabriel García
See García Márquez, Gabriel

José Luis Martín 1921-
A professor of Spanish and Spanish-American literature, Martín has written several works of literary criticism.

Luis Martín 1927-
Martín, a professor of Ibero-American history, is the author of *The Intellectual Conquest of Peru,* and *Daughters of the Conquistadores*.

Julio A. Martínez 1931-
A long-time librarian, Martínez is the author of such scholarly works as *A Bibliography of Writings on Plato* and *Dictionary of Twentieth-Century Cuban Literature*.

Max Martínez 1943-
Martínez is a Texas-born writer whose works include *Monologue of the Bolivian Major,* and *Schoolland*.

Tomás Eloy Martínez
A professor of Latin American literature, Argentine writer Martínez is best known for his *Novela de Perón,* translated as *The Perón Novel*.

Carlos Martínez Moreno 1917-1986
Martínez Moreno was a criminal lawyer, journalist, and author of *El infierno,* a novel focusing on military suppression in 1960s Uruguay.

José Martínez Ruiz 1873-1967
As Azorín, one of Spain's leading essayists of the Generation of '98, Martínez Ruiz attempted to capture the true essence of Spain in his works.

Julio Marzán 1946-
Márzan has written the play "When Is a Pigeon a Dove?" and edited *Inventing a Word: An Anthology of Twentieth-Century Puerto Rican Poetry.*

Francisco Matos Paoli 1915-
Matos Paoli has written numerous volumes of poetry on metaphysical and nationalist themes, including *Luz de los héroes* and *Song of Madness.*

Robert C. Medina 1924-
Medina is the author of two novels, *Two Ranges* and *Fabián no se muere: novela de amor,* which explore Chicano culture within American society.

Concha Meléndez 1892-
An authority on Spanish-American literature, Meléndez has written studies of Puerto Rican literature, travel books, and poetry.

Carlos Mellizo 1942-
Mellizo is active both as a translator of works into Spanish as well as an author of short fiction. His collections include *Historia de Sonia y otras historias* and *Los cocodrilos.*

Miguel Méndez M. 1930-
Although not well known to English-speaking Americans, Méndez M. is acclaimed by critics as perhaps the foremost Chicano novelist writing today.

Ramón Menéndez Pidal 1869-1968
Spanish literary historian and philologist Menéndez Pidal served for over thirty years as the head of the prestigious Royal Spanish Academy.

Doris Meyer 1942-
American editor, scholar, and anthologist of Hispanic literature, Meyer is the editor of *Contemporary Women Authors of Latin America.*

Mistral, Gabriela
See Godoy Alcayaga, Lucila

Nicholasa Mohr 1935-
A Puerto Rican-American, Mohr is the author of young-adult fiction which realistically describes life as a member of a Hispanic minority in New York City.

Enrique Molina 1910-
Molina is an Argentine-born surrealistic poet.

Augusto Monterroso 1921-
A resident of Mexico, Monterroso has written essays, scholarly studies, and fiction.

Marco Antonio Montes de Oca 1932-
Montes de Oca is a Mexican poet whose verse is acclaimed for its surrealist style and use of symbols.

José Montoya 1932-
Painter and poet José Montoya is the founder of the Rebel Chicano Art Front, a group organizing readings and exhibitions of Chicano work.

Pat Mora 1942-
Mora is the award-winning author of the poetry volumes *Chants* and *Borders.*

Cherríe Moraga 1952-
Moraga is an American-born Chicana who uses her poetry, plays, and essays to explore her ethnic background and her lesbian feminism.

Alejandro Morales 1944-
Professor of Latin American and Chicano literature, Morales documents Chicano culture in structurally complex and stylistically innovative novels.

Angel Luis Morales 1919-
Morales, a former professor at the University of Puerto Rico, has written critical studies of Spanish-American literature.

Jorge Luis Morales 1930-
Considered among Puerto Rico's finest poets, Morales has published such verse collections as *Metal y piedra: Poemas, 1949-1951* and *Decir del propio ser.*

Arturo Morales Carrión 1913-1989
Cuban-born Morales Carrión served in the State Department during the Kennedy administration before becoming president of the University of Puerto Rico in 1973.

César Moro 1903-1956
Peruvian poet César Moro was co-founder of the surrealist journal, *The Use of Words.*

Carlos Morton 1947-
Morton is an essayist, poet, playwright, and actor whose work frequently questions stereotypes of the Chicano-Latino living in the United States.

Daniel Moyano 1930-
An Argentine fiction writer, Moyano is the author of several short stories and novels such as *El trino del diablo,* translated as *The Devil's Trill.*

Manuel Mujica Láinez 1910-1984
An Argentinian novelist, Mujica Láinez's fantastic and satirical work was sometimes compared to that of Gabriel García Márquez.

Angelina Muniz 1936-
Muniz is the author of *Vilano al viento, Enclosed Garden,* and the Premio Xavier Villarrutia-winning *Huerto sellado, huerto cerrado.*

Luis Muñoz Marín 1898-1980
A journalist, essayist, and poet, Muñoz Marín was the first elected governor of Puerto Rico.

Murena, H. A.
See Alvarez Murena, Héctor Alberto

Muro, Amado
See Seltzer, Chester E.

Alvaro Mutis 1923-
Mutis writes poetry and fiction that presents characters who despair over the violence and apparent futility of twentieth-century life.

Gregory Nava 1949-
Screenwriter and director Nava is best known for the highly praised 1984 film, "El Norte." His other films include "The Confessions of Ammans" and "A Time of Destiny."

Julian Nava 1927-
A former U.S. ambassador to Mexico, Nava has spent much of his career in the field of education.

Pablo Neruda 1904-1973
Nobel Prize winner Neruda was regarded as the premier 20th-century Latin American poet for works which celebrated erotic love, the natural world, and social responsibility.

Amado Nervo 1870-1919
Considered one of Mexico's top modernist poets, Nervo is known for his works dealing with religion, philosophy, and mysticism.

Josefina Niggli 1910-
Niggli has produced such respected novels as *Mexican Village* and *Step Down, Elder Brother.*

Jorge Niosi 1945-
An Argentine now living in Canada, Niosi is a sociologist who has examined the United States' economic decline.

Lino Novás Calvo 1905-1983
Author of the 1933 novel *El negrero,* Novás Calvo has also written award-winning short stories included in *La luna nona y otros cuentos* and *Cayo Canas.*

Salvador Novo 1904-1974
A prolific, versatile writer, Novo influenced Mexican literature with his poetry, plays, travelogues, histories of Mexico, innovative essays, and works of criticism.

Novoa, Juan Bruce
See Bruce-Novoa, Juan D.

Silvina Ocampo 1906-
Wife of author Adolfo Bioy Casares and sister of Victoria Ocampo, Silvina Ocampo is an accomplished poet, short story writer, and artist.

Victoria Ocampo 1890-1979
The "grande dame" of Argentine letters, Ocampo wrote extensively but is most remembered for her work as founding editor of the influential literary review, *Sur.*

Juan Carlos Onetti 1909-
Onetti is a journalist, novelist, and a writer of short stories whose work has been praised for its innovative quality.

Héctor H. Orjuela 1930-
Orjuela is a poet, critic, novelist and educator from Colombia.

Olga Orozco 1920-
Argentine writer Orozco has written several collections of poetry, including *Cantos a berenice* and *En el revés del cielo.*

José Ortega y Gasset 1883-1955
An influential Spanish philosopher known for *Revolt of the Masses* and *The Dehumanization of Art,* Ortega y Gasset worked for the cultural revitalization of Spain.

Philip D. Ortego y Gasca 1926-
Ortego y Gasca, a professor of English and Spanish, edited *We Are Chicanos: An Anthology of Mexican-American Education.*

Adalberto Ortiz 1914-
Ortiz, an Ecuadorian poet, novelist, and short story writer, is considered one of the leading Afro-Hispanic authors of South America.

Miguel Antonio Otero 1859-1944
The first Hispanic governor of a southwestern territory, Otero led New Mexico in its first push for statehood.

Henricus Luis Pacheco 1947-
Pacheco, who also goes by the name Henry L. Pacheco, is author of a book of poems entitled *The Kindred/La Familia.*

José Emilio Pacheco 1939-
A highly esteemed Mexican author, Pacheco has written fiction and poetry exploring the metaphysical aspects of time and experience.

Heberto Padilla 1932-
The 1971 imprisonment of Padilla, one of the finest poets to emerge in Castro's Cuba, aroused international protest.

Raymond V. Padilla 1944-
Padilla, a professor of foreign languages and educational policy, has edited and contributed to several works on bilingual education.

Gloria M. Pagan Ferrer 1921-
Writing under the pseudonym Marigloria Palma, Pagan Ferrer is an award-winning Puerto Rican poet.

Luis Palés Matos 1898-1959
Palés Matos was the most prominent member of a prominent Puerto Rican family of poets.

Palma, Marigloria
See Pagan Ferrer, Gloria M.

Américo Paredes 1915-
Paredes is a noted authority on Chicano folklore. Among his major works is *With His Pistol in His Hand: A Border Ballad and Its Hero.*

Nicanor Parra 1914-
A champion of accessible poetry written in colloquial Spanish, this Chilean anti-poet has become a major influence on Hispanic poetry by denouncing elitist aesthetics.

Emilio J. Pasarell 1891-?
Pasarell is the author of an extensive study of Puerto Rican theatre entitled *Orígenes y desarrollo de la afición teatral en Puerto Rico.*

Ricardo Pau-Llosa 1954-
Cuban-born poet and Latin American art historian Pau-Llosa won the Anhinga Poetry Prize in 1983 for *Sorting Metaphors.*

Roberto J. Payró 1867-1928
Payró's novels are laced with satire and reveal his dissatisfaction with the corruption and hypocrisy of Argentine government officials and business leaders.

Octavio Paz 1914-
A former Mexican diplomat, Paz has received most of the Hispanic world's major literary prizes for his essays and poetry.

Carlos Pellicer 1899-1977
Pellicer, a Mexican diplomat, museum director, and university professor, was known for his sensuous, exuberant poetry.

Benito Pérez Galdós 1843-1920
Considered the greatest Spanish novelist since Cervantes, Galdós (usually known by his maternal surname) spawned a rebirth of the novel in nineteenth-century Spain.

Alberto Pérez-Gómez 1949-
Mexican-born Pérez-Gómez is an author and lecturer on architecture.

Monelisa L. Pérez-Marchand 1918-
A former professor at the University of Puerto Rico, Pérez-Marchand has written many essays on the intellectual history of Mexico and her homeland.

Cristina Peri Rossi 1941-
Peri Rossi is a Uruguayan poet, novelist, and short story writer best known to English-language readers for her complex psychological novel *The Ship of Fools.*

Pedro Pietri 1943-
Pietri is an American poet and playwright whose poetry includes *Puerto Rican Obituary* and *Traffic Violations.* Among his plays is *The Masses Are Asses.*

Virgilio Piñera 1912-
Cuban author, editor, and translator Piñera wrote such plays as *Cold Air* and "El flaco y el gordo," the short story collection *Cuentos fríos,* and the novel *Peque as maniobras.*

Miguel Piñero 1946-1988
While incarcerated in Sing Sing, Piñero began writing plays, "Short Eyes: The Killing of a Sex Offender by the Inmates of the House of Detention Awaiting Trial."

Agueda Pizarro 1941-
Colombian poet Pizarro has written *Aquí beso yo, Labio adicto,* and the bilingual volume *Sombraventadorañ Shadowinner.*

Elena Poniatowska 1933-
Poniatowska, a respected journalist who has contributed to several of Mexico's finest newspapers, has also written many books of fiction and nonfiction.

Portillo, José López
See López Portillo, José

Estela Portillo Trambley 1936-
Portillo Trambley is a Chicana playwright and fiction writer whose works express feminist, ethnic, and non-political themes.

Renato Prada Oropeza 1937-
The award-winning novel *Los fundadores del alba,* a character study of the Latin American guerilla, is Prada Oropeza's best-known work.

Pedro Prado 1886-1952
Prado's innovations in free verse and prose poetry opened up Chilean literature to experimentation, influencing Nobel winners Pablo Neruda and Gabriela Mistral.

Manuel Puig 1932-
An exile from his native Argentina, Puig produces novels such as *The Kiss of the Spider Woman* that are funny, ironic, and serious in their indictment of modern society.

Anthony Quinn 1915-
Quinn is an Academy Award-winning actor, an artist, and a writer who describes his life and career in a 1972 autobiography *The Original Sin.*

Leroy V. Quintana 1944-
Quintana won the American Book Award in 1982 for his collection of poems, *Sangre* ("Blood"). His other collections include *The Reason People Don't Like Mexicans.*

José Quintero 1924-
Panamanian-born Quintero gained renown in the U.S. as a director of plays by Eugene O'Neill. His memoirs, *If You Don't Dance They Beat You,* were published in 1974.

Jacinto Quirarte 1931-
Quirarte is an American professor and scholar who specializes in Chicano and Hispanic-American art.

Horacio Quiroga 1878-1937
A short story master, Quiroga described violence and death in Argentina's Misiones jungle in collections such as *South American Jungle Tales.*

Gregory Rabassa 1922-
Rabassa's translations of novels by Cortázar, García Márquez, and other Latin American writers has brought world-wide attention to the region's fiction.

Susan E. Ramirez 1946-
A professor of history, Ramirez has written acclaimed books on colonial Spanish America.

Diana Ramírez de Arellano 1919-
This highly acclaimed poet and educator, the daughter of a Puerto Rican journalist, became Puerto Rico's poet laureate in 1958.

Rafael W. Ramírez de Arellano 1884-
This Puerto Rican historian and educator founded the University of Puerto Rico's Historical Museum.

John Rechy 1934-
Of Scottish-Mexican descent, Rechy is best known for his novel *City of Night,* published in 1963 and now regarded as a modern classic.

Mercedes Rein
Rein has written several books of criticism on Hispanic literature.

Alfonso Reyes 1889-1959
Reyes is a distinguished Hispanic writer of poetry, fiction, and a wide range of nonfiction.

Carlos José Reyes 1941-
Columbian playwright Reyes has written such dramas as *Soldados, La piedra de la felicidad,* and *Dulcita y el burrito.*

Carlos Reyles 1868-1938
Reyles was an Uruguayan novelist who wrote *Beba, La raza de Caín, El gaucho Florido,* and *El embrujo de Sevilla,* translated as *Castanets.*

Evaristo Ribera Chevremont 1896-1976
Credited with introducing European innovations into Puerto Rican poetry, Ribera Chevremont spread enthusiasm for new poetic forms through the newspaper La Democracia.

Ríos, Isabella
See López, Diana

Geraldo Rivera 1943-
Host of the syndicated "Geraldo" television show, Rivera is one of the most recognized broadcast journalists in the United States.

José Eustasio Rivera 1889-1928
A lawyer and writer, Rivera is remembered for his novel, *The Vortex,* which is considered a masterpiece.

Tomás Rivera 1935-1984
Poet and novelist Rivera's early experiences as a migrant laborer became important to his work.

Augusto Roa Bastos 1917-
Roa Bastos, an esteemed Paraguayan author best known for his 1974 novel *Yo el supremo,* ended his exile in 1989 after the toppling of the Stroessner regime.

Mireya Robles 1934-
A prize-winning poet and essayist, Cuban-born Robles has been an educator and a spokesperson for Chicano women writers.

Richard Rodriguez 1944-
Rodriguez's 1982 autobiography *Hunger of Memory* excited praise and criticism for its negative views of affirmative action and bilingual education.

Hugo Rodríguez-Alcalá 1917-
Rodríguez-Alcalá is a Paraguayan-American poet and scholar whose works include the study *El arte de Juan Rulfo* and the verse collection *Palabras de los días.*

Emir Rodríguez Monegal 1921-1985
Rodríguez Monegal was a prolific writer whose canon includes several volumes of criticism on contemporary Hispanic writers.

Jaime E. Rodríguez Ordonez 1940-
Rodríguez Ordonez is an Ecuadorean-American historian who specializes in studies of the transformation of Latin America from colonialism to independence.

Arnold R. Rojas 1896(?)-1988
A former *vaquero,* Rojas chronicled the life and lore of these cowboys in regional classics such as *California Vaquero* and *Last of the Vaqueros.*

Guillermo Rojas 1938-
Rojas has written many articles, book reviews, and stories for a variety of periodicals. He edited *Chicano Studies: Nuevos Horizontes* in 1988.

Manuel Rojas 1896-1973
Argentine Rojas won acclaim for his verse and short stories, as well as for the novels *La ciudad de las césares* and *Mejor que el vino.*

Octavio I. Romano 1932-
Author, poet, editor, and social scientist, Romano has served as head of the publishing firm Tonatiuh-Quinto Sol International in Berkeley, California.

José Rubén Romero 1890-1952
Ambassador, political advisor, and novelist Romero penned *The Futile Life of Pito Pérez,* a best-seller in Mexico for over twenty-five years.

Orlando Romero 1945-
Of Hispanic and Indian descent, Romero's family has lived in Nambé, New Mexico, for three generations.

Francisco A. Rosales 1942-
Rosales is an American educator whose works include *Hispanics and the Humanities in the Southwest* and *Houston: A Twentieth Century Urban Frontier.*

Cesáreo Rosa-Nieves 1901-1974
A versatile Puerto Rican writer, Rosa-Nieves was an active participant in such literary movements as Noismo, Vanguardismo, Criollismo, and Ensueñismo.

María del Rosario Green 1941-
Rosario Green, a professor of economics and social studies, has written several books on international economics.

Ramón Eduardo Ruiz 1921-
Ruiz is a historian whose studies of the Cuban and Mexican revolutions correct previous misconceptions and provide important insights on current events.

Juan Rulfo 1918-1986
Although he produced only two books of importance, Mexican writer Rulfo was one of the most celebrated practitioners of the magic realism genre.

Ernesto Sábato 1911-
Sábato is best known for his novels, surreal looks at Argentine life, and his essays, critical views of that country's military strongmen.

Jaime Sabines 1925(?)-
Mexican poet Sabines often explores the theme of rural immigrants whose innocence is threatened by the violence and uproar of Mexico City.

Dalmiro A. Sáenz 1926-
Argentine writer Sáenz writes of the spiritual and moral struggles facing humankind in a violent world in works such as *Setenta veces siete.*

Jim Sagel 1947-
Descended from a Russian family, Sagel writes about the Chicanos of northern New Mexico, where he has lived since 1969.

Gustavo Sainz 1940-
Sainz is a best-selling Mexican novelist whose translated works include *Gazapo* and *The Princess of the Iron Palace,* both set in present-day Mexico City.

Floyd Salas 1931-
In and out of jail during adolescence and early adulthood, Salas has since forged a career as a creative writing instructor and author.

Sebastián Salazar Bondy 1924-1965
Peruvian playwright, poet, essayist, and critic, Salazar Bondy wrote *Lima, la Horrible,* a depiction of his nation's capital as a city of poverty and shantytowns.

Luis Omar Salinas 1937-
An American poet of Mexican descent, Salinas is known for his surrealistic vision. His works include *Crazy Gypsy* and *The Sadness of Days.*

Julian Samora 1920-
Samora is professor of sociology whose scholarly works include *Los Mojados: The Wetback Story* and *Gunpowder Justice: A Reassessment of the Texas Rangers.*

Florencio Sánchez 1875-1910
Sánchez was a notable Uruguayan playwright whose realistic works include *La gringa* and *Barranca abajo.*

George I. Sanchez 1906-1972
Sanchez, a professor of Latin American education, wrote *Forgotten People,* a historical and sociological study of the Hispanic community of New Mexico.

Luis Rafael Sánchez 1936-
Puerto Rican Sánchez is best known for his plays "The Passion of Antígona Pérez," "Almost the Soul," "Quintuplets," and for his novel *Macho Camacho's Beat.*

Sánchez, Oscar Arias
See Arias Sánchez, Oscar

Ricardo Sánchez 1941-
Sánchez sharply criticizes racism in the United States in writings, including *Canto y grito mi liberación* and *Hechizospells.*

Thomas Sanchez 1944-
Native Californian Sanchez has written several novels, including *Mile Zero,* which are marked by a poetic vision that encompasses larger issues such as racial oppression.

Virginia Sanchez-Korrol
Sanchez-Korrol is a professor of Puerto Rican Studies and has written on the struggles of Puerto Ricans living in the United States.

Milcha Sanchez-Scott
Sanchez-Scott is an American playwright associated with the Latino Theater Lab of the Los Angeles Theater Center.

Nicomedes Santa Cruz 1925-
Santa Cruz is an Afro-Peruvian poet whose rhythmic poems celebrate the black experience in Latin America and promote human rights and brotherhood.

Severo Sarduy 1937-
Sarduy, a noted Cuban fiction writer and literary critic, is best-known for the experimental novel *Cobra,* for which he received the French Prix Medicis.

Carlos Saura 1932-
Saura is considered one of the most talented Spanish filmmakers of a generation which grew up under Franco's dictatorship.

Isabel Schon 1940-
This Mexican-American professor of library science has published several studies of children's literature in Spanish.

Manuel Scorza 1928-1983
Exiled Peruvian Scorza wrote "La guerra silenciosa" series, a mix of history and fantasy that depicts the struggle between the Creoles and the Indians of Peru.

Chester E. Seltzer 1915-1971
Seltzer wrote short fiction under the pseudonym Amado Muro. Though not Hispanic himself, his stories capture the essence of Mexican culture.

Ramón J. Sender 1902-1982
Sender, known for his intense, realistic technique and socially compassionate style, was one of the few contemporary Spanish novelists of his time who achieved world-wide recognition.

Ramón Sender Barayón 1934-
Sender Barayón, the son of Spanish novelist Ramón J. Sender, wrote *A Death in Zamora,* the tale of his mother's execution during the Spanish Civil War.

Setien, Miguel Delibes
See Delibes Setien, Miguel

Beverly Silva 1935-
An author of poetry and fiction that reflects minority and women's issues, Silva has also co-edited the collection *Nosotras: Latina Literature Today.*

Antonio Skármeta 1940-
A Chilean author living in exile in Germany, Skármeta writes novels, short stories, and screenplays that reveal the sociopolitical turmoil in his native land.

Carlos Solórzano 1922-
Solórzano is a Mexican playwright, novelist, essayist and the former director of Mexico's National Theatre.

Roberto Sosa 1930-
Sosa is a leading Honduran poet and cultural leader whose work has been banned by the Honduran government.

Gary Soto 1952-
Soto's poetry and prose memoirs reflect his working-class Mexican-American background and have been praised for their structure and overall coherence.

Pedro Juan Soto 1928-
Puerto Rican journalist and professor Soto has written a play that was produced on NBC-TV, as well as short stories and novels.

Shirlene A. Soto 1947-
Soto is an American educator whose writings include *The Mexican Woman* and *The Emergence of the Modern Mexican Woman, 1910-1940.*

Raymond D. Souza 1936-
Souza, a professor of Spanish, has written *Major Cuban Novelists: Innovation and Tradition.*

Luis Spota 1925-1985
Spota was one of Mexico's most popular novelists for works such as *The Wounds of Hunger, Almost Paradise* and *The Cat's Laugh.*

Alfonsina Storni 1892-1938
One Argentina's first feminists, Storni is best known for her books of poetry, including *Languidez, Mundo de siete pozos,* and *Mascarilla y trébol.*

Virgil Suarez 1962-
Born in Cuba, Suarez immigrated to the United States with his family at the age of eight. His first novel, *Latin Jazz,* was published in 1989.

Guillermo Sucre 1933-
Sucre is a Venezuelan literary critic and poet.

Carmen Tafolla 1951-
Tafollo has earned critical praise for her poems about the people of the barrio.

Paco Ignacio Taibo II 1949-
President of the International Association of Crime Writers, Mexican author Taibo has written numerous tales of mystery in addition to several volumes of history.

Piri Thomas 1928-
Thomas, a Negrito of black and Puerto Rican ancestry, is noted for his three autobiographies—*Down These Mean Streets; Saviour, Saviour, Hold My Hand;* and *Seven Long Times.*

Jacobo Timerman 1923-
Timerman is the author of *Prisoner without a Name, Cell without a Number,* an account of his imprisonment and torture for promoting human rights in Argentina.

Aurelio Tío 1907-
Tío is a Puerto Rican historian who is known for his research into the early history of his native country.

José Acosta Torres 1925-
This Chicano educator and writer of short stories has also founded classes in citizenship and arts and crafts for members of the Mexican-American community.

Jaime Torres Bodet 1902-1974
An accomplished Mexican statesman, writer, and educator, Torres Bodet was director-general of UNESCO and in 1966 received Mexico's National Prize for Literature.

Arnulfo D. Trejo 1922-
Trejo's reference works on Chicano librarians and scholars are important contributions to a field previously described only by Anglo observers.

José Triana 1932(?)-
One of Latin America's most promising young dramatists in the 1960s, Triana wrote the award-winning *La noche de los asesinos (The Criminals).*

Sabine R. Ulibarrí 1919-
Acclaimed author and educator Ulibarrí writes poetry and short stories which depict the culture and history of his native New Mexico.

Luz María Umpierre 1947-
A Puerto Rican-born scholar and poet who teaches in the U.S., Umpierre is interested in Puerto Rican literature, women writers, and gay and lesbian writing.

Miguel de Unamuno 1864-1936
Considered by some the leading thinker of Spain's "Generation of 1898," Unamuno was a prolific writer of poetry, fiction, drama, and essays.

David Unger 1950-
Co-director of the Latin American Writers Institute and Book Fair, Guatemalan-born Ungar is the author of translations and a volume of poetry.

Alberto H. Urista 1947-
Considered the poet laureate of the Chicanos, Urista, who writes under the pseudonym Alurista, often composes poems that mix Spanish, English, and other dialects.

Rodolfo Usigli 1905-1979
Considered one of the founders of modern Mexican drama, Usigli is most widely known for a series of plays, including *El gesticulador* ("The Imposter").

Arturo Uslar Pietri 1906-
Uslar Pietri, who was active in Venezuelan politics, is known for poetic and vivid historical novels such as *The Red Lances,* a South American literary classic.

Luis Valdez 1940-
Valdez's credits as both writer and director include the plays "Dark Root of a Scream" and "Zoot Suit," as well as the movie "La Bamba."

Luisa Valenzuela 1938-
Valenzuela depicts the madness of Argentine politics in her technically complex novels and short stories, including *Strange Things Happen Here* and *A Lizard's Tale.*

Vallejo, Antonio Buero
See Buero Vallejo, Antonio

César Vallejo 1892-1938
A Peruvian expatriate hailed as one of Latin America's best poets, Vallejo forged a unique language in response to the suffering he saw around him and endured himself.

Alejandro Varderi 1960-
A Venezuelan of Catalan descent, Varderi is the author of essays, stories, and novels.

Mario Vargas Llosa 1936-
Peru's most prominent novellist for works such as *The War of the End of the World,* Vargas Llosa was the losing candidate in his country's 1990 presidential election.

Richard Vásquez 1928-
Vásquez is the author of *Chicano,* a 1970 best-selling novel often used in high school and college Chicano literature courses.

José Vázquez Amaral 1913-1987
Vázquez Amaral was a noted translator of American poetry into Spanish, especially that of Walt Whitman and Ezra Pound.

Carlos G. Velez-Ibanez 1936-
Velez-Ibanez, a professor of anthropology, has written on cultural, anthropological, and ethnographical issues in relation to the Mexican and Chicano peoples.

Marcio E. Veloz Maggiolo 1936-
A respected anthropologist in the Dominican Republic, Veloz Maggiolo has also published novels of Dominican history.

Bernardo Verbitsky 1907-
Argentine writer Verbitsky's novels of social realism tell of Jewish life in modern South America, focusing in particular on life in the slums of Buenos Aires.

Javier de Viana 1868-1926
Uruguayan writer Viana's realistic tales of hard-living gauchos were successful in debunking earlier romantic notions of them.

Idea Vilariño 1920-
Vilariño is an Uruguayan poet whose work belongs to the tradition erotic poetry cultivated by Delmira Agustini and Gabriela Mistral.

Alma Luz Villanueva 1944-
An acclaimed Chicana poet, Villanueva often writes of the search for personal and female identity within the confines of modern culture.

Tino Villanueva 1941-
A poet, short story writer, and critic, Villanueva first gained recognition for *Hay otra voz Poemas,* poems combining social realism and poetic imagery.

José Antonio Villarreal 1924-
Through his book *Pocho*—widely acknowledged as the forerunner of the "Chicano" novel—Villarreal explores various aspects of the Mexican-American experience.

Víctor E. Villaseñor 1940-
Villaseñor, a Chicano author, has written the coming-of-age novel *Macho!* and *Jury: The People vs. Juan Corona,* a nonfiction work exploring the American justice system.

Xavier Villaurrutia 1903-1950
Villaurrutia's poetry, especially *Nostalgia de la muerte,* and his stage plays helped establish him as an important figure among the Mexican literati of the 1920s and '30s.

David Viñas 1929(?)-
Viñas is an award-winning writer whose novels, including *Cayó sobre su rosto* and *Un dios cotidiano,* reflect the political and social turmoil of Argentina.

Cynthio Vitier 1921-
Vitier, who writes as Cintio Vitier, is considered one of the most important literary critics and anthologists in Cuba today.

Egon Wolff 1926-
Wolff, a Chilean playwright, is the author of *Ninamadre, Los invasors, Paper Flowers: A Play in Six Scenes,* and "Discípulos del miedo."

Agustín Yáñez 1904-1980
An esteemed Mexican public servant, educator, and writer, Yáñez is best known for the novel *The Edge of the Storm,* regarded as a classic in Mexican literature.

José Yglesias 1919-
A bilingual American of Cuban and Spanish descent, José Yglesias is a respected novelist and author of short stories and works of nonfiction.

Bernice Zamora 1938-
Feminist poet Zamora cares about reinterpreting relationships, whether they are sexual or racial.

Manuel Zapata Olivella 1920-
Colombian physician and psychiatrist Zapata Olivaeea is known for advocating freedom from repression for blacks and other races in his novels, plays, and short stories.

Iris M. Zavala 1936-
Zavala is a Puerto Rican-born scholar, poet, and author
of novellas, who holds the chair of Hispanic literatures
at Rijksuniversiteit Utrecht in the Netherlands.

Raúl Zurita 1951-
Chilean poet Zurita's works reflect his experience of
the American-supported military coup in Chile in
1973.

Hispanic Writers

ACOSTA, Oscar Zeta 1935(?)-

PERSONAL: Born April 8, c. 1935.

CAREER: Worked as an attorney in late 1960s; writer.

WRITINGS:

The Autobiography of a Brown Buffalo (novel), Straight Arrow Books, 1972.
The Revolt of the Cockroach People (novel), Straight Arrow Books, 1973.

Work anthologized in *Voices of Aztlán: Chicano Literature of Today,* edited by Dorothy E. Harth and Lewis M. Baldwin, Mentor, 1974. Contributor to periodicals, including *Con Safos.*

SIDELIGHTS: Oscar Zeta Acosta is a curious figure in Hispanic literature. After financing his own law-school education, he began working as an attorney in the late 1960s and became known for his successful defenses of Chicanos in cases involving discrimination. He published his first novel, *The Autobiography of a Brown Buffalo,* in 1972. This fictionalized account of Acosta's own turbulent life—which involved drug abuse, alcoholism, and poverty—prompted comparisons to Henry Miller and Jack Kerouac, other writers who had similarly mined their own experiences in books at once both impressive and provocative. Acosta ended his first book by renouncing drugs and alcohol and exploring his Mexican roots. In his second novel, *The Revolt of the Cockroach People,* Acosta resumes his tale and relates the more volatile aspects of life among Hispanics in late 1960s Los Angeles. Here protagonist Buffalo Zeta Brown succumbs to madness after discovering that fellow Hispanics have betrayed their own people by becoming police informers.

The Revolt of the Cockroach People, which appeared in 1973, is Acosta's most recent book. In the early 1970s he vanished in Mexico and has yet to reappear.

BIOGRAPHICAL/CRITICAL SOURCES:

BOOKS

Dictionary of Literary Biography, Volume 82: *Chicano Writers, First Series,* Gale, 1989.
Simmen, Edward, *The Chicano: From Caricature to Self-Portrait,* Mentor, 1971.

PERIODICALS

Denver Quarterly, fall, 1981.
Explorations in Ethnic Studies, July, 1981.
Journal of General Education, Volume 35, number 4, 1984.
Latin-American Literary Review, spring-summer, 1977.
Nation, April 13, 1974.
Rolling Stone, December, 1977.
Saturday Review, December, 1972.

*   *   *

ACUÑA, Rodolfo
See ACUÑA, Rodolfo F(rancis)

*   *   *

ACUÑA, Rodolfo F(rancis) 1932-
(Rodolfo Acuña, Rudy Acuña)

PERSONAL: Born May 18, 1932, in Los Angeles, Calif.; son of Francisco and Alicía (Elías) Acuna; married Guadalupe Compean, 1984; children: (former marriage) Frank, Walter; Angela. *Education:* California State University, Los Angeles, B.A. (social science), 1957, B.A. (general), 1958, M.A., 1962; University of Southern California, Ph.D., 1968. *Politics:* "Radical." *Religion:* Catholic.

ADDRESSES: Office—Department of Chicano Studies, California State University, Northridge, 18111 Nordhoff St., Northridge, Calif. 91324.

CAREER: Worked as columnist for the *Los Angeles Herald-Examiner;* California State University, Northridge, professor of Chicano Studies, 1969—. Member of board of Labor/Community Strategy Center; member of Committee in Solidarity With the People of El Salvador.

AWARDS, HONORS: Community service award from Liberty Hill Foundation; Rockefeller Humanities fellowship; Ford grant; outstanding scholar awards from American Council of Learned Societies and National Association of Chicano Studies; award from University of Guadalajara/state of Jalisco (Mexico) for contributions to border research.

WRITINGS:

(Under name Rudy Acuña) *The Story of the Mexican Americans: The Men and the Land,* American Book Co., 1969.

(With Peggy Shackelton, under name Rudy Acuña) *Cultures in Conflict: Problems of the Mexican Americans* (children's textbook), Charter School Books, 1970.

(Under name Rudy Acuña) *A Mexican-American Chronicle,* American Book Co., 1971.

(Under name Rodolfo Acuña) *Occupied America: The Chicano's Struggle Toward Liberation,* Canfield Press, 1972, 3rd edition, Harper, 1987.

Sonoran Strongman: Ignacio Pesquiera and His Times, University of Arizona Press, 1974.

A Community under Siege: A Chronicle of Chicanos East of the Los Angeles River, 1945-1975, University of California, Los Angeles, Chicano Studies Research Center, 1984.

Contributor to periodicals, including *Arizona and the West, Los Angeles Times,* and *Texas Observer,* and to the Pacific News Service.

WORK IN PROGRESS: A collection of previously published newspaper essays on Los Angeles in the 1980s; *When the Moment Comes: The Revolt of the Mexican Cotton Pickers, 1933.*

SIDELIGHTS: Professor of Chicano studies at the University of California, Northridge, Rodolfo F. Acuña is the author of several books and textbooks on Chicano and Mexican history. He is perhaps best known for *Occupied America: The Chicano's Struggle Toward Liberation,* a historical study in which he argues that the United States's acquisition of the Southwest from Mexico was an act of imperialism. Referring to the Chicano population in the United States as an "internal colony," Acuña contends that Mexican Americans continue to suffer the effects of economic exploitation and racism perpetrated upon them by an Anglo majority. "My purpose is to bring about an awareness . . . of the forces that control and manipulate seven million people in this country," he notes in the book. "If Chicanos can become aware of *why* they are oppressed and *how* the exploitation is perpetuated, they can work more effectively toward ending their colonization." Acuña told *CA* that in later editions of *Occupied America* he "broke with the internal colonial model, giving a more materialist interpretation."

Occupied America elicited contrasting responses from reviewers. Some critics found the book lacking in objectivity, while others appreciated the book's challenge to traditional historical interpretations of the Chicano experience. Writing in the *Western Historical Quarterly,* Victor C. Dahl, for example, called the work "an angry polemic," and charged that it "abounds with generalizations defying either substantiation or refutation." On the other hand, Robert W. Blew's *Southern California Quarterly* review of *Occupied America* praised the study's scholarly content and found it to contain "an intimacy and vigor that is frequently lacking in secondary studies." Blew declared that Acuña "has presented a provocative, stimulating, and challenging interpretation and view of the history of the southwestern portion of the United States." Similarly impressed were Carrol Hernandez and Nathaniel N. Wagner, who concluded in the *International Migration Review* that while Acuña's perspective may be unpopular, he "is trying to rectify myths and distortions that came about as a result of the 'objective academic' writing of past American historians."

BIOGRAPHICAL/CRITICAL SOURCES:

BOOKS

Acuña, Rodolfo, *Occupied America: The Chicano's Struggle Toward Liberation,* Canfield Press, 1982.
Contemporary Literary Criticism, Volume 2, Gale, 1974.

PERIODICALS

International Migration Review, Volume 7, number 4, 1973.
Los Angeles Times Book Review, January 20, 1985.
Southern California Quarterly, fall, 1973.
Western Historical Quarterly, July, 1973.

*   *   *

ACUÑA, Rudy
See ACUÑA, Rodolfo F(rancis)

*   *   *

ADAME, Leonard 1947-

PERSONAL: Born September 2, 1947, in Fresno, Calif. *Education:* California State University, Fresno, B.A., M.A.

ADDRESSES: Home—Fresno, Calif.

CAREER: Poet. Former instructor, La Raza Studies Department, California State University, Fresno.

WRITINGS:

(Contributor) Luis Omar Salinas and Lillian Faderman, editors, *From the Barrio: Chicano Anthology,* Canfield (San Francisco, Calif.), 1973.

(Contributor) *Entrance: Four Chicano Poets,* Greenfield Review (Greenfield Center, N.Y.), 1975.

(Contributor) Faderman and Barbara Bradshaw, editors, *Speaking for Ourselves: American Ethnic Writing,* Scott, Foresman, 1975.

Cantos pa' la memoria (title means "Songs for Memory"), Mango Publications (San Jose, Calif.), 1979.

(Contributor) Toni Empringham, editor, *Fiesta in Aztlán: An Anthology of Chicano Poetry,* Capra, 1981.

(Contributor) Laurence Perrine, editor, *Literature, Structure, Sound and Sense,* 4th edition, Harcourt, 1983.

(Contributor) Jon Veinberg and Ernesto Trejo, editors, *Piecework: Nineteen Fresno Poets,* Silver Skates (Albany, Calif.), 1987.

Contributor to periodicals, including *American Poetry Review, Backwash, Greenfield Review, Oyez Review,* and *Revista Chicano-Riqueña.*

BIOGRAPHICAL/CRITICAL SOURCES:

BOOKS

Dictionary of Literary Biography, Volume 82: *Chicano Writers, First Series,* Gale, 1989.
Veinberg, Jon, and Ernesto Trejo, editors, *Piecework: Nineteen Fresno Poets* (contains interview), Silver Skates, 1987.

*   *   *

ADOUM, Jorge Enrique 1926-

ADDRESSES: Home—Paris, France.

CAREER: Writer. Worked as director of Casa de la Cultura Ecuatoriana (publishers), national director of Ecuadorian culture, and secretary of Institute of Theatre and Folklore in Ecuador.

AWARDS, HONORS: Ecuadorian National Prize for Poetry, for *El enemigo y la mañana;* Poetry prize from Casa de las Américas, for *Dios trajo la sombra.*

WRITINGS:

Poderes; o, El libro que divinizia, Editorial Fernández, 1940.
Las llaves del reino, Quito, 1942.
Ecuador amargo (verse), Casa de la Cultura Ecuatoriana, 1949.
Los cuadernos de la tierra (verse; includes "Los orígenes" and "El enemigo y la mañana"), Casa de la Cultura Ecuatoriana, 1952, revised edition (includes Dios trajo la sombra and Eldorado y las occupaciones nocturnas; also see below), Editorial Casa de la Cultura Ecuatoriana, 1963.
Poesía del siglo XX: Rilke, Claudel, Lubicz-Milosz, Hughes, Eliot, Nicolás, Guillén, Maiacovski, García Lorca, Vallejo, Hikmet, Neruda (criticism), Editorial Casa de la Cultura Ecuatoriana, 1957.
(Editor) José de la Cuadra, Obras completas, Editorial Casa de la Cultura Ecuatoriana, 1958.
Dios trajo la sombra (verse), Casa de la Cultura Ecuatoriana, 1959.
Eldorado y las ocupaciones nocturnas (verse), Editorial Casa de la Cultura Ecuatoriana, 1961.
(Contributor) Paulo de Carvalho Neto, editor, Folklore de Lican y Sicalpa, Casa de la Cultura Ecuatoriana, 1962.
(Editor) José de la Cuadra, Cuentos, Casa de las Américas, 1970.
Do aprendiz e seus mistérios, Editora Pensamento, 1972.
Do companheiro e seus mistérios, Editora Pensamento, 1972.
Esta é a maconario, Editora Pensamento, 1972.
Informe personal sobre la situación, J. Giménez-Arnau, 1973.
Adonai: Novela iniciátes do colegio dos magos, Editora Pensamento, 1973.
As chaves do reino interno; ou, O conhecimento de si mesmo, Editora Pensamento, 1978.
Entre Marx y una mujer desnuda: Texto con personajes, Siglo Veintiuno, 1978.
No son todos los que están, Editorial Seix Barral, 1979.
Teatro, la subida a los infiernos, 1976, Casa de la Cultura Ecuatoriana, 1981.
Ecuador, imágenes de un pretérito presente, Editorial El Conejo, 1981.
La gran literatura ecuatoriana del 30, Editorial El Conejo, 1984.

Also author of Yo me fui por la tierra con tu nombre (verse), Notas del hijo pródigo, and Relato del extranjero (verse).

* * *

AGOSIN, Marjorie 1955-

PERSONAL: Born in 1955 in Bethesda, Md.; daughter of M. and Frida Agosín; married John Wiggins, 1977; children: Joseph Daniel. Education: Indiana State University, Ph.D., 1982.

ADDRESSES: Office—Department of Spanish, Wellesley College, Wellesley, Mass. 02181.

CAREER: Writer; associate professor of Spanish at Wellesley College.

AWARDS, HONORS: Fulbright fellow in Argentina; Good Neighbor Award from the National Association of Christians and Jews.

WRITINGS:

Conchalí (poetry), illustrations by Della Collins Cook, Senda Nueva, 1980.
Las desterradas del paraíso: Protagonistas en la narrativa de María Luisa Bombal, Senda Nueva, 1983.
Brujas y algo más (poetry), Latin American Literary Review Press, 1984, translation by Cola Franzen published in dual-language edition as Witches and Other Things, 1985.

Pablo Neruda, translated by Lorraine Ross, Twayne, 1986.
Silencio e imaginación: Metáforas de la escritura femenina, Katún, 1986.
Hogueras (poetry), Universitaria, 1986.
(Editor and contributor with Elena Gascón-Vera and Joy Renjilian-Burgy) María Luisa Bombal: Apreciaciones críticas, Bilingüe, 1987.
Scraps of Life, the Chilean Arpilleras: Chilean Women and the Pinochet Dictatorship, translated by Franzen, Red Sea Press, 1987.
Women of Smoke, translated by Naomi Lindstrom, edited by Yvette E. Miller, Latin American Literary Review Press, 1988, published as Mujeres de humo, 1989.
(With Inés Dolz Blackburn) Violeta Parra, santa de pura greda: Un estudio de su obra poética, Planeta, 1988.
Zones of Pain (poetry), translated by Franzen, White Pine, 1988.
(Editor) Landscapes of a New Land: Fiction by Latin American Women, White Pine, 1989.
Bonfires, Bilingual Review Press, 1990.

Also author of Mothers of Plaza de Mayo.

WORK IN PROGRESS: Sargasso, a book of poetry.

SIDELIGHTS: Marjorie Agosín told CA: "To write is to dare to be vulnerable."

BIOGRAPHICAL/CRITICAL SOURCES:

PERIODICALS

Hispania, March, 1987, September, 1987.
Los Angeles Times Book Review, December 24, 1989.
World Literature Today, winter, 1982.

* * *

AGUILA, Pancho 1945-

PERSONAL: Birth-given name Roberto Ignacio Zelaya, changed in 1968; born September 6, 1945, in Managua, Nicaragua; immigrated to United States, 1947; son of Ignacio and Esperanza (Solis) Zelaya. Education: Studied college courses at Soledad Prison, 1972, and at Folsom Prison College Program, 1975.

ADDRESSES: Home—c/o Esperanza Solis, 3341 18th St., San Francisco, Calif. 94110.

CAREER: Poet. Read poetry at coffeehouses in San Francisco, Calif., until 1968; sentenced to life in prison, 1969, inmate at Folsom Prison, Represa, Calif., 1969-86, escaped from prison and recaptured five months later, 1972. Chairman of writing workshop at Folsom Prison, 1975-77.

WRITINGS:

POETRY, UNLESS OTHERWISE NOTED

Hi-jacked, Twin Window, 1975.
Dark Smoke, Second Coming Press, 1976.
Anti-Gravity, Aldebaran Review, 1976.
The Beast Has Come (prose), Cloud House, 1978.
Clash, Poetry for the People, 1980.

Contributor to periodicals, including Ins and Outs Journal, Haight-Ashbury Literary Quarterly, Kite, Prison Literacy, and Coyote.

WORK IN PROGRESS: First Passage, fifty poems dedicated to the Sandinista cultural cause; Latin American Themes, fifty poems.

SIDELIGHTS: Pancho Aguila once commented: "My writing has been shaped by the rhythms of street life, by the struggles on the Continent of the Americas, and mostly by the world at large, violently born to a new atomic era in 1945. The poetic spirit in me crystalized into the poem in 1967, when I wrote and read in Haight-Ashbury coffeehouses. Since imprisonment in 1969, a fugitive period in 1972, and seven years of solitary units, I've continued to evolve the poetry and consciousness of this art and our planet. This is why I prophesy that as we enter the end of the century a blackness will engulf us, or a brilliant sun of a new horizon. Survival of the planet, of the global civilization, is the historical task. To write is to further the cause of the continuation of new flowers, new heights, new people, a race to civilize technological, destructive madness—the only poem."

* * *

AGUILAR, Ricardo
See AGUILAR MELANTZON, Ricardo

* * *

AGUILAR MELANTZON, Ricardo   1947-
(Ricardo Aguilar)

PERSONAL: Born September 16, 1947, in El Paso, Tex.; son of Lorenzo and Marta Didín (Melantzón) Aguilar; married Rosa María Quevedo, 1967; children: Rosa María, Gabriela. *Education:* University of Texas at El Paso, B.A., 1971, M.A., 1972; University of New Mexico, Ph.D., 1976. *Politics:* "Progresista." *Religion:* Roman Catholic.

ADDRESSES: Home—Ciudad Juárez, Chihuahua, Mexico. *Office*—Department of Languages and Linguistics, University of Texas at El Paso, Box 261, El Paso, Tex. 79968.

CAREER: University of Texas at El Paso, instructor in Spanish, 1974-75; University of Washington, Seattle, lecturer in Chicano studies, 1975-77; University of Texas at El Paso, director of Chicano studies and assistant vice-president for academic affairs, 1977-80, professor of Spanish and creative writing, 1977—.

MEMBER: Association of Teachers of Spanish and Portuguese, Asociación Mexicana de Críticos y del Periodismo.

AWARDS, HONORS: National Research Council/Ford Foundation postdoctoral fellow, 1983; José Fuentes Mares Mexican National Prize for literature from Secretaría de Educación Pública, Programa Cultural Fronterizo, and the Universidad Autónoma de Ciudad Juárez, 1987, for *Madreselvas en flor;* National Endowment for the Arts fellow, 1988.

WRITINGS:

UNDER NAME RICARDO AGUILAR, EXCEPT AS NOTED

Caravana enlutada (poetry), Pájaro Cascabel (Mexico City), 1975.
En son de lluvia (poetry), Inba/Transterra (Mexico City), 1980.
(Editor with Armando Armengol and Oscar U. Somoza) *Palabra nueva: Cuentos chicanos,* Texas Western Press, 1984.
Efraín Huerta, Sainz Luiselli (Mexico City), 1984.
(Editor with Armengol and Sergio D. Elizondo) *Palabra nueva: Poesía chicana,* Dos Pasos, 1985.
(Editor with Armengol and Elizondo) *Palabra nueva: Cuentos chicanos II,* Dos Pasos, 1987.
(Under name Ricardo Aguilar Melantzón) *Madreselvas en flor* (autobiographical narrative), Universidad Veracruzana (Xalapa, Mexico), 1987.
Glosario del caló de Ciudad Juárez, Joint Border Research Institute, New Mexico State University, 1989.

Aurelia, Gobierno del Estado de Querétaro, 1990.
José Fuentes Mares, Universidad Autónoma de Ciudad Juárez, 1990.

Contributor to periodicals, including *Caracol, Cuadernos Americanos, La Semana de Bellas Artes,* and *Revista Chicano-Riqueña.* Editor of Chicano literary journal *Metamórfosis;* member of editorial boards of *Plural de Excélsior* and *Entorno.*

WORK IN PROGRESS: Research on María del Rayo Monteagudo.

SIDELIGHTS: Ricardo Aguilar Melantzón told *Hispanic Writers:* "I think it's important for Chicano literature to have those writers who have not caved in to the 'American' market—in other words, those of us who still continue to write in Spanish—to have the opportunity to be read. Unfortunately, many of us have not been published in the United States or translated into English. Ours may be a different voice, a difficult expression to assimilate at first reading, for we are truly 'bilingual' and 'bicultural' and often express ourselves in various forms of slang. Yet we represent a population, a large community that lives and works close to the border. It has never been very chic, nor is this type of writing valued in many creative writing circles, mainly because those who write in the mainstream have a language block or a cultural one. A colleague once told me that 'good poetry' should be devoid of passion, and that 'good narrative should never be autobiographical' and should never include any words that are not part of the standard language. She was speaking of how literature should tend toward the universal and how the 'regional' was somehow below par. I wonder how she would explain Pablo Neruda's or Gabriel García Márquez's passion and localism, or the early Spanish/Moorish 'Jarchas.' Why should the expression of an eminently plural movement such as ours be constrained to express its most important ideas, feelings, and vision in the language of the colonizer?"

BIOGRAPHICAL/CRITICAL SOURCES:

BOOKS

Chicano Literature: A Reference Guide, Greenwood Press, 1985.
Lomelí, Francisco A., and Donaldo W. Urioste, *Chicano Perspectives in Literature: A Critical and Annotated Bibliography,* Pajarito Publications, 1976.

PERIODICALS

Ahora, August 17, 1987.
Americas Review, summer, 1988.
Cuarto Poder, December, 1989.
Cultura Norte, May, 1988.
El Fronterizo, May 28, 1986, July 27, 1988.
El Popular, July 17, 1986.
El Sol Veracruzano, August 6, 1987.
El Universal, July 4, 1987.
La Jornada, February 16, 1985, May 4, 1985, July 7, 1986.
La Palabra y el Hombre, October, 1987.
Revista de Cultura Mexicana, November, 1987.
Sábado de Uno Más Uno, February 1, 1986.
Siempre!, November 19, 1986.
Vista, October 8, 1988.

* * *

AGUILERA MALTA, Demetrio   1909-1981

PERSONAL: Born May 24, 1909, in Guayaquil, Ecuador; died in 1981; immigrated to Mexico; son of Demetrio and Teresa (Malta) Aguilera; married Velia Márquez Ramos (an actress),

September 17, 1957; children: Ciro, Adda de Manosalvas, Marlene de Davalos. *Education:* Attended the University of Guayaquil, 1928-29.

ADDRESSES: Home—Tercera Pocita 32, Mexico City 17, Mexico.

CAREER: Writer, 1930—. Worked as a newspaper reporter in Guayaquil, Ecuador; held several administrative and diplomatic posts with the government of Ecuador, including undersecretary of education, 1937, charge d'affairs in Chile, 1948, and cultural attache in Brazil, 1949; visiting professor at numerous colleges and universities, including University of Mexico, University of Guatemala, University of Panama, University of Rio de Janeiro, Howard University, Scripps College, and University of California at Irvine.

MEMBER: Latin American Community of Writers, Pan American Union.

AWARDS, HONORS: Literary Merit Medal from the Republic of Ecuador; Cruzeiro do Sul award from Brazil.

WRITINGS:

NOVELS

Don Goyo, Editorial Cenit (Madrid), 1933, translation by John Brushwood and Carolyn Brushwood published as *Don Goyo,* Humana, 1980.

C. Z. (Canal Zone): Los yanquis en Panama, Ediciones Ercilla (Santiago de Chile), 1935.

¡Madrid! Reportaje novelado de una retaguardia heroica (title means "Madrid! Novelized Report on a Heroic Rearguard"), Ediciones Ercilla, 1937.

La isla virgen (title means "The Virgin Isle"), Vera & Cia (Guayaquil), 1942.

Una cruz en la Sierra Maestra (title means "A Cross in the Sierra Maestra"), Editorial Sophos (Buenos Aires), 1960.

La caballeresa del sol: El gran amor de Bolívar, Ediciones Guadarrama (Madrid), 1964, translation by Willis Knapp Jones published as *Manuela,* Southern Illinois University Press, 1967.

El Quijote de El Dorado: Orellana y el río de las Amazonas, (title means "The Quixote of Eldorado: Orellana and the Amazon River"), Ediciones Guadarrama, 1964.

Un nuevo mar para el rey: Balboa, Anayansi, y el Océano Pacífico (title means "A New Sea for the King: Balboa, Anayansi, and the Pacific Ocean"), Ediciones Guadarrama, 1965.

Siete lunas y siete serpientes, Fondo de Cultura Económica (Mexico City), 1970, translation by Gregory Rabassa published as *Seven Moons and Seven Serpents,* University of Texas Press, 1979.

El secuestro del general (title means "The General's Kidnapping"), J. Mortiz (Mexico City), 1973, translation by Peter Earle published as *Babelandia,* Humana, 1985.

Jaguar, Editorial Grijalbo (Mexico City), 1977.

Requiem para el diablo (title means "Requiem for the Devil"), J. Mortiz, 1978.

PLAYS

España leal (three-act; title means "Loyalist Spain"), Talleres Gráficos de Educación (Quito), 1938.

(With Willis Knapp Jones) *Sangre azul* (three-act), Pan American Union (Washington, D.C.), 1948, translation by the authors published simultaneously in English as *Blue Blood.*

El tigre (one-act; title means "The Tiger"; also see below), Editorial Casa de la Cultura Ecuatoriana (Quito), 1956.

Trilogía ecuatoriana: Teatro breve (title means "Ecuadoran Trilogy: Short Plays"; contains "Honoranos" ["Honorariums"], "Dientes Blancos" ["White Teeth"], and "El tigre" ["The Tiger"]), Ediciones de Andrea (Mexico City), 1959.

Infierno negro (two-act; title means "Black Hell"), Universidad Veracruzana (Jalapa, Mexico), 1967.

Teatro completo (title means "Complete Plays"), Finisterre (Mexico City), 1970.

Also author of *Lázaro,* published in *Revista del Colegio Nacional Vicente Rocafuerte,* Volume 18, number 53 (Guayaquil), 1941; *El pirata fantasma* (title means "The Phantom Pirate"), published in *Dos comedias fáciles,* 1950; *Una mujer para cada acto* (title means "A Woman for Each Act"), 1960; and *Muerte, S.A.* (title means "Death, Inc."), 1968.

SHORT STORIES

(With Enrique Gil Gilbert and Joaquin Gallegos Lara) *Los que se van: Cuentos del cholo y del montuvio* (title means "The Ones Who Leave: Stories of the *Cholo* and the Mountain"), Hispanoamérica, Zea y Paladines (Guayaquil), 1930.

(With Manuel Mejía Valera) *El cuento actual latinoamericano* (title means "The Contemporary Latin American Short Story"), Ediciones de Andrea, 1973.

Hechos y leyendas de nuestra América: Relatos hispanoamericanos (title means "Legends and Events of Our America: Stories of Hispanic America"), Departamento del Distrito Federal, Secretaria de Obras y Servicios (Mexico City), 1975.

NONFICTION

Leticia: Notas y comentarios de un periodista ecuatoriano (title means "Leticia: Notes and Commentary by an Ecuadoran Journalist"), Talleres Gráficos Benedetti (Panama City), 1932.

(With Juan Aguilera Malta, Fausto Aguilera Malta, and Fernando Aguilera Malta) *Guayaquil 70: Metrópoli dinámica* (title means "Guayaquil 70: Dynamic City"), Publicaciones Aguilera Malta (Guayaquil), 1970.

Author of short pamphlets on political and historical topics; contributor of articles and stories to newspapers and magazines.

SIDELIGHTS: Ecuadoran novelist and playwright Demetrio Aguilera Malta first attracted notice in 1930 with a collection of short stories he published in the anthology *Los que se van: Cuentos del cholo y del montuvio.* The book, written with Enrique Gil Gilbert and Joaquin Gallegos Lara, was a kind of manifesto for the Grupo de Guayaquil, an assembly of young, socially conscious, realist writers intent on giving voice to the needs and aspirations of the country's neglected *cholos,* or peasants, of Ecuador's Guayas coastal region. Aguilera Malta's stories were acclaimed for their sensitive depiction of an often harsh and violent world, and they prepared the ground for his two major realist novels set in the Guayas region, *Don Goyo* and *La isla virgen.*

The protagonist of *Don Goyo* is a tough old *cholo* patriarch of mixed Spanish and Indian descent. He fights a losing battle with powerful white men whose economic interests threaten to usurp *cholo* land and destroy the natives' harmonious relationship with nature. In death and defeat, Don Goyo takes on a legendary status, symbolizing the fate of the Indian in countless tragedies played out all over the Americas. In *La isla virgen,* set on a coastal island, this epochal conflict takes an unusual twist. Assisted by the powerful jungle and wild animals, the *cholos* succeed in beating back the forces of "progress," proving that the will of the virgin earth is stronger than that of man.

Aguilera Malta's interest in political and social themes is further reflected in his numerous historical novels. ¡Madrid! is a semifictional account of the author's personal experience as a reporter with a Republican unit defending Madrid during the Spanish Civil War. Una cruz en la Sierra Maestro is set during the Cuban Revolution and forms the first volume of Aguilera Malta's "Episodios americanos" series on Latin American historical topics. Other titles in the series include El Quijote de El Dorado and Un nuevo mar para el rey, which imaginatively reconstruct the American adventures of the sixteenth-century Spanish explorers Francisco de Orellana and Vasco Núñez de Balboa, respectively. La caballeresa del sol, Aguilera Malta's most successful historical novel, is a portrait of Manuela Sáenz de Thorne, a little-known military officer, political adviser, and mistress of nineteenth-century Latin American independence leader Simón Bolívar.

Aguilera Malta is also well known in his native country as a playwright whose numerous dramatic works cover a broad thematic and stylistic range. Among his best-received dramas are the realistic tragedy "Lázaro," about an idealistic schoolteacher, and "Infierno negro," a highly expressionistic allegory on the subject of black oppression throughout history. The latter play is structured as a series of flashbacks in the appalling career of the late Horridus Nebus, who tried to solve the "black problem" in the mythical town of Nylonpolis by setting up a factory to make sausage of black flesh. Resurrected after his death and made to stand trial before black survivors, Horridus is condemned to live like his victims as a "wandering Negro" among white people, until such time as a black brotherhood is established. The play's surreal narrative is embellished on the stage with symbolic masks and a liturgical accompaniment of African music mixed with quotes from contemporary poets.

Surrealistic expressionism similarly characterizes Aguilera Malta's later novels, notably Siete lunas y siete serpientes, published in the United States in 1979 as Seven Moons and Seven Serpents. Set in the mythical coastal city of Santorontón in an unnamed South American country, the narrative recalls the cholo-wilderness theme of the author's earliest work generalized into the timeless and universal struggle between the forces of good and evil. Moving back and forth in time, Aguilera Malta depicts the "magical-realist" foundations of the jungle village and the bizarre and complex relationships of its current inhabitants. The book's colorful characters include Father Candido, the village priest; his talkative companion; the Burned Christ, an effigy that occasionally comes down from the cross but refuses to interfere in human affairs; Candido's godson Candelario Mariscal, a marauding colonel with the power to turn himself into a crocodile; Crisóstomo Chalena, a local entrepreneur who makes a pact with the Devil and seizes control of the town's water supply; and the sorcerer's daughter Dominga, who nightly fights with a serpent that threatens her virginity. Aguilera Malta's style mirrors this magical yet sensually concrete world with "rhythmic, onomatopoeic lyricism, earthy dialogue, and stream-of-consciousness technique molded into an admixture of African, Indian, and Christian myths," observed Clementine Rabassa in Books Abroad. The result, concluded Washington Post Book World reviewer Donald Yates, "is a multi-faceted allegory whose final resolution points toward the affirmation of tolerance and forgiveness."

BIOGRAPHICAL/CRITICAL SOURCES:

BOOKS

Luzuriaga, Gerardo Aurelio, Demetrio Aguilera Malta: Dramaturgo, University of Iowa Press (Iowa City), 1970.

PERIODICALS

Books Abroad, spring, 1971.
Hispania, December, 1986.
Latin American Theatre Review, spring, 1970.
Times Literary Supplement, January 11, 1980.
Washington Post Book World, December 23, 1979.
World Literature Today, summer, 1965, spring, 1968, summer, 1979.

* * *

AGUSTINI, Delmira   1886-1914

PERSONAL: Born in 1886 (one source says 1890), in Montevideo, Uruguay; murdered by spouse in 1914.

CAREER: Writer.

WRITINGS:

Los cálices vacíos (verse; includes selections from El libro blanco and Cantos de la mañana; also see below), O. M. Bertani, 1913, reprinted, Centro Editor de América Latina, 1968.
Poesías (verse), Editorial Cervantes, 1923.
Los astros del abismo, M. García, 1924.
El rosario de Eros, M. García, 1924.
Por campos de ensueño, B. Bauzá, 1927.
Poesías (verse), C. García, c. 1940.
Obras poéticas, Talleres Gráficos de Institutos Penales, 1940.
Poesías completas, edited by Alberto Zum Felde, Editorial Losada, 1944, 4th edition, 1971.
Antología, edited by Esther de Cáceres, Ministerio de Instrucción Pública y Previsión Social, 1965.
Correspondencia íntima (correspondence), edited by Sergio Visca, Biblioteca Nacional, Publicaciones del Departamento de Investigaciones (Montevideo), 1969.
Poesías completas, edited by Manuel Alvar, Labor, 1971.
Selección poética, Editorial Kapelusz, 1980.

Also author of El libro blanco (verse), 1907, and Cantos de la mañana (verse), 1910.

BIOGRAPHICAL/CRITICAL SOURCES:

BOOKS

Bonada Amigo, Roberto, Delmira Agustini en la vida y en la poesía, J. Masa, 1964.
Visca, A. S., and others, La poesía de Delmira Agustini, Fundación de Cultura Universitaria, 1968.

PERIODICALS

Américas, January-February, 1987.

* * *

ALAS (y UREÑA), Leopoldo (Enrique García)   1852-1901
(Clarín)

PERSONAL: Born April 25, 1852, in Zamora, Spain; died of tuberculosis, June 13, 1901, in Oviedo, Spain; son of a government official; married Onofre García Argüelles. *Education:* University of Oviedo, B.A., 1869, J.D., 1871; University of Madrid, doctor of laws, 1877.

CAREER: Author and literary critic, 1877-1901; University of Zaragoza, Zaragoza, Spain, professor of political economics, 1882-83; University of Oviedo, Oviedo, Spain, professor of law, 1883-1901.

WRITINGS:

FICTION; UNDER PSEUDONYM CLARIN

Pipá (novella), [Spain], 1879, 3rd edition, published with additional short story, F. Fé, 1886, reprinted, Cátedra, 1982.

La regenta (novel; title means "The Regent's Wife"), [Spain], 1884, reprinted, Cátedra, 1984, translation by John Rutherford published under name Leopoldo Alas as *La regenta,* University of Georgia Press, 1984.

Insolación (novella; title means "Sunshine"), [Spain], 1889.

Su único hijo, F. Fé, 1890, reprinted with introduction and notes by Carolyn Richmond, Espasa-Calpe, 1979, translation by Julie Jones published under name Leopoldo Alas as *His Only Son,* Louisiana State University Press, 1981.

Cuesta abajo (novella; title means "Downhill"), [Spain], 1890, reprinted, Júcar, 1985.

Doña Berta [and] *Cuervo* [and] *Superchería* (novellas), F. Fé, 1892, reprinted, Taurus, 1980.

El señor y lo demás (short stories; title means "The Gentleman and the Rest"), [Spain], 1892, reprinted, Sopena (Buenos Aires), 1941.

Cuentos morales (short stories), [Spain], 1896, reprinted, Mases, 1984, translation by Kenneth A. Stackhouse published as *The Moral Tales,* George Mason University Press, 1988.

El gallo de Sócrates (short stories; title means "Socrates's Rooster"), Maucci, 1901, reprinted, Espasa-Calpe, 1973.

¡Adiós, "Cordera"! y otros cuentos, Tor (Buenos Aires), 1939, reprinted, Escolar, 1983.

Also author of the drama *Teresa,* 1895, published with *Avecilla* and *El hombre de los estrenos,* Castalia, 1975.

CRITICISM; UNDER PSEUDONYM CLARIN

Solos de Clarín, F. Fé, 1881, reprinted, Alianza, 1971.

Folletos literarios (title means "Literary Pamphlets"), F. Fé, 1886-91.

Ensayos y revistas (title means "Essays and Reviews"), M. Fernández y Lasanta, 1892.

Palique (title means "Small Talk"), [Spain], 1893, Labor, 1973.

Also author of *La literatura en 1881,* with Armando Palacio Valdés, 1882; *Sermón perdido,* 1885; *Nueva campaña,* 1887; and *Mezclilla,* 1897.

COLLECTIONS; UNDER PSEUDONYM CLARIN

Obras selectas (selected works), edited by Juan Antonio Cabezas, Biblioteca Nueva, 1947.

Cuentos (includes "El pecado original"), selected by José M. Martínez Cahero, Gráficas Summa, 1953.

Preludios de "Clarín," selected by Jean-Francois Botrel, Diputación de Asturias, Instituto de Estudios Asturianos, 1972.

Obra olvidada: Artículos de crítica (title means "Forgotten Work: Critical Articles"), selected with an introduction by Antonio Ramos-Gascón, Júcar, 1973.

Selección de ensayos (selected essays), Círculo de Amigos de la Historia, 1974.

Treinta relatos (title means "Thirty Stories"), Espasa-Calpe, 1983.

Relatos breves (selected stories), Castalia, 1986.

Essays, criticism, short stories, and novels collected in *Obras completas,* four volumes, 1913-29. Novellas and short stories collected in numerous other editions. Works also published in multi-title volumes.

OTHER

(With Demófilo de Buen and Enrique R. Ramos) *De la usucapión* (legal study), Imprenta Ibérica de E. Maestre, 1916.

La publicidad y los bienes muebles (legal study), Imprenta Ibérica de E. Maestre, 1920.

Leopoldo Alas: Teoría y crítica de la novela española (title means "Leopoldo Alas: Theory and Criticism of the Spanish Novel"), edited by Sergio Beser, Laia, 1972.

SIDELIGHTS: Leopoldo Alas, who wrote under the pseudonym "Clarín" (the Spanish term for "bugle"), is considered one of Spain's greatest modern authors. Celebrated in his own day for his literary criticism, Alas is best known to contemporary readers as the author of *La regenta,* a novel of moral conflict and adultery set in a provincial Spanish town. Alas's fiction, which includes short stories and several novellas, is characterized by sharp social satire, a preoccupation with moral and philosophical doubt, and a virtuosic command of narrative structure. The author's existential pessimism and eye for the comically absurd is popular among modern readers, and new editions and translations of his works have proliferated in recent years.

In an article for *Romanic Review,* Frank Durand observed that Alas's preoccupations as a fiction writer were intimately linked to his critical ethos. As the most influential literary critic of his day, Alas apparently felt an almost messianic calling to raise Spain's cultural level and improve the quality of its literature. Reflecting the country's cultural isolation, political turmoil, and economic stagnation, Spain's literature in the mid-nineteenth century was romantic and sentimental, with little originality. Wielding a pugnaciously sarcastic pen, Alas composed a torrent of criticism attacking writing that, in his opinion, pandered to the forces of ignorance, superstition, and injustice in Spanish society. The critic was especially disdainful of mediocre intellectuals, whom he felt had vulgarized important new ideas. Not surprisingly, Alas's criticism made him many enemies, some of whom exacted their revenge when he later published his own fiction.

Stylistically, Alas was an outspoken partisan of naturalism, the literary movement founded by his great contemporary, French novelist Emile Zola. An outgrowth of positivism—a philosophy which holds that true knowledge is logical, verifiable, and based on information that can be observed by the senses—and scientific determinism, literary naturalism emphasizes detached observation of social reality. Alas embraced naturalism as a potent force for revivifying Spanish literature; he identified his own writings and the works of such realist contemporaries as Benito Pérez Galdós, Armando Palacio Valdés, and Emilia Pardo Bazán with this movement. But, as critic William E. Bull pointed out in *PMLA,* the Spanish version of naturalism was considerably less radical than the French original. Alas, for example, adopted the naturalistic technique of detailed, neutral observation, but he shied away from Zola's frank language and blunt descriptions of unpleasant scenes. Alas and the other Spanish realists also tended to place greater emphasis on free will and individual moral responsibility in their works, while, in the writings of French naturalists, environmental factors usually determined characters' behavior.

Alas's literary intentions are best revealed in his first novel, *La regenta,* a pessimistic satire of decadence in Spain that is generally recognized as his masterpiece. An epic work originally published in two volumes, the novel is set in the provincial town of Vetusta and centers on Ana Ozores, a beautiful and intelligent young woman who is married to a retired judge, Don Víctor Quintanar. An orphan raised indifferently by a pair of spinster aunts, Ana craves intimacy and loving attention but receives little from the kindly but rather detached and self-centered Quintanar, who is many years her senior. She also feels alienated from the gossipy, pettily decadent world of her upper-class acquaintances and yearns for spiritual meaning in her life. The *magistral* Don Fermín de Pas, Vetusta's most powerful Catholic church official, becomes Ana's personal confessor. Himself lonely and loveless, Don Fermín immediately identifies with Ana; despite the fact that he is a priest and she is a married woman, his spiritual affection turns to physical love for her. His desires are even further frustrated by the arrival on the scene of Vetusta's local playboy, Don Alvaro Mesía. Alas masterfully describes Ana's psychological torment as she tries to sublimate her unsatisfied sexual yearnings into spiritual goals, a struggle that ends in disillusionment when she discovers that Don Fermín—her spiritual mentor—loves her as a woman. She surrenders to the persistent and seductive Don Alvaro, setting off a tragic chain of events that ends with her husband's death in a duel and her own public humiliation and abandonment.

Alas sets this personal tragedy in a richly textured social and physical milieu evoked in naturalistic style. Indeed, the narrative spans only thirty-six hours in its first three hundred pages as the author details everyday life in his fictional city, a thinly-disguised surrogate for his hometown of Oviedo. "By that time," remarked a *Times Literary Supplement* reviewer, "we know exactly what it was like to live in Vetusta, with its eternal rain pouring down from leaden skies and its tedious, claustrophobic, small-town life. . . . The dense and massive authenticity of *La regenta* makes it a fascinating social document." Alas spends much of his time satirizing the town's leading citizens, some of whom he sketched so transparently that, upon its initial publication in 1884, the novel scandalized Oviedo. Commenting on the author's portrait of corrupt and hypocritical church officials, gossipy society matrons, conceited and dimwitted young bachelors, and the childishly dogmatic members of the local atheists' club, the *Times Literary Supplement* critic noted: "Alas's dissections of personalities are masterly in their humor, or their cruelty, or, more rarely, in their compassion, and we quickly learn to appreciate his special talent for captivating portrayals of dull and unimaginative people." Alas creates an oppressive social atmosphere in which mediocrity, pretension, hypocrisy and lasciviousness affect all who live in it, even the sensitive and high-minded "la regenta."

Alas's achievement in melding brilliant social satire with deep moral and philosophical questions in a moving tragedy prompted critic Raymond Carr, writing in the *Times Literary Supplement,* to call *La regenta* "the greatest single novel in modern Spanish literature." Critical reaction was generally unfavorable when the novel was first published, perhaps partly to avenge Alas's many attacks on Spanish letters. Pérez Galdós and other prominent writers rose to his defense, however, and *La regenta* sold well before lapsing into relative obscurity in later years. A new generation of critics helped revive the novel in the 1960s and a widely-praised version of the book appeared in English translation in 1984.

Satire is also abundant in Alas's second novel, *Su único hijo* (*His Only Son*), but "it is a softened, more kindly technique of satiric expression than that employed in *La regenta,*" observed Robert Avrett in *Hispania.* Bonifacio Reyes, the novel's protagonist, is a meek and ineffectual man who takes refuge from his shrewish wife, Emma, by playing the flute and daydreaming about a romanticized Spanish past. Passion finally touches him in the person of the singer Serafina, with whom he has an affair that provokes Emma to her own infidelity. Emma becomes pregnant and

bears a son, fulfilling Bonifacio's deep longing to be a father. But the boy's questionable paternity strains Bonifacio's traditional concept of fatherhood. Matured by his ultimate acceptance of the paternal role, he devotes himself to his family with an anguishing but admirable faith. "As in *La regenta,*" Frances Wyers Weber remarked in the *Bulletin of Hispanic Studies,* "the vision that underlies Alas's second novel is the baseness of the material world and the futility of all attempts to escape from it into a purely spiritual realm."

The author's short stories and novellas make similar use of satire to probe moral and philosophical questions. "El pecado original" ("The Original Sin") imagines the discovery of a formula that will allow one man and his progeny to become immortal if the rest of the human race undergoes a painful and costly operation. Don Angel Cuervo, the protagonist of "Cuervo" ("Crow"), thrives on the deaths of others, attending funerals to remind himself of his own good health. In "El caballero de la mesa redonda" ("The Knight of the Round Table"), Don Mamerto Anchoriz charms his friends at a vacation spa with superficial pleasantries until a serious illness leaves him unable to entertain. Abandoned and alone, he reflects bitterly on his own indifferent and egotistical life.

Alas's novella *Superchería* has been cited as a stunning and exemplary philosophical exploration. The work describes the reluctant metamorphosis of Nicolás Serrano, a rigidly rational and skeptical philosopher who initially suffers life as a series of "frauds" but eventually comes to terms with the mysteries and limitations in his own nature and the world around him. Writing in the *Bulletin of Hispanic Studies,* Nicolas G. Round praised "the mature understanding of the possibilities of human character" that makes *Superchería* "the fine story it is; the other features which command respect—philosophical seriousness, psychological finesse, comic vigour, descriptive beauty, range and assurance of tone, skilled and intricate plotting, mastery of the particular form—are all dependent on this initial maturity. It is evidence of the highest artistry that a work successfully embodies in its form what it conveys in its meaning."

BIOGRAPHICAL/CRITICAL SOURCES:

BOOKS

Alas, Leopoldo, *La regenta,* translated by John Rutherford, University of Georgia Press, 1984.
Beser, Sergio, *Leopoldo Alas, crítico literario,* Gredos, 1970.
Brent, Albert, *Leopoldo Alas and "La regenta": A Study in Nineteenth-Century Spanish Prose Fiction,* The Curators of the University of Missouri, 1951.
Rutherford, John, *Leopoldo Alas: "La regenta,"* Grant & Cutler, 1974.
Twentieth Century Literary Criticism, Volume 29, Gale, 1988.
Valis, Noel M., *The Decadent Vision in Leopoldo Alas,* Louisiana State University Press, 1981.
Varela Jácome, Benito, *Leopoldo Alas: "Clarín,"* Edaf, 1980.

PERIODICALS

Bulletin of Hispanic Studies, July, 1966, January, 1970.
Hispania, May, 1924.
Novel: A Forum on Fiction, spring, 1983.
PMLA, June, 1942.
Romanic Review, February, 1965.
Romanische Forschungen, Number 1/2, 1969.
Times Literary Supplement, January 12, 1967, June 1, 1984.

—*Sketch by Curtis Skinner*

ALCAYAGA, Lucila Godoy
  See GODOY ALCAYAGA, Lucila

*   *   *

ALEGRIA, Ciro 1909-1967

PERSONAL: Born November 4, 1909, in Trujillo, Peru; died of a heart attack, February 17, 1967, in Lima, Peru; son of José Alegría Lynch and Herminia Bazán Lynch. *Education:* Attended Colegio Nacional de San Juan, Trujillo, and University of Trujillo.

CAREER: Writer. *El Norte,* Trujillo, Peru, newspaper reporter, 1926-27 and 1930-31; construction worker, 1928-30; joined Aprista Party and participated in 1931 revolt; imprisoned, 1931-33; exiled to Chile, 1934; lived in the United States, 1941-48; teacher at University of Puerto Rico during the 1950s; returned to Peru and joined Acción Popular Party, 1960, serving in Chamber of Deputies, beginning 1963. *Wartime service:* Worked for Office of War Information and Coordinator of Inter-American Affairs, World War II.

AWARDS, HONORS: First prize, Nascimento (publishers) Contest, 1935, for *La serpiente de oro;* first prize, Latin-American Novel Contest, Pan-American Union/Farrar & Rinehart/ *Redbook* Magazine, 1941, for *El mundo es ancho y ajeno.*

WRITINGS:

La serpiente de oro (novel), Nascimento, 1935, translation by Harriet de Onís published as *The Golden Serpent,* Farrar & Rinehart, 1943.
Los perros hambrientes (novel; title means "The Starving Dogs"), Zig-Zag, 1939.
La leyende del nopal (for children), Zig-Zag, 1940.
El mundo es ancho y ajeno (novel), Ercilla, 1941, translation by Onís published as *Broad and Alien Is the World,* Farrar & Rinehart, 1941.
Novelas completas (collected novels), Aguilar, 1959.
Duelo de caballeros; cuentos y relatos (short stories), Populibros Péruanos, 1963.
Panki y el guerrero (for children), [Lima], 1968.
Gabriela Mistral íntima, compiled by Dora Varona, Universo, 1968.
La ofrenda de piedra, compiled by Varona, Universo, 1968.
Sueño y verdad de América, compiled by Varona, Universo, 1969.
Lázaro (novel), Losada, 1973.
La revolución cubana: Un testimonio personal, Peisa, 1973.
Mucha suerte con harto palo: Memorias, edited by Varona, Losada, 1976.
Siete cuentos quirománticos (stories), Varona, 1978.
El dilema de Krause: Penitenciaría de Lima (novel), Varona, 1979.
El sol de los jagurares, Varona, 1979.
Fábulas y leyendas americanas, Espasa-Calpe, 1982.
Relatos (stories), Alianza, 1983.

Contributor of poems and stories to various periodicals in Peru.

SIDELIGHTS: Peruvian Ciro Alegría expressed a concern for the Indians of his native country through his writing and political activity. The son of Spanish-Irish parents, Alegría grew up alongside the Indians of the Marañon River and as a young man became involved in the *Aprista* party, which advocated social and economic reforms, particularly with regard to the country's poorer classes. Alegría's political involvement led to his impris-

onment and eventually his exile to Chile, where he began to write of his boyhood home. In *La serpiente de oro* (translated as *The Golden Serpent*), Alegría related the trials of a tribe of Indians as they "adapt their skills and philosophies to the rough demands of their life," Mildred Adams summarized in the *New York Times.* Carleton Beals, who called *The Golden Serpent* "a strong and beautiful book," noted in his *Book Week* review that Alegría's tale "has the firm texture of things and people loved and understood, and at the same time is epic in its setting and scope."

Alegría was best known, however, for *El mundo es ancho y ajeno,* a book which brought him fame in the United States when it won the Pan American Union's Latin-American Novel Contest. Translated as *Broad and Alien Is the World,* the novel concerns a group of North Andean Indians whose way of life is destroyed when powerful landowners move into the area and exploit the land and local work force. The book was compared to John Steinbeck's *The Grapes of Wrath,* and while *New Yorker* reviewer Clifton Fadiman noted that the book could be termed "a class-warfare novel," he stated that "it is very different from the mechanical mintings of our own early nineteen-thirties. There is more poetry than dogma in it." Milton Rugoff similarly observed the theme of class conflict in *Broad and Alien Is the World,* but noted in *Books* that "what makes it so satisfying . . . is not symbolism, but fullness, authenticity, compassion. . . . Rich and strange, the material almost always justifies itself."

Other reviewers, including Fadiman and *Nation* contributor M. J. Benardete, found *Broad and Alien Is the World* somewhat congested with detail. As Benardete commented, "Story and thesis do not get in each other's way, but the overwhelming regional knowledge of the author considerably retards the flow." Nevertheless, the critic admitted that "the abundance of songs, fables, fairy tales, and legends in the novel gives it a folksy tang which sustains it and makes it a memorable introduction to Peru and the Indians." "The narrative is both easy and intricate," P. M. Jack claimed in his *New York Times* review. "The dozen stories of various village characters are sharply focused in themselves, yet they melt into the total life of the community, which is everything." Jack went on to remark that "it is not enough to say that this is the novel through which every reader will understand something fundamental in South America, though that is true and important; it is a fine work of the imagination." As critic John Dos Passos, one of the Latin-American Novel Contest judges, stated in the committee's citation: "I can say without any hesitation that *El mundo es ancho y ajeno* is one of the most impressive novels I've ever read in Spanish."

BIOGRAPHICAL/CRITICAL SOURCES:

BOOKS

Onís, Harriet de, editor, *The Golden Land,* Knopf, 1948.

PERIODICALS

Books, November 9, 1941.
Book Week, October 31, 1943.
Nation, November 29, 1941.
New Yorker, November 15, 1941.
New York Times, November 16, 1941, October 3, 1943.
New York Times Book Review, March 30, 1941, June 22, 1941.
Saturday Review of Literature, March 29, 1941.

OBITUARIES:

PERIODICALS

New York Times, February 18, 1967.

ALEGRIA, Claribel 1924-

PERSONAL: Born May 12, 1924, in Estelí, Nicaragua; lived in exile with her family in Santa Ana, El Salvador; immigrated to United States, 1943; married Darwin J. Flakoll (a writer), 1947. *Education:* Received B.A. from George Washington University.

ADDRESSES: c/o University of California Press, 2223 Fulton St., Berkeley, Calif. 94720.

CAREER: Poet, novelist, and essayist.

AWARDS, HONORS: Cenizas de Izalco was a finalist in the Seix Barral competition, Barcelona, Spain, 1964; Casa de las Américas poetry award, 1978, for *Sobrevivo.*

WRITINGS:

Anillo de silencio (poetry; also see below), Botas (Mexico), 1948.
Suite (poetry), Brigadas Líricas (Argentina), 1951.
Vigilias (poetry; also see below), Ediciones Poesía de América (Mexico), 1953.
Acuario (poetry; also see below), Editorial Universitaria (Santiago, Chile), 1955.
Tres cuentos (children's stories), illustrations by Agustín Blancovaras, El Salvador Ministerio de Cultura, 1958.
Huésped de mi tiempo (poetry; also see below), Américalee (Buenos Aires, Argentina), 1961.
(Editor and translator with husband, Darwin J. Flakoll) *New Voices of Hispanic America,* Beacon Press, 1962.
Vía única (poetry; title means "One Way"; includes *Auto de fé* and *Comunicación a larga distancia*), Alfa (Montevideo), 1965.
(With Flakoll) *Cenizas de Izalco* (novel), Seix Barral (Barcelona, Spain), 1966, translation by Flakoll published as *Ashes of Izalco,* Curbstone Press/Talman, 1989.
Aprendizaje (includes poetry from *Anillo de silencio, Vigilias, Acuario, Huésped de mi tiempo,* and *Vía única*), Universitaria de El Salvador, 1970.
(Translator with Flakoll) Mario Benedetti, editor, *Unstill Life: An Introduction to the Spanish Poetry of Latin America,* Harcourt, 1970.
Pagaré a cobrar y otros poemas, Ocnos (Barcelona), 1973.
El detén (novel; also see below), Lúmen (Barcelona), 1977.
Sobrevivo (poetry; title means "I Survive"), Casa de las Américas (Cuba), 1978.
(With Flakoll) *La encrucijada salvadoreña* (historical essays), CIDOB (Barcelona), 1980.
(With Flakoll) *Cien poemas de Robert Graves* (anthology), Lúmen, 1981.
Suma y sigue (anthology), Visor (Madrid), 1981.
(With Flakoll) *Nuevas voces de norteamérica* (anthology; parallel text in English and Spanish), Plaza & Janés (Barcelona), 1981.
Flores del volcán/Flowers From the Volcano (anthology; parallel text in English and Spanish), translation by Carolyn Forché, University of Pittsburgh Press, 1982.
(With Flakoll) *Nicaragua: La revolución sandinista; Una crónica política, 1855-1979* (history), Ediciones Era, (Mexico), 1982.
(With Flakoll) *No me agarran viva: La mujer salvadoreña en lucha,* Ediciones Era, 1983.
Poesía viva (anthology), Blackrose Press (London), 1983.
Albúm familiar (novel; title means "Family Album"; also see below), Editorial Universitaria Centroamericana (San Jose, Costa Rica), 1984.
Pueblo de Dios y de mandinga: Con el asesoriamiento científico de Slim (also see below), Ediciones Era, 1985.

Pueblo de Dios y de mandinga (contains *El detén, Albúm familiar,* and *Pueblo de Dios y de mandinga*), Lumén, 1986.
Despierta mi bien despierta, UCA Editores (San Salvador, El Salvador), 1986.
Luisa en el país de la realidad/Luisa in Realityland (parallel text in English and Spanish), translation by Flakoll, Curbstone Press/Talman, 1987.
(Contributor) Doris Meyer, editor, *Lives on the Line: The Testimony of Contemporary Latin American Authors,* University of California Press, 1988.
Mujer del río/Woman of the River (poetry; parallel test in English and Spanish), translation by Flakoll, University of Pittsburgh Press, 1989.

SIDELIGHTS: Claribel Alegría was born in Nicaragua and spent her childhood in exile in El Salvador. Alegría lived in the United States, Mexico, Chile, Uruguay, and Majorca, Spain, before returning to her native Nicaragua upon the victory of the Sandinista Front for National Liberation (FSLN) in 1979. According to Jan Clausen in the *Women's Review of Books,* Alegría represents a writer of "an educated class which is relatively privileged by Central American standards, yet has suffered enough at the hands of repressive oligarchs who represent North American imperial interests to be acutely sensitized to the plight of workers and campesinos." Alegría has been writing poetry since 1948; however, most North American readers were introduced to her writing through *Flowers From the Volcano,* a bilingual collection of poetry drawn from more than two decades of work. Helene J. F. De Aguilar, in a *Parnassus* essay, quotes translator Carolyn Forché from her preface to this collection: "In her poems, we listen to the stark cry of the human spirit, stripped by necessity of its natural lyricism, deprived of the luxuries of cleverness and virtuosity enjoyed by poets of the north." Calling the poems neither easy nor comfortable, a *Publishers Weekly* contributor writes that although the poems "ask us to share the loss of friends and country, to stand witness to torture and violent death," there is a spirit of hope in them as well, "of belief in the power of the word and in the value of one human memory."

Praised for her ability to "speak of political realities with an impassioned objectivity," as a *Library Journal* contributor remarks about *Woman of the River,* Alegría is also lauded for the way in which her "language delights and astounds in its presence as words, sounds, and images," as Sinda Gregory writes in the *American Book Review* about *Luisa in Realityland.* A novel that blends poetry and prose in telling about the coming of age of a young girl in El Salvador, *Luisa in Realityland* "moves the reader through a narrative mixing present with past, dreams with reality, the personal with the political," comments Gregory, concluding that it is a "complexly textured piece of literature which is as concerned with modes of perception as with that which is perceived and just as dependent on the resonance between images as on the images themselves."

BIOGRAPHICAL/CRITICAL SOURCES:

BOOKS

Benedetti, Mario, editor, *Unstill Life: An Introduction to the Spanish Poetry of Latin America,* Harcourt, 1970.
Meyer, Doris, editor, *Lives on the Line: The Testimony of Contemporary Latin American Authors,* University of California Press, 1988.

PERIODICALS

American Book Review, July, 1988.
Library Journal, April 1, 1989.

Los Angeles Times Book Review, November 15, 1987, December 17, 1989.
New Statesman, April 24, 1987.
New York Times Book Review, November 5, 1989.
Parnassus, spring, 1985.
Publishers Weekly, October 22, 1982.
Times Educational Supplement, May 29, 1987.
Women's Review of Books, October, 1984.
World Literature Today, spring, 1988.

* * *

ALEGRIA, Fernando 1918-

PERSONAL: Born September 26, 1918, in Santiago, Chile; son of Santiago Alegría Toro and Julia Alfaro; married Carmen Letona Melendez, January 29, 1943; children: Carmen, Daniel, Andres, Isabel. *Education:* Bowling Green State University, M.A., 1941; University of California, Berkeley, Ph.D., 1947.

ADDRESSES: Home—55 Arlmonte Dr., Berkeley, Calif. 94707. *Office*—Department of Spanish and Portuguese, Stanford University, Stanford, Calif. 94305.

CAREER: University of Chile, Santiago, Chile, professor of Spanish, 1939; Bowling Green State University, Bowling Green, Ohio, Extension Division, instructor in Spanish, 1940-41; University of California, Berkeley, instructor, 1947-49, assistant professor, 1949-55, associate professor, 1955-63, professor of Spanish and Portuguese, 1964-67; Stanford University, Stanford, Calif., professor of Spanish, 1967-87, professor of Portuguese, 1976-87, professor emeritus, 1987—. Consultant in Spanish American literature, UNESCO, 1968. Cultural attaché in Chilean Embassy, Washington, D.C.

MEMBER: Instituto Internacional de Literatura Iberoamericana, American Association of Teachers of Spanish, Sociedad de Escritores (Chile).

AWARDS, HONORS: Latin American Prize of Literature, 1943, for *Lautaro: Joven libertador de Arauco;* Guggenheim fellow, 1947-48; Premio Atenea and Premio Municipal (both Chile), for *Caballo de copas.*

WRITINGS:

Recabarren, Antares, 1938.
Ideas estéticas de la poesía moderna, Multitud, 1939.
Leyenda de la ciudad perdida, Zig-Zag, 1942.
Lautaro: Joven libertador de Arauco (juvenile fiction), Zig-Zag, 1943, 5th edition, 1965.
Ensayo sobre cinco temas de Tomás Mann, Funes, 1949.
Camaleón, Ediapsa, 1951.
La poesía chilena: Orígenes y desarollo del siglo XVI al XIX, University of California Press, 1954.
Walt Whitman en Hispanoamérica, Studium, 1954.
El poeta que se volvió gusano, Cuadernos Americanos, 1956.
Caballo de copas, Zig-Zag, 1957, 2nd edition, 1961, reprinted, Casa de las Américas, 1981, translation by Carlos Lozano published as *My Horse González,* Casa de las Américas, 1964.
Breve historia de la novela hispanoamericana, Studium, 1959, 2nd edition published as *Historia de la novela hispanoamericana,* De Andrea, 1965, published as *Nueva historia de la novela hispanoamericana,* Ediciones del Norte, 1985.
El cataclismo (short stories), Nascimento, 1960.
Las noches del cazador, Zig-Zag, 1961.
Las fronteras del realismo: Literatura chilena del siglo XX, Zig-Zag, 1962, 2nd edition published as *La literatura chilena del siglo XX,* 1967.

(Editor) *Novelistas contemporáneos hispanoamericanos,* Heath, 1964.
Mañana los guerreros (novel), Zig-Zag, 1964.
Viva Chile M!, Editorial Universitaria (Santiago), 1965.
(Editor and translator) Rene Marill, *Historia de la novela moderna,* Union Tipográfica Editorial Hispano Americana, 1966.
Genio y figura de Gabriela Mistral, Editorial Universitaria de Buenos Aires, 1966.
La novela hispanoamericana, siglo XX, Centro Editor de América Latina, 1967.
(Translator with others) Nicanor Parra, *Poems and Antipoems,* edited by Miller Williams, New Directions, 1967.
Los días contados (novel), Siglo XXI, 1968.
Ten Pastoral Psalms (poetry; bilingual edition; English versions by Bernardo Garcia and Matthew Zion), Kayak, 1968.
Como un árbol rojo, Editora Santiago, 1968.
La maratón del Palomo (short stories), Centro Editor de América Latina, 1968.
Los mejores cuentos de Fernando Alegría, edited with prologue by Alfonso Calderón, Zig-Zag, 1968.
La literatura chilena contemporánea, Centro Editor de América Latina, 1969.
Instructions for Undressing the Human Race/Instrucciones para desnudar a la raza humana (poem; bilingual edition; English version by Matthew Zion and Lennart Bruce; also see below), Kayak, 1969.
Amerika (manifiestos de Vietnam), Editorial Universitaria, 1970.
(With others) *Literatura y praxis en América Latina,* Monte Avila Editores, 1974.
Retratos contemporáneos, Harcourt, 1979.
Coral de guerra, Nueva Imagen, 1979.
El paso de los gansos, Laia, 1980.
The Chilean Spring, translated by Stephen Fredman, Latin American Literary Review Press, 1980.
(Contributor of poetry) Moraima de Semprún Donahue, *Figuras y contrafiguras en la poesía de Fernando Alegría,* Latin American Literary Review Press, 1981.
(Author of prologue) Pablo Neruda, *Canto general,* 2nd edition, Biblioteca Ayacucho, 1981.
(Editor and contributor) *Chilean Writers in Exile: Eight Short Novels,* Crossing Press, 1982.
Una especie de memoria, Editorial Nueva Imagen, 1983.
Changing Centuries: Selected Poems of Fernando Alegría (includes selections from *Instrucciones para desnudar a la raza humana*), translated by Stephen Kessler, Latin American Literary Review Press, 1984, 2nd edition, 1988.
Los trapecios, Ediciones Agua Pesada, 1985.
The Funhouse, translated by Kessler, Arte Publica, 1986.

Also author of *La venganza del general, La prensa, Literatura y revolución,* 1970, and *Allende: Mi vecino, el presidente,* 1989, translation published as *Allende: My Neighbor, the President,* 1990.

SIDELIGHTS: "The most distinguished Chilean writer living in the United States," reports Victor Perera in the *Nation,* "is the critic and novelist Fernando Alegría, who was [former Chilean President Salvador] Allende's cultural attaché in Washington." Noted for his important critical works on Latin American literature, his poetry, and his novels, Alegría has been living in exile since a military junta overthrew Allende's government on September 11, 1973. *The Chilean Spring,* Alegría's fictionalized account of a young photographer's ordeal and death at the hands of the junta, is a "tribute to a modestly heroic photographer [that] becomes a poignant elegy to a nation whose future has been taken from it," declares *New York Times Book Review* contributor Jeffrey Burke. "That Mr. Alegría accomplishes so much so effectively in so few pages," Burke continues, "is a remarkable achievement."

BIOGRAPHICAL/CRITICAL SOURCES:

BOOKS

Epple, Juan Armando, *Nos reconoce el tiempo y silba su tonada* (interview), Ediciones LAR, 1987.

PERIODICALS

Books Abroad, winter, 1970.
Carleton Miscellany, Number 3, 1969.
Chicago Review, Number 1, 1968, January/February, 1971.
Nation, February 11, 1978.
New York Times Book Review, May 11, 1980.
Poetry, March, 1970.

* * *

ALEGRIA, Ricardo E(nrique) 1921-

PERSONAL: Born April 14, 1921, in San Juan, P.R.; son of José S. and Celeste (Gallardo) Alegría; married Mela Pons (an artist), December 7, 1947; children: Ricardo, José Francisco. *Education:* University of Puerto Rico, B.A., 1943; University of Chicago, M.A., 1947; Harvard University, graduate study, 1953-55. *Religion:* Roman Catholic.

ADDRESSES: Home—San José 101, San Juan, P.R. 00901. *Office*—Department of History, University of Puerto Rico, Río Piedras, P.R. 00901.

CAREER: University of Puerto Rico, Río Piedras, associate professor of history, 1947-55, professor of anthropology and history, 1955—; director of archaeological museum and research center, 1947-55; Instituto de Cultura Puertorriqueña (Institute of Puerto Rican Culture), San Juan, director, 1955-73. Director, Office of Cultural Affairs, San Juan, 1973-76.

MEMBER: American Anthropological Association (fellow), Society for American Archaeology.

AWARDS, HONORS: Guggenheim Foundation fellow, 1953-55; Doctorate Honoris Causae, humanities, Catholic University (Puerto Rico), 1971; Doctorate Honoris Causae, law, New York University, 1971; National Trust for Historic Preservation award, 1973; Ph.D., University of Puerto Rico, 1974.

WRITINGS:

Historia de nuestros indios, illustrated by wife, Mela Pons de Alegría, Sección de Publicaciones e Impresos, Departamento de Instrucción (San Juan, Puerto Rico), 1950, 8th edition, Colección de Estudios Puertorriqueños (San Juan), 1972, translation by C. Virginia Matters published as *History of the Indians of Puerto Rico,* 1970.
La fiesta de Santiago apóstol en Loíza Aldea, prologue by Fernando Ortiz, Artes Gráficas (Madrid), 1954.
El Instituto de Cultura Puertorriqueña: Los primeros cinco años, 1955-1960, Instituto de Cultura Puertorriqueña (San Juan), 1960.
El tema del café en la literatura puertorriqueña, Instituto de Cultura Puertorriqueña, 1965.
(With others) *Café,* Instituto de Cultura Puertorriqueña, 1967.
(Collector and editor) *Cuentos folklóricos de Puerto Rico,* Editorial El Ateneo (Buenos Aires), 1967.

(Selector and adaptor) *The Three Wishes: A Collection of Puerto Rican Folktales,* translated by Elizabeth Culbert, illustrated by Lorenzo Homar, Harcourt, 1968.
Descubrimiento, conquista y colonización de Puerto Rico, 1493-1599, Colección de Estudios Puertorriqueños, 1969, translation published as *Discovery, Conquest and Colonization of Puerto Rico, 1493-1599,* 1971.
El fuerte de San Jerónimo del Boquerón, Instituto de Cultura Puertorriqueña, 1969.
A History of Our Indians, Urban Media Materials, 1970.
Apuntes en torno a la mitología de los indios taínos de las Antillas Mayores y sus orígenes suramericanos, Centro de Estudios Avanzados de Puerto Rico y el Caribe, Museo del Hombre Dominicano (Santo Domingo, Dominican Republic), 1978.
Las primeras representaciones gráficas del indio americano, 1493-1523, Centro de Estudios Avanzados de Puerto Rico y el Caribe, Instituto de Cultura Puertorriqueña, 1978.
El Instituto de Cultura Puertorriqueña, 1955-1973: Dieciocho años contribuyendo a fortalecer nuestra conciencia nacional, Instituto de Cultura Puertorriqueña, 1978.
Fort of San Jeronimo del Boqueron, Gordon Press, 1979.
Institute of Puerto Rican Culture, Gordon Press, 1979.
Utuado Ceremonial Park, Gordon Press, 1979.
Cristobal Colón y el tesoro de los indios taínos de La Española, Fundación García Arévalo (Santo Domingo), 1980.
El uso de la incrustación en la escultura de los indios antillanos, Centro de Estudios Avanzados de Puerto Rico y el Caribe/ Fundación García Arévalo, 1981.
Las primeras noticias sobre los indios caribes, Editorial Universidad de Puerto Rico/Centro de Estudios Avanzados de Puerto Rico y el Caribe, 1981.
Ball Courts and Ceremonial Plazas in the West Indies, Yale University Publications in Anthropology, 1983.
(With Lucas Morán Arce and others) *Historia de Puerto Rico,* Librotex (San Juan), 1985, 2nd revised and enlarged edition, 1986.

Also author of *Cacicazgo among the Aborigines of the West Indies,* 1947, and *La población aborigen antillana y su relación con otras áreas de América,* 1948. Contributor of articles on archaeology and folklore to journals in Puerto Rico, the United States, and Mexico, including *Revista del Instituto de Cultura Puertorriqueña, American Antiquity,* and *Revista Mexicana de Estudios Antropológicos.*

SIDELIGHTS: Ricardo E. Alegría is a noted Puerto Rican historian and anthropologist who, from 1955 through 1973, served as director of the prominent Instituto de Cultura Puertorriqueña (Institute of Puerto Rican Culture).

WORK IN PROGRESS: Writing on the folklore and history of Puerto Rico and on archaeology of the West Indies.

BIOGRAPHICAL/CRITICAL SOURCES:

PERIODICALS

Book World, August 17, 1969.
Horn Book, August, 1969.
New York Times Book Review, May 4, 1969.

* * *

ALEIXANDRE, Vicente 1898-1984

PERSONAL: Born April 26, 1898, in Seville, Spain; died of kidney failure and shock from intestinal hemorrhage, December 14, 1984, in Madrid, Spain; son of Cirilo (an engineer) and Elvira (Merlo) Aleixandre. *Education:* Attended University of Seville;

University of Madrid, license in law and diploma in business, both 1919.

CAREER: Poet and writer, 1925-84. Central School of Commerce, Madrid, Spain, associate professor, 1919-21; Residencia de Estudiantes, Madrid, teacher of business terminology, 1921; worked for Ferrocarriles andaluces (railroad company), 1921-25. Lecturer at Oxford University and University of London, 1950, and in Morocco, 1953.

MEMBER: Real Academia Española, American Association of Teachers of Spanish and Portuguese (honorary fellow), Hispanic Society of America, Monde Latin Academy (Paris); corresponding member of Malaga Arts Academy, Academy of Science and Arts (Puerto Rico), and Hispanic-American Academy (Bogotá).

AWARDS, HONORS: National Literary Prize (Spain), 1933, for *La destrucción o el amor;* Spanish Critics' Prize, 1963, 1969, and 1975; Nobel Prize in Literature, Swedish Academy, 1977; Grand Cross of the Order of Carlos III, 1977; Gold Medal of the City of Madrid, 1984.

WRITINGS:

IN ENGLISH TRANSLATION; POEMS

La destrucción o el amor, Signo (Madrid), 1935, 2nd edition, 1967, translation by Stephen Kessler of selected poems published as *Destruction or Love: A Selection From La destrucción o el amor of Vicente Aleixandre,* Green Horse Three (Santa Cruz, Calif.), 1976.

Mundo a solas, Clan (Madrid), 1950, translation by Lewis Hyde and David Unger published as *World Alone/Mundo a solas* (bilingual edition), Penmaen Press (Great Barrington, Mass.), 1982.

Poems (bilingual edition), translations by Ben Belitt, Alan Brilliant, and others, Department of English, Ohio University, 1969.

Vicente Aleixandre and Luis Cernuda: Selected Poems (bilingual edition), translations by Linda Lehrer and others, Copper Beach Press (Providence, R.I.), 1974.

The Cave of Night: Poems (bilingual edition), translation by Joef frey Bartman, Solo Press (San Luis Obispo, Calif.), 1976.

Twenty Poems, edited by Hyde, translations by Hyde and Robert Bly, Seventies Press (Madison, Minn.), 1977.

Poems-Poemas (bilingual edition), Unicorn Press, 1978.

A Longing for the Light: Selected Poems of Vicente Aleixandre, edited by Hyde, translations by Kessler and others, Harper, 1979.

The Crackling Sun: Selected Poems of the Nobel Prize Recipient, 1977, translated and introduced by Louis Bourne, Sociedad General Española de la Librería (Madrid), 1981.

A Bird of Paper: Poems of Vicente Aleixandre, translated by Willis Barnstone and David Garrison, Ohio University Press, 1982.

IN SPANISH; POEMS

Ambito (title means "Ambit"), Litoral (Málaga), 1928, reprinted, Raiz (Madrid), 1950.

Espadas como labios (title means "Swords Like Lips"; also see below), Espasa-Calpe (Madrid), 1932, reprinted, Losada (Buenos Aires), 1957.

Pasión de la tierra (title means "Passion of the Earth"; also see below), Fabula (Mexico), 1935, revised edition, Adonais (Madrid), 1946, critical edition with notes and commentary by Luis Antonio de Villena, Narceu, 1976.

Sombra del paraíso (also see below), Adan (Madrid), 1944, reprinted, Castalia, 1976, translation by Hugh Harter published as *Shadow of Paradise: Sombra del paraíso,* University of California Press, 1987.

Poemas paradisiacos (title means "Poems of Paradise"; includes selections from *Sombra del paraíso*), [Málaga], 1952, 3rd edition, edited by José Luis Cano, Cátedra, 1981.

Nacimiento último (title means "Final Birth"), Insula (Madrid), 1953.

Historia del corazón (title means "History of a Heart"), Espasa-Calpe, 1954, critical edition with prologue by Cano, 1983.

Antigua casa madrileña (title means "Ancient Madrid House"; also see below), Hermanos Bedia (Santander, Spain), 1961.

Picasso (long poem) [Málaga], 1961.

En un vasto dominio (title means "In a Vast Dominion"; includes *Antigua casa madrileña*), Revista de Occidente, 1962.

Retratos con nombres (title means "Portraits With Names"), El Bardo, 1965.

Poemas de la consumación (title means "Poems of Consummation"), Plaza y Janés (Barcelona), 1968.

Sonido de la guerra, Fomento de Cultura Ediciones (Valencia), 1972.

Diálogos del conocimiento (title means "Dialogues of Knowledge"), Plaza y Janés, 1974.

OMNIBUS VOLUMES IN SPANISH

Mis poemas mejores (title means "My Best Poems"), Gredos (Madrid), 1956, revised edition, 1976.

Espadas como labios [and] *Pasión de la tierra,* Losada, 1957, critical edition with notes and introduction by Cano, Castalia, 1977.

Poemas amorosos: Antología (title means "Love Poems: Anthology"), Losada, 1960.

Poesías completas (title means "Complete Poems"), introduction by Carlos Bousoño, Aguilar, 1960.

Presencias (title means "Presences"; limited edition), Seix Barral (Barcelona), 1965.

Obras completas (title means "Complete Works"), introduction by Bousoño, Aguilar, 1968, revised edition published in two volumes, 1977.

Poesía superrealista (title means "Surrealistic Poetry"), Barral Editores, 1971.

Antología del mar y de la noche (title means "Anthology of the Sea and the Night"), edited by Javier Lostale, Al-Borak, 1971.

Antología total (title means "Total Anthology"), compiled by Pere Gimferrer, Seix Barral, 1975.

Antología poética (title means "Poetry Anthology"), edited by Leopoldo de Luis, Castalia, 1976.

Aleixandre para niños (title means "Aleixandre for Children"; juvenile), Ediciones de la Torre (Madrid), 1984.

AUTHOR OF PROLOGUE IN SPANISH

Bousoño, *La primavera de la muerte,* Adonais, 1946.
Gregoria Prieto, *Poesía en línea,* Adonais, 1948.
Fernando Charry Lara, *Nocturnos y otros sueños,* [Bogotá], 1948.
Adonais: Segunda antología, Rialp (Madrid), 1962.

CONTRIBUTOR TO ANTHOLOGIES

Eleanor Laurelle Turnbull, editor, *Contemporary Spanish Poetry: Selections From Ten Poets* (bilingual edition), Johns Hopkins University Press, 1945.

Penguin Book of Spanish Verse, Penguin, 1956.

Willis Barnstone, editor, *Modern European Poetry,* Bantam, 1966.

Hardie St. Martin, editor, *Roots and Wings, Poetry From Spain: A Bilingual Anthology,* Harper, 1976.

OTHER

Algunos caracteres de la poesía española contemporánea (title means "Some Characteristics of Contemporary Spanish Poetry"; criticism), Imprenta Góngora (Madrid), 1955.

Los encuentros (title means "The Meetings"; critical/biographical sketches), Guadarrama (Madrid), 1958.

(Contributor) Francisco Sabadett López, *Desnudos*, [Valladolid], 1961.

(Author of epilogue) Federico García Lorca, *Obras completas*, Aguilar, 1963.

(Contributor) José Angeles, editor, *Estudios sobre Antonio Machado*, Ariel, 1977.

Contributor of poetry and articles to Spanish journals. Co-editor, *Revista de Economía*, 1920-22; staff member, *La Semana Financiera* (financial magazine), ending 1927.

SIDELIGHTS: Poet Vicente Aleixandre was a member of Spain's Generation of 1927, which Manuel Durán described in a *World Literature Today* essay as "perhaps the brightest and most original poetic generation in twentieth-century Western Europe." Along with Aleixandre, the group included many of modern Spain's most influential writers, such as Jorge Guillén, Gerardo Diego, and Rafael Alberti.

Although nearly unknown outside his native country before receiving the Nobel Prize for Literature in 1977, Aleixandre had much in common with the generation's best-known poet, Federico García Lorca. The two men were from the same region in Spain—the southernmost Andalusia—and revealed the same sources of inspiration in their poetry: Spanish writing of the fifteenth and sixteenth centuries, popular folk rhythms of their native Andalusia, and surrealism. But, while Lorca's death at the hands of Franco's forces at the beginning of the Spanish Civil War catapulted him into international recognition, Aleixandre's name was known only in Spanish circles. He survived both having his house nearly destroyed in a Civil War bomb attack—an autographed book of Lorca's was one of the only items recovered from his gutted library—and having his work banned by government censors for nearly five years after the war to become one of Spain's most prominent poets.

Most critics of Aleixandre's work commented on the thematic and stylistic evolution evident in his poetry. In *Contemporary Spanish Poetry (1898-1963)*, for example, Carl W. Cobb noted that in Aleixandre's early poems the poet "rejected the historical and social world around him and created from his elemental passions a vast domain of cosmic and telluric forces anterior to man himself." In contrast, Cobb described the poet's later work as being focused "directly in the historical reality of his pueblo, his 'people.'"

Other critics, such as Diana Der Hovanessian, Arthur Terry, and Kessel Schwartz, echoed Cobb's assessment. In the *Christian Science Monitor*, for instance, Der Hovanessian noted: "Some of [Aleixandre's] early poetry might tax a reader with its mysticism and disjointed style. But Aleixandre's poetry loses much of the disconnectedness in later years, and begins to address people directly." Terry similarly stated in the *Times Literary Supplement* that while Aleixandre's early poems were "Surrealist-influenced," in later poems "emphasis shifts to the contemplation of man in his human context." Schwartz described the poet's work in *Vicente Aleixandre* as a movement from "the chaotic maelstrom" of his early work to a new poetry in which Aleixandre "became aware of historical man, the temporal man, that is, man in time and space."

Dario Fernández-Morera explained the transformation in Aleixandre's poetry in light of the dramatic change in Spanish society following the Civil War. In *Symposium* the critic stated: "Before [the war], poets had lived in an atmosphere of continuity, of relative intellectual security; therefore they could be concerned with their own psyches rather than with the world they lived in. . . . But the growing turmoil made this attitude no longer feasible."

The selection of Aleixandre as a Nobel laureate was controversial, since the complexity of his surrealistic poetry made it unintelligible to many critics and most readers. A *Washington Post* writer quoted a translated line of poetry from Aleixandre's second book, *Pasión de la tierra* (title means "Passion of the Earth") as an example of what the reviewer called Aleixandre's "puzzling" verse: "To sleep when my time comes on a conscience without a pillowcase."

G. G. Brown referred to the same book of poetry in *A Literary History of Spain* as "a collection of largely incomprehensible prose-poems, whose private subconscious ramblings Aleixandre tried to excuse later by calling them Freudian." And in *A Longing for the Light: Selected Poems of Vicente Aleixandre*, Lewis Hyde noted that the poems in *Pasión de la tierra* were "written in an almost hermetic dream-language."

According to Hyde, Aleixandre agreed with critics who called *Pasión de la tierra* difficult, but he nevertheless defended the book's worth. Hyde translated the poet's comments: "I have always thought I could see in its chasm-like layers the sudden start of my poetry's evolution, which, from its earliest, has been . . . a longing for the light. This book has therefore produced in me a double, complicated feeling: of aversion, because of its difficulty, which contradicts the call, the appeal it makes to basic levels, common to all of us; and of affection, for the maternal *humus* from which it grew."

Although Fernández-Morera pointed out that "Aleixandre's surrealist phase is perhaps [his] most publicized," the poet's Nobel Prize was awarded largely for his later, more accessible, work. This was evident, Pablo Beltran de Heredia observed in the *Texas Quarterly*, "when [the Swedish Academy] stated, during the award ceremonies, that the work of this Spanish poet 'illuminates the condition of man in the cosmos and in our present-day society.'"

Cobb noted that "it is perhaps with a feeling of relief that the reader turns from the difficult and turbulent world of Aleixandre's first period . . . to the quieter and simpler but no less moving world of his second phase. . . . His major theme becomes human solidarity, with compassion toward all human beings living in time." Cobb singled out *Historia del corazón* (title means "History of the Heart") published in 1954 as Aleixandre's first book of this new style of poetry. Abandoning the obscurity of his early poems, Aleixandre came to believe that poetry was essentially communication. In general, the prose-poems gave way to what a *New York Times* writer called "carefully cadenced free verse." The nightmarish images were replaced by portraits of everyday life. According to Durán, "*Historia del corazón* is basically the story of a love affair, in its daily moments of joy and anguish, and also the story of a growing awareness, a solidarity: the poet realizes that he is only one member of a vast society, the Spanish people, and that ultimately he is a part of mankind."

Beltran de Heredia pointed out that Aleixandre expressed a fondness for this simpler poetry, preferring *Historia del corazón* among his books and—from that same collection—"En la plaza" (title means "On the Square") among his poems. Both

Santiago Daydi-Tolson in *The Post-Civil War Spanish Poets* and Durán emphasized the importance of this same poem. Aleixandre "uses the image of the public square," Daydi-Tolson observed, "to represent the greatness of human solidarity." According to the critic, the plaza, the axis around which society revolves in every Spanish city, is the perfect embodiment of the essence of Spanish life. In the symbol of the public square the poet "feels and understands this essential communal quality of man's existence."

Durán saw the poem as an encapsulated portrait of Aleixandre's evolution from personal to communal poet. Durán explained the imagery of the poem: "After being long confined in his room, the poet goes out into the street, to the square, in order to mingle with other human beings and be part of humanity." Durán illustrated his point with a translation from the poem: "It is a beautiful feeling, beautifully humble and buoyant, life-giving and deep,/ to feel yourself beneath the sun among other people."

Aleixandre is important for his own poetry but also for his influence on the poetry of subsequent generations. As one of the few poets to remain in Spain during the Civil War, he was a symbol of hope to younger poets. In a *New York Times Book Review* essay, Robert Bly suggested that after the war "the younger writers felt abandoned, dead, in despair. It turned out that Aleixandre's decision to stay helped all that. He represented the wild energy still alive on Spanish soil."

A *London Times* writer noted that although Aleixandre "was privately distressed at the low quality of verse of Falangist poets [members of Franco's party], . . . he encouraged them as he encouraged every other poet, seeking with a noble magnanimity of spirit to unify all factions. He worked behind the scenes to obtain the release of imprisoned writers, and was more responsible than any other single person for creating the relaxed [Spanish] censorship of the middle and late 1960s, which led to better things."

In Aleixandre's prologue to the second edition of *La destrucción o el amor,* the Spaniard summarized his ideas on poets and poetry. The prologue, written in 1944 shortly before the poet began work on *La historia del corazón* and translated by David Pritchard in the *Paris Review,* ends with a short explanation of Aleixandre's poetics. "Some poets . . .," he wrote, "are poets 'of the few.' They are artists . . . who address themselves to men by attending, so they say, to exquisite and narrow obsessions. . . . Other poets . . . address themselves to what is permanent in man. Not to the details that set us apart, but to the essence that brings us together. . . . These poets are radical poets and they speak to what is primordial, to what is elemental in humanity. They cannot *feel* themselves to be poets of the few. I am one of these."

BIOGRAPHICAL/CRITICAL SOURCES:

BOOKS

Aleixandre, Vicente, *Twenty Poems,* edited by Lewis Hyde, Seventies Press, 1977.
Aleixandre, Vicente, *A Longing for the Light: Selected Poems of Vicente Aleixandre,* edited by Lewis Hyde, Copper Canyon Press, 1985.
Alonso, Dámaso, *Ensayos sobre poesía española,* Revista de Occidente, 1946.
Bousoño, Carlos, *La poesía de Vicente Aleixandre,* Insula, 1950, revised edition, 1977.
Brown, G. G., *A Literary History of Spain,* Barnes & Noble, 1972.

Cabrera, Vicente and Harriet Boyer, editors, *Critical Views on Vicente Aleixandre's Poetry,* Society of Spanish and Spanish-American Studies (Lincoln, Neb.), 1979.
Cobb, Carl W., *Contemporary Spanish Poetry (1898-1963),* Twayne, 1976.
Contemporary Literary Criticism, Gale, Volume 9, 1978, Volume 36, 1986.
Daydi-Tolson, Santiago, editor, *Vicente Aleixandre: A Critical Appraisal,* Bilingual Press, 1981.
Daydi-Tolson, Santiago, *The Post-Civil War Spanish Poets,* Twayne, 1983.
Jiménez, José Olivio, *Cinco poetas del tiempo,* Insula, 1964.
Jiménez, José Olivio, *Vicente Aleixandre: Una aventura hacia el conocimiento,* Ediciones Jucar (Madrid), 1982.
Ley, Charles David, *Spanish Poetry Since 1939,* Catholic University of America Press, 1962.
Morris, C. B., *A Generation of Spanish Poets: 1920-1936,* Cambridge University Press, 1969.
Schwartz, Kessel, *Vicente Aleixandre,* Twayne, 1970.

PERIODICALS

Christian Science Monitor, January 2, 1980.
Hispania, May, 1967.
Hispanic Journal, fall, 1982.
Hudson Review, winter, 1978-79.
Nation, March 4, 1978.
New Republic, December 24-31, 1977.
Newsweek, October 17, 1977.
New York Times, October 7, 1977.
New York Times Book Review, October 30, 1977.
Paris Review, fall, 1978.
Parnassus: Poetry in Review, fall/winter, 1979.
Poetry, April, 1980.
Symposium, summer, 1979.
Texas Quarterly, winter, 1978.
Time, October 17, 1977.
Times (London), December 15, 1984.
Times Literary Supplement, May 17, 1957, November 2, 1958, July 10, 1969, May 23, 1975.
Washington Post, December 15, 1984.
World Literature Today, spring, 1975.

OBITUARIES:

PERIODICALS

AB Bookman's Weekly, January 21, 1985.
Chicago Tribune, December 26, 1984.
Los Angeles Times, December 16, 1984.
Time, December 24, 1984.
Times (London), December 15, 1984.

—*Sketch by Marian Gonsior*

* * *

ALEJANDRO, Carlos F(ederico) Díaz
See DIAZ-ALEJANDRO, Carlos F(ederico)

* * *

ALLENDE, Isabel 1942-

PERSONAL: Surname is pronounced "Ah-*yen*-day"; born August 2, 1942, in Lima, Peru; daughter of Tomás (a Chilean diplomat) and Francisca (Llona Barros) Allende; married Miguel Frías (an engineer), September 8, 1962 (divorced, 1987); married William Gordon (a lawyer), July 17, 1988; children: (first marriage) Paula, Nicolás; Scott (stepson). *Education:* Graduated from a private high school in Santiago, Chile, at age 16.

ADDRESSES: Home—15 Nightingale Lane, San Rafael, Calif. 94901. *Agent*—Carmen Balcells, Diagonal 580, Barcelona 21, Spain.

CAREER: United Nations Food and Agricultural Organization, Santiago, Chile, secretary, 1959-65; *Paula* (magazine), Santiago, journalist, editor, and advice columnist, 1967-74; *Mampato* (magazine), Santiago, journalist, 1969-74; Canal 13/Canal 7 (television station), television interviewer, 1970-75; worked on movie newsreels, 1973-75; Colegio Marroco, Caracas, Venezuela, administrator, 1979-82; writer. Guest teacher at Montclair State College, N.J., spring, 1985, and University of Virginia, fall, 1988; Gildersleeve Lecturer, Barnard College, spring, 1988; teacher of creative writing, University of California, Berkeley, spring, 1989.

AWARDS, HONORS: Quality Paperback Book Club New Voice Award nomination, 1986, for *The House of the Spirits; Los Angeles Times* Book Prize nomination, 1987, for *Of Love and Shadows; Eva Luna* was named one of *Library Journal*'s Best Books of 1988.

WRITINGS:

Civilice a su troglodita: Los impertinentes de Isabel Allende (humor), Lord Cochran (Santiago), 1974.
La casa de los espíritus, Plaza y Janés (Barcelona), 1982, translation by Magda Bogin published as *The House of the Spirits,* Knopf, 1985.
La gorda de porcelana (juvenile; title means "The Fat Porcelain Lady"), Alfaguara (Madrid), 1984.
De amor y de sombra, Plaza y Janés, 1984, translation by Margaret Sayers Peden published as *Of Love and Shadows,* Knopf, 1987.
Eva Luna, Plaza y Janés, 1987, translation by Peden published under same title, Knopf, 1988.

Also author of several plays and stories for children. Author of weekly newspaper column for *El Nacional* (Caracas), 1976-83.

WORK IN PROGRESS: Stories of Eva Luna, a collection of short stories.

SIDELIGHTS: When Chilean president Salvador Allende was assassinated in 1973 as part of a military coup against his socialist government, it had a profound effect on his niece, novelist Isabel Allende. "I think I have divided my life [into] before that day and after that day," Allende told *Publishers Weekly* interviewer Amanda Smith. "In that moment, I realized that everything was possible—that violence was a dimension that was always around you." At first, Allende and her family didn't believe that a dictatorship could last in Chile; they soon found it too dangerous to remain in the country, however, and fled to Venezuela. Although she had been a noted journalist in Chile, Allende found it difficult to get a job in Venezuela and didn't write for several years; but after receiving word from her grandfather, a nearly one-hundred-year-old man who had remained in Chile, she began to write again in a letter to him. "My grandfather thought people died only when you forgot them," the author explained to Harriet Shapiro in *People.* "I wanted to prove to him that I had forgotten nothing, that his spirit was going to live with us forever." Allende never sent the letter to her grandfather, who soon died, but her memories of her family and her country became the genesis of *The House of the Spirits,* her first novel. "When you lose everything, everything that is dear to you . . . memory becomes more important," Allende commented to

Mother Jones writer Douglas Foster. With *The House of the Spirits,* the author added, "[I achieved] the recovery of those memories that were being blown by the wind, by the wind of exile."

Following three generations of the Trueba family and their domestic and political conflicts, *The House of the Spirits* "is a novel of peace and reconciliation, in spite of the fact that it tells of bloody, tragic events," claims *New York Times Book Review* contributor Alexander Coleman. "The author has accomplished this not only by plumbing her memory for the familial and political textures of the continent, but also by turning practically every major Latin American novel on its head," the critic continues. The patriarch of the family, Esteban Trueba, is a strict, conservative man who exploits his workers and allows his uncompromising beliefs to distance him from his wife and children, even in the face of tremendous events.

Allende's grand scope and use of fantastic elements and characters have led many critics to place *The House of the Spirits* in the category of the Latin American novel of "magic realism," and they compare it specifically to Nobel winner Gabriel García Márquez's *One Hundred Years of Solitude.* "Allende has her own distinctive voice, however," notes a *Publishers Weekly* reviewer; "while her prose lacks the incandescent brilliance of the master's, it has a whimsical charm, besides being clearer, more accessible and more explicit about the contemporary situation in South America." In contrast, *Village Voice* contributor Enrique Fernández believes that "only the dullest reader can fail to be distracted by the shameless cloning from *One Hundred Years of Solitude.* . . . Allende writes like one of the many earnest minor authors that began aping Gabo after his success, except she's better at it than most." Although Lori M. Carlson agrees that *The House of the Spirits* is too reminiscent of García Márquez's masterpiece, she writes in *Review* that "Allende's novel does remain compelling, nevertheless. Technique is polished, imagination full." "Isabel Allende is very much under the influence of Gabriel García Márquez, but she is scarcely an imitator," remarks the *Washington Post Book World*'s Jonathan Yardley, concluding that "she is most certainly a novelist in her own right and, for a first novelist, a startlingly skillful, confident one."

While *The House of the Spirits* contains some of the magic realism that is characteristic of much Latin American fiction, it is counterbalanced by the political realities that Allende recounts. *Times Literary Supplement* reviewer Antony Beevor states that whereas the early chapters of *The House of the Spirits* seem "to belong firmly in the school of magical realism," a closer reading "suggests that Isabel Allende's tongue is lightly in her cheek. It soon becomes clear that she has taken the genre to flip it over," the critic elaborates. "The metaphorical house, the themes of time and power, the *machista* violence and the unstoppable merry-go-round of history: all of these are reworked and then examined from the other side—from a woman's perspective." Other critics, however, fault Allende for trying to combine the magical and the political; Richard Eder of the *Los Angeles Times* feels that the author "rarely manages to integrate her magic and her message," while *Nation* contributor Paul West says that the political story is "the book Allende probably wanted to write, and would have had she not felt obliged to toe the line of magical realism." But others maintain that the contrast between the fantastic and political segments is effective, as Harriet Waugh of the *Spectator* explains: "[The] magic gradually dies away as a terrible political reality engulfs the people of the country. Ghosts, the gift of foretelling the future and the ability to make the pepper and salt cellars move around the dining-room table cannot survive terror, mass-murder and torture."

Christian Science Monitor reviewer Marjorie Agosin presents a similar assessment: "Part of the [book's] power comes from the fact that real events form the background for the fictional story. The unbridled fantasy of the protagonists and their enchanted spirits is played out against the story of the demented and tragic country once free, now possessed by the evil spirits of a military dictatorship." When members of the Trueba family become increasingly involved in their nation's politics, "Allende here begins to exercise her skills as a journalist as she evokes the turbulent events she witnessed during the Marxists' electrifying rise and precipitous fall," remarks Patricia Blake in her *Time* review. "Not surprisingly, magic subsides and realism takes over. Allende deftly turns her characters into archetypes of Latin America's left and right." Despite this metaphorical aspect, notes Beevor, "there is too much humanity in her book for the characters to become ossified by symbolism; the story-telling is so natural that one risks overlooking the richness of allusion." "Finally," concludes *New York Times* critic Christopher Lehmann-Haupt, "what is fabulous in the story works to give it its extraordinary character. . . . It is also these spirits that help to lift the novel out of the realm of local political allegory, and lend it a feeling of extraterritorial truth." *The House of the Spirits* does contain a certain amount of rather predictable politics, but the only cause it wholly embraces is that of humanity, and it does so with such passion, humor and wisdom that in the end it transcends politics," asserts Yardley; "it is also a genuine rarity, a work of fiction that is both an impressive literary accomplishment and a mesmerizing story fully accessible to a general readership."

Although *The House of the Spirits* includes political approaches similar to other Latin American works, it also contains "an original feminist argument that suggests [a] women's monopoly on powers that oppose the violent 'paternalism' from which countries like Chile continue to suffer," according to *Chicago Tribune* contributor Bruce Allen. Alberto Manguel likewise considers important Allende's "depiction of woman as a colonial object," as he writes in the Toronto *Globe and Mail*, a depiction reinforced by Esteban Trueba's cruel treatment of his wife, daughter, and female workers. But despite the concentration on female characters and "the fact that Esteban rapes, pillages, kills and conspires, he never entirely loses the reader's sympathy," comments Waugh. "It is a remarkable achievement to make the old monster lovable not just to his wife, daughter, and granddaughter, and the other women in his life, but also to the reader," Philip Howard contends in the London *Times*. "It is a fair-minded book, that pities and understands people on both sides of the politics." Allen concurs: "The most remarkable feature of this remarkable book is the way in which its strong political sentiments are made to coexist with its extravagant and fascinating narrative. . . . Despite its undeniable debt to 'One Hundred Years of Solitude,' " the critic concludes, *The House of the Spirits* "is an original and important work; along with García Márquez's masterpiece, it's one of the best novels of the postwar period, and a major contribution to our understanding of societies riddled by ceaseless conflict and violent change. It is a great achievement, and it cries out to be read."

With *Of Love and Shadows,* which *Detroit Free Press* contributor Anne Janette Johnson calls "a frightening, powerful work," Allende "proves her continued capacity for generating excellent fiction. She has talent, sensitivity, and a subject matter that provides both high drama and an urgent political message." The novel begins "matter-of-factly, almost humorously," with the switching of two baby girls, as Charles R. Larson describes it in the *Detroit News*. The story becomes more complex, however,

when one of the babies grows up to become the focus of a journalist's investigation; after a reporter and photographer expose the political murder of the girl, they are forced to flee the country. "And so," Larson observes, "Allende begins with vignettes of magical realism, only to pull the rug out from under our feet once we have been hooked by her enchanting tale. What she does, in fact, is turn her story into a thriller." "Love and struggle a la 'Casablanca'—it's all there," Gene H. Bell-Villada likewise states in the *New York Times Book Review*. "Ms. Allende skillfully evokes both the terrors of daily life under military rule and the subtler form of resistance in the hidden corners and 'shadows' of her title." But while political action comprises a large part of the story, "above all, this is a love story of two young people sharing the fate of their historical circumstances, meeting the challenge of discovering the truth, and determined to live their life fully, accepting their world of love and shadows," Agosin declares. With *Of Love and Shadows* "Allende has mastered the craft of being able to intertwine the turbulent political history of Latin America with the everyday lives of her fictional characters caught up in recognizable, contemporary events."

Rosemary Sullivan, however, feels that Allende is not as successful in blending magical and realistic elements in this novel; she remarks in the Toronto *Globe and Mail* that "Allende has some difficulty getting her novel started because she has to weave two stories separately, and seems to be relying initially too much on her skills as a journalist." *New York Times* critic Michiko Kakutani similarly relates that the book is "more literal in a way that points up the author's tendency to cast everything in terms of white and black, good and evil, love and shadows." This leads to what Beevor perceives as a lack of "emotional distance"; the author's characters, "in spite of their lack of depth, are all perfectly convincing until she burdens them with interior monologues, giving them superfluous roles in a Greek chorus." But Johnson believes that Allende's characters, "major and minor, brim with the vagaries of human nature. Allende hops from one personality to another . . . with a gentle grace that is quite endearing," the critic continues. "When her tale descends to horror, which inevitably it must, she never relinquishes the warm, confiding tone, like that used between old friends." "One of [the book's] many strengths is that Allende sees no person and no issue in simplistic terms," Yardley likewise contends; "she always tries to understand what makes people think and behave as they do, even when she disagrees with them or dislikes them, and thus her work contains depths of empathy and compassion rarely found in fiction that embraces a political cause. . . . [Allende] is a writer of deep conviction, but she knows that in the end it is people, not issues, who matter most," the critic concludes. "The people in *Of Love and Shadows* are so real, their triumphs and defeats are so faithful to the truth of human existence, that we see the world in miniature. This is precisely what fiction should do."

"Fears that Isabel Allende might be a 'one-book' writer, that her first success . . . would be her only one, ought to be quashed by *Eva Luna*," asserts Abigail E. Lee in the *Times Literary Supplement*. "The eponymous protagonist and narrator of this, her third novel, has an engaging personality, a motley collection of interesting acquaintances and an interesting angle on political upheavals in the unnamed Latin American republic in which she lives." Born illegitimate and later orphaned, Eva Luna, a script-writer and storyteller, becomes involved with a filmmaker—Rolf Carlé, an Austrian emigre haunted by his Nazi father—and his subjects, a troop of revolutionary guerrillas. "In 'Eva Luna,' Allende moves between the personal and the political, between realism and fantasy, weaving two exotic coming-of-age stories—

Eva Luna's and Rolf Carlé's—into the turbulent coming of age of her unnamed South American country," Elizabeth Benedict summarizes in Chicago *Tribune Books*. Switching between the stories of the two protagonists, *Eva Luna* is "filled with a multitude of characters and tales," recounts *Washington Post Book World* contributor Alan Ryan. Allende's work is "a remarkable novel," the critic elaborates, "one in which a cascade of stories tumbles out before the reader, stories vivid and passionate and human enough to engage, in their own right, all the reader's attention and sympathy."

Perhaps due to this abundance of stories and characters, John Krich thinks that "few of the cast of characters emerge as distinctive or entirely believable," as he comments in the *New York Times Book Review*. "Too often, we find Eva Luna's compatriots revealed through generalized attributions rather than their own actions. . . . Is this magic realism a la García Márquez or Hollywood magic a la Judith Krantz? We can only marvel at how thin the line becomes between the two, and give Ms. Allende the benefit of the doubt." London *Times* writer Stuart Evans, however, praises Allende's "range of eccentric or idiosyncratic characters who are always credible," and adds: "Packed with action, prodigal in invention, vivid in description and metaphor, this cleverly plotted novel is enhanced by its flowing prose and absolute assurance." "*Eva Luna* is a great read that *El Nobel* [García Márquez] couldn't hope to write," claims Dan Bellm in the *Voice Literary Supplement*, for the women "get the best political debate scenes, not the men." Lee also sees a serious political side to the novel, noting "an interesting juxtaposition in *Eva Luna* of feminism and revolutionary politics. . . . In all the depictions of women and their relationships with men, though, one feels not a militant or aggressive feminism—rather a sympathetic awareness of the injustices inherent in traditional gender roles." The critic continues, remarking that *Eva Luna* "is an accomplished novel, skilfully blending humour and pathos; its woman's perspective on Latin American is a refreshing one, but it is enjoyable above all for its sensitivity and charm." "Reading this novel is like asking your favorite storyteller to tell you a story and getting a hundred stories instead of one . . . and then an explanation of how the stories were invented . . . and then hearing the storyteller's life as well," concludes Ryan. "Does it have a happy ending? What do you think?"

MEDIA ADAPTATIONS: The House of the Spirits will be filmed in English by Bille August, the Danish director of "Pelle the Conqueror."

BIOGRAPHICAL/CRITICAL SOURCES:

BOOKS

Coddou, Marcelio, editor, *Los libros tienen sus propios espíritus: Estudios sobre Isabel Allende,* Universidad Veracruzana, 1986.
Contemporary Literary Criticism, Volume 39, Gale, 1986.

PERIODICALS

Chicago Tribune, May 19, 1985.
Christian Science Monitor, June 7, 1985, May 27, 1987.
Detroit Free Press, June 7, 1987.
Detroit News, June 14, 1987.
Globe and Mail (Toronto), June 24, 1985, June 27, 1987.
Los Angeles Times, February 10, 1988.
Los Angeles Times Book Review, June 16, 1985, May 31, 1987.
Mother Jones, December, 1988.
Nation, July 20, 1985.
New Statesman, July 5, 1985.
Newsweek, May 13, 1985.

New York Review of Books, July 18, 1985.
New York Times, May 2, 1985, May 20, 1987, February 4, 1988.
New York Times Book Review, May 12, 1985, July 12, 1987, October 23, 1988.
People, June 10, 1985, June 1, 1987.
Publishers Weekly, March 1, 1985, May 17, 1985.
Review, January-June, 1985.
Spectator, August 3, 1985.
Time, May 20, 1985.
Times (London), July 4, 1985, July 9, 1987, March 22, 1989, March 23, 1989.
Times Literary Supplement, July 5, 1985, July 10, 1987, April 7-13, 1989.
Tribune Books (Chicago), October 9, 1988.
U.S. News and World Report, November 21, 1988.
Village Voice, June 7, 1985.
Voice Literary Supplement, December, 1988.
Washington Post Book World, May 12, 1985, May 24, 1987, October 9, 1988.

—*Sketch by Diane Telgen*

*   *   *

ALONSO, Dámaso   1898-1990

PERSONAL: Born October 22, 1898, in Madrid, Spain; died of a respiratory ailment, January 24, 1990, in Madrid, Spain; married Eulalia Galvarriato (a writer), 1929. *Education:* Received LL.L, M.A., Ph.D., and Litt.D. from University of Madrid.

ADDRESSES: Home—Ave. Alberto Alcocer 23, Madrid 16, Spain.

CAREER: Centro de Estudios Históricos, Madrid, Spain, professor, 1923-36; University of Valencia, Valencia, Spain, professor of Spanish language and literature, 1933-39; University of Madrid, Madrid, professor of Romance philology, 1939-68; writer. Lecturer and visiting professor at universities throughout the world, including Berlin, Cambridge, Columbia, Harvard, Johns Hopkins, London, Stanford, and Yale universities.

MEMBER: International Association of Hispanists (president), Royal Spanish Academy of the Language (president, 1968-1982; director emeritus), Royal Academy of History, Higher Council for Scientific Research, American Association of Teachers of Spanish and Portuguese, Hispanic Society of America, American Philosophical Society, Modern Language Association, Modern Humanities Research Association (president).

AWARDS, HONORS: Premio Nacional de Literatura, c. 1935, for *La lengua poética de Góngora;* award from the Royal Spanish Academy of the Language, c. 1942, for *La poesía de San Juan de la Cruz;* Premio Miguel de Cervantes from Spain's Ministerio de Cultura, 1978; numerous honorary degrees from universities, including Oxford University and the universities of San Marcos, Bordeaux, Hamburg, Freiburg, Rome, Massachusetts, and Leeds.

WRITINGS:

NONFICTION

(Editor) Desiderius Erasmus, *El Enquiridión; o, Manual del caballero cristiano,* Consejo Superior de Investigaciones Científicas, Instituto Miguel de Cervantes (Madrid), 1932, reprinted, 1971.
La lengua poética de Góngora, S. Aguirre (Madrid), 1935, 3rd edition, Consejo Superior de Investigaciones Científicas, Instituto Miguel de Cervantes, 1961.
Poesía española, antología, [Madrid], 1935 (also see below).

(Editor) Luis Carrillo de Sotomayor, *Poesías completas,* Signo (Madrid), 1936.

(Editor) *Poesía de la edad media y poesía de tipo tradicional* (originally published as first volume of *Poesía española, antología*), Losada (Buenos Aires), 1942.

La poesía de San Juan de la Cruz (desde esta ladera), Consejo Superior de Investigaciones Científicas, Instituto Antonio de Nebrija (Madrid), 1942.

Ensayos sobre poesía española, Revista de Occidente (Madrid), 1944.

Vida y obra de Medrano (about Francisco de Medrano), Volume 1: *Estudio,* Volume 2 (editor, with Stephen Reckert): *Edición crítica,* Consejo Superior de Investigaciones Científicas, Instituto Miguel de Cervantes, 1948-58.

Poesía y novela de España: Conferencias, Departamento de Extensión Cultural, Universidad Nacional Mayor de San Marcos (Lima), 1949.

Poesía española, ensayo de métodos y límites estilísticos: Garcilaso, fray Luis de León, San Juan de la Cruz, Góngora, Lope de Vega, Quevedo, Gredos, 1950.

(With Carlos Bousoño) *Seis calas en la expresión literaria española (prosa, poesía, teatro),* Gredos, 1951, 2nd edition, 1956, 3rd edition, 1963.

Poetas españoles contemporáneos, Gredos, 1952, 3rd edition, 1965.

La primitiva épica francesa a la luz de una Nota Emilianense, Consejo Superior de Investigaciones Científicas, Instituto Miguel de Cervantes, 1954.

Estudios y ensayos gongorinos, Gredos, 1955, reprinted, 1982.

(Editor and author of prose version) Luis de Góngora y Argote, *Las soledades* (originally published in 1927), Sociedad de Estudios y Publicaciones (Madrid), 1956, reprinted, Alianza (Madrid), 1982.

Menéndez Pelayo, crítico literario, Gredos (Madrid), 1956.

Antología: Creación, edited by Vicente Gaos, Escelicer (Madrid), 1956.

Antología: Crítica, edited by Gaos, Escelicer, 1956.

(Editor, with José M. Blecua) *Antología de la poesía española: Poesía de tipo tradicional,* Gredos, 1956, 2nd edition, 1964.

En la Andalucía de la e: Dialectología pintoresca, [Madrid], 1956.

De los siglos oscuros al de Oro: Notas y artículos a través de 700 años de letras españolas, Gredos, 1958, reprinted, 1982.

El Fabio de la "Epístola moral": Su cara y cruz en Méjico y en España, Real Academia de la Historia, 1959 (also see below).

Dos españoles del Siglo de Oro (includes *El Fabio de la "Epístola moral"*), Gredos, 1960.

Góngora y el "Polifemo," Gredos, 1960, 4th edition published in two volumes, 1961, 5th edition published in three volumes, 1967, 6th edition, 1974, 7th edition, 1985.

Primavera temprana de la literatura europea: Lírica, épica, novela, Guadarrama (Madrid), 1961.

Cuatro poetas españoles: Garcilaso, Góngora, Maragall, Antonio Machado, Gredos, 1962.

(Editor, with wife, Eulalia Galvarriato de Alonso) *Para la biografía de Góngora: Documentos desconocidos,* Gredos, 1962.

(Editor and author of prose version) Luis de Góngora y Argote, *Romance de Angélica y Medoro,* Ediciones Acies (Madrid), 1962.

Del siglo de Oro a este siglo de siglas: Notas y artículos a través de 350 años de letras españolas, Gredos, 1962.

(Author of introduction) *Antología de poetas ingleses modernos,* Gredos, 1963.

(With others) *Homenaje a don Ramón Carande,* Sociedad de Estudios y Publicaciones, 1963.

(With Galvarriato) *Poesías completas y comentarios en prosa a los poemas mayores* (poetry of San Juan de la Cruz), Aguilar (Madrid), 1963.

(With Luis Rosales) *Pasión y muerte del Conde de Villamediana* (debate), Real Academia Española (Madrid), 1964.

(With Pedro Laín Entralgo) *La amistad entre el médico y el enfermo en la Edad Media* (debate), Real Academia de la Historia (Madrid), 1964.

(With Martín de Riquer) *Vida caballeresca en la España del siglo XV* (debate), Real Academia Española, 1965.

(With Galvarriato and Luis Rosales) *Primavera y flor de la literatura hispánica,* 4 volumes, Selecciones de Reader's Digest, 1966.

Cancionero y romancero español, Salvat (Madrid), 1969, reprinted, 1985.

La novela cervantina, Universidad Internacional Menéndez Pelayo (Santander), 1969.

(With others) *Homenaje a Menéndez Pidal,* Prensa de la Universidad de Madrid (Madrid), 1969.

Libro de índices, Gredos, 1969.

En torno a Lope: Marino, Cervantes, Benavente, Góngora, los Cardenios, Gredos, 1972.

Obras completas, Gredos, Volume 1: *Estudios lingüísticos peninsulares,* 1972, Volume 2: *Estudios y ensayos sobre literatura,* c. 1974.

(Editor) *Antología de Góngora,* Gredos, 1974.

La Epístola moral a Fabio, de Andrés Fernández de Andrada: Edición y estudio, Gredos, 1978.

(Author of essay) Vicente Gaos, *Obra poética completa,* Institución Alfonso el Magnánimo, Diputación Provincial de Valencia (Valencia), 1982.

(With others) Federico García Lorca, *Llanto por Ignacio Sánchez Mejias* (critical study of the work by Lorca), Casona de Tudanca (Santander), 1982.

(With Gerardo Diego and Luis Rosales) *Antonio Machado: Conferencias pronunciadas en la Fundación Universitaria Española,* Fundación Universitaria Española, 1983.

Reflexiones sobre mi poesía, Universidad Autónoma de Madrid (Madrid), 1984.

Antología de nuestro monstruoso mundo: Duda y amor sobre el Ser Supremo, edited by Margarita Smerdou Altolaguirre, Cátedra (Madrid), 1985.

Also author of *El viento y el verso,* 1925, *La tragicomedia de Don Duardos* (critical study of the work by Gil Vicente), 1942, and *Un poeta madrileñista, latinista y francesista en la mitad del siglo XVI,* c. 1957; author of *La poesía del Petrarca e il petrarchismo,* Italian edition published by L.S. Olschki, 1959.

POETRY

Hombre y dios, [Málaga], 1955 (also see below).

Hijos de la ira: Diario íntimo (originally published c. 1944), Espasa-Calpe (Buenos Aires), 1946, reprinted, Castalia (Madrid), 1986, translation by Elias L. Rivers published in a bilingual edition as *Hijos de la ira/Children of Wrath,* Johns Hopkins University Press, 1970.

Oscura noticia [and] *Hombre y dios* (first title originally published in 1944), Espasa-Calpe (Madrid), 1959.

Poemas escogidos, Gredos, 1969.

Antología poética, edited by José Luis Cano, Plaza y Janés (Esplugas de Llobregat), 1973.

Antología poética, edited by Philip W. Silver, Alianza, 1979.

Vida y obra (contains *Poemas puros: Poemillas de la ciudad* and *Hombre y dios*), Caballo Griego para la Poesía (Madrid), 1984.

Also author of *Poemas puros: Poemillas de la ciudad,* 1921, and *Gozos de la vista,* 1970.

OTHER

Translator of works from English into Spanish, including *A Portrait of the Artist as a Young Man,* by James Joyce, *Marie Antoinette,* by Hilaire Belloc, and the poetry of Gerard Manley Hopkins.

SIDELIGHTS: Dámaso Alonso was widely hailed in his native Spain for both his works of literary criticism and his poetry. As a critic, he was without equal in twentieth-century Spain. He was perhaps best known for his studies on the poetry of Spain's Golden Age—the sixteenth and seventeenth centuries. Alonso's edition of Luis de Góngora's poem, "Soledades," which included a prose version that explained the meaning of a poem long considered incomprehensible, rescued both Góngora and his poem from oblivion. Among the other poets that Alonso examined are Saint John of the Cross, Garcilaso, and Fray Luis de León. Eventually, Alonso's criticism encompassed the entire range of Spanish literature—early and modern, poetry and prose.

As a poet, Alonso was an instrumental part of the renaissance of Spanish poetry that occurred in the decades after the civil war of 1936 to 1939. Alonso first began to publish his poetry during the 1920s, when he was a member of the group of poets known as the "Generation of 1927," a group that included Federico García Lorca and Rafael Alberti. It wasn't until the 1940s, however, that Alonso began to attract attention as a major poet. In his two most important collections of poetry, *Hijos de la ira* and *Oscura noticia*—both published in the mid-1940s—the author examines humanity's "search for religious and personal transcendence on the one hand, and [its] temptation to egotism, pettiness and destruction on the other," as Andrew P. Debicki notes in his biography *Dámaso Alonso.* As a testament to his importance as a poet, Alonso was awarded the 1978 Miguel de Cervantes prize, Spain's highest literary honor.

In addition to his works of poetry and criticism, Alonso was a respected translator. His own writings have been translated into several languages, including English, German, Portuguese, and Italian.

BIOGRAPHICAL/CRITICAL SOURCES:

BOOKS

Contemporary Literary Criticism, Volume 14, Gale, 1980.
Debicki, Andrew P., *Dámaso Alonso,* Twayne, 1970.
Homenaje a Dámaso Alonso, El Club (Madrid), 1978.

PERIODICALS

Times Literary Supplement, May 31, 1974.

OBITUARIES:

PERIODICALS

New York Times, January 27, 1990.
Times (London), January 27, 1990.
Washington Post, January 27, 1990.

*   *   *

ALURISTA
  See URISTA, Alberto H.

ALVAREZ, Alejandro Rodríguez   1903-1965
  (Alejandro Casona)

PERSONAL: Born March 23, 1903, in Besullo, Asturias, Spain; died of a heart attack, September 17, 1965, in Madrid, Spain; son of Gabino Rodríguez (a teacher) and Faustina (a teacher; maiden name, Alvarez) Alvarez; married Rosalía Martín (deceased). *Education:* Attended University of Murcia, 1920-22; graduated from Escuela Superior del Magisterio, 1926.

CAREER: Schoolmaster; elementary school superintendent, Valle de Arán, two years; inspector of schools; founder of children's theatre, El Pájaro Pinto ("The Painted Bird"); director of touring theatre company, Teatro del Pueblo, 1937-39; writer, 1939-63.

AWARDS, HONORS: National prize for literature, 1932, for juvenile adaptations of myths; Lope de Vega Prize, 1933, for "La sirena varada."

WRITINGS:

PRODUCED PLAYS

"El crimen de Lord Arturo" (three-act drama; title means "The Crime of Lord Arthur"), first produced in Havana, 1938.
"Romance de Dan y Elsa" (three-act comedy; title means "Romance of Dan and Elsa"), first produced in Caracas at Teatro Nacional, June 17, 1938.
"Sinfonía incabada" (three-act drama; title means "Unfinished Symphony"), first produced in Montevideo at Teatro Solis, May 21, 1940.
(With Francisco Madrid) "María Curie" (dramatic biography; title means "Marie Curie"), first produced in Buenos Aires at Teatro Smart, 1940.
"¡A Belén, pastores!" (title means "To Bethlehem, Shepherds"), first produced in Montevideo at Parque Rodó, December, 1951.
"Siete gritos en el mar" (three-act comedy; title means "Seven Cries in the Sea"), first produced in Buenos Aires at Teatro Politeama, March 14, 1952.
"Carta de una desconocida" (monologue; title means "Letter of an Unknown Woman"), first produced in Porto Alegre, Brazil, at Teatro Sao Pedro, May 9, 1957.
"Tres diamantes y una mujer" (title means "Three Diamonds and a Woman"), first produced in Buenos Aires, 1961.

Also author of one-act plays, "Sancho Panza en la isla Baratoria" (comedy; title means "Sancho Panza on the Island of Baratoria"), and "Entremés del mancebo que casó con mujer brava" (comedy; title means "Interlude of the Cripple who Married a Fierce Woman"), both produced at Teatro del Pueblo. Author of additional plays, including "La Flauta del Sapo," 1937; "Romance en tres noches," 1938; "Farsa y justicia del corregidor" (title means "Farce and Justice of the Magistrate"), "Farsa del cornudo apaleado" (comedy; title means "Farce of the Thrashed Cuckold"), and "Fablilla del secreto bien guardado" (comedy; title means "Little Fable of the Well-Kept Secret"), all 1949; "Tres diamantes y una mujer," 1961; and "El lindo Don Gato" (title means "The Handsome Mr. Gato").

PUBLISHED PLAYS

(Under pseudonym Alejandro Casona) *Nuestra Natacha: Comedia en tres actos el segundo dividido en tres cuadros* (also see below; title means "Our Natasha"; three-act comedy; includes one-act play, "La balada de Atta Troll," first produced in Barcelona, 1935), Editorial Magisterio Español (Madrid), 1936, Editorial Losada (Buenos Aires), 1970.

(Adaptor; under pseudonym Alejandro Casona) *Otra vez el diablo; cuento de miedo en tres jornadas y un amanecer* (also see below; title means "The Devil Again"; three-act play; first produced at Teatro Español, April 26, 1935), Universidad Nacional (Mexico), 1937, reprinted, Ediciones Alfil, 1965.

(Under pseudonym Alejandro Casona) *La dama del alba* (also see below; four-act ballad; title means "The Lady of the Dawn"; first produced in Buenos Aires at Teatro Avenida, November 3, 1944), Editorial Losada, 1944, Escelicer, 1971.

(Under pseudonym Alejandro Casona) *Retablo jovial; cinco farsas en un acto* (also see below), El Ateneo (Buenos Aires), 1949.

(Under pseudonym Alejandro Casona) *Los árboles mueren de pie, comedia en tres actos, el tercero dividido en dos cuadros* (also see below; three-act comedy; title means "The Trees Die Standing"; first produced in Buenos Aires at Teatro Ateneo, April 1, 1949), B. U. Chiesino (Buenos Aires), 1950, reprinted, Escelicer (Madrid), c. 1971.

(Under pseudonym Alejandro Casona) *La sirena varada* (also see below; title means "The Siren Castaway"; three-act comedy; first produced in Madrid at Teatro Español, March 17, 1934), edited by Ruth C. Gillespie, Appleton-Century-Crofts, 1951.

(Under pseudonym Alejandro Casona) *Prohibido suicidarse en primavera; comedia en tres actos* (also see below; three-act comedy; title means "Suicide Prohibited in the Springtime"; first produced in Mexico City at Teatro Arbeu, June 12, 1937), Librería Renacimiento, 1951.

(Under pseudonym Alejandro Casona) *La barca sin pescador* (also see below; three-act comedy; first produced in Buenos Aires at Teatro Liceo, July 24, 1945), edited by José A. Balseiro and J. Rüs Owre, illustrations by Lily Gruen, Oxford University Press, 1955, reprinted, Escelicer (Madrid), 1971, published as *The Boat without a Fisherman,* translation by David Stanley, Wellington College, University of Guelph, 1970.

(Under pseudonym Alejandro Casona) "Corona de amor y muerte; Doña Inés de Castro" (also see below; three-act dramatic legend; title means "The Crown of Love and Death"; first produced in Buenos Aires at Teatro Odeón, March 8, 1955), published as *Corona de amor y muerte,* edited by Balseiro and Owre, Oxford University Press, 1960.

"La molinera de Arcos" (five-scene musical interlude), first produced in Buenos Aires at Teatro Argentino, June 19, 1947), published as *La molinera de Arcos y Sinfonía inacabada* (title means "The Wife of the Miller of Arcos"), Editorial Losada, 1964.

(Under pseudonym Alejandro Casona) *La tercera palabra; comedia en tres actos* (three-act comedy; title means "The Third World"; first produced in Buenos Aires at Teatro Odeón, May 29, 1953), Ediciones Alfil, 1965.

(Adaptor) *Las tres perfectas casadas; comedia en tres actos* (three-act comedy; title means "The Three Perfect Married Women"; first produced in Buenos Aires at Teatro Avenida, May, 1941), Ediciones Alfil, 1966.

(Under pseudonym Alejandro Casona) *La casa de los siete balcones; comedia en tres actos* (also see below; three-act comedy; title means "The House with Seven Balconies"; first produced in Buenos Aires at Teatro Liceo, April 12, 1957), Ediciones Alfil, 1966.

(Under pseudonym Alejandro Casona) *La llave en el desván; comedia dramática en tres actos* (three-act comedy; title means "The Key in the Loft"; first produced at Teatro Ateneo, June 1, 1951), Ediciones Alfil, 1967.

(Under pseudonym Alejandro Casona) *El caballero de las espuelas de oro* (play; title means "The Knight of the Golden Spurs"), edited by Balseiro and Eliana Suárez-Rivero, Oxford University Press, 1968.

OTHER

(Translator) *El Kálevala, la epopeya nacional de Finlandia,* Losada, 1944.

(Under pseudonym Alejandro Casona) *Obras completas,* prologue by Federico Carlos Sáinz de Robles, Aguilar (Mexico), 1954.

Flor de leyendas; lecturas literarias para niños (also see below), Editorial "Orión" (Mexico), 1961.

(Contributor; under pseudonym Alejandro Casona) Pedro Calderón de la Barca, *L'acalde de Zalaméa,* [Paris], 1962.

(Editor) Gabriel Tellez, *El burlador de Sevilla,* Editora Nacional (Madrid), 1966.

(Under pseudonym Alejandro Casona) *Antología,* Coculsa (Madrid), 1968.

(Under pseudonym Alejandro Casona) *Vida de Francisco Pizarro,* illustrations by Oscar Estruga, Aguilar, 1969.

Also author of film scripts, including *Our Natacha,* 1943, and *The Mary Celeste,* 1944, and of poems, including *El peregrino de la barba florida* (title means "The Pilgrim with the Flowing Beard") and *La flauta del sapo* (title means "The Flute of the Toad"), 1930. Author of stories, essays, articles, and lectures.

PLAY COLLECTIONS

(Under pseudonym Alejandro Casona) *La sirena varada, Prohibido suicidarse en primavera, Entremés del mancebo que casó con mujer brava,* Editorial Losada, 1941.

(Under pseudonym Alejandro Casona) *Nuestra Natacha. Otra vez el diablo,* Editorial Losada, 1943.

(Under pseudonym Alejandro Casona) *Teatro: La sirena varada. La barca sin pescador. Los árboles mueren de pie,* Editorial Losada 1951, reprinted, 1973.

(Under pseudonym Alejandro Casona) *La sirena varada. Las tres perfectas casadas, Entremés del mancebo que casó con mujer brava,* Losada (Buenos Aires), 1957.

(Under pseudonym Alejandro Casona) *Teatro: La dama del alba. Retablo jovial. La tercera palabra,* Editorial Losada, 1964.

Obras completas (three volumes), edited by F. C. Sáinz de Robles, [Buenos Aires and Madrid], 1964-65.

(Under pseudonym Alejandro Casona) *El caballero de las espuelas de oro. Retablo jovial,* Espasa-Calpe (Madrid), 1965.

Número homenaje a Alejandro Casona: La sirena varada, Nuestra Natacha, Sinfonía incabada, Ediciones Alfil, 1966.

Teatro selecto de Alejandro Casona (includes *La sirena varada, Prohibido suicidarse en primavera, Los árboles mueren de pie, La casa de los siete balcones, El caballero de las espuelas de oro,* and *Nuestra Natacha*), Escelicer (Madrid), 1966.

(Under pseudonym Alejandro Casona) *Flor de leyendas. La sirena varada. La dama del alba. La barca sin pescador,* prologue by Antonio Magaña-Esquivel, Editorial Porrúa, 1972.

Lady of the Dawn; Love, Death and a Crown (translation of *La dama del alba* and *Corona de amor y muerte*), prologue and translation by Graciela Miranda de Graves, Albatros Ediciones (Valencia), 1972.

Teatro (three volumes; includes *La sirena varada, La barca sin pescador, Los árboles mueren de pie, Prohibido suicidarse en primavera, Siete gritos en el mar, Corona de amor y muerte,*

La dama del alba, Retablo jovial, and *La tercera palabra*), Editorial Losada, 1973.

Work has appeared in anthologies, including *The Genius of the Spanish Theater,* translated by B. Roman and R. O'Brien, edited by O'Brien, 1964; *Modern Spanish Theatre,* edited by Michael Benedikt and George E. Wellwarth, 1968; and *The Modern Spanish Stage: Four Plays,* edited by Marion P. Holt, 1970.

SIDELIGHTS: Spanish playwright Alejandro Rodríguez Alvarez, better known as Alejandro Casona, was a friend of dramatist Federico García Lorca. A supporter of the Spanish Republic, Casona left Spain in 1937 during the Civil War; he subsequently traveled to France and Mexico and eventually moved to Buenos Aires, where he lived for twenty-five years. The success of his productions in Argentina encouraged him to return to his homeland in 1962, and there the plays he had written in South America during the thirties and forties become the dominating voice in the Spanish theatre.

Casona's plays dealt with ethical concerns that included duty and self-sacrifice for the sake of love and truth. "Throughout Casona's works runs a preoccupation with spiritual crises, often created by social problems, and revealing keen psychological understanding, tender human sympathy, and profound moral concern," wrote William H. Shoemaker in the foreword to *Nuestra Natacha.* He added, "An uncommon sensitiveness to these things has combined with a lyrical tendency and with the irresistible attraction of other-worldly Death and the Devil to make most of his plays non-realistic fantasies."

An example of Casona's fusion of the unreal with the everyday was *The Siren Castaway,* his first commercial success. It introduced a prostitute who struggles with her sanity, and believes she is a beached mermaid who has been captured and forced to live on land. Like most of Casona's works, this play showed that real satisfaction in life can only be found by abandoning make-believe worlds and facing reality. In *Modern Language Journal,* A. Wallace Woolsey commented on Casona's unusual approach to drama: "The psychological approach is not new to drama and literature in general, but Casona seems to have evolved something almost unique in his technique. He has drawn upon his knowledge of medieval folklore and witchcraft, modern psychology and his own knowledge of man gained from life and observation."

Nuestra Natacha is Casona's only purely social play, and shows the ideals of the Spanish reformers of the pre-Franco years. In another issue of *Modern Language Journal,* Melissa A. Cilley stated the play's theme, which is common to Casona's work: "In work and responsibility lies real happiness and that steadfast devotion to duty brings about a moral and spiritual self-reliance that is necessary for a satisfying life." James R. Stamm wrote in *A Short History of Spanish Literature* that Casona's plays always included a happy ending, "always an opening of new hope and new possibilities in the last act." He concluded that while "such gentle sentiments can hardly produce high tragedy or gripping drama, but Casona can be delightful when taken on his own terms."

BIOGRAPHICAL/CRITICAL SOURCES:

BOOKS

Casona, Alejandro, *Nuestra Natacha,* edited by William H. Shoemaker, D. Appleton-Century, 1947.
Contemporary Literary Criticism, Volume 49, Gale, 1988.
Stamm, James R., *A Short History of Spanish Literature,* New York University Press, 1979.

PERIODICALS

Modern Language Journal, November, 1947, February, 1954.

* * *

ALVAREZ, Lynne

ADDRESSES: Home—347 West 57th St., Apt. 18C, New York, N.Y. 10025.

CAREER: Poet and playwright.

WRITINGS:

The Dreaming Man (poems), Waterfront Press, 1984.

Contributor to periodicals, including *Niagara, New Letters, Colorado State Review,* and *City.*

PLAYS

"El Guitarrón," published in *On New Ground: Contemporary Hispanic American Plays,* Theatre Communications Group, 1987.

Also author of unpublished and unproduced plays "Mundo," "Hidden Parts," "The Reincarnation of Jamie Brown," "Thin Air: Tales From a Revolution," and "The Wonderful Tower of Humbert Lavoignet."

BIOGRAPHICAL/CRITICAL SOURCES:

PERIODICALS

Village Voice, April 23, 1985.

* * *

ALVAREZ MURENA, Héctor Alberto 1923- (H. A. Murena)

PERSONAL: Born February 14, 1923, in Buenos Aires, Argentina.

ADDRESSES: San José 910, Buenos Aires, Argentina.

CAREER: University of Buenos Aires, Buenos Aires, Argentina, lecturer in philosophy, 1968—.

WRITINGS:

UNDER NAME H. A. MURENA

La vida nueva (poetry), Sudamericana (Buenos Aires), 1951.
El juez (title means "The Judge"; play), Sudamericana, 1953.
El pecado original de América (title means "The Original Sin of America"; essay collection), Sur (Buenos Aires), 1954.
La fatalidad de los cuerpos (title means "Fatality of Bodies"; first novel in "Story of a Day" trilogy), Sur, 1955.
El centro del infierno (short stories), Sur, 1956.
Las leyes de la noche (second novel in "Story of a Day" trilogy), Sur, 1958, translation by Rachel Caffyn published as *The Laws of the Night,* Scribner, 1970.
El círculo de los paraísos (poetry), Sur, 1958.
El escándalo y el fuego, Sudamericana, 1959.
Homo atomicus (essay collection), Sur, 1961.
Ensayos sobre subversión (essay collection), Sur, 1962.
Relámpago de la duración, Losada (Buenos Aires), 1962.
(With Francisco Ayala) *La evasión de los intelectuales* (essay collection), Centro de Estudios y Documentación Sociales (Mexico), 1963.
El demonio de la armonía (poetry), Sur, 1964.
Los herederos de la promesa (title means "Heirs of the Promise"; third novel in "Story of a Day" trilogy), Sur, 1965.

Epitalámica (title means "Epithalamic"; novel), Sudamericana, 1969.

El nombre secreto: Ensayos (essay collection), Monte Avila (Caracas, Venezuela), 1969.

Polispuercón, Sudamericana, 1970.

Caína muerte (novel), Sudamericana, 1971.

El coronel de caballería y otras relatos (short stories), Tiempo Nuevo (Caracas), 1971.

La cárcel de la mente (essay collection), Emecé (Buenos Aires), 1971.

La metáfora y lo sagrado, Tiempo Nuevo (Buenos Aires), 1973.

El águila que desaparece, Alfa Argentina (Buenos Aires), c. 1975.

Folosofía, Monte Avila, 1976.

(With D. J. Vogelmann) *El secreto claro: Diálogos,* edited by Sara Gallardo and Vogelmann, Fraterna (Buenos Aires), c. 1978.

Also author of short story collection *Primer testamento,* 1946, novel *Nímas Nímenos,* 1969, and *F. G.: Un bárbaro entre la belleza,* 1972.

SIDELIGHTS: Argentine author H. A. Murena is noted for his essay collections and novels that explore existential problems of Latin American life. An author who has also written poetry, short stories, and a play, Murena first gained widespread attention with the 1954 publication of his essay collection *El pecado original de América.* This volume argues that in their search for freedom and independence from the Old World, Latin Americans committed the "original sin" of cutting themselves off from European values, which could have provided the cultural guidance that Murena feels is missing in the New World. Murena is also known for detailing the loneliness and suffering inherent in modern existence in his novel trilogy "Story of a Day," which includes *La fatalidad de los cuerpos, Las leyes de la noche,* and *Los herederos de la promesa.*

BIOGRAPHICAL/CRITICAL SOURCES:

BOOKS

Foster, William David and Virginia Ramos Foster, editors, *Modern Latin American Literature,* Volume 2, Ungar, 1975.

Foster, William David, editor, *A Dictionary of Contemporary Latin American Authors,* Center for Latin American Studies, Arizona State University, 1975.

Ward, Philip, editor, *The Oxford Companion to Spanish Literature,* Clarendon Press, 1978.

* * *

AMORIM, Enrique (Manuel) 1900-1960

PERSONAL: Born in 1900 in Salto, Uruguay; died in 1960.

CAREER: Writer.

WRITINGS:

Tangarupá (un lugar de la tierra) cuentos (stories; includes "Tangarupá"; also see below), Claridad (Buenos Aires), 1925.

Tráfico: Buenos Aires; cuentos y notas, Latina (Buenos Aires), 1927, reprinted as *Buenos Aires y sus aspectos,* Galerna (Buenos Aires), 1967.

La trampa del pajonal: Cuentos y novelas (main title means "The Trap in the Straw Patch"), L. J. Rosso (Buenos Aires), 1928, reprinted, Ediciones del Río de la Plata (Montevideo, Uruguay), 1962.

Visitas al cielo (poems), M. Gleizer (Buenos Aires), 1929.

La carreta: Novela de quitanderas y vagabundos (novel; main title means "The Cart"), Claridad, c. 1932, reprinted, Losada (Buenos Aires), 1969.

El paisano Aguilar (novel; title means "The Peasant Aguilar"), Montevideo (Buenos Aires), 1934, reprinted, Casa de las Américas (Havana), 1964.

La edad despareja (novel; title means "The Uneven Age"), Claridad, 1938.

El caballo y su sombra (novel), Club de Libro A.L.A. (Buenos Aires), 1941, translation by Richard L. O'Connell and James Graham Luján published as *The Horse and His Shadow,* Scribner, 1943.

La luna se hizo con agua (novel; title means "The Moon Was Made from Water"), Claridad, 1944.

El asesino desvelado (title means "The Unmasked Assassin"), Emecé Editores (Buenos Aires), 1945, reprinted, Librería Huemul (Buenos Aires), 1981, student edition, adapted by J. Chalmers Herman and Agens Marie Brady, published as *El asesino desvelado del "Séptimo círculo" por Enrique Amorim,* Houghton, 1952.

Nueve lunas sobre Neuquén (title means "Nine Moons over Neuquén"), Lautaro (Buenos Aires), 1946.

Primero de mayo, Adelante (Montevideo), 1949.

La segunda sangre [and] *Pausa en la selva* [and] *Yo voy más lejos,* Conducta (Buenos Aires), 1950.

La victoria no viene sola, Bolsa de los Libros (Montevideo), 1952.

Feria de farsantes (novel), Futuro (Buenos Aires), 1952.

Después del temporal (stories), Quetzal (Buenos Aires), 1953.

Sonetos del amor en octubre, Botella al Mar (Buenos Aires), 1954.

Todo puede suceder (novel; title means "Everything Can Happen"), Vir (Montevideo), 1955.

Corral abierto (novel; title means "Open Corral"), Losada, 1956.

Los montaraces: Las leyendas, las supersticiones, han entenebrecido el suelo de América (novel; main title means "The Backwoods Men"), Goyanarte (Buenos Aires), 1957, reprinted, Arca (Montevideo), 1973.

La desembocadura (novel; title means "The Outlet"), Losada, 1958.

Don Juan 38: Pasatiempo en tres actos, Montevideo, 1959.

Eva Burgos (novel), Alfa (Montevideo), 1960.

Temas de amor, Instituto Amigos del Libro Argentino (Buenos Aires), 1960.

Mi patria: Poemas (poems), Ediciones Papel de Poesía (Montevideo), 1960.

Los pájaros y los hombres (title means "Birds and Men") [and] *El Mayoral* [and] *Vaqueros de la cordillera,* Galería Libertad (Montevideo), 1960.

Para decir la verdad: Antología, 1920-1960, selected by Hugo Rodríguez Urruty, Aquí, Poesía (Montevideo), 1964.

Los mejores cuentos (stories), selected by Angel Rama, Arca, 1967.

La plaza de las carretas, Nuevo Mundo (Montevideo), 1967.

Tangarupá, Arca, 1967.

Horizontes y bocacalles, Arca, 1968.

El ladero, y otros cuentos (stories), Centre de Recherches Hispaniques (Paris), 1969, reprinted as *El ladero y varios cuentos,* 1970.

Miel para la luna y otros relatos, "Cerno" Paysandú, 1969.

(With others) *Antología de la poesía amorosa* (anthology of love poetry), Perseo (Buenos Aires), 1971.

El Quiroga que yo conocí, Arca/Calicanto (Montevideo), 1983.

Also author of novel *Zanga,* 1952; author of short books of poetry.

SIDELIGHTS: Considered one of the great Uruguayan novelists and short story writers, Enrique Amorim wrote of the towns and people of the pampas in Argentina and Uruguay, in the area of the Río de la Plata. Amorim's knowledge of the area came from his experiences on his family's *estancia* (ranch) in northern Uruguay where, as Harley D. Oberhelman noted in *Books Abroad,* "at his father's side he became interested in the destinies of the sad, passive, frugal people who toiled in the fields." While Amorim's writing was criticized by some for being uneven, he was acclaimed as an innovative, lively storyteller who displayed, according to Oberhelman, "a sympathetic understanding of the plains people and an appreciation of the spectacular beauty of the motionless landscape." In *Carnet crítico* (translated for *Modern Latin American Literature*), Ricardo Latcham stated that "no Uruguayan writer of the twentieth century possessed the amazing vitality of Enrique Amorim." Latcham called Amorim "a profound master of the themes of rural Uruguay," and cited his "capacity for renovation, the constant freshness of his art, and the beautiful mixture of fantasy and reality that flows through his novels and short stories."

BIOGRAPHICAL/CRITICAL SOURCES:

BOOKS

Foster, David William and Virginia Ramos Foster, *Modern Latin American Literature,* Ungar, 1975.
Latcham, Ricardo, *Carnet crítico,* Alfa, 1962.
Mose, K. E. A., *Enrique Amorim: The Passion of a Uruguayan,* Plaza Mayor Ediciones, 1972.

PERIODICALS

Books Abroad, spring, 1960.
Book Week, August 22, 1943.
Nation, September 4, 1943.
New York Times, August 15, 1943.
Weekly Book Review, August 8, 1943.

* * *

ANAYA, Rudolfo A(lfonso) 1937-

PERSONAL: Born October 30, 1937, in Pastura, N.M.; son of Martín (a laborer) and Rafaelita (Mares) Anaya; married Patricia Lawless (a counselor), July 21, 1966. *Education:* Attended Browning Business School, 1956-58; University of New Mexico, B.A. (English), 1963, M.A. (English), 1968, M.A. (guidance and counseling), 1972.

ADDRESSES: Home—5324 Canada Vista N.W., Albuquerque, N.M. 87120. *Office*—Department of English, University of New Mexico, Albuquerque, N.M. 87131.

CAREER: Public school teacher in Albuquerque, N.M., 1963-70; University of Albuquerque, Albuquerque, N.M., director of counseling, 1971-73; University of New Mexico, Albuquerque, associate professor, 1974-88, professor of English, 1988—. Teacher, New Mexico Writers Workshop, summers, 1977-79. Lecturer, Universidad Anahuac, Mexico City, Mexico, summer, 1974; lecturer at other universities, including Yale University, University of Michigan, Michigan State University, University of California, Los Angleles, University of Indiana, and University of Texas at Houston. Board member, El Norte Publications/Academia; consultant.

MEMBER: Modern Language Association of America, American Association of University Professors, National Council of Teachers of English, Trinity Forum, Coordinating Council of Literary Magazines (vice president, 1974-80), Rio Grande Writers Association (founder and first president), La Academia Society, La Compañía de Teatro de Albuquerque, Multi-Ethnic Literary Association (New York, N.Y.), Before Columbus Founda-

tion (Berkeley, Calif.), Santa Fe Writers Co-op, Sigma Delta Pi (honorary member).

AWARDS, HONORS: Premio Quinto Sol literary award, 1971, for *Bless Me, Ultima;* University of New Mexico Mesa Chicana literary award, 1977; City of Los Angeles award, 1977; New Mexico Governor's Public Service Award, 1978 and 1980; National Chicano Council on Higher Education fellowship, 1978-79; National Endowment for the Arts fellowships, 1979, 1980; Before Columbus American Book Award, Before Columbus Foundation, 1980, for *Tortuga;* New Mexico Governor's Award for Excellence and Achievement in Literature, 1980; literature award, Delta Kappa Gamma (New Mexico chapter), 1981; D.H.L., University of Albuquerque, 1981; Corporation for Public Broadcasting script development award, 1982, for "Rosa Linda"; Award for Achievement in Chicano Literature, Hispanic Caucus of Teachers of English, 1983; Kellogg Foundation fellowship, 1983-85; D.H.L., Marycrest College, 1984; Mexican Medal of Friendship, Mexican Consulate of Albuquerque, N.M., 1986.

WRITINGS:

Bless Me, Ultima (novel; also see below), Tonatiuh International, 1972.
Heart of Aztlán (novel), Editorial Justa, 1976.
Bilingualism: Promise for Tomorrow (screenplay), Bilingual Educational Services, 1976.
(Editor with Jim Fisher, and contributor) *Voices from the Rio Grande,* Rio Grande Writers Association Press, 1976.
(Contributor) Charlotte I. Lee and Frank Galati, editors, *Oral Interpretations,* 5th edition, Houghton, 1977.
(Contributor) *New Voices 4 in Literature, Language and Composition,* Ginn, 1978.
(Author of introduction) Sabine Ulibarri, *Mi abuela fumaba puros,* Tonatiuh International, 1978.
(Contributor) *Anuario de letras chicanas,* Editorial Justa, 1979.
(Contributor) *Grito del sol,* Quinto Sol Publications, 1979.
Tortuga (novel), Editorial Justa, 1979.
"The Season of La Llorona" (one-act play), first produced in Albuquerque, N.M., at El Teatro de la Compañía de Albuquerque, October 14, 1979.
(Translator) *Cuentos: Tales from the Hispanic Southwest, Based on Stories Originally Collected by Juan B. Rael,* edited by José Griego y Maestas, Museum of New Mexico Press, 1980.
(Editor with Antonio Márquez) *Cuentos Chicanos: A Short Story Anthology,* University of New Mexico Press, 1980.
(Editor with Simon J. Ortiz) *A Ceremony of Brotherhood, 1680-1980,* Academia Press, 1981.
The Silence of the Llano (short stories), Tonatiuh/Quinto Sol International, 1982.
The Legend of La Llorona (novel), Tonatiuh/Quinto Sol International, 1984.
The Adventures of Juan Chicaspatas (epic poem), Arte Público, 1985.
A Chicano in China (nonfiction), University of New Mexico Press, 1986.
The Faralitos of Christmas: A New Mexican Christmas Story (juvenile), New Mexico Magazine, 1987.
Lord of the Dawn: The Legend of Quetzacoatl, University of New Mexico Press, 1987.
(Editor) *Voces: An Anthology of Nuevo Mexicano Writers,* University of New Mexico Press, 1987.
"Who Killed Don José" (play), first produced in Albuquerque, N.M., at La Compañía Menval High School Theatre, July, 1987.

"The Farolitos of Christmas" (play), first produced in Albuquerque, N.M., at La Compañía Menval High School Theatre, December, 1987.

Selected from "Bless Me, Ultima," Literary Volumes of New York City, 1989.

(Editor with Francisco Lomelí) *Aztlán: Essays on the Chicano Homeland,* El Norte, 1989.

(Editor) *Tierra: Contemporary Fiction of New Mexico* (short story collection), Cinco Puntos, 1989.

Author of unproduced play "Rosa Linda," for the Corporation for Public Broadcasting; author of unpublished and unproduced dramas for the Visions Project, KCET-TV (Los Angeles). Contributor of short stories, articles, essays, and reviews to periodicals in the United States and abroad, including *La Luz, Bilingual Review-Revista Bilingüe, New Mexico Magazine, La Confluencia, Contact II, Before Columbus Review, L'Umano Avventura, 2 Plus 2,* and *Literatura Uchioba;* contributor to *Albuquerque News.* Editor, *Blue Mesa Review;* associate editor, *American Book Review,* 1980-85, and *Escolios;* regional editor, *Viaztlán* and *International Chicano Journal of Arts and Letters;* member of advisory board, *Puerto Del Sol Literary Magazine.* Anaya's manuscript collection is available at the Zimmerman Museum, University of New Mexico, Albuquerque.

SIDELIGHTS: Best known for his first novel, *Bless Me, Ultima,* Rudolfo A. Anaya's writing stems from his New Mexican background and his fascination with the oral tradition of Spanish *cuentos* (stories). The mystical nature of these folk tales has had a significant influence on his novels, which portray the experiences of Hispanics in the American Southwest. But the novelist's books are also about faith and the loss of faith. As Anaya explains in his *Contemporary Authors Autobiography Series* entry, his education at the University of New Mexico caused him to question his religious beliefs, and this, in turn, led him to write poetry and prose in order to "fill the void." "I lost faith in my God," Anaya writes, "and if there was no God there was no meaning, no secure road to salvation. . . . The depth of loss one feels is linked to one's salvation. That may be why I write. It is easier to ascribe those times and their bittersweet emotions to my characters."

Bless Me, Ultima, "a unique American novel that deserves to be better known," in *Revista Chicano-Riqueña* contributor Vernon Lattin's opinion, leans heavily on Anaya's background in folklore in its depiction of the war between the evil Tenorio Trementina and the benevolent *curandera* (healer) Ultima. Several critics, such as *Latin American Literary Review*'s Daniel Testa, have praised Anaya's use of old Spanish-American tales in his book. "What seems to be quite extraordinary," avers Testa, " . . . is the variety of materials in Anaya's work. He intersperses the legendary, folkloric, stylized, or allegorized material with the detailed descriptions that help to create a density of realistic portrayal."

The novel is also a *bildungsroman* about a young boy, named Antonio, who grows up in a small village in New Mexico around the time of World War II. Most of Antonio's maturation is linked with a struggle with his religious faith and his trouble in choosing between the nomadic way of life of his father's family, and the agricultural lifestyle of his mother's. Reviewers of *Bless Me, Ultima* have lauded Anaya for his depiction of these dilemmas in the life of a young Mexican-American. For example, in *Chicano Perspectives in Literature: A Critical and Annotated Bibliography,* authors Francisco A. Lomelí and Donaldo W. Urioste call this work "an unforgettable novel . . . already becoming a classic for its uniqueness in story, narrative technique and struc-

ture." And *America* contributor Scott Wood remarks: "Anaya offers a valuable gift to the American scene, a scene which often seems as spiritually barren as some parched plateau in New Mexico."

Anaya's next novel, *Heart of Aztlán,* is a more political work about a family that moves from a rural community to the city; but as with its predecessor, Anaya mixes in some mystical elements along with the book's social concern for the Chicano worker in capitalist America. Reception of this second book has been somewhat less enthusiastic than it was for *Bless Me, Ultima.* Marvin A. Lewis observes in *Revista Chicano-Requeña* that "on the surface, the outcome [of *Heart of Aztlán*] is a shallow, romantic, adolescent novel which nearly overshadows the treatment of adult problems. The novel does have redeeming qualities, however, in its treatment of the urban experience and the problems inherent therein, as well as in its attempt to define the mythic dimension of the Chicano experience." Similarly, *World Literature Today* critic Charles R. Larson feels that *Heart of Aztlán,* along with *Bless Me, Ultima,* "provide[s] us with a vivid sense of Chicano Life since World War II."

Tortuga, Anaya's third novel, continues in the mythical vein of the author's other works. The novel concerns a young boy who must undergo therapy for his paralysis and wear a body cast, hence his nickname "Tortuga," which means turtle. "Tortuga," however, also "refers . . . to the 'magic mountain' (with a nod here to Thomas Mann) that towers over the hospital for paralytic children," according to Angelo Restivo in *Fiction International.* While staying at the Crippled Children and Orphans Hospital, Tortuga becomes more spiritually and psychologically mature, and the novel ends when he returns home after his year-long ordeal. As with the novelist's other books, *Tortuga* is a story about growing up; indeed, *Bless Me, Ultima, Heart of Aztlán,* and *Tortuga* form a loosely-tied trilogy that depicts the Hispanic experience in America over a period of several decades. As the author once told *CA,* these novels "are a definite trilogy in my mind. They are not only about growing up in New Mexico, they are about life."

All of Anaya's novels attempt to find the answers to life's questions, doing so from the perspective of his own personal cultural background. "If we as Chicanos do have a distinctive perspective on life," he tells John David Bruce-Novoa in *Chicano Authors: Inquiry by Interview,* "I believe that perspective will be defined when we challenge the very basic questions which mankind has always asked itself: What is my relationship to the universe, the cosmos? Who am I and why am I here? If there is a Godhead, what is its nature and function? What is the nature of mankind?" These questions echo the doubts that the author has had all his life, and that he links closely to American mythology. Anaya explains to Bruce-Novoa, "All literature, and certainly Chicano literature, reflects, in its more formal aspects, the mythos of the people, and the writings speak to the underlying philosophical assumptions which form the particular world view of culture. . . . In a real sense, the mythologies of the Americas are the only mythologies of all of us, whether we are newly arrived or whether we have been here for centuries. The land and the people force this mythology on us. I gladly accept it; many or most of the American newcomers have resisted it."

BIOGRAPHICAL/CRITICAL SOURCES:

BOOKS

Bruce-Novoa, John David, *Chicano Authors: Inquiry by Interview,* University of Texas Press, 1980.

Contemporary Authors Autobiography Series, Volume 4, Gale, 1986.
Contemporary Literary Criticism, Volume 23, Gale, 1983.
Dictionary of Literary Biography, Volume 82: *Chicano Writers, First Series,* Gale, 1989.
Lomelí, Francisco A. and Donaldo W. Urioste, *Chicano Perspectives in Literature: A Critical and Annotated Bibliography,* Pajarito, 1976.

PERIODICALS

America, January 27, 1973.
American Book Review, March-April, 1979.
Fiction International, Number 12, 1980.
Hispania, September, 1985.
La Luz, May, 1973.
Latin American Literary Review, spring-summer, 1978.
Revista Chicano-Riqueña, spring, 1978, summer, 1981.
University of Albuquerque Alumni Magazine, January, 1973.
University of New Mexico Alumni Magazine, January, 1973.
World Literature Today, spring, 1979.

—*Sketch by Kevin S. Hile*

*   *   *

ANDERSON IMBERT, Enrique   1910-

PERSONAL: Born February 12, 1910, in Córdoba, Argentina; immigrated to United States, 1947, naturalized citizen, 1953; son of José Enrique and Honorina (Imbert) Anderson; married Margot Di Clerico (a librarian), March 30, 1935; children: Carlos, Anabel (Mrs. Jack Himelblau). *Education:* National University of Buenos Aires, M.A., 1940, Ph.D., 1946.

ADDRESSES: Home—20 Elizabeth Rd., Belmont, Mass. 02178. *Office*—Harvard University, Cambridge, Mass. 02138.

CAREER: Universidad de Tucumán, Tucumán, Argentina, professor of Spanish literature, 1940-47; University of Michigan, Ann Arbor, assistant professor, 1947-48, associate professor, 1948-51, professor of Spanish literature, 1951-65; Harvard University, Cambridge, Mass., Victor S. Thomas Professor of Hispanic American Literature, 1965—. Visiting associate professor, Princeton University, 1950.

MEMBER: American Academy of Arts and Sciences, Academia Argentina de Letras.

AWARDS, HONORS: Buenos Aires City Hall literary prize, 1934, for manuscript of novel *Vigilia;* Guggenheim fellow, 1954-55.

WRITINGS:

IN ENGLISH TRANSLATION

Historia de la literatura hispanoamericana, two volumes, Fondo de Cultura Económica (México), 1954-61, 8th edition, 1979, translation of 2nd edition by J. V. Falconieri published in one volume as *Spanish-American Literature: A History,* Wayne State University Press, 1963, revised translation by Elaine Mallery published in two volumes, 1966.
El grimorio, Editorial Losada (Buenos Aires), 1961, translation by Isabel Reade published as *The Other Side of the Mirror,* Southern Illinois University Press, 1966.
Vigilia [and] *Fuga,* Editorial Losada, 1962, translation by Esther Whitmarsh Phillips published as *Fugue,* Coronado Press, 1967.
El gato de cheshire, Editorial Losada, 1965, translation published as *The Cheshire Cat,* Thunder City, 1980.

IN SPANISH

La flecha en el aire, La Vanguardia (Buenos Aires), 1937, reprinted, Editorial Gure (Buenos Aires), 1972.
Tres novelas de Payró con pícaros en tres miras, Facultad de Filosofía y Letras, Universidad de Tucuman, 1942.
Ensayos, privately printed, 1946.
Ibsen y su tiempo, Yerba Buena (La Plata), 1946.
Las pruebas del caos, Yerba Buena, 1946.
El arte de la prosa en Juan Moltavo, El Colegio de México, 1948, 2nd edition, Talleres Gráficos de Editorial Bedout, 1974.
Estudios sobre escritores de América, Editorial Raigal (Buenos Aires), 1954.
(Editor with Lawrence B. Kiddle) *Viente cuentos hispanoamericanos del siglo viente,* Prentice-Hall, 1956.
La crítica literaria contemporánea, Editorial Platania (Buenos Aires), 1957.
Los grandes libros de Occidente y otros ensayos, Ediciones de Andrea (México), 1957.
¿Qué es la prosa?, Editorial Columba (Buenos Aires), 1958, 4th edition, 1971.
El cuento español, Editorial Columba, 1959.
Crítica interna, Editorial Taurus (Madrid), 1961.
(Editor with Kiddle) *Viente cuentos españoles del siglo viente,* Prentice-Hall, 1961.
Los domingos del profesor, Editorial Cultura (México), 1965.
La originalidad de Rubén Darío, Centro Editor de América Latina (Buenos Aires), 1967.
Genio y figura de Sarmiento, Editorial Universitaria (Buenos Aires), 1967.
Análisis de "Tabare," Centro Editor de América Latina, 1968.
Análisis de "Fausto," Centro Editor de América Latina, 1968.
La sandía y otros cuentos, Editorial Galerna (Buenos Aires), 1969.
Una aventura amorosa de Sarmiento, Editorial Losada, 1969.
Métodos de crítica literaria, Revista de Occidente (Madrid), 1969, published as *La crítica literaria: Métodos y problemas,* Alianza Editorial (Madrid), 1984.
(Compiler with Eugenio Florit) *Literatura hispanoamericana,* Holt, 1970.
La locura juega al ajedrez, Siglo XXI Editores (México), 1971.
Estudios sobre letras hispánicas, Editorial Libros de México, 1974.
La botella de Klein, Centro Argentino P.E.N. Club Internacional (Buenos Aires), 1975.
El realismo mágico y otros ensayos, Monte Avila (Caracas), 1976.
El leve Pedro (short stories), Alianza Tres (Madrid), 1976.
Cuentos en miniatura (short stories), Equinoccio (Caracas), 1976.
Victoria, Editorial Emece (Buenos Aires), 1977.
Los primeros cuentos del mundo, Ediciones Marymar (Buenos Aires), 1977.
(Contributor) Jorge Lafforgue and Jorge B. Rivera, compilers, *Asesinos de papel,* Calicanto Editorial (Buenos Aires), 1977.
Las comedias de Bernard Shaw, Universidad Nacional Autónoma de México, 1977.
Teoría y técnica del cuento, Ediciones Marymar, 1979.
En el telar del tiempo, Volume I: *El mentir de las estrellas,* Editorial Emece (Buenos Aires), 1979, Volume II: *El estafador se jubila: La locura juega al ajedrez,* Corregidor (Buenos Aires), 1985, Volume III: *La botella de Klein: Dos mujeres y un Julian,* Corregidor, 1980, Volume V: *El tamaño de las brujas,* Corregidor, 1986.
La prosa: Modalidades y usos, Marymar, 1984.
Páginas selectas de Anderson Imbert, Celtia (Buenos Aires), 1985.

Nuevos estudios sobre letras hispanas, Kapelusz (Buenos Aires), 1986.

WORK IN PROGRESS: El anillo de Mozart, stories; *El pasado por venir,* a novel.

* * *

ANDRADE, Jorge Carrera
   See CARRERA ANDRADE, Jorge

* * *

ANDROVAR
   See PRADO (CALVO), Pedro

* * *

APODACA, Rudy S(amuel) 1939-

PERSONAL: Born August 8, 1939, in Las Cruces, N.M.; son of Raymond and Elisa (a homemaker; maiden name Alvarez) Apodaca; married Nancy Ruth Mitcham, January 16, 1967; children: Cheryl Ann, Carla Renee, Cynthia Lynn, Rudy Samuel. *Education:* New Mexico State University, B.S., 1961; Georgetown University, J.D., 1964.

ADDRESSES: Office—New Mexico Court of Appeals, P.O. Box 2008, Santa Fe, N.M. 87504-2008.

CAREER: Private practice of law, Las Cruces, N.M., 1964-1986; New Mexico Court of Appeals, Santa Fe, appellate judge, 1987—; writer. Attorney for Citizens Bank of Las Cruces, 1975-85. *Military service:* U.S. Army, 1964-66; became captain.

WRITINGS:

The Waxen Image (novel), Titan Publishing, 1977.

Also author of an unproduced screenplay and unpublished novel, both titled "A Rare Thing," 1984.

WORK IN PROGRESS: A thriller screenplay; a fictional examination of three generations of a family.

SIDELIGHTS: Rudy S. Apodaca is a Chicano lawyer, judge, and writer. Fueled by his experiences as a Hispanic youth living in New Mexico, he developed an interest in civil rights issues and pursued a career in law. Apodaca published his first novel, *The Waxen Image,* in 1977. Blending elements of the fantastic and the real, the novel features an aging American scientist who, after developing a drug that restores his youth, becomes the leader of a drug subculture in a New Mexico town. Mysterious deaths and disappearances occur as the town falls victim to moral decline. Though not widely reviewed, *The Waxen Image* is considered a provocative, if somewhat uneven, suspense novel. Apodaca has also written "A Rare Thing," an unpublished novel and screenplay about a teenage boy growing up in New Mexico. The youth in the coming-of-age story is forced into manhood by circumstances not of his own choosing.

Apodaca told *CA:* "I love to write creatively—to express myself through the written word. I wish I had more time to devote to the craft, but I find myself occupied with my other work, which sometimes seems overpowering. As an appellate judge, I author court opinions and decisions, a process that entails legal and technical writing. But such writing has its limits and does not permit the writer to make use of his imagination or give him the license to create characters, theme, and plot. However, there are no set limits to where our imagination will take us in the craft of creative writing. Writing, to me, provides an escape."

BIOGRAPHICAL/CRITICAL SOURCES:

BOOKS

Dictionary of Literary Biography, Volume 82: *Chicano Writers, First Series,* Gale, 1989.

* * *

AQUINO, Luis Hernández
   See HERNANDEZ AQUINO, Luis

* * *

ARAGON, Luis Cardoza y
   See CARDOZA y ARAGON, Luis

* * *

ARCINIEGAS, Germán 1900-

PERSONAL: Born December 6, 1900, in Bogotá, Colombia; son of Rafael (a farmer) and Aurora (Angueyra) Arciniegas; married Gabriela Vieira, November 19, 1926; children: Aurora, Gabriela Mercedes. *Education:* Universidad Nacional, Bogotá, Colombia, LL.D., 1924. *Politics:* Liberal. *Religion:* Roman Catholic.

ADDRESSES: Home—Calle 92 10-21, Bogotá, Colombia. *Office*—Facultad de Filosofía y Letras, Universidad de los Andes, Cra. 1E-18A-10, Bogotá, Colombia. *Agent*—ALA Agencia Latinoamericana, P.O. Box 343790, Coral Gables, Fla. 33134.

CAREER: Universidad Nacional, Bogotá, Colombia, professor of sociology, 1925-28; *El Tiempo,* Bogotá, editor, 1928-30, London correspondent, 1930-33, editor-in-chief, 1933-39, director, 1939; Government of Colombia, vice-consul in London, 1930, charge d'affaires in Buenos Aires, 1939-41, Minister of Education, 1941-42, 1945-46, ambassador to Italy, 1959-62, to Israel, 1960-62, to Venezuela, 1967-70, and to Vatican City, 1976-78; Universidad de los Andes, Faculty of Philosophy and Letters, Bogotá, dean, 1979—. Member of Colombian Parliament, 1933-34, 1939-40, 1957-58. Visiting professor, Columbia University, 1943, 1948-57, University of Chicago, 1944, Mills College, 1945, and University of California at Berkeley, 1945. Director, *Cuadernos,* Paris, 1963-65; founder, Museo de Arte Colonial, Bogotá; director, Ediciones Colombia; codirector, *Revista de América.*

MEMBER: Colombian Academy of Letters (Academia Colombiana de la Lengua), Colombian Academy of History (Academia Colombiana de Historia; president, 1980—), National Institute for Arts and Letters (honorary associate), corresponding member of academy of letters of Spain, Cuba, Mexico, and Venezuela, American Committee for Cultural Freedom (former vice-president).

AWARDS, HONORS: Dag Hammarsjkold Prize, 1967; honorary doctorate, Mills College.

WRITINGS:

WORKS IN ENGLISH TRANSLATION

Jiménez de Quesada, Editorial ABC (Bogotá), 1939, translation by Mildred Adams published as *The Knight of the El Dorado: The Tale of Don Gonzalo Jiménez de Quesada and His Conquest of New Granada, Now Called Colombia,* Viking, 1942, reprinted, Greenwood Press, 1968, new Spanish edition published as *El Caballero de El Dorado,* Primer Festival del Libro Colombiano, 1958.

Los alemanes en la conquista de América, Editorial Losada (Buenos Aires), 1941, translation by Angel Flores published as

Germans in the Conquest of America, Macmillan, 1943, reprinted, Hafner, 1971.

(Editor) *The Green Continent: A Comprehensive View of Latin America by Its Leading Writers,* translation by Harriet de Onís and others, Knopf, 1944, reprinted, 1963.

Biografía del Caribe, Editorial Sudamericana (Buenos Aires), 1945, 10th edition, 1973, translation by de Onís published as *Caribbean, Sea of the New World,* Knopf, 1946.

The State of Latin America, translation by de Onís, Knopf, 1952.

Amerigo y el Nuevo Mundo, Editorial Hermes (Mexico), 1955, 2nd edition, 1956, translation by de Onís published as *Amerigo and the New World: The Life and Times of Amerigo Vespucci,* Knopf, 1955, reprinted, Octagon, 1978.

El continente de siete colores: Historia de la cultura en la América Latina, Editorial Sudamericana, 1965, 2nd edition, 1970, translation by Joan MacLean published as *Latin America: A Cultural History,* Knopf, 1967, condensation of Spanish edition published as *Latinoamérica: El continente de siete colores,* edited by Cecil D. McVicker and Osvaldo N. Soto, Harcourt, 1967.

(Contributor) Cole Blasier, editor, *Constructive Change in Latin America,* University of Pittsburg Press, 1968.

(With John S. Knight) *The Twilight of the Tyrants,* Center for Latin American Studies, Arizona State University, 1973.

América en Europa, Editorial Sudamericana, 1975, translation by wife, Gabriela Arciniegas, and Victoria Arana published as *America in Europe: A History of the New World in Reverse,* Harcourt, 1986.

Fernando Botero, translation by Gabriela Arciniegas, Abrams, 1977.

WORKS IN SPANISH

El estudiante de la mesa redonda, J. Pueyo (Madrid), 1932, 4th edition, Ediciones Ercilla (Santiago), 1937, reprinted, Plaza & Janés Editores-Colombia, 1982.

La universidad colombiana, Imprenta Nacional (Bogotá), 1932.

Memorias de un congresista, Editorial Cromos (Bogotá), 1933.

Diario de un peatón, Imprenta Nacional, 1936.

América, tierra firme, Ediciones Ercilla, 1937, 3rd edition, Editorial Sudamericana, 1966.

Los comuneros, Editorial ABC, 1938, 2nd edition, Zig-Zag (Santiago), 1967.

¿Qué haremos con la historia?, Imprente Lehmann (Costa Rica), 1940.

En el país del rascacielos y las zanahorias, Librería Suramérica (Bogotá), 1945.

Este pueblo de América, Fondo de Cultura Económica (Mexico), 1945.

(Editor) *El pensamiento vivo de Andrés Bello,* Editorial Losada, 1946, reprinted, Plaza & Janés Editores-Colombia, 1981.

En medio del camino de la vida, Editorial Sudamericana, 1949, 3rd edition, 1964.

Entre la libertad y el miedo, Ediciones Cuadernos Americanos (Mexico), 1952, 10th revised edition, Editorial Sudamericana, 1958.

Italia, guía para vagabundos, Editorial Sudamericana, 1957, 5th edition, 1965.

América mágica: Los hombres y los meses, Editorial Sudamericana, 1959, 2nd edition, 1961.

América mágica II: Las mujeres y las horas, Editorial Sudamericana, 1961.

(Editor) Ricardo Arenales, *El Terremoto de San Salvador,* 2nd edition, Ministry of Education (San Salvador), 1961.

(Contributor) *Tres ensayos sobre nuestra América,* Biblioteca Cuadernos (Paris), c. 1962.

Colombia, Unión Panamericana (Washington), 1962.

El mundo de la bella Simonetta, Editorial Sudamericana, 1962.

Cosas del pueblo: Crónica de la historia vulgar, Editorial Hermes, 1962, published as *Este pueblo de América,* Secretaría de Educación Pública, Dirección General de Divulgación (Mexico), 1974.

Entre el Mar Rojo y el Mar Muerto: Guía de Israel, E.D.H.A.S.A. (Barcelona), 1964.

Temas de Arciniegas: Invitación a conversar, leer y escribir, edited by McVicker and Soto, Harcourt, 1967.

(Contributor) Marco Aurelio Alamazán, *Claroscuro,* Ultramar (Mexico), 1967.

Genio y figura de Jorge Isaacs, Editorial Universitaria de Buenos Aires, 1967, 2nd edition, 1970.

(Compiler) *Colombia: Itinerario y espíritu de la independencia, según los documentos principales de las revolución,* Editorial Norma (Cali), 1969.

Medio mundo entre un zapato: De Lumumba en el Congo a las brujas en Suecia, Editorial Sudamericana, 1969, 2nd edition, 1971.

Nuevo diario de Noé, Monte Avila (Caracas), 1969.

Nuevo imagen del Caribe, Editorial Sudamericana, 1970, 2nd edition, 1972.

Roma secretísima, Anaya (Salamanca), 1972.

Copérnico: Un hijo de América, Editorial de el Colegio Nacional (Mexico), 1973

Popas in Romania/Estancia en Rumania (text in Romanian and Spanish), Pentru Turism (Bucharest), 1974.

Páginas escogidas (1932-1973), Gredos (Madrid), 1975.

(Editor) *El Zancudo,* Editora Arco, 1975.

(Editor) *Antología de León de Greiff,* Instituto Colombiana de Cultura, Subdirección de Comunicaciones Culturales, División de Publicaciones, 1976.

Galileo mira a América, Instituto Español de Cultura (Rome), 1977.

(Editor) Fernando Lorenzana, *Recuerdos de vida: Diario de su viaje a Bogotá en 1832 y su correspondencia con el primer representante de Colombia en Roma,* Instituto Caro y Cuervo (Bogotá), 1978.

El revés de la historia, Plaza & Janés Editores-Colombia, 1980.

Bolívar, de Cartegena a Santa Marta, Banco Tequendama (Bogotá), 1980.

20,000 comuneros hacia Santa Fe, Editorial Pluma (Bogotá), 1981.

Los pinos nuevos, Editorial Boliviana Internacional, 1982.

Bolívar, el hombre de la gloria, Ediciones Tercer Mundo (Colombia), 1983.

Bolívar y la revolución, Planeta (Bogotá), 1984.

De Pio XII a Juan Pablo II: Cinco Papas que han conmovido al mundo, Planeta, 1986.

OTHER

Contributor to newspapers and magazines, including *La Prensa, La Nación,* and *Cuadernos Americanos.* Editor of *Amerique Latine,* 1974—, *La Revista de la Indias,* and *Correo de los Andes.*

SIDELIGHTS: In *America in Europe: A History of the New World in Reverse,* Colombian historian, journalist, and diplomat Germán Arciniegas "argues that the influence of the New World on the Old has been neglected by historians" and sets out to promote another perspective, summarizes John Gross in the *New York Times.* Drawing examples ranging from the era of Columbus to more recent times, Arciniegas presents "comparisons [that] are rarely invidious and usually serve to correct the common historical underestimation of Americans' achievements," describes *New Yorker* contributor Naomi Bliven. "For example, he reminds us that [South American revolutionary general Simón] Bolívar commanded victorious armies over areas as vast as those Napoleon commanded." Because the scope of his subject is so broad, the author "has set himself a daunting task," comments Gross. "To measure its full extent would indeed be to calculate the incalculable. But Mr. Arciniegas, a veteran Colombian man of letters, is too shrewd to let himself get drawn into attempting an exhaustive survey. Instead, he concentrates on a few major themes and episodes." And while *Atlantic Monthly* contributor Phoebe-Lou Adams comments that the author's evidence "depends on mass and variety rather than upon strict demonstration of cause and effect," she admits that "it is impressively presented and impossible to ignore."

Although he praises the author's overall approach, Gross also contends that Arciniegas "tends to be unduly lyrical about romantic nationalism and revolutions in general, where a little analysis might have been in order." In addition, "his chapter on romanticism itself occasionally threatens to take off into the clouds." But Bliven thinks that the book "abounds in mental openings," especially in Arciniegas's chapter on the Romantic movement, which "rethinks a whole library." *America in Europe* is "intellectual history at its most entertaining," continues the critic. The book is "so saturated with the cultural heritage of the west that it seems effortless, even playful." And while Gross remarks that "every so often you feel the author's rhetoric has got the better of him," the critic admits that "for the most part it is rhetoric animated by ideas, and backed up by substantial learning." Concludes the critic: "The result is an unusually stimulating book, its novelty enhanced—for North American readers—by a Latin American viewpoint."

BIOGRAPHICAL/CRITICAL SOURCES:

BOOKS

Arciniegas, Germán, *Memorias de un congresista,* Editorial Cromos, 1933.
Cobo Borda, Juan Gustavo, *Arciniegas de cuerpo entero,* Planeta, 1987.
Córdova, Federico, *Vida y obra de Germán Arciniegas,* [Havana], 1950.

PERIODICALS

Atlantic Monthly, March, 1986.
New Statesman, October 24, 1969.
New Yorker, May 5, 1986.
New York Times, March 7, 1986.
New York Times Book Review, October 17, 1943, May 18, 1952.
Spectator, October 18, 1969.
Times Literary Supplement, December 4, 1969, March 25, 1977.

*   *   *

ARELLANO, Diana Ramírez de
    See RAMIREZ de ARELLANO, Diana (T. Clotilde)

*   *   *

ARELLANO, Rafael W(illiam) Ramírez de
    See RAMIREZ de ARELLANO, Rafael W(illiam)

*   *   *

ARENAS, Reinaldo 1943-

PERSONAL: Born July 16, 1943, in Holguín, Oriente, Cuba; immigrated to United States, 1980; son of Antonio and Oneida (Fuentes) Arenas. *Education:* Attended Universidad de la Habana, 1966-68, and Columbia University.

ADDRESSES: Home—328 West 44th St., Apt. 63, New York, N.Y. 10036. *Agent*—Thomas Colchie, 700 Fort Washington Ave., New York, N.Y. 10040.

CAREER: Writer. Jose Martí National Library, Havana, Cuba, researcher, 1963-68; Instituto Cubano del Libro (Cuban Book Institute), Havana, editor, 1967-68; *La Gaceta de Cuba* (official Cuban monthly literary magazine), Havana, journalist and editor, 1968-74; imprisoned by the Castro government, c. 1974-76, served time in State Security Prison, 1974, El Murro (prison), Havana, 1974, and Reparto Flores (rehabilitation camp), 1976; visiting professor of Cuban literature at International University of Florida, 1981, Center for Inter-American Relations, 1982, and Cornell University, 1985; guest lecturer at Princeton University, Georgetown University, Washington University (St. Louis), Stockholms Universitet, Cornell University, and Universities of Kansas, Miami, and Puerto Rico.

MEMBER: Center for Inter-American Relations.

AWARDS, HONORS: First mention in Cirilo Villaverde contest for best novel, Cuban Writers' Union, 1965, for *Celestino antes del alba;* named best novelist published in France by *Le Monde,* 1969, for *El mundo alucinante;* Cintas Foundation fellow, 1980; Guggenheim fellow, 1982; Wilson Center fellow, 1988.

WRITINGS:

Celestino antes del alba (novel), Union de Escritores, 1967, translation by Andrew Hurley published as *Singing from the Well,* Viking, 1987, revised Spanish edition published as *Cantando en el pozo,* Argas Vergara, 1982.
El mundo alucinante (novel), Diógenes, 1969, translation by Gordon Brotherston published as *Hallucinations: Being an Account of the Life and Adventures of Friar Servando Teresa de Mier,* Harper, 1971, new translation by Hurley published as *The Ill-Fated Peregrinations of Fray Servando,* Avon, 1987.
Con los ojos cerrados (short stories), Arca, 1972.
Le palais des tres blanches mouffettes (novel; French translation of Spanish original; title means "The Palace of the Very White Skunks"), Editions du Seuil (Paris), 1975, first published in Spanish as *El palacio de las blanquísimas mofetas,* Monte Avila, 1980.
La vieja Rosa (novel; also see below), Librería Cruz del Sur, 1980.
Termina el desfile (short stories), Seix Barral, 1981.
Homenaje a Angel Cuadra, Solar, 1981.
El central (poem), Seix Barral, 1981, translation by Anthony Kerrigan published as *El Central: A Cuban Sugar Mill,* Avon, 1984.
Otra vez el mar (novel), Argos, 1982, translation by Hurley published as *Farewell to the Sea,* Viking, 1986.
Arturo, la estrella más brillante (also see below), Montesinos, 1984.
Necesidad de libertad (essays), Kosmos, 1985.
Persecución: Cinco piezas de teatro experimental, Ediciones, 1986.
Graveyard of the Angels (novel), translated by Alfred MacAdam, Avon, 1987.
La loma del ángel, DADOR, 1987.
El portero (novel; title means "The Doorman"), Presses de la Renaissencse, 1988.

Old Rosa: A Novel in Two Stories (contains *La vieja Rosa* and *Arturo, la estrella más brillante*), translation by Hurley and Ann T. Slater, Grove, 1989.

Contributor of articles and short stories to numerous periodicals, including *El Universal* and *Miami Herald*. Editorial advisor to *Mariel, Noticias de Arte, Unveiling Cuba, Caribbean Review,* and *Linden Lane.*

WORK IN PROGRESS: Antes jue anuchezca, memoirs; *El asalto,* a novel; *Viaje a la Habana,* three short novels.

SIDELIGHTS: Internationally acclaimed writer Reinaldo Arenas was one of more than 140,000 Cuban citizens who left their Latin American homeland for the United States in 1980 during a mass exodus known as the Mariel boat lift. Cuban president Fidel Castro exported to the Florida coast certain natives of Cuba, including common criminals, artists, members of the literati, and other perceived adversaries of the state, in an effort to squelch opposition to his Communist regime. In an interview with F. O. Geisbut for *Encounter,* Arenas admitted that as a writer and a homosexual, he was considered "an enemy of the revolution," guilty of a twofold crime against his country. The author was imprisoned by the Castro government, he further explained to Geisbut, for his alleged display of disrespect "for the rules of the official literature [and] of conventional morality." While Arenas now lives and writes in New York City, he landed on the American mainland on May 5, 1980, with nothing but pajamas and a spare shirt. His manuscripts were confiscated by the Cuban government before he left the island.

As a teenager Arenas joined the resistance movement against the regime of Fulgencio Batista y Zaldivar, then president of Cuba. The author explained in the *Encounter* interview that the Cuban people wanted to topple Batista's totalitarian government and thus fought "against the tyrant in power rather than for Fidel Castro," the young revolutionary leader who led an unsuccessful revolt against the president in 1953. By 1959 Batista had fled Cuba, and, within two years, Castro established a Communist state there, replacing the previous Batista dictatorship with his own brand of totalitarianism. It was within an atmosphere of fierce social and political scrutiny that Arenas composed his first novel, *Celestino antes del alba,* in the mid-1960s.

Translated in 1987 as *Singing from the Well,* the book is an evocation of the fantastic visions experienced by a mentally impaired boy growing up in Cuba's rural poverty. Illegitimate and raised in the turbulent environment created by his cruel grandparents, the child has trouble distinguishing fantasy from reality and imagines, among other things, that he can fly to the safety of the clouds when threatened by his ax-wielding grandfather. The boy finds consolation through his relationship with his cousin (or alter ego), a poet named Celestino who carves verses on trees. While several critics reported difficulty differentiating between dream sequences and periods of realism in the book, most regarded *Singing from the Well* as a novel of hope and an exceptional literary debut for Arenas. One *Times Literary Supplement* reviewer commented, "There is . . . a great deal of social significance in the child's pathetic longing for affection in so unsympathetic an environment." Commenting on his first novel in an interview with Ana Roca for *Américas,* Arenas referred to the story as "the revolt of a poet who wants to create in a completely violent medium."

Arenas's second novel, *El mundo alucinante,* also blends the fantastic with the real, this time in the form of a fictionalized biography. Translated as *Hallucinations,* the book chronicles the life of nineteenth-century Mexican monk and adventurer Fray Servando Teresa de Mier, who suffered torture and persecution in his fight for Mexico's independence from Spain. Imprisoned for suggesting that Mexico was a Christian country prior to the arrival of the Spanish, Servando is sentenced to a lifelong quarantine in Spain. He manages an unbelievable series of escapes from his captors only to fight in an ultimately doomed revolution. "Servando's real crime," theorized Alan Schwartz in *Washington Post Book World,* "is his refusal to be demoralized in a world completely jaded and dedicated to the exploitation of power and wealth."

Arenas defended *Hallucinations* against claims by several critics that the surrealistic rendering of Servando's exploits should have more closely approximated the monk's actual adventures. "True realism," the author told Roca, "is fantasy, the fantastic, the eclectic. It knows no bounds." Arenas further maintained that the depiction of Servando he envisioned could only be accomplished by weaving historical fact with fantasy: "My aim was to portray this compelling personality as a part of the American myth, the New World myth . . . part raving madman and part sublime, a hero, an adventurer, and a perennial exile." Schwartz conceded that any flaws in Arenas's "ambitious technique" were "overshadowed by [the author's] madcap inventiveness, the acid satire, and the powerful writing."

The anti-revolutionary implications of *Hallucinations* led to the banning of the book in Cuba by the Castro government. "What emerges [from the novel]," asserted a *Times Literary Supplement* reviewer, "is at least as much a disenchanted view of Man himself as of revolution in the abstract." Servando finds that the movement for Mexican independence meets with only token victory. By the end of the book, the ghosts of the old regime greet the new revolutionary leaders with a haunting, "We welcome you." Arenas implies that, as in Cuba, the new regime in Mexico will only perpetuate an unjust order. Yet in spite of the apparent bleakness of its vision, the *Times Literary Supplement* reviewer allowed, "The narrative . . . is an accomplished and bizarrely entertaining piece of work."

The manuscript of Arenas's 1982 novel *Otra vez el mar,* translated as *Farewell to the Sea,* was twice confiscated by the Cuban authorities. After being arrested in 1974 for his supposed social deviancy, the author spent time in a reeducation camp; following unsuccessful attempts to reconstruct the novel's plot while in jail, Arenas finally rewrote the book for the third time soon after reaching the United States in 1980. In the *Encounter* interview Arenas described *Farewell to the Sea* as a depiction of "the secret history of the Cuban people."

Set on a beach resort just outside of Havana, the novel parallels Cuba's tumultuous political events with the impact of those events on the nation's citizenry. Hector and his unnamed wife reflect on their lives, hopes, and disappointments since the fall of the Batista government. The first portion of the book is a lengthy interior monologue in which the woman expresses her feelings of emptiness and her desire for, as well as distance from, her husband. Speaking of both life under Castro and life in a passionless marriage, she muses, "The terrible becomes merely monotonous." Hector's thoughts are documented in the second section through a long sequence of dreamlike poetry revealing his outrage over Cuba's failed revolution and his own homosexual longings. After engaging in a sexual encounter with a boy from a nearby beach cottage, Hector hurls seething invectives at his young lover: "You will live your whole life pleading, begging pardon of the whole world for a crime you haven't committed, and doesn't even exist. . . . You will be the world's shame." Hector's verbal abuse leads to the boy's suicide.

While several critics were disappointed by what Michael Wood, writing in the *New York Review of Books,* termed an overly "obsessive and . . . prolix" anticommunist demeanor in the book, virtually every critic acknowledged the power and beauty of Arenas's words. In an article for *Saturday Review,* Anthony DeCurtis called *Farewell to the Sea* "a stunning literary tour-de-force." And Jay Cantor stated in the *New York Times Book Review,* "Mr. Arenas is not interested in ordinary realistic drama. He wants to give the reader the secret history of . . . emotions, the sustaining victories of pleasure and the small dishonesties that callous the soul."

Having emerged from a totalitiarian milieu that he described in *Encounter* as one holding that "there's nothing more dangerous than new ideas," Arenas continues to garner worldwide attention and praise as an eminent writer who—in the tradition of fantastic Latin American fiction—depicts the reality of life in contemporary Cuba. Commenting in the Toronto *Globe and Mail* on the effect of the author's writings, Alberto Manguel observed, "Reinaldo Arenas' Cuba is a dreamworld of repeatedly frustrated passions." The critic further theorized that the writer's works have turned Castro into a "literary creation," rendering the dictator "immortal" and "condemn[ing him] to repeat [his] sins for an eternity of readers."

Arenas told *CA:* "Being an isolated child growing up on a farm very far from people and civilization and under very poor conditions was an important motivating factor in my becoming a writer. In my books I try to communicate my happiness and my unhappiness, my solitude and my hope.

"Since the publication of my novel *El mundo alucinante* in Mexico in 1969, all of my writings have been prohibited in Cuba. In spite of Marxist censorship, however, I managed to keep on writing and was able to send four other novels out of Cuba. Though many of my works have been published all over the world and translated into French, English, Dutch, German, Italian, Japanese, Portuguese, and Turkish, I have not been able to receive any royalties, because Cuba does not have a copyright law.

"In May of 1980 I, together with 125,000 men, women, and children, left Cuba. I thank God now that I am living in freedom. I know that life in the United States is not easy, but I will struggle and keep writing. I am living in New York City, and hope to stay there a while. Still, every day I miss Cuba. I think the best (and the only) way we have for keeping our country alive is in working on our roots."

BIOGRAPHICAL/CRITICAL SOURCES:

BOOKS

Arenas, Reinaldo, *Hallucinations: Being an Account of the Life and Adventures of Friar Servando Teresa de Mier,* translated by Gordon Brotherston, Harper, 1971.
Arenas, Reinaldo, *Farewell to the Sea,* translated by Andrew Hurley, Viking, 1986.
Bejar, Eduardo, *La textualidad de Reinaldo Arenas,* [Madrid], 1988.
Contemporary Literary Criticism, Volume 41, Gale, 1987.
Rozencvaig, Perla, *The Work of Reinaldo Arenas,* [Mexico], 1986.

PERIODICALS

Américas, September, 1981, January-February, 1982.
Chicago Tribune, January 26, 1986.
Chicago Tribune Book World, September 5, 1971.
Encounter, January, 1982.
Globe and Mail (Toronto), June 21, 1986.
Listener, April 22, 1971.
New York Review of Books, March 27, 1986.
New York Times Book Review, August 29, 1971, November 24, 1985.
San Francisco Review of Books, May-June, 1985.
Saturday Review, November-December, 1985.
Times Literary Supplement, April 30, 1970, May 7, 1971, May 30, 1986.
Washington Post Book World, September 5, 1971.

*   *   *

AREVALO MARTINEZ, Rafael   1884-1975

PERSONAL: Born July 25, 1884 in Guatemala City, Guatemala; died on June 12, 1975, in Guatemala City, Guatemala; son of Rafael Arévalo Arroyo (a lawyer) and Mercedes Martínez Pineda; married Evangelina Andrade Díaz, 1911; children: four sons and three daughters.

CAREER: Writer. National Library of Guatemala, Guatemala City, Guatemala, director, 1926-45. Delegate to Panamerican Union, Washington, D.C., 1945-46. Worked as a teller at Banco Agrícola; held several teaching positions.

MEMBER: Spanish Royal Academy (corresponding member).

AWARDS, HONORS: First prize in *Electra* short story contest, 1909, for "Mujer y niños"; Great Cross of Rubén Darío (Nicaragua) and Order of the Quetzal (Guatemala), both 1958.

WRITINGS:

FICTION

El hombre que parecía un caballo (title means "The Man Who Looked Like a Horse"; also see below), 1914, Compañia General de Artes Gráficas (Madrid), 1931, reprinted, Universitaria Centroamericana (San José, Costa Rica), 1982.
Una vida: Novela corta (title means "A Life: Short Novel"), Electra (Guatemala City), 1914.
El hombre que parecía un caballo, y El ángel (title means "The Man Who Looked like a Horse and The Angel"; also see below), Ayestas (Guatemala City), 1920.
Manuel Aldano (La lucha por la vida) (autobiographical novel), Gutenberg (Guatemala City), 1922.
El señor Monitot (title means "Mr. Monitot"; short stories), Sánchez & de Guise (Guatemala City), 1922.
La Oficina de Paz de Orolandia: Novela del imperialismo yanqui (title means "The Office of Peace in Goldland: Novel of Yankee Imperialism") Sánchez & de Guise, 1925, condensed edition, Landívar, 1966.
Las noches en el palacio de la nunciatura (title means "Nights in the Palace of the Nunciature"), Sánchez & de Guise, 1927.
La signatura de la esfinge (narración de J. M. Cendal, profesor universitario) (title means "The Sign of the Sphinx [Narration by J. M. Cendal, University Professor]"; short stories), G. M. Staebler (Guatemala City), 1933.
El mundo de los maharachías (title means "The World of the Maharachias"; novel), Muñoz Plaza (Guatemala), 1939.
Viaje a Ipanda (title means "Trip to Ipanda"; sequel to *El mundo de los maharachías*; novel), Centro (Guatemala City), 1939.
Hondura (novela) (title means "Depth [Novel]"), [Guatemala], 1947.
El hombre que parecía un caballo y otros cuentos, Universitaria (Guatemala City), 1951.
El embajador de Torlania (title means "The Ambassador of Torlania"; novel), Landívar, 1960.

Cratilo y otros cuentos (title means "Cratylus, and Other Stories"; short stories), Universidad de San Carlos (Guatemala), 1968.

Cuatro contactos con lo sobrenatural y otros relatos (title means "Four Contacts with the Supernatural and Other Tales"), Landívar, 1971.

Also author of *El trovador colombiano* (sequel to *El hombre que parecía un caballo*), 1914; also author of short story, "Mujer y niños."

POETRY

Las rosas de Engaddí (title means "The Roses of Engedi"; also see below), 1918, Sánchez & de Guise, 1923.

Llama (title means "Flame"), Renacimiento (Guatemala City), 1934.

Por un caminito así (title means "Along a Path Such as This"), Unión Tipográfica (Guatemala City), 1947.

Poemas, 1901-1959, Landívar, 1958.

Poemas, Nacional, 1965.

Selección poética, José de Pineda Ibarra (Guatemala), 1975.

Also author of *Juglerías,* 1911, *Maya,* 1911, *Los atormentados* (title means "The Tormented"), 1914, and *35 poemas,* 1944.

OTHER

El hombre que parecía un caballo y Las rosas de Engaddí, Sánchez & de Guise, 1927.

Los duques de Endor: Drama en tres actos y en verso (title means "The Duke and Duchess of Endor: Three-Act Drama in Verse"; play), Centro (Guatemala City), 1940.

Influencia de España en la formación de la nacionalidad centroamericana (title means "Spain's Influence in the Formation of the Central American Nationality"), Nacional (Guatemala City), 1943.

Nietzsche el conquistador (La doctrina que engendró la segunda guerra mundial) (title means "Nietzsche, The Conqueror [The Doctrine that Begat the Second World War]"), Sánchez & de Guise, 1943.

¡Ecce Pericles! (biography), Nacional, 1945, reprinted, Universitaria Centroamericana, 1983.

Concepción del cosmos (title means "Conception of the Cosmos"), Landívar (Guatemala), 1954, published with an additional chapter, c. 1956.

El hijo pródigo: Drama en tres actos y en verso (title means "The Prodigal Son: Three-Act Drama in Verse"; play), [Guatemala], 1956.

Obras escogidas: Prosa y poesía—50 años de vida literaria (title means "Chosen Works: Prose and Poetry—50 Years of Literary Life"), Universitaria, 1959.

Rafael Arévalo Martínez: Homenaje del Instituto Guatemalteco-Americano al cumplirse cincuenta años de vida literaria de este gran escritor guatemalteco (title means ". . . Homage by the Guatemalan-American Institute Upon the Completion of the Fiftieth Year of Literary Life by this Great Guatemalan Writer"; contains an anthology of his work), [Guatemala], 1959.

Cuentos y poesías, edited by Carlos García Prada, Iberoamericanas (Madrid), 1961.

Narración sumaria de mi vida; o, historia de una varita de virtudes (title means "Narration of My Life; or, Story of a Magician's Wand"), Landívar, 1968.

Founding editor of *Juan Chapín,* 1913-15; staff member, became editor of *Centro América* (official publication of International Central American Office), 1915-20; on editorial staff of *La República.*

SIDELIGHTS: Credited with introducing modernism into Guatemala's literary environment, poet, novelist, short-story writer, and essayist Rafael Arévalo Martínez has been dubbed a modernist, post-modernist, surrealist, and precursor of magic realism by critics. His unique brand of fiction, which sports some characteristics of all the groups to which its creator has been assigned, stood in sharp contrast to the work of most other Guatemalan authors who had continued to cultivate nineteenth-century modes of writing long after much of the rest of the Hispanic world. While his countrymen wrote in the manner of the romantics or *costumbristas,* emphasizing historical or picturesque scenes of peasant life, Arévalo Martínez inaugurated a series of psycho-zoological tales with the publication in 1915 of *El hombre que parecía un caballo* ("The Man Who Looked Like a Horse"), a work that appears in nearly every anthology of Latin American literature.

Much to his distress, Arévalo Martínez was known throughout his life as the author of this story written very early in his career. In *Rafael Arévalo Martínez,* María A. Salgado noted that "literary critics have concurred with creative writers in acclaiming [*El hombre que se parecía un caballo*] as one of the most powerful and original expressions in Spanish American literature." She quoted Chile's Nobel Prize winner Gabriela Mistral as writing in a letter to Arévalo Martínez that this early work was "one of the perfect readings that life has afforded me." Similarly, in his *Spanish-American Literature: A History,* Enrique Anderson-Imbert called it "the most original story of [Arévalo Martínez's] generation." The critic likened the work's "nightmarish and poetic atmosphere" to that produced in Franz Kafka's fiction.

The character described by the title of the piece is reportedly a mocking portrait of the Colombian poet Miguel Angel Osorio (who was in real life one of Arévalo Martínez's friends). The action of the story—which is minimal—deals with the growing relationship between the author-narrator and a Mr. Aretal. The narrator notices that Aretal takes on aspects of different horses depending on the day and the mood he is in. Slowly it occurs to him that Aretal has no personality of his own but is merely a reflection of those who surround him. The tale ends when, as Salgado noted, "Aretal, realizing that the narrator has captured his true essence, 'kicks' him on the forehead and quickly 'gallops' away."

The story provoked intense critical study and seemed even to fascinate its author who himself offered several analyses of the work. To Arévalo Martínez, an understanding of the story did not necessarily include identification of the title character (he denied any deliberate attempt at a caricature), but instead concentration on two key passages. Salgado quotes the essential paragraphs Arévalo Martínez singled out, including the following portion in English translation: "Besides, the soul of Mr. Aretal was no longer blue like mine. Then I understood that what I had loved in Mr. Aretal was my own blue!" According to Salgado, Arévalo Martínez interprets these words as revealing that the true meaning of the story is the discovery that God can be found in each person's inner being. Salgado noted that this theme could be found in many examples of modernist writing and concluded, "The formal and thematic perfection of 'The Man Who Looked Like a Horse' shows how adept [Arévalo Martínez] had become at casting his interior visions into tangible images."

Additional fictional works of Arévalo Martínez which feature animals include *El trovador colombiano* ("The Colombian Troubadour"), which has a man-dog for its main character, and *El mundo de los maharachías* ("The World of the Maharachias"), which tells the story of a shipwrecked sailor who finds himself in a world populated by very intelligent creatures who look like monkeys. Other works introduce the reader to men who resemble tigers or elephants. Salgado speculated that Arévalo Martínez's use of animals to portray his characters may be related to the Central-American Indian concept of the *nahual*. According to Indian tradition, each man has a corresponding animal spirit or *nahual* (much like the North American Indian totem) which acts as that person's link to the protective spirit of the universe. Salgado commented that what Arévalo Martínez was able to accomplish with his use of animals in his stories was "the penetration of his subject and the capture of his very essence" in much the same way that the *nahual* was said to contain the characteristic traits of the particular person to whom it corresponded.

Arévalo Martínez's ability to reveal the inner workings of his characters' minds through the use of animal analogies in his psycho-zoological tales, especially in *El hombre que parecía un caballo*, was perhaps his major contribution to Hispanic literature. His double handicaps of being of very poor health throughout his life (he suffered chronic neurasthenia) and coming from a country which lacked an active literary environment during the time he was most productive explain why his works are not better known today.

BIOGRAPHICAL/CRITICAL SOURCES:

BOOKS

Anderson-Imbert, Enrique, *Spanish-American Literature: A History,* Volume 2: *1910-1963,* 2nd edition revised and updated by Elaine Malley, Wayne State University Press, 1969.
Salgado, María A., *Rafael Arévalo Martínez,* Twayne, 1979.

—*Sketch by Marian Gonsior*

*   *   *

ARGUEDAS, José María   1911-1969

PERSONAL: Born January 18, 1911, in Andahuaylas, Peru; committed suicide, November 28, 1969, in Lima, Peru; son of Victor Manuel (a provincial traveling judge) and Doña Victoria (Altamirano) Arguedas; married Celia Bustamente Vernal, 1939. *Education:* Received doctorate from University of San Marcos, Lima.

ADDRESSES: Apartado Postal 43, Lima, Peru.

CAREER: Post office employee in Lima, Peru, 1932-37; arrested and imprisoned for organizing a demonstration against an Italian fascist general at University of San Marcos, 1937; National University, Sicuani, Peru, teacher of Spanish, 1939-41; head of department of folklore and popular arts at Ministry of Public Education, beginning 1945; director of Institute of Ethnological Studies at Peruvian Museum of Culture, beginning 1951; National Museum of History, director of Institute of Ethnological Studies, beginning 1953, director of museum, 1964-69; University of San Marcos, Lima, professor of regional cultures of Peru, 1959-69. Member of a commission to reform secondary education in Peru, 1940. Director of the Casa de la Cultura, 1963-64. Professor of Quechua at Universidad Nacional Agraria, 1963-69. Lecturer.

AWARDS, HONORS: Inca Garcilaso Prize, 1968.

WRITINGS:

IN ENGLISH

Canciones y cuentos del pueblo quechua, Editorial Huascaran (Lima), 1949, translation by Ruth Walgreen Stephan pub-

lished as *The Singing Mountaineers: Songs and Tales of the Quechua People,* University of Texas Press, 1957.
Los ríos profundos (novel), Editorial Losada (Buenos Aires), 1958, translation by Frances H. Barraclough published as *Deep Rivers,* University of Texas Press, 1978.
Yawar fiesta (novel; title means "Blood Feast"), CIP (Lima), 1941, reprinted, Editorial Universitaria (Santiago), 1968, translation by Barraclough, University of Texas Press, 1985.

OTHER

Agua (short stories; title means "Water"), [Peru], 1935.
(Translator from the Quechua) *Canto kechwa* (title means "Quechua Song"), Ediciones Club del Libro Peruano, 1938.
Runa yupay, Comisión Central del Censo, 1939.
Cusco, Corporación Nacional de Turismo (Lima), 1947.
(Editor with Francisco Izquierdo Ríos) *Mitos, leyendas y cuentos peruanos,* Ediciones de la Dirección de Educación Artística y Extensión Cultural (Lima), 1947, second edition, 1970.
Cuentos mágico-realistas y canciones de fiestas tradicionales: Folklore del valle del Mantaro, provincias de Jauja y Concepción, Editora Médica Peruana (Lima), 1953.
Diamantes y pedernales (short stories; title means "Diamonds and Gems"), Mejía & P. L. Villanueva (Lima), 1954.
Las comunidades de España y del Perú (title means "The Communities of Spain and Peru"), University of San Marcos, 1954.
Evolución de las comunidades indígenas, [Lima], 1957.
El arte popular religioso y la cultura mestiza, Revista del Museo Nacional (Lima), 1958.
(Author of introduction) *Bibliografía del folklore peruano,* Instituto Panamericano de Geografía e Historia (Mexico City), 1960.
El sexto (novel; title means "The Sixth One"), Mejía, 1961.
La agonía de Rasu Niti (novel), Populibros Peruanos (Lima), c. 1964.
Todas las sangres (novel; title means "All the Races"), Editorial Losada, 1964.
(Translator from the Quechua) *Poesía quechua* (title means "Quechua Poetry"), Editorial Universitaria de Buenos Aires, 1966.
(Translator from the Quechua) Francisco de Avila, *Dioses y hombres de Huarochirí* (title means "Gods and Men of Huarochirí"), Museo Nacional de Historia y el Instituto de Estudios Peruanos, 1966.
Amor mundo y otros relatos (short stories), Arca (Montevideo), 1967.
El zorro de arriba y el zorro de abajo (novel; title means "The Fox From Above and the Fox From Below"), Editorial Losada, 1971.
Temblar/Katatay, INC, 1972.
El forastero y otros cuentos (short stories), Sandino (Montevideo), 1972.
Páginas escogidas (selected works), Editorial Universo, 1972.
Cuentos olvidados, Ediciones Imágenes y Letras, 1973.
(Contributor) Mario Vargas Llosa, *La novela,* América Nueva, 1974.
Relatos completos (complete short stories), Editorial Losada, 1974.
Formación de una cultura nacional indoamericana (addresses, essays, and lectures), compiled by Angel Rama, Siglo XXI Editores (Mexico), 1975.
Señores e indios: Acerca de la cultura quechua (essays, addresses, and lectures), Arca, 1976.

Editor of *Palabra,* a literary review.

SIDELIGHTS: Ever since Francisco Pizarro conquered the Incas in 1533, Peru has had two cultures, Indian and Hispanic. For centuries the Indian civilization had been forgotten, ignored, or misunderstood by scholars and writers. In the 1920s, however, a new literary wave which emphasized native rather than European culture swept Latin America. Called the indigenous movement, it attracted a number of Peruvian authors, among whom the most famous was José María Arguedas.

Arguedas championed the cause of the Quechua Indians, who were descendants of the Incas. Born in a city where the vast majority of people spoke Quechua, Arguedas learned to speak Quechua before he spoke Spanish. Because his mother died when he was only three, he was often cared for by his family's Quechua servants, for whom he developed a deep affection and respect. When Arguedas was a teenager, he began to accompany his father, a traveling lawyer, on his journeys. As the two men traveled through many remote regions in Peru, they became acquainted with some of the Indian serfs who were working for large landowners. For a time the young Arguedas worked on one of the haciendas, where he befriended the serfs and came to sympathize with their oppression.

Having gained such an intimate look at Quechua life and culture, Arguedas was shocked when he first began reading Peruvian fiction. In most of the literature written at that time, the Andean Indians were mere cardboard characters, depicted either as noble savages or as violent people whose ways could never be understood by white men. Even those writings which were sympathetic to the Indians' plight disturbed Arguedas, for they presented a stereotyped image of landowners as cruel and inhuman. In his own writing, Arguedas sought to show the complexity of both peoples.

Agua, Arguedas's first book, is a collection of three stories. The narratives, which are semi-autobiographical, are all told from the point of view of a child who sympathizes with the Indians whom he describes. The most notable feature of *Agua* is its style. In this book, Arguedas began to develop a language that would show the interrelationship between the Indian and Hispanic cultures of Peru. Although the book is written in Spanish, it is liberally sprinkled with Quechua expressions. The Quechua syntax is applied to the Spanish language to further emphasize the connection between the two cultures.

Arguedas's style was to become more skilled with time. Commenting on the development of his style, Phyllis Rodríguez-Peralta wrote: "For the bilingual Arguedas it was impossible to convey the essence of the Indian in either traditional Spanish or in a dialect concocted for picturesque effects. Indeed his laborious search for a valid style of speech inserts a unique tone in his writing. . . . By the time Arguedas reaches his major novels, the intertwining of Quechua and Spanish is handled so magnificently that the reader himself is aware of the psychological and artistic distinctions of language."

Among Arguedas's major novels are *Yawar fiesta* and *Todas las sangres.* In *Yawar fiesta,* the authorities prohibit their Indian subjects from practicing a primitive version of bullfighting at the Yawar fiesta. Instead the magistrates hire a professional bullfighter, who panics and flees from the ring. The courageous Indian who carries on the bullfight is killed. The novel points out that the so-called civilized element of society can be even more savage than the Indians whom it scorns. *Todas las sangres* deals with the rivalry between two brothers, a farmer and a mine owner, but the book extends far beyond their personal struggles. Rodríguez-Peralta termed *Todas las sangres* "a vast sociological document which focuses on the latent unrest in all social strata of Peruvian society."

Although Arguedas's work is highly regarded in his own country, few of his books have been translated into English. The first novel, *Los ríos profundos* (*Deep Rivers*), bears many similarities to Arguedas's own life: Ernesto, the protagonist, is the son of an itinerant lawyer. Raised by Indian servants and appreciative of their folkways, the boy undergoes an identity crisis when he attends a Catholic boarding school where most of the students have nothing but disdain for the Indians. "The book movingly dramatizes the difference between the worlds of the Indian and the Spaniard, and so is an essential part of the canon of the new Latin-American literature," noted a critic for *New Yorker.* "The violation of the Indians' dignity by the harsh imposition of Spanish order is made both tangible and inevitable." A commentator for the *Virginia Quarterly Review* also lauded *Deep Rivers:* "Arguedas is dramatic rather than dogmatic in his portrayal of social forces, and his use of Quechua songs and his vivid descriptions of landscape and wildlife give the novel charm and power. Notable is his evocation of Ernesto's magical perception of things, the 'deep river' of Indian consciousness that underlies the whole novel."

Arguedas's scholarly work went hand in hand with his literary ventures. An anthropologist, he wrote a dissertation comparing the Andean Indians of Puquio, Peru, with the residents of some isolated communities in Spain. He published a number of works on Peruvian folklore and translated Quechua songs and folktales into Spanish. As director of several museums in Peru, he had access to a wealth of information about Indian culture. In 1950 and 1951 he delivered a series of lectures, "The Problems of Peruvian Culture," which provoked much commentary. The reforms that Arguedas advocated in these lectures and in his writings were slow in coming, and as his final book reveals, he gradually began to lose hope that change would ever be effected.

Arguedas's last novel, *El zorro de arriba y el zorro de abajo* ("The Fox From Above and the Fox From Below"), was published posthumously. As Wolfgang A. Luchting explained, the "above" in the title refers to the Sierra, where the Indians have lived for centuries; "below" refers to Chimbote, a boom town on the coast to which the Indians flock to get jobs. The novel, which is incomplete, consists of narrative sections interspersed with segments from Arguedas's diary. The despair evinced in this novel over the continued exploitation of the Indians is perhaps what drove Arguedas to take his own life in 1969. Luchting wrote of *El zorro* and its creator: "Julio Ortega has made the best observation: this is a novel written to defeat death; but death won. All in all, a novel replete with defects, as is all Arguedas's fiction, but defects one feels ashamed to point out, for one feels that by criticizing one again destroys life, that of the author's memory and perhaps of a vital myth. *El zorro* is in parts deeply moving and disturbing: it proves that writing can be living, or even death. Arguedas was a very great man, and this book proves it."

BIOGRAPHICAL/CRITICAL SOURCES:

BOOKS

Contemporary Literary Criticism, Gale, Volume 10, 1979, Volume 18, 1981.

PERIODICALS

Best Sellers, November, 1978.
Books Abroad, autumn, 1972.
Hispania, May, 1972, March, 1978.
New Yorker, October 16, 1978.

Times Literary Supplement, March 17, 1966.
Virginia Quarterly Review, autumn, 1978.
Washington Post Book World, July 9, 1978.
World Literature Today, winter, 1977, winter, 1978.

*   *   *

ARGUETA, Manlio 1936-

PERSONAL: Born November 24, 1936 (one source lists 1935), in San Miguel, El Salvador.

ADDRESSES: Home—San José, Costa Rica. *Office*—c/o Vintage Books, 201 East 50th St., New York, N.Y. 10022.

CAREER: Poet and novelist.

AWARDS, HONORS: Certamen Cultural Centroamericano award, 1968, for *El valle de las hamacas;* Casa de las Américas Prize, 1977.

WRITINGS:

En el costado de la luz (poems), Editorial Universitaria de El Salvador (San Salvador, El Salvador), 1968.
El valle de las hamacas (novel), Editorial Sudamericana (Buenos Aires, Argentina), 1970.
Caperucita en la zona roja, Casa de las Américas (Havana, Cuba), 1977.
Un día en la vida (novel), UCA Editores (San Salvador), 1980, translation by Bill Brow published as *One Day of Life,* Aventura/Vintage Books, 1983.
(Editor, annotator, and author of prologue) *Poesía de El Salvador,* Editorial Universitaria Centroamericana (San José, Costa Rica), 1983.
Cuzcatlán: Donde bate la mar del sur (novel), Editorial Guaymuras (Tegucigalpa, Honduras), 1986, translation by Clark Hansen published as *Cuzcatlán: Where the Southern Sea Beats,* Aventura/Vintage Books, 1987.

SIDELIGHTS: "El Salvador's most renowned writer," according to Jim Miller in *Newsweek,* exiled poet and novelist Manlio Argueta is best known in the United States for two novels of social protest, *Un día en la vida* (1980), translated as *One Day of Life,* and *Cuzcatlán: Donde bate la mar del sur* (1986), translated as *Cuzcatlán: Where the Southern Sea Beats.* Set against the backdrop of El Salvador's prolonged civil war, both books testify to the experiences of Salvadoran peasants as they struggle for survival and rights in the face of violence and murderous repression. Argueta particularly focuses on the brutal and secretive campaign of Salvadoran military officials as they wage—with the purported complicity of the U.S.-backed Salvadoran government—death squads, beatings, and "disappearances" among the peasantry. The charges brought by Argueta against the government and military, in addition to his open support of the guerrilla rebel cause, have made life in El Salvador particularly dangerous for him. He has lived in exile in Costa Rica since 1980, when the Salvadoran authorities halted the printing of his novel *One Day of Life* and ordered confiscation of all existing copies. Prior to his exile, Argueta had been arrested and expelled from El Salvador numerous times for his involvement in various political causes.

Argueta's critical reception in the United States has been mixed, hovering between what Raymond A. Paredes in the *Los Angeles Times Book Review* describes as being "praised by some as courageous and moving but more frequently . . . dismissed as awkward and crudely propagandistic." Reviewers commend Argueta's novels as authentic, compassionate portrayals of the plight of El Salvador's peasants, yet he also draws criticism for an overtly political, one-sided, dimension to his narratives. In a review of *One Day of Life* for the *New Republic,* Christopher Dickey praises Argueta for presenting Salvadoran peasants "as something more than political ciphers," yet adds, "there is a great deal about this book, alas, that is so obvious, so banal, so plainly bad as literature and so potentially misleading as politics and sociology, that one hesitates to praise it at all." Nick Caistor in the *New Statesman* addresses this aspect in terms of Argueta being an exiled Central American writer. "Cut off from his natural audience, Argueta has to imagine a public for himself, and is unsure how much he can take for granted at either the linguistic or the cultural level," Caistor writes. "The pitfall is obvious: that of becoming over-simple or over-didactic, as the writer strives to inform a foreign audience how things are his country, rather than being able to share with them feelings about experiences that have a common base." Despite such shortcomings, Argueta's books, according to Caistor, are valuable in offering "an irreplaceable testimony of the struggle in his country and in the rest of Central America to create freer and more just societies."

Argueta's first book in English translation, *One Day of Life,* recounts twelve hours in the life of a peasant grandmother, Lupe Fuentes, as she reflects on her family, superstitions, religion, and the encompassing violence and poverty that grips her existence. Praising Argueta's evocation of the modern Salvadoran peasant, Grace Ingoldby writes in the *New Statesman* that "the story is a sad one, delicately told, revealing not only Lupe's fate as she is caught in the cross-fire of civil war but also (and as remote from our understanding) the peasant life of birds and flowers and dust, the colours of a country woven in a blanket, infant mortality, hunger, water, a precious commodity offered as a symbolic, superstitious gift to friends and enemies alike." Lupe's story is interspersed with other monologues which likewise provide details and insight into the violence permeating Salvadoran life. Included are accounts by her fifteen-year-old granddaughter Adolfina—hunted by the police for participating in a political demonstration—in addition to a neighbor girl who has survived a bus massacre with Adolfina, and Private Martínez, a member of the military who grew up as Lupe's neighbor. The reader discovers many horrors, recounted in an almost commonplace manner, including the fact that Lupe's son has been murdered and decapitated, her daughter-in-law crippled from a beating, and her husband kidnapped, tortured, and dragged through town by the police. "The events this testimonial novel depicts—the oppression, torture and murder of *campesinos* [peasants] by the 'Special Forces'—have a grim predictability," notes Allen Josephs in the *New York Times Book Review,* while Kevin Cully writes in the London *Tribune* that "we are at last offered a glimpse of what that awful, savage war must be like from the point of view of the peasants who bear the brunt of it."

Other reviewers likewise praise Argueta for his authentic portrayal of the violence committed against Salvadoran peasants. "In a one-room building behind the archbishop's offices in San Salvador there are high-piled stacks of depositions recording what is known about the last hours in the lives of thousands of people lost to El Salvador over the last four years. . . . At its best, *One Day of Life,*" according to Dickey, "reads as if it were written from those files and drawn from those grisly images." Dickey adds that when it "works, this book does what virtually no other volume or newspaper story or television report in the United States has even begun to do. It renders the Salvadoran peasant visible." In addition to documenting the plight of peasants caught in the war, *One Day of Life* also depicts, according to Dickey, "the intimate presence of a repressive system that feeds on the violence." Miller concurs, commending *One Day of Life* for "document[ing] a side of the conflict in El Salvador that is rarely reported in America—the squalor, government terror and understandable thirst for vengeance that turn peasants into revolutionaries." The novel also shows how members of death squads can rise from the ranks of the peasants themselves. Private Martínez, the son of Lupe's neighbor, has been recruited by the military and brainwashed into turning against his own people. Argueta provides "insight into the minds of [the] brutalised Civil Guard through the letters that one of them writes home," writes Cully. "Reading the letters is depressing because they throw into sharp focus the fear and suspicion that the authorities harbour toward their own people. The man is himself a peasant but after months with his 'foreign' instructors he regards his own people with icy contempt."

A number of reviewers fault the narrowness of *One Day of Life,* what Miller describes as Argueta's "crude moralizing." Miller elaborates: "The book's conclusion is gruesome, its message about as subtle as a clenched fist. 'They'—as the guardsmen are called—are mindless macho brutes. The poor villagers, in stark contrast, are pious, industrious, upright. In case anyone has missed the point, Lupe declares that 'we're all innocent. The only ones at fault for the bad things that are happening are the authorities.'" Dickey calls *One Day of Life* a "painfully awkward work that teeters somewhere between art and polemic, truth and lies. It calls itself a novel, but its roots are in propaganda . . . , [displaying] the tendency to turn your opponents into demons and your allies into angels." Josephs, noting the book "seldom transcends the literal recording of misery," comments that "readers seeking the particulars of that suffering will find this record rewarding, but those searching for larger discussion of the dilemma facing El Salvador will have to look elsewhere." Other reviewers, however, find simplicity appropriate to *One Day of Life.* "Lupe's story tells of the silent erosion of normal behavior, the effects of intimidation and terror that mark . . . a prolonged period of civil war, and of lessons learnt the hard way," explains Ingoldby: "Christian goodness must no longer be confused with resignation; stoicism in the face of horror (her son's severed head on a pole) is not only dignified but advisable—never show your fear. Rights are something that Lupe must learn to understand and to fight for, a new way of enduring, a significant if small-scale step forward."

In his next novel, *Cuzcatlán: Where the Southern Sea Beats,* Argueta broadens his exploration of El Salvador's political turmoil by putting it in a historical perspective. Argueta sets the tone in the novel's introduction, according to Paredes, "with quotations from a Spanish conquistador and a contemporary military officer to dramatize El Salvador's long record of violence and tyranny, often at the hands of foreign interlopers and their lackeys." *Cuzcatlán* spans four generations, between 1932 and the early 1980s, of a Salvadoran peasant family named Martínez, weaving various episodes of oppression in Salvadoran history. Interspersed in Argueta's story are the 1932 government massacre of 30,000 peasants—many forced to dig their own graves before being executed—the burning of peasant crops by soldiers for fear of them being supplied to government insurgents, the seizure of peasant farms by large plantation developers, and the poisoning of workers in El Salvador's indigo dye factories. "Argueta has a store of knowledge to transmit," observes Caistor, "and occasionally seems only too aware that his is one of the few voices from El Salvador which can rescue its lived history from becoming simply news items." According to Alfred J. Mac Adam in the *New York Times Book Review,* Argueta divides *Cuzcatlán*

into two "discourses: in one he denounces the plight of the peasants; in the other he recreates the personality of these people who have existed only to be exploited, first by Spanish *conquistadors* and now by home-grown agricultural capitalists." The reviewer calls *Cuzcatlán* "an up-to-date avatar of a tradition that dates back to colonial times: the socio-political defense of the bottom dogs—Indians and blacks—and the vindication of their culture."

Reviewers again were mixed on Argueta's achievements in *Cuzcatlán,* often focusing on the novel's characterization and structural limitations. Paredes writes that "the action is not emplotted but strung together in a series of sketches narrated across several generations by members of the Martínez clan, each of whom represents a predictable type of character: the martyred patriarch; the timid non-participant, forced finally to take a stand against government brutality and repression; the amoral military henchman corrupted by 'gringo' ideas, and the contemporary feminist revolutionary eager to demonstrate resourcefulness and courage equal to that of any man. Argueta's use of a flashback technique to position his narrators at various points during the historical span of the novel is sometimes heavy-handed. And nowhere is the prose of 'Cuzcatlán' anything much more than workmanlike." Jason Wilson in the *Times Literary Supplement* comments that "Argueta provides a minimal plot involving two female characters with the same name, and a forcibly conscripted brother who returns to his village as a minor despot. But he avoids psychological explanations, preferring to convey the innocence of these suffering survivors through sudden poetic description, intent, for the most part, on rousing the reader's sympathy and illuminating his passive characters' consciousness." Other reviewers remarked on the political nature of the novel. Mac Adam calls *Cuzcatlán* "a prose mosaic, a mix of times and voices. Mr. Argueta tries to balance what the Italian philosopher and critic Benedetto Croce called 'non-poetry,' language used for practical purposes such as moralizing, with 'poetry,' or language that expresses intuitions about the human spirit. We sympathize with Mr. Argueta's peasants and are indeed moved to side with them against their oppressors, but we do not respond to the text as a work of art."

Reviewers praised, nonetheless, Argueta's ability to authentically portray the perspective of Salvadoran peasants. "Spanish-American writers like Miguel Angel Asturias and José María Arguedas have tried to reproduce the way . . . non-Occidental peoples think, how their religion both sustains them and personalizes their universe, and how their communal society is victimized by the Western market economy," notes Mac Adam. Argueta "transforms these themes into a bitter yet resolutely hopeful pastoral: this novel is the history of the Martínez family and, like so many Latin American novels, demonstrates the belief that the family is the only enduring social institution in a world of constant political and economic upheaval." Paredes concludes that "Argueta writes warmly of family and romantic love and, like other Latin American writers, evokes the rich folkloric heritage—superstitions, legends, proverbs, and such—that bind people in a common culture. . . . There are even moments of inspired humor in 'Cuzcatlán' . . . [in which Argueta] makes his most appealing point: that the Salvadoran people will somehow endure and outlast their enemies."

BIOGRAPHICAL/CRITICAL SOURCES:

BOOKS

Contemporary Literary Criticism, Volume 31, Gale, 1985.

PERIODICALS

America, January 14, 1984.
Hispania, December, 1971.
Los Angeles Times Book Review, June 14, 1987.
New Republic, November 21, 1983.
New Statesman, December 11, 1987.
Newsweek, September 26, 1983.
New York Times Book Review, October 2, 1983, July 26, 1987.
Times Literary Supplement, January 8, 1988.
Tribune (London), May 11, 1984.

—*Sketch by Michael E. Mueller*

*   *   *

ARIAS, Ron(ald Francis) 1941-

PERSONAL: Born November 30, 1941, in Los Angeles, Calif.; son of Armando (an army officer) and Emma Lou (a homemaker; maiden name, Estrada) Arias; married Joan Londerman (an business executive), April 1, 1966; children: Michael. *Education:* Attended Oceanside-Carlsbad College (now Mira Costa College), 1959-60, University of Barcelona, Spain, 1960, University of California, Berkeley, 1960-61, and National University, Buenos Aires, Argentina, 1962; University of California, Los Angeles, B.A., 1967, M.A., 1968. *Politics:* Independent. *Religion:* "None."

ADDRESSES: Home—283 Weed Ave., Stamford, Conn. 06902. *Office*—*People* Magazine, Time and Life Building, Rockefeller Center, New York, N.Y. 10020. *Agent*—Reid Boates, 44 Mountain Ridge Rd., Wayne, N.J. 07470.

CAREER: Buenos Aires Herald, Buenos Aires, Argentina, reporter, 1962; community development volunteer with Peace Corps in Cuzco, Peru, 1963-64; writer for Copley Newspapers and for national and international wire services, 1960s; *Caracas Daily Journal,* Caracas, Venezuela, reporter, 1968-69; Inter-American Development Bank, Washington, D.C., editor for agency publications, 1969-71; San Bernardino Valley College, San Bernardino, Calif., instructor, 1971-80, associate professor of English, until 1985; Crafton Hills College, Yucaipa, Calif., instructor in English and journalism, 1980-84; *People* magazine, New York, N.Y., senior writer, 1986—. Member of the board of directors of the National Endowment for the Arts coordinating council of literary magazines, 1979-80.

MEMBER: Newspaper and Magazine Writers Guild.

AWARDS, HONORS: Scholarship to study journalism in Buenos Aires, Argentina, from Inter-American Press Association, 1962; Machris Award for journalistic excellence from Los Angeles Press Club, 1968; writer's fellowship from California Arts Commission, 1973; Chicano Literary Contest first place award in fiction from University of California, Irvine, 1975, for short story "The Wetback"; Modern Language Association fellowship, 1975; National Book Award nomination for fiction, 1976, for *The Road to Tamazunchale.*

WRITINGS:

The Road to Tamazunchale (novel), West Coast Poetry Review, 1975.
Five against the Sea (nonfiction), New American Library, 1989.

Also author of short stories, including "El mago," 1970, "The Interview" and "Stoop Labor," both 1974, "The Wetback," "A House on the Island," and "The Story Machine," all 1975, "The Castle" and "El señor del chivo," both 1976, "Chinches," 1977,

"The Boy Ate Himself" and "The Chamizal Express," both 1980; author of the play "The Interview," adapted from the author's short story, 1979; author of screenplays, including "Jesús and the Three Wise Guys"; author of television scripts.

Work represented in anthologies, including *The Chicanos: Mexican American Voices,* edited by Ed Ludwig and James Santibáñez, Penguin Books, 1971; *First Chicano Literary Contest Winners,* edited by Juan Villegas, Spanish and Portuguese Department, University of California, 1975; and *Cuentos Chicanos: A Short Story Anthology,* edited by Rudolfo A. Anaya and Antonio Márquez, revised edition, University of New Mexico Press, 1984.

Contributor to periodicals, including the *New York Times, Quarry West, Bilingual Review/Revista Bilingüe, Latin American Literary Review, Journal of Ethnic Studies, Revista Chicano-Riqueña, Nuestro, Christian Science Monitor, Nation,* and *Los Angeles Times.*

WORK IN PROGRESS: Nonfiction project, tentatively titled *The Secret Man: The Search for My Real Father;* researching Latin America and third-world situations and themes.

SIDELIGHTS: Ron Arias is a journalist and short story writer whose widely acclaimed debut novel, *The Road to Tamazunchale,* distinguished him as a leading Chicano writer of "magic realism," a literary form popularized by Gabriel García Márquez that blends reality with fantasy. Influenced by García Márquez's *One Hundred Years of Solitude,* Arias related to Juan Bruce-Novoa in *Chicano Authors: Inquiry by Interview* the novel's effect on him: "For me, García-Márquez transformed, *deepened* reality in so many of its aspects—tragic, humorous, adventurous, wondrous. The work was alive, entertaining at every word. There was nothing sloppy, facile, overly clever, belabored, preachy—all the things I detest in literature." Arias's own style of magic realism is a mixture of precise, journalistic descriptions, and stream-of-consciousness writing, which often centers on magical figures who can manipulate reality. Bruce-Novoa contended that even more important than Arias's stylistic affinities with magic realism are his achievements as "a skilled, patient craftsman, with a healthy sense of irony about himself and the world. . . . [H]e shares the current—we could say modern—sense of literature as one enormous text, interrelated and consciously self-referential."

Though he has written several short stories, Arias is best known for his novel, *The Road to Tamazunchale.* Nominated for a National Book Award, the novel is about the final days of a retired encyclopedia salesman named Fausto Tejada. In order to understand and accept his impending death Fausto makes an imaginative journey to Tamazunchale, a Mexican village which in the book symbolizes the final resting place after death. The story opens with an ailing and despondent Fausto peeling off his skin; not until his niece Carmela enters the room does the reader learn that Fausto has actually been playing with a wad of Kleenex. Still, the incident functions as the first in a series of events in which the boundaries between reality and illusion, past and present, and life and death are clouded: Fausto travels to sixteenth-century Lima; he helps an Inca shepherd move his flock off the Los Angeles freeway; he leads hundreds of men across the Mexican-American border; he finds himself in a play called "The Road to Tamazunchale"; and, finally, he joins friends and neighbors on a cosmic picnic where he is reunited with his deceased wife. The events culminate with Fausto accepting his inevitable demise, though exactly when this occurs is ambiguous. As quoted in *Chicano Literature: A Reference Guide,* Vernon Lattin explained in *American Literature* that even after Fausto apparently dies, "the novel continues for one more chapter without suggestions of distortion or logical violation. Fausto and his friends continue as in the past: there is no funeral or burial; the logic of the world and the dichotomy of life and death have been transcended, and the road to Tamazunchale has become a sacred way for Everyman to follow."

The Road to Tamazunchale won favorable reviews. Calling Arias's novel "skillful and imaginative," *Los Angeles Times Book Review* contributor Alejandro Morales defended the book's status as a Chicano classic because of its "magical realistic imagination, its precise crisp prose, its relationship to the 'new reality' of Spanish American fiction and its compassionate treatment of death, its central theme." Morales concluded that Arias offers "a new social reality and a new vision of the American literary mosaic in which [he himself] must now be recognized." *Chicano Literature* noted that Eliud Martínez lauded Arias in the *Latin American Literary Review* for examining universal themes and capturing distinctly Chicano speech patterns. Moreover, Martínez asserted that "no Chicano novel before *Tamazunchale* has tapped the artistic resources of the modern and contemporary novel (and the arts) in a comparable way, deliberately and intuitively."

Arias told *Hispanic Writers:* "My Mexican family heritage and continuing travel abroad, especially in Latin American countries for magazine story assignments, are strong inspirations for my writing. My work in the Peace Corps with the Andean poor also gave me an abiding insight into the world of basic survival, which is the theme of my own favorite writing projects."

BIOGRAPHICAL/CRITICAL SOURCES:

BOOKS

Bruce-Novoa, Juan, *Chicano Authors: Inquiry by Interview,* University of Texas Press, 1980.
Dictionary of Literary Biography, Volume 82, *Chicano Writers, First Series,* Gale, 1989.
Martínez, Julio A. and Francisco A. Lomelí, editors, *Chicano Literature: A Reference Guide,* Greenwood Press, 1985.

PERIODICALS

American Literature, Number 50, 1979.
Latin American Literary Review, Number 4, 1976, Number 5, 1977.
Los Angeles Times Book Review, April 12, 1987.
New Mexico Humanities Review, Volume 3, number 1, 1980.
Revista Chicano-Riqueña, Volume 5, number 4, 1977, Volume 10, number 3, 1982.

* * *

ARIAS SANCHEZ, Oscar 1941-

PERSONAL: Born September 13, 1941, in Heredia, Costa Rica; son of Juan Rafael Arias Trejos and Lilian Sánchez (coffee plantation owners); married Margarita Penón Góngora (a biochemist); children: Silvia Eugenia, Oscar Felipe. *Education:* Attended Colegio Saint Francis and Boston University; University of Costa Rica, licenciatura en ambas, 1967; University of Essex, master of political science, 1967, Ph.D., 1969; attended London School of Economics and Political Science, London. *Politics:* Liberación Nacional.

ADDRESSES: Home—Casa Presidencial, San José, Costa Rica. *Office*—Oficina del Presidente, San José, Costa Rica.

CAREER: University of Costa Rica, San José, professor of political science, 1969-72; Republic of Costa Rica, member of eco-

nomic council, 1970-72, minister of national planning and political economy, 1972-77, member of legislative assembly as representative of Heredia, 1978-81; campaigner for presidential candidate Luis Alberto Monge, 1981-82; Republic of Costa Rica, presidential candidate, 1984-86, president, 1986—. Partido de Liberación Nacional (national liberation party), international secretary, 1975-79, general secretary, 1979-84. Banco Central de Costa Rica, member of board of directors, 1970-77, vice-president of board of directors, 1970-72; member of ad hoc commission of National University of Heredia, 1972-74; member of board of directors of Technological Institute, Costa Rica, 1974-77; member of National Council of University Rectors, 1974-77; member of board of directors of International University Exchange Fund, Switzerland, 1976; member of North-South Roundtable, Rome, 1977; Costa Rican representative at congresses of Socialist International.

AWARDS, HONORS: Premio Nacional de Ensayo, 1971, for *Grupos de presión en Costa Rica;* Nobel Peace Prize, 1987.

WRITINGS:

Significado del movimiento estudiantil en Costa Rica, Ciudad Universitaria Rodrigo Facio, 1970.
Grupos de presión en Costa Rica (nonfiction; title means "Pressure Groups in Costa Rica"), Costa Rica, 1971.
¿Quién gobierna en Costa Rica? Un estudio del liderazgo formal en Costa Rica, Editorial Universitaria, 1974.
(With others) *Planificación y desarrollo regional y local latinamericano* (essays), CEDAL (San José, Costa Rica), 1975.
Democracia, independencia y sociedad latinoamericana, CEDAL, 1977.
Los caminos para el desarrollo de Costa Rica (essays), CEDAL, 1977.
Nuevos rumbos para el desarrollo costarricense, Editorial Universitaria, 1979.

Author of *Costa Rica in the Year 2000,* 1977. Contributor of articles to periodicals.

SIDELIGHTS: President of Costa Rica, a small, politically neutral Central American democracy sandwiched between Nicaragua and Panama, Oscar Arias Sánchez won the 1987 Nobel Peace Prize for his continuing efforts to establish a peace treaty with Nicaragua, Guatemala, Honduras, and El Salvador, four neighbors torn by civil war. The product of a country that abolished its army in 1948, Arias Sánchez has persistently worked for peace in the region, convinced that negotiation, not war, is the best means for achieving it. Although his approach has had its critics, notably in the administration of U.S. President Ronald Reagan, Arias Sánchez's "positions on Central American issues have become the standards by which many people in Congress and elsewhere have come to judge United States policy," remarked Elaine Sciolino in the *New York Times.*

BIOGRAPHICAL/CRITICAL SOURCES:

BOOKS

Contemporary Heroes and Heroines, Gale, 1990.

PERIODICALS

Commonweal, May 9, 1986, December 4, 1987.
Nation, December 20, 1986.
New Republic, November 9, 1987.
Newsweek, October 26, 1987, January 11, 1988.
New York Times, October 14, 1987, August 7, 1988, April 5, 1989.
People, November 9, 1987.

Time, June 29, 1987, September 28, 1987, October 5, 1987, October 26, 1987.

* * *

ARIDJIS, Homero 1940-

PERSONAL: Born April 6, 1940, in Mexico; married Betty Ferber, March 14, 1965; children: two daughters. *Education:* Received degree from Universidad Nacional Autónoma de México, 1961.

ADDRESSES: Home—Sierra Jiutepec 155 B, Lomas Barrilaco, México 11010, D.F. México.

CAREER: Writer. Editor in chief of *Correspondencias,* Mexico, 1957-61; assistant editor of *Diálogos,* 1966. Visiting lecturer at University of Indiana, 1969, and New York University, 1969-71; director of Festival Internacional de Poesía, 1981, 1982, and 1987.

MEMBER: P.E.N., Poetas Mexicanos.

AWARDS, HONORS: Xavier Villaurrutia Prize, 1964; Guggenheim fellowships, 1966 and 1979; Commander of Royal Order of the Polar Star, Sweden, 1986; Premio de Novela Novedades, 1988.

WRITINGS:

Musa roja (poetry), [México], 1958.
Los ojos desdoblados (poetry), La Palabra, 1960.
Ta, i.e. La tumba de Filidor, La Palabra, 1961.
Antes del reino (poetry), Era, 1963.
La difícil ceremonia (poem), Pájaro Cascabel, 1963.
Mirándola dormir: Seguido de Pavana por la amada presente, J. Mortiz, 1964.
Perséfone (novel), J. Mortiz, 1967, translation by wife, Betty Ferber, published as *Persephone,* Vintage, 1986.
Los espacios azules (poetry), J. Mortiz, 1968, bilingual English-Spanish edition with introduction by Kenneth Rexroth published as *Los espacios azules/Blue Spaces: Selected Poems of Homero Aridjis,* Scabury Press, 1974.
Ajedrez—Navegaciones (poems and short sketches), Siglo Veintiuno, 1969.
La poeta niño: Narración, Fondo de Cultura Económica, 1971.
(Editor) *Seis poetas latinoamericanos de hoy,* Harcourt, 1972.
El encantador solitario, Fondo de Cultura Económica, 1972.
Quemar las naves, J. Mortiz, 1975.
Sobre una ausencia, Barral Editores (Barcelona), 1976.
Antología (poetry), selected by Cristina Peri Rossi, Lumen, 1976.
Vivir para ver, J. Mortiz, 1977.
Espectáculo del año dos mil (play), J. Mortiz, 1981.
Exaltation of Light (poetry), bilingual English-Spanish edition with translations by Eliot Weinberger, Boa Editions, 1981.
(Editor) *Antología del Primer Festival International de Poesía, Morelia, 1981,* J. Mortiz, 1982.
Construir la muerte (poetry), J. Mortiz, 1982.
Playa nudista: El último ádan (short stories), Argos Vergara, 1982.
1492, Vida y tiempos de Juan Cabezón de Castilla (novel), Siglo Veintiuno, 1985.
Obra poética, 1960-1986 (poetry), J. Mortiz, 1987.
Memorias del nuevo mundo, Editorial Diana, 1988.

Also author of *Imágenes para el fin del milenio* (poetry), 1986. Work represented in anthologies, including *República de poetas: Antología de poesía,* edited by Sergio Mandragón, M. Casillas Editores, 1985. Contributor to periodicals.

SIDELIGHTS: Deemed "one of Mexico's greatest living poets" by Ana María Hernández in *World Literature Today,* Homero Aridjis is the author of numerous volumes of poetry, several novels, and plays that are extremely popular in Mexico. Aridjis is known for his lyrical style and his emphasis on the theme of the redeeming nature of human love.

BIOGRAPHICAL/CRITICAL SOURCES:

BOOKS

Rodríguez Monegal, Emir, editor, *The Borzoi Anthology of Latin American Literature,* Volume 2: *The Twentieth Century—From Borges and Paz to Guimarres Rosa and Donoso,* Knopf, 1986.

PERIODICALS

Times Literary Supplement, June 18, 1970.
World Literature Today, autumn, 1978, winter, 1983, summer, 1983, summer, 1986, summer, 1988.

* * *

ARLT, Roberto (Godofredo Christophersen) 1900-1942

PERSONAL: Born April 4, 1900, in Buenos Aires, Argentina; died of a heart attack, July 26, 1942, in Buenos Aires, Argentina; married first wife, c. 1923 (died, c. 1929); married Elizabeth Shine, 1939; children: (first marriage) Mirta. *Education:* Self-educated; attended Naval School of Mechanics, c. 1919-20.

ADDRESSES: Home—Buenos Aires, Argentina. *Office*—El Mundo, Buenos Aires, Argentina.

CAREER: Writer, 1914-42; *El Mundo* (daily), Buenos Aires, Argentina, columnist, 1929-42. Secretary to writer and publisher Ricardo Güiraldes, Buenos Aires, 1925-27; Arna (inventing business), Buenos Aires, founder, 1941-42. Employed as a book store clerk, apprentice to a tinsmith, painter, mechanic, vulcanizer, brick factory manager, newspaper manager, and port worker. *Military service:* Served in Argentine armed forces, c. 1919-20.

AWARDS, HONORS: The Seven Madmen won a municipal prize, 1929.

WRITINGS:

El juguete rabioso (novel; title means "The Rabid Plaything"), Editorial Latina, 1926, recent edition, Centro, 1981.
Los siete locos (novel), first published in 1929, recent edition, with introduction by daughter, Mirta Arlt, Fabril, 1968, translation by Naomi Lindstrom published as *The Seven Madmen,* Godine, 1984.
Los lanzallamas (novel; title means "The Flamethrowers"), Claridad, 1931, recent edition, Losada, 1977.
El amor brujo (novel; title means "Love the Sorcerer"), first published in 1932, recent edition, Losada, 1980.
El jorobadito (short stories; title means "The Little Hunchback"), first published in 1933, recent edition, with introduction by M. Arlt, Fabril, 1968.
Aguafuertes porteñas (fifty newspaper columns; title means "Porteño Etchings"), first published in 1933, recent edition, Hyspamerica, 1986.
Aguafuertes españolas (essays; title means "Spanish Etchings"), L. J. Rosso (Buenos Aires), 1936, recent edition, with introduction by M. Arlt, Fabril, 1971.

El criador de gorilas (short stories; title means "The Gorilla
    Breeder"), first published in 1941, recent edition, Losada,
    1982.
Nuevas aguafuertes porteñas (title means "New Porteño Etch-
    ings"), selected by Pedro G. Orgambide, Hachette, 1960.
Novelas completas y cuentos (complete novels and short stories),
    prologue by M. Arlt, three volumes, Fabril, 1963.
Saverio el cruel [and] *La isla desierta* (plays; titles mean "Saverio
    the Cruel" and "The Desert Island"), EUDEBA, 1965.
Teatro completo (complete plays; contains "Trescientos mi-
    llones" [title means "The Three Hundred Million"; first
    produced by El Teatro del Pueblo, 1932]; and "El fabricante
    de fantasmas" [title means "The Ghost Manufacturer"]),
    introduction by M. Arlt, two volumes, Schapire, 1968.
Un viaje terrible (long story; title means "The Terrible Jour-
    ney"), first published in journal *Nuestra Novela*, 1941, re-
    printed, edited with an introduction by Adolfo Prieto,
    Tiempo Contemporáneo, 1968.
El traje del fantasma, Edicom, 1969.
Regreso (story), prologue by Alberto Vanasco, Corregidor, 1972.
Obra completa (complete works), preface by Julio Cortázar, two
    volumes, Lohlé, 1981.
Estoy cargada de muerte y otros borradores, (stories first pub-
    lished in journals *Mundo Argentino* and *El Hogar*, 1926-39),
    Torres Agüero (Buenos Aires), 1984.

Works represented in anthologies, including *Cuatro escritores ar-
gentinos*, [Buenos Aires], 1965; and *Dos panoramas del cuento*,
Centro, 1972. Selected short stories appear in English-language
volumes, including "Ester Primavera" in *Doors and Mirrors: Fic-
tion and Poetry From Spanish America, 1920-1970*, edited by
Hortense Carpenter and Janet Brof, Grossman; "One Sunday
Afternoon" in *The Eye of the Heart: Short Stories From Latin
America*, edited by Barbara Howes, Bobbs-Merrill; and "Small-
Time Property Owners" in *Contemporary Latin American Short
Stories*, edited by Pat M. Mancini, Fawcett. Selected works pub-
lished in various collections. Contributor to periodicals, includ-
ing *Mundo Argentino*, *Nuestra Novela*, and *El Hogar*.

SIDELIGHTS: Roberto Arlt was a prolific and versatile Argentine novelist, short story writer, playwright, and journalist. Although he wrote four novels, two collections of short stories, volumes of essays, and about seven plays, only one work, his experimental and wholly original novel *Los siete locos*, has been
translated into English, as *The Seven Madmen*. Arlt was condemned by contemporary reviewers who considered his works
of fiction vulgar. General readers, however, applauded his writings, particularly his weekly newspaper column, "Aguafuertes
porteñas" ("Porteño Etchings"), in which he addressed social
and political issues that deeply concerned lower and middle class
Argentineans. In an attempt to impel the Spanish language into
the modern age, Arlt consistently used slang and informal grammar in his works, and his writings influenced the trend toward
the antiliterary in Hispanic literature begun in the 1960s.

Arlt was born in 1900 in Buenos Aires to German immigrants
who spoke Spanish laced with Italian and German. Although he
was expelled from school as "useless" at the age of eight, he read
widely and published his first story at fourteen. He left home two
years later and worked at odd jobs while aspiring to be a writer.
He published his first novel, *El juguete rabioso* ("The Rabid
Plaything"), in 1926, and although it garnered little attention
from established critics it found a youthful audience. The novel
concerns a man who idolizes historical bandits; when he emulates them, however, he fails miserably, capable of only stealing
canes and billiard balls from Buenos Aires cafes. Arlt was a frequent patron of these taverns, particularly the cafe La Puñalada,

whose seedy denizens—"outcast weirdos" according to David
William Foster in *Review: Latin American Literature and Arts*—
inspired characters in his works.

Arlt published his second—and most notable—novel, *The Seven
Madmen*, in 1929. *The Seven Madmen* and its sequel *Los lanzallamas* ("The Flamethrowers") features the neurotic antihero
Erdosain, considered by some the epitome of the alienated man
in twentieth-century society. After he loses his job because of
petty theft and his wife leaves him for another man, Erdosain—
searching for meaning to his life—joins a mysterious coterie of
misfits. Led by the Astrologer, the society is plotting to take over
the country and subsequently institute a utopian dictatorship
that will lift the people from their economic exploitation and
spiritual malaise. The scheme turns out to be only an elaborate
hoax against Erdosain, and after he witnesses an execution and
murders his mistress, he commits suicide.

"The reader's first reaction to [*The Seven Madmen*] is complete
disorientation," Foster noted in *Currents in the Contemporary
Argentine Novel*, because "the controlling consciousness of the
novel [is] Erdosain's muddled perspective on reality." Arlt's confusing narrative is a deliberate manifestation of Erdosain's own
bewildered involvement with the society, whose members and
plotting he does not understand. In *The Seven Madmen* and *Los
lanzallamas* the reader is not given any background information
on Erdosain; his character is revealed only through present actions. Ironies and loose ends abound; time sequences are often
unclear (sometimes the reader does not know if an event actually
happened or was hallucinated); and elaborate trivial detail is
presented while significant information is withheld. Finally, even
seemingly straightforward storytelling passages in the books
make the reader suspicious.

"The key to an understanding of [*The Seven Madmen* and *Los
lanzallamas*]" according to Foster in *Currents*, "lies in the essential nature of Erdosain as one anguished soul who may well be
a figure of Everyman." Arlt later commented that the characters
in these novels "are tied or bound together by desperation," as
quoted by Aden W. Hayes in *Romance Notes*. Arlt continued:
"The desperation in them originates, more than from material
poverty, from another factor: the disorientation that, after the
Great War, has revolutionized the conscience of men, leaving
them empty of ideals and hopes. . . . [T]he anguish of these
men is born in their internal sterility."

The Seven Madmen won a municipal award but drew the censure
of critics who, failing to appreciate the novel's experimental and
expressionistic tendencies, read it as a realistic book and lam-
basted its poor grammar, composition, and craftsmanship. "If
anyone ever actually believed that this novel was realistic," Paul
Gray wrote in a 1984 issue of *Time*, "then life in the Argentine
capital must once have been unimaginably weird." Arlt's subject
matter and style did not fit the traditional aesthetic concept of
beauty upheld by established Spanish literary critics and authors, many of whom were still extolling the virtues of cowboys
on the vanishing Argentine frontier. Arlt dwelt on the least
pleasant aspects of urban life: "The setting sun lit up the most
revolting inner recesses of the sloping street," Gray quoted *The
Seven Madmen*. According to Foster in the *Review*, his novels
depict, with "appalling fidelity," the horrid conditions in which
Argentineans were forced to live. In the prologue to *Los lanzallamas*, quoted by Lee Dowling in *Review*, Arlt answered and in-
dicted his detractors, particularly the wealthy and genteel establishment writers: "It is said of me that my writing is poor. That
may be . . . often I have wanted to compose a novel that would
consist of panoramic scenes like Flaubert's. But today, amid the

babble of an inevitably crumbling social edifice, it is impossible to linger over embroidery."

Many of Arlt's contemporary readers admired his linguistic audacity. During the 1920s and 1930s, when academics were calling for purity and uniformity in the Spanish language, Arlt, along with other avant-garde writers, proposed the "derhetoricizing" of what they considered a pompous, florid, and stodgy literary idiom that lacked the resources for innovation and invention. Thus his characters and narrators use colloquialisms common to middle- and lower-class Spanish, and he was the first novelist to consistently write with the familiar form of "you," *voseo,* rather than the acceptable literary form of "you." In "The Language of the Argentines," translated for *Review* from his collection *Aguafuertes porteñas,* Arlt condemned those demanding linguistic purity, criticizing "the absurdity of trying to straightjacket in a prescriptive grammar the constantly changing, new ideas of a people."

In 1932 Arlt published his last novel, *El amor brujo* ("Love the Sorcerer"), about a man who attempts to inject his life with scenes duplicated from novels he read in his youth, only to be jarred by the harsh contrast between his life and his fantasies. His other fiction includes two collections of short stories, *El jorobadito* ("The Little Hunchback"), published in 1933, and *El criador de gorilas* ("The Gorilla Breeder"), published in 1941. Arlt's stories resemble his longer fiction in their confusing chronology, fragmentation, and chaos, as well as their portrayal of warped personalities in a disintegrating society.

Arlt also tried his hand at play writing. He wrote his first play, "Los 300 Millones" ("The Three Hundred Million"), in 1932, and like many of his later dramas it explores the constant tension between the real and illusory worlds and is peopled by grotesque and surreal figures that often appear more lifelike than the principal characters. In "Los 300 Millones" a poor servant girl relieves the tedium of her life by fantasizing about what she would do if she inherited three hundred million pesos; she is brought back to reality usually by the sound of her patroness's voice. When her patroness's drunken son enters her room in an attempt to seduce her when she is about to meet her fantasy son-in-law, the shocking disparity between her daydreams and the sordidness of real life impels her to kill herself.

Arlt wrote two other plays in 1936 dealing with the interplay between fantasy and reality. In "Saverio el cruel" ("Saverio the Cruel") a group of rich young pranksters ask a timid dairyman, Saverio, to pose as a brutal colonel. They claim that one of the girls, Susana, believes herself to be a princess pursued by him and he must act out her fantasy to set her free. Although Saverio reluctantly agrees, he soon becomes immersed in his role, even buying a guillotine to eliminate his enemies. He is eventually informed of the hoax and returns to his normal self, but Susana, unable to return to reality, shoots and kills Saverio. "El fabricante de fantasmas" ("The Ghost Manufacturer") focuses on a fantasizing author who murders his wife and is condemned to the distorted, nightmarish world in his mind—peopled by a hangman, prostitute, cripple, and hunchback.

Although he tried his hand at various literary genres, Arlt's greatest popularity came through his journalism. From 1929 until his death in 1942 Arlt wrote a column called "Porteño Etchings" for the newspaper *El Mundo.* The column provided for him a forum to express his views on society, economics, and politics and was enormously successful—the paper sold twice as many copies on the day his column appeared. Today it is considered an invaluable chronicle of a decade of Argentine life. Juan Carlos Onetti, in the preface to *Los siete locos,* translated in *Re-*

view, explained "the journalistic triumph" of the "Porteño Etchings": "The common man, the petty and smaller-than-petty bourgeois of the streets of Buenos Aires, the office worker, the owner of a rundown business, the enormous mass of burned-out, bummed-out cases, could read their own thoughts, sorrows, their pallid hopes, intuited and stated in their everyday language."

Arlt's works influenced innovative Spanish writers such as Gabriel García Márquez and Jorge Luis Borges, although they received little critical recognition during his lifetime. Since the 1960s his books have been enthusiastically accepted by Argentine writers who see in Arlt a proponent of antiliterary and antiestablishment writing. Beginning in 1968 a number of his books were reissued, many—including *El juguete rabioso, El jorobadito,* and *Aguafuertes españolas*—with introductions by his daughter, Mirta. Complete collections of his novels, short stories, and plays have been recently published by such influential houses as Hachette and Fabril. Importantly, Lindstrom translated *The Seven Madmen* in 1984, introducing Arlt's original vision to the English-speaking world.

AVOCATIONAL INTERESTS: Inventing.

BIOGRAPHICAL/CRITICAL SOURCES:

BOOKS

Flint, Jack M., *The Prose Works of Roberto Arlt: A Thematic Approach,* University of Durham, 1985.
Foster, David William, *Currents in the Contemporary Argentine Novel: Arlt, Mallea, Sabato, and Cortázar,* University of Missouri Press, 1975.
Lindstrom, Naomi, *Literary Expressionism in Argentina: The Presentation of Incoherence,* Center for Latin American Studies, Arizona State University, 1977.
Twentieth-Century Literary Criticism, Volume 29, Gale, 1988.

PERIODICALS

Journal of Spanish Studies: Twentieth Century, winter, 1977.
Latin American Literary Review, spring-summer, 1976.
Review: Latin American Literature and Arts, fall, 1982.
Romance Notes, fall, 1980.
Time, August 27, 1984.

—*Sketch by Carol Lynn DeKane*

* * *

ARMAND, Octavio Rafael 1946-

PERSONAL: Born in 1946 in Guantánamo, Cuba; immigrated to United States, c. 1960, naturalized citizen. *Education:* Rutgers University, B.A., 1968, M.A., 1972, Ph.D., 1975.

ADDRESSES: Home—Caracas, Venezuela; and Elmhurst, N.Y. *Office*—Bennington College, Bennington, Vt. 05201.

CAREER: Affiliated with Bennington College, Bennington, Vt. Visiting professor at University of Michigan, fall, 1988.

WRITINGS:

Horizonte no es siempre lejanía (poems), Las Américas, 1970.
El pájaro de lata, first published by Editorial San Juan, 2nd edition, 1973.
Raíces al viento, Editorial San Juan, 1974.
Entretes, Gráfica Urex, 1974.
Piel menos mía, Escolios, 1976, 2nd edition, 1979.
Cosas pasan (1975) (poems), Monte Avila Editores, 1976.
América en su literatura, first published by Editorial Universitaria (San Juan), 2nd edition, 1978.

Raíz y ala, first published by Editorial San Juan, 2nd edition, 1979.

(Editor) *Mark Strand: Viente poemas* (title means "Mark Strand: Twenty Poems"), Fundarte, 1979.

Como escribir con erizo, 1976, Asociación de Escritores de México, 1979.

Superficies, Monte Avila Editores, 1980.

Razón y pasión de Sor Juana Inés de la Cruz, first published by Editorial Porrúa, 3rd edition, 1980.

Biografía para feacios, Pre-Textos, 1981.

(Editor and author of introduction) *Toward an Image of Latin American Poetry* (bilingual anthology), Logbridge-Rhodes, 1982.

El grillo gruñón, Editorial Universitaria, 1984.

With Dusk, translated by Carol Maier, Logbridge-Rhodes, 1984.

Origami, Fundarte, 1987.

Also author of *Entre testigos: 1971-1973,* 1974, and *Narrativa hispanoamericana actual,* 1980. Contributor of poems and articles to literary journals in the United States and Latin America. Founder and editor of *Escandalar,* 1978—.

BIOGRAPHICAL/CRITICAL SOURCES:

PERIODICALS

World Literature Today, winter, 1986, autumn, 1988.

*   *   *

AROZARENA, Marcelino   1912-

PERSONAL: Born in 1912 in Cuba.

CAREER: Poet.

WRITINGS:

Canción negra sin color (poetry), anthologized in *Orbita de la poesía afrocubana, 1928-1937,* edited by Ramón Guirao, Talleres de Ucar, García y cía, 1938, reprinted, Kraus Reprint, 1970; Unión de Escritores y Artistas de Cuba (Havana), 1966, recent edition, 1983.

SIDELIGHTS: Marcelino Arozarena is a black Cuban poet who writes of Afro-Cuban folklore. Hailed for his use of rich lyricism, the author is best known for his *Canción negra sin color,* a poetry collection documenting the black experience. The work, which exalts black heritage while calling for social revolution and universal brotherhood, has been praised as enlightening.

BIOGRAPHICAL/CRITICAL SOURCES:

BOOKS

Jackson, Richard L., *The Black Image in Latin American Literature,* University of New Mexico Press, 1976.

*   *   *

ARREOLA, Juan José   1918-

PERSONAL: Born September 12, 1918, in Ciudad Guzmán, Jalisco, Mexico. *Education:* Studied theater in Paris, France, 1945, and at the College of Mexico.

ADDRESSES: Agent—c/o Grijalbo, Ave. Granjas 82, Mexico 16, DF.

CAREER: Professional actor in Mexico City, Mexico; writer. Founder of literary journals; conductor of writers' workshops.

AWARDS, HONORS: First prize in INBA Drama Festival, for play "La hora de todos."

WRITINGS:

Gunther Stapenhorst: Viñetas de Isidoro Ocampo, [Mexico], 1946.

Varia invención (short stories), Tezontle (Mexico), 1949 (also see below).

Confabulario (short stories), Fondo de Cultura Económica, 1952, 2nd edition published with *Varia invención* as *Confabulario y Varia invención, 1951-1955,* 1955, 3rd edition published with *Bestiario* (also see below) and *Punta de plata* (also see below) as *Confabulario total, 1941-1961,* 1962, translation by George D. Schade published as *Confabulario and Other Inventions,* University of Texas Press, 1964.

La hora de todos: Juguete cómico en un acto (one-act play), Los Presentes (Mexico), 1954.

Bestiario (short stories and vignettes; title means "Bestiaries"), Universidad Nacional Autónoma de México, 1958.

Punta de Plata (short stories), [Mexico], 1958.

(Editor) *Cuadernos del unicornio* (Spanish-American literature), [Mexico], 1958-60.

La feria (novel), Joaquín Mortiz (Mexico), 1963, translation by John Upton published as *The Fair,* University of Texas Press, 1977.

(Compiler) *Lectura en voz alta* (translations of literature into Spanish), Porrúa (Mexico), 1968.

Antología de Juan José Arreola, introduced and selected by Jorge Arturo Ojeda, Oasis (Mexico), 1969.

Cuentos (short stories), Casa de las Américas (Havana), 1969.

Palindroma (short stories, vignettes, and a one-act play; title means "Palindrome"), Joaquín Mortiz, 1971.

Mujeres, animales, y fantasías mecánicas, Tusquets (Barcelona), 1972.

La palabra educación, Secretaría de Educación Pública (Mexico), 1973.

(With others) *Zoo en cuarta dimensión* (short stories), Samo (Mexico), 1973.

Y ahora, la mujer, Utopía (Mexico), 1975.

(Editor) Fernando Pereznieto Castro, *La ciudad de Querétaro* (in English and Spanish), Joaquín Mortiz, 1975.

Inventario, Grijalbo (Mexico), 1976.

Confabulario personal, Bruguera (Barcelona), 1980.

Estas páginas mías (anthology; includes stories originally published in *Confabulario y Varia invención, 1951-1955*), Fondo de Cultura Económica, 1985.

Editor of literary magazines, including *Pan* and *Eos,* during the 1940s.

SIDELIGHTS: Juan José Arreola is "a true man of the twentieth century, an eclectic," according to *Hispania* contributor Seymour Menton, "who at will can draw upon the best of all who have preceded him in order to create truly masterful works of art which in turn will be seized upon by others." Arreola has written a novel, plays, and numerous short pieces, some of which are easily identified as short stories and others that defy strict literary definition. In those works that break with literary tradition, critics have considered the lack of such devices as conventional plots or character development not carelessness, but ingenious and essential features of Arreola's unique style. Furthermore, reviewers have noted, the numerous literary and biblical allusions found throughout Arreola's writings provide a unifying aspect to his otherwise dissimilar works.

Arreola's best-known collection of short stories and sketches is probably *Confabulario,* which was first published in 1952 and, after being expanded twice, was published in English translation as *Confabulario and Other Inventions.* Selections from *Confabu-*

lario were also included in a later Spanish collection, *Estas páginas mías,* which was published in 1985. Among the pieces reviewers have lauded are "Verily, Verily I Say Unto You" and "The Disciple." The story "Verily, Verily I Say Unto You" alludes to the biblical warning that a camel can pass through the eye of a needle more easily than a rich person can enter heaven. In the tale a scientist devises a costly method—which would be financed by wealthy people—to disintegrate a camel and thus allow it to pass through a needle. The scientist reasons that if he and the rich people can make the camel go through the needle, they will go to heaven. In his introduction to *Confabulario and Other Inventions,* translator George D. Schade described Arreola's often cynical portrayals of human shallowness and greed, such as the one in "Verily, Verily I Say Unto You": "With mordant descriptions, pungent attacks, or sly irony, [Arreola] shows how silly mankind is, how outrageous man's behavior and antics are, how one is at the mercy of a world and society that more often seems to care for what is trivial and ephemeral than for what is essential."

"The Disciple" reveals Arreola's artistic, rather than social, concerns; in the story, an art teacher draws an outline for his pupil and calls the outline "beauty." The teacher then creates a splendid picture by filling in the outline, but he explains that he has destroyed beauty and subsequently burns the picture. Menton considered the story a reflection of Arreola's sentiments about literature as well as other forms of art. The reviewer explained in his *Hispania* article, as quoted in *Modern Latin American Literature,* "Arreola's message is, of course, that true beauty lies in suggestion only. Once a work of art goes beyond suggesting beauty, it loses its charm."

Arreola's 1963 novel *La feria* (*The Fair*) exemplifies the writer's theory of artistic and literary aesthetics. Like many of Arreola's shorter works, *The Fair* lacks the well-defined characters and plots of conventional fiction. Instead, the novel develops from related and unrelated scenes, partial conversations, and portions of letters and diaries; it suggests plot and character instead of depicting them outright. "Yet the totality of the work has body, literary development, and novelistic scope," assessed Joseph Sommers in *Books Abroad,* as quoted by *Modern Latin American Literature.* The novel's fragmented parts coalesce, Sommers explained, to portray the life cycle of a Mexican village, from its founding in colonial times to its deterioration in the present age. It concludes with a fabulous display of fireworks set off by vandals, which, instead of providing harmless entertainment, kills several onlookers. "If this symbolism implies anguish and cynicism," wrote Sommers, "these qualities are mediated by the author's understanding and sympathy for the complexity of human problems. His sensitive use of language . . . and his wry tone of bitter humor are the basis for the literary unity of this novel."

BIOGRAPHICAL/CRITICAL SOURCES:

BOOKS

Arreola, Juan José, *Confabulario and Other Inventions,* translated and introduced by George D. Schade, University of Texas Press, 1964.
Foster, David William and Virginia Ramos Foster, editors, *Modern Latin American Literature,* Ungar, 1975.

PERIODICALS

Books Abroad, autumn, 1964.
Hispania, September, 1959.

ARRUFAT, Antón B. 1935-

PERSONAL: Born in 1935 in Cuba.

CAREER: Writer.

AWARDS, HONORS: Theatre Prize from Union of Writers, for "Los siete contra Tebas."

WRITINGS:

(Editor) *Nuevos cuentistas cubanos,* Casa de las Américas, 1961.
En claro (verse), Ediciones la Tertulia, 1962.
(Editor) *Guarachas cubanas, curiosa recopilación desde las mas antiguas hasta las mas modernas, según la edición de 1882,* Empresa Consolidada de Artes Gráficas, 1963.
Mi antagonista, y otras observaciones, Ediciones Revolución, 1963.
Repasa final (verse), Ediciones Revolución, 1964.
Teatro (plays; includes "El caso se investiga" [produced in 1957], "El vivo al pollo" [produced in 1961], "El último tren" [produced in 1963], "La repetición" [produced in 1963], and "La zona cero"), Unión de Escritores y Artistas de Cuba, 1963.
(Editor) August Strindberg, *Teatro* (plays), Editora del Consejo Nacional de Cultural, Editorial Nacional de Cuba, 1964.
Todos los domingos (play), Ediciones Revolución, 1965.
Escrito en las puertas, Unión de Escritores y Artistas de Cuba, 1968.
Los siete contra Tebas (play), Unión de Escritores y Artistas de Cuba, 1968.
La caja está cerrada, Editorial Letras Cubanas, 1984.
La huella en la arena, Editorial Letras Cubanas, 1986.
La tierra permanente, Editorial Letras Cubanas, 1987.

Also author of *Antología del teatro bufo,* 1963. Contributor to periodicals, including *Ciclón* and *Orígenes.* Staff member of *Casa de las Américas.*

BIOGRAPHICAL/CRITICAL SOURCES:

BOOKS

Lyday, Leon F. III, and George Woodyard, *Dramatists in Revolt: The Contemporary Latin American Theatre,* University of Texas Press, 1975.

*   *   *

ARTEL, Jorge 1909-

PERSONAL: Original name Agapito de Arcos; born April 27, 1909, in Cartagena, Colombia.

CAREER: Poet and novelist. Worked as journalist, lawyer, and diplomat. Lecturer at Princeton University and Columbia University.

WRITINGS:

Tambores en la noche (poems), Editora Bolívar, 1940, reprinted, University of Guanajuato (Mexico), 1956.
Poemas con botas y banderas, prologue by Jorge Turner, Universidad del Atlántico, 1972.
No es la muerte, es el morir (novel), Ecoe Ediciones, 1979.
Antología poética, Ecoe Ediciones, 1979.

BIOGRAPHICAL/CRITICAL SOURCES:

BOOKS

Jackson, Richard L., *The Black Image in Latin American Literature,* University of New Mexico Press, 1976.

Lewis, Marvin A., *Afro-Hispanic Poetry, 1940-1980: From Slavery to "Negritud" in South American Verse,* University of Missouri Press, 1983.

* * *

ASIN, Alfredo Quíspez
See MORO, César

* * *

ASIN, César Quíspez
See MORO, César

* * *

ASTURIAS, Miguel Angel 1899-1974

PERSONAL: Surname pronounced "As-*too*-ree-ahs"; born October 19, 1899, in Guatemala City, Guatemala; stripped of Guatemalan citizenship and forced into exile in Argentina, 1954; Guatemalan citizenship restored, 1966; died June 9, 1974, in Madrid, Spain; son of Ernesto (a supreme court magistrate, later an importer) and María (Rosales) Asturias; married Clemencia Amado; married second wife, Blanca Mora y Araujo; children: Rodrigo, Miguel Angel. *Education:* Universidad de San Carlos de Guatemala, Doctor of Laws, 1923; attended the Sorbonne, University of Paris, 1923-28.

CAREER: Diplomat and writer. Left Guatemala for political reasons, 1923; European correspondent for Central American and Mexican newspapers, 1923-32; returned to Guatemala, 1933; founded and worked as broadcaster for radio program "El Diario del Aire" and worked as a journalist, c. 1933-42; elected deputy to Guatemalan national congress, 1942; member of Guatemalan diplomatic service, 1945-54, cultural attaché to Mexico, 1946-47, and to Argentina, 1947-51, minister-counselor to Argentina, 1951-52, diplomat in Paris, 1952-53, ambassador to El Salvador, 1953-54; correspondent for Venezuelan newspaper *El Nacional* and adviser to Editorial Losada publishers in Argentina, 1954-62; member of cultural exchange program Columbianum in Italy, 1962; Guatemalan ambassador to France, 1966-70. Co-founder of Universidad Popular de Guatemala (a free evening college), 1921, and of Asociación de Estudiantes Universitarios (Unionist party group).

MEMBER: International PEN.

AWARDS, HONORS: Premio Gálvez for dissertation, and Chavez Prize, both 1923; Prix Sylla Monsegur, 1931, for *Leyendas de Guatemala;* Prix du Meilleur Roman Etranger, 1952, for *El señor presidente;* International Lenin Peace Prize from U.S.S.R., 1966, for *Viento fuerte, El papa verde,* and *Los ojos de los enterrados;* Nobel Prize for literature from Swedish Academy, 1967.

WRITINGS:

POETRY

Rayito de estrella (title means "Little Starbeam"), privately printed, 1925.
Emulo lipolidón, Typografía América (Guatemala), 1935.
Anoche, 10 de marzo de 1543, Ediciones del Aire (Guatemala), 1943.
Poesía sien de alondra, preface by Alfonso Reyes, Argos (Buenos Aires), 1949.
Ejercicios poéticos en forma de soneto sobre temas de Horacio, Botella al Mar (Buenos Aires), 1951.
Bolívar, El Salvador (San Salvador), 1955.

Nombre custodio, e imagen pasajera, La Habana, 1959.
Clarivigilia primaveral (anthology), Losada (Buenos Aires), 1965.

Also author of *Fantomina,* 1935, *Sonetos,* 1936, *Alclasán,* 1939, *Fantomina,* 1940, and *Con el rehén en los dientes,* 1946.

NOVELS

El señor presidente, Costa-Amic (Mexico), 1946, critical edition, Editions Klincksieck (Paris), 1978, translation by Frances Partridge published as *The President,* Gollancz, 1963, published as *El Señor Presidente,* Atheneum, 1964 (also see below).
Hombres de maíz, Losada, 1949, reprinted, 1968, translation by Gerald Martin published as *Men of Maize,* Delacorte, 1975.
Viento fuerte (first volume in "Banana Trilogy"), Ministerio de Educación Pública (Guatemala), 1950, translation by Darwin Flakoll and Claribel Alegria published as *The Cyclone,* Owen, 1967, translation by Gregory Rabassa published as *Strong Wind,* Delacorte, 1968.
El papa verde (second volume in "Banana Trilogy"), Losada, 1954, reprinted, 1973, translation by Rabassa published as *The Green Pope,* Delacorte, 1971.
Los ojos de los enterrados (third volume in "Banana Trilogy"), Losada, 1960, translation by Rabassa published as *The Eyes of the Interred,* Delacorte, 1973.
Mulata de tal, Losada, 1963, translation by Rabassa published as *Mulata,* Delacorte, 1967 (published in England as *The Mulatta and Mr. Fly,* Owen, 1967).

PLAYS

Soluna: Comedia prodigiosa en dos jornados y un final, Ediciones Losange (Buenos Aires), 1955 (also see below).
La audiencia de los confines: Crónica en tres andanzas, Ariadna (Buenos Aires), 1957 (also see below).
Teatro: Chantaje, Dique seco, Soluna, La audiencia de los confines (collected plays), Losada, 1964.

OTHER

(Translator with J. M. González de Mendoza) *Anales de los xahil de los indios cakchiqueles,* c. 1925, 2nd edition, Tipografía Nacional, 1967.
(Translator from the French with González de Mendoza) Georges Raynaud, *Los dioses, los héroes y los hombres de Guatemala antigua, o, el libro del consejo, Popol-vuh de los indios quichés,* Paris-America (Paris), 1927, 2nd edition published as *Popul-vuh, o libro del consejo de los indios quichés,* Losada, 1969.
La arquitectura de la vida nueva (lectures; title means "The Building of a New Life"), Goubaud, 1928.
Leyendas de Guatemala (collection of Indian tales), preface by Paul Valery, Ediciones Oriente (Madrid), 1930, reprinted, Losada, 1957 (also see below).
Weekend en Guatemala (short stories), Goyanarte (Buenos Aires), 1956.
(Editor) *Poesía precolombiana* (collection of Aztec and Mayan poetry), Fabril (Buenos Aires), 1960.
(With Jean Mazon and F. Diez de Medina) *Bolivia: An Undiscovered Land,* translated by Frances Hogarth-Gaute, Harrap, 1961.
El alhajadito (poem and children's stories), Goyanarte, 1961, translation by Martin Shuttleworth published as *The Bejeweled Boy,* Doubleday, 1971 (also see below).
(Editor) *Páginas de Rubén Darío,* Universitaria de Buenos Aires, 1963.
Rumania, su nueva imagen, Universidad Veracruzana, 1964.

Juan Girador, Centre de Recherches de l'Institut d'Etudes Hispaniques, 1964.

El espejo de Lida Sal, Siglo Veintiuno Editores (Mexico), 1967.

(Translator from the Rumanian) *Antología de la prosa rumana,* Losada, 1967.

Latinoamérica y otros ensayos, Guadiana de Publicaciones (Madrid), 1968.

(With Pablo Neruda) *Comiendo en Hungría* (poems and sketches), Lumen (Barcelona), 1969, translation by Barna Balogh revised by Mary Arias and published as *Sentimental Journey around the Hungarian Cuisine,* Corvina (Budapest), 1969.

Maladrón: Epopeya de los Andes verdes, Losada, 1969.

Héctor Poleo, Villand & Golanis (Paris), 1969.

The Talking Machine (juvenile), translated by Beverly Koch, Doubleday, 1971.

Viernes de dolores, Losada, 1972.

América: Fábula de fábulas y otros ensayos (essays), compiled with preface by Richard J. Callan, Monte Avila (Caracas), 1972.

Sociología guatemalteca: El problema social del indio, (dual language edition, including original Spanish text followed by English text titled *Guatemalan Sociology: The Social Problem of the Indian*), English translation by Maureen Ahern, introduction by Callan, Arizona State University Center for Latin American Studies, 1977.

Tres de cuatro soles, preface by Marcel Bataillon, introduction and notes by Dorita Nouhaud, Fondo de Cultura Económica (Madrid), 1977.

Sinceridades (essays), edited by Epaminondas Quintana, Académica Centroamericana (Guatemala), 1980.

El hombre que lo tenía todo, todo, todo, illustrations by Jacqueline Duheme, Bruguera (Barcelona), 1981.

Viajes, ensayos y fantasías (selected articles), Losada, 1981.

Founder of periodical *Tiempos Nuevos,* 1923; contributor to periodicals.

Work collected in omnibus volumes, including *Obras escogidas,* Aguilar (Madrid), 1955; *Obras completas,* three volumes, Aguilar, 1967; *Antología de Miguel Angel Asturias,* edited by Pablo Palomina, Costa-Amic, 1968; *Miguel Angel Asturias: Semblanza para el estudio de su vida y obra, con una selección de poemas y prosas,* Cultural Centroamericana Librería Proa (Guatemala), 1968; *El problema social del indio y otros textos,* edited by Claude Couffon, Centre de Recherches de l'Institut d'Etudes Hispaniques, 1971; *Novelas y cuentos de juventud,* edited by Couffon, Centre de Recherches de l'Institut d'Etudes Hispaniques, 1971; *Mi mejor obra,* Organización Editorial Novaro (Mexico), 1973, reissued as *Lo mejor de mi obra,* 1974; *Tres obras* (includes *Leyendas de Guatemala, El alhajadito,* and *El señor presidente*), introduction by Arturo Uslar Pietri, notes by Giuseppe Bellini, Biblioteca Ayacucho (Caracas), 1977.

SIDELIGHTS: Guatemalan statesman and Nobel laureate Miguel Angel Asturias is best known for the novels *El señor presidente,* about a Latin American dictator, and *Hombres de maíz,* about the conflicts between Guatemalan native Indians and land-exploiting farmers, as well as for a trilogy of novels about the Latin American banana industry. His writing—an extensive canon of fiction, essays, and poetry—often blends Indian myth and folklore with surrealism and satiric social commentary, and is considered to evidence his compassion for those unable to escape political or economic domination. "My work," Asturias promised when he accepted the 1967 Nobel Prize for literature, "will continue to reflect the voice of the peoples, gathering their myths and popular beliefs and at the same time seeking to give birth to a universal consciousness of Latin American problems."

Asturias was born in 1899 in Guatemala City, Guatemala, just one year after the country succumbed to the dictatorship of Manuel Estrada Cabrera. Asturias's father, a supreme court magistrate, lost his position in 1903, when he refused to convict students who protested against Estrada Cabrera's totalitarian regime. Consequently, Asturias's family was forced to leave the city for a rural area in Guatemala, where the young Asturias's interest in his country's Indian and peasant customs perhaps originated. Although his family returned to Guatemala City four years later, Asturias had nonetheless suffered the first of the many personal disruptions that autocracy and political unrest would cause throughout his career.

After attending secondary school, Asturias entered the Universidad de San Carlos to study law. As a college student, he was politically active, participating in demonstrations that helped to depose Estrada Cabrera and then serving as court secretary at the dictator's trial. Asturias also helped to found both a student association of Guatemala's Unionist party and the Universidad Popular de Guatemala, an organization that provided free evening instruction for the country's poor. In 1923, as the military gained strength and Guatemala's political climate worsened, Asturias took his law degree and shortly thereafter founded the weekly newspaper *Tiempos Nuevos,* in which he and several others began publishing articles decrying the new militarist government. Asturias fled the country the same year, his own life in danger after a colleague on the paper's writing staff was assaulted.

Asturias lived for the next five months in London, spending much of his time learning about Mayan Indian culture at the British Museum. He moved then to Paris, where he supported himself for several years as European correspondent for Mexican and Central American newspapers while he studied ancient Central American Indian civilizations at the Sorbonne. There he completed a dissertation on Mayan religion and translated sacred Indian texts, including the *Popol-vuh* and the *Anales de los xahil.*

In Paris Asturias also began his literary career. Associating with such avant-garde French poets as Andre Breton and Paul Valery, Asturias was introduced to the techniques and themes of the surrealist literary movement, which would become important elements of his writing style. In 1925 Asturias privately published *Rayito de estrella,* a book of poetry, and later, his *Leyendas de Guatemala,* a critically acclaimed collection of Indian stories and legends recalled from childhood, garnered him the 1931 Prix Sylla Monsegur.

Asturias returned to Guatemala in 1933 after further travel in Europe and the Middle East. He spent the next ten years working as a journalist and poet while Guatemala operated under the military dictatorship of Jorge Ubico Casteñeda. He also founded and worked as a broadcaster for the radio program "El Diario del Aire," and between 1935 and 1940, he published several more volumes of poetry, including *Emulo lipolidón, Sonetos, Alclasán,* and *Fantomina.* Asturias first entered politics in 1942 with his election as deputy to the Guatemalan national congress. Three years later, after the fall of the Casteñeda regime and the installation of the new president, Juan José Arévalo, Asturias joined the Guatemalan diplomatic service. The more liberal policies of the new government proved important for the author, both politically and artistically. Under Arévalo's rule, Asturias served in several ambassadorial posts in Mexico and Argentina from the early 1940s until 1952. In addition, the more tolerant atmosphere made it possible for Asturias to publish his first novel, *El señor presidente,* in 1946.

Asturias began writing *El señor presidente* while he was a law student at San Carlos University. Based on his own and others' memories of the Estrada Cabrera administration, the novel was first conceived as a short story about a ruthless dictator—reportedly Estrada Cabrera himself—and his schemes to dispose of a political adversary in an unnamed Latin American country usually identified as Guatemala. Asturias had developed the story through numerous revisions into a novel and completed it in the early 1930s, when publication of the book under Ubico Casteñeda's rule would have been too dangerous.

Translated as *The President* in 1968, *El señor presidente* was acclaimed for portraying both totalitarian government and its damaging psychological effects. Drawing from his experiences as a journalist writing under repressive conditions, Asturias employed such literary devices as satire to convey the government's transgressions and used surrealistic dream sequences to demonstrate the police state's impact on the individual psyche. Asturias also made use of colloquial Latin American dialogue to render realistically the varying perspectives of the country's social classes. Asturias's stance against all forms of injustice in Guatemala caused critics to view the author as a compassionate spokesman for the oppressed. "Asturias . . . does not see the drama of his people from the outside, as a dilettante, . . . but from the inside, as a participant," noted *Les Temps Modernes* contributor Manuel Tuñón de Lara, for example. And a *Times Literary Supplement* review, also commenting on Asturias's success in portraying the country's unique political circumstances, asserted that *El señor presidente* presents "Latin American problems according to their merits and not according to preconceived stereotypes."

Proclaimed by *Los Angeles Times Book Review* contributor Eduardo Galeano as "the best novel about dictators ever written in Latin America," *El señor presidente* especially elicited praise for its representation of severe political repression. Critics expressing this view included T. B. Irving, who wrote in the *Inter-American Review of Bibliography* that Asturias "has achieved in a splendid manner a grotesque and almost asphyxiating conception of the total state." "Asturias leaves no doubt about what it is like to be tortured, or what it is like to work for a man who is both omnipotent and depraved," applauded the *Times Literary Supplement* reviewer. "When the reader puts down the novel," Irving remarked, "he does so with a feeling of compassion and, at the same time, relief that he has not had to live through similar circumstances."

Three years after the publication of *El señor presidente,* while serving as Guatemalan cultural attaché in Buenos Aires, Argentina, Asturias completed and published *Hombres de Maíz,* the first of his novels explicitly to evoke the mythology of his country's ancient past. Translated as *Men of Maize* in 1975, the book abandons *El señor presidente*'s satiric approach for a poetic, surrealistic treatment of the struggle between the Guatemalan *indigenista,* or highland Indians, and the *ladinos,* peasants who, much like their conquering Spanish ancestors, attempt to usurp Indian territory in order to raise commercial corn crops. The story unfolds from the point of view of the *indigenista,* whose ancient beliefs teach that the first human was made from corn and that the grain is therefore sacred and must be grown only for tribal use. When their resistance leader, Gaspar Ilóm, is assassinated, the Indians place a curse on their enemies, beginning a series of events that becomes part of the Indian mythological heritage. According to Joseph Sommers in the *Journal of Inter-*

American Studies, "the reader sees briefly . . . the concrete situation which gives rise to myth. Then . . . he witnesses the formation of legends, as the novel traces their spread and elaboration into full-fledged folklore."

While *Men of Maize* was coolly received at the time of its publication in 1949, many critics have come to view the work as Asturias's masterpiece—his most successful integration of the social and the artistic. Reviewers especially admired the author's portrayal of the contrasting *indigenista* and *ladino* conceptions of the world. "At one level," noted *Washington Post Book World* reviewer Patrick Breslin, the book is "symbolic of the Spanish conquest itself. The social and economic order violently introduced by the Spanish four and a half centuries ago is still tenuous, not only in the highlands of Guatemala, but throughout the Andes of South America as well." Other readers, such as Sommers, who criticized what he saw as the author's "baroque profusion of imagery" and frequent use of "expressive but difficult localism," praised Asturias's surrealistic combination of myth and reality as an original and insightful portrait of Indian attitudes. *Men of Maize,* Sommers explained, "transcends the former stereotype of superficial realism and frequently elementary social protest."

During his diplomatic assignments in Argentina, Asturias also worked on what has come to be known to English-speaking readers as his "Banana Trilogy"—three novels about the Latin American banana industry. Consisting of *Viento fuerte, El papa verde,* and *Los ojos de los enterrados,* the trilogy focuses on the conflicts between the labor force in an unidentified country (taken again by critics to be Guatemala), and Tropical Banana, Inc., a North American conglomerate commonly accepted as a portrait of the real-life United Fruit Company. *Viento fuerte,* translated as *The Strong Wind,* relates the attempts of the main character, former Tropical Banana official Lester Mead, to bring about cooperation between the native growers and the company by urging fairness over profit. *El papa verde,* the second volume of the trilogy translated as *The Green Pope,* depicts Mead's continued and ultimately unsuccessful efforts to convince the head of Tropical Banana—the "Green Pope"—to offer banana growers a stable market and fairer prices for their crops. The final novel, *Los ojos de los enterrados,* translated as *The Eyes of the Interred,* deals with the spread of the banana industry's turmoil into the political arena through a general strike that helps depose the country's president. Although the "Banana Trilogy" was not as critically acclaimed as either *El señor presidente* or *Hombres de maíz,* it earned Asturias the International Lenin Peace Prize from the Soviet Union, who honored the works' stance against capitalist imperialism.

Working for the government of Arévalo's successor Jacobo Arbenz Guzmán in 1953, Asturias was sent as Guatemalan ambassador to El Salvador to try to prevent Salvadorean rebels from invading Guatemala. Although he had enlisted the Salvadorean government's aid, the rebels, with backing from the United States, nonetheless invaded Guatemala and overthrew Arbenz Guzmán. Because of his support for the defeated leader, Asturias was stripped of his citizenship and exiled in 1954. Asturias later incorporated details from these Salvadorean events in his 1956 collection of stories titled *Weekend en Guatemala.*

Asturias lived in exile, working in Argentina as a journalist for the Caracas, Venezuela, newspaper *El Nacional* until 1962, when he traveled to Italy as part of a cultural exchange program. During this period he continued to write, completing scholarly studies and publishing lectures, children's stories, and another novel, *Mulata de tal.* Asturias did not recover his Guatemalan

citizenship until the election of president César Méndes Montenegro's moderate government in 1966, when he accepted a job
as French ambassador, the position in which he remained until
1970. Throughout his life of service and exile, Asturias remained
committed to exposing through his writing the injustice and oppression plaguing his fellow Guatemalans. For his efforts, he was
awarded the 1967 Nobel Prize for literature. "Latin American
literature is still a literature of combat," Asturias once declared,
as quoted by Robert G, Mead, Jr., in the *Saturday Review*. "The
novel is the only means I have of making the needs and aspirations of my people known to the world."

MEDIA ADAPTATIONS: El señor presidente was made into a
film of the same title by Imago Producciones, Argentina.

BIOGRAPHICAL/CRITICAL SOURCES:

BOOKS

Anderson-Imbert, Enrique, *Spanish American Literature: A His-
tory,* translation by John V. Falconiere, Wayne State Uni-
versity Press, 1963.
Callan, Richard, *Miguel Angel Asturias,* Twayne, 1970.
Contemporary Literary Criticism, Gale, Volume 3, 1975, Volume
8, 1978, Volume 13, 1980.
Dardon, Hugo Cerezo, editor, *Coloquio con Miguel Angel Astu-
rias,* Universitario, 1968.
Miquel Angel Asturias en la literatura, Istmo (Guatemala), 1969.
Meyer, Doris, *Lives on the Line: The Testimony of Contemporary
Latin American Authors,* University of California Press,
1988.

PERIODICALS

Inter-American Review of Bibliography, April-June, 1965.
Journal of Inter-American Studies, April, 1964.
Les Temps Modernes, November, 1954.
Los Angeles Times Book Review, May 28, 1989.
New Statesman, October 25, 1963, September 29, 1967, April 22,
1988.
New York Review of Books, May 22, 1969.
New York Times, October 20, 1967, January 2, 1971, June 10,
1974.
New York Times Book Review, November 19, 1967, January 26,
1979.
Saturday Review, January 25, 1969.
Times Literary Supplement, October 18, 1963, September 28,
1967, November 19, 1971.
Washington Post Book World, August 17, 1975.

OBITUARIES:

PERIODICALS

Newsweek, June 24, 1974.
New York Times, June 10, 1974.
Time, June 24, 1974.
Washington Post, June 10, 1974.

—*Sketch by Emily J. McMurray*

*   *   *

AVALLE-ARCE, Juan Bautista de 1927-
(Luis Galvez de Montalvo, Gabriel Goyeneche)

PERSONAL: Surname is pronounced "Ah-*vah*-yay *Ar*-say";
born May 13, 1927, in Buenos Aires, Argentina; came to U.S.,
1948; son of Juan Bautista (a senator) and María (Martina)
Avalle-Arce; married Constance M. Marginot, August 20, 1956
(died, 1969); married Diane Janet Pamp (a writer), August 29,

1969; children: (first marriage) Juan Bautista Alejandro Guadalupe III, María Martina, Alejandro Alcantara; (second marriage) María la Real Alejandra, Fadrique Martín Manuel. *Education:* Attended Colegio Nacional de Buenos Aires, 1941-47,
and Universidad de Buenos Aires, 1942-47; Harvard University,
A.B., 1951, M.A., 1952, Ph.D., 1955; Ohio State University,
postdoctoral fellow, 1958-59. *Politics:* Carlist. *Religion:* Catholic.

ADDRESSES: Home—"Etxeberria," 4640 Oak View Rd., Santa
Yuez, Calif. 93460. *Office*—Department of Spanish, University
of California, Santa Barbara, Santa Barbara, Calif. 93106.

CAREER: Ohio State University, Columbus, assistant professor,
1955-57, associate professor of Romance languages, 1957-61,
acting chairman of department, 1960; Smith College, Northampton, Mass., professor of Spanish, 1961-65, Sophia Smith Professor of Hispanic Studies, 1965-69, chairman of department,
1966-69, director of graduate studies, 1961-69; University of
North Carolina at Chapel Hill, William Rand Kenan, Jr. Professor of Spanish, 1969-84; University of California, Santa Barbara,
professor, 1984—. Visiting scholar in the humanities at University of Bridgeport, 1968, University at Georgia, 1972, University
of Virginia, 1976, Universidad de Salamanca, Universidad de
Cádiz, Universidad de Alicante, and Fundación Juan March
(Madrid). Lecturer at various universities in the U.S., Asia, and
Europe. Member of editorial board of Tamesis Books. Consultant for several university presses, including those of Princeton
University, University of Texas, and University of California.
Member of national board of advisors, Instituto Cultural His-
pánico; member of advisory board, Bryn Mawr College. Cultural
correspondent, Radio Nacional de España, Euskadiko
Erradio (Basque Government Radio).

MEMBER: Instituto Internacional de Literatura Iberoamericana, Academia Argentina de Letras, Hispanic Society of America, Modern Humanities Research Association, Renaissance Society of America, Council of Graduate Schools, Academy of Literary Stories (founding member), Real Sociedad Vascongada de
Amigos del País, Asociación Internacional de Hispanistas
(founding member), Sociedad de Bibliofilos Españoles, Centro
de Estudios Jacobeos (Santiago), Centre d'Etudes Superieures de
Civilisation Medievale (Universite de Poitiers), Cervantes Society of America (president, 1980), Society of Spanish and Spanish
Americans (honorary fellow).

AWARDS, HONORS: Premio Literario del Centro Gallego,
1948, for "Rosalía de Castro: A Critical Study"; Susan Anthony
Potter Literary Prize, Harvard University, 1951, for "The Po-
etry of Jorge de Montemayor"; grants from American Philo-
sophical Society, 1958 and 1963, American Council of Learned
Societies, 1962 and 1967-68, and National Endowment for the
Humanities, 1967-68 and 1978-80; Guggenheim fellow, 1960-61;
Bonsoms Medal from the government of Spain, 1962, for critical
works on Cervantes; Diploma of Merit, Universita delle Arte
(Italy); Medal *au merit,* Kyoto University for Foreign Affairs
(Japan); created Marqués de la Lealtad for Teutonic Order of the
Levant Trust.

WRITINGS:

Conocimiento y vida en Cervantes, Imprenta Universitaria (Buenos Aires), 1959.
La novela pastoril española, Revista de Occidente (Madrid),
1959.
Deslindes cervantinos, Edhigar (Madrid), 1961.
El Inca Garcilaso en sus comentarios, Gredos (Madrid), 1963,
2nd edition, 1970.

Bernal Frances y su romance, Imprenta Universitaria (Barcelona), 1966.

Don Juan Valera: Morsamor, Labor (Barcelona) 1970.

Temas hispánicos medievales, Gredos, 1972.

(Editor with E. C. Riley) *Suma cervantina,* Longwood Publishing, 1973.

El cronista Pedro de Escavias: Una vida del siglo XV, University of North Carolina Press, 1974.

Nuevos deslindes cervantinos, [Barcelona], 1975.

Las memorias de Gonzalo Fernández de Oviedo, two volumes, University of North Carolina Press, 1975.

Don Quijote como forma de vida, [Madrid], 1976.

(Editor) *Don Quijote de la Mancha,* two volumes, [Madrid], 1983.

(Editor) Lope de Vega, *Las hazañas del segundo David,* [Madrid], 1984.

(Editor) García Rodríguez de Montalvo, *Amadís de Gaula,* two volumes, [Barcelona], 1984.

La Galatea de Cervantes: Cuatrocientos años después, Juan de la Cuesta, 1985.

Lecturas, Scripta Humanística, 1987.

OTHER

(Author of prologue and notes) Miguel de Cervantes Saavedra, *La Galatea,* two volumes, Espasa-Calpe (Madrid), 1961, 2nd edition, 1968.

(Author of prologue and notes) Gonzalo Fernández de Oviedo, *El sumario de historia natural,* Anaya (Madrid), 1962.

(Author of introduction and notes) Miguel de Cervantes Saavedra, *Three Exemplary Novels: El licenciado vidriera, El casamiento engañoso, El coloquio de los perros,* Dell, 1964.

(Contributor) German Bleiberg and E. L. Fox, editors, *Spanish Thought and Letters in the Twentieth Century,* Vanderbilt University Press, 1966.

(Contributor) A. N. Zahareas, editor, *Ramón del Valle-Inclán: A Critical Appraisal of His Life and Works,* Las Américas, 1968.

(Editor and author of introduction and notes) Miguel de Cervantes Saavedra, *Los trabajos de Persiles y Sigismunda,* Castalia (Madrid), 1969.

(Editor and author of introduction and notes) Miguel de Cervantes Saavedra, *Ocho entremeses,* Prentice-Hall, 1970.

(Author of prologue and notes) Lope de Vega, *El peregrino,* Castalia, 1972.

Also author, under pseudonym Luis Galvez de Montalvo, of "The Poetry of Jorge de Montemayor"; author, under pseudonym Gabriel Goyeneche, of several lyric poems. Contributor of more than 250 articles, essays, and poems to numerous periodicals and journals, including *Hispanic Review, Romance Philology, Bulletin of Hispanic Studies, Hispanofila, Insula, Boletín de la Real Academia Española, Cuadernos Hispanoamericanos, Romance Notes,* and *Filología.* Editor, *Studies in the Romance Languages and Literatures;* contributing editor, *McGraw-Hill Encyclopedia of World Biography* and *Diccionario Enciclopédico Salvat Universal.* Member of editorial board, *Hispanic Review, Crítica Hispánica, Anales Cervantinos, Anales Galdosianos, Romance Monographs,* and *Romance Notes.*

WORK IN PROGRESS: Don Fadrique Enríquez: Vida y obras.

SIDELIGHTS: Juan Bautista de Avalle-Arce told *CA* he "cannot remember having had an interest other than books (except horses); probably reading Don Quixote at age 7-8 got me as affected by literature as he was. The traditional values and way of life are vital to me. Being Baifitt Grand Cross of the Sovereign Military Teutonic Order of the Levant and its Grand Prior is

proof." Avalle-Arce has traveled extensively in the Americas, Europe, Asia, and Africa, and knows Basque, French, Italian, Portuguese, German, Guarani, Latin, Greek, and Arabic in addition to his native Spanish.

AVOCATIONAL INTERESTS: Fox-hunting, polo, breaking and training hunting horses, cooking, wine tasting.

*   *   *

AVENDAÑO, Fausto   1941-

PERSONAL: Born June 5, 1941, in Culiacán, Sinaloa, Mexico. *Education:* San Diego State University, B.A., 1967; University of Arizona, M.A., 1970, Ph.D., 1973; additional postgraduate study at National University of Mexico and University of Lisbon.

ADDRESSES: Office—Department of Spanish and Portuguese, California State University, Sacramento, Calif. 95819.

CAREER: Professor of Spanish and Portuguese at California State University, Sacramento. Member of Bilingual Crosscultural Specialist Credential Task force; member of Luso-American Education Foundation Task Force; director of Luso-American Literary Fund. *Military Service:* Served in U.S. Army.

MEMBER: American Association of Teachers of Spanish and Portuguese, Association of Mexican-American Educators, Mexican American Educational Association (Sacramento), Sigma Delta Pi.

AWARDS, HONORS: Fulbright fellowhip, 1983; Ford Foundation fellowship; grants from Gulbenkian Foundation and California State University Foundation.

WRITINGS:

El corrido de California (title means "The Ballad of California"; three-act play), Editorial Justa (Berkeley), 1979.

(Contributor) Arnulfo Trejo, editor, *The Chicanos: As We See Ourselves,* University of Arizona Press, 1979.

(Contributor) Oscar U. Somoza, editor, *Nueva narrativa chicana,* (title means "The New Chicano Narrative"), Editorial Diógenes (Mexico City), 1983.

(Contributor) Ricardo Aguilar, Armando Armengol, and Somoza, editors, *Palabra nueva: Cuentos Chicanos* (title means "The New Word: Chicano Stories"), Texas Western, 1984.

(Contributor) Armando Miguélez, editor, *Saguaro,* Mexican American Studies, University of Arizona, 1985.

(Contributor) Aguilar, Armengol, and Sergio D. Elizondo, editors, *Palabra nueva,* Dos Pasos (El Paso), 1985.

(Contributor) Helena Viramontes, editor, *Cenzontle,* Bilingual/Editorial Bilingüe, 1987.

(Editor) *Literatura hispana de los Estados Unidos* (title means "Hispanic Literature of the United States"), ETL-Hispanic (Sacramento), 1987.

Also author of play, "Abrahán Salazar," of novel, *The Chicken Tenders,* and of essays, articles, translations, and short stories, including "El forastero," 1984, and "Juan González, poeta," 1985; contributor of short stories to periodicals, including *El Grito, Obsidian, Revista de la Universidad de México,* and *Revista Chicano-Riqueña.*

SIDELIGHTS: Considered among Chicano literature's foremost scholars, Fausto Avendaño is best known for his short stories and for his historical play, *El corrido de California* ("The Ballad of California"). It explores the effects of the 1846 American invasion of Alta (upper) California on a Mexican family living there.

(California was not admitted into the Union until 1850, following the Mexican-American War.) The protagonist, Don Gerónimo, is the mayor of a small town who is torn between accepting the Americans' presence or resisting their force. His son, however, advocates resistence, and dies in the Battle of San Pascual. Don Gerónimo eventually realizes that he must fight against the new order and defend his people; the play closes as he leads them into battle.

The work was praised for its well-drawn characters, its successful blend of historical fact and dramatic tension, and its role as a foundation for historical Chicano theater in the United States.

BIOGRAPHICAL/CRITICAL SOURCES:

PERIODICALS

Explicación de textos literarios, spring, 1981.

* * *

AZORIN
See MARTINEZ RUIZ, José

* * *

AZUELA, Arturo 1938-

PERSONAL: Born in 1938.

CAREER: Novelist. Professor of mathematics and the history of science at National Autonomous University of Mexico; teacher at universities in Mexico, Western Europe, and the United States. Journalist.

AWARDS, HONORS: Premio de Ciencias y Artes for literature, 1988.

WRITINGS:

NOVELS

El tamaño del infierno, J. Mortiz (Mexico), 1973.
Un tal José Salomé, J. Mortiz, 1975.
Manifestación de silencios, J. Mortiz, 1979, translation by Elena C. Murray published as *Shadows of Silence,* University of Notre Dame Press, 1985.
La casa de las Mil Virgenes, Argos Vergara (Barcelona), 1983.
El don de la palabra, Plaza & Janés Editores (Barcelona), 1984.
Narradores de la Revolución mejicana, Editorial Revolución (Madrid), 1986.

SIDELIGHTS: Arturo Azuela is a Mexican novelist whose book *Shadows of Silence* is considered among the best of literature concerning the 1968 student-led upheavals against the Mexican government. The grandson of novelist Mariano Azuela, the young Azuela grew up in a household that encouraged literary and political learning. Although as an adult he chose a career in teaching mathematics and science, he later, at the age of thirty-six, began writing political novels. Writing "was the result of a long and unconscious process," Azuela told Larry Rohter in the *New York Times Book Review.* "While I was teaching math and writing journalism in my spare time, the idea was growing and growing. . . . I experienced the movement of 1968 with great intensity and saw how political and public issues interacted in people's lives."

Azuela's early novels include *El tamaño del infierno* and *Un tal José Salomé.* It was not until the 1979 publication of *Manifestación de silencios*—appearing in English translation six years later as *Shadows of Silence*—that Azuela earned widespread acclaim.

Set in Mexico City during the 1960s and 1970s, the work focuses on a group of friends consisting mostly of writers. While they consider themselves intellectuals and political revolutionaries, the characters spend much of their time drinking and dancing, and their political activism is insubstantial. "They measure their political commitment in terms of how long they can resist the various temptations to sell out," described Jonathan Kendell in the *New York Times Book Review.* Although the group is generally passionless, one character named José soars into a jealous rage and kills an acquaintance of his girlfriend. He flees to Paris in exile, and his friends imagine him a political hero. José's exile, though, is decidedly unglamorous, and it is only a matter of time before he returns to leading an apathetic lifestyle in Mexico.

Favorably reviewing *Shadows of Silence,* Kendell wrote that "few recent books of this [political] genre match its sharp writing, subtlety and insights." Calling the book "remarkable," the reviewer also admired Azuela's skillful prose: "[He] has little trouble shifting from leisurely dialogue to taut narrative or dreamy introspection." Kendell concluded that Azuela "is well acquainted with the struggles of Latin American exiles, and his description of their life abroad adds an international dimension rarely seen in Mexican literature. But his novel's real strengths are the vivid depiction of an explosively growing Mexico City, its embattled intellectuals and the powerful, sophisticated political system that seduces opponents, tolerates their minor transgressions or effortlessly silences them."

Azuela is also the author of later novels that include *La casa de las Mil Virgenes, El don de la palabra,* and *Narradores de la Revolución mejicana.* In 1988 he earned Mexico's prestigious Premio de Ciencias y Artes for literature.

BIOGRAPHICAL/CRITICAL SOURCES:

PERIODICALS

New York Times Book Review, July 21, 1985.

* * *

AZUELA, Mariano 1873-1952
(Beleño)

PERSONAL: Born January 1, 1873, in Lagos de Moreno, Jalisco, Mexico; died of a heart attack, March 1, 1952, in Mexico City, Mexico; buried in the Rotonda de Hombres Ilustres, Mexico City, Mexico; son of Evaristo Azuela and Paulina González; married Carmen Rivera; children: Salvador, Mariano, Carmen, Julia, Paulina, María de la Luz, Augustín, Esperanza, Antonio, Enrique. *Education:* Faculty of Medicine and Pharmacy of Guadalajara, degree of doctor, 1898.

ADDRESSES: Home—Mexico City, Mexico.

CAREER: Physician, 1898-1952, and writer, 1907-1952. Director of public education in Jalisco province under government of Francisco ("Pancho") Villa. *Wartime service:* Physician with Villa's army during Mexican Revolution.

AWARDS, HONORS: National Prize for Literature, 1949; *The Underdogs* won a prize for drama, 1950.

WRITINGS:

NOVELS AND NOVELLAS

María Luisa, first published in 1907, 2nd edition, Botas, 1938.
Los fracasados (title means "The Failures"), first published in 1908, 4th edition, Botas, 1939.
Mala yerba: Novela de costumbres nacionales, first published in 1909, reprinted, R. Terrazas, 1924, translation by Anita

Brenner published as *Marcela: A Mexican Love Story,* foreword by Waldo Frank, Farrar & Rinehart, 1932.

Andrés Pérez, maderista, Botas, 1911.

Sin amor, first published in 1912, 2nd edition, Botas, 1945.

Los de abajo: Novela de la revolución mexicana, first published in 1916, translation by E. Munguía, Jr., published as *The Under Dogs,* preface by Carleton Beals, illustrations by J. C. Orozco, Brentano's, 1929; published as *The Underdogs: A Novel of the Mexican Revolution,* foreword by Harriet de Onís, illustrations by Orozco, New American Library, 1963; translation by Frances K. Hendricks and Beatrice Berler published as *The Underdogs* in *Two Novels of the Mexican Revolution: The Trials of a Respectable Family and The Underdogs,* Principia Press of Trinity University, 1963 (also see below).

Los caciques, first published in 1917, translation by Lesley Byrd Simpson published as *The Bosses* in *Two Novels of Mexico: The Flies. The Bosses,* University of California Press, 1956 (also see below).

Las moscas [and] *Domitilo quiere ser diputado* [and] *De cómo al fin lloró Juan Pablo,* Tip de A. Carranza e Hijos, 1918, translation of *Las moscas* by Simpson published as *The Flies* in *Two Novels of Mexico: The Flies. The Bosses,* University of California Press, 1956 (also see below).

Las tribulaciones de una familia decente, first published in 1918, 2nd edition, Botas, 1938, translation by Hendricks and Berler published as *The Trials of a Respectable Family* in *Two Novels of the Mexican Revolution: The Trials of a Respectable Family and The Underdogs,* Trinity University Press, 1963 (also see below).

La malhora, first published in 1923, 3rd edition published with 2nd edition of *El desquite,* Botas, 1941 (also see below).

El desquite, first published in 1925, 2nd edition published with 3rd edition of *La malhora,* Botas, 1941.

La luciérnaga, Espasa-Calpe (Madrid), 1932, translation by Hendricks and Berler published as *The Firefly* in *Three Novels of Mariano Azuela,* Trinity University Press, 1979 (also see below).

Pedro Moreno, el insurgente: Biografía novelada, Ediciones Ercilla (Santiago, Chile), 1935.

Precursores, Ediciones Ercilla, 1935.

El camarada Pantoja, Botas, 1937.

San Gabriel de Valdivias, comunidad indígena, Ediciones Ercilla, 1938.

Regina Landa, Botas, 1939.

Avanzada, Botas, 1940.

Nueva burguesía, Club del Libro Amigos del Libro Americano (Buenos Aires), 1941, recent edition, Secretaria de Educación Pública, Cultura, Fondo de Cultura Económica, 1985.

El padre don Agustín Rivera, Botas, 1942.

La marchanta, Seminario de Cultura Mexicana, Secretaria de Educación Pública, 1944.

La mujer domada, El Colegio Nacional, 1946.

Sendas perdidas, Botas, 1949.

La maldición, Fondo de Cultura Económica, 1955.

Esa sangre, Fondo de Cultura Económica, 1956.

Also author of *Madero: Biografía novelada.*

WORKS IN TRANSLATION

Two Novels of Mexico: The Flies. The Bosses, translation with preface by Simpson, University of California Press, 1956.

Two Novels of the Mexican Revolution: The Trials of a Respectable Family and The Underdogs, translation by Hendricks and Berler, introduction by Hendricks, Principia Press of Trinity University, 1963.

Three Novels by Mariano Azuela (contains *The Trials of a Respectable Family, The Underdogs,* and *The Firefly*), translation by Hendricks and Berler, introduction by Luis Leal, Trinity University Press, 1979.

OTHER

Teatro: Los de abajo, El buho en la noche, Del llano hnos. (plays), Botas, 1938.

Cien años de novela mexicana (criticism), Botas, 1947.

Obras completas (title means "Complete Works"), three volumes, prologue by Francisco Monterde, Fondo de Cultura Económica, 1958-60, recent edition, 1976.

Introducción al estudio del amparo: Lecciones, Departamento de Bibliotecas, Universidad de Nuevo León, 1968.

Epistolario y archivo, compiled with notes and appendices by Berler, Centro de Estudios Literarios, Universidad Nacional Autónoma de México, 1969.

Also author of works under the pseudonym Beleño. Contributor to periodicals.

SIDELIGHTS: Mariano Azuela was one of the leading writers of twentieth-century Mexico and the foremost chronicler of that country's revolution. During his forty-year literary career he wrote more than twenty novels describing the volatile Mexican political scene, including *Las tribulaciones de una familia decente* (*The Trials of a Respectable Family*), and an account of his experiences with Francisco ("Pancho") Villa's army of revolutionaries, *Los de abajo* (*The Underdogs*). A physician, he dedicated his life to alleviating the suffering of the poor and oppressed, and through his novels he strove to rectify social inequality. His works, imbued with his pessimistic view of Mexico's future, expose the sources of the oppression that brought about the revolution, the false idealism and brutality of many of the politicians and military leaders during the war years, and the anarchy that pervaded postrevolutionary Mexican society.

Azuela was originally compelled to write by the desperate conditions he encountered while practicing medicine in the Mexico City slums. His first novel, *María Luisa,* was based on a story about a woman forced to choose between becoming a factory worker or a student's mistress. The composition of this novice work, published in 1907 when Azuela was thirty-four, displays the strengths and weaknesses of his subsequent writings. While creating vivid social and cultural scenes, he pays little attention to plot and structure. He forms his characters by concentrating on a few actions or other outstanding physical features, a technique some critics contend is dangerously close to caricature. And his characters, though well-rounded, are often stereotypical: villains are rich, conservative, and ruthless, while heroes are poor and seek only social equality. Although he wrote about both the lower and middle classes throughout Mexico, most commentators label his provincial characters—rich and poor— his most believable and interesting.

María Luisa also displays Azuela's hallmark use of dialogue. The author is consistently praised for mimicking speech patterns and idioms particular to specific social classes, professions, and provinces. He writes with few subordinate clauses, and his sentence structure is straightforward but lyrical, especially when describing nature and, ironically, the horrors of war. He is also noted for his concision. Jefferson Rea Spell in *Contemporary Spanish-American Fiction* assessed that it is Azuela's "mastery of the art of selection and condensation . . . whether he is describing nature, persons, or the man-made world," that distinguishes him as a literary artist.

In his early novels—*Los fracasados* ("The Failures"), *Mala yerba* (*Marcela: A Mexican Love Story*), and *Sin amor*—Azuela outlines the social and political circumstances that led to the revolution. *Los fracasados* excoriates Porfirio Díaz, Mexico's notoriously corrupt dictator who, during his thirty-five year tenure, rewarded his political allies with lands taken from the peasants. Azuela condemns the provincial landowners and the middle class—Díaz's chief supporters—by satirizing their greed and pettiness. Some critics, including Spell, however, complained that in the novel Azuela seems "less concerned with telling a story than with exposing the iniquity of certain inhabitants of Alamos." Although reviewers found the novel technically and artistically lacking, most agreed with Spell, who claimed that the work "is significant in that it portrays the intolerable conditions in a Mexican town that gave rise to the brutality of the underlings when they rose a few years later against their masters."

Azuela continued his attack on rural bourgeois society in *Marcela* and *Sin amor*, two books exploring the differences between the wealthy landowners and the wretched peasants who worked the estates. Spell noted that *Sin amor* successfully depicts "the great gulf between those that have and those that have not; the resentment of the latter toward the former; and the scorn of the wealthy for the poor."

Azuela's novels written during the Mexican Revolution unflinchingly portray war and display his growing disgust as the violence escalated. The revolution began with Díaz's overthrow by liberal leader Francisco I. Madero in 1910, and Madero's subsequent assassination by an opposing faction. During the consequent struggle for succession, which lasted seven years and embroiled the whole country, Azuela supported Villa. When the guerrilla army led by Venustiano Carranza gained the upper hand in government, however, Azuela was forced to flee with Villa's band to Texas. After the war Azuela returned to Mexico, where he practiced medicine and chronicled the revolution in five novels, *Andrés Pérez, maderista, The Underdogs, Los caciques* (*The Bosses*), *Las moscas* (*The Flies*), and *The Trials of a Respectable Family*.

Andrés Pérez, maderista recounts the chaos and confusion of the initial battles of the revolution and analyzes the various motives of some of Madero's followers, including an altruistic ideologist, a landowner whose property had been seized, and a political opportunist. "Ideologically, [*Andrés Pérez, maderista*] is one of his most significant novels," John E. Englekirk and Lawrence B. Kiddle observed in their introduction to Azuela's *Los de abajo*. "Conceived during those very months when Azuela already foresaw the tragic turn the revolt of the idealist Madero was soon to take, . . . it is the work of one who boldly, fearlessly, and prophetically [decried the revolution]."

The Underdogs, considered Azuela's masterwork, followed. He wrote it in 1915 while a fugitive in El Paso, Texas, with Villa's band. By presenting the experiences of a common soldier during the conflict, Azuela condemned the gratuitous violence, the sociopolitical forces that drove the Mexican people into poverty, and the opportunism that contradicted the goals of the revolution. The novel follows poor country boy Demetrio Macías's rise to the rank of general in Villa's revolutionary army. Opening in a battle in Juchipila Canyon, where Demetrio's forces deftly triumph, the drama and violence escalate until Macías is killed in the same canyon. Azuela depicts him as being defeated by the same forces—corruption and greed—that were bastardizing the revolution.

Azuela's despair for the future of his country permeates *The Underdogs*. Citing the "brutality" of many of his scenes, *Bookman*

contributor Carleton Beals likened Azuela's writing to that of Russian revolutionary author Maxim Gorki. The critic pointed out, however, that the Mexican shares "Gorki's terrific pessimism [but] none of [his] revolutionary optimism." Spell also remarked on *The Underdogs*'s "intense and varied emotive power," extrapolating: "while the author arouses pity for the downtrodden peasants, he also horrifies the reader with the crimes that some of them, in their ignorance and bestiality, commit." Beals noted that Azuela's "language is the language of reality . . . crude, often vile, truculent, fiendish."

The Bosses is a pessimistic account of life in a small western town owned and run by a family of wealthy Díaz supporters who viciously defend their privileged position by making war against the peasants. "Azuela is writing in white-hot anger against the cruelty and injustice of a system," Lesley Byrd Simpson wrote in the preface to *Two Novels of Mexico*, "and uses the effective device of extreme caricature to point up his thesis." Spell agreed, noting that Azuela's apparent intention for writing *The Bosses*—to expose the oppressors—applies to all of his novels of the war in general: "Through the injustice that it lays bare, the book affords a vindication, in a measure, of those who committed the most shocking atrocities against the lives and property of the privileged classes when the Revolution broke."

Azuela continues in the same vein with *The Flies*, considered one of his finest works. The action opens as a panicked throng of middle-class merchants are crowding onto trains in a Mexico City railway station to escape imminent slaughter by guerrilla leader Alvaro Obregón's ferocious troops. Throughout the night the characters reveal their thoughts and fears, and, Simpson wrote, condemn themselves. "The choppy, fragmentary dialogue," the critic noted, "the abrupt shifts, the callousness of some, the maudlin drunkenness of others, and the prodigious silliness of the frightened mother and her gold-digging family, together give us an etching of civil war not easily forgotten."

Azuela's last war novel, *Trials of a Respectable Family*, is an uncharacteristically sensitive study of the plight of the bourgeoisie during the revolution. Some critics surmise he wrote this novel after realizing that during war "good" men are as capable of atrocities as "bad" men. When affluent provincials heard reports of slaughters and pilfering by the revolutionaries, they fled to Mexico City, where they faced hardship in a city overrun by barbarous gangs. Azuela portrays the refugees' suffering as ennobling. Today *Trials of a Respectable Family* is considered second only to *The Underdogs* in the canon of Mexican revolutionary literature, although when it was published in 1918—directly following the revolution—it was ignored by critics who were perhaps unwilling to review a book sympathetic to the bourgeoisie.

Some critics claim that Azuela next produced three experimental novels, *La malhora, El desquite*, and *La luciérnaga* (*The Firefly*), in response to this lack of contemporary critical attention. Published in 1923, 1925, and 1932, these novels are difficult to read, due to thick, obscure, and sometimes incomprehensible imagery, heavy symbolism, and distorted sentence structure. "Azuela's striving for inordinate effects has definitely marred the work," Englekirk and Kiddle assessed in their critique of *La malhora*. They also complained that Azuela's continual digressions overwhelmed the main narrative threads. Other commentators noted that Azuela's dialogue was exaggerated and ill-suited to his characters.

Yet the sentiment that *La malhora, El desquite*, and *The Firefly* purvey, critical of postrevolutionary society, is undoubtedly true to Azuela's social philosophy. According to Englekirk and Kiddle, "the picture Azuela paints for us here is a somber one indeed

. . . in the sordidness and the physical and mental degeneracy it portrays." His last radical novel, *The Firefly*, is his only work that can be called a psychological study. In it he contrasts two brothers, a guilt-ridden thief and a drug addict.

Azuela abandoned his experimental style and addressed national problems clearly in his next novels, *El camarada Pantoja, San Gabriel de Valdivias, Regina Landa, Avanzada*, and *Nueva burguesía*, which are nonetheless steeped in his characteristic pessimism. In subsequent works he shifted his focus away from society to the individual, a trend foreshadowed in *The Firefly*. In these works, *La marchanta, La mujer domada, Sendas perdidas, La maldición, Esa sangre*, and *Madero*, he forsakes his depiction of traditional provincial life for an exploration of hectic urban life.

Luis Leal suggested in *Mariano Azuela* that these latest novels are his least effective, perhaps due to Azuela's becoming "a stern critic of new social order" rather than remaining "an objective recorder of social change." A probable cause for his change in style was his growing disillusionment with Mexico's notoriously corrupt government. Critics contend that Azuela's literary reputation rests not on his plots or imagery or characterization, but on his ability to analyze Mexico's changing social and political scene and its players.

BIOGRAPHICAL/CRITICAL SOURCES:

BOOKS

Azuela, Mariano, *Los de abajo: Novela de la revolución mexicana*, edited with introduction by John E. Englekirk and Lawrence B. Kiddle, reprinted, Prentice-Hall, 1971.
Azuela, Mariano, *Two Novels of Mexico: The Flies. The Bosses*, translated with preface by Lesley Byrd Simpson, University of California Press, 1956.
Leal, Luis, *Mariano Azuela*, Twayne, 1971.
Robe, Stanley Linn, *Azuela and the Mexican Underdogs*, University of California Press, 1979.
Spell, Jefferson Rea, *Contemporary Spanish-American Fiction*, reprinted, Biblo & Tannen, 1968.
Twentieth-Century Literary Criticism, Volume 3, Gale, 1980.

PERIODICALS

Bookman, May, 1929.
Books Abroad, autumn, 1953.
Hispania, February, 1935, February, 1952, May, 1967, March, 1972, December, 1980.
Modern Language Journal, May, 1951, October, 1968.
New Republic, October 23, 1929.

—*Sketch by Carol Lynn DeKane*

B

BABIN, María Teresa 1910-

PERSONAL: Born May 31, 1910, in Ponce, Puerto Rico; married, 1964. *Education:* University of Puerto Rico, B.A., 1931, M.A., 1939; Columbia University, Ph.D., 1951.

ADDRESSES: Home—Morzagaray 266, San Juan, P.R. 00901. *Office*—Department of Puerto Rican Studies, Center for Advanced Studies on Puerto Rico, P.O. Box S-4467, Old San Juan, P.R. 00904.

CAREER: Teacher of Spanish and French in high schools in New York, Pennsylvania, and Puerto Rico, 1932-40; University of Puerto Rico, Río Piedras, associate professor of Spanish and chairman of department, 1940-45; Hunter College (now of the City University of New York), New York City, instructor of Romance languages, 1946-50; New York University, Washington Square College, New York City, assistant professor of Spanish, 1951-61; chairman of Spanish program and coordinator of special program for talented students, Puerto Rico Department of Education, 1963-66; Herbert H. Lehman College of the City University of New York, Bronx, N.Y., professor of Puerto Rican studies and chairman of department, 1969-72; City University of New York Graduate Center, New York City, professor of Spanish, 1970-78, professor emeritus, 1978—. Director, School of the Air, WIPR, Department of Education, 1936-38; lecturer at Instituto Puertorriqueño, New York, and at university centers, 1969-74. Consultant to Pan American Union, Washington, D.C., 1952-53, Ford Foundation, 1969-74, and New York Department of Education, 1970.

MEMBER: Modern Language Association of America, Hispanic Society of America (corresponding member).

AWARDS, HONORS: Instituto de Literatura Puertorriqueña literary prize, 1954; Ateneo Puertorriqueño literary prize, 1955; Unión Mujeres Americanas literary prize (Guatemala), 1962; Literary Prize of the Year, Instituto Puertorriqueño, 1970.

WRITINGS:

Introducción a la cultura hispánica, Heath, 1949.
El mundo poético de Federico García Lorca, Biblioteca de Autores Puertorriqueños, 1954.
García Lorca: Vida y obra, Las Américas (New York), 1955.
Fantasía boricua: Estampas de mi tierra, Las Américas, 1956, 2nd edition, Santander, 1960, reprinted, Cultural (San Juan), 1982.

Panorama de la cultura puertorriqueña, Las Américas, 1958.
La hora colmada: Fábula teatral en dos actos, Santander, 1960.
Jornadas literarias; temas de Puerto Rico (essays), Rumbos (Barcelona), 1967.
Siluetas literarias; once ensayos (essays), Rumbos, 1967.
La obra en prosa de Llorens Torres, Cultural, 1969.
La cultura de Puerto Rico, brief edition, Instituto de Cultura Puertorriqueña, 1970, translation by Barry Luby published as *The Puerto Ricans' Spirit: Their History, Life and Culture,* Collier, 1971.
(Editor with Stan Steiner) *Borinquen: An Anthology of Puerto Rican Literature,* Knopf, 1974.
La poesía gallega de García Lorca, Sin Nombre (San Juan), 1974.
(Author of introduction) *Puerto Rican Authors: A Biobibliographic Handbook,* Scarecrow, 1974.
Estudios lorquianos, University of Puerto Rico Press, 1976.
Genio y figura de Nemesio R. Canales, Biblioteca de Autores Puertorriqueños, 1978.
(Author of commentary) Carlos M. Passalacqua, *Noche; Fuente: Poesía,* 2nd edition, Universitaria, 1981.
La barca varada: Veinticuatro cantos, Orígenes (Madrid), 1982.
(Contributor) Arturo Morales Carrión, *Puerto Rico, a Political and Cultural History,* Norton, 1983.

Also author of *La prosa mágica de García Lorca* and *Las voces de tu voz,* both 1962. Contributor to newspapers and professional journals, including *Brújula, Puerto Rico Ilustrado, La Nueva Democracia,* and *El Mundo.*

* * *

BACA, Jimmy Santiago 1952-
(José Santiago Baca)

PERSONAL: Born in 1952; married wife, Beatrice (a therapist); children: Antonio, Gabriel. *Education:* Self-educated; received G.E.D.

ADDRESSES: Home—Albuquerque, N.M.

CAREER: Writer. Gives poetry readings.

AWARDS, HONORS: American Book Award for poetry from Before Columbus Foundation, 1988, for *Martín and Meditations on the South Valley.*

WRITINGS:

Immigrants in Our Own Land: Poems, Louisiana State University Press, 1979.
Swords of Darkness (poetry), Mango Publications, 1981.
What's Happening (poetry), Curbstone Press, 1982.
Martín and Meditations on the South Valley (poetry), introduction by Denise Levertov, New Directions, 1987.
Black Mesa Poems, New Directions, 1989.

Contributor of poetry to periodicals, including *Mother Jones.*

WORK IN PROGRESS: In the Way of the Sun, the first novel in a trilogy; a play.

SIDELIGHTS: Jimmy Santiago Baca, an ex-convict who taught himself to read while in prison, is a highly acclaimed poet who won the prestigious American Book Award in 1988. Admired for his use of rich imagery and lyrical language, Baca, unlike a growing number of "prison writers" who inject their works with rage and desolation, writes poems dealing with spiritual rebirth and triumph over tragedy. "You really don't have time to be angry," Baca explained his attitude to Beth Ann Krier in the *Los Angeles Times.* "If you compare a life to daytime photography, my life has been more like nighttime photography. My life as a background has had darkness; the only way to survive the darkness is to have my soul flash. I'm too busy trying to capture the aspects of myself in the dark."

Of Chicano and Apache Indian descent, Baca lived with a grandparent after his parents divorced and abandoned him at the age of two. By the time he was five, Baca's mother had been murdered by her second husband, his father was dead of alcoholism, and Baca was in a New Mexico orphanage. Fleeing the institution when he was eleven, Baca was reduced to a life on the street. He soon abused drugs and alcohol and, by age twenty, was convicted of drug possession (a crime, he later told Krier, he did not commit). Sentenced to serve several years in a maximum security prison in Arizona, Baca would ultimately spend four years in isolation and receive electric shock treatments for a combative nature.

Despite his hardship, Baca did not lose spirit. Rather, he became intellectually invigorated during his incarceration period, teaching himself to read and write. He later divulged to Krier: "[In prison], I saw all these Chicanos going out to the fields and being treated like animals. I was tired of being treated like an animal. I wanted to learn how to read and to write and to understand. . . . I wanted to know how to function in this world. Why was I so ignorant and deprived? . . . The only way of transcending was through language and understanding. Had I not found the language, I would have been a guerrilla in the mountains. It was language that saved [me]." Baca began writing poetry and, at the behest of a fellow inmate, sent his works to *Mother Jones* magazine. "I took a wild chance," he related to Krier, "I didn't even know how to put the stamp on the envelope and address it." His determination was rewarded when poet and professor Denise Levertov, then poetry editor of *Mother Jones,* printed Baca's poems in the periodical. Judging Baca a talented writer, Levertov began corresponding with the inmate and eventually found a publisher for his first book.

Baca's *Immigrants in Our Own Land* appeared in 1979. The collection of poems, highlighting the splendor of human existence amidst the desolate surroundings of prison life, met with rave reviews. A *Kliatt* critic, for example, found Baca's poems "astonishingly beautiful" for their "celebration of the human spirit in extreme situations." Writing in the *American Book Review,* Ron Arias commended the poet's skill and versatility: "At times

[Baca] can be terse, narrowly focused, directly to the point. . . . Other times he can resemble an exuberant Walt Whitman in the long-lined rhythm and sweep of his emotions—expansive, wordy, even conversational." The critic concluded that Baca "is a freshly aggressive poet of many abilities. . . . His is a gifted, young vision, and judging from this collection, I get the feeling he is just warming up. I look forward to more."

Baca produced another work, the ten-poem collection *What's Happening,* in 1982. While less well-received than his first effort, the book garnered praise for its subject matter concerning both the Chicano and prison experience. Michael Hogan writing in the *American Book Review* found Baca's focus on racial oppression, exploitation of laborers, and the horrors of state-run penitentiaries "powerful"; yet he also agreed with other reviewers, deciding that the poems showed a "tendency toward looseness and the prosaic. . . . There is entirely too much telling and too little showing." Hogan, however, praised some of the poems' "wry humor" and "disarming ingenuousness," deducting that Baca "is a gifted poet and has a natural lyricism in the best of his work." The reviewer declared: "One hopes to see the promise of his first book realized . . . in a future, better-crafted volume."

Baca's next work, 1987's *Martín and Meditations on the South Valley,* met with outstanding success, earning the American Book Award for poetry. A semiautobiographical work that critics termed a novel in verse, the book chronicles the life of Martín, an orphaned "detribalized" Apache who sojourns across the United States in search of permanence and meaning in his life. Intended to convey the sometimes traumatic Chicano experience in America, *Martín and Meditations on the South Valley* details the protagonist's sense of abandonment and displacement. "Your departure uprooted me mother," writes Baca in the book, "Hallowed core of a child / your absence whittled down / to a broken doll / in a barn loft. The small burned area of memory, / where your face is supposed to be, / moons' rings pass through / in broken chain of events / in my dreams." Although enduring emotional pain, the narrator, by book's end, finds spiritual comfort.

Critics found much to praise in *Martín and Meditations on the South Valley.* While several recognized the work as a forceful sociological and cultural document, Liam Rector in the *Hudson Review* also deemed the poetry volume "a page-turner." He explained: "It's . . . a powerful orchestration and revision of a narrative and lyrical admixture . . . with an utterly compelling dramatic form." Commending Baca's descriptions, drawn with "great telescopic accuracy and poignance," the reviewer called *Martín and Meditations on the South Valley* "a book of great complicity, maturity, and finally responsibility. . . . It is a contemporary hero tale."

The success of *Martín and Meditations on the South Valley* brought international attention to the former prison inmate, who found himself in demand for teaching positions and poetry readings; he also enjoyed the publication of another book, *Black Mesa Poems,* in 1989. Despite his impressive accomplishments, Baca claims to maintain the humble attitude he first fostered while in prison. Proclaiming to Krier that producing poetry still "comes down to my act of sitting down in my little room and writing what's in my heart," Baca elaborated: "I have been hailed by some of the most severe critics in the country. It doesn't mean anything. . . . I just try to stay within the rules of the earth, within the boundaries of dignity. I don't do anything for money. . . . I live on a day-to-day basis. . . . In prison, I didn't know if I was going to be alive from day to day."

BIOGRAPHICAL/CRITICAL SOURCES:

BOOKS

Martín and Meditations on the South Valley, New Directions, 1987.

PERIODICALS

American Book Review, January, 1982, November, 1983.
Commonweal, December 5, 1980.
Hudson Review, summer, 1988.
Kliatt, spring, 1980.
Los Angeles Times, February 15, 1989.

—Sketch by Janice E. Drane

*   *   *

BACA, José Santiago
  See BACA, Jimmy Santiago

*   *   *

BAEZ, Joan (Chandos) 1941-

PERSONAL: Born January 9, 1941, in Staten Island, N.Y.; daughter of Albert V. (a physicist) and Joan Chandos (a drama teacher; maiden name, Bridge) Bacz; married David Victor Harris, March, 1968 (divorced, 1973); children: Gabriel Earl. Education: Studied drama at Boston University Fine Arts School, 1958.

ADDRESSES: Home—Woodside, Calif. Office—Diamonds Rust Productions, Inc., P.O. Box 1026, Menlo Park, Calif. 94026.

CAREER: Learned to play the guitar at age fourteen and sang in a high school choir, Palo Alto, Calif.; first performed in public, playing the guitar and singing folk ballads with other amateurs at Club 47, a coffeehouse in Cambridge, Mass., 1958-60; performed regularly in coffeehouses around Harvard Square in Cambridge and Boston, Mass., 1958-60; appeared at The Gate of Horn, a folk-nightclub in Chicago, Ill., 1958, when she was noticed by Bob Gibson and invited to play at the Newport (R.I.) Folk Festival in the summer of 1959; performed again at the Newport Folk Festival in 1960; recordings for Vanguard Records, 1960-72; has toured colleges and concert halls around the United States (first Carnegie Hall concert, 1962), 1961—; numerous concert tours in Europe, 1965—; concert tours in Japan, 1966 and 1982, Latin America, 1981, and Israel, 1988; extensive television appearances and speaking tours for anti-militarism, United States and Canada, 1967-68; arrested for civil disobedience opposing draft, October and December, 1967; recordings for A & M Records, 1972-76, for Portrait Records, 1977-79, for CBS International, 1980, for Ariola France, 1983, and for Gold Castle Records, 1987. Founded the Institute for the Study of Nonviolence, Palo Alto, Calif. (now the Resource Center for Nonviolence, Santa Cruz, Calif.), 1965; founded Humanitas International, 1979, president, 1979—. Starred with David V. Harris in film "Carry It On" (title song also sung by Baez), New Film Company Production, 1970; also appeared in documentary film "There But for Fortune: Joan Baez in Latin America," 1982, and in a documentary produced for German television, "Music Alone Is Not Enough."

MEMBER: Amnesty International (member of national advisory board, 1973—).

AWARDS, HONORS: Award from Chicago business executives for work for peace, 1971; Thomas Merton Award for commitment to peace, 1975; August 2, 1975, named "Joan Baez Day" in Atlanta, Georgia; public service award for work on behalf of abused children, 1977; Bay Area Music award for top female vocalist in the San Francisco Bay area, 1978 and 1979; Jefferson Award for public service, 1980; award from Americans for Democratic Action, 1982; Lennon Peace Tribute Award, 1982.

WRITINGS:

Daybreak, Dial, 1968.
(With David V. Harris) Coming Out, Pocket Books, 1971.
And a Voice to Sing With, Summit Books, 1987.

MUSIC COMPOSITIONS

Joan Baez Songbook, Ryerson Music, 1964.
And Then I Wrote. . . ., Big Three Music, 1979.

SOUND RECORDINGS

Folksingers 'round Harvard Square, Veritas Recordings, 1959.
Joan Baez, Vanguard, 1960.
Joan Baez, Volume II, Vanguard, 1961.
Joan Baez in Concert, Vanguard, 1962.
Joan Baez in Concert, Part II, Vanguard, 1963.
Joan Baez/five, Vanguard, 1964.
Farewell, Angelina, Vanguard, 1965.
Noel, Vanguard, 1966.
Joan, Vanguard, 1967.
Baptism, Vanguard, 1968.
Any Day Now (songs by Bob Dylan), Vanguard, 1969.
(With Mimi and Richard Farina) Memories, Vanguard, 1969.
One Day at a Time, Vanguard, 1969.
David's Album, Vanguard, 1969.
Joan Baez—The First Ten Years, Vanguard, 1970.
Carry It On (sound track), Vanguard, 1970.
Woodstock (sound track), Cotillion, 1970.
Celebration at Big Sur (sound track), Twentieth Century-Fox, 1971.
Celebration, Ode, 1971.
Blessed Are . . ., Vanguard, 1971.
The Joan Baez Ballad Book, Vanguard, 1972.
Big Sur Folk Festival (One Hand Clapping), Columbia, 1972.
Come From the Shadows, A & M Records, 1973.
Hits/Greatest and Others, Vanguard, 1973.
Gracias a La Vida, A & M Records, 1974.
Contemporary Ballad Book, Vanguard, 1974.
Diamonds and Rust, A & M Records, 1975.
From Every Stage, A & M Records, 1976.
Gulf Winds, A & M Records, 1976.
Love Song Album, Vanguard, 1976.
Blowin' Away, Portrait, 1977.
Best of Joan C. Baez, A & M Records, 1977.
Honest Lullaby, Portrait, 1979.
Joan Baez Twenty-four Juglio 1970, Portrait, 1979.
Joan Baez in Italy, Portrait, 1979.
Joan Baez Live in Japan, Portrait, 1979.
Joan Baez—European Tour, CBS International, 1980.
Very Early Joan, Vanguard, 1982.
Recently, Gold Castle Records, 1987.

Other recordings include Tribute to Woody Guthrie, Warner Brothers; Folk Festival at Newport '59, Vanguard; Newport Broadside '63, Vanguard; The Newport Folk Festival Evening Concerts, Volume I and II, Vanguard; The Lucid Interval, Center for Study of Democratic Institutions; Earl Scruggs, His Family and Friends, Columbia; Save the Children, Jeffrey Shurtleff/State Farm; and the sound tracks Sacco and Vanzetti, RCA; Si-

lent Running, Decca; *Metamorphosis,* Sanrio Films; *Renaldo and Clara,* 1978; *Banjo Man.*

SIDELIGHTS: Joan Baez, sometimes known as "Queen of the Folksingers," has gained national attention as much for her political activism as for her music. Baez became aware of social injustice early in life, when the dark skin she inherited from her Mexican father drew racial slurs from her schoolmates. Her commitment to pacifism also originated with her father, a physicist whose belief in nonviolence led him to give up lucrative work in the defense industry. As Joan Baez writes in *And a Voice to Sing With,* her father's decision meant that she and her sisters "would never have all the fine and useless things little girls want when they are growing up. Instead we would have a father with a clear conscience. Decency would be his legacy to us."

Baez began to develop her singing in childhood, as a way of winning acceptance from her peers. She taught herself to play "House of the Rising Sun" on a guitar from Sears, Roebuck, and practiced her vibrato by tapping on her throat while singing in the shower. When the Baez family moved to Cambridge, Massachusetts, in 1958, Joan found an excellent outlet for her budding talent. Folk music was becoming something of a mass taste at the time and could be heard in many of the area's coffeehouses. Baez began to frequent these, both to listen and to sing. Within a year she made her professional debut in front of thirteen thousand people at the Newport Folk Festival, where she transfixed the crowd with her pure, high soprano and down-to-earth stage presence. Overnight she became a celebrity.

A national tour followed her remarkable appearance at Newport. While on that tour, Baez discovered that blacks were not admitted to her performances at white colleges in the South. To counter this segregation policy, she embarked in 1962 on a tour of all black colleges in Nashville, Atlanta, Mobile, Tuscaloosa, and other major Southern cities. In 1963 she refused to perform on the ABC-TV program "Hootenanny" because the network had blacklisted her fellow folksinger, Pete Seeger. The following year she informed the Internal Revenue Service that she would not pay the sixty percent of her taxes destined to be used for defense spending. Actions such as these, combined with her celebrity status, made Joan Baez a national figurehead for the emerging protest movements of the 1960s.

Baez herself considered her work for social change more important than her performing career, and she limited her singing engagements to have more time for civil rights and antiwar demonstrations. Although her pacifism made her a hero to some, Baez's stance drew the ire of political conservatives. The Daughters of the American Revolution refused to let her perform at Constitution Hall in Washington, D.C., due to her "unpatriotic activities." Army bases all over the world banned her albums. She was jailed twice for her part in antiwar demonstrations, and her then-husband, draft resistance leader David Harris, began a three-year jail term just months after their marriage.

To those who supported Baez and her causes, her "remarkably pure voice seemed to stand for the integrity of her generation," writes Margot Hentoff in the *New York Review of Books.* Her popularity assured the success of her first book, *Daybreak,* a brief collection of autobiographical sketches that appeared in 1968. Richard Goldstein discounts *Daybreak* as "at once a poorly written and badly organized book" in the *New York Times Book Review,* although he admits that the book is "not without its charms. . . . As a work of sensitive gossip, delicately phrased, 'Daybreak' can make enchanting filler on an empty afternoon." Other reviewers take Baez's book much more seriously than does Goldstein, however. The *New York Times*'s Christopher Leh-

mann-Haupt calls *Daybreak* "an impressionistic prose-poem"; he believes that Baez uses an unconventional form in "a bold attempt to describe the growth and beliefs of a profoundly committed advocate of nonviolence." Baez's prose is highly praised by Henry S. Resnik in *Saturday Review.* He comments: "In a dozen pages she makes her mother so unforgettably vivid that any novelist could envy the artlessness. She writes about her relationships with her father and with Ira, her closest soulmate, so honestly, so profoundly, that the narrative would be embarrassing if it weren't incredibly delicate. . . . Super patriots will continue to see her as a threat but *Daybreak* is a jewel of American folklore—it captures the America of our dreams."

Baez found her popularity waning in the 1970s, as folk music went out of vogue and the national mood grew more conservative. But even while her career suffered a setback, she remained as strongly dedicated as ever to her ideals. Promoting the cause of Amnesty International, forming the human rights committee Humanitas International, working for nonviolent reform in Central America, and rallying for nuclear disarmament were just a few of her activities in the 1970s and 1980s. Commenting on recent political events to *Chicago Tribune* interviewer Iain Blair, Baez said, "It's very depressing to me that the social and political activism of the '60s has given way to the selfish materialism of the '80s, and for that I blame the [Reagan] administration." Discussing her image with Patrick Connolly in another *Chicago Tribune* interview, Baez laughed and said: "Some people still picture me with a dress made out of hopsack with a peace symbol on it, sitting on railroad tracks with a bucket of organic honey on my lap. . . . That's the stereotype of a dumb nonviolent activist I've spent years trying to do something about." Of her unswerving devotion to pacifism, she told Connolly, "I'm not a utopian fool. I see the world full of conflicts and we have a right to our differences. But we should have a law saying we don't kill over differences. We can't keep giving medals for murder."

In 1985 Joan Baez found herself back in the international spotlight when she was asked to open Live-Aid, a rock concert intended to raise money for famine victims. In 1987 she released her first American album in eight years. It included original compositions, gospel staples, a South African song entitled "Asimbonanga," and cover versions of songs popularized by Dire Straits, U2, and Peter Gabriel. In 1987 she also published a second volume of autobiography, *And a Voice to Sing With.* Stylistically less experimental than *Daybreak, And a Voice to Sing With* is called "a frank, open-hearted memoir" by the *New York Times*'s Stephen Holden. While *Daybreak* was an impressionistic portrait of Baez's early life, *And a Voice to Sing With* is a straightforward account of her life as a star and an activist. Todd Gitlin assesses it in the *Los Angeles Times Book Review:* "It is written in a human voice, and if that voice is a gushing and unmodulated one, at least it does not sound manufactured. [Baez] reaches her vivid best when she writes about her visit to Hanoi during Christmas, 1972, when she found herself under the ferocious bombardment that President Nixon had decided upon as an exercise in diplomacy. She starts off self-dramatizing, but her narrative takes on force as she sinks into details, glossing over neither her own fear nor the absurdity of her situation."

Barbara Goldsmith concludes that *And a Voice to Sing With* provides readers with valuable social history as well as a look at the singer's life. "Ms. Baez's 20 year metamorphosis from popular folk singer to 80's survivor provides an instructional tale from which one could extrapolate the changes in values in our society in the past two decades," writes Goldsmith in the *New York Times Book Review.* "She reminds us of who we once were before we replaced hard realities with easily malleable images. But because she is all too human and longs to recapture the success she once enjoyed, she also provides, perhaps unwittingly, a peculiarly poignant and American story of how an artist addicted to the adoration of the public endeavors to recut her values and become sophisticated, if not cynical, in the manipulation of the media in order to survive. Ms. Baez's voyage to the 80's becomes emblematic of the artist's struggle to accommodate to our present age of celebrity."

In 1988 Baez brought her message of nonviolence to Israel where she pleaded with both Israelis and Palestinians to end their fighting and their "dialogue of death." Though she said she did not fully understand the complexities of the problems regarding the Israeli occupation of land the Palestinians claim is theirs, Baez spoke with groups from both sides and performed a concert in Tel Aviv that benefitted the Peace Now organization. Baez's trip to Israel, moreover, exemplifies the strength of her ongoing, international commitment to the kind of political activism that made her famous in the 1960s. In a 1987 interview published in *Rolling Stone*, Baez related how she finds the stamina to continue fighting for social change in a world fraught with problems: "There's this wonderful British expression I use: 'Bash on, regardless!' What that means is you don't stop because [the state of the world looks] grim. What are you going to do? Lie down and die of depression?"

BIOGRAPHICAL/CRITICAL SOURCES:

BOOKS

Baez, Joan, *Daybreak*, Dial, 1968.
Baez, Joan, *And a Voice to Sing With*, Summit Books, 1987.
Didion, Joan, *Slouching Towards Bethlehem*, Dell, 1968.

PERIODICALS

Atlantic, October, 1968.
Book World, September 8, 1968.
Cambridge Thirty-eight, April, 1961.
Chicago Tribune, May 30, 1982, June 21, 1987, June 28, 1987.
Christian Century, September 4, 1968.
Christian Science Monitor, October 3, 1968, September 9, 1969.
Detroit Free Press, April 14, 1969, April 4, 1986.
Los Angeles Times, September 14, 1982, June 14, 1987, May 30, 1988.
Los Angeles Times Book Review, June 21, 1987.
Nation, September 23, 1968.
Newsweek, November 27, 1961, September 2, 1968, March 29, 1971, November 3, 1975, July 20, 1987.
New Yorker, August 23, 1969.
New York Review of Books, November 7, 1968.
New York Times, September 18, 1968, January 26, 1969, June 18, 1972, July 8, 1987.
New York Times Book Review, September 8, 1968, June 21, 1987.
Reporter, January 4, 1962.
Rolling Stone, November 5, 1987.
Saturday Review, September 7, 1968.
Show Business Illustrated, January 23, 1962.
Time, June 1, 1962, November 23, 1962, April 5, 1968, July 25, 1969, June 15, 1970.
Village Voice, February 22, 1968, July 24, 1969, August 28, 1969.
Washington Post, June 5, 1968, July 5, 1987.
Washington Post Book World, June 7, 1987.

BALSEIRO, José Agustín 1900-

PERSONAL: Born August 23, 1900, in Barceloneta, Puerto Rico; son of Rafael and Dolores (Romos-Casellas) Balseiro; married Mercedes Pedreira, March 3, 1924; children: Yolanda Buchanon, Liliana Mees. *Education:* University of Puerto Rico, LL.B., 1921.

ADDRESSES: Home—408 Valencia 4, Coral Gables, Fla. 33134.

CAREER: University of Illinois, Urbana, professor of romance languages, 1930-33 and 1936-38; University of Puerto Rico, Río Piedras, visiting professor of Spanish literature, 1933-36; U.S. delegate to First International Congress on Teaching Iber-American Literature, 1938; U.S. representative to First International American Conference on Libraries and Publications, 1939; senator-at-large to Puerto Rican Senate, 1942-44; University of Miami, Coral Gables, Fla., professor of Hispanic literature, 1946-67; University of Arizona, Tucson, visiting professor of Spanish literature, 1967-72. Consultant on Hipanic literature at University of Miami. Summer lecturer, Northwestern University, 1937, Duke University, 1947, 1949, and 1950, Inter-American University, Puerto Rico, 1957-63, University of Mexico, 1959, University of North Carolina at Chapel Hill, 1973, Bryn Mawr College, 1973, Yale University, 1973, and Emory University, 1975. U.S. State Department, International Educational Exchange Program, lecturer in South America, 1954, in Spain and England, 1955-56, and in Puerto Rico, 1956; member of U.S. consultative committee of UNESCO, 1957; vice-president of Fourth Congress of the Academies of the Spanish Language, 1964.

MEMBER: International Institute of Ibero-American Literature (president, 1955-57), North American Academy of Spanish Languages, Modern Language Association of America (president of contemporary Spanish literature section, 1938), National Association of Authors and Journalists (honorary member), Spanish Royal Academy of Language (corresponding member), Spanish-American Academy of Sciences and Arts, Colombian Academy of Letters (corresponding member), Instituto Sarmiento of Argentina, Puerto Rican Academy.

AWARDS, HONORS: Spanish Royal Academy prize for best collection of essays of the year, 1925, for *El vigía*, Volume 1; Litt.D., Inter-American University, 1950; Sc.D., Catholic University, Chile, 1954; L.H.D., Belmont Abbey, 1962; Litt.D., Catholic University, Puerto Rico, 1972; diploma of honor, Mexican Academy of Letters; D.H.L., Polytechnic Institute of Puerto Rico; decorated commander of the Order of Queen Isabel La Católica, Spain; member of the Order of Vasco Núñez de Balboa, Panama.

WRITINGS:

IN ENGLISH

Eugenio María de Hostos: Hispanic America's Public Servant, [Coral Gables, Fla.], 1949.
The Americas Look at Each Other, translated by Muna Muñoz Lee, University of Miami Press, 1969.
(Editor) *The Hispanic Presence in Florida*, E. A. Seeman, 1976.

POETRY

Flores de primavera (title means "Flowers of Spring"), [San Juan], 1919.
Las palomas de Eros (title means "The Doves of Eros"), [Madrid], 1921.

Al rumor de la fuente (title means "To the Murmur of the Fountain"), [San Juan], 1922.

La copa de Anacreonte (title means "The Crown of Anacreon"), Editorial Mundo Latino (Madrid), 1924.

Música cordial (title means "Friendly Music"), Editorial Lex (Havana), 1926.

Sonetos (title means "Sonnets"), [San Juan], 1933.

La pureza cautiva (title means "Captive Purity"), Editorial Lex, 1946.

Saudades de Puerto Rico (title means "Homesickness for Puerto Rico"), Aguilar, 1957.

Vísperas de sombras y otros poemas (title means "Eves of Shadow and Other Poems"), Ediciones de Andre (Mexico), 1959.

NOVELS

La maldecida (title means "The Cursed Woman"), [Madrid], 1922.

La ruta eterna (title means "The Eternal Way"), [Madrid], 1926.

En vela mientras el mundo duerme (title means "Vigil While the World Sleeps"), Mnemosyne Publishing, 1969.

La gratitud humana, Mnemosyne Publishing, 1969.

Also author of *El sueño de Manon,* 1922.

EDITOR

Novelistas españoles modernos (title means "Modern Spanish Novelists"), Macmillan, 1933, 8th revised and enlarged edition, University of Puerto Rico Press, 1977.

(With J. Riis Owre and others) Alejandro Casona, *La barca sin pescador* (title means "The Boat without a Fisherman"), Oxford University Press, 1955.

(With Owre) Casona, *Corona de amor y muerte* (title means "Crown of Love and Death"), Oxford University Press, 1960.

(With Eliana Suárez-Rivero) Casona, *El caballero de las espuelas de oro* (title means "The Cowboy of the Golden Spurs"), Oxford University Press, 1968.

OTHER

El vigía (title means "The Watchman"), Volume 1, Editorial Mundo Latino, 1925, Volume 2, [Madrid], 1926, reprinted, Biblioteca de Autores Puertorriqueños, 1956, Volume 3, [San Juan], 1942.

El Quijote de la España contemporánea: Miguel de Unamuno (title means "The Quixote of Contemporary Spain"), E. Giménez, 1935.

Blasco Ibáñez, Unamuno, Valle Inclán y Baroja, cuatro individualistas de España (title means "Four Spanish Individualists"), University of North Carolina Press, 1949.

Mediciones físicas: Cálculo de errores, aproximaciones, métodos gráficos (title means "Physical Measurements: Calculation of Errors, Approximations, Graphic Methods"), Librería Machette (Buenos Aires), 1956.

Expresión de Hispanoamérica (title means "Expression of Spanish America"), Instituto de Cultura Puertorriqueña, Volume 1, 1960, Volume 2, 1963, 2nd edition, 1970.

Seis estudios sobre Rubén Darío (title means "Six Studies About Ruben Dario"), Editorial Gredos (Madrid), 1967.

Contributor to periodicals, including *Cuadernos Americanos, Nosotros, Hispanic Review,* and *La Torre.* Editor of numerous Spanish periodicals.

SIDELIGHTS: Although trained in law, a talented musician whose compostitions have been performed at Carnegie Hall, and once asked to play professional baseball, José Agustín Balseiro set out at a young age to become a writer. While living in Spain, he was rewarded by the early publication of his first book of poems. Novels as well as works of criticism followed, and as his reputation grew, Balseiro's profession expanded to include the teaching of languages and literature. Eventually, he came to be regarded world-wide as a kind of cultural ambassador. Since the 1930s, Balseiro has lectured internationally. His topics have included the philosophies and biographies of poets, public leaders, artists, and musicians. His focus has always been on the connections between the Hispanic and American cultures, and critics have acknowledged Balseiro's importance to people both within and without the Spanish-speaking world.

During a lecture at the University of Miami in the 1950s, Balseiro explained the reason for his emphasis on internationalism. *Miami Herald* staff writer Sandy Flickner quotes the author's speech: "The nearer we approach our neighbors by the disinterested paths of art, literature, scholarship, and open-hearted friendship, the sooner will we demolish the prejudices that hamper the constructive development of human nature." In his honor, the University of Miami established the José A. Balseiro Award, an essay contest, in 1967.

BIOGRAPHICAL/CRITICAL SOURCES:

PERIODICALS

Miami Herald, April 29, 1974.

*   *   *

BANCHS, Enrique J.   1888-1968

PERSONAL: Born 1888 in Buenos Aires, Argentina; died in 1968.

CAREER: Poet and journalist.

WRITINGS:

El cascabel del halcón, 1909, revised edition, Centro Editor de América Latina (Buenos Aires), 1968.

Lecturas, [Buenos Aires], 1920.

Poemas selectos, edited by F. Monterde, [Mexico], 1921.

Cantos del anochecer, 1908-1955, [Buenos Aires], 1966.

Obra poética, Academia Argentina de Letras (Buenos Aires), 1973.

Prosas, Academia Argentina de Letras, 1983.

Also author of *Las barcas,* 1907, *El libro de los elogios,* 1908, *Oda a los padres de la patria,* 1910, and *La urna* (sonnets), 1911. Contributor to periodical *Nosotros.*

SIDELIGHTS: A very popular Argentinian lyricist, Enrique J. Banchs wrote classic verse in modernist style on the traditional themes of passion, death, beauty, and nature.

*   *   *

BARAYON, Ramón Sender
See SENDER BARAYON, Ramón

*   *   *

BARRIO, Raymond   1921-

PERSONAL: Born August 27, 1921, in West Orange, N.J.; son of Saturnino and Angelita (Santos) Barrio; married Yolanda Sánchez Ocio, February 2, 1957; children: Angelita, Gabriel, Raymond, Jr., Andrea, Margarita. *Education:* Attended University of Southern California, 1941-43, and Yale University,

1943-44; University of California, Berkeley, B.A., 1947; Art Center College of Los Angeles, B.P.A., 1952. *Politics:* Humanist. *Religion:* Humanist.

ADDRESSES: P.O. Box 1076, Guerneville, Calif. 95446.

CAREER: Taught art at Los Angeles county adult education schools in Burbank, Calif., and at Ventura College, Ventura, Calif.; art instructor at colleges and universities in California, including University of California, Santa Barbara, 1963-65, West Valley College, Saratoga, 1969-72, De Anza College, Cupertino, 1972, Skyline College, San Bruno, 1972, Foothill College, Los Altos Hills, 1975-77, and Sonoma State University, Rohnert Park, 1985-86; writer. Owner and operator of Ventura Press. Art work has been displayed in more than eighty national exhibitions. *Military service:* U.S. Army, 1943-46; served in Europe.

AWARDS, HONORS: Creative Arts Institute faculty grant from University of California, 1964-65.

WRITINGS:

The Big Picture (art manual), self-illustrated, Ventura, 1967, published as *Experiments in Modern Art,* Sterling, 1968.
Art: Seen (drawings and commentary), self-illustrated, Ventura, 1968.
The Plum Plum Pickers (novel), self-illustrated, Ventura, 1969, 2nd edition, Bilingual Review/Press, 1984.
Selections From Walden, self-illustrated, Ventura, 1970.
Prism: Essays in Art, self-illustrated, Ventura, 1970.
The Fisherman's Dwarf (juvenile), self-illustrated, Ventura, 1970.
Mexico's Art and Chicano Artists, self-illustrated, Ventura, 1975.
The Devil's Apple Corps: A Trauma in Four Acts, self-illustrated, Ventura, 1976.
Political Portfolio (commentary), Ventura, 1985.
Carib Blue (novel), Ventura, 1990.

Contributor to anthologies. Contributor of weekly column "Barrio's Political Estuary" to local and national periodicals. Contributor of articles to art magazines and fiction to literary quarterlies.

SIDELIGHTS: When Raymond Barrio's novel *The Plum Plum Pickers* was turned down by every publishing house to which he offered it, he published it himself. In less than two years the "social proletarian" novel, as Adorna Walia calls it in *Bilingual Journal,* was an underground classic and had sold more than ten thousand copies. At that point Harper & Row publishers took another look at Barrio's story of a Chicano migrant family and published it. Since then *The Plum Plum Pickers* has sold twenty-two thousand copies and has been included in numerous high school and college level anthologies. Barrio repurchased the rights to the book in 1976.

Examining the lives of Manuel Gutiérrez, his family, and other migrant workers in *The Plum Plum Pickers,* Barrio gives the reader "a study of the persistent exploitation of the stoop-workers, the migrant laborers in Santa Clara County," writes Walia. "Barrio has an unusually good understanding," continues the reviewer, "of the psychology of groveling foremen and managers who maintain their positions by oppressing those below them. He skillfully employs irony when he writes of the 'clear' consciences of Anglo executives and growers who sleep peacefully unaware of the misery of the migrants in their orchards because they leave the most sordid tasks to their Mexican overseers." Linda Gray in the *Penninsula Bulletin* comments that Barrio, "with uncompromising clarity, opens up the lives that are lived almost on the subterranean level. He understands the plight of the Chicanos."

In *The Plum Plum Pickers* Barrio details the frustration the migrant worker feels: "The competition was not between pickers and growers, . . . it was between pickers. . . . Between the poor and the hungry, the desperate and the hunted, the slave and the slave, slob against slob, the depraved and himself. You were your own terrible boss. That was the cleverest part of the whole thing. The picker his own bone picker, his own willing built-in slave driver. Pick fast, pick hard, pick furious, pick, pick, pick. They didn't need straw bosses studying your neck to see if you kept bobbing up and down to keep your picking pace up. Like the barn-stupid chicken, you drove yourself to do it."

More than an examination of migrant life, *The Plum Plum Pickers* is an indictment of the economic system that perpetuates the exploitation of the migrants, the Chicanos, and the illegal aliens who are often recruited to do the picking. "*The Plum Plum Pickers* is both an ode to and a denunciation of California and the United States—an ode because California has some of the most fertile land in the world, and a denunciation because of the labor exploitation by the agricombines which perpetuate the migrant slavery," states Walia. "Everyone gets rich from the fertile lands of California except the pickers. The corporation heads view the migrants as refuse." However, Gray notes, despite *The Plum Plum Picker*'s strong indictment of the way in which migrant workers are treated and "although deep with sadness, the book avoids moroseness through its fine satire of the local growers and politicians. A meeting of 'socially-conscious' corporation wives and a governor being dubbed 'Howlin' Mad' are good examples."

Barrio is also praised for his skillful prose in *The Plum Plum Pickers.* "Barrio's language is lyrical, a stream of consciousness that gathers poetic momentum through use of newscopy, graffiti, and excerpts from a government pamphlet of 'How to Pick Canning Tomatoes,' " says Gray. Walia considers "the dialogues that imitate the speech of the migrant workers [to be] particularly effective, because of their black humor. As his workers speak, they often garble their words, and their malapropisms are humorous in an ironic way. Through dialogue, Barrio reveals the twisted thinking of landowners and company owners; their rationalizations and self-justifications. He apes the language of American politicians exposing them in all their hypocrisy."

As evidenced in *The Plum Plum Pickers,* Barrio is concerned with inequalities he perceives in a capitalist system. He told *HW:* "Our modern America is suffering from a hideous disease called superaffluence. Mechanization, specialization, and modern technology are all linked together, eroding and destroying America's fine moral spirit. American multinational corporations conspire to drain all the resources they can rob from Third World countries, causing their misery, underdevelopment, and famine.

"Young writers coming through our schools see the tremendous production of great blockbuster million-dollar best-sellers. Some use up great amounts of energy trying to figure out how to jump aboard that luscious circus wagon. It can be done, by a very few, but the price is devastating—the destruction of one's very soul.

"Young writers are the key to humanity's survival. As a lifelong teacher, artist, and writer, I do my best to persuade young people coming up to ignore the siren ululations of the money merchant and to learn to listen to their own private drummer. To thine own self be true. Integrity above all. The most ignorant rural dweller can possess more integrity than the head of a great corporation—and often does. Therein lies the hope a young person needs to carry out his dreams, visions, ideals, and mission.

"To the question, 'What do you hope to achieve through the books you write?,' my answer is: the salvation of humanity. Nothing less. I would hope that that would serve as a role model for the idealistic young."

The Plum Plum Pickers has been translated into German.

BIOGRAPHICAL/CRITICAL SOURCES:

BOOKS

Barrio, Raymond, *The Plum Plum Pickers,* Ventura, 1969.

PERIODICALS

Bilingual Journal, fall, 1982.
Penninsula Bulletin, December 11, 1976.
Top of the News, January, 1969.

* * *

BARRIOS, Eduardo 1884-1963

PERSONAL: Born October 25, 1884, in Valparaíso, Chile; died September 13, 1963, in Santiago, Chile; son of Eduardo Barrios Achurra (an army officer) and Isabel Hudtwalcker de Barrios; married Deifiria Passa, 1910 (marriage dissolved); married Carmen Rivadeneira, 1920; children: (first marriage) Raúl, Roberto; (second marriage) Carmen, Gracia, Angélica. *Education:* Attended military school in Chile.

CAREER: Writer. Worked as a salesman, rubber prospector, ice factory worker, circus performer, and bookkeeper in a nitrate factory; secretary to pro-Rector, University of Santiago, beginning 1909; shorthand reporter, Chilean Congress, beginning 1912; Guardian of Intellectual Property, 1925, and General Supervisor, 1927-31 and 1953-59, of National Library; Minister of Education, 1927-28 and 1953-59; manager of La Marquesa ranch, Leyda, Chile, 1937-43.

MEMBER: PEN (Chile; co-founder), Chilean Academy, Argentine Academy (corresponding member), Los Diez.

AWARDS, HONORS: Literary prize from Chilean government, 1910, for "Mercaderes en el templo"; Chilean National Prize for Literature, 1946; Atenea Prize from University of Concepción, 1949, for *Gran señor y rajadiablos.*

WRITINGS:

PLAYS

"Mercaderes en el templo," first produced June 7, 1911.
"Por el decoro" (also see below), first produced May 2, 1913.
"Lo que niega la vida" (also see below), first produced August 28, 1914.
"Vivir" (also see below), first produced in 1916.
Teatro escogido (collection; contains "Vivir," "Por el decoro," and "Lo que niega la vida"), Zig-Zag (Santiago), 1947.

FICTION

Del natural (stories), [Iquique], 1907.
Un perdido (novel), Chilena, 1918, reprinted, Zig-Zag, 1967.
El niño que enloqueció de amor (short works), Nascimento (Santiago), 1920, published as *El niño que enloqueció de amor. ¡Pobre feo! Papá y mamá,* 1957, reprinted, Losada, 1982.
Páginas de un pobre diablo (stories), Nascimento, 1923.
El hermano asno (novel), Agencia General de Librería y Publicaciones, 1923, reprinted, Losada, 1975, translation by Ed-

mundo García Girón published as *Brother Asno,* Las Américas (New York), 1969.
Tamarugal (novel and stories), Nascimento, 1944.
Gran señor y rajadiablos (novel), Nascimento, 1948, reprinted, Andrés Bello, 1983, published with author's note, Aguilar, 1961.
Los hombres del hombre (novel), Nascimento, 1950, reprinted, Losada, 1978.

COLLECTIONS

Y la vida sigue . . . (includes previously unpublished stories), prologue by Gabriela Mistral, Tor (Buenos Aires), 1925.
Cuatro cuentos, edited by Seymour Resnick, Harper, 1951.
Obras completas (collected works), two volumes, Zig-Zag, 1962.
El niño que enloqueció de amor, y otros cuentos, edited by Resnick, Las Américas, 1966.

OTHER

Also editor, with Roberto Meza Fuentes, of collections of the work of Rubén Darío, 1922, and Amado Nervo, *Sus mejores poemas,* Nascimento. Translation of short story "Papá y Mamá" by Willis Knapp Jones published as "Papa and Mama" in *Poet Lore,* 1922. Contributor to periodicals, including *Revista de "Los Diez," Pluma y Lápiz, Pacífico Magazine, La Mañana,* and *Zig-Zag.* Editor, *Atenea,* beginning 1925.

SIDELIGHTS: Eduardo Barrios was a writer with a "peculiar talent for the narration of reverie and self-analysis—the essence of his psychological fiction and the source, undoubtedly, of his reputation as one of the great novelists of Chile," Ned J. Davison asserted in his study *Eduardo Barrios.* After his early fiction, which focused on the sensual aspects of life, and his dramatic work, which dealt with social themes, Barrios turned his attention "to the individual personality, and society [became] simply a backdrop before which is played out the intensely individual and personal struggles of his protagonists," Davison noted. With the publication of the novella "El niño que enloqueció de amor" ("The Child Who Was Maddened by Love"), Barrios emerged as an influential figure on the Latin American literary scene. Told through the diary entries of a young boy, the novella follows the child's disintegration into madness as his unhealthy romantic interest in an older woman is thwarted. With its attention to the boy's reaction to feelings he doesn't understand, "El niño que enloqueció de amor" "is probably the earliest example in Spanish America of such total concentration on the inner life of a novelistic protagonist," the critic added, a psychological emphasis Barrios would continue throughout his career.

In what is generally acknowledged as his masterpiece, *El hermano asno* (published in English as *Brother Asno*), for example, Barrios relates the story of two Franciscan monks beset by spiritual self-doubt: Lázaro, a worldly man unsure whether he is fit for religious service; and Rufino, who despite his asceticism and miraculous acts believes he is unworthy. The result, as James W. Brown described it in *Hispania,* is "a lyrical story, with stunning beauty of description and a touching sentimental portrait of subtle characterization." Nevertheless, the critic continued, *Brother Asno* "leaves unsettled questions regarding the issues it stirs up." Because the novel is told entirely through Lázaro's diary entries, *Brother Asno* is "a sophisticated work that contains a pattern of narrative irony which lies within and possibly even undermines the same thorny ideological questions that it raises," Brown elaborated. As a result, Davison concluded, *Brother Asno*'s "fascinating interplay of these various views [of the characters] and the paradox of human identity which emerges from them contribute greatly to the quality and fame of the story. It is not surprising that many critics consider this novel to be Barrios' finest work."

BIOGRAPHICAL/CRITICAL SOURCES:

BOOKS

Davison, Ned J., *Eduardo Barrios,* Twayne, 1970.
Walker, John, *Metaphysics and Aesthetics in the Works of Eduardo Barrios,* Tamesis (London), 1983.

PERIODICALS

Hispania, Number 42, 1959, Number 58, 1975, December, 1988.

*   *   *

BARRIOS, Pilar E.   1889-

PERSONAL: Born in 1889 in Uruguay.

CAREER: *Nuestra Raza* magazine, San Carlos and Montevideo, Uruguay, co-founder, 1917, editor, beginning 1917, staff member, 1933-48. Co-founder, 1936, and secretary, Indigenous Black party, Uruguay.

WRITINGS:

Piel negra: Poesías (1917-1947) (also see below; poems; title means "Black Skin"), Nuestra Raza (Montevideo), 1947.
Mis cantos (also see below; poems), Comité Amigos del Poeta (Montevideo), 1949.
Campo afuera: Poemas (also see below; poems), Minerva (Montevideo), 1959.
The Poetic Works of Pilar E. Barrios: Piel negra, Mis cantos, Campo afuera, Kraus Reprints, 1959.

Contributor of poems and essays to magazines, including *Nuestra Raza, Revista Uruguay,* and *Direcciones.*

SIDELIGHTS: "Pilar [E.] Barrios—as poet, the editor of [*Nuestra Raza,*] and an intellectual committed to the progress of Afro-Uruguayans—expressed his sentiments concerning their problems on many occasions," stated Marvin A. Lewis in *Afro-Hispanic Poetry, 1940-1980: From Slavery to "Negritud" in South American Verse.* Barrios founded *Nuestra Raza* ("Our Race") with his brother and sister in 1917, and the journal quickly became a popular outlet for many black writers of the era. Barrios himself published "some of [his] earliest poems, dedicated to love, nature, poetry, and patriotism" in the periodical; later, however, "as he became more involved in the worldwide struggle against racism, war, and fascism, the tone of Barrios's poems changed noticeably," related Lewis. This involvement in social issues also extended to the poet's participation in the Indigenous Black party, a political group devoted to raising black consciousness in Uruguay.

The issues of race and social injustice are prominent in much of Barrios's work, yet they are not the sum total of his poetry. He is "fond," as Richard L. Jackson described, of "modernist verse and escapist allusions"; nevertheless, the critic added in *The Black Image in Latin American Literature,* "Barrios, like many black writers who rose to prominence in this century, continues to identify in *Mis cantos* . . . with black [anxieties], while expressing at the same time his solidarity or fraternal bond with other races." Lewis similarly noted that Barrios is "a multifaceted poet and not just a writer who pens black verse." In *Piel Negro,* for example, "Barrios struggles to reconcile art, social reality, and the Afro-Uruguayan experience, but he arrives at the conclusion that poetry certainly has a critical social function that does not remove it from the realm of artistic creation," Lewis

stated. The critic concluded: "Barrios recognized early on that positive values must first be found in blackness before the transition could be made to being just another Uruguayan," and his accomplishments as a literary and political figure "were all steps in that direction."

BIOGRAPHICAL/CRITICAL SOURCES:

BOOKS

Jackson, Richard L., *The Black Image in Latin American Literature,* University of New Mexico Press, 1976.
Lewis, Marvin A., *Afro-Hispanic Poetry, 1940-1980: From Slavery to "Negritud" in South American Verse,* University of Missouri Press, 1983.

*   *   *

BASS, Nelson Estupiñán
    See ESTUPIÑAN BASS, Nelson

*   *   *

BASTOS, Augusto (Antonio) Roa
    See ROA BASTOS, Augusto (Antonio)

*   *   *

BELEÑO
    See AZUELA, Mariano

*   *   *

BELLI, Carlos Germán   1927-

PERSONAL: Born September 15, 1927, in Lima, Peru. *Education:* Catholic University and National University of San Marcos, graduate with degrees in literature.

ADDRESSES: Home—Las Palomas 330, Lima 18, Peru.

CAREER: Poet and translator. Currently a professor at Universidad de San Marcos, Lima, Peru; *Comercio,* Lima, columnist.

AWARDS, HONORS: National Poetry Prize, 1962; Guggenheim Foundation Award for Poetry, 1970, 1987.

WRITINGS.

POETRY

Poemas (also see below), [Lima], 1958.
Dentro y fuera (also see below), Escuela Nacional de Bellas Artes (Lima), 1960.
¡Oh hada cibernética! (also see below), [Lima], 1961, enlarged edition, 1962.
El pie sobre el cuello (also see below), de la Florida, 1964.
Por el monte abajo (also see below), de La Rama Florida (Lima), 1966.
El pie sobre el cuello (contains *Poemas, Dentro y fuera, ¡Oh hada cibernética!, El pie sobre el cuello,* and *Por el monte abajo*), Editorial Alfa, 1967.
Sextinas y otros poemas, Universitaria (Santiago, Chile), 1970.
¡Oh hada cibernética! (contains a selection of earlier poems and the collection *El libro de los nones*), El Timonel (Lima), 1971.
"Poemas de Carlos Germán Belli" (sound recording of Belli reading a selection of his poems), Discos Smith, c. 1975.
En alabanza del bolo alimenticio, Premiá (Mexico), 1979.
Asir la forma que se va, Cuadernos del Hipocampo (Lima), 1979.
Canciones y otros poemas, Premiá, 1982.

El buen mudar (also see below), [Madrid], 1986.
Más que señora humana, [Lima], 1986.
El buen mudar (contains poems from book of same title and additional prose), [Lima], 1987.
En el restante tiempo terrenal, Perla (Lima), 1988.
Antología personal, [Lima], 1988.

OTHER

(Translator) Murilo Mendes, *29 poemas,* Centro de Estudios Brasileños (Lima), 1978.
(Translator) Antonio Fantinato, *Poemas,* Centro de Estudios Brasileños, 1984.
Boda de la pluma y la letra (anthology), Ediciones Cultura Hispánica, Instituto de Cooperación Iberoamericana, 1985.
(Translator) Alberto Da Costa e Silva, *Poemas,* Centro de Estudios Brasileños, 1986.

Also author of *Carlos Germán Belli: Antología crítica.* Contributor to anthologies. Contributor to periodicals, including *Amaru, Golpe de Dados,* and *Hispamérica.*

SIDELIGHTS: Carlos Germán Belli has been called one of the most original hispanic poets writing today. Using a combination of technological terminology, seventeenth-century Spanish Golden Age diction and meter, and colloquial Peruvian, Belli "creates a poetry in which individual feeling is at odds with the modern world," according to one *Times Literary Supplement* reviewer. His poems use irony and black humor to comment bitterly on the social injustices in his native Peru brought about by bureaucracy and technology. However, he also extrapolates this outrage to address his nihilistic view of mankind's destiny as a whole. More recently, his poetry has assumed a metaphysical tone.

BIOGRAPHICAL/CRITICAL SOURCES:

PERIODICALS

Times Literary Supplement, December 7, 1967, August 27, 1971.

*   *   *

BENAVENTE (y MARTINEZ), Jacinto   1866-1954

PERSONAL: Born August 12, 1866, in Madrid, Spain; died July 14, 1954, in Madrid, Spain; son of Mariano Benavente (a pediatrician) and Venancia Martínez. *Education:* Studied law at University of Madrid, 1882-85.

CAREER: Writer. Director of Teatro Español, beginning 1920. Actor; founder with Porredón, of a children's theatre, 1909. President of Spanish Theater Commission (advisory body of Central Theater Council), beginning 1936. Lecturer.

MEMBER: Royal Spanish Academy (became honorary member, 1946).

AWARDS, HONORS: Piquer Prize, Royal Spanish Academy, 1912; Nobel Prize in literature, Swedish Academy, 1922; made honorary citizen of New York City, Columbia University and Instituto de las Américas, 1923; named "Hijo Predilecto" ("Favorite Son") of Madrid, 1924; Grand Cross of King Alfonso XII (Spain), 1924; Mariano de Cavia Prize for best newspaper article of 1947, 1948.

WRITINGS:

IN ENGLISH TRANSLATION

"El nido ajeno" (three-act play; also see below), first produced in Madrid at Teatro de la Comedia, October 6, 1894, translation published as "Another's Nest" in *Nineteenth Century Spanish Plays,* edited by L. E. Brett, [New York], 1935.

"La gobernadora" (three-act play), first produced in Madrid at Teatro de la Comedia, October 8, 1901, translation by John Garrett Underhill published as *The Governor's Wife: A Comedy in Three Acts,* R. G. Badger (Boston), 1913.

"La noche de sábado" (five-act play), first produced in Madrid at Teatro Español, October 26, 1903, translation by Underhill published as *Saturday Night: A Novel for the Stage, in Five Tableaux,* R. G. Badger, 1918, translation by Underhill published under same title with introduction by Underhill, Scribner, 1926.

"No fumadores", first produced in Madrid at Teatro de Lara, March 3, 1904, translation by Underhill published as *No Smoking: A Farce in One Act,* Baker, 1935.

"El encanto de una hora" (one-act dialogue; also see below), first produced in Madrid at Teatro de la Princesa, December 30, 1905, translation by Underhill published as *The Magic of an Hour: A Comedy in One Act,* Baker, 1935.

La sonrisa de Gioconda, 1908, translation by John Armstrong Herman published as *The Smile of Mona Lisa: A Play in One Act,* R. G. Badger, 1915.

El marido de su viuda: Comedia en un acto (first produced in Madrid at Teatro del Príncipe Alfonso, October 19, 1908), R. Velasco (Madrid), 1908, translation by Underhill published as *His Widow's Husband: A Comedy in One Act,* Baker, 1935.

De cerca: Comedia en un acto (first produced in Madrid at Teatro de Lara, April 10, 1909), Hernando, 1909, translation by Underhill published as *At Close Range: A One-Act Play,* Samuel French, 1936.

El príncipe que todo lo aprendió en los libros: Comedia en dos actos y siete cuadros (children's fantasy; first produced in Madrid at Teatro del Príncipe Alfonso, December 20, 1909), Artes Gráficas Mateu, 1910, reprinted, Cervantes, 1966, published under title *El príncipe que todo lo aprendió en los libros,* with notes, exercises, and vocabulary by Aurelio M. Espinosa, World, 1918, translation by Underhill of original Spanish edition published as *The Prince Who Learned Everything out of Books: A Fairy Play in Three Acts and Five Scenes,* R. G. Badger, 1919.

La malquerida (three-act drama), first produced in Madrid at Teatro de la Princesa, December 12, 1913; produced in English translation as "The Passionflower" in New York City, c. 1920), edited with introduction, notes, and vocabulary by Paul T. Manchester, Crofts, 1941, translation by Underhill published as "The Passionflower" in *Twenty-five Modern Plays,* edited by S. M. Tucker and A. S. Downer, 3rd edition, 1953.

Los intereses creados: Comedia de polichinelas en dos actos, tres cuadros y un prólogo, (three-act play with prologue; first produced in Madrid at Teatro de Lara, December 9, 1907; produced in English translation as "The Bonds of Interest," in New York City, April 19, 1919; produced in English translation as "The Bias of the World" in London), 4th edition, Nuevo Mundo (Madrid), 1914, reprinted, Fournier, 1950, translation by Underhill published as *The Bonds of Interest,* preface by Underhill, Scribner, 1929, translation by Underhill published as *The Bonds of Interest. Los intereses creados.* (bilingual edition), edited and revised by Hymen Alpern, Ungar, 1967.

La Verdad (dialogue; first produced in Madrid at Teatro de la Comedia), 1915, translation by Underhill published as *The Truth: A Play in One Act,* Baker, 1935.

Plays (contains "His Widow's Husband," "The Bonds of Interest," "The Evil Doers of Good," and "La malquerida"), edited and translated by Underhill, Scribner, 1917.

Plays: Second Series (contains "No Smoking," "Princess Bebé," "The Governor's Wife," and "Autumnal Rose"), edited and translated by Underhill, Scribner, 1919.

"La fuerza bruta" (two-act musical comedy), first produced in Madrid at Teatro de la Zarzuela, 1919, translation by Underhill published as *Brute Force: A Comedy in Two Acts,* Samuel French, 1935.

Plays: Third Series (contains "The Prince Who Learned Everything out of Books," "Saturday Night," "In the Clouds," and "The Truth"), edited and translated by Underhill, Scribner, 1923.

Plays: Fourth Series (contains "The School of Princesses," "A Lady," "The Magic of an Hour," and "Field of Ermine"), edited and translated by Underhill, Scribner, 1924.

(Contributor) Lope de Vega, *Four Plays,* translated by Underhill with a critical essay by Benavente, Scribner, 1936, reprinted, Hyperion Press (Westport, Conn.), 1978.

PUBLISHED PLAYS; IN SPANISH

Teatro fantástico (contains "Comedia italiana" [title means "Italian Comedy"; two scenes], "El criado de Don Juan" [title means "Don Juan's Servant"; also see below], "La senda del amor" [title means "The Path of Love"; one-act comedy for marionettes], "La blancura de Pierrot" [title means "The Whiteness of Pierrot"; one-act pantomine], "Cuento de primavera" [title means "Spring Story"; two-act], "Amor de artista" [title means "Artist's Love"; one-act], "Modernismo" [title means "Modernism"; one-act], and "El encanto de una hora" [title means "The Magic of an Hour"; also see below]), 1892, reprinted, Fortanet (Madrid), 1905.

Los malhechores del bien (two-act; first produced in Madrid at Teatro de Lara, December 1, 1905), edited with introduction, notes and vocabulary by Irving A. Leonard and Robert K. Spaulding, Macmillan, 1933, reprinted, 1961.

Las cigarras hormigas (title means "The Harvest Flies"; three-act; first produced in Madrid at Teatro de la Comedia, December 24, 1905), edited with notes and vocabulary by University of Michigan Sociedad Hispánica, C. W. Graham, 1923.

Los buhos: Comedia en tres actos (title means "The Owls: Three-Act Play"; first produced in Madrid at Teatro de Lara, February 8, 1907), Hernando, 1908.

Hacia la verdad: Escenas de la vida moderna, en tres cuadros (title means "Toward the Truth: Scenes from Modern Life, in Three Scenes"; first produced in Madrid at Teatro del Príncipe Alfonso, December 23, 1908), Hernando, 1909.

La escuela de las princesas: Comedia en tres actos (title means "The School of Princesses: Play in Three Acts"; first produced in Madrid at Teatro de la Comedia, October 14, 1909), R. Velasco, 1910.

La señorita se aburre: Comedia en un acto, basada en una poesía de Tennyson (title means "The Princess Is Bored: One-Act Play, Based on a Poem by Tennyson"; first produced in Madrid at Teatro del Príncipe Alfonso, December 1, 1909), R. Velasco, 1910.

La losa de los sueños: Comedia en dos actos (title means "The Graveyard of Dreams: Two-Act Play"; comedy; first produced in Madrid at Teatro de Lara, November 9, 1911), Nuevo Mundo (Madrid), 1911.

El collar de estrellas: Comedia en cuatro actos (title means "The Necklace of Stars: Four-Act Play"; first produced in Ma-

drid at Teatro de la Princesa, March 4, 1915), R. Velasco (Madrid), 1915.

Campo de armiño: Comedia en tres actos (title means "Field of Ermine: Three-Act Play"; drama; first produced in Madrid at Teatro de la Princesa, February 14, 1916), R. Velasco and V. H. de Sanz Calleja (Madrid), 1916.

La ciudad alegre y confiada: Comedia en tres cuadros y un prólogo, considerados como tres actos (title means "The Joyous and Confident City: Play in Three Scenes and A Prologue, Considered as Three Acts"; sequel to "Los intereses creados"; first produced in Madrid at Teatro de Lara, May 18, 1916), R. Velasco, 1916.

Los cachorros: Comedia en tres actos (three-act; first produced in Madrid at Teatro de la Princesa, March 8, 1918), V. H. de Sanz Calleja, 1918.

La fuerza bruta: Comedia en un acto y dos cuadros (one act; first produced in Madrid at Teatro de Lara, November 19 1908), Hernando, 1909.

Lecciones de buen amor: Comedia en tres actos (title means "Lessons in Good Love: Three-Act Play"; first produced in Madrid at Teatro Español, April 2, 1924), Hernando, 1924.

La otra honra: Comedia en tres actos (title means "The Other Honor: Three-Act Play"; first produced in Madrid at Teatro de Lara, September 19, 1924), Hernando, 1924.

La virtud sospechosa: Comedia en tres actos (title means "Suspect Virtue: Three-Act Play"; comedy; first produced in Madrid at Teatro Fontalba, October 20, 1924), Hernando, 1924.

Alfilerazos: Comedia en tres actos (title means "Pinpricks: Comedy in Three Acts"; first produced in Buenos Aires at Teatro Avenida, June 18, 1924; produced in Madrid at Teatro del Centro, October 5, 1925), Hernando, 1925.

Los nuevos yernos: Comedia en tres actos (title means "The New Sons-in-Law: Three-Act Play"; comedy; first produced in Madrid at Teatro Fontalba, October 2, 1925), Hernando, 1925.

La mariposa que voló sobre el mar: Comedia en tres actos (title means "The Butterfly that Flew over the Sea: Three-Act Play"; comedy; first produced in Madrid at Teatro Fontalba, September 22, 1926), Hernando, 1926.

La noche iluminada: Comedia de magia en tres actos (title means "The Illuminated Night: Three-Act Magical Comedy"; first produced in Madrid at Teatro Fontalba, December 22, 1927), Hernando, 1927.

El hijo de Polichinela: Comedia en un prólogo y tres actos (comedy; first produced in Madrid at Teatro de Lara, April 16, 1927), Hernando, 1927.

El demonio fué antes ángel: Comedia en tres actos (title means "The Devil Used to Be an Angel: Three-Act Play"; comedy; first produced in Madrid at Teatro Calderón, February 18, 1928), Hernando, 1928.

¡No quiero, no quiero!: Comedia en tres actos (title means "I Don't Want To, I Don't Want To: Three-Act Play"; first produced in Madrid at Teatro Fontalba, March 10, 1928), Hernando, 1928.

Pepa Doncel: Comedia en tres actos y dos cuadros (title means "Pepa Doncel: Play in Three Acts and Two Scenes"; first produced in Madrid at Teatro Calderón, November 21, 1928), Hernando, 1928.

Para el cielo y los altares: Drama en tres actos, divididos en trece cuadros, y un epílogo (title means "For Heaven and the Altars: Three-Act Drama, Divided into Thirteen Scenes and an Epilogue"), Hernando, 1928.

Vidas cruzadas: Cinedrama en dos partes, dividida la primera en diez cuadros, y la segunda en tres y un epílogo (title means "Crossed Lives: A Screenplay in Two Parts, the First Divided into Ten Scenes, and the Second into Three and an Epilogue"; first produced in Madrid at Teatro de la Reina Victoria, March 30, 1929), Hernando, 1929.

Los andrajos de la púrpura: Drama en cinco actos (title means "Purple Tatters: Drama in Five Acts"; first produced in Madrid at Teatro Muñoz Seca, November 6, 1930), Hernando, 1930.

Literatura: Comedia en tres actos (title means "Literature: Play in Three Acts"; first produced in Madrid at Teatro Alcázar, April 4, 1931), Hernando, 1931.

De muy buena familia: Comedia en tres actos (title means "From a Very Good Family: Three-Act Play"; comedy; first produced in Madrid at Teatro Muñoz Seca, March 11, 1931), Hernando, 1931.

La melodía del jazz-band: Comedia en un prólogo y tres actos (title means "The Jazz Band's Melody: Play with a Prologue and Three Acts"; comedy; first produced in Madrid at Teatro Fontalba, October 30, 1931), Hernando, 1931.

Cuando los hijos de Eva no son los hijos de Adán: Comedia en tres actos (title means "When Eve's Sons Are Not Adam's: Three-Act Play"; based on Margaret Kennedy's novel, *The Constant Nymph*; comedy; first produced in Madrid at Teatro Calderón, November 5, 1931), Hernando, 1931.

Santa Rusia, primera parte de una trilogía (title means "Holy Russia, First Part of a Trilogy"; first produced in Madrid at Teatro Beatriz, October 6, 1932), Imprenta Helénica (Madrid), 1932.

La duquesa gitana: Comedia de magia en cinco actos divididos en diez cuadros (title means "The Gypsy Duchess: Magic Comedy in Five Acts Divided in Ten Scenes"; fist produced in Madrid at Teatro Fontalba, October 28, 1932), Imprenta Helénica, 1932.

La moral del divorcio: Conferencia dialogada, dividida en tres partes (title means "The Moral of Divorce: Lecture in Dialogue, Divided into Three Parts"; first produced in Madrid at Teatro de la Avenida, November 4, 1932), Imprenta Helénica, 1932.

La verdad inventada: Comedia en tres actos (title means "The Invented Truth: Three-Act Play"; comedy; first produced in Madrid at Teatro de Lara, October 27, 1933), Artes Gráficas (Madrid), 1933.

El rival de su mujer: Comedia en tres actos (title means "His Wife's Rival: Three-Act Play"; comedy; first produced in Buenos Aires at Teatro Odeón, 1933), Artes Gráficas, 1934.

El pan comido en la mano: Comedia en tres actos (title means "Bread Eaten from the Hand: Three-Act Play"; comedy; first produced in Madrid at Teatro Fontalba, January 12, 1934), Artes Gráficas, 1934.

Ni al amor ni al mar: Drama en cuatro actos y un epílogo (title means "Neither to Love nor to the Sea: Drama in Four Acts and an Epilogue"; first produced in Madrid at Teatro Español, January 19, 1934), Artes Gráficas, 1934.

Memorias de un madrileño: Puestas en acción en cinco cuadros (title means "Memories of a Man from Madrid: Performed in Five Scenes"; five-act moving tableaux; first performed in Madrid at Teatro de Lara, November 8, 1934), Artes Gráficas, 1934.

La novia de nieve: Comedia en un prólogo y tres actos (title means "The Snow Bride: Three-Act Play with a Prologue"; comedy; first produced in Madrid at Teatro Español, November 29, 1934), Artes Gráficas, 1934.

"No juguéis con esas cosas": Comedia en tres actos (title means " 'Don't Play with Those Things': Three-Act Play "; comedy; first produced in Madrid at Teatro Esclava, January 18, 1935), Artes Gráficas, 1935.

Cualquiera lo sabe: Comedia en tres actos (title means "Anyone Knows That: Three-Act Play"; comedy; first produced in Madrid at Teatro de la Comedia, February 13, 1935), Artes Gráficas, 1935.

Also author of *La princesa sin corazón* (title means "The Heartless Princess"; one-act horror play), 1908; *¡A ver qué hace un hombre!* (title means "Let's See What a Man Does!"), 1909; *Caridad* (title means "Charity"; monologue; first produced in Madrid at Teatro Real, February 3, 1911; one-act), 1918; *¡Si creerás tú que es por mi gusto!* (title means "If You Think I Want It This Way!"; one-act dialogue), 1925; *A las puertas del cielo* (title means "At the Gates of Heaven"; one-act dialogue), 1927; *La culpa es tuya* (title means "It's Your Fault"; three-act comedy; first produced in San Sebastián, Spain, August, 1942, produced in Madrid at Teatro de la Zarzuela, September 17, 1942), 1943; *La enlutada* (title means "The Mourner"; three-act; first produced in Saragossa, Spain at Teatro Principal, October 16, 1942), 1943; *El demonio del teatro* (title means "The Demon of the Theatre"; three-act comedy; first produced in Madrid at Teatro Cómico, October 28, 1942), 1943; *Al servicio de su majestad imperial* (title means "In the Service of His Imperial Majesty"; one-act comedy), 1947; *La vida en verso* (title means "Life in Verse"; three-act comedy; first produced in Madrid at Teatro de la Infanta Isabel, November 9, 1951), 1953; *El lebrel del cielo* (title means "The Hound of Heaven"; three-act comedy; based on Francis Thompson's poem of the same title; first produced in Madrid at Teatro Calderón, April 25, 1952), 1953. Plays also published in numerous collections.

PLAY PRODUCTIONS; IN SPANISH

"Gente conocida" (title means "People of Importance"; four-act drama), first produced in Madrid at Teatro de la Comedia, October 21, 1896.

"El marido de la Téllez" (title means "The Tellez Woman's Husband"; one-act), first produced in Madrid at Teatro de Lara, February 13, 1897.

"De alivio" (title means "On Comfort"; one-act monologue), first produced in Madrid at Teatro de la Comedia, February 27, 1897.

"Don Juan" (based on the play by Moliere; five-act), first produced in Madrid at Teatro de la Princesa, October 31, 1897.

"La farándula" (title means "Bombastic Actors"; two-act), produced in Madrid at Teatro de Lara, November 30, 1897.

"La comida de las fieras" (title means "The Wild Beasts' Banquet"; three-act; also see below), first produced in Madrid at Teatro de la Comedia, November 7, 1898.

"Teatro feminista" (title means "Feminist Theatre"; one-act), first produced in Teatro de la Comedia, December 28, 1898.

(Adapter) "Cuento de amor" (title means "Love Story"; based on Shakespeare's "Twelfth Night"; three-act drama), first produced in Madrid at Teatro de la Comedia, March 11, 1899.

"Operación quirúgica" (title means "Surgery"; one-act), first produced in Madrid at Teatro de Lara, May 4, 1899.

"Despedida cruel" (title means "Cruel Farewell"; one-act), first produced in Madrid at Teatro de Lara, December 7, 1899.

"La gata de Angora" (title means "The Angora Cat"; four-act), first produced in Madrid at Teatro de la Comedia, March 31, 1900.

"Viaje de instrucción" (title means "The Journey of Instruction"; one-act musical comedy), first produced in Madrid at Teatro Alhambra, April 6, 1900.

"Por la herida" (title means "Through Affliction"; one-act drama), first produced in Madrid at Teatro de Novedades, July 15, 1900.

"Modas" (title means "Fashions"; one-act farce), first produced in Madrid at Teatro de Lara, January 18, 1901.

"Lo cursi" (title means "Vulgarity"; three-act drama), first produced in Madrid at Teatro de la Comedia, January 19, 1901.

"Sin querer" (title means "In Perfect Innocence"; one-act comic sketch), first produced in Madrid at Teatro de la Comedia, March 3, 1901.

"Sacrificios" (title means "Sacrifices"; three-act drama), first produced in Madrid at Teatro de Novedades, July 19, 1901.

"El primo román" (three-act), first produced in Saragossa, November 12, 1901.

"Amor de amar" (title means "Love of Loving"; two-act), first produced in Madrid at Teatro de la Comedia, February 24, 1902.

"¡Libertad!" (title means "Liberty!"; three-act; based on a play by Santiago Rusiñol y Prats), first produced in Madrid at Teatro de la Comedia, March 17, 1902.

"En tren de los maridos" (title means "In the Husbands' Retinue"; two-act comedy), first produced in Madrid at Teatro de Lara, April 18, 1902.

"Alma triunfante" (title means "Triumphant Soul"; three-act drama), first produced in Madrid at Teatro de la Comedia, December 2, 1902.

"El automóvil" (title means "The Automobile"; two-act), first produced in Madrid at Teatro de Lara, December 19, 1902.

"Los favoritos" (title means "The Favorites"; one-act), first produced in Seville, March 20, 1903.

"El hombrecito" (title means "The Manikin"; three-act), first produced in Madrid at Teatro de la Comedia, March 23, 1903.

"Por qué se ama" (title means "Why One Loves"; one-act), first produced in Madrid at Teatro Español, October 26, 1903.

"Al natural" (title means "No Affectation"; two-act), first produced at Madrid at Teatro de Lara, November 20, 1903.

"La casa de la dicha" (title means "The House of Happiness"; first produced in Barcelona at Teatro Intimo, December 9, 1903.

"El dragón de fuego" (title means "The Fire Dragon"; three-act drama with epilogue), first produced in Madrid at Teatro Español, March 16, 1904.

"Rosas de otoño" (title means "Autumnal Roses"; three-act drama), first produced in Madrid at Teatro Español, April 13, 1905.

"El susto de la condesa" (title means "The Countess's Terror"; one-act dialogue), first produced in Madrid at Teatro Español, November 15, 1905.

"Cuento inmoral" (title means "Immoral Story"; one-act monologue), first produced in Madrid at Teatro Español, November 15, 1905.

"La sobresalienta" (title means "The Understudy"; one-act lyrical farce), first produced in Madrid at Teatro Español, December 23, 1905.

"El encanto de una hora" (title means "The Magic of an Hour"; dialogue), first produced in Madrid at Teatro de la Princesa, December 30, 1905.

"Más fuerte que el amor" (title means "Stronger than Love"; four-act drama), first produced in Madrid at Teatro Español, February 22, 1906.

"La princesa Bebé" (title means "Princess Bebe"; four-act), first produced in Madrid at Teatro Español, March 31, 1906.

"El amor asusta" (title means "Love Shocks"; one-act), first produced in Madrid on January 10, 1907.

"Abuela y nieta" (title means "Grandmother and Granddaughter"; one-act dialogue), first produced in Madrid at Teatro de Lara, February 21, 1907.

"La copa encantada" (title means "The Enchanted Cup"; one-act musical comedy), first produced in Madrid at Teatro de la Zarzuela, March 16, 1907.

"Todos somos unos" (title means "All Are One"; one-act lyrical farce), first produced in Madrid at Teatro Esclava, September 21, 1907.

"La historia de Otelo" (title means "The Story of Othello"; one-act), first produced in Madrid at Teatro de Apolo, October 11, 1907.

"Los ojos de los muertos" (title means "The Eyes of the Dead"; three-act drama), first produced in Madrid at Teatro de la Princesa, November 7, 1907.

"Señora Ama" (three-act), first produced in Madrid at Teatro de la Princesa, February 22, 1908.

"De pequeñas causas . . ." (title means "From Small Beginnings . . ."; one-act), first produced in Madrid at Teatro de la Princesa, March 14, 1908.

"Por las nubes" (title means "In the Clouds"; two-act; also see below), first produced in Madrid at Teatro de Lara, January 20, 1909.

"El último minué" (title means "The Last Minuet"; one-act comedy), first produced in Madrid at Teatro Benavente, October 23, 1909.

"Ganarse la vida" (title means "Earning a Living"; one-act), first produced in Madrid at Teatro del Príncipe Alfonso, December 20, 1909.

"El nietecito" (title means "The Little Grandson"; one-act), first produced in Teatro del Príncipe Alfonso, January 27, 1910.

"El criado de Don Juan" (title means "Don Juan's Servant"; one-act), first produced in Madrid at Teatro Español, March 29, 1911.

"La losa de los sueños" (title means "The Graveyard of Dreams"; two act comedy), first produced in Madrid at Teatro de Lara, November 9, 1911.

"La propia estimación" (title means "Proper Esteem"; three-act), first produced in Madrid at Teatro de la Comedia, December 22, 1915.

"La mal que nos hacen" (title means "The Evil Done to Us"; three-act), first produced in Madrid at Teatro de la Princesa, March 23, 1917.

"La Inmaculada de los Dolores" (title means "Our Lady of Sorrow"; three-act dramatic novel), first produced in Madrid at Teatro de Lara, April 30, 1918.

"La ley de los hijos" (title means "The Children's Law"; three-act drama), first produced in Madrid at Teatro de la Zarzuela, December 23, 1918.

"Por ser con todos leal, ser para todos traidor" (title means "Loyalty to All Through Treachery to All"; three-act drama), first produced in Madrid at Teatro del Centro, March 5, 1919.

"La vestal de Occidente" (title means "The Vestal of the West"; four-act drama), first produced in Madrid at Teatro de Lara, March 29, 1919.

"La honra de los hombres" (title means "The Honor of Men"; two-act comedy), first produced in Madrid at Teatro de Lara, May 2, 1919.

(Adapter) "El audaz" (five-act drama; based on the novel of the same title by Benito Pérez Galdós), first produced in Madrid at Teatro Español, December 6, 1919.

"La Cenicienta" (title means "Cinderella"; three-act), first produced in Madrid at Teatro Español, December 20, 1919.

"Y va de cuento" (title means "And Once Upon a Time"; four-act fantasy with prologue), first produced in Madrid on December 23, 1919.

"Una señora" (title means "A Lady"; three-act dramatic novel), first produced in Madrid at Teatro del Centro, January 2, 1920.

"Una pobre mujer" (title means "A Poor Woman"; three-act drama), first produced in Madrid at Teatro de la Princesa, April 3, 1920.

"Más allá de la muerte" (title means "Beyond Death"; three-act drama), first produced in Buenos Aires, August, 1922.

"Por qué se quitó Juan de la bebida" (title means "Why Juan Quit Drinking"; monologue), first produced in Montevideo, Uruguay at Teatro Soles, August 30, 1922.

"Un par de botas" (title means "A Pair of Boots"; one-act comedy), first produced in Madrid at Teatro de la Princesa, May 24, 1924.

"Nadie sabe lo que quiere; o, El bailarín y el trabajador" (title means "Nobody Knows What He Wants; or, The Dancer and the Laborer"; three-act comedy), first produced in Madrid at Teatro Cómico, March 14, 1925.

"El suicidio de Lucerito" (title means "Lucerito's Suicide"; one-act comedy), first produced in Madrid at Teatro Alcázar, July 17, 1925.

"Los amigos del hombre" (title means "Man's Friends"; four-act farce), produced in Madrid at Teatro de la Avenida, November 3, 1930.

"Aves y pájaros" (title means "Birds and Fowl"; two-part), first produced in Madrid at Teatro de Lara, October 20, 1940.

"Lo increíble" (title means "The Incredible"; three-act comedy), first produced in Madrid at Teatro de la Comedia, October 25, 1940.

"Abuelo y nieto" (title means "Grandfather and Grandson"; one-act dialogue), produced in San Sebastián, Spain, at Teatro del Príncipe, August 29, 1941.

"Y amargaba. . ." (title means "And It Was Bitter . . ."; three-act comedy), first produced in Madrid at Teatro de la Zarzuela, November 19, 1941.

"La última carta" (title means "The Last Letter"; three-act comedy), first produced in Madrid at Teatro Alcázar, December 9, 1941.

"La honradez de la cerradura" (title means "The Integrity of the Lock"; three-act comedy), first produced in Madrid at Teatro Español, April 4, 1942.

"Al fin, mujer" (title means "Finally, Woman"; three-act comedy), first produced in San Sebastián, Spain at Teatro del Príncipe, September 13, 1942, produced in Madrid at Teatro Alcázar, November 17, 1942.

"¡Hija del alma!" (title means "Daughter of My Soul!"; one-act), first produced in Madrid at Teatro de Lara, September 17, 1942.

"Don Magín, él de las magias" (title means "Don Magin, the Magician"; three-act comedy), first produced in Barcelona at Teatro Barcelona, March 26, 1944, produced in Madrid at Teatro Alcázar, January 12, 1945.

"Los niños perdidos en la selva" (title means "Children Lost in the Forest": four-act dramatic novel), first produced in Madrid at Teatro de la Infanta Beatriz, April 14, 1944.

"Espejo de grandes" (title means "Mirror of the Great"; one-act), first produced October 12, 1944, produced in Madrid at Teatro de Lara, June 11, 1946.

"Nieve en mayo" (title means "Snow in May"; four-act dramatic poem), first produced in Madrid at Teatro de la Zarzuela, January 19, 1945.

"La ciudad doliente" (title means "The Suffering City"; three-act comedy), first produced in Madrid at Teatro de la Comedia, April 14, 1945.

"Titania" (three-act comedy), first produced in Buenos Aires, September 25, 1945, first produced in Madrid at Teatro Calderón, November 8, 1946.

"La infanzona" (title means "The Noblewoman"; three-act drama), first produced in Buenos Aires, December 6, 1945, produced in Madrid at Teatro Calderón, January 10, 1947.

"Abdicación" (title means "Abdication"; three-act comedy), first produced in Madrid at Teatro de Lara, March 27, 1948.

"Divorcio de almas" (title means "Divorce of Souls"; three-act comedy), first produced in Madrid at Teatro Fontalba, September 30, 1948.

"Adoración" (title means "Adoration"; two-act dramatic comedy with prologue), first produced in Madrid at Teatro Cómico, December 3, 1948.

"Al amor hay que mandarlo al colegio" (title means "Love Should be Sent to School"; comedy with four episodes), first produced in Madrid at Teatro de Lara, September 29, 1950.

"Su amante esposa" (title means "His Lover-Wife"; three-act comedy), first produced in Madrid at Teatro de la Infanta Isabel, October 20, 1950.

"Tú una vez, y el diablo diez" (title means "You Once, the Devil Ten Times"; three-act comedy), first produced in Valladolid, Spain at Teatro Lope de Vega, October 23, 1950, produced in Madrid at Teatro de la Infanta Isabel, March 27, 1951.

"Mater imperatrix" (three-act dramatic comedy), first produced in Barcelona at Teatro de la Comedia, November 29, 1950, first produced in Madrid at Teatro de la Comedia, January 30, 1951.

"Ha llegado Don Juan" (title means "Don Juan Has Arrived"; two-act comedy with prologue), first produced in Barcelona at Teatro de la Comedia, April 12, 1952.

"Servir" (title means "To Serve"; two-act comedy with interlude), first produced in Madrid at Teatro María Guerrero, January 22, 1953.

"El alfiler en la boca" (title means "A Pin in the Mouth"; three-act comedy), first produced in Madrid at Teatro de la Infanta Isabel, February 13, 1953.

"Almas prisioneras" (title means "Imprisoned Souls"; two-act drama with prologue), first produced in Madrid at Teatro Alvarez Quintero, February 26,1953.

"Caperucita asusta al lobo" (title means "Little Red Riding-Hood Frightens the Wolf "; three-act), first produced in Madrid at Teatro de la Infanta Isabel, September 23, 1953.

"Hijos padres de sus padres" (title means "Sons Fathers of their Fathers"; three-act comedy), first produced in Madrid at Teatro de Lara, February 11, 1954.

"El marido de bronce" (three-act comedy), first produced in Madrid at Teatro de la Infanta Isabel, April 23, 1954.

OTHER

Cartas de mujeres (title means "Women's Letters"; fictional letters), 1893, reprinted, Espasa-Calpe, 1965.

Figulinas (sketches), Fortanet, 1898.

(Translator) Alexandre Dumas *pere,* "Mademoiselle de Belle-Isle" (five-act play), first produced in Valladolid, Spain, October 20, 1903.

(Translator) Edward Bulwer-Lytton, "Richelieu" (five-act drama), first produced in Mexico City, March 15, 1904.

(Translator) Emile Augier, "Buena boda" (title means "A Good Marriage"; three-act), first produced in Madrid at Teatro de Sociedad, 1905.

Vilanos (sketches), Fortanet, 1905.

El teatro del pueblo (title means "The People's Theatre"), F. Fé (Madrid), 1909.

(Translator) Paul Hervieu, "El destino manda" (title means "Destiny Commands"; two-act drama; translation of "Le destin est maitre"), first produced in Madrid at Teatro de la Princesa, March 25, 1914.

(Translator) George C. Hazelton and Harry Benrimo, "La túnica amarilla" (title means "The Yellow Tunic"; three-act), first produced in Madrid at Teatro de la Princesa, April 22, 1916.

Los niños (title means "The Children"; anthology), Hesperia (Madrid), 1917.

"La Mefistófela" (title means "Mephistopheles"; three-act comic operetta), first produced in Madrid at Teatro de la Reina Victoria, April 29, 1918.

Conferencias (title mean "Lectures"), Hernando, 1924.

Pensamientos (title means "Thoughts"), Hernando, 1931.

De sobremesa: Crónicas (title means "After-Dinner Conversation: Chronicles"), F. Fé (Madrid), 1940.

Plan de estudios para una escuela de arte escénico, Aguilar, 1940.

Así piensan los personajes de Benavente (title means "Benavente's Characters Think Thusly"; excerpts from his writings), edited by José María Viqueira, Aguilar, 1958.

Recuerdos y olvidos (memorias) (title means "Things Recalled and Forgotten: Memories"), Aguilar, 1959.

Las terceras de ABC (selections of contributions to *ABC*), edited by Adolfo Prego, Prensa Española, 1976.

Editor of *El año germanófilo* (title means "The Germanic Year"; symposium), 1916; also author of unpublished and unproduced play, "El bufón de Hamlet" (title means "The Buffoon of Hamlet"). Also translator of "King Lear" by Shakespeare published as *El rey Lear,* 1911. Weekly columnist, *El Imparcial,* 1908-12. Contributor to *ABC* (Madrid newspaper). Editor, *La Vida Literaria* (magazine).

SIDELIGHTS: Dramatist Jacinto Benavente was the dominant force in Spanish drama during the first third of the twentieth-century. He produced nearly two hundred works for stage and in 1922 was granted the Nobel Prize for literature. Although extremely popular during the early years of his career, many critics noted a decline in Benavente's theatre beginning shortly before he won the highly coveted award. In a *World Literature Today* essay chronicling the Nobel prizes received by Hispanic authors throughout the history of the award, Manuel Durán seemed to summarize modern thought on the playwright when he wrote: "Another prize was squandered in 1922. The laurel went that year to playwright Jacinto Benavente, whose vast production is now mostly obsolete and was already out of phase with modern times when the medallion was conferred." However slighted by today's critics, Benavente's impact on Spanish theatre and the high esteem in which he was held by the theatre-going public and critics of his day cannot be denied.

Son of a well-respected pediatrician (a bust of whom can be found in Madrid's *Buen Retiro* park), Benavente showed an early interest in theatre and as a boy he often wrote short skits to be performed for his young friends. Besides attending plays produced on the stages of Madrid, he read voraciously all the theatre he could find. When as a teenager he learned several foreign languages, he began to read plays by foreign authors, especially those by Shakespeare, in their original languages. Although he studied law for a time, his true career was in the theatre and he soon became an actor with a professional company based in Madrid. (Later in life he stated on numerous occasions that he would have preferred to have been an actor rather than a playwright and often appeared in the cast of his own productions.)

In the late 1880s he began to regularly submit plays to Emilio Mario, a family friend and director of Madrid's famous Teatro de la Comedia. Mario rejected nearly a dozen of the fledgling dramatist's efforts until finally consenting to produce a three-act play entitled "El nido ajeno" ("Another's Nest") in 1894. Although the work was virtually ignored by critics, Benavente's next offering, "Gente conocida" ("People of Importance") won for the playwright an adoring public.

"Gente conocida" introduced to Madrid a type of theatre completely different from that in vogue at the time. Spanish theatre was under the spell of Spain's first Nobel Prize winner, José Echegaray (who won the award in 1904), a playwright whose work was characterized by exaggerated melodrama, grandiloquent verses, and artificiality. Although Benavente confessed a deep admiration for the older playwright, his own theatre was in direct contrast to that of Echegaray. "Benavente's theater . . . meant a reaction against the anachronistic, turn-of-the-century Romanticism of Echegaray," wrote Marcelino C. Peñuelas in *Jacinto Benavente.* "Against a background of the affected gesture, the hollow voice, the melodramatic, declamatory and solemn tone, the violence of passion and the traditional concept of honor, appear the theater of clever conversation in a confidential, ironic and satirical tone which Benavente succeeded in popularizing."

Critics John Van Horne and Walter Starkie both group Benavente's plays produced from 1894 to 1901 as the author's first period. This phase is marked by what Starkie referred to in *Jacinto Benavente,* his 1924 biography of the author, as "the Toledo blade of satire." In these plays Benavente satirized the decadent upper and middle classes of Madrid and Moraleda, the playwright's fictional version of a provincial town of the countryside surrounding the Spanish capital. Productions of this period include, "La farándula," which compares the empty speech of politicians to the meaningless line of actors; "La comida de las fieras," which explores what happens to a wealthy family when it loses its fortune; and "La gobernadora," which reveals the intrigue behind small town politics.

In these first plays Benavente showed a tendency to imitate several French authors with whose work he was familiar, including Alfred Capus, Mauric Donnay, and Henry Lavedan. All three were playwrights who wrote satirical works about French society. Critics who noted this influence, along with Benavente's obvious rejection of the norm for Spanish theatre of the time established by Echegaray, accused Benavente of not being a true Spanish playwright. "Perhaps without his knowing it, he is more foreign than Spanish," commented José Vila Selma in his *Benavente: Fin de siglo* which Peñuelas quoted in English translation. Vila Selma continued, "Whatever is new in Benavente's theater is something which singularly sets itself apart from the traditional course." In an essay included in *The Theatre, the Drama, the Girls* George Jean Nathan seemed to side with Vila Selma's assessment when he accused Benavente of copying many of his plays from a variety of Italian, French, German sources.

Benavente's theatre reflected his cosmopolitan life-style: He had traveled extensively through Europe and, because he was fluent in several languages, was familiar with several European literatures. Differing with Vila Selma and Nathan, some critics saw these influences in Benavente's theatre as a reason to praise the playwright for bringing fresh material into the tradition-bound Spanish theatre. "It was he," *Books Abroad* contributor Robert G. Sánchez pointed out, "who brought to the Spanish stage all the currents of the European theater of the first quarter of the century." Julius Brouta, and others, likened Benavente to several of the best dramatists on the European scene. In comments published in *Drama* Brouta wrote, "Benavente is, in many respects, the Bernard Shaw of Spain. Like Shaw, he is a disciple of Ibsen; like him, an iconoclast, a reformer, a teacher, a preacher, and his dialectics are hardly less efficient or his spirit less brilliant." Elsewhere in the same essay, Brouta noted that Benavente's ironic touch was "similar to that of Anatole France." In a comparison with another European author, *Topic* contributor Alfredo Marquerie found Benavente "had much in common with Oscar Wilde."

While admitting to the European influences in Benavente's theatre, other critics, including Storm Jameson and Starkie, found his work to be firmly rooted in that of the seventeenth-century Spanish playwright Lope de Vega, known as the father of Spanish drama, and who represented the very essence of *lo español.* Starkie noted: "Many of [Benavente's] enemies have made it an accusation against him that he introduced foreign ideals which caused the decline of true Spanish art. To those, however, who examine carefully Benavente's drama, it will become plain that foreign influences did not altogether hide the Spanish dramatist who counted back his literary descent to Lope de Vega." In a similar vein, Jameson observed in an essay in his *Modern Drama in Europe,* "The work of Jacinto Benavente is in the highest tradition of the Spanish drama. . . . The creative genius of Lope de Vega informed his vision of reality." "Cosmopolitan as he may be in theories," Van Horne wrote in his introduction to *Tres Comedias: 'Sin querer,' 'De pequeñas causas . . .,' 'Los intereses creados,'* "his nature is essentially and intensely Spanish."

Benavente's witty dialogue and fertile imagination won over skeptical actors, critics, and public. The second phase of his career, which in Starkie's estimation covered the years 1901 to 1914, brought the playwright his greatest triumphs. In 1905 he was acclaimed by Madrid's theatrical community with a festival in his honor which concluded with the public reading of a tribute by the great Spanish novelist Benito Pérez Galdós. Two plays from this period, "Los intereses creados" ("The Bonds of Interest") and "La malquerida" ("The Passionflower"), were successfully produced in English translation on the New York stage. These plays show Benavente's evolution from the social satire of his first period to a broader scope, including a wide variety of theatrical genres, but often focusing on comedy with a moral tone.

Considered Benavente's masterpiece, "The Bonds of Interest" is a three-act comedy based on the Italian *commedia dell'arte.* This dramatic genre consisted of a improvisational skit performed by actors filling the roles of stock characters, including "the beautiful young lady," her "suitor," "the Doctor," and others. Later versions also included "Polichinelle," who survived to modern times as Punch in Punch and Judy shows, and "Harlequin," known for his unique costume. Benavente's play tells the story of the handsome Leander's attempt to dupe an entire city into thinking he is a wealthy aristocrat traveling incognito. After falling in love with the beautiful Sylvia, daughter of Polichinelle, Leander tells her of his true identity. Meanwhile, Leander's servant, Crispín, who is unaware of his master's confession, contrives to have the whole town and Sylvia turn against Polichinelle. The comedy ends happily with Crispín forced to admit his lies and Sylvia stepping forward to address the audience, declaring that although we are often selfishly ruled by "bonds of interest," the power of love is there to redeem us.

Sylvia's closing statement embodies an important facet of Benavente's view of life as presented in his work: the value of love and tolerance in combating society's evils. In his introduction to

Plays, Benavente's chief translator John Garrett Underhill wrote, "The subject of Jacinto Benavente is the struggle of love against poverty, of obligation against desire, of imputed virtue against the consciousness of sin." Jameson commented on the same aspect of Benavente's work, noting "The other side of the dramatist's passionate indignation is love, love towards the oppressed, the thwarted and the maimed of life. . . . Men are to be pitied, but they are also to be loved. Through the dynamic force of love they will be set free, not from pain, but from despair and the isolation of defeat." "Love stands forth prominently in Benavente as the principle dynamic factor," Brouta concluded.

Many of the plays of Benavente's second period explore the problems of married life. Included in this group is "La Malquerida" ("The Passionflower"), one of the plays individually cited for merit in the Nobel prize presentation address given by the then-chairman of the Nobel Committee of the Swedish Academy, Per Hallstroem. This three-act peasant drama of provincial life focuses on the relationship between Estebán and Acacia, his wife Raimunda's daughter from her first marriage. The play ends tragically with the death of Raimunda at Estebán's hands. Such was the success of the first production of the play in 1913 that Benavente was carried home in triumph by enthusiastic theatre-goers. Sánchez called it "a powerful and fascinating melodrama, a landmark in the modern Spanish theater."

In "La Malquerida," as in many of his plays, Benavente focuses his attention on his female characters. Dubbed a feminist for his portrayals of strong females, he expressed his interest in female characterization in one of his first works, *Cartas de mujeres,* a volume of letters purported to be written by women. "In these letters," Starkie observed, "he tries to plumb the depths of the Spanish woman's soul." Unlike some Spanish dramatists who insisted in their works on the centuries-old concepts of honor and machismo, according to Brouta, Benavente "stoutly espoused the rights of woman, the idea of equality of the sexes, and pointed out the moral obligation which matrimony imposes upon man." He was also fond of poking fun at one of Spain's national heroes, Don Juan, the professional seducer. "Rosas de otoño" and "Señora Ama," which each deal with how a woman married to a philandering husband deals with his infidelity, are just two of his works in which his interest in feminine psychology is apparent.

At the beginning of his career, Benavente was seen as a reformer of the Spanish stage and a revealer of the hypocrisy of Spanish society. Because of this revolutionary beginning, Benavente is often included by many critics as a member of Spain's Generation of '98, a loosely knit group of writers who broke with the members of the preceding generation in hopes of avoiding a disaster similar to the one Spain suffered in 1898 when it lost all of its overseas empire. By the time the playwright had entered his third period, starting in 1914, his plays had changed so that characters, and not reform, had became their focus. Speaking of this last phase of Benavente's career Starkie commented, "His heroes and heroines in most cases tend to become mere mechanical symbols of an abstract thought. In many cases also he falls into sentimentality, and mistakes rhetoric for art." He seemed to be writing for that very portion of society that he previously had so bitterly satirized.

When Benavente was awarded the Nobel in 1922, members of the Generation of '98, who previously had held him in high esteem as one of their own, protested vehemently. Peñuelas explained that although Benavente had indeed reformed Spanish theatre, at least technically, "he never came to experience the artistic and human anxieties which appeared at the turn of the century in Europe and in Spain with the writers of the Generation of '98." Because of Benavente's failure to continue on the path of revision suggested by his early works, nearly all his plays remain essentially bound to the Spanish society in which they were originally written. As Peñuelas concluded: "Although Benavente undoubtedly influenced twentieth-century Spanish writers, the best of his followers oriented their works in other directions and Benavente's theater was soon out of date."

BIOGRAPHICAL/CRITICAL SOURCES:

BOOKS

Benavente, Jacinto, *Plays,* edited and translated by John Garrett Underhill, Scribner, 1917.
Benavente, Jacinto, *Tres comedias: "Sin querer," "De pequeñas causas . . .," "Los intereses creados,"* edited by John Van Horne, Heath, 1918.
Jameson, Storm, *Modern Drama in Europe,* Collins, 1920.
Nathan, George Jean, *The Theatre, the Drama, the Girls,* Knopf, 1921.
Noble Prize Library: Asturias, Benavente, Bergson, Helvetica Press, 1971.
Peñuelas, Marcelino C., *Jacinto Benavente,* Twayne, 1968.
Starkie, Walter, *Jacinto Benavente,* Oxford University Press, 1924.
Twentieth-Century Literary Criticism, Volume 3, Gale, 1980.
Vila Selma, José, *Benavente: Fin de siglo,* Rialp, 1952.

PERIODICALS

Books Abroad, winter, 1955.
Drama, November, 1915.
Topic, spring, 1968.
World Literature Today, spring, 1988.

OBITUARIES:

PERIODICALS

Newsweek, July 26, 1954.
New York Times, July 15, 1954.
Publishers Weekly, August 7, 1954.
Time, July 26, 1954.

—*Sketch by Marian Gonsior*

* * *

BENEDETTI, Mario 1920-
(Damocles)

PERSONAL: Born September 14, 1920, in Paso de los Toros, Tacuarembo, Uruguay; son of Brenno Benedetti and Matilde Farrugia; married Luz López. *Education:* Attended the Colegio Alemán.

CAREER: Accountant in Montevideo, Uruguay; organizer and director of a literary research center in Cuba, 1969-71; writer.

WRITINGS:

ESSAYS AND LECTURES

Peripecia y novela, [Montevideo], 1948.
Marcel Proust y otros ensayos, Número (Montevideo), 1951.
El país de la cola de paja, Asir (Montevideo), 1960.
(Under pseudonym Damocles) *Mejor es meneallo,* Alfa (Montevideo), 1961.
Literatura uruguaya siglo XX, Alfa, 1963, revised 2nd edition, 1969.
(With others) *Sobre Julio Cortázar,* [Havana], 1967.
Letras del continente mestizo, Arca (Montevideo), 1967.
Sobre artes y oficios, Alfa, 1968.

Cuaderno cubano, Arca, 1969, revised 2nd edition, 1971.
(With others) *Nueve asedios a García Márquez,* Universitaria (Santiago), 1969.
(With others) *Literatura y arte nuevo en Cuba,* Estela (Barcelona), 1971.
(With others) *Rodó: Parábolas y textos escogidos,* Fundación Editorial Unión del Magisterio (Montevideo), 1971.
Crítica cómplice, Instituto Cubano del Libro (Havana), 1971.
(With Angel Rama) *Cielitos y diálogos patrióticos* (about Bartolomé Hidalgo), Biblioteca de Marcha (Montevideo), 1971.
Crónicas del 71, Arca, 1972.
El escritor latinoamericano y revolución posible, Alfa Argentina (Buenos Aires), 1974.
El ejercicio del criterio: Crítica literaria, 1950-1970, Nueva Imagen (Mexico City), 1981.
Escritos políticos, Arca, 1985.

FICTION AND POETRY

Esta mañana (short stories), [Montevideo], 1949, published as *Esta mañana y otros cuentos* (also see below), Arca, 1967.
El último viaje y otros cuentos (short stories), Número, 1951.
Quién de nosostros (novel), Alfa, 1953.
Poemas de la oficina (poetry), Número, 1956.
Montevideanos (also see below; short stories), Alfa, 1959.
La tregua (novel), Alfa, 1960, translation by Benjamin Graham published as *The Truce,* Harper, 1969.
Poemas del hoyporhoy (poetry), Alfa, 1961.
Inventario (poetry), Alfa, 1963, revised 3rd edition published as *Inventario 67,* 1967, revised 4th edition published as *Inventario 70,* 1970; revised 5th edition published as *Inventario,* Alfa Argentina, 1974.
Gracias por el fuego (novel), Alfa, 1965.
Contra los puentes levadizos (poetry), Alfa, 1966.
Antología natural (poetry), Alfa, 1967.
A ras de sueño (poetry), Alfa, 1967.
La muerte y otras sorpresas (also see below; short stories), Siglo XXI (Mexico City), 1968.
(With others) *Montevideo en cuentas* (short stories), Arca, 1968.
Cuentos completos (short stories; contains *Esta mañana y otros cuentos, Montevideanos,* and *La muerte y otras sorpresas*), Universitaria, 1970.
El cumpleaños de Juan Angel (novella in verse), Siglo XXI, 1971.
(With others) *Cuentos de la revolución* (short stories), Giron (Montevideo), 1971.
Letras de emergencia (poetry and prose), Alfa Argentina, 1973.
Poemas de otros (poetry), Alfa Argentina, 1974.
(With others) *Siete cuentos de hoy* (short stories), Sandino (Montevideo), 1974.
Cotidianas (poetry), Siglo XXI, 1979.
Pedro y el capitán: Pieza en cuatro partes, Nueva Imagen, 1979.
Poesía trunca: Poesía latinoamericana revolucionaria (poetry), Visor (Madrid), 1980.
Viento del exilio (poetry), Nueva Imagen, 1981.
Antología poética (poetry), Alianza (Madrid), 1984.
Geografías (short stories and poetry), Nueva Imagen, 1984.
Noción de patria: Próximo prójimo (poetry), Visor, 1985.

Also author of *La víspera indeleble,* 1945, and *Sólo mientras tanto,* 1950.

A collection of the author's poems and short stories was recorded by Benedetti and released as an album, *Mario Benedetti: Poemas y cuentos.*

PLAYS

El reportaje (also see below), Marcha (Montevideo), 1958.

Ida y vuelta (also see below), Talía (Buenos Aires), 1963.
Dos comedias (contains *El reportaje* and *Ida y vuelta*), Alfa, 1968.

EDITOR

Narradores rumanos (Rumanian short stories), Alfa, 1965.
(And author of prologue) Rubén Darío, *Poesías* (poetry), Casa de las Américas (Havana), 1967.
(And author of prologue) *Poemas de amor hispanoamericanos* (poetry), Arca, 1969.
(With Antonio Benítez Rojo) *Quince relatos de la América Latina* (essays), Casa de las Américas, 1970.
(With Benítez Rojo) J. J. Fernández de Lizardi and others, *Un siglo del relato latinoamericano* (short stories), Casa de las Américas, 1976.
(And author of prologue) *Jóvenes de esta América* (essays and lectures), Casa de las Américas, 1978.
Roque Dalton, *Poesía* (poetry), Casa de las Américas, 1980.

Also editor of *Naturaleza viva: Introducción a la poesía hispanoamericana,* translation by Darwin J. Flakoll and Claribel Alegría published as *Unstill Life: An Introduction to the Spanish Poetry of Latin America,* Harcourt, 1969.

OTHER

Genio y figura de José Enrique Rodó, Universitaria de Buenos Aires, 1966.
Datos para el viudo, Galerna (Buenos Aires), 1967.
Los poetas comunicantes (interviews), Biblioteca de Marcha, 1972.
(With others) *Onetti* (literary criticism), Biblioteca de Marcha, 1973.
Hasta aquí, La Línea (Buenos Aires), c. 1974.
Daniel Viglietti (musical criticism), Júcar (Madrid), 1974.
La casa y el ladrillo, Siglo XXI, 1976.
Con y sin nostalgia, Siglo XXI, 1977.
El recurso del supremo patriarca (literary criticism), Nueva Imagen, 1979.
Notas sobre algunas formas subsidiarias de la penetración cultural, Tierra Adentro (Mexico City), 1979.
El escritor y la crítica en el contexto del subdesarrollo, Universidad Nacional Autónoma de México (Mexico City), 1979.
Primavera con una esquina rota, Nueva Imagen, 1982.
(With Hélder Camara) *Escritos sobre la teología de la liberación en Latinoamérica,* Instituto de Estudios Latinoamericanos (Buenos Aires), 1984.
El desexilio, y otras conjeturas, Nueva Imagen, 1985.
La cultura, ese blanco móvil, División Publicaciones y Ediciones, Universidad de la República (Montevideo), 1985.
Cultura entre dos fuegos, División Publicaciones y Ediciones, Universidad de la República, 1986.
Preguntas al azar, Nueva Imagen, 1986.
Yesterday y mañana, Arca, 1987.
Subdesarrollo y letras de osadia, Alianza, 1987.
Recuerdos olvidados, Trilce (Montevideo), 1988.

Contributor to *Panorama histórico-literario de nuestra América,* by América Díaz Acosta and others, Casa de las Américas, 1982. Journalist for *Marcha,* a weekly periodical in Montevideo; literary, film, and theater critic for *El Diario, Tribuna Popular,* and *La Mañana,* Montevideo.

BIOGRAPHICAL/CRITICAL SOURCES:

BOOKS

Alfaro, Hugo, *Mario Benedetti: Detrás de un vidrio claro,* Trilce (Montevideo), 1986.

PERIODICALS

New York Times Book Review, October 19, 1969, November 9, 1969.
Times Literary Supplement, December 7, 1967, June 20, 1968, September 18, 1970, August 6, 1976.

* * *

BENEDETTO, Antonio di
See di BENEDETTO, Antonio

* * *

BENEKE, Walter 1923-

PERSONAL: Born in 1923 in El Salvador.

CAREER: Playwright. Cultural attaché for El Salvador serving in Madrid, Spain.

WRITINGS:

PLAYS

El paraíso de los imprudentes (three-act), Ministerio de Cultura (San Salvador), 1956, second edition published in *El paraíso de los imprudentes* [and] *Funeral Home* (also see below), Ministerio de Educación (San Salvador), 1974.
Funeral Home (three-act), Ministerio de Cultura, 1959, 5th edition, Ministerio de Educación, 1982.

* * *

BENITEZ, Fernando 1911-

PERSONAL: Born in 1911 in Mexico.

ADDRESSES: Agent—c/o Ediciones Era, Apdo 74-092, 09080 México, DF, México.

CAREER: Journalist.

WRITINGS:

TRANSLATED WORKS

La ruta de Hernán Cortés, Fondo de Cultura Económica (Mexico), 1950, reprinted, 1983, translation published as *In the Footsteps of Cortés,* Pantheon, 1952.
La vida criolla en el siglo XVI (history), El Colegio de México, 1953, published as *Los primeros mexicanos: La vida criolla en el siglo XVI,* Era (Mexico), 1962, translation by Joan MacLean published as *The Century After Cortés,* University of Chicago Press, 1965.
El agua envenenada (novel), Fondo de Cultura Económica, 1961, translation by Mary E. Ellsworth published as *The Poisoned Water,* foreword by J. Cary Davis, Southern Illinois University Press, 1973.
En la tierra mágica del peyote (essays; originally published as part of *Los indios de México* [also see below]), [Mexico], 1968, reprinted, Era, 1971, translation by John Upton published as *In the Magic Land of Peyote,* introduction by Peter T. Furst, University of Texas Press, 1975.

UNTRANSLATED WORKS

Caballo y Dios: Relatos sobre la muerte (contains "Caballo y Dios," "Otoño," "Una muerte," "Dos mineros," "El teniente incorregible," "Un extraño personaje," and "La sombra amarilla"), Leyenda (Mexico), 1945.
Morelia: Textos de Fernando Benítez, Ediciones de Arte (Mexico), 1948.

China a la vista (travel), Cuadernos Americanos (Mexico), 1953.

Ki: El drama de un pueblo y de una planta, Fondo de Cultura Económica, 1956.

El rey viejo (fiction), Fondo de Cultura Económica, 1959.

La batalla de Cuba, Era, 1960.

Viaje a la Tarahumara (travel book), Era, 1960.

La última trinchera, Era, 1963.

Los hongos alucinantes, Era, 1964.

La ruta de la libertad (history), [Mexico], 1964.

Los indios de México (essays; title means "Indians of Mexico"), Era, 1967.

Tierra incógnita (originally published as part of *Los indios de México*), Era, 1972.

Historia de un chamán cora (originally published as part of *Los indios de México*), Era, 1973.

Viaje al centro de México, Fondo de Cultura Económica, 1975.

Lázaro Cárdenas y la Revolución Mexicana, three volumes, Fondo de Cultura Económica, 1977-78.

(Editor) *Entrevistas con un solo tema: Lázaro Cárdenas* (essays), Facultad de Ciencias Políticas y Sociales, Universidad Nacional Autónoma de México, 1979.

La ciudad de México, 1325-1982 (history), three volumes, Salvat, 1981-82, published as *Historia de la ciudad de México,* nine volumes, 1984.

Los demonios en el convento: Sexo y religión en la Nueva España (biography), Era, 1985.

El libro de los desastres, Era, 1988.

BIOGRAPHICAL/CRITICAL SOURCES:

PERIODICALS

Nation, September 26, 1966.

*   *   *

BERNAL, Vicente J. 1888-1915

PERSONAL: Born December 15, 1888, in Costilla, N.M.; died of a brain hemorrhage, April 28, 1915, in Dubuque, Iowa. *Education:* Attended Dubuque German College and Academy (now University of Dubuque), in mid-1910s.

ADDRESSES: Home—Dubuque, Iowa.

CAREER: Writer.

WRITINGS:

Las primicias (verse and prose; title means "The First Fruits"), edited by brother, Luis E. Bernal, and Robert N. McLean, Telegraph-Herald (Dubuque), 1916.

SIDELIGHTS: Vicente J. Bernal is known for *Las primicias,* a bilingual—Spanish and English—collection of poetry and prose. Bernal spent his childhood in New Mexico, and many of his poems reflect the longing he felt for Spanish culture after moving to Iowa, where he attended Dubuque German College and Academy (now University of Dubuque). He wrote many of his English-language verses between 1913 and 1915 while he was still studying in Dubuque. These English poems—thirty-four of which appear in *Las primicias*—are particularly prized for their literary sensibility and moving articulation. Before he could enter the Dubuque Seminary, Bernal died of a brain hemorrhage in 1915. *Las primicias* appeared the next year.

BIOGRAPHICAL/CRITICAL SOURCES:

BOOKS

Dictionary of Literary Biography, Volume 82: *Chicano Writers,* Gale, 1989.

PERIODICALS

La Aurora, January 18, 1939.

LULAC News, September, 1938.

*   *   *

BIOY CASARES, Adolfo 1914-
(Javier Miranda, Martín Sacastru, pseudonyms; H[onorio] Bustos Domecq, B. Lynch Davis, B. Suárez Lynch, joint pseudonyms)

PERSONAL: Surname appears in some sources as Bioy-Casares; born September 15, 1914, in Buenos Aires, Argentina; son of Adolfo Bioy and Marta Casares; married Silvina Ocampo (a writer), 1940; children: Marta.

ADDRESSES: Home—Posadas 1650, 1112 Buenos Aires, Argentina.

CAREER: Writer.

AWARDS, HONORS: Premio Municipal de la Ciudad de Buenos Aires, 1940, for *La invención de Morel;* Segundo Premio Nacional de Literatura (Argentina), 1963, for *El lado de la sombra;* Primer Premio Nacional de Literatura (Argentina), 1969, for *El gran serafín;* Gran Premio de Honor, Argentine Society of Writers, 1975; Premio Mondello, 1984, for *Historias fantásticas;* Premio Internacional Literario IILA (Rome), 1986, for *Historias fantásticas* and *Historias de amor.*

WRITINGS:

IN ENGLISH TRANSLATION

La invención de Morel (novel; also see below), prologue by Jorge Luis Borges, Losada (Buenos Aires), 1940, reprinted, Alianza (Madrid), 1981, translation by Ruth L. C. Simms published with her translation of *La trama celeste* (also see below) as *The Invention of Morel, and Other Stories from "La trama celeste,"* University of Texas Press, 1964, reprinted, 1985.

(Editor with wife, Silvina Ocampo, and Borges, and author of foreword) *Antología de la literatura fantástica* (title means "Anthology of Fantastic Literature"), Sudamericana (Buenos Aires), 1940, enlarged edition with postscript by Bioy Casares, 1965, translation of revised version published as *The Book of Fantasy,* introduction by Ursula K. Le Guin, Viking, 1988.

(With Borges, under joint pseudonym H. Bustos Domecq) *Seis problemas para don Isidro Parodi* (short stories), Sur (Buenos Aires), 1942, translation by Norman Thomas di Giovanni published under authors' real names as *Six Problems for Don Isidro Parodi,* Dutton, 1983.

El perjurio de la nieve (short stories), Emecé, 1945, translation by Simms published as *The Perjury of the Snow,* Vanishing Rotating Triangle (New York), 1964.

Plan de evasión (novel), Emecé, 1945, reprinted, 1977, translation by Suzanne J. Levine published as *A Plan for Escape,* Dutton, 1975.

La trama celeste (short stories; title means "The Celestial Plot"), Sur, 1948, reprinted as *La trama celeste y otros relatos,* Centro (Buenos Aires), 1981, translation by Simms published with her translation of *La invención de Morel* as *The Invention of Morel, and Other Stories from "La trama celeste,"* University of Texas Press, 1964, reprinted, 1985.

El sueño de los héroes (novel), Losada, 1954, reprinted, Alianza, 1976, translation by Diana Thorold published as *The Dream of Heroes,* Dutton, 1988.

(Editor and translator with Borges) *Cuentos breves y extraordinarios: Antología,* Raigal (Buenos Aires), 1955, revised and enlarged edition, Losada, 1973, translation by Anthony Kerrigan published as *Extraordinary Tales,* Souvenir Press, 1973.

(With Borges) *Crónicas de Bustos Domecq,* Losada, 1967, translation by di Giovanni published as *Chronicles of Bustos Domecq,* Dutton, 1976.

Diario de la guerra del cerdo (novel), Emecé, 1969, translation by Gregory Woodruff and Donald A. Yates published as *Diary of the War of the Pig,* McGraw, 1972.

Dormir al sol (novel), Emecé, 1973, translation by Levine published as *Asleep in the Sun,* Persea Books, 1975.

La aventura de un fotógrafo en La Plata (novel), Emecé, 1985, translation by Levine published as *Adventures of a Photographer,* Dutton, 1989.

IN SPANISH; SHORT STORIES

(Under pseudonym Martín Sacastru) *Diecisiete disparos contra lo provenir* (title means "Seventeen Shots Against the Future"), Editorial Tor (Buenos Aires), 1933.

Caos, Viau & Zona (Buenos Aires), 1934.

Luis Greve, muerto, Destiempo (Buenos Aires), 1937.

Las vísperas de Fausto, La Perdiz (Buenos Aires), 1949.

Historia prodigiosa (title means "Prodigious History"), Obregón (Mexico), 1956, enlarged edition, Emecé, 1961.

Guirnalda con amores: Cuentos (title means "A Garland of Love: Stories"), Emecé, 1959, reprinted, 1978.

El lado de la sombra (title means "The Shady Side"), Emecé, 1962.

El gran serafín, Emecé, 1967.

Historias de amor (title means "Love Stories"), Emecé, 1972.

Historias fantásticas (title means "Fantastic Stories"), Alianza, 1976.

El héroe de las mujeres, Emecé, 1978.

Historias desaforadas, Alianza, 1986.

IN SPANISH; WITH JORGE LUIS BORGES

(Under joint pseudonym H. Bustos Domecq) *Dos fantasías memorables* (short stories), Oportet & Haereses, 1946, reprinted under authors' real names with notes and bibliography by Horacio Jorge Becco, Edicom (Buenos Aires), 1971.

(Under joint pseudonym B. Suárez Lynch) *Un modelo para la muerte* (novel; title means "A Model for Death"), Oportet & Haereses, 1946.

Los orilleros [and] *El paraíso de los creyentes* (screenplays; titles mean "The Hoodlums" and "The Believers' Paradise"; first screenplay produced as an Argentine film, directed by Ricardo Luna, 1975), Losada, 1955, reprinted, 1975.

(And with Hugo Santiago) *Les Autres: Escenario original* (screenplay; produced as a French film directed by Santiago, 1974), C. Bourgois (Paris), 1974.

Nuevos cuentos de Bustos Domecq (short stories), Librería de la Ciudad, 1977.

IN SPANISH; EDITOR OR COMPILER WITH BORGES

(And with Ocampo) *Antología poética argentina* (title means "Anthology of Argentine Poetry"), prologue by Borges, Sudamericana, 1941.

(And translator with Borges) *Los mejores cuentos policiales* (title means "The Best Detective Stories"), Emecé, 1943, reprinted, Alianza, 1972.

(And translator with Borges) *Los mejores cuentos policiales: Segunda serie,* Emecé, 1951.

(And author of prologue, notes, and glossary with Borges) *Poesía gauchesca* (title means "Gaucho Poetry"), two volumes, Fondo de Cultura Económica, 1955.

Libro del cielo y del infierno (anthology; title means "Book of Heaven and Hell"), Sur, 1960, reprinted, 1975.

Also editor with Borges of series of detective novels, "The Seventh Circle," for Emecé, 1943-56.

IN SPANISH; OTHER

Prólogo (title means "Prologue"; miscellany), Editorial Biblos (Buenos Aires), 1929.

La nueva tormenta; o, La vida multiple de Juan Ruteño (title means "The New Storm; or, The Multiple Life of Juan Ruteño"; novel), Destiempo, 1935.

La estatua casera (miscellany), Ediciones del Jacaranda (Buenos Aires), 1936.

(With Ocampo) *Los que aman, odian* (title means "Those Who Love, Hate"; novel), Emecé, 1946.

Adolfo Bioy Casares (anthology), edited by Ofelia Kovacci, Ediciones Culturales Argentinas, Ministerio de Educación y Justicia, Dirección General de Cultura, 1963.

La otra aventura (title means "The Other Adventure"; essays), Galerna (Buenos Aires), 1968, reprinted, Emecé, 1986.

Adversos milagros: Relatos (anthology), prologue by Enrique Pezzoni, Monte Avila (Caracas), 1969.

Memoria sobre la pampa y los gauchos (title means "Remembrance of the Pampa and the Gauchos"; essay), Sur, 1970, reprinted, Emecé, 1986.

(Under pseudonym Javier Miranda) *Breve diccionario del argentino exquisito,* Barros Merino, 1971, enlarged edition with new prologue published under author's real name, Emecé, 1978.

Páginas de Adolfo Bioy Casares seleccionadas por el autor (title means "Pages by Adolfo Bioy Casares Selected by the Author"), preface by Alberto Lagunas, Celtia, 1985.

Contributor with Borges, under joint pseudonym B. Lynch Davis, to *Los Anales de Buenos Aires,* 1946-48. Editor with Borges of *Destiempo* (literary magazine), 1936.

SIDELIGHTS: Although in his native Argentina Adolfo Bioy Casares is a respected author of novels and short stories, his fame in the United States is largely due to his collaborative efforts with his more famous countryman, the late Jorge Luis Borges. The two met when Bioy Casares was seventeen, Borges nearly fifteen years his senior. However, Bioy Casares was already a published author and their mutual interest in books filled in whatever gap the difference in age might have meant otherwise. Within a few years of their meeting, they began to write together. Their first joint effort was a commercial pamphlet about yogurt (the Bioy Casares family owned a large dairy ranch and yogurt was one of their products). "That pamphlet was a valuable lesson to me," Bioy Casares recalls in Emir Rodríguez Monegal's *Jorge Luis Borges: A Literary Biography.* "After writing it, I was a different writer, more experienced and skillful. Any collaboration with Borges is the equivalent of years of work."

Rodríguez Monegal quotes Borges as saying that when the two writers worked together on their later fiction "a third man, Honorio Bustos Domecq, emerged and took over." Borges's biographer explains: "Borges and Bioy [Casares] had been replaced by their own creations. A new writer had been born, a writer who ought to be called 'Biorges' because he was neither Borges nor Bioy [Casares], and because he did not stick to one pseudonym." The pseudonym Honorio Bustos Domecq was a combination of the names of two of their great-grandfathers, as were their other pen names, B. Suárez Lynch and B. Lynch Davis. "In a 1964 interview," *Washington Post Book World* contributor Donald A. Yates notes, "Borges offered this insight into the nature of the collaboration. 'We wrote somewhat for each other and since everything happened in a joking mood, the stories turned out so involved, so baroque, that it was difficult to understand them. At first we made jokes, and in the end jokes on jokes. It was a kind of algebraic contest: jokes squared, jokes cubed. . . .'"

At first, the stories and novel which Bioy Casares and Borges wrote together were not very well received in Argentina. When Victoria Ocampo (whose magazine, *Sur,* published the first of the stories in 1942) learned that the Bustos Domecq stories were written by two men, she was appalled that a pseudonymous—and, therefore, frivolous—work had been connected with her serious literary journal. But, eventually, the stories of the Bioy Casares/Borges collaboration attracted the appropriate readers and recognition. As Rodríguez Monegal notes: "The readers [of the original works] did not realize that a joke could be serious, and that irony and parody are among the deadliest forms of criticism. The gap between readers and authors was unbridgeable. Not until Bustos Domecq's first book was reissued a quarter of a century later would it be read by readers who could see its point."

Both *Six Problems for Don Isidro Parodi* and *Chronicles of Bustos Domecq* have been applauded by U.S. reviewers. Some critics delight in the books' humor; others are impressed by the authors' social criticism. In the *New Republic* Clarence Brown refers to *Chronicles of Bustos Domecq*'s "sheer nonsensical hilarity," while in the *Atlantic* Phoebe-Lou Adams calls the same book "hilariously awful and a great creation." In the *Chicago Tribune Book World* Denis Lynn Heyck finds *Six Problems for Don Isidro Parodi* "an extremely funny book. . . . [It] mercilessly exposes Argentine pretentiousness, pseudo-cosmopolitanism, and shallow nativism. . . . And it caricatures those Argentines, and others who live life as if it were bad literature."

In *Six Problems for Don Isidro Parodi,* six people come to Isidro Parodi's jail cell for solutions to their problems. Rodríguez Monegal notices the irony in the "fact that the detective [is] himself in jail (convicted of a murder committed by somebody who had very good connections both with the local authorities and the police.)" Each story is a parody of a particular type of Argentine personality. The first problem, for instance, is proposed by Achilles Molinari, who Yates says represents "the foppish journalist," while the second pokes fun at members of the Argentine Academy of Letters.

Chronicles of Bustos Domecq (published under the authors' real names but purported to be written by Bustos Domecq) is a collection of tongue-in-cheek vignettes of characters from Argentine literary and artistic circles. One piece deals with the poet F. J. C. Loomis, who writes poems containing only one word because of his dislike of metaphors. In *Time* Paul Gray notes that Bustos Domecq explains the poor reception of Loomis's poem "Beret" was due "to the demands it makes on the reader of having to learn French." Other writers or artists Bustos Domecq describes in the short sketches include Adalberto Vilaseco, who repeatedly publishes the same poem, each time with a different title, and artist Antarctic A. Garay, who sets up pieces of junk and invites onlookers to admire the spaces between the numerous items—a concept he calls "concave sculpture."

In these works Bioy Casares and Borges disguise their social criticism with humor. Their complex parodies of the tragically "funny" Argentine society—one in which an author of Borges's stature was "promoted" by the national government from his library post to inspector of chickens and rabbits—deal with false

appearances and the acceptance of them as a normal part of Argentine life. They paint a world which Gray describes as "invariably monstrous; [full of] novels and poems that cannot be read, art that cannot be seen, architecture—freed from the 'demands of inhabitability'—that cannot be used." Plot complexity, humor, and the importance of appearances—constants in the work produced by Bioy Casares and Borges—are also found in Bioy Casares's solo efforts.

In Rodríguez Monegal's *Review* essay on Bioy Casares the critic refers to "the almost unbearable complexity of *A Plan for Escape* and the stories of *The Celestial Plot.*" The plots of *The Invention of Morel* and *Asleep in the Sun* are also somewhat complicated. In *The Invention of Morel,* for instance, the narrator is shipwrecked on what he believes to be a deserted island, but soon discovers a group of people on the island with him. After falling in love with one of them, Faustine, he discovers that she and her friends are merely images projected by a machine. Hopelessly in love, he attempts to become part of the film the machine is projecting. *Asleep in the Sun* tells the story of a man named Bordenave who sends his neurotic wife to a clinic only to have her come back "inhabited" by someone else's personality.

Some critics contend that these complex plots add to the humor of Bioy Casares's work. In *Nation,* for example, Richard Kostelanetz calls *The Invention of Morel* "marvelously comic" because of the narrator's repeated attempts to establish a relationship with a woman who does not exist. In the *Bulletin of Hispanic Studies* D. P. Gallagher refers to Bioy Casares's novels and short stories as "comic masterpieces whose fundamental joke is the gap that separates what his characters know from what is going on." Bordenave's efforts to get his wife out of the clinic are funny because they are rewarded with the return of her body but not of her spirit. This humor, like that in the parodies written with Borges, is a double-edged humor which carries bitterness along with the laughter it inspires.

Toronto *Globe and Mail* contributor Alberto Manguel calls Bioy Casares's work "extraordinary adventures told in a voice that is subtle, interesting and wise." According to Manguel, the reader who discovers Bioy Casares's fiction enters "further into the world of a writer who will, in time, come to be read as one of the wisest interpreters of our unfathomable and bewildering existence." The complex humor of the absurd tales produced by Bioy Casares and Borges, like that of Bioy Casares's solo works, serves to point to a possible better society in which our senses—and our governments—can be trusted to tell us the truth about our world and in which the artist and writer can produce truly meaningful works of artistic expression.

MEDIA ADAPTATIONS: Alain Resnais's film, "Last Year at Marienbad," was based on *A Plan for Escape;* three of the stories in *Six Problems for Don Isidro Parodi* were dramatized for radio broadcast by the British Broadcasting Corporation.

BIOGRAPHICAL/CRITICAL SOURCES:

BOOKS

Contemporary Literary Criticism, Gale, Volume 4, 1975, Volume 8, 1978, Volume 13, 1980.
Rodríguez Monegal, Emir, *Jorge Luis Borges: A Literary Biography,* Dutton, 1978.

PERIODICALS

Atlantic, April, 1976, January, 1979, April, 1981.
Bulletin of Hispanic Studies, July, 1975.
Chicago Tribune Book World, April 19, 1981.
Globe and Mail (Toronto), January 21, 1989.

Nation, October 11, 1965.
New Republic, June 5, 1976.
Review, fall, 1975.
Time, March 29, 1976.
Washington Post Book World, April 19, 1981.

—*Sketch by Marian Gonsior*

* * *

BLADES, Rubén 1948-

PERSONAL: Born July 16, 1948, in Panama City, Panama; son of Rubén Darío (a police detective) and Anoland Benita (an actress and singer; maiden name, Bellido de Luna) Blades; married Lisa A. Lebenzon (an actress), December 13, 1986. *Education:* Instituto Nacional, Panama, B.A., 1966; University of Panama, lic. in law and political science, 1973; Harvard University, LL.M., 1985. *Religion:* Roman Catholic.

ADDRESSES: Office—c/o David Maldonado Management, 1674 Broadway, Ste. 703, New York, N.Y. 10019. *Agent*—Paul Schwartman, International Creative Management, 8899 Beverly Hills Blvd., Los Angeles, Calif. 90048.

CAREER: Composer, singer, actor, and writer. Banco Nacional, Panama City, Panama, member of legal staff, 1973-74; Fania Records, New York City, recording artist and legal advisor, 1973-83; Elektra Records, New York City, recording artist, 1984—. Songwriter and performer with Pete Rodriguez, with the Willie Colón Combo, and as solo artist; composer of music for films, including "Q & A," 1990. Actor in films, including "Crossover Dreams," 1985, "The Milagro Beanfield War," 1988, and "The Two Jakes," 1990.

MEMBER: American Society of Composers, Authors, and Publishers (ASCAP), National Academy of Recording Arts and Sciences, Screen Actors Guild, American Federation of Television and Radio Artists, Harvard Law School Association (vice-president, 1984-85), Colegio Nacional de Abogados (Panamanian law association).

AWARDS, HONORS: Named honorary citizen, City of Chicago, 1984; *Time* magazine "Top Ten Albums of the Year" list, 1984, for *Buscando América,* and 1985, for *Escenas;* New York Award, 1985, for *Buscando América,* and 1986, for *Escenas;* New York Music Awards for Best Ethnic/International Act and Best Latin Act, *New York Post,* 1986; Grammy Award for Best Tropical Latin Performance, National Academy of Recording Arts and Sciences, 1986, for *Escenas.*

WRITINGS:

RECORDINGS

(With the Willie Colón Combo) *Metiendo Mano,* Fania, 1976.
(With the Willie Colón Combo) *Siembra,* Fania, 1977.
(With the Willie Colón Combo) *Canciones del Solar de los Aburridos,* Fania, 1982.
Maestra Vida, Fania, c. 1982.
Buscando América, Elektra, 1984.
Escenas, Elektra, 1985.
Agua de Luna, Elektra, 1987.
Nothing but the Truth, Elektra, 1988.

OTHER

(With León Ichaso and Manuel Arce) "Crossover Dreams" (screenplay), Miramax, 1985.

Contributor of book reviews and articles to periodicals, including *Village Voice;* author of political columns for Panamanian newspapers, including *La Estrella de Panamá.*

WORK IN PROGRESS: Three more recordings for Elektra.

SIDELIGHTS: Ever since he started writing and recording songs in the late sixties, Rubén Blades has been an innovator in the Latino music world. "An intellectual who maintains passionate ties to street-level Latino culture, Mr. Blades has been compared to such thoughtful pop-rock composers as Bruce Springsteen, Jackson Browne, and Paul Simon," Stephen Holden of the *New York Times* reports. At a time when salsa musicians mostly sung of dancing and good times, "Blades made the argument for a change in subject matter as a means of changing the stereotypes [of Latin Americans]," Pete Hamill relates in a *New York* article. Blades's lyrics are literate—the 1987 album *Agua de Luna* was inspired by the stories of Nobel winner Gabriel García Márquez—and deal with political and social concerns and everyday life in the barrio. Indeed, the artist feels so strongly about his lyrics being understood that he has translations included with his albums. The quality of his writing, along with his transforming of salsa "into what he terms an 'urban sound,' with instrumental trappings borrowed from rock and jazz," writes Anthony DePalma in the *New York Times,* has brought Blades popularity with critics and fans, Latinos and Anglos alike.

While Blades appreciates the success he has enjoyed outside the Latino community, he hasn't made a concerted attempt to "cross over" into mainstream popularity. "I find the whole idea of crossover dangerous, because it implies the abandonment of one base for another," he told Holden. Blades elaborated, saying that most "crossover" attempts fail because "they were either seeking to escape their own backgrounds or trying to cash in," he continued. "The attempts have been forced, rather than natural, and when the elements don't match, you have performers who end up looking like fools."

This concern about forsaking one's heritage became the genesis for the 1985 film "Crossover Dreams," which Blades co-wrote and starred in. The movie follows the attempts of a salsa singer, Rudy Veloz, to break into the mainstream music scene; in the process of pursuing stardom, however, Rudy abandons his friends and subsequently has no one to support him when he fails. While the plot of the story is "one of the hoariest clichés—the artist struggling for recognition and success," as *Washington Post* writer Richard Harrington observes, the film is "a big-hearted snapshot of life in East Harlem and its vibrant musical subculture."

Chicago Tribune movie critic Gene Siskel likewise states that "even though 'Crossover Dreams' treads familiar territory in its dramatic structure, the specific Latino terrain is as fresh as is [Blades,] its genuinely charismatic star." "As in pop songs, familiarity can give the artist an emotional edge, can be a tool for greater economy," explains *Los Angeles Times* reviewer Michael Wilmington. The film "might have had a better, subtler, fresher script, with somewhat deeper characterizations—but it doesn't necessarily need it. There are too many elements that keep it fresh . . . most of all, the wizardly economy of the storytelling." Wilmington concludes that the film "is hot, lyrical, spicy and soulful. . . . Anyone who passes it up is missing a rich, body- and heart-satisfying treat."

With his increased visibility as an actor and the recording of his first album in English, Blades has been the target of accusations that he is forsaking his Latino origins. In answer to these criticisms, Blades told *Time* writer Bill Barol: "You don't have to leave your background behind in order to see what's on the other side. The proposition is simple: let's talk. Let's meet in the middle someplace, and then we'll walk together." Blades views *Nothing but the Truth* as an attempt to allow Anglo audiences to share in his native music and culture; as DePalma quoted him as saying in concert: "I'm going to speak in English . . . , but don't accuse me of selling out or anything. These people [Anglos] came here to share our culture with us, and this will help them understand what we're trying to do."

In addition, Blades has frequently commented that English is also a part of the Latino tradition, whether it comes from the Afro-Cuban calypso music he heard as a child or the American rock 'n' roll popular in Panama when he was teenager. "I want people to acknowledge the possibilities of a Latin artist fully—meaning we can do English, too," Blades told *Rolling Stone* writer David Fricke. He accepts, however, that his unconventional career moves might cost him. As he explained to *Time*'s Guy D. Garcia, "I will never be a superstar. My role is to be different, to do what others won't do, and, as a result, my fortunes will always fluctuate. I will always be viewed with suspicion by some, though not by all, because I move against the current."

"I've always believed that music can do more than offer escape—it can help bring people together to change their lives," the singer remarked to Holden. Blades also hopes someday to express his concerns through political action in addition to his music. "Eventually I'll return to Panama and the odds are good I'll run for office," he told Barol. "I'll participate in some way. There's a need there for figures people can trust." Blades believes his experience in law (he is a member of the Panamanian bar and has a degree from Harvard) and his regular political commentaries (published in Panamanian newspapers) provide him with a legitimate background for public office. And he realizes that his singing can only do so much, as he noted to DePalma: "I made a foundation of talking and singing about people's lives. I'm proud of that and proud of my singing. But I can't sing forever with the world exploding around me."

AVOCATIONAL INTERESTS: Baseball, soccer, boxing, dominoes, collecting toy soldiers, old books, reading.

BIOGRAPHICAL/CRITICAL SOURCES:

BOOKS

Contemporary Musicians, Volume 2, Gale, 1990.

PERIODICALS

Chicago Tribune, October 4, 1985.
Los Angeles Times, October 2, 1985.
Newsweek, September 9, 1985.
New York, August 19, 1985.
New York Times, August 18, 1985, June 21, 1987.
Rolling Stone, April 23, 1987.
Time, July 11, 1988, January 29, 1990.
Village Voice, March 5, 1985.
Washington Post, October 11, 1985.

—*Sketch by Diane Telgen*

*   *   *

BLANCO FOMBONA, Rufino   1874-1944

PERSONAL: Born June 17, 1874, in Caracas, Venezuela; died in 1944.

CAREER: Politician, novelist, short story writer, publisher, and poet. Consul for Venezuela and Peru in Philadelphia, Pa., beginning 1894; attache in The Hague, Netherlands, beginning 1896; consul for Dominican Republic in Boston, Mass., beginning 1899; consul in Amsterdam, Netherlands, 1901-04; governor of state of Amazonas, Venezuela, beginning 1905; secretary to Venezuelan Chamber of Deputies, 1909; imprisoned for opposition to Venezuelan president Juan Vicente Gómez, 1909-10, exiled, 1914; founded publishing house of América in Madrid, Spain, 1915; civil governor of Navarre, Spain, 1934-37; returned to Venezuela; president, State of Miranda, Venezuela, 1937-39; minister of Spain to Uruguay, 1939.

WRITINGS:

Cuentos de poeta, Imprenta Americana, 1900.
Más allá de los horizontes (poems), Viuda de R. Serra, 1903.
El hombre de hierro (novel), Tipografía Americana, 1907.
Letras y letrados de Hispano-América, Sociedad de Ediciones Literarias y Artísticas, 1908.
La evolución política y social de Hispano-América, B. Rodríguez, 1911.
Judas capitolino, Imprenta de E. Garnier, 1912.
Cuentos americanos (dramas mínimos) juicios críticos de mm. Henri Barbusse y J. Ernest-Charles, Garnier Hermanos, 1913.
La lámpara de Aladino: Notículas, Renacimiento, 1915.
Grandes escritores de América, Renacimiento, 1917.
Cancionero del amor infelix, Editorial América, 1918.
Pequeña ópera lírica: Trovadores y trovas, Editorial América, 1919.
The Man of Gold, translated by Isaac Goldberg, Brentano's, 1920, published as *El hombre de oro,* edited by Virgil A. Warren, Oxford University Press, 1948.
Dramas mínimos, Biblioteca Nueva, 1920.
La máscara heroica (novel), Editorial Mundo Latino, 1923.
La espada del samuray, Editorial Mundo Latino, 1924.
La mitra en la mano (novel), 2nd edition, Editorial América, 1927.
Tragedias grotescas: Novelines de la fe, del amor, de la maldad y de la estupidez, Editorial América, 1928.
Diario de mi vida, 1904-1905, Ibero-Americana de Publicaciones, 1929.
Motivos y letras de España, Renacimiento, 1930.
La bella y la fiera (novel), Renacimiento, 1931.
Camino de imperfección: Diario de mi vida (1906-1913), Editorial América, 1933.
El secreto de la felicidad (novel), Editorial América, 1933.
El espejo de tres faces, Ediciones Ercilla, 1937.
El pensamiento vivo de Bolívar, Editorial Losada, 1942.
Dos años y medio de inquietud, [Caracas], 1942.
El espíritu de Bolívar (ensayo de interpretación psicológica), Impresores Unidos, 1943.
Mazorcas de oro, Impresores Unidos, 1943.
Mocedades de Bolívar: El héroe antes del heroísmo, Dirección de Cultura, Ministerio de Educación Nacional de Venezuela, 1945.
(Compiler) Simón Bolívar, *Bolívar, pintado por sí mismo,* Editora Nacional, 1955.
El conquistador español del siglo XVI: Ensayo de interpretación, Ediciones Edime, 1956.
Obras selectas, selected by Edgar Gabaldón Márquez, Ediciones EDIME, 1958.
(Editor) Simón Bolívar, *Tres excritos,* Ediciones del Ministerio de Educación, 1959.
Crítica de la obra de Gonzálezs Prada, Fondo de Cultura Popular, 1966.

Cartas de Blanco-Fombona a Unamuno, edited by Marcos Falcón Briceño, INCIBA, 1968.

Bolívar y la guerra a muerte: Epoca de Boves, 1813-1814, Ministerio de Educación, Departamento de Publicaciones, 1969.

(Contributor) *Rufino Blanco Fombona y sus coterráneos* (correspondence), compiled by Rafael Ramón Castellanos V, [Bogotá], 1970.

(Contributor) *Un sueño en el exilio (Carmen Luisa López de Vicena)* (correspondence), compiled by Rafael Ramón Castellanos V, Editorial Kelly, 1971.

Rufino Blanco Fombona íntimo, selected by Angel Rama, Monte Avila Editores, 1975.

(Author of prologue and notes) Felipe Larrazábal, *Bolívar,* edited by José Agustín Catalá, Ediciones Centauro, 1975.

Rufino Blanco Fombona (collection), compiled by Norberto Galasso, El Cid Editor, 1977.

(Editor) Simón Bolívar, *Pensamiento vivo del Libertador,* Ediciones Centauro, 1977.

General en jefe Rafael Urdaneta, Archivo General de la Nación, 1979.

(Editor) Carlos Pereyra, *El crimen de Woodrow Wilson,* Librería de M. Porrúa, 1981.

Ensayos históricos, Biblioteca Ayacucho, 1981.

Also author of *Autores americanos juzgados por españoles,* Casa Editorial Hispano-Americana. Contributor to *La Voz* and *El Sol.*

SIDELIGHTS: Rufino Blanco Fombona was a Venezuelan diplomat whose writings reflected his long service and political ideas. Many of his novels deal with corruption in politics; *El hombre de oro* looks at unscrupulous Venezuelan politicians, while *La mitra en la mano* examines the career of an ambitious priest. Some of his bitterness may have stemmed from his long exile from Venezuela during the dictatorship of Juan Vicente Gómez.

* * *

BLASCO IBAÑEZ, Vicente 1867-1928

PERSONAL: Born January 29, 1867, in Valencia, Spain; died January 28, 1928, in Menton, France; originally buried in France, reinterred in 1933 in Valencia, Spain; son of Gaspar Blasco Teruel and Ramona Ibáñez Martínez; married María Blasco del Cacho, November 8, 1891 (died, January, 1925); married Elena Ortúzar Bulnes, October, 1925; children: (first marriage) Mario, Libertad, Julio César, Sigfriedo. *Education:* University of Valencia, licentiate in civil and canonical law, 1888.

ADDRESSES: Home and office—Menton, France.

CAREER: Writer. Secretary to novelist Manuel Fernández y González, Madrid, Spain, beginning 1883. Legislative delegate for six terms; founder of Blasquista party.

AWARDS, HONORS: Honorary degree from George Washington University, Washington, D.C., 1920; Legion d'Honneur (France).

WRITINGS:

NOVELS

¡Viva la república! (Roméu el guerrillero) (novel in four volumes), Sempere, 1892, Volume 1: *En el crater del volcán,* Volume 2: *La hermosa Liejesa,* Volume 3: *La explosión,* Volume 4: *Guerra sin cuartel.*

Arroz y tartana (also see below), Sempere, 1894, reprinted, Plaza & Janés (Barcelona), 1976, translation by Stuart Edgar Gummon published as *The Three Roses,* Dutton, 1932.

Flor de mayo (includes four stories published in *Cuentos valencianos;* also see below), Sempere, 1896, reprinted, Plaza & Janés, 1978, translation by Arthur Livingston published as *The Mayflower: A Tale of the Valencian Seashore,* Dutton, 1921.

La barraca: Novela (also see below), Sempere, 1898, reprinted, Plaza & Janés, 1977, edited with introduction, notes, and vocabulary by Hayward Keniston, Holt, 1910, translation by Francis Haffkin Snow and Beatrice M. Mekota of original Spanish edition published as *The Cabin,* Knopf, 1917, translation published with a new introduction by John Garrett Underhill, 1938, reprinted, Fertig, 1975.

Entre naranjos (title means "Among the Orange Trees"), Prometeo, 1900, reprinted, Plaza & Janés, 1978, translation by Isaac Goldberg and Arthur Livingston published as *The Torrent,* Dutton, 1921.

Sónnica la cortesana, Sempere, 1901, reprinted, Plaza & Janés, 1978, translation by Frances Douglas published as *Sónnica,* Duffield, 1912.

Cañas y barro (also see below), Prometeo, 1902, reprinted, Plaza & Janés, 1978, translation by Issac Goldberg published as *Reeds and Mud,* Dutton, 1928, translation by Lester Beberfall published as *Reeds and Mud,* Branden Press (Boston), 1966.

La catedral (title means "The Cathedral"), Prometeo, 1903, reprinted, Plaza & Janés, 1976, translation by Mrs. W. A. Gillespie published as *The Shadow of the Cathedral,* Constable (London), 1909, Dutton, 1919.

El intruso, Prometeo, 1904, reprinted, Plaza & Janés, 1978, translation by Mrs. W. A. Gillespie published as *The Intruder,* Dutton, 1928.

La voluntad de vivir (title means "The Will to Live"), Prometeo, 1904, reprinted, Planeta (Barcelona), 1953.

La bodega, Sempere, 1905, translation by Goldberg published as *The Fruit of the Vine,* Dutton, 1919.

La horda, Sempere, 1905, translation by Mariano Joaquín Lorente published as *The Mob,* Dutton, 1927.

La maja desnuda (title means "The Nude Maja"), Prometeo, 1906, reprinted, Plaza & Janés, 1977, translation by Hayward Keniston published as *Woman Triumphant,* with an introductory note by the author, Dutton, 1920, translation by Frances Partridge published as *The Naked Lady,* Elek (London), 1969.

Sangre y arena (also see below), Sempere, 1908, reprinted, Plaza & Janés, 1976, translation by Frances Douglas published as *The Blood of the Arena,* A. C. McClurg (Chicago), 1911, translation by Mrs. W. A. Gillespie published as *Blood and Sand,* Simpkin, Marshall & Co., 1913, Dutton, 1919, published as *The Matador,* Nelson, 1918, edition based on Mrs. Gillespie's translation published as *Blood and Sand: The Life and Loves of a Bullfighter, A New English Version of the Novel,* Dell, 1951, translation by Frances Partridge published as *Blood and Sand,* Ungar, 1958.

Los muertos mandan, Prometeo, 1909, translation by Frances Douglas published as *The Dead Command,* Duffield, 1919, abridged Spanish edition edited by Frederick Augustus Grant Cowper and John Thomas Lister, Harper, 1934.

Luna Benamor (includes "El último león" and other stories; also see below), Prometeo, 1909, reprinted, Plaza & Janés, 1978, translation by Isaac Goldberg published under same title, J. W. Luce (Boston), 1919.

Los Argonautas: Novela, Prometeo, 1914, reprinted, Plaza & Janés, 1978.

Los cuatro jinetes del Apocalipsis, Prometeo, 1916, reprinted, Plaza & Janés, 1976, translation by Charlotte Brewster Jordan published as *The Four Horsemen of the Apocalypse,* Dutton, 1918, reprinted, 1962.

Mare Nostrum, Prometeo, 1918, reprinted, Plaza & Janés, 1977, translation by Jordan published as *Our Sea,* Dutton, 1919.

Los enemigos de la mujer, Prometeo, 1919, reprinted, Planeta, 1961, translation by Irving Brown published as *The Enemies of Women,* Dutton, 1920.

La tierra de todos (title means "Everyone's Land"), Prometeo, 1921, translation by Leo Ongley published as *The Temptress,* Dutton, 1923.

El paraíso de las mujeres (title means "The Paradise of Women"), Prometeo, 1922, reprinted, Plaza & Janés, 1978.

El comediante Fonseca, Rivadeneyra (Madrid), 1923.

La reina Calafia, Prometeo, 1923, reprinted, Plaza & Janés, 1978, translation published as *Queen Calafia,* Dutton, 1924.

El Papa del mar (also see below), Prometeo, 1925, translation by Arthur Livingston published as *The Pope of the Sea: An Historical Medley,* Dutton, 1927.

A los pies de Venus (los Borgia): Novela (sequel to *El Papa del mar*), Prometeo, 1926, reprinted, Prometeo (Mexico City), 1944, translation by Livingston published as *The Borgias; or, At the Feet of Venus,* Dutton, 1930.

Mademoiselle Norma, [Madrid], 1927.

El conde Garci-Fernández, reprinted, Cosmopolis, c. 1928.

En busca del Gran Kan (Cristóbal Colón) (title means "In Search of the Great Khan [Christopher Columbus]"), Prometeo (Valencia), 1929, reprinted, Plaza & Janés, 1978, translation by Livingston published as *Unknown Lands: The Story of Columbus,* Dutton, 1929.

El caballero de la Virgen (Alonso de Ojeda), Prometeo, 1929, reprinted, Planeta, 1959, translation by Livingston published as *Knight of the Virgin,* Dutton, 1930.

El fantasma de las alas de oro, Prometeo, 1930, translation by Livingston published as *The Phantom with Wings of Gold,* Dutton, 1931.

COLLECTIONS

Fantasías (leyendas y tradiciones) (title means "Fantasies [Legends and Traditions]"; short stories), Prometeo, 1887.

El adiós de Schubert (title means "Schubert's Goodbye"; short stories), Prometeo, 1888.

Cuentos valencianos (title means "Valencian Tales"), Prometeo, 1896, reprinted, Plaza & Janés, 1978.

La condenada (cuentos) (title means "The Condemned Woman [Stories]"; includes "En el mar" and other stories), Prometeo, 1900, published as *La condenada y otros cuentos,* Espasa-Calpe, 1960.

The Last Lion and Other Tales (translation of stories included in *Luna Benamor*), Four Seas (Boston), 1919.

El préstamo de la difunta (title means "The Loan of the Dead Woman"; stories; also see below), Prometeo, 1920, edited with introduction, notes, and vocabulary by George Baer Fundenburg and John F. Klein, Century, 1925.

Novelas de la costa azul (title means "Novellas of the Blue Coast"), Prometeo, 1924.

The Old Woman of the Movies, and Other Stories (translation of stories included in *El préstamo de la difunta*), Dutton, 1925.

Obras completas (title means "Complete Works"), eleven volumes, Prometeo, 1925-34, expanded edition published in three volumes, Aguilar, 1946, reprinted, 1964.

Siete cuentos de Vicente Blasco Ibáñez, edited with introduction, notes, and vocabulary by Sturgis E. Leavitt, Holt, 1926.

The Mad Virgins, and Other Stories (translation of stories from *El préstamo de la difunta* and other collections), Butterworth, 1926.

Novelas de amor y de muerte (title means "Novellas of Love and Death"), Prometeo, 1927.

La araña negra (title means "The Black Spider"), eleven volumes, Cosmopolis (Madrid), 1928, published in two volumes, A. T. E. (Barcelona), 1975.

Cuentos escogidos (title means "Selected Stories"), edited by J. Bayard Morris, Dent, 1932.

Tres novelas valencianas: Arroz y tartana, La barraca, Cañas y barro, Plenitud (Madrid), 1958.

OTHER

Historia de la revolución española (desde la guerra de la independencia a la restauración en Sagunto) 1808-1874 (title means "History of the Spanish Revolution [from the War of Independence to the Restauration in Sagunto] 1808-1874"), three volumes, Enciclopedia Democrática (Barcelona), 1892, reprinted, Cosmopolis, 1930.

París, impresiones de un emigrado (title means "Paris, An Emmigrant's Impressiones"), Prometeo, 1893.

El juez (title means "The Judge"; play), Ripollés, 1894.

En el país del arte (tres meses en Italia) (travel), Pellicers (Valencia), 1896, reprinted, Plaza & Janés, 1980, translation by Douglas published as *In the Land of Art,* Dutton, 1923.

(Translator from the French and author of preface) Onesime Reclús and J. J. E. Reclús, *Novísima geografía universal,* six volumes, La Novela Ilustrada (Madrid), 1906-07.

Oriente (title means "East"; travel), Prometeo, 1907, reprinted, Plaza & Janés, 1980.

(Translator from the French) Ernesto Laviss and Alfredo Rambaud, *Novísima historia univeral, dirigida a partir del siglo IV,* fifteen volumes, Prometeo, 1908-30.

Argentina y sus grandezas (title means "Argentina and Her Grandeurs"; travel), Española Americana (Madrid), 1910.

Historia de la guerra europea de 1914 (title means "History of the European War of 1914"), Prometeo, thirteen volumes, 1914-19.

(Translator from the French) J. C. Mardrus, *El libro de los mil y una noches,* twenty-three volumes, Prometeo, 1915.

The Bull Fight (Spanish and English text; extract from *Sangre y arena*), translation by C. D. Campbell, Harrap, 1919.

El militarismo mejicano: Estudios publicados en los principales diarios de los Estados Unidos (contains articles originally published in US newspapers), Prometeo, 1920, reprinted, Plaza & Janés, 1979, translation by José Padín and Arthur Livingston published as *Mexico in Revolution,* Dutton, 1920.

Vistas sudamericanas (title means "South American Views"; excerpts), edited by Carolina Marcial Dorado, Ginn, 1920.

Una nación secuestrada (El terror militarista en España), J. Dura (Paris), 1924, translation by Leo Ongley published as *Alfonso XIII Unmasked: The Military Terror of Spain,* Dutton, 1924.

Blasco Ibáñez: Paisajista (title means "Blasco Ibáñez: Landscape Artist"; contains excerpts from his works), edited by Camille Pitollet, Vuibert (Paris), 1924.

La vuelta al mundo de un novelista (memoirs), three volumes, Prometeo, 1924-25, reprinted, Planeta, 1958, translation by Leo Ongley and Arthur Livingston published as *A Novelist's Tour of the World,* Dutton, 1926.

Lo que será la república española: Al país y al ejército (title means "What the Spanish Republic Will Become; To the Country and to the Army"), La Gutenberg (Valencia), 1925.

Por España y contra el rey, Excelsior (Paris), 1925.

Estudios literarios (title means "Literary Studies"; essays chiefly on French authors), Prometeo, 1933.

Discursos literarios (title means "Literary Lectures"), Prometeo, 1966.

Crónicas de viaje (title means "Travel Chronicles"), Prometeo, 1967.

Contra la Restauración: Periodismo político, 1895-1904 (articles previously published in *El Pueblo*), compiled by P. Smith, Nuestra Cultura (Madrid), 1978.

Founding editor, *El Pueblo* (Valencian newspaper), beginning 1891.

SIDELIGHTS: A novelist, politician, and adventurer who enjoyed worldwide fame during the first part of the twentieth century, Vicente Blasco Ibáñez remains a controversial figure in Spanish literature. Blasco Ibáñez was a nonconformist committed to political and social action and to the toppling of the Spanish Monarchy that ruled Spain during his lifetime; he pursued these goals both directly as a political activist and indirectly through several of his novels. In his youth his rebellious spirit caused his expulsion from school, and as Ricardo Landeira has pointed out in *The Modern Spanish Novel, 1898-1936,* "this incident of rebelliousness marks the beginning of a chronicled biography that reads like an adventure story worthy of Blasco [Ibáñez] the novelist." Repeatedly in his early adulthood he was incarcerated for his outspoken criticism of the government. By the author's own account, his stays in Spanish jails numbered as many as thirty.

No less evident than his nonconformist spirit was Blasco Ibáñez's strong literary and journalistic inclination. As a young student, he compiled short stories and news items for circulation among his classmates and wrote an original short story for submission to a literary competition. Blasco Ibáñez later founded *El Pueblo,* a liberal newspaper which served as a vehicle for his political ideas and in which he also published short stories and novels in serialized form. Yet throughout his young adult years he compromised his reputation as a writer by moving farther and farther into the realm of political and social activism, a fact that at least partially explains Blasco Ibáñez's often unfavorable treatment in Spanish literary histories. In many ways he represented a new literary phenomenon: he shattered the traditional model of the passive intellectual who did not take sides.

Blasco Ibáñez's early novels and short stories, all set in his native Valencia, stand as highly original and significant artistic contributions to modern Spanish literature. In his early works, Blasco Ibáñez proved himself a natural storyteller and a master of descriptive technique in the Naturalistic and Impressionistic modes. Often referred to as his "Valencian cycle" or "regional works," the novels included in this group are *Arroz y tartana* (*The Three Roses,* 1894), *Flor de mayo* (*The Mayflower,* 1896), *La barraca* (*The Cabin,* 1898), *Entre naranjos* (*The Torrent,* 1900), and *Cañas y barro* (*Reeds and Mud,* 1902). Also belonging to this group are such short story collections as *Cuentos valencianos* ("Valencian Tales," 1896) and *La condenada y otros cuentos* ("The Condemned Woman, and Other Stories," 1900).

In these early works Blasco Ibáñez treated subjects and settings with which he had had direct contact and revealed an acute understanding of regional social problems. Elements of Naturalism—deterministic themes (such as the human being's subjugation to the natural elements), a focus on the common individual and his struggle for survival in a hostile or uncaring society, and an essential note of pessimism—color these works. But what often separates them from conventional Naturalistic narratives is the quality of the struggle depicted. Blasco Ibáñez's characters often take on heroic proportions; they are rarely Naturalism's

sickly, feeble men and women, predisposed to failure because of their physical makeup or their heredity.

In his regional works Blasco Ibáñez created an artistic canvas that captured the quintessential aspects of the people of Valencia as they lived and worked at the turn of the century. *The Three Roses* portrays the materialistic aspirations of the bourgeoisie; *The Mayflower* and *Reeds and Mud* depict the lives of the people associated with the fishing industry so important to the region; *The Cabin* vividly recreates the hardships of the farmer; and *The Torrent,* which uses the Valencian orange groves as a poetic backdrop, addresses the conflict between materialistic or political aspirations and the desire for purity and beauty.

These novels represent significant contributions to Spanish Naturalism and Realism for several reasons. Blasco Ibáñez surpassed many of his contemporaries such as Jose María Pereda and Pedro Antonio de Alarcón who, in keeping with the *costumbrista* mode of literature with its focus on customs, types, and characteristic scenes of a particular region, created a rather superficial, romantic image of society. Although Blasco Ibáñez did make extensive use of local color and picturesque details, these features never constituted the final objective of his writing. In *Historia social de la literatura española,* Carlos Blanco Aguinaga comments on this dimension of Blasco Ibáñez's works, stating that "the characteristic Spanish *costumbrista* novel . . . never offers a realistic critical analysis of social conflicts nor a progressive interpretation of those conflicts that one finds in these works of Blasco Ibáñez."

The Mayflower illustrates Blasco Ibáñez's combining of local color and realistic social analysis. In this novel the *costumbrista* stamp appears in the extensive references to and description of local customs (for example, religious processions and the practice of inaugurating new boats) and in the vision of the fishermen's and fisherwomen's everyday dealings at sea and in the fish market. But the overriding theme of the novel concerns the tremendous danger to which the fishermen must expose themselves and the small compensation they receive from society. In the final episode of the novel, the village witnesses the destruction of a fishing boat during a terrifying storm, and Tía Picores, a wise elder of the town and in many ways a living monument of the region's psychological and spiritual makeup—stoic, proud, hardworking, moral, and peace-loving—conveys Blasco Ibáñez's theme. When the boat has finally crashed against the rocks, and hope has faded for a possible sole survivor (a young child who has been equipped with a life preserver and thrown from the ship), Tía Picores turns away to face the city and cries out: "And after this they'll come to the Fishmarket, the harlots, and beat you down, and beat you down! And still they'll say fish comes high, the scullions! And cheap 't would be at fifty, yes, at seventy-five a pound!"

Along with this thematic consideration Blasco Ibáñez's early works embody a stylistic feature that also proves original to fiction in the Naturalistic mode: the use of simile and metaphor to create a dramatic tension between the character and his environment. *The Cabin* is exemplary in this respect. In an article appearing in *Hispania,* Douglas Rogers summarizes this technique: "The suggestive power of the similes rings so emphatically throughout the novel that the 'as if' situations are as though converted into effective power, and the sense of a huge, all-controlling destiny, where there once were Greek and Roman Gods, swallows up the smaller intellectual concept of socio-political determinism."

Blasco Ibáñez records and dramatically evokes vivid sensations. In so doing, he imbues nature with an often very poetic sense of mystery and power. This quality in Blasco Ibáñez's works is often obscured by Naturalistic features, such as determinism and a belief in the destructive power of man's base instincts, which, to be sure, are present in Blasco Ibáñez's works. But the poetic quality is just as important since the sea, the earth, and the other natural elements described in the fiction are intrinsically poetic. Nature is a cruel, destructive force; it is also something marvelous and beautiful.

Thematically, the presentation of nature in these terms emphasizes the tragic dimension of the works since the characters are victims of their own courses of action and not mere toys of impersonal, destructive, deterministic forces. Blasco Ibáñez's characters are strong-willed and healthy individuals, who in refusing to accept their human limitations and to pay heed to warnings ultimately bring about their own downfall. In *The Mayflower,* for example, the protagonist decides to set sail in the storm, knowing that he is placing himself and his crew in great danger. When he realizes his mistake, he relies upon his abilities as a seaman and makes a desperate but failing attempt to defy the elements.

A variation on this theme appears in one of Blasco Ibáñez's most famous short stories, "En el mar" ("At sea"). Here, the protagonist sets out to catch a huge tuna, and when a storm threatens, the character blindly but boldly moves forward, venturing far out into the sea. After a preliminary encounter with the fish, which nearly results in his boat being capsized, a clear warning to the would-be hero, the protagonist is even more determined to catch his prey. He finally succeeds, though at a terrible price: his young son is thrown from the boat during the violent struggle with the fish and is given up for dead. Yet another example of this bold behavior appears in *The Cabin* as a newly arrived farmer decides to cultivate a parcel of land that all the other farmers of the region, joined together in a spirit of solidarity, have sworn to abandon in protest of the unjust treatment and death of the farmer who previously occupied that land. As in the previous narratives, the protagonist is given several warnings but nevertheless persists in his endeavour, even if it means placing his family in great danger. When his cabin is finally burned down, he is forced to leave.

Bernardo Suárez in a *Cuadernos hispanoamericanos* essay states that "nature as it is presented in *The Cabin* . . . is a favorable agent . . . a type of paradise." The notion of paradise helps define man's relationship to nature, a subject that manifests itself repeatedly in Blasco Ibáñez's regional novels and short stories. These works artistically convey man as a primitive being exiled from a mythic paradise; providing a chronicle of the social and historical changes that were taking place in Spain at the turn of the century, the regional fiction depicts the lives of individuals caught between present and past, between, on the one hand, the realities of a mechanized economy, government intervention, and a social gospel of "progress" and, on the other, the futile yearning to regain harmony with nature.

In terms of narration, Blasco Ibáñez wrote in an objective omniscient mode, often relying on dialogue and indirect discourse to maintain his distance from the work and thereby producing, as Sherman H. Eoff declares in *The Modern Spanish Novel,* "an unusually strong singleness of narrative effect." In adopting the omniscient voice Blasco Ibáñez remained faithful to Naturalism, which in theory sought to emulate the laboratory setting of the scientist to insure objectivity and to obtain a "truer" sense of reality. But he rarely made use of Naturalism's encyclopedic descriptive approach, where even the most minute detail is recorded. And in spite of his predominantly objective tone, Blasco

Ibáñez often playfully interacted with his characters by adding a humorous comment or juxtaposing images that end an ironic quality to his prose. He did not make extensive use of irony, especially as a narrative framework, but it does appear in several novels and short stories; for example, in "El último león" ("The Last Lion"), a masterful sketch portraying an anachronistic Valencian artisan who champions the cause of tradition (dressing like a legendary lion in a religious procession) in a world which has long since disassociated itself from its noble, legendary past. In such instances the reader encounters compassion, admiration, and humor in the narrator's characterization, but there is no romantic idealization or nostalgic appeal as in the typical *costumbrista* writer.

After the regional works, Blasco Ibáñez wrote a series of novels which are commonly referred to as his "thesis cycle." Each of these novels bore a specific ideological orientation and sought to denounce a particular aspect of Spanish society. Much more political than the preceding works, these novels are generally considered artistically inferior to the Valencian cycle. If the early works present a realistic image of society in its many aspects, the thesis cycle addresses specific problems articulated through the struggle of the worker (the proletariat) for economic and political emancipation. *La catedral* (*In the Shadow of the Cathedral,* 1903) seeks to unveil the retrogressive effect of the Catholic Church on the Spaniard; *El intruso* (*The Intruder,* 1904) deals with the problems of the mine workers in northern Spain; *La horda* (*The Mob,* 1905) focuses on the conditions of the inhabitants of Madrid's ghettos; and *La bodega* (*The Fruit of the Vine,* 1905) is an expose of southern Spain's sherry industry, which on the one hand exploits Spanish workers and on the other produces the widely consumed alcohol that ultimately enslaves them by inhibiting their intellectual growth. Other novels can also be loosely classified within this group: *La maja desnuda* (*Woman Triumphant,* 1906) examines the manner in which artistic talent is stifled by capitalistic influences, and *Sangre y arena* (*Blood and Sand,* 1908), the best novel of this group, portrays the bullfighter as a victim of society and tradition. Using as a setting the Balearic Islands, *Los muertos mandan* (*The Dead Command,* 1909) addresses the problem of social barriers and racial prejudices, a theme that reappears in *Luna Benamor* (1909).

Although these works risk being viewed as nothing more than propagandistic documents, they also significantly contribute to modern Spanish literature. Examined in the specific historical context from which they were conceived, they represent an important development in what would later become the contemporary novel of Social Realism. Transitional works, they break with the Naturalistic model by replacing the unique protagonist with the collective protagonist and by discarding the individual focus on a particular scene or situation for a larger historical vision of the worker's universal struggle for equality and justice through socialism. In the novels of the thesis cycle, actual events and social movements are recognizable; for example, the 1892 peasant uprising in southern Spain is incorporated into *The Fruit of the Vine.* One might even say that through his creation of this group of novels Blasco Ibáñez could be considered the father of the modern Spanish novel. This opinion is advanced by Raphael Bosch who declares in *La novela española del siglo XX* that Blasco Ibáñez helped inaugurate "an open novel, attentive to the immediate reality, urgent, common, in opposition to the closed action and the more or less explored characters, all as protagonists, characteristic in the nineteenth century."

The cycle of thesis novels might also be considered important for the light it casts on Blasco Ibáñez's relationship with the universally acclaimed group of Spanish writers known as the Generation of 1898, a group to which he technically belonged by virtue of his birthdate. This group included such prominent philosophical and literary figures as Miguel de Unamuno and Pío Baroja, but critics have commonly excluded Blasco Ibáñez from this circle on aesthetic grounds: the Generation of 1898 espoused an innovative and experimental style of writing whereas Blasco Ibáñez continued to pursue the traditional, realistic manner.

All of these writers, however, including Blasco Ibáñez, were deeply concerned with the fate of Spain; they saw the once vast and mighty Spanish empire quickly decline when, defeated by the United States in the Spanish-American War of 1898, it lost its last territorial possessions and whatever remained of its world power. Both Blasco Ibáñez and the members of this group wanted to remedy the ills of Spain by introducing national reforms. To this end, Blasco Ibáñez proposed the formation of an Academy of Arts and Letters similar to that in France. Initially, the response of the Generation of 1898 was positive, and the Academy was in fact formed, if only in theory. Eduardo Betoret-Paris has observed in an article published in *Hispania* that "not only [was] there a lot in common between the concerns of Blasco [Ibáñez] and those of the most distinguished components of the Generation of 1898, but these members also [accepted] Blasco [Ibáñez]'s leadership in these enterprises, perhaps because they [knew] that Blasco [Ibáñez did] not suffer from the so often referred to *abulia* (apathy)," a common symptom experienced by these writers.

If in his thesis novels Blasco Ibáñez was primarily concerned with criticizing contemporary society, in most of his subsequent novels his goal was quite different: he conceived a monumental work of several volumes in which he would present to the world an account of Spain's glorious past, focusing on figures and events that were not well known. This phase of historical vindication might well have represented a desire on Blasco Ibáñez's part to balance the negative image of Spain elaborated in his previous novels. On the other hand, the historical framework also allowed him to incorporate his life experiences outside of Spain, especially since many of the themes he treated dealt with voyages, conquest, and discovery. Blasco Ibáñez had traveled extensively, giving speeches wherever he went, often about Spain. In many ways he himself was both the Columbus protagonist of *En busca del Gran Kan* (*Unknown Lands: The Story of Columbus,* 1929) and the character Alonso de Ojeda, one of Columbus's ship commanders during his second voyage to the Americas, in *El caballero de la Virgen* (*The Knight of the Virgin,* 1929). Like them, he was engaged in a "mission"; he was spreading Spanish culture throughout the Spanish speaking Americas and the United States as well. Other characters presented in these works are less convincing as historical figures: the Spanish Benedict XIII, Avignon pope during the Church schism in *El papa del mar* (*The Pope of the Sea,* 1925), and the Borgias, also Spanish popes, in *A los pies de Venus (los Borgias)* (*The Borgias; or, At the Feet of Venus,* 1926).

Blasco Ibáñez was at the pinnacle of his success during this later period of his life, having a sure platform and an international audience, but this position of renown ultimately proved detrimental to the artistic quality of these works. In most of these writings, his artistry gave way to a formulaic approach to literature in which he wrote to a thesis or endeavored to produce bestsellers. His later books are often marred by incongruous and extraneous elements of romance and intrigue, unrealistic descriptions, and anachronisms. Such works pleased the uncritical reader of commercial fiction but did little to enhance Blasco Ibáñez's reputation in literary circles. His early, regional works,

however, continue to be held in great esteem by readers throughout the world.

MEDIA ADAPTATIONS: La tierra de todos was adapted for a stage production by L. Linares Becerra, 1927; *Blood and Sand* and *The Four Horsemen of the Apocalypse* were made into films of the same titles starring Rudolph Valentino, produced by Paramount Pictures; *The Four Horsemen of the Apocalypse* was made into a film starring Glenn Ford and Charles Boyer, 1961; four other novels were also made into U.S. films.

BIOGRAPHICAL/CRITICAL SOURCES:

BOOKS

Bell, Aubrey F. G., *Contemporary Spanish Literature,* Knopf, 1925.
Blanco Aguinaga, Carlos, and others, *Historia social de la literatura española,* Castalia, 1978.
Bosch, Rafael, *La novela española del siglo XX,* Volume 1, Las Américas, 1970.
Cejador y Frauca, Julio, *Historia de la lengua y literatura castellana,* Volume 9, Revista de Archivos, Biliotecas y Museos, 1918.
Day, A. Grove, and Edgar C. Knowlton, *Vicente Blasco Ibáñez,* Twayne, 1972.
Eoff, Sherman H., *The Modern Spanish Novel: Comparative Essays Examining the Philosophical Impact of Science on Fiction,* New York University Press, 1961.
Landeira, Ricardo, *The Modern Spanish Novel, 1898-1936,* Twayne, 1985.
Twentieth-Century Literary Criticism, Volume 12, Gale, 1984.

PERIODICALS

Cuadernos hispanoamericanos, May, 1981.
Hispania, Volume 53, number 1, 1969, Volume 53, number 4, 1970.

*   *   *

BODET, Jaime Torres
See TORRES BODET, Jaime

*   *   *

BOMBAL, María Luisa   1910-1980

PERSONAL: Born June 8, 1910, in Viña del Mar, Chile; died May 6, 1980, in Chile; married Count Raphael de Saint-Phalle (a Wall Street financier), c. 1945. *Education:* Attended Ecole Notre Dame de l'Assomption, Lycée La Bruyere, and the Sorbonne, University of Paris.

CAREER: Writer. Worked as a screenwriter for Sonofilm in Argentina, 1937-40. Chilean representative to the International PEN conference held in the United States, 1940.

MEMBER: International PEN.

AWARDS, HONORS: Annual prize from the Chilean Academy of Arts and Letters, 1977, for *La historia de María Griselda;* municipal prize from the city of Santiago, Chile, 1942, for the novella *La amortajada.*

WRITINGS:

La última niebla (novella; title means "The Final Mist"; originally published alone, 1935; subsequent editions also contain the short stories "El árbol" and "Las islas nuevas"),

2nd edition, Nascimento, 1941, 8th edition, Editorial Orbe, 1975, translation of title story, revised with husband, Raphael de Sainte-Phalle, published separately as *The House of Mist,* Farrar, Straus, 1947.

La amortajada (novella), Sur, 1938, reprinted, Editorial Universitaria, 1981, translation by Bombal published as *The Shrouded Woman,* Cassell, 1950.

(Translator) Jules Supervielle, *La desconocida del Sena,* Editorial Losada, 1962.

La historia de María Griselda, Editorial "El Observador," 1976.

OMNIBUS VOLUMES

La última niebla (contains *La última niebla,* "El árbol," "Las islas nuevas," and "Lo secreto"), introduction by Amado Alonso, Andina, 1981.

La última niebla, El arbol, Las islas nuevas, Lo secreto: Textos completos, Editorial Andrés Bello, 1982.

New Islands, and Other Stories (contains "The Final Mist," "The Tree," "Braids," "The Unknown," and "New Islands"), translated by Richard and Lucia Cunningham, preface by Jorge Luis Borges, Farrar, Straus, 1982.

La última niebla [and] *La amortajada,* Seix Barral, 1984.

La amortajada; y, El arbol, Zig-Zag, 1984.

SIDELIGHTS: María Luisa Bombal was one of the most esteemed Latin American writers of the twentieth century. Although she produced only a small body of work during her lifetime and was relatively unknown in English-speaking countries until after her death, Bombal is credited with changing the style, tone, and substance of Hispanic literature. Her avant-garde works—considered early examples of feminist writing—deviated from the exaggeratedly masculine, regionalistic, and realistic trends that dominated South American fiction through the 1930s. Composed in reaction to the confines of her patriarchal society, Bombal's lyrical prose writings center on women who escape their lonely, unfulfilled existences through fantasy.

A native Chilean of Argentine and German descent, Bombal wrote the bulk of her fiction during the mid-1930s while living in Chile. Her works, which are characterized by the use of powerful imagery, recurring themes, and fantastic symbolism, illuminate the conflicts of being a woman, especially in a South American society dominated by males. Bombal composed her first novella, *La última niebla,* at the kitchen counter of an apartment she shared with poet Pablo Neruda and his wife in Buenos Aires. The story was first published in Spanish in 1935; twelve years later, it was revised, enlarged, and published in English as *The House of Mist.* Set in South America, the tale revolves around Helga, a woman who resorts to a dream life for satisfaction after realizing that her new husband, Daniel, remains devoted to his dead wife; the novella is titled for the white mist that rolls up from the lagoon where Daniel's first wife was drowned. Helga finds the fog suffocating, as indicated in a passage from the story excerpted in the *New York Times Book Review:* "[It enshrouds and obscures] the color of the walls, the contours of the furniture, entwining itself in my hair, clinging to my body, smothering everything . . . everything."

American critics found the tale somewhat oversentimentalized but nonetheless intriguing. In a review for the *New York Times* Richard Sullivan noted, "Bombal's heroine dwells far too steadily on her raptures," but conceded that the book's "familiar substance [is] ingeniously twisted"; he judged *The House of Mist* to be "dexterous, amoral, delicate," and suffused with "a kind of engaging breathlessness of manner."

Bombal's 1938 novella *La amortajada* is an unusual story told from the point of view of a dead woman. Ana María reflects on her life, her loves, and her feelings of hopelessness as she lies in state at her own funeral. Several critics praised Bombal for her insightful portrait of human conflict and stunning use of lush prose. Marjorie Brace, reviewing the English translation of the work (titled *The Shrouded Woman*) for the *Saturday Review,* commented that the story was at once "amazingly horrid and uncommonly dreadful." She went on to describe Bombal's writing as "a kind . . . seldom produced in [the United States], the ideology of which does not encourage a mysticism of destructiveness." Argentine novelist and art critic Marta Traba, writing in *Américas,* dubbed Bombal's work "the literature of despair." According to Traba, "Death is welcome, not as a romantic figure but as a practical solution" for Ana María in *La amortajada,* as "it separates her from those who used, ignored, or humiliated her" during her life.

In 1941 Bombal shot and seriously wounded Eulogio Sánchez Errazuriz, her anticommunist lover. She was jailed and, upon Errazuriz's recovery, banished from Chile. Bombal then immigrated to the United States. In an article for *Américas* Cuban art critic José Gómez-Sicre recalled his affiliation with Bombal, which began in 1944 when they were introduced by a mutual friend. Gómez-Sicre, Bombal, and Cuban painter Mario Carreño—who had an unrequited romantic interest in the author—spent the winter of 1944 together, watching old films shown at New York City's Museum of Modern Art. They passed cold afternoons in neighborhood bars, debating and discussing topics that ranged from the chances for a democratic victory in World War II to the new trends in European cinema. Gómez-Sicre related, "María Luisa reasoned that the only way to get warm on those freezing February [days] was to have a properly chilled and decidedly dry martini. . . . She could handle four with no difficulty."

Although a Hollywood studio had purchased the rights to *La última niebla* and asked Bombal to compose the script, the film version was never produced. This disappointment, suggested Gómez-Sicre, along with her predisposition to melancholia, may have contributed to Bombal's eventual battle with alcoholism. She remained in the United States until her husband, Raphael de Saint-Phalle, died in 1970. Ten years after returning to Chile, the writer died in her sleep and "like [the corpse in] *La amortajada,*" noted Gómez-Sicre, was cremated.

Bombal's English-speaking audience expanded after her death with the release of *New Islands, and Other Stories* in 1982. Containing the English translation of five stories, including the original, unlengthened version of *La última niebla* published as *The Final Mist,* the entire collection is informed by the author's preoccupation with the powers of the imagination. "Of earth and sea and sky," wrote Bombal as quoted by James Polk in the *Nation,* "I know an infinity of small and magic secrets." One enchanting story in the *New Islands* volume, "The Unknown," is about a pirate ship lost in a whirlpool at the bottom of the sea. A frequently anthologized piece titled "The Tree" chronicles a woman's growing alienation from her husband. The man "is emotionally dead, incapable of responding to her need for love," noted Rona Berg in the *Voice Literary Supplement.* As excerpted by Ronald De Feo in the *New York Times Book Review,* the closing lines of "The Tree" capture Bombal's basic philosophy: "It may be that true happiness lies in the conviction that one has irremediably lost happiness. It is only then that we can begin to live without hope or fear, able finally to enjoy all the small pleasures, which are the most lasting."

New Islands was well received in the United States. Critics were particularly impressed by Bombal's ability to elicit empathy in her readers. Berg stated, "We drown in silence along with [the author's] characters," and asserted, "Bombal's writing is subtle and beautiful, sensual, yet restrained. . . . It has the rhythm of somnolent breathing. Her tone emulates the murmur of the subconscious."

Bombal's reactionary writings changed the face of Hispanic fiction and prefigured magic realism—a South American literary movement whose fiction aims to depict imaginary and fantastic scenes in a realistic way. Having influenced a later generation of Spanish writers, including Carlos Fuentes, Gabriel García Márquez, and José Donoso, Bombal remains, according to some observers, the most innovative female voice in twentieth-century Latin American literature.

BIOGRAPHICAL/CRITICAL SOURCES:

PERIODICALS

Américas, February, 1981.
Nation, December 11, 1982.
New York Times Book Review, April 13, 1947, December 19, 1982.
Saturday Review, May 1, 1948.
Times Literary Supplement, December 9, 1983.
Voice Literary Supplement, October, 1982.

—*Sketch by Barbara Carlisle Bigelow*

* * *

BONDY, Sebastián Salazar
See SALAZAR BONDY, Sebastián

* * *

BORGES, Jorge Luis 1899-1986
(F[rancisco] Bustos; joint pseudonyms: H[onorio] Bustos Domecq, B. Lynch Davis, B. Suárez Lynch)

PERSONAL: Born August 24, 1899, in Buenos Aires, Argentina; died June 14, 1986, in Geneva, Switzerland, of liver cancer; buried in Plainpalais, Geneva, Switzerland; son of Jorge Guillermo Borges (a lawyer, teacher, and writer) and Leonor Acevedo Suárez (a translator); married Elsa Astete Millán, September 21, 1967 (divorced, 1970); married María Kodama, April 26, 1986. *Education:* Attended College Calvin, Geneva, Switzerland, 1914-18.

ADDRESSES: Home—Geneva, Switzerland.

CAREER: Writer. Miguel Cané branch library, Buenos Aires, Argentina, municipal librarian, 1937-46; teacher of English literature at several private institutions and lecturer in Argentina and Uruguay, 1946-55; National Library, Buenos Aires, director, 1955-73; University of Buenos Aires, Buenos Aires, professor of English and U.S. literature, beginning 1956. Visiting professor or guest lecturer at numerous universities in the United States and throughout the world, including University of Texas, 1961-62, University of Oklahoma, 1969, University of New Hampshire, 1972, and Dickinson College, 1983; Charles Eliot Norton Professor of Poetry, Harvard University, 1967-68.

MEMBER: Argentine Academy of Letters, Argentine Writers Society (president, 1950-53), Modern Language Association of America (honorary fellow, 1961-86), American Association of Teachers of Spanish and Portuguese (honorary fellow, 1965-86).

AWARDS, HONORS: Buenos Aires Municipal Literary Prize, 1928, for *El idioma de los argentinos;* Gran Premio de Honor from Argentine Writers Society, 1945, for *Ficciones, 1935-1944;* Gran Premio Nacional de la Literatura (Argentina), 1957, for *El Aleph;* Prix Formentor from International Congress of Publishers (shared with Samuel Beckett), 1961; Commandeur de l'Ordre des Lettres et des Arts (France), 1962; Ingram Merrill Foundation Award, 1966; Matarazzo Sobrinho Inter-American Literary Prize from Bienal Foundation, 1970; nominated for Neustadt International Prize for Literature, *World Literature Today* and University of Oklahoma, 1970, 1984, and 1986; Jerusalem Prize, 1971; Alfonso Reyes Prize (Mexico), 1973; Gran Cruz del Orden al mérito Bernando O'Higgins from Government of Chile, 1976; Gold Medal from French Academy, Order of Merit from Federal Republic of Germany, and Icelandic Falcon Cross, all 1979; Miguel de Cervantes Award (Spain) and Balzan Prize (Italy), both 1980; Ollin Yoliztli Prize (Mexico), 1981; T. S. Eliot Award for Creative Writing from Ingersoll Foundation and Rockford Institute, 1983; Gold Medal of Menéndez Pelayo University (Spain), La Gran Cruz de la Orden Alfonso X, el Sabio (Spain), and Legion d'Honneur (France), all 1983; Knight of the British Empire. Recipient of honorary degrees from numerous colleges and universities, including University of Cuyo (Argentina), 1956, University of the Andes (Colombia), 1963, Oxford University, 1970, University of Jerusalem, 1971, Columbia University, 1971, and Michigan State University, 1972.

WRITINGS:

POETRY

Fervor de Buenos Aires (title means "Passion for Buenos Aires"), Serantes (Buenos Aires), 1923, revised edition, Emecé, 1969.
Luna de enfrente (title means "Moon across the Way"), Proa (Buenos Aires), 1925.
Cuaderno San Martín (title means "San Martin Copybook"), Proa, 1929.
Poemas, 1923-1943, Losada, 1943, 3rd enlarged edition published as *Obra poética, 1923-1964,* Emecé, 1964, translation published as *Selected Poems, 1923-1967* (bilingual edition; also includes prose), edited, with an introduction and notes, by Norman Thomas di Giovanni, Delacorte, 1972.
Seis poemas escandinavos (title means "Six Scandinavian Poems"), privately printed, 1966.
Siete poemas (title means "Seven Poems"), privately printed, 1967.
El otro, el mismo (title means "The Other, the Same"), Emecé, 1969.
Elogio de la sombra, Emecé, 1969, translation by di Giovanni published as *In Praise of Darkness* (bilingual edition), Dutton, 1974.
El oro de los tigres (also see below; title means "The Gold of Tigers"), Emecé, 1972.
Siete poemas sajones/Seven Saxon Poems, Plain Wrapper Press, 1974.
La rosa profunda (also see below; title means "The Unending Rose"), Emecé, 1975.
La moneda de hierro (title means "The Iron Coin"), Emecé, 1976.
Historia de la noche (title means "History of Night"), Emecé, 1977.
The Gold of Tigers: Selected Later Poems (contains translations of *El oro de los tigres* and *La rosa profunda*), translated by Alastair Reid, Dutton, 1977.
La cifra, Emecé, 1981.

Also author of *Los conjurados* (title means "The Conspirators"), 1985.

ESSAYS

Inquisiciones (title means "Inquisitions"), Proa, 1925.

El tamaño de mi esperanza (title means "The Measure of My Hope"), Proa, 1926.

El idioma de los argentinos (title means "The Language of the Argentines"), M. Gleizer (Buenos Aires), 1928, 3rd edition (includes three essays by Borges and three by Jose Edmundo Clemente), Emecé, 1968.

Figari, privately printed, 1930.

Las Kennigar, Colombo (Buenos Aires), 1933.

Historia de la eternidad (title means "History of Eternity"), Viau y Zona (Buenos Aires), 1936, revised edition published as *Obras completas*, Volume 1, Emecé, 1953, reprinted, 1978.

Nueva refutación del tiempo (title means "New Refutation of Time"), Oportet y Haereses, 1947.

Aspectos de la literatura gauchesca, Número (Montevideo), 1950.

(With Delia Ingenieros) *Antiguas literaturas germánicas*, Fondo de Cultura Económica (Mexico), 1951, revised edition with María Esther Vázquez published as *Literaturas germánicas medievales*, Falbo, 1966, reprinted, Emecé, 1978.

Otras inquisiciones, Sur (Buenos Aires), 1952, published as *Obras completas*, Volume 8, Emecé, 1960, translation by Ruth L. C. Simms published as *Other Inquisitions, 1937-1952*, University of Texas Press, 1964.

(With Margarita Guerrero) *El "Martín Fierro,"* Columba, 1953, reprinted, Emecé, 1979.

(With Bettina Edelberg) *Leopoldo Lugones*, Troquel (Buenos Aires), 1955.

(With Guerrero) *Manual de zoología fantástica*, Fondo de Cultura Económica, 1957, translation published as *The Imaginary Zoo*, University of California Press, 1969, revised Spanish edition with Guerrero published as *El libro de los seres imaginarios*, Kier (Buenos Aires), 1967, translation and revision by di Giovanni and Borges published as *The Book of Imaginary Beings*, Dutton, 1969.

La poesía gauchesca (title means "Gaucho Poetry"), Centro de Estudios Brasileiros, 1960.

(With Vázquez) *Introducción a la literatura inglesa*, Columba, 1965, translation by L. Clark Keating and Robert O. Evans published as *An Introduction to English Literature*, University Press of Kentucky, 1974.

(With Esther Zemborain de Torres) *Introducción a la literatura norteamericana*, Columba, 1967, translation by Keating and Evans published as *An Introduction to American Literature*, University Press of Kentucky, 1971.

(With Alicia Jurado) *¿Qué es el budismo?* (title means, "What Is Buddhism?"), Columba, 1976.

Nuevos ensayos dantescos (title means "New Dante Essays,") Espasa-Calpe, 1982.

SHORT STORIES

Historia universal de la infamia, Tor (Buenos Aires), 1935, revised edition published as *Obras completas*, Volume 3, Emecé, 1964, translation by di Giovanni published as *A Universal History of Infamy*, Dutton, 1972.

El jardín de senderos que se bifurcan (also see below; title means "Garden of the Forking Paths"), Sur, 1941.

(With Adolfo Bioy Casares, under joint pseudonym H. Bustos Domecq) *Seis problemas para Isidro Parodi*, Sur, 1942, translation by di Giovanni published under authors' real names as *Six Problems for Don Isidro Parodi*, Dutton, 1983.

Ficciones, 1935-1944 (includes *El jardín de senderos que se bifurcan*), Sur, 1944, revised edition published as *Obras completas*, Volume 5, Emecé, 1956, reprinted, with English introduction and notes by Gordon Brotherson and Peter Hulme, Harrap, 1976, translation by Anthony Kerrigan and others published as *Ficciones*, edited and with an introduction by Kerrigan, Grove, 1962 (published in England as *Fictions*, John Calder, 1965), reprinted, Limited Editions Club (New York), 1984.

(With Bioy Casares, under joint pseudonym H. Bustos Domecq) *Dos fantasías memorables*, Oportet & Haereses, 1946, reprinted under authors' real names with notes and bibliography by Horacio Jorge Becco, Edicom (Buenos Aires), 1971.

El Aleph, Losada, 1949, revised edition, 1952, published as *Obras completas*, Volume 7, Emecé, 1956, translation and revision by di Giovanni in collaboration with Borges published as *The Aleph and Other Stories, 1933-1969*, Dutton, 1970.

(With Luisa Mercedes Levinson) *La hermana de Eloísa* (title means "Eloisa's Sister"), Ene (Buenos Aires), 1955.

(With Bioy Casares) *Crónicas de Bustos Domecq*, Losada, 1967, translation by di Giovanni published as *Chronicles of Bustos Domecq*, Dutton, 1976.

El informe de Brodie, Emecé, 1970, translation by di Giovanni in collaboration with Borges published as *Dr. Brodie's Report*, Dutton, 1971.

El matrero, Edicom, 1970.

El congreso, El Archibrazo, 1971, translation by di Giovanni in collaboration with Borges published as *The Congress* (also see below), Enitharmon Press, 1974, translation by Alberto Manguel published as *The Congress of the World*, F. M. Ricci (Milan), 1981.

El libro de arena, Emecé, 1975, translation by di Giovanni published with "The Congress" as *The Book of Sand*, Dutton, 1977.

(With Bioy Casares) *Nuevos cuentos de Bustos Domecq*, Librería de la Cuidad, 1977.

Rosa y azul (contains "La rosa de Paracelso" and "Tigres azules"), Sedmay (Madrid), 1977.

Veinticinco agosto 1983 y otros cuentos de Jorge Luis Borges (includes interview with Borges), Siruela, 1983.

OMNIBUS VOLUMES

La muerte y la brújula (stories; title means "Death and the Compass"), Emecé, 1951.

Obras completas, ten volumes, Emecé, 1953-67, published as one volume, 1974.

Cuentos (title means "Stories"), Monticello College Press, 1958.

Antología personal (prose and poetry), Sur, 1961, translation published as *A Personal Anthology*, edited and with foreword by Kerrigan, Grove Press, 1967.

Labyrinths: Selected Stories and Other Writings, edited by Donald A. Yates and James E. Irby, preface by Andre Maurois, New Directions, 1962, augmented edition, 1964, reprinted, Modern Library, 1983.

Nueva antología personal, Emecé, 1968.

Prólogos (title means "Prologues"), Torres Agüero (Buenos Aires), 1975.

(With others) *Obras completas en colaboración* (title means "Complete Works in Collaboration"), Emecé, 1979.

Narraciones (stories), edited by Marcos Ricardo Bamatán, Cátedra, 1980.

Borges: A Reader (prose and poetry), edited by Emir Rodríguez Monegal and Reid, Dutton, 1981.

Ficcionario: Una antología de sus textos, edited by Rodríguez Monegal, Fondo de Cultura Económica, 1985.

Textos cautivos: Ensayos y reseñas en "El Hogar" (1936-1939) (title means "Captured Texts: Essays and Reviews in 'El Hogar' [1936-1939]"), edited by Rodríguez Monegal and Enrique Sacerio-Gari, Tusquets, 1986.

El aleph borgiano (chiefly book reviews which appeared in journals, 1922-84), edited by Juan Gustavo Cobo Borda and Martha Kovasics de Cubides, Biblioteca Luis-Angel Arango (Bogotá), 1987.

Biblioteca personal: Prólogos, Alianza, 1988.

OTHER

(Author of afterword) Ildefonso Pereda Valdés, *Antología de la moderna poesía uruguaya,* El Ateneo (Buenos Aires), 1927.

Evaristo Carriego (biography), M. Gleizer, 1930, revised edition published as *Obras completas,* Volume 4, Emecé (Buenos Aires), 1955, translation by di Giovanni published as *Evaristo Carriego: A Book about Old Time Buenos Aires,* Dutton, 1984.

(Translator) Virginia Woolf, *Orlando,* Sur, 1937.

(Editor with Pedro Henríquez Ureña) *Antología clásica de la literatura argentina* (title means "Anthology of Argentine Literature"), Kapelusz (Buenos Aires), 1937.

(Translator and author of prologue) Franz Kafka, *La metamorfosis,* [Buenos Aires], 1938, reprinted, Losada, 1976.

(Editor with Bioy Casares and Silvina Ocampo) *Antología de la literatura fantástica* (title means "Anthology of Fantastic Literature"), with foreword by Bioy Casares, Sudamericana, 1940, enlarged edition with postscript by Bioy Casares, 1965, translation of revised version published as *The Book of Fantasy,* with introduction by Ursula K. Le Guin, Viking, 1988.

(Author of prologue) Bioy Casares, *La invención de Morel,* Losada, 1940, reprinted, Alianza, 1981, translation by Simms published as *The Invention of Morel and Other Stories,* University of Texas Press, 1964, reprinted, 1985.

(Editor with Bioy Casares and Ocampo and author of prologue) *Antología poética argentina* (title means "Anthology of Argentine Poetry"), Sudamericana, 1941.

(Translator) Henri Michaux, *Un bárbaro en Asia,* Sur, 1941.

(Compiler and translator with Bioy Casares) *Los mejores cuentos policiales* (title means "The Best Detective Stories"), Emecé, 1943, reprinted, Alianza, 1972.

(Translator and author of prologue) Herman Melville, *Bartleby, el escribiente,* Emecé, 1943, reprinted, Marymar (Buenos Aires), 1976.

(Editor with Silvina Bullrich) *El compadrito: Su destino, sus barrios, su música* (title means "The Buenos Aires Hoodlum: His Destiny, His Neighborhoods, His Music"), Emecé, 1945, 2nd edition, Fabril, 1968.

(With Bioy Casares, under joint pseudonym B. Suárez Lynch) *Un modelo para la muerte* (novel; title means "A Model for Death"), Oportet & Haereses, 1946.

(Compiler and translator with Bioy Casares) *Los mejores cuentos policiales: Segunda serie,* Emecé, 1951.

(Editor and translator with Bioy Casares) *Cuentos breves y extraordinarios: Antología,* Raigal (Buenos Aires), 1955, revised and enlarged edition, Losada, 1973, translation by Kerrigan published as *Extraordinary Tales,* Souvenir Press, 1973.

(With Bioy Casares) *Los orilleros* [and] *El paraíso de los creyentes* (screenplays; titles mean "The Hoodlums" and "The Believers' Paradise"; "Los orilleros" produced by Argentine director Ricardo Luna, 1975), Losada, 1955, reprinted, 1975.

(Editor and author of prologue, notes, and glossary with Bioy Casares) *Poesía gauchesca* (title means "Gaucho Poetry"), two volumes, Fondo de Cultura Económica, 1955.

(Translator) William Faulkner, *Las palmeras salvajes,* Sudamericana, 1956.

(Editor with Bioy Casares) *Libro del cielo y del infierno* (anthology; title means "Book of Heaven and Hell"), Sur, 1960, reprinted, 1975.

El hacedor (prose and poetry; Volume 9 of *Obras completas;* title means "The Maker"), Emecé, 1960, translation by Mildred Boyer and Harold Morland published as *Dreamtigers,* University of Texas Press, 1964, reprinted, 1985.

(Editor and author of prologue) *Macedonio Fernández,* Culturales Argentinas, Ministerio de Educación y Justicia, 1961.

Para las seis cuerdas: Milongas (song lyrics; title means "For the Six Strings: Milongas"), Emecé, 1965.

Diálogo con Borges, edited by Victoria Ocampo, Sur, 1969.

(Translator, editor, and author of prologue) Walt Whitman, *Hojas de hierba,* Juárez (Buenos Aires), 1969.

(Compiler and author of prologue) Evaristo Carriego, *Versos,* Universitaria de Buenos Aires, 1972.

Borges on Writing (lectures), edited by di Giovanni, Daniel Halpern, and Frank MacShane, Dutton, 1973.

(With Bioy Casares and Hugo Santiago) *Les Autres: Escenario original* (screenplay; produced in France and directed by Santiago, 1974), C. Bourgois (Paris), 1974.

(Author of prologue) Carlos Zubillaga, *Carlos Gardel,* Júcar (Madrid), 1976.

Cosmogonías (title means "Cosmogonies"), Librería de la Ciudad, 1976.

Libro de sueños (transcripts of Borges's and others' dreams; title means "Book of Dreams"), Torres Agüero, 1976.

(Author of prologue) Santiago Dabove, *La muerte y su traje,* Calicanto, 1976.

Borges—Imágenes, memorias, diálogos, edited by Vázquez, Monte Avila, 1977.

Adrogué (prose and poetry), privately printed, 1977.

(Editor with María Kodama) *Breve antología anglosajona,* Emecé, 1979.

Borges oral (lectures), edited by Martín Mueller, Emecé, 1979.

Siete noches (lectures), Fondo de Cultura Económica, 1980, translation by Weinberger published as *Seven Nights,* New Directions, 1984.

(Compiler) Paul Groussac, *Jorge Luis Borges selecciona lo mejor de Paul Groussac,* Fraterna (Buenos Aires), 1981.

(Compiler and author of prologue) Francisco de Quevedo, *Antología poética,* Alianza, 1982.

(Compiler and author of introduction) Leopoldo Lugones, *Antología poética,* Alianza, 1982.

(Compiler and author of prologue) Pedro Antonio de Alarcón, *El amigo de la muerte,* Siruela (Madrid), 1984.

(With Kodama) *Atlas* (prose and poetry), Sudamericana, 1984, translation by Kerrigan published as *Atlas,* Dutton, 1985.

En voz de Borges (interviews), Offset, 1986.

Libro de diálogos (interviews), edited by Osvaldo Ferrari, Sudamericana, 1986, published as *Diálogos últimos,* 1987.

Editor with Bioy Casares of series of detective novels, "The Seventh Circle," for Emecé, 1943-56. Contributor, under pseudonym F. Bustos, to *Crítica* (Buenos Aires), 1933. Contributor, with Bioy Casares under joint pseudonym B. Lynch Davis, to *Los anales de Buenos Aires,* 1946-48. Founding editor of *Prisma* (mural magazine), 1921; founding editor of *Proa* (Buenos Aires literary revue), 1921, and, with Ricardo Güiraldes and Pablo Rojas Paz, 1924-26; literary editor of weekly arts supplement of *Crítica,* beginning 1933; editor of biweekly "Foreign Books and

Authors" section of *El Hogar* (magazine), 1936-39; co-editor with Bioy Casares of *Destiempo* (literary magazine), 1936; editor of *Los anales de Buenos Aires* (literary journal), 1946-48.

SIDELIGHTS: "Jorge Luis Borges [was] a great writer," noted French author Andre Maurois in his preface to the Argentine poet, essayist, and short story writer's *Labyrinths: Selected Stories and Other Writings,* "who . . . composed only little essays or short narratives. Yet they suffice for us to call him great because of their wonderful intelligence, their wealth of invention, and their tight, almost mathematical style. Argentine by birth and temperament, but nurtured on universal literature, Borges [had] no spiritual homeland."

Borges was nearly unknown in most of the world until 1961 when, in his early sixties, he was awarded the Prix Formentor—the International Publishers Prize—an honor he shared with Irish playwright Samuel Beckett. Before winning the award, according to Gene H. Bell-Villada in *Borges and His Fiction: A Guide to His Mind and Art,* "Borges had been writing in relative obscurity in Buenos Aires, his fiction and poetry read by his compatriots, who were slow in perceiving his worth or even knowing him." The award made Borges internationally famous: a collection of his short stories, *Ficciones,* was simultaneously published in six different countries, and he was invited by the University of Texas to come to the United States to lecture, the first of many international lecture tours.

Borges's international appeal was partly a result of his enormous erudition which is apparent in the multitude of literary allusions from cultures around the globe contained in his writing. "The work of Jorge Luis Borges," Anthony Kerrigan wrote in his introduction to the English translation of *Ficciones,* "is a species of international literary metaphor. He knowledgeably makes a transfer of inherited meanings from Spanish and English, French and German, and sums up a series of analogies, of confrontations, of appositions in other nations' literatures. His Argentinians act out Parisian dramas, his Central European Jews are wise in the ways of the Amazon, his Babylonians are fluent in the paradigms of Babel." In the *National Review* Peter Witonski commented: "Borges' grasp of world literature is one of the fundamental elements of his art."

The familiarity with world literature evident in Borges's work was initiated at an early age, nurtured by a love of reading. His paternal grandmother was English, and, consequently, since she lived with the Borgeses, English and Spanish were spoken in the family home. Jorge Guillermo Borges, Borges's father, had a large library of English and Spanish books in which his son, whose frail constitution made it impossible to participate in more strenuous activities, spent many hours. "If I were asked to name the chief event in my life," Borges stated in "An Autobiographical Essay" that originally appeared in the *New Yorker* and was later included in *The Aleph and Other Stories, 1933-1969,* "I should say my father's library."

Under his grandmother's tutelage, Borges learned to read English before he could read Spanish. Among the first books he read were works in English by Twain, Poe, Longfellow, Stevenson, and Wells. In Borges's autobiographical essay he recalled reading even the great Spanish masterpiece, Cervantes's *Don Quixote,* in English before reading it in Spanish. Borges's father encouraged writing as well as reading: Borges wrote his first story at age seven, and, at nine, saw his Spanish translation of Oscar Wilde's "The Happy Prince" published in a Buenos Aires newspaper. "From the time I was a boy . . . ," Borges noted in his autobiographical essay, "it was tacitly understood that I had to fulfill the literary destiny that circumstances had denied my father. This was something that was taken for granted. . . . I was expected to be a writer."

Borges became a writer whose works were compared to those of many others, Franz Kafka and James Joyce in particular, but whose style was unique. Critics were forced to coin a new word—Borgesian—to capture the magical world invented by the Argentine master. As Jaime Alazraki noted in *Jorge Luis Borges,* "As with Joyce, Kafka, or Faulkner, the name of Borges has become an accepted concept; his creations have generated a dimension that we designate 'Borgesian.' " And, in *Atlantic,* Keith Botsford declared: "Borges is . . . an international phenomenon, . . . a man of letters whose mode of writing and turn of mind are so distinctively his, yet so much a revealed part of our world, that 'Borgesian' has become as commonplace a neologism as the adjectives 'Sartrean' or 'Kafkaesque.' "

Perhaps the most profound consequence of this Borgesian style was the dramatic change it engendered in Latin American literature. "As [Mexican novelist] Carlos Fuentes remarked," according to Bell-Villada in *Nation,* "without Borges the modern Latin American novel simply would not exist." In *Jorge Luis Borges* George R. McMurray explained that "prior to 1950, the vast majority of Latin American novelists relied on traditional realism to depict life in their native lands and convey messages of social protest. Borges not only liberated Latin American literature from documentation but also restored imagination as a major fictional ingredient." Borges's greatest accomplishment, James E. Irby notes in his introductory remarks to *Labyrinths,* was to rise above the regionalism favored by the writers of his time and "to transmute his circumstances into an art as universal as the finest in Europe."

U.S. writers did not escape Borges's influence. "The impact of Borges on the United States writing scene," commented Bell-Villada, "may be almost as great as was his earlier influence on Latin America. The Argentine reawakened for us the possibilities of farfetched fancy, of formal exploration, of parody, intellectuality, and wit." Bell-Villada specifically noted Borges's presence in works by Robert Coover, Donald Barthelme, and John Gardner. Another important novelist, John Barth, confessed Borges's influence in his own novels. The critic concluded that Borges's work paved "the way for numerous literary trends on both American continents, determining the shape of much fiction to come. By rejecting realism and naturalism, he . . . opened up to our Northern writers a virgin field, led them to a wealth of new subjects and procedures."

The foundation of Borges's literary future was laid in 1914 when the Borgeses took an ill-timed trip to Europe. There, the outbreak of World War I stranded them temporarily in Switzerland, where Borges studied French and Latin in school, taught himself German, and began reading the works of German philosophers and expressionist poets. He was also introduced to the poetry of Walt Whitman in German translation and soon began writing poetry imitative of Whitman's style. "For some time," Rodríguez Monegal wrote in *Borges: A Reader,* "the young man believed Whitman was poetry itself."

After the war the Borgeses settled in Spain for a few years. During this extended stay Borges published reviews, articles, and poetry and became associated with a group of avant-garde poets called Ultraists (named after the magazine, *Ultra,* to which they contributed). Upon Borges's return to Argentina, in 1921, he introduced the tenets of the movement—they believed, for example, in the supremacy of the metaphor—to the Argentine literary scene. His first collection of poems, *Fervor de Buenos Aires,* was written under the spell of this new poetic movement. Although in his autobiographical essay he expressed regret for his "early Ultraist excesses" and in later editions of *Fervor de Buenos Aires* eliminated more than a dozen poems from the text and considerably altered many of the remaining poems, Borges still saw some value in the work. In his autobiographical essay he noted, "I think I have never strayed beyond that book. I feel that all my subsequent writing has only developed themes first taken up there; I feel that all during my lifetime I have been rewriting that one book."

One poem from the volume, "El truco" (a card game), for example, seems to testify to the truth of Borges's statement. In the piece he introduced two themes that appear over and over again in his later writing: circular time and the idea that all people are but one person. "The permutations of the cards," Rodríguez Monegal observed in *Jorge Luis Borges: A Literary Biography,* "although innumerable in limited human experience, are not infinite: given enough time, they will come back again and again. Thus the cardplayers not only are repeating hands that have already come up in the past. In a sense, they are repeating the former players as well: they are the former players."

The decade from 1920 to 1930 was a period of intense activity for Borges. Not only did he publish seven books—four collections of essays and three of poetry—but he also founded three magazines and contributed to nearly a dozen other publications. But although these early works met with some success, it was his work in fiction that would bring him worldwide fame. As McMurray noted, Borges's "highly original short stories—the most important written during the 1940s and early 1950s— . . . made him one of the most widely acclaimed writers of our time."

Illusion is an important part of Borges's fictional world. In *Borges: The Labyrinth Maker,* Ana María Barrenechea called it "his resplendent world of shadows." But illusion is present in his manner of writing as well the fictional world he describes. In *World Literature Today,* William Riggan quoted Icelandic author Sigurdur Magnusson's thoughts on this aspect of Borges's work. "With the possible exception of Kafka . . . ," Magnusson stated, "no other writer that I know manages, with such relentless logic, to turn language upon itself to reverse himself time after time with a sentence or a paragraph, and effortlessly, so it seems, come upon surprising yet inevitable conclusions."

Because of Borges's choice of words and the way he used them, the reader is never sure about the possible outcome of the work until he has finished reading it. But, even then, subsequent readings often reveal subtle shades of meaning or entirely new conclusions. In "The South," for example, one cannot be certain if the protagonist, Juan Dahlmann, dies in his hospital bed or in a knife duel. In "The Shape of the Sword" the reader listens to the narrator tell the story of a despicable traitor and only in the last lines of the story does he learn that the narrator is actually talking about himself. The reader cannot even be certain that once he has finished a Borges story that what he read was actually a story. Borges's short narrative "The Approach to al-Mu'tasim," written as a book review of a non-existent book, was originally published in a collection of essays, *Historia de la eternidad.* Even the writer's friends were fooled by the story: Adolfo Bioy Casares, with whom Borges collaborated on many projects, tried to order the book under review from its alleged publisher in London (Borges had used the name of an actual publishing house in the text). Borges didn't acknowledge the hoax until five years later when the story was published in a fiction collection. But the apparent reality of "The Approach to al-Mu'tasim" is not unique to that story. As D. P. Gallagher noted in *Modern Latin American Literature:* "The stories often look

real. Borges indeed always deploys illusionists' tricks to make them look so, before demolishing them as fictions. The stories are full of scholarly footnotes, references to real people, precise dates, all sorts of devices designed to give an appearance of reality to extraordinary things. Borges himself appears as a character in several stories and so do some of his friends."

Borges expertly blended the traditional boundaries between fact and fiction and between essay and short story and he was similarly adept at obliterating the border between other genres as well. In a tribute to Borges which appeared in the *New Yorker* after the Argentine's death in 1986, Mexican poet and essayist Octavio Paz wrote: "He cultivated three genres: the essay, the poem, and the short story. The division is arbitrary. His essays read like stories, his stories are poems; and his poems make us think, as though they were essays." In *Review,* Ambrose Gordon, Jr., similarly noted, "His essays are like poems in their almost musical development of themes, his stories are remarkably like his essays, and his poems are often little stories." Borges's "Conjectural Poem," for example, is very much like a short story in that it is an account of the death of one of his ancestors, Francisco Narciso de Laprida. Another poem, "The Golem," is a short narrative relating how Rabbi Low of Prague created an artificial man.

To deal with the problem of actually determining to which genre a prose piece by Borges might belong, Martin S. Stabb proposed in *Jorge Luis Borges* that the usual manner of grouping all of Borges's short fiction as short stories was invalid. Stabb instead divided the Argentine's prose fiction into three categories which took into account Borges's tendency to blur genres: " 'essayistic' fiction," "difficult-to-classify 'intermediate' fiction," and those pieces deemed "conventional short stories." Other reviewers saw a comparable division in Borges's fiction but chose to emphasize the chronological development of his work, noting that his first stories grew out of his essays, his "middle period" stories were more realistic, while his later stories were marked by a return to fantastic themes.

Others commentators on Borges's work chose to avoid classification by genre altogether and concentrated instead on thematic studies. This could be done quite easily for many of Borges's poetic themes, for example, are also found in his work in prose. In *Spanish American Literature: A History* Enrique Anderson-Imbert lists some of the motifs commonly found in Borges's poetry as "time, the meaning of the universe, [and] the personality of man." These same major concerns are found in Borges's essays and fiction as well. When used to examine Borges's short stories, this method recalls Borges's own insistence on exploring fantastic literature based on four key elements. "Borges once claimed that the basic devices of all fantastic literature are only four in number: the work within the work, the contamination of reality by dream, the voyage in time, and the double," Irby explained. "These are both his essential themes—the problematical nature of the world, of knowledge, of time, of the self—and his essential techniques of construction."

When dealing with a body of work as rich and multifaceted as Borges's, a combination of both interpretive methods seems to impart the most accurate picture of Borges's fiction. Stabb began his study of Borges's "essayistic fiction" with this explanation: "These, and other pieces like them, are often based on readily identified philosophic notions, though many of the personalities used by Borges to make his points are fictional. In none of them is there any real narrative: several are based on invented literary notes describing fictitious authors and their works. It would not be difficult to imagine most of them cast in the form of a traditional essay." In *The Narrow Act: Borges' Art of Illusion*, Ronald J. Christ noted that these characteristics listed by Stamm are very common in Borges. He remarked, "The point of origin for most of Borges' fiction is neither character nor plot, considered in the traditional sense; but instead, a proposition, an idea, a metaphor." Stabb included in this type of fiction the stories "Funes the Memorious," "Pierre Menard, Author of the *Quixote*," and "Three Versions of Judas." These stories elaborate a multitude of ideas, including the uselessness of unordered knowledge, the impossibility of originality in literature, and the true nature of Jesus.

"Funes the Memorious," listed in Richard Burgin's *Conversations with Jorge Luis Borges* as one of the Argentine's favorite stories, is about Ireneo Funes, a young man who cannot forget anything. His memory is so keen that he is surprised by how different he looks each time he sees himself in a mirror because, unlike the rest of us, he can see the subtle changes that have taken place in his body since the last time he saw his reflection. The story is filled with characteristic Borgesian detail. Funes's memory, for instance, becomes excessive as a result of an accidental fall from a horse. In Borges an accident is a reminder that man is unable to order his existence because the world has a hidden order of its own. Alazraki saw this Borgesian theme as "the tragic contrast between a man who believes himself to be the master and maker of his fate and a text or divine plan in which his fortune has already been written." The deliberately vague quality of the adjectives Borges typically uses in his sparse descriptive passages is also apparent: Funes's features are never clearly distinguished because he lives in a darkened room, he was thrown from his horse on a dark "rainy afternoon," and the horse itself is described as "blue-gray"—neither one color or the other. "This dominant chiaroscuro imagery," commented Bell-Villada, "is further reinforced by Funes's name, a word strongly suggestive of certain Spanish words variously meaning 'funereal,' 'ill-fated,' and 'dark.' " The ambiguity of Borges's descriptions lends a subtle, otherworldly air to this and other examples of his fiction.

Bell-Villada noted another important aspect of the story. When the narrator visits Funes he finds the young man reciting from memory a portion of an actual book, an ancient Roman text entitled *Natural History* written by Pliny, which deals with memory. This is an example of what Bell-Villada called "a typical hall-of-mirrors effect: someone with a perfect memory reciting from memory a passage on memory." According to Bell-Villada "the hall-of-mirrors effect" is comparable to "the work within a work" device mentioned by Borges as essential to fantastic fiction. "Borges is especially renown," Bell-Villada continued, "for his use of . . . the work of art within a work of art. Some of his most celebrated tales ('Pierre Menard,' 'Tlon, Uqbar, Orbis Tertius') deal with nonexistent books and authors. Borges even has a special essay, 'Partial Magic in the *Quixote*,' which deals with a kind of derivative: those works in which a literary character finds himself depicted in a book or a play."

In "Partial Magic in the *Quixote*" (also translated as "Partial Enchantments of the *Quixote*") Borges describes several occasions in world literature when a character reads about himself or sees himself in a play, including episodes from Shakespeare's plays, an epic poem of India, Cervantes's *Don Quixote*, and *The One Thousand and One Nights*. "Why does it disquiet us to know," Borges asked in the essay, "that Don Quixote is a reader of the *Quixote*, and Hamlet is a spectator of *Hamlet*? I believe I have found the answer: those inversions suggest that if the characters in a story can be readers or spectators, then we, their readers, can be fictitious."

With his analysis of this literary device Borges offered his own interpretation of what John Barth referred to in the *Atlantic* as "one of Borges' cardinal themes." Barrenechea explained Borges's technique, noting: "To readers and spectators who consider themselves real beings, these works suggest their possible existence as imaginary entities. In that context lies the key to Borges' work. Relentlessly pursued by a world that is too real and at the same time lacking meaning, he tries to free himself from its obsessions by creating a world of such coherent phantasmagorias that the reader doubts the very reality on which he leans." For example, in one of Borges's variations on "the work within a work," Jaromir Hladik, the protagonist of Borges's story "The Secret Miracle," appears in a footnote to another of Borges's stories, "Three Versions of Judas." The note refers the reader to the *Vindication of Eternity*, a work said to be written by Hladik. In this instance, Borges used a fictional work written by one of his fictional characters to lend an air of erudition to another fictional work about the works of another fictional author.

Borges took "the work within a work" device one step further than any of the examples he spoke of in "Partial Magic in the *Quixote*." One of his favorite literary allusions was to what he referred to as the six-hundred-and-second night of *A Thousand and One Nights*. On this night, Borges recalled, due to a copyist error, Scheherezade began to tell the Sultan the story of *A Thousand and One Nights* by mistake. Although Borges often referred to this episode, it is just another of his *ficciones*, never having been actually included in the original Arabic text. Thus, each time Borges talks about the episode, he is telling a tale about a fictional character telling a tale about telling a tale. As Barth pointed out, the episode is "a literary illustration of the *regressus in infinitum* [the infinite regression], as are almost all of Borges' principal images and motifs." It is as if two mirrors faced each other on the wall, each endlessly reflecting the reflection of the other.

The effect of referring to a work familiar to his readers in one of his stories and then making up a story about it lends an atmosphere of reality to Borges's fiction. A similar effect is created by the footnotes found in several of Borges's stories such as "Three Versions of Judas" and "Pierre Menard, Author of the *Quixote*." The use of footnotes is an example of how Borges blended essay and fiction to create his "essavistic fiction." Both stories, just like Borges's "Approach to al-Mu'tasim," were written as book reviews of works written by Borges's fictional authors and, thus, differ sharply in form and content from the traditional short story.

These intrusions of reality on the fictional world are characteristic of Borges's work. He also uses a device, which he calls "the contamination of reality by dream," to produce the same effect of uneasiness in the reader as "the work within the work" but through directly opposite means. Two examples of stories using this technique are "Tlon, Uqbar, Orbis Tertius" and "The Circular Ruins." The first, which Stabb included in his "difficult-to-classify 'intermediate' fiction," is one of Borges's most discussed works. It tells the story, according to Barrenechea, "of an attempt of a group of men to create a world of their own until, by the sheer weight of concentration, the fantastic creation acquires consistency and some of its objects—a compass, a metallic cone—which are composed of strange matter begin to appear on earth." By the end of the story, the world as we know it is slowly turning into the invented world of Tlon. Stabb called the work "difficult-to-classify" because, he commented, "the excruciating amount of documentary detail (half real, half fictitious) . . . make[s] the piece seem more like an essay" than a short story. There are, in addition, footnotes and a postscript to the story as well as an appearance by Borges himself and references to several other well-known Latin American literary figures, including Borges's friend, Bioy Casares.

"The Circular Ruins," which Stabb considered a "conventional short story," describes a very unconventional situation. (The story is conventional, however, in that there are no footnotes or real people intruding on the fictive nature of the piece.) In the story a man decides to dream about a son until the son becomes real. Later, after the man accomplishes his goal, much to his astonishment, he discovers that he in turn is being dreamt by someone else. "The Circular Ruins" includes several themes seen throughout Borges's work, including man's attempt to establish order in a chaotic universe, the infinite regression, the symbol of the labyrinth, and the idea of all men being one.

The futility of any attempt to order the universe, seen in "Funes the Memorious" and in "The Circular Ruins," is also found in "The Library of Babel" where, according to Alazraki, "Borges presents the world as a library of chaotic books which its librarians cannot read but which they interpret incessantly." The library was one of Borges's favorite images, often repeated in his fiction. In another work, Borges uses the image of a chessboard, however, to elaborate the same theme. In his poem "Chess," he speaks of the king, bishop, and queen who "seek out and begin their armed campaign." But, just as the dreamer dreams a man and causes him to act in a certain way, the campaign is actually being planned by someone other than the members of royalty. "They do not know it is the player's hand," the poem continues, "that dominates and guides their destiny." In the last stanza of the poem Borges uses the same images to suggest the infinite regression: "God moves the player, he in turn, the piece. / But what god beyond God begins the round / of dust and time and sleep and agonies?" Another poem, "The Golem," which tells the story of an artificial man created by a rabbi in Prague, ends in a similar fashion: "At the hour of anguish and vague light, / He would rest his eyes on his Golem. / Who can tell us what God felt, / As he gazed on His rabbi in Prague?" Just as there is a dreamer dreaming a man, and beyond that a dreamer dreaming the dreamer who dreamt the man, then, too, there must be another dreamer beyond that in an infinite succession of dreamers.

The infinite doubling effect inherent in the image of the dreamer who dreams a dreamer and the contrast between a chaotic universe and the order sought by man evoke an image that will be forever linked with Borges's name: the labyrinth. Like the mirror facing the mirror, "the labyrinth is born of duplication," John Sturrock observed in *Paper Tigers: The Ideal Fictions of Jorge Luis Borges,* "of the postulation of an alterative to a given reality, and founded on duplication thereafter." Alazraki concluded: "The labyrinth expresses both sides of the coin: it has an irreversible order if one knows the solution (the gods, God) and it can be at the same time a chaotic maze if the solution constitutes an unattainable secret (men). The labyrinth represents to a greater or less degree the vehicle through which Borges carries his world view to almost all his stories."

The title of the story "The Circular Ruins" suggests a labyrinth. In another story, "The Babylon Lottery," Stabb commented, "an ironically detached narrator depicts life as a labyrinth through which man wanders under the absurd illusion of having understood a chaotic, meaningless world." Labyrinths or references to labyrinths are found in nearly all of Borges's fiction. The labyrinthine form is often present in his poems, too, especially in Borges's early poetry filled with remembrances of wandering the labyrinth-like streets of old Buenos Aires.

In "The Circular Ruins" Borges's returns to another favorite theme: circular time. This theme embraces another device mentioned by Borges as typical of fantastic literature: time travel. Borges's characters, however, do not travel through time in machines; their travel is more on a metaphysical, mythical level. Circular time—a concept also favored by Nietzsche, one of the German philosophers Borges discovered as a boy—is apparent in many of Borges's stories, including "Three Versions of Judas," "The Garden of the Forking Paths," "Tlon, Uqbar, Orbis Tertius," "The Library of Babel," and "The Immortal." It is also found in another of Borges's favorite stories, "Death and the Compass," in which the reader encounters not only a labyrinth but a double as well. Stabb offered the story as a good example of Borges's "conventional short stories."

"Death and the Compass" is a detective story. Erik Lonnrot, the story's detective, commits the fatal error of believing there is an order in the universe that he can understand. When Marcel Yarmolinsky is murdered, Lonnrot refuses to believe it was just an accident; he looks for clues to the murderer's identity in Yarmolinsky's library. Red Scharlach, whose brother Lonnrot had sent to jail, reads about the detective's efforts to solve the murder in the local newspaper and contrives a plot to ambush him. The plan works because Lonnrot, overlooking numerous clues, blindly follows the false trail Scharlach leaves for him.

The final sentences—in which Lonnrot is murdered—change the whole meaning of the narrative, illustrate many of Borges's favorite themes, and crystalize for the reader Borges's thinking on the problem of time. Lonnrot says to Scharlach: " 'I know of one Greek labyrinth which is a single straight line. Along that line so many philosophers have lost themselves that a mere detective might well do so, too. Scharlach, when in some other incarnation you hunt me, pretend to commit (or do commit) a crime at A, then a second crime at B . . . , then a third crime at C. . . . Wait for me afterwards at D. . . . Kill me at D as you now are going to kill me at Triste-le-Roy.' 'The next time I kill you,' said Scharlach, 'I promise you that labyrinth, consisting of a single line which is invisible and unceasing.' He moved back a few steps. Then, very carefully, he fired."

"Death and the Compass" is in many ways a typical detective story, but this last paragraph takes the story far beyond that popular genre. Lonnrot and Scharlach are doubles (Borges gives us a clue in their names: *rot* means red and *scharlach* means scarlet in German) caught in an infinite cycle of pursuing and being pursued. "Their antithetical natures, or inverted mirror images," McMurray observed, "are demonstrated by their roles as detective/criminal and pursuer/pursued roles that become ironically reversed." Rodríguez Monegal concluded: "The concept of the eternal return . . . adds an extra dimension to the story. It changes Scharlach and Lonnrot into characters in a myth: Abel and Cain endlessly performing the killing."

Doubles, which Bell-Villada defined as "any blurring or any seeming multiplication of character identity," are found in many of Borges's works, including "The Waiting," "The Theologians," "The South," "The Shape of the Sword," "Three Versions of Judas," and "Story of the Warrior and the Captive." Borges's explanation of the story "The Theologians" (included in his collection, *The Aleph and Other Stories, 1933-1969*) reveals how a typical Borgesian plot involving doubles works: "In 'The Theologians' you have two enemies," Borges told Burgin in an interview, "and one of them sends the other to the stake. And then they find out somehow they're the same man." In a *Studies in Short Fiction* essay Robert Magliola noticed that "almost every story in *Dr. Brodie's Report* is about two people fixed in some sort of dramatic opposition to each other." In two pieces, "Borges and I" (also translated as "Borges and Myself") and "The Other," Borges appears as a character along with his double. In the former, Borges, the retiring Argentine librarian, contemplates Borges, the world-famous writer. It concludes with one of Borges's most-analyzed sentences: "Which of us is writing this page, I don't know."

Some critics saw Borges's use of the double as an attempt to deal with the duality in his own personality: the struggle between his native Argentine roots and the strong European influence on his writing. They also pointed out what seemed to be an attempt by the author to reconcile through his fiction the reality of his sedentary life of an almost-blind scholar with the longed for adventurous life of his dreams based on that led by his famous ancestors who actively participated in Argentina's wars for independence. This latter tendency is especially evident in "The South," a largely autobiographical story about a library worker who, Bell-Villada noted, like Borges, "is painfully aware of the discordant strains in his ancestry."

The double is also based on what Alazraki called "the pantheistic notion that one man is all men." This suggests, Alazraki observed, "the negation of individual identity, or more exactly, the reduction of all individuals to a general and supreme identity which contains all." Borges developed this theme starting with his very first book. One of its earliest manifestations occurs in Borges's introduction to the 1923 edition of *Fervor de Buenos Aires,* which Norman Thomas di Giovanni quoted in *Selected Poems, 1923-1967.* Borges wrote: "If in the following pages there is some successful verse or other, may the reader forgive me the audacity of having written it before him. We are all one; our inconsequential minds are much alike, and circumstances so influence that it is something of an accident that you are the reader and I am the writer . . . of my verse." Other glimpses of the theme occur in the stories, "Tlon, Uqbar, Orbis Tertius" and "Everything and Nothing." In a footnote to "Tlon, Uqbar, Orbis Tertius" Borges noted: "All men are the same man. All men who repeat a line from Shakespeare *are* William Shakespeare." "Everything and Nothing," which considers the life of a British actor and playwright, also deals with the oneness of all men and recalls Borges's fondness for the image of the infinite number of dreamers from "The Circular Ruins." "Before or after dying" the playwright confronts God saying, "I who have been so many men in vain want to be one and myself." God replies, "Neither am I anyone; I have dreamt the world as you dreamt your work, my Shakespeare, and among the forms in my dream are you, who like myself are many and no one."

The idea that all men are one, which Anderson-Imbert observed calls for the "obliteration of the I," is perhaps Borges's farthest step towards a literature devoid of realism. In this theme we see, according to Christ, "the direction in Borges' stories away from individual psychology toward a universal mythology." This explains why so few of Borges's characters show any psychological development; instead of being interested in his characters as individuals, Borges typically uses them only to further his philosophical beliefs.

All of the characteristics of Borges's work, his blending of genres, confusion of the real and the fictive, his favorite themes and symbols, seem to come together in one of his most quoted passages, the final paragraph of his essay "A New Refutation of Time." While in *Borges: A Reader* Rodríguez Monegal called the essay Borges's "most elaborate attempt to organize a personal system of metaphysics in which he denies time, space, and the individual 'I,'" Alazraki noted that it contains a summation of Borges's belief in "the heroic and tragic condition of man as dream and dreamer."

"Our destiny . . . ," wrote Borges in the essay, "is not horrible because of its unreality; it is horrible because it is irreversible and ironbound. Time is the substance I am made of. Time is a river that carries me away, but I am the river; it is a tiger that mangles me, but I am the tiger; it is a fire that consumes me, but I am the fire. The world, alas, is real; I, alas, am Borges."

MEDIA ADAPTATIONS: "Emma Zunz," a short story, was made into a movie called "Días de odio" ("Days of Wrath") by Argentine director Leopoldo Torre Nilsson, 1954, a French television movie directed by Alain Magrou, 1969, and a film called "Splits" by U.S. director Leonard Katz, 1978; "Hombre de la esquina rosada," a short story, was made into an Argentine movie of the same title directed by René Mugica, 1961; Bernardo Bertolucci based his "La strategia de la ragna" ("The Spider's Stratagem"), a movie made for Italian television, on Borges's short story "El tema del traidor y del héroe," 1970; Héctor Olivera, in collaboration with Juan Carlos Onetti, adapted Borges's story "El muerto" for the Argentine movie of the same name, 1975; Borges's short story "La intrusa" was made into a Brazilian film directed by Carlos Hugo Christensen, 1978; three of the stories in *Six Problems for Don Isidro Parodi* were dramatized for radio broadcast by the British Broadcasting Corporation.

BIOGRAPHICAL/CRITICAL SOURCES:

BOOKS

Alazraki, Jaime, *Jorge Luis Borges,* Columbia University Press, 1971.

Anderson-Imbert, Enrique, *Spanish-American Literature: A History,* Volume 2: *1910-1963,* 2nd edition, Wayne State University Press, 1969.

Barrenechea, Ana María, *Borges: The Labyrinth Maker,* translated by Robert Lima, New York University Press, 1965.

Bell-Villada, Gene H., *Borges and His Fiction: A Guide to His Mind and Art,* University of North Carolina Press, 1981.

Borges, Jorge Luis, *Ficciones,* translated by Anthony Kerrigan and others, edited and with an introduction by Kerrigan, Grove Press, 1962.

Borges, Jorge Luis, *Labyrinths: Selected Stories and Other Writings,* edited by Donald A. Yates and James E. Irby, New Directions, 1964.

Borges, Jorge Luis, *The Aleph and Other Stories, 1933-1969,* translated and revised by Norman Thomas di Giovanni in collaboration with Borges, Dutton, 1970.

Borges, Jorge Luis, *Selected Poems, 1923-1967,* translated and edited, with an introduction and notes, by Norman Thomas di Giovanni, Delacorte Press, 1972.

Borges, Jorge Luis, *Borges: A Reader,* edited by Emir Rodríguez Monegal and Alastair Reid, Dutton, 1981.

Burgin, Richard, *Conversations with Jorge Luis Borges,* Holt, 1969.

Christ, Ronald J., *The Narrow Act: Borges' Art of Illusion,* New York University Press, 1969.

Contemporary Literary Criticism, Gale, Volume 1, 1973, Volume 2, 1974, Volume 3, 1975, Volume 4, 1975, Volume 6, 1976, Volume 8, 1978, Volume 9, 1978, Volume 10, 1979, Volume 13, 1980, Volume 19, 1981, Volume 44, 1987, Volume 48, 1988.

Dictionary of Literary Biography: Yearbook, 1986, Gale, 1987.

Gallagher, D. P., *Modern Latin American Literature,* Oxford University Press, 1973.

McMurray, George R., *Jorge Luis Borges,* Ungar, 1980.

Rodríguez Monegal, Emir, *Jorge Luis Borges: A Literary Biography,* Dutton, 1978.

Stabb, Martin S., *Jorge Luis Borges,* Twayne, 1970.

PERIODICALS

Atlantic, January, 1967, August, 1967, February, 1972, April, 1981.

Nation, December 29, 1969, August 3, 1970, March 1, 1971, February 21, 1972, October 16, 1972, February 21, 1976.

National Review, March 2, 1973.

Review, spring, 1972, spring, 1975, winter, 1976, January-April, 1981, September-December, 1981.

Studies in Short Fiction, spring, 1974, winter, 1978.

World Literature Today, autumn, 1977, winter, 1984.

Yale Review, October, 1969, autumn, 1974.

OBITUARIES:

PERIODICALS

Detroit News, June 15, 1986, June 22, 1986.

Los Angeles Times, June 15, 1986.

Nation, June 28, 1986.

New Republic, November 3, 1986.

New Yorker, July 7, 1986.

New York Review of Books, August 14, 1986.

New York Times, June 15, 1986.

Publishers Weekly, July 4, 1986.

Time, June 23, 1986.

USA Today, June 16, 1986.

Washington Post, June 15, 1986.

—*Sketch by Marian Gonsior*

*   *   *

BORNSTEIN-SOMOZA, Miriam   1950-

PERSONAL: Born in 1950 in Puebla, Mexico. *Education:* University of Arizona, Ph.D., 1982.

ADDRESSES: Home—Denver, Colo.

CAREER: Poet.

WRITINGS:

Bajo cubierta (title means "Undercover"; poetry), Scorpion (Tucson), 1976.

Poetry represented in *Siete poetas,* Scorpion, 1978, and *Flor y Canto IV and V: An Anthology of Chicano Literature,* Flor y Canto Committee (Albuquerque, N.M.), 1980. Contributor to periodicals, including *Hojas Poéticas, La Palabra,* and *Revista Chicano-Riqueña.*

BIOGRAPHICAL/CRITICAL SOURCES:

BOOKS

Martínez, Julio A. and Francisco A. Lomelí, editors, *Chicano Literature: A Reference Guide,* Greenwood Press, 1985.

*   *   *

BOSCH (GAVIÑO), Juan   1909-

PERSONAL: Born in 1909 in the Dominican Republic. *Education:* Attended school in La Vega and Santo Domingo, Dominican Republic.

CAREER: Writer and politician. Founder and president of Partido Revolucionario Dominicano, 1939-1966. President of Do-

minican Republic, February-September, 1963 (deposed in military coup). Professor at Institute of Political Science of Costa Rica.

AWARDS, HONORS: Short story award from FNAC Foundation (France), 1988.

WRITINGS:

FICTION

La mañosa: Novela de las revoluciones (novel), El Diario (Santiago, Dominican Republic), 1936.

Camino real (short stories), El Diario, 1937.

Dos pesos de agua (short stories), privately printed (Havana), 1941.

Ocho cuentos (short stories), [Havana], 1947.

La muchacha de La Guaira (short stories), Nascimento (Santiago, Chile), 1955.

Cuento de Navidad, Ercilla (Santiago, Chile), 1956.

Cuentos escritos en el exilio y apuntes sobre el arte de escribir cuentos (short stories), Librería Dominicana (Santo Domingo), 1962.

Más cuentos escritos en el exilio (short stories), Librería Dominicana, 1964.

Cuentos escritos ante del exilio (short stories), Edición Especial (Santo Domingo), 1974.

El oro y la paz (novel), [Santo Domingo], 1977.

Cuentos (short stories), Casa de Las Américas (Havana), 1983.

NONFICTION

Indios: Apuntes históricos y leyendas, La Nación (Santo Domingo), 1935.

Mujeres en la vida de Hostos, conferencia, Asociación de Mujeres Graduadas de la Universidad de Puerto Rico (San Juan), 1938.

Cuba: La isla fascinante, Universitaria (Santiago, Chile), 1955.

Trujillo: Causas de una tiranía sin ejemplo, Las Novedades (Caracas), 1959 (also see below).

Apuntes para una interpretación de la historia costarricense, Eloy Morua Carrillo (San Jose, Costa Rica), 1963, reprinted as *Una interpretación de la historia costarricense,* Juricentro (San Jose), 1980.

(With Adolfo López Mateos) *Un nuevo planteamiento de las relaciones entre México y la República Dominicana,* La Justicia (Mexico City), 1963.

Crisis de la democracia de América en la República Dominicana; Centro de Estudios y Documentación Sociales (Guadalquivir), 1964, translation published as *The Unfinished Experiment: Democracy in the Dominican Republic,* Praeger, 1965.

Tres artículos sobre la Revolución Dominicana, Partido Revolucionario Dominicano (Mexico City), 1965.

Páginas para la historia, Librería Dominicana, 1965.

Bolívar y la guerra social, Jorge Alvarez (Buenos Aires), 1966.

Teoría del cuento: Tres ensayos (essays), Universidad de los Andes, Facultad de Humanidades y Educación, Escuela de Letras, Centro de Investigaciones Literarias (Mérida, Venezuela), 1967.

El pentagonismo: Sustituto del imperialismo, Publicaciones Ahora (Santo Domingo), 1967, translation by Helen R. Lane published as *Pentagonism: A Substitute for Imperialism,* Grove Press, 1968.

Composición social dominicana: Historia e interpretación, [Santo Domingo], 1970.

De Cristóbal Colón a Fidel Castro: El Caribe, frontera imperial, Alfaguara (Madrid), 1970.

El próximo paso: Dictadura con respaldo popular, Impresora Arte y Cine (Santo Domingo), 1970.

Breve historia de la oligarquía, Impresora Arte y Cine, 1971.

Tres conferencias sobre el feudalismo, Talleres Gráficos (Santo Domingo), 1971.

(Author of prologue) Federico García Godoy, *El derrumbe,* La Universidad Autónoma de Santo Domingo, 1975.

Viaje a los antípodas, Alfa y Omega (Santo Domingo), 1978.

Artículos y conferencias, Alfa y Omega, 1980.

(With others) *Abril* (essays), Alfa y Omega, 1980.

(With others) *Coronel Fernández Domínguez: Fundador del movimiento militar constitucionalista* (essays), Cosmos (Santo Domingo), 1981.

La Revolución de Abril (essays; first published in periodical *Vanguardia del Pueblo,* 1979), Impresora Mercedes (Santo Domingo), 1981.

Clases sociales en la República Dominicana (essays; first published in periodicals *Vanguardia del Pueblo* and *Política—Teoría y Acción,* beginning in 1974), Corripio (Santo Domingo), 1982.

La guerra y la restauración, Corripio, 1982.

El partido: Concepción, organización y desarrollo (essays), Alfa y Omega, 1983.

Capitalismo, democracia y liberación nacional (essays; first published in periodical *Vanguardia del Pueblo,* 1978-83), Alfa y Omega, 1983.

(With Narciso Isa Conde) *El problema de las alianzas* (essays; first published in periodicals *Vanguardia del Pueblo* and *Hablan los Comunistas,* 1983), Ediciones de Taller (Santo Domingo), 1983.

La fortuna de Trujillo (excerpts from *Trujillo: Causas de una tiranía sin ejemplo*), Alfa y Omega, 1985.

La pequeña burguesía en la historia de la República Dominicana (essays; first published in periodical *Vanguardia del Pueblo,* 1984-85), Alfa y Omega, 1985.

Capitalismo tardío en la República Dominicana, Alfa y Omega, 1986.

Las dictaduras dominicanas, Alfa y Omega, 1988.

BIOGRAPHY

Hostos, el sembrador, Trópico (Havana), 1939, reprinted, Huracán (Río Piedras, Puerto Rico), 1976.

Simón Bolívar: Biografía para escolares, Escolar (Caracas), 1960.

David: Biografía de un rey, Librería Dominicana, 1963, translation by John Marks published as *David: The Biography of a King,* Hawthorn Books, 1966.

El Napoleón de las guerrillas, Alfa y Omega, 1977 (also see below).

Judas Iscariote: El calumniado, Alfa y Omega, 1978.

(With Luis Cordero Velásquez) *Juan Vicente Gómez: Camino del poder,* Humboldt (Caracas), 1982.

Máximo Gómez: De Monte Cristi a la gloria; tres años de guerra en Cuba (includes *El Napoleón de las guerrillas*), Alfa y Omega, 1986.

BIOGRAPHICAL/CRITICAL SOURCES:

BOOKS

Alexander, Robert J., editor, *Biographical Dictionary of Latin American and Caribbean Political Leaders,* Greenwood Press, 1988.

BRITO, Aristeo 1942-

PERSONAL: Born October 20, 1942, in Ojinaga, Chihuahua, Mexico; dual U.S.-Mexican citizen until 1967; became U.S. citizen, 1967. *Education:* Sul Ross State University, B.A., 1965; University of Arizona, M.A., 1967, Ph.D., 1978.

ADDRESSES: Home—2740 West Aurora Dr., Tucson, Ariz. 85746. *Office*—Department of Spanish, Pima Community College, 2202 West Anklam Rd., Tucson, Ariz. 85709.

CAREER: Farm worker until c. 1960; Pima Community College, Tucson, Ariz., 1970—, began as instructor, became professor in Spanish and Chicano literature and department chairperson. Guest professor at educational institutions, including University of Arizona and University of California at Santa Barbara. English teacher for Alpine Community Center in Texas, 1964-65, and for Migrant Opportunity Program in Tucson, Arizona, 1969; consultant for Southwestern Cooperative Language Laboratory, 1969; adviser for U.S. Office of Education, 1971; regional director and consultant for Congreso Nacional de Asuntos Colegiales in Washington, D.C., 1980-86; translator for AZTLAN Language Services and Arizona State Department, both 1982—. Delegate to Modern Language Association, 1971-73, and member of the association's commission on minority groups, 1976-79.

AWARDS, HONORS: Grants from National Endowment for the Humanities, 1973-74, and National Endowment for the Arts, 1977; WESTAF award, 1990.

MEMBER: National Association for Bilingual Education, American Association of Community and Junior Colleges, Modern Language Association of America, American Association of Teachers of Spanish and Portuguese, Arizona Association of Mexican American Education, League of Latin American Citizens.

WRITINGS:

Cuentos y poemas de Aristeo Brito (title means "Short Stories and Poems of Aristeo Brito"), Fomento Literario (Washington, D.C.), 1974.

El diablo en Texas: Literatura chicana (novel), Peregrinos (Tucson, Ariz.), 1976.

Contributor of poems and short stories to periodicals, including *La Luz,* and to anthologies. Editor of bilingual literary magazine *Llueve Tlaloc,* 1986—.

SIDELIGHTS: Aristeo Brito told *HW:* "The power of the word and the creative energy it generates has always been a mystery to me. However, I do not write for the purpose of understanding that mystery. I write so that perhaps, on occasion, I might achieve some of that magic."

BIOGRAPHICAL/CRITICAL SOURCES:

BOOKS

Martínez, Julio A. and Francisco A. Lomelí, editors, *Chicano Literature: A Reference Guide,* Greenwood Press, 1985.

PERIODICALS

Latin American Literary Review, spring-summer, 1977.
Revista Chicano-Requeña, autumn, 1977, summer, 1978.
World Literature Today, autumn, 1977.

BRUCE-NOVOA
See BRUCE-NOVOA, Juan D.

* * *

BRUCE-NOVOA, John David
See BRUCE-NOVOA, Juan D.

* * *

BRUCE-NOVOA, Juan D. 1944-
(Bruce-Novoa, John David Bruce-Novoa)

PERSONAL: Born June 20, 1944, in San José, Costa Rica; immigrated to the United States, 1945, naturalized U.S. citizen; son of James H. Bruce (a coffee importer) and Dolores Novoa; married, 1969; children: one. *Education:* Regis College, Denver, Colo., B.A. (cum laude), 1966; University of Colorado, Boulder, M.A., 1968, Ph.D., 1974.

ADDRESSES: Home—535 Inwood Dr., Santa Barbara, Calif. 93111. *Office*—Department of Foreign Languages, Trinity University, 715 Stadium Dr., San Antonio, Tex. 78284.

CAREER: University of Colorado, Boulder, instructor in Spanish, 1967-72, Denver, instructor in Spanish, 1972-74; Yale University, New Haven, Conn., former assistant professor of Spanish, beginning 1974, director of undergraduate studies in Latin American studies; University of California, Santa Barbara, instructor and associate director of Center for Chicano Studies, 1983-85; Trinity University, San Antonio, Tex., member of foreign language department, 1985—. Mexican prose annotator for Library of Congress, 1977—. Member, Movimiento Estudiantil Chicano de Aztlán.

MEMBER: Modern Language Association of America, American Association of Teachers of Spanish and Portuguese, Popular Culture Association.

AWARDS, HONORS: Fellow of National Chicano Committee for Higher Education, 1978; Fullbright scholarship, 1983.

WRITINGS:

(Contributor) Felipe Ortego and David Conde, editors, *The Chicano Literary World—1974,* New Mexico Highlands University, 1975.
Inocencia perversa/Perverse Innocence (poem), Baleen Press, 1976.
(Author of afterword) Juan García Ponce, *Entry Into Matter: Modern Literature and Reality,* Applied Literature Press, 1976.
Canto al pueblo: An Anthology of Experiences II, edited by Leonardo Carrillo and others, Penca (San Antonio, Tex.), 1978.
Chicano Authors: Inquiry by Interviews, University of Texas Press, 1980.
Chicano Poetry: A Response to Chaos, University of Texas Press, 1982.
La literatura chicana a través de sus autores, Siglo Veintiuno Editores, 1983.

Work represented in anthologies, including *Christmas Anthology,* edited by Teresinha Pereira, Backstage Book Stores, 1975, and *El quetzal emplumece,* edited by Carmela Montalvo, Mexican American Cultural Center (San Antonio), 1976. Contributor of articles, poems, and stories to literature and ethnic studies journals and literary magazines, including *Mango, Riversedge, Puerto del Sol,* and *Xalman.* Editor of *La Luz* and *South Western Literature.*

SIDELIGHTS: Poet and short story writer Juan D. Bruce-Novoa asserted in *The Chicano Literary World—1974* that "no one would deny the predominance of the Mexican and the American influences [on Chicano literature]; yet, we are neither, as we are not Mexican-American. I propose that we are the space (not the hyphen) between the two, the intercultural nothing of that space. . . . Chicano art is the space created by the tensions of all its particular manifestations. It is the nothing of that continuous space where all possibilities are simultaneously possible and all achieved products are simultaneously in relationship, creating one unit. We may concentrate on one, but it is only a particular surface leading to the space of all: the impersonal, continuous nothing." Because of this belief, "Bruce-Novoa's poetry is not Chicano poetry in the sense that there are no social concerns, no specific Chicano themes or brown consciousness," according to *Revista Chicano-Riqueña* contributor Arthur Ramírez. As for his prose, Juanita Luna Lawhn explains in the *Dictionary of Literary Biography* that the author "develops a thesis that Chicano literature should not be limited to its own social or ethnic space, but that it should have an intertextual dialogue with all literatures."

Bruce-Novoa's manuscript collection is kept at the Nettie Lee Benson Collection, Latin American Collection, University of Texas at Austin.

BIOGRAPHICAL/CRITICAL SOURCES:

BOOKS

Dictionary of Literary Biography, Volume 82: *Chicano Writers,* Gale, 1989.
Ortego, Felipe, and David Conde, editors, *The Chicano Literary World—1974,* New Mexico Highland University, 1975.

PERIODICALS

Revista Chicano-Riqueña, fall, 1977.
World Literature Today, spring, 1981, spring, 1983.

* * *

BUENAVENTURA, Enrique 1925-

PERSONAL: Born in 1925 in Cali, Colombia.

CAREER: Worked as manual laborer, sailor, literature teacher, and journalist, before 1955; Experimental Theater of Cali, Cali, Colombia, founder and leader, beginning in 1955; affiliated with Cali School of Fine Arts, until 1969.

AWARDS, HONORS: UNESCO Prize, 1965, for *La tragedia del rey Christophe;* prize for drama from Casa de las Américas, 1980, for *Historia de una bala de plata.*

WRITINGS:

PLAYS; SEPARATE WORKS OR PRODUCTIONS

En la diestra de Dios Padre (title means "In the Right Hand of God the Father"; based on Tomás Carrasquilla's retelling of a folktale), first produced in 1960.
La tragedia del rey Christophe (title means "The Tragedy of King Christophe"), first produced in 1963.
Un réquiem por el Padre Las Casas (title means "Requiem for Father Las Casas"), first produced in 1963.
La trampa (title means "The Trap"), first produced in 1966.
Los papeles del infierno (title means "Documents from Hell"; assembly of shorter works, generally one-acts, sometimes considered separately; has at various times included *La maestra* ["The Schoolteacher"], *La autopsia* ["The Autopsy"], *La*

requisa, La tortura ["Torture"], *El entierro, La orgía* ["The Orgy"], *El menú,* and *El sueño* ["The Dream"]), first produced in 1968.

Tirano Banderas (title means "Tyrant Banderas"; based on the novel of the same title by Ramón Valle-Inclán), first produced in 1969.

Historia de una bala de plata (title means "Tale of a Silver Bullet"), Casa de las Américas (Havana, Cuba), 1980.

Author or co-author of additional plays and play adaptations. Author of adaptation of Sophocles's "Oedipus Rex" and of "El fantoche lusitano," based on a work by Peter Weiss.

PLAYS IN OMNIBUS VOLUMES

Teatro (includes *Un réquiem por el Padre Las Casas, La tragedia del rey Christophe,* and *En la diestra de Dios Padre*), Tercer Mundo (Bogotá, Colombia), 1963.

(With others) *Voices of Change in the Spanish American Theater* (includes *In the Right Hand of God the Father*), edited by William I. Oliver, University of Texas Press, 1971.

(With others) *The Orgy: Modern One-Act Plays From Latin America* (includes *The Orgy* and *The Schoolteacher*), edited and translated by Gerardo Luzuriaga and Robert S. Rudder, University of California, Los Angeles, Latin American Center, 1974.

Teatro (includes *Los papeles del infierno, El menú, La orgía, Soldados,* and *En la diestra de Dios Padre*), introduction by Carlos José Reyes, Instituto Colombiano de Cultura (Bogotá), 1977.

Teatro (includes *En la diestra de Dios Padre, Los papeles del infierno, La maestra, La tortura, La audiencia, La autopsia, La orgía, El menú,* and *Vida y muerte del Fantoche Lusitano*), Casa de las Américas, 1980.

SIDELIGHTS: Colombian dramatist Enrique Buenaventura is well known in the Latin American theater world as an advocate of innovative drama that encourages social change. Deeply concerned that the United States exercises undue influence over the culture of his region, he has sought to bring a distinctively Latin American content to his works. His plays often dramatize events in the political history of Latin America and attack the failures of its traditional oligarchical regimes.

After holding a wide variety of jobs during his twenties, Buenaventura founded the Experimental Theater in his hometown of Cali in 1955. The next few years saw production of his first major play, *En la diestra de Dios Padre* (*In the Right Hand of God the Father*). Based on Tomás Carrasquilla's retelling of a folktale, the work centers on Peralta, a warmhearted common man who receives five wishes from God and tries to use them to solve the world's problems. When Peralta abolishes poverty, sickness, and death, however, new troubles arise. "The [play's] irony," wrote George McMurray in *Spanish American Writing Since 1941,* "stems from the inability of God, who naively allied himself with the all-to-human Peralta, to perfect his flawed universe." *In the Right Hand of God the Father* was brought to Europe by Colombian actors and staged in Paris and other cities to great acclaim. Soon thereafter Buenaventura wrote two of his best-known historical dramas. *Un réquiem por el Padre Las Casas* ("Requiem for Father Las Casas") shows the ill-fated efforts of a priest to intercede with Spanish colonists on behalf of the Indians. *La tragedia del rey Christophe* ("The Tragedy of King Christophe") shows the downfall of Henri Christophe, a Haitian revolutionary hero of the early 1800s. After gaining renown as a fighter for Haitian independence, Christophe betrays his own ideals by proclaiming himself king and emulating the decadence of French

royalty. The play received the UNESCO Prize for drama in 1965.

During the late 1960s Buenaventura's work became more iconoclastic, as he experimented with theatrical styles and became openly critical of the society around him. His 1966 drama *La trampa* ("The Trap"), for example, is outwardly a portrait of the regime of Guatemalan dictator Jorge Ubico. By implication, however, as McMurray suggested, the play is also a portrait of some Colombian leaders. In 1967 Buenaventura released a group of short plays, known collectively as *Los papeles del infierno* ("Documents from Hell"), that forthrightly condemned the state of contemporary Colombian society. As the author wrote in a preface to the work, quoted in *Latin American Theatre Review,* the plays comprise "a testimony of twenty years of violence and undeclared civil war" that plagued Colombia during *la violencia,* a period of political turmoil that lasted from the 1940s to the 1960s. To strengthen his message, observers suggest, Buenaventura employed the deliberately shocking "theater of cruelty" style advocated by French drama theorist Antonin Artaud. Among the plays considered part of *Las papeles del infierno* are *La maestra* (*The Schoolteacher*), in which a teacher testifies from beyond the grave about how she was raped by government soldiers and lost the will to live; *La tortura,* in which a government torturer makes brutality a part of his marriage; and *La autopsia,* in which a coroner who signs false autopsies to hide state-sponsored terrorism must inspect the corpse of his own son. In *La orgía* (*The Orgy*), one of the culminating works of the collection, an old woman offers food and money to beggars if they will entertain her by impersonating her past lovers. As the beggars appear in borrowed finery, they parody four leading components of Colombia's longstanding oligarchy: the aristocracy, the politicians, the military, and the Catholic church.

As the result of political controversy, by 1969 the Experimental Theater had been stripped of its government subsidy; Buenaventura and his followers were expelled from the local School of Fine Arts by order of the government of Cali and the Cuaca Valley. But under Buenaventura's leadership, the Experimental Theater continued successfully as an independent organization. It has since become known as a pioneer in collective production, in which the traditional hierarchy of the theater is de-emphasized and directors, actors, playwrights, and technicians work together to create their plays.

Two of the company's productions, each scripted and directed by Buenaventura, received high praise from Wolfgang Luchting in *Latin American Theatre Review.* Both productions were marked by heavy political exhortation, Luchting noted, but in each case the work was done "intelligently and *professionally.*" "Buenaventura is, I think, a very great director," the reviewer observed. "With a minimum of props and costumes he devises [stage] effects that are astounding." In keeping with such a highly visual style, the actors vividly physicalized their roles, displaying an aptitude for such skills as mime and even acrobatics. Luchting continued: "What they offer and how they perform and make use of the public's receptivity, for politics or for simple entertainment, is so engaging, so well orchestrated . . . that even the 'esthetes' cannot really criticize it; at least not the *theatricality* of it." The skill and self-assurance of both the actors and the director, the reviewer declared, placed them on a level of accomplishment far above the norm for experimental theaters in Latin America.

In a 1980 interview for *Theater,* Buenaventura looked back on the changing goals of Latin American playwrights such as himself, who wanted to foster a socially relevant alternative to commercial theater. "At first, we sought audiences made up of workers, of what is generally considered a popular audience," he recalled. However, he said, "experience has taught us that we can't base all our efforts on getting the working masses to go to the theater because they don't go"—whether in the Third World, in the West, or in Marxist Cuba. "Yet, this isn't new," he continued, adding, "Marx knew he had to write for the workers but, did they read him? Of course not." Accordingly, Buenaventura observed, "Our relationship with the viewing public has become rather 'polemic.' We now seek to engage the audience in the fundamental problems of our countries."

As the 1980s began, Buenaventura was at work on a new trilogy of historical dramas, according to Ana María Hernández of *World Literature Today*. The first play in the series was the prize-winning *Historia de una bala de plata* ("History of a Silver Bullet"). Here the author returned to the early years of Haitian independence, showing the difficulties that plagued its original slave revolt, from American intriguers to feuding revolutionaries. According to Hernández, Buenaventura planned to cap the trilogy with a drama of the Cuban Revolution.

BIOGRAPHICAL/CRITICAL SOURCES:

BOOKS

Jones, Willis Knapp, *Behind Spanish American Footlights*, University of Texas Press, 1966.
McMurray, George R., *Spanish American Writing Since 1941: A Critical Survey*, Ungar, 1987.

PERIODICALS

Latin American Theatre Review, fall, 1975, spring, 1976, spring, 1979.
Theater, fall/winter, 1980.
World Literature Today, summer, 1981.

—Sketch by Thomas Kozikowski

*   *   *

BUENDIA, Manuel
  See GIRON, Manuel Buendía Téllez

*   *   *

BUERO VALLEJO, Antonio 1916-

PERSONAL: Surname listed in some sources as Buero-Vallejo; born September 29, 1916, in Guadalajara, Spain; son of Francisco Buero (a military engineer) and Cruz Vallejo; married Victoria Rodríguez (an actress), 1959; children: Carlos, Enrique. *Education:* San Fernando School of Fine Arts, Madrid, Spain, 1934-36.

ADDRESSES: Home and office—Calle General Díaz Porlier 36, Madrid 28001, Spain.

CAREER: Playwright, 1949—. Lecturer at universities in the United States, 1966; speaker at Symposium on Spanish Theater, University of North Carolina at Chapel Hill, 1970.

MEMBER: International Committee of the Theatre of the Nations, Hispanic Society of America (corresponding member), American Association of Teachers of Spanish and Portuguese (honorary fellow), Society of Spanish and Spanish-American Studies (honorary fellow), Modern Language Association (honorary fellow), Deutscher Hispanistenverband (honorary fellow), Sociedad General de Autores de España, Real Academia Española, Ateneo de Madrid (honorary fellow), Círculo de Bellas Artes de Madrid (honorary fellow).

AWARDS, HONORS: Premio Lope de Vega, 1949, for "Historia de una escalera"; Premio Amigos de los Quintero, 1949, for "Las palabras en la arena"; Premio María Rolland, 1956, for "Hoy es fiesta," 1958, for "Un soñador para un pueblo," and, 1960, for "Las Meninas"; Premio Nacional de Teatro, 1957, for "Hoy es fiesta," 1958, for "Las cartas boca abajo," 1959, for "Un soñador para un pueblo," and 1980; Premio Marcha de Teatro, 1959, for "Hoy es fiesta"; Premio de la crítica de Barcelona, 1960, for "Un soñador para un pueblo"; Premio Larra, 1962, for "El concierto de San Ovidio"; Premio Leopoldo Cano, 1966, 1970, 1972, 1974, and 1976; Medalla de Oro del Espectador y la crítica, 1967, 1970, 1974, 1976, 1977, 1981, 1984, and 1986; Premio Mayte and Premio Foro Teatral, both 1974; Medalla de Oro "Gaceta illustrada," 1976; Officier des Palmes Academiques de France, 1980; Premio Ercilla and Medalla "Valle-Inclán" de la Asociación de Escritores y Artistas, both 1985; Premio Pablo Iglesias and Premio Miguel de Cervantes, both 1986; Medalla de Oro e Hijo Predilecto de Guadalajara, 1987.

WRITINGS:

IN ENGLISH TRANSLATION

En la ardiente oscuridad: Drama en tres actos (title means "In the Burning Darkness: Three-Act Drama"; first produced in Madrid at Teatro Nacional María Guerrero, December 1, 1950; also see below), Alfil (Madrid), 1951, reprinted, Escelicer (Madrid), 1970, critical Spanish edition edited by Samuel A. Wofsy, Scribner, 1954.
La tejedora de sueños: Drama en tres actos (title means "The Dream Weaver: Three-Act Drama"; first produced in Madrid at Teatro Español, January 11, 1952; also see below), Alfil, 1952, translation by William I. Oliver published as "The Dreamweaver" in *Masterpieces of the Modern Spanish Theatre*, edited by Robert W. Corrigan, Collier Books, 1967.
Las Meninas: Fantasía velazqueña en dos partes (title means "The Ladies-in-Waiting: Velazquen Fantasy in Two Parts"; first produced at Teatro Español, December 9, 1960; first published in *Primer Acto*, January, 1961; also see below), Alfil, 1961, critical Spanish edition edited by Juan Rodríguez Castellano, Scribner, 1963, translation by Marion Peter Holt published as *Las Meninas: A Fantasy*, Trinity University Press, 1987.
El concierto de San Ovidio: Parábola en tres actos (title means "The Concert at Saint Ovide: Three-Act Parable"; first produced in Madrid at Teatro Goya, November 16, 1962; first published in *Primer Acto*, December, 1962; also see below), Alfil, 1963, critical Spanish edition edited by Pedro N. Trakas, Scribner, 1965, translation by Farris Anderson of original Spanish version published as *The Concert at Saint Ovide*, Pennsylvania State University Press, 1967, Anderson's translation also published in *The Modern Spanish Stage: Four Plays*, edited by Holt, Hill & Wang, 1970.
El tragaluz: Experimento en dos partes (title means "The Skylight: Two-Part Experiment"; first produced in Madrid at Teatro Bellas Artes, October 7, 1967; first published in *Primer Acto*, November, 1967; also see below), Alfil, 1968, critical Spanish edition edited by Anthony M. Pasquariello and Patricia W. O'Connor, Scribner, 1977, translation by O'Connor of original Spanish version published as "The Basement Window" in *Plays of Protest from the Franco Era*, Sociedad General Española de la Librería (Madrid), 1981.

La doble historia del doctor Valmy: Relato escénico en dos partes (title means "The Double Case-History of Doctor Valmy: Story with Scenes, in Two Parts"; first produced in English translation in Chester, England, at Gateway Theatre, November 22, 1968; first produced in Spanish in Madrid at Teatro Benavente, January 29, 1976; first published in *Artes hispánicas/Hispanic Arts* [bilingual; English translation by Anderson], 1967), edited and annotated by Alfonso M. Gil, Center for Curriculum Development (Philadelphia), 1970, critical Spanish edition edited by William Giuliano, Scribner, 1986.

El sueño de la razón: Fantasía en dos actos (title means "The Sleep of Reason: Two-Act Fantasy"; first produced in Madrid at Teatro de la Reina Victoria, February 6, 1970; also see below), Escelicer, 1970, critical Spanish edition edited by John C. Dowling, Center for Curriculum Development, 1971.

"La fundación" (title means "The Foundation"; two parts; also see below), first produced in Madrid at Teatro Fígaro, January 15, 1974.

Three Plays (contains "The Sleep of Reason," "The Foundation," and "In the Burning Darkness"), translation by Holt, Trinity University Press, 1985.

IN SPANISH; PLAYS

"Las palabras en la arena: Tragedia en un acto" (title means "Words in the Arena: Tragedy in One Act"; also see below), first produced at Teatro Español, December 19, 1949.

Historia de una escalera: Drama en tres actos (title means "Story of a Stairway: Three-Act Drama"; first produced at Teatro Español, October 14, 1949; also see below), José Janés (Barcelona), 1950, critical Spanish edition edited by José Sánchez, Scribner, 1955, reprinted, 1971, critical Spanish edition edited by H. Lester and J. A. Zabalbeascoa Bilbao, University of London Press, 1963.

La señal que se espera: Comedia dramática en tres actos (title means "The Expected Sign: Three-Act Dramatic Comedy"; first produced in Madrid at Teatro de la Infanta Isabel, May 21, 1952), Alfil, 1952.

Casi un cuento de hadas: Una glosa de Perrault, en tres actos (title means "Almost a Fairy Tale: Three-Act Variation on Perrault"; first produced in Madrid at Teatro Alcázar, January 10, 1953), Alfil, 1953, reprinted, Narcea, 1981.

El terror inmóvil: Fragmentos de una tragedia irrepresentable (title means "Motionless Terror: Fragments of An Unrepresentable Tragedy"), Alfil, 1954.

Madrugada: Episodio dramático en dos actos (title means "Daybreak: Two-Act Dramatic Episode"; first produced at Teatro Alcázar, December 9, 1953; also see below), Alfil, 1954, critical Spanish edition edited by Donald W. Bleznick and Martha T. Halsey, Blaisdell (Waltham, Mass.), 1969.

Irene o el tesoro: Fabula en tres actos (title means "Irene; or, The Treasure: Three-Act Fable"; first produced at Teatro Nacional María Guerrero, December 14, 1954; also see below), Alfil, 1955.

Aventura en lo gris: Drama en dos actos únidos por un sueño increíble (title means "Adventure in Grayness: Drama in Two Acts United by an Incredible Dream"; first published as "Aventura en lo gris: Dos actos grises, únidos por un sueño increíble" [subtitle means "Two Gray Acts, United by an Incredible Dream"] in *Teatro: Revista internacional de la escena* [Madrid], January-March, 1954), Puerta del Sol, 1955, revised edition published as *Aventura en lo gris: Dos actos y un sueño* (subtitle means "Two Acts and a Dream";

first produced in Madrid at Teatro Recoletas, October 1, 1963), Alfil, 1964.

Hoy es fiesta: [Tragi]comedia en tres actos (title means "Today Is a Holiday: Three-Act [Tragi]comedy"; first produced at Teatro Nacional María Guerrero, September 20, 1956; also see below), Alfil, 1957, reprinted, Almán, 1978, critical Spanish edition edited by J. E. Lyon, Harrap, 1964, Heath, 1966.

Las cartas boca abajo: Tragedia española en dos partes, y cuatro cuadros (title means "The Cards Face Down: Spanish Tragedy in Two Parts and Four Scenes"; first produced at Teatro de la Reina Victoria, November 5, 1957; also see below), Alfil, 1958, critical Spanish edition edited by Felix G. Ilarraz, Prentice-Hall, 1967.

Un soñador para un pueblo: Versión libre de un episodio histórico, en dos partes (title means "A Dreamer for the People: A Version of a Historical Episode, in Two Parts"; first produced at Teatro Español, December 18, 1958; also see below), Alfil, 1959, critical Spanish edition edited by Manuela Manzanares de Cirre, Norton, 1966.

Llegada de los dioses (title means "The Gods' Arrival"; first produced in Madrid at Teatro Lara, September 17, 1971; also see below), Aguilar, 1973.

"La detonación" (two parts; title means "The Detonation"; also see below), first produced at Teatro Bellas Artes, September 20, 1977.

"Jueces en la noche" (two parts; title means "Judges in the Night"; also see below), first produced at Teatro Lara, October 2, 1979.

"Caimán" (two parts; title means "Alligator"; also see below), first produced at Teatro de la Reina Victoria, September 10, 1981.

Diálogo secreto (two parts; title means "Secret Dialogue"; first produced in San Sebastian, Spain, at Teatro Victoria Eugenia, August 6, 1984), Espasa-Calpe, 1985.

Lázaro en el laberinto (two parts; title means "Lazarus in the Labyrinth"; first produced at Teatro Maravillas, December 18, 1986), Espasa Calpe, 1987.

Also author of unpublished plays "Historia despiada" and "Otro juicio de Salomón," both before 1949, and "Una extraña armonía," 1957.

OMNIBUS VOLUMES

Historia de una escalera [and] *Las palabras en la arena,* Alfil, 1952, reprinted, Escelicer, 1974.

Teatro, Losada (Buenos Aires), Volume 1: *En la ardiente oscuridad, Madrugada, Hoy es fiesta, Las cartas boca abajo,* 1959, Volume 2: *Historia de una escalera, La tejedora de sueños, Irene o el tesoro, Un soñador para un pueblo,* 1962.

Teatro selecto: Historia de una escalera, Las cartas boca abajo, Un soñador para un pueblo, Las Meninas, El concierto de San Ovidio, edited by Luce Moreau-Anabal, Escelicer, 1966.

Buero Vallejo: Antología teatral (contains fragments of "Historia de una escalera," "En la ardiente oscuridad," and "Irene o el tesoro"), Coculsa (Madrid), 1966.

Dos dramas de Buero Vallejo: Aventura en lo gris [and] *Las palabras en la arena,* edited by Isabel Magana Schevill, Appleton-Century-Crofts, 1967.

En la ardiente oscuridad [and] *Irene o el tesoro,* Magisterio Español (Madrid), 1967.

Teatro: Hoy es fiesta, Las Meninas, [and] *El tragaluz* (includes interviews and critical essays by others), Taurus (Madrid), 1968.

El tragaluz [and] *El sueño de la razón,* Espasa-Calpe, 1970.

El concierto de San Ovidio [and] *El tragaluz,* edited by Ricardo Domenech, Castalia, 1971.

En la ardiente oscuridad [and] *Un soñador para un pueblo,* Espasa-Calpe, 1972.

Historia de una escalera [and] *Llegada de los dioses,* Salvat, 1973.

Historia de una escalera [and] *Las Meninas,* prologue by Domenech, Espasa-Calpe, 1975.

La doble historia del Doctor Valmy [and] *Mito* (also see below), prologue by Francisco García Pavón, Espasa-Calpe, 1976.

La tejedora de sueños [and] *Llegada de los dioses,* edited by Luis Iglesias Feijoo, Catedra, 1976.

La detonación [and] *Las palabras en la arena,* Espasa-Calpe, 1979.

Jueces en la noche [and] *Hoy es fiesta,* prologue by Feijoo, Espasa-Calpe, 1981.

Caimán [and] *Las cartas boca abajo,* Espasa-Calpe, 1981.

CONTRIBUTOR

Charles Davillier, *Viaje por España,* Castilla (Madrid), 1949.

Don Juan y el teatro en España: Fotografías de Juan Gyenes, Mundo Hispánico (Madrid), 1955.

Informaciones: Extraordinario teatral del sábado de gloria, [Madrid], 1956.

Guillermo Díaz-Plaja, editor, *El teatro: Enciclopedia del arte escénico,* Noguer (Barcelona), 1958.

Homenaje a Vicente Aleixandre, El Bardo (Barcelona), 1964.

CONTRIBUTOR TO "TEATRO ESPAÑOL" SERIES; EDITED BY F. C. SAINZ DE ROBLES

Teatro español, 1949-1950 (includes "Historia de una escalera"), Aguilar, 1951.

. . . *1950-1951* (includes "En la ardiente oscuridad"), Aguilar, 1952.

. . . *1951-1952* (includes "La tejedora de sueños"), Aguilar, 1953.

. . . *1953-1954* (includes "Madrugada"), Aguilar, 1955.

. . . *1954-1955* (includes "Irene o el tesoro"), Aguilar, 1956.

. . . *1957-1958* (includes "Las cartas boca abajo"), Aguilar, 1959.

. . . *1958-1959* (includes "Un soñador para un pueblo"), Aguilar, 1960.

. . . *1960-1961* (includes "Las Meninas"), Aguilar, 1962.

. . . *1962-1963* (includes "El concierto de San Ovidio"), Aguilar, 1964.

. . . *1967-1968* (includes "El tragaluz"), Aguilar, 1969.

. . . *1969-1970* (includes "El sueño de la razón"), Aguilar, 1971.

. . . *1971-1972* (includes "Llegada de los dioses"), Aguilar, 1973.

. . . *1973-1974* (includes "La fundación"), Aguilar, 1975.

CONTRIBUTOR TO ANTHOLOGIES

Fernando Díaz-Plaja, editor, *Teatro español de hoy: Antología (1939-1958),* Alfil, 1958, 2nd edition published as *Teatro español de hoy: Antología (1939-1966),* Alfil, 1967.

Antonio Espina, editor, *Las mejores escenas del teatro español e hispano-americano,* Aguilar, 1959.

Festival de la literatura española contemporánea, Volume 4: *Teatro,* Tawantinsuyu (Lima, Peru), 1960.

Teatro: Buero Vallejo, Delgado Benavente y Alfonso Sastre, Tawantinsuyu, 1960.

Richard E. Chandler and Kessel Schwartz, editors, *A New Anthology of Spanish Literature,* Louisiana State University Press, 1967.

Robert W. Corrigan, editor, *Masterpieces of the Modern Spanish Theatre,* Collier, 1967.

Diego Marín, editor, *Literatura española,* Holt, 1968.

Walter T. Pattison and Bleznick, editors, *Representative Spanish Authors,* 3rd edition, Volume 2, Oxford University Press, 1971.

Spanische Stuecke, Henschelverlag (Berlin), 1976.

Años difíciles, Bruguera, 1977.

TRANSLATOR OF PLAYS

William Shakespeare, *Hamlet: Príncipe de Dinamarca* (first produced at Teatro Español, December 15, 1961), Alfil, 1962.

Bertolt Brecht, *Madre Coraje y sus hijos: Una crónica de la Guerra de los Treinta Años* (first produced at Teatro Bellas Artes, October 6, 1966), Alfil, 1967.

Also translator of "Vildanden" by Henrik Ibsen, first produced as "El pato silvestre" at Teatro Nacional María Guerrero.

OTHER

(Author of prologue) Juan B. Devoto and Alberto Sábato, *Un responso para Lázaro,* Almafuerte (Buenos Aires), 1956.

Mito: Libro para una ópera (title means "Myth: Book for an Opera"; first published in *Primer Acto,* November-December, 1968), Alfil, 1968.

Tres maestros ante el público (biographical essays; title means "Three Masters before the Public"), Alianza, 1973.

Also author of screenplays and of sound recording *Me llamo Antonio Buero Vallejo* (title means "My Name is Antonio Buero Vallejo"), Discos Aguilar (Madrid), 1964. Contributor to periodicals, including *Correo Literario, Primer Acto, Revista de Occidente, Pipirijaina, Cuadernos de Agora,* and *Estreno.*

SIDELIGHTS: "The 1949-1950 theatrical season represents a turning point in Spanish drama," writes Martha T. Halsey in *Antonio Buero Vallejo,* "because of the new direction represented by" Buero Vallejo's play "Historia de una escalera" ("Story of a Stairway"). Although this was the Spanish playwright's first produced play, its impact, according to Marion Peter Holt in *The Contemporary Spanish Theater (1949-1972),* was comparable to that of Arthur Miller's "Death of a Salesman," which triumphed on the American stage during the same season. Not only were both plays popular and critical successes during their first theater runs, but they were also tragic portrayals of everyday existence in their respective societies.

The effect of Buero Vallejo's play on Spanish drama is described in an Arturo del Hoyo essay which Holt translates (it first appeared in the Spanish literary review *Insula* shortly after "Historia de una escalera" opened). "From the first moments of the performance," del Hoyo notes, "the spectator was aware that *Story of a Stairway,* with its sense of dramatic values, was what had been needed in our theater to help free itself from paralysis, from mediocrity. For since 1939 the Spanish theater had been living among the ruins of the past."

Spanish theater had been living "among the ruins" caused by the bloody Spanish civil war, which devastated the country from 1936 to 1939. Joelyn Ruple's *Antonio Buero Vallejo: The First Fifteen Years* gives a picture of the bleak state of postwar Spanish theater: "During the years immediately following the war the government used the theater and movies for propaganda. There were translations of works from other countries, presentations of the Spanish classics, and some works by contemporary writers, but works censored and in general of limited value."

Strict censorship caused many writers to produce light, inoffensive works rather than risk government reprisals. "The early postwar years," Halsey explains, "had been characterized by a new type of escape theater, termed 'theater of evasion,' which renounced any purposeful interpretation of reality in favor of adventures of a strictly imaginative nature."

However, when Buero Vallejo (who had been studying painting) decided to become a playwright after the war, government censorship and the general evasiveness of Spanish plays of the period were not his most important concerns. He was an ex-prisoner, having been sentenced to death—later commuted to six years imprisonment—for his activities with the Republican (Loyalist) army during the war. But, whereas many writers chose to flee Fascist rule, Buero Vallejo decided instead to remain in Spain and produce plays. While he chose not to overtly attack Spanish authorities in his works, his plays nevertheless subtly protest Spain's repressive society.

Because of Buero Vallejo's technique of veiled criticism, Francis Donahue lists the playwright in *Books Abroad* as the leader of the Spanish "Theater of Commitment." "Spain's Theater of Commitment," Donahue remarks, "is a non-political, political theater, for it makes its impact by indirect means. The antagonist in the Theater of Commitment is the Establishment. To point out specifically the nature of that antagonist . . . would mean the play would remain unstaged. . . . The cause of the evil conditions remains unspecified, but implied: The Spanish Establishment."

Buero Vallejo's first play, "En la ardiente oscuridad" ("In the Burning Darkness"), is a good example of his theater in general and shows how a playwright of the Theater of Commitment voices criticism in his or her work. According to Halsey the play "contains much of the thematics and symbolism more fully developed in [Buero Vallejo's] later works." Holt concurs, noting, "A consideration of *In the Burning Darkness* . . . is fundamental to an understanding of the playwright's ideas and dramatic techniques."

Although Buero Vallejo may seem to avoid the issue of government oppression in, for example, "In the Burning Darkness" because he writes about a school for the blind, his meaning is subtly revealed. The play tells the story of Ignacio's arrival at the school and how his anger at being blind disrupts the formerly tranquil life of the students. Ruple explains the social protest inherent in the play: "In ['In the Burning Darkness'] we find a philosophical or religious struggle within the protagonist as he pleads to society to look about and see the conditions under which it actually exists, to stop pretending that all is right with the world. . . . He . . . protests a lethargic society which refuses to recognize and reject a dictator." In *The Tragic Stages of Antonio Buero Vallejo*, Robert L. Nicholas agrees that this play, and many of Buero Vallejo's other works, can be viewed in terms of two levels: the surface story and its underlying philosophical truth. "As the play develops," he notes, "it becomes clear that physical blindness is symbolic of spiritual blindness and that a longing for truth, and not physical sight, is the real source of Ignacio's torment."

Many of Buero Vallejo's plays deal with a quest for the truth and the fate of those who look for it in a society blind to its own tragic reality. The seekers of truth in his plays are often "visionaries," according to Holt in his introduction to *Three Plays,* who look "beyond the present reality to a more enlightened future." Ignacio, the blind "trouble-maker" of "In the Burning Darkness," is such a visionary. In three later plays, Buero Vallejo chooses as protagonists figures from Spanish history—the painters Diego de Silva Velázquez and Francisco José de Goya, and the writer Mariano José de Larra. The three plays in which these historical characters appear—"Las Meninas" ("The Ladies-in-Waiting"), "El sueño de la razón" ("The Sleep of Reason"), and "La detonación" ("The Detonation"), respectively—deal with, as Halsey comments in *Hispanic Journal,* "the role of the intellectual in a repressive society."

"Las Meninas" takes its name from Velázquez's masterpiece, a 10' x 9' painting of five-year-old Princess Margarita and other members of Philip IV's royal household. The painting has fascinated art critics for centuries because the wonderful portrait of the princess also includes the shadowy images of Spain's king and queen in a background mirror. Buero Vallejo's play explores the political and social implications of the painting, and "the painter," observes Nicholas, ". . . is portrayed as the lonely intellectual who attacks all that is false and unjust in seventeenth-century Spanish society." According to Nicholas, "Las Meninas" "is a . . . plea for justice. More than that, it is a call to responsibility for the intelligentsia. Buero [Vallejo] has pictorially revived a moment in history in order to address and indict his contemporaries. . . . *Las Meninas* is a direct yet subtly conceived attack against censorship."

Nicholas, Halsey, and Ruple comment on the importance of a scene in the play in which Pedro, a half-blind beggar, reacts to Velásquez's preliminary sketch for *Las Meninas*. Ruple translates Pedro's words: "Yes, I think I understand. A serene picture, but containing all the sadness of Spain. Anyone who sees these creatures will understand how irredeemably condemned they are to suffer. They're living ghosts whose truth is death. Whoever sees them in the future will notice it with terror." By implication, Buero Vallejo suggests that under Franco's repression Spaniards of the twentieth century are also "irredeemably condemned to suffer."

"El sueño de la razón" takes its name from a late eighteenth-century etching by Goya entitled *El sueño de la razón produce monstruos* ("The Sleep of Reason Produces Monsters"). The etching carries the caption: "Imagination abandoned by reason produces impossible monsters; united with her, she is the mother of the arts and the source of their wonders." The etching is a self-portrait of the artist asleep at his desk while evil-looking winged creatures hover about his head and a large cat-like animal watches him with glowing eyes. The terror depicted in the etching is masterfully portrayed in Buero Vallejo's play, according to critics. Through a variety of techniques he captures the misery of the great artist left totally deaf by illness and under constant threat of harassment or death from the authorities. The playwright uses projections of the "Black Paintings"—strange dark scenes with which Goya covered the interior walls of his country house—to express his emotional turmoil.

Holt refers to a characteristic Buero Vallejo dramatic device introduced in "In the Burning Darkness" and later refined in "The Sleep of Reason." This technique, which the playwright calls "interiorización" ("interiorization") appears in the earlier play in a scene that makes Ignacio's blindness startlingly real to the audience. While Ignacio speaks of his horror at being blind, the stage lights begin to dim until the entire theater is completely dark. The darkness lasts through four or five lines of dialogue before the lights are turned on again.

In "The Sleep of Reason" Buero Vallejo forces the audience to experience Goya's deafness: in the latter's presence the actors mouth their lines of dialogue but make no sound. To simulate the artist's inner anguish, amplified heartbeats and the noise of flapping wings fill the theater, but only Goya reacts to them—

they are not heard by the other characters. To heighten the drama, the projections of Goya's "Black Paintings" flash across the stage in an ever increasing tempo.

Holt comments: "The momentary dimming of the stage and houselights to a point of absolute darkness in one crucial scene of *In the Burning Darkness* is a far cry from the frequent scenes of silently mouthed dialogue or the visual and aural bombardment of the audience with projections and amplified sounds in *The Sleep of Reason*. . . . The audience is drawn into the mind of a character or into a crucial dramatic situation with intensified personal identification, as the proscenium barrier is bridged and momentarily ceases to exist."

Halsey refers to the techniques of interiorization as "psychic participation." She concludes that through interiorization in both "In the Burning Darkness" and in "The Sleep of Reason," Buero Vallejo produces "a more authentic participation in the reality of the tragedy." According to Halsey the reality in both of these plays "is symbolic, for the blindness portrayed represents . . . man's lack of spiritual vision and the deafness, his alienation or estrangement from his fellow human beings."

The protagonist of Buero Vallejo's "La detonación" ("The Detonation"), Mariano José de Larra, is a visionary similar to the playwright's Ignacio, Velázquez, and Goya. Larra lived during the early 1800s, another period of political struggle in Spain characterized by strict censorship. Just as during Buero Vallejo's time, writers of Larra's era tried to avoid direct confrontation with the authorities by writing comedies. Larra refused to do so, writing instead satirical essays in which he attacked almost every facet of society. In *Hispanic Journal* Halsey calls Larra an "author surrogate." She notes: "Larra stated that to write in Madrid was to weep. Buero [Vallejo] no doubt experienced the same sentiment during the Franco era and initial transition period" after the dictator's death.

In spite of tremendous obstacles, Buero Vallejo achieved success as a playwright from the very beginning of his career. "The Sleep of Reason" is probably his most notable play; after being acclaimed in Madrid it was subsequently produced in a number of European countries. In 1974, it became the first Buero Vallejo play to be produced professionally in the United States. In *The Contemporary Spanish Theater* Holt calls "The Sleep of Reason" "one of the most impressive achievements of [Buero Vallejo's] career" and later adds: "With this play Buero [Vallejo] . . . sustained his right to be included among the major international writers of his day."

In a *Hispania* essay, Patricia W. O'Connor comments that because of Buero Vallejo's position as a highly respected playwright, Spanish censors have given him "relatively few problems" during his long career. But, almost all of his plays underwent at least a few *tachaduras,* or cuts, before they were allowed to be produced. "Aventura en lo gris" ("Adventure in Gray"), for example, although written in 1953, was not performed in Spain until 1963 and then only after extensive revision. The playwright's 1964 work "La doble historia del doctor Valmy" ("The Double Case-History of Doctor Valmy"), which deals with the torture of political prisoners, was not performed in Spain until 1976, after the death of Franco.

Even with the lifting of censorship in the post-Franco era, Buero Vallejo continues to deal with social issues in his plays. He writes about the tragic nature of man in order to hope for a better society. Nicholas observes: "Buero [Vallejo] is no genius—he is not a Goya; he is just an honest, courageous playwright who tries to expose social injustice, and a good, humble man who seeks to understand human suffering. Each is an endless task."

Buero Vallejo told *CA:* "After three years of war and six long years in prison, I had fallen so far behind in my painting studies that I gave them up, and set out to write for the theatre because, naturally, I had also loved the theatre since I was a child. Under Franco's strict censorship this undertaking proved even more difficult, but a set of favorable circumstances permitted me to continue onward. For me and for others, this censorship was a challenge, not just an obstacle, and I wasn't the only one to accept it. Poets, novelists, essayists, and other dramatists tried to convince the Spanish people (and themselves) that, although frequently very painful, a critical and reformative literature was possible in spite of all the environmental and administrative obstacles.

"In regards to the theatre, the official, unwritten watchwords were patriotism, escapism, moralism, and as much laughter as possible. Therefore, one had to do the opposite: tragedy which revealed instead of concealed the fact that one's destiny is a result of human and social factors instead of fate; a denunciation of injustices and frauds, a defense of liberty. And one had, at the same time, to produce serious experiences. Others will say to what extent each of us has attained these goals; perhaps they'll explain it tomorrow when the biases against this literature, which remain very strong, have been dismantled sociologically. I believe undeniably that, between all of us, something, and perhaps even a lot, has been gained. And because of this, our nation also had more support for resistance, hope and clear thinking.

"The Greek tragedians, Shakespeare, Cervantes, Calderón, Unamuno, Ibsen, Pirandello, Brecht have been, among others, my teachers, and their imprint can be observed in my theatre. Although less frequently noted, but perhaps even more important in some of my works, is the presence of Wells and Kafka. As a poet-friend of mine says about himself, I am also a 'child of well-known parents.' My originality, if I have any, is not based on denying them."

MEDIA ADAPTATIONS: "Madrugada" was made into a film.

AVOCATIONAL INTERESTS: Painting.

BIOGRAPHICAL/CRITICAL SOURCES:

BOOKS

Bejel, Emilio F., *Lo moral, lo social y lo metafísico en el teatro de Buero Vallejo,* Florida State University, 1970.
Buero Vallejo, Antonio, *Teatro: Hoy es fiesta, Las Meninas* [and] *El tragaluz,* Taurus, 1968.
Buero Vallejo, Antonio, *Three Plays,* edited and translated by Marion Peter Holt, Trinity University Press, 1985.
Contemporary Literary Criticism, Gale, Volume 15, 1980, Volume 46, 1988.
Corrigan, Robert W., *Masterpieces of the Modern Spanish Theatre,* Collier, 1967.
Domenech, Ricardo, *El teatro de Buero Vallejo,* Gredos, 1973.
Feijoo, Luis Iglesias, *La trayectoria dramática de Antonio Buero Vallejo,* University of Santiago, 1982.
Halsey, Martha T., *Antonio Buero Vallejo,* Twayne, 1973.
Holt, Marion Peter, *The Modern Spanish Stage: Four Plays,* Hill & Wang, 1970.
Holt, Marion Peter, *The Contemporary Spanish Theater (1949-1972),* Twayne, 1975.
Nicholas, Robert L., *The Tragic Stages of Antonio Buero Vallejo,* Estudios de Hispanófila, 1972.

Ruple, Joelyn, *Antonio Buero Vallejo: The First Fifteen Years,* Eliseo Torres & Sons, 1971.

PERIODICALS

Books Abroad, summer, 1969.
Hispania, March, 1968, September, 1968, December, 1968, May, 1969, September, 1969, December, 1969, September, 1971, December, 1972, May, 1973, September, 1974, September, 1978.
Hispanic Journal, spring, 1984, fall, 1986.
Hispanófila, May, 1970.
Modern Drama, September, 1977.
Modern Language Journal, February, 1972, January, 1973, December, 1978, spring, 1984, fall, 1986.
Revista de estudios hispánicos, November, 1969, May, 1978.

* * *

BULLRICH (PALENQUE), Silvina 1915-

PERSONAL: Born in Argentina in 1915; daughter of a cardiologist; married first husband, c. 1935 (divorced); married Marcelo Dupont, c. 1952 (deceased, 1956); children: one son (first marriage).

CAREER: Writer. Member of Argentine National Arts Foundation.

AWARDS, HONORS: Premio Municipal de la Ciudad de Buenos Aires, 1943, for *La redoma del primer ángel: Crónica de los años cuarenta.*

WRITINGS:

NOVELS

Calles de Buenos Aires (title means "The Streets of Buenos Aires"), 1939, reprinted, Emecé, 1979.
Sáloma (title means "Salome"), A. Contreras (Buenos Aires), 1940.
Su vida y yo, Espasa-Calpe (Buenos Aires), 1941.
La redoma del primer ángel: Crónica de los años cuarenta (title means "The First Angel's Flask: Chronicle of the Forties"), prologue by Bullrich, Emecé, 1943, reprinted, 1979.
La tercera versión (title means "The Third Version"; also see below), Emecé, 1944, reprinted, S. Rueda (Buenos Aires), 1969.
Bodas de cristal (title means "Crystal Wedding Anniversary"; also see below), Sudamericana, 1953, reprinted, 1973.
Teléfono ocupado (title means "The Line Is Busy"; also see below), Goyanarte, 1955, published with author's corrections, Emecé, 1971.
Mientras los demás viven (title means "While the Rest Live"; also see below), Sudamericana, 1958.
El hechicero (title means "The Witch"; also see below), Goyanarte, 1961.
Un momento muy largo (title means "A Very Long Moment"; also see below), Sudamericana, 1961.
Los burgueses (title means "The Bourgeoisie"), Sudamericana, 1964.
Los salvadores de la patria (title means "The Saviors of the Fatherland"), Sudamericana, 1965.
Tres novelas: Bodas de cristal, Mientras los demás viven, Un momento muy largo, Sudamericana, 1966.
La creciente (title means "The Flood"), Sudamericana, 1967.
Mañana digo basta (title means "Tomorrow I'll Say Enough"), Sudamericana, 1968.
La tercera versión; Bodas de cristal, Selectas (Buenos Aires), 1969.

Hágase justicia, 1970, published as *Será justicia,* Sudamericana, 1976.
El calor humano (title means "Human Warmth"), 2nd edition, Merlín (Buenos Aires), 1970.
Carta abierta a los hijos (title means "Open Letter to the Children"), Emecé, 1970.
Los monstruos sagrados (title means "The Sacred Monsters"), Sudamericana, 1971.
Los pasajeros del jardín (title means "The Passengers in the Garden"), Emecé, 1972.
Mal don (title means "Bad Gift"), Emecé, 1973.
Su excelencia envió el informe, Emecé, 1974.
Te acordarás de Taormina (title means "You Will Remember Taormina"), Emecé, 1975.
Reunión de directorio (title means "The Board of Directors' Meeting"), Sudamericana, 1977.
Los despiados, Emecé, 1978.
Escándalo bancario (title means "Bank Scandal"), Emecé, 1980.
Después del escándalo, Emecé, 1981.
¿A qué hora murió el enfermo? (title means "At What Time Did the Sick One Die?"), Emecé, 1984.
La bicicleta (title means "The Bicycle"), Emecé, 1986.

OTHER

Vibraciones (title means "Vibrations"; poems), [Buenos Aires], 1935.
(Editor with Jorge Luis Borges) *El compadrito: Su destino, sus barrios, su música* (title means "The Buenos Aires Hoodlum: His Destiny, His Neighborhoods, His Music"), prologue by Borges, Emecé, 1945, 2nd edition, Fabril, 1968.
Historia de un silencio (title means "Story of a Silence"; short stories), Folia (Buenos Aires), 1949, enlarged edition, Merlín, 1971.
George Sand (biography), 2nd edition, Emecé, 1963.
Historias inmorales (title means "Immoral Stories"; short stories), Sudamericana, 1965.
Carta a un joven cuentista (title means "Letter to a Young Story Teller"), S. Rueda, 1968.
El mundo que yo ví: Documentos de época a través de los viajes (1949-1976) (title means "The World that I Saw: Documents of an Era through Travel [1949-1976]"; travel), Merlín, 1969.
La aventura interior (title means "The Inner Adventure"; essays), Merlín, 1970.
Entre mis veinte y treinta años (title means "Between My Twentieth and Thirtieth Years"; anthology), Emecé, 1970.
La mujer argentina en la literatura (monograph), Centro Nacional de Documentación e Información Educativa (Buenos Aires), 1972.
Un hombre con historia (title means "A Man With a Past"; contains two short stories: the title story and "Lo demás es mentira" [title means "Anything Else Is a Lie"]), Merlín, 1973.
Silvina Bullrich (selections from her works), edited by Nicolás Cócaro, Ediciones Culturales Argentinas, 1979.
Mis memorias (title means "My Memories"; autobiography), Emecé, 1980.
Flora Tristán, la visionaria, RIESA, 1982.
La mujer postergada, Sudamericana, 1982.
Páginas de Silvina Bullrich (title means "Pages by Silvina Bullrich"; selections from her work), Celtia (Buenos Aires), 1983.
Cuento cruel, Abril, 1983.
La Argentina contradictoria (collection of pieces which originally appeared in *La Nación*), Emecé, 1986.

Cuando cae el telón, Emecé, 1987.

Translator of works by French authors, including Simone de Beauvoir, Guy de Maupassant, George Sand, and Prosper Merimee. Contributor to periodicals, including *La Nación.*

SIDELIGHTS: Silvina Bullrich has been an extremely popular author in her native Argentina for over forty years. Although not particularly acclaimed by critics, Bullrich is well known for her best-selling novels which she divides into three phases of development: early works (1935-49), sentimental novels (1951-61), and works of maturity (1964 to present). In Erica Fouman-Smith's extensive essay on Bullrich appearing in *Contemporary Women Authors of Latin America* the critic analyzes the feminist content of Bullrich's novels, noting an evolution in her thinking from an optimistic point of view to a more pessimistic and satiric vision of Argentine life. Although her outlook has changed over the years, the content of Bullrich's novels has remained the same: her works focus on the problems of women forced to live in the shadow of Argentina's male-oriented society.

Bodas de cristal ("Crystal Wedding Anniversary"), an example of Bullrich's second phase of novels, is one of the writer's most successful works and has been reprinted several times and translated into several languages. It features one of Bullrich's characters as a first-person narrator, a technique which became typical of most of her later works. *Bodas de cristal* tells the story of a nameless Wife, her husband Luis, and his three mistresses, Elena, Susana, and Isabel. The novel contains many of Bullrich's most important themes, including the inferior status of women in Argentina. Being nameless, the Wife can be just another object for her husband to possess and, at the same time, she can stand for every woman. Frouman-Smith quotes in English translation a statement by one of Luis's mistresses through whom Bullrich comments on the desperateness of the female condition: "Oh, the eternal, constant female inferiority. Oh, the prolonged shout that goes on unceasingly from adolescence to maturity that is motherhood! What man could carry that dependency, that submission."

In Bullrich's mature works she continues her examination of the plight of Argentine women, but she couples this theme with social satire on the general deterioration of Argentine society. In an example of her fiction from this period, *Reunión de directorio* ("The Board of Directors' Meeting"), Bullrich creates the island nation of La Enjoyada as a stand-in for Argentina and through Cecilia, the female narrator-protagonist of the novel, comments on her own country's ills. Cecilia appears to be the only member of the Board of Directors of the Directory of Central Planning who appears to see the social reality that surrounds her. Her experiences echo Bullrich's own frustrating activities as a board member of the Argentine National Arts Foundation during the repressive dictatorship of Juan Perón. The fictional Board ponders the huge amount of money needed to ready the country for the World Cup Figure Skating Competition, even though the citizens lack adequate sanitary supplies and reliable electrical systems, just as the Argentine government spent an equal sum of money to host the World Cup of Soccer in 1978 instead of providing badly needed social services. Frouman-Smith notes that the pessimistic attitude prevalent in Bullrich's most recent fiction allows only an unhappy ending to this novel: "Despite another revolution and a new president, everything returns to its former, unhappy condition. Cecilia is once again on the Board of Directors listening for plans for a new subway system (the country is so small it is hardly visible on a map), and large hotels with swimming pools (despite abundant, natural beaches)."

Although lacking international acclaim, Bullrich continues to write novels that are well received in her country. She believes

such an absence of recognition is the typical fate of an Argentine woman writer as she notes in her essay *La mujer en la literatura argentina* ("Woman in Argentine Literature"), which Frouman-Smith quotes in English translation. Bullrich maintains that women writers "were the artificers of the famous 'boom' of the Argentine novel, but when the time comes to reap the benefits, men's hands stretch out ahead of ours, they are longer and greedier." Frouman-Smith concludes her thoughts on Bullrich's fiction with the observation that "Bullrich has demonstrated, for more than forty years, a serious and sincere commitment to writing. Her depiction of women within a particular milieu is penetrating, revealing and universal in nature."

BIOGRAPHICAL/CRITICAL SOURCES:

BOOKS

Bullrich, Silvina, *Bodas de cristal,* Sudamericana, 1953.
Bullrich, Silvina, *La mujer en la literatura argentina,* Centro Nacional de Documentación e Información Educativa, 1972.
Meyer, Doris, and Margarite Fernández Olmos, editors, *Contemporary Women Authors of Latin America,* Brooklyn College Press, 1983.

*   *   *

BUÑUEL, Luis   1900-1983

PERSONAL: Born February 22, 1900, in Calanda, Spain; died of cirrhosis of the liver, July 29, 1983, in Mexico City, Mexico; son of Leonardo (a landowner) and María (Portoles) Buñuel; married Jeanne Rucar, 1934; children: Rafael, Juan Luis. *Education:* Attended University of Madrid, 1920-23, and Academie du Cinema, 1925.

ADDRESSES: Office—Greenwich Film Production, 72 Avenue des Champs-Elysees 75008, Paris, France.

CAREER: Writer, producer, and director of motion pictures. Director of motion pictures in Mexico, including "Las hurdes" (documentary; released in the U.S. as "Land Without Bread"), 1932, "Gran casino," 1947, "El gran calavera" (released in the U.S. as "The Great Madcap"), 1949, "Susana" (also released in the U.S. as "The Devil and the Flesh"), 1951, "La hija del engaño" (released in the U.S. as "Daughter of Deceit"), 1951, "Una mujer sin amor," 1951, "La ilusión viaja en tranvía" (released in the U.S. as "Illusion Travels by Streetcar"), 1953. Worked as actor and assistant to Jean Epstein on "Mauprat," 1926, "La sirene du tropiques," 1927, and "The Fall of the House of Usher," 1928; language dubber for Warner Bros., in Paris, France, 1932-34, and Spain, 1935; executive producer in Spain, 1935-36; technical adviser for Metro-Goldwyn-Mayer in Hollywood, Calif., on uncompleted motion picture, "Cargo of Innocence," 1938; assistant on anti-Nazi film projects for Museum of Modern Art in New York, N.Y., 1940; filmmaker for U.S. Army, 1940-43; language dubber for Warner Bros., in Hollywood, 1944-46.

AWARDS, HONORS: Best director award from Cannes Film Festival and International Critics' Prize, both 1951, both for "Los olvidados"; best avant-garde film award from Cannes Film Festival, 1952, for "Subida al cielo"; special international jury prize from Cannes Film Festival, 1958, for "Nazarín"; *hors concours* recognition from Cannes Film Festival, 1960, for "The Young One"; Golden Palm from Cannes Film Festival, 1961, for "Viridiana"; Golden Lion of St. Mark from Venice Film Festival, 1967, for "Belle de jour"; Order of the Yugoslav Flag, 1971: Academy Award for best foreign language film from Academy of Motion Picture Arts and Sciences, 1972, for "Le Charm discret de la bourgeoisie"; and other film awards.

WRITINGS:

SCREENPLAYS IN ENGLISH; AND DIRECTOR

(With Julio Alejandro) *Viridiana* (produced in Spain by Gustavo Alatriste and Uninci Films 59, 1961; also see below), Interspectacles, 1962.

(With Alejandro) *El angel exterminador* (title means "The Exterminating Angel"; produced in Mexico by Uninci Films 59, 1962; also see below), Ayma, 1964.

(With Alejandro) *Nazarín* (produced in Mexico by Manuel Barbachano Ponce, 1958; adapted from the novel by Benito Pérez Galdós; also see below), Belgium Ministre de l'Education National et de la Culture, Service Cinematographique, 1967.

(With Salvador Dali) *L'Age d'or* [and] *Un Chien andalou* (title of former means "The Golden Age," produced in France by Vicomte de Noailles, 1930; title of latter means "An Andalusian Dog," co-produced in France with Dali, 1928), translated by Marianne Alexandre from the unpublished French manuscripts, Simon & Schuster, 1968.

(With Alejandro) *Three Screenplays: Viridiana, The Exterminating Angel, Simon of the Desert* (latter by Buñuel only, produced in Mexico as "Simón del desierto" by Gustavo Alatriste, 1965; also see below), Orion Press, 1970.

(With Jean-Claude Carriere) *Belle de jour* (produced in France by Paris Film Production, 1966; adapted from the novel by Joseph Kessel), translated by Robert Adkinson from the unpublished French manuscript, Simon & Schuster, 1971.

(With Alejandro) *Tristana* (produced in Spain by Epoch Film, Talia Film, Selentia Cinematográfica, and Les Films Corona, 1970, adapted from the novel by Pérez Galdós), translated by Nicholas Fry from the unpublished French manuscript, Simon & Schuster, 1971.

(With Alejandro and Luis Alcoriza) *The Exterminating Angel, Nazarín, and Las Olvidados* (latter co-written with Alcoriza, produced in Mexico by Ultramar Films, 1950; also see above), translated by Fry from the unpublished French translations of the Spanish manuscripts, Simon & Schuster, 1972.

UNTRANSLATED WORKS; AND DIRECTOR

Un Chien andalou (poems and stories), [Spain], c. 1927.

(With Alcoriza) *Los náufragos de la calle de la providencia,* [Mexico], 1958.

(With Carriere) *Le Journal d'une femme de chambre* (screenplay; produced in France by Speva-Filmalliance-Filmsonor-Dear, 1964; released in U.S. as "The Diary of a Chambermaid"; adapted from the novel by Octave Mirbeau), Seuil, 1971.

(With Carriere) *El discreto encanto de la burguesía* (screenplay; produced in France as "Le Charme discret de la bourgeoisie" by Greenwich Productions, 1972; released in U.S. as "The Discreet Charm of the Bourgeoisie"), Ayma, 1973.

(With Carriere) *El fantasma de la liberte* (screenplay; produced in France as "Le Fantome de la liberté" by Greenwich Productions, 1974; released in U.S. as "The Phantom of Liberty"), Ayma, 1975.

UNPUBLISHED SCREENPLAYS IN ENGLISH; AND DIRECTOR

(With Philip Roll) "Robinson Crusoe" (adapted from the novel by Daniel Defoe), Ultramar Films, 1954.

(With H. B. Addis) "The Young One" (adapted from Peter Matthiesen's novel *Travellin' Man*), Producciones Olmeca, 1960.

UNPUBLISHED SCREENPLAYS IN SPANISH; AND DIRECTOR

(With Alcoriza) "El Bruto," International Cinematográfica, 1952.

(With Alcoriza) "El" (also released in U.S. as "This Strange Passion"; adapted from a novel by Mercedes Pinto), Nacional Film, 1952.

"Cumbres borrascosas" (also released as "Abismos de pasión"; adapted from the novel *Wuthering Heights,* by Emily Bronte), Tepeyac, 1953.

(With Alcoriza) "El río y la muerte" (adapted from the novel by Miguel Alvarez Acosta), Clasa Films Mundiales, 1954.

(With Eduardo Ugarte) "Ensayo de un crimen" (released in U.S. as "The Criminal Life of Archibaldo de la Cruz"; adapted from a story by Rodolfo Usigli), Alianza Cinematográfica, 1955.

(With Alcoriza, Louis Sapin, and Charles Dorat) "La Fievre monte a El Pao" (title means "Fever Mounts in El Paso"; adapted from the novel by Henri Castillou), C.I.C.C., Cite Films, Indus Films, Terra Films, Cormoran Films, and Cinematográfica Filmex, 1959.

UNPUBLISHED SCREENPLAYS IN FRENCH; AND DIRECTOR

(With Jean Ferry) "Cela s'appelle l'aurore" (title means "It's Called the Dawn"; adapted from the novel by Emmanuel Robles), Les Films Marceau and Laetitia Film, 1955.

(With Alcoriza, Raymond Queneau, and Gabriel Arout) "La Mort en ce jardin" (title means "Death in This Garden"), Dismage and Teperac, 1956.

(With Carriere) "La Voie lactée" (released in U.S. as "The Milky Way"), Greenwich Film Productions and Medusa, 1969.

(With Carriere) "Cet obscur objet du desir" (released in U.S. as "That Obscure Object of Desire"; suggested from the novel, *La Femme et le pantin,* by Pierre Louys), Serge Silberman, 1977.

OTHER

My Last Sigh (autobiography), translated by Abigail Israel, Knopf, 1983.

SIDELIGHTS: Luis Buñuel once told an interviewer, "I'm . . . an atheist, thank God." The comment is an apt example of both Buñuel's obsession and disdain for religion as well as his desire to elicit doubletakes from his audience. In his films, Buñuel welds his love-hate attitude towards religion with an ability to jar audiences, especially those from the upper class, into realizing that the world is not entirely safe or predictable. His first film, "An Andalusian Dog," shocked audiences with its opening depiction of a woman's eye being sliced with a straight razor. Buñuel called it "a desperate appeal to violence and crime." But in a career that spans more than fifty years, he has tempered his disposition to violence by directing his talents towards indictments of the bourgeoisie and the Church. He has persisted in his efforts to eliminate complacency and expose the corruption inherent in social convention. "The final sense of my films is this: to repeat, over and over again, in case anyone forgets it or believes the contrary, that we do not live in the best of all possible worlds," he contends.

Buñuel first became interested in art as a student of entomology in Madrid where he met such artists as José Ortega y Gasset, Federico García Lorca, and Salvador Dali. Buñuel and Dali became close friends and began attending films together. After the two established Spain's first film club, however, Buñuel moved to Paris and enrolled in the Academie du Cinema. He subsequently obtained an apprenticeship with filmmaker Jean Epstein on two motion pictures, "Mauprat" and "The Fall of the House of Usher." Through Epstein, Buñuel befriended several artists involved in surrealism, including spokesman Andre Breton and painters such as Pablo Picasso, Max Ernst, Giorgio de Chirico, and Joan Miró. The group met informally in cafes throughout Paris, and their discussions helped Buñuel develop his own philosophy of art.

Inspired by the surrealists, Buñuel rushed back to Spain to fetch Dali. Together they returned to Paris and began work on a film scenario. The two agreed early in the venture to avoid conventional narrative techniques. Instead, they decided to use symbols and images from dreams to create a "poetic" effect similar to that being achieved on canvas by Breton, Ernst, and other surrealists. Their efforts resulted in "An Andalusian Dog," a silent, twenty-five-minute film that defied interpretation. It alternately shocked, humored, and confused the audience with a barrage of bizarre images: a character with ants emerging from a hole in his hand; another man hauling a piano weighted by the bodies of two dead horses; and an androgynous bicyclist who, upon toppling over on a curb, leaves only a single, severed hand at the site of his accident. Buñuel, expecting a violent reaction from the opening-night audience, had smuggled rocks into the theatre for his own protection. To his surprise, though, the crowd erupted into applause following the showing.

Throughout the following weeks, Buñuel and Dali were confronted with numerous interpretations of their film, all of which they denied. "The plot is the result of CONSCIOUS *psychic automatism,*" Buñuel insisted, "and, to that extent, it does not attempt to recount a dream, although it profits by a mechanism analogous to that of dreams." He explained that he and Dali selected the images at random, deliberately discarding anything that could be construed as relevant to a logical storyline. "The motivation of the images was . . . purely irrational," claimed Buñuel. "They are mysterious and inexplicable to the two collaborators as to the spectator. NOTHING, in the film, SYMBOLIZES ANYTHING."

Embarrassed by the enthusiastic reception accorded "An Andalusian Dog" by the bourgeoisie they had sought to offend, Buñuel and Dali began work on a second film, "The Golden Age," to rectify the situation. Their collaboration was short-lived, however, for Buñuel, upon discovering that Dali had fallen in love with their producer's wife, accused her of disrupting the filmmakers' relationship and tried to strangle her on the first day of shooting. Outraged, Dali stormed from the set and never returned.

"The Golden Age," as completed by Buñuel, proved quite different from its predecessor. Buñuel abandoned the random imagery of "An Andalusian Dog" in favor of a fairly coherent, though extremely disturbing, narrative. The film chronicles the efforts of two lovers to reunite despite the bourgeoisie's attempts to keep them apart. In the first scene, Buñuel compares the bourgeoisie to the scorpion and cuts from a glimpse of the latter to the lovers coupling in the sand. They are suddenly separated by celebrants attending an inaugural address who claim that the couple's moans are annoying the speaker. The film then proceeds to follow the protagonist in his quest for his lover. He encounters characters who reveal the hypocrisy and ennui that symbolize, for Buñuel, the decadence of bourgeois life. When the lovers are finally reunited, the film accelerates into a series of surrealist images depicting age and death. The film ends with Christ escorting fellow revelers from the Marquis de Sade's castle, where they've just participated in an orgy.

Despite the overt and deliberately offensive depiction of social values as practiced by hypocritical bourgeoisie, "The Golden

Age" was shown without incident at its premier. On the second night, however, fights broke out in the audience and viewers hurled inkwells at the screen. After the showing, audience members vented their anger by destroying paintings by Dali, Ernst, and Miró on display in the theatre lobby. For Buñuel, who had considered himself an outsider among his surrealist contemporaries after the bourgeoisie's approval of "An Andalusian Dog," "The Golden Age" was an immense triumph.

"The Golden Age" was shown for two months before French censors yielded to public pressure and banned it. Buñuel became the target of right-wing critics eager to preserve the social status quo. Richard-Pierre Bodin wrote: "A film called *L'Age d'Or*—in which I defy any qualified authority to detect the slightest artistic merit—multiplies (in public showings!) its crop of utterly obscene, repugnant, and tawdry episodes. Country, family, religion are dragged through the mire. All those who saved the grandeur of France, all those who have faith in the future of a race which has enlightened the whole world, all those Frenchmen who have been chosen to protect you against the poison of rotten entertainment, now ask what you think of the job our censorship is doing."

In the wake of this violent reaction, numerous other writers rose to Buñuel's defense. His most celebrated supporter, Henry Miller, wrote, "They have called Buñuel everything—traitor, anarchist, pervert, defamer, iconoclast. But lunatic they have not called him. True, it is lunacy he portrays in his film, but it is not of his making. This stinking chaos which for a brief hour or so is amalgamated under his magic wand, this is the lunacy of man's achievements after ten thousand years of civilization."

Although it elicited dramatic responses from viewers, "The Golden Age" was relatively ignored by film scholars until the 1960s, when Buñuel's rejuvenated career sparked a renewed interest in his early works. Its stature then rose to that of classics such as "Potemkin" and "Citizen Kane," and Carlos Fuentes hailed it as "the greatest of the surrealist films and one of the most personal and original works in the history of the cinema."

While the controversy over "The Golden Age" raged in Paris, Buñuel was in Hollywood studying sequences from American films. He was drawn to the film capital by Metro-Goldwyn-Mayer (MGM) with the understanding that he would be permitted to make a film for the studio. The opportunity, however, never arose, and Buñuel returned to Spain in 1932.

His next film, "Land Without Bread," revealed few of the surrealist elements that characterized his previous films. In detailing the plight of an impoverished Spanish village, he replaced surrealism with realism. Buñuel called it "a simple documentary" and declared: "I didn't invent anything. Pierre Unik wrote a scientific, statistical text. We merely wished to show the most abject region of Spain."

"Land Without Bread" was Buñuel's only film during the next fifteen years. After the political uprising in Spain, he obtained work dubbing dialogue for Warner Brothers in Paris and then returned to Hollywood to work for MGM on a project that was eventually abandoned. In 1940, he was hired by the Museum of Modern Art. One of his tasks there was to re-edit footage from the pro-Nazi films of Leni Riefenstahl for use as American propaganda. But as Buñuel recalled: "Riefenstahl's images were so damned good and impressive . . . that the effect would be the contrary of what we were aiming at. . . . Audiences would be overpowered and come out feeling that German might be irresistible." The project was terminated at President Roosevelt's request.

He left the museum soon afterwards when Dali, in *The Secret Life of Salvador Dali,* revealed that Buñuel was both anti-Catholic and a member of the French Communist party. Buñuel later told Carlos Fuentes that he "resigned . . . to avoid embarrassing my good friends [at the museum]." He also recalled his final meeting with Dali. "I had decided to give him a good beating," he claimed. "But when I saw him walk down the lobby, I felt a surge of sympathy for the man, too many fond memories came back, our youth. . . . So I just called him a son of a bitch and told him our friendship was over. He looked nonplused and said, 'Luis, you understand that my remarks were not intended to hurt you, but to publicize myself.' I've never seen him since."

During the mid-1940s Buñuel resumed his work with Warner Brothers. He developed a number of film projects, including one with Man Ray, but was unable to finance them. In 1947 he moved from California to Mexico to begin work on an adaptation of García Lorca's "The House of Bernarda Alba." That project also failed to develop into a film, but that same year Buñuel was hired by a Mexican producer to work in that country as a director.

He directed several films that were essentially showcases for popular actors. In the midst of these mediocre ventures, however, Buñuel made "Los olvidados," an intense and graphic depiction of slum life in Mexico City. The film is often gruesome in its action, for in proposing that life is essentially a struggle, Buñuel unflinchingly presented torture, rape, and incest. Many critics, including Andre Bazin, defended Buñuel's grim portrayal as part of his surrealist heritage. "It is not possible to avoid touching on the surrealism in Buñuel's films," wrote Bazin in a review of "Los olvidados." "He is . . . one of the rare valuable representatives of this mode. . . . His surrealism is a part of the rich and fortunate influence of a totally Spanish tradition. . . . It reflects a tragic sense of life, which these painters expressed through the ultimate human degradations. . . . But their cruelty, too, served only as a measure of their trust in mankind itself, and in their art."

Buñuel followed "Los olvidados" with several more entertaining films, including "The Devil and the Flesh" and "The Daughter of Deceit." When an interviewer remarked to Buñuel during the 1960s that many of his early films in Mexico were rather mediocre, Buñuel responded that even his less-ambitious works reflected his philosophy. "I have made several frankly bad pictures," he confessed, "but not once did I compromise my moral code. . . . My bad films were always decent. I am against conventional morality."

Throughout the 1950s Buñuel was saddled with miniscule budgets and often untrained actors. He nevertheless produced several films that rank among his finest works. In 1952 he made "El," the story of an obsessively jealous bourgeois poet. The following year he directed "Illusion Travels by Streetcar." This film begins with two trolley operators refusing to scrap their dilapidated car. They take the car on an unscheduled run but are unable to convince passengers that they are taking a "joy ride." Soon the car is overrun with characters, each of whom insists on paying fare. The conductor refuses to accept their money, however, for fear that he will be accused of robbery. This conflict results in a parody of freedom as the right to pay for that which is free. As Jean Delmas noted: "All the riders insist on paying, each for his own personal reason, and each resents the fact that in the society they live in, nothing can be free without being suspect. At this level, comedy becomes philosophy."

Buñuel's next film was an adaptation of Emily Bronte's *Wuthering Heights,* a novel that was particularly prized by his surrealist

clan during the 1920s. Unfortunately, the small budget and inconsistent casting undermined the eerie romanticism Buñuel was attempting to evoke. He later dismissed it as "a bad film."

Buñuel fared much better with his next effort, an adaptation of Daniel Defoe's *Robinson Crusoe.* Supplied with American actors and financial backing, he managed to sustain a sense of isolation throughout Crusoe's solitary life on the island while at the same time delving into his subconscious and his past. A particularly memorable scene occurs when the exasperated Crusoe shouts God's name from the mountain top, but hears only his own voice echoing in response. Emilio García Riera called this film "a great triumph" for Buñuel. "One could say that the character of Robinson has been created especially for Buñuel," he observed. "For it is precisely through exceptional characters, alienated by circumstance from the elemental norms of common sense and customary morality, that Buñuel often penetrates into the mysterious, and therefore poetical, regions of the human being."

In 1955, Buñuel explored the relationship between sex and death in "The Criminal Life of Archibaldo Cruz." Cruz possesses a magic box that, when touched, causes the death of anyone he wishes. As a child, his first target is his wet-nurse. Later, he instigates the deaths of a number of people who are subjects in his sexual fantasies. He becomes guilt ridden and confesses to the police, but is released when it becomes impossible to prove that his victims perished through his actions. When he finally attempts to actually murder a woman, he is foiled by a bizarre mishap. He then falls in love with the woman and marries her. "The one point which makes it outstanding is the portrait of the central figure Buñuel offers us," contended Riera. "This central character is really an assassin who wishes and enjoys the death of his fellow beings and who, nevertheless, is quite innocent before the eyes of society; innocent to such a point that when the film ends, he is moving toward the enjoyment of a happy and peaceful future."

Three years later Buñuel made "Nazarín," which many critics consider one of his finest achievements. It details a priest's struggle to live a Christ-like existence. After suffering excommunication for sheltering a whore, Nazarín wanders about the Mexican countryside and unintentionally causes many catastrophes. As Louis Seguin explained, Buñuel "gives rein fully to his unfrocked priest in the certainty that, rejected by the Church, but always inhabited by a desperate love of God and men, he can only do what he does: sow fire and murder in his wake." Despite constant failure, though, Nazarín persists in his efforts to lead a Christian life. "What counts for Buñuel is that Nazarín applies to his own life the perception enunciated by Jesus," wrote Joan Mellen, "and like Jesus he is a man willing to stand up to the repressive ruling order." Buñuel contended: "If Christ were to return, they'd crucify him again. It is possible to be *relatively* Christian, but the *absolutely* pure, the absolutely innocent man—he's bound to fail. . . . I am sure that if Christ came back, the Church, the powerful churchmen, would condemn Him again."

By film's end, Nazarín has rejected the Church and turned against it. Disillusioned, he is offered a pineapple by a sympathetic woman, and the look on his face reveals that he has found a new faith: in humanity. Penelope Gilliatt wrote, "When Nazarín, the failed Christ figure, is on the road and is offered a pineapple, symbol of help and charity, one feels a flash of hope for loosening of human bondage." By putting his faith in humanity, according to Gavin Lambert, Nazarín "finds a reality with which to replace an illusion, and the film itself goes beyond protest to reach affirmation." Ado Kyrou came to a similar conclusion, finding "Nazarín" not merely a renunciation of Christianity but also a celebration of humanity. "This film places love and its Christian caricature in confrontation," wrote Kyrou. "Buñuel contrasts those who love with a man who adores a nonexistent being. 'Love your neighbor,' says the man of the Christian myth. 'Love women and your companions,' says Buñuel. The first precept leads to ideological wails, to resignation; the second, to love and rebellion." Kyrou concluded by calling the film one "charged with dynamite, hope, love and certainty—a film addressed to mankind."

Buñuel returned to Spain in 1961 to direct "Viridiana," his first film in that country since "Las hurdes." Ranked by many critics as one of his finest films, "Viridiana" is a variation on the faith-in-humanity theme of "Nazarín." A devout woman, Viridiana is duped by her bizarre uncle into believing that she has lost her virginity on the eve of her entry into the convent. Though she plans to leave her uncle's estate immediately, she suddenly becomes its owner when her uncle commits suicide. She decides to accept her new role and converts the home into a haven for beggars and cripples. But the vagrants simply exploit Viridiana's Christian charity without embracing Christian tenets. While Viridiana is away one evening, the ingrates stage a raucous banquet and orgy. When she returns to find the house in shambles and the beggars either drunk, sleeping, or fighting, several of them overpower her and rape her. The film ends with Viridiana joining a card game as her belongings, including a cross, nails, and a crown of thorns, burn outside.

Because Buñuel submitted "Viridiana" to Spanish censors in sections, they never perceived the anti-Christian emphasis. When it was shown in Cannes at the film festival, it was a huge success and was awarded the Golden Palm. But Spanish officials responded with outrage to the film's content. The film was banned and its censors fired from their positions. Even the pope condemned it. Buñuel, however, was baffled by the criticism. "It was not my intention to blaspheme," he responded, "but of course Pope John XXIII knows more than I do about these things." He also addressed charges that he had seemed to make a film that justified maliciousness. "I am also reproached for my cruelty," he said. "Where is it in the film? The novice proves her humanity. The old man, a complicated human being, is capable of kindness towards human beings and towards a lowly bee whose life he doesn't hesitate to rescue." Regarding Viridiana's transformation, he added: "I don't see why people complain. My heroine is more of a virgin at the denouement than she was at the start." Perhaps David Robinson summed up Buñuel's attitude best when he wrote, "The film's total effect is invigorating rather than depressing because Buñuel values them all alike as men, and likes them all because they are funny and human."

Despite critical acclaim, "Viridiana" was also banned in France, and Buñuel once again found himself amid controversy. His reaction was to return to Mexico to make another film, "The Exterminating Angel." It concerns a group of bourgeois Mexicans who meet together after attending an opera and find themselves unable to leave the premises. The doors of the home are open; the guests simply cannot leave. No explanation is given. What results, however, is a complete breakdown in the social order cherished by the bourgeois. Hunger and thirst become the primary motivation for the characters' actions, and tension becomes violence. "Coarseness, violence and filth have become our inseparable companions," Buñuel commented. "Death is better than this abject promiscuity." But the trapped figures in "The Exterminating Angel" do not die. They finally escape from the house and flee to a church. But as Buñuel exposes the restrictions imposed by class society as affectations and mannerisms, which

conceal the animal-like will to survive that makes all people equal, he similarly indicts organized religion. At film's end, the bourgeois characters discover themselves unable to leave the church. "The implication," declared Randall Conrad, "is that to be free they will now have to kill their host, God."

Buñuel traveled to France for his next film, "The Diary of a Chambermaid." The film details the encounters of Celestine, a chambermaid, with a variety of characters, including Monteil, her employer, who enjoys seducing the chambermaids and firing his rifle; Madame Monteil, a compulsive hygienic who abstains from sex because of the pain it causes her; Captain Mauger, a soldier living with his common-law wife, Rose, whom he eventually evicts in order to pursue Celestine; and Joseph, the coachman whom Celestine loves but whom she nonetheless turns in to the police for having murdered a young girl. Throughout the film, Celestine uses her charms to the best advantage, encouraging Monteil, Captain Mauger, and Joseph with their romantic notions. Ultimately, as Peter Harcourt noted, she makes the wrong decision. "She sits on her bed, impatient with Mauger's unctuousness," he wrote, "biting her little finger as she recognizes her fate." He added that "there is no sense of divine retribution. The dice have simply rolled the wrong way." The film concludes with Joseph in a cafe watching a Fascist rally. Having been found not guilty by the court, he is now a supporter of the Fascists in Paris. Tom Milne called the last scene "a brilliantly ominous evocation, not only of the imminent rise of Hitler, but of the reverberations which still smolder under the surface today." Similarly, Conrad summarized "The Diary of a Chambermaid" as "Buñuel's strongest politically," and acknowledged it as "a global expression of the pessimism which is after all inherent in Buñuel's vision."

Buñuel returned to Mexico for "Simon of the Desert." The film is based loosely on the life of St. Simon Stylites, a preacher who spoke from a small platform overlooking the desert. More brutally funny than his previous efforts, "Simon of the Desert" reveals the uselessness of Christianity in a world that prizes love over abstract faith, action over prayer. In one scene, Simon performs a miracle, restoring an amputee's hands. The onlookers judge Simon's deed as unimpressive. The former amputee immediately uses his restored limbs to strike his child. Eventually, Simon accompanies Satan, who, as an alluring woman, had previously tempted him, to a bar filled with frenzied teenage dancers. Simon is confronted with the failure of his own actions and preachings to deter humanity from sin.

When Buñuel finally settled in France in 1966, he focused his attentions on the destructiveness of social conventions. In "Belle de jour," he depicts Severin, a woman whose Catholic beliefs were so deeply ingrained that she was incapable of consummating her marriage. She resorts instead to fantasies in which she is degraded by her husband and coachmen. Finally, she decides to overcome her guilt-produced fears by working during the day as a prostitute for an affluent madam. She soon learns, however, that the sex her clients desire involves the enactment of their fantasies. When she does enjoy what appears to be a sexually satisfying relationship, it is with a gangster who follows her home. Fearing that her husband will discover everything, she urges the visitor to leave. The film ends with the gangster shooting her husband before being killed by the police. The husband survives, though blinded and paralyzed. He has learned of his wife's actions from a friend who discovered her at the brothel. Severin assures him that she no longer has any sexual fantasies, at which point he rises from his wheelchair and suggests they take a vacation. Severin then gazes out the window and hears the coachmen's bells that signify a resumption of the fantasies.

With the enormous critical acclaim that was accorded "Belle de jour," Buñuel finally began to receive recognition as one of the world's greatest filmmakers. He began a series of collaborations with producer Serge Silberman and fellow screenwriter Jean-Claude Carriere. In 1969, Buñuel directed "The Milky Way," in which he traced the history of Christianity through the adventures of two travelers. Throughout the film, Buñuel tests the validity of Christian dogma. Oswaldo Capriles called the film "a single-minded, coherent compendium of the devastating reasons for opposing religion as an historical phenomenon, as rational thought, and as providing transcendence."

Buñuel's next film, "Tristana," is a reworking of the sexual repression theme of "Belle de jour." Tristana is a woman totally deprived of freedom by her guardian, Don Lope. An aristocratic lecher, Don Lope adheres to a double standard that permits him the sexual license he paranoically denies Tristana. "The only way to keep a woman honest," Don Lope insists, "is to break her leg and keep her home." Tristana rebels against her mentor by eloping with a young artist. She returns within two years, however, unmarried and disease-stricken. Because of her affliction, her leg is amputated. She takes to teasing a mute lad. As Joan Mellen noted, "Tristana is a woman whose sexuality has been perverted by a fear of seduction by an older, forbidding father figure, and who can now respond only to the brutal and the perverse." In the end, Tristana finally rids herself of Don Lope by opening the bedroom window for the now sickly guardian and allowing the cold air to cause a fatal heart attack.

There is little sense of victory in Don Lope's death. As Buñuel implies in film after film, the parasitic Christian customs and social conventions he exposes are too deeply ingrained in society to become vulnerable to his cinematic assaults. Mellen wrote that "Buñuel has relentlessly and brilliantly exposed the destruction of the individual by a corrupt, hypocritical moral code which makes no pretense of improving a society in which class animosities are deepening and brutality is growing." For Buñuel, true freedom involves the choice of the individual to separate from society. This is a choice society guarantees but, by its parasitic nature, cannot grant. "Group solidarity was a tremendous thing among the surrealists," Buñuel related. "Breton would call us in to sit in judgment if we deviated from the group morality. I learned then that being free is not doing whatever you want, but acting in solidarity with friends you love and respect. But then, by choosing a certain morality, you are not really free at all. Only crypto-Fascists pretend they are ideologically free. Surrealism taught me that man is never free yet fights for what he can never be. That is tragic."

The notion of freedom as a destructive and deceiving element in society is embellished in Buñuel's next two films "The Discreet Charm of the Bourgeoisie" and "The Phantom of Liberty." In the former, several bourgeois characters find themselves unable to finish their extravagant meals. Buñuel's contention seems to be that the bourgeoisie's wealth affords them no greater escape from a repressive society. Raymond Durgnat declared that "Buñuel has selected only those meals whose bill of fare—or circumstances, or relationships with dream, love, or business—illustrates how a round of dinner parties can do as little to preserve their participants from the emptiness which society has sowed within their hearts as communing with nature could do to redeem the Victorian middle class from its materialism."

In "The Phantom of Liberty," Buñuel begins with a reenactment of the action depicted in Francisco Goya's painting, "The Third of May," as a firing squad executes a group of enemy soldiers. But whereas Goya's work is a passionate plea for peace, Buñuel's film exposes the absurdness of that plea. "Down with freedom!" shout the executioners' targets. "Long live the chains!" Throughout the remainder of the film, Buñuel reveals how society's faith in Christianity and social conventions perpetuates an order that often spawns absurd and criminal actions. In the final sequence, police charge a group of protesters who shout the same epithets as the victims in the initial sequence. For Buñuel, history's lessons are useless: by denying the past and perpetuating a social order that promotes destruction, humanity imprisons itself.

Buñuel's last film during the 1970s, "That Obscure Object of Desire," is a variation on the theme previously explored in both "The Exterminating Angel" and "The Discreet Charm of the Bourgeoisie." In this film, the object of desire is the virginity of Conchita, a young Spanish woman being pursued by Mathieu, a French businessman. For Mathieu, Conchita's sexual cooperation is always on the verge of acquisition. He tries to use his powers as her employer for seductive purposes, but she quits her job. When Mathieu tries to bribe Conchita's mother into delivering her to him, Conchita becomes incensed and leaves the city. Eventually, Mathieu and Conchita live together, but she continues to withhold herself from him. She then convinces him to give her a home of her own. After doing so, she insults him by feigning sexual intercourse with another man while Mathieu watches through an iron gate. Conchita returns to Mathieu's home the next day, though, and reveals that what he witnessed the previous night was only a simulation. Mathieu then beats her. The film ends with Mathieu and Conchita apparently reconciled, strolling arm-in-arm through a shopping district when a bomb planted by terrorists detonates and kills them.

"That Obscure Object of Desire" is one of Buñuel's many subtle exposes of the bourgeois mentality. Mathieu is not concerned with Conchita, except as a vehicle through which he can prove his power over women. Neither is Mathieu interested in the terrorists whose actions serve as a background to the film. Conchita, however, is as much to blame for her predicament as Mathieu. She teases Mathieu and manipulates his desire in order to further her own material worth. For her, the terrorists are simply another instrument she can use in her relationship with Mathieu. Ultimately, both Mathieu and Conchita fall victim to the terrorists who refuse to accept the parasitic social order maintained by the couple.

Since the mid-1960s, Buñuel has refused to acknowledge any long-range filmmaking projects. He seems content simply listening to classical music and studying insects. "I like idleness," he told an interviewer. "I enjoy my days without doing anything. I am never bored." But he also laments the silence that has existed between Dali and himself since 1930. "I do hope I can invite him to drink a glass of champagne before we both die." In 1975 he finally convinced himself to hang a portrait Dali had painted during the 1920s. "Thirty-five years is too long for a fight."

Buñuel's feelings towards the cinema have also changed during his fifty years as a filmmaker. In 1953 he contended that "in the hands of a free spirit, the cinema is a magnificent and dangerous weapon." But in 1974, with the release of "The Phantom of Liberty," he reiterated Breton's last words to him and acknowledged that "it is no longer possible to scandalize people as we did in 1930." Buñuel also mentioned that he hopes the cinema will "give us the ease of a quest for pleasure and inquiry which isn't followed by the pounding hooves of guilt." He told Gilliatt, "It's guilt we must escape from, not God."

AVOCATIONAL INTERESTS: Classical music, entomology.

BIOGRAPHICAL/CRITICAL SOURCES:

BOOKS

Contemporary Literary Criticism, Volume 16, Gale, 1981.
Durgnat, Raymond, *Luis Buñuel,* University of California Press, 1967, revised edition, 1978.
Francisco Aranda, J., *Luis Buñuel: A Critical Biography,* translated by David Robinson, Da Capo Press, 1976.
Gould, Michael, *Surrealism in Cinema,* A. S. Barnes, 1976.
Harcourt, Peter, *Six European Directors,* Viking, 1972.
Kyrou, Ado, *Buñuel: An Introduction,* Simon & Schuster, 1963.
Matthews, J. H., *Surrealism in Film,* University of Michigan Press, 1971.
Mellen, Joan, editor, *The World of Luis Buñuel,* Oxford University Press, 1978.
Miller, Henry, *The Cosmological Eye,* New Directions, 1939.
Rebolledo, Carlos, *Luis Buñuel,* Editions Universitaires, 1964.
Stauffacher, Frank, *Art in Cinema,* Arno, 1968.

PERIODICALS

American Scholar, summer, 1973.
Cineaste, Volume VII, number 3, 1976.
Etudes Cinematographiques, spring, 1963.
Film Comment, May-June, 1975.
Film Culture, summer, 1960, spring, 1962, summer, 1966.
Film Quarterly, spring, 1960, spring, 1967, winter, 1970-71, summer, 1975.
Jeune Cinema, February, 1966.
Le Figaro, December 7, 1930.
Los Angeles Times, November 2, 1983, November 18, 1983.
New Yorker, December 5, 1977.
New York Times, November 3, 1972, February 25, 1973, October 16, 1977, June 10, 1979, September 28, 1983, December 27, 1983.
New York Times Magazine, March 1, 1973.
Positif, March, 1961, July, 1962.
Show, April, 1970.
Sight and Sound, January-March, 1954, summer, 1962, autumn, 1964.
Society, July-August, 1973.
Times (London), January 26, 1984.
Village Voice, May 2, 1968, May 9, 1968, May 5, 1980.
Washington Post, November 5, 1983.
Yale French Studies, summer, 1956.

OBITUARIES:

PERIODICALS

Chicago Tribune, July 31, 1983.
Detroit News, July 31, 1983.
Los Angeles Times, July 30, 1983.
Newsweek, August 8, 1983.
New York Times, July 31, 1983.
Time, August 8, 1983.
Times (London), August 1, 1983.
Washington Post, August 1, 1983.

*   *   *

BURCIAGA, José Antonio 1940-

PERSONAL: Born August 23, 1940, in El Chuco, Tex.; son of José Cruz and María Guadalupe Fernandez Burciaga; married Cecilia Preciado, 1972; children: Lupita, Efrain, Conchita, Margarita, Raul. *Education:* University of Texas at El Paso, B.A., 1968; attended Corcoran School of Art, 1970-71, Juarez-Lincoln Center of Antioch University, 1973-74, and San Francisco Art Institute, 1974.

ADDRESSES: Home and office—P.O. Box 3729, Stanford, Calif. 94305.

CAREER: Project director of Multicultural Task Force, San Mateo County Arts Council, San Mateo, Calif.; Stanford University, Stanford, Calif., resident fellow, 1985—. Founder of Diseños Literarios (publishing company), Menlo Park, Calif. Artist, with solo shows all over the United States, including Central Intelligence Agency, Chicano Library at Stanford University, and Foothill College. Board member of United Nations Association of San Francisco. *Military service:* U.S. Air Force, 1960-64.

MEMBER: Concilio de Arte Popular de California (Califas Chicano Art Council).

WRITINGS:

(With Bernice Zamora) *Restless Serpents* (poems and drawings), Diseños Literarios, 1976.
Drink cultura refrescante (poems and drawings), Mango Publications, 1979.
(With Emy López) *Versos para Centroamérica,* Diseños Literarios, 1981.
Weedee Peepo: A Collection of Essays (bilingual in Spanish and English), Pan American University Press, 1988.

Works represented in anthologies, including *Canto al Pueblo: An Anthology of Experiences,* edited by Leonardo Carrillo, Antonio Martínez, Carol Molina, and Marie Wood, Penca (San Antonio), 1978; *Flor y Canto IV and V: An Anthology of Chicano Literature,* edited by José Armas, Bernice Zamora, and Michael Reed, Pajarito, Flor y Canto V Committee (Albuquerque), 1978; *Linguistics for Students of Literature,* edited by Elizabeth Closs Traugott and Mary Louise Pratt, Harcourt, 1980; *Chicanos: Antología histórica y literaria,* edited by Tino Villanueva, Fondo de Cultura Económica, 1980; *Nueva Narrativa Chicana,* edited by Oscar U. Somoza, Editorial Diógenes, 1983; and *Palabra Nueva: Cuentos Chicanos,* edited by Ricardo Aguilar, Armando Armengol, and Somoza, Texas Western, 1984.

Contributor of fiction, poetry, and articles to periodicals, including *Texas Monthly, Denver Quarterly, Grito del Sol, Maize, Escolios, La Luz, Mango, Vórtice, Semana de Bellas Artes, Imagine, Revista Chicano-Riqueña, Caracol, Vista, San Jose Mercury News, Christian Science Monitor,* and *Los Angeles Times.*

WORK IN PROGRESS: Wachuseh, a collection of essays; *Spilling the Beans,* an autobiography; a collection of short stories.

BIOGRAPHICAL/CRITICAL SOURCES:

BOOKS

Dictionary of Literary Biography, Volume 82: *Chicano Writers, First Series,* Gale, 1989.

PERIODICALS

San Francisco Chronicle, March 9, 1978.

*   *   *

BUSTOS, F(rancisco)
See BORGES, Jorge Luis

BUSTOS DOMECQ, H(onorio)
   See BIOY CASARES, Adolfo
   and BORGES, Jorge Luis

C

CABALLERO, Manuel 1931-
(Jason Elchamo, Sebastian Hemeze)

PERSONAL: Born December 5, 1931, in Caracas, Venezuela; son of Francisco (a journalist) and María Antonieta (a homemaker; maiden name, Agüero) Caballero; married Hanni Ossott (a poet), October 9, 1980. *Education:* Attended University of Paris, 1953-56; Universidad Central de Venezuela, licenciate in history, 1963; University of London, Ph.D., 1985. *Politics:* Socialist.

ADDRESSES: Home—Avenida Leopoldo Aguerrevere, Residencias "Caroni," Apt. 61-A, Sante Fe Norte, Caracas 1080, Venezuela. *Office*—Escuela de Historia, Universidad Central de Venezuela, Ciudad Universitaria Los Chaguaramos, Apdo Postal 104, Caracas 1051, Venezuela.

CAREER: El Nacional (newspaper), Caracas, Venezuela, columnist, 1958—; *Clarín* (newspaper), Caracas, journalist, 1962-64; Universidad Central de Venezuela, Caracas, professor of history, 1965—, director of School of History, 1975-78, chairman of Department of Historical Theory and Methodology, 1979—, director of Faculty of Humanities and Education Press, 1982-87. Founding member of political party Movimiento al Socialismo, 1970, congressional representative, 1973-83. Member of board of directors of Center for Studies on Development (CENDES), 1986-87.

MEMBER: Foreign Press Association of London, Colegio Nacional de Periodistas, Asociación Venezolana para el Avance de la Ciencia.

AWARDS, HONORS: National award for journalism, 1979.

WRITINGS:

(Co-author) *El concepto de la historia en Laureano Vallenilla Lanz,* Universidad Central de Venezuela (Caracas), 1966.
El desarrollo desigual del socialismo y otros ensayos polémicos, Fuentes (Caracas), 1970.
Betancourt: Populismo y petroleo en Venezuela, Centro Editor de América Latina (Buenos Aires), 1972.
El mundo no se acaba en diciembre, Centauro (Caracas), 1973.
Sobre autonomía, reforma y política en la Universidad Central de Venezuela, 1827-1958, Universidad Central de Venezuela, 1973.

(Co-author) *La izquierda venezolana y las elecciones de 1973,* Síntesis Dos Mil (Caracas), 1974.
Rómulo Betancourt, Centauro, 1977.
La Internacional Comunista y América Latina: La sección venezolana, Siglo XXI (Mexico City), 1978.
Ve y toma el libro que está abierto en la mano del angel, Ateneo de Caracas, 1979.
El 18 de octubre de 1945, Libros al día (Caracas), 1979.
La pasión de comprender: Ensayos de historia (y de) política, Ariel-Seix Barral Venezolana (Barcelona and Caracas), 1983.
Latin America and the Comintern, 1919-1943, Cambridge University Press, 1986.
El discurso del desorden, Alfadil (Caracas), 1987.
Las Venezuelas del siglo veinte, Grijalbo (Caracas), 1988.

Also author of *El nombre de la cosa,* Pomaire (Caracas), and *El orgullo de leer,* ANH-El Libro Menor (Caracas). Contributor to books, including *Cartas hiperbóreas,* Congreso de la República, 1975; *Venezuela 1979, examen y futuro,* Ateneo de Caracas, 1980; *1984: ¿A dónde va Venezuela?,* Planeta, 1984; and *Gómez, gomecismo y antigomecismo,* Fondo Editorial de Humanidades-Tropykos, 1987.

Contributor to periodicals, inlcuding *Papel Literario, Diario de Caracas, Bohemia,* and *Nueva Sociedad.* Also contributor to periodicals under pseudonyms Jason Elchamo and Sebastian Hemeze.

WORK IN PROGRESS: A biography of Juan Vicente Gómez, dictator of Venezuela from 1908 to 1935.

SIDELIGHTS: Manuel Caballero told *CA:* "It is not easy to describe my career as an intellectual because it was never my specific intention to develop a 'career' as such. In that sense I am not different from a good number of other Latin American writers, artists, and even scholars of my generation or previous ones. It also explains why, although I began to write at an early age, I did not publish except in the press until relatively late in my career, just as I also began my university career at a relatively late date, when I was already well known as a journalist who specialized in political and literary commentaries. As a natural consequence of my political concern, I have been actively engaged in politics since adolescence and was imprisoned and later exiled for a number of years, most of which were spent in France."

BIOGRAPHICAL/CRITICAL SOURCES:

PERIODICALS

Times Literary Supplement, April 17, 1987.

* * *

CABALLERO CALDERON, E.
See CABALLERO CALDERON, Eduardo

* * *

CABALLERO CALDERON, Eduardo 1910-
(E. Caballero Calderón)

PERSONAL: Born March 6, 1910, in Bogotá, Colombia. *Education:* Attended Universidad Externado de Colombia.

ADDRESSES: Calle 37, No. 19-07, Bogotá, D.E., Colombia.

CAREER: Writer and diplomat. Colombian Embassy, Lima, Peru, secretary, 1937-40; business official in Madrid, Spain, 1946-48; Congress, Bogotá, Colombia, representative, 1958-61; ambassador to UNESCO, Paris, 1962-66; editor of *El Tiempo,* 1966; served as mayor of Tipacoque, Colombia.

MEMBER: Colombian Academy, Royal Spanish Academy (corresponding member).

AWARDS, HONORS: Eugenio Nadal Prize, 1965, for *El buen salvaje.*

WRITINGS:

Caminos subterráneos, ensayo de interpretación del paisaje (essay), Santafé (Bogotá, Colombia), 1936.
Tipacoque: Estampas de provincia (short stories), Talleres Gráficos Mundo al Día (Bogotá), 1941, reprinted, Oveja Negra (Bogotá), 1983.
Suramérica, tierra del hombre (essays), originally published c. 1941, reprinted, Guadarrama (Madrid, Spain), 1956.
(Under name E. Caballero Calderón) *El arte de vivir sin soñar* (novel), Siglo XX (Bogotá), 1943.
Discurso leído en el acto de su recepción por el señor don Eduardo Caballero Calderón y contestación del señor don Eduardo Guzmán Esponda (lecture), Imprenta Nacional (Bogotá), 1944.
(Editor) *Cervantes en Colombia,* Patronato del IV Centenario de Cervantes (Madrid), 1948.
(Editor) *Confesión del sufrimiento: La vida íntima de Dostoyewski, Amiel, Wilde, M. Bashkirtseff, Zweig* (diaries), Librería Suramérica (Bogotá), 1948.
Diario de Tipacoque, photographs by Luis B. Ramos, ABC (Bogotá), 1950, reprinted, Oveja Negra, 1983.
Ancha es Castilla (travel), Kelly (Bogotá), 1950, published as *Ancha es Castilla: Guía espiritual de España,* Guadarrama, 1954.
Cartas colombianas (essays), Kelly, 1951.
El Cristo de espaldas (novel), Losada (Buenos Aires, Argentina), 1952, reprinted, Oveja Negra, 1983.
Siervo sin tierra (novel), originally published in 1954, reprinted, Destino (Barcelona, Spain), 1967.
(With Herbert Boy, under name E. Caballero Calderón) *Una historia con alas* (correspondence), Guadarrama, 1955.
Americanos y europeos (essays), Guadarrama, 1957.
Breviario del "Quijote" (essays), Aguado (Madrid), 1957.
(With Enrique Caballero Escovar and Lucas Caballero) *Rabo de Paja: Handel, Trilladora, Suaita* (essays), Iqueima (Bo-

gotá), 1962, also published as *Por el liberalismo y contra Castro: Rabo de paja,* 1962.
(Under name E. Caballero Calderón) *Manuel Pacho* (novel), Bedout (Medellín, Colombia), c. 1963, reprinted, Destino, 1966.
Obras (collected works), Bedout, 1963-64.
Memorias infantiles, 1916-1924 (novel), Bedout, 1964.
El buen salvaje (novel), Destino, 1966.
Bogotá: Guía turística oficial (guidebook), Empresa Colombiana de Turismo (Bogotá), c. 1968.
Caín (novel), Destino, 1969.
El nuevo príncipe: Ensayo sobre las malas pasiones (essay), Revista (Madrid), 1969.
El almirante niño. El rey de Roma. El caballito de Bolívar (stories), Banco Cafetero de Colombia (Bogotá), 1969.
Los hijos del sol. El pastor de puercos. La traición de Francisquillo (stories), illustrations by Luis Caballero Holguín, Banco Cafetero de Colombia, 1969.
Tres cuentos infantiles: Todo por un florero, El corneta llanero, El zapatero soldado (stories), Banco Cafetero de Colombia, 1969, also published as *Todo por un florero El corneta llanero El zapatero soldado,* 1969.
Yo, el alcalde (soñar un pueblo para después gobernarlo): Tipacoque, 1969-1971, photographs by Abdu Eljaiek, Talleres Gráficos del Banco de la República (Bogotá), 1971.
El amirante niño y otros cuentos (stories), Instituto Colombiano de Cultura (Bogotá), 1972.
El buen salvaje. Vicente Soto. La zancada. José María Sanjuán. Réquiem por todos nosotros, Destino, 1972.
Los campesinos, Ministerio de Educación Nacional, Instituto Colombiano de Cultura, 1974.
Azote de Sapo (novel), Rodas (Madrid), 1975.
Historia de dos hermanos, Pomaire (Barcelona), 1977.
Hablamientos y pensadurías, Talleres Gráficas de PROGRAFF (Bogotá), 1979.
El cuento que no se puede contar, Plaza y Janés (Bogotá), 1981.

Also author of *Latinoamérica, un mundo por hacer,* 1944, *Historia privada de los colombianos* (essays), 1949, and *La penúltima hora* (novel), 1953.

BIOGRAPHICAL/CRITICAL SOURCES:

PERIODICALS

Times Literary Supplement, May 5, 1966.

* * *

CABEZAS (LACAYO), Omar 1951(?)-

PERSONAL: Born c. 1951 in Nicaragua.

CAREER: Worked for Nicaraguan Government as chief of Council of Higher Education, as chief of Office of National Security, and as vice-minister of Office of Interior, beginning in 1979. Member of Sandinista National Liberation Front, beginning in 1968.

AWARDS, HONORS: Prose award from Casa de las Américas for *La montaña es algo más que una inmensa estepa verde.*

WRITINGS:

La montaña es algo más que una inmensa estepa verde (autobiography), Siglo Veintiuno (Mexico City), 1982, translation by Kathleen Weaver published as *Fire From the Mountain: The Making of a Sandinista,* introduction by Carlos Fuentes, Crown, 1985.
(With Dora María Tellez) *La insurrección de las paredes: Pintas y graffiti de Nicaragua,* Editorial Nueva Nicaragua, 1984.

SIDELIGHTS: In *La montaña es algo más que una inmensa estepa verde* (*Fire From the Mountain: The Making of a Sandinista*), Nicaraguan official Omar Cabezas describes his early years as a member of the Sandinista National Liberation Front (FSLN). In 1968, when Cabezas joined the organization, the FSLN was a small, leftist movement committed to overthrowing the existing Nicaraguan Government—long controlled by the Somoza family and supported by the United States. Within a decade, the FSLN—named after the famous Nicaraguan guerrilla Augusto César Sandino—joined with other opposition elements in Nicaragua and toppled the Somoza regime. The Sandinistas, emerging from the revolution as the most powerful of the opposition groups, gained control of the new Nicaraguan Government. During the 1980s, Cabezas was appointed to several government posts and was awarded the rank of *comandante,* the highest in the Sandinista military.

Before the success of the revolution, though, the FSLN was barely able to survive as an opponent of the Somoza government. After Cabezas became a member in 1968, he spent the next several years as a student activist, recruiting members at the university in León, Nicaragua. This task proved extremely difficult, since the students knew that to criticize the Somoza government could mean imprisonment and death. In 1974, Cabezas decided to join a small group of Sandinistas living in the mountains of Nicaragua. Although the FSLN hoped to launch guerrilla attacks against the Nicaraguan army, the group remained too small to make an impact on the army. Since the army was unwilling to seriously pursue the Sandinistas, Cabezas and his fellow fighters never engaged in direct combat with the army during the year that the author spent in the mountains. Instead of fighting government soldiers, the Sandinistas fought disease and desertion. In his book, Cabezas reveals how difficult that struggle was, and how precarious the FSLN's existence. The author notes, however, that after surviving their exile in the mountains, the Sandinistas forged a stronger cohesiveness and a more intense commitment to their cause.

Because *Fire From the Mountain* is in large part a political document, reviewers of the book tended to focus less on the book's literary merits than on its political content. Some critics expressed their opposition to the U.S. Government, which during the 1980s openly supported an armed rebellion against the Sandinistas simply because of the latter's leftist ideology. Accordingly, such reviewers commended Cabezas for revealing the Sandinistas as decent people committed only to improving the living conditions of their fellow Nicaraguans. Writing in the *Los Angeles Times Book Review,* Ariel Dorfman commented that "though Sandinistas like [Cabezas] have been branded the enemy by the President of the United States, Americans who read his story with an open mind may find it difficult to say, after finishing it, 'This man is my enemy. This man must be eliminated.'" Critics of different political persuasions reacted differently to the book. For example, in a review for *New Republic,* former Sandinista Xavier Arguello wrote of his opposition to the cause to which the book is devoted. Questioning Cabezas's respect for "liberty and democracy," Arguello noted that "a truly democratic socialism, creative and free, which the Sandinistas once promised, exists only as a myth for the consumption of . . . foreigners who after brief visits to Nicaragua return to their own countries to defend a system they do not truly know and would never themselves accept if by some misfortune they were forced to endure it."

Regardless of their political opinions, though, reviewers reacted favorably to the book's literary qualities. Some critics praised the chatty, informal tone of writing that Cabezas uses, achieved in part because the author dictated most of the text to a tape recorder. Others noted the tension and drama that he is able to create. Arguello, for his part, conceded that *Fire From the Mountain* is both interesting and largely accurate. "With a sense of humor all his own, and at times a distinctly poetic quality," stated Arguello, "Cabezas portrays the Sandinista forces very much as they really were in their early years, during their long physical and emotional struggle to survive as a small guerrilla army in the northern mountains of Somoza's Nicaragua." Similarly, Dorfman praised "the author's extraordinary sense of humor, the irreverence and earthiness of his language, [and] the sensuality of his imagery" and commented that "even for those who disagree with the author's politics . . . his story is fascinating."

BIOGRAPHICAL/CRITICAL SOURCES:

BOOKS

Cabezas, Omar, *Fire From the Mountain: The Making of a Sandinista,* Crown, 1985.

PERIODICALS

Los Angeles Times Book Review, June 16, 1985.
Nation, May 10, 1986.
New Republic, February 24, 1986.
New York Times Book Review, June 30, 1985.
Times Literary Supplement, October 25, 1985.
Washington Post Book World, July 14, 1985.

* * *

CABRERA, Lydia 1900-

PERSONAL: Born May 20, 1900, in Havana, Cuba; came to United States, 1960. *Education:* Studied at L'Ecole du Louvre, Paris, 1927 and 1930.

ADDRESSES: Home—8716 S.W. 5th Terrace, Miami, Fla. 33174.

CAREER: Writer.

AWARDS, HONORS: Honorary doctorates from Denison University, 1977, Redlands University, 1981, and Florida International University.

WRITINGS:

Cuentos negros de Cuba (title means "Black Stories from Cuba"; short stories; also see below), La Verónica (Havana), 1940, 2nd edition, Ramos (Madrid), 1972, first published in French translation by Francis de Miomandre from the original Spanish manuscript, 1936.
¿Por qué? Cuentos negros de Cuba (title means "Why? Black Stories from Cuba"; also see below), C.R. (Havana), 1948, 2nd edition, Ramos, 1972.
El monte, igbo finda, ewe orisha, vititi nfinda: Notas sobre las religiones, la magia, las supersticiones y el folklore de los negros criollos y del pueblo de Cuba, C.R., 1954, 5th edition, Ultra Graphics, 1975.
(Compiler) *Refranes de negros viejos* (title means "Sayings of Old Blacks"), C.R., 1955, revised edition, C.R. (Miami), 1970.
Anagó: Vocabulario lucumí (el yoruba que se habla en Cuba), C.R. (Havana), 1957, 2nd edition, Ediciones (Gaithersburg, Md.), 1986.
(Author of preface and notes) Pierre Verger, *Cuba: 196 Photos* (French, Spanish, and English text), Casa Belga (Havana), 1958.
La sociedad secreta Abakuá, narrada por viejos adeptos, C.R. (Havana), 1959, revised edition, 1970.

Cuentos negros de Cuba (selections from *Cuentos negros de Cuba* and *¿Por qué? Cuentos negros de Cuba*), Nuevo Mundo (Havana), 1961.

Otán iyebiyé: Las piedras preciosas, Universal, 1969.

Ayapá: Cuentos de Jicotea (short stories), Universal, 1971.

La laguna sagrada de San Joaquín, R (Madrid), 1973.

Yemayá y Ochún (Kariocha, Iyalorichas y Olorichas), [Madrid], 1974.

Anaforuana: Ritual y símbolos de la iniciación en la sociedad secreta Abakuá, R, 1975.

Francisco y Francisca: Chascarrillos de negros viejos, Peninsular Printing (Miami), 1976.

La regla kimbisa del Santo Cristo del Buen Viaje, Peninsular Printing, 1977.

Itinerarios del insomnio, Trinidad de Cuba, Peninsular Printing, 1977.

Reglas de Congo: Palo Monte Mayombé, Peninsular Printing, 1979.

Koekó, Iyawó, aprende novicia: Pequeño tratado de regla Lucumí, Ultra Graphics (Miami), 1980.

Cuentos para adultos niños y retrasados mentales, Ultra Graphics, 1983.

Vocabulario congo, Universal, 1985.

La medicina popular de Cuba: Médicos de antaño, curanderos, santeros y paleros de hogaño, Ultra Graphics, 1984.

Los animales en el folklore y la magia de Cuba (title means "Animals in Cuban Folklore and Magic"), Ediciones, 1988.

La lengua sagrada de los nañigos (title means "The Sacred Language of the Nañigos"), Ediciones, 1988.

Supersticiones y buenos consejos (title means "Superstitions and Good Advice"), Ediciones, 1988.

Author of story translated by Suzanne Jill Levine as "Obbara Lies But Doesn't Lie" published with essay "Lydia Cabrera: An Intimate Portrait" by Ana María Simo, Intar Latin American Gallery, 1984. Contributor of stories and tales to journals in France and Cuba.

SIDELIGHTS: A Cuban-born resident of Miami, Florida, Lydia Cabrera writes of the Afro-Cuban culture which has fascinated her since early childhood. Her collections of Afro-Cuban legends and folklore are important for their literary impact as well as for their contribution to anthropological and enthnological studies of her native island. Her nonfiction works include an investigation into the secret Nañigo society of Cuba, a study of the folk medicine practiced by Cuban *santeros* (medicine men), and a compilation of Afro-Cuban folk beliefs concerning the magical properties of certain precious stones and metals. Cabrera's fictional pieces, based on the Afro-Cuban tales she heard while growing up in Cuba, are told in a simple manner imitative of that of an oral storyteller. Talking in an interview with Suzanne Jill Levine published in *Review* about her first Cuban stories written while in Paris, Cabrera notes, "In a way, I began to discover the island from the banks of the Seine, and I thought that Cuba had a great deal to express, that it was an unexplored country. I still think it's an unexplored country for the Cubans."

BIOGRAPHICAL/CRITICAL SOURCES:

PERIODICALS

Review, January-April, 1982.

CABRERA INFANTE, G(uillermo) 1929-
(G. Cain, Guillermo Cain)

PERSONAL: Born April 22, 1929, in Gibara, Cuba; immigrated to London, England, 1966; naturalized British citizen; son of Guillermo Cabrera López (a journalist) and Zoila Infante; married Marta Calvo, August 18, 1953 (divorced, October, 1961); married Miriam Gómez, December 9, 1961; children: (first marriage) Ana, Carola. *Education:* Graduated from University of Havana, Cuba, 1956. *Politics:* "Reactionary on the left." *Religion:* Catholic.

ADDRESSES: Home—53 Gloucester Rd., London SW7, England. *Agent*—Carmen Balcells, Diagonal 580, Barcelona 21, Spain.

CAREER: Writer. School of Journalism, Havana, Cuba, professor of English literature, 1960-61; Government of Cuba, Cuban embassy, Brussels, Belgium, cultural attache, 1962-64, charge d'affaires, 1964-65; scriptwriter for Twentieth-Century Fox and Cupid Productions, 1967-72. Visiting professor, University of Virginia, spring, 1982.

MEMBER: Writers Guild of Great Britain.

AWARDS, HONORS: Asi en la paz como en la guerra was nominated for Prix International de Literature (France), 1962; unpublished manuscript version of *Tres tristes tigres* won Biblioteca Breve Prize (Spain), 1964, and was nominated for Prix Formentor—International Publishers Prize, 1965; Guggenheim fellowship for creative writing, 1970; Prix du Meilleur Livre Etranger (France), 1971, *Tres tristes tigres.*

WRITINGS:

FICTION

Asi en la paz como en la guerra: Cuentos (title means "In Peace as in War: Stories"), Revolución (Havana), 1960.

Vista del amanecer en el trópico, Seix Barral (Barcelona, Spain), 1965, translation by Suzanne Jill Levine published as *View of Dawn in the Tropics,* Harper, 1978.

Tres tristes tigres (novel), Seix Barral, 1967, translation by Donald Gardner, Levine, and the author published as *Three Trapped Tigers,* Harper, 1971.

La Habana para un infante difunto, Seix Barral, 1979, translation by Levine and the author published as *Infante's Inferno,* Harper, 1984.

FILM CRITICISM

(Under pseudonym G. Cain) *Un oficio del siglo veinte* (title means "A Twentieth-Century Job"; film reviews originally published in magazine *Carteles;* also see below), Revolución, 1963.

Arcadia todas las noches (title means "Arcadia Every Night"), Seix Barral, 1978.

OTHER

(Editor) *Mensajes de libertad: La España rebelde—Ensayos selectos,* Movimiento Universitario Revolucionario (Lima, Peru), 1961.

"Vanishing Point" (screenplay), Twentieth-Century Fox, 1970.

(Translator into Spanish) James Joyce, *Dublineses* (title means "The Dubliners"), Lumen (Barcelona), 1972.

O, Seix Barral, 1975.

Exorcismos del esti(l)o (title means "Summer Exorcisms" and "Exorcising Style"; English, French, and Spanish text), Seix Barral, 1976.

Holy Smoke (nonfiction; English text), Harper, 1986.

Also author of screenplay, "Wonderwall," 1968, and of unfilmed screenplay, "Under the Volcano," based on Malcolm Lowry's novel of the same title. Also translator of stories by Mark Twain, Ambrose Bierce, Sherwood Anderson, Ernest Hemingway, William Faulkner, Dashiell Hammett, J. D. Salinger, Vladimir Nabokov, and others. Work is represented in many anthologies. Contributor to periodicals, including *New Yorker, New Republic, El País* (Spain), and *Plural* (Mexico). *Carteles* (Cuban magazine), film reviewer under pseudonymn G. Cain, 1954-60, fiction editor, 1957-60; editor of *Lunes* (weekly literary supplement of Cuban newspaper, *Revolución*), 1959-61.

WORK IN PROGRESS: Cuerpos divinos (title means "Heavenly Bodies"), a novel about women and writing.

SIDELIGHTS: Talking about his award-winning first novel *Tres tristes tigres,* translated as *Three Trapped Tigers,* Cuban-born writer Guillermo Cabrera Infante tells Rita Guibert in *Seven Voices:* "I would prefer everyone to consider the book solely as a joke lasting about five hundred pages. Latin American literature errs on the side of excessive seriousness, sometimes solemnity. It is like a mask of solemn words, which writers and readers put up with by mutual consent."

In the novel, we hear the voices of a group of friends as they take part in the nightlife of pre-Castro Havana. The friends take turns narrating the story using the colloquial speech of the lower-class inhabitants of that city. Told from so many perspectives using the language of such a small population group, the narrative is not always easy to follow. Elias L. Rivers explains in *Modern Language Notes:* "While some passages are readily accessible to any reader, others are obscured by Cuban vernaculars in phonetic transcription and by word-plays and allusions of many different kinds. A multiplicity of 'voices' engage in narrative, dialogue and soliloquy. [The novel] is a test which fascinates as it eludes and frustrates; the over-all narrative sense is by no-means obvious."

The importance of spoken language in *Three Trapped Tigers* is apparent even in the book's title, which in its English version repeats only the alliteration found in the Spanish title and not the title's actual meaning. Inside the book, the emphasis on sound continues as the characters pun relentlessly. There are so many puns in the book that *New Republic* contributor Gregory Rabassa maintains that in it Cabrera Infante "established himself as the punmaster of Spanish-American literature." Appearing most often are literary puns, including such examples as "Shame's Choice" used to refer to James Joyce, "Scotch Fizzgerald" for Scott Fitzgerald and "Somersault Mom" for Somerset Maugham. In another example, a bongo player—a member of the group of friends whose exploits are followed in the novel—is called "Vincent Bon Gogh."

If the emphasis on spoken rather than written language makes complete understanding of the novel difficult, it has made translating nearly impossible. Comparison of the Spanish, English and French editions of the book prove that readers of each language are not reading the same text. "What Cabrera [Infante] has really done," comments Roger Sale in the *New York Review of Books,* "is to write, presumably with the help of his translators, three similar but different novels." Because of the word play, Sale continues, "quite obviously no translation can work if it attempts word-for-word equivalents."

Playing with words is also an important part of Cabrera Infante's next novel, *Infante's Inferno,* and his nonfiction work, *Holy Smoke.* The latter—Cabrera Infante's first book written originally in English—tells the history of the cigar and describes famous smoking scenes from literature and film. Unlike the nearly universal acclaim received for *Three Trapped Tigers,* critics were unable to reach a consensus on these two works. While some praised Cabrera Infante's continued use of puns as innovative, other had grown tired of the Cuban's verbal contortions.

Commenting on *Infante's Inferno* in the *New York Review of Books* Michael Wood complains that Cabrera Infante's relentless punning "unrepentedly mangles language and hops from one tongue to another like a frog released from the throat. Some of the jokes are . . . terrible. . . . Others are so cumbersome, so fiendishly worked for, that the noise of grinding machinery deafens all the chance of laughter." *New York Review of Books* contributor Josh Rubins has similar problems with *Holy Smoke.* He comments, "In *Holy Smoke* . . . the surfeit of puns seems to arise not from mania . . . , but from mere tic. Or, worse yet, from a computer program."

Other reviewers are not so harsh in their criticism. In Enrique Fernández's *Voice Literary Supplement* review of *Infante's Inferno,* for example, the critic observes that the novel is written in "an everyday Cuban voice, unaffected, untrammeled [and], authentic." John Gross of the *New York Times* hails Cabrera Infante as a master in the use of language. Commenting on *Holy Smoke,* he claims: "Conrad and Nabokov apart, no other writer for whom English is a second language can ever have used it with more virtuousity. He is a master of idiomatic echoes and glancing allusions; he keeps up a constant barrage of wordplay, which is often outrageous, but no more outrageous than he intends it to be."

Three Trapped Tigers established Cabrera Infante's reputation as a writer of innovative fiction, a reputation that some critics find justified by his later work. Cabrera Infante once described his literary beginnings to *CA:* "It all began with parody. If it were not for a parody I wrote on a Latin American writer who was later to win the Nobel Prize, I wouldn't have become a professional writer and I wouldn't qualify to be here at all. My parents wanted me to go to University and I would have liked to become a doctor. But somehow that dreadful novel crossed my path. After reading a few pages (I just couldn't stomach it all, of course) and being only seventeen at the time, I said to myself, 'Why, if that's what writing is all about—*anch'io sono scrittore* [I am also a writer]!' To prove I too was a writer I wrote a parody of the pages I had read. It was a dreadfully serious parody and unfortunately the short story I wrote was taken by what was then the most widely-read publication in Latin America, the Cuban magazine, *Bohemia.* They paid me what at the time I considered a fortune and I was hooked: probably hooked by fortune, probably hooked by fame but certainly hooked by writing."

AVOCATIONAL INTERESTS: Birdwatching, old movies.

BIOGRAPHICAL/CRITICAL SOURCES:

BOOKS

Contemporary Literary Criticism, Gale, Volume 5, 1976, Volume 25, 1983, Volume 45, 1987.
Gallagher, David Patrick, *Modern Latin American Literature,* Oxford University Press, 1973.
Guibert, Rita, *Seven Voices,* Knopf, 1973.
Nelson, Ardis L., *Cabrera Infante in the Menippean Tradition,* Juan de la Cuesta (Newark, Delaware), 1983.
Souza, Raymond D., *Major Cuban Novelists: Innovation and Tradition,* University of Missouri Press, 1976.
Tittler, Jonathan, *Narrative Irony in the Contemporary Spanish-American Novel,* Cornell University Press, 1984.

PERIODICALS

Book World, October 3, 1971.
Commonweal, November 12, 1971.
London Review of Books, October 4-17, 1984, February 6, 1986.
Los Angeles Times, June 6, 1984.
Modern Language Notes, March, 1977.
Nation, November 4, 1978.
New Republic, July 9, 1984.
Newsweek, October 25, 1971.
New Yorker, September 19, 1977.
New York Review of Books, December 16, 1971, June 28, 1984, May 8, 1986.
New York Times Book Review, October 17, 1971, May 6, 1984, March 2, 1986.
Observer, September 2, 1984, October 13, 1985, December 21, 1986.
Paris Review, spring, 1983.
Review, January 10, 1972.
Time, January 10, 1972.
Times Literary Supplement, April 18, 1968, October 12, 1984, August 26, 1986.
Village Voice, March 25, 1986.
Voice Literary Supplement, April 18, 1968, October 12, 1984, August 29, 1986.
Washington Post Book World, January 28, 1979, May 27, 1984.
World Literature Today, spring, 1977, summer, 1981.

* * *

CAIN, G.
See CABRERA INFANTE, G(uillermo)

* * *

CAIN, Guillermo
See CABRERA INFANTE, G(uillermo)

* * *

CALDERON, Eduardo Caballero
See CABALLERO CALDERON, Eduardo

* * *

CALVO, Lino Novás
See NOVAS CALVO, Lino

* * *

CAMPA, Arthur L(eon) 1905-

PERSONAL: Born February 20, 1905, in Guaymas, Mexico; naturalized U.S. citizen; son of Daniel and Delfina (Lopez) Campa; married Lucille Cushing, April 23, 1943; children: Mary Del (Mrs. Larry Price), Danielle Lucille (Mrs. Michael M. Kiley), Arthur Leon, Jr., Celia Nita (Mrs. Rick Hamm), David Louis. *Education:* University of New Mexico, B.A., 1928, M.A., 1930; Columbia University, Ph.D., 1940. *Politics:* Republican. *Religion:* Protestant.

ADDRESSES: *Home*—2031 South Madison, Denver, Colo. 80210. *Office*—Department of Modern Languages, University of Denver, Denver, Colo. 80210.

CAREER: Albuquerque High School, Albuquerque, N.M., chairman of department of modern languages, 1928; Columbia University, New York, N.Y., instructor in Spanish, 1930-31; University of New Mexico, Albuquerque, instructor, 1932-33, assistant professor, 1935-37, associate professor, 1937-41, professor of modern languages, 1942-46; University of Denver, Denver, Colo., 1946—, began as professor of modern languages, chairman of department, and director of Center for Latin American Studies, became professor emeritus, chairman of Division of languages and Literature, 1946-50. Lecturer in Spain, U.S Department of State, 1953-54; cultural attache, U.S. Embassy, Lima, Peru, 1955-57; training project director and Denver University liaison officer, Peace Corps. President, National Folk Festival Association, Inc., Washington, D.C. *Military service:* U.S. Army Air Forces, 1942-45; served in European theater; became major; received Bronze Star Medal and ten campaign stars.

MEMBER: American Association of Teachers of Spanish and Portuguese, Modern Language Association of America, American Anthropological Association, American Folklore Society (councillor), American Dialect Society, National Folklore Festival Association (president), Rocky Mountain Modern Language Association, Colorado Authors League, Colorado Folklore Society (president, 1953), Westerners (Denver Posse), Pan American Club of Denver (president, 1948, 1952).

AWARDS, HONORS: Spanish Arts Foundation fellow, 1932; Rockefeller research grant, 1933-34; Guggenheim fellowship, 1952; Top Hand Award of Colorado Authors League for nonfiction article, 1955 and 1964, and for non-fiction book, 1963.

WRITINGS:

Acquiring Spanish, Macmillan, 1944.
Spanish Folk-Poetry in New Mexico, University of New Mexico Press, 1946.
Treasure of the Sangre de Cristos: Tales and Traditions of the Spanish Southwest, University of Oklahoma Press, 1963.
Hispanic Folklore Studies of Arthur Campa: An Original Anthology, edited by Carlos Coates, Arno, 1976.
Hispanic Culture in the Southwest, University of Oklahoma Press, 1979.
Sayings and Riddles in New Mexico, Borgo Press, 1982.
Spanish Religious Folktheatre in the Southwest, Borgo Press, 1982.

Also author of more than seventy monographs, bulletins, and articles for folklore and other professional journals. Editor, *Westerners Roundup* (monthly magazine).

* * *

CAMPOBELLO, Nellie (Francisca Ernestina) 1912-

PERSONAL: Born in 1912 in Mexico.

ADDRESSES: c/o Compañía General de Ediciones, Selector, Mier y Pesado 128, Col de Valle, 03100 México; and University of Texas Press, Box 7819, Austin, Tex. 78713-7819.

CAREER: Writer. Founder and overseer, with sister Gloria Campobello, of National School of Dance.

WRITINGS:

Cartucho: Relatos de la lucha en el norte de México, Integrales (Mexico), 1931, revised edition, Iberoamericana de Publicaciones (Mexico), 1940, translation by Doris Meyer and Irene Matthews published in tandem with *My Mother's Hands* (also see below) as *Cartucho,* University of Texas Press, 1988.
Las manos de mamá, Juventudes de Izquierda (Mexico), 1937, 2nd edition, illustrations by José Clemente Orozco, Villa

Ocampo (Mexico), 1949, translation by Doris Meyer and Irene Matthews published in tandem with *Cartucho* as *My Mother's Hands,* University of Texas Press, 1988.

Apuntes sobre la vida militar de Francisco Villa, Iberoamericana de Publicaciones, 1940.

(With sister, Gloria Campobello) *Ritmos indígenas de México,* [Mexico], 1940.

Tres poemas (three poems), Compañía General de Ediciones (Mexico), 1957.

Mis libros (collected works), illustrations by José Clemente Orozco, Compañía General de Ediciones, 1960.

Also author of poetry collections *Yo, por Francisca* and *Abra en la roca.*

SIDELIGHTS: Nellie Campobello is known for her portrayals, mainly through fictionalized autobiography, of the Mexican Revolution, which the author witnessed as a child. The vignettes in her 1931 book, *Cartucho: Relatos de la lucha en el norte de México,* feature such individuals as Campobello's mother and Francisco Villa, a revolutionary leader who is often regarded as an outlaw but is defended by Campobello. The author again portrays her mother in *Las manos de mamá,* a laudatory work that depicts Campobello's mother as a constant source of strength and hope during the difficult revolutionary years. *Cartucho* and *Las manos de mamá* were translated into English and published together as *Cartucho* [and] *My Mother's Hands* in 1988. A collection of the author's works was published in Spanish in 1960 as *Mis libros.*

* * *

CANDELARIA, Cordelia (Chávez) 1943-

PERSONAL: Born September 14, 1943, in Deming, N.M.; daughter of Ray (a road construction worker) and Addie Trujillo Chávez; married José Fidel Candelaria, 1961; children: Clifford. *Education:* Fort Lewis College, B.A., 1970; University of Notre Dame, M.A., 1972, Ph.D., 1976.

ADDRESSES: *Office*—Department of English, University of Colorado, Box 226, Boulder, Colo. 80309.

CAREER: Idaho State University, Pocatello, assistant professor of English, 1975-77; University of Colorado, Boulder, assistant professor of English and Chicano literature, 1978—. Program officer for National Endowment for the Humanities, 1976-77; humanities program adviser for National Council of Mayors, 1981. Member of board of directors of New World Foundation and National Council of La Raza, both 1978—; consultant to Danforth Foundation. Chairperson of South Bend Human Rights Commission, 1973.

MEMBER: American Association of University Professors, Modern Language Association of America, National Chicano Teachers of English, Mexican American Women's National Association, Women's Political Caucus, Panel of American Women, Organization of Teachers of English to Speakers of Other Languages, Society for Values in Higher Education (fellow), Rocky Mountain Modern Language Association, Notre Dame English Association, Common Cause.

AWARDS, HONORS: Woodrow Wilson fellow, 1970; Mellon fellow at Aspen Institute for Humanistic Studies, 1977-78; grant from Southern Fellowship Fund, 1979-80.

WRITINGS:

(Contributor) Julian Samora, editor, *A History of the Mexican-American People,* University of Notre Dame Press, 1977.
Ojo de la cueva/Cave Springs (poems), Maize Press, 1984.

(Contributor) Teresinha Pereira, editor, *International Poetry Yearbook,* International Book, 1985.
Chicano Poetry: A Critical Introduction, Greenwood Press, 1986.
Baseball in American Literature, Greenwood Press, 1989.

Contributor of poems and articles to literature journals, including *Rocky Mountain Review, Grito del sol, Rendezvous, Poe Studies,* and *Agenda.*

WORK IN PROGRESS: *Rainbow in Black and White,* a poetry collection.

BIOGRAPHICAL/CRITICAL SOURCES:

BOOKS

Dictionary of Literary Biography, Volume 82: *Chicano Writers,* Gale, 1989.

* * *

CANDELARIA, Nash 1928-

PERSONAL: Born May 7, 1928, in Los Angeles, Calif.; son of Ignacio N. (a railway mail clerk) and Flora (Rivera) Candelaria; married Doranne Godwin (a fashion designer), November 27, 1955; children: David, Alex. *Education:* University of California, Los Angeles, B.S., 1948. *Politics:* "I usually seem to vote for the person who doesn't get elected." *Religion:* "Non-church-going monotheistic and cultural Christian."

ADDRESSES: *Home and office*—1295 Wilson St., Palo Alto, Calif. 94301.

CAREER: Don Baxter, Inc. (pharmaceutical firm), Glendale, Calif., chemist, 1948-52; *Atomics International,* Downey, Calif., technical editor, 1953-54; Beckman Instruments, Fullerton, Calif., promotion supervisor, 1954-59; Northrup-Nortronics, Anaheim, Calif., in marketing communications, 1959-65; Hixon & Jorgensen Advertising, Los Angeles, Calif., account executive, 1965-67; Varian Associates, Inc. (in scientific instruments), Palo Alto, Calif., advertising manager, 1967-82; freelance writer, 1982-85; Daisy Systems Corp., Mountain View, Calif., marketing writer, 1985-87; Hewlett-Packard Co., Palo Alto, Calif., marketing writer, 1987—. *Military service:* U.S. Air Force, 1952-53; became second lieutenant.

AWARDS, HONORS: *Not by the Sword* was a finalist in the Western Writers of America Spur Award competition, 1982, and received the Before Columbus Foundation American Book Award, 1983.

WRITINGS:

Memories of the Alhambra (novel), Cíbola Press, 1977.
(Contributor) Gary D. Keller and Francisco Jiménez, editors, *Hispanics in the United States: An Anthology of Creative Literature,* Bilingual Press, Volume 1, 1980, Volume 2, 1982.
Not by the Sword (novel), Bilingual Press, 1982.
(Contributor) Nicholas Kanellos, editor, *A Decade of Hispanic Literature: An Anniversary Anthology,* Arte Público, 1982.
Inheritance of Strangers (novel), Bilingual Press, 1984.
The Day the Cisco Kid Shot John Wayne (short stories), Bilingual Press, 1988.

Contributor of short stories to *Bilingual Review;* contributor to *Science.* Editor, *VIA.*

WORK IN PROGRESS: *Leonor Park,* a novel about land, greed, and sibling rivalry in the U.S. Hispanic southwest of the 1920s.

SIDELIGHTS: Nash Candelaria writes: "*Memories of the Alhambra* is about the Chicano heritage myth of being descendants of conquistadors, the unsolvable dilemma of Hispanics from the state of New Mexico who acknowledge their European heritage and may not accept their American Indian heritage. . . . *Not by the Sword* is a look at the Mexican War (1846-48) from the point-of-view of New Mexicans, who became Americans by conquest. *Inheritance of Strangers,* a sequel to *Not by the Sword,* looks at the aftermath of the Mexican War forty years later, and the problems of assimilation; it focuses on the futility of revenge and the difficulty of forgiveness by a conquered people. *The Day the Cisco Kid Shot John Wayne* is a collection of twelve stories that give insight into and understanding of the Hispanic experience in the United States and its interface with the dominant Anglo culture.

"I am a descendant of one of the founding families of Albuquerque, New Mexico, and an ancestor, Juan, authored a history of New Mexico in 1776. Although I was born in California, I consider myself a New Mexican by heritage and sympathy. My writing is primarily about Hispanic Americans, trying, through fiction, to present some of their stories to a wider audience that may only be aware of them as a 'silent minority.' "

AVOCATIONAL INTERESTS: The arts and family, reading, and the stock market.

BIOGRAPHICAL/CRITICAL SOURCES:

BOOKS

Meier, Matt S., *Mexican American Biographies: A Historical Dictionary, 1836-1987,* Greenwood Press, 1988.

PERIODICALS

Best Sellers, August, 1977, May, 1983.
Carta Abierta, Number 9, 1977.
De Colores, Nos. 1 and 2, 1980.
New Mexico Magazine, September, 1977.
Western American Literature, Volume 34, number 2, 1978, Spring, 1984.

*   *   *

CARBALLIDO, Emilio 1925-

PERSONAL: Born May 22, 1925, in Córdoba, Veracruz, Mexico; son of Francisco Carballido and Blanca Rosa Fentanes; children: Juan de Diós. *Education:* Universidad Nacional Autónoma de México, 1945-49. *Politics:* Third positionist. *Religion:* Roman Catholic.

CAREER: Universidad Veracruzana, Xalapa, Mexico, subdirector of Escuela de Teatro, 1954, member of Editorial Council, beginning in 1959, Faculty of Philosophy and Letters, professor, 1960-61; Instituto Nacional de Bellas Artes, Escuela de Arte Teatral, Mexico City, Mexico, professor, beginning in 1955; Ballet Nacional A.C., Mexico, literary adviser, beginning in 1957, public relations representative on European and Asian tours, 1957-58; Instituto Politécnico Nacional, Mexico City, Departamento de Difusión Cultural, staff member, 1960-74, Taller de Composición Dramática, director, 1969-74; Universidad Nacional Autónoma de México, Mexico City, professor of dramatic theory and composition and head of Seminario de Teatro Mexicano, 1965-68. Visiting professor at Rutgers University, 1965-66, and University of Pittsburgh, 1970-71.

MEMBER: Sindicato de Trabajadores de la Producción Cinematográfica (secretary, Sección de Autores y Adaptadores).

AWARDS, HONORS: Second prize in Concurso Nacional de Teatro, 1950, for "La zona intermedia: Auto sacramental"; Rockefeller fellowship, New York, N.Y., 1950; Centro Mexicano de Escritores fellowship, 1951-52 and 1955-56; second prize in libretto contest, Opera Nacional, 1953, for "El pozo"; first prize in Universidad Nacional Autónoma de México contest, 1954, for "La hebra de oro"; *El Nacional* prize, 1954, for *La danza que sueña la tortuga;* first prize in theatre, Festival Regional, Instituto Nacional de Bellas Artes, 1955, and Ruiz de Alarcón Critics' Prize for the best work of 1957, both for "Felicidad"; *El Nacional* prize, 1958, for "El día que se soltaron los leones"; Premio de los Críticos No-asociados for the best work of 1960, for "El relojero de Córdoba"; Menorah de Oro prize for best film continuity of 1961, for "Macario"; Instituto Internacional de Teatro prize, Mexican branch, 1962, and honorable mention, Paris, 1963, both for "Medusa"; *Casa de las Américas* prize, 1962, for *Un pequeño día de ira;* Ruiz de Alarcón Prize for best play of the year, 1966, for *Yo también hablo de la rosa,* and 1968, for "Medusa"; *El Heraldo* prize, 1967, for "Te juro, Juana, que tengo ganas," and 1975, for "Las cartas de Mozart"; Asociación de Críticos y Cronistas prize, 1976, for *Un pequeño día de ira.*

WRITINGS:

PLAYS

"La triple porfía" (title means "The Triple Cross"; one-act farce), first produced in Mexico City, Mexico, at Escuela de Arte Teatral, Instituto Nacional de Bellas Artes, 1949.

"El triángulo sutil" (title means "The Subtle Triangle"; one-act farce), privately produced in Mexico City, 1949.

"La zona intermedia: Auto sacramental" (also see below; first produced in Mexico City at Teatro Latino, 1950), translation by Margaret Sayers Peden published as "The Intermediate Zone" in *The Golden Thread and Other Plays* (also see below).

"Escribir, por ejemplo" (title means "To Write, For Example"; monologue; also see below) first produced in Mexico City at Teatro del Caracol, 1950.

"Rosalba y los llaveros" (title means "Rosalba and the Turnkeys"; three-act comedy; also see below), first produced in Mexico City at Palacio de Bellas Artes, 1950.

"La sinfonía doméstica" (title means "The Domestic Symphony"; three-act comedy), first produced in Mexico City at Teatro Ideal, 1953.

(With Sergio Magaña) "El viaje de Nocresida" (three-act juvenile comedy), first produced in Mexico City at Palacio de Bellas Artes, 1953.

"Felicidad" (title means "Happiness"; three-act; first produced in Mexico City at Teatro Reforma, 1955), published in *Concurso Mexicano de Teatro: Obras premiadas,* Instituto Nacional de Bellas Artes, 1956.

La danza que sueña la tortuga (title means "The Dance the Turtle Dreams About"; three-act comedy; first produced as "Palabras cruzadas" in Mexico City at Teatro de la Comedia, 1955), Fondo de Cultura Económica, 1957.

(With Luisa Bauer and Fernando Wagner) "Cinco pasos al cielo" (title means "Five Steps to Heaven"; three-act juvenile comedy), first produced in Mexico City at Palacio de Bellas Artes, 1959.

"La hebra de oro" (three-act; first produced in Mexico City at Teatro Reforma, 1959), translation by Peden published as "The Golden Thread" in *The Golden Thread and Other Plays* (also see below).

"Selaginela" (monologue; also see below), first produced in Mexico City at Teatro de la Feria del Libro, 1959.

115

"El censo" (comedy; also see below), first produced in Mexico City at Teatro de la Feria del Libro, 1959; produced in New York City by Repertorio Español, 1977.

Las estatuas de marfil (title means "The Ivory Statues"; three-act; first produced in Mexico City at Teatro Ofelia, 1960), Universidad Veracruzana, 1960.

"El relojero de Córdoba" (two-act comedy, first produced in Mexico City at Teatro del Bosque, 1960), translation by Peden published as "The Clockmaker from Cordoba" in *The Golden Thread and Other Plays* (also see below).

"La lente maravillosa" (juvenile), first produced in Mexico City at Teatro Orientación, 1960.

"El jardinero y los pájaros" (title means "The Gardener and the Birds"; juvenile), first produced in Mexico City at Teatro Orientación, 1960.

"Guillermo y el nahual" (juvenile), first produced in Mexico City at Teatro Orientación, 1960.

"Homenaje a Hidalgo" (pageant with actors, dance company, chorus, soloists, and symphony orchestra), with music by Rafael Elizondo, first produced in Mexico City at Palacio de Bellas Artes, 1960, expanded version produced in Mexico City at Plaza de la Alhóndiga, 1965.

"Teseo" (tragicomedy; first produced in Mexico City at Teatro Xola, 1962), published in *La Palabra y el Hombre,* Number 24, 1962, translation by Peden published as "Theseus" in *The Golden Thread and Other Plays* (also see below).

"Parasitas" (monologue; also see below), first produced in German as "Die Parasiten" in Kiel, West Germany, at Theatre of the State Capital, 1963.

"La perfecta casada" (title means "The Perfect Wife"; one-act; also see below), first produced in Xalapa, Mexico, at Teatro del Estado, 1963.

"El día que se soltaron los leones" (three-act farce; first produced in Havana at Teatro del Sótano, 1963; also see below), translation by William Oliver published as "The Day They Let the Lions Loose" in *New Voices in Latin American Theatre,* University of Texas Press, 1971.

"¡Silencio, pollos pelones, ya les van a echar su maíz. . .!" (farce; first produced in Ciudad Juárez, Mexico, at Teatro de Seguro Social, 1963; produced in Mexico City at Teatro Urueta, 1964; translation by Ruth S. Lamb produced as "Shut Up, You Plucked Chickens, You're Going to Be Fed!" in Claremont, Calif., at Scripps College, 1969), Aguilar, 1963.

"Los hijos del capitán Grant" (three-act melodrama for children, based on a novel by Jules Verne), first produced in Mexico City by Compañía Estudiantil de la Preparatoria Número 5 at their theatre, 1964, produced in Mexico City at Palacio de Bellas Artes, 1966.

"Medusa" (five-act tragicomedy; also see below), first produced in English translation by Mary Madiraca under same title in Ithaca, N.Y., at Cornell University, 1966.

Yo también hablo de la rosa (first produced in Mexico City at Teatro Jiménez Rueda, 1966; translation by Myrna Winer produced as "I Also Speak about the Rose" in Northridge, Calif., at San Fernando Valley State College, 1972), Departamento de Teatro, Instituto Nacional de Bellas Artes, 1966, 2nd edition, 1970, translation by Oliver published as "I Too Speak of the Rose" in *Drama and Theatre,* Number 1, 1970.

"Te juro, Juana, que tengo ganas" (title means "I Swear to You, Joan, I Want To"; farce; first produced in Mexico City at Teatro del Granero, 1967; produced in New York City by the Repertorio Español, 1977), published in *La Palabra y el Hombre,* Number 35, 1965.

"Almanaque de Juárez" (dramatic collage-spectacle), first produced in Mexico City at Teatro del Bosque, 1968.

"¡Tianguis!" (spectacle), first produced in Mexico City at Auditorio Nacional, 1968.

Las noticias del día (title means "The News of the Day"; dialogue), Colección Teatro de Bolsillo, 1968.

Un pequeño día de ira (first produced in Havana on Cuban television, 1969; produced in Mexico City, 1976; translation by Peden produced as "A Short Day's Anger" in Pittsburgh, Pa., at University of Pittsburgh, 1970), Casa de las Américas (Havana), 1962.

"Un vals sin fin por el planeta" (title means "An Endless Waltz around the Planet"; comedy), directed by Carballido, first produced in Mexico City at Teatro Orientación, 1970.

Acapulco, los lunes (title means "Acapulco, On Mondays"; farce; first produced in Mexico City at Teatro Antonio Caso, 1970), Sierra Madre, 1969.

"La fonda de las siete cabrillas" (farce, based on "Don Bonifacio" by Manuel Eduardo de Gorostiza), first produced in Mexico City by Compañía Popular de la Ciudad de México, 1970.

"Conversación entre las ruinas," first produced in English translation by Myra Gann as "Conversation Among the Ruins" in Kalamazoo, Mich., at Kalamazoo College, 1971; produced in New York City at Puerto Rican Traveling Theater, June, 1989.

"Las cartas de Mozart," first produced in Mexico City at Teatro Jiménez Rueda, 1975.

"Nahui Ollin" (commissioned by Consejo Nacional de Cultura, Venezuela), first produced in Caracas, Venezuela, 1977.

"Rose of Two Aromas," translation by Peden, produced in New York City at Puerto Rican Traveling Theater, March, 1987.

Also author, with Luisa Josefina Hernández, of "Pastores de la ciudad" (also see below), first produced at Teatro Universitario de Puebla.

PLAY COLLECTIONS

La zona intermedia: Auto sacramental [and] *Escribir, por ejemplo,* Colección Teatro Mexicano, 1951.

La hebra de oro (contains "La hebra de oro" and "El lugar y el boro" [translation by Peden published as "The Time and the Place: Dead Love" in *The Golden Thread* (also see below)]), Imprenta Universitaria, Universidad Nacional Autónoma de México, 1957.

D.F. (title means "Federal District"; contains nine one-act plays: "Misa primera," "Selaginela," "El censo," "Escribir, por ejemplo," "El espejo [English translation by Margaret Sayers Peden published as "The Mirror" in *The Golden Thread and Other Plays* (also see below)], "Hipolito," "Tangentes," "Parasitas," and "La medalla"), Colección Teatro Mexicano, 1957, 2nd edition published with preamble and five additional plays (also contains: "La perfecta casada," "Paso de madrugada," "El solitario en octubre," "Un cuento de Navidad," and "Pastores de la ciudad"), Universidad Veracruzana, 1962, revised and enlarged edition published as *D.F.: 26 obras en un acto* (title means "Federal District: 26 One-Act Works"), Grijalbo, 1978.

Teatro (contains "El relojero de Córdoba," "Medusa," "Rosalba y los llaveros", and "El día que se soltaron los leones"), Fondo de Cultura Económica, 1960, French & European Publications, 1969.

The Golden Thread and Other Plays (contains "The Mirror," "The Time and the Place: Dead Love," "The Glacier," "The Wine Cellar," "The Golden Thread," "The Intermediate Zone," "The Clockmaker from Cordoba," and "Theseus"), translation and introduction by Peden, University of Texas Press, 1970.

Tres comedias (contains "Un vals sin fin por el planeta," "La danza que sueña la tortuga," and "Felicidad"), Extemporáneos, 1981.

OTHER

La veleta oxidada (title means "The Rusty Weathervane"; novel), Los Presentes (Mexico), 1956.

El norte (novel), Universidad Veracruzana, 1958, translation by Peden published as *The Norther,* with introduction by Peden, University of Texas Press, 1968.

La caja vacía (title means "The Empty Box"; short stories), Fondo de Cultura Económica, 1962.

"Macario" (filmscript), Azteca, 1968.

Las visitaciones del diablo: Folletín romántico en XV partes (novel; also see below), J. Mortiz (Mexico), 1965, 2nd edition, 1969.

El sol (novel), J. Mortiz, 1970.

(Compiler) *Teatro joven de México* (anthology), Novaro, 1973.

(Compiler and contributor) *El arca de Noé* (anthology), Secretaria de Educación Pública, 1974.

Los zapatos de fierro (novel), J. Mortiz, 1977.

Tiempo de ladrones: La historia de Chucho el Roto, Grijalbo, 1983.

El tren que corría, Fondo de Cultura Económica, 1984.

(Compiler) *Nueve obras jóvenes,* Mexicanos Unidos, 1985.

(Editor) *Avanzada: Más teatro joven,* Mexicanos Unidos, 1985.

Also author of play "Auto del juicio final" (title means "Auto of the Judgment Day"); and of filmscripts, including "Felicidad" (adapted from his play of the same title), "Los novios," "Las visitaciones del diablo" (adapted from his novel of the same title), "Rosa Blanca," "El águila descalza," and "La torre de marfil." Also author of ballets "El invisible" and "Ermesinda," both first produced in Mexico City at Palacio de Bellas Artes, 1952, and of operas "Misa de seis," first produced at Palacio de Bellas Artes, 1962, and "El pozo." Contributor to anthologies. Contributor of plays to *Revista de Bellas Artes, Revista de la Universidad de México, Novedades, El Nacional,* and *America: Revista Antológica;* contributor of stories to *Texas Quarterly* and *Izvestia* (Moscow). Founder and director of *Tramoya,* a theater quarterly published by Universidad Veracruzana, beginning in 1975.

SIDELIGHTS: Acclaimed Mexican playwright and novelist Emilio Carballido is a member of the group of Mexican playwrights responsible for a revitalization of their country's theater during the 1950s and 1960s. Discarding the traditional realist techniques prevalent in the dramas of the time, Carballido's plays often contain surrealistic and fantastic elements. One such work is his prize-winning "Hebra de oro" (translated as "The Golden Thread") which deals with two elderly women who stubbornly believe that their grandson will one day return from his foreign travels. Several of Carballido's best-known plays, including "Rosalba y los llaveros," "La danza que sueña la tortuga," and "Felicidad," are psychological studies of the problems of Mexico's middle class.

MEDIA ADAPTATIONS: "El censo" was produced on Spanish television in 1970, and "Yo también hablo de la rosa" was produced on French television in 1973; several of Carballido's other plays, including "Felicidad," "La danza que sueña la tortuga," and "El relojero de Córdoba," have also been adapted for production on Spanish television.

CARDENAL (MARTINEZ), Ernesto 1925-

PERSONAL: Born January 20, 1925, in Granada, Nicaragua; son of Rodolfo and Esmerelda (Martínez) Cardenal. *Education:* Attended University of Mexico, 1944-48, and Columbia University, 1948-49. *Politics:* "Christian-Marxist."

ADDRESSES: Home—Carretera a Masaya Km. 9 1/2, Apt. A-252, Managua, Nicaragua.

CAREER: Ordained Roman Catholic priest, 1965. Poet and author; formerly Minister of Culture in Nicaragua.

AWARDS, HONORS: Christopher Book Award, 1972, for *The Psalms of Struggle and Liberation;* Premio de la Paz grant, Libreros de la República Federal de Alemania, 1980.

WRITINGS:

Ansias lengua de la poesía nueva nicaragüense (poems), [Nicaragua], 1948.

Gethsemani, Ky. (poems), Ecuador 0°0'0', 1960, 2nd edition, with foreword by Thomas Merton, Ediciones La Tertulia (Medellín, Colombia), 1965.

Epigramas: Poemas, Universidad Nacional Autónoma de Mexico, 1961.

Hora 0 (poems), Revista Mexicano de Literatura, 1960.

(Translator and editor at large with Jorge Montoya Toro) *Literatura indígena americana: Antología,* Editorial Universidad de Antioquía (Medellín), 1964.

(Translator with José Coronel Urtecho) *Antología de la poesía norteamericana,* Aguilar (Madrid), 1963, Alianza (Madrid), 1979.

Oración por Marilyn Monroe, y otros poemas, Ediciones La Tertulia, 1965, reprinted, Editorial Nueva Nicaragua-Ediciones Monimbó, 1985, translation by Robert Pring-Mill published as *Marilyn Monroe and Other Poems,* Search Press, 1975.

El estrecho dudoso (poems), Ediciones Cultura Hispánica (Madrid), 1966, Editorial Nueva Nicaragua-Ediciones Monimbó, 1985.

Antología de Ernesto Cardenal (poems), Editora Santiago (Santiago, Chile), 1967.

Poemas de Ernesto Cardenal, Casa de las Américas (Havana), 1967.

Mayapan (poem), Editorial Alemania (Managua, Nicaragua), 1968.

Salmos (poems), Institución Gran Duque de Alba (Avila, Spain), 1967, Ediciones El Pez y la Serpiente (Managua, Nicaragua), 1975, translation by Emile G. McAnany published as *The Psalms of Struggle and Liberation,* Herder & Herder, 1971, translation from the sixth edition of 1974 by Thomas Blackburn and others published as *Psalms,* Crossroad Publishing, 1981.

Homenaje a los indios americanos (poems), Universidad Nacional Autónoma de Nicaragua, 1969, Laia (Madrid), 1983, translation by Carlos Altschul and Monique Altschul published as *Homage to the American Indians,* Johns Hopkins University Press, 1974.

Vida en el amor (meditations; with foreword by Thomas Merton), Lohlé (Buenos Aires), 1970, translation by Kurt Reinhardt published as *To Live is to Love,* Herder & Herder, 1972 (published in England as *Love,* Search Press, 1974), translation by Dinah Livingstone published as *Love,* Crossroad Publishing, 1981.

La hora cero y otros poemas, Ediciones Saturno, 1971, translation by Paul W. Borgeson and Jonathan Cohen published as

Zero Hour and Other Documentary Poems, edited by Donald D. Walsh, New Directions, 1980.

Antología: Ernesto Cardenal, edited by Pablo Antonio Cuadra, Lohlé, 1971, 2nd edition, Universidad Centroamericana, 1975.

Poemas, Editorial Leibres de Sinera, 1971.

Poemas reunidos, 1949-1969, Dirección de Cultura, Universidad de Carabobo, 1972.

(And translator) *Epigramas* (with translations from Catullus and Martial), Lohlé, 1972.

En Cuba, Lohlé, 1972, translation published as *In Cuba,* New Directions, 1974.

Canto nacional, Siglo Veintiuno (Mexico), 1973.

Oráculo sobre Managua, Lohlé, 1973.

(Compiler and author of introduction) *Poesía nicaragüense,* Casa de las Américas, 1973, 4th edition, Editorial Nueva Nicaragua, 1981.

Cardenal en Valencia, Ediciones de la Dirección de Cultura, Universidad de Carabobo (Venezuela), 1974.

El Evangelio en Solentiname (also see below), Ediciones Sigueme, 1975, Editorial Nueva Nicaragua-Ediciones Monimbó, 1983, translation by Donald D. Walsh published as *The Gospel in Solentiname,* Orbis Books, 1976 (published in England as *Love in Practice: The Gospel in Solentiname,* Search Press, 1977), reprinted in four volumes, Orbis Books, 1982.

Poesía escogida, Barral Editores, 1975.

La santidad de la revolución (title means "The Sanctity of the Revolution"), Ediciones Sigueme, 1976.

Poesía cubana de la revolución, Extemporáneos, 1976.

Apocalypse, and Other Poems, translation by Thomas Merton, Kenneth Rexroth, Mireya Jaimes-Freyre, and others, New Directions, 1977.

Antología, Laia (Barcelona, Spain), 1978.

Epigramas, Tusquets (Barcelona), 1978.

Catulo-Marcial en versión de Ernesto Cardenal, Laia, 1978.

Canto a un país que nace, Universidad Autónoma de Puebla, 1978.

In der Nacht Leuchten die Wrer: Gedichte, Aufbau-Verlag, 1979.

Antología de poesía primitiva, Alianza, 1979.

Nueva antología poética, Siglo Veintiuno, 1979.

La paz mundial y la Revolución de Nicaragua, Ministerio de Cultura, 1981.

Tocar el cielo, Lóguez, 1981.

(With Richard Cross) *Nicaraugua: La Guerra de liberación der Befreiungskrieg,* Ministerio de Cultura de Nicaragua, c. 1982.

Los campesinos de Solentiname pintan el Evangelio, Monimbó, c.1982.

(Translator from the German) Ursula Schulz, *Tu paz es mi paz,* Editorial Nueva Nicaragua-Ediciones Monimbó, 1982.

(Contributor) *Entrüstet Euch!: Für Frieden und völerverstandigung; Katholiken gegen Faschismus und Krieg* (essays on nuclear disarmament), Rdrberg, 1982.

La democratización de la cultura, Ministerio de Cultura, 1982.

Nostalgia del futuro: Pintura y buena noticia en Solentiname, Editorial Nueva Nicaragua, 1982.

Evangelio, pueblo, y arte (selections from *El Evangelio en Solentiname*), Lóguez, 1983.

Waslala: Poems, translated by Fidel López-Criado and R. A. Kerr, Chase Avenue Press, 1983.

Antología: Ernesto Cardenal, Editorial Nueva Nicaragua-Ediciones Monimbó, 1983.

Poesía de la nueva Nicaragua, Siglo Veintiuno, 1983.

The Gospel in Art by the Peasants of Solentiname (translated from *Bauern von Solentiname malen des Evangelium,* selections from *El Evangelio en Solentiname*), edited by Philip and Sally Sharper, Orbis Books, 1984.

(Contributor) Teófilo Cabestrero, *Ministros de Dios, ministros del pueblo: Testimonio de tres sacerdotes en el Gobierno Revolucionario de Nicaragua, Ernesto Cardenal, Fernando Cardenal, Miguel d'Escoto,* Ministerio de Cultura, 1985.

Vuelos de Victoria, Visor (Madrid), 1984, Editorial Universitaria, (León, Nicaragua), 1987, translation by Marc Zimmerman published as *Flights of Victory: Songs in Celebration of the Nicaraguan Revolution,* Orbis Books, 1985.

Quetzalcóatal, Editorial Nueva Nicaragua-Ediciones Monimbó, 1985.

Nuevo cielo y tierra nueva, Editorial Nueva Nicaragua-Ediciones Monimbó, 1985.

With Walker in Nicaragua and Other Early Poems, 1949-1954, translated by Cohen, Wesleyan University Press, 1985.

(Compiler and author of introduction) *Antología: Azarias H. Pallais,* Nueva Nicaragua, 1986.

From Nicaragua with Love: Poems 1979-1986, translated by Cohen, City Lights Press, 1986.

Contributor to *Cristianismo y revolución,* Editorial Quetzal (Buenos Aires), and *La Batalla de Nicaragua,* Bruguera Mexicana de Ediciones (Mexico).

SIDELIGHTS: Ernesto Cardenal is a major poet of the Spanish language well-known in the United States as a spokesman for justice and self-determination in Latin America. Cardenal, who recognizes that poetry and art are closely tied to politics, used his poetry to protest the encroachments of outsiders in Nicaragua and supported the revolution that overthrew Somoza in 1979. Once the cultural minister of his homeland, Cardenal spends much of his time as "a kind of international ambassador," notes Richard Elman in the *Nation.*

Victor M. Valle, writing in the *Los Angeles Times Calendar,* cites Cardenal's statement, "There has been a great cultural rebirth in Nicaragua since the triumph of the revolution. A saving of all of our culture, that which represents our national identity, especially our folklore." Literacy and poetry workshops established throughout the "nation of poets," as it has been known since the early twentieth century, are well-attended by people whose concerns had been previously unheard. Most workshops are led by government-paid instructors in cultural centers, while others convene in police stations, army barracks, and workplaces such as sugar mills, Valle reports. In these sessions, Romantic and Modern poetry is considered below standard; Cardenal also denigrates socialist realism, which he says "comes from the Stalinist times that required that art be purely political propaganda." The "greatest virtue" of Cardenal's own poems, says a *Times Literary Supplement* reviewer, "is the indirectness of Cardenal's social criticism, which keeps stridency consistently at bay." In addition, says the reviewer, Cardenal's poems "are memorable and important both for their innovations in technique and for their attitudes." In this way they are like the works of Ezra Pound, whose aesthetic standards Cardenal promotes.

Review contributor Isabel Fraire demonstrates that there are many similarities between Cardenal's poetry and Pound's. Like Pound, Cardenal borrows the short, epigrammatic form from the masters of Latin poetry Catullus and Martial, whose works he has translated. Cardenal also borrows the canto form invented by Pound to bring "history into poetry" in a manner that preserves the flavor of the original sources—a technique Pablo Neruda employed with success. Cardenal's use of the canto form "is much more *cantabile*" than Pound's *Cantos,* says Fraire. "We get passages of a sustained, descriptive lyricism . . . where the intense beauty and harmony of nature or of a certain social order or life style are presented." Pound and Cardenal develop similar themes: "the corrupting effect of moneymaking as the overriding value in a society; the importance of precision and truthfulness in language; the degradation of human values in the world which surrounds us; [and] the search through the past (or, in Cardenal's poetry, in more 'primitive' societies, a kind of contemporary past) for better world-models." Fraire also points out an important difference between the two: "Cardenal is rooted in a wider cultural conscience. Where Pound seems to spring up disconnected from his own contemporary cultural scene and to be working against it, Cardenal is born into a ready-made cultural context and shared political conscience. Cardenal's past is common to all Latin Americans. His present is likewise common to all Latin Americans. He speaks to those who are ready and willing to hear him and are likely to agree on a great many points."

Cardenal's early lyrics express feelings of love, social criticism, political passion, and the quest for a transcendent spiritual life. Following his conversion to Christianity in 1956, Cardenal studied to become a priest in Gethsemani, Kentucky, with Thomas Merton, the scholar, poet, and Trappist monk. While studying with Merton, Cardenal committed himself to the practice of nonviolence. He was not allowed to write secular poetry during this period, but kept notes in a journal that later became the poems in *Gethsemani, Ky.* and the spiritual diary in prose, *Vida en el amor.* Cardenal's stay in Kentucky was troubled by illness; he finished his studies in Cuernevaca, Mexico, where he was ordained in 1965. While there, he wrote *El estrecho dudoso* and other epic poems that discuss Central America's history.

Poems collected in *With Walker in Nicaragua and Other Early Poems, 1949-1954* look at the history of Nicaragua which touches upon the poet's ancestry. During the 1800s, the William Walker expedition from the United States tried to make Nicaragua subservient to the Southern Confederacy. According to legend, a defector from that expedition married into Cardenal's family line. Incorporating details from Ephraim George Squier's chronicles of that period, Cardenal's poem "With Walker in Nicaragua" "is tender toward the invaders without being sentimental," Elman observes. "This is political poetry not because it has a particular rhetorical stance but because it evokes the distant as well as the more recent historical roots of the conflict in Central America," Harris Schiff relates in the *American Book Review.* The poet identifies with a survivor of the ill-fated expedition in order to express the contrast between the violent attitudes of the outsiders and the beauty of the tropical land they hoped to conquer. "The theme of the gringo in a strange land," as Elman puts it, an essentially political topic, is developed frequently in Cardenal's work.

Later poems become increasingly explicit regarding Cardenal's political sympathies. "Zero Hour," for example, is his "single greatest historical poem about gringoism, a patriotic epic of sorts," says Elman. The poem's subject is the assassination of revolutionary leader César Augusto Sandino, who used guerilla tactics against the United States Marines to force them to leave Nicaragua in 1933. "It's a poem of heroic evocation in which the death of a hero is also seen as the rebirth of nationhood: when the hero dies, green herbs rise where he has fallen. It makes innovative use of English and Spanglais and is therefore hard to translate, but . . . it is very much a work of national consciousness and unique poetic expression," Elman relates.

Moving further back in time to reclaim a common heritage for his countrymen, Cardenal recaptures the quality of pre-Columbian life in *Homage to the American Indians.* These descriptions of Mayan, Incan and Nahuatl ways of life present their attractiveness in comparison to the social organization of the present. In these well-crafted and musical poems written at the end of the 1960s, the poet praises "a way of life which celebrates peace above war and spiritual strength above personal wealth. One has a strong sense when reading Cardenal that he is using the American Indian as a vehicle to celebrate those values which are most important to him as a well-educated Trappist monk who has dedicated himself to a life of spiritual retreat," F. Whitney Jones remarks in the *Southern Humanities Review.* That the poems are didactic in no way impedes their effectiveness, say reviewers, who credit the power of the verses to Cardenal's mastery of poetic technique.

The use of Biblical rhetoric and prosody energizes much of Cardenal's poetry. *El estrecho dudoso,* like the Bible, "seeks to convince men that history contains lessons which have a transcendent significance," James J. Alstrum maintains in *Journal of Spanish Studies: Twentieth Century.* Poems in *Salmos,* written in the 1960s, translated and published as *The Psalms of Struggle,* echo the forms and the content of the Old Testament psalms. Cardenal's psalms are updated to speak to the concerns of the oppressed in the twentieth century. "The vocabulary is contemporary but the . . . sheer wonder at the workings of the world, is biblical," Jack Riemer observes in *Commonweal.* "Equally memorable are those Psalms in which Cardenal expresses his horror at the cruelty and the brutality of human life. His anguished outcries over the rapaciousness of the greedy and the viciousness of the dictators are the work of a man who has lived through some of the atrocities of this century."

As the conflict between the Nicaraguan people and the Somoza government escalated, Cardenal became convinced that without violence, the revolution would not succeed. "In 1970 he visited Cuba and experienced what he described as 'a second conversion' which led him to formulate his own philosophy of Christian Marxism. In 1977 the younger Somoza destroyed the community at Solentiname and Cardenal became the field chaplain for the Sandinista National Liberation Front," reports Robert Hass in the *Washington Post Book World.* Poems Cardenal wrote during that "very difficult time in his country"—collected in *Zero Hour and Other Documentary Poems*—are less successful than the earlier and later work, says Hass, since "there is a tendency in them to make of the revolution a symbol that answers all questions." Some reviewers have found the resulting combination of Biblical rhetoric and Marxist revolutionary zeal intimidating. For example, Jascha Kessler, speaking on KUSC-FM radio in Los Angeles, California in 1981, commented, "It is clearly handy to be a trained priest, and to have available for one's poetry the voices of Amos, Isaiah, Hosea and Jeremiah, and to mix prophetic vision with the perspectives of violent revolutionary Marxist ideology. It makes for an incendiary brew indeed. It is not nice; it is not civilized; it is not humane or sceptical or reasonable. But it is all part of the terrible heritage of Central Latin America." Also commenting on *Zero Hour and Other Documentary Poems, American Book Review* contributor Harold Jaffe suggests, "Although the manifest reality of Cardenal's Central America is grim, it's future—which to Cardenal is as 'real' as its present—appears eminently hopeful. Furious or revolted as Cardenal is over this or that dreadful inequity, he never loses hope. His love, his faith in the disadvantaged, his great good humor, his enduring belief that communism and Christ's communion are at root the same—these extraordinary convictions resound throughout the volume."

"Though Cardenal sees no opposition between Marxism and the radical gospel, neither is he a Moscow-line communist," Mary Anne Rygiel explains in *Southern Humanities Review.* Rygiel cites the poem "Las tortugas" (title means "The Turtles") to demonstrate that Cardenal's reference to "communism" as the order of nature might better be understood as "communalism," a social organization of harmonious interdependence founded on spiritual unity. The poet-priest's social vision stems from his understanding of "the kingdom of God," Lawrence Ferlinghetti notes in *Seven Days in Nicaragua Libre.* "And with [Cardenal's] vision of a primitive Christianity, it was logical for him to add that in his view the Revolution would not have succeeded until there were no more masters and no more slaves. 'The Gospels,' he said, 'foresee a classless society. They foresee also *the withering away of the state*' [Ferlinghetti's emphasis]."

In the 1980s, Pope John Paul II reprimanded Cardenal for promoting a liberation theology that the prelate found divergent from Roman Catholicism. Alstrum notes, however, that *El estrecho dudoso* "reaffirms the Judeo-Christian belief that there is an inexorable progression of historical events which point toward the ultimate consummation of the Divine Word. Cardenal himself views his poetry as merely the medium for his hopeful message of the transformation of the old order into a new and more just society in which the utopian dreams and Christian values of men . . . can finally be realized." Cardenal founded the Christian commune Solentiname on an island in Lake Nicaragua near the Costa Rican border to put that dream into practice.

Some critics feel that the political nature of Cardenal's poetry precludes its appreciation by a sophisticated literary audience. Reviewers responded to the 1966 volume *El estrecho dudoso,* for example, as an attack on the Somoza dynasty while neglecting "the intricate artistry with which Cardenal has intertwined the past and present through myth and history while employing both modern and narrative techniques in his poem," asserts Alstrum. Others point out that Cardenal's work gains importance to the extent that it provides valuable insights into the thinking of his countrymen. Cardenal's poetry, which he read to audiences in the United States during the seventies, was perhaps more informative and accessible than other reports from that region, Kessler concluded in 1981, soon after Nicaraguan revolutionaries ousted the Somoza regime. "It may well be that Cardenal's poems offer us a very clear entrance into the mentality of the men we are facing in the . . . bloody guerilla warfare of Central America," Kessler suggested. More recently, a *New Pages* reviewer comments, "We can learn some contemporary history, [and] discover the feelings and thoughts of the people who were involved in Nicaragua's revolution by reading Cardenal's poems. And once we know what the revolution 'felt' like, we'll be a lot smarter, I believe, than most . . . who . . . make pronouncements about Nicaragua's threat to the free world."

BIOGRAPHICAL/CRITICAL SOURCES:

BOOKS

Bhalla, Alok, *Latin American Writers: A Bibliography with Critical Biographical Introductions,* Envoy Press, 1987.
Brotherston, Gordon, *Latin American Poetry: Origins and Presence,* Cambridge University Press, 1975.
Cardenal, Ernesto, *Zero Hour and Other Documentary Poems,* edited by Donald D. Walsh, New Directions, 1980.
Contemporary Literary Criticism, Volume 31, Gale, 1985.

Ferlinghetti, Lawrence, *Seven Days in Nicaragua Libre,* City Lights Books, 1984.

PERIODICALS

America, November 6, 1976.
American Book Review, summer, 1978, January, 1982, January-February, 1982, September, 1985.
Commonweal, September 17, 1971.
Journal of Spanish Studies: Twentieth Century, spring & fall, 1980.
Los Angeles Times Calendar, January 8, 1984.
Nation, March 30, 1985.
New Leader, May 4, 1981.
New Pages, Volume 10, 1986.
New Republic, October 19, 1974, April 9, 1977.
Parnassus, spring-summer, 1976.
Review, fall, 1976.
Southern Humanities Review, winter, 1976, winter, 1988.
Times Literary Supplement, July 12, 1974, August 6, 1976.
Voice Literary Supplement, September, 1982.
Washington Post Book World, June 23, 1985.
World Literature Today, spring, 1983.

OTHER

Kessler, Jascha, "Ernesto Cardenal: 'Zero Hour and other Documentary Poems' " (radio broadcast), KUSC-FM, Los Angeles, Calif., April 15, 1981.

—*Sketch by Marilyn K. Basel*

*   *   *

CARDENAS, Reyes 1948-

PERSONAL: Born January 6, 1948, in Seguin, Tex.

ADDRESSES: c/o P.O. Box 531, 756 Fourth St., Seguin, Tex.

CAREER: Writer.

WRITINGS:

Chicano Territory (poems), Rifan, 1975.
Survivors of the Chicano Titanic, introduction by Juan Rodríguez, illustrations by David Ellis, Place of Herons (Austin, Tex.), 1981.
I Was Never a Militant Chicano (poems), Relámpago Books Press (Austin), 1986.

Also author of short poetry collection *Anti-bicicleta haiku,* 1976; author, with Cecilio García-Camarillo and Carmen Taffola, of poetry collection *Get Your Tortillas Together,* 1976. Author of novel *Los Pachucos and La Flying Saucer.* Contributor of poems to periodicals, including *El Grito* and *Caracol,* and to anthologies, including *Floricantos II.*

*   *   *

CARDOSO, Onelio Jorge 1914-1986

PERSONAL: Born in 1914 in Calabazar de Sagua, Las Villas, Cuba; died May 29, 1986, in Havana, Cuba.

CAREER: Short story writer. Worked as teacher, darkroom technician, and radio scriptwriter before 1959; staff member, National Culture Council, Cuba, beginning 1959; writer, *Bohemia* (newsmagazine).

AWARDS, HONORS: First prize, literary contest, 1936; numerous other literary prizes and honors.

WRITINGS:

El cuentero, Universidad Central de Las Villas, 1958.
El pueblo cuenta (stories), [Havana], 1961.
Cuentos completos (anthology), Ediciones R, 1962, enlarged edition, Instituto del Libro, 1969.
Gente de pueblo, Universidad Central de Las Villas, 1962, reprinted, Letras Cubanas, 1980.
La otra muerte del gato (stories), UNEAC (Unión Nacional de Escritores y Artistas de Cuba), 1964.
Iba caminando (stories), Granma, 1966.
Abrir y cerrar los ojos, UNEAC, 1969.
El autor y su obra, edited with an introduction by Angelina Gavilán, Dirección Nacional de Educación General MINED, 1973.
El hilo y la cuerda (stories), UNEAC, 1974.
Cuentos (stories), Arte y Literatura, 1975.
La melipona, Arte y Literatura, 1977.
Caballito blanco, Gente Nueva, 1978.
Cuentos completos (stories), Ediciones de la Torre, 1981.
Gente de un nuevo pueblo, Giron, 1981.
Cuentos escogidos (stories), Letras Cubanas, 1981.
Los indocubanos, Gente Nueva, 1982.
La cabeza en la almohada, Letras Cubanas, 1983.
Negrita, Gente Nueva, 1984.

* * *

CARDOZA y ARAGON, Luis   1904-

PERSONAL: Born in 1904, in Antigua, Guatemala.

CAREER: Poet, art critic, and essayist. Founder, with Raúl Leiva, Otto-Raúl González, and others, of literary magazine *Revista de Guatemala.*

AWARDS, HONORS: Premio Rubén Darío, 1986.

WRITINGS:

Luna-park (poetry), Imprimerie Sainte-Catherine (Bruges), 1924.
Maelstrom (poetry), [Paris], 1926.
Torre de Babel (poetry; title means "Tower of Babel"), [Havana], 1930.
El somnámbulo (poetry), [Mexico City], 1937.
La nube y el reloj (art criticism), Universidad Nacional Autónoma, 1940.
Apolo y Coatlicue: Ensayos mexicanos de espina y flor, Ediciones de la Serpiente Emplumada, 1944.
Retorno al futuro: Moscú (travel), Letras de México, 1946.
Pintura mexicana contemporánea (art criticism), Universitaria, 1953.
Guatemala, las líneas de tu mano, Fondo de Cultura Económica, 1955, 3rd edition, 1975.
La revolución guatemalteca (nonfiction), Ediciones Pueblos Unidos (Montevideo), 1956.
Orozco (art criticism), Universidad Nacional Autónoma de México, 1959, 2nd edition, 1974.
Nuevo mundo (essays), Universidad Veracruzana, 1960.
México: Pintura activa (art criticism; text in Spanish and English), Ediciones Era, 1961.
México: Pintura de hoy (art criticism), Fondo de Cultura Económica, 1964.
Círculos concéntricos, Universidad Veracruzana, 1967.
Dibujos de ciego, Siglo XXI Editores, 1969.
Pequeña sinfonía del nuevo mundo (selected poems and prose), Universidad Nacional Autónoma de México, 1969.
Quinta estación (poetry), Universitaria Centroamericana, 1972.

Poesías completas y algunas prosas (poetry and prose), Tezontle (Mexico), 1977.
Malevich (art monagraphs), Universidad Nacional Autónoma de México, 1983.

* * *

CARDOZO-FREEMAN, Inez   1928-

PERSONAL: Born February 19, 1928, in Merced, Calif. *Education:* Received B.A., M.A., and Ph.D. from Ohio State University.

ADDRESSES: Office—Department of Comparative Studies, Newark Campus, Ohio State University, University Dr., Newark, Ohio 43055.

CAREER: Professor of Romance languages at Ohio State University, Columbus; professor of comparative studies at Ohio State University, Newark Campus; writer.

MEMBER: American Folklore Society, La Raza Unida de Ohio, Ohio Folklore Society, Mid-Ohio Women's Studies Consortium.

AWARDS, HONORS: Fellow of National Endowment for the Humanities, 1973.

WRITINGS:

(Contributor) Claire Farrer, editor, *Women and Folklore,* University of Texas Press, 1976.
The Joint: Language and Culture in a Maximum Security Prison, C. C Thomas, 1984.

Contributor to professional journals.

* * *

CARPENTIER (y VALMONT), Alejo   1904-1980
(Jacqueline)

PERSONAL: Born December 26, 1904, in Havana, Cuba; died after a long illness, April 24, 1980, in Paris, France; son of Jorge Julian Carpentier y Valmont (an architect); married Andrea Esteban. *Education:* Attended Universidad de Habana.

ADDRESSES: Home—Apartado 6153, Havana, Cuba. *Office*—Embassy of Cuba, 3 rue Scribe, Paris 4e, France.

CAREER: Journalist, editor, educator, musicologist, and author. Worked as a commercial journalist in Havana, Cuba, 1921-24; *Cartels* (magazine), Havana, editor in chief, 1924-28; Foniric Studios, Paris, France, director and producer of spoken arts programs and recordings, 1928-39; CMZ radio, Havana, writer and producer, 1939-41; Conservatorio Nacional, Havana, professor of history of music, 1941-43; traveled in Haiti, Europe, the United States and South America in self-imposed exile from his native Cuba, 1943-59; Cuban Publishing House, Havana, director, 1960-67; Embassy of Cuba, Paris, cultural attache, beginning 1966.

AWARDS, HONORS: Prix du Meilleur Livre Etranger (France), 1956, for *The Lost Steps* (*Los pasos perdidos*); Cino del duca Prize, 1975; Prix Medici, 1979.

WRITINGS:

NOVELS, UNLESS OTHERWISE NOTED

Poemes des Antilles (poetry), [Paris], 1929.
Ecue-yambo-ó!, [Paris], 1933, reprinted, Editorial Xanadu (Buenos Aires), 1968.

La música en Cuba (music history), Fondo de Cultura Económica (Mexico), 1946, reprinted, Editorial Letras Cubanas (Havana), 1979.

El reino de este mundo, originally published in 1949, Organización Continental de Los Festivales del Libro (Havana), 1958, 7th edition, Seix Barral (Barcelona), 1978, translation by Harriet de Onís published as *The Kingdom of This World,* Knopf, 1957.

Los pasos perdidos, Ibero Americana de Publicaciones (Mexico), 1953, enlarged edition, Editorial de Arte y Literatura (Havana), 1976, translation by de Onís published as *The Lost Steps,* Knopf, 1956, new edition with introduction by J. B. Priestly, Knopf, 1967.

El acoso, Editorial Losada (Buenos Aires), 1956, new edition with introduction by Mercedes Rein, Biblioteca de Marcha (Montevideo), 1972, translation by Alfred MacAdam published as *The Chase,* Farrar, Straus, 1989.

Guerra del tiempo: Tres relatos y una novela, Compañía General de Ediciones, 1958, translation by Frances Partridge published as *The War of Time,* Knopf, 1970.

El siglo de las luces, Compañía General de Ediciones (Mexico), 1962, 8th edition, Seix Barral, 1979, translation by John Sturrock published as *Explosion in a Cathedral,* Little, Brown, 1963.

El camino de Santiago (short story), Editorial Galema (Buenos Aires), 1967.

Tientos y diferencias, Arca (Montevideo), 1967, 3rd enlarged edition, 1973.

Literatura y conciencia política en América Latina (essays), edited by A. Corazón, [Madrid], 1969.

(Author of text) *La ciudad de las columnas* (architectural study of Havana; photographs by Paolo Gasparini), Editorial Lumen (Barcelona), 1970.

Viaje a la semilla y otros relatos (short stories), Editorial Nascimento (Santiago), 1971.

El derecho de asilo; dibujos de Marcel Berges, Editorial Lumen, 1972.

Los convidados de plata, Sandino (Montevideo), 1972.

Concierto barroco, Siglo XXI Editores (Mexico), 1974, 8th edition, 1979, translation by Asa Zatz published as *Concierto Barroco,* Country Oak Books, 1988.

El recurso del método, Editorial Arte y Literatura (Havana), 1974, 16th edition, Siglo XXI Editores, 1978, translation by Partridge published as *Reasons of State,* Knopf, 1976.

Novelas y relatos, Unión de Escritores y Artistas de Cuba (Havana), 1974.

Cuentos cubanos, Laia (Barcelona), 1974.

América Latina en su musica, UNESCO (Havana), 1975.

Letra y solfa, Síntesis Dosmil (Caracas), 1975.

El acoso [and] *El derecho de asilo* (collection), Editora Latina (Buenos Aires), 1975, published as *Dos novelas,* Editorial Arte y Literatura, 1976.

Crónicas (collection of articles), Editorial Arte y Literatura, 1975.

Razón de ser: Conferencias, Ediciones del Rectorado (Caracas), 1976.

Visión de América (essays), Ediciones Nemont (Buenos Aires), 1976.

Cuentos, Editorial Arte y Literatura, 1977.

Bajo el signo de La Cibeles: Crónicas sobre España y los españoles, 1925-1937, Editorial Nuestra Cultura (Madrid), 1979.

La consagración de la primavera, Siglo XXI de España (Madrid), 1979, 5th edition, 1979.

El arpa y la sombra, Siglo XXI Editores, 1979.

El adjetivo y sus arrugas, Editorial Galerna, 1980.

La novela latinoamericana en vísperas de un nuevo siglo y otros ensayos (essays), Siglo XXI Editores, 1981.

Works also published in various multi-title volumes.

Author of oratorio, "La Passion noire," first performed in Paris in the 1920s. Also author of librettos; author of two sound recordings, both produced by Casa de las Américas, "Alejo Carpentier narraciones" (cassette), and "Alejo Carpentier lee sus narraciones." Former columnist for *El Nationale* (Caracas). Contributor of articles on politics, literature, and musicology to numerous publications, including *Revolutions Surrealist.* Former editor, under pseudonym Jacqueline, of fashion section of Havana publication; former editor, *Iman* (Paris).

SIDELIGHTS: Although considered a major literary force in his native Latin America, Cuban Alejo Carpentier did not achieve widespread recognition with the American reading public. His prose examines historico-political factors as they relate to Latin American life and cultural development. In his writing, "Carpentier searches for the marvelous buried beneath the surface of Latin American consciousness, where African drums still beat and Indian amulets rule; in depths where Europe is only a vague memory of a future still to come," asserted Roberto González Echevarría in his *Alejo Carpentier: The Pilgrim at Home.* Echevarría continued: "On the one hand, Carpentier maintains that the baroque nature of Latin American literature stems from the necessity to name for the first time realities that are outside the mainstream of Western culture. On the other, he states that what characterizes Latin American reality is its stylelessness, which results from its being an amalgam of styles from many cultural traditions and epochs: Indian, African, European, Neoclassical, Modern, etc."

Carpentier's relative obscurity in the United States may have been related to the broad spectrum of knowledge he displayed in his writing, according to critics. Commented Gene H. Bell in the *New Boston Review:* "Out of a dozen or so major [South American] authors (Borges and García Márquez are the best-known here), Alejo Carpentier remains the one least recognized in these parts. . . . Some readers may be put off by Carpentier's displays of learning, an encyclopedism that ranges over anthropology, history, geography, botany, zoology, music, folk and classical, the arts, visual and culinary, and countless forgotten novels and verse—in all an erudition easily rivaling that of Borges." Yet despite Carpentier's immense scholarship, Bell perceived a universal quality in the author's writing, noting, "Precisely because . . . of national differences, however, Carpentier's novel[s] (like those of Fuentes or García Márquez) can furnish already interested Americans more insight into the social dislocations of the Southern continent than many a Yankee Poli Sci professor could."

Most critics familiar with Carpentier's work applauded the scholarly qualities that Bell enumerated, yet others criticized these very elements. The *New York Times Book Review*'s Alexander Coleman commented that Carpentier's early books were "often pretty heavy going, what with their tiresome philosophizing and heavily laid-on historical panoplies." Alan Cheuse concurred in *Review,* observing that some "readers may have decided that indeed the reasons for Carpentier's failure to capture an audience here are the same reasons put forth by the earliest reviewers: that his fiction is too 'erudite,' that he is more a 'cultural historian' than a novelist, . . . or that he is a 'tiresome philosophizer.'" However, Paul West remarked, also in *Review,* that "Carpentier is a master of both detail and mass, of both fixity and flux." West continued, "He can not only describe: he can describe what no-one has seen; and, best, he seems to have the hypothetical gift of suggesting, as he describes."

Carpentier's writing encompasses numerous styles and techniques. The *New York Review of Books*'s Michael Wood remarked that Carpentier "is interested not in myth but in history, and his method is to plunge us circumstantially into an earlier period, before, during, and after the First World War." Cheuse noted: "Intelligence and erudition are certainly present . . . in Carpentier's fiction. But so are sex, violence, political uproar, war, revolution, voyages of exploration, naturalist extravaganzas, settings ranging from ancient Greece to contemporary New York City, and characters running the gamut from the simple Haitian protagonist of *The Kingdom of This World* to the worldly wise, word-weary Head of State [in *Reasons of State*], . . . all of this comprising a complex but highly variegated and appealing fictional matrix."

Carpentier's themes often illustrate an awareness of broad social issues. Bell noted in the *New Boston Review* that "Carpentier's fiction regularly depicts individuals swept—often against their wishes—into the larger social struggle; they thereby become participants in history and embody the conflicts of their times." Echevarría asserted that "the plot in Carpentier's stories always moves from exile and fragmentation toward return and restoration, and the overall movement of each text is away from literature into immediacy." Echevarría further explained the historical relevance of Carpentier's themes: "The persistence of the structure and thematics of fall and redemption, of exile and return, of individual consciousness and collective conscience, stems from a constant return to the source of modern Latin American self-awareness."

Many critics found *Reasons of State* and *The Lost Steps* among Carpentier's best efforts. *Reasons of State* (*El recurso del método*) deals with a Francophile South American dictator attempting to rule the fictitious Nueva Cordoba from his Paris home, periodically returning to his country to control revolutionary outbreaks. Bell stated, "This is no drama of the individual soul, but an imaginative evocation of the material and cultural forces of history." He added: "*Reasons of State* is not a psychological study in tyranny. . . . Carpentier rather places the Dictator (who is actually something of a cultural-historical caricature) within a broader global process, shows how the petty brutalities of South American politics ultimately interlock with European and, later, U.S. interests."

Reviewers saw *Reasons of State* as a departure in style from earlier Carpentier books. The *New York Times Book Review*'s Coleman commented: "*Reasons of State* is something different—a jocular view of imaginative idealism, repressive power and burgeoning revolution, all done with breezy panache. Once again Carpentier has shown how canny and adept a practitioner he can be in mediating between the many realms which his own life has touched upon." Bell concurred, noting that the novel "exhibits a new lightness of touch, a wry and rollicking humor."

Carpentier's *The Lost Steps* (*Los pasos perdidos*) "is considered his masterpiece," wrote Ruth Mathewson in the *New Leader*. The novel, which contains autobiographical elements, "represents an attempt at unification and synthesis, if only because it is centered on a continuous and reflexive narrative presence," suggested author Echevarría. Like his other novels which deal with historical analysis, *The Lost Steps* also exhibits historical aspects. Gregory Rabassa observed in the *Saturday Review* that "Carpentier digs into the past: it almost seems as if he cannot get away from it, even in his novel *The Lost Steps*, which is contem-

porary in time but is really a search for origins—the origin first of music and then of the whole concept of civilization."

In an overall summation of Carpentier's work, Echevarría stated, "History is the main topic in Carpentier's fiction, and the history he deals with—the history of the Caribbean—is one of beginnings or foundations." Echevarría concluded that, "In a sense, as in *The Lost Steps,* Carpentier's entire literary enterprise issues from the desire to seize upon that moment of origination from which history and the history of the self begin simultaneously—a moment from which both language and history will start, thus the foundation of a symbolic code devoid of temporal or spatial gaps."

BIOGRAPHICAL/CRITICAL SOURCES:

BOOKS

Contemporary Literary Criticism, Gale, Volume 8, 1978, Volume 11, 1979, Volume 38, 1986.
Echevarría, Roberto González, *Alejo Carpentier: The Pilgrim at Home,* Cornell University Press, 1977.
Harss, Luis and Barbara Dohmann, *Into the Mainstream,* Harper, 1967.
Rodríguez Monegal, Emir, *Narradores de esta América,* Alfa, 1963.
Sentata aniversario de Alejo Carpentier, La Habana, 1975.

PERIODICALS

Books Abroad, spring, 1959.
New Boston Review, fall, 1976.
New Leader, July 5, 1976.
New Statesman, May 28, 1976.
New York Review of Books, December 9, 1976.
New York Times Book Review, May 2, 1976.
PMLA, spring, 1963.
Review, fall, 1976.
Saturday Review, May 29, 1976.
Studies in Short Fiction, winter, 1971.
UNESCO Courier, January, 1972, June, 1973.

OBITUARIES:

PERIODICALS

New York Times, April 26, 1980.
Times (London), April 26, 1980.

*   *   *

CARRERA ANDRADE, Jorge   1903-1978

PERSONAL: Born September 18, 1903, in Quito, Ecuador; died December, 1978, in Quito, Ecuador. *Education:* Attended Colegio Menjia, Universidad Central del Ecuador, and Universidad de Barcelona.

CAREER: Poet, essayist, and diplomat.

WRITINGS:

La guirnalda del silencio (poems), Imprenta Nacional (Quito, Ecuador), 1926.
Boletines de mar y tierra (poems), Cervantes (Barcelona, Spain), 1930.
Latitudes; Viajes, hombres, lecturas, América (Quito), 1934.
El tiempo manual (poems), Ediciones Literatura (Madrid), 1935.
Rol de la manzana; Poesías (1926-1929), Espasa-Calpe (Madrid), 1935.
La hora de las ventanas iluminadas (poems), Ercilla (Santiago, Chile), 1937.

Guía de la joven poesía ecuatoriana, Asia América (Tokyo), 1939.

Registro del mundo; Antología poética, 1922-1939, [Quito], 1940.

Microgramas (precedidos de un ensayo y seguidos de una selección de haikais japoneses), Asia América, 1940.

País secreto, poemas, Edición del Autor (Tokyo), 1940.

To the Bay Bridge/Canto al puente de Oakland (original text in Spanish) English translation by Eleanor L. Turnbull, Office of Pan-American Relations, Hoover Library on War, Revolution & Peace, Stanford University, 1941.

Mirador terrestre, la república del Ecuador encrucijada cultural de América, Las Américas (Forest Hills, New York), 1943.

Lugar de origen (poems), [Caracas, Venezuela], 1945.

Poesías escogidas, Ediciones Suma (Caracas), 1945.

Registro del mundo, antología poética, 1922-1939, Séneca (Mexico), 1945.

Canto a las fortalezas volantes: Cuaderno del paracaidista (poems), Ediciones Destino (Caracas), 1945.

Secret Country, Poems (parallel text in Spanish and English), translation by Muna Lee, Macmillan, 1946.

Visitor of Mist, translation by G. R. Coulthard, Williams & Norgate (London), 1950.

(Editor) *Poesía francesa contemporánea,* Casa de la Cultura Ecuatoriana (Quito), 1951.

La tierra siempre verde (el Ecuador visto por los cronistas de Indias, los corsarios y los viajeros ilustres), Ediciones Internacionales (Paris), 1955.

(Editor) Carlos Henrique Pareja, *Los mejores versos de la poesía ecuatoriana,* [Buenos Aires], 1956.

Edades poéticas, 1922-1956, Casa de la Cultura Ecuatoriana, 1958.

Moneda del forastero; Monnaie de l'étranger, G. Chambelland (Dijon, France), 1958.

El camino del sol; Historia de un reino desaparecido, Casa de la Cultura Ecuatoriana, 1959.

Galería de místicos y de insurgentes; La vida intelectual del Ecuador durante cuatro siglos, 1555-1955, Casa de la Cultura Ecuatoriana, 1959.

Pedreira das almas; o telescópio, Livraria Agir (Rio de Janeiro), 1960.

Viaje por países y libros; o, Paseos literarios, Casa de la Cultura Ecuatoriana, 1961.

Mi vida en poemas; Ensayo autocrítico seguido de una selección poética, Ediciones Casa del Escritor (Caracas), 1962.

Sus primeros poemas, Lírica Hispana (Caracas), 1962.

El fabuloso reino de Quito, Casa de la Cultura Ecuatoriana, 1963.

Hombre planetario (poems), Casa de la Cultura Ecuatoriana, 1963.

Presencia del Ecuador en Venezuela; Escritos varios, entrevistas, discursos, Colón (Quito), 1963.

Carrera Andrade en la Academia; Dos discursos, Casa de la Cultura Ecuatoriana, 1963.

Floresta de los guacamayos (poems), illustrations by Leoncio Sáenz, Nicaragüense (Managua), 1964.

Retrato cultural del Ecuador, Centre de Recherches de l'Institut d'Etudes Hispaniques (Paris), 1965.

A moratória, Livraria Agir, 1965.

Vereda da salvacao, Brasiliense (Sao Paulo, Brazil), 1965.

Retrato cultural del Ecuador/Cultural Portrait of Ecuador, Gulf Oil Corp. (Pittsburgh, Pa.), c. 1966.

Interpretaciones hispanoamericanas, Casa de la Cultura Ecuatoriana, 1967.

Las relaciones culturales entre el Ecuador y Francia, Ministerio de Educacíon Pública (Quito), 1967.

Poesía última, Las Américas, 1968.

El volcán y el colibrí; Autobiografía, J. M. Cajica, Jr. (Puebla, Mexico), 1970.

Selected Poems of Jorge Carrera Andrade, translation by H. R. Hays, State University of New York Press (Albany), 1972.

Reflections on Spanish-American Poetry, translation by Don C. Bliss and Gabriela de C. Bliss, State University of New York Press, 1973.

Obra poética completa, Casa de la Cultural Ecuatoriana, 1976.

SIDELIGHTS: As both a diplomat in Ecuador's foreign service and an intermittent expatriate living in exile, Jorge Carrera Andrade travelled extensively throughout the world, recording his observations in numerous essays. An eminent poet as well, Carrera Andrade composed brief, imagistic poems noted for a sympathetic understanding of the human condition. He also translated the works of other writers into Spanish and adapted Japanese *haiku* into Spanish in a form called *micrograma.*

BIOGRAPHICAL/CRITICAL SOURCES:

BOOKS

Pellicer, C., *Three Spanish American Poets: Pellicer, Neruda, and Andrade,* Sage Books (Albuquerque, N.M.), 1942.

PERIODICALS

Books Abroad, autumn, 1941, April, 1943.
PMLA, Volume 76, 1961.
Poetry, February, 1942.
World Literature Today, spring, 1979.

* * *

CARRION, Arturo Morales
See MORALES CARRION, Arturo

* * *

CASACCIA, Gabriel
See CASACCIA BIBOLINI, G(abriel)

* * *

CASACCIA BIBOLINI, G(abriel) 1907-
(Gabriel Casaccia)

PERSONAL: Born in 1907 in Asunción, Paraguay; immigrated to Argentina, 1935.

CAREER: Writer.

AWARDS, HONORS: Argentinean Kraft Prize, c. 1963, for *La llaga;* prize from Argentinean weekly *Primera Plana,* c. 1966, for *Los exiliados.*

WRITINGS:

Hombres, mujeres y fantoches (novel), El Ateneo (Buenos Aires), 1930.

UNDER NAME GABRIEL CASACCIA

El bandolero (play), Atlántida, 1932.

El guajhú (stories), Proventas (Buenos Aires), 1938, recent edition, Castañeda, 1978.

El pozo (stories), first published in 1938, 2nd edition, augmented, J. Alvarez (Buenos Aires), 1967.

Mario Pareda (novel), Librería del Colegio (Buenos Aires), 1939.

La babosa (novel), first published in 1952, 4th edition, El Lector (Asuncion), 1983.

La llaga, G. Kraft (Buenos Aires), 1964, recent edition, El Lector, 1987.

Los exiliados, Sudamericana, 1966, recent edition, El Lector, 1983.
Los herederos (novel), Planeta (Barcelona), 1975.
Los Huertas, Ediciones NAPA, 1981.
Cuentos completas, El Lector, 1984.

BIOGRAPHICAL/CRITICAL SOURCES:

PERIODICALS

World Literature Today, autumn, 1982.

* * *

CASARES, Adolfo Bioy
See BIOY CASARES, Adolfo

* * *

CASONA, Alejandro
See ALVAREZ, Alejandro Rodríguez

* * *

CASTANEDA, Carlos 1931(?)-

PERSONAL: Author gives birthdate and place as December 25, 1931, in Sao Paulo, Brazil; cites Castaneda as an adopted surname. Immigration records list name as Carlos César Aranha Castaneda, birthdate as December 25, 1925, and place as Cajamarca, Peru; son of C. N. and Susana (Aranha) Castaneda; came to United States in 1951. Other sources list birthdate from 1925 to late 1930s. *Education:* University of California, Los Angeles, B.A., 1962, M.A., 1964, Ph.D., 1970.

ADDRESSES: Home—308 Westwood Plaza, B101, Los Angeles, Calif. 90024. *Office*—c/o Simon & Schuster, Inc., 1230 Avenue of the Americas, New York, N.Y. 10020. *Agent*—Ned Brown, 407 North Maple Dr., Beverly Hills, Calif. 90210.

CAREER: Anthropologist.

WRITINGS:

The Teachings of Don Juan: A Yaqui Way of Knowledge, University of California Press, 1968.
A Separate Reality: Further Conversations with Don Juan, Simon & Schuster, 1971.
Journey to Ixtlan: The Lessons of Don Juan, Simon & Schuster, 1972.
Tales of Power, Simon & Schuster, 1974.
Trilogy (three volumes), Simon & Schuster, 1974.
Don Juan Quartet (boxed set; includes *The Teachings of Don Juan: A Yaqui Way of Knowledge, A Separate Reality: Further Conversations with Don Juan, Journey to Ixtlan: The Lessons of Don Juan,* and *Tales of Power*), Simon & Schuster, 1975.
The Second Ring of Power, Simon & Schuster, 1977.
The Eagle's Gift, Simon & Schuster, 1981.
The Fire from Within, Simon & Schuster, 1984.
The Power of Silence: Further Lessons of Don Juan, Simon & Schuster, 1987.

SIDELIGHTS: Carlos Castaneda's recorded experiences as an apprentice to Don Juan, a Yaqui Indian *brujo,* or sorcerer, are detailed in his many books, all of which deal with becoming a Yaqui "man of knowledge." According to Castaneda, Don Juan sensed in the younger man "the possibility of a disciple and proceeded to introduce him, by way of rigorous curriculum, into

realms of esoteric experience which clash disconcertingly with our prevailing scientific conception of reality," writes *Nation* contributor Theodore Roszak in a review of the author's first book, *The Teachings of Don Juan: A Yaqui Way of Knowledge.* The world through which Don Juan wished to lead Castaneda initially included using hallucinogenic drugs in order to attain certain experiences, although as the books progress, other means are used to reach different levels of consciousness.

A Separate Reality: Further Conversations with Don Juan records Castaneda's subsequent visits with Don Juan and his continuing visits to other phases of the intangible world. *Natural History* contributors William and Claudia Madsen feel the book's strength lies in its presentation of sorcery: "In his haunting story, [Castaneda] draws you into the weird world of witches—a world you will never be able to explain or forget. . . . Castaneda's work is unique because it reveals an inside view of how witchcraft works." However, *New York Times Book Review* contributor William Irwin Thompson thinks that by concentrating on the narrative instead of striving for an anthropological report, Castaneda's style becomes more readable. Throughout his books, the author shows himself as an occasional bungler and reports his teacher's often harsh criticism of his mistakes. Thompson notes this and remarks that Castaneda "can parody himself and mock his own ignorance without ever tilting the balance away from Don Juan toward himself. The tone is . . . perfect for the book."

Journey to Ixtlan: The Lessons of Don Juan concentrates on how a sorcerer becomes a "man of power" through "seeing" instead of using the ordinary means of perception, "looking." In *Book World,* Barry Corbet notes: "*Ixtlan* marks an enormous change in Castaneda. . . . His reporting is warm, human and perceptive. The extraordinary thing is that the book represents very little new teaching from don Juan, but is the result of Castaneda's new ability to discern the best of the earlier teachings. This is a book of rejects, all the field notes he previously considered irrelevant. And it is this material which makes *Ixtlan* such staggeringly beautiful reading. . . . *Journey to Ixtlan* is one of the important statements of our time." A *Times Literary Supplement* contributor, however, feels that Castaneda has drawn too close to his subject, and has "rejected the objective and scientific approach to [his] subject-matter in favour of an extravagant empathy with the human object of [his] studies." While a *Time* contributor, like many other critics, finds Don Juan himself puzzling, he appreciates the *Journey to Ixtlan:* "Indeed, though [Don Juan] is an enigma wrapped in mystery wrapped in a tortilla, [Castaneda's books are] beautifully lucid. [His] story unfolds with a narrative power unmatched in other anthropological studies. . . . In detail, it is as thoroughly articulated a world as, say, Faulkner's Yoknapatawpha County. In all the books, but especially in *Journey to Ixtlan,* Castaneda makes the reader experience the pressure of mysterious winds and the shiver of leaves at twilight, the hunter's peculiar alertness to sound and smell."

Tales of Power continues with Castaneda's mysterious experiences, although this book centers more on the pupil's dealings with the unseen than with the lessons of his master. Michael Mason, however, writes in the *New Statesman* that Castaneda's ideas may not be as unusual as they seem: "Ideas from European existentialism pervade the book more than Castaneda's admirers might care to recognise," Mason claims. He adds: "*Tales of Power* is not a work of mysticism." Mason also voices an objection to seeing Castaneda as a student of Yaqui spiritism: "The awkwardness arises of how Castaneda can be achieving enlightenment if he is such a spiritual clodhopper." *New York Times Book Review* contributor Elsa First finds the tale more convincing, however: "This is a splendid book, for all that it may seem ungainly, at times ponderous, at others overwrought. . . . [*Tales of Power*] could well be read as a farcical picaresque epic of altered states of consciousness. . . . One of the finest things in [*Tales of Power*], however stylized or fictional it may be, is the convincing portrait of a spiritual teacher working away at his student's tendency to 'indulge' in self-dramatization and self-pity."

Despite the factual presentation of Castaneda's books, many critics have debated whether Don Juan really exists. *New York Times Book Review* Paul Riesman sees them as scholarly works: "Taken together—and they should be read in the order they were written—[Carlos Castaneda's books] form a work which is among the best that the science of anthropology has produced." In another *New York Times Book Review* article, however, Joyce Carol Oates states another view: "I realize that everyone accepts them as anthropological studies, yet they seem to me remarkable works of art, on the Hesse-like theme of a young man's initiation into 'another way' of reality." And Dudley Young, also writing in the *New York Times Book Review,* questions Don Juan's credibility: "Since we are given virtually no information about the Don's credentials as a sorcerer (or indeed about his family or friends) it is very difficult to decide whether his symbology has genuine ethnic roots in Yaqui culture, whether he is just a more or less harmless crank, or whether he was seeking a corrupting kind of power over his disciple. . . . But Mr. Castaneda nowhere considers this possibility." Other reviewers, however, have dismissed the question of Don Juan's origins as irrelevant. According to *Washington Post* contributor Joseph McLellan: "The material in Castaneda's books is probably rooted in some sort of objective or hallucinatory experience—not cynically invented. If he had made it all up, as some observers have suggested, he could surely have produced something more interesting and coherent; something in which he is not seen so constantly as a dimwitted blunderer. Seen in context with other mystical writings, Castaneda's work seems less eccentric and its authenticity seems less dubious. . . . But by the same token, his work becomes less interesting—simply an exotic variant on fairly well-known themes."

Other critics have voiced different objections to Castaneda's writings. Weston LaBarre, in *Seeing Castaneda: Reactions to the "Don Juan" Writings of Carlos Castaneda,* questions the disciple's memory: "The long disquisition of Don Juan and the detailing of each confused emotional reaction of the author, . . . imply either total recall, novelistic talent, or a tape recorder." And in *Horizon,* Richard de Mille brings up what he considers important inconsistencies: "First, the so-called field reports contradict each other. Carlos meets a certain witch named La Catalina for the first time in 1962 and *again* for the first time in 1965. . . . A second kind of proof arises from absence of convincing detail and presence of implausible detail. . . . A third kind of proof is found in [Don] Juan's teachings, which combine American Indian folklore, oriental mysticism, and European philosophy. Indignantly dismissing such a proof, [Don] Juan's followers declare that enlightened minds think alike in all times and places, but there is more to the proof than similar ideas; there are similar words." But according to Joshua Gilder in his *Saturday Review* article on *The Eagle's Gift:* "It isn't necessary to believe to get swept up in Castaneda's other-worldly narrative; like myth it works a strange and beautiful magic beyond the realm of belief. . . . Sometimes, admittedly, one gets the impression of a con artist simply glorifying in the game—even so, it is a con touched by genius."

BIOGRAPHICAL/CRITICAL SOURCES:

BOOKS

Contemporary Literary Criticism, Volume 12, Gale, 1980.
LaBarre, Weston, *Seeing Castaneda: Reactions to the "Don Juan" Writings of Carlos Castaneda,* edited by Daniel C. Noel, Putnam, 1976.

PERIODICALS

American Anthropologist, Volume 71, number 2, 1969.
Book World, October 22, 1972, November 17, 1974.
Horizon, April, 1979.
Nation, February 10, 1969.
Natural History, June, 1971.
New Statesman, June 27, 1975.
New York Times Book Review, September 29, 1968, February 13, 1972, October 22, 1972, November 26, 1972, October 27, 1974, January 22, 1978.
Psychology Today, December, 1977.
Saturday Review, May, 1981.
Time, November 6, 1972, March 5, 1973.
Times Literary Supplement, June 15, 1973.
Washington Post, December 18, 1987.

—Sketch by Jani Prescott

* * *

CASTELLANOS, Rosario 1925-1974

PERSONAL: Born in 1925 in Mexico City, Mexico; died 1974 in an accidental electrocution. *Education:* Attended National University, Mexico City.

CAREER: Worked at Institute of Arts and Sciences, Tuxtla, Mexico, and at National Indigenist Institute, Mexico City, Mexico; held chair in comparative literature at National University, Mexico City; served as Mexico's ambassador to Israel.

WRITINGS:

De la vigilia estéril (poems), Ediciones de "América," 1950.
Sobre cultura femenina, Ediciones de "América," 1950.
Tablero de damas (one-act play), Revista América, 1952.
Poemas (1953-1955), [D. F.], 1957.
Balún-Canán (novel), Fondo de Cultura Económica, 1957, translation by Irene Nicholson published as *The Nine Guardians,* Faber, 1959, Vanguard, 1960.
Al pie de la letra (poems), Universidad Veracruzana (Xalapa, Mexico), 1959.
Salomé y Judith: Poemas dramáticos, Editorial Jus, 1959.
Lívida luz (poems), Universidad Nacional Autónoma de México, 1960.
Oficio de tinieblas (novel), Fondo de Cultura Económica, 1962.
Los convidados de agosto (story collection), Era, 1964.
La novela mexicana contemporánea y su valor testimonial, Instituto Nacional de la Juventud, c. 1965.
Juicios sumarios (essays), Universidad Veracruzana, 1966.
Rostros de México, photographs by Bernice Kolko, Universidad Nacional Autónoma de México, 1966.
El mar y sus pescaditos (literary criticism), Secretaria de Educa-ción Pública, 1968.
Materia memorable, Universidad Nacional Autónoma de México, 1969.
Album de familia (story collection), Joaquín Mortiz, 1971.
Poesía no eres tú; obra poética: 1948-1971, Fondo de Cultura Económica, 1972.
Mujer que sabe latín (literary criticism), Secretaria de Educación Pública, 1973.

Ciudad Real (story collection), Novaro, 1974.
El eterno femenino (play), Fondo de Cultura Económica, 1975.
El uso de la palabra (essays), Excélsior, 1975.
Bella dama sin piedad y otros poemas, Fondo de Cultura Económica, 1984.
Rosario Castellanos, el verso, la palabra y el recuerdo, Instituto Cultural Mexicano-Israeli, Costa-Amic Editores, 1984.
Meditation on the Threshold (text in English and Spanish), Bilingual Press, 1988.
The Selected Poems of Rosario Castellanos (text in English and Spanish), Bilingual Press, 1988.
A Rosario Castellanos Reader, translation by Maureen Ahern, University of Texas Press, 1988.

SIDELIGHTS: Rosario Castellanos was one of Mexico's leading feminists. Her concern for the plight of women was matched by her commitment to the nation's Indians. Raised in Comitán, Chiapas, in southern Mexico, Castellanos often wrote of the region and its Indian inhabitants. Mary S. Vásquez wrote in *Hispania* that since Castellanos's death in 1974, "there has been a proliferation of homage sessions and other tributes, together with numerous theses and dissertations on Castellanos topics, particularly in Mexico and the United States."

BIOGRAPHICAL/CRITICAL SOURCES:

BOOKS

Ahern, Maureen and Mary Seale Vásquez, editors, *Homenaje a Rosario Castellanos,* Albatros, 1980.
Meyer, Doris, editor, *Lives on the Line: The Testimony of Contemporary Latin American Authors,* University of California Press, 1988.
Miller, Beth, *Rosario Castellanos: Una conciencia feminista en México,* Universidad Autónoma de Chiapas, 1983.

PERIODICALS

Hispania, September, 1986.

OBITUARIES:

PERIODICALS

AB Bookman's Weekly, October 7, 1974.

*   *   *

CASTILLO, Ana (Hernandez Del)   1953-

PERSONAL: Born June 15, 1953, in Chicago, Ill. *Education:* Northeastern Illinois University, B.A., 1975.

CAREER: Writer, 1975—. Instructor in ethnic studies at Santa Rosa Junior College, Santa Rosa, Calif.

MEMBER: Association of the Latino Brotherhood of Artists (Chicago, Ill.), Movimiento Artístico Chicano, La Junta de Sociólogos.

WRITINGS:

Zero Makes Me Hungry (poetry), Scott, Foresman, 1975.
i close my eyes (to see) (poetry), Washington State University, 1976.
Otro canto (poetry), Alternativa Publications (Chicago, Ill.), c. 1977.
The Invitation, privately printed, 1979.
Keats, Poe, and the Shaping of Cortazar's Mythopoesis, Benjamins North America, 1981.
Women Are Not Roses, Arte Público, 1984.
The Mixquiahuala Letters (novel), Bilingual Press, 1986.

(Editor with Cherrie Moraga) *This Bridge Called My Back,* ISM Press (San Francisco, Calif.), 1988, Spanish translation by Castillo and Norma Alarcon published as *Este puente, mi espalda: Voces de mujeres tercermundistas en los Estados Unidos,* 1988.
My Father Was a Toltec: Poems, West End Press (Albuquerque, N.M.), 1988.

Contributor to *Revista Chicano-Riqueña, Spoon River Quarterly, River Styx,* and *Maize.*

SIDELIGHTS: Ana Castillo's epistolary novel *The Mixquiahuala Letters* explores the changing role of Hispanic women in the United States and Mexico during the 1970s and 1980s and the reaction many conservative Hispanic and Anglo men have toward their liberation. Comprised of thirty-eight letters written over a ten-year period from Teresa, a California poet, to a college friend, Alicia, a New York artist, the novel chronicles their relationship and travels together to Mexico as well as the women's separate personal lives. Castillo created three possible versions of Teresa and Alicia's story—for the "Conformist," the "Cynic," and the "Quixotic"—by numbering the letters and supplying varying orders in which to read them, each with a different tone and resolution.

BIOGRAPHICAL/CRITICAL SOURCES:

PERIODICALS

Choice, May, 1987.
Hispania, May, 1988.

*   *   *

CASTRO (y QUESADA), Américo   1885-1972

PERSONAL: Born May 4, 1885, in Rio de Janeiro, Brazil; died July 26, 1972, in Spain; son of Antonio and Carmen (Quesada) Castro; married Carmen Madinaveitia, 1911; children: Carmen, Luis. *Education:* Attended University of Granada, 1900-1905, and University of Paris, 1905-1908; University of Madrid, Ph.D., 1913.

CAREER: University of Madrid, Madrid, Spain, professor, 1913-36; professor at University of Wisconsin, 1937-39; professor at University of Texas, 1939-40; Princeton University, Princeton, N.J., professor of Spanish, 1940-53, Ford Emeritus Professor, 1953-72; University of California, La Jolla, professor, beginning in 1953. Founder of University of Madrid's Research Center for Humanistic Studies; advisor to Guggenheim Memorial Foundation, 1938-46. Visiting professor at University of Buenos Aires, 1923-24 and 1936-37, at Columbia University, 1924, and at University of Berlin, 1930-31; honorary professor at University of La Plata, Chile; special professor of Spanish at University of Houston, 1956.

MEMBER: Modern Language Association, Medieval Academy of America, Hispanic Society of America (honorary member), Academia Argentina de Letras.

AWARDS, HONORS: Officer de la Legion d'Honneur; honorary degrees from University of Poitiers, 1935, University of Paris, 1936, University of Rio de Janeiro, 1946, and Princeton University.

WRITINGS:

(Editor with Federico de Onís) *Fueros leonesses te Zamora, Salamance, Ledesma y Alba de Tormes,* [Madrid], 1916.
La enseñanza del español en España, V. Suárez, 1922 (Madrid), reprinted, 1959.
Lengua enseñanza y literatura (ebozos) (essays), V. Suárez, 1924.

El pensamiento de Cervantes, Hernando (Madrid), 1925, revised edition with notes by Castro and Julio Rodríguez-Puértolas, Noguer (Barcelona), 1972.
Santa Teresa, y otros ensayos, Historia Nueva (Madrid), 1929.
Cervantes, Reider (Paris), 1931.
Glosarios latino-españoles de la edad media, Hernando, 1936.
Iberamérica, su presente y pasado, Dryden Press (New York), 1941, 2nd edition, 1946.
La peculiaridad lingüística rioplatense y su sentido histórico, Losada (Buenos Aires), 1941, 2nd edition, Taurus (Madrid), 1961.
Lo hispánico y el erasmismo: Los prólogos al "Quijote", Facultad de Filosofía y Letras de la Universidad de Buenos Aires, Instituto de Filología, 1942.
España en su historia: Cristianos, moros y judíos, Losada, 1948, translation by Edmund L. King published as *The Structure of Spanish History,* Princeton University Press, 1954, translation by Willard F. King and Selma Margaretten published as *The Spaniards: An Introduction to Their History,* University of California Press, 1971.
Aspectos del vivir hispánico: Espiritualismo, mesianismo, actitud personal en los siglos XIV al XVI, Cruz del Sur (Santiago), 1949, reprinted, 1970.
Iberoamérica, su historia y su cultura, edited by Raymond S. Willis, Dryden Press, 1954, 3rd edition, 1956.
La realidad histórica de España, Porrúa (Mexico), 1954, 4th edition, Holt, 1971.
Semblanzas y estudios españoles, edited by Juan Marichal, [Princeton, N.J.], 1956.
Hacia Cervantes (criticism), Taurus, 1957, 3rd edition, 1967.
Santiago de España, Emecé (Buenos Aires), 1958.
Origen, ser y existir de los españoles, Taurus, 1959, revised edition published as *Los españoles: Cómo llegaron a serlo,* 1965.
De la edad conflictiva, Taurus, 1961, also published as *El Drama de la honra en España y en su literatura,* 3rd edition published as *De la edad conflictive: Crisis de la cultura española en el siglo XVII,* 1972.
La Celestina como contienda literaria: Castas y casticismos, Revista de Occidente (Madrid), 1965.
Cervantes y los casticismos españoles, Alfaguara (Madrid), 1967, reprinted with notes by Paulino Garagorri, Alianza (Madrid), 1974.
Español, palabra extranjera: Razones y motivos, Taurus, 1970.
Teresa la Santa: Gracián y los separatismos con otros ensayos, Alfaguara, 1972.
Sobre el nombre y el quién de los españoles, Taurus, 1973.
An Idea of History: Selected Essays of Américo Castro, translated and edited by Stephen Gilman and Edmund L. King, introduction by Roy Harvey Pearce, Ohio State University Press, 1977.

BIOGRAPHICAL/CRITICAL SOURCES:

PERIODICALS

Times Literary Supplement, February 25, 1972, December 1, 1972.

OBITUARIES:

PERIODICALS

New York Times, July 27, 1972.

* * *

CATALA, Rafael 1942-

PERSONAL: Born September 26, 1942, in Las Tunas, Cuba; came to United States in 1961; son of Rafael Enrique (a business-

man) and Caridad (Gallardo) Catalá. *Education:* New York University, B.A., 1970, M.A., 1972, Ph.D., 1982.

ADDRESSES: Home—c/o P.O. Box 450, Corrales, N.M. 87048.

CAREER: Poet, editor, and educator. Lafayette College, Easton, Pa., instructor of languages, 1977-79; writer, 1979-84; Seton Hall University, South Orange, N.J., assistant professor of modern languages, 1983-84; Lafayette College, Cintas fellow, 1984-85, assistant professor, 1985-87; full-time writer, 1987—. Director of Racata Literary Workshop, City University of New York, spring, 1983.

MEMBER: International Institute of Ibero-American Literature, Society for Literature and Science, American Association of Teachers of Spanish and Portuguese, Modern Language Association of America, Pacific Coast Council of Latin American Studies.

AWARDS, HONORS: Penfield fellowship from New York University, 1974-75.

WRITINGS:

Caminos/Roads (bilingual edition with English translation by Nancy Sebastiani), Hispanic Press, 1972.
Círcula cuadrado, Anaya-Las Américas, 1974.
(Co-author) *Ojo sencillo/Triqui-traque,* Editorial Cartago, 1975.
(With Luis Jiménez, Gladys Zaldivar, Concepción Alzola, Arthur Natella) *Cinco aproximaciones a la narrativa hispanoamericana contemporánea,* Playor, 1977.
(With others) *Estudios de Historia, Literatura y Arte Hispánicos,* Ediciones Insula, 1977.
(Contributor) *Azor en vuelo,* Volume 5, Rondas, 1981.
Copulantes, Luna Cabeza Caliente, 1981, 2nd edition, Prisma, 1986.
(Contributor) *Hispanics in the United States: An Anthology of Creative Literature,* Bilingual Press Review, 1982.
(Contributor) *Literatures in Transition: The Many Voices of the Caribbean Area,* Ediciones Hispamérica-Montclair State College, 1982.
(Editor with Robertoluis Lugo) *Soles emellis,* Prisma, 1983.
(Contributor) *Esta urticante pasión de la pimienta,* Prisma, 1983.
(Contributor) *Los Paraguas Amarillos,* Ediciones del Norte, 1983.
Cienciapoesía, Prisma, 1986.
Para una lectura americana del barroco mexicano: Sor Juana Inén de la Cruz y Sigüenza-y-Góngora, Institute of Ideologies and Literature, University of Minnesota, 1987.
Letters to a Student: Preparation for the Experience, Corrales Infinite Way Study Group, 1988.
(Contributor) *Poetas Cubanos en Nueva York,* Betania, 1988.
(Contributor) *El Jardín También es Nuestro,* SLUSA Press, 1988.
Sufficient Unto Itself Is the Day, Corrales Infinite Way Study Group, 1989.

Editor of "Index of American Periodical Verse" series, Scarecrow, 1981—. Work featured on videotape "First Symposium on New Tendencies in Latin American Literature," produced by Adelphi University, 1983. Contributor of poetry and essays to numerous periodicals, including *Norte, Lyra, EducaAcción, El Diario, Boreal, Septagon, New York Times, Publication of the Society for Literature and Science, Revista Iberamericana,* and *Catalyst.* Editor, *Rom[ḿ]nica,* 1973-75 and *Ometeca: Literature and Science,* 1988—. Associate editor of *Cuadernos de Poética,* 1987—.

WORK IN PROGRESS: *Cienciapoesía II; Towards a Theoretical Construct of Science and Poetry: A Unified View.*

SIDELIGHTS: Rafael Catalá told *CA:* "For me writing is an act of listening, as if I were an instrument of a universal text that is unfolding. I am a tool through which this text comes forth into expression.

In his book, *Cienciapoesía,* Catalá introduces the concept of sciencepoetry—the process of unifying or linking the humanities and science. Catalá explains in an article for the *Publication of the Society for Literature and Science:* "Science and the humanities, as the expression of human consciousness, are one. In order to have a balanced world view, both must be taken into account as a reasoning and as an intuitive process. In order to do this, we must learn to discern the commonality of principles that unifies both sub-systems of thought. I have named this process *cienciapoesía* (sciencepoetry—one word). It is the process where the sciences and the humanities, recognizing each other as one, meet in men and women as one body."

BIOGRAPHICAL/CRITICAL SOURCES:

PERIODICALS

Publication of the Society for Literature and Science, March, 1987.

* * *

CELA, Camilo José 1916-
(Matilde Verdu)

PERSONAL: Surname pronounced *Say*-lah; born May 11, 1916, in Iria Flavia, La Coruña, Spain; son of Camilo (a customs official and part-time writer) and Camila Enmanuela (Trulock Bertorini) Cela; married María del Rosario Conde Picavea, March 12, 1944; children: Camilo José. *Education:* Attended University of Madrid, 1933-36, and 1939-43.

ADDRESSES: *Home*—La Bonanova, 07015 Palma de Mallorca, Spain, and Madrid, Spain.

CAREER: Writer; publisher of *Papeles de Son Armadans* (literary monthly), 1956-79. Lecturer in England, France, Latin America, Belgium, Sweden, Italy, and the United States. *Military service:* Served in Spanish Nationalist Army during Spanish Civil War, 1936-39; became corporal.

MEMBER: Real Academia Española, Premio Nacional de Literatura, Premio Príncipe de Asturias, Real Academia Gallega, Hispanic Society of America, American Association of Teachers of Spanish and Portuguese (honorary fellow, 1966—).

AWARDS, HONORS: Premio de la crítica, 1955, for *Historias de Venezuela: La Catira;* Spanish National Prize for Literature, 1984, for *Mazurca para dos muertos;* honorary doctorates from Syracuse University, 1964, University of Birmingham, 1976, University of Santiago de Compostela, 1979, University of Palma de Mallorca, 1979, John F. Kennedy University (Buenos Aires), and Interamericana University (Puerto Rico).

WRITINGS:

IN ENGLISH TRANSLATION

La familia de Pascual Duarte (novel), Aldecoa (Madrid), 1942, reprinted, Destino (Barcelona), 1982, translation by John Marks published as *Pascual Duarte's Family,* Eyre & Spottiswoode, 1946, translation by Anthony Kerrigan published as *The Family of Pascual Duarte,* Little, Brown, 1964, reprinted, 1990, Spanish/English version by Herma Briffault published as *Pascual Duarte and His Family,* Las Américas Publishing, 1965.

Pabellón de reposo (novel; first published serially in *El Español,* March 13 to August 21, 1943), illustrations by Suárez de Arbol, Afrodisio Aguado (Madrid), 1943, reprinted, Destino, 1977, Spanish / English version by Briffault published as *Rest Home,* Las Américas Publishing, 1961.

Las botas de siete leguas: Viaje a la Alcarría, con los versos de su cancionero, cada uno en su debido lugar (travel; also see below), Revista de Occidente, 1948, reprinted, Destino, 1982, published as *Viaje a la Alcarría,* Papeles de Son Armadans, 1958, reprinted, 1976, translation by Frances M. López-Morillos published as *Journey to the Alcarría,* University of Wisconsin Press, 1964, reprinted, Atlantic Monthly Press, 1990.

Caminos inciertos: La colmena (novel), Emecé (Buenos Aires), 1951, published as *La colmena,* Noguer (Barcelona), 1955, reprinted, Castalia (Madrid), 1984, translation by I. M. Cohen and Arturo Barea published as *The Hive,* Farrar, Straus, 1953, reprinted, 1990.

Mrs. Caldwell habla con su hijo (novel), Destino, 1953, reprinted, 1979, translation by Jerome S. Bernstein published as *Mrs. Caldwell Speaks to Her Son,* Cornell University Press, 1968.

Also author of *Avila* (travel), 1952, revised edition, 1968, translation by John Forrester published under same title, 1956.

NOVELS

Nuevas andanzas y desventuras de Lazarillo de Tormes, y siete apuntes carpetovetónicos (title means "New Wanderings and Misfortunes of Lazarillo de Tormes"; first published serially in *Juventud,* July 4 to October 18, 1944), La Nave (Madrid), 1944, reprinted, Noguer, 1975.

Santa Balbina 37: Gas en cada piso (novella; title means "Santa Balbina 37, Gas in Every Flat"; also see below), Mirto y Laurel (Melilla, Morocco), 1952, 2nd edition, 1977.

Timoteo, el incomprendido (novella; title means "Misunderstood Timothy"; also see below), Rollán (Madrid), 1952.

Café de artistas (novella; also see below), Tecnos (Madrid), 1953.

Historias de Venezuela: La catira (title means "Stories of Venezuela: The Blonde"), illustrations by Ricardo Arenys, Noguer, 1955, published as *La catira,* 1966.

Tobogán de hambrientos (title means "Toboggan of Hungry People"), illustrations by Lorenzo Goñi, Noguer, 1962.

Vísperas, festividad y octava de San Camilo del año 1936 en Madrid (title means "Eve, Feast and Octave of San Camilo's Day, 1936, in Madrid"), Alfaguara, 1969, Noguer, 1981.

Oficio de tinieblas 5; o, Novela de tesis escrita para ser cantada por un coro de enfermos (title means "Ministry of Darkness 5; or, Novel with a Thesis Written to Be Sung by a Chorus of Sick People"), Noguer, 1973.

Mazurca para dos muertos (title means "Mazurka for Two Bad People"), Ediciones del Norte (Hanover, N.H.), 1983.

Cristo versus Arizona (title means "Christ versus Arizona"), Seix Barral (Barcelona), 1988.

Also author of *Los cipreses creen en Dios* (title means "The Cypresses Believe in God").

STORIES

Esas nubes que pasan (title means "The Passing Clouds"; also see below), Afrodisio Aguado, 1945, reprinted, Espasa-Calpe (Madrid), 1976.

El bonito crimen del carabinero, y otras invenciones (stories; title means "The Neat Crime of the Carabiniere and Other Tales"; one chapter first published in *Arriba,* April 25, 1946; also see below), José Janés (Barcelona), 1947, published as *El bonito crimen del carabinero,* Picazo, 1972.

Baraja de invenciones (title means "Pack of Tales"; also see below), Castalia (Valencia), 1953.

Historias de España: Los ciegos, los tontos, illustrations by Manuel Mampaso, Arión (Madrid), 1958, new enlarged edition published in four volumes as *A la pata de palo* (title means "The Man with the Wooden Leg"), illustrations by Goñi, Alfaguara, Volume 1: *Historias de España* (title means "Stories of Spain"), 1965, Volume 2: *La familia del Héroe; o, Discurso histórico de los últimos restos; ejercicios para una sola mano,* 1965, Volume 3: *El ciudadano Iscariote Reclús* (title means "Citizen Iscariote Reclús"), 1965, Volume 4: *Viaje a U.S.A.* (title means "Trip to the U.S.A."), 1967, published in one volume as *El tacatá oxidado: Florilegio de carpetovetonismos y otras lindezas,* Noguer, 1973.

Los viejos amigos, two volumes, illustrations by José María Prim, Noguer, 1960-61, 3rd edition, 1981.

Gavilla de fábulas sin amor (title means "A Bundle of Loveless Fables"), illustrations by Pablo Picasso, Papeles de Son Armadans (Palma de Mallorca), 1962, reprinted, 1979.

Once cuentos de fútbol, illustrations by Pepe, Nacional (Madrid), 1963.

Toreo de salón: Farsa con acompañamiento de clamor y murga, photographs by Oriol Maspons and Julio Ubiña, Editorial Lumen (Barcelona), 1963, reprinted, 1984.

Izas, rabizas y colipoterras: Drama con acompañamiento de cachondeo y dolor de corazón, photographs by Juan Colom, Editorial Lumen, 1964, reprinted, 1984.

Nuevas escenas matritenses (title means "New Scenes of Madrid"), seven volumes, photographs by Enrique Palazuela, Alfaguara, 1965-66, published in one volume as *Fotografías al minuto,* Organización Sala (Madrid), 1972.

La bandada de palomas (juvenile), illustrations by José Correas Flores, Labor, 1969.

Cuentos para leer después del baño, La Gaya Ciencia (Barcelona), 1974.

Rol de cornudos, Noguer, 1976.

El espejo y otros cuentos, Espasa-Calpe, 1981.

TRAVEL

Del Miño al Bidasoa: Notas de un vagabundaje (title means "From the Mino to the Bidasoa: Notes of a Vagabondage"), Noguer, 1952, reprinted, 1981.

Vagabundo por Castilla (title means "Vagabond in Castile"), Seix Barral, 1955.

Judíos, moros y cristianos: Notas de un vagabundaje por Avila, Segovia y sus tierras (title means "Jews, Moors, and Christians: Notes of a Vagabondage through Avila, Segovia, and Their Surroundings"), Destino, 1956, reprinted, 1979.

Primer viaje andaluz: Notas de un vagabundaje por Jaén, Córdoba, Sevilla, Huelva y sus tierras (title means "First Andalusian Trip: Notes on a Vagabondage through Jaen, Cordoba, Seville, Huelva, and Their Surroundings"), illustrations by José Hurtuna, Noguer, 1959, reprinted, 1979.

Cuaderno del Guadarrama (title means "Guadarrama Notebook"), illustrations by Eduardo Vicente, Arión, 1959.

Páginas de geografía errabunda (title means "Pages of Wandering Geography"), Alfaguara, 1965.

Viaje al Pirineo de Lérida: Notas de un paseo a pie por el Pallars Sobirá, el Valle de Arán y el Condado de Ribagorza, Alfaguara, 1965.

Madrid, illustrations by Juan Esplandíu, Alfaguara, 1966.

Calidoscopio callejero, marítimo y campestre de C.J.C. para el reino y ultramar, Alfaguara, 1966.

La Mancha en el corazón y en los ojos, EDISVEN (Barcelona), 1971.

Balada del vagabundo sin suerte y otros papeles volanderos, Espasa-Calpe, 1973.

Madrid, color y siluta, illustrations by Estrada Vilarrasa, AUSA (Sabadell, Spain), 1985.

Nuevo viaje a la Alcarría, three volumes, Información y Revistas (Madrid), 1986.

Also author of *Barcelona,* 1970.

OMNIBUS VOLUMES

El molino de viento, y otras novelas cortas (title means "The Windmill and Other Short Novels"; contains *El molino de viento, Timoteo, el incomprendido* [also see below], *Café de artistas* [also see below], and *Santa Balbina 37: Gas en cada piso*), illustrations by Goñi, Noguer, 1956, reprinted, 1977.

Mis páginas preferidas (selections), Gredos (Madrid), 1956.

Nuevo retablo de don Cristobita: Invenciones, figuraciones y alucinaciones (stories; contains *Esas nubes que pasan, El bonito crimen del carabinero,* and part of *Baraja de invenciones*), Destino, 1957, reprinted, 1980.

Obra completa (title means "Complete Works"), fourteen volumes, Destino, 1962-83.

Las compañías convenientes y otros figimientos y cegueras (stories; title means "Suitable Companions and Other Deceits and Obfuscations"), Destino, 1963, reprinted, 1981.

Café de artistas y otros cuentos, Salvat/Alianza, 1969.

Timoteo el incomprendido y otros papeles ibéricos, Magisterio Español, 1970.

Obras selectas (includes *La familia de Pascual Duarte, Viaje a la Alcarría, La colmena, Mrs. Caldwell habla con su hijo, Iazas, rabizas y colipoterras,* and *El carro de heno; o, El inventor de la guillotina*), Alfaguara, 1971.

Prosa, edited by Jacinto-Luis Guereña with notes and commentaries, Narcea (Madrid), 1974.

Café de artistas y otros papeles volanderos, Alce (Madrid), 1978.

Also author of *Antología,* 1968.

OTHER

Mesa revuelta (essays) Ediciones de los Estudiantes Españoles, 1945, new and expanded edition (includes text of *Ensueños y figuraciones*), Taurus (Madrid), 1957.

Pisando la dudosa luz del día: Poemas de una adolescencia cruel (poems; title means "Treading the Uncertain Light of Day"), Zodíaco (Barcelona), 1945, new corrected and expanded edition, Papales de Son Armadans, 1963.

(Under pseudonym Matilde Verdu) *San Juan de la Cruz,* [Madrid], 1948.

El gallego y su cuadrilla y otros apuntes carpetovetónicos (title means "The Galician and His Troupe and Other Carpeto-Vettonian Notes"), Ricardo Aguilera (Madrid), 1949, 3rd edition corrected and enlarged, Destino, 1967.

Ensueños y figuraciones, Ediciones G.P., 1954.

La rueda de los ocios (title means "The Wheel of Idle Moments"), Mateu (Barcelona), 1957, reprinted, Alfaguara, 1972.

La obra literaria del pintor Solana: Discurso leído ante la Real Academia Española el día 26 de mayo de 1957 en su recepción pública por el Excmo. Sr. D. Camilo José Cela y contestación del Excmo. Sr. D. Gregorio Marañón, Papeles de Son Armadans (Madrid), 1957, reprinted, 1972.

Cajón de sastre (articles) Cid (Madrid), 1957, reprinted, Alfaguara, 1970.

Recuerdo de don Pío Baroja (title means "Remembrance of Pío Baroja"), illustrations by Eduardo Vicente, De Andrea (Mexico City), 1958.

La cucaña: Memorias (memoirs) Destino, 1959, portion printed as *La rosa,* Destino, 1979.

(Editor) *Homenaje y recuerdo a Gregorio Marañón (1887-1960),* Papeles de Son Armadans, 1961.

Cuatro figuras del 98: Unamuno, Valle Inclán, Baroja, Azorín, y otros retratos ensayos españoles, Aedos (Barcelona), 1961.

El solitario: Los sueños de Quesada (title means "The Solitary One"), illustrations by Rafael Zabaleta, Papeles de Son Armadans, 1963.

Garito de hospicianos; o, Guirigay de imposturas y bambollas (articles; title means "Poorhouse Inmates; or, Jargon Frauds and Sham"), Noguer, 1963, reprinted, Plaza & Janés, 1986.

(Author of prologue) Tono y Rafael Florez, *Memorias de mi: Novela,* Biblioteca ca Nueva, 1966.

(With Cesáreo Rodríguez Aguilera) *Xam* (illustrated art commentary), Daedalus (Palma de Mallorca), 1966.

Diccionario secreto (title means "Secret Dictionary"), Alfaguara, Volume 1, 1968, Volume 2, 1972.

María Sabina (dramatic poem; also see below), Papeles de Son Armadans, 1967, 2nd edition bound with *El carro de heno; o, El inventor de la guillotina* (play; also see below), Alfaguara, 1970.

Poesía y cancioneros, [Madrid], 1968.

Homenaje al Bosco, I: El carro de heno; o, El inventor de la guillotina, Papeles de Son Armadans, 1969.

Al servicio de algo, Alfaguara, 1969.

La bola del mundo: Escenas cotidianas, Organización Sala (Madrid), 1972.

A vueltas con España, Seminarios y Ediciones (Madrid), 1973.

Cristina Mallo (monograph), Theo (Madrid), 1973.

Diccionari manual castellá-catalá, catalá-castellá, Bibliograf (Barcelona), 1974.

Enciclopedia de eroticismo (title means "Encyclopedia of Eroticism"), D. L. Sedmay (Madrid), 1977.

(Adaptor) Fernando de Rojas, *La Celestina puesta respetuosamente en castellano moderno por Camilo José Cela quien añadió muy poco y quitó aún menos* (title means "La Celestina Put Respectfully into Modern Castilian by Camilo Jose Cela Who Added a Little and Took Out Even Less"), Destino, 1979.

Los sueños vanos, los ángeles curiosos, Argos Vergara (Barcelona), 1979.

Los vasos comunicantes, Bruguera (Barcelona), 1981.

Las compañías convenientes y otros figimientos y cegueras, Destino, 1981.

Vuelta de hoja, Destino, 1981.

Album de taller (art commentary), Ambit (Barcelona), 1981.

(Editor and author of prologue) Miguel de Cervantes Saavedra, *El Quijote,* Ediciones Rembrandt (Alicante, Spain), 1981.

El juego de los tres madroños, Destino, 1983.

El asno de Buridán (articles), El País (Madrid), 1986.

Also author of *San Camilo,* 1936, reprinted, 1969, *La bandada de palmoas,* 1969, and, with Alfonso Canales, *Crónica del cipote de Archidona* (first published as *La insólita y gloriosa hazaña del cipote de Archidona*), 1977. Author of poems "Himno a la muerte" (title means "Hymn to Death"), 1938, and *Dos romances de ciego,* 1966.

SIDELIGHTS: While not widely known in the United States, 1989 Nobel laureate Camilo José Cela has played a pivotal role in twentieth-century Spanish literature. Upon awarding the prize to Cela, the Swedish Academy praised the author "for a rich and intensive prose, which with restrained compassion forms a challenging vision of man's vulnerability," relates Sheila Rule for the *New York Times.* In the same article, Rule reports Julio Ortego's statement that "Cela represents the searching for a better literature from the Franco years, through the democratic experiments and into European Spain. At the same time, he remained very Spanish, keeping the cultural traditions of Spanish art and literature in his writing. He didn't follow a European literature, but developed his own style, and so, in his way, symbolized Spain's going through a long period of adjustment." Throughout the Franco regime, Cela suffered from heavy governmental censorship. Many of his books were banned outright or later removed from the shelves: the second edition of *Pascual Duarte* was seized; the censor found it "nauseating," and *The Hive* was initially published in South America. D. W. McPheeters maintains in *Camilo José Cela* that, in spite of such opposition, Cela "has always had the courage to express himself frankly, even forthrightly, . . . which has led to problems with an overly squeamish censorship."

Cela's stylistic development has moved from the more traditional *Pascual Duarte* to the innovative fiction of his later novels. McPheeters sees Cela as "dedicated to a constant trying of various forms . . . of fiction in a search for the one that best suits him and . . . what he has to say concerning the human situation. He [is] an outspoken critic of traditional forms of the novel and the restrictions which [some] would impose upon the creative artist." Cela's first novel, *The Family of Pascual Duarte,* has been called the most widely read Spanish novel since *Don Quixote.* It was published in the early 1940s, a time when "the Spanish novel . . . had virtually ceased to exist as a worthy genre," attests McPheeters. "Almost single-handedly, Cela [gave the genre] new life and international significance." Many critics have noted that Cela's national prominence and international fame is a result of the popularity of *The Family of Pascual Duarte* and a later novel, *The Hive.* McPheeters agrees, stating that while *Pascual Duarte,* Cela's first novel, "secured a wide foreign acceptance," *The Hive* "assured his place as one of Europe's outstanding novelists."

Pascual Duarte relates the life of a convicted murderer awaiting execution. It is introduced as a prison letter to an old family friend, but the reader soon becomes immersed in a first-person narrative. Pascual responds to a life of poverty and frustration through killing: his dog, his horse, his wife's lover, and finally, his mother, fall victim to his rage. "A deceptive objectivity masks the presentation of cruel and monstrous scenes, including murder and matricide," *Michigan Quarterly Review* contributor Francis Donahue describes. "In a taut style, with emotion carefully reined, Cela evokes an atmosphere of extreme brutality, one which a nation suffering from the after-effects of a brutal civil war could readily understand and believe." But some reviewers find such intense scenes hinder any identification with the main character. "Pascual Duarte speaks of suffering and ferocity so appalling as to be almost beyond the reach of our sympathy. They stun even more than they horrify," resolves *Saturday Review* contributor Emile Capouya. However, Pierre Courtines in *America* insists that the book is worth the reader's effort: "The dialogues between Cela's leading characters are rapid and dramatic, and his language is rich in imagery that reveals many popular traditions. Cela has combined realism with poetry, and his novel expresses the 'tragic sense of life,' so much a part of the Spanish character."

Some critics, as I. S. Bernstein states in his introduction to *Mrs. Caldwell Speaks to Her Son,* credit Cela with the invention of "tremendismo," a type of fiction which dwells on the darker side of life—the distasteful, the grotesque and the vulgar. Although in his prologue to the Spanish version of *Mrs. Caldwell Speaks to Her Son,* Cela denies this paternity, tremendista elements are abundant in *Pascual Duarte.* As an example of tremendismo, McPheeters translates a portion of the struggle in which Pascual kills his mother: "I was able to bury the blade in her throat. . . . Blood squirted out in a torrent and struck me in the face. It was warm like a belly and tasted the same as the blood of a lamb." Other gruesome incidents fill the pages of the novel; in one scene Pascual's retarded brother's ears are eaten off by a pig. This type of detail—meant to shock the placid reader—is present in a lesser degree or non-existent in some of Cela's novels, but even so, a *Times Literary Supplement* critic calls Cela's works "perversely restricted to a pathology of human decay and loneliness." His *Mazurca para dos muertos,* for example, concludes with a six-page postmortem examination of a cadaver. Even Cela's nonfiction works such as *Enciclopedia de eroticismo* (the title means "Encyclopedia of Eroticism") and *Diccionario secreto,* which contains definitions of vulgar words, are written in defiance of Spain's traditionalist moral code.

The Hive led critics to compare Cela with John Dos Passos, particularly to Dos Passos's novel *Manhattan Transfer,* which characterizes frenetic Manhattan life. Comparisons between the two novels are based on the large number of characters introduced in both works and by the novelists' similarly cinematographic styles. In both novels, the shifting time sequence is similar to the filmmaker's flashback. But while David W. Foster concedes in *Forms in the Work of Camilo José Cela* that an analogy can be made between the two techniques, he notes: "Cela's perspective goes much beyond that of the camera in what it is able to record. It is, in effect, all inclusive, omniscient, and omnipresent."

The Hive is frequently seen as Cela's greatest work. In *Books Abroad,* Jacob Ornstein and James Y. Causey note that "Spanish criticism has been almost unanimous in acclaiming this novel as Cela's masterpiece, both for its vigorous simplicity and for the author's artistry in evoking the atmosphere of Madrid during the final days of World War II and the years immediately following." *The Hive*'s publication was typical of Cela's struggle with the censors, as it was banned in Spain and printed in Buenos Aires in 1952; William D. Montalbano reports in the *Los Angeles Times* that Cela autographed copies "a bitter chronicle of a bitter time." *Nation* contributor Maxwell Geismar finds *The Hive* "suffused with anger and bitterness at society in Madrid." The novel portrays the lives of 346 characters during three days in Madrid in the winter of 1943, when the city was facing intense hardship. Although only forty-eight of *The Hive*'s characters play a significant role in the plot, their appearances and disappearances are more important than the story itself. As Foster notes, "[*The Hive*] is one continuous interplay of people. Although chronology is fragmented, the novel is able to develop a world based upon the activities of individuals." And a *Times Literary Supplement* contributor finds that "in spite of the author's literary theories which confuse the reader with an enormous gallery of characters presented in very short passages, *The Hive* is a work of art of great power."

While *The Hive,* as Foster remarks, "has stood as a sort of beacon for Cela's fiction, the one novel to which most critics turn with . . . admiration," Cela has continued producing innovative and award-winning novels. The author "has chosen," Foster points out, "to make his career one of a complete reexamination and reconsideration of the novel as an art form." Foster classifies

most of Cela's novels since *Mrs. Caldwell Speaks to Her Son* as experimental. Among the characteristics most prominent in Cela's later work are the decreasing emphasis plot—the sequence of cause and effect is discarded—and an increasing emphasis on artificial patternings of events. Some of his more original novels besides *Mrs. Caldwell* include *Tobogán de hambrientos, Vísperas, festividad y octava de San Camilo del año 1936 en Madrid* (usually referred to as *San Camilo, 1936*), and *Oficio de tinieblas 5.* However, McPheeters believes that these later works may be less accessible to the general reader. He mentions that *Pascual Duarte* and *The Hive* "continue to influence contemporary Spanish writers, but certain innovations in his other works may not gain rapid acceptance."

Mrs. Caldwell contains excerpts from the letters of a mentally disturbed woman to her dead son. McPheeters finds that *Mrs. Caldwell* "is about as much an antinovel as has yet been conceived in Spain." The theme is incest, one ideally suited to Cela's fiction because of its shock value. The form is equally unexpected: although only slightly longer than two hundred pages, it contains two hundred and twelve chapters. There is no connection between the chapters (except for chapters fourteen and sixty) and no reason for ending the novel other than the illegibility of the last of the "Letters from the Royal Hospital for the Insane."

The form and content of *Tobogán de hambrientos, San Camilo, 1936,* and *Oficio de tinieblas 5* are also out of the ordinary. *Oficio de tinieblas,* for example, has no capital letters, while *San Camilo, 1936* has no paragraphs. *Tobogán de hambrientos,* Foster notes, "employs many of the devices of the new novel, especially in its use of pattern and in the rejection of chronology, definable plot, and unified points of view." The book is divided into two hundred units. These two hundred are in turn divided in half and labeled in ascending, then, at the half-way point, in descending numerical order. Each narrative unit presents a new individual or group of individuals and the characters from the first half of the book reappear in the corresponding chapters of the second half.

Except for the epilogue, *San Camilo, 1936* is a young student's continuous stream of consciousness. Again, in content and form the book is far removed from the traditional novel. The book's opening chapter, for instance, includes a list of Madrid's brothels, complete with addresses and names of proprietresses. A *Times Literary Supplement* reviewer remarks on the novel's unusual style: "[Cela] reinforces his . . . contempt for petit-bourgeois credulity by quoting an enormous variety of patent medicine advertisements, [and] making astonishingly free with his sexual and other carnal references, indeed, the language of [the book] is scabrous." While noting Cela's emphasis on "the erotic, obscene and scatological" in *San Camilo, 1936, Hispania* contributor Robert Louis Sheehan also observes the "stylistic innovations" present in the novel, including "the rhythmic reiteration of names, clauses, [and] phrases," the "use of one-paragraph chapters, run-on sentences, and frequent use of commas in place of periods."

Today the name of Camilo José Cela is associated with the rebirth of the Spanish novel, and with experimentation in its form and content. *Pascual Duarte* is credited with starting a new school of Spanish literature, while *The Hive* brought a new cinematographic technique to literature, which Margaret E. W. Jones in *The Contemporary Spanish Novel, 1939-1975* believes "suggested new possibilities in [the] elasticity of novelistic form." Jones also confirms the author's sense of exploration, and claims that "Cela has consistently been at the forefront of new movements in the contemporary novel since the 1940s." And Cela himself sums up his feelings on his favorite genre in the dedication to *Journey to the Alcarría*—which Jones quotes—"Anything goes in the novel, as long as it's told with common sense."

MEDIA ADAPTATIONS: The Hive was filmed by director Mario Camus; *The Family of Pascual Duarte* was filmed by director Ricardo Franco.

AVOCATIONAL INTERESTS: Collecting wine bottles, stamps, and literary myths.

BIOGRAPHICAL/CRITICAL SOURCES:

BOOKS

Cela, Camilo José, *Caminos inciertos: La colmena,* Noguer, 1955.
Cela, Camilo José, *Mrs. Caldwell Speaks to Her Son,* translated and with introduction by J. S. Bernstein, Cornell University Press, 1968.
Chandler, Richard E. and Kessel Schwartz, *A New History of Spanish Literature,* Louisiana State University Press, 1961.
Contemporary Authors Autobiography Series, Volume 10, Gale, 1989.
Contemporary Literary Criticism, Gale, Volume 4, 1975, Volume 13, 1980.
Foster, David W., *Forms in the Work of Camilo José Cela,* University of Missouri Press, 1967.
Ilie, Paul, *La novelística de Camilo José Cela,* Gredos, 1963.
Jones, Margaret E. W., *The Contemporary Spanish Novel, 1939-1975,* Twayne, 1985.
Kirsner, Robert, *The Novels and Travels of Camilo José Cela,* University of North Carolina Press, 1964.
McPheeters, D. W., *Camilo José Cela,* Twayne, 1969.

PERIODICALS

America, November 7, 1964.
Books Abroad, spring, 1953, winter, 1971.
Christian Science Monitor, January 14, 1965.
Hispania, March, 1965, March, 1966, September, 1966, September, 1967, May, 1972.
Los Angeles Times, November 2, 1989.
Michigan Quarterly Review, summer, 1969.
Nation, November 14, 1953.
New Statesman, February 19, 1965.
New Yorker, January 30, 1965.
New York Times, October 20, 1989.
New York Times Book Review, May 26, 1968.
Observer, February 14, 1965.
Saturday Review, November 23, 1964.
Spectator, February 19, 1965.
Times Literary Supplement, February 2, 1965, February 25, 1965, May 27, 1965, November 11, 1965, February 12, 1970, April 2, 1970, November 5, 1971, February 11, 1972.
Washington Post, October 20, 1989.
World Literature Today, autumn, 1977, summer, 1982, autumn, 1984.

* * *

CERNUDA (y BIDON), Luis 1902-1963

PERSONAL: Born September 21, 1902, in Seville, Spain; immigrated to United States, 1947; immigrated to Mexico, 1952; died of a heart attack, November 6, 1963, in Mexico City, Mexico; son of a military engineer. *Education:* Attended University of Se-

ville, 1919-25; received doctorate in law from University of Madrid; graduate study at the Center for Historical Studies at University of Madrid.

CAREER: Poet and literary critic. University of Toulouse, Toulouse, France, lecturer in Spanish language and literature, 1929-30; worked in a Madrid bookstore; served in diplomatic and other posts for the Spanish Republican government in Madrid, Valencia, Paris, and London, c. 1936-38; took political exile in Great Britain, 1938, and taught Spanish language and literature at Glasgow University, Cambridge University, and the Instituto Español (London); professor of Spanish at Mount Holyoke College, South Hadley, Mass., 1947-52.

WRITINGS:

POETRY

Perfil del aire (title means "Profile of the Air"), originally published, 1927, expanded edition published as *Perfil del aire, con otras obras olvidadas e inéditas documentos y epistolario,* Tamesis (London), 1971.
Egloga, elegía, oda (title means "Eclogue, Elegy, Ode"), originally published, 1928, limited edition with color lithographs by Gregorio Prieto, Ediciones de Arte y Bibliofilia (Madrid), 1970.
La invitación a la poesía (title means "An Invitation to Poetry"), M. Altolaguirre, 1933, reprinted, Barral (Barcelona), 1975.
La realidad y el deseo (title means "Reality and Desire"), Ediciones del Arbol (Madrid), 1936, augmented editions published by Editorial Séneca (Mexico City), 1940, and Tezontle Editores (Mexico City), 1958, 4th edition published as *La realidad y el deseo (1924-1962),* Fondo de Cultura Económica (Mexico City), 1965 (also see below).
Ocnos, originally published, 1942, revised edition, Insula (Madrid), 1949, reprinted, Taurus (Madrid), 1979.
Como quien espera el alba [and] *La realidad y el deseo* (title of former means "As One Awaiting Dawn"), Losada (Buenos Aires), 1947.
Variaciones sobre tema mexicano (title means "Variations on a Mexican Theme"), Porrúa y Obregón (Mexico City), 1952.
Desolación de la quimera (title means "The Desolation of the Chimera"), J. Mortiz (Mexico City), 1962.
Antología poética, selected by Rafael Santos Torroella, Plaza & Janés (Barcelona), 1970.
The Poetry of Luis Cernuda, bilingual English/Spanish text edited by Anthony Edkins and Derek Harris, New York University Press, 1971.
Poesía completa, Barral, 1974.
Antología poética, selected by Philip Silver, Alianza (Madrid), 1975. *Selected Poems of Luis Cernuda,* bilingual English/ Spanish text edited and translated by Reginald Gibbons, University of California Press, 1977.
Sonetos clásicos sevillanos (title means "Classic Sonnets of Seville"), El Observatorio (Madrid), 1986.

Also author of poetry volumes *Un río, un amor* (title means "A River, a Love"), 1929, *Los placeres prohibidos* (title means "The Forbidden Pleasures"), 1931, *Donde habite el olvido* (title means "Where Forgetfulness Dwells"), 1934, *Invocaciones* (title means "Invocations"), 1934-35, *Las nubes* (title means "The Clouds"), 1940, *Vivir sin estar viviendo* (title means "To Live Without Living"), 1949, and *Con las horas contadas* (title means "Your Hours Are Numbered"), 1956. Poems also published together in other collections.

OTHER

Trés narraciones (short stories), Ediciones Imán (Buenos Aires), 1948.

Estudios sobre poesía española contemporánea (criticism; title means "Studies in Contemporary Spanish Poetry"), Guadarrama (Madrid), 1957.

Pensamiento poético en la lírica inglesa: Siglo XIX (criticism; title means "Poetic Thought in the English Lyrical Tradition of the Nineteenth Century"), Imprenta Universitaria (Mexico City), 1958.

Poesía y literatura (criticism; title means "Poetry and Literature"), Barral, 1960.

Poesía y literatura II (criticism), Barral, 1964.

Crítica, ensayos y evocaciones (criticism; title means "Criticism, Essays, and Evocations"), edited by Luis Maristany, Barral, 1970.

(Translator) *Poemas de Friedrich Hoelderlin* (title means "The Poems of Friedrich Hoelderlin"), Visor (Madrid), 1974.

Prosa completa (title means "Complete Prose Works"), edited by Harris and Maristany, Barral, 1975.

Epistolario inédito (title means "Unpublished Letters"), Servicio de Publicaciones del Ayuntamiento (Seville), 1981.

Translator of Shakespeare's play *Troilus and Cressida*. Contributor to literary journals, including *Revista de Occidente, Octubre, Ahora,* and *El Lochador*. Works represented in anthologies.

SIDELIGHTS: A member of the so-called "Generation of 1927" of Spanish modernist poets, Luis Cernuda wrote frank verses of homosexual love and metaphysical pessimism. His poetry is distinguished by its starkly solitary and individualistic spirit, its sharp social criticism, and its unrelenting self-examination in spare and colloquial language. Cernuda's work, the Mexican poet Octavio Paz observed in a critical essay in *On Poets and Others,* "is one of the most impressive personal testimonies to this truly unique situation of modern man: we are condemned to a promiscuous solitude and our prison is as large as the planet itself."

While Cernuda's pessimistic world-view has often been attributed to an introverted and sensitive character, critics also speculate that his melancholic, defiant poetic voice resulted from a painful sense of isolation brought about by his open homosexuality and years spent in exile abroad. Cernuda began writing poetry while still a law student at the University of Madrid. He became a protege of the poet Pedro Salinas, who helped him publish his first verse collection, *Perfil del aire* ("Profile of the Air") in 1927. The poet's highly refined lyric verses showed the influence of Salinas and his contemporary Jorge Guillén, among others, and received only a lukewarm reception. Cernuda began finding his distinctive voice in two collections of surrealist-influenced poetry, *Un río, un amor* ("A River, a Love," 1929) and *Los placeres prohibidos* ("The Forbidden Pleasures," 1931). In these books, the poet experimented with incongruous word juxtapositions and spontaneous derivations from chance stimuli to express his sexual and metaphysical turmoil.

These verses also introduce a number of recurrent themes in Cernuda's work: desire and its relationship to love and reality; the hopeless search for wholeness and a yearning for oblivion; a deep hostility to the city and its imprisoning social conformity; and a keen appreciation of the transcendent mystery of nature. Also present in the poetry are themes of the poet's homoeroticism, in defiance of his time and culture. "For Cernuda, love is a break with the social order and a joining with the natural world," wrote Octavio Paz. "He exalted as man's supreme experience the experience of love."

Cernuda published two additional important, surrealist-influenced collections in the mid-1930s, *Donde habite el olvido* ("Where Forgetfulness Dwells") and *Invocaciones* ("Invocations"), before issuing the first edition of his definitive work, *La realidad y el deseo* ("Reality and Desire"), in 1936. A collection of new and previously published verse, this book was revised and expanded in subsequent editions to include most of Cernuda's poetry. Critics have pointed out that *La realidad y el deseo* can be read as the poet's emotional and spiritual autobiography. The book also illuminates Cernuda's stylistic development over the years.

A predominant theme in *La realidad y el deseo* is exile—both the spiritual exile Cernuda always felt in Spanish society and the physical exile he experienced after the Spanish Civil War. "Spain as a problem pervades *La realidad y el deseo* from beginning to end," Michael Ugarte observed in *Modern Language Notes.* The poet excoriates such hallowed Spanish institutions as the patriarchal family and the Catholic Church and decries the backwardness, intolerance, and violence he finds in his homeland. Yet in many poems from the collections *Las nubes* ("The Clouds") and *Como quien espera el alba* ("As One Awaiting Dawn"), Cernuda also reveals a deep, nostalgic longing for the Andalusian gardens and sea of his childhood. Along with many of his contemporaries in literature and the arts, Cernuda left Spain shortly before the Republican defeat in 1939 and spent the remainder of his life in exile in Europe, the United States, and Mexico.

Some critics suggest that a deep sense of metaphysical exile underlies Cernuda's moral, sexual, and political estrangement. The poet's understanding of human existence as essentially exile is reflected in his large canon of verse. Cernuda directs his gaze inwardly, to the raw truth of his longings and desires, and he arrests time by capturing the ephemeral but eternal instants when desire and the world are one. Cernuda found some of these moments in sexual love, contemplating the ceaseless cycle of nature and engaging in the creative process. Such pursuits are the subject of many of his poems.

Stylistically, Cernuda emancipated himself from the French literary influences that dominated his major contemporaries and sought inspiration from English and German romanticism, particularly William Wordsworth, Samuel Taylor Coleridge, John Keats, and Friedrich Hoelderlin. T. S. Eliot was a strong influence on his later work. Despite his bleak themes and restrained, understated imagery, Cernuda remained essentially a lyric and romantic poet. His verses often take the form of a monologue/dialogue with himself, and he uses a range of mythical, historical, and imaginative personae to sound his constant themes.

In addition to his poetic work, Cernuda wrote several volumes of critical essays on poetry and literature, including *Estudios sobre poesía española contemporánea* ("Studies in Contemporary Spanish Poetry") and *Poesía y literatura* ("Poetry and Literature"). The Spanish poet, who died in 1963, also translated a selection of poems by Hoelderlin and Shakespeare's play *Troilus and Cressida,* among other works.

BIOGRAPHICAL/CRITICAL SOURCES:

BOOKS

Barnette, Douglas, *El exilio en la poesía de Luis Cernuda,* Sociedad de Cultura Valle-Inclán, 1984.

Coleman, Alexander, *Other Voices: A Study of the Late Poetry of Luis Cernuda,* University of North Carolina Press, 1969.

Contemporary Literary Criticism, Volume 54, Gale, 1989.

Harris, Derek, *Luis Cernuda: A Study of the Poetry,* Tamesis, 1973.

Paz, Octavio, *On Poets and Others,* translated by Michael Schmidt, Seaver Books, 1986.

Quirarte, Vicente, *La poética del hombre dividido en la obra de Luis Cernuda,* Universidad Nacional Autónoma de México (Mexico City), 1985.

Silver, Philip, *"Et in Arcadia Ego": A Study of the Poetry of Luis Cernuda,* Tamesis, 1965.

PERIODICALS

Journal of Spanish Studies: Twentieth Century, Volume 6, number 2, 1978. *Modern Language Notes,* Volume 101, number 2, 1986.

Parnassos: Poetry in Review, Volume 9, number 1, 1981.

Romance Notes, Volume 19, number 2, 1978.

Times Literary Supplement, July 8, 1965, July 7, 1972.

—*Sketch by Curtis Skinner*

* * *

CERVANTES, Lorna Dee 1954-

PERSONAL: Born August 6, 1954, in San Francisco, Calif. *Education:* Received B.A. from San Jose State University; graduate study at University of California, Santa Cruz.

ADDRESSES: Home—10410 Doris Ave., San Jose, Calif. 95127. *Office*—Mango Publications, 329 South Willard, San Jose, Calif. 95126.

CAREER: Founder and editor in chief of Mango Publications, San Jose, Calif.; writer.

AWARDS, HONORS: Grant from the National Endowment for the Arts, 1979.

WRITINGS:

Emplumada (poems), University of Pittsburgh Press, 1981.

Also author of unpublished poetry collection "Bird Ave." Contributor of poems to magazines, including *Samisdat, ¿Qué tal?, London Meadow Quarterly,* and *Revista Chicano-Riqueña.*

SIDELIGHTS: Through her writings, Chicana poet Lorna Dee Cervantes evokes the cultural clash that Americans of Mexican descent frequently face. Her first published poetry collection, *Emplumada,* includes verses of mourning, acceptance, and renewal and offers poignant commentary on the static roles of class and sex, especially among Hispanics. Characterized by simplicity of language and boldness of imagery, the work has earned considerable critical acclaim.

BIOGRAPHICAL/CRITICAL SOURCES:

BOOKS

Dictionary of Literary Biography, Volume 82: *Chicano Writers, First Series,* Gale, 1989.

Lomelí, Francisco A. and Donaldo W. Urioste, *Chicano Perspectives in Literature: A Critical and Annotated Bibliography,* Pajarito Publications, 1976.

Sánchez, Marta Ester, *Contemporary Chicana Poetry: A Critical Approach to an Emerging Literature,* University of California Press, 1985.

* * *

CHACON, Eusebio 1869-1948

PERSONAL: Born September 16, 1869, in Peñasco, New Mexico; died 1948; married, 1891; wife's maiden name: Barela. *Education:* University of Notre Dame, LL.B., 1889.

ADDRESSES: Home and office—Trinidad, Colo.

CAREER: Lawyer and translator-interpreter for U.S. courts in Colorado, beginning 1891. English teacher at Colegio Guadalupano in Durango, Mexico.

WRITINGS:

El hijo de la tempestad; Tras la tormenta la calma: Dos novelitas originales (title means "The Son of the Storm; The Calm After the Storm: Two Original Short Novels"), Tipografía de *El Boletín Popular* (Santa Fe, N.M.), 1892.

Also author of essays, editorials, and poetry. Contributor to series, "Las Dos Repúblicas de Denver."

SIDELIGHTS: Although Eusebio Chacón was for years ignored by critics, a revived interest in Chicano studies in the 1970s led to a rediscovery of his work nearly three decades after his death. His two novels—believed to be the first written in Spanish in the New Mexico-Colorado region—show Chacón's attempt to take traditional Spanish literary models, including the stories of Don Quixote and Don Juan, and place them in a Southwestern milieu.

* * *

CHAVEZ, Angélico
See CHAVEZ, Manuel

* * *

CHAVEZ, Denise (Elia) 1948-

PERSONAL: Born August 15, 1948, in Las Cruces, N.M.; daughter of E. E. (an attorney) and Delfina (a teacher; maiden name, Rede) Chávez; married Daniel Zolinsky (a photographer and sculptor), December 29, 1984. *Education:* New Mexico State University, B.A., 1971; Trinity University, San Antonio, Tex., M.F.A., 1974; University of New Mexico, M.A., 1984. *Politics:* Democrat. *Religion:* Roman Catholic.

ADDRESSES: Home and office—1524 Sul Ross, Houston, Tex. 77006.

CAREER: Northern New Mexico Community College, Espanola, instructor in English, 1975-77; playwright, 1977—; University of Houston, Houston, Tex., assistant professor of drama, 1988—. Instructor at American School of Paris, 1975-77; past member of faculty at College of Santa Fe; teacher at Radium Springs Center for Women, a medium security prison; gives readings and workshops. Writer in residence at La Compañia de Teatro, Albuquerque, N.M., and Theatre-in-the-Red, Santa Fe, N.M.; artist in residence at Arts With Elders Program, Santa Fe and Las Cruces; co-director of senior citizen workshop in creative writing and puppetry at Community Action Agency, Las Cruces, 1986-89.

MEMBER: National Institute of Chicana Writers (founding member), Santa Fe Writers Cooperative.

AWARDS, HONORS: New Mexico State University, Best Play Award, 1970, for "The Wait"; Steele Jones Fiction Award, 1986, for short story "The Last of the Menu Girls"; grants from New Mexico Arts Division, 1979-80, 1981, and 1988; award from Doña Ana Human Services Consortium, 1981; grants from National Endowment for the Arts, 1981 and 1982, and Rockefeller Foundation, 1984; creative writing fellowship from University of New Mexico, 1982; creative artist fellowship from the Cultural Arts Council of Houston, 1990.

WRITINGS:

Life Is a Two-Way Street (poetry anthology), Rosetta Press, 1980.
The Last of the Menu Girls (stories), Arte Público, 1986.
Face of an Angel, Arte Público, 1990.
(With Georgia McInnis) *The Red Dress* (photographic essay with text), Arte Público, 1990.
Dear Juanita (creative writing handbook for young people), Arte Público, in press.
Descansos: An Interrupted Journey (photographic essay with text), Arte Público, in press.
Río Grande Family (history), Arte Público, in press.

Work represented in anthologies, including *An Anthology of Southwestern Literature,* University of New Mexico Press, 1977; *An Anthology: The Indian Río Grande,* San Marcos Press, 1977; *Voces: An Anthology of Nuevo Mexicano Writers,* El Norte Publications, 1987. Contributor to periodicals, including *Americas Review, New Mexico, Journal of Ethnic Studies,* and *Revista Chicano-Riqueña.*

PLAYS

"Novitiates" (one-act), first produced in Dallas, Tex., at Dallas Theater Center, spring, 1971.
"Elevators" (one-act), first produced in Santa Fe, N.M., at Munn Theater, spring, 1972.
"The Flying Tortilla Man" (one-act), first produced in Espanola, N.M., at Northern New Mexico Community College, spring, 1975.
"The Mask of November" (one-act), first produced in Espanola at Northern New Mexico Community College, November, 1977.
"Nacimiento" (one-act; title means "Birth"), first produced in Albuquerque, N.M., at Kimo Theater, December, 1979.
"The Adobe Rabbit" (one-act), first produced in Taos, N.M., at Taos Community Auditorium, summer, 1979.
"Santa Fe Charm" (one-act), first produced in Santa Fe at Armory for the Arts, February, 1980.
"Sí, hay posada" (one-act; title means "Yes, There Is Shelter"), first produced in Albuquerque at Kimo Theater, December, 1980.
"El santero de Córdova" (one-act; title means "The Woodcarver of Córdova"), first produced in Albuquerque at Fiesta Artesana, August, 1981.
(With Nita Luna) "Hecho en México" (one-act; title means "Made in Mexico"), first produced in Santa Fe at El Sanctuario de Guadalupe, 1982.
"The Green Madonna" (one-act), first produced in Santa Fe at Armory for the Arts, December, 1982.
"La morenita" (one-act; title means "The Dark Virgin"), first produced in Las Cruces, N.M., at Immaculate Heart of Mary Cathedral, June, 1983.
"¡Francis!" (one-act), first produced in Las Cruces at Immaculate Heart of Mary, 1983.
"How Junior Got Throwed in the Joint" (one-act), first produced in Santa Fe at Penitentiary of New Mexico, 1981.
"El más pequeño de mis hijos" (one-act; title means "The Smallest of My Children"), first produced in Albuquerque at Kimo Theater, December, 1983.
"Plaza" (one-act), first produced in Albuquerque at Kimo Theater, summer, 1984.
"Novena narrativas" (one-woman show; title means "The Novena Narratives"), first produced in Taos at Our Lady of Guadalupe Church, 1986.

"The Step" (one-act), first produced in Houston, Tex., at Museum of Fine Arts, May, 1987.
"Language of Vision" (one-act), first produced in Albuquerque at Albuquerque Convention Center, August, 1987.
"The Last of the Menu Girls" (one-act; adapted from Chávez's short story of the same title), first produced in Houston at Ripley House, March, 1990.

Also author of the produced play "The Wait," c. 1970, and of unproduced plays "Mario and the Room María," 1974, "Rainy Day Waterloo," 1976, "The Third Door" (trilogy), 1979, "Cruz Blanca, the Story of a Town," 1981, "Plague-Time," 1984, and "The Mask of November," 1976.

SIDELIGHTS: Denise Chávez told *HW:* "I consider myself a performance writer. My training in theater has helped me to write roles that I myself would enjoy acting. My characters are survivors, and many of them are women. I feel, as a Chicana writer, that I am capturing the voice of so many who have been voiceless for years. I write about the neighborhood handymen, the waitresses, the bag ladies, the elevator operators. They all have something in common: they know what it is to love and to be merciful. My work as a playwright is to capture as best as I can the small gestures of the forgotten people, the old men sitting on park benches, the lonely spinsters inside their corner store. My work is rooted in the Southwest, in heat and dust, and reflects a world where love is as real as the land. In this dry and seemingly harsh and empty world there is much beauty to be found. That hope of the heart is what feeds me, my characters."

*   *   *

CHAVEZ, Fray Angélico
See CHAVEZ, Manuel

*   *   *

CHAVEZ, John R(ichard) 1949-

PERSONAL: Born January 12, 1949, in Pasadena, Calif.; son of Manuel (a laborer) and Andrea (a homemaker; maiden name, Quiroz) Chávez; married Lorena Poirier (a homemaker), August 11, 1984. *Education:* California State University, Los Angeles, B.A. (English), 1971, M.A. (English), 1972, B.A. (Spanish), 1975; University of Michigan, M.A. (American culture), 1978, Ph.D., 1980. *Politics:* Democrat. *Religion:* Roman Catholic.

ADDRESSES: Office—Department of History, Texas A & M University, College Station, Tex. 77843.

CAREER: California State University, Los Angeles, lecturer in Chicano studies, 1980-81; California State University, Long Beach, lecturer in Mexican-American studies, 1981-84; University of Michigan, Ann Arbor, visiting assistant professor of American culture and director of Latino studies program, beginning 1984; currently affiliated with Department of History, Texas A & M University, College Station.

AWARDS, HONORS: Pulitzer Prize nomination, 1984, for *The Lost Land: The Chicano Image of the Southwest.*

WRITINGS:

The Lost Land: The Chicano Image of the Southwest, University of New Mexico Press, 1984.
(Contributor) Julio A. Martínez and Francisco A. Lomelí, editors, *Chicano Literature: A Reference Guide,* Greenwood Press, 1985.

Contributor to *Magill's Literary Annual* and *Campo Libre.*

WORK IN PROGRESS: Research on the image of the Southwest in the Chicano novel.

SIDELIGHTS: John R. Chávez writes: "*The Lost Land* is a history of Mexican Americans that traces their image of the Southwest and themselves from earliest times to the present. My interests in Chicano history, literature, and language stem from my own ethnic background."

AVOCATIONAL INTERESTS: Travel (Mexico and Europe, especially Spain).

* * *

CHAVEZ, Manuel 1910-
(Angélico Chávez, Fray Angélico Chávez)

PERSONAL: Name in religion, Fray Angélico Chávez; born April 10, 1910, in Wagon Mound, N.M.; son of Fabián (a carpenter) and Nicolasa (a teacher; maiden name, Roybal) Chávez. *Education:* Attended Franciscan seminaries in Cincinnati, Ohio, and Detroit, Mich.

CAREER: Entered Franciscan religious order, 1929; ordained Roman Catholic priest, 1937; missionary among Pueblo Indians in New Mexico, 1937-72; laicized, 1972; writer, 1972—. Lecturer at University of Albuquerque, 1972-74. Member of board of regents of Museum of New Mexico, 1946-57. *Military service:* U.S. Army, Infantry, chaplain, 1943-46 and 1951-52; served in Pacific theater and Germany; became major.

AWARDS, HONORS: Catholic Poetry Award from Catholic Poetry Society of New York, 1948, for body of lyric poetry; award from National Council of Christians and Jews, 1963; literary award from governor of New Mexico, 1976, for body of literature. Honorary degrees from University of New Mexico, 1947 and 1974, University of Albuquerque, 1963, and Southern University of New Mexico, 1975.

WRITINGS:

UNDER NAME ANGELICO CHAVEZ, EXCEPT AS NOTED

(Under name Fray Angélico Chávez) *Clothed with the Sun* (poems), Rydal, 1939.
(Under name Fray Angélico Chávez; and illustrator) *New Mexico Triptych* (short stories), St. Anthony Guild Press, 1940, reprinted under name Angélico Chávez, Gannon, 1976.
Seraphic Days: Franciscan Thoughts and Affections on the Principal Feasts of Our Lord and Our Lady and All the Saints of the Three Orders of the Seraph of Assisi (meditations), edited by Sebastian Erbacher, Duns Scotus College, 1940.
Eleven Lady-Lyrics, and Other Poems, St. Anthony Guild Press, 1945.
The Single Rose (poems), Los Santos Bookshop, 1948.
Our Lady of the Conquest (nonfiction), Historical Society of New Mexico, 1948.
La Conquistadora: The Autobiography of an Ancient Statue (nonfiction), St. Anthony Guild Press, 1954, reprinted, Sunstone Press, 1983.
Origins of New Mexico Families in the Spanish Colonial Period (nonfiction), Historical Society of New Mexico, 1954, reprinted, Gannon, 1982.
(With E. B. Adams) *The Missions of New Mexico, 1776,* University of New Mexico Press, 1956.
Archives of the Archdiocese of Santa Fe, Academy of American Franciscan History, 1957.
From an Altar Screen; El retablo: Tales From New Mexico (short stories), Farrar, Straus, 1957, published as *When the Santos Talked: A Retable of New Mexico Tales,* Gannon, 1977.

The Virgin of Port Lligat (poems), Academy Library Guild, 1959.
(And illustrator) *The Lady from Toledo* (historical novel), Academy Guild Press, 1960.
Coronado's Friars: The Franciscans in the Coronado Expedition (nonfiction), Academy of American Franciscan History, 1968.
Selected Poems, with an Apologia, Press of the Territorian, 1969.
(Editor and translator) *The Oroz Codex; or, Relation of the Description of the Holy Gospel Province in New Spain, and the Lives of the Founders and Other Note-Worthy Men of Said Province Composed by Fray Pedro Oroz, 1584-1586,* Academy of American Franciscan History, 1972.
The Song of Francis, Northland Press, 1973 (published in England under name Fray Angélico Chávez as *The Song of St. Francis,* Sheldon Press, 1978).
My Penitente Land: Reflections on Spanish New Mexico, University of New Mexico Press, 1974, 2nd edition, Gannon, 1979.
The Lord and New Mexico, Archdiocese of Santa Fe, 1975.
(Translator) *The Domínguez-Escalante Expedition, 1776,* Brigham Young University Press, 1976.
But Time and Chance: The Story of Padre Martínez of Taos, 1793-1867 (nonfiction), Sunstone Press, 1981.
Tres Macho, He Said: Padre Gallegos, New Mexico's First Congressman, Gannon, 1985.
(Under name Fray Angélico Chávez) *The Short Stories of Fray Angélico Chávez,* University of New Mexico Press, 1987.

Work represented in *Best Poems,* J. Cape, 1938, 1940, and 1941. Contributor of articles, poems, and reviews to history and literary journals.

WORK IN PROGRESS: Books on southwestern history.

SIDELIGHTS: Manuel Chávez told *CA:* "I have loved English literature since childhood. I started publishing poetry and prose in my teens. I left the Franciscan order and active priesthood at age sixty-two, obviously not for wine, women, and song at that age, but because of having outgrown former ideals. I started a new life, as happy as the first, with no regrets for the past."

BIOGRAPHICAL/CRITICAL SOURCES:

BOOKS

Dictionary of Literary Biography, Volume 82: *Chicano Writers, First Series,* Gale, 1989.

* * *

CHEVREMONT, Evaristo Ribera
See RIBERA CHEVREMONT, Evaristo

* * *

CHOCANO, José Santos 1875-1934

PERSONAL: Born May 15, 1875, in Lima, Peru; killed December 13, 1934, in Santiago, Chile. *Education:* Studied briefly at University of San Marcos.

CAREER: Poet. Member of Peruvian diplomatic mission to Madrid, Spain, 1905-08.

AWARDS, HONORS: Publicly crowned National Poet of Peru, 1922.

WRITINGS:

Alma América: Poemas indo-españoles, V. Suárez (Madrid), 1906, reprinted, Editorial Nuevos Rumbos, 1958.

¡Fiat lux! Poemas varios, P. Ollendorff (Paris), 1908.

La selva virgen: Poemas y poesías, Garnier Hermanos (Paris), 1909.

Poesías completas: Iras santas, En la aldea, Azahares, Selva virgen, Poemas, 3rd edition, Maucci (Barcelona), 1910.

El conflicto personal de la revolución mexicana: Examen crítico de todo lo que ha dicho el ciudadano Carranza, [El Paso, Tex.], 1914.

Poesías: Alma América, Fiat lux, Oro de Indias, C. García (Montevideo), 1920.

Ayacucho y los Andes: Canto IV de "El hombre-sol," trazo de una epopeya panteísta, [Lima], 1924, reprinted, c. 1975.

El escándalo de Leticia ante las conferencias de Río de Janeiro (los engaños hechos al pueblo peruano por los explotadores de su patriotismo), Talleres Gráficos de "La Nación" (Santiago), 1933.

Primicias de "Oro de Indias": Poemas neo-mundiales; Tierras mágicas, Las mil y una noches de América, Alma de virrey, Corazón aventurero, Siglo XX (Santiago), 1934.

Spirit of the Andes, translated by Edna Worthley Underwood, Mosher Press, 1935, reprinted, Gordon Press, 1977.

Poemas del amor doliente, preface by Alfonso Navarro, Nascimento (Santiago), 1937.

Oro de Indias, four volumes, Volume I: *Pompas solares,* Volume II: *Fantasía errante,* Volume III: *Sangre incaíca: Estampas newyorkinas y madrileñas,* Volume IV: *Nocturnos intensos,* Nascimento, 1939-41.

Memorias: Las mil y una aventuras, Nascimento, 1940.

El alma de Voltaire y otras prosas, Nascimento, 1940.

Selección de poesías: Alma América, Fiat lux, Oro de Indias y otras poesías, two volumes, C. García & Sons (Montevideo), 1941.

Selecciones poéticas, Camacho Roldán and Sons (Bogota), 1941.

José Santos Chocano: Sus mejores versos, La Gran Colombia, 1944.

Páginas de oro de José Santos Chocano: Poesías inéditas escritas desde los doce años, publicadas en zincograbados con sus respectivas transcripciones, Empresa Editorial Rímac, 1944.

Obras completas, edited by Luis Alberto Sánchez, Aguilar, 1954.

Las mejores poesías de Chocano, edited by Francisco Bendezú, Patronato del Libro Peruano, 1956.

Los mejores versos de José Santos Chocano, Editorial Nuestra América (Buenos Aires), 1957.

Poesías, prologue by Luis Fabio Xammar, 3rd edition, W. M. Jackson (Buenos Aires), 1957.

Alma América: Poemas, edited by Francisco Bendezú, Editorial Nuevos Rumbos, 1958.

Las mejores poesías de Chocano: Poemas escogidos, with biography by J. Jiménez Borja, 2nd edition, Editora Latinoamericana (Lima), 1958.

Chocano: Poesía, edited by Luis Alberto Sánchez, Patronato del Libro Universitario, Universidad Nacional Mayor de San Marcos, 1959.

Antología poética, edited by Alfonso Escudero, 4th edition, Espasa-Calpe, 1962.

José Santos Chocano: Sus mejores poemas, Editora Paracas, 1962.

Chocano: Antología, edited by Julio Ortega, Editorial Universitaria (Lima), 1966.

Puerto Rico lírico, Cooperativa de Artes Gráficas Romualdo Real (San Juan), 1967.

Sus mejores poesías, edited by Francisco Bendezú, Editorial Bendezú, 1968.

Alma de América, edited by Alberto Tauro, Editorial Jurídica (Lima), c. 1969.

Poemas: Poesía de siempre, Horizonte, c. 1969.

Los cien mejores poemas de José Santos Chocano, edited by Antonio Castro Leal, Aguilar, 1971.

Antología poética, edited by Tomás G. Escajadillo, Editorial Universo (Lima), 1972, reprinted as *Antología poética: Edición-homenaje centenario, 1875-1975,* Librería Studium (Lima), 1975.

Antología: José Santos Chocano, edited by Carlos Germán Belli, Ediciones Peisa, 1974.

Muestrario lírico del Tomo II: Primicias de Oro de Indias, Siglo XX, c. 1978.

Also author of *En la aldea* (poems), 1895; *Iras santas* (poems), 1895; *La epopeya del Morro,* 1899; *El derrumbe,* 1899; *El canto del siglo,* 1901; *El fin de Satán y otros poemas* (title means "The End of Satan and Other Poems"), 1901; and *Cantos del Pacífico,* 1904. Author of dramatic pieces. Work represented in anthologies.

BIOGRAPHICAL/CRITICAL SOURCES:

BOOKS

Aguilar Machado, Margarita, *José Santos Chocano: Sus últimos años,* Aranciba Hermanos, 1964.

Chocano, José Santos, *Las mejores poesías de Chocano,* Editora Latinoamericana, 1958.

Chocano, José Santos, *Selección de poesías: Alma América, Fiat lux, Oro de Indias y otras poesías,* two volumes, C. García & Sons, 1941.

Sánchez, L. A., *Aladino o Vida y obra de José Santos Chocano,* 1960.

*   *   *

CHUMACERO, Alí 1918-

PERSONAL: Born in 1918 in Acaponeta, Nayarit, Mexico.

CAREER: Writer.

WRITINGS:

(Editor) *Poesía romántica,* Universidad Nacional Autónoma de México, 1941, reprinted, 1973.

Páramo de sueños, [Mexico], 1944 (also see below).

Imágenes desterradas, Stylo (Mexico), 1948 (also see below).

Palabras en reposo, Fondo de Cultura Económica (Mexico), 1956.

Páramo de sueños [followed by] *Imágenes desterradas,* Universidad Nacional Autónoma de México, 1960.

(Editor with Miguel Capistrán and Luis Mario Schneider, and author of prologue) Xavier Villarrutia, *Obras: Poesía, teatro, prosas varias, crítica,* Fondo de Cultura Económica, 1966.

Acerca del poeta y su mundo (lecture), Academia Mexicana, 1965.

(Author of introduction) Francisco Zuniga, *Zuniga,* Tudor, 1969.

Poesía completa, Premia (Mexico), 1981.

Los momentos críticos, Fondo de Cultura Económica, 1987.

Also author of *El viaje de la tribú.* Co-editor of *Poesía en movimiento: México, 1915-1966,* 4th edition, 1970. Member of editorial board of *Tierra Nueva,* 1940-42.

BIOGRAPHICAL/CRITICAL SOURCES:

BOOKS

Rodríguez Monegal, Emir, editor, *The Borzoi Anthology of Latin American Literature,* Volume 2: *The Twentieth Century—*

From Borges and Paz to Guimaraes Rosa and Donoso, Knopf, 1986.

PERIODICALS

World Literature Today, spring, 1988.

* * *

CISNEROS, Antonio 1942-

PERSONAL: Born December 27, 1942, in Lima, Peru. *Education:* Attended Catholic University, Lima; National University of San Marcos, Ph.D., 1974.

CAREER: Poet and essayist. Teacher of literature at University of Huamanga, Ayacucho, Peru, 1965, University of Southampton, Southampton, England, 1967-70, University of Nice, Nice, France, 1970-72, and University of San Marcos, Lima, Peru, beginning in 1972; University of Budapest, Budapest, Hungary, exchange professor, 1974-75.

AWARDS, HONORS: Peruvian National Poetry Prize, 1965, for *Comentarios reales;* Cuban Casa de las Américas prize, 1968, for *Canto ceremonial contra un oso hormiguero.*

WRITINGS:

POETRY

Destierro, [Lima, Peru], 1961.
David, El Timonel (Lima), 1962.
Comentarios reales (title means "Royal Commentaries"; also see below), Ediciones de la Rama Florida and Ediciones de la Biblioteca Universitaria, 1964.
Canto ceremonial contra un oso hormiguero (title means "Ceremonial Song Against the Anteater"; also see below), Casa de las Américas (Havana), 1968.
The Spider Hangs Too Far From the Ground (contains selections from *Comentarios reales* and *Canto ceremonial contra un oso hormiguero*), translated by Maureen Ahern, William Rowe, and David Tipton, Cape Goliard (London), 1970.
Agua que no has de beber (also see below), CMB Ediciones (Barcelona), 1971.
Como higuera en un campo de golf (also see below), Instituto Nacional de Cultura (Lima), 1972.
El libro de Dios y los húngaros (also see below), illustrations by David Herskovitz, Libra-1 (Lima), 1978.
(Contributor) *Cuatro poetas: Víctor García Robles, Antonio Cisneros, Pedro Shimose, Armando Tejada Gómez,* Casa de las Américas, 1979.
At Night the Cats (bilingual text; contains selections from *Comentarios reales, Canto ceremonial contra un oso hormiguero, Agua que no has de beber, Como higuera en un campo de golf, El libro de Dios y los húngaros,* and *La crónica del Niño Jesús;* also see below), edited and translated by Ahern, Rowe, and Tipton, Red Dust, 1985.
Monólogo de la casta Susana y otros poemas, Instituto Nacional de Cultura, 1986.

Also author of *La crónica del Niño Jesús,* 1981. Contributor to anthologies.

OTHER

Author of essays.

WORK IN PROGRESS: Los hijos de Albion, a collection of essays on British poetry.

SIDELIGHTS: An award-winning Peruvian poet, Antonio Cisneros is internationally acclaimed for his satirical works challenging the established values and conventions of his native country. The author first attracted literary attention with the poetry volumes *Comentarios reales* and *Canto ceremonial contra un oso hormiguero,* works exploring alternative interpretations of history and myth. Proceeding to produce such collections as *Agua que no has de beber, Como higuera en un campo de golf,* and *At Night the Cats,* Cisneros has consistently won critical approval for his precise language, evocative imagery, and irreverent and ironic humor. Deeming the author "the most distinguished poet now writing in Peru," Jack Schmitt in the *Los Angeles Times Book Review* further proclaimed: "Cisneros . . . is today one of the major poets of all Spanish America."

Studying literature at the Catholic University in Lima, Cisneros later received a doctorate degree from the National University of San Marcos. He sought to broaden his experiences through travel and, in addition to teaching literature in his native Peru, has taught at foreign universities in England, France, and Hungary. Many critics attribute Cisneros' fresh perspective on his own country to his multi-cultural experiences. "Cisneros is the product of over ten years of travel between London, Nice and Budapest; the political unrest of the 60s in his own country and abroad; and a keen sense of literary technique," explained Gloria F. Waldman in *Hispania.* "He brings his own ironic, gently critical voice to the exotic settings he evokes."

Cisneros produced the poetry collections *Destierro* and *David* in the early 1960s, but it was not until the appearance of *Comentarios reales* that the poet earned international recognition. Published when Cisneros was twenty-two years old, the work offers sardonic views of Peruvian history. In doing so, *Comentarios reales* was considered significant for its departure from traditionally repressive twentieth-century Peruvian poetry, and the work garnered Peru's National Poetry Prize in 1965. Reviewing the poems of *Comentarios reales* when many of them appeared in a 1970 volume titled *The Spider Hangs Too Far From the Ground,* a *Times Literary Supplement* writer thought the pieces "terse and irreverent." The reviewer extolled, for example, such poems as "Dead Conquerors" for not mythologizing past warriors, quoting: "Shat upon by scorpions & spiders few / survived their horses." "As for the nineteenth century," the critic continued, "all that remains are a few grotesque monuments and allegories. . . . Ants, vultures, rocks, red cactus are the elements of [a] pitiless landscape in which neither history nor environment can offer shelter."

Cisneros enjoyed continued success with his next volume, *Canto ceremonial contra un oso hormiguero,* winner of the Cuban Casa de las Américas prize in 1968. While this volume branches out to embrace Cisneros' remembrances of travels and experiences in Ayacucho and England, it nonetheless casts a critical eye on culture and history. Discussing the poems of *Canto ceremonial* (some of which also appeared in *The Spider Hangs Too Far From the Ground*), the *Times Literary Supplement* critic considered "Chronicle of Lima" one of the volume's finest poems; in it, "history and organic growth have been halted and distorted. The poet's Lima is a place of accidental, historical fragments, of absurd superimposed modernity, 'the jungle of cars, a sexless snake of no known species'—a city whose seasons have been altered by the cutting down of forests, where the sea is only visible in rust, where rivers have dried up and 'a white furry veil protects you from the open sky.'"

Cisneros' subsequent poetry volumes further destroy myth, legend, history, and culture through his hallmark satirical voice. *Agua que no has de beber,* containing twenty-two poems written between the years 1964 and 1966, was published in 1971, and the poet's *Como higuera en un campo de golf* appeared in 1972. Selections from these two volumes, as well as those from *Comentarios reales* and *Canto ceremonial* and Cisneros' more recent productions, 1978's *El libro de Dios y los húngaros* and 1981's *La crónica del Niño Jesús,* all appear in *At Night the Cats;* this bilingual anthology containing seventy-six poems was published in 1985.

"For those not previously familiar with Antonio Cisneros' original voice, . . . *At Night the Cats* is an excellent introduction," wrote Waldman. Widely praised for its excellent translation and its choice selections that capture the essence of Cisneros' voice and style, the book gave critics another opportunity to extol Cisneros' craftsmanship. "His early poems, characterized by their epigrammatic brevity, are lean and taut, precise in language and ironic in tone," declared Schmitt. Discussing Cisneros' later works, the reviewer praised the author's "intensely poetic imagination; his stunning images and metaphors, often surreal; his incisive irony and droll humor, sometimes wistful, often self-mocking; his personal, confessional tone; his decorum and reserve, so typical of Peruvians, and also his passion and tenderness." Waldman concurred and compared Cisneros to such famed twentieth-century Hispanic poets as the irreverent Nicanor Parra, the historically astute Pablo Neruda, and the melancholic César Vallejo. Waldman concluded by deeming *At Night the Cats* a "highly valuable volume . . . that will surely make new and old readers smile, and sometimes even laugh out loud, cause indignation at ancient and present injustices, and delight, as good poetry does."

Cisneros' poetry has appeared in numerous anthologies in such languages as French, German, Russian, Danish, and Ukrainian.

BIOGRAPHICAL/CRITICAL SOURCES:

BOOKS

Cisneros, Antonio, *The Spider Hangs Too Far From the Ground,* Cape Goliard, 1970.

PERIODICALS

Hispania, September, 1987.
Los Angeles Times Book Review, October 27, 1985.
Times Literary Supplement, August 21, 1970.

—*Sketch by Janice E. Drane*

*   *   *

CISNEROS, Sandra

ADDRESSES: Home—6525 North Sheridan Rd., Chicago, Ill. 60626.

CAREER: Writer.

AWARDS, HONORS: American Book Award from Before Columbus Foundation, 1985, for *The House on Mango Street.*

WRITINGS:

Bad Boys (poems), Mango Publications, 1980.
The House on Mango Street (young adult), Arte Público, 1983.
The Rodrigo Poems, Third Woman Press, 1985.
My Wicked, Wicked Ways, Third Woman Press, 1987.

Contributor to periodicals, including *Imagine, Contact II,* and *Revista Chicano-Riqueña.*

CLARIN
See ALAS (y UREÑA), Leopoldo (Enrique García)

*   *   *

COFER, Judith Ortiz 1952-

PERSONAL: Born February 24, 1952, in Hormigueros, P.R.; immigrated to United States, 1956; daughter of J. M. (in U.S. Navy) and Fanny (Morot) Ortiz; married Charles John Cofer (in business), November 13, 1971; children: Tanya. *Education:* Augusta College, B.A., 1974; Florida Atlantic University, M.A., 1977; attended Oxford University, 1977.

ADDRESSES: P.O. Box 938, Louisville, Ga. 30434. *Office*—Mercer University College, Forsyth, Ga. 31029. *Agent*—Berenice Hoffman Literary Agency, 215 West 75th St., New York, N.Y. 10023.

CAREER: Bilingual teacher at public schools in Palm Beach County, Fla., 1974-75; Broward Community College, Fort Lauderdale, Fla., adjunct instructor in English, 1978-80, instructor in Spanish, 1979; University of Miami, Coral Gables, Fla., lecturer in English, 1980-84; University of Georgia, Athens, instructor in English, 1984-87, Georgia Center for Continuing Education, instructor in English, 1987-88; Macon College, instructor in English, 1988-89; Mercer University College, Forsyth, Ga., special programs coordinator, 1990. Adjunct instructor at Palm Beach Junior College, 1978-80. Conducts poetry workshops and gives poetry readings. Member of regular staff of International Conference on the Fantastic in Literature, 1979-82; member of literature panel of Fine Arts Council of Florida, 1982; member of administrative staff of Bread Loaf Writers' Conference, 1983 and 1984.

MEMBER: Poetry Society of America, Poets and Writers, Associated Writing Programs.

AWARDS, HONORS: Scholar of English Speaking Union at Oxford University, 1977; fellow of Fine Arts Council of Florida, 1980; Bread Loaf Writers' Conference, scholar, 1981, John Atherton Scholar in Poetry, 1982; grant from Witter Bynner Foundation for Poetry, 1988, for *Letters From a Caribbean Island;* National Endowment for the Arts fellowship in poetry, 1989.

WRITINGS:

Latin Women Pray (chapbook), Florida Arts Gazette Press, 1980.
The Native Dancer (chapbook), Pteranodon Press, 1981.
Among the Ancestors (chapbook), Louisville News Press, 1981.
"Latin Women Pray" (three-act play), first produced in Atlanta at Georgia State University, June, 1984.
Peregrina (poems), Riverstone Press, 1986.
Terms of Survival (poems), Arte Público, 1987.
(Contributor) *Triple Crown: Chicano, Puerto Rican and Cuban American Poetry* (trilogy; contains Cofer's poetry collection *Reaching for the Mainland*), Bilingual Press, 1987.
The Line of the Sun (novel), University of Georgia Press, 1989.
Silent Dancing (personal essays), Arte Público, 1990.

Also author of the poetry collection *Letters From a Caribbean Island.* Work represented in anthologies, including *Hispanics in the U.S.,* Bilingual Review/Press, 1982; *Latina Writers; Revista Chicano-Riqueña;* and *Heath Anthology of Modern American Literature.* Contributor of poems to magazines, including *Southern Humanities Review, Poem, Prairie Schooner, Apalachee Quarterly, Kansas Quarterly,* and *Kalliope.* Poetry editor of *Florida Arts Gazette,* 1978-81; member of editorial board of *Waves.*

SIDELIGHTS: An accomplished author of several books of poetry in the early 1980s, Judith Ortiz Cofer garnered praise for the poetic quality of her first novel, *The Line of the Sun*, published in 1989. Writing in the *New York Times Book Review*, Roberto Márquez commended the "vigorous elegance" of the novel's language and called Cofer "a prose writer of evocatively lyrical authority, a novelist of historical compass and sensitivity." The first half of *Line of the Sun* depicts the poor village of Salud, Puerto Rico, and introduces the characters Rafael Vivente and his wild brother-in-law, Guzmán. *Los Angeles Times Book Review* contributor Sonja Bolle noted that the author's eye for detail "brings alive the stifling and magical world of village life." The second part of the novel follows Rafael to Paterson, New Jersey, where his daughter Marisol, the story's narrator, grows up. Marisol's father encourages her to become wholly American, but her mother advises her to adopt the customs and values of Puerto Rico. Marisol learns about her heritage mainly through the stories told by her family, which often focus on her Uncle Guzmán, the "demon child"; his arrival at her New Jersey home helps Marisol to balance the American and Puerto Rican aspects of her identity. Though Márquez criticized parts of the plot as contrived, he proclaimed Cofer as "a writer of authentic gifts, with a genuine and important story to tell."

Cofer told *CA:* "The 'infinite variety' and power of language interest me. I never cease to experiment with it. As a native Puerto Rican, my first language was Spanish. It was a challenge, not only to learn English, but to master it enough to teach it and—the ultimate goal—to write poetry in it.

"My family is one of the main topics of my poetry; the ones left behind on the island of Puerto Rico, and the ones who came to the United States. In tracing their lives, I discover more about mine. The place of birth itself becomes a metaphor for the things we all must leave behind; the assimilation of a new culture is the coming into maturity by accepting the terms necessary for survival. My poetry is a study of this process of change, assimilation, and transformation."

BIOGRAPHICAL/CRITICAL SOURCES:

PERIODICALS

Los Angeles Times Book Review, August 6, 1989.
New York Times Book Review, September 24, 1989.

* * *

COLON, Jesús 1901-

PERSONAL: Born in 1901 in Puerto Rico.

CAREER: Writer; educator.

WRITINGS:

A Puerto Rican in New York, and Other Sketches, Mainstream Publishers, 1961, 2nd edition, illustrated by Ernesto Ramos Nieves, International Publishers, 1982.
(Translator) Kenneth B. Hoyt, *Fundamentos básicos de career education*, U.S. Government Printing Office, Department of Health, Education, and Welfare, Office of Education, 1979.

SIDELIGHTS: Jesús Colón's 1961 collection *A Puerto Rican in New York* is among the first works of Hispanic literature to depict the immigrant experience. Colón has been credited with creating a modulated narrative voice that reflects a blend of Anglo and Hispanic cultures.

COLORADO (CAPELLA), Antonio J(ulio) 1903-

PERSONAL: Born February 13, 1903, in San Juan, Puerto Rico; son of Rafael Colorado D'Assoy (a photographer) and Lorenza Capella Martínez; married Isabel Laguna Matienzo (a social worker), 1938; children: Antonio, Isabelita, Rafael. *Education:* University of Puerto Rico, B.A., 1932; Clark University, M.A., 1933; Universidad Central, Madrid, Spain, Ph.D., 1934. *Politics:* Popular Democratic Party. *Religion:* Roman Catholic.

ADDRESSES: Home—821 Vesta St., Río Piedras, Puerto Rico 00923.

CAREER: Writer, U.S. Department of State, 1942-43; University of Puerto Rico, Río Piedras Campus, professor and dean of faculty of social science, 1943-46, director of university press, 1946-48; Department of Education of Puerto Rico, Río Piedras, director of department of press, 1948-55; president, Labor Relations Board of Puerto Rico, 1962-69. Writer, translator, and literary critic.

MEMBER: Academia Puertorriqueña de la Lengua Española (treasurer), Academia de Artes y Ciencias (Puerto Rican branch), Ateneo Puertorriqueño, Fundación Puertorriqueña de las Humanidades (member of board of directors), Quinto Centenario del Descubrimiento de Puerto Rico.

WRITINGS:

(Collaborator) *New World Guides to Latin American Republics*, Duell, Sloan & Pearce, 1943.
Puerto Rico y tú; libro de estudios sociales para la escuela elemental, Prentice-Hall, 1948.
Noticia y pulso del movimiento político puertorriqueño (bound with *Noticia acerca del pensamiento político de Puerto Rico* by Lidio Cruz Monclova), Orión, 1955.
Luis Palés Matos, el hombre y el poeta, Rodadero, 1964.
The First Book of Puerto Rico, Watts, 1964, 3rd edition, 1978.
Puerto Rico: La tierra y otros ensayos, Editorial Cordillera, 1972.

TRANSLATOR

Breve historia de los Estados Unidos, Ginn & Co., 1953.
La canción verde, Troutman, 1956.
Nuestro mundo a través de las edades, Prentice-Hall, 1959.
La política puertorriqueña y el nuevo trato, University of Puerto Rico Press, 1960, translation published as *Puerto Rican Politics and the New Deal*, 1976.
América de todos, Rand McNally, 1963.
El árbol de la violeta, Troutman, 1964.

OTHER

Also author of *Haití Intervenido*, 1934. Editor, *Diario de Puerto Rico*, 1948-50. Contributor to *Asomante, Puerto Rico Ilustrado, El Mundo, El Imparcial, La Torre*, and other periodicals.

WORK IN PROGRESS: Semblanzas; Ensayos y conferencias; Crítica literaria; Campañas políticas.

SIDELIGHTS: Antonio J. Colorado told *CA* that he is interested in journalism, labor relations, political science, and sociology. He has traveled through Central and northern South America, Spain, France, Santo Domingo, the Caribbean Islands, Cuba, the United States, and Canada.

* * *

CORPI, Lucha 1945-

PERSONAL: Born April 13, 1945, in Jáltipan, Veracruz, Mexico; immigrated to United States; married. *Education:* Received

B.A. from University of California, Berkeley, and M.A. from San Francisco State University.

ADDRESSES: Home—Oakland, Calif. *Office*—Clinton Park Adult School, 655 East 14th St., Oakland, Calif. 94606.

CAREER: University of California, Berkeley, vice-chair of Chicano Studies executive committee, 1970-71, coordinator of Chicano Studies Library, 1970-72; Oakland Public Neighborhood Centers, Oakland, Calif., teacher of English as a second language, 1973—; writer. Founding member of Aztlán Cultural, 1971, and Centro Chicano de Escritores, 1980; member of Oakland Museum and of Latin American Commission.

MEMBER: California Association of Teachers of English as a Second Language.

AWARDS, HONORS: Fellow of National Endowment for the Arts, 1979-80; winner of *Palabra nueva* literary contest, 1983, for short story, "Los cristos del alma" ("The Martyrs of the Soul").

WRITINGS:

(With Elsie Alvarado de Ricord and Concha Michel) *Fireflight: Three Latin American Poets,* translation from Spanish by Catherine Rodríguez-Nieto, Oyez, 1976.
Palabras de mediodía: Noon Words (poems; text in English and Spanish; translation from Spanish by Catherine Rodríguez-Nieto), El Fuego de Aztlán, 1980.
Delia's Song (novel), Arte Público, 1988.

Author of short stories, including "Los cristos del alma." Work represented in anthologies, including *The Other Voice: Twentieth-Century Women's Poetry in Translation,* edited by Joanna Bankier and others, Norton, 1976; *Chicanos: Antología histórica y literaria,* edited by Tino Villanueva, Fondo de Cultura Económica, 1980; and *Palabra nueva: Cuentos chicanos,* edited by Ricardo Aguilar and others, Texas Western Press, 1984. Contributor of poems and stories to periodicals, including *De colores* and *El Fuego de Aztlán.*

SIDELIGHTS: Mexican-born writer Lucha Corpi immigrated to the United States with her husband at the age of nineteen. Primarily a poet, Corpi writes in Spanish, but her work has been translated into English. Her book of poems, *Palabras de mediodía: Noon Words,* describes and contrasts three places familiar to Corpi—Jáltipan, the sunny, friendly coastal town where she was born, the less genial San Luis Potosí, a town in central Mexico where she moved at the age of nine, and the United States. The poems set in the United States often feature homey scenes of domestic activities such as ironing and cleaning. Corpi writes particularly about women—frequently depicting characters trapped in tragic situations. She also focuses on the repression of women's sexual desires in Mexican culture. *Delia's Song,* Corpi's first novel, may be based on some of the author's own experiences; its main character chooses to part from her family in order to attend college in California, and ultimately decides to become a writer.

BIOGRAPHICAL/CRITICAL SOURCES:

BOOKS

Dictionary of Literary Biography, Volume 82, Gale, 1989.
Sánchez, Marta Ester, *Contemporary Chicana Poetry: A Critical Approach to an Emerging Literature,* University of California Press, 1985.

CORTAZAR, Julio 1914-1984
(Julio Denís)

PERSONAL: Born August 26, 1914, in Brussels, Belgium; held dual citizenship in Argentina and (beginning 1981) France; died of a heart attack February 12, 1984, in Paris, France; son of Julio José and María Herminia (Descotte) Cortázar; married former spouse Aurora Bernárdez, August 23, 1953. *Education:* Received degrees in teaching and public translating; attended Buenos Aires University.

CAREER: Writer. High school teacher in Bolívar and Chivilcoy, both in Argentina, 1937-44; teacher of French literature, University of Cuyo, Mendoza, Argentina, 1944-45; manager, Argentine Publishing Association (Cámara Argentina del Libro), Buenos Aires, Argentina, 1946-48; public translator in Argentina, 1948-51; free-lance translator for UNESCO, Paris, France, 1952-84. Member of jury, Casa de las Américas Award.

AWARDS, HONORS: Prix Médicis, 1974, for *Libro de Manuel;* Rubén Darío Order of Cultural Independence awarded by Government of Nicaragua, 1983.

WRITINGS:

FICTION

Bestiario (stories; title means "Bestiary"; also see below), Sudamericana (Buenos Aires), 1951, reprinted, 1983.
Final del juego (stories; also see below), Los Presentes (Mexico), 1956, expanded edition, Sudamericana, 1964, reprinted, 1983.
Las armas secretas (stories; title means "The Secret Weapons"; also see below), Sudamericana, 1959, reprinted, Cátedra (Madrid), 1983.
Los premios (novel), Sudamericana, 1960, reprinted, Ediciones B, 1987, translation by Elaine Kerrigan published as *The Winners,* Pantheon, 1965, reprinted, 1984.
Historias de cronopios y de famas, Minotauro (Buenos Aires), 1962, reprinted, Alfaguara, 1984, translation by Paul Blackburn published as *Cronopios and Famas,* Pantheon, 1969.
Rayuela (novel), Sudamericana, 1963, reprinted, 1984, translation by Gregory Rabassa published as *Hopscotch,* Pantheon, 1966, reprinted, 1987.
Cuentos (collection), Casa de las Américas (Havana), 1964.
Todos los fuegos el fuego (stories), Sudamericana, 1966, reprinted, 1981, translation by Suzanne Jill Levine published as *All Fires the Fire, and Other Stories,* Pantheon, 1973, reprinted, 1988.
La vuelta al día en ochenta mundos (essays, poetry, and stories), Siglo Veintiuno (Mexico), 1967, reprinted, 1984, translation by Thomas Christensen published as *Around the Day in Eighty Worlds,* North Point Press, 1986.
El perseguidor y otros cuentos (stories), Centro Editor para América Latina (Buenos Aires), 1967, reprinted, Bruguera, 1983.
End of the Game, and Other Stories, translated by Blackburn (includes stories from *Final del juego, Bestiario,* and *Las armas secretas*), Pantheon, 1967, published as *Blow-Up, and Other Stories,* Collier, 1968, reprinted, Pantheon, 1985.
Ceremonias (collection), Seix Barral, 1968, reprinted, 1983.
62: Modelo para armar (novel), Sudamericana, 1968, translation by Rabassa published as *62: A Model Kit,* Pantheon, 1972.
Ultimo round (essays, poetry, and stories; title means "Last Round"), Siglo Veintiuno, 1969, reprinted, 1984.
Relatos (collection), Sudamericana, 1970.
La isla a mediodía y otros relatos (contains twelve previously published stories), Salvat, 1971.

Libro de Manuel (novel), Sudamericana, 1973, translation by Rabassa published as *A Manual for Manuel,* Pantheon, 1978.

Octaedro (stories; title means "Octahedron"; also see below), Sudamericana, 1974.

Antología (collection), La Librería, 1975.

Fantomas contra los vampiros multinacionales (title means "Fantomas Takes on the Multinational Vampires"), Excelsior (Mexico), 1975.

Los relatos (collection), four volumes, Alianza, 1976-1985.

Alguien que anda por ahí y otros relatos (stories), Alfaguara (Madrid), 1977, translation by Rabassa published as *A Change of Light, and Other Stories* (includes *Octaedro;* also see below), Knopf, 1980.

Territorios, Siglo Veintiuno, 1978.

Un tal Lucas, Alfaguara, 1979, translation by Rabassa published as *A Certain Lucas,* Knopf, 1984.

Queremos tanto a Glenda, Alfaguara, 1980, translation by Rabassa published as *We Love Glenda So Much, and Other Tales* (also see below), Knopf, 1983.

Deshoras (short stories), Alfaguara, 1982.

We Love Glenda So Much [and] *A Change of Light,* Vintage, 1984.

TRANSLATOR

Alfred Stern, *Filosofía de la risa y del llanto,* Imán (Buenos Aires), 1950.

Lord Houghton, *Vida y cartas de John Keats,* Imán, 1955.

Marguerite Yourcenar, *Memorias de Adriano,* Sudamericana, 1955.

Edgar Allan Poe, *Obras en prosa,* two volumes, Revista de Occidente, 1956.

Poe, *Cuentos,* Editorial Nacional de Cuba, 1963.

Poe, *Aventuras de Arthur Gordon Pym,* Instituto del Libro (Havana), 1968.

Poe, *Eureka,* Alianza (Madrid), 1972.

Daniel Defoe, *Robinson Crusoe,* Bruguera, 1981.

Also translator of works by G. K. Chesterton, Andre Gide, and Jean Giono, published in Argentina between 1948 and 1951.

OTHER

(Under pseudonym Julio Denís) *Presencia* (poems; title means "Presence"), El Bibliófilo (Buenos Aires), 1938.

Los reyes (play; title means "The Monarchs"), Gulab y Aldabahor (Buenos Aires), 1949, reprinted, Alfaguara, 1982.

(Contributor) *Buenos Aires de la fundación a la angustia,* Ediciones de la Flor (Buenos Aires), 1967.

(With others) *Cuba por argentinos,* Merlín (Buenos Aires), 1968.

Buenos Aires, Buenos Aires (includes French and English translations), Sudamericana, 1968.

Viaje alrededor de una mesa (title means "Trip around a Table"), Cuadernos de Rayuela (Buenos Aires), 1970.

(With Oscar Collazos and Mario Vargas Llosa) *Literatura en la revolución y revolución en la literatura,* Siglo Veintiuno, 1970.

(Contributor) *Literatura y arte nuevo en Cuba,* Estela (Barcelona), 1971.

Pameos y meopas (poetry), Editorial Libre de Sivera (Barcelona), 1971.

Prosa del observatorio, Lumen (Barcelona), 1972.

La casilla de los Morelli (essays), edited by José Julio Ortega, Tusquets, 1973.

Convergencias, divergencias, incidencias, edited by Ortega, Tusquets, 1973.

(Author of text) *Humanario,* La Azotea (Buenos Aires), 1976.

(Author of text) *Paris: Ritmos de una ciudad,* Edhasa (Barcelona), 1981.

Paris: The Essence of an Image, Norton, 1981.

(With Carol Dunlop) *Los autonautas de la cosmopista,* Muchnik (Buenos Aires), 1983.

Nicaragua tan violentamente dulce (essays), Nueva Nicaragua, 1983.

Argentina: Años de almbradas culturales (essays), edited by Saúl Yurkiévich, Muchnik, 1984.

Nada a pehuajó: Un acto; Adiós, Robinson (plays), Katún, 1984.

Salvo el crepúsculo (poems), Nueva Imagen, 1984.

Textos políticos, Plaza y Janés, 1985.

Divertimento, Sudamericana/Planeta, 1986.

El examen, Sudamericana/Planeta, 1986.

Nicaraguan Sketches, Norton, 1989.

Contributor to numerous periodicals, including *Revista Iberoamericana, Cuadernos Hispanoamericanos, Books Abroad,* and *Casa de las Américas.*

SIDELIGHTS: Argentine author Julio Cortázar was "one of the world's greatest writers," according to novelist Stephen Dobyns. "His range of styles," Dobyns wrote in the *Washington Post Book World,* "his ability to paint a scene, his humor, his endlessly peculiar mind makes many of his stories wonderful. His novel *Hopscotch* is considered one of the best novels written by a South American."

A popular as well as a critical success, *Hopscotch* not only established Cortázar's reputation as a novelist of international merit but also, according to David W. Foster in *Currents in the Contemporary Argentine Novel,* prompted wider acceptance in the United States of novels written by other Latin Americans. For this reason many critics, such as Jaime Alazraki in *The Final Island,* viewed the book as "a turning point for Latin American literature." A *Times Literary Supplement* reviewer, for example, called *Hopscotch* "the first great novel of Spanish America."

Still other critics, including novelists José Donoso and C. D. B. Bryan, saw the novel in the context of world literature. Donoso, in his *The Boom in Spanish American Literature: A Personal History,* claimed that *Hopscotch* "humanized the novel." Cortázar was a writer, Donoso continued, "who [dared] to be discursive and whose pages [were] sprinkled with names of musicians, painters, art galleries, . . . movie directors[, and] all this had an undisguised place within his novel, something which I would never have dared to presume to be right for the Latin American novel, since it was fine for [German novelist] Thomas Mann but not for us." In the *New York Times Book Review,* Bryan stated: "I think *Hopscotch* is the most magnificent book I have ever read. No novel has so satisfactorily and completely and beautifully explored man's compulsion to explore life, to search for its meaning, to challenge its mysteries. Nor has any novel in recent memory lavished such love and attention upon the full spectrum of the writer's craft."

Cortázar attempted to perfect his craft by constant experimentation. In his longer fiction he pursued, as Leo Bersani observed in the *New York Times Book Review,* both "subversion and renewal of novelistic form." This subversion and renewal was of such importance to Cortázar that often the form of his novels overshadowed the action that they described. Through the form of his fiction Cortázar invited the reader to participate in the writer's craft and to share in the creation of the novel.

Hopscotch is one such novel. In *Into the Mainstream: Conversations with Latin-America Writers,* Luis Harss and Barbara Dohmann wrote that *Hopscotch* "is the first Latin American novel which takes itself as its own central topic or, in other words, is essentially about the writing of itself. It lives in constant metamorphoses, as an unfinished process that invents itself as it goes, involving the reader in such a way to make him part of the creative impulse." Thus, *Hopscotch* begins with a "Table of Instructions" that tells the reader that there are at least two ways to read the novel. The first is reading chapters one to fifty-six in numerical order. When the reader finishes chapter fifty-six he can, according to the instructions, stop reading and "ignore what follows [nearly one hundred more short chapters] with a clean conscience." The other way of reading suggested by the instructions is to start with chapter seventy-two and then skip from chapter to chapter (hence, the title of the book), following the sequence indicated at the end of each chapter by a number which tells the reader which chapter is next. Read the second way, the reader finds that chapter 131 refers him to chapter fifty-eight, and chapter fifty-eight to chapter 131, so that he is confronted with a novel that has no end. With his "Table of Instructions" Cortázar forces the reader to write the novel while he is reading it.

Cortázar's other experimental works include *62: A Model Kit* (considered a sequel to *Hopscotch*), *A Manual for Manuel, Ultimo round* ("Last Round"), and *Fantomas contra los vampiros multinacionales* ("Fantomas Takes on the Multinational Vampires"). *62: A Model Kit* is based on chapter sixty-two of *Hopscotch* in which a character, Morelli, expresses his desire to write a new type of novel. "If I were to write this book," Morelli states, "standard behavior would be inexplicable by means of current instrumental psychology. Everything would be a kind of disquiet, a continuous uprooting, a territory where psychological causality would yield disconcertedly."

In *62: A Model Kit* Cortázar attempted to put these ideas into action. Time and space have no meaning in the novel: although it takes place in Paris, London, and Vienna, the characters move and interact as if they are in one single space. The characters themselves are sketchily presented in fragments that must be assembled by the readers; chapters are replaced by short scenes separated by blank spaces on the pages of the novel. Cortázar noted in the book's introduction that once again the reader must help create the novel: "The reader's option, his personal montage of the elements in the tale, will in each case be the book he has chosen to read."

A Manual for Manuel continues in the experimental vein. Megan Marshall described the book in *New Republic* as "a novel that merges story and history, a supposed scrapbook of news clippings, journal entries, diagrams, transcripts of conversations, and much more." The book, about the kidnapping of a Latin American diplomat by a group of guerillas in Paris, is told from the double perspective of an unnamed member of the group, who takes notes on the plans for the kidnapping, and a nonmember of the group, Andres, who reads the notes. Periodically, these two narrations are interrupted by the inclusion of English-, French-, and Spanish-language texts reproduced in the pages of the novel. These texts, actual articles collected by Cortázar from various sources, form part of a scrapbook being assembled for Manuel, the child of two of the members of the group. On one page, for example, Cortázar reprinted a statistical table originally published in 1969 by the U.S. Department of Defense that shows how many Latin Americans have received military training in the United States. The reader reads about the compilation of the scrapbook for Manuel, while at the same time reading the scrapbook and reacting to the historical truth it contains.

Other such experimentation is found in *Ultimo round*, a collection of essays, stories, and poetry. William L. Siemens noted in

the *International Fiction Review* that this book, like *Hopscotch* and *62: A Model Kit*, "is a good example of audience-participation art." In *Ultimo round*, he declared, "it is impossible for the reader to proceed in a conventional manner. Upon opening the book the reader notes that there are two sets of pages within the binding, and he must immediately decide which of them to read first, and even whether he will go through by reading the top and then the bottom of page one, and so on."

Cortázar's brief narrative *Fantomas contra los vampiros multinacionales* is yet another experiment with new forms of fiction. It presents, in comic book form, the story of a "superhero," Fantomas, who gathers together "the greatest contemporary writers" to fight the destructive powers of the multinational corporations. Chilean Octavio Paz, Italian Alberto Moravia, and American Susan Sontag, along with Cortázar himself, appear as characters in the comic book. Although short, the work embodies several constants in Cortázar's fiction: the comic (the comic book form itself), the interplay of fantasy and reality (the appearance of historical figures in a fictional work), and a commitment to social activism (the portrayal of the writer as a politically involved individual). These three elements, together with Cortázar's experiments with the novelistic form, are the basic components of his fiction.

Cortázar explained how these elements function together in his essay "Algunos aspectos del cuento" ("Some Aspects of the Story"), which Alazraki quoted in *The Final Island*. His work, Cortázar claimed, was "an alternative to that false realism which assumed that everything can be neatly described as was upheld by the philosophic and scientific optimism of the eighteenth century, that is, within a world ruled more or less harmoniously by a system of laws, of principles, of causal relations, of well defined psychologies, of well mapped geographies. . . . In my case, the suspicion of another order, more secret and less communicable [was one of the principles guiding] my personal search for a literature beyond overly naive forms of realism." Whatever the method, whether new narrative forms, unexpected humor, incursions into fantasy, or pleas for a more humane society, Cortázar strove to shake the reader out of traditional ways of thinking and seeing the world and to replace them with new and more viable models. Dobyn explained in the *Washington Post Book World*, "Cortázar wants to jolt people out of their self-complacency, to make them doubt their own definition of the world."

Cortázar's last full-length work of fiction, *A Certain Lucas*, for example, "is a kind of sampler of narrative ideas, a playful anthology of form, including everything from parables to parodies, folk tales to metafictions," as Robert Coover describes it in the *New York Times Book Review*. Including chapters with such titles as "Lucas, His Shopping," "Lucas, His Battles with the Hydra," and "Lucas, His Pianists," the book "builds a portrait, montage-like, through a succession of short sketches (humorous set-pieces, really) full of outrageous inventions, leaping and dream-like associations and funny turns of phrase," states *Los Angeles Times Book Review* critic Charles Champlin. "Lucas is not Cortázar," Dobyns suggests in the *Washington Post Book World*, "but occasionally he seems to stand for him and so the book takes on an autobiographical quality as we read about Lucas' friends, his struggles with himself, his dreams, his tastes, his view of writing." The result, writes Champlin, might appear to be "no more than a series of extravagant jokes, [and] it would be an exceptional passing entertainment but no more than that. Yet under the cover of raillery, self-indicting foolishness and extremely tall tales," the critic continues, "Cortázar is discovered to be a thoughtful, deep-feeling man, impassioned, sentimental, angry, complicated, a philosopher exploring appearances vs. realities is the way of philosophers ever." "What we see in Lucas and in much of Cortázar's work is a fierce love of this earth, despite the awfulness, and a fierce respect for life's ridiculousness," concludes Dobyns. "And in the midst of this ridiculousness, Cortázar dances . . . and that dance comforts and eases our own course through the world."

This ridiculousness, or humor, in Cortázar's work often derived from what a *Time* reviewer referred to as the author's "ability to present common objects from strange perspectives as if he had just invented them." Cortázar, declared Tom Bishop in *Saturday Review*, was "an intellectual humorist. . . . [He had] a rare gift for isolating the absurd in everyday life [and] for depicting the foibles in human behavior with an unerring thrust that [was] satiric yet compassionate."

Hopscotch is filled with humorous elements, some of which Saúl Yurkiévich listed in *The Final Island*. He included "references to the ridiculous, . . . recourse to the outlandish, . . . absurd associations, . . . juxtaposition of the majestic with the popular or vulgar," as well as "puns, . . . [and] polyglot insults." *New York Times* writer John Leonard called absurdity "obligatory" in a work by Cortázar and gave examples of the absurd found in *A Manual for Manuel*, such as "a turquoise penguin [is] flown by jet to Argentina; the stealing of 9,000 wigs . . . and obsessive puns." In an interview with Evelyn Picon Garfield, quoted in *Books Abroad*, Cortázar called *Cronopios and Famas* his "most playful book." It is, he continued, "really a game, a very fascinating game, lots of fun, almost like a tennis match."

This book of short, story-like narratives deals with two groups of creatures described by Arthur Curley in *Library Journal* as the "warm life-loving cronopios and practical, conventional famas . . . imaginary but typical personages between whom communication is usually impossible and always ridiculous." One portion of the book, called "The Instruction Manual," contains detailed explanations of various everyday activities, including how to climb stairs, how to wind a clock, and how to cry. In order to cry correctly, the author suggested thinking of a duck covered with ants. With these satiric instructions Cortázar, according to Paul West in *Book World*, "cleanses the doors of perception and mounts a subtle, bland assault on the mental rigidities we hold most dear." By forcing us to think about everyday occurrences in a new way, Cortázar, Malva E. Filer noted in *Books Abroad*, "expresses his rebellion against objects and persons that make up our everyday life and the mechanical ways by which we relate to them." Filer continued: "In Cortázar's fictional world [a] routine life is the great scandal against which every individual must rebel with all his strength. And if he is not willing to do so, extraordinary elements are usually summoned to force him out of this despicable and abject comfort."

These "extraordinary elements" enter into the lives of Cortázar's characters in the form of fantastic episodes which interrupt their otherwise normal existences. Alexander Coleman observed in *Cinco maestros: Cuentos modernos de Hispanoamérica* ("Five Masters: Modern Spanish-American Stories"): "Cortázar's stories start in a disarmingly conversational way, with plenty of local touches. But something always seems to go awry just when we least expect it." "Axolotl," a short story described by novelist Joyce Carol Oates in the *New York Times Book Review* as her favorite Cortázar tale, begins innocently: a man describes his trips to the Parisian botanical gardens to watch a certain type of salamander called an axolotl. But the serenity ends when the narrator admits, "Now I am an axolotl." In another story, a woman has a dream about a beggar who lives in Budapest (a city the woman has never visited). The woman ends up actually going to Budapest where she finds herself walking across a bridge as the beggar woman from her dream approaches from the opposite side. The two women embrace in the middle of the bridge and the first woman is transformed into the beggar woman—she can feel the snow seeping through the holes in her shoes—while she sees her former self walk away. In yet another story, a motorcyclist is involved in a minor traffic accident and suddenly finds himself thrown back in time where he becomes the victim of Aztec ritual sacrifice. Daniel Stern noted in *Nation* that with these stories and others like them "it is as if Cortázar is showing us that it is essential for us to reimagine the reality in which we live and which we can no longer take for granted."

Although during the last years of his life Cortázar was so involved with political activism that Jason Weiss described him in the *Los Angeles Times* as a writer with hardly any time to write, the Argentine had early in his career been criticized "for his apparent indifference to the brutish situation" of his fellow Latin Americans, according to Leonard. Evidence of his growing political preoccupation is found in his later stories and novels. Leonard observed, for instance, that *A Manual for Manuel* "is a primer on the necessity of revolutionary action," and William Kennedy in the *Washington Post Book World* noted that the newspaper clippings included in the novel "touch[ed] the open nerve of political oppression in Latin America." Many of the narratives in *A Change of Light, and Other Stories* are also politically oriented. Oates described the impact of one story in the *New York Times Book Review*. In "Apocalypse at Solentiname," a photographer develops his vacation photographs of happy, smiling people only to discover pictures of people being tortured. Oates commented, "The narrator . . . contemplates in despair the impotence of art to deal with in any significant way, the 'life of permanent uncertainty . . . [in] almost all of Latin America, a life surrounded by fear and death.' "

Cortázar's fictional world, according to Alazraki in *The Final Island*, "represents a challenge to culture." This challenge is embedded in the author's belief in a reality that reaches beyond our everyday existence. Alazraki noted that Cortázar once declared, "Our daily reality masks a second reality which is neither mysterious nor theological, but profoundly human. Yet, due to a long series of mistakes, it has remained concealed under a reality prefabricated by many centuries of culture, a culture in which there are great achievements but also profound aberrations, profound distortions." Bryan further explained these ideas in the *New York Times Book Review*: Cortázar's "surrealistic treatment of the most pedestrian acts suggest[ed] that one way to combat alienation is to return to the original receptiveness of childhood, to recapture this original innocence, by returning to the concept of life as a game."

Cortázar confronted his reader with unexpected forms, with humor, fantasy, and unseemly reality in order to challenge him to live a more meaningful life. He summarized his theory of fiction (and of life) in an essay, "The Present State of Fiction in Latin America," which appeared in *Books Abroad*. The Argentine concluded: "The fantastic is something that one must never say good-bye to lightly. The man of the future . . . will have to find the bases of a reality which is truly his and, at the same time, maintain the capacity of dreaming and playing which I have tried to show you . . . , since it is through those doors that the Other, the fantastic dimension, and the unexpected will always slip, as will all that will save us from that obedient robot into which so many technocrats would like to convert us and which we will not accept—ever."

MEDIA ADAPTATIONS: The story "Las babas del diablo," from the collection *Las armas secretas* was the basis for Michaelangelo Antonioni's 1966 film "Blow Up."

AVOCATIONAL INTERESTS: Jazz, movies.

BIOGRAPHICAL/CRITICAL SOURCES:

BOOKS

Alazraki, Jaime and Ivar Ivask, editors, *The Final Island: The Fiction of Julio Cortázar,* University of Oklahoma Press, 1978.

Boldy, Steven, *The Novels of Cortázar,* Cambridge University Press, 1980.

Coleman, Alexander, editor, *Cinco maestros: Cuentos modernos de Hispanoamérica,* Harcourt, Brace & World, 1969.

Contemporary Literary Criticism, Gale, Volume 2, 1974, Volume 3, 1975, Volume 5, 1976, Volume 10, 1979, Volume 13, 1980, Volume 15, 1980, Volume 33, 1985, Volume 34, 1985.

Donoso, José, *Historia personal del "boom,"* Anagrama (Barcelona), 1972, translation by Gregory Kolovakos published as *The Boom in Spanish American Literature: A Personal History,* Columbia University Press, 1977.

Foster, David W., *Currents in the Contemporary Argentine Novel,* University of Missouri Press, 1975.

Garfield, Evelyn Picon, *Julio Cortázar,* Ungar, 1975.

Garfield, Evelyn Picon, *Cortázar por Cortázar* (interviews), Universidad Veracruzana, 1981.

Giacoman, Helmy F., editor, *Homenaje a Julio Cortázar,* Anaya, 1972.

Harss, Luis and Barbara Dohmann, *Into the Mainstream: Conversations with Latin-American Writers,* Harper, 1967.

Prego, Omar, *La fascinación de las palabras* (interviews), Muchnik, 1985.

Vásquez Amaral, José, *The Contemporary Latin American Narrative,* Las Américas, 1970.

PERIODICALS

America, April 17, 1965, July 9, 1966, December 22, 1973.
Atlantic, June, 1969, October, 1973.
Books Abroad, fall, 1965, winter, 1968, summer, 1969, winter, 1970, summer, 1976.
Book World, August 17, 1969.
Casa de las Américas, numbers 15-16, 1962.
Chicago Tribune, September 24, 1978.
Chicago Tribune Book World, November 16, 1980, May 8, 1983.
Christian Science Monitor, August 15, 1967, July 3, 1969, December 4, 1978.
Commentary, October, 1966.
El País, April 19, 1981.
Hispania, December, 1973.
Hudson Review, spring, 1974.
International Fiction Review, January, 1974, January, 1975.
Library Journal, July, 1967, September, 1969, September 15, 1980.
Listener, December 20, 1979.
Los Angeles Times, August 28, 1983.
Los Angeles Times Book Review, December 28, 1980, June 12, 1983, May 27, 1984.
Nation, September 18, 1967.
National Review, July 25, 1967.
New Republic, April 23, 1966, July 15, 1967, October 21, 1978, October 25, 1980.
New Yorker, May 18, 1965, February 25, 1974.
New York Review of Books, March 25, 1965, April 28, 1966, April 19, 1973, October 12, 1978.
New York Times, November 13, 1978, March 24, 1983.
New York Times Book Review, March 21, 1965, April 10, 1966, June 15, 1969, November 26, 1972, September 9, 1973, November 19, 1978, November 9, 1980, March 4, 1984, May 20, 1984.
Novel: A Forum on Fiction, fall, 1967.
Review of Contemporary Fiction (special Cortázar issue), fall, 1983.
Revista Iberoamericana, July-December, 1973.
Saturday Review, March 27, 1965, April 9, 1966, July 22, 1967, September 27, 1969.
Time, April 29, 1966, June 13, 1969, October 1, 1973.
Times Literary Supplement, October 12, 1973, December 7, 1979.
Virginia Quarterly Review, spring, 1973.
Washington Post Book World, November 18, 1973, November 5, 1978, November 23, 1980, May 1, 1983, June 24, 1984.
World Literature Today, winter, 1977, winter, 1980.

OBITUARIES:

PERIODICALS

Chicago Tribune, February 14, 1984.
Globe and Mail (Toronto), February 18, 1984.
Los Angeles Times, February 14, 1984.
New York Times, February 13, 1984.
Times (London), February 14, 1984.
Voice Literary Supplement, March, 1984.
Washington Post, February 13, 1984.

*   *   *

COSTANTINI, Humberto   1924(?)-1987

PERSONAL: Born c. 1924 in Buenos Aires, Argentina; died of cancer, June 7 (one source says May 31), 1987, in Buenos Aires, Argentina; married wife, Nela; children: Violeta Paroldo, Ana Prego, Daniel.

CAREER: Writer.

AWARDS, HONORS: First prize for narrative from Casa de las Américas, 1979, for *De dioses, hombrecitos y policías;* Premio Municipal from the city of Buenos Aires for *Una vieja historia de caminantes* and *Háblenme de Funes.*

WRITINGS:

De por aquí nomás (short stories), Stilcograf, 1958.
Un señor alto, rubio, de bigotes (short stories), Stilcograf, 1963.
Tres monólogos, Falbo, 1964.
Cuestiones con la vida (poetry), Canto y Cuento, 1966.
Una vieja historia de caminantes (short stories; title means "An Old Story About Travelers"), Centro Editor de América Latina, 1967.
Háblenme de Funes (short stories), Sudamericana, 1970 (also see below).
Libro de Trelew, Granica, 1973.
Más cuestiones con la vida (poetry), Papeles de Buenos Aires, c. 1974.
Bandeo (short stories), Granica, 1975 (also see below).
De dioses, hombrecitos y policías, Nueva Imagen (Mexico City), 1979, reprinted, Bruguera, 1984, translation by Toby Talbot published as *The Gods, the Little Guys, and the Police,* Harper, 1984.
Háblenme de Funes (short stories; title means "Talk to Me About Funes"; contains collections *Háblenme de Funes* and

Bandeo and additional story, "La llegada"), Nueva Imagen, 1980, reprinted, Centro Editor de América Latina, 1983.

La larga noche de Francisco Sanctis (novel), Bruguera, 1984, translation by Norman Thomas di Giovanni published as *The Long Night of Francisco Sanctis,* Harper, 1985.

En la noche, Bruguera, 1985.

Also author of plays.

SIDELIGHTS: Argentine Humberto Costantini distinguished himself as an imaginative writer of Latin American satire. His works frequently depict the tumultuous political history of his native country, focusing in particular on the effect of the turmoil on ordinary citizens. The author of novels, short stories, poetry, and plays, Costantini is best known in English literary circles for the political satire *De dioses, hombrecitos y policías,* translated as *The Gods, the Little Guys, and the Police,* and the provocative novel *La larga noche de Francisco Sanctis,* translated as *The Long Night of Francisco Sanctis.*

A blend of humor and pathos, Costantini's fiction reflects the hopes and fears of his compatriots. His short story collections of the 1970s, most notably *Háblenme de Funes,* are rich in their evocations of Argentine history, legend, and culture. The title story, "Háblenme de Funes," for instance, recalls everyday life in Buenos Aires in the 1940s, after army colonel Juan Domingo Perón assumed power. Perón was elected president of Argentina three years after the 1943 military overthrow of Ramón S. Castillo. With his charismatic wife, Eva, Perón succeeded in establishing a popular dictatorship. But economic troubles and the 1952 death of Eva—who had been a champion of the country's lower classes—contributed to his expulsion from office in 1955.

After vacillating between military and civilian rule in the 1950s and 1960s, Argentina entered a period of violent paramilitary oppression. Professed and suspected leftists and members of the Argentine intelligentsia became targets of a governmental crusade designed to stifle opposition. By the mid-1970s, such dissenters (now known as "the disappeared ones") began to vanish without a trace, becoming victims of a frenzied and murderous regime. Following the "disappearance" of a close friend, Costantini fled to Mexico in 1977, living there in self-imposed exile for six years. During that time, he wrote *The Gods, the Little Guys, and the Police.*

Banned by Argentina's military government, *The Gods, the Little Guys, and the Police* was published in Mexico in 1979. The satiric novel illuminates both the absurdity of oppression and the capriciousness of fate through a darkly comedic plot: In arbitrary retaliation for the death of a vicious Argentine general in war-torn Buenos Aires, an angered Hades decides that twelve unprofound but well-intentioned poets should be sacrificed. Three deities, working to protect the bungling poets, inspire them with a redemptive wisdom that renders their executioners powerless. The poets are saved from certain death, but another twelve innocent citizens are subsequently chosen to take their place.

As Lydia Hunt noted in the *New York Times Book Review,* through *The Gods, the Little Guys, and the Police* "Costantini stresses . . . the role chance or randomness plays as an indiscriminate instrument of repression." According to S. R. Wilson in *Latin American Literary Review,* Costantini places the fate of the poets in the hands of an arbitrarily vengeful god from hell because "politically organized death simply cannot be comprehended by any other means." While some critics viewed the novel's ending—the ultimate deliverance of the twelve poets from the hands of death—as a striking prolongation of the absur-

dity theme, several dissenting reviewers were disappointed with the contrived resolution. David T. Haberly, writing in *Review: Latin American Literature and Arts,* asserted: "The novel is a technical tour de force, but Costantini's cleverness and his verbal brilliance . . . seem designed, in the end, to evade reality rather than to confront and comprehend it." *The Gods, the Little Guys, and the Police* was finally released in the author's native land in 1984, after the establishment of rule there by free election.

Costantini returned to Argentina in 1983, following the election of Raúl Alfonsín as president. The author's last novel, published first in Argentina and translated as *The Long Night of Francisco Sanctis* in 1985, offers further commentary on Argentine politics. The story takes place in Buenos Aires on a single day in the fall of 1977. Sanctis, a head accountant for a wholesaling firm, dabbled in left-wing politics as a university student and is confronted seventeen years later by Elena Vaccaro, an acquaintance from school who implores him to warn two unsuspecting men of their impending "disappearance." *The Long Night of Francisco Sanctis* turns on the title character's struggle to reconcile his instinct for self-preservation with a sense of responsibility to his seemingly doomed comrades. Commenting in the *New York Times Book Review* on the moral implications raised in Costantini's work, Margery Resnick concluded: "The originality of this taut, compassionate novel lies in its refusal to portray the protagonist's situation as a dark night of the soul. . . . [*The Long Night of Francisco Sanctis*] shows the inevitability of personal moral choices even for those determined to remain uninvolved."

A significant number of Costantini's writings remain inaccessible to English-speaking readers. His reputation in the United States rests almost exclusively on his two translated novels. While the author's fiction deals mainly with the social and political uprisings affecting Argentine citizens, most critics concede that his canon as a whole is informed by a universal understanding of human nature. Upon learning in 1986 that he was afflicted with terminal cancer, Costantini, as recounted in the *Chicago Tribune,* announced: "I am going to die creating, surrounded by friends, in my homeland."

BIOGRAPHICAL/CRITICAL SOURCES:

BOOKS

Contemporary Literary Criticism, Volume 49, Gale, 1988.

PERIODICALS

Christian Science Monitor, May 23, 1984.
Globe and Mail (Toronto), August 31, 1985.
Latin American Literary Review, fall-winter, 1981.
London Review of Books, April 23, 1987.
Los Angeles Times, September 7, 1984.
New Statesman, March 13, 1987.
New Yorker, September 22, 1986.
New York Times Book Review, April 29, 1984, October 6, 1985.
Review: Latin American Literature and Arts, January-June, 1986.
Time, July 9, 1984.
World Literature Today, winter, 1981, summer, 1981.

OBITUARIES:

PERIODICALS

Chicago Tribune, June 11, 1987.
New York Times, June 13, 1987.
Washington Post, June 13, 1987.

—Sketch by Barbara Carlisle Bigelow

CREDO, Alvaro J. de
   See PRADO (CALVO), Pedro

* * *

CRUZ, Arturo, Jr. 1954(?)-

PERSONAL: Born c. 1954 in Nicaragua; son of Arturo Cruz, Sr. (a banker and political leader). *Education:* Attended Institute of Development Studies, Sussex, England and Johns Hopkins University.

CAREER: Worked for the foreign affairs branch of the Nicaraguan government under the Sandinistas, 1978-82; worked as political adviser for Contra movement in Washington, D.C., beginning in 1982; writer.

WRITINGS:

Nicaragua's Continuing Struggle: In Search of Democracy, edited by James Finn, Freedom House, 1988.
Memoirs of a Counterrevolutionary, Doubleday, 1989.

SIDELIGHTS: Arturo Cruz, Jr., has written two books about the political struggles in Nicaragua. After studying at England's Institute of Developmental Studies and at Johns Hopkins University, he returned to his country in 1978 to support the newly installed communist Sandinista government. Cruz became disillusioned by the Sandinistas, however, when he determined that the new regime was more concerned with establishing military power and alliances with other communist countries than with instituting social and economic reforms. Consequently, he joined his father, also a former Sandinista, in working for the Contras, a counterrevolutionary faction attempting to oust the Sandinistas. Cruz later resigned from the Contra movement as well; he recounts his experiences in *Memoirs of a Counterrevolutionary* and presents his views on Nicaraguan politics in *Nicaragua's Continuing Struggle.*

BIOGRAPHICAL/CRITICAL SOURCES:

BOOKS

Cruz, Arturo, Jr., *Memoirs of a Counterrevolutionary,* Doubleday, 1989.

PERIODICALS

Los Angeles Times Magazine, April 19, 1987.
New York Times Book Review, October 15, 1989.

* * *

CRUZ, Gilbert R(alph) 1929-
   (Gilberto Rafael Cruz)

PERSONAL: Born December 6, 1929, in San Antonio, Tex.; son of Gilbert and Hilaria (Rivas) Cruz; children: Andrés Antonio, Miguel Luis. *Education:* Attended Assumption Seminary, 1949-55, and Catholic University of America, 1962; St. Mary's University of San Antonio, B.A., 1968, M.A., 1970; St. Louis University, Ph.D., 1974. *Politics:* Democrat. *Religion:* Roman Catholic.

CAREER: St. John's Seminary, San Antonio, Tex., member of faculty, 1967; Pan American University, Edinburg, Tex., assistant professor of history, 1970-71 and 1973-81; National Park Service, San Antonio Missions National Historical Park, park historian, beginning 1981. Visiting professor, University of Texas at San Antonio, summer, 1978. Consultant to school districts in Texas, 1971-78.

MEMBER: American Studies Association, Southwestern Council of Latin American Studies, Texas State Historical Association, Texas Association of College Teachers, Society of Texas Social Science Teachers (director, 1979-80), Texas Catholic Historical Society, Texas Association of Chicanos in Higher Education, Phi Alpha Theta.

AWARDS, HONORS: Bishop Steven A. Leven Award, Archdiocese of San Antonio, Texas, 1964; O'Connor Presidio La Bahia Award, Sons of Republic of Texas, 1970 and 1975; faculty research grant, Pan American University; Fulbright grant to Colombia, 1979.

WRITINGS:

Our Lady Queen of the Americas: A Religious Drama on the Historical Events of Guadalupe, Artes Gráficas (San Antonio, Tex.), 1956.
(Compiler with Jane Mitchell Talbot) *A General Bibliography for Research in Mexican-American Studies: The Decade of the Sixties to the Present,* Pan American University, 1972.
(Compiler with Talbot) *A Comprehensive Chicano Bibliography, 1960-1972,* foreword by Edward Simmen, Jenkins Publishing, 1973.
(With Martha Oppert Cruz) *A Century of Service: The History of the Catholic Church in the Lower Rio Grande Valley,* United Printers and Publishers (Harlingen, Tex.), 1979.
(With James A. Irby) *Texas Bibliography,* Eakin Publications, 1982.
San Antonio Missions National Historical Park: A Commitment to Research, Lebco Graphics, 1983.
(Editor) *Proceedings of the 1984 and 1985 San Antonio Missions Research Conferences,* Lebco Graphics, 1986.
Let There Be Towns: Spanish Municipal Origins in the American Southwest, 1610-1810, Texas A & M University Press, 1988.

Contributor of reviews and articles to periodicals.

* * *

CRUZ, Gilberto Rafael
   See CRUZ, Gilbert R(alph)

* * *

CRUZ, Nicomedes Santa
   See SANTA CRUZ (GAMARRA), Nicomedes

* * *

CRUZ, Víctor Hernández 1949-

PERSONAL: Born February 6, 1949, in Aguas Buenas, P.R.; son of Severo and Rosa Cruz; children: Ajani. *Education:* Attended high school in New York, N.Y.

ADDRESSES: P.O. Box 40148, San Francisco, Calif. 94140.

CAREER: Poet. Guest lecturer at University of California, Berkeley, 1969; San Francisco State University, San Francisco, Calif., instructor, beginning 1973.

AWARDS, HONORS: Creative Artists public service award, 1974, for *Tropicalization.*

WRITINGS:

Papa Got His Gun!, and Other Poems, Calle Once Publications, 1966.
Doing Poetry, Other Ways, 1968.
Snaps (poems), Random House, 1969.

(Editor with Herbert Kohl) *Stuff: A Collection of Poems, Visions, and Imaginative Happenings from Young Writers in Schools—Open and Closed,* Collins & World, 1970.
Mainland (poems), Random House, 1973.
Tropicalization (poems and prose), Reed, Canon, 1976.
The Low Writings, Lee/Lucas Press, 1980.
By Lingual Wholes, Momo's, 1982.
Rhythm, Content and Flavor: New and Selected Poems, Arte Público, 1989.

Work has been included in anthologies, including *An Anthology of Afro-American Writing,* Morrow, 1968, and *Giant Talk: An Anthology of Third World Writings,* Random House, 1975. Contributor to *Evergreen Review, New York Review of Books, Ramparts, Down Here,* and *Revista del Instituto de Estudios Puertorriqueños.* Former editor, *Umbra.*

WORK IN PROGRESS: A novel, for Random House.

SIDELIGHTS: Víctor Hernández Cruz wrote: "My family life was full of music, guitars and conga drums, maracas and songs. My mother sang songs. Even when it was five below zero in New York she sang warm tropical ballads." He continued: "My work is on the border of a new language, because I create out of a consciousness steeped in two of the important world languages, Spanish and English. A piece written totally in English could have a Spanish spirit. Another strong concern in my work is the difference between a tropical village, such as Aguas Buenas, Puerto Rico, where I was born, and an immensity such as New York City, where I was raised. I compare smells and sounds, I explore the differences, I write from the center of a culture which is not on its native soil, a culture in flight, living half the time on memories, becoming something totally new and unique, while at the same time it helps to shape and inform the new environment. I write about the city with an agonizing memory of a lush tropical silence. This contrast between landscape and language creates an intensity in my work."

In a *New York Times Book Review* of *By Lingual Wholes,* Richard Elman remarks: "Cruz writes poems about his native Puerto Rico and elsewhere which often speak to us with a forked tongue, sometimes in a highly literate Spanglish. . . . He's a funny, hard-edged poet, declining always into mother wit and pathos: 'So you see, all life is a holy hole. Bet hard on that.'" And Nancy Sullivan reflects in *Poetry* magazine: "Cruz allows the staccato crackle of English half-learned, so characteristic of his people, to enrich the poems through its touching dictional inadequacy. If poetry is arching toward the condition of silence as John Cage and Susan Sontag suggest, perhaps this mode of inarticulateness is a bend on the curve. . . . I think that Cruz is writing necessary poems in a period when many poems seem unnecessary."

BIOGRAPHICAL/CRITICAL SOURCES:

PERIODICALS

New York Times Book Review, September 18, 1983.
Poetry, May, 1970.

* * *

CRUZ MONCLOVA, Lidio 1899-

PERSONAL: Born July 13, 1899, in Río Piedras, P.R.

ADDRESSES: c/o University of Puerto Rico Press, Box 23322, UPR Station, Río Piedras, P.R. 00931-3322.

CAREER: Educator, lawyer, historian, and writer. University of Puerto Rico, Río Piedras, professor of Puerto Rican history,

1923-25, lecturer on Puerto Rican history and literature, beginning 1933; practiced law, 1924-33.

MEMBER: Puerto Rico Historical Society, Puerto Rico Cultural Society, Puerto Rican Young Radical Society, Puerto Rico Atheneum, José Gautier Benítez Literary Society (president, 1917), Aurora Society (president, 1919).

AWARDS, HONORS: Prize from Puerto Rico Atheneum, 1922, for *Folklore de Puerto Rico;* Atheneum Prize for journalism, 1945; various prizes for literature, 1952, 1959, and 1964.

WRITINGS:

Historia de Puerto Rico: Siglo XIX, 6 volumes, University of Puerto Rico Press, 1952, 2nd edition, 1970.
Historia del año de 1887, University of Puerto Rico Press, 1958, 3rd edition, 1970.
Luis Muñoz Rivera: Diez años de su vida política, Instituto de Cultura Puertorriqueña, 1959.
Noticia acerca del pensamiento político de Puerto Rico, 1808-1952 (bound with *Noticia y pulso del movimiento político puertorriqueño* by Antonio J. Colorado), Editorial Orión, 1955.
(Editor and author of introduction) Luis Muñoz Rivera, *Obras completas,* 4 volumes, Instituto de Cultura Puertorriqueña, 1960.
(With Reece B. Bothwell) *Los documentos. . . , "¿Que Dicen?,"* University of Puerto Rico Press, 1960, 2nd edition, 1974.
Baldorioty de Castro: Su vida, sus ideas, Instituto de Cultura Puertorriqueña, 1966.
El grito de lares, Instituto de Cultura Puertorriqueña, 1968.
(With Arturo Morales Carrión) *La abolición de la esclavitud,* Asociación Pro Democracia Española, 1974.
El libro y nuestra cultura literaria, Colegio Universitario del Sagrado Corazón, 1974.

Also author of *Folklore de Puerto Rico.*

* * *

CUADRA, Pablo Antonio 1912-

PERSONAL: Born in 1912 in Managua, Nicaragua; son of a cattle rancher; married Adilla Bendana in 1935; children: five. *Education:* Received B.A.; studied law.

ADDRESSES: Office—Asociación "Libro Libre," Apartado Postal 1154-1250, Escazú, Costa Rica.

CAREER: Worked variously as cattle rancher, farmer, and sawmill operator; taught poetry at universities in United States and South America until 1950; *La Prensa* (newspaper), Managua, Nicaragua, co-editor, 1954-78, editor, 1978—. Instructor in Central American poetry at University of Texas at Austin.

AWARDS, HONORS: Rubén Darío Prize for Central American verse, 1959, for *El jaguar y la luna.*

WRITINGS:

POETRY

Poemas nicaragüenses, 1930-1933 (title means "Nicaraguan Poems"), Nascimento (Santiago, Chile), 1934.
Canto temporal, poema (title means "Temporal Song"), Cuaderno del Taller San Lucas (Granada, Nicaragua), 1943.
El jaguar y la luna (also see below; title means "The Jaguar and the Moon"), [Managua, Nicaragua], 1959, published in dual-language edition, English translation by Thomas Merton, Unicorn Press, 1974.
Poesía: Selección 1929-1962, Cultura (Madrid, Spain), 1964.

Poesía escogida, Universidad Nacional Autónoma de Nicaragua (León), 1968.

Cantos de Cifar y del mar dulce (also see below; title means "Songs of Cifar and the Sweet Sea"), Institución Gran Duque de Alba, Diputación Provincial (Avila, Spain), 1971, 3rd edition, enlarged, Academia Nicaragüense (Managua), 1979.

Doña Andreita y otros retratos, Poesía de Venezuela (Caracas), 1971.

Tierra que habla: Antología de cantos nicaragüenses (title means "Talking Land"), Editorial Universitaria (San José, Costa Rica), 1974.

Introduzione alla terra promessa: Antologia poetica (in Spanish and Italian), edited by Franco Cerutti, Edizioni Accademia (Milan, Italy), 1976.

Esos rostros que asoman en la multitud, Ediciones El Pez y la Serpiente (Managua), 1976.

Songs of Cifar and the Sweet Sea: Selections from the "Songs of Cifar," 1967-1977 (in Spanish and English), translation by Grace Schulman and Ann McCarthy de Zavala, Columbia University Press, 1979.

Siete árboles contra el atardecer (title means "Seven Trees Against the Dusk"), preface by Guillermo Yepes Boscán, Ediciones de la Presidencia de la República (Caracas), 1980.

Canciones de pájaro y señora; y, Poemas nicaragüenses, Libro Libre (San José, Costa Rica), 1983.

Cuaderno del sur; Canto temporal; Libro de horas, Libro Libre, 1984.

Poemas con un crepúsculo a cuestas; Epigramas; El jaguar y la luna, Libro Libre, 1984.

La ronda del año: Poemas para un calendario, Libro Libre, 1988.

The Birth of the Sun: Selected Poems, 1935-1985, translation by Steven F. White, Unicorn Press, 1988.

Also author of *Poemas con un crepúsculo a cuestas* (title means "Poems Bearing a Twilight"), 1949. Poems represented in anthologies, including *Poets of Nicaragua: A Bilingual Anthology, 1918-1979,* edited and translated by Steven F. White, Unicorn Press, 1982.

NONFICTION

Hacia la cruz del sur (essays), Comisión Argentina de Publicaciones e Intercambio (Buenos Aires), 1938.

Promisión de México, y otros ensayos (essays), Jus (Mexico), 1945.

Torres de Dios: Ensayos sobre poetas (essays), Academia Nicaragüense, 1958.

(Contributor) Mariano Fiallos Gil, *Panorama universitario mundial: Crónicas y comentarios de la Tercera Conferencia Mundial de Universidades celebrada en la Ciudad Universitaria de México,* Ediciones de la Universidad (León), 1961.

Otro rapto de Europa: Notas de un viaje (essays), Ediciones El Pez y La Serpiente, 1976.

Torres de Dios: Ensayos literarios y memorias del movimiento de vanguardia (essays), Ediciones El Pez y La Serpiente/Prensa Literaria, 1986.

Aventura literaria del mestizaje y otros ensayos (essays), Libro Libre, 1988.

OTHER

Breviario imperial, Cultura española (Madrid), 1940.

Entre la cruz y la espada, Instituto de Estudios Políticos (Madrid), 1946.

Elegías, [Madrid], 1957.

(Editor) *Los cuentos de Tío Coyote y Tío Conejo, cuentos de camino: Estudio preliminar de Pablo Antonio Cuadra,* Academia Nicaragüense, 1957.

Por los caminos van los campesinos (play), [Managua], 1958, reprinted, Ediciones El Pez y La Serpiente, 1982.

(Compiler, with Eduardo Zepeda Henríquez) Rubén Darío, *Antología poética,* Hospicio (León), 1966.

Escrito a máquina (title means "Typewritten"), Volume 1: *El nicaragüense,* Union (Managua), 1967, revised and enlarged edition, Distribuidora Cultural Nicaragüense (Managua), 1968.

Agosto: Cuento, Editorial & Distribuidora Cultural Centroamericana (Managua), 1969.

(Editor and author of introduction) Ernesto Cardenal, *Antología,* Lohlé (Buenos Aires), 1971.

(Editor) *Tío Coyote y Tío Conejo: Tradición oral nicaragüense,* illustrations by Ana María Dueñas, Editorial Universitaria, 1976.

(With Francisco Pérez Estrada) *Muestrario del folklore nicaragüense,* Banco de América, 1978.

Obras completas de Pablo Antonio Cuadra: Obras en prosa, four volumes, Libro Libre, 1986-88.

Author of *La tierra prometida* (title means "The Promised Land"), 1952, and *Libro de horas* (title means "The Book of Hours"), 1956. Editor of *Vanguardia,* 1930-32, *Cuadernos del Taller San Lucas,* 1943-51, and *El Pez y La Serpiente,* 1961—.

SIDELIGHTS: Pablo Antonio Cuadra is considered a leading poet of the Nicaraguan *vanguardia,* a literary movement born in the early 1930s that sought to renew and affirm that country's literature and to merge with the international literary vanguard. Cuadra's collection *Poemas nicaragüenses: 1930-1933,* highlighting the speech, customs, and objects of ordinary Nicaraguan life, was the movement's first poetic publication. His subsequent books, some written during his self-imposed exile in Mexico, Spain, and the United States, further celebrate the land and people of Nicaragua and, according to critics, transcend them through Cuadra's use of a wide poetic tradition that includes non-Latin writers such as Walt Whitman and Ezra Pound. Cuadra also became prominent in Nicaraguan journalism, editing reviews such as *Vanguardia,* beginning in the 1930s, and joining Pedro Joaquin Chamorro as co-editor of *La Prensa,* deemed Nicaragua's most important newspaper, in 1954. Upon Chamorro's assassination in 1978 Cuadra became sole editor of the paper, but he remains best known as one of Nicaragua's greatest poets.

BIOGRAPHICAL/CRITICAL SOURCES:

BOOKS

Balladares, José Emilio, *Pablo Antonio Cuadra: La palabra y el tiempo,* Libro Libre, 1986.

*   *   *

CUZA MALE, Belkis 1942-

PERSONAL: Born in 1942 in Guantánamo, Oriente, Cuba; came to United States; married Herberto Padilla (a writer), 1968; children: Ernesto; stepchildren: Giselle, María, Carlitos. *Education:* University of Havana, licentiate degree, 1967.

ADDRESSES: Home—103 Cuyler Rd., Princeton, N.J. 08540.

CAREER: Journalist, editor, biographer, and poet. Journalist for the newspaper *Granma,* 1966-68; editor of the literary publication of the Artists and Writers Guild of Cuba, *La Gaceta de*

Cuba, 1968-79; co-founder of *Linden Lane Magazine,* 1982, editor, 1982—.

AWARDS, HONORS: Honorable mentions in the Casa de las Américas literary competition, 1962, for *El viento en la pared,* and 1963, for *Tiempos de sol.*

WRITINGS:

El viento en la pared (poetry), Universidad de Oriente (Santiago, Cuba), 1962.
Tiempos de sol (poetry), El Puente (Havana, Cuba), 1963.
Cartas a Ana Frank (poetry), Unión Nacional de Escritores y Artistas de Cuba (Havana, Cuba), 1963.
(Editor) Mario Sobrino Martínez, *Cuatro Leguas a La Habana,* Unión de Escritores y Artistas de Cuba, 1978.
El clavel y la rosa (biography), Cultura Hispánica and Instituto de Cooperación Iberoamericana, 1984.

Woman on the Front Lines (selections from *Juego de damas* and *El patio de mi casa;* dual text in English and Spanish), English translation by Pamela Carmell, Unicorn Press, 1987.

Also author of *Los alucinados,* 1963, *Juego de damas,* and *El patio de mi casa.* Work represented in anthologies, including poems in English translation in *Open to the Sun,* edited by Nora Jacquez Wieser, 1979. Contributor to Cuban and American journals.

SIDELIGHTS: Belkis Cuza Malé is a Cuban-born poet who lives in the United States. Cuza Malé's poems often take the form of imaginative dialogues and letters between the poet and such figures as British novelist Virginia Woolf and Holocaust victim and diarist Anne Frank. With her husband, Herberto Padilla, a respected Cuban author once jailed for criticizing the Cuban government in his writings, Cuza Malé also edits *Linden Lane Magazine,* a journal the couple founded to publish works of Cuban-American writers.

D

DAMOCLES
See BENEDETTI, Mario

* * *

DARIO, Rubén 1867-1916

PERSONAL: Name originally Felíx Rubén García y Sarmiento; born January 18, 1867, in Metapa, Nicaragua; died February 6, 1916, in León, Nicaragua; married Rafaela Contrera, 1890 (died, 1892); married Francisca Sánchez; children: two sons (one from each marriage). *Education:* Attended a Jesuit school.

CAREER: Writer and poet. Began work as a journalist for newspapers in Santiago and Valparaíso, Chile, and Buenos Aires, Argentina, c. 1881. Became correspondent for *La Nación,* Buenos Aires, and other Latin American papers in Latin America; Paris, France; and Madrid, Spain. Founder, with Gilberto Freyre, of *Revista de América,* 1896. Also served in various diplomatic and representative posts for Colombia and Nicaragua.

WRITINGS:

Primeras notas (title means "First Notes"), Tipografía Nacional, 1888.

Azul (poetry and short prose; title means "Blue"), [Chile], 1888, reprinted, Espasa-Calpe (Madrid), 1984 (also see below).

Los raros (literary biography and critical essays; title means "The Rare Ones"), 1893, reprinted, Universidad Autónoma Metropolitana (Mexico), 1985 (also see below).

Prosas profanas (title means "Profane Prose"), 1896, reprinted, introduction and notes by Ignacio M. Zuleta, Castalia (Madrid), 1983 (also see below).

Castelar, B. R. Serra (Madrid), 1899.

España contemporánea (title means "Contemporary Spain"), Garnier (Paris), 1901, reprinted, Lumen, 1987 (also see below).

Cantos de vida y esperanza, Los cisnes, y otros poemas (title means "Songs of Life and Hope, The Swans, and Other Poems"), [Madrid], 1905, reprinted, Nacional (Mexico), 1957 (also see below).

El canto errante (poetry; title means "The Wandering Song"), M. Perez Villavicencio (Madrid), 1907, reprinted, Espasa-Calpe, 1965 (also see below).

El viaje a Nicaragua; e, Intermezzo tropical (travel writings), Biblioteca "Ateneo" (Madrid), 1909, reprinted, Ministerio de Cultura, 1982 (also see below).

Poema del otoño y otros poemas (title means "Poem of Autumn and Other Poems"), Biblioteca "Ateneo," 1910, Espasa-Calpe, 1973 (also see below).

Muy antiguo y muy moderno (poetry; title means "Very Old and Very Modern"), Biblioteca Corona (Madrid), 1915.

El mundo de los sueños: Prosas póstumas (title means "The World of Dreams: Posthumous Prose"), Librería de la Viuda de Pueyo (Madrid), 1917.

Sol del domingo (title means "Sunday Sun"), Sucesores de Hernando (Madrid), 1917.

Alfonso XIII y sus primeras notas (addresses, essays, lectures and biographical text; title means "Alfonso the Thirteenth and His Principal Notes"), R. Darío Sánchez (Madrid), 1921.

Baladas y canciones (title means "Ballads and Songs"), prologue by Andrés González-Blanco, Biblioteca Rubén Darío Hijo (Madrid), 1923.

Sonetos (title means "Sonnets"), Biblioteca Rubén Darío (Madrid), 1929.

En busca del alba (poetry; title means "In Search of Dawn"), Arístides Quillet (Buenos Aires), 1941.

Brumas y luces (poetry; title means "Fogs and Lights"), Ediciones Argentinas "S.I.A.," 1943.

Wakonda: Poemas, Guillermo Kraft (Buenos Aires), 1944.

"El ruiseñor azul": Poemas inéditos y poemas olvidados (title means "The Blue Nightingale: Unpublished and Forgotten Poems"), prologue by Alberto Ghiraldo, Talleres Gráficos Casa Nacional del Niño, c. 1945.

Quince poesías (title means "Fifteen Poems"), illustrated by Mallol Suazo, Argos (Barcelona), 1946.

Cerebros y corazones (biographical sketches; title means "Minds and Hearts"), Nova (Buenos Aires), 1948.

La amargura de la Patagonia (novella; title means "The Grief of Patagonia"), Nova (Buenos Aires), 1950.

El manto de Ñangasasú (novella; title means "The Cloak of Ñangasasú"), S.A.C.D.I.C., 1958.

El sapo de oro (novella; title means "The Golden Toad"), G. Kraft (Buenos Aires), 1962.

Also author of *Epístolas y poemas* (title means "Epistles and Poems"), 1885; *Abrojos* (poetry; title means "Thorns"), 1887; *Canto épico a las glorias de Chile* (poetry; title means "Epic Song to the Glories of Chile"), 1887; *Emelina* (novel), with Eduardo Poirier, 1887; *Las rosas andinas: Rimas y contra-rimas* (title means "Andean Roses: Rhymes and Counter-Rhymes"), with Rubén Rubí, 1888; *Rimas* (title means "Poems"), 1888; *Pere-*

grinaciones (travel writings; title means "Journeys"), 1901 (also see below); *Oda a Mitre* (poetry; title means "Ode to Mitre"), 1906 (also see below); *Canto a la Argentina y otros poemas* (title means "Song to Argentina and Other Poems"), c. 1910 (also see below); *Historia de mis libros* (title means "The Story of My Books"), 1912; *Caras y caretas* (title means "Faces and Masks"), 1912; *Vida de Rubén Darío, escrita por él mismo* (title means "The Life of Rubén Darío, Written By Himself"), 1916; *Edelmira* (fiction), edited by Francisco Contreras, c. 1926; and *El hombre de oro* (title means "The Golden Man"), Zig-Zag.

Fiction and verse also published in numerous anthologies and collections.

IN ENGLISH

Eleven Poems, introduction by Pedro Henríquez Ureña, translation by Thomas Walsh and Salomón de la Selva, Putnam, 1916, revised edition published as *Eleven Poems of Rubén Darío: Bilingual Edition,* Gordon, 1977.

Selected Poems of Rubén Darío, introduction by Octavio Paz, translated by Lysander Kemp, University of Texas Press, 1965, reprinted, 1988.

COLLECTIONS

Obras completas (title means "Complete Works"), twenty-two volumes, edited by author's son, Rubén Darío Sánchez, illustrations by Enrique Ochoa, Mundo Latino (Madrid), Volume 1: *La caravana pasa* (poetry; title means "The Caravan Passes"), prologue by Ghiraldo, 1917; Volume 2: *Prosas profanas,* 1917; Volume 3: *Tierras solares* (travel writings; title means "Lands of the Sun"), 1917; Volume 4: *Azul,* 1917; Volume 5: *Parisiana,* 1917; Volume 6: *Los raros,* 1918; Volume 7: *Cantos de vida y esperanza, Los cisnes, y otros poemas,* 1920; Volume 8: *Letras* (addresses, essays, lectures), 1918; Volume 9: *Canto a la Argentina, Oda a Mitre, y otros poemas,* 1918; Volume 10: *Opiniones,* 1918; Volume 11: *Poema del otoño y otros poemas,* 1918; Volume 12: *Peregrinaciones,* 1918; Volume 13: *Prosas políticas: Las repúblicas americanas* (title means "Political Prose: The American Republics"), 1918; Volume 14: *Cuentos y crónicas* (title means "Stories and Chronicles"), 1918; Volume 15: *Autobiografía,* 1918; Volume 16: *El canto errante,* 1918; Volume 17: *El viaje a Nicaragua, e historia de mis libros* (title means "The Trip to Nicaragua and the Story of My Books"), 1919; Volume 18: *Todo al vuelo* (title means "All On the Fly"), 1919; Volume 19: *España contemporánea,* 1919; Volume 20: *Prosa dispersa* (title means "Random Prose"), 1919; Volume 21: *Lira póstuma* (title means "Posthumous Verse"), 1919; Volume 22: *Cabezas: Pensadores y artistas, políticos* (biographical essays; title means "Heads: Thinkers, Artists, Politicians"), 1919.

Obras poéticas completas (title means "Complete Poetic Works"), twenty-one volumes, edited by Ghiraldo and González-Blanco, [Madrid], 1923-29, new edition edited by A. Méndez Plancarte, [Madrid], 1952.

Cuentos completos (title means "Complete Stories"), edited with notes by Ernesto Mejía Sánchez, preliminary study by Raimundo Lida, Fondo de Cultura Económica (Mexico), 1950, reprinted, 1983.

Poesías completas (title means "Complete Poems"), two volumes, edited by Alfonso Méndez Plancarte, 1952, revised edition edited by Antonio Oliver Belmás, 1967.

Several volumes of Darío's *Obras completas* were reissued separately during the 1980s. Works collected in other volumes, including *Obra poética* (title means "Poetic Works"), four vol-

umes, 1914-1916; *Textos socio-políticos,* [Managua], 1980; *Poesías escogidas,* 1982; and *Cuentos fantásticos,* Alianza (Madrid), 1982.

SIDELIGHTS: Nicaraguan writer Rubén Darío ranks among the most esteemed and enduring figures in South American literature. A journalist, critic, poet and author of short stories, he is credited with both founding and leading the *modernista* literary movement, which ended a period of creative latency among Spanish-language writers. Darío is probably best remembered for his innovative poetry, noted for its blending of experimental rhymes and meters with elements of French and Italian culture, classical literature, and mythology.

A bright and inquisitive child, Darío displayed a propensity for poetry while he was still quite young. His aunt, who raised him after the separation of his parents, nurtured his literary aspirations, and his early interest in journalism led to his association with members of the European and South American intelligentsia. By the turn of the twentieth century, Darío had taken his place among the literary and cultural elite and, as a foreign correspondent and diplomat, had become a symbol of a new bohemianism in Latin America. Stephen Kinzer, writing in the *New York Times,* summarized the author's career as that of a "vagabond poet who . . . influence[d] Latin American and Spanish literature forever and dazzle[d] Europe as no provincial ever had."

Though generally dismissed by critics as an uninspired and predictable contribution to the romance genre, *Emelina*—one of Darío's earliest writings and his only novel—offers a glimpse at the artistry that the poet would perfect in his 1888 volume *Azul* ("Blue"), a work that revolutionized Spanish letters. The poetry and short prose in *Azul* marks a deliberate break with the conventions of Romanticism, a bold experimentation with line and meter construction, and an introduction to Darío's celebration of literature as an *alcázar interior* ("tower of ivory"), a dreamlike shelter dedicated to pure art. Another collection, *Prosas profanas* ("Profane Prose"), first published in 1896, is a masterful, melodic display of the poet's fascination with Symbolism. The 1905 volume *Cantos de vida y esperanza* ("Songs of Life and Hope"), however, reveals a change in Darío's orientation as an artist—a move away from the idealistic "ivory tower" toward the global concerns of political and humanistic unity and nationalism among Hispanics. In *Studies in Spanish-American Literature,* Isaac Goldberg asserted: "*Cantos de vida y esperanza* is the keystone of Darío's poetical arch. It most exemplifies the man that wrote it; it most reveals his dual nature, his inner sincerity, his complete psychology; it is the artist at maturity."

Darío remains largely unknown among English-speaking readers, mainly because of the difficulty in translating his poetry while preserving the unique rhythms and linguistic nuances that the works possess in their original form. However, two volumes of the author's poems are available in English, and several critics have noted that the universality of Darío's themes precludes the problem of accessibility. Commenting on Darío's widespread appeal, Goldberg rated the poet among "the consecrated few who belong to no nation because they belong to all." And S. Griswold Morley, writing in *Dial,* concluded: "What cannot be denied is that Darío, single-handed, initiated a movement in Spain that affects today nearly every branch of literary art; that he renovated the technique of both poetry and prose; that he made his own many diverse styles; and that his verse is often so inevitable as to touch the finality of art."

BIOGRAPHICAL/CRITICAL SOURCES:

BOOKS

Darío, Rubén, *Eleven Poems of Rubén Darío,* introduction by Pedro Henríquez Ureña, translated by Thomas Walsh and Salomón de la Selva, Putnam, 1916.

Darío, Rubén, *Selected Poems of Rubén Darío,* introduction by Octavio Paz, translated by Lysander Kemp, University of Texas Press, 1965.

Ellis, Keith, *Critical Approaches to Rubén Darío,* University of Toronto Press, 1974.

Fiore, Dolores Ackel, *Rubén Darío in Search of Inspiration: Greco-Roman Mythology in His Stories and Poetry,* Las Américas Publishing Co., 1963.

Fitzmaurice-Kelly, James, *Some Masters of Spanish Verse,* Oxford University Press, 1924.

Goldberg, Isaac, *Studies in Spanish-American Literature,* Brentano's, 1920.

Peers, E. Allison, *A Critical Anthology of Spanish Verse,* University of California Press, 1949.

Twentieth-Century Literary Criticism, Volume 4, Gale, 1981.

Watland, Charles D., *Poet-Errant: A Biography of Rubén Darío,* Philosophical Library, 1965.

PERIODICALS

Dial, June 14, 1917.
Hispania, March, 1919, May, 1966.
Latin American Literary Review, spring, 1973.
New York Times, January 18, 1987.
Poetry, July, 1916.

*   *   *

DAVILA, Virgilio   1869-1943

PERSONAL: Born January 28, 1869, in Toa Baja, Puerto Rico; died August 22, 1943, in Bayamón, Puerto Rico; children: José Antonio.

CAREER: Writer. Worked as schoolteacher, agriculturalist, and politician.

WRITINGS:

Patria (verse), Boletín Mercantil, 1903, reprinted with prologue by M. González García, Cordillera, 1969.

Viviendo y Amando (verse), 1912, reprinted with prologue by Romualdo Real, Cordillera, 1963.

Aromas del terruño (verse), 1916, reprinted, Cordillera, 1963.

Pueblito de antes (verse), 1917, reprinted with critical notes by Cesáres Rosa-Nievas, Cordillera, 1967.

Un libro para mis nietos, 1923, reprinted, Cordillera, 1963.

Obras completas, Instituto de Cultura Puertorriqueña, 1964, translation published as *Complete Works of Virgilio Dávila,* Gordon Press, 1979.

Pipo, poemas infántiles (verse), Cordillera, 1968.

Contributor to periodicals, including *Almanaque Aguinaldo de la Isla de Puerto Rico* and *El Carnaval.*

SIDELIGHTS: Virgilio Dávila is known for his modernist poems about life in Puerto Rico.

*   *   *

DAVIS, B. Lynch
See BIOY CASARES, Adolfo and BORGES, Jorge Luis

De LEON, Nephtalí   1945-

PERSONAL: Born May 9, 1945, in Laredo, Tex.; son of Francisco De León Cordero (a migrant worker) and María Guadalupe De León-González (a migrant worker); children: Aidé. *Education:* Attended Texas Technological University, Our Lady of the Lake University of San Antonio, Instituto de Alianza Francesa, and University of Mexico City.

ADDRESSES: Home—1411 Betty Dr., San Antonio, Tex. 78224.

CAREER: La Voz de los Llanos (bilingual weekly journal; title means "The Voice of the Plains"), Lubbock, Tex., editor, 1968-73; free-lance poet, writer, painter, and sculptor, c. 1973—. President of Le Cercle Francais; director of Teatro Chicano del Barrio; vice-chairperson of American Civil Liberties Union, and Ciudadanos Pro Justicia Social. Has given poetry readings on television. *Military service:* U.S. Army.

MEMBER: Hispanic Writers Guild, Revolución Artística y Acción Social, Royal Chicano Air Force (affiliate), Congreso de Artistas Cósmicos de Aztlán (affiliate).

AWARDS, HONORS: Ford fellowship, 1975; award from Canto al Pueblo Commission, 1976; award from National Hispanic Writers Guild, 1977; first place award from Le Cercle Francais.

WRITINGS:

(And illustrator) *Chicanos: Our Background and Our Pride* (essays), Trucha Publications, 1972.

Five Plays (contains "The Death of Ernesto Nerios," "¡Chicanos! The Living and the Dead," "Play Number Nine," "The Judging of Man," and "The Flies"), Totinem Publications, 1972 (also see below).

(And illustrator) *Chicano Poet: With Images and Visions of the Poet* (poetry; includes "Coca Cola Dream" [also see below]), Trucha Publications, 1973.

"The Flies" (play), first produced in El Paso, Tex., at University of Texas at El Paso, 1973.

(And illustrator) *I Will Catch the Sun* (for children; first produced in San Antonio, Tex., at Our Lady of the Lake University's Thiry Auditorium, 1979), Trucha Publications, 1973.

(And illustrator) *Coca Cola Dream* (poetry), Trucha Publications, 1973, 2nd edition, 1976.

I Color My Garden (for children), Tri-County Housing (Shallowater, Tex.), 1973.

"¡Chicanos! The Living and the Dead" (play), first produced in Hagerman, N.M., 1974.

"Play Number Nine," first produced in Boulder, Colo., at University of Colorado, 1976.

"El tesoro de Pancho Villa" (play), first produced in Lubbock, Tex., 1977.

"La muerte de Ernesto Nerios" (play; also titled "The Death of Ernesto Nerios"), first produced in San Antonio, Tex., at San Pedro Playhouse, 1978.

Tequila Mockingbird; or, The Ghost of Unemployment (play), Trucha Publications, 1979.

(With Carlos González and Alfredo Alemán) *El Segundo de Febrero* (historical play for children), Centro Cultural Aztlán, 1983.

Guadalupe Blues (poetry), privately printed, 1985.

Sparky y su Gang (for children), Nosotros, 1985.

Artemia: La Loca del River Walk: An Allegory of the Arts in San Antonio, Educators' Roundtable, 1986.

El pollito amarillo: Baby Chick Yellow, Educators' Roundtable, 1987.

Also author of *Hey, Mr. President Man: On the Eve of the Bicentennial,* Trucha Publications, 1975, *Poems by Nephtalí,* 1977, and *Getting It Together,* 1980. Contributor to anthologies, including *We Are Chicanos: An Anthology of Mexican-American Literature,* edited by Philip D. Ortego, Washington Square Press, 1973; *Floricanto,* edited by Mary Ann Pacheco, University of California, Los Angeles, 1974; *Floricanto II,* University of Texas, Austin, 1975; and *El Quetzal Emplumece,* edited by Carmela Montalvo and others, Mexican-American Cultural Center (San Antonio, Tex.), 1976. Contributor of articles and poems to periodicals, including *Texas Observer, Reverberations, American Dawn, La Luz, Noticias, New Blood, Grito del Sol, New Morning, El Regional, El Sol of Houston, La Voz de Texas, Floricanto, Caracol, El Tecolote, La Guardia, Tiempo,* and *Canto al Pueblo.*

SIDELIGHTS: Nephtalí De León is a Chicano writer of poems, plays, essays, and children's stories. A sculptor and painter, he has also illustrated many of his books. Although these diverse artistic activities keep him busy, De León nonetheless considers himself a Chicano activist first. His passion for justice and equality for his people formed during childhood when as a migrant worker in Texas he witnessed the cruel treatment of illegal aliens by American border patrolmen. As an adult activist, De León has primarily focused his efforts on improving the quality of education for young Chicanos by writing books for them and by working with school systems in the Southwest. In addition, De León has supported Chicanos by helping establish Trucha Publications, a small press founded in 1970 by barrio residents of Lubbock, Texas, for the purpose of supporting emerging Chicano writers. Trucha published many of De León's early books, most of which center on the author's interest in promoting equal opportunity for Chicanos. "De León writes mainly to express the dreams, desires, and aspirations of the Chicano people," wrote Jean S. Chittenden in *Dictionary of Literary Biography.* "His motivation in writing is to give an honest and truthful representation of the plight of the Chicano, which he sees as the result of a historical process."

Whether based on historical events or his own musings, De León's writings advocate Chicano liberation from all forms of repression. His play "¡Chicanos! The Living and the Dead," for instance, involves Chicano protestors rallying against the abuses of Americans and their system of government; "Play Number Nine" compares the mythological Prometheus, who is seeking physical freedom, with the Chicanos seeking cultural freedom through improved education; and "The Flies" equates downtrodden Chicanos with squashed flies. De León's call for liberation continues in his poetry, where his imaginative works typically promote a world of peace and happiness beyond the life of injustice and discrimination Chicanos often experience in America. One of his more notable poems, "Coca Cola Dream," attacks American materialism for preventing humans from achieving Christian kindness and a full understanding of each other. De León made his own contribution to a better understanding between cultures by publishing many of his works in bilingual and bicultural editions, including the children's book *I Color My Garden,* which is used in many schools.

BIOGRAPHICAL/CRITICAL SOURCES:

BOOKS

Dictionary of Literary Biography, Volume 82: *Chicano Writers, First Series,* Gale, 1989.

DELGADO, Abelardo B(arrientos) 1931-

PERSONAL: Born November 27, 1931, in La Boquilla de Conchos, Chihuahua, Mexico; immigrated to United States, 1943; naturalized citizen, 1954; son of Vicente Delgado (a rancher and cattleman) and Guadalupe Barrientos; married Dolores Estrada, October 11, 1953; children: Ana, Alicia, Arturo, Alfredo, Angela, Amelia, Abbie, Andie. *Education:* University of Texas at El Paso, B.S., 1962; graduate study at University of Texas at El Paso, 1972, and at University of Utah, Salt Lake City, 1974-77.

ADDRESSES: Home—6538 Eaton St., Arvada, Colo. 80003. *Office*—Bueno Center for Multicultural Education, School of Education, Campus Box 249, University of Colorado, Boulder, Colo. 80309-0249; and Aims Community College, South Campus, 260 College Ave., Fort Lupton, Colo. 80621

CAREER: Held various positions in construction and restaurant work, 1950-55; Our Lady's Youth Center, El Paso, Tex., special activities and employment director, 1955-64; Colorado Migrant Council, Denver, executive director, 1969-71; University of Texas at El Paso, Special Services Program, executive director and faculty member, 1971-72; Northwest Chicano Health Task Force, Seattle, Wash., executive director, 1973-74; University of Utah, Salt Lake City, instructor, 1974-77; Colorado Migrant Council, Farmerworker Data Network, Wheat Ridge, Colo., project director, 1977-81; Colorado Migrant Council, Henderson, Colo., special services/parent involvement coordinator, 1981-84, executive director, 1985; House of Neighborly Services, Inc., Brighton, Colo., adult basic education director, 1986-88; Aims Community College, South Campus, Fort Lupton, Colo., instructor, 1986—; St. Thomas Seminary, Denver, instructor, 1986—; Denver Metro State College, Denver, instructor, 1986—; University of Colorado, Bueno Center for Multicultural Education, Boulder, instructor and curriculum specialist, 1986—. Consultant to Interstate Research Associates, Washington, D.C., 1973, and Adrienne Hynes Associates, Denver, 1988—. Former area education director of New Mexico's statewide migrant program. Has given numerous poetry readings. Founder and president of Barrio Publications, 1970—.

AWARDS, HONORS: Tonatiuh Prize for literature, 1978, for *Letters to Louise;* Mayor's Award for Literature, Denver, Colo., 1988; first prize for poetry from *El Paseño* (newspaper), El Paso, Tex., 1988.

WRITINGS:

Chicano: Twenty-five Pieces of a Chicano Mind (poetry), Barrio (Denver), 1969.
The Chicano Movement: Some Not Too Objective Observations (essays), Colorado Migrant Council (Denver), 1971.
(Editor with Ricardo Sánchez and contributor) *Los cuatro: Abelardo Delgado, Reymundo "Tigre" Pérez, Ricardo Sánchez, Juan Valdez (Magdaleno Avila)—Poemas y reflecciones de cuatro chicanos* (poetry), Barrio, 1971.
Mortal Sin Kit (chapbook), Idaho Migrant Council, 1973.
Bajo el sol de Aztlán: Veinticinco soles de Abelardo (title means "Under the Sun of Aztlán: Twenty-five Suns of Abelardo"; poetry), Barrio, 1973.
It's Cold: Fifty-two Cold-Thought Poems of Abelardo, Barrio (Salt Lake City), 1974.
A Thermos Bottle Full of Self-Pity: Twenty-five Bottles of Abelardo (poetry), Barrio (Arvada, Colo.), c. 1975.
Reflexiones: Sixteen Reflections of Abelardo (poetry and short stories), Barrio (Salt Lake City), 1976.

Here Lies Lalo: Twenty-five Deaths of Abelardo (poetry), Barrio (Salt Lake City), 1977, revised edition, Barrio (Arvada), 1979.

Under the Skirt of Lady Justice: Forty-three Skirts of Abelardo (poetry), Barrio (Denver), 1978.

Siete de Abelardo, Barrio (Arvada), 1979.

Totoncaxihuitl, a Laxative: Twenty-five Laxatives of Abelardo (poetry and fiction), Barrio (Arvada), 1981.

Letters to Louise (novel), Tonatiuh-Quinto Sol International, 1982.

Unos perros con metralla (Some Dogs with a Machine-gun): Twenty-five Dogs of Abelardo (poetry), Barrio, 1982.

Also author of *A Quilt of Words: Twenty-five Quilts of Abelardo,* c. 1976, *Reflexiones. . . .* (poetry), *Seven Abelardos,* and of plays. Contributor to numerous anthologies, including *Canto al Pueblo: Antología,* Arizona Canto al Pueblo IV, Comité Editorial, 1980, and *Chicanos: Antología histórica y literaria,* Fondo de Cultura Económica, 1980. Contributor to periodicals. Founder and editor of *La Onda Campesina* (newsletter) and *Farmworker Journal,* both Denver; editor-at-large, *La Luz* (magazine), Denver.

SIDELIGHTS: Although the author of several of Chicano literature's most popular poems, including "Stupid America," "La Causa," and "The Organizer," Abelardo B. Delgado's books are not widely known or reviewed largely due to nearly all of them being published on a small-scale by the author's own Barrio Publications. Undaunted by a lack of approval from mainstream publishers, Delgado (known to his friends as "Lalo") has established his reputation on the strength of numerous personal appearances throughout the United States. While his dramatic poetry readings help to increase Delgado's popularity, they also enable him to spread his message of social justice for Mexican-Americans and other minority groups.

The desire to promote social reform has been a major theme in Delgado's poetry since 1969 when his first collection, *Chicano: Twenty-five Pieces of a Chicano Mind,* appeared during the height of the Chicano Movement. In this work Delgado explores the many concepts that define Mexican-American culture, such as *chicanismo, carnalismo* (brotherhood), and machismo, while examining the impact on Chicano society of the migrant, the undocumented worker, and living in the barrio. Writing about the collection in a *Dictionary of Literary Biography* essay, Donaldo W. Urioste claims, "Delgado is at his best when he advocates social justice, human dignity, and equality for Chicanos, and when he angrily condemns those forces—be they social or cultural, Anglo or Chicano—that work against these ideals." Urioste quotes from Delgado's "Stupid America" as an example of the poet's socially motivated work. The poem begins: "stupid america, see that chicano / with a big knife / on his steady hand / he doesn't want to knife you / he wants to sit on a bench / and carve Christfigures . . . ."

One of the many difficulties associated with the Chicano culture about which Delgado writes is the use of Spanish in a nation where the majority speak only English. Delgado himself writes in a combination of Spanish and English typical of many Mexican-American authors. In an interview with Juan David Bruce-Novoa appearing in *Chicano Authors: Inquiry by Interview,* Delgado calls bilingualism a "trademark" of Chicano expression. "Chicano literature's main characteristic," the poet observes, "is that it is a literature that is naturally at ease in the way that Chicanos express themselves, and that is a natural bilingualism, with the influence of English naturally predominant, as that is the language in which all Chicanos are educated. . . . To write using

natural bilingual style is a very vivid affirmation that we are here, that we are alive and well, thinking and writing in both idiomas [languages]."

Delgado's papers are part of the Nettie Lee Benson Collection in the Latin American Collection of the University of Texas at Austin.

BIOGRAPHICAL/CRITICAL SOURCES:

BOOKS

Bruce-Novoa, Juan David, *Chicano Authors: Inquiry by Interview,* University of Texas Press, 1980.
Dictionary of Literary Biography, Volume 82: *Chicano Writers, First Series,* Gale, 1989.

*   *   *

DELIBES, Miguel
See DELIBES SETIEN, Miguel

*   *   *

DELIBES SETIEN, Miguel   1920-
(Miguel Delibes)

PERSONAL: Born October 17, 1920, in Valladolid, Spain; son of Adolfo (a professor) and María (Setien) Delibes; married Angeles de Castro Ruiz, April 23, 1946 (died November, 1974); children: Miguel, Angeles, Germán, Elisa, Juan, Adolfo, Camino. *Education:* Hermanos Doctrina Cristiana, Bachillerato; Universidad de Valladolid, Doctor en Derecho (law), 1944; attended Escuela Altos Estudios Mercantiles, and Escuela Periodismo. *Religion:* Roman Catholic.

ADDRESSES: Home—Dos de Mayo 10, Valladolid, Spain. *Agent*—Ediciones Destino, Consejo de Ciento 425, Barcelona 9, Spain.

CAREER: Novelist and writer. Teacher of mercantile law, University de Valladolid, Valladolid, Spain. Director, El Norte de Castilla, Valladolid. Visiting professor, University of Maryland, 1964. *Military service:* Spanish Navy, 1938-39.

MEMBER: Real Academia Española, Hispanic Society.

AWARDS, HONORS: Nadal Prize, 1947, for *La sombra del ciprés es alargada;* Ministry of Information Cervantes Prize (Spanish national prize for literature), 1955, for *Diario de un cazador;* Critics Prize (Spain), 1963; Asturias Prize, 1982.

WRITINGS:

UNDER NAME MIGUEL DELIBES; NOVELS, EXCEPT AS INDICATED

La sombra del ciprés es alagarda (also see below; title means "The Cypress's Shadow is Long"), Ediciones Destino, 1948, reprinted, 1979.
Aún es de día, Ediciones Destino, 1949, 2nd edition, 1962, reprinted, 1982.
El camino (also see below; title means "The Road"), Ediciones Destino, 1950, reprinted, 1984, self-illustrated edition, Holt, 1960, translation by Brita Haycraft published as *The Path,* John Day, 1961.
Mi idolatrado hijo Sisí (also see below), Ediciones Destino, 1953, reprinted, 1980.
El loco (novella; also see below), Editorial Tecnos, 1953.
La partida (fiction; includes "La Partida," "El refugio," "Una peseta para el tranvía," "El manguero," "El campeonato,"

"El traslado," "El primer pitillo," "La contradicción," "En una noche así," and "La conferencia"), L. de Caralt, 1954, 2nd edition, Alianza Editorial, 1969, reprinted, 1982.

Diario de un cazador, Ediciones Destino, 1955, reprinted, 1980.

Siestas con viento sur (novellas; includes "La mortaja," "El loco," "Los nogales," and "Los railes"), Ediciones Destino, 1957, 2nd edition, 1967.

Diario de un emigrante, Ediciones Destino, 1958, reprinted, 1977.

La hoja roja, Ediciones Destino, 1959, 3rd edition, 1975.

Las ratas, Ediciones Destino, 1962, 7th edition, 1971, Harrap, 1969.

Obra completa (includes "Prólogo," "La sombra de ciprés es alargada," "El camino," and "Mi idolatrado hijo Sisí"), Part 1, Ediciones Destino, 1964.

Cinco horas con Mario, Ediciones Destino, 1966, 9th edition, 1975, translation by Frances M. López-Morillas published as *Five Hours with Mario,* Columbia University Press, 1989.

La Mortaja (novellas; also see above; includes "La mortaja," "El amor propio de Juanito Osuna," "El patio de vecindad," "El sol," "La fé," "El conejo," "La perra," and "Navidad sin ambiente"), Alianza Editorial, 1969, 2nd edition, 1974.

Parábola del náufrago, Ediciones Destino, 1969, 3rd edition, 1971, translation by López-Morillas published as *The Hedge,* Columbia University Press, 1983.

Mi mundo y el mundo: Selección antológica de obras del autor, *para niños de 11 a 14 años,* Miñon, 1970.

Smoke on the Ground, translation by Alfred Johnson, Doubleday, 1972.

El príncipe destronado, Ediciones Destino, 1973, reprinted, 1982.

Las guerras de nuestros antepasados, Ediciones Destino, 1974, 5th edition, 1979.

El disputado voto del señor Cayo, Ediciones Destino, 1978.

Los santos inocentes, Planeta, 1981.

Tres pájaros de cuenta, Miñon, 1982.

Cartas de amor de un sexagenario voluptuoso, Ediciones Destino, 1983.

El tesoro, Ediciones Destino, 1985.

377A, madera de héroe, Ediciones Destino, 1987.

NONFICTION

Un novelista descubre América, Editora Nacional, 1956.

La barbería, Portada de Coll, O. P. Ediciones, 1957.

Castilla, Editorial Lumen, 1960, published as *Viejas historias de Castilla la Vieja,* Ediciones Destino, 1964, 3rd edition, 1974, Alianza Editorial, 1982.

Por esos mundos: Sudamérica con escala en las Canarias, Ediciones Destino, 1971, 2nd edition, 1972.

La caza de la perdiz roja, Editorial Lumen, 1963, 2nd edition, 1975.

Europa: Parada y fonda, Ediciones Cid, 1963, reprinted, Plaza & Janés, 1981.

El libro de la caza menor, Ediciones Destino, 1964, 3rd edition, 1973.

USA y yo, Ediciones Destino, 1966, Odyssey, 1970.

Vivir al día (also see below), Ediciones Destino, 1968, 2nd edition, 1975.

(Contributor) Susanne Filkau, editor, *Historias de la guerra civil,* Edition Langewiesche-Brandt, 1968.

La primavera de Praga, Alianza Editorial, 1968.

Con la escopeta al hombro (also see below), Ediciones Destino, 1970, 2nd edition, 1971.

Un año de mi vida (also see below), Ediciones Destino, 1972.

La caza en España, Alianza Editorial, 1972.

Castilla en mi obra, Editorial Magistero Español, 1972.

S.O.S.: El sentido del progreso desde mi obra, Ediciones Destino, 1975.

Aventuras, venturas, y desventuras de un cazador a rabo, Ediciones Destino, 1976.

Mis amigas las truchas, Ediciones Destino, 1977.

Castilla, lo castellano y los castellanos, Editorial Planeta, 1979.

Las perdices del domingo, 2nd edition, Ediciones Destino, 1981.

Dos viajes en automóvil: Suecia y Paises Bajos, Plaza & Janés, 1982.

El otro fútbol, Ediciones Destino, 1982.

La censura de prensa en los años 40, y otros ensayos, Ambito, 1985.

Castilla habla, Ediciones Destino, 1986.

OTHER

César Alonso de los Ríos, *Conversaciones con Delibes,* Emesa (Madrid), 1971.

Javier Goñi, *Cinco horas con Miguel Delibes,* Anjana, 1985.

Also author of another volume of *Obra completa,* which includes "Vivir al día," "Con la escopeta al hombro," and "Un año de mi vida," for Ediciones Destino. Author of television plays *Tierras de Valladolid,* 1966, *La mortaja,* and *Castilla, esta es mi tierra,* 1983.

SIDELIGHTS: Miguel Delibes Setien is considered one of Spain's most important novelists; his work is distinguished by its stark realism, rural subject matter, and well-developed characters. Ronald Schwartz explains in *Spain's New Wave Novelists: 1950-1974,* "Delibes has been always considered a major novelist whose career is constantly developing, growing in quantity and quality, and becoming more prestigious because of his consistent use of Realism and his attachment to rural themes, which display a variety of character types. . . . Critics acknowledge his skepticism, pessimism, reactionary vision of nature, his love for the man of instinct, of nature in contrast to a 'civilized' product, in short, his negative view of progress and 'civilization,' his black humor and cold intellectualism."

A recurrent theme in fiction by Delibes is the message that technological and social changes brought about during the twentieth century have resulted in the alienation and repression of the individual. As they find their places in the world of business, many of his characters feel isolated. This is perhaps best seen in *The Hedge,* a novel in which a sensitive clerk degenerates into a fearful person who will do almost anything—even resort to violence—to maintain his sense of material security. At first, "Jacinto is scared of losing his job, of having children and having to raise them to be either victims or executioners in a pitiless society," Toby Talbot relates in the *New York Times Book Review.* Sent by an authoritarian official to be rehabilitated after questioning the difference between zero and the letter "O" in the documents he transcribes, Jacinto notices that a thick hedge separates him from the rest of the world. The hedge depicts "the encroachment of an Orwellian state," Talbot explains, and Jacinto's degeneration shows that the end result of the encroachment is "the dehumanization of man, victimized by his own progress, specialization and conformity. And along with it comes the disintegration of thought and language," two activities eventually dominated and regulated by the state.

Five Hours with Mario, a novel regarded as a masterpiece by some critics, also shows the human fight for liberty and dignity against oppressive forces. The narrator Carmen's husband has just died and we listen as she critically reviews their life together. Reduced to poverty for daring to confront the repressive authorities, her husband had failed to improve her material standard of living. While berating him, she exhibits her own failure to live up to her stated ideals. Delibes thus criticizes many aspects of traditional and modern life in Spain. In addition, the novel "addresses lost words, last words and listening—important issues in a country that is now free to examine its conscience and its recent history," *New York Times Book Review* critic Arthur J. Sabatini comments.

The realism and themes of nature in Delibes Setien's work have been widely praised. Schwartz believes that the author demonstrates "an enormous capacity to capture within his writings the essence of nature by means of his starkly Realist style." In the *New York Times Book Review*, Martin Levin constrasts the "charming and nostalgic" view of nature rendered by "Anglo-Saxon novels" to the harsh atmosphere of *Smoke on the Ground*. "The land is wretchedly poor," he writes, "the climate is harsh, and the atmosphere has a haunting, 19th-century bleakness, although it is set in the age of moon missions." Schwartz believes that with the "harmonious" combination of "humor, tenderness, nature and tragedy" evident in Delibes Setien's later work, he is "reviving the theme of nature as a literary element indispensable to the human condition and portraying this harmony through his extremely personal style."

MEDIA ADAPTATIONS: Some of Delibes Setien's works have been adapted for Spanish television. Feature-length film adaptations of his work include "Retrato de familia," based on his novel *Mi idolatrado hijo Sisí*, filmed in 1975, "La guerra de papa," produced in 1978, and based on the novel *El príncipe destronada*, and "The Holy Innocents," directed by Mario Camus. *Cinco horas con Mario* has also been filmed.

BIOGRAPHICAL/CRITICAL SOURCES:

BOOKS

Alonso de los Ríos, César, *Conversaciones con Delibes,* Emesa (Madrid), 1971.
Contemporary Literary Criticism, Gale, Volume 8, 1978, Volume 18, 1981.
Díaz, Janet W., *Delibes,* Twayne, 1971.
Estudios sobre Delibes, Universidad Complutense, 1983.
Gullón, Agnes, *La novela experimental de Delibes,* Taurus, 1981.
Schwartz, Ronald, *Spain's New Wave Novelists: 1950-1974,* Scarecrow Press, 1976.
Umbral, Francisco, *Delibes,* Emesa, 1970.

PERIODICALS

Antioch Review, June, 1973.
Booklist, February 15, 1971.
Hispania, December 1971, December, 1972, March, 1974, May, 1974, May, 1976.
New York Times Book Review, August 20, 1972, December 11, 1983, January 22, 1989.
Times Literary Supplement, April 20, 1967, June 11, 1970.
World Literature Today, summer, 1977.

* * *

DENEVI, Marco 1922-

PERSONAL: Born May 12, 1922, in Sáenz Pena, Argentina; son of Valerio José and María Eugenia (Buschiazzo) Denevi. *Education:* Received bachelor's degree from Colegio Nacional de Buenos Aires, 1939; received law degree from University of Buenos Aires, 1956.

ADDRESSES: Home—657 Pastorini Sáenz Oena, Buenos Aires, Argentina.

CAREER: Dramatist and writer.

AWARDS, HONORS: Kraft award, 1955; National Theater Award (Argentina), 1958; *Life en Español* prize for the best Latin American short novel from *Life* magazine for *Ceremonia secreta,* and Martín Fierro Award, both 1960; Argentores Award, 1962.

WRITINGS:

Rosaura a las diez (novel), Kraft, 1955, translation by Donald A. Yates published as *Rosa at Ten O'Clock,* Holt, 1964.
Los expedientes (three-act play), Talía, 1957, revised version, 1978.
El emperador de la China (one-act play), Aguaviva, 1960 (also see below).
Ceremonia secreta y otros cuentos de América Latina premiados en el concurso literario de Life en español (novel), Doubleday, 1961 (also see below), translation by Harriet de Onís published as *Secret Ceremony,* Time, 1961, published as *Ceremonia secreta y otros cuentos,* edited by Donald A. Yates, Macmillan, 1965.
Falsificaciones (stories), Universitaria de Buenos Aires, 1966.
Un pequeño café, Calatayud Editor, 1966.
El emperador de la China y otros cuentos (stories), Librería Huemul, 1970.
Parque de diversiones (novel; title means "Amusement Park"), Emecé, 1970.
Los asesinos de los días de fiesta, Emecé, 1972.
Antología precoz, selected with prologue by Edmundo Concha, Universitaria, 1973.
Hierba del cielo (stories), Corregidor, 1973.
Salón de lectura (selected works), Librería Huemul, 1974.
Los locos y los cuerdos, Librería Huemul, 1975.
Reunión de desaparecidos, Macondo Ediciones, 1977.
Parque de diversiones II, Macondo Ediciones, 1979.
Obras completas (collected works), five volumes, Corregidor, 1980.
Araminta, o, el poder, el laurel, y siete extrañas desapariciones, CREA, 1982.
Robotobor, Abril, 1983.
Páginas de Marco Denevi, Celtia, 1983.
Manuel de historia, Corregidor, 1985.
Enciclopedia secreta de una familia argentina, Sudamericana, 1986.

Also author of the play "El cuarto de la noche," 1962.

SIDELIGHTS: Marco Denevi is an Argentine novelist, dramatist, and short-story writer best known for his detective novel *Rosaura a las diez*. A tale of a girl's death in a shabby hotel in Buenos Aires, the book is admired for its surprise ending; its English translation, *Rosa at Ten O'Clock,* was published in 1964.

BIOGRAPHICAL/CRITICAL SOURCES:

PERIODICALS

World Literature Today, winter, 1989.

* * *

DENIS, Julio
See CORTAZAR, Julio

* * *

DIAZ, Jorge 1930-

PERSONAL: Born in 1930 in Rosario, Argentina; naturalized Chilean citizen; immigrated to Spain, 1965.

CAREER: Playwright. Originally worked as an architect.

WRITINGS:

PLAYS

El cepillo de dientes; o, Náufragos en el parque de atracciones (also see below; two-act; first produced in Santiago, Chile, 1961), Center for Curriculum Development (Philadelphia), 1971.

"Un hombre llamado Isla," first produced in Santiago, 1961.

Réquiem por un girasol (also see below; first produced in Santiago, 1961), U.S. Ministry of Education, 1963.

"El velero en la botella" (also see below), first produced in Santiago, 1962.

El lugar donde mueren los mamíferos (two-act; first produced in Santiago, 1963), [Santiago], 1963.

"Variaciones para muertos de precusión," first produced in Santiago, 1964.

"El nudo ciego," first produced in Santiago, 1965.

La víspera de degüello (contains *El cepillo de dientes; o, Náufragos en el parque de atracciones, Réquiem por un girasol,* and one-act comedy *La víspera de degüello*), Taurus (Madrid), 1967.

Topografía de un desnudo: Esquema para una indagación inútil (two-act), Editora Santiago (Santiago), 1967.

(Contributor) *Teatro difícil* (play collection; contains *La pancarta*), Escelicer (Madrid), 1971.

El velero en la botella [and] *El cepillo de dientes; o, Náufragos en el parque de atracciones,* Universitaria (Santiago), 1973, 8th edition, 1983.

Os anxos cómense crús, music by Vittorio Cintolesi, Galaxia (Vigo, Spain), 1973.

Algo para contar en Navidad, Don Bosco (Barcelona), 1974.

El locutorio (also see below; bound with *El cerco de la peste* by José González Torices), [Valladolid, Mexico], 1976.

Mata a tu prójimo como a ti mismo (also see below), Cultura Hispánica (Madrid), 1977.

Teatro, ceremonias de la soledad (contains *El locutorio, Mata a tu prójimo como a ti mismo,* and *Ceremonia ortopédica*), foreword and biographical notes by Juan Andrés Piña, Nascimento (Santiago), 1978.

Las cicatrices de la memoria (finale, allegro ma non troppo), Cultura Hispánica, Instituto de Cooperación Iberoamericana (Madrid), 1986.

La otra orilla, Junta de Comunidades de Castilla-La Mancha (Spain), c. 1988.

Also author of play "La orgástula."

OTHER

(With Manuel Barrera and Gustavo Aranda) *El cambio en una empresa del APS,* Instituto de Economía y Planificación (Santiago), c. 1973.

Contributor to *Mapochos, Teatro,* and *Conjunto.*

SIDELIGHTS: An architect by training, Jorge Díaz became interested in the theater while working on set designs. His plays are now best known for their humor and witty dialogue, which are emphasized over characterization. The humor in his plays is often black and makes use of irony and satire to comment on politics and society.

*   *   *

DIAZ-ALEJANDRO, Carlos F(ederico)   1937-1985

PERSONAL: Born July 18, 1937, in Havana, Cuba; died of pneumonia, July 17, 1985, in New York, N.Y.; son of José Díaz.

Education: Miami University (Ohio), B.S., 1957; Massachusetts Institute of Technology, Ph.D., 1961.

CAREER: Yale University, New Haven, Conn., assistant professor, 1961-65, professor of economics, 1970-83; University of Minnesota—Minneapolis, associate professor of economics, 1965-70; Columbia University, New York, N.Y., professor of economics, 1983-85. Visiting professor at Pontificia Universitaria Catholica Rio de Janeiro, 1971; visiting scholar at Nuffield College, Oxford, 1975-76. Consultant to Organization of American States, 1962-63; consultant to Pan American Union's Interamerican Commission Alliance for Progress, 1965-66; member of Commission for International Development (Pearson Commission), 1968-69; adviser to United Nations Economic Commission for Latin America, 1976-79; member of Council on Foreign Relations, beginning in 1977; member of advisory board for American Economics Association's Economic Institute, 1977-80; appointed to president's Bipartisan Commission on Central America (Kissinger Commission), 1983; member of Rockefeller Foundation's Academic Panel Consultative Group for International Economic Monetary Affairs.

MEMBER: American Economics Association.

AWARDS, HONORS: Guggenheim fellowship, 1967-68.

WRITINGS:

Exchange-Rate Devaluation in a Semi-Industrialized Country: The Experience of Argentina, 1955-1961, MIT Press, 1966.

Essays on the Economic History of the Argentine Republic, Yale University Press, 1970.

(Contributor) G. K. Helleiner, editor, *A World Divided: The Less Developed Countries in the International Economy,* CUP, 1975.

Foreign Trade Regimes and Economic Development: Colombia, Columbia University Press, 1976.

(Editor with S. Teitel and V. E. Tokman) *Política económica en centro y periferia: Ensayos en homenaje a Felipe Pazos,* Fondo de Cultura Económica, 1976.

(Contributor) R. G. Hawkins, editor, *The Economic Effects of Multinational Corporations,* JAI Press, 1979.

(Contributor) R. Thorp, editor, *Latin America in the 1930s: The Role of the Periphery in World Crisis,* Macmillan, 1984.

International Trade, Investment, Macro Policies, and History, Elsevier Science, 1987.

Trade, Development, and the World Economy, Blackwell, 1988.

Contributor to professional journals, including *Journal of International Economics.* Co-editor of *Journal of Development Economics,* 1976-85.

BIOGRAPHICAL/CRITICAL SOURCES:

PERIODICALS

New York Times, September 6, 1983.

OBITUARIES:

PERIODICALS

Los Angeles Times, July 25, 1985.
New York Times, July 20, 1985.

*   *   *

DIAZ MIRON, Salvador   1858-1928

PERSONAL: Born in 1858 in Veracruz City, Mexico; died in 1928.

CAREER: Poet. Political journalist, 1874-76.

WRITINGS:

Poesías, [Xalapa, Mexico], 1886.

Lascas, Editorial-América, (Madrid), c. 1917, recent edition edited with introduction by Manuel Sol T., Universidad Veracruzana, 1987.

Salvador Díaz Mirón: Sus mejores poemas, introduction by R. Blanco-Fombona, Editorial-América, (Madrid), 1928.

Selección de poemas, Editorial Orientaciones, 1932.

Poesías completas, edited with introduction by Antonio Castro Leal, Porrúa, 1941.

Salvador Díaz Mirón, selection and notes by Roberto Blanco Moheno, Secretaría de Educación Pública, (Mexico), 1947.

Prosa, compiled and with introduction by Leonardo Pasquel, [Mexico], 1954.

Antología, Novaro-México, 1962.

Sus mejores poesías (anthology), El Libro Español, 1963.

Los cien mejores poemas, edited with introduction by Antonio Castro Leal, Aguilar (Mexico), 1969.

Antología, selected by Francisco Monterde, Fondo de Cultura Económica, 1979.

Poesías de Salvador Díaz Mirón, selected by Armando Rodríguez, Libro-Mex Editores, 1980.

La giganta y otros poemas, Fondo de Cultura Económica and Secretaría de Educación Pública Cultura, 1984.

Also author of political speeches and the unpublished *Astillas* and *Triunfos.*

SIDELIGHTS: Salvador Díaz Mirón was a Mexican poet who aspired to holding political office, but more than once his campaign ended with his incarceration for attempted murder.

BIOGRAPHICAL/CRITICAL SOURCES:

BOOKS

Méndez Plancarte, Alfonso, *Díaz Mirón, poeta y artífice,* Antigua Librería Robredo, (Mexico), 1954.

*   *   *

DIAZ PLAJA, Guillermo   1909-1984

PERSONAL: Surname appears in some sources as Díaz-Plaja; born in May 24, 1909, in Manresa, Barcelona, Spain; died of kidney cancer, July 27, 1984, in Barcelona, Spain; marrried Concepción Taboada, 1935; children: five children. *Education:* University of Madrid, Ph.D., 1931.

ADDRESSES: Home—Calle Fernando Agullo 8, Barcelona, Spain.

CAREER: Writer. Instructor of language and literature at University of Barcelona. Director of Instituto Nacional del Libro Español; director of Instituto del Teatro and Museo de Arte Escénico, both Barcelona. Councillor for national education. Director of *San Jorge* (magazine). Lecturer in Europe, the United States and Africa.

MEMBER: Real Academia Española, Spanish Society of Literary Critics (president), Real Academia de Buenas Letras (Barcelona), Consejo Superior de Investigaciones Científicas, Hispanic Society of America (honorary), American Association of Teachers of Spanish and Portuguese (honorary).

AWARDS, HONORS: Premio Nacional de Literatura, 1935, for *Introducción al estudio del romanticismo español;* Premi d'Assaig "Ciutat de Barcelona," 1961, for *Viatge a l'Atlantida i retorn a Itaca: Una interpretació de la cultura catalana;* Premio Internacional de Poesía; Premio Pedro Enríquez Ureña; Comendador de las Ordenes de Isabel la Católica y de Alfonso X, el Sabio; Gran Oficial de la Orden de Rubén Darío; Cavaliere della Ordine della Repubblica Italiana; Officer of the Order of Arts and Letters (France).

WRITINGS:

IN ENGLISH TRANSLATION

Historia de la literatura española a través de la crítica y de los textos, two volumes, La Espiga (Barcelona), 1942, translation by Hugh A. Harter published as *A History of Spanish Literature,* New York University Press, 1971.

IN CATALAN

L'avantguardisme a Catalunya i altres notes de crítica, La Revista (Barcelona), 1932.

De literatura catalana: Estudis i interpretacions, Selecta (Barcelona), 1956.

Papers d'identitat (limited edition), L'Espiga (Barcelona), 1959.

Viatge a l'Atlantida i retorn a Itaca: Una interpretació de la cultura catalana, Destino (Barcelona), 1962.

La defenestració de Xenius, Andorra, 1967.

(Editor and author of introduction) Juan Maragall, *Poemes* (bilingual French-Catalan edition), Ministere des Affairs Etrangeres (Madrid), 1968.

Les petites histories i altres proses seguides del llibre de poemes "Le claus," Táber (Barcelona), 1969.

Primers assaigs, primers viatges, 1929-1935, La Paraula Viva (Barcelona), 1974.

Sota la llum d'Ausias, L'Espiga, 1979.

IN SPANISH

Rubén Darío: La vida, la obra, notas críticas, Sociedad General de Publicaciones (Barcelona), 1930, reprinted, Editora Nacional (Mexico), 1957.

(Editor and author of prologue) *Visiones contemporáneas de España (textos descriptivos),* Librería Bosch, 1935.

Introducción al estudio del romanticismo español, Espasa-Calpe (Madrid), 1936, 3rd edition, 1967.

El arte de quedarse solo, y otros ensayos, Juventud (Barcelona), 1936.

(Editor and author of prologue) *Garcilaso y la poesía española (1536-1936),* Universidad de Barcelona, 1937.

La poesía lírica española, Labor (Barcelona), 1937, 2nd edition published as *Historia de la poesía lírica española,* 1948.

La ventana de papel (ensayos sobre el fenómeno literario), Apolo (Barcelona), 1939.

El espíritu del barroco: Tres interpretaciones, Apolo, 1940, reprinted, Crítica (Barcelona), 1983.

Teoría e historia de los géneros literarios, lengua española y literatura: Cuatro curso, La Espiga, 1940.

Primer cuaderno de sonetos, [Cádiz], 1941.

Historia del español: La evolución del lenguaje desde sus orígenes hasta hoy, La Espiga, 1941.

La poesía y el pensamiento de Ramón de Basterra, Juventud (Barcelona), 1941.

Hacia un concepto de la literatura española, Austral (Buenos Aires), 1942.

(Editor, author of prologue, and translator from Catalan) *Cuentistas catalanes contemporáneos,* Aguilar (Madrid), 1944, 2nd edition, 1959.

Esquema de historia del teatro, [Barcelona], 1944, Instituto del Teatro, 1964.

Ensayos escogidos, Aguilar, 1944.

(Editor and author of prologue) Pedro de Lorenzo, *La sal perdida,* Nacional (Madrid), 1947.

Nuevo asedio a Don Juan, Sudamericana (Barcelona), 1947.

Federico García Lorca: Estudio crítico, G. Kraft (Buenos Aires), 1948.

Vacación de estío (poetry), [Madrid], 1948.

Cartas de navegar: Pequeña geografía lírica, A. Aguado (Madrid), 1949.

(Editor) *Historia general de las literaturas hispánicas,* introduction by Ramón Menéndez Pidal, five volumes, Barna (Barcelona), 1949-58, volume 6: *Literatura contemporánea,* Vergara (Barcelona), 1968.

Modernismo frente a noventa y ocho: Una introducción a la literatura española del siglo XX, prologue by Gregorio Marañón, Espasa-Calpe, 1951, 2nd edition, 1966.

Poesía y realidad: Estudios y aproximaciones, Revista de Occidente (Madrid), 1952.

Don Quijote en el país de Martín Fierro, Cultura Hispánica (Madrid), 1952.

La voz iluminada: Notas sobre el teatro a través de un cuarto de siglo, Instituto del Teatro (Barcelona), 1952.

Defensa de la crítica y otras notas, Barna, 1953.

Vencedor de mi muerte: Poemas, Insula (Madrid), 1953.

Federico García Lorca: Su obra e influencia en la poesía española, Espasa-Calpe (Buenos Aires), 1954.

Historia de la literatura universal y española de acuerdo con los nuevos programas oficiales para el 5 [-6] curso de enseñanza media, two volumes, La Espiga, 1954.

Veinte glosas en memoria de Eugenio d'Ors, Sección de Prensa de la Diputación Provincial de Barcelona, 1955.

Los métodos literarios a través de la imagen y el ejemplo, Ciordia y Rodríguez (Buenos Aires), 1955, 2nd edition, 1960.

El estilo de San Ignacio y otras páginas, Noguer (Barcelona), 1956.

El reverso de la belleza, Barna, 1956.

Registro de horizontes: Poesía y meditación del viaje, Destino, 1956.

Martí desde España, Librería Selecta (Havana), 1956.

El poema en prosa en España: Estudio crítico y antología, G. Gili (Barcelona), 1956.

(Editor and author of prologue) *Antología mayor de la literatura española,* four volumes, Labor, 1958-61.

Juan Ramón Jiménez en su poesía, Aguilar, 1958.

Setenta comentarios de textos de literatura española, argentina, y americana: Fides, patria, amor, literae, Ciordia (Buenos Aires), 1958.

(Editor) *El Teatro: Enciclopedia del arte escénico,* Noguer (Barcelona), 1958.

(Editor and author of prologue) Gustavo Adolfo Bécquer, *Obras,* Vergara, 1962.

Cuestión de límites: Cuatro ejemplos de estéticas fronterizas, Revista de Occidente, 1963.

La literatura hispánica contemporánea a través de la crítica y de los textos, La Espiga, 1963.

El estudio de la literatura: Los métodos históricos, Sayma (Barcelona), 1963.

El viajero y su luz, Argos (Barcelona), 1963.

Las estéticas de Valle Inclán, Gredos, 1965.

El arco bajo las estrellas: Ruta lírica de Cataluña a Santiago, 2nd edition, Ediciones de San Jorge (Barcelona), 1965.

(Editor) *Lazarillo de Tormes. Vida del Buscón don Pablos,* Porrúa (Mexico), 1965.

La literatura universal, prologue by Angel Valbuena Prat, Danae (Barcelona), 1965.

Ensayos elegidos, Revista de Occidente, 1965.

Belén lírico, limited edition, Librería Anticuaria El Guadalhorce (Málaga), 1966.

La soledad caminante: Poemas del norte de América, limited edition, Librería Anticuaria El Guadalhorce, 1966.

Zoo (poetry), limited edition, Librería Anticuaria El Guadalhorce, 1966.

Memoria de una generación destruída, 1930-1936 (memoirs), prologue by Julián Marías, Delos-Aymá (Barcelona), 1966.

Trópicos: Geografías de Asia y América, Prometeo (Valencia), 1966.

Las lecciones amigas, EDHASA (Barcelona), 1967.

La letra y el instante: Anotaciones a la actualidad cultural, 1961-1963, Nacional, 1967.

Africa por la cintura: Etiopía, Kenia, Tanzania, Uganda: Notas a un safari fotográfico, Juventud (Barcelona), 1967.

(Editor and author of prologue) *Azorín y los libros,* Instituto Nacional del Libro Español, 1967.

Con variado rumbo: De la ruta de Mío Cid a la invención de Brasilia, Planeta, 1967.

(Editor and contributor) Rafael María Baralt, *Obras literarias publicadas e inéditas,* Atlas (Madrid), 1967.

La literna intermitente: Anotaciones a la actualidad cultural, Prensa Española, 1967.

Los monstruos y otras literaturas, Plaza y Janés, 1967.

Poesía junta, 1941-1966, Losada, 1967.

La creación literaria en España: Primera bienal de crítica, 1966-1967, Aguilar (Madrid), 1968.

(Editor and author of prologue) *De las jarchas a Juan del Encina: Tesoro breve de las letras hispánicas,* five volumes, Magisterio Español (Madrid), 1968.

Soliloquio y coloquio: Notas sobre lírica y teatro, Gredos, 1968.

Discursos para sordos, EMESA (Madrid), 1968.

Figuras y paisajes, Táber, 1969.

España en su literatura, Salvat (Madrid), 1969.

El oficio de escribir, Alianza (Madrid), 1969.

América vibra en mí (poetry), Cultura Hispánica (Madrid), 1969.

(Editor and contributor) Luciano Doddoli and Manlio Maradei, *Historia del mundo contemporáneo de Hiroshima al espacio,* Nauta (Barcelona), 1969.

El calendario inútil: Notas a la actualidad cultural, 1967-1968, EMESA, 1970.

Agenda para una política cultural, R. Grandío (Oviedo), 1970.

Los paraísos perdidos: La actitud "hippy" en la historia, Seix Barral (Barcelona), 1970.

Hispanoamérica en su literatura, Salvat, 1970.

(Editor and author of prologue) *Papeles inéditos y dispersos de Ramón de Basterra,* M.A.E. (Madrid), 1970.

El barroco literario, Columba, 1970.

Al filo del novecientos: Estudios de intercomunicación hispánica, Planeta (Barcelona), 1971.

(Editor and author of prologue) Ramón de Basterra, *Llama romance,* Diputación de Vizcaya (Bilbao), 1971.

Cien libros españoles: Poesía y novela, 1968-1970, Anaya (Salamanca), 1971.

La cultura como noticia: Política, tiempo, rostros, literatura, máscaras, formas, mapas—1969-1970, DOPESA (Barcelona), 1971.

España, un modo de ser, Teide (Barcelona), 1972.

Leo, luego existimos (contains articles previously published in *La Vanguardia*), Ediciones 29 (Barcelona), 1972.

Obras selectas, AHR (Barcelona), 1972.

(Editor and author of prologue) *Crónicas de Indias,* Salvat, 1972.

Culturalismo y creación poética, Revista de Occidente, 1972.

Las llaves, La Isla de los Ratones (Santander), 1972.

Poemas de Oceanía, Institución "Fray Bernardino de Sahagún" (León), 1972.

El intelectual y su libertad, Seminarios y Ediciones (Madrid), 1972.

Poesía en treinta años (1941-1971), Plaza y Janés, 1972.

Europeo en el exilio: Crónica del acontecer cultural, 1972, Picazo (Barcelona), 1973.

Consideración del libro: Crónicas de 1972 (Año Internacional del Libro de UNESCO), Nacional, 1973.

Los élites españolas, Cuadernos para el Diálogo (Madrid), 1973.

Poemas en el mar de Grecia, Delegación Nacional de Cultura (Salamanca), 1973.

Ensayos sobre literatura y arte, Aguilar, 1973.

Poemas y canciones del Brasil, Cultura Hispánica, 1974.

El libro ayer, hoy y mañana, Salvat, 1974.

El ocio atento, Narcea (Madrid), 1974.

Al pie de la poesía: Páginas críticas 1971-1973, Nacional, c. 1974.

En torno a Azorín: Obra selecta temática, Espasa-Calpe (Madrid), 1975.

Tratado de las melancolías españolas, Sala (Madrid), 1975.

Estructura y sentido del novecentismo español, Alianza (Madrid), 1975.

Vanguardismo y protesta en la España de hace medio siglo, J. Batlló (Barcelona), 1975.

Conciencia del otoño (also see below), Oriens (Madrid), 1975.

Mentalizar sobre la región: Una posibilidad llamada Cataluña, DOPESA (Barcelona), 1976.

Literatura española: Comentario de textos, La Espiga, 1976.

España en sus espejos, Plaza y Janés, 1977.

En torno a Cervantes, EUNSA (Pamplona), 1977.

Atlas lírico seguido de Conciencia del otoño, Plaza y Janés, 1978.

Las ínsulas extrañas: Viaje por las cinco partes del mundo, Plaza y Janés, 1978.

Literatura y contorno vital, Bello (Valencia), 1978.

Retrato de un escritor, Pomaire (Barcelona), 1978.

China en su laberinto, Plaza y Janés, 1979.

Sociología cultural del postfranquismo, Plaza y Janés, 1979.

Goya en sus cartas y otros escritos, Heraldo de Aragón (Zaragoza), 1980.

La contracultura y otras alarmas, Plaza y Janés, 1980.

El encanto de Europa, Plaza y Janés, 1981.

El combate por la luz, Espasa-Calpe, 1981.

Lo social en Eugenio d'Ors y otros estudios, Ediciones del Cotal (Barcelona), 1982.

El campo en la literatura española, Banco de Crédito Agrícola (Madrid), 1982.

Ensayos sobre comunicación cultural, Espasa-Calpe, 1984.

Entre la vida y los libros, Argos Vergara, 1984.

Mis viajes por Europa, Mundo Actual de Ediciones (Barcelona), 1984.

Foreign editor for *Modern Drama.* Regular contributor to *ABC* (Madrid) and *La Vanguardia* (Barcelona).

SIDELIGHTS: Guillermo Díaz Plaja was one of Spain's best-known literary historians as well as being an accomplished poet, essayist, and literary critic. Born in the Spanish province of Catalonia, Díaz Plaja wrote in Catalan, the language native to the region, as well as Spanish, publishing more that 150 books. An extremely versatile writer, he was known to Spanish school children as the editor or author of textbooks used for decades in Spanish literature classes, enjoyed by Spanish adults who read his lively contributions to two major Spanish newspapers, *ABC* and *La Vanguardia,* and respected by Hispanists world-wide for his important studies of nearly every aspect of Spanish literature.

OBITUARIES:

PERIODICALS

Chicago Tribune, August 1, 1984.
New York Times, July 30, 1984.
Washington Post, August 1, 1984.

* * *

DIAZ VALCARCEL, Emilio 1929-

PERSONAL: Born October 16, 1929, in Trujillo Alto, P.R. *Education:* Attended University of Puerto Rico, Río Piedras, beginning in 1954.

ADDRESSES: *Agent*—c/o Editorial Cultural, Apdo 21056, Río Piedras Station, P.R. 00928.

CAREER: Employed with Puerto Rico Division of Community Education, Publications Unit. *Military service:* Served with U.S. Army in Korea.

AWARDS, HONORS: Awards from Puerto Rico Atheneum, 1956, for "La última sombra," and 1958, for "Sol negro"; award from Institute of Puerto Rican Literature, 1958, for "El asedio"; finalist in Seix Barral contest, 1972, for *Figuraciones en el mes de marzo.*

WRITINGS:

"Una sola puerta hacia la muerte" (play), broadcast on WIPR-TV, 1957.

"El asedio," y otros cuentos (short stories), Arrecife (Mexico), 1958.

Proceso en diciembre (fiction; contains "Proceso en diciembre," "El soldado Damián Sánchez," "El asalto," "Andrés," "La sangre inútil," "La evasión," "El hijo," "Los héroes," and "El regreso"), Taurus (Madrid, Spain), 1963.

El hombre que trabajó el lunes (short stories; contains "El hombre que trabajó el lunes," "La culpa," "María," "El alcalde," and "Sol negro"), Era (Mexico), 1966.

Napalm, Zero (Madrid), 1970.

Panorama (narraciones 1955-1967), Editorial Cultural (Río Piedras, P.R.), 1971.

Figuraciones en el mes de marzo (novel), Seix Barral (Barcelona, Spain), 1972, translation by Nancy A. Sebastiani published as *Schemes in the Month of March,* Bilingual Press, 1979.

Inventario (novel), Editorial Cultural, 1975.

Harlem todos los días (novel), Huracán (San Juan, P.R.), 1978.

Mi mamá me ama, Seix Barral, 1981.

La visión del mundo en la novela: Tiempo de silencio, de Luis Martín-Santos, University of Puerto Rico Press, 1982.

Dicen que de noche tú no duermas, Editorial Cultural, 1985.

BIOGRAPHICAL/CRITICAL SOURCES:

PERIODICALS

Washington Post, December 6, 1979.

* * *

di BENEDETTO, Antonio 1922-

PERSONAL: Born in 1922 in Argentina.

CAREER: Editorial secretary for *Los Andes* (daily newspaper), Mendoza, Argentina; stringer for *La nación* (daily newspaper), Buenos Aires, Argentina.

AWARDS, HONORS: Twelve Latin American literary prizes.

WRITINGS:

Mundo animal (title means "Animal World"), 1953, Compañía General Fabril Editora (Buenos Aires, Argentina), 1971.

El pentágono: Novela en forma de cuentos (novel), Doble P. (Buenos Aires), 1955, published as *Annabella: Novela en forma de cuentos,* Orión (Buenos Aires), 1974.

Zama (novel), Doble P., 1956.

Grot: Cuentos claros (short stories), [Mendoza, Argentina], 1957.

Declinación y ángel (short stories), introduction by Luis Emilio Soto, Biblioteca Pública San Martín (Mendoza), 1958.

El cariño de los tontos (short stories), Goyanarte (Buenos Aires), 1961.

El silenciero (novel; title means "The Silencer"), Troquel (Buenos Aires), 1964.

Two Stories (in English and Spanish; contains "Abandonment and Passivity" and "Horse in the Saltflat"), Voces Edition (Mendoza), 1965.

Los suicidas (novel; title means "The Suicides"), Sudamericana (Buenos Aires), 1969.

Cuentos claros (short stories; contains "Enroscado," "Falta de vocación," "As," "El juicio de Dios," and "No"), Galerna (Buenos Aires), 1969.

El juicio de Dios: Antología de cuentos (short story anthology), edited by Alberto Cousté, Orión, 1975.

Caballo en el salitral (title means "Horse in the Saltflat"), Bruguera (Barcelona, Spain), 1981 (also see above).

SIDELIGHTS: Antonio di Benedetto, who has worked for Argentine newspapers, has won a number of literary awards for his experimental fiction. Regarded as an existentialist, he writes of nameless, isolated men, apparently ordinary except for their acute awareness of their insignificance in the world. Di Benedetto's use of stylistic experimentation in works such as the story "Abandonment and Passivity" and the novel *Zama* has suggested to some reviewers an affinity with the French "new novel" writers, and he has earned favorable comparisons to esteemed Argentine writers such as Julio Cortázar and Ernesto Sábato.

BIOGRAPHICAL/CRITICAL SOURCES:

BOOKS

Barufaldi, Rogelio, and others, editors, *Moyano, di Benedetto, Cortázar,* Colmegna (Rosario, Argentina), 1968.

Lorenz, Guenter W., *Die zeitgenoessiche Literatur in Lateinamerika,* Erdmann Verlag (Tuebingen, West Germany), 1971.

PERIODICALS

Davar, January-March, 1964.
Nueva crítica, Number 1, 1970.

*   *   *

DIEGO (CENDOYA), Gerardo   1896-1987

PERSONAL: Born October 3, 1896, in Santander, Spain; died July 8, 1987, in Madrid, Spain. *Education:* Studied with the Jesuits in Bilbao, Spain; attended University of Salamanca and University of Madrid; graduate in romance philology, 1916. *Politics:* Nationalist. *Religion:* Catholic.

CAREER: Anthologist, poet, and musicologist. Taught in Spain as a professor of literary criticism in Soria, Gijón, Santander, and Madrid. Lectured on music and performed piano recitals throughout Europe, Asia, and South America. Founder of literary magazines *Carmen* and *Lola.*

MEMBER: Academia Española.

AWARDS, HONORS: Literary contest prize, *La Revista General,* 1918; co-recipient, National Prize for Literature (Spain), 1925.

WRITINGS:

POEMS

El romancero de la novia (first edition published in 1920), new edition, Hispánica, 1944.

Soria, limited edition, [Valladolid, Spain], 1923, 2nd edition, illustrated by Pedro de Matheu, A. Zuñiga, 1948.

Viacruces, [Santander, Spain], 1931, 2nd edition, Agora, 1956.

Fábula de Equis y Zeda, Alcancía (Mexico City), 1932.

Poemas adrede, Alcancía, 1932, new edition, Hispánica, 1943.

Angeles de Compostela (also see below; first published in 1940), new edition, Gráficas Valera, 1961.

Gerardo Diego: Primera antología de sus versos (poetry collection), Espasa-Calpe, 1941, 6th edition, 1964.

La sorpresa, Instituto Antonio de Nebrija, 1944.

Poemas, edited and with a prologue by Manuel Altolaguirre, Secretaría de Educación Pública, 1948.

Hasta siempre: Geografía, canciones, epístoles y retratos dedicatorias y hojas de álbum, varia: 1925-1941, [Madrid], 1949.

La luna en el desierto y otros poemas, [Santander], 1949.

Limbo, El Arca, 1951.

Variación, illustrated by Enrique Núñez-Castelo, R. Millán, 1952.

Biografía incompleta, Ediciones Cultura Hispánica, 1953, 2nd edition, illustrated by Jose Caballero, 1967.

Amazona, Agora, 1955, 2nd edition, 1956.

Egloga de Antonio Bienvida, Taller de Artes Gráficas de los Hermanos Bedia, 1956.

Paisaje con figuras, Ediciones de los Papeles de son Armadans, 1956.

Amor solo, Espasa-Calpe, 1958.

Canciones a Violante, Ediciones Punta Europa, 1959.

Glosa a Villamediana, [Madrid], 1961.

La rama, La Isla de los Ratones, 1961.

Mi Santander, mi cuna, mi palabra, [Santander], 1961.

Sonetos a Violante, La Muestra, 1962.

La suerte o la muerte, [Madrid], 1963.

Nocturnos de Chopin, Bullón, 1963.

Lope y Ramón, Editora Nacional, 1964.

El Jándalo, [Madrid], 1964.

Poesía amorosa, Plaza & Janés, 1965.

"El Cordobés" dilucidado (also see below), 1966.

"El Cordobés" dilucidado y Vuelta del peregrino (also see below), Ediciones de la Revista Occidente, 1966.

Preludio, aria y coda a Gabriel Fauré, Taller de Artes Gráficas de G. Bedia, c. 1967.

Segunda antología de sus versos (1941-1967), Espasa-Calpe, 1967.

Antología poética, 1918-1969, Dirección General de Enseñanza Media y Profesional, 1969.

Antología (primer cuaderno: 1918-1940), Anaya, 1970.

La fundación del querer, La Isla de los Ratones, 1970.

Versos divinos, Fundación Conrado Blanco, 1970.

Versos escogidos, Gredos, 1970.

Clausura e volo (in Spanish and Italian), edited with an introduction by M. C. D'Arrigo-Bona, Guanda, 1970.

Poesía de creación, Seix Barral, 1974.

Angeles de Compostela y Vuelta del peregrino (also see below), studies, notes, and commentary by Arturo del Villar, Narcea, 1976.

Poemas menores, Alianza, 1980.

Also author of *Iniciales,* 1918, *Imagen,* 1922, *Manual de espumas,* 1924, 2nd edition, 1941, *Versos humanos,* 1925, *Romances,* 1941, *Alondra de verdad,* 1941, and *Vuelta del peregrino,* 1967.

OTHER

Antología poética en honor de Góngora desde Lope de Vega a Rubén Darío, Revista de Occidente, 1927.
(Editor) *Poesía española contemporánea, 1901-1934* (poetry anthology), Signo, 1932, 6th edition, Taurus, 1972.
(With Joaquín Rodrigo and Federica Sopeña) *Diez años de música en España: Musicología, intérpretes, compositores,* Espasa-Calpe, 1949.
La pintura de Eduardo Vicente, Biblioteca José María de Pereda, 1949.
(With Joaquín Calvo-Sotelo) *El tiempo y su mudanza en el teatro de Benavente,* [Madrid], 1955.
(Translator) *Tántalo: Versiones poéticas* (poetry collection), Agora, 1960.
(With Juan Antonio de Zunzunegui) *En torno de don Pío Baroja y su obra,* Diputación de Vixcaya, 1960.
Nuevo excorzo de Góngora, Publiciones de la Universidad Internacional Menéndez Pelayo, 1961.
El cerezo y la palmera: Retablo escénico en forma tríptico, Ediciones Alfil, 1964.
(Author of introduction) Federico García Lorca, *Casidas* (poems from Lorca's *El diván de Tamarit*), Ediciones de Arte y Bibliofilia, 1969.
(Editor) Concha Espina, *Edición antológica de Concha Espina,* Institución Cultural de Cantabria, Diputación Provincial, 1970.
(With Ignacio Aguilera and Francisco Bueno Arús) *Ramón Sánchez Díaz, 15 octubre, 1869-15 octubre, 1969,* Instituto de Literatura, 1970.
Cementerio civil, Plaza & Janés, 1972.
Manuel Machada, poeta (criticism), Nacional, 1974.
Un jándalo en Cádiz, Caja de Ahorros, c. 1974.
El poeta Manuel Machada: Conferencia pronunciada en la Fundación Universitaria Española con motivo del centenario del poeta el día 11 junio de 1974, Fundación Universitaria Española, 1975.
(Editor and author of introduction) León Felipe Camino Galicia, *Obra poética escogida,* Espasa-Calpe, 1975.
Dieciocho pintores españoles contemporáneos vistos por un poeta, Ibérico Europea de Ediciones, c. 1975.
(Editor and author of introduction) Lope de Vega, *Rimas,* Taurus, 1979.
Crítica y poesía (criticism), Ediciones Júcar, 1984.

Also author of *Menéndez Pelayo en la historia literaria,* 1956.

SIDELIGHTS: Primarily known as the editor of *Poesía española contemporánea, 1901-1934,* Gerardo Diego was "an anthologist of extraordinary authority and usefulness," according to his London *Times* obituary. Scholars generally regarded Diego's work as an anthologist to be his major contribution to literature, but he was also a productive poet, contributing to the revival of the sonnet and *décima,* a Spanish stanza form consisting of ten octosyllabic lines that was popular in the Baroque age. "As a technician" of poetic form, attests the *Times* writer, "Diego was second to none."

However, Diego is not considered to be a major Spanish poet because of his adherence to traditional styles. He was, nevertheless, involved in several of the poetic movements of his time. For example, along with Vicente Huidobro and Juan Larrea, Diego was one of the founders of the Spanish theory of *creacionismo.* This school emphasized the use of creative and free imagery without regard for realism. Diego's poetry was also influenced by *ultraísmo,* the Spanish school of poetry which combined cubism, futurism, expressionism, and other forms into an all-encompassing style, and neogongorism, an extremely complex style that employs obscure imagery, conceits, and neologisms. Diego's masterwork is considered to be *Versos humanos,* which won the National Prize for Literature in 1925, along with *Marinero en tierra* by Rafael Alberti. Subsequent collections by the poet, such as *La sorpresa* and *Biografía incompleta,* follow in the footsteps of *Versos humanos.* During his later period, Diego's poetry became increasingly religious and personal, and works like *Angeles de Compostela* employed a combination of his earlier styles.

OBITUARIES:

PERIODICALS

Times (London), July 10, 1987.

*   *   *

DOBLES, Fabián 1918-

PERSONAL: Born in 1918 in San Antonio de Belén, Costa Rica.

CAREER: Novelist, poet, and short-story writer.

AWARDS, HONORS: Premio Centroamericano, 1945, for poetry collection *Verdad del agua y del viento;* Premios Nacionales Aquileo J. Echeverría from Costa Rica Ministerio de Cultura, 1967; Premio Nacional de la Cultura Magón from Costa Rica Ministerio de Cultura, 1968.

WRITINGS:

Ese que llaman pueblo (novel), Letras Nacionales (San José, Costa Rica), 1942, 5th edition, Editorial Costa Rica (San José), 1982.
Aguas turbias (novel), Trejos Hermanos (San José), 1943, reprinted, Editorial Costa Rica, 1983.
Una burbuja en el limbo (novel), L'Atelier (San José), 1946, 4th edition, Editorial Costa Rica, 1978.
La rescoldera, L'Atelier, 1947.
El sitio de las abras (novel), originally published in 1950, 2nd edition, Editorial Costa Rica, 1970, 6th edition, 1976.
Historias de Tata Mundo (short stories), Trejos Hermanos, 1955, 2nd edition published under same title with *El maijú, y otras historias de Tata Mundo* (also see below), Editorial Costa Rica, 1966, 8th edition, 1979.
El maijú, y otras historias de Tata Mundo (short stories), Trejos Hermanos, 1957, published with *Historias de Tata Mundo* as *Historias de Tata Mundo,* 2nd edition, Editorial Costa Rica, 1966, 8th edition, 1979.
El violín y la chatarra (short stories), P. Presbere, 196-.
Los leños vivientes (novel), [San José], 1962, 2nd edition, Editorial Costa Rica, 1979.
(With Mario Picado) *Yerbamar* (poetry), Impr. Tormo (San José), 1965.
En el San Juan hay tiburón (novel), L'Atelier, 1967.
Cuentos de Fabián Dobles (short stories), Universitaria Centroamericana (San José), 1971.

Also author of poetry collection *Verdad del agua y del viento,* 1949, and novel *El targua,* 1960.

SIDELIGHTS: Fabián Dobles is an award-winning Costa Rican author whose novels, short stories, and poetry reflect his concern for social justice for the poor.

BIOGRAPHICAL/CRITICAL SOURCES:

BOOKS

Foster, David William, editor, *A Dictionary of Contemporary Latin American Authors,* Center for Latin American Studies, Arizona State University, 1975.

Ward, Philip, editor, *The Oxford Companion to Spanish Literature,* Clarendon Press, 1978.

* * *

DOMECQ, H(onorio) Bustos
See BIOY CASARES, Adolfo and BORGES, Jorge Luis

* * *

DONOSO (YAÑEZ), José 1924-

PERSONAL: Born October 5, 1924, in Santiago, Chile; son of José Donoso (a physician) and Alicia Yáñez; married María del Pilar Serrano (a translator), 1961. *Education:* Attended University of Chile, beginning in 1947; Princeton University, A.B., 1951.

ADDRESSES: Home—Santiago, Chile.

CAREER: Writer, journalist, and translator. Shepherd in southern Chile, 1945-46; dockhand in Buenos Aires, Argentina, c. 1946; Kent School, Santiago, Chile, English teacher, c. 1953; Catholic University of Chile, Santiago, professor of conversational English, beginning in 1954; worked in Buenos Aires, 1958-60; *Ercilla* (weekly newsmagazine), Santiago, journalist with assignments in Europe, beginning in 1960, editor and literary critic, beginning in 1962; University of Chile, Santiago, lecturer at school of journalism, beginning in 1962; *Siempre* (periodical), Mexico City, Mexico, literary critic, 1965; University of Iowa, Dubuque, teacher of writing and modern Spanish American literature at Writers' Workshop, 1965-67; Colorado State University, Fort Collins, teacher, 1969.

AWARDS, HONORS: Santiago Municipal Short Story Prize, 1955, for *Veraneo y otros cuentos;* Chile-Italia Prize for journalism, 1960; William Faulkner Foundation Prize, 1962, for *Coronación;* Guggenheim awards, 1968 and 1973; Critics Award for best novel in Spanish, 1979, for *Casa de campo.*

WRITINGS:

Veraneo y otros cuentos (title means "Summertime and Other Stories"), privately printed (Santiago, Chile), 1955.

Dos cuentos (title means "Two Stories"), Guardia Vieja, 1956.

Coronación (novel), Nascimento, 1957, Seix Barral, 1981, translation by Jocasta Goodwin published as *Coronation,* Knopf, 1965.

El charleston (short stories; title means "The Charleston"), Nascimento, 1960.

Los mejores cuentos de José Donoso (short stories; title means "The Best Stories of José Donoso"), Zig-Zag, 1965.

Este domingo (novel), Zig-Zag, 1965, translation by Lorraine O'Grady Freeman published as *This Sunday,* Knopf, 1967.

El lugar sin límites (novella; title means "The Place Without Limits"), J. Moritz (Mexico), 1966, translation by Suzanne Jill Levine and Hallie D. Taylor published as *Hell Has No Limits* in *Triple Cross,* Dutton, 1972.

(Editor with William A. Henkin and others) *The Tri-Quarterly Anthology of Contemporary Latin American Literature,* Dutton, 1969.

El obsceno párajo de la noche (novel), Seix Barral, 1970, translation by Hardie St. Martin and Leonard Mades published as *The Obscene Bird of Night,* Knopf, 1973.

Cuentos (title means "Stories"), Seix Barral, 1971, translation by Andrée Conrad published as *Charleston and Other Stories,* David Godine, 1977.

Historia personal del "boom" (memoir), Anagrama (Barcelona), 1972, translation by Gregory Kolovakos published as *The Boom in Spanish American Literature: A Personal History,* Columbia University Press, 1977.

Tres novelitas burguesas (title means "Three Bourgeois Novellas"), Seix Barral, 1973, translation by Andrée Conrad published as *Sacred Families: Three Novellas,* Knopf, 1977.

Casa de campo (novel), Seix Barral, 1978, translation by David Pritchard and Suzanne Jill Levine published as *A House in the Country,* Knopf, 1984.

El jardín de al lado (novel; title means "The Garden Next Door"), Seix Barral, 1981.

La misteriosa desparición de la Marquesita de Loria (novel; title means "The Mysterious Disappearance of the Young Marchioness of Loria"), Seix Barral, 1981.

Poemas de un novelista (poems), Ganymedes (Santiago), 1981.

Cuatro para Delfina (novellas; title means "Four for Delfina"), Seix Barral, 1982.

La desesperanza (novel; title means "Despair"), Seix Barral, 1986, translation by Alfred MacAdam published as *Curfew,* Weidenfeld & Nicolson, 1988.

(Contributor) Doris Meyer, editor, *Lives on the Line: The Testimony of Contemporary Latin American Authors,* University of California Press, 1988.

Translator into Spanish of numerous works, including *The Life of Sir Arthur Conan Doyle* by John Dickson Carr and *Last Tales* by Isak Dinesen, and, with wife, María del Pilar Serrano, of *The Scarlet Letter* by Nathaniel Hawthorne and *Les Personnages* by Françoise Malet-Joris. Contributor of articles and short stories to periodicals, including *Américas, mss.* (Princeton University), and *Review.*

WORK IN PROGRESS: A work set in the coal-mining community of Chile, excerpted in *Review,* January-June, 1988, under the title "The Fish in the Window."

SIDELIGHTS: "I fear simplification more than anything," said Chilean novelist José Donoso in *Partisan Review.* Donoso's novels, noted for their complexity and insistent pessimism, seem to embody his observation that life, society, and writing are each an "adventure into [a] mad, dark thing." Donoso has often been ranked among the finest Latin American authors of the twentieth century; he has been hailed as a master by Mexican novelist Carlos Fuentes and Spanish filmmaker Luis Buñuel, two of his most renowned contemporaries. "He is an extraordinarily sophisticated writer," wrote *Newsweek*'s Walter Clemons, "in perfect control of time dissolves, contradictory voices, gritty realism and hallucinatory fugues."

Observers suggest that Donoso's concern with the complexity of life is particularly appropriate to the situation in his homeland. Chile, which appeared to be a moderate, stable democracy for most of the twentieth century, erupted in violent political conflict in the 1970s. The country lurched abruptly from the Marxist government of Salvador Allende to the brutal conservative dictatorship of General Augusto Pinochet. From the time his first novels appeared in the 1950s, Donoso was praised for his sense of the strained relations between rich and poor that underlay Chilean society. The author is reluctant, however, to be viewed as a social commentator: he seems determined, in both his life and his work, to avoid the didacticism he has seen in politics. "Ideologies and cosmogonies are alien to me," he stated in *Lives on the Line*. "Their life is too short and they are too soon proved wrong, their place immediately taken by another explanation of the world." Accordingly, as Donoso observed in *Review*, "I'm not interested in the novels of ideas. . . . If I write a novel, it won't be to express an idea I saw in an essay."

Writers of the Chilean left, Donoso suggested, have repeatedly challenged his political standoffishness; sometimes, he observed in *Nation*, he has been "denounced . . . as decadent bourgeois." But Donoso's many admirers suggest that his pessimistic outlook, even his refusal to offer a solution to the problems that he surveys in his work, reflects an acute awareness of the breadth and depth of human suffering. As Z. Nelly Martínez explained in *Books Abroad:* "Beyond the social reality and its multiple stratification, Donoso probes into life's duality of good and evil, order and chaos, life and death, and examines man's inability to reconcile both sides of existence. Therein lies the tragedy; for, despite man's effort to build an illusion of order, life's anarchy eventually overcomes him." In much of the author's work, as Martínez observed, "madness, abdication to chaos, becomes the only alternative." Against such all-encompassing pain, Donoso seems to offer hope primarily in the form of intellectual understanding. "Kicking people in the shins gets you nowhere," he said in the *New York Times Book Review*. "Understanding gets you much farther."

Donoso was born into a family that kept a tenuous foothold in Chile's respectable upper middle class. His father "was a young physician more addicted to horse racing and to playing cards than to his profession," the author recalled in *Review*. His mother, who "somehow coped," came from "the ne'er-do-well branch of a *nouveau riche* family." The father used family connections to get a newspaper job, but he was fired; thereafter he became house physician to three decrepit great-aunts whose fortunes he hoped to inherit. When the aunts died, the Donosos inherited nothing. But soon they were sheltering other relatives, including an irresponsible uncle and Donoso's grandmother, who lived with the family for ten years while slowly succumbing to insanity. "The gradual process of [my grandmother's] deterioration, intertwined with lightning flashes of memory and family lore . . . is one of the episodes that has most marked my life," Donoso declared, "not because I loved this old woman but because her madness brought the ironies of family life and the horrors of aging and dying so cruelly into focus." He became a high-school truant and then a dropout, associating with bums and spending a year as a shepherd in the remote grasslands of southern Chile. In his early twenties he returned home and resumed his education, rejecting the traditional careers open to "an upper middle-class boy" by becoming an undergraduate English major.

Donoso describes his literary development in the memoir *Historia personal del "boom"* (*The Boom in Spanish American Literature: A Personal History*). The book introduces readers to one of the most renowned periods in Spanish American Literature— the "Boom," a flowering of literary activity during the 1960s—by showing its relationship to Donoso's own life. As an aspiring author in the 1950s, Donoso relates in his memoir, he shared with other young writers throughout Latin America the sense of being "asphyxiated" by the provincial cultural environment of his native land. Great authors of the past such as Mexico's Manuel Azuela, who saw the novel as a practical way to discuss contemporary social problems, seemed to members of Donoso's generation like "statues in a park." The earnest, simple style that such "grandfathers" had made popular seemed to rob the novel of creativity and expressiveness. The region's publish-

ers, too poor to take risks on new talent, preferred to reprint literary classics and popular foreign works; accordingly, Donoso and his peers had difficulty getting published, often had to sell copies of their books on their own, and found it difficult to obtain each others' work in print. For role models, Donoso declares, writers of his generation looked beyond the Hispanic world. Some authors he mentions, including William Faulkner and Henry James, were subtle stylists who experimented with the conventions of the novel, showing, for instance, how a character's point of view could affect their perception of reality. Others, including Franz Kafka and Albert Camus, were critics of human nature who seemed to have little hope of reform: their works showed isolated individuals grappling with an uncaring and fundamentally absurd society. By the late 1950s and early 1960s, Donoso began to see such innovative writing in novels by his peers, notably Cuba's Alejo Carpentier and Mexico's Carlos Fuentes. Such works, Donoso recalls, were "a spur to my envy, to my need to emulate," and they confirmed his sense that "the baroque, the distorted, the excessive could all increase the possibilities of the novel."

In his first novel, *Coronación* (*Coronation*), Donoso combined traditional realism with the more complex personal vision that would emerge in his later works. The book's main character is an affluent old woman who lives with her servants in a mansion; her vivid delusions and curses frighten her grandson, a repressed middle-aged bachelor. The old woman, Donoso admitted, is a portrait of his insane grandmother, and some relatives were indignant at the resemblance. Reviewers in Chile praised *Coronation* as a realistic depiction of that country's society, especially, recalled Donoso in *The Boom*, "the decadence of the upper class." Wishing to transcend realism, Donoso found such praise frustrating. The resolution of the novel, he suggested, was designed to challenge traditional literary style. The book's climax largely abandons the restraints of realism by dwelling on madness and the grotesque. The old woman, costumed and crowned by her maids during a drunken prank, dies convinced she has already gone to heaven. The grandson, confronting his mortality and his unfulfilling life, concludes that God himself must have been mad to create such a world and then follows his grandmother into insanity. *Coronation* brought Donoso an international reputation and won the 1962 William Faulkner Foundation Prize, established in Faulkner's will to encourage the translation of outstanding Latin American fiction into English.

Donoso's second novel, *Este domingo* (*This Sunday*), with its themes of upper-class decay and incipient chaos, has often been likened to *Coronation*. Many reviewers considered the later work a significant advance for Donoso, showing greater subtlety, impact, and stylistic sophistication. "As Donoso sees it," wrote Alexander Coleman in the *New York Times Book Review*, "the rich are different because they cannot live without the underworld of the poor to exploit and command." Don Alvaro is an affluent, middle-aged professional who has grown up weak and ineffective, but has kept a sense of virility by making a chambermaid his mistress. His wife Chepa, who has an obsessive need to minister to others, becomes the domineering patroness to a paroled murderer still drawn toward a life of crime. The novel's climax occurs when Chepa, unhappy with the parolee's conduct, seeks him out in the slum where he lives; she is hounded by poor neighborhood children and collapses on a trash heap. Throughout the book Donoso experiments with differing points of view, showing parts of the story through the eyes of its obsessive participants, and part through the eyes of a young relative of Alvaro, too naive to understand the underlying brutality of the world around him. Noting Donoso's "cool and biting intelligence," Coleman praised the author's "perfect balance between compulsion and control as he exorcises his infernally driven characters."

Donoso delved much further into obsession and fantasy with his novella *El lugar sin límites* (*Hell Has No Limits*), written at about the same time as *This Sunday.* The work is set in an isolated small town owned by Don Alejo, a powerful, all-knowing, selfish aristocrat whom many reviewers saw as the satirical embodiment of an unfeeling God. The main character is Manuela, whose delusions about being a lithe, young female dancer are lavishly echoed by the story's narration; in fact, however, Manuela is an aging male transvestite who works as a dancer in his daughter's bordello and uses fantasy to transcend his absurd existence. The story culminates in violence when Pancho, a virile male truckdriver attracted to Manuela, lashes out against his own underlying homosexuality by savagely assaulting the transvestite. Biographer George McMurray considered *Hell Has No Limits* a powerful comment on the futility of human aspirations, so pessimistic as to approach nihilism. The author's intentions, McMurray explained, "are to undermine traditional values, reveal the bankruptcy of reason, and jar the reader onto new levels of awareness by exposing the other side of reality." McMurray found the story one of Donoso's most accomplished works.

During the 1960s Donoso moved beyond the intellectual confines of Chile to become part of a growing international community of Latin American writers—major figures of the Boom—who knew each other as friends and colleagues and shared moral support, ideas, and interesting books. At a 1962 conference of such writers he became close friends with Carlos Fuentes; after attending another conference in Mexico two years later, Donoso began more than a dozen years of voluntary exile from his homeland. He wrote *Hell Has No Limits* while renting a house from Fuentes in Mexico, taught for two years at the University of Iowa's prestigious Writers Workshop, then settled in Spain. Meanwhile he went through numerous drafts of a novel far more lengthy, intricate, and allusive than his previous efforts. Its title came from a letter that young Henry James received from his father Henry Sr., warning about life's underlying chaos. "Life is no farce," the letter advised: "the natural inheritance of everyone who is capable of spiritual life is an unsubdued forest where the wolf howls and the obscene bird of night chatters."

When *El obsceno párajo de la noche* (*The Obscene Bird of Night*) finally emerged in 1970, reviewers found it both masterful and indescribable—"How do you review a dream?" asked Wolfgang Luchtig in *Books Abroad.* The novel is narrated by Humberto, an unsuccessful writer who becomes the retainer to a decaying aristocratic family and the tutor of their only son and heir. The child, monstrously deformed, is seen by his father as an emblem of chaos and is surrounded by freaks so that he will seem "normal." Eventually Humberto apparently flees to one of the family's charitable ventures—a decrepit convent that houses some of society's castoff women, ranging from the elderly to young orphans. Throughout the novel past and present are confusingly intermingled, and characters undergo bizarre transformations, sometimes melting into one another. Humberto appears as a deaf-mute servant in the convent; is apparently transformed into a baby by the old women, who often seem to be witches; and is finally sealed in a bundle of rags and thrown onto a fire, where he turns to ashes as the book ends.

Observers such as McMurray suggest that the novel should not be viewed as a "story" in the conventional sense, but as an outpouring of the deranged mind of its narrator, Humberto. According to such a view, Humberto is a schizophrenic, driven mad, perhaps, by his lack of success; his narration is disordered because he freely mixes reality with his fantasies, fears, and resentments of the world. Humberto's many transformations reflect his disintegrating personality, as he picks up and discards various identities in an effort to define himself; his bizarre demise, in which he is cut off from the world and then destroyed, represents the madman's final withdrawal from reality. In *Review* Donoso said that while the narrator is hardly autobiographical in a literal sense, "he is the autobiography of my fears, of my fantasies"; interestingly, the author finished his book while recovering from an episode of near-madness, brought on by a traumatic ulcer operation and the administration of pain-killing drugs. "Basically I don't know what my novel is about," Donoso also observed. "It's something that has happened to me rather than something I've written." "Donoso does not offer us . . . a novel simply to read," explained *Review*'s John J. Hassett, "but one to experience in which we are continuously called upon to give the text some order by discovering its unities and its repetitions." Many commentators ranked *The Obscene Bird of Night* among the best novels of the Boom era, which ended in the early 1970s; Donoso was favorably compared with Gabriel García Márquez, a Boom author who eventually won the Nobel Prize.

Until the 1980s Donoso continued to reside primarily in Spain. After he finished *The Obscene Bird of Night,* his writing began to change: his style became less hallucinatory and his narratives were less concerned with the Chilean aristocracy. Some of his work was set in Spain, including *Tres novelitas burguesas* (*Sacred Families*), novellas that portray that country's upper middle class with a blend of fantasy and social satire, and *El jardín de al lado* ("The Garden Next Door"), which features a novelist-in-exile who is haunted by his past. Throughout his years in Spain, Donoso reported in *Lives on the Line,* he found it impossible to cut his emotional ties to Chile. He did not feel nostalgia, he continued, but rather "the *guilt of absence*" or the "guilt of not being connected with action." His dilemma was heightened because he remained abroad by choice while Pinochet established his dictatorship. "All of us who lived abroad during that period who didn't have to," he explained in *Vogue,* "have a terrible feeling of guilt" because "we didn't share in the history of Chile during a very important time."

In the mid-1970s Donoso resolved to discuss Chile's turmoil in a novel, which became *Casa de campo* (*A House in the Country*). Aware that he was cut off from the daily life of Chileans—including the way they spoke—he wrote about them indirectly, creating what reviewers called a political allegory. Once more Donoso set his book in an aristocratic household. When the estate's owners leave on an excursion, their children (perhaps representing the middle class) and exploited Indians from the surrounding area (perhaps the working class) take over and wreak havoc. They are led by an aristocratic uncle (Salvador Allende?) who may be insane or may be the victim of injustice at the hands of his relatives. When the owners return, they use servants to ruthlessly re-establish order and then proclaim—despite all the bitterness they have engendered—that nothing has changed since they first left. Though some reviewers faulted the novel for being too intellectual and emotionally detached, others found it highly relevant and involving. "The combination of literary grace, political urgency and a fierce and untethered imagination," wrote Charles Champlin in the *Los Angeles Times Book Review,* "give Donoso and 'A House in the Country' the power of an aimed projectile."

By the mid-1980s Donoso had resettled in Chile, and in 1986 he produced a more direct study of life under Pinochet in the novel *La desesperanza* (*Curfew*). Though the book describes both Pinochet's torturers and the dispossessed poor, its principal focus is the country's well-educated, dispirited political left. The two main characters—a onetime revolutionary and a political folk-singer who fled to Paris—share deep feelings of guilt because they were not punished as much by the regime as were other left-ists. Their old comrades, meanwhile, seem paralyzed by infighting, didacticism, and bitterness. The book was highly praised by prominent American critics and, notably, by Jacobo Timerman, an Argentine journalist respected worldwide as an eloquent victim of political oppression. "Donoso is a moderate who has written a revolutionary novel," Timerman observed in *Vogue;* in *New Yorker* he wrote that "it is a relief, finally, to read a work of Chilean literature in which none of the characters are above history or appear to dominate it." *Curfew,* reviewers suggested, displays the deep personal flaws of leftists and rightists alike: by avoiding simple conclusions, the novel makes plain that Chile abounds in uncertainty and despair. In contrast to its reception abroad, *Curfew* was viewed rather coolly by many Chilean intellectuals. "The book doesn't flag-wave" or "present an alternative," Donoso explained in *Vogue,* and "people would respect me much more if it did." However, he observed, "I'm not a crusader. I'm not a hero. I'm just a man who is very hurt, and who wants change."

BIOGRAPHICAL/CRITICAL SOURCES:

BOOKS

Contemporary Literary Criticism, Gale, Volume 4, 1975, Volume 8, 1978, Volume 11, 1979, Volume 32, 1985.
Donoso, José, *The Boom in Spanish American Literature: A Personal History,* Columbia University Press, 1977.
Forster, Merlin H., editor, *Tradition and Renewal: Essays on Twentieth-Century Latin American Literature and Culture,* University of Illinois Press, 1975.
MacAdam, Alfred J., *Modern Latin American Narratives: The Dreams of Reason,* University of Chicago Press, 1977.
McMurray, George R., *José Donoso,* Twayne, 1979.
Meyer, Doris, editor, *Lives on the Line: The Testimony of Contemporary Latin American Authors,* University of California Press, 1988.
Schwartz, Ronald, *Nomads, Exiles, and Emigres: The Rebirth of the Latin American Narrative, 1960-80,* Scarecrow Press, 1980.

PERIODICALS

Américas, June 9, 1984, November/December, 1987.
Book Forum, summer, 1977.
Books Abroad, winter, 1968, winter, 1972, spring, 1972, spring, 1975.
Christian Science Monitor, June 27, 1973, June 2, 1988.
Commonweal, September 21, 1973, May 18, 1984.
Contemporary Literature, Volume 28, number 4, 1987.
Essays in Literature, spring, 1975.
Hispania, May, 1972.
Hudson Review, winter, 1978, winter, 1989.
Journal of Spanish Studies: Twentieth Century, winter, 1973.
Los Angeles Times Book Review, February 5, 1984, May 15, 1988.
Modern Fiction Studies, winter, 1978.
Nation, March 11, 1968, June 11, 1973, February 11, 1978.
New Leader, October 1, 1973.
New Statesman, June 18, 1965, March 1, 1974.
Newsweek, June 4, 1973.
New Yorker, June 16, 1973, April 30, 1984, November 2, 1987, June 13, 1988.
New York Review of Books, April 19, 1973, December 13, 1973, August 4, 1977, July 18, 1985.

New York Times Book Review, March 14, 1965, November 26, 1967, December 24, 1972, June 17, 1973, June 26, 1977, February 26, 1984, May 29, 1988.
Partisan Review, fall, 1974, number 1, 1982, number 2, 1986.
PMLA, January, 1978.
Punch, April 18, 1984.
Review, fall, 1973, January-May, 1984.
Revista de Estudios Hispánicos, January, 1975.
Saturday Review, March 13, 1965, December 9, 1967, January 23, 1971, July 9, 1977.
Spectator, June 18, 1965.
Studies in Short Fiction, winter, 1971.
Symposium, summer, 1976.
Time, April 23, 1965, July 30, 1973, June 27, 1977, February 20, 1984.
Times Literary Supplement, July 1, 1965, October 12, 1967, February 22, 1968, July 2, 1971, February 10, 1978, April 6, 1984.
Village Voice, March 27, 1984.
Vogue, May, 1988.
Washington Post Book World, May 27, 1973, August 14, 1977, February 26, 1984, May 22, 1988.
World Literature Today, autumn, 1977, spring, 1981, summer, 1982, winter, 1983.

—*Sketch by Thomas Kozikowski*

*   *   *

DORFMAN, Ariel 1942-

PERSONAL: Born May 6, 1942, in Buenos Aires, Argentina; naturalized Chilean citizen, 1967; exiled from Chile, 1973; came to United States, 1980; son of Adolfo (an economist, engineer, and adviser to the government of Argentina) and Fanny (a Spanish literature teacher; maiden name, Zelicovich) Dorfman; married María Angélica Malinarich (an English teacher and social worker), January 7, 1966; children: Rodrigo, Joaquín. *Education:* University of Chile, Licenciado en filosofía con mención en literatura general (summa cum laude), 1967.

ADDRESSES: Home—Durham, N.C.; and Santiago, Chile. *Office*—Department of International Studies, Duke University, Durham, N.C. 27706. *Agent*—Andrew Wylie, 250 West 57th St., Suite 2106, New York, N.Y. 10017.

CAREER: University of California, Berkeley, research scholar, 1968-69; University of Chile, Santiago, Chile, professor of Spanish-American studies, 1970-73; Sorbonne, University of Paris, Paris, France, maitre des conferences reemplacant of Spanish-American literature, 1975-76; University of Amsterdam, Amsterdam, Holland, chief research scholar at Spaans Seminarium, 1976-80; Woodrow Wilson Center for International Scholars, Washington, D.C., fellow, 1980-81; Institute for Policy Studies, Washington, D.C., visiting fellow, 1981-84; Duke University, Durham, N.C., visiting professor during fall semesters, 1984-89, research professor of literature and Latin American studies, 1989—. Visiting professor at University of Maryland, College Park, 1983. Guest on television and radio news programs, including "All Things Considered," "Nightline," "This Week With David Brinkley," "Crossfire," "This Morning," "Nightwatch," and "Larry King Live"; lecturer.

MEMBER: International P.E.N., National Writers' Union, Sociedad de Escritores Chilenos, Drama Guild.

AWARDS, HONORS: Award for best screenplay from Chile Films, 1972, for unproduced film "Balmaceda"; Premio Ampliado Sudamericana from *La Opinión* (Buenos Aires newspaper), 1973, for *Moros en la costa;* New American Plays award from Kennedy Center-American Express, 1988, for the play "Widows"; honorary degree from Illinois Wesleyan University, 1989.

WRITINGS:

NOVELS

Moros en la costa (title means "The Coast Is Not Clear in Chile"), Sudamericana, 1973, translation by George R. Shivers published as *Hard Rain,* Readers International, 1990.

Viudas, Siglo XXI, 1981, translation by Stephen Kessler published as *Widows,* Pantheon Books, 1983 (also see below).

La última canción de Manuel Sendero, Siglo XXI, 1983, translation by Dorfman and Shivers published as *The Last Song of Manuel Sendero,* Viking, 1987.

Mascara, Viking, 1988.

OTHER

El absurdo entre cuatro paredes: El teatro de Harold Pinter (criticism; title means "Enclosures at the Absurd: Harold Pinter's Theatre"), Universitaria, 1968.

Imaginación y violencia en América (essays; title means "Imagination and Violence in Latin America"), Universitaria, 1970.

(With Armand Mattelart) *Para leer al Pato Donald,* Siglo Vientiuno Argentina, 1972, translation by David Kunzle published as *How to Read Donald Duck: Imperialist Ideology in the Disney Comic,* International General, 1975, 2nd edition, 1984.

Ensayos quemados en Chile: Inocencia y neocolonialismo (essays; title means "Essays Burnt in Chile: Innocence and Neocolonialism"), Ediciones de la Flor, 1974.

(With Manuel Jofré) *Superman y sus amigos del alma* (essays; title means "Superman and His Cronies"), Galerna, 1974.

Culture et resistance au Chili (essays; title means "Culture and Resistance in Chile"), Institut d'Action Culturelle, 1978.

La última aventura del Llanero Solitario (essays; title means "The Last Adventure of the Lone Ranger"), Universitaria Centroamericana (Costa Rica), 1979.

Cría ojos (short stories), Nueva Imagen, 1979, translation by Dorfman and Shivers published as *My House Is on Fire* (includes "Reader"), Viking, 1990 (also see below).

(Contributor) *El intelectual y el estado, Venezuela-Chile* (essays; title means "The Intellectual and the State, Venezuela-Chile"), University of Maryland, 1980.

Pruebas al canto (poems; title means "Soft Evidence"), Nueva Imagen, 1980.

Reader's nuestro que estás en la tierra: Ensayos sobre el imperialismo cultural (essays; title means "Our Readers That Art on Earth"), Nueva Imagen, 1980, translation by Clark Hansen published as *The Empire's Old Clothes: What the Lone Ranger, Babar, and Other Innocent Heroes Do to Our Minds* (includes three previously unpublished essays in English), Pantheon Books, 1983.

Missing (poems), translated by Edie Grossman, Amnesty International British Section, 1982.

Hacia liberación del lector latinoamericano (essays), Ediciones del Norte, 1984.

Patos, elefantes y héroes: La infancia como subdesarrollo (essays; title means "On Ducks, Elephants, and Heroes"), Ediciones de la Flor, 1985.

Dorando la píldora (stories; title means "The Medicine Goes Down"), Ediciones del Ornitorrinco, 1985.

Pastel de choclo (poetry), Sinfronteras, 1986, translation by Dorfman and Grossman published as *Last Waltz in Santiago and Other Poems of Exile and Disappearance* (includes some poems originally published in *Missing*), Penguin, 1988 (also see above).

"Widows," two-act play based on Dorfman's novel of the same name; first produced in Williamstown, Mass., at the Williamstown Theatre Festival, 1988.

Missing Continents, Pantheon, in press.

Also author of unproduced screenplay "Balmaceda," 1972, and of "Reader," a play based on Dorfman's short story of the same name. Contributor of articles, stories, and editorials to periodicals, including *Harper's, Nation, New York Times, Los Angeles Times, Village Voice, Washington Post,* and *New York Times Sunday Magazine.*

WORK IN PROGRESS: A detective novel that "grounds some characters of *Mascara* in contemporary Chile," and an epic novel set in California in the mid-nineteenth century; both will be written in Spanish for Pantheon.

SIDELIGHTS: Argentinean-born author, journalist, and scholar Ariel Dorfman is best known for his opposition to political oppression in Chile. Since his 1973 expulsion from his adopted country for his outspoken resistance to the harsh policies of dictator Augusto Pinochet, Dorfman has produced poetry, nonfiction, short stories, and three acclaimed novels that probe the terror of dictatorship and the despair of exile. According to Robert Atwan in the *New York Times Book Review,* Dorfman's fiction displays his "ability to create methods of storytelling that enact, not merely record, a political vision, [and] that fuse both the political and the literary imaginations."

Dorfman was born in Argentina in 1942 to a family well acquainted with the pain of exile: his Jewish grandparents had escaped the pogroms in Eastern Europe, and his father, an economist, fled Argentina and took a job in New York City at the United Nations when Dorfman was two years old. Dorfman and his family spent ten years in the United States before they returned to South America, settling in Chile in 1954. Although initially averse to leaving New York, Dorfman grew to love his new country; he completed his education, married, and in 1967 became a naturalized Chilean citizen.

Dorfman established himself in Chile as a writer, publishing his first novel, *Moros en la costa,* and several nonfiction studies. These included a critical analysis of the works of English playwright Harold Pinter, a book of essays on the Latin American novel, and a 1972 collaboration with Armand Mattelart titled *Para leer al Pato Donald,* which was widely reviewed in English. Translated as *How to Read Donald Duck: Imperialist Ideology in the Disney Comic,* the book is an examination of the ways Donald Duck and other Disney characters subtly transmit capitalist ideology to their Latin American audiences, with whom the cartoons are extremely popular. A later study translated as *The Empire's Old Clothes: What the Lone Ranger, Babar, and Other Innocent Heroes Do to Our Minds* presents Dorfman's analysis of how American children's literature and popular culture also project dominant values.

Dorfman worked as an activist, journalist, and writer in Chile until 1973, when Salvador Allende's democratically elected Marxist government was overthrown by Pinochet in a U.S.-supported coup, resulting in Allende's death and the expulsion of thousands of intellectuals, writers, clergymen, and politicians from the country. After receiving death threats and witnessing the burning of his books in Santiago, Dorfman was expelled from

Chile. Devastated by the loss of his citizenship and appalled by the intimidation and violence perpetrated on his countrymen by the Pinochet regime, Dorfman, after a brief stay in Argentina, settled in France. There he worked for the Chilean resistance movement in Paris and, later, taught Spanish-American literature at the Sorbonne.

After a two-year period in which his distress over his country's turmoil blocked his creativity and left him unable to write, Dorfman composed a group of poems expressing his thoughts about the atrocities—which included torture, murder, and abductions—he knew were still occurring in his homeland. The poems, which were published in an English collection titled *Missing* in 1982, center on *desaparecidos,* people deemed subversive by the Chilean government and abducted ("disappeared") by secret agents. In the collection Dorfman describes the effects this practice has upon the families of the disappeared; one poem conveys the conflicting emotions of parents who receive word from a prison camp veteran that their son—whom they feared dead—is still alive but being tortured. "I discovered a way in which I could become a meeting ground of the living and the dead—a way to give voice to the missing, which was also a metaphor for the whole country and what had been irretrievably lost," Dorfman later told Leslie Bennetts of the *New York Times.* "All of my poems are ways of giving voices to those who have disappeared and those who are left behind; I am a bridge between them. Words become a way of returning to your country—a cemetery, but also a resurrection ground."

Dorfman left France in 1976 for a position as chief research scholar at the University of Amsterdam, remaining there until 1980, when he accepted a Woodrow Wilson fellowship in Washington, D.C. He returned to fiction writing, voicing his deep concern for the disappeared in a second novel, *Viudas* (*Widows*). Knowing that its highly sensitive subject would probably prevent the book's publication in Chile, he devised an elaborate scheme to have *Viudas* printed first in Europe. Using the pseudonym Eric Lohmann, Dorfman included in the manuscript a foreword—which claimed to be written by Lohmann's son—explaining that the book's author was a World War II Danish resistance fighter who had set the story in Greece in order to have it safely published in his homeland. *Viudas*'s foreword also stated that Lohmann had been killed by the Nazi secret police just days after the book's completion, and that Lohmann's son had only recently found and published the manuscript. Dorfman then planned to have the novel published first in Danish, French, or German and subsequently issued at home as a Spanish translation of the European novel. "That double distancing—of mediation through an author who was not me and a country which was not my own—allowed me to write an allegory which is simultaneously realistic, [and] a literary solution to the problem of how to write about overwhelming horror and sorrow," the author explained in an interview with Peggy Boyers and Juan Carlos Lertora in *Salmagundi.* At the last minute, however, Dorfman's Spanish-language publisher backed out; the novel was ultimately released, under Dorfman's real name, by the Mexican firm Siglo XXI in 1981.

Translated in 1983, *Widows* is set in a Greek village under the control of Nazi soldiers during World War II, and it centers on Sofia Angelos, a village peasant woman whose husband, father, and son have been "disappeared" by the military regime. Given no information about their menfolk's safety or whereabouts, Sofia and the other peasant women—whose male relatives have also been abducted—rise in opposition to the soldiers when Sofia claims an unidentifiable corpse that has washed up on the river bank is her father and demands the right to bury him.

Widows was acclaimed for its political relevance as well as for its powerful portrayal of the grief and emotional strain that disappearances put on the families of the missing. Alan Cheuse, for example, in his *New York Times Book Review* critique, compared the book's intensity and scope to that of such Greek tragedies as *Antigone* and *The Trojan Women,* and he praised *Widows*'s "emotional amplitude and political resonance." Noting especially its "sharply observed details of the bereaved . . . who suffer . . . painfully," Cheuse asserted that the reader "moves [through the novel] as if in a dream of outrage among its tombs of love." *Times Literary Supplement* contributor Nicholas Rankin also admired Dorfman's work, applauding the way the author bypassed the "realist clutter of local detail" in order to create "a tragedy of universal application."

Dorfman followed *Widows* with the 1983 *La última canción de Manuel Sendero,* a lengthy novel that explores the larger implications of repression and exile through several complexly interwoven narratives. "There's fantasy," Dorfman said of the book in an interview with Richard J. Meislin in the *New York Times Book Review,* "but also the very harsh terror of reality. Writers of Latin American literature, especially my generation, are constantly being pulled between two poles: what you would call the dictatorship of everyday life and the imagination of things that might come and come be." Translated as *The Last Song of Manuel Sendero,* the work unfolds through several perspectives, mainly that of unborn fetuses who have been organized into a revolt—in the form of a mass refusal to emerge from their mothers' wombs. Much of the novel contains the generation's discussions about whether it is better to shun a world full of violence and fear or to risk birth in order to solve human problems. The babies, according to Dorfman, also serve as the book's principal metaphor. "They are the utopia that are inside each of us," the author affirmed in a *Los Angeles Times* interview with Mona Gable. "There are millions of people who are born and never born—they don't leave any change in the world. To read the novel means I want people to come away with a sense of what is unborn inside them." Other narratives in *The Last Song of Manuel Sendero* include the realistic dialogue between David and Felipe, exiled Chilean cartoonists living in Mexico and collaborating on a comic strip for their fellow expatriates; the lives of characters within David and Felipe's comic strip; and notes and scholarly commentary from a course in "Prehistoric Amerspanish III," given thirty thousand years in the future.

Critical response to *The Last Song of Manuel Sendero* was generally favorable, with reviewers commenting both on the book's complexity and on Dorfman's success in blending his political and artistic concerns. Judith Freeman, for example, in the *Los Angeles Times Book Review,* stated: "This is a demanding book, but for those who make the effort it requires, the result is a ride on a parabolic roller coaster of timely and humanitarian thought." Earl Shorris's *New York Times Book Review* critique expressed a similar assessment, noting that "after the complications of plot and puzzle have done their work, the richness of invention breaks through." Concluded Pat Aufderheide in the *Boston Review:* "every page, every insistent act of imagination is an act of resistance against the death-in-life of political oppression and the life-on-hold of exile."

In 1983, ten years after Dorfman was forced to leave Chile, Pinochet's government softened its attitude somewhat towards many of the nation's exiles, and Dorfman was allowed to return to the country temporarily; he began to split his time between living in Santiago and teaching as a visiting professor at North Carolina's Duke University. He persisted, however, in voicing his criticism of Pinochet's dictatorial policies during the next five years, both in articles and editorials in American and international publications as well as during appearances on American news programs. Although Dorfman has been given permission to return to Chile, unsettling incidents (such as Chilean news reports announcing Dorfman's death and Dorfman's unexplained detention and expulsion from the Santiago airport, after which he was temporarily refused entry into the country in 1987) have made his full-time residence there unlikely as long as Pinochet remains in power.

In the late 1980s Dorfman published another volume of poetry titled *Last Waltz in Santiago and Other Poems of Exile and Disappearance* and *My House Is on Fire,* a translation of earlier short stories. He also completed the thriller *Mascara* in 1988. Written in English and considered the least overtly political of Dorfman's novels, the story centers on personal identity as it is created, controlled, changed, and escaped by three characters—an anonymous loner who works as a photographer for an obscure government agency, an amnesiac woman with multiple personalities, and a manipulative plastic surgeon—whose monologues form the book's three sections. *Mascara* was well received by critics, who admired its compelling narration, suspenseful plot, and ambiguous ending and compared it to the fiction of German novelists Guenter Grass and Franz Kafka. *Mascara,* noted Atwan, "is an intricately layered book [that] can be read as an ominous fairy tale, a literary horror story, a post-modern version of Jekyll and Hyde. But the book is also a parable of human identity and paranoia engendered by authoritarian politics."

Despite the uncertainty about his permanent return to Chile, Dorfman continues to protest—both in print and in person—repression and brutality in his homeland and elsewhere. He also remains optimistic that the situation in Chile will improve. "My literature *should* be the literature of despair," Dorfman concluded to Geoffrey Stokes in the *Voice Literary Supplement,* "but always, not because I desire it, but because it comes out, I find myself telling the story of human beings who have managed to rescue dignity from the midst of terror."

BIOGRAPHICAL/CRITICAL SOURCES:

BOOKS

Contemporary Literary Criticism, Volume 48, Gale, 1988.

PERIODICALS

Books Abroad, June 27, 1978.
Boston Review, April, 1987.
Chicago Tribune, March 18, 1987.
Chicago Tribune Book World, July 17, 1983.
Globe and Mail (Toronto), March 4, 1989.
Harper's, December, 1989.
Los Angeles Times, August 7, 1987, August 16, 1987, September 16, 1987.
Los Angeles Times Book Review, June 12, 1983, April 5, 1987, October 30, 1988.
Nation, February 11, 1978, September 24, 1983, October 18, 1986.
New York Times, February 17, 1987, April 14, 1988, October 8, 1988.
New York Times Book Review, May 8, 1983, July 24, 1983, February 15, 1987, November 6, 1988.
Publishers Weekly, October 21, 1988.
Salmagundi, spring/summer, 1989.
Spectator, July 26, 1975.
Times Literary Supplement, June 11, 1971, December 9, 1983.
Voice Literary Supplement, September, 1982, April, 1987.
Washington Post, August 25, 1988.
Washington Post Book World, June 12, 1983, April 5, 1987.

—*Sketch by Emily J. McMurray*

*   *   *

DRAGUN, Osvaldo 1929-

PERSONAL: Born in 1929 in Entre Ríos province, Argentina. *Education:* Studied law during 1950s.

CAREER: Playwright and screenwriter. Affiliated with Teatro Independente Popular Fray Mocho, during 1950s.

AWARDS, HONORS: Drama prizes from Casa de las Américas, 1961, for *Historias para ser contadas,* and 1966, for *Heroica de Buenos Aires.*

WRITINGS:

PLAYS

La peste viene de Melos (three-act; title means "The Plague Comes From Melos"), Ariadna (Buenos Aires), 1956.
Tupac Amarú (three-act), Losange (Buenos Aires), 1957.
Historias para ser contadas (trilogy of one-acts; title means "Stories to Be Told"; contains *Historia de un flemón, una mujer, y dos hombres* ["The Story of an Abscess, a Woman, and Two Men"], *Historia de cómo nuestro amigo Panchito González se sintió responsable de la epidemia de peste en Africa del Sur* ["The Story of How Our Friend Panchito González Felt Responsible for the Plague Epidemic in South Africa"], and *Historia del hombre que se convirtió en perro* ["The Story of a Man Who Turned Into a Dog"]), Talía (Buenos Aires), 1957, translation of latter two one-acts published in *The Orgy: Modern One-Act Plays From Latin America,* edited and translated by Gerardo Luzuriaga and Robert S. Rudder, University of California, Los Angeles, Latin American Center, 1974, translation of complete work by Joe and Graciela Rosenberg published in *Texas A & I University Studies,* November, 1976.
Los de la mesa 10, published with *Historia para ser contadas,* 1957 (also see above).
El jardín del infierno (title means "The Garden of Hell"), published in *Revista de la Escuela de Arte Teatral, Number 5,* 1961, CEAL (Buenos Aires), 1966.
Y nos dijeron que éramos inmortales, Universidad Veracruzana (Xalapa, Mexico), 1962, Monteagudos (Buenos Aires), 1963, translation by Alden J. Green published as *And They Told Us We Were Immortal* in *The Modern Stage in Latin America,* edited by George Woodyard, Dutton, 1971.
Milagro en el Mercado Viejo (one act), Producciones Norte (Buenos Aires), 1963, translation by Joe and Graciela Rosenberg published as *Miracle in the Old Market* in *Texas A & I University Studies,* November, 1979.
Teatro (collected plays; includes *Historia de mi esquina* ["Story of My Corner"]), Davalos/Hernández (Buenos Aires), 1965.
Amoretta (two-act), Carro de Tespis (Buenos Aires), 1965.
Heroica de Buenos Aires (title means "Epic of Buenos Aires"), Casa de las Américas (Havana, Cuba), 1966, Astral (Buenos Aires), 1967.
El amasijo (title means "The Hodgepodge"), Calatayud (Buenos Aires), 1968.
¡Un maldito domingo! [and] *Y nos dijeron que éramos inmortales* [and] *Milagro en el Mercado Viejo,* Taurus (Madrid, Spain), 1968.
Historias con cárcel, published in *Caminos del teatro latinoamericano,* Casa de las Américas, 1973.

¡Arriba corazón!, Teatro Municipal General San Martín (Buenos Aires), 1987.

Author of additional plays, including *Una mujer por encomienda, Historia del escritor que metieron preso, Sonata popular,* and (with Andrés Lizárraga) *Desde el 80.* Author of adaptation of Alejandro Berruti's play *Madre tierra.* Also author of film and television screenplays.

SIDELIGHTS: Osvaldo Dragún was considered one of the most talented young playwrights to emerge in Argentina in the 1950s and 1960s. He played an important role in the rise of small, innovative theaters that appeared in Buenos Aires during that time, particularly the Teatro Independiente Popular Fray Mocho, which premiered several of his early works. His plays are notable for their wide variety of styles, ranging from social realism and historical dramas to absurdism.

The author began his career with two major works on historical themes. *La peste viene de Melos* ("The Plague Comes From Melos") depicts an episode from ancient Greek history, during which Athens—supposedly a progressive democracy—invaded the peaceful island of Melos for selfish national advantage. Observers believe that the work is a commentary on interventions by the United States in Latin America. *Tupac Amarú* is set in eighteenth-century Peru and tells the story of an Indian leader who became a martyr for the independence of his people.

Dragún may be best known for a trilogy of one-act plays from the late 1950s entitled *Historias para ser contadas* ("Stories to Be Told"). Reviewers link these works to the French theater of the absurd, which dramatizes the futility of human existence by placing characters in bizarre, grimly comic situations. The trilogy culminates with *Historia del hombre que se convirtió en perro* (*The Story of a Man Who Turned Into a Dog*), in which the title character, desperate and unemployed, accepts a humiliating job as a guard dog and soon forgets he is human. Two decades after *Historias para ser contadas* was first produced, Enisberto Jaraba-Pardo told readers of *Américas* that the work had been staged throughout both Europe and the New World and had attained the status of a classic.

Dragún's later works tend to be grimmer, less metaphorical accounts of the struggles of individuals to survive in contemporary Argentina. *Y nos dijeron que éramos inmortales* (*And They Told Us We Were Immortal*) features a young soldier who returns to his family deeply disillusioned, having witnessed the death of one comrade-at-arms and the crippling of another. In *Amoretta,* a forty-year-old widow and a man ten years her junior fall in love and must endure the resentment of friends and relatives. *Heroica de Buenos Aires* ("Epic of Buenos Aires") is modeled on Bertolt Brecht's play *Mother Courage and Her Children,* according to Joelyn Ruple of *Books Abroad.* Just as Brecht's Mother Courage strains to provide for her children, only to lose them to the chaos of Germany's Thirty Years' War, so does Dragún's María strive to make her children rich, only to see them become arrogant strangers because of their wealth. Both *Heroica de Buenos Aires* and *Historias para ser contadas* won prestigious recognition from Casa de las Américas, the Cuban government publishing house.

BIOGRAPHICAL/CRITICAL SOURCES:

BOOKS

Jones, Willis Knapp, *Behind Spanish American Footlights,* University of Texas Press, 1966.
Lyday, Leon F. and George W. Woodyard, *Dramatists in Revolt: The New Latin American Theater,* University of Texas Press, 1976.

McMurray, George R., *Spanish American Writing Since 1941: A Critical Survey,* Ungar, 1987.

PERIODICALS

Américas, September, 1979.
Books Abroad, spring, 1967.
Comparative Drama, fall, 1969.
Hispania, December, 1956.
Latin American Literary Review, fall, 1978.
Latin American Theatre Review, spring, 1972, fall, 1979, spring, 1983.
Prairie Schooner, summer, 1965.
Theatre Arts, February, 1959.

*   *   *

DUNCAN, Quince 1940-

PERSONAL: Born December 5, 1940, in San José, Costa Rica. *Education:* Religious study for two years; university study for three years.

CAREER: Short story writer, novelist, and essayist. Speaker on black culture and literature.

MEMBER: Costa Rican Authors Association (past secretary), Circle of Costa Rican Poets.

AWARDS, HONORS: Second prize in literary contest sponsored by Editorial Costa Rica; Premios Nacionales Aquileo J. Echeverría in novel category, Ministerio de Cultura, Juventud, y Deportes, 1979.

WRITINGS:

Una canción en la madrugada (stories), Editorial Costa Rica (San José), 1970, 3rd edition, 1981.
Hombres curtidos (novel), Cuadernos de Arte Popular (San José), 1971.
(With Carlos Meléndez Chaverri) *El negro en Costa Rica* (anthology), Editorial Costa Rica, 1972, 8th edition, 1981.
Los cuatro espejos (novel), Editorial Costa Rica, 1973.
La rebelión pocomía y otros relatos (stories), Editorial Costa Rica, 1976.
La paz del pueblo, Editorial Costa Rica, 1978.
Final de calle (novel), Editorial Costa Rica, 1979, 2nd edition, 1981.
(With others) *Cultura negra y teología,* Editorial Departamento Ecuménico de Investigaciones (San José), 1986.
(With Lorein Powell) *Teoría y práctica del racismo,* Editorial Departamento Ecuménico de Investigaciones, 1988.

Also author of *El pozo y una carta,* 1969, and *Bronce,* 1970. Contributor of weekly literary column to newspaper *Pueblo;* contributor of articles to periodicals, including *Exelsior.* Member of editorial boards and director of literary magazines.

SIDELIGHTS: Quince Duncan is one of Central America's best-known black writers. Born of Jamaican ancestry in San José, Costa Rica, the author is acclaimed for conveying the aspirations, culture, and social problems of his country's black citizens to an audience outside of Central America. Pointing out the neglect Costa Rican blacks have suffered, Duncan's works aim to dispel the misconception that black citizens in that country are inferior to whites. In the anthology *El negro en Costa Rica,* for example, Duncan and co-author Carlos Meléndez Chaverri relate the prejudices that blacks face in a predominantly white Costa Rican population; the authors also emphasize both the desire of blacks to develop an individual culture and their aspirations to hold the same privileges as their white counterparts. *El negro en Costa Rica* has been praised as a valuable reference source documenting the black experience in Costa Rica.

Duncan is also the author of novels and stories that strive to eliminate the negative image surrounding black Costa Ricans. His 1973 novel *Los cuatro Espejos,* for instance, relates the author's frustration with black superstitions and certain barbaric rites which he believes contribute to the race's own oppression; Duncan conveys in the novel, though, that a measure of ignorance within the black Costa Rican community persists because blacks are denied access to proper educational facilities.

BIOGRAPHICAL/CRITICAL SOURCES:

BOOKS

Jackson, Richard L., *The Black Image in Latin American Literature,* University of New Mexico Press, 1976.

* * *

DURAN, Roberto (Tinoco) 1953-

PERSONAL: Born May 13, 1953, in Bakersfield, Calif.; son of Pedro H. (a farm labor contractor) and Guadalupe Tinoco (a cannery worker) Durán; married Anna Hough, February, 1982 (separated, 1988); children: Deserie, Marcella. *Education:* Attended San José City College, 1972-74; San José State University, B.S.W., 1985. *Politics:* Democrat. *Religion:* Catholic.

ADDRESSES: Home and office—2212 Quimby Rd., San José, Calif. 95122.

CAREER: Poet. Barrio Leadership Training Program, San José, Calif., youth supervisor, summer, 1982; Mosquitos Boys Club, San José, recreation manager, summer, 1985; Western Homes for Youth, San Martin, Calif., house counselor, summer, 1987; Vida Nueva, San José, program attendant, summers, 1989—. Consultant for Mid-Peninsula Conversion Project, 1983; liaison for East San José jobs in energy. Secretary for Alcoholics Anonymous. Active in United Farmworkers Organization. Gives poetry readings.

AWARDS, HONORS: Received first place in contest sponsored by El Tecolote Literary Review for Poetry, San Francisco, Calif., 1982.

WRITINGS:

A Friend of Sorrow, privately printed, 1980.
(With Judith Ortiz Cofer and Gustavo Pérez Firmat) *Triple Crown* (poetry), Bilingual Press, 1987.

Contributor of poems to periodicals, including *Quarry West* and *Traces.*

WORK IN PROGRESS: A poetry collection tentatively titled *Up and Down the New Downtown;* a series of essays and short stories about the judicial system and drug abuse in certain communities.

SIDELIGHTS: Roberto Durán is a Chicano poet who wrote *Triple Crown* with fellow poets Judith Ortiz Cofer and Gustavo Pérez Firmat. Writing from the perspective of a Chicano farmworker, Durán was praised for employing in the book strong metaphor and highly charged emotions. Reviewers generally found *Triple Crown* to be a valuable collection relating the hispanic experience.

Durán has also earned acclaim for his many poetry readings. "Though my poetry is my personal perception, I like to share it with others," the author told John Ramos in *El Observador.* Durán, who writes of such topics as drug abuse, police brutality, immigration, discrimination, and the justice system, related to Ramos, "I can't change things, but I can be vocal about the truth." Critics praise his readings for relating serious topics with a measure of hope.

Durán told *HW:* "My current manuscript deals with issues and social economic realities as they affect the plight of the homeless, working poor, etcetera, of Santa Clara, California. I take a humorous yet serious look at the diversity of the Santa Clara Valley—its impact on its residents, their interaction (or noninteraction, as the case may be)—and issues of crime and punishment, especially as they relate to minorities."

BIOGRAPHICAL/CRITICAL SOURCES:

PERIODICALS

El Observador, July 30, 1986.

E

ECHEGARAY (y EIZAGUIRRE), José (María Waldo) 1832-1916
(Jorge Hayaseca y Eizaguirre)

PERSONAL: Born in 1832 in Madrid, Spain; died in 1916 in Madrid, Spain.

CAREER: Spanish mathematician, engineer, statesman, and playwright. Worked as a professor of hydraulics, School of Civil Engineering, Madrid, Spain; held several government posts during the Spanish revolutionary period, 1868-1874; lived briefly as an exile in Paris, France; returned to Spain in 1874. Former Minister of Finance for Spain; founder of the Bank of Spain.

AWARDS, HONORS: Elected to Royal Spanish Academy, 1894; recipient, with Frédéric Mistral, of the Nobel Prize for literature, 1904.

WRITINGS:

PLAYS

(Under pseudonym Jorge Hayaseca y Eizaguirre) *El libro talonario* (also see below; one-act), [Spain], 1874, 3rd edition, José Rodríguez (Madrid), 1881, microcard edition, Falls City Press (Louisville, Ky.), 1968.

La esposa del vengador (also see below; three-act; title means "The Wife of the Avenger"), José Rodríguez, 1874.

En el puño de la espada (also see below; three-act), [Madrid], 1875, 3rd edition, José Rodríguez, 1876, microcard edition, Falls City Microcards (Louisville, Ky.), 1960.

O locura ó santidad (also see below; three-act; title means "Folly or Saintliness"; first produced at Teatro Español, January 22, 1877), Imprento de J. M. Ducazcal (Madrid), 1877, translation by Ruth Lansing published as *Madman or Saint,* R. G. Badger (Boston), 1912.

El gladiator de Ravena: Imitación de las últimas escenas de la tragedia alemana de Federico Halm (Munch de Bellinghaussen), T. Fortanet (Madrid), 1877, microcard edition, Falls City Press, 1968.

Como empieza y come acaba (three-act), T. Fortanet, 1877, microcard edition, Falls City Press, 1968.

Ni la paciencia de Job (three-act), José Rodríguez, 1879, microcard edition, Falls City Microcards, 1959.

Mar sin orillas (three-act), José Rodríguez, 1880, microcard edition, Falls City Microcards, 1960.

La muerte en los labios (also see below; three-act; first produced at Teatro Español, November 30, 1880), José Rodríguez, 1880, 9th edition, Sucesores de Rodríguez y Odriózola, 1897, microcard edition, Falls City Microcards, 1959.

El gran galeoto (also see below; three-act; produced in the United States as *The World and His Wife;* produced in England as *Calumny*), [Spain], 1881, edited with introduction, notes, and vocabulary by Aurelio M. Espinosa, C. A. Koehler & Co. (Boston), 1903, translation by Hannah Lynch published as *The Great Galeoto: A Play in Three Acts,* introduction by Elizabeth R. Hunt, Doubleday, 1914, new and revised edition, Knopf, 1918, reprinted, Las Américas (New York), 1964.

Haroldo el Normado (three-act), José Rodríguez, 1881, microcard edition, Falls City Press, 1970.

Conflicto entre dos deberes (three-act), Cosme Rodríguez (Madrid), 1883, microcard edition, Falls City Press, 1968.

Correr en pos de un ideal (three-act), Cosme Rodríguez, 1883, microcard edition, Falls City Press, 1968.

En el pilar y en la cruz (three-act), Cosme Rodríguez, 1883, microcard edition, Falls City Press, 1968.

Un milagro en Egipto (three-act), Cosme Rodríguez, 1883, microcard edition, Falls City Press, 1968.

La peste de Otranto (three-act), José Rodríguez, 1884, microcard edition, Falls City Microcards, 1960.

Piensa mal . . . ¿y acertarás? (also see below), first produced in Spain, February 5, 1884.

Obras dramáticas escogidas (contains *La esposa del vengador, En el puño de la espada, O locura ó santidad, En el seno de la muerte, La muerte en los labios,* and *El gran galeoto*), 12 volumes, Imprento de Tello (Madrid), 1884-1905.

Mancha que limpia (also see below; four-act), [Spain], 1885, José Rodríguez, 1895, microcard edition, Falls City Press, 1968.

Vida alegre y muerte triste (three-act), José Rodríguez, 1885.

Dos fanatismos (three-act), José Rodríguez, 1887, reprinted on microcards, Falls City Microcards, 1959.

Manantial que no se agota (three-act), José Rodríguez, 1889, microcard edition, Fall City Press, 1968.

Los rigidos (three-act), José Rodríguez, 1889, microcard edition, Falls City Press, 1970.

Siempre en ridículo, [Spain], 1890, translation by T. Walter Gilkyson published as *Always Ridiculous: A Drama in Three Acts,* R. G. Badger, 1916.

Un crítico incipiente: Capricho en tres actos y en prosa sobre crítica dramática, José Rodríguez, 1891, microcard edition, Falls City Microcards, 1960.

Irene de Otranto (three-act opera), music by Emilio Serrano, José Rodríguez, 1891, microcard edition, Falls City Press, 1968.

El hijo de Don Juan, [Spain], 1892, translation by James Graham published as *The Son of Don Juan: An Original Drama in Three Acts; Inspired by the Reading of Ibsen's Work Entitled "Gengangere,"* Roberts Brothers (Boston), 1895, reprinted, Little, Brown, 1918.

Mariana: An Original Drama in Three Acts and an Epilogue, [Spain], 1892, translated by Graham, Roberts Brothers, 1895.

A la orilla del mar (three-act; first performed in Spain at Teatro de la Comedia, December 12, 1893), R. Velasco, 1903.

The Great Galeoto; Folly or Saintliness: Two Plays, translated by Hannay Lynch, L. Wolffe & Co. (Boston), 1895, reprinted, Fertig, 1989.

El estigma (three-act), E. Odriózola (Madrid), 1896.

El prólogo de un drama (also see below; one-act), E. Odriózola, 1896, microcard edition, Falls City Press, 1970.

El poder de la impotencia (three-act), José Rodríguez, 1897, edited with introduction, notes, and vocabulary by Aurelio M. Espinosa, Schoenhof (Boston), 1906.

La duda (also see below), [Spain], 1898.

El loco dios (four-act; title means "The Insane Gods"), [Spain], 1900, translation by Hunt published in *Poet Lore* as *The Madman Divine (El loco dios),* 1908.

Sic vos non vobis; ó, La última limosna (also see below; three-act), R. Velasco (Madrid), 1905, microcard edition, Falls City Press, 1970.

A fuerza de arrastrarse (also see below), [Spain], 1905.

Silencio de muerte (three-act), R. Velasco, 1906, microcard edition, Falls City Press, 1970.

El preferido y los cenicientos, [Spain], 1908.

Tierra baja (three-act), R. Velasco, 1909, microcard edition, Falls City Press, 1968.

El primer acto de un drama (continuation of *El prólogo de un drama*), R. Velasco, 1914, microcard edition, Falls City Press, 1970.

La rencorosa (three-act), R. Velasco, 1915, microcard edition, Falls City Press, 1970.

Lo sublime en lo vulgar (three-act), R. Velasco, 1918, microcard edition, Falls City Press, 1970.

Teatro escogido (contains *El libro talonario, La última noche, En el puño de la espada, O locura ó santidad, En el seno de la muerte, La muerte en los labios, El gran galeoto, Piensa mal . . . ¿y acertarás?, De mala raza, Sic vos non vobis: o, La última limosna, Mancha que limpia, La duda,* and *A fuerza de arrastrarse*), introduction by Amando Lázaro Ros, Aguilar (Madrid), 1955.

Also author of *La realidad y el delirio.*

OTHER

Teoría matemática de la luz, Imprenta de la Viuda de Agualo (Madrid), 1871.

Disertaciones matemáticas sobre la cuadratura del círculo, el método de Wantzel, y la división de la circunferencia en partes iguales (mathematics), Imprento de la Viuda é Hijo de D. E. Aguado (Madrid), 1887.

Algunas reflexiones generales sobre la crítica y el arte literario [Spain], 1894.

Discursos leídos ante la Real Academia Española (lectures), Imprenta de los Hijos de J. A. García (Madrid), 1894.

Discurso leído en la Universidad central en la solemne inauguración del curso académico de 1905 á 1906 (mathematical physics), Colonial (Madrid), 1905.

Cuentos (short stories), [Spain], 1912.

(Translator of Spanish text) Angel Guimerá, *Marta of the Lowlands (Terra baixa)* (also see below), English text translation by Wallace Gillpatrick, introduction by John Garrett Underhill, Doubleday, 1914.

Recuerdos (autobiography), three volumes, Ruiz Hermanos (Madrid), 1917.

(Translator) Guimerá, *Tierra baja* (three-act play; translation of *Terra baixa*), illustrated by Mauricio de Vassal, Orbis (Barcelona), 1930.

SIDELIGHTS: Regarded as an important link in the history of Spanish drama, the plays of José Echegaray recall the romantic style of the nineteenth century, while also foreshadowing the socially conscious plays of the twentieth. Writing both romantic and naturalistic plays, the author drew large audiences during the three decades that followed his first popular work, *La esposa del vengador* ("The Wife of the Avenger"). Critics, however, felt that Echegaray's romances were too melodramatic and that his naturalistic plays were too contrived and suffered from lack of characterization. Consequently, some reviewers objected to the Nobel Prize committee's decision to honor the playwright in 1904. Frank W. Chandler summarized Echegaray this way in his *Modern Continental Playwrights:* Echegaray "delights to portray high-strung characters, intense hysterical souls, driven by passion or idea. He shows the individual struggling with himself or against social institutions. He loves the moral, the heroic, the perfervid. He is a natural rhetorician, less poetic than theatric. At his worst, Echegaray sinks to the level of extravagant melodrama; at his best, he rises to the heights with such original creations as *Folly or Saintliness* and *The Great Galeoto.*"

Part of Echegaray's success, according to Nora Archibald Smith in *Poet Lore,* may be attributed to his entering "upon the dramatic arena at a critical time, when the political disorder and disturbance which followed the revolution of 1868 were paralleled by similar disorder and disturbance upon the stage." Spanish drama had begun to seek its own individuality after a period when it followed the style of the French classicists and needed a playwright to spearhead this change. Echegaray's first works, such as *La esposa del vengador,* were romances in the same vein as *Romeo and Juliet.* Later, with the rise in popularity of dramas about social issues, the playwright also began to address this concern; but "he did so without in any way forsaking the Romantic tradition," noted E. Allison Peers in his *A History of the Romantic Movement in Spain.*

A major influence of Echegaray's social dramas was Norwegian playwright Henrik Ibsen, a point that was readily acknowledged by Echegaray and even noted directly in his play *The Son of Don Juan: An Original Drama in Three Acts; Inspired by the Readings of Ibsen's Work Entitled "Gengangere."* But although both *The Son of Don Juan* and Ibsen's "Gengangere" ("Ghosts") are studies of a character's decline into madness and contain other similarities in plot and dialogue, a number of critics argued that they are indeed completely different works. Bernard Shaw pointed out in a *Saturday Review* article that the cause of insanity in Ibsen's play is due to outside pressures of society beyond the protagonist's control, while in *The Son of Don Juan* Echegaray places all the blame on the main character himself. "Indeed," noted Shaw, "had Echegaray adapted Ibsen's moral to the conditions of domestic life and public opinion in Spain, the process would have destroyed all the superficial resemblances to

'Ghosts' which has led some critics hastily to describe Echegaray's play as a wholesale plagiarism.''

Other Echegaray plays, such as *El loco dios* ("The Insane Gods"), also reveal the playwright's debt to Ibsen. As *Sewanee Review* contributor Ruth Lee Kennedy warned, however, not all resemblances in the author's plays are attributable to Ibsen's influence. In Echegaray's *Piensa mal . . . ¿y acertarás?*, for example, the "symbolic story of a wounded bird . . . immediately recalls the use of the wild duck in Ibsen's drama of that name." But *Piensa mal* was staged in early 1884, three years before Echegaray could have read Ibsen's *The Wild Duck.*

Besides *The Son of Don Juan*, other well-known Echegaray plays include *O locura ó santidad* ("Folly or Saintiness") and *El gran galeoto* ("The Great Galeoto"), which are "undoubtedly two of Echegaray's best," in *Academy* critic Wentworth Webster's opinion. Both plays are about the destructive powers of public opinion. In *The Great Galeoto*, the author begins with the story of Francesca and Paolo from Dante's *Inferno*, and adds a twist in which the couple's pure love is destroyed by slanderous rumors. In a similar manner, Lorenzo, the protagonist in "Folly or Saintliness" is declared insane by those who cannot understand his high moral principles. Critics like Webster considered the first acts in "Folly or Saintliness" "excellent," but the critic felt the story's resolution suffers when Lorenzo's fate is decided by the destruction of an important document that would vindicate him. "And thus, instead of the solution of the moral problem being laid before us, we have only the more commonplace result, that the world's sentence . . . on a man's sanity may depend on a mere accident."

When considering the lasting relevance of Echegaray's plays, some critics regarded his works as dated. Others, though, took more into consideration the time period in which he wrote. "To get any evaluation of the works of the Spaniard," remarked Kennedy, "his drama should be compared with what was being written in England, France, Italy, and Germany from 1874 to 1884. . . . [By] 1881 Echegaray had written both *O locura ó santidad* and *El gran galeoto*, dramas that certainly, from the standpoint of technique, bear comparison with anything written during that decade." Echegaray "is usually classified as a neoromanticist," Wilma Newberry summarized in *PMLA*, "he is accused of being too melodramatic . . . [and] is called anachronistic and is criticised for blocking the Spanish realist movement." But, Newberry proposed, "Echegaray's true position in the procession of dramatists who have made important contributions to the history of ideas should be reevaluated. Although some aspects of his work may seem anachronistic at the end of the nineteenth century, in many ways he looks forward to the twentieth century, while often drawing inspiration from the great literature of the past."

BIOGRAPHICAL/CRITICAL SOURCES:

BOOKS

Chandler, Frank W., *Modern Continental Playwrights*, Harper, 1931.
Echegaray, José, *The Great Galeoto: A Play in Three Acts*, Doubleday, 1914.
Echegaray, José, *The Son of Don Juan: An Original Drama in Three Acts; Inspired by the Reading of Ibsen's Work Entitled "Gengangere,"* Little, Brown, 1918.
Jameson, Storm, *Modern Drama in Europe*, Collins, 1920.
Peers, E. Allison, *A History of the Romantic Movement in Spain*, Volume 2, Cambridge University Press, 1940.

Shaw, Donald L., *The Nineteenth Century*, Barnes & Noble, 1972.
Twentieth Century Literary Criticism, Volume 4, Gale, 1981.

PERIODICALS

Academy, November 2, 1895.
PMLA, March, 1966.
Poet Lore, May-June, 1909.
Saturday Review, April 27, 1895, June 1, 1901.
Sewanee Review, October-December, 1926.

—*Sketch by Kevin S. Hile*

*   *   *

ELCHAMO, Jason
See CABALLERO, Manuel

*   *   *

El HUITLACOCHE
See KELLER, Gary D.

*   *   *

ELIZONDO, Sergio
See ELIZONDO (DOMINGUEZ), Sergio D(anilo)

*   *   *

ELIZONDO (DOMINGUEZ), Sergio D(anilo) 1930-
(Sergio Elizondo)

PERSONAL: Born April 29, 1930, in El Fuerte, Sinaloa, Mexico; immigrated to United States, 1950, naturalized citizen, 1955; son of Cristino Santiago (a teacher and school principal) and Feliciana (Domínguez) Elizondo; married Sharon Mowrey (a high school teacher), 1958 (marriage ended, 1971); married Szylvia Nagy (a college professor), September, 1982 (marriage ended, September, 1984); children: Sean Santiago, Mark. *Education:* Attended Teacher's College at Sinaloa, 1947; Findlay College, B.A., 1958; University of North Carolina at Chapel Hill, M.A., 1961, Ph.D., 1964.

ADDRESSES: Home—La Mesa, Calif. *Office*—Department of Foreign Languages, New Mexico State University, Box 3L, Las Cruces, N.M. 88003.

CAREER: University of North Carolina, Chapel Hill, instructor in Spanish, 1961-62; University of Texas at Austin, instructor, 1963-64, assistant professor of Spanish, 1964-68; California State College, San Bernardino, associate professor of Spanish, 1968-71; Western Washington State College (now University), Bellingham, dean of College of Ethnic Studies, 1971-72; New Mexico State University, Las Cruces, professor of foreign languages, 1972—, department chair, 1972-75, director of Instituto de Estudios Chicanos-Latinoamericanos, 1975—. Program coordinator and visiting professor at various universities, 1962—. *Military service:* U.S. Army, 1954-56; served in West Germany; became private first class.

MEMBER: American Association of Teachers of Spanish and Portuguese, Poets and Writers, Rocky Mountain Modern Language Association.

AWARDS, HONORS: Grants from Ford Foundation, 1971, New Mexico State University, 1973, and National Endowment for the Arts, 1982.

WRITINGS:

(Under name Sergio Elizondo) *Perros y antiperros: Una épica chicana* (title means "Dogs and Antidogs: A Chicano Epic"; poetry; bilingual edition), English translation by Gustavo Segade, Quinto Sol, 1972.

(Under name Sergio Elizondo) *Libro para batos y chavalas chicanas* (title means "A Book for Chicano Guys and Girls"; poetry; bilingual edition), English translation by Edmundo García Girón, Justa, 1977.

(Under name Sergio Elizondo) *Rosa, la flauta* (title means "Rose, the Flute"; short stories), Justa, 1980.

(With Richard W. Tyler) *The Characters, Plots, and Settings of Calderon's Comedias,* Society of Spanish and Spanish-American Studies (Lincoln, Neb.), 1981.

Muerte en una estrella (title means "Death on a Star"; novel), Tinta Negra, 1984.

(Editor with Ricardo Aguilar and Armando Armengol) *Palabra nueva: Poesía chicana* (anthology of Mexican-American fiction), Dos Pasos, 1985.

(Editor with Aguilar and Armengol) *Palabra nueva: Cuentos chicanos II* (anthology of Mexican-American fiction), Dos Pasos, 1987.

Suruma (novel), Dos Pasos, 1990.

Editor of Dos Pasos Editores, Inc., 1985—.

SIDELIGHTS: Sergio D. Elizondo is the Mexican-American author of two volumes of poetry, a collection of short stories, and two novels. Each of his works addresses aspects of the Chicano movement, which he considers an "awakening" or "renaissance" among Americans of Mexican descent, as he told interviewer Juan D. Bruce-Novoa in *Chicano Authors.* Elizondo began to write creatively while a student at Findlay College, which he attended during the 1950s after immigrating (at first illegally, then legally) to the United States. Although the desire for a publisher and an audience at first prompted the bilingual author to write in English, he says he eventually switched to Spanish because his native language gave him more satisfaction. Elizondo denies that Chicano literature must be written in either one of the two languages; as he told Bruce-Novoa, "The literature of the Chicano [should be written in] the language that is most suited to the writer, the one he feels more comfortable with." He expressed, however, his disappointment in the dearth of Spanish-language literature in the United States. Acting on that dissatisfaction, Elizondo promotes such literature not only through his poetry and fiction but also through his teaching at New Mexico State University and his editorial work with Dos Pasos Editores, a Texas publisher of Spanish-language writings.

Elizondo's first two works, both poetry volumes, were published during the 1970s as Spanish-English editions. The first collection, *Perros y antiperros: Una épica chicana,* translates as "Dogs and Antidogs: A Chicano Epic" and describes conflicts between Anglos (the "dogs" of the title) and Chicanos (the "antidogs"). A Chicano narrator recounts the history of Mexico, particularly the Anglos' nineteenth-century invasions into Hispanic territories, in the first several poems, and he affirms his devotion to his fellow Chicanos throughout the volume. "To a Chicano reader," observed Ana Perches in *Dictionary of Literary Biography,* "the message of the book is to trust his fellow Chicanos and to learn (or relearn) his history, heritage, and the Spanish language so as to reject the Anglo world." By stressing the incompatibility of Mexican-American and Anglo-American societies, noted a *Chicano Literature* reviewer, *Perros y antiperros* conveys "a strong rejection of the melting pot concept."

Libro para batos y chavalas chicanas, which means "A Book for Chicano Guys and Girls," continues Elizondo's treatment of Chicano concerns but is considered less strident than *Perros y antiperros. Libro para batos y chavalas chicanas* contains poetry inspired by a woman the author had loved, explained Perches, and includes depictions of passion, wisdom, and philosophy. "This work is Elizondo's most autobiographical expression," the critic remarked. "Lyrical in tone," according to the *Chicano Literature* reviewer, the poetry conjures images of sand and the desert and water and the sea in illustrating beauty and sensuality.

The short stories in *Rosa, la flauta* ("Rose, the Flute"), while described as less nationalistic than Elizondo's poetry, employ Chicano subjects to explore universal themes. Lost innocence is depicted in the title story, which comprises the thoughts of a young flutist who loses her musical skill when she loses her virginity. An actual Chicano strikers' march is described from the point of view of a sunflower in "Las flores," and metaphysical discussions of creation, space, and energy take place in the stories "Ur" and "Lugar." Commenting on the diversity of Elizondo's writings, the *Chicano Literature* reviewer wrote that "although he is one of the strongest promoters of cultural nationalism and Chicano awareness, his writing evinces metaphysical preoccupations which are absent from most Chicano fiction."

Elizondo's 1984 novel, *Muerte en una estrella* ("Death on a Star"), strongly recalls the social protest evident in his first volume of poetry, according to Perches. The action is based on the true story of two Chicano boys who attend a circus in Texas and are shot by police officers. Few details are provided about the events leading to the shooting, and much of the novel consists of a dialogue between the two dying teenagers, as well as their personal reminiscences. Valentín, the older of the two, proves to be a defiant young man who was raised in poverty and without love. Oscar, whose character is more fully developed, grew up working alongside his migrant parents and, through them, adopted a strong desire to improve life for his family and other Chicanos. His methods differ from his father's, though, for while Oscar advocates joining farmers who strike for better working conditions, his father believes such strikers would only be considered unruly by Anglos and thus ignored or rebuffed with even worse conditions. Elizondo offers no conclusion about which opinion is better; he merely presents the different viewpoints as they exist among Chicanos.

Perches called attention to Elizondo's "ethnocentric view of Chicano culture," which she found evident in *Muerte en una estrella,* and she quoted an explanation the author gave for his focus: "We are ethnocentric because it is a way of showing that we have something valid, that we are human, that we are worth something." Recognizing Elizondo's role as a political artist, Bruce-Novoa described the writer as a "cultured poet [who] garners the cries of the people, distills an essential sentiment, synthesizes a common language, and creates for the *pueblo* its song." The reviewer in *Chicano Literature* likewise recognized the cultural focus of the author's writings and concluded, "Elizondo's main achievement is to have given poetic voice to the Chicano's collective search for identity and historical consciousness."

Elizondo told *Hispanic Writers:* "I still want to be a musician, a performer, a composer, a dancer, and a painter. Most of my brothers are musicians, as are my sons, but I must reconcile and accept my limitations as a musicologist. In my fantasies I am all of the above, but mostly as metaphors in my mind. Now I write to make up for all those persons I am not, and I have found I can do it. The best of my head leads me away from this delightful and frightful wave of life, and into labyrinths of my own making, and I pretend to always have the strength of will and determination to usually come out and start all over again, either daily or consecutively, and pretend that I still am intact.

"To write is to fill up with the images and ideas of one's choice. One may try to be original, and it is not easy; there's always someone more talented and disciplined than I. I must settle for novel forms and modes; that is to say, work like a good jobber and demonstrate talent, if possible, through discipline. The point ought to be to offer all this to other persons out there, the public, for good reasons: to entertain and possibly to edify; or if not this, to offer again any sets of possible variables for a joyful life. One may write to give a greater dimension to life, either mine or yours. If it's mine, it always leaves me a little bit more satisfied, as if one were loved. Why not?

"Love moves us to do fine things. In this case, devices of the craft are silent agents of it, I believe; for one ought not to expect the reader to believe or accept the wisdom of the paternal author. But if the reception has been positive, the craftsman has done the work for at least one of its intended purposes. The writer could stand a little modesty and hope rather than expect; it might save a measure of embarrassment.

"The other ethical aspect of the writer's craft could be construed as the opposite of love; or else, what would one do with the hateful or the hate-filled? Here, the honest craftsman may serve as the executioner of society and, from time to time, mop up the scene of reproachable characters. In any case, it's form and style that determine whether there has been success or failure in the effort. A certain degree of redemptive qualities could be recommended; I, for one, would like to ascribe to myself such presumption; I believe it can be done in many ways, but always under the most difficult factor in the craft: discipline, doing it right so that strangers may possibly understand what the writer is trying to render.

"Now: perhaps the record should speak better than the author."

BIOGRAPHICAL/CRITICAL SOURCES:

BOOKS

Bruce-Novoa, Juan D., *Chicano Authors: Inquiry by Interview,* University of Texas Press, 1980.
Dictionary of Literary Biography, Volume 82: *Chicano Writers, First Series,* Gale, 1989.
Martínez, Julio A. and Francisco A. Lomelí, editors, *Chicano Literature: A Reference Guide,* Greenwood Press, 1985.

—*Sketch by Christa Brelin*

*   *   *

ENAMURADO CUESTA, Jose 1892-

PERSONAL: Born October 7, 1892 in Yauco, Puerto Rico. *Politics:* Member of Puerto Rico Communist Party.

CAREER: U. S. customs inspector, 1916-1929; member of Executive Congress for Independence, 1946; editor of *Puerto Rico Libre* (newspaper); held offices in Puerto Rico Communist Party. *Military service:* U. S. Calvary, 1918-30; became captain.

WRITINGS:

Porto Rico, Past and Present: The Island after Thirty Years of American Rule, Eureka Printing, 1929, reprinted, Arno Press, 1975.
Pedernales, Ponce Printing, 1931.

El imperialismo yanqui y la revolución en el Caribe, Editorial Campos, 1936, 2nd edition, Editorial Puerto Rico Libre, 1966.
Con sangre roja (poemas de revolución), Impr. Soltero, 1946.
Euforia, Impr. Arroyo, 1949.
Manuel María Corchado y Juarbe, auténtico liberal puertorriqueño, Editorial Puerto Rico Libre, 1955.
La princesa y el oso blanco: Versos carcelarios, Editorial Puerto Rico Libre, 1955.
Fuera de la ley: Denuncia de la hipócrita tiranía "democrática" en Puerto Rico, Editorial Puerto Rico Libre, 1957.
Salve hispania, Editorial Puerto Rico Libre, 1958.
Estampas del vivac, Editorial Puerto Rico Libre, 1962.
Puerto Rico se nacionaliza: No se "Americaniza," Editorial Puerto Rico Libre, 1970.
Protohistoria e historia de Puerto Rico, Editorial Edil, 1971.

*   *   *

ESPINOSA, Aurelio M(acedonio)   1880-1958

PERSONAL: Born September 12, 1880, in Carneo, Colo.; died September 4, 1958, in Stanford, Calif.; son of Celso and Rafaela (Martínez) Espinosa; married Margarita García, June 14, 1905; children: María Margarita, Aurelio Macedonio, Jr., José Manuel, María Josefita, Ramón. *Education:* University of Colorado, Ph.B., 1902, M.A., 1904; University of Chicago, Ph.D., 1909.

CAREER: University of New Mexico, Albuquerque, professor of modern languages, 1902-10; Stanford University, Stanford, Calif., began as assistant professor, became associate professor and professor of Spanish, 1910-47, head of department, 1932-47. Fellow and instructor at University of Chicago, 1908-09.

MEMBER: American Association of Teachers of Spanish and Portuguese (co-founder, 1915; president, 1928), American Folklore Society (president, 1923-24), Hispanic Society of America (corresponding member), Real Academia Española de la Lengua (corresponding member), Real Academia Hispano-Americana de Ciencias y Artes (corresponding member), Mexican Society of Geography and Statistics (honorary member), Chile Folklore Society (honorary member), Institut Historique et Heraldique de France, Philological Association of the Pacific Coast (president, 1929), New Mexico Historical Society (honorary member).

AWARDS, HONORS: Decorated Knight Commander of Royal Order of Isabella the Catholic, 1922; Litt.D. from University of San Francisco, 1930; LL.D. from University of New Mexico, 1934.

WRITINGS:

(Translator into Spanish) David Starr Jordan, *La cosecha humana* (title means "The Human Harvest"), [Madrid], 1912.
(With Clifford G. Allen) *Elementary Spanish Grammar, With Practical Exercises for Reading, Conversation, and Composition,* American Book Co., 1915.
(Translator) *El imperio invisible* (title means "Unseen Empire"), [Barcelona], 1915.
Elementary Spanish Reader, With Practical Exercises for Conversation, B. H. Sanborn, 1916.
Advanced Spanish Composition and Conversation, B. H. Sanborn, 1917.
(Editor) *El folklore de Oaxaca,* G. E. Stechert, 1917.
First Spanish Reader, With Grammatical and Conversational Exercises, B. H. Sanborn, 1920.
(With Clifford G. Allen) *Beginning Spanish: Direct Method,* American Book Co., 1921.

(Editor) *Cuentos populares españoles: Recogidos de la tradición oral de España y publicados con una introducción y notas comparativas,* three volumes, Stanford University Press, 1923-26, reprinted, one volume, AMS Press, 1967, 3rd edition published as *Cuentos populares de España,* Espasa-Calpe, 1965.

Elementary Spanish Conversation and Composition, Allyn & Bacon, 1924.

(Editor and author of notes and exercises) *Cuentos, Romances y Cantares: A Collection of Spanish Popular Tales, Ballads, and Songs,* Allyn & Bacon, 1925.

Lecciones de literatura española, Stanford University Press, 1927, revised edition published as *Historia de la literatura española: Breve resumen,* Oxford University Press, 1939.

Easy Spanish Conversation: Spanish Anecdotes, Short Stories, and Other Materials, With Exercises for Conversation and Oral Practice, B. H. Sanborn, 1927.

(With John A. Sellards) *Easy French Composition and Conversation,* B. H. Sanborn, 1927.

Estudios sobre el español de Nuevo Méjico, two volumes, Universidad de Buenos Aires, 1930.

El romancero español: Sus orígenes y su historia en la literatura universal, V. Suárez (Madrid), 1931.

España en Nuevo Méjico: Lecturas elementales sobre la historia de Nuevo Méjico y su tradición española, Allyn & Bacon, 1937.

España: Lecciones elementales sobre la historia de la civilización española, Oxford University Press, 1937.

Conchita Argüello: Historia y novela californiana, Macmillan, 1938.

(Editor) *Romancero de Nuevo Méjico,* Consejo Superior de Investigaciones Científicas (Madrid), 1953.

(Contributor) *Spanish and Portuguese Languages in the United States,* Arno, 1980.

The Folklore of Spain in the American Southwest: Traditional Spanish Folk Literature in Northern New Mexico and Southern Colorado, edited by J. Manuel Espinosa, University of Oklahoma Press, 1985.

Also author of *Primer of Spanish Pronunciation,* with Tomas T. Tomas, 1926. Contributor to scholarly journals. Editor of *Hispania,* 1918-25; associate editor of *Journal of American Folklore.*

BIOGRAPHICAL/CRITICAL SOURCES:

PERIODICALS

Hispania, March, 1959.
Journal of American Folklore, October, 1959.

* * *

ESPINOSA, Aurelio M(acedonio), Jr. 1907-

PERSONAL: Born May 3, 1907, in Albuquerque, N.M.; son of Aurelio Macedonio (a professor of Romance languages) and Margarita (Garcia) Espinosa; married wife, 1942; children: three. *Education:* Stanford University, A.B., 1927, A.M., 1928; University of Madrid, D.Phil. y Let., 1932.

ADDRESSES: Home—632 Foothill, Stanford, Calif. 94305.

CAREER: Stanford University, Stanford, Calif., instructor in Romanic languages, 1927-29; Center for Historical Studies, Madrid, Spain, research associate, 1929-36; Harvard University, Cambridge, Mass., instructor in Romance languages, 1936-46; Stanford University, Stanford, Calif., assistant professor, 1946-49, associate professor, 1949-55, professor of Romanic languages, 1955-72, professor emeritus, 1972—. Acting associate professor at University of Michigan, 1953; visiting professor at University of Oregon, 1960. Collaborator on *Linguistic Atlas of the Iberian Peninsula,* 1932-36. *Military service:* U.S. Army, 1942-46; became lieutenant colonel.

MEMBER: Modern Language Association of America, American Association of Teachers of Spanish and Portuguese, American Folklore Society, Royal Spanish Academy (corresponding member), Philological Association of the Pacific Coast.

AWARDS, HONORS: Order of Alfonso the Wise of Spain, 1956.

WRITINGS:

Arcaísmos dialectales: La conservación de "s" y "z" sonoras en Cáceros y Salamanca, Hernando (Madrid), 1935.

(Editor) *Cuentos castellanos, recogidos de la tradición oral moderna,* Oxford University Press, 1937.

(Editor) *Cuentitos fáciles,* Oxford University Press, 1939.

Cuentos populares de Castilla, recogidos de la tradición oral y publicados con una introducción, Espasa-Calpe Argentina, 1946.

(Editor) *El español de hoy: Contemporary Spanish Readings With Direct-Method Exercises in Conversation and Composition,* Dryden, 1952.

(With Richard L. Franklin and Klaus A. Mueller) *Spanish for Schools and Colleges,* four volumes, Heath, 1966.

(With Franklin and Mueller) *Cultura, conversación y repaso,* Heath, 1967, revised edition published as *Cultura hispánica: Temas para hablar y escribir,* 1972.

(With Laurel H. Turk) *Foundation Course in Spanish,* first published by Heath, 2nd edition, 1970, 4th edition (with Turk and Carlos A. Solé, Jr.), 1978, 5th edition (with Turk and María-Paz Haro), 1981, 6th edition, annotated, 1985.

(With Turk) *Mastering Spanish,* Heath, 1971, 4th edition, 1983.
(With Turk) *Lecturas hispánicas,* Heath, 1972.
(With John P. Wonder) *Gramática analítica,* Heath, 1976.
(With León Gambetta) *Spanish for Doctors and Nurses,* Editorial Excelsior Corp., 1976.

Contributor to scholarly journals. Associate editor of *Hispania,* 1942-47.

* * *

ESTUPIÑAN BASS, Nelson 1915-

PERSONAL: Born in 1915 in Esmeraldas, Ecuador.

CAREER: Novelist and poet.

WRITINGS:

Cuando los guayacanes florecían (novel), Cultura, 1954, third edition, Editorial El Conejo (Quito), 1983, translation by Henry J. Richards published as *When the Guayacans Were in Bloom,* afterword by Richards, Afro-Hispanic Institute (Washington, D.C.), 1987.

Canto negro por la luz: Poemas para negros y blancos, Editorial Rumiñahui (Quito), 1954.

Timarán y Cuabú: Cuaderno de poesía para el pueblo, Cultura, 1956.

El paraíso (novel), Cultura, 1958, second edition, two volumes, 1985.

El último río (novel), Cultura, 1966.
Las huellas digitales: Poemas, Cultura, 1971.
Las tres carabelas: Poesía, relato, teatro, Editorial Gregorio (Portoviejo), 1973.
Senderos brillantes, Cultura, 1974.
Las puertas del verano (novel), Cultura, 1978.
Toque de queda, Cultura, 1978.

El desempate: Cuaderno de poesía para el pueblo, Editorial Gregorio, 1980.

Bajo el cielo nublado, Cultura, 1981.

(Editor) Luis Vargas Torres, *Vargas Torres en la poesía y en la prosa* (anthology), Cultura, 1987.

Contributor to periodicals, including *Norte.*

SIDELIGHTS: Nelson Estupiñán Bass is a novelist and poet who writes of black life in his native province of Esmeraldas, in northwest Ecuador. Many of his works, including the poems of *Canto negro por la luz* and his novel *El último río,* celebrate Afro-Hispanic heritage and call for an end to racial prejudice among all men. Estupiñán Bass's other works include the poetry collections *Timarán y Cuabú* and *El desempate* and the novels *Las*

puertas del verano, El paraíso,* and *Cuando los guayacanes florecían,* which Henry J. Richards translated into English in 1987 as *When the Guayacans Were in Bloom.*

BIOGRAPHICAL/CRITICAL SOURCES:

BOOKS

Jackson, Richard L., *The Black Image in Latin American Literature,* University of New Mexico Press, 1976.

*   *   *

EYNHARDT, Guillermo
  See QUIROGA, Horacio (Sylvestre)

F

FERNANDEZ, Roberto G. 1951-

PERSONAL: Born September 24, 1951, in Sagua la Grande, Cuba; immigrated to United States, 1961; naturalized citizen, 1972; son of José Antonio (a certified public accountant) and Nelia G. (a homemaker; maiden name, López) Fernández; married Elena Reyes (a psychologist), July 7, 1978 (divorced, April 26, 1983; remarried Elena Reyes, 1990); children: Tatiana. *Education:* Florida Atlantic University, B.A., 1970, M.A., 1973; Florida State University, Ph.D., 1977. *Religion:* Roman Catholic.

ADDRESSES: Home—Tallahassee, Fla. *Office*—Department of Modern Languages, Florida State University, Tallahassee, Fla. 32306.

CAREER: Florida State University, Tallahassee, instructor of Spanish literature, 1975-78; University of South Alabama, Mobile, assistant professor of Spanish, 1978-80; Florida State University, associate professor of Spanish and Spanish literature, 1980—.

MEMBER: American Association of Teachers of Spanish and Portuguese, Modern Language Association of America, Associated Writing Programs, Florida Arts Council.

AWARDS, HONORS: Florida Artist fellowship and Cintas fellowship, both 1986-87, for fiction writing; writer in residence at University of Texas at El Paso, 1989; King-Chavez-Parks Visiting Professorship at Western Michigan University, 1990.

WRITINGS:

Cuentos sin rumbos, Ediciones Universal, 1975.
El jardín de la luna, Ediciones Universal, 1976.
La vida es un special (novel), Ediciones Universal, 1981.
(With José B. Fernández) *Indice bibliográfico de autores cubanos (Diáspora, 1959-1979),* Ediciones Universal, 1983.
La montaña rusa (novel), Arte Público, 1985.
Raining Backwards (novel), Arte Público, 1988.

Contributor to periodicals, including *Apalachee Quarterly, Florida Review, Linden Lane,* and *West Branch.*

WORK IN PROGRESS: Nellie, a novel, publication expected in 1992.

SIDELIGHTS: Roberto G. Fernández told *Hispanic Writers:* "*Raining Backwards,* the novel, is the first Cuban-American piece that focuses on the Miami area and the zany characters it has produced and continues to produce. This book is about myths—the myths created by immigrants to explain why they are here and how they fit into this life."

Fernández's first novel in English, *Raining Backwards,* is an experimental, multilayered work. Characters ranging from a cheerleader to the Pope tell their stories through letters, poetry, recipes, advertisements, telephone calls, and other media. *New York Times Book Review* contributor Andrei Codrescu criticized *Raining Backwards* as being "merely quaint because it makes little use of fresh or original language," but later summarized the book as "an affectionate autobiographical memoir cast in a rather fantastic shape by a talented, developing writer." Comparing Fernández to such literary giants as James Joyce and Jonathan Swift, Dawn Kolokithas's *San Francisco Chronicle* review found *Raining Backwards* to be "a zany, unpredictable book that keeps its readers interested and surprised. . . . It is a story told with honesty, outrageous wit and a vigorous imagination of the possible."

BIOGRAPHICAL/CRITICAL SOURCES:

PERIODICALS

Hispanic, March, 1989.
New York Times Book Review, August 14, 1988.
Philadelphia Inquirer, December 6, 1988.
San Francisco Chronicle, April 14, 1988.
USA Today, January 3, 1989.
Vista, September 3, 1988.

* * *

FERNANDEZ, Vicente García Huidobro
See HUIDOBRO FERNANDEZ, Vicente García

* * *

FERNANDEZ MENDEZ, E.
See FERNANDEZ MENDEZ, Eugenio

* * *

FERNANDEZ MENDEZ, Eugenio 1924-
(E. Fernández Méndez)

PERSONAL: Born July 11, 1924, in Cayey, P.R.

ADDRESSES: Office—Department of Sociology, University of Puerto Rico, P.O.B. N, Río Piedras, P.R. 00931.

CAREER: University of Puerto Rico, Río Piedras, professor of anthropology, chair of sociology department, and director of University of Puerto Rico Press. Chairman of board of directors of Institute of Puerto Rican Culture, 1956—.

WRITINGS:

Filiación y sentido de una isla: Puerto Rico; cuatro ensayos en busca de una comunidad auténtica (essays), Editorial del Departamento de Instrucción Pública, Estado Libre Asociado de Puerto Rico (San Juan), 1955, revised edition published as *Puerto Rico, filiación y sentido de una isla: Cuatro ensayos en busca de una comunidad auténtica,* Ariel (San Juan), 1980.

Portrait of a Society: A Book of Readings on Puerto Rican Sociology, University of Puerto Rico, 1956.

Salvador Brau y su tiempo: Drama y paradoja de una sociedad (biography), Universidad de Puerto Rico, 1956.

(Author of introduction) Salvador Brau, *Disquisiciones sociológicas, y otros ensayos* (essays), Universidad de Puerto Rico, 1956.

(Editor under name E. Fernández Méndez) *Crónicas de Puerto Rico desde la conquista hasta nuestros días* (anthology), two volumes, Ediciones del Gobierno, Estado Libre Asociado de Puerto Rico (San Juan), 1957, published under author's full name as *Crónicas de Puerto Rico, desde la conquista hasta nuestros días, 1493-1955,* Universidad de Puerto Rico, 1969.

Tres siglos, Ateneo Puertorriqueño (San Juan), 1958.

Criterios de la periodización cultural de la historia, Universidad Nacional de México, 1959.

La identidad y la cultura: Críticas y valoraciones en torno a Puerto Rico, El Cemí (San Juan), 1959, revised and enlarged edition published as *La identidad y la cultura: Críticas y valoraciones en torno a la historia social de Puerto Rico,* Instituto de Cultura Puertorriqueña (San Juan), 1965.

(Editor) Luis Muñoz Rivera, *Obras completas* (complete works), four volumes, Instituto de Cultura Puertorriqueña (San Juan), 1960.

Ensayos de antropología popular (essays), Universidad de Puerto Rico, 1961, revised and enlarged edition, 1966.

Conceptos fundamentales de antropología física, Universitaria, Universidad de Puerto Rico, 1964.

Historia de la cultura en Puerto Rico, 1493-1960, Rodadero (Puerto Rico), 1964.

Las encomiendas y la esclavitud de los indios de Puerto Rico, 1508-1550, Escuela de Estudios Hispano-Americanos, Consejo Superior de Investigaciones Científicas, 1966.

The Sources on Puerto Rican Culture History: A Critical Appraisal, El Cemí, 1967.

(Editor) *Antología de la poesía puertorriqueña* (anthology), El Cemí, 1968.

Historia cultural de Puerto Rico, 1493-1968, El Cemí, 1970.

Proceso histórico de la conquista de Puerto Rico (1508-1640), Instituto de Cultura Puertorriqueña, 1970.

The Haitian Primitivism (in English, French, and Spanish), Galerie Georges S. Nader (Port-au-Prince, Haiti), 1972.

Art and Mythology of the Taino Indians of the Greater West Indies, El Cemí, 1972.

Antropología, psiquiatría y el porvenir del hombre, El Cemí, 1972.

Viaje histórico de un pueblo: La evolución puertorriqueña, introduction by Abel Plenn, Troutman Press, 1972.

(Editor) *Antología del pensamiento puertorriqueño, 1900-1970* (anthology), two volumes, Universitaria, Universidad de Puerto Rico, 1975.

Autodefinición del hombre a través de una visión humanística de la antropología y la psiquiatría, [Río Piedras], 1979.

Luis Muñoz Rivera, hombre visible, Biblioteca de Autores Puertorriqueños, 1982.

Also author of *Unidad y esencia del Ethos Puertorriqueños,* three volumes, 1954. Contributor to *Asomante, El Mundo, La Torre,* and *Revista del Instituto de Cultura Puertorriqueña.*

* * *

FERNANDEZ MORENO, Baldomero   1886-1950

PERSONAL: Born in Buenos Aires, Argentina, 1886; died, 1950; children: César. *Education:* Studied medicine and qualified as a doctor, 1912.

CAREER: Doctor, 1917-24; literature teacher; poet.

WRITINGS:

Versos de negrita (poems), 1920, reprinted, Editorial Deucalión, 1956.

Nuevos poemas: Ciudad, Intermedio provinciano, Campo argentino, Editorial Tor (Buenos Aires), 1921.

El hogar en el campo (poems), Editorial Tor, 1923.

Décimas (poems), [Buenos Aires], 1928.

Poesía, L. J. Rosso (Buenos Aires), 1928.

Ultimo cofre de negrita (poems), L. J. Rosso, 1929.

Dos poemas: La tertulia de los viernes, Epístola de un verano, El Ateneo (Buenos Aires), 1935.

Seguidillas (poems), El Ateneo, 1935.

Romances (poems), El Ateneo, 1936.

Continuación, Espasa-Calpe Argentina (Buenos Aires), 1938.

Tres poemas de amor, J. Castro Barrera (Buenos Aires), 1941.

Antología, 1915-1940, Espasa-Calpe Argentina, 1941.

Yo, médico, yo, catadrático (poems), Ediciones Anaconda (Buenos Aires), 1941.

Buenos Aires; ciudad, pueblo, campo (poems), G. Kraft (Buenos Aires), 1941.

Las azoteas. Las tapias. Los peones (poems), Fontefrida (Buenos Aires), 1943.

La patria desconocida; páginas de vida, Emecé Editores (Buenos Aires), 1943.

La mariposa y la viga, aire aforístico, aire confidencial (aphorisms and apothgems), Editora y Distribuidora del Plata (Buenos Aires), 1947.

Parva. Xilografías de Víctor Delhez (poems), G. Kraft, 1949.

Viaje del Tucumán, El Balcón de Madera (Buenos Aires), 1949.

Penumbra. Libro de Marcela (poems), Editorial Losada, 1951.

La mariposa y la viga; selección y nota de Raúl Gustavo Aguirre, Ediciones Poesía Buenos Aires, 1955.

Poemas del Uruguay, Editorial Perrot, 1957.

Vida; memorias de Fernández Moreno, G. Kraft, 1957.

La patria desconocida. Selección, Kapelusz (Buenos Aires), 1958.

Las cien mejoras poesías, illustrations by Raúl Soldi, Editorial Universitaria (Buenos Aires), 1961.

San José de Flores, Cuadernos de Buenos Aires, 1963.

Córdoba y sus sierras (poems), prologue and notes by Clara Fernández Moreno, Kapelusz, 1961.

Guía caprichosa de Buenos Aires, Editorial Universitaria de Buenos Aires, 1965.

Poesía y prosa, Centro Editor de América Latina, 1968.

Vida y desaparición de un médico, Editorial Kapelusz, 1968.

La mariposa y la viga (aphorisms and apothgems), R. Alonso (Buenos Aires), 1968.

Obra poética, Huemul (Buenos Aires), 1969.
Baldomero Fernández Moreno, poesía y prosa, Centro Editor de
   América Latina, 1980.
Antología de antologías, Ciudad de La Habana (Cuba), 1984.

Also author of *Las iniciales del misal,* 1915, *Intermedio provinciano,* 1916, *Ciudad,* 1917, *Campo argentino,* 1919, *Aldea española,* 1925, and *El hijo* (poems), 1928; author of aphorisms and
apothgems, *La mariposa y la viga; selección y nota de Raúl Gustavo Aguirre,* Ediciones Poesía Buenos Aires, 1955.

*   *   *

FERNANDEZ MORENO, César   1919-

PERSONAL: Born November 26, 1919, in Buenos Aires, Argentina. *Education:* Received law degree from University of Buenos
Aires.

ADDRESSES: Home—Cuba No 60, Havana 4, Cuba. *Office*—
551 Calzada, Havana 4, Cuba.

CAREER: Poet, literary critic, and editor. Instituto Histórico,
Buenos Aires, Argentina, director, 1963-65; Museum and Library Alberdi, Buenos Aires, director, 1965-66; UNESCO,
Paris, France, beginning in 1967, regional head of Office for Culture in Latin America and the Caribbean, beginning in 1973. Director of the review *Zona.*

MEMBER: Sociedad Argentina de Escritores.

AWARDS, HONORS: Municipal Poetry Prize, 1940, for *Gallo
ciego;* Second National Prize of Literary Criticism, 1958; humanities fellowship from National Fund of Arts, 1959; Poetry Prie
León de Greiff, 1968.

WRITINGS:

Gallo ciego (poems), [Buenos Aires], 1940.
El alegre ciprés (poems), Fontefrida (Buenos Aires), 1941.
La palma de la mano, Fontefrida, 1947.
Viente años después, Losada (Buenos Aires), 1953.
Introducción a Fernández Moreno, Emecé (Buenos Aires), 1956.
Esquema de Borges, Perrot (Buenos Aires), 1957.
Poemas del Uruguay (poems), Perrot, 1957.
Sentimientos (poems), Emecé, 1960.
Argentino hasta la muerta, 2nd edition, Sudamericana (Buenos
   Aires), 1967, revised edition, Centro Editor de América La-
   tina, 1982.
Los aeropuertos, Sudamericana, 1967.
La realidad y los papeles, Aguilar (Madrid), 1967.
(Compiler with Horacio Jorge Becco) *Antología lineal de la poe-
   sía argentina,* Gredos (Madrid), 1968.
Ambages (poems), Monte Avila, 1972.
(Editor and author of introduction) *América Latina en su litera-
   tura,* Unesco, 1972, English translation by Mary G. Berg
   published as *Latin America in Its Literature,* edited by Iván
   Schulman, Holmes & Meier, 1980.
Argentina, with photographs by Simón Feldman, Destino (Bar-
   celona), 1972.
¿Poetizar o politizar? (essays), Losada, 1973.
Introducción a la poesía, Fondo de Cultura Económica (Mexico),
   1973.
La vuelta de Franz Moreno, Mortiz (Mexico), 1975.
Buenos Aires me vas a matar (poems), Siglo XXI, 1977, revised
   edition, Casa de las Américas (Havana, Cuba), 1982.
Sentimientos completos, Ediciones de la Flor, (Buenos Aires),
   1981.

Also author of *Romance de valle verde.* Contributor to periodicals.

SIDELIGHTS: César Fernández Moreno's early poetry was traditional in form and romantic in its depiction of the author's native Argentina; later works employed surrealism and the use of
irony in examining Argentine society.

*   *   *

FERNANDEZ RETAMAR, Roberto   1930-

PERSONAL: Born in 1930 in Havana, Cuba. *Education:* Studied
literature in Havana, Cuba, Paris, France, and London, England.

ADDRESSES: Office—Universidad de la Habana, Calle San Lázaro esq. L, Vedado, Havana 4, Cuba.

CAREER: Worked variously as instructor at Yale University,
New Haven, Conn., diplomat in Paris, France, and professor at
University of Havana, Havana, Cuba. Editor of literary review
published by Casa de las Américas.

MEMBER: Union of Writers and Artists of Cuba (secretary).

WRITINGS:

Patrias, 1949-1951 (poems), [Havana, Cuba], 1952.
La poesía contemporánea en Cuba (1927-1953) (essays), Orí-
   genes (Havana), 1954.
Alabanzas, conversaciones, 1951-1955 (poems), El Colegio de
   México, 1955.
Idea de la estilística (essays), Universidad Central, Departa-
   mento del Relaciones Culturales (Santa Clara, Cuba), 1958.
(Editor with Fayad Jamís) *Poesía joven de Cuba* (poetry), Orga-
   nización Continental de los Festivales del Libro (Havana),
   1959.
(Author of text) Samuel Feijóo, *Dibujos,* Consejo Nacional de
   Cultura, Ministerio de Educación (Havana), 1961.
Papelería (essays), Universidad Central, Dirección de Publica-
   ciones, 1962.
Con las mismas manos, 1949-1962 (poems), Unión de Escritores
   (Havana), 1962.
Historia antigua (poems), Tertulia (Havana), 1964.
(Editor) Rubén Martínez Villena, *Orbita de Rubén Martínez Vi-
   llena,* Unión de Escritores, 1964.
Antología de poetas españoles del siglo XX (essays), Editorial Na-
   cional de Cuba, Universitaria (Havana), 1965.
(Editor) José Martí, *Páginas escogidas,* Universitaria, 1965.
(Editor) Pablo Neruda, *Poesías* (poems), Casa de las Américas
   (Havana), 1965.
Poesía reunida: 1948-1965 (collected poems), Unión (Havana),
   1966.
Buena suerte viviendo, Era (Mexico), 1967.
Ensayo de otro mundo (essays), Instituto del Libro (Havana),
   1967, revised edition, Universitaria (Santiago, Chile), 1969.
(Editor) Ernesto Ché Guevara, *Obra revolucionaria,* Era, 1967.
(Editor) *Cinco escritores de la revolución rusa,* Instituto del
   Libro, 1968.
Introducción a Cuba: La historia, Instituto del Libro, 1968.
(Editor) Alfonso Reyes, *Ensayos* (essays), Casa de las Américas,
   1968.
A quien pueda interesar (poesía, 1958-1970) (poems), Siglo XXI
   (Mexico), 1970.
Algo semejante a los monstruos antediluvianos (poems), Saturno
   (Barcelona), 1970, published as *Qué veremos arder,* Unión
   de Escritores, 1970.
(Editor) José Martí, *Nuestra América,* Ariel (Barcelona), 1970.
Calibán: Apuntes sobre la cultura en nuestra América (essays),
   Diógenes (Mexico), 1971.
Lectura de Martí (essays), Nuestro Tiempo (Mexico), 1972.

El son de vuelo popular, Unión de Escritores, 1972.

Cuaderno paralelo (poems), Unión de Escritores, 1973.

Sobre la crítica de Martí (essays), Bello (Santiago), 1973.

(Editor) José Martí, *Cuba, Nuestra América, los Estados Unidos,* Siglo XXI, 1973.

(With Domingo L. Bordoli and Angel Rama) *Martí: Valoraciones críticas,* Fundación (Montevideo, Uruguay), 1973.

Circunstancia de poesía, Crisis (Buenos Aires), 1974.

(Editor) Jacques Roumain, Pedro Mir, and Jacques Viau, *Poemas de una isla y de dos pueblos,* Casa de las Américas, 1974.

Para una teoría de la literatura hispanoamericana y otras aproximaciones, Casa de las Américas, 1975.

Revolución nuestra, amor nuestro (poems), Arte y Literatura (Havana), 1976.

Introducción a José Martí, Centro de Estudios Martianos/Casa de las Américas, 1978.

Nuestra América y el occidente, Universidad Nacional (Mexico), 1978.

Calibán y otros ensayos: Nuestra América y el mundo, Arte y Literatura, 1979, translation by Edward Baker published as *Caliban and Other Essays,* University of Minnesota Press, 1989.

Cuba hasta Fidel; y, Para leer al Ché, Letras Cubanas (Havana), 1979.

Also author of poetry volume *Elegía como un himno.* Work represented in *Three Cuban Poets: "In the Turmoil of the People,"* edited and translated by Roger Prentice, Canadian-Cuban Friendship Committee, 1967.

*   *   *

FERRATER-MORA, José 1912-

PERSONAL: Born October 30, 1912, in Barcelona, Spain; came to United States, 1947; became naturalized citizen, 1960; son of Maximiliano and Carmen (Mora) Ferrater; married, 1940; children: James. *Education:* Institute of Maragall, Barcelona, B.A., 1932; University of Barcelona, Licenciado en Filosofía, 1936.

ADDRESSES: Home—1518 Willowbrook Lane, Villanova, Pa. 19085. *Office*—Department of Philosophy, Bryn Mawr College, Bryn Mawr, Pa. 19010.

CAREER: University of Chile, Santiago, professor, 1943-47; Bryn Mawr College, Bryn Mawr, Pa., lecturer, 1949-51, associate professor, 1951-56, professor of philosophy, 1956-75, Fairbank Professor of Humanities, 1975-81, professor emeritus, 1981—, chairman of philosophy department, 1971. Visiting professor, Princeton University, 1951-52, Johns Hopkins University, 1955-56, and Temple University, 1970-71.

MEMBER: Institute Internationale de Philosophie, American Philosophical Association, Association for Symbolic Logic, Hispanic Society of America (honorary member).

AWARDS, HONORS: Guggenheim fellowship, 1947-49; American Council of Learned Societies fellowship, 1963-64; D.Litt., Autonomous University of Barcelona, Universidad Nacional de Educación a Distancia, University of Colombia, National University of Uruguay, University of Mendoza, University of Tucuman, University of Salta, and Central University of Barcelona.

WRITINGS:

Cóctel de verdad, Ediciones Literatura (Madrid), 1935.

Diccionario de filosofía, four volumes, Editorial Atlante (Mexico), 1941, 6th edition, 1979.

Unamuno: Bosquejo de una filosofía, Editorial Losada (Buenos Aires), 1944, Alianza Editorial, 1985, translation by Philip Silver published as *Unamuno: A Philosophy of Tragedy,* University of California Press, 1962, reprinted, Greenwood Press, 1981.

Las formas de la vida catalana, Ediciones de la Agrupacio, 1944, 4th edition, 1972.

Variaciones sobre el espíritu, Editorial Sudamericana (Buenos Aires), 1945.

La ironia, la muerte y la admiración, Cruz del Sur (Mexico), 1946.

El hombre en la encrucijada, Editorial Sudamericana, 1952, 2nd edition, 1965.

Cuatro visiones de la historia universal: San Agustin, Vico, Voltaire, Hegel, Editorial Sudamericana, 1952, 6th edition, 1971.

Lógica matemática, Fondo de Cultura Económica (Buenos Aires), 1955, 4th edition, 1967.

Cuestiones disputadas: Ensayos de filosofía, Revista de Occidente (Madrid), 1955.

Ortega y Gasset: An Outline of His Philosophy, Bowes & Bowes, 1956, Yale University Press, 1957, revised edition, 1963.

¿Qué es la lógica?, Editorial Columbia (Buenos Aires), 1957, 3rd edition, 1965.

Man at the Crossroads, translation by Willard R. Trask, Beacon, 1957.

La filosofía en el mundo de hoy, Revista de Occidente, 1959, 2nd edition, c. 1963.

Philosophy Today: Conflicting Tendencies in Contemporary Thought, Columbia University Press, 1960.

Una mica de tot, Editorial Moll (Palma de Mallorca), 1961.

El ser y la muerta: Bosquejo de filosofía integracionista, Aguilar (Madrid), 1962, translation published as *Being and Death: An Outline of Integrationist Philosophy,* University of California Press, 1965.

(With T. A. Brody, J. D. García Bacca, and Henry Margenau) *Symposium sobre información y comunicación,* Universidad Nacional Autónoma de México, 1963.

Obras selectas, two volumes, Ediciones de la Revista de Occidente, 1967.

El ser y el sentido, Ediciones de la Revista de Occidente, 1967.

La filosofía actual, Alianza Editorial, 1969, 4th edition, 1982.

De Joan Oliver a Pere Quart, Ediciones 62 (Barcelona), 1969.

Indagaciones sobre el lenguaje, Alianza Editorial, 1970.

Els mots i els homes, Ediciones 62, 1970.

El hombre y su medio y otros ensayos, Veinteuno de España (Madrid), 1971.

Las palabras y los hombres, Ediciones Peninsul, 1972.

Las crisis humanas, Salvat, 1972, reprinted, Alainza Editorial, 1983.

Cambio de marcha en la filosofía, Alianza Editorial, 1974.

Cine sin filosofía, Esti-Arte Ediciones, c. 1974.

De la materia a la razón, Alianza Editorial, 1979.

Siete relatos capitales, Editorial Planeta, 1979.

Etica aplicada: Del aborto a la violencia, Alianza Editorial, 1981.

Claudia, mi Claudia, Alianza Editorial, 1982.

El mundo del escritor, Editorial Critica, 1983.

Fundamentos de filosofía, Alianza Editorial, 1985.

Modos de hacer filosofía, Critica (Barcelona), 1985.

Voltaire en Nueva York, Alianza Editorial, 1985.

Ventana al mundo, Anthropos, 1986.

Hecho en Corona, Alianza Editorial, 1986.

El juego de la verdad, Destino, 1988.

Regreso del infierno, Destino, 1989.

BIOGRAPHICAL/CRITICAL SOURCES:

BOOKS

Cohn, Priscilla, editor, *Transparencies: Philosophical Essays in Honor of J. Ferrater-Mora,* Humanities, 1981.

*   *   *

FERRE, Rosario 1942-

PERSONAL: Born July 28, 1942, in Ponce, Puerto Rico; daughter of Luis (an engineer) and Lorenza Ramírez Ferré; married Benigno Trigo (a merchant), 1960 (divorced); children: Rosario, Benigno, Luis. *Education:* University of Maryland, Ph.D., 1986. *Religion:* Catholic.

ADDRESSES: Agent—Tomás Colchie, 5 Rue de la Villette, Paris, France 75019.

CAREER: Writer. Founder and director of *Zona de carga y descarga,* a Latin American journal devoted to new Puerto Rican literature.

WRITINGS:

Papeles de Pandora, Joaquín Mortiz (Mexico), 1976.
El medio pollito: Siete cuentos infántiles, Ediciones Huracán (Río Piedras, Puerto Rico), 1976.
La muñeca menor/The Youngest Doll (bilingual edition), illustrations by Antonio Martorell, Ediciones Huracán, 1979.
Sitio a Eros: Trece ensayos literarios, Joaquín Mortiz, 1980.
La mona que le pisaron la cola, Ediciones Huracán, 1981.
Los cuentos de Juan Bobo, Ediciones Huracán, 1981.
Fábulas de la garza desangrada, Joaquín Mortiz, 1982.
La caja de cristal, La Máquina de Escribir (Mexico), 1982.
Maldito amor (title means "Cursed Love,"), Joaquín Mortiz, 1986, revision and translation by Ferré published as *Sweet Diamond Dust,* Ballantine, 1988.
El acomodor: Una lectura fantástica de Felisberto Hernández, Fondo de Cultura Económica, 1986.
Sonatinas, Ediciones Huracán, 1989.
El árbol y sus sombras, Fondo de Cultura (Mexico), 1989.

CONTRIBUTOR

Teresa Mindez Faith, editor, *Contextos: Literarios hispanoamericanos,* Holt, 1985.
Anthology of Contemporary Latin American Literature, 1960-1984, Farleigh Dickinson University Press, 1986.
Lives on the Line: The Testimony of Contemporary Latin American Authors, University of California Press, 1988.
Reclaiming Medusa: Short Stories by Contemporary Puerto Rican Women, Spinsters Aunt Lute (San Francisco, Calif.), 1988.
Marie-Lisa Gazarian Gautier, editor, *Interviews with Latin American Writers,* Dalkey Archive Press, 1989.

Selections from Ferré's writings have also been anthologized in *Ritos de iniciación: Tres novelas cortas de Hispanoamérica,* a textbook for intermediate and advanced students of college Spanish, by Grinor Rojo, and *Anthology of Women Poets.*

SIDELIGHTS: Rosario Ferré represents "a pleasant paradox," writes Alan Cheuse in the *Chicago Tribune:* "that one of the most engaging young Latin American fiction writers at work today is a U.S. citizen." In her collection of a novella and three stories entitled *Sweet Diamond Dust,* "Ferré shows off her linguistic talent as well as her inventiveness by giving us her own English version of the book," Cheuse continues. He calls Ferré "a mature writer" and *Sweet Diamond Dust,* "a fine debut."

BIOGRAPHICAL/CRITICAL SOURCES:

PERIODICALS

Chicago Tribune, January 13, 1989.

*   *   *

FERRER, Gloria M. Pagan
See PAGAN FERRER, Gloria M.

*   *   *

FIGUEROA (MERCADO), Loida 1917-

PERSONAL: Born October 6, 1917, in Yauco, P.R.; daughter of Agustín (a cane cutter) and Emeteria (Mercado) Figueroa; married third husband, José Nelson Castro, November 14, 1953 (divorced, 1957); children: Eunice, María Antonia, Rebeca, Avaris (daughters). *Education:* Polytechnic Institute, San Germán, P.R., B.A. (magna cum laude), 1941; Columbia University, M.A., 1952; Universidad Central de Madrid, Ph.D., 1963. *Politics:* "Independentist." *Religion:* Protestant.

ADDRESSES: Box 456, San Antonio, Aguadilla, P.R. 00752.

CAREER: Teacher in elementary and high schools, 1942-57; Guánica High School, Guánica, P.R., acting principal, 1947, 1955; University of Puerto Rico, Mayaguez, professor of Puerto Rican history, 1957-74; Brooklyn College of the City University of New York, Brooklyn, N.Y., professor of Puerto Rican history, 1974-77. Writer and lecturer.

MEMBER: PEN, Asociación Histórica Puertorriqueña, Association of Caribbean Historians, Asociación de Historiadores Latinoamericanos y del Caribe, Sociedad de Autores Puertorriqueños, Club de Puerto Rico, National Audubon Society, Phi Alpha Theta.

AWARDS, HONORS: Yale University fellow, 1975.

WRITINGS:

Acridulces (poems), Rodríquez Lugo, 1947.
Arenales (novel), Rumbos, 1961, 2nd edition, 1985.
Breve historia de Puerto Rico, Edil, Volume 1: *Desde sus comienzos hasta 1800,* 1968, Volume 2: *Desde 1800 a 1892,* 1969, 4th edition of Volumes 1 and 2 published together as *Breve historia de Puerto Rico,* Part 1, 1971, Part 2: *Desde 1892-1900,* 1976, translation of Part 1 published as *History of Puerto Rico From the Beginning to 1892,* Anaya Book Co., 1972.
Tres puntos claves: Lares, idioma, soberania, Edil, 1972.
La histografía de Puerto Rico, Paraninfo (Madrid), 1975.
El caso de Puerto Rico a nivel international, Edil, 1980.
(Biographical editor) Emilio Godinez Sosa, editor, *Hostos, ensayos inéditos* (booklet), Edil, 1987.
(With Vicente Reynal) *Biografías de hombres y mujeres ilustres de Puerto Rico,* Edil, 1988.
(With Jim Blaut) *La cuestión nacional y el colonialismo,* Claridad, 1988.

Contributor to *Revista de Historia.* Editor of *Atenea* (journal).

WORK IN PROGRESS: Mesa revuelta, an essay anthology (includes "Una Isla en el mar de los caribes" and "Conociendo a Vieques," a travel chronicle).

SIDELIGHTS: Loida Figueroa once told *CA:* "A speech by the late Juan B. Soto. Chancellor of the University of Puerto Rico, given during my high school commencement exercises in 1934 induced me to change my purpose to be a nurse, prompting me instead to continue studying all the way to PhD. The aim was attained in 1963.

"I wrote poems when I was young, but I have abandoned this genre since 1958. I have written one novel, but others rumble in my brain. I cannot direct my pen to write them on account of my involvement in historical writings. I have continued on this track because the majority of our people do not know their own history, and historians in Puerto Rico are few."

She added: "I began to write *Breve historia de Puerto Rico* (not so brief now) because there was no adequate textbook for the course I was asked to teach in the University. I continued writing it and will continue again soon, because even persons on the street ask me when I am going to publish the next volume."

* * *

FIGUEROA, Pablo 1938-

PERSONAL: Born January 26, 1938, in Santurce, Puerto Rico; son of Sotero and Natividad (Dávila) Figueroa. *Education:* City College of the City University of New York, B.A., 1962.

ADDRESSES: Home and office—321 West 22nd St., New York, N.Y. 10011.

CAREER: New York Public Library, New York City, technical assistant, 1965-70; free-lance television producer for National Broadcasting Co., New York City, 1971—. Photographer and theatrical director.

WRITINGS:

Enrique (novel for children), Hill & Wang, 1971.
(With W. D. Halls and R. J. Griggs) *Physics,* Council for Cultural Cooperation, Council of Europe, 1972.
"El King Cojo" (play), first produced Off-Off-Broadway by INTAR, 1973.
Teatro: Hispanic Theatre in New York City, 1920-1976, Alliance, 1977.
"Dolores" (screenplay), New York Committee for Hispanic Families and Children, 1989.

Television programs include "Bienvenido Means Welcome," "We, Together," and "The Hispanic Policeman." Writer of filmstrip, "Los Puertorriqueños," and other materials on Puerto Rico.

WORK IN PROGRESS: Cofresi, a short novel for children.

SIDELIGHTS: Pablo Figueroa commented: "Believe in no ideology, a few people and all children. Interested in all aspects of the communication arts."

* * *

FLORES, Angel 1900-

PERSONAL: Born October 2, 1900, in Barceloneta, P.R.; son of Nepomuceno (in business) and Paula (a teacher; maiden name, Rodríguez) Flores; married Kate Mann (a writer), 1936; children: Ralph, Juan, Barbara Flores Dederick. *Education:* New York University, A.B., 1923; Lafayette College, A.M., 1925; Cornell University, Ph.D., 1947.

ADDRESSES: Home—P.O. Box 4833, Albuquerque, N.M. 87196.

CAREER: Union College, Schenectady, N.Y., instructor in Spanish, 1924-25; Rutgers University, New Brunswick, N.J., instructor in Spanish language and literature, 1925-29; editor of *Alhambra,* 1929-30; Cornell University, Ithaca, N.Y., instructor in Spanish, 1930-33; editor of *Literary World,* 1934-45; Queens College of the City University of New York, Flushing, N.Y., assistant professor, 1945-47, associate professor, 1948-52, professor of romance languages and comparative literature, 1952-70, professor emeritus, 1970—. Visiting professor at University of Wisconsin (now University of Wisconsin—Madison), 1953-54; professor at Graduate Center of the City University of New York, 1968-70. Editor of Dragon Press, 1931-33. Member of Pan American Union's Division of Intellectual Cooperation, 1941-45.

MEMBER: Instituto Internacional de Literatura Iberoamericana.

WRITINGS:

IN ENGLISH

Spanish Literature in English Translation, H. W. Wilson, 1926.
Lope de Vega: Monster of Nature, Brentano's, 1930, re-printed, Kennikat, 1969.
(With M. J. Benardete) *Cervantes across the Centuries: A Quadricentennial Volume,* Dryden, 1947, reprinted, Gordian, 1969.
Masterpieces of the Spanish Golden Age, Rinehart, 1957.
The Medieval Age, Dell, 1963.
The Literature of Spanish America, five volumes, Las Américas, 1966-69.
Ibsen: Four Essays, Haskell Booksellers, 1970.
(With Helene M. Anderson) *Masterpieces of Spanish American Literature,* two volumes, Macmillan, 1972.
A Bibliography of Spanish-American Writers, 1609-1974, Gordian, 1975.
A Kafka Bibliography, 1908-1976, Gordian, 1976.
The Problem of "The Judgment": Eleven Approaches to Kafka's Story, Gordian, 1977.

EDITOR; IN ENGLISH

(With Benardete) *The Anatomy of Don Quixote,* Dragon Press, 1932.
(With Dudley Poore) *Fiesta in November: Stories From Latin America,* Houghton, 1942.
The Kafka Problem: An Anthology of Criticism about Franz Kafka, New Directions, 1946, revised edition, Gordian, 1975.
Spanish Writers in Exile, Bern Porter, 1947, reprinted, 1977.
Great Spanish Stories, Modern Library, 1956.
An Anthology of French Poetry from Nerval to Valery, Doubleday, 1958.
(With Homer Swander) *Franz Kafka Today,* University of Wisconsin Press, 1958, revised edition, Gordian, 1977.
Nineteenth-Century German Tales, Doubleday, 1959.
Spanish Stories (in Spanish and English), Bantam, 1960, 8th edition, 1979.
An Anthology of German Poetry from Hoelderlin to Rilke, Doubleday, 1960.
An Anthology of Spanish Poetry from Garcilaso to García Lorca, Doubleday, 1961.
Great Spanish Short Stories, Dell, 1962.
Spanish Drama, Bantam, 1962.
An Anthology of Medieval Lyrics, Modern Library, 1962.
Giacomo Leopardi, *Leopardi: Poems and Prose,* Greenwood Press, 1966, reprinted, 1987.
The Kafka Debate: New Perspectives for Our Times, Gordian, 1977.

Explain to Me Some Stories of Kafka, Gordian, 1983.

(With wife, Kate Flores) *The Defiant Muse: Hispanic Feminist Poems from the Middle Ages to the Present,* Feminist Press, 1986.

TRANSLATOR INTO ENGLISH

José E. Rodó, *The Motives of Proteus,* Brentano's, 1928.

Ramón Gómez de la Serna, *Movieland,* Macaulay, 1930.

Miguel de Unamuno, *Three Exemplary Novels and a Prologue,* A. & C. Boni, 1930, reprinted, Grove Press, 1987.

Miguel A. Menéndez, *Nayar,* Farrar & Rinehart, 1942.

German Arciniegas, *Germans in the Conquest of America,* Macmillan, 1943.

Benjamin Subercaseaux, *Chile: A Geographic Extravaganza,* Macmillan, 1943, reprinted, Haffner, 1971.

Pablo Neruda, *Selected Poems,* privately printed, 1944.

Neruda, *Residence on Earth and Other Poems,* New Directions, 1946.

Neruda, *Tres cantos materiales: Three Material Songs,* East River Editions, 1948.

Jaime Sabartes, *Picasso: An Intimate Portrait,* Prentice-Hall, 1948.

Humberto Díaz Casanueva, *Requiem,* Grupo Fuego, 1958.

(With Esther S. Dillon) Baldomero Lillo, *The Devil's Pit,* UNESCO Collection of Representative Works, 1959.

Esteban Echeverría, *The Slaughter House,* Las Américas, 1959.

Neruda, *Nocturnal Collection: A Poem,* [Madison, Wis.], 1966.

IN SPANISH

(Translator) T. S. Eliot, *Tierra baldia* (title means "The Waste Land"), Editorial Cervantes, 1930, reprinted, Ocnos, 1973.

(With Alberto Vásquez) *Paisaje y hombres de América,* Dryden, 1947.

Historia y antología del cuento y la novela en Hispanoamérica, Las Américas, 1959.

First Spanish Reader, Bantam, 1964.

La literatura de España, Las Américas, 1970.

Aproximaciones a César Vallejo (title means "Approaches to César Vallejo"), two volumes, Las Américas, 1971.

Aproximaciones a Octavio Paz (title means "Approaches to Octavio Paz"), Mortiz, 1974.

Aproximaciones a Pablo Neruda (title means "Approaches to Pablo Neruda"), Ocnos, 1974.

Orígenes del cuento hispanoamericana (title means "Origins of the Spanish-American Short Story"), Premiá, 1979.

Selecciones españolas (title means "Spanish Selections"), Macmillan, 1979.

Realismo mágico (title means "Magical Realism"), Premiá, 1981.

César Vallejo (biography), Premiá, 1981.

Narrativa hispanoamericana: Historia y antología (title means "Spanish-American Fiction: History and Anthology"), Siglo XXI, 1981.

Expliquémonos a Kafka, Siglo XXI, 1983.

El realismo mágico en el cuento hispanoamericano, Premiá, 1985.

Nuevas aproximaciones a Pablo Neruda, Fondo de Cultura Económica, 1987.

Also author of volumes devoted to Jorge Luis Borges and other Hispanic writers.

BIOGRAPHICAL/CRITICAL SOURCES:

PERIODICALS

New York Times Book Review, May 3, 1987.

FLORIT (y SANCHEZ de FUENTES), Eugenio 1903-

PERSONAL: Born October 15, 1903, in Madrid, Spain; immigrated to Cuba, 1918; immigrated to the United States, 1940; naturalized U.S. citizen, 1960; son of Ricardo (a law clerk) and María (a poet; maiden name, Sánchez de Fuentes) Florit. *Education:* Instituto La Habana, B.A., 1922; University of Havana, LL.D., 1926.

CAREER: Official in Cuban Exterior Ministry, 1927-40; Cuban Consular Service, New York City, consular official, 1940-45; Columbia University, New York City, instructor, 1942-45, professor at Barnard College, 1945-69, professor emeritus of Spanish, 1969—. Writer of poetry, essays, and literary criticism. Taught at Spanish summer school of Middlebury College, 1944-64.

MEMBER: Academia Norteamericana de la Lengua Española, Real Academia de la Lengua (correspondent member), Academia Chilena de la Lengua (correspondent member), Modern Language Association of America, Hispanic Society of America, Association of Professors of Spanish and Portuguese, Cruzada Educativa Cubana.

AWARDS, HONORS: Received medal from La Salle College, 1963, for distinguished contributions to Christian writing, scholarship, and research; Mitre Medal from Hispanic Society of America, 1969; Prize of Literature from Institute of Puerto Rico, 1972; award from Spanish Literary Society, Southern Connecticut College, 1978; Guadalupe Medal from St. John's University.

WRITINGS:

IN ENGLISH

(Editor) *Invitation to Spanish Poetry,* Dover, 1965.

(Editor and translator) *Spanish Poetry: A Selection from the Cantar de Mío Cid to Miguel Hernández,* Dover, 1971.

(Editor and translator) William D. Servodidio, *The Quest for Harmony,* Society of Spanish and Spanish-American Studies, 1979.

POETRY: IN SPANISH

Treinta y dos poemas breves (title means "Thirty-two Short Poems"), [Havana], 1927.

Trópico (title means "Tropic"), Revista de Avance, 1930.

Doble acento (title means "Double Accent"), Ucacia, 1937.

Reino (title means "Kingdom"), Ucar, García, 1938.

Cuatro poemas de Eugenio Florit (title means "Four Poems by Eugenio Florit"), Ucar, García, 1940.

Poema mío: poesía completa (title means "My Poem: Complete Poetry"), Letras de México, 1947.

(Editor and translator) *Antología de la poesía norteamericana contemporánea* (title means "Anthology of Contemporary North American Poetry"), Unión Panamericana, 1955.

Asonante final, y otros poemas (title means "Last Assonant, and Other Poems"), Orígenes, 1955.

Alfonso Reyes: la poesía (title means "The Poetry of Alfonso Reyes"), Hispanic Institute in the United States, 1956.

Antología poética (1930-1955) (title means "An Anthology of My Poems, 1930-1955"), prologue by Andrés Iduarte, Instituto Internacional de Literatura Ibero-Americana, 1956.

(Editor with Enrique Anderson Imbert) *Literatura hispanoamericana: antología e introducción histórica* (title means "Spanish-American Literature: Anthology and Historical Introduction"), Holt, 1960.

Siete poemas (title means "Seven Poems"), Cuadernos Julio Herrera y Reissig, 1960.

Tres autos religiosos (title means "Three Religious Short Plays"), Palma de Mallorca, 1960.

(With Beatrice P. Patt) *Retratos de Hispanoamérica* (title means "Portraits of Spanish America"), Holt, 1962.

(Editor) *Cien de las mejores poesías españolas* (title means "One Hundred of the Best Spanish Poems"), Las Américas, 1965.

Hábito de esperanza: poemas, 1936-1964 (title means "A Cloak of Hope, 1936-1964"), Insula, 1965.

(Editor)*José Martí: Versos,* edited by José Martí, Las Américas, 1965.

(Editor and author of introduction and notes) Federico García Lorca, *Obras escogidas* (title means "Selected Works"), Dell, 1965.

Concordancias de la obra poética de Eugenio Florit (title means "Concordances of the Poetical Works of Eugenio Florit"), edited by Alice M. Pollin, New York University Press, 1967.

(Compiler with José Olivio Jiménez) *La poesía hispanoamericana desde el modernismo* (title means "Spanish American Poetry Since Modernism"), Appleton-Century-Crofts, 1968.

Antología penúltima (title means "Penultimate Anthology"), prologue by José Olivio Jiménez, Plenitude, 1970.

(Editor) *Antología poética (1898-1953)* (title means "An Anthology of Poems (1898-1953)"), Biblioteca Nueva, 1971.

De tiempo y agonía (title means "Of Time and Agony"), introduction by Amelia Agostini de del Río, Roberto Esquenazi-Mayo, and Jiménez, Revista de Occidente, 1974.

Versos pequeños (1938-1975) (title means "Short Poems (1938-1975)"), El Marco, 1979.

Obras completas, edited by Luis González-del-Valle and Roberto Esquenazi-Mayo, Society of Spanish and Spanish-American Studies, Volume 1, 1982, Volume 2, 1983, Volume 3, 1983, Volume 4, in press.

Castillo interior y otros versos, Universal, 1987.

A pesar de todo, Universal, 1987.

Tercero sueño y otros versos, Universal, 1989.

OTHER

Poesía casi siempre: ensayos literarios (title means "Mostly Poetry: Literary Essays"), Mensaje, 1978.

Poesía en José Martí, Juan Ramon Jiménez, Alfonso Reyes, Federico García Lorca y Pablo Neruda: cinco ensayos (title means "The Poetry of José Martí, Juan Ramon Jiménez, Alfonso Reyes, Federico García Lorca, and Pablo Neruda: Five Essays"), Universal, 1978.

Also author of literary criticism, essays, and reviews to scholarly journals. Editor of *Revista Hispánica Moderna,* 1960-69.

AVOCATIONAL INTERESTS: Music, painting.

BIOGRAPHICAL/CRITICAL SOURCES:

BOOKS

Burnshaw, Stanley, *The Poem Itself,* Holt, 1960.

Florit, Eugenio, *Antología penúltima,* prologue by José Olivio Jiménez, Plenitude, 1970.

PERIODICALS

Hispania, May, 1969, May, 1972, September, 1972.

*   *   *

FOMBONA, Rufino Blanco
See BLANCO FOMBONA, Rufino

FORNES, Maria Irene 1930-

PERSONAL: Born May 14, 1930, in Havana, Cuba; immigrated to the United States, 1945; naturalized U.S. citizen, 1951; daughter of Carlos Luis (a public servant) and Carmen Hismenia (Collado) Fornes. *Education:* Attended public schools in Havana, Cuba. *Politics:* Democrat. *Religion:* Catholic.

ADDRESSES: Home—One Sheridan Sq., New York, N.Y. 10014. *Agent*—Helen Merrill, 435 West 23th St. #1A, New York, N.Y. 10011.

CAREER: Playwright, 1960—. Painter in Europe, 1954-57; textile designer in New York City, 1957-60. Director of her plays, including "Tango Palace," "The Successful Life of 3," "The Annunciation," "Molly's Dream," "Aurora," "Cap-a-Pie," "Fefu and Her Friends," "Washing," "Eyes on the Harem," "Evelyn Brown (A Diary)," "Life Is Dream," "A Visit," "The Danube," "Abingdon Square," "Sarita," "Mud," "Cold Air," "The Conduct of Life," "A Matter of Faith," and "Lovers and Keepers." Founding member and president, New York Theatre Strategy, 1973-78. Teacher with Theatre for the New City, New York City, 1972-73, Padua Hills Festival, Claremont, Calif., 1978—, INTAR (International Arts Relations), New York City, 1981—, and at numerous universities and theatre festivals in the United States.

MEMBER: Dramatists Guild, ASCAP, League of Professional Theatre Women, Society of Stage Directors and Choreographers.

AWARDS, HONORS: John Hay Whitney Foundation fellowship, 1961; Centro Mexicano de Escritores fellowship, 1962; Obie Award (Off-Broadway theatre award) for distinguished playwriting (and direction), 1965, for "Promenade" and "The Successful Life of 3," 1977, for "Fefu and Her Friends," 1984, for "The Danube," "Mud," and "Sarita," and 1988, for "Abingdon Square"; Yale University fellowships, 1967, 1968; Cintas Foundation fellowship, 1967; Boston University-Tanglewood fellowship, 1968; Rockefeller Foundation grants, 1971, 1984; Guggenheim fellowship, 1972; Creative Artist Public Service grants, 1972, 1975; National Endowment for the Arts grants, 1974, 1984; Obie Award for distinguished direction, 1979, for "Eyes on the Harem"; Obie Award for sustained achievement, 1982; Obie Award for best new play, 1985, for "The Conduct of Life"; American Academy and Institute of Arts and Letters Award in Literature, 1985; Playwrights U.S.A. Award, 1986, for translation of "Cold Air."

WRITINGS:

PLAYS

"The Widow" (published as "La Viuda" in *Cuatro Autores Cubanos*), Casa de las Américas (Havana), 1961.

"There! You Died" (also see below) first produced in San Francisco at Actor's Workshop, November 19, 1963; title changed to "Tango Palace" (also see below), first produced on double bill with "The Successful Life of 3" in Minneapolis at Firehouse Theatre, January 22, 1965; produced in New York City at Theatre Genesis, 1973.

"The Successful Life of 3" (also see below), first produced on double bill with "Tango Palace" at Firehouse Theatre, January 22, 1965; produced Off-Broadway at Sheridan Square Playhouse Theatre, March 15, 1965.

"Promenade" (musical; also see below), music by Al Carmines, first produced Off-Off-Broadway at Judson Poets' Theatre, April 9, 1965; produced Off-Broadway at Promenade Theatre, June 4, 1969.

The Office (first produced on Broadway at Henry Miller's Theatre, April 21, 1966 [preview performances; never officially opened]), Establishment Theatre Co., 1965.

"A Vietnamese Wedding" (also see below), first produced in New York City at Washington Square Methodist Church, February 4, 1967; produced Off-Broadway at La Mama Experimental Theatre, April 12, 1969.

"The Annunciation," first produced on double bill with "The Successful Life of 3" at Judson Poets' Theater, May, 1967.

"Dr. Kheal" (also see below), first produced at Judson Poets' Theater, April 3, 1968; produced in London, 1969.

"The Red Burning Light: or Mission XQ3" (also see below), first produced in Zurich, Switzerland, for Open Theatre European Tour, June 19, 1968; produced at La Mama Experimental Theatre, April 12, 1969.

"Molly's Dream" (also see below), music by Cosmos Savage, first produced Off-Off-Broadway at New York Theatre Strategy, 1968.

Promenade and Other Plays (includes "Tango Palace," "The Successful Life of 3," "Promenade," "A Vietnamese Wedding," "Dr. Kheal," "The Red Burning Light: or Mission XQ3," and "Molly's Dream"), Winter House, 1971, reprinted, PAJ Publications, 1987.

"The Curse of the Langston House," first produced in Cincinnati at Playhouse in the Park, October, 1972.

"Aurora," first produced at New York Theatre Strategy, 1974.

"Cap-a-Pie," music by José Raul Bernardo, first produced Off-Off-Broadway at INTAR (International Arts Relations), May, 1975.

"Washing," first produced Off-Off-Broadway at the Theatre for the New City, November 11, 1976.

"Lolita in the Garden," first produced at INTAR, 1977.

"Fefu and Her Friends," first produced at New York Theatre Strategy, May 5, 1977; produced Off-Broadway at the American Place Theater, January 6, 1978; published in *Wordplays 1*, PAJ Publications, 1981.

"In Service," first produced in Claremont, Calif., at the Padua Hills Festival, 1978.

"Eyes on the Harem," first produced at INTAR, April 23, 1979.

"Evelyn Brown (A Diary)," first produced at Theatre for the New City, April 3, 1980.

(Adaptor) Federico García Lorca, "Blood Wedding," produced at INTAR, May 15, 1980.

(Adaptor) Pedro Calderón de la Barca, "Life Is Dream," produced at INTAR, May 28, 1981.

"A Visit," first produced at the Padua Hills Festival, 1981; produced at Theatre for the New City, December 24, 1981.

"The Danube" (also see below), first produced at the Padua Hills Festival, 1982; produced at Theatre for the New City, February 17, 1983; produced at the American Place Theater, March 11, 1984.

"Mud" (also see below), first produced at the Padua Hills Festival, 1983; produced at Theatre for the New City, November 10, 1983.

"Sarita" (musical; also see below), music by Leon Odenz, first produced at INTAR, January 18, 1984.

"No Time," first produced at the Padua Hills Festival, 1984.

"The Conduct of Life" (also see below), first produced at Theatre for the New City, February 21, 1985.

(Adaptor and translator) Virgilio Piñera, *Cold Air* (produced at INTAR, March 27, 1985), Theatre Communications Group, 1985.

Maria Irene Fornes: Plays (includes "Mud," "The Danube," "Sarita," and "The Conduct of Life"), preface by Susan Sontag, PAJ Publications, 1986.

"A Matter of Faith," first produced at Theatre for the New City, March 6, 1986.

Lovers and Keepers (three one-act musicals; first produced at INTAR, April 4, 1986), music by Tito Puente and Fernando Rivas, Theatre Communications Group, 1987.

"Drowning" (one-act; adapted from Anton Chekhov's story of the same title; produced with six other one-act plays under collective title "Orchards"), first produced Off-Broadway at Lucille Lortel Theater, April 22, 1986; published in *Orchards*, Knopf, 1986.

"Art," first produced at Theatre for the New City, 1986.

"The Mothers" (also see below), first produced at the Padua Hills Festival, 1986.

"Abingdon Square," first produced the American Place Theater, October, 1987.

(Adaptor) Chekhov, "Uncle Vanya," produced Off-Broadway at the Classic Stage Company, December, 1987.

"Hunger" (also see below), first produced Off-Off-Broadway by En Garde Productions, 1989.

"And What of the Night" (includes "Hunger," "Springtime," "Lust," and "Charlie" [previously "The Mothers"]), first produced in Milwaukee, Wis., at Milwaukee Repertory, 1989.

Also author of "The Anatomy of Inspiration."

SIDELIGHTS: "One would almost think," writes the *Chicago Tribune*'s Sid Smith, that playwright and director Maria Irene Fornes "was a hot young New York experimentalist—indeed, in a sense, she is and always will be. Her work spans decades, but she endures as a refreshing influence." Smith comments that although Fornes has won six "Obie" awards for her plays Off-Broadway, she is "one of the art form's most cherished secrets. Ask playgoers about her, and they are apt to answer with a blank look. Mention Fornes to those who work in the theater, and their faces light up." As Wynn Handman of the American Place Theatre told *New York*'s Ross Wetzsteon, "She's clearly among the top five playwrights in America today. [But] playwrights like Irene, whose work haunts and resonates rather than spelling everything out, almost never receive immediate recognition." Although they frequently deal with human and even "political" issues, "Fornes's plays are whimsical, gentle and bittersweet, and informed with her individualistic intelligence," states Bonnie Marranca in *American Playwrights: A Critical Survey.* "Virtually all of them have a characteristic delicacy, lightness of spirit, and economy of style. Fornes has always been interested in the emotional lives of her characters, so human relationships play a significant part in the plays." The critic adds that Fornes "apparently likes her characters, and often depicts them as innocent, pure spirits afloat in a corrupt world which is almost absurd rather than realistic. . . . Political consciousness is present in a refined way."

It is not Fornes's subjects, however, that make her work unconventional; as the playwright told Kathleen Betsko and Rachel Koenig in *Interviews with Contemporary Women Playwrights,* "I realized that what makes my plays unacceptable to people is the form more than the content. My content is usually not outrageous. . . . What makes people vicious must be the form." This form is influenced by diverse factors, "neither theatre nor literature but certain styles of painting and the movies," notes Susan Sontag in her preface to *Maria Irene Fornes: Plays.* "But unlike similarly influenced New York dramatists, her work did not eventually become parasitic on literature (or opera, or movies). It was never a revolt against theatre, or a theatre recycling fantasies encoded in other genres." The critic continues by remarking that "Fornes is neither literary nor anti-literary. These are not cerebral exercises or puzzles but the real questions."

Fornes's first major critical success was "Promenade," a musical which debuted in 1965 and contributed to her first Obie Award. "The play mixes wit and compassion, humor and tenderness, zaniness and social satire as prisoners named 105 and 106 journey from prison out into the world and back again," describes Phyllis Mael in a *Dictionary of Literary Biography* essay. While much of the play's action concerns the comic conflict between the prisoners and the rich and powerful people they meet, it is Fornes's lyrics that "comment on unrequited love, the abuse of power, the injustice of those who are supposed to uphold the law, and the illogical and random nature of life," adds Mael. "In a work that is really more a choreographed oratorio than a conventional musical," comments Stephen Holden in the *New York Times,* "the music and language are reduced to artful basics, as in the Virgil Thomson-Gertrude Stein operas." Because of this lack of conventional plot, "there may be those who will question the slightness of the story line," maintains *New York Times* critic Clive Barnes, "but there will be more, many, many more who will glory in the show's dexterity, wit and compassion. Miss Fornes's lyrics, like her book, seem to have a sweetly irrelevant relevance." Marranca similarly observes that "*Promenade* has the joie de vivre, the disregard for external logic and spatial convention, the crazy-quilt characters that one associates with the plays of Gertrude Stein. . . . The satire seems almost effortless because the playwright's touch is so playful and laid back. Yet Fornes makes her point, and there's no confusion as to whose side she is on in this comedy of manners." As Barnes concludes in his review: "One definition of 'Promenade' might be that it is a protest musical for people too sophisticated to protest."

"Fefu and Her Friends," Fornes's next major success, ventures even farther into new dramatic forms. Set in one house where eight women are meeting, "the play has no plot in the conventional sense, and the characters are presented as fragments," remarks Marranca. "Though there is much about them that Fornes keeps hidden, the play—seeming at first like realism—is purposely set in the realm of the mysterious and abstract. By setting the play in a home, and then offering a narrative that subverts realistic conventions, Fornes plays ironically with domestic space, and the notion of domestic drama." The playwright presents a further innovation by having the audience separate and move out of the main theatre to view four separate scenes in different areas of the house. "[But] the conceit is more than just a gimmick," writes David Richards in the *Washington Post.* "Fornes, you see, is literally asking her audience to 'track down' her characters. . . . Theater-goers are being transformed into sleuths." The result of this fragmentation, claims Richard Eder in the *New York Times,* is that " 'Fefu' is the dramatic equivalent of a collection of poems. Each conversation, each brief scene tries to capture an aspect of the central, anguished vision."

This reformation of traditional staging has disturbed some critics, however. Walter Kerr believes that there is too much emphasis on the structure of the play; he states in the *New York Times* that while "everyone finally gets to see every scene, though not in the same sequence . . . this does not matter for the play is not going anywhere; *you* are." The critic also comments that "if I lasted as long as I did, it was because I kept hoping during my constant journeyings that I *might* find a play in the very next room." But others, such as *Washington Post* contributor Lloyd Grove, find that this complicated staging is effective: "You're close enough to touch the characters in action, and suddenly on intimate-enough terms with them to grasp what they're about." Mael similarly believes that "these close-ups (another example

of Fornes's use of cinematic style) enable members of the audience to experience the women's relationship in a more intimate manner than would be possible on a proscenium stage." And Richards feels that "the strength of this production is that it has you thinking, 'If only I could look into one more room, catch one more exchange, come back a minute later.' In short, it lures you into a labyrinth of the mind." "*Fefu and Her Friends* has the delicacy of tone and economical style of Fornes's earlier plays," concludes Marranca. "[But] what makes this play stand apart— and ahead—of the others is, more than the inclusiveness of the experiment in text and performance, the embodiment of a deeply personal vision."

"Ever since *Fefu and Her Friends* Maria Irene Fornes has been writing the finest realistic plays in this country," asserts Marranca in *Performing Arts Journal.* "In fact, one could say that *Fefu* and the plays that followed it . . . have paved the way for a new language of dramatic realism, and a way of directing it." The critic explains: "Fornes brings a much needed intimacy to drama, and her economy of approach suggests another vision of theatricality, more stylized for its lack of exhibitionism." Calling Fornes "America's truest poet of the theatre," a *Village Voice* critic observes that in 1985 Obie-winner "The Conduct of Life," the author "takes on a subject so close to the bones of our times you'd think it unapproachable." "The Conduct of Life" follows the family life of a torturer who works for a fascist Latin American government. Although "we don't think of the fascist classes in Latin America bothering with disgust or introspection or moral concern," remarks Paul Berman in the *Nation,* ". . . of course they do, and no doubt they ask [questions] much the way Fornes shows this officer's unhappy wife asking in *The Conduct of Life,* with agonies of soul and eventually with a gun. And what is this, by the way, if not the spirit of our time?"

In presenting the internal and external conflicts of these characters, Fornes uses "a dozen or so vignettes, some lasting only a moment or two, that are punctuated by lighting that fades slowly," describes Herbert Mitgang of the *New York Times.* The critic adds that "these theatrical punctuation marks are the equivalent of the ellipses that some poets and novelists use, and abuse, to tell the reader: At this point it's time to think about the wisdom of what is being said." Thus "the play conjures a lot of tension, mostly by keeping the scenes tight and disciplined and unsettlingly short," states Berman. "The dialogue and staging seem almost to have been cropped too close . . . [but] sometimes the cropping pares away everything but the musing of a single voice, and these monologues are the most effective aspect of all." Although he finds some faults with the play, Berman concludes that "*The Conduct of Life* is incomparably more serious than any of the new plays on Broadway and will surely stand out in memory as a bright spot of the season." And another *Village Voice* critic presents a comparable assessment, calling Fornes's work "as important and as entertaining as any you're likely to see this year."

"Fornes's work goes to the core of character," writes Marranca. "Instead of the usual situation in which a character uses dialogue or action to explain what he or she is doing and why, her characters exist in the world by their very act of trying to understand it. In other words, it is the characters themselves who appear to be thinking, not the author having thought." Sontag also praises the playwright, commenting that "Fornes's work has always been intelligent, often funny, never vulgar or cynical; both delicate and visceral. Now it is something more. . . . The plays have always been about wisdom: what it means to be wise. They are getting wiser." "Working for more than [thirty] years in Off-Broadway's unheralded spaces," declares Marranca, "Fornes is an exemplary artist who through her writing and teaching has created a life in the theatre away from the crass hype that attends so many lesser beings. How has she managed that rare accomplishment in this country's theatre—a career?" Explains the critic: "What is admirable about Fornes is that she is one of the last real bohemians among the writers who came to prominence in the sixties. She never changed to fit her style to fashion. She has simply been writing, experimenting, thinking. Writers still have to catch up to her." The critic concludes that "if there were a dozen writers in our theatre with Fornes's wisdom and graciousness it would be enough for a country, and yet even one of her is sometimes all that is needed to feel the worth of the enormous effort it takes to live a life in the American theatre."

A manuscript collection of Fornes's work is located at the Lincoln Center Library of the Performing Arts in New York City.

BIOGRAPHICAL/CRITICAL SOURCES:

BOOKS

Betsko, Kathleen and Rachel Koenig, *Interviews with Contemporary Women Playwrights,* Beech Tree Books, 1987.
Contemporary Literary Criticism, Volume 39, Gale, 1986.
Dictionary of Literary Biography, Volume 7: *Twentieth-Century American Dramatists,* Gale, 1981.
Fornes, Maria Irene, *Maria Irene Fornes: Plays,* PAJ Publications, 1986.
Marranca, Bonnie and Gautam Dasgupta, *American Playwrights: A Critical Survey,* Volume 1, Drama Books Specialists, 1981.

PERIODICALS

Chicago Tribune, June 14, 1969, February 8, 1988.
Hispanic, July, 1988.
Los Angeles Times, July 9, 1987.
Nation, April 6, 1985.
Newsweek, June 4, 1969.
New York, June 23, 1969, March 18, 1985.
New York Times, April 17, 1968, June 5, 1969, June 6, 1969, February 22, 1972, January 14, 1978, January 22, 1978, April 25, 1979, December 30, 1981, October 25, 1983, March 13, 1984, March 20, 1985, April 17, 1986, April 23, 1986, October 17, 1987, December 15, 1987.
Performing Arts Journal, Number 1, 1984.
Village Voice, April 21, 1966, April 17, 1969, March 19, 1985, March 26, 1985.
Washington Post, July 9, 1983, July 15, 1983.

—*Sketch by Diane Telgen*

* * *

FREYRE, Ricardo Jaimes
See JAIMES FREYRE, Ricardo

* * *

FUENTES, Carlos 1928-

PERSONAL: Born November 11, 1928, in Panama City, Panama; Mexican citizen; son of Rafael Fuentes Boettiger (a career diplomat) and Berta Macías Rivas; married Rita Macedo (a movie actress), 1959 (divorced, 1969); married Sylvia Lemus (a television journalist), 1973; children: (first marriage) Cecilia; (second marriage) Carlos Rafael, Natasha. *Education:* National University of Mexico, LL.B., 1948; graduate study, Institute des Hautes Etudes, Geneva, Switzerland. *Politics:* Independent leftist.

ADDRESSES: Home—716 Watchung Rd., Bound Brook, N.J. 08805.

CAREER: Writer. International Labor Organization, Geneva, Switzerland, began as member, became secretary of the Mexican delegation, 1950-52; Ministry of Foreign Affairs, Mexico City, Mexico, assistant chief of press section, 1954; National University of Mexico, Mexico City, secretary and assistant director of cultural dissemination, 1955-56; head of department of cultural relations, 1957-59; Mexico's ambassador to France, 1975-77. Fellow at Woodrow Wilson International Center for Scholars, 1974. Norman Maccoll Lecturer, Cambridge University, 1977; Virginia Gildersleeve Professor, Barnard College, 1977; Henry L. Tinker Lecturer, Columbia University, 1978; lecturer or visiting professor at University of Mexico, University of California at San Diego, University of Oklahoma, University of Concepción in Chile, University of Paris, University of Pennsylvania, Harvard University, and George Mason University.

MEMBER: American Academy and Institute of Arts and Letters (honorary).

AWARDS, HONORS: Centro Mexicano de Escritores fellowship, 1956-57; Biblioteca Breve Prize from Seix Barral (publishing house; Barcelona), 1967, for *Cambio de piel;* Xavier Villaurrutia Prize (Mexico), 1975; Rómulo Gallegos Prize (Venezuela), 1977, for *Terra Nostra;* Alfonso Reyes Prize (Mexico), 1979, for body of work; National Award for Literature (Mexico), 1984, for "Orchids in the Moonlight"; nominated for *Los Angeles Times* Book Award in fiction, 1986, for *The Old Gringo;* Miguel de Cervantes Prize from Spanish Ministry of Culture, 1987; Rubén Darío Order of Cultural Independence (Nicaragua) and literary prize of Italo-Latino Americano Institute, both 1988, for *The Old Gringo;* honorary degrees from numerous colleges and universities, including Columbia College, Chicago State University, Harvard University, and Washington University.

WRITINGS:

NOVELS

La región más transparente, Fondo de Cultura Económica, 1958, translation by Sam Hileman published as *Where the Air Is Clear,* Ivan Obolensky, 1960, Hileman's translation published as *Where the Air Is Clear: A Novel,* Farrar, Straus, 1982.
Las buenas consciencias, Fondo de Cultura Económica, 1959, translation published as *The Good Conscience,* Ivan Obolensky, 1961, reprinted, Farrar, Straus, 1981.
La muerte de Artemio Cruz, Fondo de Cultura Económica, 1962, reprinted, 1983, translation by Hileman published as *The Death of Artemio Cruz,* Farrar, Straus, 1964.
Aura (also see below), Era, 1962, reprinted, 1982, translation by Lysander Kemp, Farrar, Straus, 1965.
Zona sagrada, Siglo XXI, 1967, translation by Suzanne Jill Levine published as *Holy Place* (also see below), Dutton, 1972.
Cambio de piel, Mortiz, 1967, translation by Hileman published as *A Change of Skin,* Farrar, Straus, 1968.
Cumpleaños, Mortiz, 1969, translation published as "Birthday" in *Holy Place & Birthday: Two Novellas,* Farrar, Straus, in press.
Terra Nostra (also see below), Seix Barral, 1975, translation by Levine, afterword by Milan Kundera, Farrar, Straus, 1976.
La cabeza de hidra, Mortiz, 1978, translation by Margaret Sayers Peden published as *Hydra Head,* Farrar, Straus, 1978.

Una familia lejana, Era, 1980, translation by Peden published as *Distant Relations,* Farrar, Straus, 1982.

El gringo viejo, Fondo de Cultura Económica, 1985, translation by Peden and Fuentes published as *The Old Gringo,* Farrar, Straus, 1985.

Christopher Unborn (translation of *Cristóbal Nonato*), Farrar, Straus, 1989.

Holy Place & Birthday: Two Novellas, Farrar, Straus, in press.

SHORT STORIES

Los días enmascarados (also see below), Los Presentes, 1954, reprinted, Era, 1982.

Cantar de ciegos (also see below), Mortiz, 1964.

Dos cuentos mexicanos (title means "Two Mexican Stories"; two short stories previously published in *Cantar de ciegos*), Instituto de Cultura Hispánica de Sao Paulo, Universidade de Sao Paulo, 1969.

Poemas de amor: Cuentos del alma, Imp. E. Cruces (Madrid), 1971.

Chac Mool y otros cuentos, Salvat, 1973.

Agua quemada (anthology), Fondo de Cultura Económica, 1981, translation by Peden published as *Burnt Water,* Farrar, Straus, 1980.

Constancia and Other Stories for Virgins, Farrar, Straus, 1989.

PLAYS

Todos los gatos son pardos (also see below), Siglo XXI, 1970.

El tuerto es rey (also see below; first produced [in French], 1970), Mortiz, 1970.

Los reinos originarios (contains "Todos los gatos son pardos" and "El tuerto es rey"), Seix Barral, 1971.

Orquídeas a la luz de la luna (first produced in English as "Orchids in the Moonlight" at American Repertory Theater in Cambridge, Mass., June 9, 1982), Seix Barral, 1982.

NONFICTION

The Argument of Latin America: Words for North Americans, Radical Education Project, 1963.

(Contributor) *Whither Latin America?* (political articles), Monthly Review Press, 1963.

Paris: La revolución de mayo, Era, 1968.

La nueva novela hispanoamericana, Mortiz, 1969.

(Contributor) *El mundo de José Luis Cuevas,* Tudor (Mexico City), 1969.

Casa con dos puertas (title means "House With Two Doors"), Mortiz, 1970.

Tiempo mexicano (title means "Mexican Time"), Mortiz, 1971.

Cervantes; o, La crítica de la lectura, Mortiz, 1976, translation published as *Don Quixote; or, The Critique of Reading,* Institute of Latin American Studies, University of Texas at Austin, 1976.

On Human Rights: A Speech, Somesuch Press (Dallas), 1984.

Latin America: At War With the Past, CBC Enterprises, 1985.

Myself With Others: Selected Essays, Farrar, Straus, 1988.

OTHER

(Editor and author of prologue) Octavio Paz, *Los signos en rotación, y otros ensayos,* Alianza, 1971.

Cuerpos y ofrendas (anthology; includes selections from *Los días enmascarados, Cantar de ciegos, Aura,* and *Terra Nostra*), introduction by Octavio Paz, Alianza, 1972.

(Author of introduction to Spanish translation) Milan Kundera, *La vida está en otra parte,* Seix Barral, 1977.

(Author of introduction) Omar Cabezas, *Fire From the Mountain,* Crown, 1988.

Collaborator on several film scripts, including "Pedro Páramo," 1966, "Tiempo de morir," 1966, and "Los caifanes," 1967. Work represented in numerous anthologies, including *Antología de cuentos hispanoamericanos,* Nueva Década (Costa Rica), 1985. Contributor to periodicals in the United States, Mexico, and France, including *New York Times, Washington Post,* and *Los Angeles Times.* Founding editor, *Revista Mexicana de Literatura,* 1954-58; co-editor, *El Espectador,* 1959-61, *Siempre,* 1960, and *Política,* 1960.

WORK IN PROGRESS: A novel about the assassination of Emiliano Zapata; a five-part television series for the Smithsonian Institution, to be called "The Buried Mirror," commemorating the 500th anniversary of Christopher Columbus's voyage, to be broadcast in the fall of 1991.

SIDELIGHTS: "Carlos Fuentes," states Robert Maurer in *Saturday Review,* is "without doubt one of Mexico's two or three greatest novelists." He is part of a group of Latin American writers whose writings, according to Alistair Reid's *New Yorker* essay, "formed the background of the Boom," a literary phenomenon Reid describes as a period in the 1960s when "a sudden surge of hither-to unheard-of writers from Latin America began to be felt among [U.S.] readers." Fuentes, however, is singled out from among the other writers of the Boom in José Donoso's autobiographical account, *The Boom in Spanish American Literature: A Personal History,* in which the Chilean novelist calls Fuentes "the first active and conscious agent of the internationalization of the Spanish American novel." And since the 1960s, Fuentes has continued his international influence in the literary world: his 1985 novel, *The Old Gringo,* for example, was the first written by a Mexican to ever appear on the *New York Times* best-seller list.

Although, as Donoso observes, early worldwide acceptance of Fuentes's novels contributed to the internationalization of Latin American literature, his work is an exploration of the culture and history of one nation, his native Mexico. Critics note the thematic presence of Mexico in nearly all Fuentes's writing. Robert Coover comments in the *New York Times Book Review* that in *The Death of Artemio Cruz,* for instance, Fuentes delineates "in the retrospective details of one man's life the essence of the post-Revolutionary history of all Mexico." Mexico is also present in Fuentes's novel *Terra Nostra,* in which, according to *Washington Post Book World* contributor Larry Rohter, "Fuentes probes more deeply into the origins of Mexico—and what it means to be a Mexican—than ever before." Fuentes's *Old Gringo*—published more than twenty years after *The Death of Artemio Cruz*—returns to the same theme as it explores Mexico's relationship with its northern neighbor, the United States.

Fuentes explains his preoccupation with Mexico, and particularly with Mexican history, in a *Paris Review* interview. "Pablo Neruda used to say," he told Alfred MacAdam and Charles Rúas, "that every Latin American writer goes around dragging a heavy body, the body of his people, of his past, of his national history. We have to assimilate the enormous weight of our past so that we will not forget what gives us life. If you forget your past, you die." Fuentes also notes that the development of the same theme in his novels unifies them so that they may be considered part of the same work. The author observes in the same interview, "In a sense my novels are one book with many chapters: *Where the Air Is Clear* is the biography of Mexico City; *The Death of Artemio Cruz* deals with an individual in that city; [and] *A Change of Skin* is that city, that society, facing the world, coming to grips with the fact that it is part of civilization and that there is a world outside that intrudes into Mexico."

Along with thematic unity, another characteristic of Fuentes's work is his innovative narrative style. In a *New Yorker* review, Anthony West compares the novelist's technique to "a rapid cinematic movement that cuts nervously from one character to another." Evan Connell states in the *New York Times Book Review* that Fuentes's "narrative style—with few exceptions—relies on the interruption and juxtaposition of different kinds of awareness." Reviewers Donald Yates and Karen Hardy also comment on Fuentes's experimental style. In the *Washington Post Book World* Yates calls Fuentes "a tireless experimenter with narrative techniques and points of view," while in *Hispania* Hardy notes that in Fuentes's work "the complexities of a human or national personality are evoked through . . . elaborate narrative devices."

Fuentes's novels *The Death of Artemio Cruz* and *Terra Nostra* are especially good examples of his experimental techniques. The first narrative deals with a corrupt Mexican millionaire who on his deathbed relives his life in a series of flashbacks. In the novel Fuentes uses three separate narrations to tell the story, and for each of these narrations he uses a different narrative person. *New York Review of Books* contributor A. Alvarez explains the three-part narration of the novel: "Cruz's story is told in three persons. 'I' is the old man dying on his bed; 'you' is a slightly vatic, 'experimental' projection of his potentialities into an unspecified future . . . ; 'he' is the real hero, the man whose history emerges bit by bit from incidents shuffled around from his seventy-one years." In John S. Brushwood's *Mexico in Its Novel: A Nation's Search for Identity,* the critic praises Fuentes's technique, commenting: "The changing narrative viewpoint is extremely effective, providing a clarity that could not have been accomplished any other way. I doubt that there is anywhere in fiction a character whose wholeness is more apparent than in the case of Artemio Cruz."

Coover observes that in *Terra Nostra* Fuentes once again uses a variety of narrators to tell his story. Commenting favorably on Fuentes's use of the "you" narrative voice in the novel, Coover writes: "Fuentes's second person [narration] is not one overheard on a stage: the book itself, rather than the author or a character, becomes the speaker, the reader or listener a character, or several characters in succession." Spanish novelist Juan Goytisolo similarly states in *Review:* "One of the most striking and most successful devices [in *Terra Nostra*] is the abrupt shift in narrative point of view (at times without the unwary reader's even noticing), passing from first-person narration to second, . . . and simultaneously rendering objective and subjective reality in one and the same passage with patent scorn for the rules of discourse that ordinarily govern expository prose." In the *Paris Review* Fuentes comments on his use of the second person narrative, calling it "the voice poets have always used and that novelists also have a right to use."

Fuentes's use of the second person narrative and other experimental techniques makes his novels extremely complex. The author's remarks in a *New York Times Book Review* interview with Frank MacShane concerning the structure of *Terra Nostra* describe the intricacy of the work: "My chief stylistic device in 'Terra Nostra' is to follow every statement by a counter statement and every image by its opposite." This deliberate duplicity by the author, along with the extensive scope of the novel, causes some reviewers to criticize *Terra Nostra* for being unaccessible to the average reader. Maurer, for instance, calls the novel "a huge, sprawling, exuberant, mysterious, almost unimaginably dense work of 800 pages, covering events on three continents from the creation of man in Genesis to the dawn of the twenty-first century," and adds that "*Terra Nostra* presents a common reader with enormous problems simply of understanding what is going on." *Newsweek*'s Peter S. Prescott notes: "To talk about [*Terra Nostra*] at all we must return constantly to five words: excess, surreal, baroque, masterpiece, [and] unreadable."

Other critics, however, have written more positive reviews, seeing *Terra Nostra* and other Fuentes works as necessarily complex. *Village Voice* contributor Jonah Raskin finds Fuentes is at his best when the novelist can "plunge readers into the hidden recesses of his characters' minds and at the same time allow language to pile up around their heads in thick drifts, until they feel lost in a blizzard of words that enables them to see, to feel, in a revolutionary way." Fuentes also defends the difficulty of his works in a *Washington Post* interview with Charles Truehart. Recalling the conversation with the Mexican author, Truehart quotes Fuentes as saying: "I believe in books that do not go to a ready-made public. . . . I'm looking for readers I would like to *make*. . . . To *win* them, . . . to *create* readers rather than to give something that readers are expecting. That would bore me to death."

While Fuentes's innovative use of theme and structure has gained the author an international reputation as a novelist, he believes that only since *Terra Nostra* has he perfected his craft. "I feel I'm beginning to write the novels I've always wanted to write and didn't know how to write before," he explains to Philip Bennett in a *Boston Globe Magazine* interview. "There were the novels of youth based on energy, and conceptions derived from energy. Now I have the conceptions I had as a young man, but I can develop them and give them their full value."

MEDIA ADAPTATIONS: Two short stories from *Cantar de ciegos* were made into films in the mid-1960s; *The Old Gringo* was adapted into a film of the same title by Fonda Films, 1989.

AVOCATIONAL INTERESTS: Reading, travel, swimming, visiting art galleries, listening to classical and rock music, motion pictures, the theater.

BIOGRAPHICAL/CRITICAL SOURCES:

BOOKS

Authors in the News, Volume 2, Gale, 1976.
Brushwood, John S., *Mexico in Its Novel: A Nation's Search for Identity,* University of Texas Press, 1966.
Contemporary Literary Criticism, Gale, Volume 3, 1975, Volume 8, 1978, Volume 10, 1979, Volume 13, 1980, Volume 22, 1982, Volume 41, 1987.
Donoso, José, *The Boom in Spanish American Literature: A Personal History,* Columbia University Press, 1977.
Plimpton, George, editor, *Writers at Work: The Paris Review Interviews, Sixth Series,* Penguin Books, 1984.

PERIODICALS

Boston Globe Magazine, September 9, 1984.
Hispania, May, 1978.
Los Angeles Times Book Review, October 27, 1985.
Newsweek, November 1, 1976.
New Yorker, March 4, 1961, January 26, 1981, February 24, 1986.
New York Review of Books, June 11, 1964.
New York Times Book Review, November 7, 1976, October 19, 1980, October 27, 1985, August 20, 1989.
Paris Review, winter, 1981.
Review, winter, 1976.
Saturday Review, October 30, 1976.
Village Voice, January 28, 1981, April 1, 1986.
Washington Post, May 5, 1988.

Washington Post Book World, October 26, 1976, January 14, 1979, August 20, 1989.

—Sketch by Marian Gonsior

*   *   *

FUENTES, Gregorio López y
See LOPEZ y FUENTES, Gregorio

*   *   *

FUSI (AIZPURUA), Juan Pablo 1945-

PERSONAL: Born September 24, 1945, in San Sebastián, Spain; son of Vincenzo and María Delores (Aizpurua) Fusi; married Eva Rodríguez. *Education:* University of Madrid, lic. in history; University of Oxford, D.Phil.

ADDRESSES: Home—Amaniel 30, E-Madrid, 8, Spain. *Office*—Biblioteca Nacional, Paseo de Recoletos 20, 28001 Madrid, Spain.

CAREER: Colegio Universitario, Madrid, Spain, lecturer in contemporary Spanish history, 1975-77; University of Oxford, St. Antony's College, Oxford, England, head of Iberian Centre, 1977-79; University of Santander, Santander, Spain, head of department of history, beginning 1979; Biblioteca Nacional, Madrid, currently director of library. Visiting professor, University of Wisconsin, 1981.

WRITINGS:

(With Raymond Carr) *Spain: Dictatorship to Democracy,* Allen & Unwin, 1979, 2nd edition, Unwin Hyman, 1981.
Franco: Autoritarismo y poder personal, El País, 1986, translation by Felipe Fernández-Armesto published as *Franco: A Biography,* Harper, 1988.

Also author of *Working Class Politics in the Basque Country 1880-1923,* 1975, and *El problema vasco en la segunda república,* c. 1988.

SIDELIGHTS: Juan Pablo Fusi's study *Franco: A Biography* has been commended for its objective assessment of the life and regime of Generalissimo Francisco Franco, who ruled Spain from 1939 until his death in 1975. *New York Times Book Review* contributor William Herrick, for example, notes that this "excellent book" is "dispassionately written and, most rare for the subject,

without ideological discoloration." Where other biographies have been politically biased, Fusi's *Franco* is "a short, balanced and intelligent account of Franco's long reign," David Gilmour summarizes in the *London Review of Books.* Including selections from the memoirs of Franco's associates, Fusi "has produced a dense and dispassionate reappraisal of Franco's career, crisply written and cool where the others are verbose and partisan," states Paul Preston in his *Times Literary Supplement* review. Fusi, "in his concise and careful study, sets out to explain the apparently contradictory elements of Franco's career."

As Gilmour explains, "the author manages to reconcile conflicting views [of Franco's regime] by deflating the arguments used by both critics and admirers. There are some contradictions in the book," the reviewer continues, but "its appraisal of Franco's achievements is more accurate and less tendentious than we used to get. Franco is presented as neither a great statesman nor a lucky adventurer but as a skilful politician without much vision—which is what he was." Preston similarly observes that in this "indispensable" narrative, "Fusi produces a convincing character study of the cold, reserved, slow-moving Franco and of that indefinable quality, so akin to good luck, his ability simply to survive by waiting for the wind to change." "The judgments of Franco and Francoism that emerge" in *Franco,* writes Edwin M. Yoder, Jr. of the *Washington Post Book World,* are "incisive but measured. Like most revisionist historians, recent chroniclers of the Franco years are beginning to detect continuities obscured by the bitter polemics and resentments of the Caudillo's time." "Any judgment of Franco must set the stability and prosperity his regime created against the persecution and misery he caused in the early years and the disregard for human rights he maintained until his death," states Gilmour. "For many years supporters and critics simply refused to acknowledge that there were two sides to his rule. It is the chief merit of Fusi's book," the critic concludes, "that it presents the contrasting features of the man and his regime clearly and dispassionately, so that an impartial judgment can at least be attempted."

BIOGRAPHICAL/CRITICAL SOURCES:

PERIODICALS

London Review of Books, February 4, 1988.
National Review, August 5, 1988.
New York Times Book Review, May 1, 1988.
Times Literary Supplement, October 3, 1986.
Washington Post Book World, May 1, 1988.

G

GALARZA, Ernest
See GALARZA, Ernesto

* * *

GALARZA, Ernesto 1905-1984
(Ernest Galarza)

PERSONAL: Born August 15, 1905, in Jalcocotán, Nayarit, Mexico; immigrated to United States, 1911, naturalized citizen, 1939; died June 22, 1984, in San Jose, Calif.; son of Ernesto (a merchant) and Henriqueta (a homemaker) Galarza; married Mae Taylor (a schoolteacher), December, 1928; children: two daughters. *Education:* Occidental College, B.A., 1927; Stanford University, M.A., 1929; Columbia University, Ph.D., 1944.

ADDRESSES: Home—1031 Franquette St., San Jose, Calif. 95125.

CAREER: Pan American Union (now Organization of American States), Washington, D.C., began as educational specialist, became chief of Division of Labor and Social Information, 1936-47; National Farm Labor Union, Sacramento Valley, Calif., director of research and education and field organizer, 1947-54; National Agricultural Workers Union, Sacramento Valley, director of research and education and field organizer in Florida, Louisiana, Texas, Arizona, and California, 1954-63; writer and lecturer. Researcher and adviser to Foreign Policy Association on Latin American Affairs; program analyst of Economic and Youth Opportunity Agency, Los Angeles, Calif.; counsel to U.S. House of Representatives Committee on Education and Labor. Consultant to Republic of Bolivia, National Farmers Union, U.S. Civil Rights Commission, Ford Foundation, Rosenberg Foundation, John Hay Whitney Foundation, Anti-Defamation League, Human Resources Corporation of San Francisco, Santa Barbara Schools, Edgewood District Schools, and Laras Fund.

Lecturer at various institutions, including universities of Denver, Texas, Minnesota, Utah, and Arizona, Claremont and Pomona colleges, John Marshall College of Law, Universidad de la Paz, Bolivia, and Universidad Nacional Autónoma de México; associate research professor at Notre Dame University; associate of graduate school of education of Harvard University. Distinguished visiting professor at San Jose State University; regents visiting professor at University of California, San Diego; honorary fellow of Oaks College at University of California, Santa Cruz. Codirector of an elementary school in Jamaica, N.Y., 1934-36; elementary school teacher; organizer and teacher at Boys Clubs. Chairman of National Committee of Classroom Teachers and of National Committee of La Raza Unida; director of organization and research of Santa Clara County Community Organization to Monitor Education; director of Studio Laboratory for Bilingual Education of San Jose Unified School District. Training counselor at Alviso Family Health Service and counselor at Alviso Community Planning Committee. Worked as a newsboy, Western Union messenger, stock clerk, farm worker, cannery laborer, camp counselor, Christmas card designer, social work aide, and court interpreter.

MEMBER: Phi Beta Kappa.

AWARDS, HONORS: Officer of Order of the Condor from Republic of Bolivia; honorary Ph.D. from Occidental College, 1971; Chicano Studies Diploma from Stanford University for service to minority students; community awards from Santa Clara County for public service.

WRITINGS:

(Under name Ernest Galarza) *The Roman Catholic Church as a Factor in the Political and Social History of Mexico,* Capital Press (Sacramento, Calif.), 1928.

(Under name Ernest Galarza) *Argentina's Revolution and Its Aftermath,* Foreign Policy Association (New York), 1931.

(Under name Ernest Galarza) *Debts, Dictatorship and Revolution in Bolivia and Peru,* Foreign Policy Association, 1931.

Thirty Poems, Yearlong School (Jamaica Estates, N.Y.), 1935.

La industria eléctrica en México, Fondo de Cultura Económica, 1941.

Labor Trends and Social Welfare in Latin America, two volumes, Pan American Union, Division of Labor and Social Information (Washington, D.C.), 1941.

Plantation Workers in Louisiana, Inter-American Education Association, 1955.

Strangers in Our Fields, Joint United States-Mexico Trade Union Committee (Washington, D.C.), 1956.

Merchants of Labor: The Mexican Bracero Story; An Account of the Managed Migration of Mexican Farm Workers in California, 1942-1960, preface by Ernest Gruening, McNally & Loftin, 1964.

(With Herman Gallegos and Julian Samora) *Mexican-Americans in the Southwest: A Report to the Ford Foundation,* 1966, published with photographs by George Ballis, McNally & Loftin, 1969.

Spiders in the House and Workers in the Field, University of Notre Dame Press, 1970.

Barrio Boy (autobiography), University of Notre Dame Press, 1971.

Bilingual Education in the San Jose Unified School District, Department of Urban Education and San Jose Model Cities, 1973.

Farm Workers and Agri-Business in California, 1947-1960, University of Notre Dame Press, 1977.

The Tragedy at Chualar, McNally & Loftin, 1977.

Kodachromes in Rhyme (poems), University of Notre Dame Press, 1982.

JUVENILE

Zoo-risa: Rimas y fotografías de Ernesto Galarza, McNally & Loftin, 1968, English companion text published as *Zoo-Fun,* Almadén (San Jose, Calif.), 1971, selections published as *Where Do Stories Come From,* Ginn and Co., 1976.

Aquí y allá en California, with own photographs, Almadén, 1971.

(With Robert E. Neitsch and Phil Wood) *Historia verdadera de una gota de miel,* with own photographs, Almadén, 1971.

Poemas párvulos (poems), illustrations by Vincent P. Rascón, arranged by Neitsch, Almadén, 1971.

Rimas tontas, illustrations by Arthur J. Schneida, arranged by Neitsch, Almadén, 1971.

La historia verdadera de una botella de leche, with own photographs, Almadén, 1972.

Mas poemas párvulos (poems), Almadén, 1972.

Poemas pe-que pe-que pe-que-ñitos: Very, Very Short Nature Poems (text in Spanish and English), with own photographs, Almadén, 1972.

Un poco de México, with own photographs, Almadén, 1972.

Chogorrom, Almadén, 1973.

Todo mundo lee, Almadén, 1973.

Also author of pamphlets *What Is Progressive Education: An Outline for Parents,* Yearlong School, 1934; *Educational Trends in Latin America,* Pan American Union, Division of Intellectual Cooperation, 1937; *The Latin American Universities in Step With History,* U.S. Government Printing Office, 1940; *Labor in Latin America,* American Council on Public Affairs (Washington, D.C.), 1942; *Economic Development of the Oakland/Mexican American Community,* 1969; and *Alviso: The Crisis of a Barrio,* Mexican American Community Services Agency (San Jose, Calif.), 1973. Author or editor of various issues of "Inter-American Reports" series, including *The Case of Bolivia, Armaments in the Western Hemisphere, Argentine Labor Under Peron, Economic Conflict in Inter-American Relations, Crisis of the Pan American Union,* and *The Cost of Living in Latin America.*

Chapters published in various books, including *Problemas Agrícolos Industriales de México,* 1958; *Plural Society in the Southwest,* University of New Mexico Press, 1972; *Ghosts in the Barrio,* Leswig Press (San Rafael), 1973; *Teaching the Bilingual,* University of Arizona Press, 1974; *Chicano Content and Social Work Education,* Council on Social Work Education, 1975; *Humanidad: Essays in Honor of George I. Sánchez,* edited by Américo Paredes, Regents of the University of California Chicano Studies Center, 1977; and *Immigrants—and Immigrants,* Greenwood Press, 1978. Contributor to periodicals, including *Nation,* and *New York Times.* Editor of "Young Reader Series" for Pan American Union, 1942.

SIDELIGHTS: Ernesto Galarza was a union leader and writer who fought tirelessly for the rights of American and Mexican farm workers. Through his many writings, including *Strangers in Our Fields, Merchants of Labor,* and *Spiders in the House and Workers in the Field,* Galarza attempted to bring an end to the exploitation of agricultural laborers by calling attention to the abuses they suffered—such as low pay and squalid living conditions at workers' camps—at the hands of the federal government and private agricultural corporations.

Galarza was born in 1905 in an Indian village in western Mexico's Sierra Madres. At the age of six he migrated north with his mother and two uncles as part of an exodus of hundreds of thousands of Mexicans who were fleeing the violence of the revolution and seeking work in the American West and Southwest. Galarza's family settled in Sacramento, California, and his uncles worked on the railroads while he attended school. Galarza learned English quickly, and, an astute student, he won a scholarship to Occidental College. After earning his bachelor's degree there he received his master's from Stanford and his doctorate from Columbia. In 1936 he moved to Washington, D.C., to join the Pan American Union (PAU) as an education specialist. He later became director of its labor and social information office. During his eleven-year tenure with the PAU he wrote numerous pamphlets discussing Latin American labor, education, and politics and the book *Labor Trends and Social Welfare in Latin America.* He resigned his position after eleven years, however, claiming that the PAU tolerated the exploitive practices of U.S. business interests against Mexican agricultural workers.

Galarza returned to the Sacramento Valley, joined the fledgling National Farm Labor Union and later the National Agricultural Workers Union, and attempted to help farm laborers in the West and Southwest who were suffering due to the mismanagement and exploitative policies of the "bracero" system. Beginning in World War II, the U.S. Government, with the cooperation of the Mexican Government, imported many Mexican contract workers, or braceros, to supplement the dwindling American agricultural work force. Some profit-minded growers, however, exclusively hired the Mexican migrants, who were forced for survival to work at a lower wage. Galarza realized that this practice was also detrimental to the welfare of domestic laborers, who, because they were not unionized, could lose their jobs to the cheaper workforce.

Galarza attempted to unionize the American and Mexican workers but his efforts were opposed by the agricultural corporations, which, Galarza told *HW* in 1984, "coordinated land, water, and labor supply with technology, mechanization and mass marketing" to enormous profits. In 1947, when Galarza and other union leaders attempted to organize a group of laborers employed by the DiGiorgio Fruit Corporation, the giant of agribusiness at the time, DiGiorgio, with congressional help, crushed their strike and sued the union and Galarza for libel. Galarza would later chronicle the devastating though not insurmountable blow to unionizing in *Spiders in the House and Workers in the Field.* Undaunted, Galarza led a strike of California tomato pickers three years later and cantaloupe pickers in 1951 and helped organize Louisiana sugar-cane workers and strawberry pickers.

Galarza next called attention to the struggle between the braceros and farm owners in *Strangers in Our Fields,* a report resulting from his tour of more than 150 migrant worker camps in California and Arizona during the 1955 harvest season. In interviews with hundreds of Mexican agricultural laborers Galarza heard stories of low wages and lack of worker representation and saw the filthy living conditions and lack of food. Galarza told *HW* that when *Strangers in Our Fields* was published, "the documented complaints provoked efforts at the highest levels of the state and federal government by agribusiness to suppress the report. They did not succeed, and the document became pivotal in the long struggle to terminate the bracero program."

Galarza continued his assault on the bracero system with *Merchants of Labor,* a 1964 exposé focusing on the agreements between the governments of Mexico and the United States and between U.S. Government officials and private industry to control the migration and wages of industrial workers. In 1964, due in part to Galarza's reports on abuse in the bracero system, the laws concerning immigration were repealed and the bracero system was forced to an end. Galarza soon retired from the union and devoted himself to community work, teaching elementary school (Galarza and the San Jose Unified School District were pioneers in bilingual education) and writing. Some of his works of this period include *Mexican Americans in the Southwest,* the history *Farm Workers and Agri-Business in California, 1947-1960,* and *The Tragedy at Chualar,* an account of an accident in which thirty-two braceros perished in an overcrowded bus that collided with a train in California. Galarza also published his autobiography, *Barrio Boy,* in 1971, focusing on his emigration from Mexico and acculturation into American life. In addition, he wrote numerous volumes for young readers, including the nursery rhyme collections *Poemas párvulos* and *Rimas tontas, La historia verdadera de una botella de leche,* in which bilingual cows tell the story of milk, and photo books about Mexico and California.

Galarza told *HW:* "*Barrio Boy* is the story of a Mexican family, uprooted from its home in a mountain village, in continuous flight from the revolutionary wind that swept Mexico after 1910. The episodes of the journey were typical of those of hundreds of thousands of refugees. They settled permanently in California and other border states. The barrio of this tale is that of Sacramento, California."

BIOGRAPHICAL/CRITICAL SOURCES:

BOOKS

Barrera, Mario and Geralda Vialpando, editors, *Action Research: In Defense of the Barrio; Interviews with Ernesto Galarza, Guillermo Flores, and Rosalio Muñoz,* Aztlán Publications, 1974.
Galarza, Ernesto, *Barrio Boy,* University of Notre Dame Press, 1971.
Meister, Dick and Amme Loftis, *A Long Time Coming: The Struggle to Unionize America's Farm Workers,* Macmillan, 1977.

PERIODICALS

New York Review of Books, August 31, 1972.

OBITUARIES:

PERIODICALS

Chicago Tribune, June 26, 1984.
New York Times, June 25, 1984.
Washington Post, June 25, 1984.

—Sketch by Carol Lynn DeKane

GALDOS, Benito Pérez
See PEREZ GALDOS, Benito

* * *

GALEANO, Eduardo (Hughes) 1940-

PERSONAL: Born September 3, 1940, in Montevideo, Uruguay; son of Eduardo Hughes and Ester Galeano; married first wife Silvia Brando, 1959; married second wife, Graciela Berro, 1962; married third wife, Helena Villagra, 1976; children: (first marriage) Veronica; (second marriage) Florencia, Claudio. *Education:* Attended school in Uruguay. *Politics:* Socialist. *Religion:* None.

ADDRESSES: c/o Susan Bergholz Literary Services, 340 West 72nd, New York, N.Y. 10023

CAREER: Marcha (weekly), Montevideo, Uruguay, editor in chief, 1961-64; *Epoca* (daily), Montevideo, director, 1964-66; University Press, Montevideo, editor in chief, 1965-73; *Crisis* (magazine), Buenos Aires, Argentina, founder, 1973, director, 1973-76; writer.

AWARDS, HONORS: Premio Casa de las Américas, 1975, for *La canción de nosotros,* and 1978, for *Días y noches de amor y de guerra;* American Book Award, 1989, for *Memory of Fire.*

WRITINGS:

Los días siguientes (novel), Alfa, 1962.
China 1964: Crónica de un desafío, Jorge Alvarez, 1964.
Los fantasmas del día del léon, y otros relatos (short stories), Arca, 1967.
Guatemala: Clave de Latinoamérica, Ediciones de la Banda Oriental, 1967, translation by Cedric Belfrage published as *Guatemala: Occupied Country,* Monthly Review Press, 1969.
Reportajes: Tierras de Latinoamérica, otros puntos cardinales, y algo más (also see below), Ediciones Tauro, 1967.
(Compiler and author of prologue) *Su majestad, el fútbol,* Arca, 1968.
Siete imágenes de Bolivia, Fondo Editorial Salvador de la Plaza, 1971.
Las venas abiertas de América Latina, Departamento de Publicaciones, Universidad Nacional de la República, 1971, 2nd edition, 1972, translation by Belfrage published as *The Open Veins of Latin America: Five Centuries of the Pillage of a Continent,* Monthly Review Press, 1973.
Crónicas latinoamericanas, Editorial Girón, 1972.
Vagamundo (short stories), Ediciones de Crisis, 1973.
La canción de nosotros (novel), Editorial Sudamericana, 1975.
Conversaciones con Raimon, Granica, 1977.
Días y noches de amor y de guerra, Editorial Laia, 1978, translation by Judith Brister published as *Days and Nights of Love and War,* Monthly Review Press, 1983.
Voces de nuestro tiempo, Editorial Universitaria Centroamericana, 1981.
Los nacimientos (first book in trilogy "Memoria del fuego"), Siglo XXI, 1982, translation by Cedric Belfrage published as *Memory of Fire: Genesis,* Pantheon, 1985.
La piedra arde, Lóguez Ediciones, 1983.
Las caras y las máscaras (second book in trilogy "Memoria del fuego"), Siglo XXI, 1984, translation by Belfrage published as *Memory of Fire: Faces and Masks,* Pantheon, 1987.
Contraseña, Ediciones del Sol, 1985.
El siglo del viento (third book in trilogy "Memoria del fuego"), Siglo XXI, 1986, translation by Belfrage published as *Memory of Fire: Century of the Wind,* Pantheon, 1988.

Aventuras de los jóvenes dioses, Kapelusz, 1986.
Nosotros decimos no: Crónicas (1963-1988), Siglo XXI, 1989.
El libro de los abrazos, Siglo XXI, 1989.

SIDELIGHTS: Eduardo Galeano has had a long and active career as a journalist, historian, and political activist. At the age of thirteen he began publishing cartoons for the Uruguayan socialist paper *El Sol.* He went on to work for the journal *Marcha* while still in his teens, and became editor in chief of that publication at twenty. When he was still in his early thirties, a right wing military coup imprisoned Galeano and later forced him to flee from Uruguay to Argentina. Still later, another coup and several death threats forced him to leave Argentina for Spain, where he lived in exile until he was permitted to return to Uruguay in 1984. Upon his arrival in Spain, he tells Sam Staggs in *Publishers Weekly,* he felt "broken in pieces. . . . I tried to create a structure from all the broken pieces of myself, like putting together a puzzle. *Days and Nights of Love and War* resulted from this open, free conversation with my own memory, as I tried to understand what had really happened and to guess who I really was."

In his memoir *Days and Nights of Love and War,* Galeano recounts and reflects on the murders, tortures, and disappearances that have become a routine part of Latin American politics. Described by Julie Schumacher in the *Nation* as "the notebook of a wandering 'people's reporter,' " *Days and Nights of Love and War* approaches its subject in an unorthodox manner, in which "the action is presented . . . through semi-related paragraphs that jump back and forth in time, place, person and mood." She maintains that *Days and Nights of Love and War* proves the author is "a magical writer in the best sense of the word," a writer whose nonfiction is able to "match the intensity and appeal of the [South American] continent's best fiction." In short, the reviewer concludes, Galeano shows in *Days and Nights of Love and War* that "the reality of Latin America is more fantastic than the lies we've been told, and that nothing is more horrible or poetic than the truth."

Galeano expands on this fragmentary approach to story in his trilogy "Memoria del fuego" ("Memory of Fire"). In the three books of the trilogy, translated as *Genesis, Faces and Masks,* and *Century of the Wind,* the author relates an anecdotal chronicle of all the Americas—North, South, and Central—from the first native myths to modern times. Drawing on a wide variety of primary sources, Galeano dramatizes some scenes in paragraph-length sketches; how God told President McKinley that the United States should retain the Philippines after the Spanish-American War, for instance, or how, when the Chiriguano Indians first learned of paper, they called it "the skin of God." In others, he reprints historic documents to form a work described by Thulani Davis in the *Voice Literary Supplement* as "historical fact written with a fiction writer's sensibilities." "The result," declares Garry Abrams in the *Los Angeles Times,* "is like a mosaic or an impressionistic painting with each dot contributing to the big picture."

Galeano combines elements of the novel, poetry, and history in "Memory of Fire." Each vignette is based on a documentary source or sources (identified by number in the book's bibliography), but Galeano has recast many of the stories in a poetic form to show the history of the Americas. He states in *Publishers Weekly* that he has reinterpreted the stories to make "the voice of my conscience and the will of my hand coincide. . . . I was looking for little stories that would reveal the great ones, the universe seen through a keyhole. The little things about little people reveal the history of America—the *masked history.*" He tells

Staggs, "I'm trying to create a synthesis of all the different ways of expressing life and reality." Talking to Magda Bogin in the *Voice Literary Supplement,* Galeano says, "I remember as a child feeling that history was locked away in a museum, and that she had to be rescued and set free so she could walk the streets and fields again at will. This implies rescuing history by means of a language capable of embracing all its dimensions, the language people on the coast of Colombia call *sentipensante*—a language capable of uniting the reasons of passion with the passions of reason."

"I do not want to write an objective work—neither wanted to nor could," Galeano writes in the preface to *Genesis.* "There is nothing neutral about this historical narration. Unable to distance myself, I take sides: I confess it and I am not sorry. However, each fragment of this huge mosaic is based on a solid documentary foundation." In an interview appearing in the *New Yorker,* Galeano calls the trilogy "highly subjective," and explains, "Back in school, history classes were terrible—boring, lifeless, empty. . . . It was as if the teachers were intentionally trying to rob us of that connection [to reality], so that we would become resigned to our present—not realize that history is something people make, with their lives, in their own present. So, you see, I tried to find a way of recounting history so that the reader would feel that it was happening right now, just around the corner—this immediacy, this intensity, which is the beauty and the *reality* of history."

"Perhaps I write because I know that the people and the things I care about are going to die and I want to preserve them alive," Galeano told *CA.* "I believe in my craft; I believe in my instrument. I can never understand how writers could write while cheerfully declaring that writing has no meaning. Nor can I ever understand those who turn words into a target for fury or an object of fetishism. Words are a weapon: the responsibility for the crime never lies with the knife. Slowly gaining strength and form, there is in Latin America a literature that does not set out to bury our own dead but to perpetuate them; that refuses to clear up the ashes and tries, on the contrary, to light the fire. Perhaps my own words may help a little to preserve for people to come, as the poet put it, 'the true name of each thing.' "

BIOGRAPHICAL/CRITICAL SOURCES:

BOOKS

Galeano, Eduardo, *Memory of Fire: Genesis,* translated by Cedric Belfrage, Pantheon, 1985.

PERIODICALS

Boston Globe, May 1, 1988, December 2, 1988.
Chicago Tribune, May 15, 1988.
Detroit News, April 26, 1987.
El Diario, April, 1986.
Globe and Mail (Toronto), March 22, 1986, May 2, 1987, June 11, 1988.
Guardian, February 5, 1986, June 13, 1986, June 15, 1988.
Los Angeles Times, May 11, 1988.
Los Angeles Times Book Review, December 29, 1985, March 15, 1987, July 17, 1988.
Los Angeles Weekly, May 27, 1988.
Nation, June 25, 1983.
New Yorker, July 28, 1986.
New York Times, May 2, 1988.
New York Times Book Review, October 27, 1985.
Publishers Weekly, January 16, 1987, April 1, 1988, June 3, 1988.
San Francisco Chronicle, May 15, 1988.

Times Literary Supplement, October 20-26, 1989.
Toronto Now, April 21, 1988.
Toronto Star, April 26, 1988.
Tribune Books (Chicago), May 15, 1988.
USA Today, July 14, 1988.
Voice Literary Supplement, March, 1983, April, 1987, May, 1988.
Washington Post Book World, April 5, 1987, May 22, 1988.

* * *

GALINDO, P.
See HINOJOSA(-SMITH), Rolando (R.)

* * *

GALLARDO, Edward

ADDRESSES: Home—54 West 16th St. (4E), New York, N.Y. 10010.

CAREER: Playwright.

AWARDS, HONORS: First prize from New York Shakespeare Festival's National Contest for Latino Plays, 1985, for "Women Without Men."

WRITINGS:

(And director) "Bernie" (one-act), produced Off-Off-Broadway at New York Theatre Ensemble, 1968.
"In Another Part of the City," produced Off-Off-Broadway at New York Theatre Ensemble, 1970.
"Women Without Men," produced Off-Broadway at Public/Susan Stein Shiva Theatre, 1985.
(Translator) Mario Vargas Llosa, "La Señorita de Tacna," produced Off-Broadway at Public/Newman Theatre, 1987.

Also author of plays "The Mugger" and "Simpson Street."

SIDELIGHTS: Edward Gallardo is an important contemporary playwright. He first distinguished himself in the late 1960s with "Bernie," a one-act monologue delivered by a suicidal mental patient. Dick Brukenfeld, in assessing this work in the *Village Voice,* deemed it "an engrossing character study." Another of Gallardo's plays, "In Another Part of the City," presents a trio of warring homosexuals, only one of whom is entirely honest about his sexuality. Brukenfeld called this play "good . . . theatre." Perhaps Gallardo's most notable play is "Women Without Men," an examination of six women and their struggles on the homefront during World War II. *New York Times* critic Mel Gussow praised "Women Without Men" as "a deeply felt dramatic document, with leavening humor."

BIOGRAPHICAL/CRITICAL SOURCES:

PERIODICALS

New York Times, July 2, 1985, August 10, 1985.
Village Voice, November 20, 1969, July 30, 1970.

* * *

GALLEGO, Laura (Matilde)   1924-

PERSONAL: Born in 1924 in Bayamón, P.R.

ADDRESSES: c/o University of Puerto Rico Press, Box 23322, UPR Station, Río Piedras, P.R. 00931-3322.

CAREER: High school teacher in Bayamón, P.R.; University of Puerto Rico, Río Piedras, professor of education, 1959—.

WRITINGS:

Celajes, 1951-1953 (poetry), Ateneo Puertorriqueño (San Juan), 1959.
(Author of commentary) José Antonio Dávila, *Poemas,* Cordillera (Bayamón, P.R.), 1964.
(Compiler with Margot Arce de Vázquez) *Lecturas puertorriqueñas* (poetry), Troutman Press, 1968.
Laura Gallego: Obra po'etica, University of Puerto Rico Press, 1972.
(With Ernesto Camilli and Luis M. Arrigoitía Rodríguez), *Habla y lengua puertorriqueña: Antología manual de práctica gramatical, ejercicios de redaccíon* (textbook), Acuario (Buenos Aires), 1972, 2nd edition, 1973.
Que voy de vuelo, Instituto de Cultura Puertorriqueña, 1979.

Also author of book of poems, *Presencia,* 1952.

* * *

GALLEGOS (FREIRE), Rómulo   1884-1969

PERSONAL: Born August 2, 1884, in Caracas, Venezuela; died April 4, 1969, in Caracas, Venezuela; son of Rómulo Gallegos Osíe and Rita Freire Guruceaga; married Teotiste Arocha Egui, April, 1912; children: Alexis, Sonia. *Education:* Attended Colegio Sucre; received B.Ph. from Central University; studied law. *Politics:* Democratic Action.

CAREER: Writer. Worked variously as accountant and railway stationmaster; co-founder and staff member of magazine *La Alborada,* beginning in 1909; Colegio Federal, Barcelona, Venezuela, faculty member, 1911; assistant principal of high school in Caracas, Venezuela, c. 1912-18; subdirector of Normal School for Men, 1918; director of Liceo Andrés Bello and professor of philosophy, beginning in 1922; Venezuelan Government, appointed senator by Juan Vicente Gómez, c. 1930, resigned, 1931; salesman for National Cash Register Co. in Spain; Municipal Council, Caracas, member, beginning in 1936, also served briefly as minister of education; elected deputy to Congress from Federal District, 1937; elected president of Venezuela, February, 1948; deposed by army, November, 1948; exiled to Cuba; returned to Venezuela in 1958. Member of National Council of Public Instruction, 1914-21.

AWARDS, HONORS: Prize from Asociación del Mejor Libro del Mes (Book-of-the-Month Club), Madrid, Spain, 1929, for *Doña Bárbara;* LL.D. from Columbia University, 1948; Gold Medal of the Liberator from Bolivarian Society, 1948.

WRITINGS:

"El milagro del año" (play), first produced c. 1914.
El último Solar (novel), originally published in 1920, published as *Reinaldo Solar,* Araluce (Barcelona, Venezuela), 1930.
La trepadora (novel), Tipografía Mercantil (Caracas, Venezuela), 1925.
Doña Bárbara (novel), Araluce, 1929, reprinted, Ayacucho (Caracas), 1982, translation by Robert Malloy, J. Cape and H. Smith, 1931.
Cantaclaro (novel), Araluce, 1934, reprinted, Espasa-Calpe (Madrid), 1982.
Canaima (novel), Araluce, 1935, reprinted, Espasa-Calpe, 1982, translation with notes by Jaime Tello, North American Association of Venezuela (Caracas), 1984.
Pobre negro (novel), Elite (Caracas), 1937.
Programa político y discursos del candidato popular, Rómulo Gallegos, Elite, 1941, reprinted, Comisión Centenario del Natalicio de Rómulo Gallegos, 1985.

El forastero (novel), Elite, 1942, published as *La primera versión de El forastero: Novela inédita,* Equinoccio (Caracas), 1980.

Sobre la misma tierra (novel), Elite, 1943, reprinted, Espasa-Calpe, 1981.

La rebelión, y otros cuentos (stories), del Maestro (Caracas), 1946, reprinted, Espasa-Calpe, 1981.

Obras completas (complete works), Lex (Havana, Cuba), 1949.

La brizna de paja en el viento (novel), Selecta (Havana), 1952.

Una posición en la vida, Humanismo (Mexico), 1954.

La doncella (drama) y El último patriota (cuentos) (play and stories), Montobar (Mexico), 1957.

Obras selectas (selected works), EDIME (Madrid), 1959.

Sus mejores cuentos (stories), Organización Continental de los Festivales del Libro, c. 1959.

Antología de Rómulo Gallegos, edited with introduction by Pedro Díaz Seijas, B. Costa-Amic (Mexico), 1966.

Cuentos venezolanos (stories), Espasa-Calpe Argentina (Buenos Aires), 1966.

Tierra bajo los pies, Alianza, 1971.

Cuentos (stories), Arte y Literatura (Havana), 1973.

Vida y literatura, Embajada de Venezuela, 1977.

Cuentos completos (complete stories), Monte Avila (Caracas), 1981.

Apreciación de Andrés Eloy Blanco: Con apéndice de textos del poeta, Gobierno del Estado Miranda (Los Teques, Venezuela), 1985.

Rómulo Gallegos, la "segura inmortalidad," Centauro (Caracas), 1985.

Pensamiento y acción política de Rómulo Gallegos, introduction by Marco Tulio Bruni Celli, [Caracas], c. 1985.

Rómulo Gallegos, multivisión, Ediciones de la Presidencia de la República, Comisión Ejecutiva Nacional para la Celebración del Centenario del Natalicio de Rómulo Gallegos, 1986.

Also author of story collection *Los aventureros,* 1913.

SIDELIGHTS: Numbered among Venezuela's finest novelists, Rómulo Gallegos became known both for his prosaic depictions of the Venezuelan prairies and for his mixed reception in political circles. Gallegos's debut novel, *El último Solar,* features thieves and ruthless politicians in a land said to reflect early twentieth-century Venezuela under the rule of dictator Juan Vicente Gómez. Gómez took no action against Gallegos for this novel or the following one, *La trepadora,* but Gallegos's third, *Doña Bárbara,* attracted a great deal of attention.

In *Doña Bárbara* Gallegos depicts the Venezuelan prairie ranches, modeling them in part after one of Gómez's; published in 1929, the book describes the rise of the character Bárbara from river boat life to head of an empire of estates. *Doña Bárbara* was widely praised and is regarded as a classic in Latin American literature. As a result of its success, Gómez named Gallegos a senator, reportedly in an attempt to curb his writing. Gallegos, however, never attended a Senate session; instead he resigned his post and went to live in the United States in 1931. Two other novels, *Cantaclaro* and *Canaima,* were written during this voluntary exile.

Gallegos returned to Venezuela in 1936 after Gómez's death and became increasingly active in politics, at the same time continuing to write. The novel *Pobre negro,* published in 1937, won acclaim for its fine writing and moving portrayal of slavery and the plight of mulattos. Gallegos's political involvement peaked in the 1940s with his election as president of a new government. Taking office in 1948, he was Venezuela's first freely elected leader, but he held the post less than a year before a military junta overthrew

his administration. Another period of exile ensued, lasting until the 1958 overthrow of Marcos Pérez Jiménez, who had led the junta. By the time of his death a decade later, Gallegos had achieved international recognition as one of his country's foremost men of letters.

OBITUARIES:

BOOKS

Current Biography, H. W. Wilson, 1969.

PERIODICALS

New York Times, April 8, 1969.
Times (London), April 6, 1969.

*   *   *

GALVEZ (BALUZERA), Manuel 1882-1962

PERSONAL: Born July 18, 1882, in Paraná, Argentina; died November 14, 1962, in Buenos Aires, Argentina; married Delfina Bunge (a writer), 1910 (died, 1952); married María Elena Gaviola Salas, 1954. *Education:* University of Buenos Aires, School of Law, diploma, 1904.

CAREER: Novelist. Founder with Ricardo Olivera of magazine *Ideas,* 1903; law clerk in criminal and correctional court in Buenos Aires, Argentina, 1903-05; inspector of secondary and normal schools, 1906-31; Argentine delegate to International Conference on Unemployment, 1910; staff member of *Nosotros,* beginning 1910; founder of Cooperativa Editorial Buenos Aires, 1917; founder with Augusto Bunge of Editorial Pax, 1919; founder of Biblioteca de Novelistas Americanos (a publishing house), 1920; founder of Argentine chapter of PEN, 1930.

MEMBER: Argentine Academy of Letters.

AWARDS, HONORS: National Prize for Literature, 1932; candidate for Nobel Prize, 1932, 1933, and 1951.

WRITINGS:

FICTION

La maestra normal (also see below), Sociedad Cooperativa Nosotros (Buenos Aires), 1914, reprinted, Losada (Buenos Aires), 1964.

El mal metafísico (also see below), Sociedad Cooperativa Nosotros, 1916, reprinted, Espasa-Calpe Argentina (Buenos Aires), 1962.

La sombra del convento (also see below), Sociedad Cooperativa Nosotros, 1917.

Nacha Regules (also see below), Pax (Buenos Aires), 1912, reprinted, Centro Editor de América Latina (Buenos Aires), 1968, translation by Leo Ongley, Dutton, 1922, reprinted, Gordon Press, 1977.

Luna de miel y otras narraciones, Biblioteca de Novelistas Americanos, 1920.

La tragedia de un hombre fuerte, Biblioteca de Novelistas Americanos, 1922, reprinted, Talleres Gráficos de la Compañía General Fabril Editora (Buenos Aires), 1961.

Historia de arrabal, illustrations by Adolfo Belloca, Agencia General de Librería y Publicaciones, 1922, reprinted, Centro Editor de América Latina, 1968.

El cántico espiritual, Agencia General de Librería y Publicaciones, 1923.

La pampa y su pasión, Agencia General de Librería y Publicaciones, 1926, reprinted, Losada, 1978.

Una mujer muy moderna, M. Gleizer (Buenos Aires), 1927.

Los caminos de la muerta, La Facultad (Buenos Aires), 1928, reprinted, Losada, 1957.

Humaitá, La Facultad, 1929, reprinted, Losada, 1959.

Jornadas de agonía, La Facultad, 1929, reprinted, Losada, 1978.

Miércoles Santo (also see below), La Facultad, 1930, reprinted, Tor, 1966, translation by Warre B. Wells published as Holy Wednesday, Bodley Head, 1934.

El gaucho de Los Cerrillos (also see below), La Facultad, 1931, reprinted, Espasa-Calpe Argentina, 1966.

El General Quiroga, La Facultad, 1932, reprinted, Theoría (Buenos Aires), 1971.

Cautiverio, Sociedad Amigos del Libro Rioplatense, (Buenos Aires), 1935.

La noche toca a su fin, Cabaut y Cía, 1935, reprinted, Theoría, 1956.

Hombres en soledad, Club del Libro (Buenos Aires), 1938, reprinted, Aguilar (Madrid), 1960.

La ciudad pintada de rojo, Instituto Panamericano de Cultura, 1948.

La muerte en las calles, El Ateneo (Buenos Aires), 1949.

Tiempo de odio y angustia, Espasa-Calpe Argentina, 1951.

Han tocado a degüello (1840-1842), Espasa-Calpe Argentina, 1951.

Bajo la garra anglo-francesa, Espasa-Calpe Argentina, 1953.

Y así cayó don Juan Manuel, Espasa-Calpe Argentina, 1954.

Las dos vidas del pobre Napoleón, Losada, 1954, edited with introduction, notes, exercises, and vocabulary by Myron I. Lichtblau, Scribner, 1963.

El uno y la multitud, Alpe (Buenos Aires), 1955.

Tránsito Guzmán, Theoría, 1956.

Perdido en su noche, Sudamericana, 1958, reprinted, 1978.

Me mataron entre todos, Emecé (Buenos Aires), 1962.

La locura de ser santo, Puma (Buenos Aires), 1967.

POETRY

El enigma interior, privately printed (Buenos Aires), 1907.

El sendero de humildad, A. Moen y Hermano (Buenos Aires), 1909.

Poemas para la recién llegada, Theoría, 1957.

DRAMA

Nacha Regules (based on the author's book of the same title), Agencia General de Librería y Publicaciones, 1924.

El hombre de los ojos azules (comedy in three acts), La Facultad, 1928.

Calibán: Tragicomedia de la vida política, privately printed (Buenos Aires), 1943.

BIOGRAPHY

Vida de Fray Mamerto Esquiú, Tor, 1933, reprinted, Guillermo Kraft, (Buenos Aires), 1962.

Vida de Hipólito Yrigoyen, Guillermo Kraft, 1939, reprinted, Universitaria de Buenos Aires, 1973.

Vida de don Juan Manuel de Rosas, El Ateneo, Librería Científica y Literaria (Buenos Aires), 1940, reprinted, Trivium, 1976.

Vida de don Gabriel García Moreno, Difusión (Buenos Aires), 1942, reprinted, Dictio (Buenos Aires), 1980.

Vida de Aparicio Saravia, Imprenta López (Buenos Aires), 1942, reprinted, Tor, 1957.

Vida de Sarmiento, Emecé, 1945, reprinted, Dictio, 1980.

José Hernández, La Universidad (Buenos Aires), 1945, reprinted, Huemul (Buenos Aires), 1964.

Don Francisco de Miranda, el más universal de los americanos, Emecé (Buenos Aires), 1947.

El santito de la toldería, la vida perfecta de Ceferino Namuncurá, Poblet (Buenos Aires), 1947, reprinted, Club de Lectores, 1976.

ESSAYS

El diario de Gabriel Quiroga: Opiniones sobre la vida argentina, A. Moen (Buenos Aires), 1910.

Argentina, Sociedad Cooperativa Nosotros, 1913, reprinted, Tor, c. 1936.

La inseguridad de la vida obrera: Informe sobre el paro forzoso, Alsina (Buenos Aires), 1913, reprinted, 1978.

El espíritu de aristocracia y otros ensayos, Agencia General de Librería y Publicaciones, 1924.

Este pueblo necesita, A. García Santos (Buenos Aires), 1934.

La Argentina en nuestros libros, Ercilla (Santiago), 1935.

España y algunos españoles, Huarpes (Buenos Aires), 1945.

El novelista y las novelas, Emecé, 1959.

MEMOIRS

Amigos y maestros de mi juventud, 1900-1910 (also see below), Guillermo Kraft, 1944, reprinted, Librería Hachette (Buenos Aires), 1961.

En el mundo de los seres ficticios (also see below), Librería Hachette, 1961.

Recuerdos de la vida literaria (contains *Amigos y maestros de mi juventud* and *En el mundo de los seres ficticios*), Librería Hachette, 1961.

Entre la novela y la historia, Librería Hachette, 1962.

En el mundo de los seres reales, Librería Hachette, 1965.

COLLECTIONS

Obras escogidas (contains *La maestra normal, El mal metafísico, La sombra del convento, Miércoles Santo, El gaucho de Los Cerrillos,* "Luna de miel," and "Una santa criatura"), M. Aguilar, 1949.

Biografías completas, two volumes, Emecé, 1962.

OTHER

La vida múltiple (arte y literatura: 1910-1916), Sociedad Cooperativa Nosotros, 1916.

Los mejores cuentos, Patria (Buenos Aires), 1919.

El solar de la raza, obra premiada por el gobierno de la República Argentina, Saturnino Calleja (Madrid), 1920.

El espiritualismo español, Bayardo (Buenos Aires), 1921.

(Translator with Roberto F. Giusti) Romain Rolland, *Clerambault,* Pax, 1921.

Holy Wednesday, translated from the Spanish by Warre B. Wells, Appleton-Century (London), 1934.

La casa colonial (text in Spanish and English), edited by Guillermo Rivera, Oxford University Press (New York), 1939.

La gran familia de los Laris, Universitaria de Buenos Aires, 1973.

Contributor of nearly four hundred articles, commentaries, and reviews to numerous journals, including *Ichthys, Criterio, Número, El Pueblo, Atlántida, Leoplán, Il Mattino d'Italia,* and *El Hogar.*

SIDELIGHTS: "By general consent, Manuel Gálvez is one of the most important figures of the modern Argentine novel because of his realistic portrayal of the social fabric of Argentine life," wrote Myron I. Lichtblau in his preface to Twayne's *Manuel Gálvez.* "He was the first complete novelist Argentina produced, as well as one of the few professional novelists in the early decades of this century. Unlike most other writers of his time, who earned their livelihood from sources other than pure literature, Gálvez devoted himself almost exclusively to his profession and was able to live from his pen." According to Lichtblau, "His novelistic art rests essentially on the desire to tell a socially significant story and create a social environment in the simplest and most intelligible terms."

BIOGRAPHICAL/CRITICAL SOURCES:

BOOKS

Anzoátegui, Ignacio B., *Manuel Gálvez*, Ediciones Culturales Argentinas, 1961.
A Century of Latin-American Thought, Harvard University Press, 1961.
Desinano, Norma, *La novelística de Manuel Gálvez*, Universidad Nacional del Litoral, 1965.
Lichtblau, Myron I., *Manuel Gálvez*, Twayne, 1972.
Olivari, Nicolas, and Lorenzo Stanchina, *Manuel Gálvez: Ensayo sobre su obra*, Agencia General de Librería y Publicaciones, 1924.
Spell, J. R., *Contemporary Spanish-American Fiction*, University of North Carolina Press, 1944.

PERIODICALS

Hispania, Volume 5, 1922.
Hispanic Review, Volume 11, number 3, 1943, Volume 12, number 3, 1944.
Modern Language Quarterly, Volume 9, number 2, 1948.

*   *   *

GALVEZ de MONTALVO, Luis
See AVALLE-ARCE, Juan Bautista de

*   *   *

GAMARRA, Eduardo (A.) 1957-

PERSONAL: Born June 10, 1957, in La Paz, Bolivia; son of Jaime (an engineer) and Elena (a homemaker; maiden name, Rodrigo) Gamarra; married Terry Faldon (a counselor), August 24, 1981; children: Jacqueline. *Education:* University of Pittsburgh, Ph.D., 1987.

ADDRESSES: Home—15133 Southwest 109th Ln., Miami, Fla. 33196. *Office*—Florida International University, Miami, Fla. 33199.

CAREER: Florida International University, Miami, assistant professor, 1986—.

MEMBER: Latin American Studies Association, American Political Science Association.

WRITINGS:

(With James M. Malloy) *Revolution and Reaction: Bolivia, 1964-1985*, Transaction Books, 1988.
(With Malloy) *Latin America and Caribbean Contemporary Record*, Holmes & Meier, 1990.

WORK IN PROGRESS: Research on stabilization and democracy in Latin America.

*   *   *

GAMBARO, Griselda 1928-

PERSONAL: Born July 28, 1928, in Buenos Aires, Argentina; daughter of a sailor and postal employee; married Juan Carlos Distéfano (a sculptor); children: Andrea, Lucas.

CAREER: Author and playwright. Office worker at publishing company, 1943, and sports club, 1947-56; drama teacher at Universidad Nacional del Litoral, Argentina, c. 1969; National Endowment for the Arts, lecturer on contemporary drama, 1973, juror in national competitions, 1973-75.

AWARDS, HONORS: National Endowment for the Arts publication prize, 1963, for *Madrigal en ciudad;* Emecé Publishers Prize, 1964, for short fiction collection *El desatino;* Argentores Prize from Society of Argentinian Authors, 1968, and first prizes from Municipality of Buenos Aires, Argentina, *Talía* magazine, and "Theatrical Broadcast News" of Municipal Radio of Buenos Aires, all for *El campo;* Argentores Prize from Society of Argentinian Authors, 1976, for *Sucede lo que pasa;* Guggenheim fellowship, 1982.

WRITINGS:

FICTION

Cuentos (short stories), Américalee (Buenos Aires), 1953.
Madrigal en ciudad (short stories), Goyanarte (Buenos Aires), 1963.
El desatino (short stories; title means "The Blunder"; includes "El desatino" and "Las paredes"), Emecé (Buenos Aires), 1965.
Un felicidad con menos pena (novel; title means "Happiness With Less Sorrow"), Sudamericana (Buenos Aires), 1968.
Nada que ver con otra historia (novel; title means "Nothing to Do With Another Story"), Noé (Buenos Aires), 1972.
La cola mágica (stories for children), De la Flor (Buenos Aires), 1975.
Ganarse la muerte (novel; title means "To Earn Death"), De la Flor, 1976.
Dios no nos quiere contentos (novel; title means "God Does Not Want Us to Be Happy"), Lumen (Barcelona), 1979.
Lo impenetrable (title means "Impenetrable"), Torres Agüero, 1984.

PLAYS

Matrimonio (title means "Marriage"), first produced in Buenos Aires, Argentina, 1965.
El desatino (two-act; title means "The Blunder"; based on her short story of the same title; first produced in Buenos Aires, 1966), Centro de Experimentación Audiovisual del Instituto Torcuato Di Tella (Buenos Aires), 1965.
Las paredes (title means "The Walls"; based on her short story of the same title; first produced in Buenos Aires, 1966), published in *Teatro: Las paredes* [and] *El desatino* [and] *Los siameses*, Argonauta (Barcelona), 1979.
Los siameses (two-act; title means "The Siamese Twins"; first produced in Buenos Aires, 1967), Insurrexit (Buenos Aires), 1967.
El campo (two-act; first produced in Buenos Aires, 1968), Insurrexit, 1967, translation by William I. Oliver published as *The Camp* in *Voices of Change in the Spanish American Theater*, University of Texas Press, 1971.
La gracia, published in *El Urogallo*, Number 17, 1972, published in *Teatro* (also see below).
Nada que ver (title means "Nothing to Do"; based on her novel *Nada que ver con otra historia;* first produced in Buenos Aires, 1972), published in *Nada que ver* [and] *Sucede lo que pasa*, Girol (Ottawa, Canada), 1983.
Sólo un aspecto (title means "Only One Aspect"; first produced in Buenos Aires, 1974), published in *La Palabra y el Hombre*, Number 8, 1973, published in *Teatro* (also see below).
El viaje, first produced in Buenos Aires, 1975.

Información para extranjeros, translation published in Italy, c. 1975, Spanish version published in *Teatro* (also see below), selected translation by Marguerite Feitlowitz published as *Information for Foreigners* in *Literary Review,* summer, 1989.

El nombre (title means "The Name"), first produced in Buenos Aires, 1976.

Sucede lo que pasa (first produced in Buenos Aires, 1976), published in *Nada que ver* [and] *Sucede lo que pasa* (also see above), published in *Teatro* (also see below).

Decir sí (title means "To Say Yes"; first produced in Buenos Aires, 1981), published in *Hispamérica,* Number 21, 1978, published in *Antología Teatro Abierto,* [Buenos Aires], 1981 (also see below).

El despojamiento, published in *Tramoya,* November-December, 1981.

La malasangre (title means "Bitter Blood"; first produced in Buenos Aires, 1982), published in *Teatro* (also see below).

Real envido (title means "Royal Bet"; first produced in Buenos Aires, 1983), published in *Teatro* (also see below).

Del sol naciente (title means "From the Rising Sun"; first performed in Buenos Aires, 1984), published in *Teatro* (also see below).

Teatro (contains *Real envido, La malasangre, Del sol naciente, Dar la vuelta, Información para extranjeros, Puesta en claro, Sucede lo que pasa, Viaje de invierno, Sólo un aspecto, La gracia, El miedo, Decir sí, Antígona furiosa,* and several short plays), three volumes, De la Flor, 1984-89.

OTHER

Conversaciones con chicos: Sobre la sociedad, los padres, los afectos, la cultura, Timerman, 1977.

Contributor of articles, reviews, and short stories to periodicals, including *Análisis, Clarín, El cronista, Ficción, Latin American Theatre Review, Mantrana, La Nación, La Opinión, Revista de la Universidad Nacional del Litoral, Sipario, Talía, Teatro Municipal,* and *Vigencia.*

SIDELIGHTS: Griselda Gambaro is considered one of the most important dramatists to emerge from Latin America during the 1960s. Her work as a whole, which includes novels and short stories, has been praised for its portrayal of vulnerable individuals struggling for dignity against an impersonal or hostile society. "I'm from a poor family," Gambaro told Evelyn Garfield for *Women's Voices From Latin America.* "Now things are much better but that circumstance marks you forever." Unable to obtain a good education from public school—let alone attend many plays—Gambaro taught herself about theater by going to the public library and reading the works of such playwrights as Eugene O'Neill, Anton Chekhov, and Luigi Pirandello. When she reached her mid-thirties her fortunes as a writer improved suddenly and dramatically. Her second volume of short stories, *Madrigal en ciudad,* won a valuable prize from Argentina's National Endowment for the Arts: publication. Recalling her big break for Kathleen Betsko and Rachel Koenig in *Interviews With Contemporary Women Playwrights,* Gambaro observed: "The prize . . . enabled me to enter the theater easily, comfortably. Nowadays young playwrights have a more difficult time." Gambaro quickly linked up with the Instituto Torcuato Di Tella, a Buenos Aires foundation for sociology and the arts that gained national renown in the 1960s as a venue for pioneering trends in art, music, and theater. Often using the Instituto's theater for performances, she released a series of four plays during the 1960s that made her a dramatist of international repute.

Each of the plays—*Las paredes* ("The Walls"), *El desatino* ("The Blunder"), *Los siameses* ("The Siamese Twins"), and *El campo* (*The Camp*)—has a notably stark and menacing atmosphere; in each, individuals are slowly and inexorably overwhelmed by social forces that seem beyond their control. To embody this confrontation on stage, as Joan Rea Boorman suggested in *Rice University Studies,* Gambaro takes commonplace pairs of characters, such as "mother-child, brother-brother, friend-friend, authority figure-subservient figure," and warps the relationship into that of tormentor and victim. The victim is generally harmless, passive, and isolated, while the tormentor is remorseless, energetic, and allied with others. Breaking with the conventions of realistic drama, the plays are not clearly set in a time or place and the actions are illogical and nightmarish: arguably, the plays' link to reality is their depiction of the effect of social tyranny on the vulnerable individual.

Las paredes begins as an unnamed Youth is held in a room for questioning by a similarly nameless Official and a Custodian. The Youth never learns the reason for his detention, nor do his jailers seem to care. They beat him occasionally, but their principal goal seems to be the destruction of his will through psychological torture. They forcibly engage the Youth in a series of irrational arguments, and he painfully submits to their verbal bullying in the mistaken belief that by surrendering his reason he can earn his freedom. The walls of the room move inward toward the Youth, signifying his steady loss of independence; at the end of the play, when the jailers are gone and the door of the room is open, the Youth is psychologically unable to leave. In *El desatino,* as Sandra Cypress wrote in *Dramatists in Revolt,* "the unidentified youth and his tormentors are replaced by a group of family and friends," making the context of the play somewhat less abstract. The main character, a man named Alfonso, loses control of his life when he awakes one morning with a huge weight on one foot. He is visited by his mother and best friend, both of whom ignore his plight and mock his sense of masculinity. Gradually Gambaro suggests that Alfonso is not only crippled by the excess weight but by his own attitudes. He claims to have a wife, but she only appears as a movie idol in a dream sequence; as the author told interviewers, the "wife" merely embodies Alfonso's unrealistic sexual fantasies. Then Alfonso snobbishly rebuffs the efforts of a poor man to free him. Freed anyway, Alfonso collapses on his bed, where his family and friends discuss him as if he were an infant.

The suggestions of physical brutality that appear in *Las paredes* and *El desatino* become blatant in *Los siameses* and *The Camp.* The main characters of *Los siameses* are two men, Ignacio and Lorenzo, who may be friends or brothers. Lorenzo repeatedly demands sympathy from Ignacio by insisting that the two are siamese twins who were later separated. At the same time, however, Lorenzo, who is cruel and sexually impotent, violently envies the popularity that Ignacio's warm-heartedness brings. Apparently convinced that he could gain greater happiness by eliminating Ignacio, Lorenzo arranges to have his "twin" savagely beaten by a succession of people, including the police. Finally, after being imprisoned for a crime he did not commit, Ignacio dies. Only after burying Ignacio does Lorenzo realize the extent of his unhappiness and loneliness. Commentators suggest that Ignacio and Lorenzo represent the good and evil sides of human nature, locked together like siamese twins.

The Camp begins as bookkeeper Martín enters a nondescript military encampment as part of his work. He is received by an increasingly boorish commander named Franco (also the name of a notorious Spanish dictator). As in *Las paredes,* events in the camp become more and more illogical, shocking, and disorienting. Franco compels Martín to witness a bizarre musical performance in which Emma, a woman dressed like a concentration-camp inmate, plays a silent piano while other residents of the camp deride her. Emma has a festering wound and seems to be in physical fear of Franco, though she insists, with unsettling cheerfulness, that at the camp she is surrounded by friends. Martín manages to take her from the camp, but he remains uneasy even in his home; as the plays ends he is visited by members of the camp staff who inject him with a tranquilizer and approach him with a branding iron.

These four dramatically powerful plays brought forth strong reactions in the theater world: Gambaro was variously praised, resented, and misunderstood. Many 1960s theater critics, Gambaro recalled years later in *Américas,* enthusiastically depicted her as a unique new talent and so engendered a "schism" between herself and other deserving Latin American dramatists. "But time does tell," she observed, "and now each of us has been assigned a proper place." Admirers from outside Argentina often labeled her a follower of European trends, to her evident discomfort. Observers noted, for example, that Gambaro's stage dialogue is simply worded and inexpressive, seemingly designed to show that her characters cannot communicate meaningfully with each other. By contrast, she employs non-verbal elements, including screams, nonsensical actions, and violence, with unsettling effectiveness. Such tactics were advocated in the early twentieth century by the influential French dramatist Antonin Artaud, whose "theater of cruelty" would shock an audience to attention by attacking the emotions as well as addressing the intellect. Artaud's ideas helped inspire the French "theater of the absurd," which puts characters in nonsensical situations in order to demonstrate the futility of human existence. Praise of Gambaro that likened her work to the theaters of cruelty or absurdity left her open to attack from some Argentines, who called her unrealistic, un-Argentine, or unconcerned with her own society.

Accordingly, in successive interviews since the 1960s Gambaro has sought to define the nature and purpose of her work in her own terms. "We come from Argentinian dramaturgy," she told Betsko and Koenig, "[from] a genre called *grotesco* [grotesque] created by a playwright named Armando Discépolo, [1887-1971]. We don't come from European absurdism, which is so metaphysical, which presents the world as a fact with inexplicable laws." Instead, as she observed in *Américas,* "Our theater . . . is more down-to-earth. It confronts a reality that seems absurd to us but that *can* be changed." While Gambaro deliberately avoids political didacticism, she can be seen as "the denouncer of passivity," as Lucia Lockert called her in *Michigan Academician.* In such a view, the finales of Gambaro's plays, in which her characters surrender to superior forces, are not counsels of despair but calls to action: Alfonso should throw off the weight of outmoded social attitudes; the Youth, Ignacio, and Martín should stand up for their dignity. "I [believe] that man . . . is a very passive being for whom it is a great effort to assume responsibility with respect to others and with respect to himself," Lockert quoted the author. "It always concerned me that people locked themselves up and did not assume responsibility, because that attitude brings us to destruction and death."

In the 1970s, as successive Argentine governments became more blatantly dictatorial, Gambaro's work more openly expressed her social concern. She wrote a highly experimental play called *Información para extranjeros* (*Information for Foreigners*) that would be performed by dividing the audience into small groups, then leading them through various rooms and hallways where scenes of torture and terrorism would be enacted. Some of the scenes were drawn from stories in Argentine newspapers about the country's political turmoil. "The spectators, deprived of the security of their usual distance as audience, [would] become living witnesses," wrote Rosalea Palma in *Latin American Theatre Review.* The author also wrote a novel, *Ganarse la muerte* ("To Earn Death"), that depicted the bleak family life of an Argentine woman. The Argentine government took notice of Gambaro. Beginning in 1973, "the army paid us 'visits' during which they looked at all the material in the house," she told Betsko and Koenig. Performances of *The Camp* were monitored overseas by Argentine intelligence, which scanned reviews for evidence that the play was considered a commentary on dictatorship. For fear of the government Gambaro destroyed her manuscript of *Information for Foreigners,* and she was able to reconstruct the play in later years only because it had already been published in Italy. (In 1989, a portion appeared in English in *Literary Review*). Finally, in 1977 *Ganarse la muerte* was banned by presidential decree, thus branding Gambaro a public enemy and effectively barring her from presenting her writings in print or on the stage. The author and her family became voluntary exiles in Europe soon thereafter and did not return to their homeland for three years.

Meanwhile Gambaro was expanding her awareness of feminist writing. As commentators have remarked, her early works show little direct comment on gender issues, and she was interested to discover that *Ganarse la muerte,* which she had conceived as a metaphor about Argentina in general, was received in France as a feminist work. She resolved to put more emphasis on assertive woman characters in her writings, including the novel *Dios no nos quiere contentos* ("God Does Not Want Us to Be Happy"), which she suggested was a metaphor for her experience as an exile. The book's main character is a woman trapeze artist called the Ecuyère; she is repeatedly abused and abandoned by the circus for which she works, but seeks it out again and again so that she can continue to perform. The Ecuyère, wrote Garfield, "perceives the sadness and hypocrisy in man's unfathomable actions and yet in the circus of life, she maintains her identity. On her trapeze high above the crowd, she perfects her abilities so that the spectators below must recognize her existence." In sharp contrast to the human warmth of the Ecuyère and her few allies is the book's narrator, who is at various times devious, willfully confusing, and self-satisfied. The resulting work, wrote William David Foster in *World Literature Today,* is "difficult to read" but "a truly original work of fiction."

By the early 1980s dictatorship began to lose its power over Argentine society, and Gambaro and her family returned to their home. In 1981 a broad spectrum of Argentina's theater community, emboldened by the government's declining fortunes, joined in protest against continuing repression by staging the Teatro Abierto ("Open Theater")—a series of nearly two dozen plays, many on political topics. Gambaro's play *Decir sí* ("To Say Yes") was published in the group's 1981 collection, *Antología Teatro Abierto.* The next year the government tried to boost its image by initiating the Falklands War, a disastrous effort to drive Great Britain from the Falkland Islands off Argentina's coast. When Britain triumphed the dictatorship fell, and Argentina began its first extended period of progressive democracy in many years. Carlos Gorostiza, formerly a "prohibited" playwright like Gambaro, became minister of culture.

As democracy prospered Gambaro welcomed the new vitality she observed in the Argentine women's movement. A political outcast no longer, she released an Argentine edition of *Information for Foreigners* and a new play called *Del sol naciente* ("From the Rising Sun") that used a Japanese setting to comment on the Falklands War. "I've earned my own space," she told Betsko and Koenig, "and have entered that suspicious, dangerous category of 'respectable' people."

BIOGRAPHICAL/CRITICAL SOURCES:

BOOKS

Betsko, Kathleen and Rachel Koenig, *Interviews With Contemporary Women Playwrights,* Beech Tree Books, 1987.

Garfield, Evelyn Picon, *Women's Voices From Latin America: Interviews With Six Contemporary Authors,* Wayne State University Press, 1985.

Lyday, Leon F. and George W. Woodyard, editors, *Dramatists in Revolt: The New Latin American Theater,* University of Texas Press, 1976.

Miller, Yvette E. and Charles M. Tatum, editors, *Latin American Women Writers: Yesterday and Today,* Latin American Literary Review, 1977.

PERIODICALS

Américas, March-April, 1985.
Books Abroad, autumn, 1968.
Hispanic Journal, spring, 1980.
Latin American Theatre Review, spring, 1968, fall, 1970, spring, 1978, fall, 1980.
Michigan Academician, winter, 1987.
Modern Drama, December, 1975, March, 1981.
Rice University Studies, winter, 1978.
World Literature Today, summer, 1980.

—*Sketch by Thomas Kozikowski*

*   *   *

GAMBOA, Harry, Jr.

ADDRESSES: c/o Los Angeles Theatre Center, 514 S. Spring St., Los Angeles, Calif. 90013.

CAREER: Playwright. Founding member of ASCO.

WRITINGS:

"Jetter's Jinx," produced in Los Angeles at the Theatre Center, 1985.

WORK IN PROGRESS: A two-act musical, on "urban issues" and "phantom culture," for the Los Angeles Theatre Center's Latino Theatre Lab.

BIOGRAPHICAL/CRITICAL SOURCES:

PERIODICALS

Los Angeles Times, May 24, 1989.

*   *   *

GARCIA, Lionel G.   1935-

PERSONAL: Born August 20, 1935, in San Diego, Tex.; son of Gonzalo Guzmán and María (Saenz) García; married Naoemi Barrera (an educational diagnostician), 1959; children: Rose, Carlos, Paul. *Education:* Texas A & M University, B.S., 1956, D.V.M., 1965.

ADDRESSES: Home—1034 Villacourt, Seabrook, Tex. 77586. *Office*—619 Kirby Rd., Seabrook, Tex. 77586.

CAREER: Texas A & M University, College Station, assistant professor of anatomy, 1966-68; practitioner of veterinary medicine in Seabrook, Tex., 1969—; writer. *Military service:* U.S. Army, 1957-58 and 1959-60.

MEMBER: International PEN, American Veterinary Medical Association, Texas Veterinary Medical Association, Harris County Veterinary Medical Association, Amnesty International.

AWARDS, HONORS: PEN Southwest Discovery prize, 1983, for work in progress *Leaving Home.*

WRITINGS:

Leaving Home (novel), Arte Público, 1985.
A Shroud in the Family (novel), Arte Público, 1987.
Hardscrub (novel), Arte Público, 1989.

Work represented in anthology *Cuentos Chicanos,* edited by Rudolfo A. Anaya and Antonio Márquez, University of New Mexico Press, 1984. Contributor of short stories to periodicals, including *Revista Chicano-Riqueña* and *Américas Review.*

WORK IN PROGRESS: A novel, tentatively titled *The Raffle;* a collection of short stories by contemporary Texas writers, titled *New Growth.*

SIDELIGHTS: Lionel G. García wrote: "As a child I feared death so much that I developed a mental technique that I was sure would keep me from dying, a discovery that would make me the only person that ever lived that would not die. Later, I came to realize that what I was doing was placing myself in a mental state in which one is separated from consciousness and everything seems possible, as in the art of fiction. It is in this state of lost consciousness that a highly imaginative writer lives while he works.

"A writer's job is to present people as they are, usually to the surprise of the reader. My job, in particular, is to present to the world the people of Mexican ancestry living in the United States. I have the best of both the Mexican and the Anglo worlds— Catholic upbringing, Protestant society, Mexican music, Mexican food, and the mentality to live life to the fullest.

"As to writing itself, a writer that looks on writing as an art form seeks neither fame nor fortune. He, as I did as a child, seeks immortality. What concerns the writer is what he has written that will be read many years after he is gone.

"We are all seeking approval from someone. Some writers look for it in the masses, writing books that sell into the millions. And they make millions. I have no criticism to make of those writers. They are very talented and are an essential part of publishing. Without them the publishing empire would topple. Other writers write for the sheer joy of writing, working in obscurity, hoping that someday someone whose opinion they respect will approve of their work.

"The ideal world, like mine as a child, would be where the writer is literary and rich and famous. But that would be asking for too much. Very few of us ever achieve that goal. So, in truth, what makes the poor literary writer happy is that he knows that one day he will be proven right and everyone else will be proven wrong—a state of paranoia. Mind you, you cannot find good writing without paranoia.

"Personally, I hate to write. I would rather dig graves with a spoon. My mind looks for excuses not to write with so much intensity that I sometimes wonder if I'll ever get started and, once started, I wonder if I'll ever get finished. I would much rather be enjoying myself at night like my friends than sitting down writing. Every day that I have to sit down to write is agony, and painfully, the more I do it the more agonizing writing becomes. I am happiest when I'm not writing. The paradox, though, is that if I don't write I don't feel that I deserve to be happy. My day is not done unless I have written.

"I have come to realize that the art of writing is the art of rewriting. I laugh out loud now when I think that in my twenties I would brag that I could write a short story in one night. And I often did. But as the saying in Spanish goes, in those days my corn was very green. Experience has taught me that nothing is ever as good as when rewritten many times.

"I write at night. It's more peaceful then. The day is done. Everything that could happen to me has happened. The only noises I hear are the crickets and the dogs barking. I try to write two to three hours every day, giving myself some days off to go do what my friends are doing—drinking, cavorting, messing around. I fool my mind by working on several pieces at the same time.

"I am a firm believer in throwing things away. Every novel and every short story that I have written has been thrown away many times."

BIOGRAPHICAL/CRITICAL SOURCES:

BOOKS

Dictionary of Literary Biography, Volume 82: *Chicano Writers, First Series,* Gale, 1989.

* * *

GARCIA, Richard A. 1941-

WRITINGS:

Selected Poetry, Quinto Sol, 1973.
Political Ideology: A Comparative Study of Three Chicano Youth Organizations, R. & E. Research Associates, 1977.
(Editor and compiler) *The Chicanos in America, 1540-1974: A Chronology and Fact Book,* Oceana, 1977.
My Aunt Otilia's Spirits/Los espíritus de mi tía Otilia, translated into Spanish by Jesús Guerrero Rea, Children's Book, 1978.

Also author of *The Making of the Mexican-American Mind, San Antonio, Texas, 1929-1941,* 1980.

* * *

GARCIA, Sam 1957-

PERSONAL: Born November 11, 1957, in El Paso, Tex.; son of Samuel (a mechanic) and Bertha (a seamstress) Garcia. *Education:* Alan Hancock College, Pacific Conservatory of the Performing Arts, A.A.; Temple University, M.F.A. *Politics:* Democrat.

ADDRESSES: P.O. Box 1768, Santa Monica, Calif. 90406.

CAREER: Playwright. Temple University, Philadelphia, Penn., acting coach and teacher, 1982-83. Member, Latino Workshop, Los Angeles Theater Center.

WRITINGS:

"The Land of Plenty" (play), produced at South Coast Repertory, Los Angeles, Calif., May, 1989.

WORK IN PROGRESS: "The Ring," a play.

* * *

GARCIA LORCA, Federico 1898-1936

PERSONAL: Commonly known by mother's surname, Lorca; born June 5, 1898, in Fuentevaqueros, Granada, Spain; executed August 19, 1936, in Víznar, Granada, Spain; son of Federico García Rodríguez (a landowner) and Vicenta Lorca (a teacher).

Education: Attended University of Granada, 1914-19; received law degree from University of Madrid, 1923; attended Columbia University, 1929.

CAREER: Writer. Artistic director, serving as director and producer of plays, for University Theater (state-sponsored traveling theater group, known as *La Barraca* ["The Hut"]), 1932-35. Director of additional plays, including *Blood Wedding,* 1933. Lecturer; illustrator, with work represented in exhibitions; musician, serving as arranger and pianist for recordings of Spanish folk songs, 1931. Helped to organize Festival of *Cante Jondo* (Granada, Spain), 1922.

WRITINGS:

POETRY

Libro de poemas (title means "Book of Poems"), Maroto (Madrid), 1921 (also see below).
Canciones (1921-1924), [Málaga, Spain], 1927, translation by Phillip Cummings published as *Songs,* Duquesne University Press, 1976 (also see below).
Primer romancero gitano (1924-1927), Revista de Occidente (Madrid), 1928, 2nd edition (and most later editions) published as *Romancero gitano,* 1929, translation by Langston Hughes published as *Gypsy Ballads,* Beloit College, 1951, translation by Rolfe Humphries published as *The Gypsy Ballads, With Three Historical Ballads,* Indiana University Press, 1953, translation by Michael Hartnett published as *Gipsy Ballads,* Goldsmith Press (Dublin), 1973, translation and commentary by Carl W. Cobb published as *Lorca's "Romancero gitano": A Ballad Translation and Critical Study,* University Press of Mississippi, 1983 (also see below).
Poema del cante jondo, Ulises (Madrid), 1931, translation by Carlos Bauer published as *Poem of the Deep Song/ Poema del cante jondo* (bilingual edition), City Lights Books, 1987 (also see below).
Llanto por Ignacio Sánchez Mejías (title means "Lament for Ignacio Sánchez Mejías"; commonly known as "Lament for the Death of a Bullfighter"), Arbol, 1935 (also see below).
Seis poemas gallegos (title means "Six Galician Poems"; written in Galician with assistance from others), Nos (Santiago de Compostela), 1935 (also see below).
Primeras canciones (title means "First Songs"), Héroe (Madrid), 1936 (also see below).
Lament for the Death of a Bullfighter, and Other Poems (bilingual edition), translation by A. L. Loyd, Oxford University Press, 1937, reprinted, AMS Press, 1978.
Diván del Tamarit (title means "Divan of the Tamarit"), published in *Obras Completas,* Losada, 1938 (also see below).
Poems, translation by Stephen Spender and J. L. Gili, Oxford University Press, 1939.
Poeta en Nueva York, Séneca (Mexico), 1940, translations published as *Poet in New York,* (bilingual edition) by Ben Belitt, introduction by Angel del Río, Grove Press, 1955, reprinted, 1983, by Stephen Fredman, Fog Horn Press, 1975, by Greg Simon and Steven F. White, Farrar, Straus, 1988 (also see below).
The Poet In New York, and Other Poems (includes "Gypsy Ballads"), translation by Rolfe Humphries, introduction by J. Bergamín, Norton, 1940.
Selected Poems of Federico García Lorca, translation by Stephen Spender and J. L. Gili, Hogarth Press (London), 1943, Transatlantic Arts (New York), 1947.
Poemas póstumos, Canciones musicales, Diván del Tamarit, Mexicanas (Mexico), 1945.

The Selected Poems of Federico García Lorca (bilingual edition), edited by Francisco García Lorca and Donald M. Allen, introduction by Francisco García Lorca, New Directions, 1955.

Lorca, translation and introduction by J. L. Gili, Penguin, 1960-65.

(With Juan Ramón Jiménez) *Lorca and Jiménez: Selected Poems,* translation by Robert Bly, Sixties Press, 1967.

Divan and Other Writings (includes "Divan of the Tamarit"), translation by Edwin Honig, Bonewhistle Press, 1974.

Lorca/Blackburn: Poems, translation by Paul Blackburn, Momo's Press, 1979.

The Cricket Sings: Poems and Songs for Children (bilingual edition), translation by Will Kirkland, New Directions, 1980.

Suites (reconstruction of a collection planned by Lorca), edited by André Belamich, Ariel (Barcelona), 1983.

Inéditos de Federico García Lorca: Sonetos del amor oscuro, 1935-1936, (title means "Unpublished Works of Federico García Lorca: Sonnets of the Dark Love, 1935-1936") compiled by Marta Teresa Casteros, Instituto de Estudios de Literatura Latinoamericana (Buenos Aires), c. 1984.

Poems represented in numerous collections and anthologies.

PLAYS

El malefico de la mariposa (two-act; title means "The Butterfly's Evil Spell"; first produced in Madrid at Teatro Esclava, March 22, 1920), published in *Obras completas,* Aguilar, 1954 (also see below).

Mariana Pineda: Romance popular en tres estampas (three-act; first produced in Madrid, Spain, at Teatro Fontalba, October, 1927; first published as *Romance de la muerte de Torrijos* in *El Día Gráfico,* June 25, 1927), Rivadeneyra (Madrid), 1928, translation by James Graham-Luján published as *Mariana Pineda: A Popular Ballad in Three Prints* in *Tulane Drama Review,* winter, 1962, translation by Robert G. Havard published as *Mariana Pineda: A Popular Ballad in Three Engravings,* Aris & Phillips, 1987 (also see below).

La zapatera prodigiosa: Farsa violenta (two-act; title means "The Shoemaker's Prodigious Wife"; first produced in Madrid at Teatro Español, 1930), published in *Obras completas* (also see below).

El público (one scene apparently missing), excerpts published in *Los Cuatro Vientos,* 1933; enlarged version published in *El público: Amor, teatro, y caballos en la obra de Federico García Lorca,* edited by R. Martínez Nadal, Dolphin (Oxford), 1970, revised edition published as *El público: Amor y muerte en la obra de Federico García Lorca,* J. Mortiz (Mexico), 1974, translation published as *Lorca's "The Public": A Study of an Unfinished Play and of Love and Death in Lorca's Work,* Schocken, 1974; Lorca's manuscript published by Dolphin, 1976; revised version published in *El público y comedia sin título: Dos obras póstumas,* 1978 (also see below).

Bodas de sangre: Tragedia (three-act; first produced in Madrid at Teatro Beatriz on March 8, 1933), Arbol, 1935, translation by José A. Weissberger produced as *Bitter Oleander* in New York City, 1935, translation by Gilbert Neiman published as *Blood Wedding,* New Directions, 1939 (also see below).

Amor de Don Perlimplín con Belisa en su jardín (title means "The Love of Don Perlimplín with Belisa, in His Garden"; first produced in Madrid on April 5, 1933), published in *Obras completas* (also see below).

Yerma: Poema trágico (three-act; first produced in Madrid on December 29, 1934), Anaconda (Buenos Aires), 1937, translation by Ian Macpherson and Jaqueline Minett published as *Yerma: A Tragic Poem* (bilingual edition), general introduction by John Lyon, Aris & Phillips, 1987 (also see below).

Retabillo de Don Cristóbal (puppet play; title means "Don Cristóbal's Puppet Show"; first produced in Buenos Aires, Argentina, at Teatro Avenida, March, 1934; revised version produced in Madrid at Feria del Libro, May 12, 1935), Subcomisariado de Propaganda del Comisariado General de Guerra (Valencia), 1938 (also see below).

Doña Rosita la soltera; o, El lenguaje de las flores: Poema granadino del novecientos, (three-act; title means "Doña Rosita the Spinster; or, The Language of Flowers: Poem of Granada in the Nineteenth Century"; first produced in Barcelona, Spain, at the Principal Palace, December, 1935), published in *Obras completas* (also see below).

Los títeres de Cachiporra: Tragecomedia de Don Cristóbal y la señá Rosita: Farsa (puppet play; title means "The Billy-Club Puppets: Tragicomedy of Don Cristóbal and Mam'selle Rosita: Farce"; first produced in Madrid at Zarzuela Theater, December, 1937), published in *Obras completas* (also see below).

Así que pasen cinco años (three-act; title means "As Soon as Five Years Pass"), published in *Obras Completas,* Losada, 1938 (also see below).

From Lorca's Theater: Five Plays (contains *The Shoemaker's Prodigious Wife, The Love of Don Perlimplín with Belisa, in His Garden, Doña Rosita the Spinster, Yerma,* and *When Five Years Pass*), translation by Richard L. O'Connell and James Graham-Luján, introduction by Stark Young, Scribner, 1941.

La casa de Bernarda Alba: Drama de mujeres en los pueblos de España (three-act; title means "The House of Bernarda Alba: Drama of Women in the Villages of Spain"; first produced in Buenos Aires at Teatro Avenida, March 8, 1945), Losada, 1944 (also see below).

Three Tragedies (contains *Blood Wedding, Yerma,* and *The House of Bernarda Alba*), translation by Richard L. O'Connell and James Graham-Luján, introduction by Francisco García Lorca, New Directions, 1947, Greenwood Press, 1977.

Comedies (contains *The Butterfly's Evil Spell, The Shoemaker's Prodigious Wife, The Love of Don Perlimplín with Belisa, in His Garden, Doña Rosita the Spinster*), translation by Richard L. O'Connell and James Graham-Luján, introduction by Francisco García Lorca, New Directions, 1954, enlarged edition published as *Five Plays: Comedies and Tragicomedies* (includes *The Billy-Club Puppets*), 1963, Penguin, 1987.

Three Tragedies (contains *Blood Wedding, Yerma,* and *The House of Bernarda Alba*), translation by Sue Bradbury, Folio Society (London), 1977.

Comedia sin título (one act of an incomplete play; also known as "El sueño de la vida" ["The Dream of Life"]; first produced in Madrid in July, 1989), published in *El público y comedia sin título: Dos obras póstumas,* 1978 (also see below).

El público [and] *Comedia sin título: Dos obras póstumas,* edited by R. Martínez Nadal and M. Laffranque, Seix Barral, 1978, translation by Carlos Bauer published as *The Public* [and] *Play Without a Title: Two Posthumous Plays,* New Directions, 1983.

The Rural Trilogy: Blood Wedding [and] *Yerma* [and] *The House of Bernarda Alba,* translation by Michael Dewell and Carmen Zapata, introduction by Douglas Day, Bantam, 1987.

Three Plays (contains *Blood Wedding, Doña Rosita the Spinster,* and *Yerma*), translation by Gwynne Edwards and Peter Luke, introduction by Edwards, Methuen, 1987.

Once Five Years Pass, and Other Dramatic Works, translation by William B. Logan and Angel G. Orrios, Station Hill Press, 1989.

Two Plays of Misalliance: The Love of Don Perlimplín [and] *The Prodigious Cobbler's Wife,* Aris & Phillips, 1989.

Also author of short dramatic sketches, including "La doncella, el marinero, y el estudiante" (title means "The Maiden, the Sailor, and the Student") and "El paseo de Buster Keaton" (title means "Buster Keaton's Stroll"), both 1928, and "Quimera" (title means "Chimera"). Adapter of numerous plays, including *La dama boba* and *Fuenteovejuna,* both by Lope de Vega. Plays represented in collections and anthologies.

OMNIBUS VOLUMES

Obras completas, (title means "Complete Works"), edited by Guillermo de Torre, Losada (Buenos Aires), 1938-46.

Obras completas, edited with commentary by Arturo de Hoyo, introductions by Jorge Guillén and Vicente Aleixandre, Aguilar, 1954, recent edition, 1986.

Obras (title means "Works"), edited with commentary by Mario Hernández, several volumes, Alianza, 1981—, 2nd edition, revised, 1983—.

OTHER

Impresiones y paisajes (travelogue), P. V. Traveset (Granada), 1918, translation by Lawrence H. Klibbe published as *Impressions and Landscapes,* University Press of America, 1987.

Federico García Lorca: Cartas a sus amigos (letters), edited by Sebastián Gasch, Cobalto (Barcelona), 1950.

García Lorca: Cartas, postales, poemas, y dibujos (includes letters and poems), edited by Antonio Gallego Morell, Monedo y Crédito (Madrid), 1968.

Deep Song, and Other Prose, translation by Christopher Maurer, New Directions, 1980.

From the Havana Lectures, 1928: "Theory and Play of the Duende" and "Imagination, Inspiration, Evasion" (lectures; bilingual edition), translation by Stella Rodriguez, preface by Randolph Severson, introduction by Rafael López Pedraza, Kanathos (Dallas, Tex.), 1981.

Selected Letters, edited with translation by David Gershator, New Directions, 1983.

How a City Sings from November to November (lecture; bilingual edition), translation by Christopher Maurer, Cadmus Editions, 1984.

Also author of the filmscript "Trip to the Moon." Illustrator of several books, including *El fin del viaje* by Pablo Neruda; drawings represented in collections, including *Federico García Lorca: Dibujos,* Ministerio de Cultura (Granada), 1986, and Helen Oppenheimer, *Lorca—The Drawings: Their Relation to the Poet's Life and Work,* F. Watts, 1987. Co-editor of *gallo* (Granada literary magazine; title means "rooster"), 1928.

SIDELIGHTS: Federico García Lorca was "a child of genius beyond question," declared Jorge Guillén in *Language and Poetry.* A Spanish poet and dramatist, Lorca was at the height of his fame in 1936 when he was executed by fascist rebels at the age of thirty-eight; in the years thereafter, Guillén suggested, the writer's prominence in European culture matched that of his countryman Pablo Picasso. Lorca's work has been treasured by a broad spectrum of the reading public throughout the world. His complete works have been reprinted in Spain almost every year since the 1950s, and observers believe he is more widely recognized in the English-speaking world than any Spanish writer except Miguel de Cervantes, author of *Don Quixote.* Lorca was familiar with the artistic innovators of his time, and his work shares with theirs a sense of sophistication, awareness of human psychology, and overall pessimism. But while his contemporaries often preferred to appeal to the intellect, Lorca gained wide popularity by addressing basic human emotions. He possessed an engaging personality and a dynamic speaking style, and he imbued his writing with a wide range of human feeling, including awe, lust, nostalgia, and despair. "Those who knew him," wrote his brother Francisco in a foreword to *Three Tragedies,* "will not forget his gift . . . of enlivening things by his presence, of making them more intense."

The public image of Lorca has varied greatly since he became famous in the 1920s. Known primarily for works about peasants and gypsies, he was quickly labeled a simple poet of rural life—an image he felt oversimplified his art. His death enraged democratic and socialist intellectuals, who called him a political martyr; but while Lorca sympathized with leftist causes, he avoided direct involvement in politics. In the years since Lorca died, his literary biographers have grown more sophisticated, revealing his complexity both as a person and as an artist. To biographer Carl Cobb, for instance, Lorca's "life and his work" display a "basic duality." Despite friends and fame Lorca struggled with depression, concerned that his homosexuality, which he hid from the public, condemned him to live as a social outcast. While deeply attached to Spain and its rural life, he came to reject his country's social conservatism, which disdained his sexuality. Arguably, Lorca's popularity grew from his conscious effort to transform his personal concerns into comments on life in general, allowing him to reach a wide audience.

During his youth Lorca experienced both Spain's traditional rural life and its entry into the modern world. Born in 1898, he grew up in a village in Andalusia—the southernmost region of Spain, then largely untouched by the modern world. Such areas were generally dominated by the traditional powers of Spanish society, including political conservatism, the Catholic church, and affluent landowners. Lorca's father, a landowning liberal, confounded his wealthy peers by marrying a village schoolteacher and by paying his workers generously. Though Lorca was a privileged child he knew his home village well, attending school with its children, observing its poverty, and absorbing the vivid speech and folktales of its peasants. "I have a huge storehouse of childhood recollections in which I can hear the people speaking," Lorca observed, according to biographer Ian Gibson. "This is poetic memory, and I trust it implicitly." The sense of lost innocence that recurs in Lorca's writings, Gibson averred, focuses on his early rural years, probably the happiest of his life.

But once Lorca moved with his parents to the Andalusian city of Granada in 1909, many forces propelled him into the modern world. Spain was undergoing a lengthy crisis of confidence, spurred by the country's defeat by the United States in the War of 1898. Some Spaniards wished to strengthen traditional values and revive past glory, but others hoped their country would moderate its conservatism, foster intellectual inquiry, and learn from more modernized countries. With his parents' encouragement Lorca encountered Spain's progressives through his schooling, first at an innovative, nonreligious secondary school, and then at the University of Granada, where he became a protege of such intellectual reformers as Fernando de los Ríos and Martín Domínguez Berrueta. By his late teens Lorca was already known as a multi-talented artist—his first book, the travelogue *Impresiones y paisajes* (*Impressions and Landscapes*), appeared before he was twenty—but he was also a poor student. Skilled as a pianist and singer, he would probably have become a musician if his parents had not compelled him to stay in school and study law. "I am a great Romantic," he wrote to a friend at the time, according to Gibson. "In a century of Zeppelins and idiotic deaths, I weep at my piano dreaming of the Handelian mist."

In 1919 Lorca's parents let him transfer to the University of Madrid, where he ignored classes in favor of socializing and cultural life. The move helped Lorca's development as a writer, however, for some of the major trends of modern European culture were just beginning to reach Spain through Madrid's intellectual community. As Western writers began to experiment with language, Madrid became a center of ultraism, which sought to change the nature of poetry by abandoning sentiment and moral rhetoric in favor of "pure poetry"—new and startling images and metaphors. Surrealism, aided by Sigmund Freud's studies of psychology, tried to dispense with social convention and express the hidden desires and fears of the subconscious mind. New ideas surrounded Lorca even in his dormitory—an idealistic private foundation, the Residencia de Estudiantes, which tried to re-create in Spain the lively intellectual atmosphere found in the residence halls of England's elite universities. At the Residencia Lorca met such talented students as Luis Buñuel and Salvador Dalí, who soon became prominent in the surrealist movement. The friendship between Lorca and Dalí became particularly close, and at times painful to both. Dalí, somewhat withdrawn in his youth, resisted becoming Lorca's lover but was clearly drawn to Lorca's ebullient personality. Lorca, who came to view Dalí with feelings of unrequited love, was impressed by his friend's audacity as a social critic and as a painter. "You are a Christian tempest," Dalí told Lorca, according to Gibson, "and you need my paganism."

Lorca's early poems, Carl Cobb suggested, show his "search . . . for a permanent manner of expression"; the results are promising but sometimes awkward. Lorca quickly showed a gift for imagery and dramatic imagination, adeptly describing, for instance, the experience of a bird being shot down by a hunter. But he had to struggle to shed the vague, overemotional style of romanticism—a difficult task because he often seemed to be making veiled comments about his unhappiness as a homosexual. For example, Lorca's poem about the doomed love of a cockroach for a butterfly became an artistic disaster when it was presented in 1920 as the play "El maleficio de la mariposa" ("The Butterfly's Evil Spell"). Lorca's Madrid audience derided the play, and even when he became a successful dramatist he avoided discussing the experience. A more successful poem, which Gibson called "one of Lorca's most moving," is "Encuentro" ("Meeting"), in which the poet speaks with the loving wife he might have known as a heterosexual. (At his death Lorca left behind many unpublished works—generally dominated by frustration or sadness—on homosexual themes, apparently presuming that the general public would not accept the subject matter.) Lorca tried many poetic forms, particularly in *Canciones* (*Songs*), which contains poems written between 1921 and 1924. He wrote several extended odes, including the "Ode to Salvador Dalí," which was widely praised as a defense of modern art although it can also be read as a love poem. The form and rhythm of music inspired a group of poems titled *Suites,* which were not published as a unified collection until 1983.

Eventually Lorca achieved great success as a poet by describing the traditional world of his childhood with a blend of very old and very contemporary writing techniques. The impetus came from his friendship with Manuel de Falla, a renowned composer who moved to Granada to savor the exotic music of Andalusia's gypsies and peasants. The two men rediscovered the gypsies' *cante jondo* or "deep song," a simple but deeply felt form of folk music that laments the struggles of everyday life. For Lorca, the ancient *cante jondo* became a model for innovative poetry: it expressed human feeling in broad terms while avoiding the rhetorical excess of romanticism. While helping Falla to organize a 1922 *cante jondo* festival that drew folk singers from throughout Spain, Lorca wrote a poetry collection titled *Poema del cante jondo* (*Poem of the Deep Song*). In these verses, Gibson observed, Lorca tried to convey the emotional atmosphere of the folk songs while avoiding the awkward pretense that he was an uneducated gypsy. Thereafter Lorca discovered that he could increase the dramatic impact of his folk-inspired poetry by using the narrative form of old Spanish ballads to tell poetic stories about gypsies and other characters; the poems could retain a twentieth-century outlook by using innovative language and a sophisticated understanding of the human mind. The resulting work, *Romancero gitano* (*Gypsy Ballads*), appeared in 1928 and soon made Lorca famous throughout the Hispanic world.

Gypsy Ballads shows Lorca at the height of his skill as a poet, in full control of language, imagery, and emotional suggestion. The characters inhabit a world of intense, sometimes mysterious, emotional experience. In the opening ballad a gypsy boy taunts the moon, which appears before him as a sexually attractive woman; suddenly the moon returns to the sky and takes the child with her, while other gypsies wail. Observers have tried to explain the ballad as everything from a comment on Lorca's sense of being sexually "different" to a metaphor for death. Some of the ballads appear to celebrate sexual vitality. In an unusually delicate poem, Lorca describes a gypsy nun who is fleetingly aroused by the sound of men on horseback outside her convent; in another a gypsy man describes his nighttime tryst with a woman by a riverbank. Much of the book conveys menace and violence: a girl runs through the night, her fear of being attacked embodied by the wind, which clutches at her dress; a gypsy is murdered by others who envy his good looks; in the final ballad, derived from the Bible, a prince rapes his sister. In his lecture "On the Gypsy Ballads," reprinted in *Deep Song and Other Prose,* Lorca suggests that the ballads are not really about gypsies but about pain—"the struggle of the loving intelligence with the incomprehensible mystery that surrounds it." "Lorca is not deliberately inflicting pain on the reader in order to shock or annoy him," wrote Roy Campbell in *Lorca,* but the poet "feels so poignantly that he has to share this feeling with others." Observers suggest that the collection describes the force of human life itself—a source of both energy and destructiveness.

The intensity of *Gypsy Ballads* is heightened by Lorca's mastery of the language of poetry. "Over the years," observed Cobb in his translation of the work, "it has become possible to speak of the 'Lorquian' metaphor or image, which [the poet] brought to fruition" in this volume. When Lorca says a gypsy woman bathes "with water of skylarks," Cobb explained, the poet has created a stunning new image out of two different words that describe something "soothing." Sometimes Lorca's metaphors boldly draw upon two different senses: he refers to a "horizon of barking dogs," for instance, when dogs are barking in the distance at night and the horizon is invisible. Such metaphors seem to surpass those of typical avant-garde poets, who often combined words arbitrarily, without concern for actual human experience. Lorca said his poetic language was inspired by Spanish peasants, for whom a seemingly poetic phrase such as "oxen of the waters" was an ordinary term for the strong, slow current of a river. Campbell stressed that Lorca was unusually sensitive to "the *sound* of words," both their musical beauty and their ability to reinforce the meaning of a poem. Such skills, practiced by Spain's folksingers, made Lorca a "musician" among poets, Campbell averred; interestingly, Lorca greatly enjoyed reading his work aloud before audiences and also presented Spanish folk songs at the piano. Reviewers often lament that Lorca's ear for language is impossible to reproduce in translation.

Lorca's newfound popularity did not prevent him from entering an unusually deep depression by 1929. Its causes, left vague by early biographers, seem to have been the breakup of Lorca's intense relationship with a manipulative lover and the end of his friendship with Dalí. At Buñuel's urging Dalí had moved to Paris, where the two men created a bizarre surrealist film titled "Un Chien andalou" ("An Andalusian Dog"). Lorca was convinced that the film, which supposedly had no meaning at all, was actually a sly effort to ridicule him. The poet, who knew no English and had never left Spain, opted for a radical change of scene by enrolling to study English at New York City's Columbia University. In New York Lorca's lively and personable manner charmed the Spanish-speaking intellectual community, but some have surmised that inwardly he was close to suicide. Forsaking his classes Lorca roamed the city, cut off from its citizens by the language barrier. He found most New Yorkers cold and inhuman, preferring instead the emotional warmth he felt among the city's black minority, whom he saw as fellow outcasts. Meanwhile he struggled to come to terms with his unhappiness and his sexuality.

The first product of Lorca's turmoil was the poetry collection *Poeta en Nueva York* (*Poet in New York*). In the book, Cobb observed, New York's social problems mirror Lorca's personal despair. The work opens as the poet reaches town, already deeply unhappy; he surveys both New York's troubles and his own; finally, after verging on hopelessness, he regathers his strength and tries to resolve the problems he has described. *Poet in New York* is far more grim and difficult than *Gypsy Ballads,* as Lorca apparently tries to heighten the reader's sense of alienation. The liveliness of the earlier volume gives way to pessimism; the verse is unrhymed; and, instead of using vivid metaphors about the natural world, Lorca imitates the surrealists by using symbols that are strange and difficult to understand. In poems about American society Lorca shows a horror of urban crowds, which he compares to animals, but he also shows sympathy for the poor. Unlike many white writers of his time, he is notably eloquent in describing the oppression of black Americans, particularly in his image of an uncrowned "King of Harlem"—a strong-willed black man humiliated by his menial job. Near the end of the collection he predicts a general uprising in favor of economic equality and challenges Christianity to ease the pain of the modern world. In more personal poems Lorca contrasts the innocent world of his childhood with his later unhappiness, alludes to his disappointments in love, and rails at the decadence he sees among urban homosexuals. He seems to portray a positive role model in his "Ode to Walt Whitman," dedicated to a nineteenth-century American poet—also a homosexual—who attempted to celebrate common people and the realities of everyday life. Lorca's final poem is a song about his departure from New York for Cuba, which he found much more hospitable than the United States. Commentators disagreed greatly about the merits of *Poet in New York,* which was not published in its entirety until after Lorca's death. Many reviewers, disappointed by the book's obscure language and grim tone, dismissed it as a failed experiment or an aberration. By contrast, Cobb declared that "with the impetus given by modern critical studies and translations, *Poet in New York* has become the other book which sustains Lorca's reputation as a poet."

Before Lorca returned to Spain in 1930, he had largely completed what many observers would call his first mature play, *El público* (*The Public*). Written in a disconcerting, surrealist style comparable to *Poet in New York,* the play confronts such controversial themes as the need for truth in the theater and for truth about homosexuality, in addition to showing the destruction of human love by selfishness and death. After his disastrous experience with "The Butterfly's Evil Spell," Lorca had spent the 1920s gradually mastering the techniques of drama, beginning with the light, formulaic Spanish genres of farce and puppet plays. From puppet theater, observers have suggested, Lorca learned to draw characters rapidly and decisively; in farces for human actors, he developed the skills required to sustain a full-length play. For instance, the farce *La zapatera prodigiosa* (*The Shoemaker's Prodigious Wife*), begun in the mid-1920s, shows Lorca's growing ease with extended dialogue and complex action. In *Amor de Don Perlimplín con Belisa en su jardín* (*The Love of Don Perlimplín with Belisa, in His Garden*), begun shortly thereafter, Lorca toys with the conventions of farce, as the play's object of ridicule—an old man with a lively young wife—unexpectedly becomes a figure of pity. By 1927 Lorca gained modest commercial success with his second professional production, *Mariana Pineda.* The heroine of this historical melodrama meets death rather than forsake her lover, a rebel on behalf of democracy. By the time the play was staged, however, Lorca said he had outgrown its "romantic" style.

Accordingly, in *The Public* Lorca proposed a new theater that would confront its audience with uncomfortable truths. As the play opens, a nameless Director of popular plays receives three visitors, who challenge him to present the "theater beneath the sand"—drama that goes beneath life's pleasing surface. The three men and the Director rapidly change costumes, apparently revealing themselves as unhappy homosexuals, locked in relationships of betrayal and mistrust. The Director then shows his audience a play about "the truth of the tombs," dramatizing Lorca's pessimistic belief that the finality of death overwhelms the power of love. Apparently the Director reshapes William Shakespeare's "Romeo and Juliet," in which young lovers die rather than live apart from each other. In *The Public* Juliet appears on stage after her love-inspired suicide, realizing that her death is meaningless and that she will now remain alone for eternity. The Director's audience riots when faced with such ideas, but some theater students, perhaps representing the future of drama, are intrigued. Back in Spain Lorca read *The Public* to friends, who were deeply shocked and advised him that the play was too controversial and surrealistic for an audience to accept. Lorca apparently agreed: he did not release the work and, according to biographer Reed Anderson, dismissed it in interviews as "a poem to be booed at." Nonetheless, Lorca observed, it reflected his "true intention."

Lorca remained determined to write plays rather than poetry, but he reached what some have called an unspoken compromise with his audience, presenting innovative theater that would not provoke general outrage. He became artistic director of the University Theater, a state-supported group of traveling players known by its Spanish nickname, *La barraca* ("The Hut"). The troupe, which presented plays from the "Golden Age" of Spanish drama in the seventeenth century, was welcomed by small villages throughout Spain that had never seen a stage performance. Lorca, who gained invaluable experience in theater by directing and producing the programs, decided that an untapped audience for challenging drama existed among Spain's common people. In a manner reminiscent of the *Gypsy Ballads,* he wrote a series of plays set among the common people of Spain, discussing such serious themes as human passion, unrequited love, social repression, the passing of time, and the power of death. Rather than shock by discussing homosexuality as in *The Public,* he focused on the frustrations of Spain's women. As the plays emerged, Lorca spoke of bringing "poetry" to the theater. But his characters often speak prose, and observers suggest he was speaking somewhat metaphorically. Like other playwrights of his time, Lorca seems to have felt that nineteenth-century dramatists' emphasis on realism—accurate settings, everyday events—distracted writers from deeper, emotional truths about human experience. To make theater more imaginative and involving, Lorca used a variety of effects: vivid language, visually striking stage settings, and heightened emotions ranging from confrontation to tension and repression. By adding such "poetry" to scenes of everyday Spanish life, he could show audiences the underlying sorrows and desires of their own lives.

In accord with such aims, Lorca's four best-known plays from the 1930s—*Doña Rosita la soltera* (*Doña Rosita the Spinster*), *Bodas de sangre* (*Blood Wedding*), *Yerma*, and *La casa de Bernarda Alba* (*The House of Bernarda Alba*)—show notable similarities. All are set in Spain during Lorca's lifetime; all spotlight ordinary women struggling with the impositions of Spanish society. *Doña Rosita* is set in the Granada middle class that Lorca knew as a teenager. In three acts set from 1885 to 1911, Lorca first revels in nostalgia for turn-of-the-century Spain, then shows Rosita's growing despair as she waits helplessly for a man to marry her. By the play's end, as Rosita faces old age as an unwanted, unmarried woman, her passivity seems as outdated as the characters' costumes. The three remaining plays, called the "Rural Trilogy," are set in isolated villages of Lorca's Spain. *Yerma*'s title character is a woman whose name means "barren land." She dutifully allows relatives to arrange her marriage, then gradually realizes, to her dismay, that her husband does not want children. Torn between her desire for a baby and her belief in the sanctity of marriage, Yerma resorts to prayer and sorcery in a futile effort to become a mother. Finally she strangles her husband in a burst of uncontrollable frustration. In *The House of Bernarda Alba,* the repressive forces of society are personified by the play's title character, a conservative matriarch who tries to confine her unmarried daughters to the family homestead for eight years of mourning after the death of her husband. The daughters grow increasingly frustrated and hostile until the youngest and most rebellious commits suicide rather than be separated from her illicit lover. *Blood Wedding* is probably Lorca's most successful play with both critics and the public. A man and woman who are passionately attracted to each other enter loveless marriages out of duty to their relatives, but at the woman's wedding feast the lovers elope. In one of the most evocative and unconventional scenes of all Lorca's plays, two characters representing the Moon and Death follow the lovers to a dark and menacing forest, declaring that the couple will meet a disastrous fate. The woman's vengeful husband appears and the two men kill each other. The play ends back at the village where the woman, who has lost both her husband and her lover, joins other villagers in grieving but is isolated from them by mutual hatred. In each of the four plays, an individual's desires are overborne by the demands of society, with disastrous results.

After *Blood Wedding* premiered in 1933, Lorca's fame as a dramatist quickly matched his fame as a poet, both in his homeland and in the rest of the Hispanic world. A short lecture tour of Argentina and Uruguay stretched into six months, as Lorca was greeted as a celebrity and his plays were performed for enthusiastic crowds. He was warmly received by such major Latin American writers as Chile's Pablo Neruda and Mexico's Alfonso

Reyes. Neruda, who later won the Nobel Prize for his poetry, called Lorca's visit "the greatest triumph ever achieved by a writer of our race." Notably, while Lorca's most popular plays have achieved great commercial success with Spanish-speaking audiences, they have been respected, but not adulated, by the English-speaking public. Some observers suggested that the strength of the plays is limited to their language, which is lost in translation. But others, including Spaniard Angel del Río and American Reed Anderson, have surveyed Lorca's stagecraft with admiration. In the opening scenes of *Blood Wedding,* for instance, Lorca skillfully contrasts the festive mood of the villagers with the fierce passions of the unwilling bride; in *Yerma* he confronts his heroine with a shepherd whose love for children subtly embodies her dreams of an ideal husband. In an article that appeared in *Lorca: A Collection of Critical Essays,* del Río wondered if the plays were too steeped in Hispanic culture for other audiences to easily appreciate.

Lorca's triumphs as a playwright were marred by growing troubles in Spain, which became divided between hostile factions on the political left and right. Though Lorca steadily resisted efforts to recruit him for the Communist party, his social conscience led him to strongly criticize Spanish conservatives, some of whom may have yearned for revenge. Meanwhile Lorca seemed plagued by a sense of foreboding and imminent death. He was shocked when an old friend, retired bullfighter Ignacio Sánchez Mejías, was killed by a bull while attempting to revive his career in the ring. Lorca's elegy—*Llanto por Ignacio Sánchez Mejías* (*Lament for the Death of a Bullfighter*)—has often been called his best poem, endowing the matador with heroic stature as he confronts his fate. Later, friends recalled Lorca's melodramatic remark that the bullfighter's death was a rehearsal for his own. In 1936 civil war broke out in Spain as conservative army officers under General Francisco Franco revolted against the liberal government. Lorca, who was living in Madrid, made the worst possible decision by electing to wait out the impending conflict at his parents' home in Granada, a city filled with rebel sympathizers. Granada quickly fell to rebel forces, who executed many liberal politicians and intellectuals. One was Lorca, who was arrested, shot outside town, and buried in an unmarked grave.

Franco's regime, which controlled all of Spain by 1939, never accepted responsibility for Lorca's death. But Lorca remained a forbidden subject in Spain for many years: "We knew there had been a great poet called García Lorca," recalled film director Carlos Saura in the *New York Times,* "but we couldn't read him, we couldn't study him." By the 1950s Lorca's work was again available in Spain, but it was still difficult to research either his life or his death. Those who knew him avoided discussing his sexuality or releasing his more controversial work; residents of Granada who knew about his execution were afraid to speak. Gradually there emerged a new willingness to understand Lorca on his own terms, and after Franco died in 1975, Lorca could be openly admired in his homeland as one of the century's greatest poets—a status he had never lost elsewhere. His legacy endures as a unique genius whose personal unhappiness enabled him to see deeply into the human heart. "When I met him for the first time, he astonished me," Guillén recalled, according to Anderson. "I've never recovered from that astonishment."

MEDIA ADAPTATIONS: Several of Lorca's plays have been adapted for opera and ballet, including *Blood Wedding, Yerma,* and *The Love of Don Perlimplín with Belisa, in His Garden. Blood Wedding* was adapted by Antonio Gades for a ballet, which was in turn adapted by Carlos Saura for a film of the same title, 1981.

BIOGRAPHICAL/CRITICAL SOURCES:

BOOKS

Adams, Mildred, *García Lorca: Playwright and Poet,* Braziller, 1977.

Allen, Rupert C., *The Symbolic World of García Lorca,* University of New Mexico Press, 1972.

Anderson, Reed, *Federico García Lorca,* Grove, 1984.

Berea, Arturo, *Lorca: The Poet and His People,* translation by Ilsa Berea, Harcourt, 1949.

Bowra, C. M., *The Creative Experiment,* Macmillan, 1949.

Byrd, Suzanne Wade, *García Lorca, La Barraca, and the Spanish National Theater,* Abra, 1975.

Campbell, Roy, *Lorca: An Appreciation of His Poetry,* Yale University Press, 1952.

Cobb, Carl W., *Federico García Lorca,* Twayne, 1967.

Cobb, Carl W., *Contemporary Spanish Poetry (1898-1963),* Twayne, 1976.

Colecchia, Francesca, editor, *García Lorca: A Selectively Annotated Bibliography of Criticism,* Garland Publishing, 1979.

Colecchia, Francesca, editor, *García Lorca: An Annotated Primary Bibliography,* Garland Publishing, 1982.

Duran, Manuel, editor, *Lorca: A Collection of Critical Essays,* Prentice-Hall, 1962.

Edwards, Gwynne, *Lorca: The Theatre Beneath the Sand,* Boyars, 1980.

García Lorca, Federico, *Three Tragedies,* translation by Richard L. O'Connell and James Graham-Luján, introduction by Francisco García Lorca, New Directions, 1947.

García Lorca, Federico, *Five Plays: Comedies and Tragicomedies,* translation by Richard L. O'Connell and James Graham-Luján, introduction by Francisco García Lorca, New Directions, 1963.

García Lorca, Federico, *Deep Song, and Other Prose,* translation by Christopher Maurer, New Directions, 1980.

García Lorca, Federico, *Lorca's "Romancero gitano": A Ballad Translation and Critical Study,* translation and commentary by Carl W. Cobb, University Press of Mississippi, 1983.

García Lorca, Federico, *Poet in New York,* translation by Greg Simon and Steven F. White, edited with an introduction by Christopher Maurer, Farrar, Straus, 1988.

García Lorca, Francisco, *In the Green Morning: Memories of Federico,* translation by Christopher Maurer, New Directions, 1986.

Gibson, Ian, *The Assassination of Federico García Lorca,* W. H. Allen, 1979.

Gibson, Ian, *Federico García Lorca: A Life,* Pantheon, 1989.

Guillén, Jorge, *Language and Poetry: Some Poets of Spain,* Harvard University Press, 1961.

Honig, Edwin, *García Lorca,* New Directions, 1944.

Laurenti, Joseph L. and Joseph Siracusa, *Federico García Lorca y su mundo: Ensayo de una bibliografía general/ The World of Federico García Lorca: A General Bibliographic Survey,* Scarecrow Press, 1974.

Lima, Robert, *The Theatre of García Lorca,* Las Américas, 1963.

Londré, Felicia Hardison, *Federico García Lorca,* Ungar, 1984.

Morris, C. B., *A Generation of Spanish Poets, 1920-1936,* Cambridge University Press, 1969.

Pollin, Alice M. and Philip H. Smith, editors, *A Concordance to the Plays and Poems of Federico García Lorca,* Cornell University Press, 1975.

Stanton, Edward F., *The Tragic Myth: Lorca and Cante Jondo,* University Press of Kentucky, 1978.

Trend, J. B., *Lorca and the Spanish Poetic Tradition,* Russell & Russell, 1971.

Twentieth-Century Literary Criticism, Gale, Volume 1, 1978, Volume 7, 1982.

Young, Howard T., *The Victorious Expression: A Study of Four Contemporary Spanish Poets,* University of Wisconsin Press, 1966.

PERIODICALS

Commonweal, November 3, 1939, April 20, 1945, August 12, 1955, September 2, 1955, October 21, 1955.

Kenyon Review, summer, 1955.

Nation, September 18, 1937, November 1, 1941, December 27, 1947.

New Republic, February 27, 1935, November 10, 1937, October 11, 1939, September 2, 1940, October 13, 1941.

New York Times, October 19, 1980, July 5, 1989.

New York Times Book Review, September 3, 1939, June 14, 1953, October 9, 1955, November 20, 1988, October 8, 1989.

Parnassus, spring, 1981.

Poetry, December, 1937, September, 1940.

Saturday Review, October 2, 1937, August 26, 1939, January 13, 1940, November 26, 1960.

Time, December 22, 1947, April 17, 1964.

Times Literary Supplement, October 16, 1937, May 27, 1939, September 2, 1965, September 2, 1977, November 21, 1980, August 2, 1984.

—*Sketch by Thomas Kozikowski*

*   *   *

GARCIA MARQUEZ, Gabriel (José) 1928-

PERSONAL: Surname pronounced "Gar-*see*-a *Mar*-kez"; born March 6, 1928, in Aracataca, Colombia; son of Gabriel Eligio García (a telegraph operator) and Luisa Santiaga Márquez Iguaran; married Mercedes Barcha, March 21, 1958; children: Rodrigo, Gonzalo. *Education:* Attended Universidad Nacional de Colombia, 1947-48, and Universidad de Cartagena, 1948-49.

ADDRESSES: Home—P.O. Box 20736, Mexico City D.F., Mexico. *Office*—Apartado Postal 20736 Deleyación Alvaro Bregon 01000, Mexico. *Agent*—Agencia Literaria Carmen Balcells, Diagonal 580, Barcelona 21, Spain.

CAREER: Worked as a journalist, 1947-65, including job with *El heraldo,* Baranquilla, Colombia; film critic and news reporter, *El espectador,* Bogotá, Colombia, Geneva, Switzerland, Rome, Italy, and Paris, France, Prensa Latina news agency, Bogotá, 1959, and as department head in New York City, 1961; writer, 1965—. Founder, Cuban Press Agency, Bogotá; Fundación Habeas, founder, 1979, president, 1979—. Mediator between Colombian government and leftist guerrillas in early 1980s.

MEMBER: American Academy of Arts and Letters (honorary fellow), Foundation for the New Latin American Film (Havana; president, 1985—).

AWARDS, HONORS: Colombian Association of Writers and Artists Award, 1954, for story "Un día después del sábado"; Premio Literario Esso (Colombia), 1961, for *La mala hora;* Chianciano Award (Italy), 1969, Prix de Meilleur Livre Etranger (France), 1969, and Rómulo Gallegos prize (Venezuela), 1971, all for *Cien años de soledad;* LL.D., Columbia University, 1971; *Books Abroad/*Neustadt International Prize for Literature, 1972; Common Wealth Award for Literature, Bank of Delaware, 1980; Nobel Prize for Literature, 1982; *Los Angeles Times* Book Prize nomination for fiction, 1983, for *Chronicle of a Death Foretold; Los Angeles Times* Book Prize for fiction, 1988, for *Love in the Time of Cholera.*

WRITINGS:

FICTION

La hojarasca (novella; title means "Leaf Storm"; also see below), Ediciones Sipa (Bogotá), 1955, reprinted, Bruguera (Barcelona), 1983.

El coronel no tiene quien le escriba (novella; title means "No One Writes to the Colonel"; also see below), Aguirre Editor (Medellín, Colombia), 1961, reprinted, Bruguera, 1983.

La mala hora (novel; also see below), Talleres de Gráficas "Luis Pérez" (Madrid), 1961, reprinted, Bruguera, 1982, English translation by Gregory Rabassa published as *In Evil Hour,* Harper, 1979.

Los funerales de la Mamá Grande (short stories; title means "Big Mama's Funeral"; also see below), Editorial Universidad Veracruzana (Mexico), 1962, reprinted, Bruguera, 1983.

Cien años de soledad (novel), Editorial Sudamericana (Buenos Aires), 1967, reprinted, Cátedra, 1984, English translation by Rabassa published as *One Hundred Years of Solitude,* Harper, 1970.

Isabel viendo llover en Macondo (novella; title means "Isabel Watching It Rain in Macondo"; also see below), Editorial Estuario (Buenos Aires), 1967.

No One Writes to the Colonel and Other Stories (includes "No One Writes to the Colonel," and stories from *Big Mama's Funeral*), translated by J. S. Bernstein, Harper, 1968.

La increíble y triste historia de la cándida Eréndira y su abuela desalmada (novella; title means "Innocent Erendira and Her Heartless Grandmother"; also see below), Barral Editores, 1972.

El negro que hizo esperar a los ángeles (short stories), Ediciones Alfil (Montevideo), 1972.

Ojos de perro azul: Nueve cuentos desconocidos (short stories; also see below), Equisditorial (Argentina), 1972.

Leaf Storm and Other Stories (includes "Leaf Storm," and "Isabel Watching It Rain in Macondo"), translated by Rabassa, Harper, 1972.

La increíble y triste historia de la cándida Eréndira y su abuela desalmada (short stories; includes *El coronel no tiene quien le escriba*), Librería de Colegio (Buenos Aires), 1975.

El otoño del patriarca (novel), Plaza & Janés Editores (Barcelona), 1975, translation by Rabassa published as *The Autumn of the Patriarch,* Harper, 1976.

Todos los cuentos de Gabriel García Márquez: 1947-1972 (title means "All the Stories of Gabriel García Márquez: 1947-1972"), Plaza & Janés Editores, 1975.

Innocent Erendira and Other Stories (includes "Innocent Erendira and Her Heartless Grandmother" and stories from *Ojos de perro azul*), translated by Rabassa, Harper, 1978.

Dos novelas de Macondo (contains *La hojarasca* and *La mala hora*), Casa de las Américas (Havana), 1980.

Crónica de una muerte anunciada (novel), La Oveja Negra (Bogotá), 1981, translation by Rabassa published as *Chronicle of a Death Foretold,* J. Cape, 1982, Knopf, 1983.

Viva Sandino (play), Editorial Nueva Nicaragua, 1982, 2nd edition published as *El asalto: El operativo con que el FSLN se lanzo al mundo,* 1983.

El rastro de tu sangre en la nieve: El verano feliz de la señora Forbes, W. Dampier Editores (Bogotá), 1982.

El secuestro: Guión cinematográfico (unfilmed screenplay), Oveja Negra, 1982.

"Eréndira" (filmscript; adapted from his novella *La increíble y triste historia de la cándida Eréndira y su abuela desalmada*), Les Films du Triangle, 1983.

Collected Stories, translated by Rabassa and Bernstein, Harper, 1984.

El amor en los tiempos del cólera, Oveja Negra, 1985, English translation by Edith Grossman published as *Love in the Time of Cholera,* Knopf, 1988.

"A Time to Die" (filmscript), ICA Cinema, 1988.

El cataclismo de Dámocles, Editorial Universitaria Centroamericana (Costa Rica), 1986.

"Diatribe of Love against a Seated Man" (play), first produced at Cervantes Theater, Buenos Aires, 1988.

El general en su laberinto (title means "The General in His Labyrinth"), Mondadori España, 1989.

NONFICTION

(With Mario Vargas Llosa) *La novela en América Latina: Diálogo,* Carlos Milla Batres (Lima), 1968, published as *Diálogo sobre la novela Latinoamericana,* Perú Andino (Lima), 1988.

El relato de un náufrago (journalistic pieces), Tusquets Editor (Barcelona), 1970, English translation by Randolph Hogan published as *The Story of a Shipwrecked Sailor,* Knopf, 1986.

Cuando era feliz e indocumentado (journalistic pieces; title means "When I Was Happy and Undocumented"), Ediciones El Ojo de Camello (Caracas), 1973.

Crónicas y reportajes (journalistic pieces), La Oveja Negra, 1978.

Periodismo militante (journalistic pieces), Son de Máquina Editores (Bogotá), 1978.

De viaje por los países socialistas: 90 dias en las "Cortina de hierro" (journalistic pieces), Ediciones Macondo (Colombia), 1978.

(Contributor) *Los sandinistas,* Oveja Negra, 1979.

(Contributor) Soledad Mendoza, editor, *Asi es Caracas,* Editorial Ateneo de Caracas, 1980.

Obra periodística (journalistic pieces), edited by Jacques Gilard, Bruguera, Volume 1: *Textos constenos,* 1981, Volumes 2-3: *Entre cachacos,* 1982, Volume 4: *De Europa y América (1955-1960),* 1983.

(With P. Mendoza) *El olor de la guayaba: Conversaciones con Plinio Apuleyo Mendoza* (interviews), La Oveja Negra, 1982, English translation by Ann Wright published as *The Fragrance of Guava,* edited by T. Nairn, Verso, 1983.

(With Guillermo Nolasco-Juarez) *Persecución y muerte de minorías: Dos perspectivas,* Juarez Editor (Buenos Aires), 1984.

(Contributor) *La Democracia y la paz en América Latina,* Editorial El Buho (Bogotá), 1986.

1928-1986, presencia de Jóvito Villalba en la historia de la democracia venezolana, Ediciones Centauro, 1986.

La aventura de Miguel Littín, clandestino en Chile: Un reportaje, Editorial Sudamericana, 1986, English translation by Asa Zatz published as *Clandestine in Chile: The Adventures of Miguel Littín,* Holt, 1987.

OTHER

Also co-author and producer of six screenplays made for Spanish television, "Fable of the Beautiful Pigeon Fancier," "I'm the One You're Looking For," "Miracle in Rome," "The Summer of Miss Forbes," "Letters from the Park," and "A Happy Sunday," together titled "Amores Difíciles" (title means "Dangerous Loves"); two screenplays, "Letters from the Park" and "Miracle in Rome" were scheduled to appear on Public Television's "Great Performance" series, 1989 and 1990. Author of weekly syndicated column.

WORK IN PROGRESS: Co-writing new works with Guerra, Duque, and director Sergio Toledo; adapting a Colombian novel, "La María," for television.

SIDELIGHTS: "I knew [*One Hundred Years of Solitude*] would please my friends more than my other [books] had," said Gabriel García Márquez in a *Paris Review* interview with Peter H. Stone. "But when my Spanish publisher told me he was going to print eight thousand copies, I was stunned because my other books had never sold more than seven hundred. I asked him why not start slowly, but he said he was convinced that it was a good book and that all eight thousand copies would be sold between May and December. Actually they were sold within one week in Buenos Aires."

Winner of the 1982 Nobel Prize for Literature, García Márquez "is one of the small number of contemporary writers from Latin America who have given to its literature a maturity and dignity it never had before," asserts John Sturrock in the *New York Times Book Review. One Hundred Years of Solitude* is perhaps García Márquez's best-known contribution to the awakening of interest in Latin American literature, for the book's appearance in Spanish in 1967 prompted unqualified approval from readers and critics. It has sold more than ten million copies, has been translated into over thirty languages and, according to an *Antioch Review* critic, the popularity and acclaim for the novel "mean that Latin American literature will change from being the exotic interest of a few to essential reading and that Latin America itself will be looked on less as a crazy subculture and more as a fruitful, alternative way of life." So great was the novel's initial popularity, writes Mario Vargas Llosa in *García Márquez: Historia de un deicido,* that not only was the first Spanish printing of the book sold out within one week, but for months afterwards Latin American readers alone would exhaust each successive printing. Translations of the novel similarly elicited enthusiastic responses from critics and readers around the world.

In this outpouring of critical opinion, which *Books Abroad* contributor Klaus Muller-Bergh refers to as "an earthquake, a maelstrom," various reviewers have termed *One Hundred Years of Solitude* a masterpiece of modern fiction. For example, Chilean poet Pablo Neruda, himself a Nobel laureate, is quoted in *Time* as calling the book "the greatest revelation in the Spanish language since the *Don Quixote* of Cervantes." Similarly enthusiastic is William Kennedy, who writes in the *National Observer* that "*One Hundred Years of Solitude* is the first piece of literature since the Book of Genesis that should be required reading for the entire human race." And Regina Janes, in her study *Gabriel García Márquez: Revolutions in Wonderland,* describes the book as "a 'total novel' that [treats] Latin America socially, historically, politically, mythically, and epically," adding that *One Hundred Years of Solitude* is also "at once accessible and intricate, lifelike and self-consciously, self-referentially fictive."

The novel is set in the imaginary community of Macondo, a village on the Colombian coast, and follows the lives of several generations of the Buendía family. Chief among these characters are Colonel Aureliano Buendía, perpetrator of thirty-two rebellions and father of seventeen illegitimate sons, and Ursula Buendía, the clan's matriarch and witness to its eventual decline. Besides following the complicated relationships of the Buendía family, *One Hundred Years of Solitude* also reflects the political, social, and economic troubles of South America. Many critics believe that the novel, with its complex family relationships and extraordinary events, is a microcosm of Latin America itself. But as *Playboy* contributor Claudia Dreifus states in her interview with the author, García Márquez has facetiously described the plot

as "just the story of the Buendía family, of whom it is prophesied that they shall have a son with a pig's tail; and in doing everything to avoid this, the Buendías *do* end up with a son with a pig's tail."

The mixture of historical and fictitious elements that appear in *One Hundred Years of Solitude* places the novel within that type of Latin American fiction that critics term magical or marvelous realism. Janes attributes the birth of this style of writing to Alejo Carpentier, a Cuban novelist and short story writer, and concludes that García Márquez's fiction follows ideas originally formulated by the Cuban author. The critic notes that Carpentier "discovered the duplicities of history and elaborated the critical concept of 'lo maravilloso americano' the 'marvelous real,' arguing that geographically, historically, and essentially, Latin America was a space marvelous and fantastic . . . and to render that reality was to render marvels." García Márquez presents a similar view of Latin America in his *Paris Review* interview with Stone: "It always amuses me that the biggest praise for my work comes for the imagination while the truth is that there's not a single line in all my work that does not have a basis in reality." The author further explained in his *Playboy* interview with Dreifus: "Clearly, the Latin American environment is marvelous. Particularly the Caribbean. . . . The coastal people were descendants of pirates and smugglers, with a mixture of black slaves. To grow up in such an environment is to have fantastic resources for poetry. Also, in the Caribbean, we are capable of believing anything, because we have the influences of all those different cultures, mixed in with Catholicism and our own local beliefs. I think that gives us an open-mindedness to look beyond apparent reality."

The first line of *One Hundred Years of Solitude* introduces the reader into this world of imagination. According to James Park Sloan in the *Chicago Tribune Book World:* "Few first lines in literature . . . have comparable force: 'Many years later, as he faced the firing squad, Colonel Aureliano Buendía was to remember that distant afternoon when his father took him to discover ice.' It contains so much of what [makes] the work magical, including a steadily toneless background in which everyday events become marvelous and marvelous events are assimilated without comment into everyday life. Equally important, it establishes a time scheme," continues the critic, which "simultaneously [looks] backward at a present seen as memory in light of that future." Gordon Brotherson also notes the magical quality of *One Hundred Years of Solitude* and the book's relationship with Carpentier's fiction. In *The Emergence of the Latin American Novel,* Brotherson refers to the "skillful vagueness" of the opening sentence and writes, "Phrases like 'many years later' and 'that distant afternoon' lead back through the prehistoric stones to a timeless world where (in an allusion to Carpentier and his magic realism) we are told many things still needed to be named."

Muller-Bergh believes that García Márquez's particular gift for inserting the magical into the real is responsible for his popularity as a writer. The critic comments that "Latin American and Spanish readers . . . as well as European critics who have heaped unprecedented praise on the author" have found that this "penchant for plausible absurdities [is] one of García Márquez's most enduring qualities." Alan Weinblatt explains the novelist's technique in the *New Republic,* noting that for García Márquez "the key to writing *One Hundred Years of Solitude* was the idea of saying incredible things with a completely unperturbed face." The author credits this ability to his maternal grandmother: "She was a fabulous storyteller who told wild tales of the supernatural with a most solemn expression on her face," he told Dreifus. "As I was growing up, I often wondered whether or not her stories were truthful. Usually, I tended to believe her because of her serious, deadpan facial expression. Now, as a writer, I do the same thing; I say extraordinary things in a serious tone. It's possible to get away with *anything* as long as you make it believable. That is something my grandmother taught me." The straightforward manner in which the author tells of Aureliano Buendía and his father going out "to discover ice" is repeated throughout the novel and throughout García Márquez's fiction. For example, in *One Hundred Years of Solitude* Remedios the Beauty ascends into heaven while outside shaking out some sheets, yellow flowers fall all night when a family patriarch dies, and when a young man dies, his blood runs through the streets of the town and into his parents' house where, avoiding the rugs, it stops at the feet of his mother. In other works, García Márquez tells of a woman "so tender she could pass through walls just by sighing" and of a general who sires five thousand children.

But along with the fantastic episodes in García Márquez's fiction appear the historical facts or places that inspired them. An episode involving a massacre of striking banana workers is based on a historical incident; in reality, García Márquez told Dreifus, "there were very few deaths . . . [so] I made the death toll 3000 because I was using certain proportions in my book." But while *One Hundred Years of Solitude* is the fictional account of the Buendía family, the novel is also, as John Leonard states in the *New York Times*, "a recapitulation of our evolutionary and intellectual experience. Macondo is Latin America in microcosm." Robert G. Mead, Jr. similarly observes in *Saturday Review* that "Macondo may be regarded as a microcosm of the development of much of the Latin American continent." Adds the critic: "Although [*One Hundred Years of Solitude*] is first and always a story, the novel also has value as a social and historical document." García Márquez responds to these interpretations in his interview with Dreifus, commenting that his work "is not a history of Latin America, it is a *metaphor* for Latin America."

The "social and historical" elements of *One Hundred Years of Solitude* reflect the journalistic influences at work in García Márquez's fiction. Although known as a novelist, the author began as a reporter and still considers himself one. As he remarked to Stone, "I've always been convinced that my true profession is that of a journalist." Janes believes that the evolution of García Márquez's individual style is based on his experience as a correspondent; in addition, this same experience leads Janes and other critics to compare the Colombian with Ernest Hemingway. "[The] stylistic transformation between *Leaf Storm* and *No One Writes to the Colonel* was not exclusively an act of will," Janes claims. "García Márquez had had six years of experience as a journalist between the two books, experience providing practice in the lessons of Hemingway, trained in the same school." And George R. McMurray, in his book *Gabriel García Márquez*, maintains that Hemingway's themes and techniques have "left their mark" on the work of the Colombian.

García Márquez has also been compared to another American Nobel-winner, William Faulkner, who also elaborated on facts to create his fiction. Faulkner based his fictional territory Yoknapatawpha County on memories of the region in northern Mississippi where he spent most of his life; García Márquez based Macondo, the town appearing throughout his fiction, on Aracataca, the coastal city of his birth. A *Time* reviewer calls Macondo "a kind of tropical Yoknapatawpha County" while *Review* contributor Mary E. Davis points out further resemblances between the two authors. Davis notes: "García Márquez concentrates on the specific personality of place in the manner of the Mississippean, and he develops even the most reprehensi-

ble of his characters as idiosyncratic enigmas." Concludes the critic: "García Márquez is as fascinated by the capacity of things, events, and characters for sudden metamorphosis as was Faulkner."

Nevertheless, *Newsweek* writer Peter S. Prescott maintains that it was only after García Márquez shook off the influence of Faulkner that he was able to write *One Hundred Years of Solitude;* in this novel the author's "imagination matured: no longer content to write dark and fatalistic stories about a Latin Yoknapatawpha County, he broke loose into exuberance, wit and laughter." Thor Vilhjalmsson similarly observes in *Books Abroad* that while "García Márquez does not fail to deal with the dark forces, or give the impression that the life of human beings, one by one, should be ultimately tragic, . . . he also shows every moment pregnant with images and color and scent which ask to be arranged into patterns of meaning and significance while the moment lasts." While the Colombian has frequently referred to Faulkner as "my master," Luis Harss and Barbara Dohmann add in their *Into the Mainstream: Conversations with Latin-American Writers* that in his later stories, "the Faulknerian glare has been neutralized. It is not replaced by any other. From now on García Márquez is his own master."

In *The Autumn of the Patriarch* García Márquez uses a more openly political tone in relating the story of a dictator who has reigned for so long that no one can remember any other ruler. Elaborating on the kind of solitude experienced by Colonel Aureliano Buendía in *One Hundred Years,* García Márquez explores the isolation of a political tyrant. "In this fabulous, dreamlike account of the reign of a nameless dictator of a fantastic Caribbean realm, solitude is linked with the possession of absolute power," describes Ronald De Feo in the *National Review.* Rather than relating a straightforward account of the general's life, however, *The Autumn of the Patriarch* skips from one episode to another, using dense and detailed descriptions. *Times Literary Supplement* contributor John Sturrock finds this approach appropriate to the author's subject; calling the work "the desperate, richly sustained hallucination of a man rightly bitter about the present state of so much of Latin America," Sturrock notes that "García Márquez's novel is sophisticated and its language is luxuriant to a degree. Style and subject are at odds because García Márquez is committed to showing that our first freedom—and one which all too many Latin American countries have lost—is of the full resources of our language." *Time* writer R. Z. Sheppard similarly comments on García Márquez's elaborate style, observing that "the theme is artfully insinuated, an atmosphere instantly evoked like a puff of stage smoke, and all conveyed in language that generates a charge of expectancy." The critic concludes: "García Márquez writes with what could be called a stream-of-consciousness technique, but the result is much more like a whirlpool."

Some critics, however, find both the theme and technique of *The Autumn of the Patriarch* lacking. J. D. O'Hara, for example, writes in the *Washington Post Book World* that for all his "magical" realism García Márquez "can only remind us of real-life parallels; he cannot exaggerate them. For the same reason," adds the critic, "although he can turn into grisly cartoons the squalor and paranoia of actual dictatorships, he can scarcely parody them; reality has anticipated him again." *Newsweek*'s Walter Clemons similarly finds the novel somewhat disappointing: "After the narrative vivacity and intricate characterization of the earlier book [*The Autumn of the Patriarch*] seems both oversumptuous and underpopulated. It is—deadliest of compliments—an extended piece of magnificent writing," concludes Clemons. But other critics believe that the author's skillful style enhances the novel; referring to the novel's disjointed narrative style, Wendy McElroy comments in *World Research INK* that "this is the first time I have seen it handled properly. Gabriel García Márquez ignores many conventions of the English language which are meant to provide structure and coherence. But he is so skillful that his novel is not difficult to understand. It is bizarre; it is disorienting," continues the critic. "But it is not difficult. Moreover, it is appropriate to the chaos and decay of the general's mind and of his world." Similarly, De Feo maintains that "no summary or description of this book can really do it justice, for it is not only the author's surrealistic flights of imagination that make it such an exceptional work, but also his brilliant use of language, his gift for phrasing and description." Concludes the critic: "Throughout this unique, remarkable novel, the tall tale is transformed into a true work of art."

"With its run-on, seemingly free-associative sentences, its constant flow of images and color, Gabriel García Márquez's last novel, *The Autumn of the Patriarch,* was such a dazzling technical achievement that it left the pleasurably exhausted reader wondering what the author would do next," comments De Feo in the *Nation.* This next work, *Chronicle of a Death Foretold* "is, in miniature, a virtuoso performance," states Jonathan Yardley of the *Washington Post Book World.* In contrast with the author's "two masterworks, *One Hundred Years of Solitude* and *The Autumn of the Patriarch,*" continues the critic, "it is slight; . . . its action is tightly concentrated on a single event. But in this small space García Márquez works small miracles; *Chronicle of a Death Foretold* is ingeniously, impeccably constructed, and it provides a sobering, devastating perspective on the system of male 'honor.' " In the novella, describes Douglas Hill in the Toronto *Globe and Mail,* García Márquez "has cut out an apparently uncomplicated, larger-than-life jigsaw puzzle of passion and crime, then demonstrated, with laconic diligence and a sort of concerned amusement, how extraordinarily difficult the task of assembling the pieces can be." The story is based on a historical incident in which a young woman is returned after her wedding night for not being a virgin; her brothers then set out to avenge the stain on the family honor by murdering the man she names as her "perpetrator." The death is "foretold" in that the brothers announce their intentions to the entire town; but circumstances conspire to keep all but Santiago Nasar, the condemned man, from this knowledge, and he is brutally murdered.

"In telling this story, which is as much about the townspeople and their reactions as it is about the key players, García Márquez might simply have remained omniscient," observes De Feo. But instead "he places himself in the action, assuming the role of a former citizen who returns home to reconstruct the events of the tragic day—a day he himself lived through." This narrative maneuvering, claims the critic, "adds another layer to the book, for the narrator, who is visible one moment, invisible the next, could very well ask himself the same question he is intent on asking others, and his own role, his own failure to act in the affair contributes to the book's odd, haunting ambiguity." This recreation after the fact has an additional effect, as Gregory Rabassa notes in *World Literature Today:* "From the beginning we know that Santiago Nasar will be and has been killed, depending on the time of the narrative thread that we happen to be following, but García Márquez does manage, in spite of the repeated foretelling of the event by the murderers and others, to maintain the suspense at a high level by never describing the actual murder until the very end." The critic explains: "Until then we have been following the chronicler as he puts the bits and pieces together ex post facto, but he has constructed things in such a way that we are still hoping for a reprieve even though we know better." "As

more and more is revealed about the murder, less and less is known," writes Leonard Michaels in the *New York Times Book Review.* "Yet the style of the novel is always natural and unselfconscious, as if innocent of any paradoxical implication."

In approaching the story from this recreative standpoint, García Márquez is once again making use of journalistic techniques. As *Chicago Tribune Book World* editor John Blades maintains, "García Márquez tells this grisly little fable in what often appears to be a straight-faced parody of conventional journalism, with its dependence on 'he-she-they told me' narrative techniques, its reliance on the distorted, contradictory and dreamlike memories of 'eyewitnesses.' " Blades adds, however, that "at the same time, this is precision-tooled fiction; the author subtly but skillfully manipulates his chronology for dramatic impact." The *New York Times*'s Christopher Lehmann-Haupt similarly notes a departure from the author's previous style: "I cannot be absolutely certain whether in 'Chronicle' Gabriel García Márquez has come closer to conventional storytelling than in his previous work, or whether I have simply grown accustomed to his imagination." The critic determines that "whatever the case, I found 'Chronicle of a Death Foretold' by far the author's most absorbing work to date. I read it through in a flash, and it made the back of my neck prickle." "It is interesting," remarks *Times Literary Supplement* contributor Bill Buford, that García Márquez has chosen to handle "a fictional episode with the methods of a journalist. In doing so he has written an unusual and original work: a simple narrative so charged with irony that it has the authority of political fable." Concludes the critic: "If it is not an example of the socialist realism [García] Márquez may claim it to be elsewhere, *Chronicle of a Death Foretold* is in any case a mesmerizing work that clearly establishes [García] Márquez as one of the most accomplished, and the most 'magical' of political novelists writing today."

Despite this journalistic approach to the story, *Chronicle of a Death Foretold* does contain some of the "magical" elements that characterize García Márquez's fiction. As Robert M. Adams observes in the *New York Review of Books,* there is a "combination of detailed factual particularity, usually on irrelevant points, with vagueness, confusion, or indifference on matters of more importance." The result, suggests Adams, is that "the investigation of an ancient murder takes on the quality of a hallucinatory exploration, a deep groping search into the gathering darkness for a truth that continually slithers away." But others find that this combination of journalistic detail and lack of explanation detracts from the novel; D. Keith Mano, for example, comments in the *National Review* that because the narrator "has been sequestered as a juror might be . . . , he cannot comment or probe: and this rather kiln-dries the novel." The critic elaborates by noting that the primary characters "are left without development or chiaroscuro. They seem cryptic and surface-hard: film characters really. . . . Beyond a Warren Report-meticulous detective reconstruction, it is hard to care much for these people. Emotion, you see, might skew our clarity." But Edith Grossman asserts in *Review* that this reconstruction is meant to be enigmatic: "García Márquez holds onto the journalistic details, the minutiae of the factual, that constitute the great novelistic inheritance of Western realism, and at the same time throws doubt on their reliability through his narrative technique and by means of the subtle introduction of mythic elements." Concludes the critic: "Once again García Márquez is an ironic chronicler who dazzles the reader with uncommon blendings of fantasy, fable and fact."

Another blending of fable and fact, based in part on García Márquez's recollections of his parents's marriage, *Love in the Time of Cholera* "is an amazing celebration of the many kinds of love between men and women," characterizes Elaine Feinstein in the London *Times*. "In part it is a brilliantly witty account of the tussles in a long marriage, whose details are curiously moving; elsewhere it is a fantastic tale of love finding erotic fulfilment in ageing bodies." The novel begins with the death of Dr. Juvenal Urbino, whose attempt to rescue a parrot from a tree leaves his wife of fifty years, Fermina Daza, a widow. Soon after Urbino's death, however, Florentino Ariza appears on Fermina Daza's doorstep; the rest of the novel recounts Florentino's determination to resume the passionate courtship of a woman who had given him up over half a century ago. In relating both the story of Fermina Daza's marriage and her later courtship, *Love in the Time of Cholera* "is a novel about commitment and fidelity under circumstances which seem to render such virtues absurd," recounts *Times Literary Supplement* contributor S. M. J. Minta. "[It is] about a refusal to grow old gracefully and respectably, about the triumph sentiment can still win over reason, and above all, perhaps, about Latin America, about keeping faith with where, for better or worse, you started out from."

Although the basic plot of *Love in the Time of Cholera* is fairly simple, some critics accuse García Márquez of over-embellishing his story. Calling the plot a "boy-meets-girl" story, Chicago *Tribune Books* contributor Michael Dorris remarks that "it takes a while to realize this core [plot], for every aspect of the book is attenuated, exaggerated, overstated." The critic also notes that "while a Harlequin Romance might balk at stretching this plot for more than a year or two of fictional time, García Márquez nurses it over five decades," adding that the "prose [is] laden with hyperbolic excess." In addition, some observers claim that instead of revealing the romantic side of love, *Love in the Time of Cholera* "seems to deal more with libido and self-deceit than with desire and mortality," as Angela Carter terms it in the *Washington Post Book World*. Dorris expresses a similar opinion, writing that while the novel's "first 50 pages are brilliant, provocative, . . . they are overture to a discordant symphony" which portrays an "anachronistic" world of machismo and misogyny. In contrast, Toronto *Globe and Mail* contributor Ronald Wright believes that the novel works as a satire of this same kind of "hypocrisy, provincialism and irresponsibility of the main characters' social milieu." Concludes the critic: "Love in the Time of Cholera is a complex and subtle book; its greatest achievement is not to tell a love story, but to meditate on the equivocal nature of romanticism and romantic love."

Other reviewers agree that although it contains elements of his other work, *Love in the Time of Cholera* is a development in a different direction for García Márquez. Author Thomas Pynchon, writing in the *New York Times Book Review*, comments that "it would be presumptuous to speak of moving 'beyond' 'One Hundred Years of Solitude' but clearly García Márquez has moved somewhere else, not least into deeper awareness of the ways in which, as Florentino comes to learn, 'nobody teaches life anything.'" Countering criticisms that the work is overemotional, Minta claims that "the triumph of the novel is that it uncovers the massive, submerged strength of the popular, the cliched and the sentimental." While it "does not possess the fierce, visionary poetry of 'One Hundred Years of Solitude' or the feverish phantasmagoria of 'The Autumn of the Patriarch,'" as *New York Times* critic Michiko Kakutani describes it, *Love in the Time of Cholera* "has revealed how the extraordinary is contained in the ordinary, how a couple of forgotten, even commonplace lives can encompass the heights and depths of grand and eternal passion. The result," concludes the critic, "is a rich commodious novel, a novel whose narrative power is matched only by its generosity of vision." "The Garcimarquesian voice we have come to recognize from the other fiction has matured, found and developed new resources," asserts Pynchon, "[and] been brought to a level where it can at once be classical and familiar, opalescent and pure, able to praise and curse, laugh and cry, fabulate and sing and when called upon, take off and soar." Concludes the critic: "There is nothing I have read quite like [the] astonishing final chapter, symphonic, sure in its dynamics and tempo. . . . At the very best [this remembrance] results in works that can even return our worn souls to us, among which most certainly belongs 'Love in the Time of Cholera,' this shining and heartbreaking novel."

Although he has earned literary fame through his fiction, García Márquez has also gained notoriety as a reporter; as he commented to Stone, "I always very much enjoy the chance of doing a great piece of journalism." The Colombian elaborated in his interview with Dreifus: "I'm fascinated by the relationship between literature and *journalism*. I began my career as a journalist in Colombia, and a reporter is something I've never stopped being. When I'm not working on fiction, I'm running around the world, practicing my craft as a reporter." His work as a journalist, however, has produced some controversy, for in it García Márquez not only sees a chance to develop his "craft," but also an opportunity to become involved in political issues. His self-imposed exile from Colombia was prompted by a series of articles he wrote in 1955 about the sole survivor of a Colombian shipwreck, for the young journalist related that the government ship had capsized due to an overloading of contraband. García Márquez has more recently written *Clandestine in Chile: The Adventures of Miguel Littín,* a work about an exile's return to the repressive Chile of General Augusto Pinochet; the political revelations of the book led to the burning of almost 15,000 copies by the Chilean government. In addition, García Márquez has maintained personal relationships with such political figures as Cuban President Fidel Castro, French President Francois Mitterand, and the late Panamanian leader General Omar Torrijos.

Because of this history of political involvement, García Márquez has often been accused of allowing his politics to overshadow his work; he has also encountered problems entering the United States. When asked by the *New York Times Book Review*'s Marlise Simons why he is so insistent on becoming involved in political issues, the author replied that "If I were not a Latin American, maybe I wouldn't [become involved]. But underdevelopment is total, integral, it affects every part of our lives. The problems of our societies are mainly political." The Colombian further explained that "the commitment of a writer is with the reality of all of society, not just with a small part of it. If not, he is as bad as the politicians who disregard a large part of our reality. That is why authors, painters, writers in Latin America get politically involved."

Despite the controversy that his politics and work stir, García Márquez's *One Hundred Years of Solitude* is enough to ensure the author "a place in the ranks of twentieth century masters," claims Curt Suplee of the *Washington Post*. The Nobel-winner's reputation, however, is grounded in more than this one masterpiece; as the Swedish Academy's Nobel citation states, "Each new work of his is received by critics and readers as an event of world importance, is translated into many languages and published as quickly as possible in large editions." "At a time of dire predictions about the future of the novel," observes McMurray, García Márquez's "prodigious imagination, remarkable compositional precision, and wide popularity provide evidence that the genre is still thriving." And as *Chicago Tribune Book World* contributor Harry Mark Petrakis describes him, García Márquez "is a magician of vision and language who does astonishing things with time and reality. He blends legend and history in ways that make the legends seem truer than truth. His scenes and characters are humorous, tragic, mysterious and beset by ironies and fantasies. In his fictional world, anything is possible and everything is believable." Concludes the critic: "Mystical and magical, fully aware of the transiency of life, his stories fashion realms inhabited by ghosts and restless souls who return to those left behind through fantasies and dreams. The stories explore, with a deceptive simplicity, the miracles and mysteries of life."

MEDIA ADAPTATIONS: "Erendira" was produced by Les Films du Triangle in 1984; "Chronicle of a Death Foretold" was filmed by Francesco Rossi in 1987; the play "El Coronel No Tiene Quien Le Escriba" was adapted from García Márquez's novel of the same title by Carlos Giménez, and was first produced Off-Broadway at the Public/Newman Theater; a play, "Blood and Champagne," has been based on García Márquez's *One Hundred Years of Solitude.*

BIOGRAPHICAL/CRITICAL SOURCES:

BOOKS

Authors & Artists for Young Adults, Volume 3, Gale, 1990.
Bestsellers 1989, Number 1, Gale, 1989.
Brotherson, Gordon, *The Emergence of the Latin American Novel,* Cambridge University Press, 1979.
Contemporary Literary Criticism, Gale, Volume 2, 1974, Volume 3, 1975, Volume 8, 1978, Volume 10, 1979, Volume 15, 1980, Volume 27, 1984, Volume 47, 1988, Volume 55, 1989.
Dictionary of Literary Biography Yearbook: 1982, Gale, 1983.
Fernández-Braso, Miguel, *Gabriel García Márquez,* Editorial Azur (Madrid), 1969.
Gabriel García Márquez, nuestro premio Nobel, La Secretaria de Información y Prensa de la Presidencia de la Nación (Bogotá), 1983.
Gallagher, David Patrick, *Modern Latin American Literature,* Oxford University Press, 1973.
Guibert, Rita, *Seven Voices,* Knopf, 1973.
Harss, Luis and Barbara Dohmann, *Into the Mainstream: Conversations with Latin-American Writers,* Harper, 1967.
Janes, Regina, *Gabriel García Márquez: Revolutions in Wonderland,* University of Missouri Press, 1981.
Mantilla, Alfonso Renteria, compiler, *García Márquez habla de García Márquez,* Renteria (Colombia), 1979.
McGuirk, Bernard and Richard Cardwell, editors, *Gabriel García Márquez: New Readings,* Cambridge University Press, 1988.
McMurray, George R., *Gabriel García Márquez,* Ungar, 1977.
Porrata, Francisco E. and Fausto Avedano, *Explicación de Cien años de soledad [de] García Márquez,* Editorial Texto (Costa Rica), 1976.
Pritchett, V. S., *The Myth Makers,* Random House, 1979.
Rodman, Selden, *Tongues of Fallen Angels,* New Direction, 1974.
Vargas Llosa, Mario, *García Márquez: Historia de un deicido,* Barral Editores, 1971.

PERIODICALS

Books Abroad, winter, 1973, summer, 1973, spring, 1976.
Book World, February 22, 1970, February 20, 1972.
Chicago Tribune, March 6, 1983.
Chicago Tribune Book World, November 11, 1979, November 7, 1982, April 3, 1983, November 18, 1984, April 27, 1986.
Christian Science Monitor, April 16, 1970.
Commonweal, March 6, 1970.
Detroit News, October 27, 1982, December 16, 1984.

El País, January 22, 1981.
Globe and Mail (Toronto), April 7, 1984, September 19, 1987, May 21, 1988.
Hispania, September, 1976.
London Magazine, April/May, 1973, November, 1979.
Los Angeles Times, October 22, 1982, January 25, 1987, August 24, 1988.
Los Angeles Times Book Review, April 10, 1983, November 13, 1983, December 16, 1984, April 27, 1986, June 7, 1987, April 17, 1988.
Nation, December 2, 1968, May 15, 1972, May 14, 1983.
National Observer, April 20, 1970.
National Review, May 27, 1977, June 10, 1983.
New Republic, April 9, 1977, October 27, 1979, May 2, 1983.
New Statesman, June 26, 1970, May 18, 1979, February 15, 1980, September 3, 1982.
Newsweek, March 2, 1970, November 8, 1976, July 3, 1978, December 3, 1979, November 1, 1982.
New York Review of Books, March 26, 1970, January 24, 1980, April 14, 1983.
New York Times, July 11, 1978, November 6, 1979, October 22, 1982, March 25, 1983, December 7, 1985, April 26, 1986, June 4, 1986, April 6, 1988.
New York Times Book Review, September 29, 1968, March 8, 1970, February 20, 1972, October 31, 1976, July 16, 1978, September 16, 1978, November 11, 1979, November 16, 1980, December 5, 1982, March 27, 1983, April 7, 1985, April 27, 1986, August 9, 1987, April 10, 1988.
Paris Review, winter, 1981.
Playboy, February, 1983.
Publishers Weekly, May 13, 1974, December 16, 1983.
Review, Number 24, 1979, September/December, 1981.
Saturday Review, December 21, 1968, March 7, 1970.
Southwest Review, summer, 1973.
Time, March 16, 1970, November 1, 1976, July 10, 1978, November 1, 1982, March 7, 1983, December 31, 1984, April 14, 1986.
Times (London), November 13, 1986, June 30, 1988.
Times Literary Supplement, April 15, 1977, February 1, 1980, September 10, 1982, July 1, 1988.
Tribune Books (Chicago), June 28, 1987, April 17, 1988.
Washington Post, October 22, 1982.
Washington Post Book World, February 22, 1970, November 14, 1976, November 25, 1979, November 7, 1982, March 27, 1983, November 18, 1984, July 19, 1987, April 24, 1988.
World Literature Today, winter, 1982.
World Press Review, April, 1982.
World Research INK, September, 1977.

—*Sketch by Marian Gonsior and Diane Telgen*

*   *   *

GARCIA PONCE, Juan 1932-

PERSONAL: Born in 1932, in Mérida, Yucatán. *Education:* Studied drama at Centro de Escritores Mexicanos.

CAREER: Writer and literary critic. Editor, *Universidad de México,* and *Revista mexicana de literatura.*

MEMBER: Centro de Escritores Mexicanos (fellow), 1957-58.

WRITINGS:

El canto de los grillos, obras en tres actos (play), Imprenta Universitaria (Mexico), 1957.
Imagen primera; cuentos (short stories), [Xalapa, Mexico], 1963.
La noche; relatos (short stories), Ediciones Era (Mexico), 1963.

Figura de paja (novel), J. Mortiz (Mexico), 1964.

Cruce de caminos (lectures and essays), Universidad Veracruzana (Mexico), 1965.

La casa en la playa (novel), J. Mortiz, 1966.

Prólogo de Emmanuel Carballo, Empresas Editoriales (Mexico), 1966.

Entrada en la materia (essays), Universidad Nacional Autonóma de México, 1968.

La aparición de lo visible (essays), Siglo XXI Editores, 1968.

Deconsideraciones (essays), J. Mortiz, 1968.

La presencia lejana, Arca, 1968.

Nueve pintores mexicanos, Ediciones Era, 1968.

Cinco ensayos (criticism), Universidad Nacional Autónoma de México, 1969.

El reino milenario, ARCA (Montevideo), 1969.

La cabaña (novel), Universidad de Guanajuato, 1969.

El nombre olvidado; novels, Ediciones Era, 1970.

Vicente Rojo, Universidad Nacional Autónoma de México, 1970.

Encuentros, Fondo de Cultura Económica (Mexico), 1972, translation by Helen Lane published as *Encounters,* introduction by Octavio Paz, Eridanos Press (Hygiene, Col.), 1989.

Thomas Mann vivo, Era (Mexico), 1972.

El gato, Editorial Sudamericana, 1974.

(With Leonora Carrington) *Leonora Carrington* (Spanish-English text), Ediciones Era, 1974.

Unión, J. Moritz, 1974.

Teología y pornografía: Pierre Klossowski en su obra, una descripción, illustrations by Pierre Klossowski, Ediciones Era, 1975.

Entry into Matter: Modern Literature and Reality, translation by David J. Parent and Bruce-Novoa; afterword by Bruce-Novoa, Applied Literature Press (Normal, Ill.), 1976.

Imagen primera, Bruguera (Barcelona), 1978.

El libro, Editorial Grijalbo (Mexico), 1978.

Cuentos, Liberta-Sumaria (Mexico), 1980.

La errancia sin fin, Anagrama (Barcelona), 1981.

Figuraciones, Fondo de Cultura Económica (Mexico), 1982.

La cabaña, Montesinos (Barcelona), 1982.

Crónica de la intervención, Bruguera, 1982.

Catálogo razonado, Premiá Editora (Mexico), 1982.

Las huellas de la voz, Ediciones Coma (Mexico), 1982.

La vida perdurable, Ediciones Coma, 1982.

El gato y otros cuentos, Fondo de Cultura Económica, 1984.

De ánima, Montesinos, 1984.

José Francisco, Gobierno del Estado de Tabasco (Villahermosa, Mexico), 1986.

Apariciones, Fondo de Cultura Económica, 1987.

Also author of monograph, *Paul Klee: dibujos,* Librería Madero, 1965; author of *Felguérez,* Universidad Nacional Autónoma de México, 1976; author of commentary for exhibition catalog, *José Luis Cuevas, su infierno terrenal,* Instituto Nacional de Bellas Artes (Mexico), 1976; author of novel, *La invitación* 1972. Contributor to *Siempre* and *Novedades.*

SIDELIGHTS: Juan García Ponce's book of short stories and one novella, *Encounters,* as translated by Helen Lane, conveys "a distinct sensibility: erotic, nostalgic, visual, refined," writes Gene H. Bell-Villada in the *New York Times Book Review.* Bell-Villada, however, finds García Ponce at his best with the novella, "The Seagull," an intense adolescent love story, which "shows a consummate artistry." Bell-Villada concludes: "The fine-grained emotion and sustained glow of 'The Seagull' are simply haunting."

BIOGRAPHICAL/CRITICAL SOURCES:

PERIODICALS

New York Times Book Review, June 25, 1989.

* * *

GARCIA ROCHA, Rina 1954-

PERSONAL: Born March 20, 1954, in Chicago, Ill.; married Thomas Rocha. *Education:* Attended Columbia College, Santa Rosa Jr. College, and Northeastern Illinois University.

ADDRESSES: *Home*—5840 West Roosevelt Rd., Chicago, Ill. 60650.

CAREER: Poet. Has given numerous poetry readings in the Chicago area, including "Latina Art Expo '77."

MEMBER: Popular Culture Association, Movimiento Artístico Chicano (MARCH).

AWARDS, HONORS: One of García Rocha's poems won publication in a national contest in 1967; Olga-Bush Journal Award; cash prize for two poems published in *Eluder.*

WRITINGS:

(Contributor) *Raza Art and Media Collective* (anthology), University of Michigan, 1977.

Eluder (poems), Alexander Books, 1980.

Contributor of poems to *Abrazo, Garland Court Review, Revista Chicano-Riqueña,* and *Hojas Poéticas.*

* * *

GARRO, Elena 1920(?)-

PERSONAL: Born c. 1920 (one source says 1917) in Mexico; married Octavio Paz (a poet).

ADDRESSES: c/o University of Texas Press, Box 7819, Austin, Tex. 78713-7819.

CAREER: Writer. Playwright for Poesía en Voz Alta (theater group; name means "Poetry Aloud"), choreographer for Teatro de la Universidad; journalist in Mexico and United States; screenwriter.

AWARDS, HONORS: Premio Hispanoamericano Xavier Villaurrutia from Sociedad Alfonsina International, 1963, for *Recollections of Things to Come.*

WRITINGS:

PLAYS

Andarse por las ramas (one-act; title means "Walking in the Treetops"), [Mexico City, Mexico], 1957 (also see below).

"Un hogar sólido," y otras piezas en un acto (title means "A Solid Home, and Other One-Act Plays"; contains "Un hogar sólido," "Los pilares de doña Blanca," "El rey mago," "Andarse por las ramas," "Ventura Allende," "El encanto, tendajón mixto," "Los perros" [title means "The Dogs"], "El árbol," "La dama boba" [title means "The Foolish Lady"], "El rastro," "Benito Fernández," and "La mudanza" [title means "The Move"]), Universidad Veracruzana (Jalapa, Mexico), 1958, published as *Un hogar sólido, y otras piezas,* illustrations by Juan Soriano, 1983.

"La señora en su balcón" (title means "The Lady on Her Balcony"), in *Teatro hispanoamericano contemporáneo,* Aguilar (Madrid, Spain), 1970.

Felipe Angeles (first produced in 1954; first published serially in *Coatl,* fall, 1967), Difusión Cultural/UNAM, 1979.

Work represented in anthologies, including *Uno, dos, tres: Tres dramas mexicanos en un acto,* edited by Jeanine Gaucher-Shultz and Alfredo O. Morales, Odyssey Press, 1971.

FICTION

Los recuerdos del porvenir (novel), Mortiz (Mexico City, Mexico), 1963, translation by Ruth L. C. Simms published as *Recollections of Things to Come,* illustrations by Alberto Beltrán, University of Texas Press, 1969.

La semana de colores (stories; title means "A Week in Colors"; contains "La semana de colores," "La culpa es de los Tlaxcaltecas" [title means "The Tlaxcaltecas Are to Blame"], "El zapaterito de Guanajuato" [title means "The Little Cobbler From Guanajuato"], ",Qué hora es . . . ?" [title means "What Time Is It . . . ?"], "El día que fuimos perros" [title means "The Day We Were Dogs"], "Antes de la guerra de Troya," "El robo de Tiztla," "El duende," "El anillo" [title means "The Ring"], "Perfecto Luna," and "El árbol"), Universidad Veracruzana, 1964.

Stories represented in anthologies, including *Contemporary Women Authors of Latin America,* edited by Doris Meyer and Margarite Fernández Olmos, Brooklyn College Press, 1983.

OTHER

Andamos huyendo Lola, Mortiz, 1980.
Testimonios sobre Mariana (first published serially in *Espejo,* 1967), Grijalbo (Mexico), 1981.
Reencuentro de personajes, Grijalbo (Mexico), 1982.
La casa junto al río, Grijalbo (Barcelona, Spain), 1983.

SIDELIGHTS: Well regarded in the Spanish-speaking world for her plays and short stories, Elena Garro is best known to English speakers as the author of the award-winning novel *Recollections of Things to Come,* first published in 1963 and translated from the Spanish in 1969. Told from the collective viewpoint of a Mexican town, the tale employs the conventions of magic realism, a genre largely associated with Latin American writers and distinguished by the occurrence of supernatural or marvelous events which the characters accept without surprise. One woman turns to stone, another stops time, escaping the town with her lover by flying away on a horse, as Garro unfolds an account "at once caustic and lyrical" of Mexican life in the early 1900s, according to *Ms.* reviewer Bell Gale Chevigny. Esteemed by Chevigny and other critics as a forerunner of Gabriel García Márquez's hugely successful novel *One Hundred Years of Solitude,* a landmark in the literature of magic realism, Garro's novel won the prestigious Premio Hispanoamericano Xavier Villaurrutia.

In *Recollections of Things to Come* Garro considers the period in Mexican history when President Plutarco Elias Calles sought to limit the power of the Catholic church, sparking a revolt by Church supporters. Garro's imaginary town takes part in the rebellion, its women conspiring to save a well-loved priest from the occupying military forces. The status of women in Mexican society is an important concern in the novel. Observed Chevigny, "The fact that magic immobilizes one woman and releases the other underscores Garro's dual vision of women: frozen by centuries of institutionalized repression, they are freer than men to imagine all possibilities." Garro also explores Mexican Indian concerns, including the victimization of Indians at the hands of conquerors and other authorities and the Aztec idea of time as cyclical, a concept that results in her characters' ability to "remember" their futures as suggested in the novel's title.

Garro's achievements in her novel and other writings make her "one of the three important pioneering women in modern Mexican fiction," in Chevigny's opinion. To a literary tradition known for its protest of socioeconomic conditions and its unique way of using the magical to examine the real, she has brought her own "poetic style, . . . originality and sense of humor," remarked Gabriela Mora in an essay in *Latin American Women Writers: Yesterday and Today.* Summarized Mora: "With demanding artistry, Garro has explored the Latin American self and society in a body of work that deserves a place alongside the better known writings of her peers."

BIOGRAPHICAL/CRITICAL SOURCES:

BOOKS

Miller, Yvette E. and Charles M. Tatum, editors, *Latin American Women Writers: Yesterday and Today,* Latin American Literary Review, 1977.

PERIODICALS

Ms., April, 1987.

* * *

GARZA, Roberto J(esus) 1934-

PERSONAL: Born April 10, 1934, in Hargill, Tex.; son of Andres (a horse trainer) and Nazaria (de la Fuente) Garza; married Idolina Alaniz (an educator), August 24, 1957; children: Robert J., Jr., Sylvia Lynn. *Education:* Texas A & I University, B.S., 1959, M.A., 1964; Oklahoma State University, Ed.D., 1975; graduate study at University of Kansas, University of Arizona, and University of Washington, Seattle. *Politics:* Democrat. *Religion:* Roman Catholic.

ADDRESSES: Home—2 Alvarado Ave. (Rancho Viejo), Brownsville, Tex. 78520. *Office*—Division of Education, Pan American University, 80 Fort Brown, Brownsville, Tex. 78520.

CAREER: High school Spanish teacher and counselor in Premont, Agua Dulce, and Alice, Tex., 1959-63, Alton, Ill., 1960-61, and Rawlins, Wyo., 1963-64; St. Joseph Junior College, St. Joseph, Mo., instructor in Spanish and chairman of department of Spanish, French, and German, 1964-65; Southwest Texas Junior College, Uvalde, instructor in Spanish and chairman of Division of Fine Arts, 1966-68; Sul Ross State University, Alpine, Tex., assistant professor of Spanish language and literature, 1968-70; Oklahoma State University, Stillwater, instructor in Spanish, 1971-72; University of Notre Dame, Notre Dame, Ind., member of faculty, 1972-73; Pan American University, Brownsville Center, Brownsville, Tex., assistant professor, 1973-76, professor of secondary education and head of Division of Education, 1977—. Psychometrist and Spanish language specialist, U.S. Peace Corps, summer, 1966; guidance counselor, Gary Job Corps, summer, 1967; administrative assistant and researcher, Associated City-County Economic Development Corp. of Hidalgo County, 1970-71; member, Texas Education Agency Accreditation Team, 1979—. *Military service:* U.S. Army, 1954-56.

MEMBER: American Association of University Professors, American Association for Higher Education, Smithsonian Associates, Texas Association of College Teachers, Sigma Iota, Phi Delta Kappa.

AWARDS, HONORS: NDEA fellowship; grants from John Hay Whitney Foundation and National Endowment for the Humanities; named an outstanding educator and leader in state of Texas by Texas House of Representatives, 1987.

WRITINGS:

(Contributor) *The Role of the Mexican-American in the History of the Southwest,* Inter-American Institute, Pan American University, 1969.
Chicano Theatre: An Anthology, University of Notre Dame Press, 1975.

Contributor to *La Luz.*

WORK IN PROGRESS: Contemporary Chicano Short Stories: An Anthology; writing on Chicano drama; research on comparative higher education systems.

SIDELIGHTS: Robert J. Garza told *CA:* "Every piece of literary work is an attempt to further find understanding and meaning to our existence in this labyrinth called life."

* * *

GASSET, José Ortega y
  See ORTEGA y GASSET, José

* * *

GEIGEL POLANCO, Vincente   1904-1979

PERSONAL: Born June 18, 1904, in Isabela, Puerto Rico; died April 30, 1979, in San Juan, Puerto Rico.

CAREER: Attorney, public official, journalist, and author. Government of Puerto Rico, San Juan, counsel to bureau of labor, 1926-30, counsel to bureau of wage claims, 1930-31, director of division of economic and social research of department of labor, 1932-36, member of senate, beginning in 1940, member of legislative delegation to Washington, D.C., 1945-47, attorney general during administration of Luis Muñoz Marín (1949-65); professor of law and social sciences at University of Puerto Rico, Río Piedras. Organizer of People's Institute of Free Education, 1936. Puerto Rican delegate to People's Peace Congress, Buenos Aires, Argentina, 1936; leader of Puerto Rican delegation to Third International Conference of Lawyers, Mexico, 1944.

MEMBER: Puerto Rico Atheneum (secretary, 1927-33, president of history section, 1934-36 and 1942-46, vice-president, 1937-38, president, 1939-41), Puerto Rican Academy of History (founding secretary, 1934), Puerto Rican Civil Liberties Union (secretary, 1936), Puerto Rican Economic Congress (member of executive committee, 1939), Institute of Puerto Rican Literature (secretary, 1939-47), Society of Puerto Rican Authors (founder; president, 1966), Puerto Rico College of Law, Puerto Rico Casino, Union Party of Puerto Rico (secretary of committee on international relations, 1931), Liberal Party (member of central committee, 1932-37), Popular Democratic Party (member of central committee, beginning in 1940), Association for Adult Education (vice president, 1937), Social Action United Front, National Congress for the Liberation of Political Prisoners, Spanish Casino.

WRITINGS:

El problema universitario: Una aproximación crítica al problema de la Universidad, Imprenta Venezuela (San Juan, Puerto Rico), c. 1941.
El despetar de un pueblo, Biblioteca de Autores Puertorriqueños, 1942.
Valores de Puerto Rico, Editorial Eugenio María de Hostos (San Juan), 1943, reprinted, Arno Press, 1975.
Bajo el signo de Géminis: Poemas de ayer y de hoy (poems), Imprenta Venezuela, 1963.

Canto de tierra adentro, Ateneo Puertorriqueño de Nueva York (New York), 1965.
Palabras de nueva esperanza (poems), [San Juan], 1969.
La mujer en la poesía de Puerto Rico en las décadas del '30 al '50, Academia Puertorriqueña de la Lengua Española, c. 1971.
La farsa del Estado Libre Asociado (collected prose pieces), Edil (Río Piedras, Puerto Rico), 1972.
El grito de Lares: Gesta de heroísmo y sacrificio, Antillana (Río Piedras), 1976.
Ensayos hostosianos, Florentia (Boston), 1976.
(Co-editor) *Antología de oradores puertorriqueños del pasado* (anthology of speeches), Instituto de Cultura Puertorriqueña, 1978.
(Editor) Clara Lair, *Obra poética,* Instituto de Cultura Puertorriqueña, 1979.
(Author of introduction) *Indice: Mensuario de historia, literatura, arte, y ciencia,* Editorial Universitaria, Universidad de Puerto Rico, 1979.

Also author of several booklets, including *The Problem of Puerto Rico: Memorial Addressed to the Hon. Franklin D. Roosevelt, President of the United States of America,* 1940.

Contributor of poems and articles to periodicals, including *Asomante, La Democracia, El Diario de Puerto Rico, Faro, El Imparcial, Hostos, El Mundo, Puerto Rico Ilustrado,* and *Vórtice.* Editor of *La Democracia,* 1926-30, and *Revista del Colegio de Abogados de Puerto Rico,* 1944-46; co-founder of *Indice,* 1929; assistant editor of *Mundo Mercantil,* 1931-33; member of editorial board of *Revista del Ateneo Puertorriqueño,* 1934-40.

SIDELIGHTS: Vincente Géigel Polanco was a prominent Puerto Rican statesman and writer. As a young man he helped to found the *noísta* school of experimental poetry and published works in that style in periodicals of the late 1920s. With Antonio Pedreira and Samuel Quiñones he founded his own literary magazine, *Indice,* in 1929. By the 1930s Géigel Polanco was playing an active role in the movement to assert Puerto Rico's rights in relation to the United States, and he joined the executive committee of the Puerto Rican Economic Congress, which sent members to Washington, D.C., to protest against failings in the island's political and economic life. One of his early publications in book form was a 1940 pamphlet titled *The Problem of Puerto Rico: Memorial Addressed to the Hon. Franklin D. Roosevelt, President of the United States of America;* shortly thereafter he produced *El despetar de un pueblo,* a historical survey of the attitudes toward nationalism among Puerto Rican leaders. After working as a public administrator during the 1920s and 1930s, the author began a successful political career, gaining election to the island's senate during the 1940s and journeying to Washington, D.C., after World War II as part of a legislative delegation that helped to redefine the U.S. role in his homeland. In 1949 Puerto Rico was allowed for the first time to elect its own governor, and Géigel Polanco served as attorney general during the ensuing sixteen-year administration of Luis Muñoz Marín. During his many years as an attorney and public official Géigel Polanco helped to protect Puerto Rican workers through the implementation of labor laws, and on his death in 1979 he was recalled by Muñoz Marín as a friend of working people.

OBITUARIES:

PERIODICALS

New York Times, May 2, 1979.
Washington Post, May 4, 1979.

GELMAN, Juan 1930-

PERSONAL: Born in 1930 in Buenos Aires, Argentina.

CAREER: Writer. Served several prison terms for leftist political militancy in Argentina.

WRITINGS:

Violín y otras cuestiones (poetry), M. Gleizer, 1956.
El juego en que andamos (poetry), Nueva Expresión, 1959.
Velorio del solo (poetry), Nueva Expresión, 1961.
Gotán (poetry), Ediciones Horizonte, 1962.
Cólera buey (poetry), Ediciones La Tertulia, 1965.
Poemas (poetry), Casa de las Américas, 1969.
Traducciones III, Galerna, 1969, reissued as *Los poemas de Sidney West,* Llibres de Sinera, 1972.
Relaciones, Ediciones La Rosa Blindada, 1973.
Obra poética (poetry collection), Corregidor, 1975.
Citas y comentarios, Visor (Madrid), 1982.
Hacia el sur, Marcha (Mexico), 1982.
La junta luz, Libros de Tierra Firme, 1985.
Interrupciones II, Libros de Tierra Firme, 1986.
Anunciaciones, Visor, 1988.
Interrupciones I, Libros de Tierra Firme, 1988.

Associated with the *El Pan Duro* and the *La Rosa Blindada* literary groups.

SIDELIGHTS: Juan Gelman is a respected Argentine poet whose works are renowned for their themes and images taken from popular culture and contemporary political issues. His original and pedantic verses express pessimism toward the present social structures in Latin America, but evince hope for revolutionary change.

BIOGRAPHICAL/CRITICAL SOURCES:

BOOKS

Rodríguez Monegal, Emir, editor, *The Borzoi Anthology of Latin American Literature,* Volume II: *The Twentieth Century— From Borges and Paz to Guimaraes Rosa and Donoso,* Knopf, 1986.

*   *   *

GERCHUNOFF, Alberto 1883-1950

PERSONAL: Born in 1883 in Ukraine; immigrated to Argentina, c. 1890; son of Jewish parents. *Education:* Self-educated.

CAREER: Manual laborer, c. late 1890s; *El Censor* (revolutionary newspaper), Rosario, Argentina, editor, beginning in 1903; *La Nación,* Buenos Aires, Argentina, journalist, c. early 1900s-1950.

WRITINGS:

Los gauchos judíos, 1910, new edition, prologue by Martiniano Leguizamón, M. Gleizer, 1936, reprinted, Aguilar, 1975, translation by Prudencio de Pereda published as *The Jewish Gauchos of the Pampas,* Abelard-Schuman, 1955, revised edition, 1959.
Cuentos de ayer, 1919, reprinted, Fraterna, 1985.
La jofaina maravillosa, Babel, 1923.
La asamblea de la bohardilla, M. Gleizer, 1925.
Historias y proezas de amor, M. Gleizer, 1926, reprinted, Emecé, 1962.
El hombre que habló en la Sorbona (essays), M. Gleizer, 1926.
Pequeñas prosas (addresses, essays, lectures), M. Gleizer, 1926.

Enrique Heine, el poeta de nuestra intimidad, Biblioteca Argentina de Buenas Ediciones Literarias, 1927.
Las imágenes del país, Talleres Gráficos de Placente & Dupuy, 1931.
Los amores de Baruj Spinoza, Biblioteca Argentina de Buenas Ediciones Literarias, 1932.
El hombre importante (novel), Montevideo, 1934, reprinted, Hachette, 1960.
La clínica del doctor Mefistófeles: moderna milagrería en diez jornadas, Ercilla (Santiago), 1937.
Entre Ríos, mi país, Futuro, 1950.
Retorno a Don Quijote, Sudamericana, 1951.
Argentina, país de advenimiento, Losada, 1952.
El pino y la palmera (addresses, essays, lectures), Sociedad Hebraica Argentina, 1952.
Buenos Aires, la metrópoli de mañana, [Buenos Aires], 1960.
Figuras de nuestro tiempo, Vernácula, 1979.
Autobiografía, Libreros y Editores del Poligono, 1983.

Portions of *Los gauchos judíos* published in *Setenta y cinco años de colonización judía en la Argentina.* Former member of editorial staff, *El País.*

SIDELIGHTS: Alberto Gerchunoff was a Russian-born Jew who became a distinguished figure in Hispanic literature. He fled to Argentina with his family at the end of the nineteenth century, during the height of the massacre of Jews in Russia. Gerchunoff engaged in years of manual labor by day and rigorous study by night before establishing himself as a prominent journalist. Though affiliated with the Buenos Aires-based *La Nación* for nearly five decades, he is probably best known as the author of *Los gauchos judíos* (*The Jewish Gauchos of the Pampas*), which was published in 1910 to commemorate Argentina's liberation from Spain a century earlier. Resembling a collection of sketches more than a novel, *The Jewish Gauchos* is a simple narrative of rural life among Jews in Argentina. As a testament to the relative ease with which Jews were absorbed into the South American prairie culture, the work serves as an insightful contrast to the hatred and prejudice Jews faced in Russia. Critics, however, have faulted Gerchunoff for his failure to address the issue of Argentine anti-Semitism in the book. In spite of the mixed critical commentary afforded the work, *The Jewish Gauchos* secured Gerchunoff's role as an enduring figure in South American literature.

BIOGRAPHICAL/CRITICAL SOURCES:

BOOKS

Stambler, Beatriz Marquis, *Vida y obra de Alberto Gerchunoff,* Albar (Madrid), 1985.

PERIODICALS

Hispania, September, 1987.

*   *   *

GIL-MONTERO, Martha 1940-

PERSONAL: Born September 27, 1940, in Córdoba, Argentina; immigrated to United States, 1976, naturalized citizen, 1989; daughter of Rosendo (a civil engineer) and Beatriz Eugenia (Premoli) Gil-Montero; married Joseph A. Page (a law professor and writer), May 18, 1984. *Education:* Escuela Normal de Profesores Alejandro Carbo, Córdoba, maestra normal, 1958; Cambridge University, lower certificate in English, 1959, certificate of proficiency in English, 1964; Goethe Institut, Radolfzell, West Germany, zeugnis, 1963; Alliance Francaise, Córdoba, diploma de capacidad in French, 1965; attended Universidad Autónoma de México, 1966, and Georgetown University, 1985. *Politics:* Democrat. *Religion:* Roman Catholic.

ADDRESSES: Home—1001 26th St. N.W., No. 808, Washington, D.C., 20037. *Agent*—Carl D. Brandt, 1501 Broadway, New York, N.Y. 10036.

CAREER: Author, editor, researcher, and lecturer, 1960—; Embassy of Argentina, Mexico City, Mexico, translator and interpreter, 1966; Embassy of Argentina, Washington, D.C., assistant to the cultural attache, 1967-69, affiliated with Press and Cultural Office, 1979-80; head of Department of International Relations of the National Council of Science and Technology of Argentina, 1969-78. Translator and interpreter for Universidad Nacional de Córdoba, 1960-63, Industrias Kayser Argentina, 1961-63, and Editorial de la Universidad de Buenos Aires, 1969-70.

WRITINGS:

Mundomujer (poetry), Fulgor (Buenos Aires), 1970.
(Translator) Herbert Matthews, *Fidel Castro,* Cuarto Poder, 1971.
(Translator) Joseph A. Page, *Perón,* Vergara, 1984.
(Translator) James A. Whelan, *Out of the Ashes,* [Chile], 1989.
Brazilian Bombshell: The Biography of Carmen Miranda, Donald I. Fine, 1989.

Also author of several monographs on international science policy for National Council of Science and Technology of Argentina, 1969-78.

WORK IN PROGRESS: "An erotic feminist historical biography."

SIDELIGHTS: Argentine-born American Martha Gil-Montero is a former Argentine government official who wrote about Latin American show business legend Carmen Miranda in *Brazilian Bombshell.* A singer of Brazilian samba music, Miranda was famous for her provocative dancing style and exotic costumes, which featured large, exotically decorated hats. Gil-Montero's book records Miranda's ascent to stardom in Brazil before she moved to the United States in 1939 to appear in such Hollywood films as "That Night in Rio" and "The Gang's All Here." Though the move boosted Miranda's career and brought her tremendous financial success, she often suffered from depression and became dependent on pills. Miranda's career waned during the late 1940s, and she died of a heart attack in 1955 at age forty-six. Gil-Montero's *Brazilian Bombshell,* however, emphasizes the positive aspects of the singer's life: "The most important part of the book is my real admiration for her music, mainly the Brazilian songs. I think that has to come back and that Americans should know about them," Gil-Montero told Rod Granger of *Inside Books.* Reviewers generally praised the biography as an important, well-researched book. Alan Ryan's comments in the *Washington Post* were typical: "Martha Gil-Montero's 'Brazilian Bombshell' is just the sort of biography Carmen Miranda deserves: affectionate and generous, yet honest and realistic."

BIOGRAPHICAL/CRITICAL SOURCES:

PERIODICALS

Chicago Tribune, June 20, 1989.
City Paper, August 4, 1989.
Inside Books, July-August, 1989.
Voice Literary Supplement, August, 1989.
Washington Post, May 29, 1989.

GIRON, Manuel Buendía Téllez   1926(?)-1984 (Manuel Buendía)

PERSONAL: Professionally known as Manuel Buendía; born c. 1926; died of gunshot wounds, May 30, 1984, in Mexico City, Mexico.

CAREER: Journalist. Columnist for *Excélsior,* Mexico City, Mexico.

WRITINGS:

Red Privada, Marcha Editores, 1981.
La CIA en México, Océano, 1983.
Los petroleros, Océano, 1983.
La ultraderecha en México, Océano, 1984.
Ejercicio periodístico, Océano, 1985.
La Santa Madra, Océano, 1985.
Los empresarios, Océano, 1986.

SIDELIGHTS: Before his assassination on May 30, 1984, Manuel Buendía Téllez Girón was one of Mexico's most widely syndicated columnists. A journalist for Mexico City's *Excélsior,* Girón wrote the paper's front-page column, "Red Privada," in which he spoke critically about drug trafficking, government corruption, and CIA activities in Mexico. His investigative pursuits also led him to write several books, including *La CIA en México* and *Los petroleros.* A successful writing career ended abruptly when Girón, after receiving death threats, was shot several times in the back while entering a Mexico City parking lot. His assailant escaped into a crowd. Girón's death is among many unsolved murder cases involving journalists in Mexico. Five years following his assassination, though, Mexican officials charged a suspect with the murder and speculate that Girón may have been killed in order to suppress information about connections between high-level government officials and drug traffickers.

BIOGRAPHICAL/CRITICAL SOURCES:

PERIODICALS

Washington Post, June 13, 1989.

OBITUARIES:

PERIODICALS

Newsweek, June 11, 1984.
Time, June 11, 1984.

* * *

GIRONDO, Oliverio   1891-1967

PERSONAL: Born in 1891 in Buenos Aires, Argentina; died in 1967; married Nora Lange (a poet).

CAREER: Writer.

WRITINGS:

Veinte poemas para ser leídos en el tranvía (poetry; title means "Twenty Poems to Be Read in a Trolley Car"), self-illustrated, [France], 1922, [Argentina], 1925 (also see below).
Interlunio (short story), illustrations by Lino Spilimbergo, Sur (Buenos Aires), 1937.
Persuasión de los días (poetry), Losada (Buenos Aires), 1942 (also see below).
Campo nuestro (poetry; title means "Our Countryside"), Sudamericana (Buenos Aires), 1946 (also see below).

(Author of text with others) *Pedro Figari, 1861-1938: Veinticinco obras del artista reproducidas en color,* Galerínas Witcomb (Buenos Aires), 1953.

En la masmédula (poetry; title means "Into the Moremarrow"), Losada, 1954 (also see below).

Oliverio Girondo, compiled by Aldo Pellegrini, Culturales Argentinas, Ministerio de Educación y Justicia (Buenos Aires), 1964.

Veinte poemas para ser leídos en el tranvía [and] *Calcomanías* [and] *Espantapájaros,* Centro Editor de América Latina (Buenos Aires), 1966 (also see below).

Obras completas, Losada, 1968.

En la masvida (poetry), Libres de Sinera (Barcelona), 1972.

Antología (includes *Veinte poemas para ser leídos en el tranvía, Calcomanías, Espantapájaros, Persuasión de los días, Campo nuestro,* and *En la masmédula*), selected by Aldo Pellegrini, Argonauta (Buenos Aires), 1986.

Also author of poetry volume whose title means "Decals," 1925, and a book whose title means "Scarecrow," 1932. Author of plays. Editor of manifest of magazine *Martín Fierro,* 1924.

SIDELIGHTS: Oliverio Girondo was a noted Argentine humorist whose avant-garde poetry challenges his country's established values and traditions. Born into an affluent family, Girondo traveled extensively throughout Europe in his youth. A member of an emerging group of experimental writers in Argentina, Girondo began writing outrageous plays in 1915. He later turned to poetry, producing his first major collection of humorous poems, *Veinte poemas para ser leídos en el tranvía,* in 1922. Interspersing travel with writing both verse and stories over the next two decades, Girondo became known for the frivolous humor he brought to his experimental works. One of the author's later volumes of verse, though, takes on a dark tone; titled *En la masmédula,* it centers on the tragedy of life and the decay and corruption of the body. Girondo died in 1967 and his works have since been collected in such volumes as *Obras completas* and *Antología.*

BIOGRAPHICAL/CRITICAL SOURCES:

BOOKS

Rodríquez Monegal, Emir, *The Borzoi Anthology of Latin American Literature,* Volume II: *The Twentieth Century—From Borges and Paz to Guimaraes Rosa and Donoso,* Knopf, 1986.

*   *   *

GIRRI, A.
See GIRRI, Alberto

*   *   *

GIRRI, Alberto 1919-
(A. Girri)

PERSONAL: Born November 27, 1919, in Buenos Aires, Argentina; son of Juan and Delfina (Scelza) Girri; married Leonor Vassena, 1958. *Education:* Attended Facultad de Filosofía y Letras, Buenos Aires.

ADDRESSES: Home—Viamonte 349, Piso 4 Letra LL, 1053 Buenos Aires, Argentina.

CAREER: Poet.

MEMBER: Society of Argentine Writers.

AWARDS, HONORS: Municipal Prize of Poetry, 1955, for *Examen de nuestra causa;* Third National Prize of Poetry, 1958, for

La penitencia y el mérito; Leopoldo Lugones Prize from Fondo Nacional de las Artes, 1960, for *La condición necesaria;* Medalla de Oro del Gobierno de Italia and Second National Prize of Poetry, both 1962, both for *Elegías italianas;* fellowships from Guggenheim Foundation, 1964 and 1977; First National Prize of Poetry, 1967, for *Envíos;* annual literary prize from Lorenzutti Foundation, 1975; First Prize for Poetry from Argentina Foundation, 1976; First Prize for Poetry from Dupuytren Foundation, 1978, for *Arbol de la estirpe humana;* Cesar Mermet Poetry Prize, 1980, for *Lo propio, lo de todos;* René Barón Prize, 1982, for *Homenaje a W. C. Williams;* First Prize for Poetry from Fortabat Foundation, 1985, for *Existenciales.*

WRITINGS:

POETRY

Playa sola, Nova (Buenos Aires), 1946.

Coronación de la espera, Botella (Buenos Aires), 1947 (also see below).

Trece Poemas, Botella, 1949 (also see below).

El tiempo que destruye, Botella, 1951.

Escándalo y soledades, Botella, 1952.

Examen de nuestra causa, Sur (Buenos Aires), 1956.

Línea de la vida, edited with a prologue by H. A. Murena, Sur, 1957.

La penitencia y el mérito, Sur, 1957 (also see below).

Propiedades de la magia, illustrations by Batlle, Sur, 1959 (also see below).

La condición necesaria, Sur, 1960.

Elegías italianas, Sur, 1962.

El ojo, Losada (Buenos Aires), 1964.

Poemas elegidos (anthology), prologue by Jorga A. Paita, Losada, 1965.

Envíos, Sudamericana (Buenos Aires), 1967.

Coronación de la espera, Trece poemas, La penitencia y el mérito, [and] *Propiedades de la magia,* Centro (Buenos Aires), 1967.

Casa de la mente, Sudamericana, 1970.

Antología temática (anthology), edited with a prologue by Enrique Pezzoni, Sudamericana, 1970.

Valores diarios, Sudamericana, 1970.

Poemas, 1946-1952, Brujula (Buenos Aires), 1970.

En la letra, ambigua selva, Sudamericana, 1972.

Poesía de observación, Sudamericana, 1973.

Quien habla no está muerto, Sudamericana, 1975.

(Under name A. Girri) *Girri & Sábat, galería personal,* illustrations by Hermenegildo Sábat, Sudamericana, 1975.

El motivo es el poema, Sudamericana, 1976.

Bestiario, illustrations by Luis Seoane, La Garza (Buenos Aires), 1976.

Obra poética, Corregidor (Buenos Aires), Volume I, 1977, Volume II, 1978, Volume III, 1980, Volume IV, 1984, Volume V, 1988.

Arbol de la estirpe humana, Sudamericana, 1978.

Lo propio, lo de todos, Sudamericana, 1980.

(And translator) *Homenaje a W. C. Williams* (includes Spanish translations of twelve poems by William Carlos Williams), Sudamericana, 1981.

Los Diez Mandamientos, illustrations by Raúl Alonso, Estudio Abierto (Buenos Aires), 1981.

Poemas: Antología, edited with a prologue by Barbara Crespo de Arnaud, Centro, 1982.

Borradores: Dibujos, poemas, illustrations by Alonso, Galería Rubbers (Buenos Aires), 1982.

Lírica de percepciones, Sudamericana, 1983.

Notas sobre la experiencia poética, Losada, 1983.

Páginas de Alberto Girri: Seleccionadas por el autor, Celtia (Buenos Aires), 1983.

Monodías, Sudamericana, 1985.

Existenciales, Sudamericana, 1986.

OTHER

(Editor and translator with William Shand) *Poesía inglesa de la guerra española,* prologue by Guillermo de Torre, Ateneo (Buenos Aires), 1947.

Misántropos, illustrations by Luis Seoane, Botella, 1953.

(Editor and translator with C. Viola Soto) *Poesía italiana contemporánea,* Raigal (Buenos Aires), 1956.

(Editor and translator with Shand) *Poesía norteamericana contemporánea,* prologue and notes by Gilbert Chase, Raigal, 1956, 3rd edition, Distribuidora Argentina, 1976.

(Editor and translator with Shand) John Donne, *Poemas de John Donne,* Culturales Argentinas (Buenos Aires), 1963.

(Compiler) *Quince poetas norteamericanos,* bilingual edition, Omeba (Buenos Aires), 1966, 2nd edition, 1969.

Un brazo de Dios (short stories), Américalee (Buenos Aires), 1966.

(Editor and translator) Wallace Stevens, *Poemas de Wallace Stevens,* bilingual edition, Omeba, 1967.

(Editor and translator with Shand) Stephen Spender, *Stephen Spender: Poemas,* Losada, 1968.

(Translator) *Cosmopolitismo y disensión: Antología de la poesía norteamericana actual,* Monte Avila (Caracas, Venezuela), 1969.

(Translator and author of prologue and notes) Robert Lowell, *Poemas de Robert Lowell,* Sudamericana, 1969.

Diario de un libro (prose), Sudamericana, 1972.

(Translator) *Versiones* (Spanish, English, American, and Japanese poetry), Corregidor, 1974.

Prosas, Monte Avila, 1977.

(Editor and translator with Enrique Pezzoni) T. S. Eliot, *T. S. Eliot: Retrato de una dama, y otras poemas,* Corregidor, 1982.

Cuestiones y razones (interviews), Fraterna (Buenos Aires), 1987.

(Translator) T. S. Eliot, *La tierra yerma,* Fraterna, 1988.

SIDELIGHTS: Alberto Girri is an award-winning Argentine poet noted for his exploration of philosophical issues. Praised for its economy of phrasing, Girri's poetry probes the fleeting nature of life, human loneliness, and the inadequacy of love to satisfactorily resolve problems of existence. In addition, his work examines the endless play between opposites, including what he feels is the irreconcilable conflict between the spiritual and material needs of humans. Rather than to escape this dualism, Girri's poetry asserts that the highest goal toward which a person can strive is to develop the courage to live amidst the chaos and ambiguity of existence.

BIOGRAPHICAL/CRITICAL SOURCES:

BOOKS

Foster, David William and Virginia Ramos Foster, editors, *Modern Latin American Literature,* Ungar, 1975.

*   *   *

GODOY ALCAYAGA, Lucila 1889-1957
(Gabriela Mistral)

PERSONAL: Born April 7, 1889, in Vicuña, Chile; died in 1957 in Hempstead, N.Y.; daughter of Jerónimo Godoy Villanueva (a schoolteacher and minstrel) and Petronila Alcayaga; children:

Yin Yin (adopted; deceased). *Education:* Attended Pedagogical College, Santiago, Chile.

CAREER: Poet and author. Primary and secondary school teacher and administrator in Chile, including position as principal of Liceo de Señoritas, Santiago, 1910-22; adviser to Mexican minister of education José Vasconcelos, 1922; visiting professor at Barnard and Middlebury colleges and the University of Puerto Rico. League of Nations, Chilean delegate to Institute of Intellectual Cooperation, member of Committee of Arts and Letters; consul in Italy, Spain, Portugal, Brazil, and the United States.

AWARDS, HONORS: Juegos Florales laurel crown and gold medal from the city of Santiago, Chile, 1914, for *Sonetos de la muerte;* Nobel Prize for literature from the Swedish Academy, 1945; honorary degree from the University of Chile.

WRITINGS:

UNDER PSEUDONYM GABRIELA MISTRAL

Desolación (poetry and prose; title means "Desolation"; also see below), preliminary notes by Instituto de las Españas, Instituto de las Españas en los Estados Unidos (New York), 1922, 2nd edition augmented by Mistral, additional prologue by Pedro Prado, Nascimento, 1923, 3rd edition, prologues by Prado and Hernán Díaz Arrieta (under pseudonym Alone), 1926, new edition with prologue by Roque Esteban Scarpa, Bello, 1979 (variations in content among these and other editions).

(Editor and contributor) *Lecturas para mujeres* (essays; also see below), introduction by Mistral, Secretaria de Educación (Mexico), 1923, 4th edition, edited with an apology by Palma Guillén de Nicolau, Porrúa (Mexico), 1967.

Ternura: Canciones de niños (title means "Tenderness"; also see below), Saturnino Calleja (Madrid), 1924, enlarged edition, Espasa Calpe, 1945, 8th edition, 1965.

Nubes blancas (poesías), y la oración de la maestra (poetry and prose; includes selections from *Desolación* and *Ternura* and complete text of "Oración de la maestra"), B. Bauzá (Barcelona), 1925.

Poesías, Cervantes (Barcelona), c. 1936.

Tala (poetry; title means "Felling"; also see below), Sur (Buenos Aires), 1938, abridged edition, Losada, 1946, reprinted with introduction by Alfonso Calderón, Bello, 1979.

Antología: Selección de la autora (includes selections from *Desolación, Tala,* and *Ternura*), selected by Mistral, prologue by Ismael Edwards Matte, ZigZag, 1941, 3rd edition published as *Antología,* prologue by Alone, 1953.

Pequeña antología (selected poetry and prose), Escuela Nacional de Artes Gráficas, 1950.

Poemas de las madres, epilogue by Antonio R. Romero, illustrations by André Racz, Pacífico, 1950.

Lagar (poetry; title means "Wine Press"), Pacífico, 1954.

Obras selectas, Pacífico, 1954.

Los mejores versos, prologue by Simón Latino, Nuestra América (Buenos Aires), 1957.

Canto a San Francisco, El Eco Franciscano, 1957.

Epistolario, introduction by Raúl Silva Castro, Anales de la Universidad de Chile, 1957.

México maravilloso (essays and poetry originally published in *Lecturas para mujeres* and periodical *El Maestro*), selected with an introduction by Andrés Henestrosa, Stylo (Mexico), 1957.

Producción de Gabriela Mistral de 1912 a 1918 (poetry, prose, and letters, most previously unpublished), edited by Silva Castro, Anales de la Universidad de Chile, 1957.

Recados: Contando a Chile, selected with prologue by Alfonso
M. Escudero, Pacífico, 1957.
Selected Poems of Gabriela Mistral, translated by Langston
Hughes, Indiana University Press, 1957.
Croquis mexicanos: Gabriela Mistral en México (contains prose
selections from *Lecturas para mujeres,* poetry, and a peda-
gogical lecture titled "Imagen y palabra en la educación"),
B. Costa-Amic (Mexico), c. 1957, reprinted, Nascimento,
1978.
Poesías completas, edited by Margaret Bates, prologues by Julio
Saavedra Molina and Dulce María Loynaz, Aguilar (Ma-
drid), 1958, 3rd edition, introduction by Esther de Cáceres,
1966.
Poema de Chile, revisions by Doris Dana, Pomaire, 1967.
Antología de Gabriela Mistral, selected with prologue by Emma
Godoy, B. Costa-Amic, 1967.
Poesías, edited with a prologue by Eliseo Diego, Casa de las
Américas, 1967.
Homenaje a Gabriela Mistral, Orfeo, 1967.
Selected Poems of Gabriela Mistral, translated by Dana, Johns
Hopkins Press, 1971.
Todas íbamos a ser reinas, Quimantú, 1971.
Antología general de Gabriela Mistral (poems, essays, and letters;
portions originally published in periodical *Orfeo,* 1969),
Comité de Homenaje a Gabriela Mistral, 1973.
Antología poética de Gabriela Mistral, selected with a prologue
by Calderón, Universitaria, 1974.
Cartas de amor de Gabriela Mistral, Bello, 1978.
Prosa religiosa de Gabriela Mistral, notes and introduction by
Luis Vargas Saavedra, Bello, 1978.
Gabriela presente, selected by Inés Moreno, Literatura Ameri-
cana Reunida, 1987.

Also author of *Sonetos de la muerte,* 1914, and "An Appeal to
World Conscience: The Genocide Convention," 1956. Author of
fables, including *Grillos y ranas,* translation by Dana published
as *Crickets and Frogs,* Atheneum, 1972, and *Elefante y su secreto,*
adaptation and translation by Dana published as *The Elephant
and His Secret,* Atheneum, 1974. Poetry for children published
as *El niño en la poesía de Gabriela Mistral,* 1978. Correspondence between Mistral and Matilde Ladrón de Guevara published as *Gabriela Mistral, "rebelde magnífica,"* 1957.

Contributor to periodicals, including *Bulletin, Commonweal,
Living Age,* and *Poetry.*

SIDELIGHTS: Nobel laureate Gabriela Mistral—whose actual
name was Lucila Godoy Alcayaga—was a prominent Latin
American poet, educator, and diplomat. A Chilean native of
Spanish, Basque, and Indian descent, she was raised in a northern rural farming community. Following the example of her father, Mistral initially pursued a career in education, beginning
as a primary school teacher at the age of fifteen. Over the next
decade, she went on to become a secondary school professor, inspector general, and ultimately a school director. A leading authority on rural education, Mistral served as an adviser to Mexican minister of education José Vasconcelos in the early 1920s.
Her background in teaching and value as an educational consultant led to her active service in the Chilean government. Mistral
is probably best known, however, for her brand of rich but unpretentious lyrical poetry.

The tragic suicide of her fiance in the early 1900s prompted Mistral to compose her first lines of melancholy verse. Within several years she completed a small body of poetry that she would
later publish under the Mistral pseudonym (which is said to be
either a tribute to poets Gabriele D'Annunzio and Frédéric Mis-

tral or a combined reference to the archangel Gabriel and the
brutal northerly wind, or "mistral," of southern France). Having
entered her *Sonetos de la muerte* ("Sonnets on Death") in a Santiago writing contest in 1914, she earned first prize and instant
fame, developing in ensuing years a reputation as one of Latin
America's most gifted poets.

Critics have noted the joint influences of biblical verse and the
works of Hindu poet Rabindranath Tagore and Nicaraguan poet
Rubén Darío on the literary development of Mistral. She frequently expressed through her verse an urgent concern for outcasts, underprivileged or otherwise impoverished people, and ancestors—the poet donated profits from her third book to Basque
children orphaned in the Spanish Civil War. Her simple, un-
adorned writings evoke a sense of mystery and isolation, centering on themes of love, death, childhood, maternity, and religion.
Mistral had turned to religion for solace in her despair over the
loss of her intended husband. Her first volume of poetry, *Desolación* ("Desolation"), is imbued with the spirit of an individual's
struggle to reconcile personal fulfillment with the will of God.
In expressing her grief and anguish throughout the collection
with characteristic passion and honesty, Mistral "talks to Christ
as freely as to a child," commented Mildred Adams in *Nation.*

Several critics on Mistral, including Adams, have suggested that
both her lover's death and her failure to bear his child inspired
in the poet a fervent dedication to children. *Ternura* ("Tenderness"), her 1924 volume of children's poetry, is a celebration of
the joys of birth and motherhood. While *Desolación* reflects the
pain of a lost love and an obsession with death, *Ternura* is generally considered a work of renewed hope and understanding. Infused with a decidedly Christian temper, the poems in the latter
collection are among the most sentimental written by Mistral,
and they evoke the poet's overriding desire to attain harmony
and peace in her life.

Correlating Mistral's treatment of the love theme with her frequent depiction of mother and child, Sidonia Carmen Rosenbaum theorized in *Modern Women Poets of Spanish America:*
"Her conception of love is . . . profoundly religious and pure.
Its purpose is not to appease desire, to satisfy carnal appetites,
but soberly to give thought to the richest, the most precious, the
most sacred heritage of woman: maternity." *Saturday Review*
contributor Edwin Honig expressed a similar view, noting that
for Mistral, "Childbearing . . . approximates a mystic condition: it is like finding union with God. . . . The experience of
gestating another life inside oneself is the supreme act of creation."

Though consistently stark, simple, and direct, Mistral's later
verse is marked by a growing maturity and sense of redemption
and deliverance. The 1938 collection *Tala* ("Felling"), according
to Rosenbaum, possesses "a serenity that reveals an emotion
more contained (whose key note is hope) and . . . an expression
less tortured" than the early works and therefore continues Mistral's path toward renewal. The poet achieved a greater objectivity in both this work and her final volume of poetry, *Lagar*
("Wine Press"), which was published in 1954. Through pure and
succinct language, *Lagar* conveys Mistral's acceptance of death
and marks her growing freedom from bitterness. Several critics
have implied that this collection—the culmination of her literary
career—is both a refinement of her simple and skillful writing
style and a testament to her strengthened faith and ultimate understanding of God. As Fernando Alegría explained in *Las fronteras del realismo: Literatura chilena del siglo XX,* "Here we have
the secret dynamism [of the poet's verse]; it contains a salvation."

In *Gabriela Mistral: The Poet and Her Work,* Margot Arce de Vázquez concluded: "[Mistral's] poetry possesses the merit of consummate originality, of a voice of its own, authentic and consciously realized. The affirmation within this poetry of the intimate 'I,' removed from everything foreign to it, makes it profoundly human, and it is this human quality that gives it its universal value."

BIOGRAPHICAL/CRITICAL SOURCES:

BOOKS

Alegría, Fernando, *Las fronteras del realismo: Literatura chilena del siglo XX,* ZigZag, 1962.
de Vázquez, Margot Arce, *Gabriela Mistral: The Poet and Her Work,* translated by Helene Masslo Anderson, New York University Press, 1964.
Foster, David William and Virginia Ramos Foster, editors, *Modern Latin American Literature,* Volume 2, Ungar, 1975.
Mistral, Gabriela, *Selected Poems of Gabriela Mistral,* translated by Doris Dana, Johns Hopkins Press, 1971.
Rosenbaum, Sidonia Carmen, *Modern Women Poets of Spanish America: The Precursors, Delmira Agustini, Gabriela Mistral, Alfonsina Storni, Juana de Ibarbourou,* Hispanic Institute in the United States, 1945.
Szmulewicz, Efraim, *Gabriela Mistral: Biografía emotiva,* Sol de Septiembre, 1967.
Taylor, Martin C., *Gabriela Mistral's Religious Sensibility,* University of California Press, 1968.
Twentieth-Century Literary Criticism, Volume 2, Gale, 1979.
Vargas Saavedra, Luis, editor, *El otro suicida de Gabriela Mistral,* Universidad Católica de Chile, 1985.

PERIODICALS

Cuadernos Americanos, September-October, 1962.
Living Age, November 29, 1924.
Nation, December 29, 1945.
Poet Lore, winter, 1940.
Saturday Review, March 22, 1958, July 17, 1971.

—*Sketch by Barbara Carlisle Bigelow*

* * *

GOLDEMBERG, Isaac 1945-

PERSONAL: Born November 15, 1945, in Chepén, La Libertad, Peru; immigrated to United States, 1964; son of Isaac (a merchant) and Eva (a merchant; maiden name, Bay) Goldemberg; married Mona Stern, December 19, 1963 (separated); children: David, Dina. *Education:* City College of the City University of New York, B.A. (magna cum laude), 1968; New York University, graduate study, 1968.

ADDRESSES: Home—515 West 110th St., Apt. 6A, New York, N.Y. 10025.

CAREER: Writer. Worked in a kibbutz in Israel, 1962-63; insurance salesman in Barcelona, Spain, 1963; New York Public Library, New York City, clerk in Jewish Division, 1965-66; Grolier, Inc., New York City, Spanish editor, 1968-69; American Book Co., New York City, Spanish editor, 1969; New York University, New York City, lecturer in Spanish, 1970—; Latin American Writers Institute at City College, New York City, director, 1987—. Coordinator, New York's Latin American Book Fair, New York City, 1985—. Writer in residence, Center for Inter-American Relations, 1981, Ollantay Center for the Arts, 1988.

MEMBER: Phi Beta Kappa.

WRITINGS:

Tiempo de silencio (poems; title means "Time for Silence"), Colección de Poesía Hispanoamericana, 1969.
(With José Kozer) *De Chepén a la Habana* (poems; title means "From Chepén to Havana"), Editorial Bayu-Menorah, 1973.
The Fragmented Life of Don Jacobo Lerner (novel), translated by Robert Picciotto, Persea Books, 1976.
(And translator with David Unger) *Hombre de paso/Just Passing Through* (poems), bilingual edition, Ediciones del Norte, 1981.
Tiempo al tiempo; o, La conversión (novel), Ediciones del Norte, 1983, translated by Hardie St. Martin, published by Persea Books as *The Conversion,* 1983, and as *Play by Play,* 1985.
La vida al contado (poems; title means "Life Paid in Cash"), Lluvia, 1989.

Contributor to Spanish- and English-language journals, including *Present Tense, Nimrod,* and *Mundo Nuevo.*

WORK IN PROGRESS: An anthology of Latin American fiction by writers living in New York; an anthology of Latin American Jewish writers; a novel.

SIDELIGHTS: Isaac Goldemberg once told *CA:* "I am a Peruvian of Jewish, Russian, English, Italian, Spanish, and Indian descent. I traveled to Israel in 1962. Then I moved to Barcelona, where I spent a year in medical school. I decided (age eighteen) I wanted to be a writer and quit medical school. I settled in New York. Prior to my return to Peru (for the first time in fifteen years) in 1976, I wrote *The Fragmented Life of Don Jacobo Lerner,* an attempt at reconstructing my own past and that of the Peruvian Jewish community at large. Even though my work deals mainly with the Jewish experience in Peru, the burdens of exile and spiritual rootlessness, I am also concerned with Peruvian life as a whole, particularly that of provincial Peru, marked by narrowness and claustrophobia. This is the world depicted in my first novel, where I attempted to draw the life of the Jewish immigrant as a tragic and heroic parody of the legend of the Wandering Jew."

Frank Macshane comments on *The Fragmented Life of Don Jacobo Lerner* in an article for the *New York Times Book Review,* writing that the world depicted by Goldemberg "is a nightmare world of frustrated hopes, of narrowness and claustrophobia where no one can afford to be generous and where people become insane and destructive. Goldemberg allows his characters to tell their own stories and interrupts these private narratives with notices, documents and newspaper headlines to give a sense of the public dimension of the life of these exiles. This technique also insures that the novel remains refreshingly free of the exotic trimmings that are often associated with Latin American fiction: it is a moving exploration of the human condition." In another review of Goldemberg's novel, Margo Jefferson says in *Newsweek* that the author "shows with great perception how history, belief and myth can burden people with more contradictions than they can bear. This insight, joined to well-observed details makes this novel a wonderfully promising debut for a gifted writer."

But Goldemberg's attempt to integrate Peruvian and Jewish concerns in *The Fragmented Life of Don Jacobo Lerner* has caused him to fall under the attack of both sectors of Peru's population. As *Village Voice* contributor Ellen Lesser observes, "When *Jacobo Lerner* appeared in Peru, a self-appointed Jewish community spokesman attacked Goldemberg as an anti-Semite. On the other side, non-Jewish Peruvian critics tended to address themselves to the novel's Jewish aspect alone." The reviewers acted "as if it were about Peruvian Jews only and not about Peru itself," the author tells Lesser. "One critic, whose name I wish to forget, said, 'What does Goldemberg have to do with Peru? Just look at his name. He doesn't represent any of our traditions.' "

In an effort to appease his critics, Goldemberg set out to write a novel that would not offend either the Peruvians or the Jews. The result was a first draft of *Play by Play* that took Goldemberg two years to compose. But, as he says in Lesser's article, "I felt the novel was very dishonest. I burned it. That was like an exorcism, a purification. Then I started writing the second version and I said exactly what the narrator wanted to say." The theme of the problems of racial integration in *Play by Play* is much like that in Goldemberg's first novel; the stories are also similar in that they end in tragedy. In *The Fragmented Life of Don Jacobo Lerner* the protagonist's inability to accept both sides of his mixed racial background results in his son's insanity, while in *Play by Play* the main character, Marcos, ultimately commits suicide. *New York Times Book Review* contributor Ariel Dorfman compares the protagonist in *Play by Play* with the "characters in the work of Proust, Philip Roth and Elias Canetti," adding that Marcos "is a fascinating addition to that group."

After spending over twenty years in New York City writing about his native country, Goldemberg now feels an urge to return to Peru. "I know I have to go back," he tells Lesser. "I had a feeling I was missing something in all my years in New York. The conditions in Peru are very difficult, but people live their lives passionately. You read the newspapers, and when there's an editorial, it is passionate. If you read the newspapers here, everybody tries to be very objective about things, and I hate that. I've had it." Lesser later adds that "while the distance of exile has helped shape Goldemberg's work so far, he's now convinced that going home will stimulate his writing, that he needs to close the circle and reconnect with his source."

BIOGRAPHICAL/CRITICAL SOURCES:

PERIODICALS

Newsweek, May 9, 1977.
New Yorker, April 4, 1977.
New York Times, May 18, 1977.
New York Times Book Review, June 12, 1977.
Times Literary Supplement, March 10, 1978.
Village Voice Literary Supplement, May, 1982.

*   *   *

GOMEZ de la SERNA, Ramón 1888-1963 (Tristán)

PERSONAL: Born on July 3, 1888 (one source says July 6), in Madrid, Spain; died on January 12, 1963, in Buenos Aires, Argentina; buried in Madrid's Panteón de Hombres Ilustres; son of Javier Gómez de la Serna y Laguna (an author and magazine editor) and Josefa Puig Coronado. *Education:* University of Madrid Law School, graduated, 1908.

CAREER: Writer. Held political post in Paris, France, 1909-11. Host of series of radio programs, Madrid, beginning 1930.

AWARDS, HONORS: Juan Paloma Award for literature, 1960; "Special" March Award, official March Award, awards from the Spanish provinces of Galicia and Catalonia, and lifetime monthly pension from Argentine Parliament in recognition of literary achievements, all 1962.

WRITINGS:

IN ENGLISH TRANSLATION

Cinelandia, Sempere (Valencia) 1923, reprinted, Nostromo, 1974, translation by Angel Flores published as *Movieland,* Macauley (New York), 1930.
Some greguerías (selections from *Greguerías* and *Flor de greguerías*; also see below), translation by Helen Granville-Barker, W. E. Rudge's Sons (New York), 1944.
Dalí, Espasa-Calpe, 1977, translation by Nicholas Fry and Elizabeth Evans published under same title, Morrow, 1979.

Contributor of stories and *greguerías* in English translation to journals, including *Broom,* May, 1922, *Criterion,* January, 1923, *Bookman,* June, 1928, and *Alhambra,* June, 1929. Also contributor in English translation to anthologies, including *The Best Continental Short Stories of 1927,* edited by R. Eaton, *Great Spanish Short Stories,* edited by J. G. Gorkin, and *The European Caravan,* edited by S. Putnam.

IN SPANISH

Entrando en el fuego (title means "Entering the Fray"), Imprenta del Diario de Avisos (Segovia), 1905.
Morbideces, El Trabajo (Madrid), 1908.
Cuento de Calleja (play), Sociedad de Autores Españoles (Madrid), 1909.
Ex-votos: Dramas (play collection), Aurora (Madrid), 1910.
La bailarina (title means "The Ballerina"), Aurora—Sociedad de Autores Españoles, 1911.
El doctor inverosímil (title means "The Unlikely Doctor"; novel), La Novela de Bolsillo (Madrid), 1914, reprinted, Destino, 1981.
El rastro (novel), Prometeo, 1915, reprinted, La Nave, 1931.
La viuda blanca y negra (title means "The Black and White Widow"; novel), Biblioteca Nueva, 1917, reprinted, Poseidón, 1943.
El circo (title means "The Circus"), Latina (Madrid), 1917, reprinted, Plaza y Janés, 1987.
Senos (title means "Bosoms"), Latina, 1917, AHR (Barcelona), 1968.
(Editor, contributor, and author of epilogue) Silverio Lanza, *Páginas escogidas e inéditas de Silverio Lanza,* Biblioteca Nueva, 1918.
Pombo, Mesón de Paños (Madrid), 1918, published as *Pombo: Biografía del célebre café y de otros cafés famosos,* Juventud (Buenos Aires), 1941, abridged edition, Juventud (Barcelona), 1960.
Greguerías, Prometeo (Valencia), 1917, enlarged edition published as *Greguerías, 1940-1945,* Espasa-Calpe (Buenos Aires), 1945, enlarged edition published as *Greguerías, selección 1910-1960,* Espasa-Calpe (Madrid), 1960.
Muestrarios (title means "Samplings"), Biblioteca Nueva, 1918.
El alba y las cosas (title means "The Dawn and Things"), Saturnino Calleja (Madrid), 1918.
Toda la historia de la Puerta del Sol (title means "The Complete History of the Puerta del Sol"), La Tribuna, 1920.
Variaciones (title means "Variations"; also see below), La Tribuna, 1920.
Virguerías (title means "Virginal Glimpses"), self-published (Madrid), 1920.
El libro nuevo (title means "The New Book"), Mesón de Paños, 1920.
Edgar Poe, Biblioteca Nueva (Madrid), 1920, revised edition published as *Edgar Poe, genio de América,* Losada, 1953.
Disparates (title means "Absurdities"), Calpe (Madrid), 1921.
Oscar Wilde, Biblioteca Nueva, 1921, reprinted, Poseidón, 1944.

El secreto del acueducto (title means "The Secret of the Aqueduct"), Biblioteca Nueva, 1922, EDHASA (Barcelona), 1962.

El incongruente: Novela grande, Calpe, 1922, reprinted, Picazo (Barcelona), 1972.

Leopoldo y Teresa, La Novela Corta (Madrid), 1922.

El gran hotel (title means "Grand Hotel"), América (Madrid), 1922.

Ramonismo (title means "Ramonism"; also see below), self-illustrated, Calpe, 1923.

El chalet de las rosas, Sempere (Valencia), 1923, reprinted, Centro (Madrid), 1975.

La quinta de Palmyra (title means "Palmyra's Country Villa"), Biblioteca Nueva, 1923, reprinted, Espasa-Calpe (Madrid), 1982.

El novelista (novela grande), Sempere, 1923, reprinted, Espasa-Calpe, 1973.

Azorín (biography), La Nave (Madrid), 1923, reprinted, Losada, 1957.

La sagrada cripta del Pombo (title means "Pombo, The Sacred Crypt"), Mesón de Paños, 1924.

La malicia de las acacias: Novelas (novel collection), Sempere, 1924.

Cuentos para niños (title means "Stories for Children"), Calpe, 1924.

Caprichos (title means "Caprices"; short sketches), La Lectura (Madrid), 1925, reprinted, Espasa-Calpe (Madrid), 1962.

El Prado, Librería (Madrid), 1925.

El drama del palacio deshabitado: Dramas (contains title play and "La utopia", "Beatriz," "La corona de hierro", and "El lunático"), América (Madrid), 1926.

Gollerías (title means "Tidbits"), self-illustrated, Sempere, 1926, expanded edition (also includes *Ramonismo* and *Variaciones*), Losada, 1946.

El torero Caracho (novel), Agencia Mundial de Librería (Madrid), 1926, reprinted, Espasa-Calpe (Madrid), 1969.

La mujer de ámbar (title means "The Amber Woman"), Biblioteca Nueva, 1927, reprinted, Espasa-Calpe (Madrid), 1968.

Seis falsas novelas (title means "Six False Novels"), Mundial (Paris), 1927, reprinted, Mondadori (Madrid), 1989.

El caballero del hongo gris: Novela humorística (title means "The Gentleman in the Grey Top Hat"; novel), Agencia Mundial de Librería, 1928, reprinted, Salvat (Madrid), 1970.

El dueño del átomo: Novelas (title means "The Master of the Atom: Novels"; collection), Historia Nueva (Madrid), 1928, reprinted, Losada, 1945.

Goya (biography), La Nave, 1928, reprinted, Consejo Nacional de Cultura (Havana), 1963.

Efigies, (biographical sketches), Oriente (Madrid), 1929, reprinted, Aguilar, 1944.

Los medios seres (title means "The Half-Beings"; play; first produced in Madrid, 1929), Prensa Moderna (Madrid), 1929.

Novísimas greguerías, 1929, E. Giménez (Madrid), 1929.

La nardo (novela grande), Ulises (Madrid), 1930, reprinted, Bruguera, 1981.

Ismos (criticism), Biblioteca Nueva (Madrid), 1931, enlarged edition, Poseidón, 1943, reprinted, Brújula (Buenos Aires), 1968.

Elucidario de Madrid, Renacimiento, 1931, 2nd edition, Artes Gráficas Municipales (Madrid), 1957.

Policéfalo y señora (title means "Polycephalous and Wife"; novel), Espasa-Calpe (Madrid), 1932.

Chao: Novela, [Barcelona], 1933.

La hiperestética (El regalo del doctor, La roja, El vegetariano): Novelas, Ulises, 1934.

Flor de greguerías, Espasa-Calpe (Madrid), 1935, expanded edition published as *Flor de greguerías, 1910-1958,* Losada, 1958.

El Greco: El visionario de la pintura, Nuestra Raza (Madrid), 1935, reprinted, Losada, 1950.

Las escaleras (also see below), Cruz y Raya (Madrid), 1935.

Los muertos y las muertas, y otras fantasmagorías (title means "Dead Men and Dead Women, and Other Phantasmagories"), Arbol (Madrid), 1935, corrected and enlarged edition, Espasa-Calpe (Madrid), 1961.

El cólera azul, Sur (Buenos Aires), 1937.

¡Rebeca!: Novela inédita, Ercilla (Santiago de Chile), 1937, reprinted, Espasa-Calpe (Madrid), 1974.

Retratos contemporáneos (title means "Contemporary Portraits"), Sudamericana, 1941.

Don Francisco de Goya y Lucientes (biography), Poseidón, 1942.

Mi tía Carolina Coronado, Emecé (Buenos Aires), 1942.

Lo cursi, y otros ensayos (also see below), Sudamericana, 1943.

El turco de los nardos, La Novela Actual (Madrid), 1943.

Don Diego de Velázquez, Poseidón (Buenos Aires), 1943.

José Gutiérrez Solana, Poseidón, 1944, reprinted, Picazo, 1972.

Don Ramón María de Valle-Inclán (biography), Espasa-Calpe (Buenos Aires), 1944, reprinted, Espasa-Calpe (Madrid), 1969.

Doña Juana la loca y otras (seis novelas superhistóricas), Clydoc (Buenos Aires), 1944.

Lope de Vega, La Universidad (Buenos Aires), 1945, published as *Lope viviente* (title means "Living Lope"), Espasa-Calpe (Buenos Aires), 1954.

Nuevos retratos contemporáneos (title means "New Contemporary Portraits"), Sudamericana, 1945.

Norah Borges (monograph), Losada (Buenos Aires), 1945.

El hombre perdido (title means "The Lost Man"), Poseidón, 1947, reprinted, Espasa-Calpe (Madrid), 1962.

Trampantojos (title means "Tricks of Whimsy"), La Cuerda Floja (Buenos Aires), 1947.

Cuentos del fin del año (title means "Stories for the End of the Year"), Clan (Madrid), 1947.

Greguerías completas, Lauro (Barcelona), 1947, published as *Total de greguerías,* self-illustrated, Aguilar, 1955.

Obras selectas, ten volumes, Plenitud (Madrid), 1947, published in one volume, with prologue by Pablo Neruda, AHR, 1971.

Explicación de Buenos Aires, Prólogo (Madrid), 1948.

Automoribundia, 1888-1948 (autobiography), Sudamericana, 1948, reprinted, Guadarrama (Madrid), 1974.

Cartas a las golondrinas (title means "Letters to the Swallows"; also see below), Juventud, 1949.

Las tres gracias (novela madrileña de invierno), Perseo (Madrid), 1949.

Interpretación del tango, Ultreya, 1949, reprinted, Albino y Asociados (Buenos Aires), 1979.

Quevedo (biography), Espasa-Calpe (Buenos Aires), 1953.

Antología: Cincuenta años de literatura, edited by Guillermo de Torre, Losada, 1955.

Cartas a mi mismo (title means "Letters to Myself"; also see below), AHR, 1956.

Nostalgias de Madrid (title means "Nostalgias of Madrid"), El Grifón de Plata (Madrid), 1956.

Obras completas (title means "Complete Works"), two volumes, AHR, 1956-57.

Mis mejores páginas literarias (title means "My Best Pages of Literature"), Gredos, 1957.

Nuevas páginas de mi vida: Lo que no dije en mi Automoribundia (autobiography), Marfil, 1957, reprinted, Alianza, 1970.

Biografías completas (title means "Complete Biographies"; collection), Aguilar, 1959.

Piso bajo: Novela (title means "Ground Floor: Novel"), Espasa-Calpe (Madrid), 1961.

Retratos completos (title means "Complete Portraits"; collection), Aguilar, 1961.

Guía del Rastro (title means "Guide to the Rastro"), with photographs by Carlos Suara, Taurus (Madrid), 1961.

Cartas a las golondrinas. Cartas a mi mismo, Espasa-Calpe, 1962.

Ensayo sobre lo cursi. Escaleras: Drama en tres actos, Cruz del Sur (Santiago de Chile), 1963.

Greguerías: Selección, introduction and selection by Gaspar Gómez de la Serna, Anaya (Salamanca), 1963.

Ramón Gómez de la Serna (selections), edited by Luisa Sofovich, [Buenos Aires], 1963.

(Editor) Ramón de Mesonero y Romanos, *Escenas matritenses* (title means "Scenes of Madrid"), Espasa-Calpe (Madrid), 1964.

Retratos contemporáneos escogidos, Sudamericana, 1968.

Caprichos póstumos, La Esquina, 1969.

Diario póstumo, Plaza y Janés, 1972.

Descubrimiento de Madrid, Cátedra (Madrid), 1974.

Also author of *El miedo al mar,* 1921, *La hija del verano,* 1922, *La gangosa,* 1922, *Por los tejados,* 1924, *En el bazar más suntuoso del mundo,* 1924, *Aquella novela,* 1924, *La fúnebre falsa,* 1925, *Hay que matar el Morse,* 1925, *El hijo del millonario,* 1927, *Siluetas y sombras,* 1934, *Ruskin, el apasionado,* 1943, and *Ventura García Calderón,* 1946. Also author of prologue to Carmen de Burgos's Spanish translation of John Ruskin's *Stones of Venice.* Columnist, *El Liberal* (Madrid newspaper), 1918-23, *El Sol,* 1923-1933, and *La Nación* (Buenos Aires newspaper), beginning 1928. Contributor, occasionally under pseudonym Tristán, to periodicals, including *La Tribuna* (Madrid daily), *Revista de Occidente* (literary journal) and *Arriba* (newspaper). Editor, *Prometeo,* beginning 1912.

WORK IN PROGRESS: Unfinished biography of Miguel de Unamuno.

SIDELIGHTS: Spanish humorist, short story writer, playwright and novelist Ramón Gómez de la Serna's literary career began while he was still in his teens. The elder Gómez de la Serna financed the publication of young Ramón's first book, *Entrando en el fuego* ("Entering the Fray"; published when he was just sixteen), used his influence to obtain a political post in Paris for his son so he could live in the city where authors such as Guillaume Apollinaire, Marcel Proust, Colette and others were writing, and later founded the literary magazine, *Prometeo,* and appointed Ramón its editor. Before the boy turned twenty, he had been honored at a literary banquet in his honor and had established himself as an innovative thinker. To many critics his subsequent work—spanning a period of nearly six decades—proved his early reputation to be justified and constituted a major contribution to Spanish letters.

One of the highlights of Gómez de la Serna's career was his invention of the *greguería* in 1911. A chance glance out of his balcony window in Madrid recalled to the writer a similar view out of a balcony on the Arno River in Florence, Italy. As he longingly tried to recreate the scene in his mind, the idea struck him that maybe the river wished it could be in another location too or that the far bank of the river might want to exchange places with the near bank. Enchanted by the humor of his thoughts,

Gómez de la Serna decided to name the concept *greguería,* a Spanish word meaning a "confused hubbub of voices." In *The Literature of the Spanish People* Gerald Brenan offered several examples of *greguerías* in English translation, including: "Stale bread is like a newly formed fossil" and "The seagulls were born from the handkerchiefs that wave goodbye in ports." Included in Rita Mazzetti Gardiol's *Ramón Gómez de la Serna* is the equation the writer used as his own definition of the term: "Humor + metaphor = *greguería.*" These semi-aphoristic pieces, which often convey brilliant poetic images, have been seen by critics as precursors to several of the vanguardist schools of thought popular in Europe during the early years of the twentieth-century.

The absurd humor of some of the *greguerías,* for example, brings to mind the writing of the surrealists who reveled in anything that would shock the staid middle-class. Gómez de la Serna attempted to do the same in his work nearly a decade before French writer Andre Breton's first surrealist manifesto. According to *Modern Fiction Studies* contributor Richard L. Jackson: "The power to startle consistently with surprising analogies is one of the major artistic achievements of the *greguería.* The expression of this surprise, shock, and astonishment is one of the main objectives of this literary 'invention.' " Brenan wrote of the *greguerías:* "The best of them reveal the secret correspondences of things, employing for this a peculiar sort of poetic intuition. This kind of writing is of course surrealism, born long before that term was invented."

Other works that demonstrated Gómez de la Serna's surrealistic tendencies include the two early volumes, *Senos* ("Bosoms") and *El circo* ("The Circus"), published in 1917, the same year in which his first collection of *greguerías* was published. Both *Senos* and *El circo* can be considered collections, too, for they each contain long lists of images associated with the theme referred to in the book's title. In the former, Gómez de la Serna describes bosoms in chapters entitled, for instance, "Bosoms in Art" and "Andalusian Bosoms." *El circo* focuses on the exciting and colorful world of the circus. This work was to provide its author with several opportunities to live out his surrealistic tendencies: Once, when honored in Madrid for the book by a traveling circus, Gómez de la Serna chose to deliver a responding lecture entitled "The Complex Beauty of the Circus" from a circus trapeze. On the occasion of a similar tribute at the Cirque d'Hiver in Paris, he spoke about elephants while perched on the back of such an animal.

In his listing of things or sensations associated with the circus, his listing of bosoms, and his listings of images in his *greguería* collections, Gómez de la Serna revealed his love of looking for the logic behind what might at first glance appear to be a seemingly unconnected series of ideas or things. He gathered what appeared to be a confused jumble of thoughts and hoped, on completion of his work, to produce an understandable whole. Gardiol considered this characteristic of Gómez de la Serna's work an echo of a similar inclination towards enumeration in the writings of Spanish essayist José Martínez Ruiz (known by his pseudonym Azorín). But while Azorín merely offered detailed descriptions of things, Gómez de la Serna granted human qualities to the objects. In *El Rastro* (which included a dedication to Azorín) Gómez de la Serna describes the sights of Madrid's lively outdoor flea market of the same name where second-hand odds and ends spread out on blankets or stretch for miles in booths. In Gómez de la Serna's hands the sea of discards takes on a life of its own, each item has a story to tell. His love of things, which might typically be construed as a characteristic of the writing of a realist, was used by the author in a vanguardist manner.

"Never is Ramón more Ramón—and less a realist—then when he seems to enjoy, to take delight in things," commented Spanish philosopher and essayist Julián Marías in an *Insula* article quoted in English translation by Gardiol.

Marías greatly admired Gómez de la Serna's work and, according to Jackson, "maintained that in Ramón's generation only three men reached the stature of genius: Ortega [y Gasset] in philosophy, Picasso in art, and Ramón in literature." All three men excelled in looking at their world in ways that upset traditional modes of thought. Gómez de la Serna, in fact, was influenced by Ortega y Gasset's views, including his theory advocating the dehumanization of art (the title of his most famous work) and an his emphasis on the microstructure—those seemingly unimportant events—of life. Gómez de la Serna dedicated his novel *El secreto del acueducto* ("The Secret of the Aqueduct") to Ortega y Gasset and the work's structure reveals his indebtedness to the philosopher's thinking: Human characters diminish in importance, as in most of Gómez de la Serna's novels, while things, in this case the great Roman aqueduct of Segovia, gain in significance. The aqueduct becomes the focus of the author's attention and, at times, he even stops his narrative to admire its beauty. Other Gómez de la Serna works, such as *Ramonismo* ("Ramonism"), *Caprichos* ("Caprices"), and *Gollerías* ("Tidbits"), celebrate Ortega y Gasset's idea of the microstructure by emphasizing minute details. .

Ramonismo, the word the author used to describe his attitude toward art and life, serves as the title to a collection of random thoughts on a variety of topics, including polka dot blouses, parrots, and awnings. In *The Generation of 1898 and After* Beatrice Patt and Martin Nozick described *ramonismo* as "an outrageously unconventional and purely arbitrary vision of facts and things." The *greguería* is perhaps the best expression of *ramonismo* and Gómez de la Serna's most enduring contribution to Spanish literature. "He proved that literary language could be richer if it used images," wrote Spanish critic Arturo Barea in *Books Abroad,* "with the same freedom as did the symbol-studded talk of the Andalusian peasants and gypsies." The "symbol-studded" speech of Andalusian country folk was what was to similarly inspire the innovative use of metaphors found in the work of García Lorca (whose first book of poetry was published a decade after Gómez de la Serna's creation of the *greguería*) and other writers of his generation and after. As Gardiol noted, "Because [Gómez de la Serna's] creative innovations succeeded in expanding the expressive powers of the image, he has been recognized as a major influence on the Spanish poets of the Generation of '25 and one of the precursors of the 'new' Spanish literature."

The Town Hall of the City of Madrid houses a museum of Ramón Gómez de la Serna memorabilia.

BIOGRAPHICAL/CRITICAL SOURCES:

BOOKS

Brenan, Gerald, *The Literature of the Spanish People: From Roman Times to the Present,* World Publishing, 1957.
Contemporary Literary Criticism, Volume 9, Gale, 1978.
Gardiol, Rita Mazzetti, *Ramón Gómez de la Serna,* Twayne, 1974.
Patt, Beatrice, and Martin Nozick, editors, *The Generation of 1898 and After,* Harper, 1960.

PERIODICALS

Books Abroad, spring, 1953.
Insula, February 15, 1957.

Modern Fiction Studies, summer, 1976.

—*Sketch by Marian Gonsior*

* * *

GOMEZ-QUIÑONES, Juan (H.) 1942-

PERSONAL: Born January 28, 1942, in Parral, Chihuahua, Mexico; immigrated to United States, 1942, naturalized citizen, 1962; son of Juan and Dolores (Quiñones) Gómez. *Education:* University of California, Los Angeles, B.A., 1962, M.A., 1964, Ph.D., 1972.

ADDRESSES: Home—507 Grande Vista Ave., Los Angeles, Calif. 90063. *Office*—History Department, University of California, Los Angeles, Los Angeles, Calif. 90024.

CAREER: California State University, San Diego (now San Diego State University), San Diego, Calif., assistant professor of history, 1968-69; University of California, Los Angeles, Los Angeles, assistant professor, 1969-73, associate professor, 1973-79, professor of history, 1979—, director of Chicano Studies Research Center, 1975—. Member of board of directors of Chicano Legal Defense Fund, 1968-69, Euclid Foundation, Los Angeles, and Los Angeles Urban Coalition, 1970-73; member of executive committee of National Chicano Council for Higher Education, 1975—; member of board of trustees of California State Universities and Colleges, 1976-84; member of Western Association of Schools and Colleges Senior Accreditation Commission, 1980-83.

MEMBER: American Association of University Professors, American Historical Association, Organization of American Historians, National Association of Chicano Social Scientists, Movimiento Estudiantil Chicano de Aztlán.

AWARDS, HONORS: Social Sciences Research Council Foreign Area fellow, 1966-68; National Endowment for the Humanities fellow, 1972-73, at University of Texas at Austin.

WRITINGS:

(Editor) *Statistical Abstract of Latin America,* Latin American Center Publications, University of California, Los Angeles (UCLA), 1964.
Fifth and Grande Vista: Poems, 1960-1973 (bilingual edition), [Austin, Texas], 1973, Editorial Mensaje, 1974.
Sembradores, Ricardo Flores Magón y el Partido Liberal Mexicano: A Eulogy and Critique, Aztlán Publications, Chicano Studies Center, UCLA, 1973, revised edition, 1977.
Piedras contra la luna, México en Aztlán y Aztlán en México: Chicano-Mexicano Relations and the Mexican Consulates, 1900-1920, An Extended Research Note, UCLA, 1973.
(Editor with Reynaldo Flores Macías) *The National Directory of Chicano Faculty and Research,* Aztlán Publications, Chicano Studies Center, UCLA, 1974.
(Editor with Roberto Cabello-Argandoña and Patricia Herrera Durán) *The Chicana: A Comprehensive Bibliographic Study,* introduction by Roberto Peter Haro, Chicano Research Library, Chicano Studies Center, UCLA, 1975.
Mexican Students por La Raza: The Chicano Student Movement in Southern California, 1967-1977, Editorial La Causa (Santa Barbara, Calif.), 1978.
(With Luis Leobardo Arroyo) *Orígenes del movimiento obrero chicano,* Era, 1978.
(With David Maciel) *Al norte del Río Bravo: Pasado lejano, 1600-1930,* Siglo Veintiuno, 1981.
Porfirio Díaz: Los intelectuales y La Revolución, Caballito, 1981.

Development of the Mexican Working Class North of the Rio Bravo: Work and Culture Among Laborers and Artisans, 1600-1900, Chicano Studies Research Center Publications, UCLA, 1982.

Also author of pamphlets *Selected Materials on the Chicano,* Mexican-American Cultural Center, UCLA, 1970; *Selected Materials for Chicano Studies,* Center for Mexican-American Studies, University of Texas at Austin, 1973; with Victor Nelson Cisneros, *Selective Bibliography on Chicano Labor Materials,* UCLA, 1974; and, with Alberto Camarillo, *Selected Bibliography for Chicano Studies,* third edition (Gómez-Quiñones was not associated with earlier editions), Aztlán Publications, Chicano Studies Center, UCLA, 1974.

Contributor of chapters to books, including *Investigaciones contemporáneas sobre historia de México,* Universidad Nacional de México, El Colegio de México, and University of Texas, 1970; *Parameters of Institutional Change: Chicano Experiences in Education,* Southwest Network (Hayward, Calif.), 1974; *Aztlán: Historia del Pueblo Chicano (1884-1910),* compiled by Maciel and Patricia Bueno, Sep Setentas (Mexico), 1975; *Contemporary Mexico: Papers of the IV International Congress of Mexican History,* University of California Press and El Colegio de México, 1975; *The Bakke Decision: The Question of Chicano Access to Higher Education,* edited by Carlos Manuel Haro, Chicano Studies Center, UCLA, 1977; and *Humanidad: Essays in Honor of George I. Sánchez,* edited by Américo Paredes, Chicano Studies Center Publications, UCLA, 1977. Poems represented in anthologies, including *Festival de Flor y Canto: An Anthology of Chicano Literature,* University of Southern California Press, 1976.

Contributor to periodicals, including *Revista Chicano-Riqueña* and *Western Historical Quarterly.* Member of editorial board of Chicano newspaper *Verdad,* San Diego, Calif., 1969; founder and co-editor of *Aztlán-Chicano Journal of the Social Sciences and the Arts,* 1970—.

* * *

GOMEZ ROSA, Alexis 1950-

PERSONAL: Born September 2, 1950, in Santo Domingo, Dominican Republic; son of Juan Francisco Gómez (a certified public accountant) and Altagracia de la Rosa de Gómez; married Barbara García Jiménez (in psychology), February 12, 1976; children: Berenice, Yelidá. *Education:* Attended Universidad Autónoma de Santo Domingo, 1970-74, and University of Massachusetts—Boston, 1983-85; State University of New York, Empire State College, B.A., 1988.

ADDRESSES: Home—514 West 176th St., New York, N.Y. 10033. *Office*—501 Fifth Ave., 4th Floor, New York, N.Y. 10016.

CAREER: Colegio Onésimo Jiménez (high school), Dominican Republic, teacher, 1972-74; copywriter for Young & Rubican advertising agency, 1974; teacher at Padre Billini High School, 1975-77; copywriter for RETHO advertising agency, 1975; publicist for Dominican Export Promotion Center, 1978-83; poetry instructor in the public schools of Boston and Dorchester, Massachusetts, 1984-85; Northern Manhattan Coalition for Immigrants Rights, New York City, community liaison, 1987-88. Journalist. Social worker with organizations and clubs of Washington Heights.

WRITINGS:

POETRY

Oficio de post-muerte, Williamsburg Print Shop, 1973.
(Contributor) *Los paraguas amarillos,* Ediciones del Norte, 1983.
High Quality, Ltd., Luna Cabeza Caliente (Santo Domingo, Dominican Republic), 1985.
(Contributor) *La poesía bisoña,* Associated University Presses, 1986.
(Contributor) *Poesía dominicana de post-guerra,* Associated University Presses, 1986.
(Contributor) *Anthology of Contemporary Latin American Literature,* Associated University Presses, 1986.
(Contributor) *Antología de la poesía hispanoamericana actual,* Siglo Veintiuno (Mexico), 1987.
Tiza & Tinta, Lluvia Editores (Lima, Peru), 1990.

Also author of *Pluroscopo* (Santo Domingo).

WORK IN PROGRESS: "New York City en tránsito de pie quebrado" (poems); "Contra la pluma la espuma."

* * *

GONZALES, Sylvia Alicia 1943-

PERSONAL: Born December 16, 1943, in Fort Huachuca, Arizona; daughter of Nazario Antonio (an accountant) and Aida (López) Gonzáles. *Education:* University of Arizona, B.A., 1966; graduate study at Antioch College, 1971-72; University of Massachusetts, Ed.D., 1974, M.A. (education), 1974. *Politics:* Democrat.

ADDRESSES: Office—Department of Mexican American Graduate Studies, San Jose State University, San Jose, Calif. 95192.

CAREER: U.S. Congress, Washington, D.C., receptionist, 1967; U.S. Civil Rights Commission, Washington, D.C., social science analyst, 1968, personnel management specialist, 1969-70; Model Cities, Tucson, Ariz., assistant coordinator, 1970-71; San Jose State University, San Jose, Calif., assistant professor of Mexican American studies and bilingual education, 1974—. Co-founder and member of board of directors, Interstate Research Associates, 1968—, and National Congress of Hispanic American Citizens (El Congreso), 1971-74; associate, Women's Institute for Freedom of the Press, 1977. Member, University of Massachusetts Center for Curriculum Studies, 1976—. Delegate-at-large, U.S. State Department International Women's Year Conference, 1977; National Institute of Education, member of Hispanic women's advisory committee and national advisory committee on desegregation and education concerns of the Hispanic community. Adviser to board of directors, Biblioteca Latino Americano, San Jose City Library, 1974-75.

MEMBER: National Association for Bilingual Education, National Women's Studies Association (executive director, 1977; member of coordinating council), National Women's Political Caucus, Mexican American Women's National Association (member of board), Conference on Inter-American Women Writers, Consortium on Peace Research, Education, and Development, United Professors of California (member of executive board, 1976).

AWARDS, HONORS: Experiment in International Living Scholarship, Argentina, 1965; Robert F. Kennedy Memorial Fellowship, 1971; Ford Foundation fellowship, 1972-74; certificate of excellence, Chicano literature contest at Chicano Cultural Center (Bakersfield, Calif.), 1975-76, for *Chicano Evolution.*

WRITINGS:

Consortium of Colleges and Universities for Chicanos and American Indians in Higher Education, U.S. Atomic Energy Commission, 1971.

(Editor) *Women in Action,* Office of Federal Programs, U.S. Civil Service Commission, 1971.

La Chicana Piensa (title means "The Chicana Thinks"), art by José Antonio Burciaga, Spartan Bookstore (San Jose State University), 1974.

(Contributor) Arnulfo Trejo, editor, *The Mexican-American—As We See Ourselves,* University of Arizona Press, 1974.

(Editor) *Que Tal Anthology,* Spartan Bookstore, 1975.

(Contributor) Phillip Ortega and Carlos Conde, editors, *The Chicano Literary World, 1974,* New Mexico Highlands University, 1975.

The Chicana Perspective: A Design for Self-Awareness, Spartan Bookstore, 1976.

(Contributor) Lipman-Blumen, editor, *Women's Research Compendium,* National Institute of Education, 1976.

(Contributor) Kathleen Blumhagen and Walter Johnson, editors, *Women's Studies Symposium,* Greenwood Press, 1977.

(Contributor) Beverly Lindsay, editor, *Comparative Perspectives of Third World Women: Social, Educational and Career Patterns,* Pennsylvania State University, 1977.

(Contributor) Dexter Fisher, editor, *The Third Woman,* Houghton, 1977.

(Contributor) Myrna Hellerman, editor, *¿Qué Pasa?,* Macmillan, 1977.

Hispanic American Voluntary Organizations, Greenwood Press, 1985.

Also author of *Chicano Evolution.* Work anthologized in *An Anthology of Bay Area Poets,* edited by C. Peeden, Stanford University, 1977. Contributor of articles and stories to periodicals, including *Ms., Caracol, La Luz, Social Science Journal, De Colores,* and *Peace Corps Training Journal;* contributor to newspapers.

WORK IN PROGRESS: A Pictorial Essay of the Hispanic Women in the United States; an autobiographical novel.

SIDELIGHTS: Sylvia Alicia Gonzáles once commented: "As a minority in this country, caught between two worlds of language, culture, and history, it was important to have a voice, particularly in the early years. My own predicament inspired me to seek, understand, and interpret the broader experience of humankind in order to find my place in the world. I grew to love people, cultures, differences, in a way that I had not been loved or accepted. I wrote of my experiences, my perceptions. I traveled throughout Latin America seeking my roots, Europe in my search for universality, and the barrios of the United States to share with my people. I love music and the arts of all peoples for the stories they have to tell."

BIOGRAPHICAL/CRITICAL SOURCES:

BOOKS

Fisher, Dexter, editor, *The Third Woman,* Houghton, 1977.

PERIODICALS

La Cosecha: Journal of the Chicano, Volume 1, number 1, 1976.
La Luz, December, 1974.

GONZALEZ, César A.
   See GONZALEZ T(RUJILLO), César A.

*   *   *

GONZALEZ, José Luis 1926-

PERSONAL: Born March 8, 1926, in Santo Domingo, Dominican Republic; immigrated to Mexico, naturalized citizen. *Politics:* Marxist.

ADDRESSES: Home—Mexico City, Mexico.

CAREER: Writer, 1943—. Professor of literature at Universidad Nacional Autónoma de México, Coyoacán, Mexico, and at Universidad de Guanajuato, Guanajuato, Mexico.

AWARDS, HONORS: Xavier Villaurrutia Prize for fiction from Sociedad Alfonsina International, 1978, for *Balada de otro tiempo.*

WRITINGS:

En la sombra (short stories), Imprenta Venezuela (San Juan, P.R.), 1943.
Cinco cuentos de sangre (short stories), foreword by Francisco Matos Paoli, Imprenta Venezuela, 1945.
En este lado (short stories), Los Presentes (Mexico), 1954.
La galería y otros cuentos, [Mexico], 1972, 2nd edition, Era, 1977.
Mambrú se fue a la guerra (y otros relatos), Mortiz, 1972.
Cuento de cuentos y once más, Extemporáneos, 1973.
En Nueva York y otras desgracias, Siglo Veintiuno Editores (Mexico), 1973, 3rd edition, revised and enlarged, Ediciones Huracán (Río Piedras, P.R.), 1981.
Novela y cuento en el siglo XX, Programa Nacional de Formación de Profesores, Asociación Nacional de Universidades e Institutos de Enseñanza Superior, 1973.
Viente cuentos y Paisa, introduction by Pedro Juan Soto, Cultural (Río Piedras), 1973.
Literatura y sociedad en Puerto Rico: De los cronistas de Indias a la generación del 98, Fondo de Cultura Económica, 1976.
(With Mónica Mansour) *Poesía negra de América,* Era, 1976.
Balada de otro tiempo, illustrated by Antonio Martorell, Nueva Imagen, 1978, translation by Asa Zatz published as *Ballad of Another Time,* Council Oak Books/Ilccatc, with the University of Tulsa, 1987.
Plebeyismo y arte en el Puerto Rico de hoy, Centro de Investigaciones Lingüístico-Literarias de la Universidad Veracruzana, Instituto de Investigaciones Humanísticas, c. 1979.
El país de cuarto pisos y otros ensayos (essays), Ediciones Huracán, 1980.
La llegada: Crónica con "ficción," Ediciones Huracán, 1980.
(Editor and author of prologue) Eugenio María de Hostos, *Textos* (title means "Selections"), SEP/UNAM (Mexico), 1982.
La tercera llamada y otros relatos, Editorial Leega (Mexico), 1983.
El oído de Dios, Cultural, 1984.
Las caricias del tigre, Mortiz, 1984.
Teresa de la Parra, 1895-1936, Offset (Xochimilco), 1987.

Also author or *El hombre de la calle,* 1948, *Paisa: Un relato de la emigración* (novela), 1950, and *The Destruction of a Nation,* 1977.

SIDELIGHTS: José Luis González is considered one of Puerto Rico's foremost authors although he was born in Santo Domingo and is a Mexican citizen. Born in 1926 to a Puerto Rican father, González was raised and educated in Puerto Rico, but when the

Mexican Government considered the prospect of becoming an American state, González became a Mexican citizen. The island still claims González for its own, however, and the themes of his many works focus on the social and political problems that affect the workers and the poor of Puerto Rico.

Although González is known primarily as a short story writer, he won the prestigious Xavier Villaurrutia Prize for fiction with his first novel, *Balada de otro tiempo,* published in 1978. The tale, translated into English as *Ballad of Another Time,* is set in Puerto Rico during the Great Depression and concerns a lovers' triangle comprised of a coffee farmer, his wife, and one of his young employees. González uses this traditional theme to great advantage, for he is able to comment on many levels of Puerto Rican society—from the poverty-stricken country folk to the revolutionary coffee-shop patrons—by following the young lovers as they flee the mountains for the coastal cities, with the humiliated husband in pursuit.

BIOGRAPHICAL/CRITICAL SOURCES:

BOOKS

Díaz Quinoñes, Arcadio, *Conversación con José Luis González,* Ediciones Huracán, 1976.

PERIODICALS

New York Times Book Review, January 31, 1988.

*   *   *

GONZALEZ-CRUSSI, F(rank) 1936-

PERSONAL: Born October 4, 1936, in Mexico City, Mexico; immigrated to United States, 1973; naturalized citizen, 1987; son of Pablo (a pharmacist) and María (a pharmacist; maiden name, Crussi) González; married Ana Luz, December 22, 1961 (divorced, 1974); married Wei Hsueh (a research pathologist), October 7, 1978; children: (first marriage) Daniel, Francis Xavier, Juliana. *Education:* Universidad Nacional Autónoma de México, B.A., 1954, M.D., 1961.

ADDRESSES: Home—2626 North Lakeview Ave., Chicago, Ill. 60614. *Office*—Department of Pathology, Children's Memorial Hospital, 2300 Children's Plaza, Chicago, Ill. 60614.

CAREER: Licensed to practice medicine in Indiana, Illinois, and Ontario; certified by American Board of Pathology, 1967, Canada Register, Ontario, 1970. Penrose Hospital, Colorado Springs, Colo., intern, 1962; St. Lawrence Hospital, Lansing, Mich., and Shands Teaching Hospital at the University of Florida, Gainesville, Fla., resident in pathology, 1963-67; Queen's University, Kingston, Ontario, assistant professor of pathology, 1967-73; Indiana University-Purdue University at Indianapolis, Ind., associate professor of pathology, 1973-78; Northwestern University, Chicago, Ill., professor of pathology, 1978—; writer. Head of laboratories at Children's Memorial Hospital, Chicago.

MEMBER: International Academy of Pathology, Society for Pediatric Pathology, American Society of Clinical Pathologists, Authors Guild, Authors League of America, Royal College of Physicians and Surgeons of Canada, Chicago Pathology Society, Society of Midland Authors.

AWARDS, HONORS: Best Nonfiction Award from the Society of Midland Authors, 1985, for *Notes of an Anatomist.*

WRITINGS:

(Editor) *Wilm's Tumor (Nephroblastoma) and Related Renal Neoplasms of Childhood,* CRC Press, 1983.
Notes of an Anatomist (essays), Harcourt, 1985.

Three Forms of Sudden Death; and Other Reflections on the Grandeur and Misery of the Body (essays; includes "Some Expressions of the Body [in Four Movements]"), Harper, 1986.
On the Nature of Things Erotic (essays), Harcourt, 1988.
The Five Senses, Harcourt, 1989.

Also author of a medical book entitled *Extragonadal Teratomas.* Contributor to numerous specialized medical journals.

SIDELIGHTS: Pathologist F. González-Crussi established himself as a noteworthy author with the publication of three nontechnical essay collections. Described as "witty" and "well-read" by Brett Singer in the *Los Angeles Times Book Review,* González-Crussi colors his informal writings with the insight he has gained from an almost three-decade career in medicine. Critics credit him with renewing the essay as a viable literary form in the twentieth century and liken his style to that of classic writers, such as Herman Melville, Michel Eyquem Montaigne, and Charles Lamb.

González-Crussi's first collection of essays, entitled *Notes of an Anatomist,* deals with a vast array of subjects, including corpses, ancient embalming techniques, the phenomenon of multiple births, bodily appendages, and natural monstrosities, from a pathologist's perspective. The volume is considered to be an unusually rich and thought-provoking first effort that artfully blends the author's personal experience and wry humor with mythic and literary references. González-Crussi spices his essays with fascinating asides: his use of allusions ranging from mention of sixteenth-century French king Henry IV's venereal diseases and Greek painter El Greco's astigmatism to the look of a Federico Fellini film prompted critic Dennis Drabelle to call him a "skilled wielder of literary references" in a review for *Washington Post Book World.*

John Gross, writing for the *New York Times,* suggested that *Notes of an Anatomist* "could also have been entitled 'A Pathologist's Apology,'" as it attempts to purge doctors who perform autopsies of their presumed callousness. González-Crussi asserted the nobility of pathologists in "The Dead as a Living," an essay from the volume that was cited in part in *Washington Post Book World:* physicians who search for the cause of their patients' deaths, explained the author, are unequaled in their "interest in the dead as dead persons, rather than abstractions." In the same excerpt, the doctor went on to argue that pathologists regard a corpse as a unique repository of clues capable of disclosing the cause of an individual human being's death. Ironically, however, the highly personal postmortem examination also reveals man's sameness in what González-Crussi, quoted by Edward Schneidman for the *Los Angeles Times Book Review,* calls "a most brutal way." The author reminds us, wrote Bruce Hepburn in an article for *New Statesman,* of the disturbing but undeniable fact that "decomposition of one sort or other is our universal fate and that it is salutary for us all to keep our latter end in mind."

Critics applauded González-Crussi's literary debut for both its form and content. D. J. Enright wrote in the *New York Times Book Review* that the essays "mix fact with speculation and gravity with humor, are rich in apposite and astounding anecdote and are elegant in expression." Schneidman echoed Enright's praise and expressed the consensus of the critics when he called the essays the "marvelously original and provocative" products of a "gifted" writer. *Notes of an Anatomist* earned González-Crussi the Best Nonfiction Award from the Society of Midland Authors in 1985.

The author's follow-up volume of essays, *Three Forms of Sudden Death; and Other Reflections on the Grandeur and Misery of the Body,* centers on issues of aging and death. Allan J. Tobin, commenting on the doctor's unconventional treatment of a seemingly somber topic, wrote in the *Los Angeles Times Book Review:* "González-Crussi deals less with the gloom of death than with the joy of life, especially of a life devoted to inquiry." Tobin suggested that just as the doctor examines physiological abnormalities in an effort to better understand normal life processes, he writes his essays in an attempt to explore timeless human mysteries: "There are only two themes worth writing . . . about," González-Crussi stated according to Tobin, "love and death, *eros* and *thanatos.*"

Three Forms of Sudden Death, which refers to death by lightning, asphyxiation, or unknown causes, intersperses thoughts on cannibalism and the female breast with a philosophical view of the human emotions in what several critics have referred to as "pithy" and "engaging" essays. While the collection was hailed as both cogent and well worth reading, it did not enjoy the exposure or popularity of its predecessor.

González-Crussi's third publication, *On the Nature of Things Erotic,* marks a departure from the scientifically inspired writings that dominated the doctor's earlier collections. The essays deal with love, desire, and seduction, achieving "something that it is not too much to call wisdom," stated John Gross, writing for the *New York Times.* Reviewers expressed a desire for the author to offer his own theories on the subjects he addresses, rather than a compilation of the thoughts of others, but were content to enjoy his intriguing accounts of ancient Greek love diagnoses, medieval Chinese seduction, and the classical view of homosexuality as a sign of high culture.

While González-Crussi has gained both critical and popular success for his reflections on human nature, he continues an active career in medicine, teaching pathology at Northwestern University in Chicago, Illinois. As an author, he is the practitioner of a long-ignored art, "a true essayist," wrote Gross in an article for the *New York Times.* By following the paths of his imagination, González-Crussi has touched upon what critics consider to be universal themes in essays of universal appeal.

González-Crussi told *HW:* "In my books, I have attempted to join science and the humanities. I would like to produce works of literature inspired on medical and biological subjects—not scientific divulgation. *Notes of an Anatomist* originated from a desire to reflect on the personal experience of a pathologist. *Three Forms of Sudden Death* attempts to be a personal statement of perplexity at the limitations and strengths of the human body."

BIOGRAPHICAL/CRITICAL SOURCES:

PERIODICALS

Los Angeles Times Book Review, July 7, 1985, December 7, 1986, March 27, 1988.
New Statesman, April 11, 1986.
New York Times, May 14, 1985, April 15, 1988.
New York Times Book Review, July 7, 1985, April 9, 1989.
Observer (London), April 13, 1986.
Vista, November 26, 1989.
Washington Post, July 5, 1985.
Washington Post Book World, April 9, 1989.

* * *

GONZALEZ MARTINEZ, Enrique 1871-1952

PERSONAL: Born 1871 in Guadalajara, Mexico; died in 1952.

CAREER: Poet. Physician and political secretary until 1911; served as Mexico's ambassador to Spain, Argentina, and Chile.

WRITINGS:

Los senderos ocultos, Librería de Porrúa Hermanos, 1915.
Jardines de Francia, Librería de Porrúa Hermanos, 1915.
La muerte del cisne, Librería de Porrúa Hermanos, 1915.
Parábolas y otras poemas, [Mexico], 1918.
Poemas escogidos, Maucci (Barcelona), c. 1920.
La palabra del viento, Ediciones México Moderno, 1921.
El romero alucinado (1920-1922), Editorial Babel, 1923.
Las señales furtivas, 1923-1924, Editorial S. Calleja, 1925.
Silentes, Librería de Porrúa Hermanos, 1926.
Poesía, 1909-1929, Espasa-Calpe, c. 1930.
Algunos aspectos de la lírica mexicana, Editorial Cultura, 1932.
Poemas truncos, Imprenta Mundial, 1935.
Ausencia y canto, Taller Poético, 1937.
Poesía, 1898-1938, Editorial "Polis," 1939.
Poemas, 1939-40, Nueva Voz, 1940.
Bajo el signo mortal, Compañia Editora y Librera, 1942.
Antología poética, Espasa-Calpe, 1943, 5th edition, 1965.
El hombre del buho, misterio de una vocación, Editorial Cultura, 1944, reprinted, Departamento de Bellas Artes del Gobierno del Estado (Guadalajara), 1973.
Segundo despertar, y otros poemas, Editorial Stylo, 1945.
(Editor) *Poesía española,* Editorial Signo, 1945.
Vilano al viento: Poemas, Editorial Stylo, 1948.
Babel, Revista de Literatura Mexicana, 1949.
La apacible locura, segunda parte de "El hombre del buho, misterio de una vocación," Cuadernos Americanos, 1951.
Tuércele el cuello al cisne, [Mexico], 1951.
El nuevo Narciso, y otros poemas, Fondo de Cultura Económica, 1952, reprinted, 1971.
Cuentos y otras paginas, Libro-Mex Editores, 1955.
Los mejores versos de González Martínez, Editorial Nuestra América, 1957.
Enrique González Martínez: Homenaje antológico, Sociedad de Amigos del Libro Mexicano, 1964.
Los cien mejores poemas, Aguilar, 1970.
Enrique González Martínez: Antología de su obra poética, Fondo de Cultura Económica, 1971.
Obras completas, [Mexico], 1971.

Also author of poetry collections *Preludios,* 1903, *Lirismos,* 1907, and *Silenter,* 1909.

SIDELIGHTS: A noted physician and diplomat, Enrique González Martínez wrote poems on such enduring themes as love, death, and acceptance. His sonnets are marked by a reflective, serious tone. This serious quality is commented on by Isaac Goldberg, who, writing in *Studies in Spanish-American Literature,* called González Martínez "an intellectual pantheist," explaining that "it is the pantheism of a modern intellect that gazes at feeling through the glasses of reason." John S. Brushwood, in his *Enrique González Martínez,* spoke of the poet's "discovery of a subtle, intuited reality" and claimed that "his poetry projects us onto the bridge that extends into intuited reality, where the aspects of time become one, where all places are the same, where all created things are joined."

Long considered an opponent of Modernism, critics came to see González Martínez as a Modernist writer himself. "The severity of González Martínez, the absence of any unforeseeable element, which is the salt of poetry, and the didacticism which tinges part of his work, have caused him to be considered the first Spanish-American poet to break with Modernism," according to Octavio Paz in *The Modern Mexican Essay.* But Paz continued: "In reality, González Martínez does not oppose Modernism; he undresses it and strips it of its trappings. . . . He redeems it, makes it conscious of itself and of its inner significance. . . . He does not repudiate Modernism, but is the only true Modernist poet Mexico has had."

BIOGRAPHICAL/CRITICAL SOURCES:

BOOKS

Brushwood, John S., *Enrique González Martínez,* Twayne, 1969.
Goldberg, Isaac, *Studies in Spanish-American Literature,* Brentano's, 1920.
Martínez, José Luis, editor, *The Modern Mexican Essay,* University of Toronto Press, 1965.

* * *

GONZALEZ PRADA, Manuel 1844-1918

PERSONAL: Born January 5, 1844 (some sources say 1848), in Lima, Peru; died July 22, 1918, in Lima, Peru; son of a distinguished Peruvian couple. *Education:* San Marcos University.

CAREER: Essayist, poet, polemicist, and educator. Fought in the War of the Pacific (1879-83) against Chile. Lived in Europe, 1885-91. Professor of literature. Director of the National Library, 1912-18. Founder of Círculo Literario (a literary and political group), which became the National Union Party.

WRITINGS:

Páginas libres (essays and speeches; also see below; contains "Conferencia en el Ateneo de Lima," "Discurso en el palacio de la Exposición," "Discurso en el teatro Olimpo," "Discurso en el entierro de Luis Márquez," "Grau," "Discurso en el Politeama," "Perú y Chile," "15 de julio," "Virgil," "Instrucción laica," "Libertad de escribir," "Propaganda y ataque," "Victor Hugo," "Renan," "Valera," "Castelar," "Los fragmentos de Luzbel," "Notas acerca del idioma," "La revolución francesca," and "La muerte y la vida"), Tipografía de P. Dupont, 1894, abridged edition, Tipografía librería de A. Quiroz Perea, 1934, corrected definitive edition, Editorial P.T.C.M., 1946, reprinted in two volumes, Ediciones Páginas Libres, 1960.
Los partidos y la Unión nacional, conferencia del señor Manuel G. Prada, Lima, 21 de agosto de 1898, Imprenta Grau (Callao, Peru), 1899.
Minúsculas (poems), Ediciones de Cien Ejemplares (Lima, Peru), 1901, 3rd edition, Librería e Imprenta "El Inca" (Lima), 1928, 4th edition, Adoración, 1986.
Manuel G. Prada: El catolicismo y la mujer; Tirada: Three Thousand ejemplares, Asociación de Propaganda Liberal, 1904.
Horas de lucha (title means "Hours of Struggle"; also see below; contains "Los partidos y la unión nacional," "Librepensamiento de acción," "El intelectual y el obrero," "Las esclavas de la iglesia," "Italia y el papado," "Nuestro periodismo," "Nuestros conservadores," "Nuestros liberales," "Nuestros magistrados," "Nuestros legisladores," "Nuestra aristocracia," "Nuestros beduinos," "Nuestros tigres," "Nuestros ventrales," "Nuestros inmigrantes," "Nuestros aficionados," "Nuestras glorificaciones," "Nuestros licenciados vidriera," "Política y religión," and "Apéndice: Dos cartas"), Tipografía "El progreso literario" (Lima), 1908, 3rd edition, includes "Nuestra indios," Tipografía "Lux" (Callao, Peru), 1935, reprinted, Editorial Universo, 1972.
Manuel G. Prada: Presbiterianas (poems), Imprenta "El Olimpo," 1909, 2nd edition, Librería e Imprenta "El Inca," 1928.

Manuel G. Prada: Exóticas, Tipografía de "El Lucero," 1911, reprinted, Tipografía de Louis Bellenand et Fils (Paris), 1933.
Bajo el oprobio (also see below), Tipografía de L. Bellenand et Fils, 1933, reprinted, Imprenta Editores Tipo-offset, 1979.
Manuel G. Prada: Trosoz de vida (poems), Talleres de L. Bellenand, 1933.
Manuel G. Prada: Baladas peruanas (poems), with prologue by Luis Alberto Sánchez, Prensas de la Editorial Ercilla, 1935, reprinted, Bendezú, 1969.
Manuel G. Prada: Anarquía, Ediciones Ercilla, 1936, 4th edition published as *Anarquía,* Editorial P.T.C.M., 1948.
Manuel G. Prada: Grafitos, edited by son, Alfredo González Prada, Tipografía de L. Bellenand et Fils, 1937.
Manuel G. Prada: Nuevas páginas libres, Ediciones Ercilla, 1937.
Manuel G. Prada: Libertarias, Tipografía de L. Bellenand et Fils, 1938.
Manuel G. Prada: Baladas, edited by A. González Prada, Tipografía de L. Bellenand et Fils, 1939.
M. González Prada: Propaganda y ataque, Ediciones Imán (Buenos Aires), 1939.
Manuel González Prada: Antología poética, edited by Carlos González Prada, Editorial Cultura, 1940.
González Prada: Pensamientos, selection and prologue by Campio Carpio, Arco Iris, 1941.
M. González Prada: Prosa menuda, Ediciones Imán, 1941.
González Prada, selection and prologue by Andrés Henestrosa, Secretaría de Educación Pública, 1943.
El tonel de Diógenes, seguido de Fragmentaria y Memoranda, Edición Tezontle (Mexico), 1945.
Florilegio: Poesía, ensayo, crítica, [Lima], 1948.
Ensayos escogidos, selection and prologue by Augusto Salazar Bondy, Patronato del Libro Peruano, 1956, 3rd revised and enlarged edition, Editorial Universo, 1970.
Sus mejores páginas, Editora Paracas, c. 1962.
Figuras y figurones: Manuel Pardo, Pierola, Romaña, José Pardo, Bendezú, 1969.
Poemas desconocidos, selection by Elsa Villanueva de Puccinelli, Ediciones de la Clépsidra, 1973.
Letrillas, Editorial Milla Batres, 1975.
Pensamiento político de González Prada (selections), Instituto Nacional de Cultura, 1975.
Antología: Páginas libertarias, Ediciones PEISA, 1975.
Páginas libres; horas de lucha, Biblioteca Ayacucho, 1976.
Manuel González Prada, Ministerio de Cultura, Juventud y Deportes, Departmento de Publicaciones, 1977.
Ortometria: Apuntes para una rítmica, Universidad Nacional Mayor de San Marcos, Dirección Universitaria de Biblioteca y Publicaciones, 1977.
Nuestros indios, Universidad Autónoma de México, 1978.
Sobre el militarismo; antología; Bajo el oprobio (selections), Editorial Horizonte, 1978.
Cantos del otro siglo, Universidad Nacional Mayor de San Marcos, Dirección Universitaria de Biblioteca y Publicaciones, 1979.
Textos (selections), SEP-UNAM, 1982.
Obras (collected works), Ediciones Copé, Departamento de Relaciones Públicas de PETROPERU, 1985.

Also author of *Poésias selectas,* Casa Editorial Franco-Iberoamericana. Translator of works by Schiller and Heine. Founding editor of numerous literary and political journals in Peru, including *Germinal.*

SIDELIGHTS: Peruvian essayist and poet Manuel González Prada became famous for speeches in which he criticized local politicians and the Roman Catholic church. Adamantly opposed to colonialism and racial discrimination against Indians, he valued freedom and equality more than the privileges that came with economic, social, or political power. His writings have inspired several generations of revolutionaries and reformers in Peru. Alfred Coester reports in *The Literary History of Spanish America* that González Prada "taught a whole generation to write well."

BIOGRAPHICAL/CRITICAL SOURCES:

BOOKS

Alexander, Robert J., editor, *Biographical Dictionary of Latin American and Caribbean Political Leaders,* Greenwood Press, 1988.

Coester, Alfred, *The Literary History of Spanish America,* Macmillan, 1919.

Mead, Robert G., *González Prada, el pensador y el prosista,* [New York], 1958.

*   *   *

GONZALEZ T(RUJILLO), César A. 1931-
(César A. González)

PERSONAL: Born January 17, 1931, in Los Angeles, Calif.; son of José A. (a chef) and Camerina (a seamstress; maiden name, Trujillo) González; married Bette Beattie (a teacher), August 30, 1969. *Education:* Gonzaga University, B.A., 1953, M.A., Ph.L., 1954; University of Santa Clara, M.S.T., S.T.L., 1961; graduate study at University of California, Los Angeles, 1962-65; graduate study at University of New Mexico, 1986. *Politics:* "Registered Democrat." *Religion:* "Practicing Catholic."

ADDRESSES: Home—7252 Caminito Carlotta, San Diego, Calif. 92120. *Office*—Chicano Studies Department, San Diego Mesa College, 7250 Mesa College Dr., San Diego, Calif. 92111.

CAREER: Instituto Regional, Chihuahua, Mexico, teacher, 1954-57; Centro Laboral México, Mexico City, worked at community development projects, 1965-68; Head Start, Los Angeles, Calif., supervisor working for civil rights and Chicano educational reform, 1968-69; Operation SER, San Diego, Calif., employment counselor, 1969-70; San Diego Mesa College, San Diego, founding chair and professor in Chicano studies department, 1970—.

MEMBER: National Association of Chicano Studies, American Federation of Teachers, La Raza Faculty Association, Chicano Federation of San Diego County, Centro Cultural de la Raza, Poets and Writers.

AWARDS, HONORS: Fulbright-Hays fellow in Peru, 1982; community service award from Chicano Federation of San Diego, 1982; member of first Chicano National Endowment for the Humanities fellowship group, 1984; outstanding instructor award from Mesa College, 1985.

WRITINGS:

(Editor, with others, under name César A. González) *What You Want to Know about English Grammar But Are Afraid to Ask: English Grammar for College Students,* San Diego Community College District, 1978.

(Editor and contributor, with others, under name César A. González) *Real Writing: English Composition for College Students,* San Diego Community College District, 1979.

Unwinding the Silence (poetry; includes "Sol Invernal," "Ancient Youth," "Damned," "In the Long Run," and "Quet-

zalcóatl and Christ"), introduction by Luis Leal, Lalo, 1987.

(Editor with Luis Alberto Urrea) *Fragmentos de Barro: The First Seven Years,* Tolteca, 1987.

(Editor and contributor) *Rudolfo A. Anaya: Focus on Criticism,* Massachusetts Bay, 1989.

Work represented in anthologies, including *First Chicano Literary Prize,* edited by Juan Villegas and others, Department of Spanish and Portuguese, University of California, Irvine, 1975; and *Southwest Tales: A Contemporary Collection,* edited by Alurista and Xelina Rojas-Urista, Maize, 1986. Contributor to periodicals, including *De Colores, Maize, Paperback Edition, Caracol, Citybender, Mesa Press,* and *Imagine.* Editor, with others, of literary contest publication *Fragmentos de Barro: Pieces of Clay,* 1976-81 and 1983.

WORK IN PROGRESS: Poetry collections *Gather These Years* and *A Family Remembering;* short fiction volume, *Santos;* collaborating with María Teresa Huerta Márquez on *Rudolfo A. Anaya,* a bio-bibliography in the series "Bio-Bibliographies in American Literature," for Greenwood Press.

SIDELIGHTS: César A. González T., who has spent much of his career teaching Chicano studies, philosophy, and English, is best known as a poet. A child during the Depression, he was deeply affected by the suffering and turmoil he witnessed, developing a strong sense of compassion for his fellow man and an awareness of the transitory nature of the world. Such feelings surface in his poetry, which is marked by its philosophical slant. In González T.'s first collection of verse, *Unwinding the Silence,* the poet explores how opposites such as good and evil can be transformed into a unity and shows how love and companionship can transcend the impermanence of the world. Observed *Dictionary of Literary Biography* contributor Ernesto Chávez Padilla, "His are songs of innocence and experience that probe life with the logical mind of the philosopher; and yet, in the end, González abandons the rigor of philosophy for the mystical precept that man can sustain contraries in his approach to the perfection of love."

González T. writes: "The Chicano movement, Chicano publications, and writing contests moved me to commit myself to writing in a dedicated and sustained way. I wanted to be part of a movement expanding the base of American literature, with its implicit redefinition of American reality.

"A great deal of what I write is done while I am on the move, sometimes at night, on a pad in the dark, by the side of the bed, writing something only when it must be written. I write in English or Spanish, at times using both languages in what Tino Villanueva has aptly called bisensitive writing. Both are public languages in the United States, with all of the attendant problems of publication. When I published my first collection, *Unwinding the Silence* with Lalo Press, I also made a linguistic statement.

"In my reading, reflection, and expression, I am fascinated by change and by the analogy of being. Hence, for all of its elusiveness, I read reality as a kaleidoscope of prisms, wherein everything is in everything. So whether we look outwards in our naming or inward from our necessarily limited apprehension of the totality of physical/psycho-moral space, we see the world which we continue to try to express through the particularity of our word.

"The poem 'Maldito/Damned' in *Unwinding the Silence* may be read as an expression of this fascination with anagogy, expressing the frustration of intuiting the whole, yet being unable to take in, comprehend, much less 'name the world,' or reality. I believe that aspirations for transcendence are not a chance hoax of nature, destined for frustration. Ending ' Maldito por no ser Dios!/ Damned, I'm not God!' there is implicit an intuition of the existence of God.

"My faith and a certain privacy are very important to me. A friend remarked recently that in my writing I often seem to slip in traces of scholasticism. I learned this in my many years of studying and working with the Jesuits. Gerard Manly Hopkins, S.J., and Pierre Teilhard de Chardin, S.J., have been great influences. Thomas Aquinas and Jacques Maritain were also important in my formative years.

"An example of deliberate philosophical intent is found in the epilogue-poem of *Unwinding the Silence*, 'A la larga/In the Long Run.' While expressing affirmative expectations for the future of Chicano literature, it asserts that in the long run 'we will be / re-membered,' as a community once scattered in moral disjunction, creating personhood. We will be 're-newed' and 're-read for / what / we with art fully make, / with prudence truly do, with wisdom thought-full speculate and / say we do ourselves freely decide' our own ideals as a community in unity. I remember Aquinas speaking of wisdom as a virtue of the speculative intellect seeking truth for its own sake, as in metaphysics or pure science. Art, he goes on to say, is the virtue proper to the intellect being used for the practical purpose of making something; prudence guides the practical intellect in doing, that is in moving the will toward deliberate, responsible choice—which is the realm of ethics. The intellect acting for the practical purpose of guiding choice is more popularly known as conscience.

"My reading includes an extensive reading of Chicano literature, with a special interest in the writings of women. There are many excellent writers. The *Quinto Sol* prize winners (Tomás Rivera, Rudolfo A. Anaya, Rolando Hinojosa-Smith, and Estela Portillo Trambley) are notable. I share Anaya's interest in archetype and myth. When he speaks of myth as 'the truth in the heart,' I read this as intuitive, dimensional human nature, common to all across time and space, and also the foundation of natural law and *ius gentium*. The Aztecs—the inheritors of millenia of indigenous wisdom—spoke of this as an innate sense of 'what is fitting, what is right.' "

BIOGRAPHICAL/CRITICAL SOURCES:

BOOKS

Dictionary of Literary Biography, Volume 82: *Chicano Writers,* First Series, Gale, 1989.

* * *

GOROSTIZA, Celestino

PERSONAL: Born in Mexico.

WRITINGS:

El color de nuestra piel: Pieza en tres actos, [Mexico], 1953, edition edited by Luis Soto-Ruiz and S. Samuel Trifilo, Macmillan, 1966.
Columna social: Comedia en tres actos, B. Costa-Amic, 1956.
(Editor) *Teatro mexicano del siglo XX,* volume 3, Fondo de Cultura Económica, 1956.
Las paradojas del teatro: Discurso de ingreso a la Academia Mexicana de la Lengua, Respuesta del Académico Salvador Novo, 1960.
Discursos de bellas artes, Instituto Nacional de Bellas Artes, Departamento de Literatura, 1964.

GOROSTIZA, José 1901-1973

PERSONAL: Born in 1901, in Villahermosa, Tabasco, Mexico; died in 1973.

CAREER: Writer. Diplomat in London, The Hague, Rome, Managua, Havana, Rio de Janeiro, Florence, and Paris, and at the United Nations.

WRITINGS:

Muerte sin fin (poem), R. Loera y Chávez, 1939, reprinted with commentary by Octavio Paz, Imprenta Universitaria (Mexico City), 1952, translation by Laura Villaseñor published as *Death Without End,* University of Texas Press, 1969.
Honor a los héroes de la independencia, La Justicia, 1957.
(With Humberto Romero) *La patria existe donde vive un Mexicano,* 2nd edition, Ediciones de la Asociación Nacional de Abogados, 1961.
Poesía, Fondo de Cultura Económica (Mexico City), 1964, reprinted as *Muerte sin fin y otras poemas,* 1983.
Prosa, edited by Miguel Capistrán, Universidad de Guanajuato, 1969.

Also author of *Canciones para cantar en las barcas* (poems; title means "Songs to Sing in Boats"), 1925. Contributor of articles, stories, translations, and reviews to periodicals, including *Contemporáneos.*

* * *

GOYENECHE, Gabriel
See AVALLE-ARCE, Juan Bautista de

* * *

GOYTISOLO, Juan 1931-

PERSONAL: Born January 5, 1931, in Barcelona, Spain; immigrated to France, 1957. *Education:* Attended University of Barcelona and University of Madrid, 1948-52.

CAREER: Writer. Worked as reporter in Cuba, 1965; associated with Gallimard Publishing Co., France. Visiting professor at universities in the United States.

AWARDS, HONORS: Received numerous awards for *Juegos de manos;* Premio Europalia, 1985.

WRITINGS:

NOVELS

Juegos de manos, Destino, 1954, recent edition, 1975, translation by John Rust published as *The Young Assassins,* Knopf, 1959.
Duelo en el paraíso, Planeta, 1955, Destino, 1981, translation by Christine Brooke-Rose published as *Children of Chaos,* Macgibbon & Kee, 1958.
El circo (title means "The Circus"), Destino, 1957, recent edition, 1982.
Fiestas, Emecé, 1958, Destino, 1981, translation by Herbert Weinstock published as *Fiestas,* Knopf, 1960.
La resaca (title means "The Undertow"), Club del Libro Español, 1958, J. Mortiz, 1977.
La isla, Seix Barral, 1961, reprinted, 1982, translation by José Yglesias published as *Island of Women,* Knopf, 1962 (published in England as *Sands of Torremolinos,* J. Cape, 1962).
Señas de identidad, J. Mortiz, 1966, translation by Gregory Rabassa published as *Marks of Identity,* Grove, 1969.

Reivindicación del Conde don Julián, J. Mortiz, 1970, Cátedra, 1985, translation by Helen R. Lane published as *Count Julian,* Viking, 1974.

Juan sin tierra, Seix Barral, 1975, translation by Lane published as *Juan the Landless,* Viking, 1977.

Makbara, Seix Barral, 1980, translation by Lane published as *Makbara,* Seaver Books, 1981.

Paisajes después de la batalla, Montesinos, 1982, translation by Lane published as *Landscapes After the Battle,* Seaver Books, 1987.

SHORT STORIES

Para vivir aquí (title means "To Live Here"), Sur, 1960, Bruguera, 1983.

Fin de fiesta: Tentativas de interpretación de una historia amorosa, Seix Barral, 1962, translation by Yglesias published as *The Party's Over: Four Attempts to Define a Love Story,* Weidenfeld & Nicolson, 1966, Grove, 1967.

TRAVEL NARRATIVES

Campos de Níjar, Seix Barral, 1960, Grant & Cutler, 1984, translation by Luigi Luccarelli published as *The Countryside of Nijar* in *The Countryside of Nijar* [and] *La chanca,* Alembic Press, 1987.

La chanca, Librería Española, 1962, Seix Barral, 1983, translation by Luccarelli published in *The Countryside of Nijar* [and] *La chanca,* Alembic Press, 1987.

Pueblo en marcha: Instantáneas de un viaje a Cuba (title means "People on the March: Snapshots of a Trip to Cuba"), Librería Española, 1963.

Crónicas sarracinas (title means "Saracen Chronicles"), Ibérica, 1982.

OTHER

Problemas de la novela (literary criticism; title means "Problems of the Novel"), Seix Barral, 1959.

Las mismas palabras, Seix Barral, 1963.

Plume d'hier: Espagne d'aujourd'hui, compiled by Mariano José de Larra, Editeurs Francais Réunis, 1965.

El furgón de cola (critical essays; title means "The Caboose"), Ruedo Ibérico, 1967, Seix Barral, 1982.

Spanien und die Spanien, M. Bucher, 1969.

(Author of prologue) José María Blanco White, *Obra inglesa,* Formentor, 1972.

Obras completas (title means "Complete Works"), Aguilar, 1977.

Libertad, libertad, libertad (essays and speeches), Anagrama, 1978.

(Author of introduction) Mohamed Chukri, *El pan desnudo* (title means "For Bread Alone"), translation from Arabic by Abdellah Djibilou, Montesinos, 1982.

Coto vedado (autobiography), Seix Barral, 1985, translation by Peter Bush published as *Forbidden Territory: The Memoirs of Juan Goytisolo,* North Point Press, 1989.

En los reinos de taifa (autobiography), Seix Barral, 1986.

(Author of commentary) Omar Khayyam, *Estances,* translation into Catalan by Ramon Vives Pastor, del Mall, 1985.

Contracorrientes, Montesinos, 1985.

Space in Motion (essays), translation by Lane, Lumen Books, 1987.

Work represented in collections and anthologies, including *Juan Goytisolo,* Ministerio de Cultura, Dirección General de Promoción del Libro y la Cinematografía, 1982. Contributor to periodicals.

SIDELIGHTS: "Juan Goytisolo is the best living Spanish novelist," wrote John Butt in the *Times Literary Supplement.* The author, as Butt observed, became renowned as a "pitiless satirist" of Spanish society during the dictatorship of Francisco Franco, who imposed his version of conservative religious values on the country from the late 1930s until his death in 1975. Goytisolo, whose youth coincided with the rise of Franco, had a variety of compelling reasons to feel alienated from his own country. He was a small child when his mother was killed in a bombing raid, a casualty of the civil war that Franco instigated to seize power from a democratically elected government. The author then grew up as a bisexual in a country dominated, in Butt's words, by "frantic machismo." Eventually, said Goytisolo in his memoir *Coto vedado* (*Forbidden Territory*), he became "that strange species of writer claimed by none and alien and hostile to groups and categories." In the late 1950s, when his writing career began to flourish, he left Spain for Paris and remained in self-imposed exile until after Franco died.

The literary world was greatly impressed when Goytisolo's first novel, *Juegos de manos* (*The Young Assassins*), was published in 1954. David Dempsey found that it "begins where the novels of a writer like Jack Kerouac leave off." Goytisolo was identified as a member of the Spanish "restless generation" but his first novel seemed as much akin to Fedor Dostoevski as it did to Kerouac. The plot is similar to Dostoevski's *The Possessed:* a group of students plot the murder of a politician but end up murdering the fellow student chosen to kill the politician. Dempsey wrote, "Apparently, he is concerned with showing us how self-destructive and yet how inevitable this hedonism becomes in a society dominated by the smug and self-righteous."

Duelo en el paraíso (*Children of Chaos*) was seen as a violent extension of *The Young Assassins.* Like Anthony Burgess's *A Clockwork Orange* and William Golding's *Lord of the Flies, Children of Chaos* focuses on the terror wrought by adolescents. The children have taken over a small town after the end of the Spanish Civil War causes a breakdown of order.

Fiestas begins a trilogy referred to as "The Ephemeral Morrow" (after a famous poem by Antonio Machado). Considered the best volume of the trilogy, it follows four characters as they try to escape life in Spain by chasing their dreams. Each character meets with disappointment in the novel's end. Ramon Sender called *Fiestas* "a brilliant projection of the contrast between Spanish official and real life," and concluded that Goytisolo "is without doubt the best of the young Spanish writers."

El circo, the second book in "The Ephemeral Morrow," was too blatantly ironic to succeed as a follow-up to *Fiestas.* It is the story of a painter who manages a fraud before being punished for a murder he didn't commit. The third book, *La resaca,* was also a disappointment. The novel's style was considered too realistic to function as a fitting conclusion to "The Ephemeral Morrow."

After writing two politically oriented travelogues, *Campos de Níjar* (*The Countryside of Nijar*) and *La chanca,* Goytisolo returned to fiction and the overt realism he'd begun in *La resaca.* Unfortunately, critics implied that both *La isla* (*Island of Women*) and *Fin de Fiesta* (*The Party's Over*) suffered because they ultimately resembled their subject matter. *The Party's Over* contains four stories about the problems of marriage. Although Alexander Coleman found that the "stories are more meditative than the full-length novels," he also observed, "But it is, in the end, a small world, limited by the overwhelming ennui of everything and everyone in it." Similarly, Honor Tracy noted, "Every gesture of theirs reveals the essence of the world, they're absolutely necessary, says another: we intellectuals operate in a vacuum. . . . Everything ends in their all being fed up."

Goytisolo abandoned his realist style after *The Party's Over.* In *Señas de identidad* (*Marks of Identity*), wrote Barbara Probst Solomon, "Goytisolo begins to do a variety of things. Obvious political statement, he feels, is not enough for a novel; he starts to break with form—using a variety of first, second and third persons, he is looking and listening to the breaks in language and . . . he begins to break with form—in the attempt to describe what he is really seeing and feeling, his work becomes less abstract." Robert J. Clements called *Marks of Identity* "probably his most personal novel," but also felt that the "most inevitable theme is of course the police state of Spain." Fusing experimentation with a firm political stance, Goytisolo reminded some critics of James Joyce while others saw him elaborating his realist style to further embellish his own sense of politics.

Reivindicación del Conde don Julián (*Count Julian*), Goytisolo's next novel, is widely considered to be his masterpiece. In it, he uses techniques borrowed from Joyce, Céline, Jean Genet, filmmaker Luis Buñuel, and Pablo Picasso. Solomon remarked that, while some of these techniques proved less than effective in many of the French novels of the 1960s, "in the hands of this Spanish novelist, raging against Spain, the results are explosive." *Count Julian* is named for a legendary Spanish nobleman who betrayed his country to Arab invaders in the Middle Ages. In the shocking fantasies of the novel's narrator, a modern Spaniard living as an outcast in Africa, Julian returns to punish Spain for its cruelty and hypocrisy. Over the course of the narration, the Spanish language itself gradually transforms into Arabic. Writing in the *New York Times Book Review,* Carlos Fuentes called *Count Julian* "an adventure of language, a critical battle against the language appropriated by power in Spain. It is also a search for a new/old language that would offer an alternative for the future."

With the publication of *Juan sin tierra* (*Juan the Landless*), critics began to see Goytisolo's last three novels as a second trilogy. However, reviews were generally less favorable than those for either *Marks of Identity* or *Count Julian.* Anatole Broyard, calling attention to Goytisolo's obsession with sadistic sex and defecation, remarked, "Don Quixote no longer tilts at windmills, but toilets." A writer for *Atlantic* suggested that the uninformed reader begin elsewhere with Goytisolo.

Even after the oppressive Franco regime was dismantled in the late 1970s, Goytisolo continued to write novels that expressed deep alienation by displaying an unconventional, disorienting view of human society. *Makbara,* for example, is named for the cemeteries of North Africa where lovers meet for late-night trysts. "What a poignant central image it is," wrote Paul West in *Washington Post Book World,* "not only as an emblem of life in death . . . but also as a vantage point from which to review the human antic in general, which includes all those who go about their daily chores with their minds below their belts." "The people [Goytisolo] feels at home with," West declared, "are the drop-outs and the ne'er do wells, the outcasts and the misfits." In *Paisajes después de la batalla* (*Landscapes After the Battle*), the author moved his vision of alienation to Paris, where he had long remained in exile. This short novel, made up of seventy-eight nonsequential chapters, displays the chaotic mix of people—from French nationalists to Arab immigrants—who uneasily coexist in the city. "The Paris metro map which the protagonist contemplates . . . for all its innumerable permutations of routes," wrote Abigail Lee in the *Times Literary Supplement,* "provides an apt image for the text itself." *Landscapes* "looked

like another repudiation, this time of Paris," Butt wrote. "One wondered what Goytisolo would destroy next."

Accordingly, Butt was surprised to find that the author's memoir of his youth, published in 1985, had a markedly warmer tone than the novels that had preceded it. "Far from being a new repudiation," Butt observed, *Forbidden Territory* "is really an essay in acceptance and understanding. . . . Gone, almost, are the tortuous language, the lurid fantasies, the dreams of violation and abuse. Instead, we are given a moving, confessional account of a difficult childhood and adolescence." Goytisolo's recollections, the reviewer concluded, constitute "a moving and sympathetic story of how one courageous victim of the Franco regime fought his way out of a cultural and intellectual wasteland, educated himself, and went on to inflict a brilliant revenge on the social system which so isolated and insulted him."

BIOGRAPHICAL/CRITICAL SOURCES:

BOOKS

Contemporary Literary Criticism, Gale, Volume 5, 1976, Volume 10, 1979, Volume 23, 1983.
Goytisolo, Juan, *Forbidden Territory,* translation by Peter Bush, North Point Press, 1989.
Schwartz, Kessel, *Juan Goytisolo,* Twayne, 1970.
Schwartz, Ronald, *Spain's New Wave Novelists 1950-1974: Studies in Spanish Realism,* Scarecrow Press, 1976.

PERIODICALS

Atlantic, August, 1977.
Best Sellers, June 15, 1974.
Los Angeles Times Book Review, January 22, 1989.
Nation, March 1, 1975.
New Republic, January 31, 1967.
New York Times Book Review, January 22, 1967, May 5, 1974, September 18, 1977, June 14, 1987, July 3, 1988, February 12, 1989.
Saturday Review, February 14, 1959, June 11, 1960, June 28, 1969.
Texas Quarterly, spring, 1975.
Times Literary Supplement, May 31, 1985, September 9, 1988, May 19, 1989, November 17, 1989.
Washington Post Book World, January 17, 1982, June 14, 1987.

*   *   *

GRACIA, Jorge J(esus) E(miliano) 1942-

PERSONAL: Born July 18, 1942, in Camagüey, Cuba; naturalized Canadian citizen, 1971; permanent U.S. resident, 1975; son of Ignacio Jesús Loreto (a pharmacist and landowner) and Leonila (a poet; maiden name, Otero) Gracia; married Norma Elida Silva (a vice president of a corporation); children: Leticia Isabel, Clarisa Raquel. *Education:* Wheaton College, B.A., 1965; University of Chicago, M.A., 1966; Pontifical Institute of Mediaeval Studies, M.S.L., 1970; University of Toronto, Ph.D., 1971.

ADDRESSES: Home—420 Berryman Dr., Amherst, N.Y. 14226. *Office*—Department of Philosophy, Baldy Hall, State University of New York at Buffalo, Buffalo, N.Y. 14260.

CAREER: State University of New York at Buffalo, assistant professor, 1971-76, associate professor, 1976-80, professor of philosophy, 1980—, chairman of department, 1980-1985, 1989-90. Visiting professor at University of Puerto Rico, 1972-73. Magister, Schola Lullistica Maioricensis, Palma de Mallorca, 1976—.

MEMBER: Societe Internationale pour l'Etude de la Philosophie Medievale, International Federation of Latin American and Caribbean Studies (president, 1987-89), American Philosophical Association, Metaphysical Society of America, Society for Medieval and Renaissance Philosophy (member of executive committee, 1986—; vice president, 1988-90; president, 1990-92), Society for Iberian and Latin American Thought (vice-president, 1985-86; president, 1986-88), Sociedad Filosófica Ibero-Americana (member of executive council, 1985—).

AWARDS, HONORS: Grants from Canada Council, 1968-71, American Council of Learned Societies, 1977, National Endowment for the Humanities, 1981-82, Academia Nacional Argentina de Ciencias and Goethe Institute, both 1983, and New York Council for the Humanities, 1987.

WRITINGS:

(Editor) *El hombre y los valores en la filosofía latinoamericana del siglo veintavo* (title means "Man and Values in Twentieth-Century Latin American Philosophy"), Fondo de Cultura Económica, 1975, 2nd edition, 1981.

(Editor and author of introduction) Francesc Eimenes, *Com usar bé de beure e menjar* (title means "How to Drink and Eat Well"), Curial, 1977.

(Editor and author of introduction) *Man and His Conduct: Philosophical Essays in Honor of Risieri Frondizi,* University of Puerto Rico Press, 1980.

(Translator and author of introduction) Francisco Suárez, *Suárez on Individuation,* Marquette University Press, 1982.

Introduction to the Problem of Individuation in the Early Middle Ages, Catholic University of America Press, 1984, revised, 2nd edition, Philosophia Press, 1988.

(Editor with others, and author of introduction) *Philosophical Analysis in Latin America,* Reidel, 1984.

(Editor and author of introduction) *Ensayos filosóficos de Risieri Frondizi,* Fondo de Cultura Económica, 1986.

(Editor and author of introduction) *Latin American Philosophy in the Twentieth Century: Man, Value, and the Search for Philosophical Identity,* Prometheus Books, 1986.

(Editor and co-author of introduction) *Filosofía e identidad cultural en América Latina* (title means "Philosophy and Cultural Identity in Latin America"), Monte Avila, 1988.

Individuality: An Essay on the Foundations of Metaphysics, State University of New York Press, 1988.

(Translator, and author of introduction, with Douglas Davis) *The Metaphysics of Good and Evil According to Suárez,* Philosophia Verlag, 1988.

(Editor) *Directory of Latin American Philosophers,* Society for Iberian and Latin American Thought, 1988.

(Editor, and author of introduction, with M. Camurati) *Philosophy and Literature in Latin America,* State University of New York, 1989.

(Editor with others) *Social Sciences in Latin America,* UB Council for International Studies and Programs, 1989.

(Editor and author of introduction) *Individuation in Scholasticism: The Later Middle Ages and the Counter-Reformation,* Philosophia Verlag, in press.

(Editor with R. Barber) *Individuality, Individuation, and Identity,* Philosophia Verlag, in press.

Contributor of more than seventy articles to periodicals, including *Review of Metaphysics, Journal of the History of Philosophy, New Scholasticism, Journal of the History of Ideas,* and *Philosophy and Phenomenological Research.* Member of numerous editorial boards.

WORK IN PROGRESS: Philosophy and Its History: Essays on Philosophical Historiography; Texts: Their Nature and Interpretation, completion expected in 1992; editing special issues of *The Philosophical Forum, The New Scholasticism,* and *Topoi.*

SIDELIGHTS: Jorge J. E. Gracia told *HW:* "My research and writing has centered on four subject areas: the Middle Ages, Latin America, metaphysics, and more recently, philosophical historiography. I was trained as a medievalist in Toronto, and therefore a great part of my work is concerned with the history of medieval thought. Most of this is technical and deals with such topics as the views of individuality developed during the period. In *Introduction to the Problem of Individuation in the Early Middle Ages,* I argue, for example, that the basic problems related to individuality, its causes and its nature, are raised for the first time in an explicit way in the early middle ages. The book on Francis Suárez [a Spanish philosopher of the 1500s], which contains a translation of his treatise on this topic as well as an extensive glossary of technical terms, argues that Suárez's views on individuality are the most sophisticated and developed to come out of the middle ages and that Suárez provides one of the most clear and systematic treatments of the topic to date.

"More recently I have been working on the theories of good and evil in late scholasticism, particularly on the views of Suárez. In the book I published with Davis on good and evil in Suárez, we present the key texts on this topic by Suárez and argue that he gives a credible defense of the traditional scholastic interpretation of evil as privation by introducing the concept of evil as a kind of disagreeability. Likewise, we find much merit in the view of good as a kind of agreeability. But we also argue that neither theory goes far enough, since neither of them develops sufficiently the relational character of value.

"After coming to Buffalo and visiting Puerto Rico for a year, I became interested in the thought and philosophy of Latin America, both because I was asked to teach a course on the subject and because I have never forgotten my ethnic background. Given the scarcity of sources available I decided, with the help of my good friend, the late Risieri Frondizi, to put together a collection of readings from Latin American philosophers centered on the themes of man and values. These themes are the areas where Latin American philosophy had made its most important contributions in the first half of this century.

"Another area of my research has been concerned with the impact that philosophical analysis, as practiced in the Anglo-American tradition, has had on Latin America. I have also been working on the crisis of philosophical identity which Latin America is undergoing. One of the most discussed issues in Latin America for the past thirty years has been the question of whether there is such a thing as a Latin American philosophy that may be idiosyncratically unique and authentic. In my book on the subject, I point out that the source of the question is a misunderstanding about the very nature of philosophy and philosophical method and that once a proper understanding of these is achieved, the problem dissolves.

"In the area of metaphysics, my main concern has been with the so-called problem of universals and individuals—the ontological categorization of two of our most basic notions. In the book on individuality I present my view that individuality has to do primarily with non-instantiability, while universality has to do with instantiability. I argue, moreover, that much of the concern with individuals and universals in the course of the history of philosophy is a result of a lack of understanding this fact as well as a lack of understanding and distinguishing the various issues involved in the notions of individuality and universality. These are the faults that flaw the work of most philosophers concerned with these issues, from Plato to Strawson.

"Finally, I recently have been reflecting on the historical work I have carried out for the past twenty years. This has raised questions in my mind about the nature of historical knowledge, the proper methodology in historical investigation, and the difficulties involved in the interpretation of texts. The result is a manuscript which argues for a philosophical approach to the history of philosophy and a new interpretation of the nature of texts."

*   *   *

GREEN, María del Rosario
    See ROSARIO GREEN (de HELLER), María del

*   *   *

GUEVARA, Ché
    See GUEVARA (SERNA), Ernesto

*   *   *

GUEVARA (SERNA), Ernesto   1928-1967
(Ché Guevara)

PERSONAL: Born June 14, 1928, in Rosario, Argentina; executed by the Bolivian army, October 9, 1967, in Higueras, Bolivia; son of Ernesto Rafael Guevara Lynch (an architect) and Celia de la Serna de Guevara; married Hilda Gadea (a Peruvian revolutionary), May, 1955 (divorced); married Aleida March (a schoolteacher); children: (first marriage) Hilda; (second marriage) Aleida. *Education:* University of Buenos Aires Medical School, doctor of medicine and surgery, 1953.

CAREER: Inspector for Guatemalan Government agrarian reform agency, 1954; military commander and medical corps director for the 26th of July Movement guerrilla organization in Cuba, 1956-59; commander of La Cabaña fortress in Havana, Cuba, 1959; official with the National Institute of Agrarian Reform in Havana, 1959; president of the National Bank of Cuba in Havana, 1959-61; minister of Industries for the government of Cuba in Havana, 1961-65; commander-in-chief of the National Liberation Army guerrilla organization in Bolivia, 1966-67.

WRITINGS:

NONFICTION

La guerra de guerrillas, Departamento de Instrucción de MIN-FAR (Havana), 1960, translation by J. P. Morray published as *Guerrilla Warfare,* Monthly Review Press, 1961.
Pasajes de la guerra revolucionaria, Unión de Escritores y Artistas de Cuba, 1963, translation published as *Episodes of the Revolutionary War,* International Publishing, 1968, revised and enlarged translation by Victoria Cruz published as *Reminiscences of the Cuban Revolutionary War,* Monthly Review Press, 1968.
Condiciones para el desarrollo económico latinoamericano (title means "The Conditions for Latin American Economic Development"), El Siglo Ilustrado (Montevideo), 1966.
Ché Guevara Speaks: Selected Speeches and Writings, edited by George Lavan, Grove, 1967.
Obra revolucionaria (title means "Revolutionary Works"), edited by Roberto Fernández Retamar, Ediciones Era (Mexico), 1967.
El diario de Ché en Bolivia: Noviembre 7, 1966, a octubre 7, 1967, Instituto de Libro, 1968, translation published as *The Diary*

of Ché Guevara; Bolivia: November 7, 1966-October 7, 1967, edited by Robert Scheer, Bantam, 1968, enlarged translation published as *The Complete Bolivian Diaries of Ché Guevara and Other Captured Documents,* edited by Daniel James, Stein & Day, 1968.
Venceremos! The Speeches and Writings of Ernesto Ché Guevara, edited and annotated with an introduction by John Gerassi, Macmillan, 1968.
(Contributor) *La economía socialista* (title means "The Socialist Economy"), Editorial Nova Terra (Barcelona), 1968.
Escritos económicos de Ernesto Ché Guevara (title means "Economic Writings of Ernesto Ché Guevara"), Ediciones Pasado y Presente (Córdoba), 1969.
Ché: Selected Works of Ernesto Guevara, edited by Rolando E. Bonachea and Nelson P. Valdes, MIT Press, 1969.
Ché Guevara on Revolution: A Documentary Overview, edited by Jay Mallin, University of Miami Press, 1969.
El libro verde olivo (title means "The Olive Green Book"), Editorial Diógenes (Mexico), 1970.
Obras, 1957-1967 (title means "Works, 1957-1967"), Casa de las Américas (Havana), 1970.
Barro y cenizas: Diálogos con Fidel Castro y el Ché Guevara (title means "Clay and Ashes: Dialogues with Fidel Castro and Ché Guevara"), Fomento Editorial (Madrid), 1971.
El hombre y el socialismo en Cuba (title means "Socialism and Man in Cuba"), Ediciones Síntesis (Buenos Aires), 1973.
La planificación socialista y su significado (title means "Socialist Planning and Its Significance"), El Tunel (Buenos Aires), 1973.
La revolución latinoamericana (title means "The Latin American Revolution"), Editorial Encuadre (Rosario, Argentina), 1973.
El socialismo y el hombre nuevo (title means "Socialism and the New Man"), edited by José Arico, Siglo Veintiuno (Mexico), 1977.
Ché Guevara and the Cuban Revolution: Writings and Speeches, Pathfinder Press/Pacific & Asia (Sydney), 1987.

Also author of numerous political pamphlets and contributor of articles to newspapers and magazines.

SIDELIGHTS: Ernesto "Ché" Guevara, the Argentine-born Marxist revolutionary, remains a potent political symbol more than twenty years after his death at the hands of the Bolivian army. The bearded, beret-clad guerrilla leader, who inspired a generation of radical youth in the 1960s with his call for "two, three, many Vietnams" to defeat United States imperialism, is still lionized by leftists all over the world as a martyr to the cause of third world revolution. Guevara's near-mythic reputation today rests largely on his military exploits and his personal example of courage, self-sacrifice, and idealism rather than any major original contributions to Marxist theory and revolutionary practice. Guevara's best-known books are a training manual titled *Guerrilla Warfare* and his posthumously published personal *Diary* recounting the ill-fated Bolivian campaign he led in 1967, but numerous collections of his speeches and articles on topics ranging from socialist morality to economic planning have also appeared over the years.

Latin America's most celebrated modern revolutionary was born into a left-leaning, middle-class family to whom he remained close in later life. As a boy, Guevara developed the severe asthma condition that would plague him throughout his life and contribute to his decision to pursue a medical career. Guevara took his doctor of medicine degree from the University of Buenos Aires in 1953 and then traveled around South and Central America, eventually settling in Guatemala, where he worked as an inspector for the agrarian land redistribution program launched by reformist President Jacobo Arbenz Guzmán. Not long after the young physician arrived in that country, a military coup organized and financed by the U.S. Central Intelligence Agency (CIA) overthrew the Arbenz government. After fruitless attempts to organize local popular resistance to the military takeover, Guevara took asylum in the Argentine Embassy, where he remained for two months before fleeing to neighboring Mexico. Guevara's first-hand experience of the coup against Arbenz deepened his anti-American sentiments and helped convince him that armed revolution was needed to carry out and defend structural reforms in Latin America.

In Mexico Guevara met the exiled Cuban brothers Fidel and Raúl Castro, who were organizing just such a revolutionary movement against the Cuban dictator Fulgencio Batista. The Argentine agreed to join the Castros' 26th of July Movement as the physician and sole non-Cuban among an expeditionary force of eighty-three guerrilla fighters who landed in Cuba from Mexico aboard the boat *Granma* in December of 1956. The Cuban army wiped out the bulk of this force immediately, but Guevara and the Castros were among the twelve survivors who managed to reach the rugged Sierra Maestra mountain range in Oriente province, where they began organizing the infrastructure for a prolonged guerrilla insurgency. Guevara, nicknamed "Ché" (an affectionate Argentine expression meaning "you") by his Cuban comrades, took up arms with the rest of the insurgents and displayed such leadership ability that he was named commander of a second guerrilla column composed of local peasant recruits. Guevara also served as a trusted political adviser to commander-in-chief Fidel Castro, headed the insurgent medical corps, and organized military training camps, a radio station, a weapons plant, and a network of schools in the guerrilla zone of control. In late 1958 Guevara's column routed a much larger and better equipped Cuban army contingent at the decisive battle of Santa Clara, which convinced Batista to resign from office and flee the country. Not long afterward, the Argentine commander led the first rebel force into Havana and sealed the revolutionary victory.

Guevara drew on his combat experience in the Sierra Maestra to write *Guerrilla Warfare*, a manual of guerrilla strategy, tactics, and logistics that was published in Cuba in 1960. In this work the author openly stated his hope that the Cuban example would trigger similar revolutions elsewhere in Latin America and argued that a dedicated guerrilla force of only a few dozen combatants could successfully initiate an insurgency virtually anywhere in the continent. Guevara's guerrilla manual found a readership not only among revolutionaries but also within the ranks of U.S. Army strategists seeking to apply lessons to the growing counter-insurgency war in South Vietnam. Guevara later wrote a series of articles describing his personal experiences in the Cuban insurgency that were published in book form as *Episodes of the Revolutionary War*. *Nation* reviewer Jose Yglesias found this collection "simple, beautiful, and politically prophetic."

Guevara held a series of important positions in the early years of the Cuban revolutionary government, serving first as military commander of Havana's La Cabaña fortress and successively as a top official of the National Institute of Agrarian Reform, president of the National Bank of Cuba, and minister of Industries. In the last two posts, Guevara (who was given the full citizenship rights of a native Cuban by the Castro government) became a leader in the immensely complex and difficult task of converting a sugar-based, capitalist economy heavily dependent on the United States into a state-run system with a more diversified pro-

duction and trading base. Guevara helped negotiate a historic trading pact with the Soviet Union, exchanging sugar for capital goods in February of 1960 and, after the United States imposed an economic boycott of the island later in the year, he traveled to other East Bloc countries to develop new commercial relations. Better versed in Marxism than Castro, Guevara had early envisioned a socialist outcome for the Cuban Revolution, and he undoubtedly encouraged the Cuban leader to take the definitive step toward a state-run system by nationalizing virtually all of the country's industry in late 1960.

As minister of industries, Guevara then confronted the daunting task of organizing, administrating, and expanding a broad range of industrial and agricultural enterprises. Determined to break Cuba from its over-reliance on sugar exports, Guevara sought to industrialize the island rapidly with support from the East Bloc in the form of generous bilateral aid and advantageous sugar prices. But Guevara believed that the emergence of a new "socialist morality" among the Cuban people would have the greatest effect in developing the island's economy in the long run. For this reason he favored moral over material incentives to raise production and advocated voluntary work programs to strengthen revolutionary consciousness and solidarity. Guevara's personal popularity and example—as minister of industries he paid himself $250 per month and worked eighty-hour weeks—did much to make the voluntary work programs a success in the early years of the revolution.

Guevara discussed his conception of the socialist "new man" and other political and social issues confronting post-capitalist society in numerous speeches and articles published in Cuban journals. He also wrote a number of papers on international economic topics still current today, such as the problem of third world foreign debt and terms of trade with the industrialized countries and the controversy over "market socialism" versus centralized planning in the non-capitalist world. Many of Guevara's major articles and speeches have been translated into English and appear in the collections *Ché Guevara Speaks* and *Venceremos! The Speeches and Writings of Ernesto Ché Guevara.*

In early 1965 Guevara resigned his post as minister of industries and mysteriously disappeared from public view. The Western media at the time speculated that the Argentine had had a falling out with Castro and was either imprisoned or executed. The world only learned the real reason for Guevara's disappearance when he was killed while leading a guerrilla column in a remote region of Bolivia more than two years later. The restless revolutionary, seeking continental support for Castro's isolated regime and convinced that most of Latin America was ripe for guerrilla insurgency, had set out to sow the seeds of regional rebellion himself. After much consideration, he chose Bolivia as an auspicious starting point for several reasons: the country's militant tin miners had led an aborted popular revolution in the early 1950s and remained a potent social force; the Bolivian army and capitalist class were relatively weak; and Bolivia's geographical position gave a guerrilla force ready access to five other South American countries where it might attempt to spread the insurgency. Guevara secretly recruited and trained a force of about fifty former Cuban army officers and Bolivian Communist party members in Cuba and then entered Bolivia disguised as an Uruguayan diplomat to launch the insurgency in the remote south-central region of Nancahuazu in October, 1966.

With historical hindsight Guevara's disastrous Bolivian campaign has been dismissed as a quixotic adventure doomed to failure from the beginning. But at the time Guevara was guided by the spectacular success of the Cuban insurgency, whose lessons had informed his book *Guerrilla Warfare* and French writer Regis Debray's theoretical study, *Revolution in the Revolution?* According to the so-called *foco* theory of guerrillaism advanced by Debray and Guevara, a small band of dedicated guerrilla fighters could serve as a catalyst for igniting revolution in third world countries where weak governments of little legitimacy enforced gross social inequality. Whether a given oppressed population had much of a history of political struggle and class consciousness was of relatively minor importance; the brute facts of poverty and oppression itself would suffice to turn the people actively against the regime once the guerrilla band had proven in battle that the political system and armed forces backing it were vulnerable. To reduce the risk of being captured and exterminated, the guerrilla force would have to operate in the remote countryside during early stages of the insurgency, but after building a strong peasant army it could begin to coordinate its actions with strikes and demonstrations by urban supporters. As in Cuba, however, military success on the battlefield rather than popular insurrection would determine the revolutionary victory and the guerrilla leadership would in effect substitute for the mobilized working class in directing the Marxist course of the revolution from above.

The *foco* theory died with Ché's army in the rugged Bolivian jungles and ravines. In his riveting chronicle of the year-long guerrilla campaign, Guevara described the hellish physical conditions and unbroken political isolation that plagued his small band of fighters from the beginning. Malaria and other diseases took a constant toll on the insurgents and the terrain supported little wildlife for food; for days on end the men ate lard as they wandered lost in the wilderness. The local peasants were suspicious of the guerrillas and Guevara failed to win any recruits to replace the men he lost steadily to illness and desertion. Miner and student organizations who sought to mobilize support for the insurgents, moreover, were brutally suppressed by security forces. The guerrillas did manage several successful ambushes against their army pursuers and at one point occupied a small town in early 1967, but they lost the offensive capability soon afterward when Guevara had to divide the force to escort some non-combatants, Debray among them, out of the region. The two guerrilla contingents never made contact again, and the escort group was betrayed by local peasants and wiped out by the Bolivian army in August. The Bolivian army encircled Ché's group and finally captured the wounded guerrilla leader on October 8. Guevara was taken to a nearby town, interrogated, and executed a day later.

BIOGRAPHICAL/CRITICAL SOURCES:

BOOKS

Cabrera, Guillermo, editor, *Memories of Ché,* translated from the Spanish by Jonathan Fried, Lyle Stuart, 1987.

Debray, Regis, *Ché's Guerrilla War,* translated from the French by Rosemary Sheed, Penguin, 1975.

Ebon, Martin, *Ché: The Making of a Legend,* Universe Books, 1969.

Galdea, Hilda, *Ernesto: A Memoir of Ché Guevara,* translated from the Spanish by Carmen Molina and Walter I. Bradbury, Doubleday, 1972.

Gonzáles, Luis J. and Gustavo A. Sánchez Salazar, *The Great Rebel: Ché Guevara in Bolivia,* translated from the Spanish by Helen Lane, Grove, 1969.

Harris, Richard, *Death of a Revolutionary: Ché Guevara's Last Mission,* Norton, 1970.

James, Daniel, *Ché Guevara: A Biography,* Stein & Day, 1969.

Konigsberger, Hans, *Future of Ché Guevara,* Doubleday, 1971.

Lavaretsky, I., *Ernesto Ché Guevara,* Progress Publishers (Moscow), 1976.

Resnick, Marvin D., *Black Beret: The Life and Meaning of Ché Guevara,* Ballantine, 1969.

Rojo, Ricardo, *My Friend Ché,* translated from the Spanish by Julian Casart, Dial, 1968.

Sauvage, Leo, *Ché Guevara: The Failure of a Revolutionary,* translated from the French by Raoul Fremont, Prentice-Hall, 1973.

Sinclair, Andrew, *Ché Guevara,* Viking, 1970.

PERIODICALS

Atlas, January, 1968.
Commonweal, April 10, 1968.
Life, October 6, 1967.
Nation, September 30, 1968, October 17, 1987.
New Republic, November 11, 1967.
New Statesman, October 20, 1967, October 7, 1978.
Newsweek, December 7, 1959, December 21, 1964, June 28, 1965.
New York Times Book Review, November 26, 1961, May 5, 1968, August 25, 1968.
New York Times Magazine, June 19, 1960, April 10, 1966, August 18, 1968.
Ramparts, July 27, 1968, August 24, 1968.
Saturday Review, August 24, 1968.
Time, August 8, 1960.

OBITUARIES:

PERIODICALS

Commonweal, October 27, 1967.
Newsweek, October 23, 1967.
New York Times, October 10, 1967, October 11, 1967.
Time, October 20, 1967.

* * *

GUIDO, Beatriz 1924-1988

PERSONAL: Born December 13, 1924, in Rosaria, Argentina; died March 4, 1988, in Madrid, Spain; daughter of Angel and Berta (Eirin) Guido; married Leopoldo Torres Nilsson (a film director), June 29, 1959. *Education:* Attended University of Buenos Aires and La Sorbonne, Paris, France.

CAREER: Writer. Argentine cultural attache in Spain.

AWARDS, HONORS: Premio Emecé, 1954, for *La casa del ángel.*

WRITINGS:

Regreso a los hilos, El Ateneo, 1947.
Estar en el mundo, El Ateneo, 1950.
La casa del ángel (novel), Emecé, 1954, translation by Joan Coyne MacLean published as *The House of the Angel,* McGraw, 1957.
La caída (novel), Losada, 1956, reprinted, 1981.
Fin de fiesta (novel), Losada, 1958.
La mano en la trampa (short stories), Losada, 1961.
El incendio y las vísperas (novel), Losada, 1964, translation by A. D. Towers published as *End of a Day,* Scribner, 1966.
(Contributor) *Memorias de infancia,* selected by Piri Lugones, J. Alvarez, 1968.
Escándalos y soledades (novel), Losada, 1970.
El ojo único de la ballena (short stories and plays), Merlín, 1971.
Los insomnes (short stories and interviews), Corregidor, 1973.
Una madre, Emecé, 1973.

(With Luis Pico Estrada and husband, Leopoldo Torre Nilsson)
El Pibe Cabeza (drama), Schapire, 1975.
Piedra libre, Galerna, 1976.
¿Quién le teme a mis temas?, Fraterna, 1977.
Todos los cuentos, el cuento, Planeta Argentina, 1979.
La invitación, Losada, 1979.
Apasionados, Losada, 1982.
Soledad y el incendiario, Abril, 1982.
Doce mujeres cuentan, La Campana, 1983.

SIDELIGHTS: Beatriz Guido was a prominent Argentine writer known for her vivid depictions of political and social conflict existing in her native country. Among her most enduring works are *La casa del ángel* (*The House of the Angel*), which offers commentary on corruption within Argentine society by focusing on a wealthy young girl's painful right of passage, and *El incendio y las vísperas* (*End of a Day*), about an aristocratic family at the close of Juan Domingo Perón's regime.

MEDIA ADAPTATIONS: Guido collaborated with her husband, director Leopoldo Torres Nilsson, on film adaptations of several of her works, including *La casa del ángel, La caída, Fin de fiesta,* and *La mano en la trampa.*

BIOGRAPHICAL/CRITICAL SOURCES:

PERIODICALS

New York Times Book Review, June 5, 1966.

* * *

GUILLEN, Jorge   1893-1984

PERSONAL: Surname is pronounced with a hard G, "Gee-lyen"; born January 18, 1893, in Valladolid, Castile, Spain; immigrated to United States, 1938; returned to Spain, 1977; died of pneumonia, February 6, 1984, in Málaga, Spain; son of Julio Guillén Saenz and Esperanza Alvarez Guerra; married Germaine Cahen, October 17, 1921 (deceased, 1947); married Irene Sismondi, October 11, 1961; children: (first marriage) Teresa, Claudio. *Education:* Studied at Maison Perreyve of the French Fathers of the Oratory, Freibourg, Germany; attended University of Madrid and University of Granada.

CAREER: Sorbonne, University of Paris, Paris, France, lecturer, 1917-23; Oxford University, Oxford, England, lecturer, 1929-31; professor at University of Murcia, Murcia, Spain; University of Seville, Seville, Spain, professor of Spanish literature, 1931-38; professor at McGill University, Montreal, Quebec; Wellesley College, Wellesley, Mass., professor, 1940-57. Gave Charles Eliot Norton Lectures in Poetry at Harvard University, 1957 and 1958. Visiting professor at other U.S. and Canadian colleges and universities, and in Mexico, Chile, and Puerto Rico.

AWARDS, HONORS: Miguel de Cervantes Prize, 1972.

WRITINGS:

IN ENGLISH

Cántico, Revista, 1928, 3rd edition published as *Cántico, fe de vida,* Litoral, 1945, recent edition, Editorial Seix Barral, 1984, translation published as *Cántico: A Selection of Spanish Poems,* edited by Norman Thomas di Giovanni, Little Brown, 1963.
Lenguaje y poesía, Revista, 1961, recent edition, Alianza, 1983, translation published as *Language and Poetry: Some Poets of Spain,* Harvard University Press, 1961.
Affirmation: A Bilingual Anthology (selections from *Aire nuestro;* also see below), edited and translated from the Spanish by Julian Palley, University of Oklahoma Press, 1968.

Guillén on Guillén: Poetry and the Poet, translated by Reginald Gibbons and Anthony L. Geist, Princeton University Press, 1979.

IN SPANISH; POETRY

Tercer cántico, limited edition, Ediciones "La Poesía Sorprendida," 1944.
El encanto de las serenas, Gráfica Panamericana, 1953.
El huerto de Melibea, Insula, 1954, recent edition, Editorial Arte y Literatura (Havana), 1982.
Maremagnum (also see below), Editorial Sudamericana, 1957.
Lugar de Lázaro, limited edition, Daido, 1957.
Clamor (contains *Maremagnum, Que van a dar en a mar,* and *A la altura de las circunstancias;* also see below), Editorial Sudamericana, 1957.
Viviendo y otros poemas, Editorial Seix Barral, 1958.
Poemas de Castilla (title means "Poems From Castile"), [Santiago, Chile], 1960.
Que van a dar en la mar (also published in *Clamor* [also see above]), Editorial Sudamericana, 1960.
Poesías (title means "Poetry"), Ediciones Mito, 1960.
Relatos, Librería Anticuaria el Guadalhorce, 1960.
Historia natural, Ediciones de los Papeles de son Armedans, 1960.
(Author of poem) Francesco Sabadell López, *Flores,* [Valladolid, Spain], 1961.
Versos (title means "Poems"), edited by Miguel Pizarro, Ediciones Meridiano, 1961.
Las tentaciones de Antonio, Santander Hermanos, 1962.
Según las horas, Editorial Universitaria, 1962.
A la altura de las circunstancias, Editorial Sudamericana, 1963 (also see below).
Clamor [and] *A la altura de las circunstancias* (both also published separately; also see above), Editorial Sudamericana, 1963.
Tréboles, Publicaciones la Isla de los Ratones, 1964.
Selección de poemas (title means "Selection of Poems"), Gredos, 1965, enlarged edition, c. 1970.
Guirnalda civil, Halty Ferguson, 1970.
Antología (title means "Anthology"), edited by José Manuel Blecna, Anaya, 1970.
Obra poética, introduction by Joaquín Casalduero, Alianza, 1970, recent edition, Alianza, 1982.
Y otros poemas (title means "And Other Poems"), Muchnik Editores, 1973.
Al margen, Visor, 1974.
Convivencia, introduction by Mario Hernández, Turner, 1975.
Antología: Aire nuestro (contains *Cántico, Clamor,* and *Homenaje*), edited by Manuel Mantero, Plaza y Janés, 1975, published in two volumes, 1977.
Plaza mayor: Antología civil, introduction by Francisco Abad Nebot, Taurus, 1977.
Mientras el aire es nuestro (anthology), edited by Philip W. Silver, Ediciones Cátedra (Madrid), 1978.
Poesía amorosa: 1919-1972, selection and introduction by Anne-Marie Couland, Cupsa (Madrid), 1978.
Serie castellana, introduction by Manuel Alvar, Caballo Griego para la Poesía (Madrid), 1978.
Algunos poemas, Institución Cultural de Cantabria, 1981.
Antología del mar, Librería Agora (Málaga), 1981.
La expresión, Sociedad de Cultura Valle-Inclán, 1981.
Poemas malagueños, Servicio de Publicaciones de la Diputación Provincial de Málaga, 1983.

Jorge Guillén para niños (for children), edited by Antonio A. Gómez Yebra, illustrations by John Rosenfeldt, Ediciones de la Torre, 1984.

Sonetos completos, A. Ubago (Granada), 1988.

Contributor of poetry to Ortega y Gasset's *Revista de Occidente.*

OTHER

Federico en persona: Semblanza y epistolario, Emece, 1959.

En torno a Gabriel Miró, breve epistolario (contains "Gabriel Miró," "Amistad y correspondencia," and "Cartas"), Ediciones de Arte y Bibliofilia, c. 1969.

El argumento de la obra (essays; contains "Una generación," "El argumento de la obra," and "Poesía integral"), Libres de Sinera, 1969, recent edition, Taurus, 1985.

(Editor) Federico García Lorca, *Obras completas* (title means "Complete Works"), Aguilar, 1969, recent edition, 1986.

La poética de Becquer, Hispanic Institute (New York, N.Y.), 1973.

(With others) *Azaña,* edited by Vicente-Alberto Sertrano and José María San Luciano, Edascal (Madrid), 1980.

Translator of *Le Cimetiere marin* by Paul Valery.

SIDELIGHTS: Before his death at the age of ninety-one, Jorge Guillén was called "beyond dispute the greatest living Spanish poet" by Jorge Luis Borges. Willis Barnstone went on to call him "one of the . . . masters of twentieth-century poetry, along with Elytis, Aleixandre, Borges, Voznesensky, Montate." Although Guillén earned a prominent position in Spanish letters and resided in the United States for many years, he is not yet widely known in the English-speaking world.

Born in Valladolid, Spain, Guillén studied in Freibourg, Germany, and at universities in Madrid and Grenada, Spain, before beginning a teaching career at the Sorbonne. He began writing in 1919 and later became associated with the "Generation of 1927," a group of Spanish poets who employed new subjects and words, untraditional rhyme and meter, strong metaphor, and pure aestheticism in their poetry. Like many Spanish artists of his time, Guillén opposed Spanish leader Generalissimo Franco's regime, and the writer exiled himself to the United States after the Spanish Civil War. He became a professor at Wellesley College, where he taught from 1941 until his retirement in 1957. He also taught at McGill, Harvard, Princeton, and Yale universities. In 1972 the government of Madrid awarded Guillén the first Miguel de Cervantes Prize, often considered the most prestigious Hispanic literary honor. This recognition marked Spain's more receptive attitude toward its expatriate artists, and the poet returned to his homeland in 1977, two years after Franco's death. Guillén died seven years later in Málaga, Spain.

Unlike many contemporary Spanish poets who voice what Miller Williams termed a "sweet pessimism," Guillén was widely praised for expressing an intense *joie de vivre* in his lyric poetry. In this regard, his style is reminiscent of classic poets of the sixteenth century: Luis de León, San Juan de la Cruz, and Luis de Góngora y Argote. Guillén's spontaneous enjoyment of each moment is expressed in the present tense, in short lines of nouns and verbs (with an emphasis on the former) ending in exclamation points.

Guillén devoted forty-seven years of work to *Antología: Aire nuestro,* which combines in a single volume the previously published *Cántico, Clamor,* and *Homenaje.* In this collection Guillén not only emphasizes the joyful aspects of life, but acknowledges the darker sides of existence. He writes of the personal pain caused by Spain's civil war and the discovery that violence is also present in the United States. Nevertheless, in all the poems, a *Times Literary Supplement* critic pointed out, Guillén's "language is purified to the point of being univocal."

Only a small representation of Guillén's poetry has been translated into English. "The very purity and exactitude of Guillén's language makes him a difficult poet to translate," noted the *Times Literary Supplement.* But Barnstone remarked that, "despite other reviews to the contrary, Guillén's poetry translates admirably well into other languages."

BIOGRAPHICAL/CRITICAL SOURCES:

BOOKS

Contemporary Literary Criticism, Volume 11, Gale, 1979.

Guillén, Jorge, *Guillén on Guillén: Poetry and the Poet,* translated by Reginald Gibbons and Anthony L. Geist, Princeton University Press, 1979.

Peak, Frances Avery, *The Poetry of Jorge Guillén,* [Princeton, N.J.], 1942.

Trend, J. B., *Jorge Guillén,* [Cambridge, Mass.], 1952.

PERIODICALS

Books Abroad, winter, 1968.
Commonweal, September 24, 1965.
Hispania, September, 1965.
Modern Language Journal, November, 1970.
New Republic, April 9, 1977.
New Statesman, April 30, 1965.
New York Times Book Review, June 20, 1965, August 18, 1968, September 12, 1968, July 3, 1977.
Poetry, October, 1967.
Times Literary Supplement, April 22, 1965, September 12, 1968.
Virginia Quarterly Review, Volume 41, autumn, 1965.

OBITUARIES:

PERIODICALS

Chicago Tribune, February 9, 1984.
Newsweek, February 20, 1984.
New York Times, February 11, 1984.
Times (London), February 8, 1984.
Washington Post, February 8, 1984.

*   *   *

GUILLEN (Y BATISTA), Nicolás (Cristobal) 1902-1989

PERSONAL: Surname pronounced "Gee-yane," with a hard *g* as in geese; born July 10, 1902, in Camagüey, Cuba; died after a long illness, July 16, 1989, in Havana, Cuba; son of Nicolás (a silversmith, newspaper editor, and politician) and Argelia (Batista) Guillén. *Education:* Attended University of Havana, 1920-21.

ADDRESSES: Home—Calle O, 22o, No. 2, Edificio Someillán, Vedado, Havana, Cuba. *Office*—Unión Nacional de Escritores y Artistas Cubanos, Calle 17, No. 351, Vedado, Havana, Cuba.

CAREER: Poet, beginning 1922. Founder and editor of *Lis* literary magazine in the early 1920s; contributor to Cuban newspapers and magazines, including *Diario de la Marina,* c. 1922-37; war correspondent in Spain for *Mediodía* magazine, 1937-38; lecturer and correspondent in Latin America and Europe in the 1940s and 1950s; served as editor in chief of *La Gaceta de Cuba* (official cultural publication of Cuban National Union of Writers and Artists). Mayoral candidate for Camagüey, 1940; senatorial candidate, La Habana Province, 1948; Ambassador of Cuba.

MEMBER: Unión Nacional de Escritores y Artistas Cubanos (president, beginning 1961), Society of Afro-Cuban Studies (founder).

AWARDS, HONORS: Stalin Prize and Lenin Peace Prize, both from the Soviet Union, 1953 and 1954; named National Poet of Cuba by Fidel Castro, 1961; honorary doctorate, 1977; Cuban Order of José Martí from the Republic of Cuba, 1981; Order of Merit from the Republic of Haiti; Order of Cyril and Methodius (first class) from the People's Republic of Bulgaria.

WRITINGS:

POEMS

Motivos de son (title means "Motifs of Sound"; also see below), 1930, special fiftieth anniversary edition, with music by Amadeo Roldan, Editorial Letras Cubanas, 1980.

Sóngoro cosongo (includes *Motivos de son* plus eight new poems), 1931, published as *Sóngoro cosongo: Poemas mulatos,* Presencia Latinoamericana, 1981.

West Indies Ltd.: Poemas, Imprenta Ucar, García, 1934.

Cantos para soldados y sones para turistas (title means "Songs for Soldiers and Sones for Tourists"), prologue by Juan Marinello, Editorial Masas, 1937, reprinted, Premiá Editora, 1985, published as *El son entero: Cantos para soldados y sones para turistas,* Editorial Losada, 1952.

España: Poema en cuatro angustias y una esperanza (title means "Spain: A Poem in Four Anguishes and a Hope"; also see below), Editorial México Nuevo, 1937.

Sóngoro cosongo y otros poemas de Nicolás Guillén, La Verónica, 1942.

El son entero: Suma poética, 1929-1946 (title means "The Entire Son: Poetic Summary"; with a letter by Miguel de Unamuno and musical notation by various composers; includes *Motivos de son, Sóngoro cosongo, West Indies Ltd., Cantos para soldados y sones para turistas,* and *España*), Editorial Pleamar, 1947, Premiá Editora, 1982.

La paloma de vuelo popular (title means "The Dove of Popular Flight"), 1958, also published, in a single volume, with *Elegías* (title means "Elegies", also see below), Editorial Losada, 1959.

Sus mejores poemas, Organización Continental de los Festivales del Libro, 1959.

¿Puedes? (title means "Can You?"; with drawings by the author), Librería La Tertulia, 1961.

Elegía a Jesús Menéndez, Imprenta Nacional de Cuba, 1962, reprinted, Editorial Letras Cubanos, 1978.

La rueda dentada (title means "The Serrated Wheel"), UNEAC (Unión Nacional de Escritores y Artistas Cubanos), 1962.

Tengo (title means "I Have"), prologue by José Antonio Portuondo, Editora del Consejo Nacional de Universidades, 1964, translation by Richard J. Carr published under same title, Broadside Press, 1974.

Poemas de amor (title means "Love Poems"), Ediciones La Tertulia, 1964.

Nadie (title means "Nobody"), Sol y Piedra, 1966.

El gran zoo, Instituto del Libro, 1967, translation by Robert Márquez published as *¡Patria o muerte! The Great Zoo and Other Poems,* Monthly Review Press, 1972.

El diario que a diario (title means "The Daily Newspaper"), UNEAC, 1972.

Poemas manuables, UNEAC, 1975.

El corazón con que vivo (title means "The Heart With Which I Live"), UNEAC, 1975.

Por qué imperialismo?: Poemas (title means "Why Imperialism?: Poems"), Ediciones Calarca, 1976.

Elegías, edited by José Mártinez Matos, illustrations by Dario Mora, UNEAC, 1977.

Por el Mar de las Antillas anda un barco de papel: Poemas para niños mayores de edad (title means "Going through the Antilles Sea in a Boat of Paper: Poems for Older Children"), illustrations by Rapi Diego, UNEAC, 1978.

Coplas de Juan Descalzo (title means "The Ballad of John Barefoot"), Editorial Letras Cubanas, 1979.

Música de camara (title means "Chamber Music"), UNEAC, 1979.

Sputnik 57, [Havana, Cuba], 1980.

Martín Morúa Delgado, ¿quién fue—?, UNEAC, 1984.

(Contributor) Elvio Romero, editor, *Despiertan las fogatas: 1950-52,* Alcándara, 1986.

Also author of *Poemas para el Che* (title means "Poems for Che"), *Buenos Dias, Fidel,* for Gráfica Horizonte.

POETRY COLLECTIONS

Cuba Libre, translated from Spanish by Langston Hughes and Ben Frederic Carruthers, illustrations by Gar Gilbert, Andersón & Ritchie, 1948.

Sóngoro cosongo, Motivos de son, West Indies Ltd., España: Poema en cuatro angustias y una esperanza, Editorial Losada, 1952.

Nicolás Guillén: Sus mejores poemas, Organización de los Festivales del Libro, 1959.

Los mejores versos de Nicolás Guillén, Editorial Nuestra América, 1961.

Antología mayor: El son entero y otros poemas, UNEAC, 1964.

Antología clave, prologue by Luis Inigo Madrigal, Editorial Nascimento, 1971.

Man-Making Words: Selected Poems of Nicolás Guillén, bilingual edition translated from the Spanish by Márquez and David Arthur McMurray, University of Massachusetts Press, 1972.

Cuba, amor y revolución: Poemas, Editorial Causachun, 1972.

Obra poética, 1920-1972 (two volumes), edited by Angel Augier with illustrations by the author, Editorial de Arte y Literatura, 1974.

Latinamericasón, Quatro Editores, 1974.

Nueva antología mayor, edited by Augier, Editorial Letras Cubanas, 1979.

Páginas vueltas: Selección de poemas y aflantes autobiográficos (title means "Turned Pages: Selected Poems and Autobiographical Notes"), Grupo Editor de Buenos Aires, 1980.

Páginas vueltas: Memorias, UNEAC, 1982.

Las grandes elegías y otros poemas, Humanities, 1984.

The Daily Daily, translated by Vera Kutzinski, University of California Press, 1989.

Also author of *Poesías completas,* 1973.

OTHER

Claudio José Domingo Brindis de Salas, el rey de las octavas (title means "Claudio José Domingo Brindis de Salas, King of the Octaves"; prose), Municipio de La Habana, 1935.

Prosa de prisa, crónicas (title means "Hasty Prose, Chronicles"; selection of journalistic articles published from 1938 to 1961), Universidad Central de las Villas, 1962, expanded edition published as *Prosa de prisa, 1929-1972* (three volumes), edited with introduction by Augier, Editorial Arte y Literatura, 1975.

El libro de las décimas, UNEAC, 1980.

El libro de los sones, Editorial Letras Cubanas, 1982.

Sol de domingo, UNEAC, 1982.

Cronista en tres épocas (title means "Journalist in Three Epochs"; selection of journalistic articles), edited by María Julia Guerra Avila and Pedro Rodríguez Gutiérrez, Editorial Política, 1984.

Works represented in anthologies, including *Some Modern Cuban Poems by Nicolás Guillén and Others,* translated from the Spanish by Manish Handy, Satyabrata Pal, 1968. *Tengo* was recorded in the 1970s and released by Consejo Nacional de Cultura.

SIDELIGHTS: Nicolás Guillén, considered a master of the "Afro-Cuban" style, also known as *Poesía negrista,* was one of twentieth-century Cuba's greatest poets. He was born in the year that Cuba achieved its independence, and his work occupied a broad spectrum, ranging from *modernista* poems to folklore, social protest, revolutionary, and experimentalist poems. Robert Márquez in the introduction to *¡Patria o muerte! The Great Zoo and Other Poems* claims that Guillén represented "the very best in Hispanic poetry and [was] at the same time the undisputed leader of an important trend in contemporary Latin American letters."

Guillén was a mulatto from the provincial middle class and initially studied law, but like many young Cubans of the time, he was forced by economic hardship to change his career to newspaper journalism. A 1930 visit to Cuba by the black American poet Langston Hughes, a leading figure in the black cultural movement known as the Harlem Renaissance, inspired Guillén to write and publish his first verse collection, *Motivos de son* ("Motifs of Sound"). A group of eight poems structured rhythmically like the son—a popular Cuban arrangement containing strong African elements and affected by dance, ballads, song rhythms, and varying speech patterns—*Motivos de son* drew on a new international interest in primitive art and African culture and became identified with the Afro-Caribbean movement in Hispanic poetry that had begun in the mid-1920s. According to Márquez, "Since his first widely acclaimed *Motivos de son* . . . [Guillén] has been regarded as the major exponent of Black poetry in the Spanish-speaking world."

Like earlier white Afro-Caribbean poets in Cuba and Puerto Rico, Guillén treated local lower-class black life as his major theme and combined onomatopoeia and African rhythms as major stylistic devices; Guillén, though, went further in both style and substance than his predecessors, who tended toward somewhat stereotypical depictions of a joyful, sensual, happy-go-lucky folk. Guillén instead wrote "from within"—as G. R. Coulthard noted in *Race and Colour in Caribbean Literature*—and subtly gave poetic voice to the lives of poverty and pathos behind the picturesque facade of Havana's black slum dwellers. Guillén was also credited with capturing the genuine dialect and speech patterns of Cuban blacks, which he blended with Yoruba African words to create a unique language that relied as much on sound and rhythm as on word sense for its meaning. But some critics, including those within the black community, disapproved of the images in *Motivos de son*. Richard L. Jackson recounted in *Black Writers in Latin America* that the publication of *Motivos de son* "was upsetting, unsettling and controversial, partly because [the poems] broke momentarily with traditional Spanish verse expression and partly because they dealt with authentic black characters, but largely because they brought to literature a new and genuine black concern, perspective, and poetic voice, which even some blacks misunderstood."

Guillén further refined his Afro-Cuban poetry in *Sóngoro cosongo,* a 1931 verse collection that quickly earned him a worldwide reputation and became widely regarded as his masterwork. Published with Guillén's lottery winnings that year, this work evinced a deeper social consciousness and still bolder style in seeking to express the tragedy, passion, and vigor of black life in Cuba. The poet moved from an implicit criticism of slum life to direct denunciations of racism and an affirmation of the roles of black men and women in building Cuban and American culture and society. Guillén sought to create a "mulatto poetry" that would reflect Cuba's true history and racial composition. Stylistically, his occasional use of the ballad form and reliance on naive, "nonsensical" imagery in *Sóngoro cosongo* showed the influence of the internationally acclaimed Spanish poet Federico García Lorca, whom Guillén had met in Cuba. Guillén's extraordinary synthesis of traditional Spanish metric forms with Afro-Cuban words, rhythms, and folkloric symbols uniquely captures the cultural flavor of the Spanish-speaking Caribbean, critics have noted.

Some poems in *Sóngoro cosongo* relied almost entirely on onomatopoeic effects and rhythm, becoming, in a sense, abstract word-paintings with no direct representational value at all—the title itself had no meaning other than its rhythmic and symbolic suggestions. Though seemingly spontaneous, these verses were in fact carefully crafted, with rigorous attention to rhyme, meter, and tonal nuances. Often recited publicly to a drum accompaniment, Guillén's Afro-Cuban verses have been set to music by the Spanish composer Xavier Montsalvatge and sung by the American mezzo-soprano Marilyn Horne.

The current of social protest running through *Sóngoro cosongo* turned deeper and swifter in *West Indies Ltd.,* published just after the 1933 revolution that deposed Cuban dictator Antonio Machado. The volume was "widely hailed as his first volume of social (as opposed to racial) protest poetry," described Jackson. In verse that was by turns satirical and bitter, Guillén depicted the often cruel and exploitative history of slavery, colonialism, and imperialism in the Antilles islands of the West Indies. In 1936 Guillén was imprisoned by the Fulgencio Batista regime, but he was subsequently released.

The poet's commitment to social change grew when he traveled to Spain in 1937 to cover the civil war for *Mediodía* magazine and participate in the anti-fascist Second International Congress of Writers for the Defense of Culture. That year he joined the Cuban Communist party (then called Popular Socialist) and wrote a long, elegiac ode to the Spanish Republic titled *España: Poema en cuatro angustias y una esperanza* ("Spain: A Poem in Four Anguishes and a Hope") that voiced his hope for humanity's communist future. Guillén also devoted most of his 1937 verse collection, *Cantos para soldados y sones para turistas* ("Songs for Soldiers and Sones for Tourists"), to social and political themes.

Guillén spent much of the next two decades in exile from Batista's regime traveling around Europe and Latin America as a lecturer and correspondent for several Cuban journals. In 1962 he published a selection of these articles under the title *Prosa de prisa* ("Hasty Prose"). Guillén's poetic output during these years was somewhat reduced, although he published a major collection titled *El son entero* ("The Entire Son") in 1947 and his first English language selection, *Cuba Libre* (co-edited and translated by Langston Hughes), that following year. Denied permission to return to Cuba by the Batista dictatorship in the 1950s, Guillén spent several years in unhappy exile in Paris, France, where he wrote *La paloma de vuelo popular* ("The Dove of Popular

Flight") and *Elegías* ("Elegies"), published together in one volume in 1958. These two works complemented each other thematically and stylistically. The first consisted mainly of broadly political—and often witty and ironical—protest poems against the Cuban dictatorship and American imperialism, while *Elegías* mourned the loss of friends and other victims of political repression in somber, lyrical tones.

The triumph of the Cuban revolution in early 1959 immediately brought Guillén back to his homeland, where he enthusiastically embraced the revolutionary cause. Already recognized as the country's greatest living poet, Guillén readily took on the role of poet laureate of the revolution. His 1964 verse collection *Tengo* ("I Have") was a joyful celebration of the revolution that read somewhat like a historical epic; the work praised the insurgent heroes, depicted major battles against Batista, showed the dictator's flight, and illustrated the Cuban victory over the American backed invasion at the Bay of Pigs. As the title suggests, Guillén also explored the new feelings of empowerment, possession, and comradeship that the revolution inspired in many poor Cubans.

The theme of social liberation was also present in Guillén's 1967 collection, *El gran zoo*. Hailed as one of Guillén's outstanding later works, *El gran zoo* marked a major stylistic shift for a poet usually identified with the Afro-Cuban style. While still showing a crystalline attention to craft, these poems relied less on rhyme and strict meter than Guillén's past work and approached free verse with spare wording and fractured images. The volume was structured thematically as a visit to a metaphorical zoo, where some of the world's curious and beautiful social, natural, and metaphysical phenomena were cataloged in individual poems. Guillén's usually direct language was more allusive and enigmatic here, and his subjects ranged from critical jabs at imperialism to taut musings on love, the forces of nature, and the ineffable mystery of being. *University of Toronto Quarterly* contributor Keith Ellis saw the work as a "blending of old forms and of revolutionary political content to achieve a new kind of poetry with no barriers between it and the people."

"Although a poet of limited resources and relatively small output, Guillén has excelled in adapting the rhythms of Cuban popular speech and Afro-Cuban music in verse that nonetheless, for all its Caribbean charm, remains essentially in the traditional Spanish mold," wrote Emir Rodríguez Monegal in *The Borzoi Anthology of Latin American Literature*. And Jackson concluded that "despite Guillén's ever-widening circle of concerns that he has pursued throughout his long career, he has never left the black man behind or out of his poetry." Finally, Márquez felt that Guillén has been "the poet of a people and his principle concern has been the creation of a poetry with a distinctively Cuban flavor, one which reflects—and helps consolidate—the Cuban national identity."

BIOGRAPHICAL/CRITICAL SOURCES:

BOOKS

Augier, Angel, *Nicolás Guillén: Notas para un estudio biográfico-crítico* (two volumes), Universidad de las Villas, 1963-64.
Coulthard, G. R., *Race and Colour in Caribbean Literature*, Oxford University Press, 1962.
Ellis, Keith, *Cuba's Nicolás Guillén: Poetry and Ideology*, University of Toronto Press, 1983.
Guillén, Nicolás, *¡Patria o muerte! The Great Zoo and Other Poems*, translated by Robert Márquez, Monthly Review Press, 1972.
Guillén, Nicolás, *Paginas vueltas: Memorias*, UNEAC, 1982.
Jackson, Richard L., *Black Writers in Latin America*, University of New Mexico Press, 1979.
Martínez Estrada, Ezequiel, *La poesía de Nicolás Guillén*, Calicanto Editorial, c. 1977.
Rodríguez, Monegal, Emir, *The Borzoi Anthology of Latin American Literature*, Volume II: *The Twentieth Century—from Borges and Paz to Guimaraes Rosa and Donoso*, Knopf, 1977.
Sardinha, Dennis, *The Poetry of Nicolás Guillén: An Introduction*, New Beacon, 1976.

PERIODICALS

Black Scholar, July/August, 1985.
Hispania, October 25, 1942.
Latin America Research Review, Volume 17, number 1, 1982.
Opportunity, January, 1946.
University of Toronto Quarterly, fall, 1975.

OBITUARIES:

PERIODICALS

Chicago Tribune, July 18, 1989.
Detroit Free Press, July 18, 1989.
Los Angeles Times, July 18, 1989.
New York Times, July 18, 1989.

*   *   *

GÜIRALDES, Ricardo (Guillermo)   1886-1927

PERSONAL: Born in Buenos Aires, Argentina, February 13, 1886; died of Hodgkin's disease in Paris, France, October 8, 1927; son of Manuel Güiraldes (ranchowner); married Adelina del Carril, 1913. *Education:* Attended college courses in architecture and law.

CAREER: Writer. Co-founder of Editorial Proa (publishing house), Buenos Aires, Argentina.

AWARDS, HONORS: Gran Premio Nacional de la Literatura (Argentina) for *Don Segundo Sombra*.

WRITINGS:

El cencerro de cristal (title means "The Crystal Cowbell"; prose and poetry), 1915, reprinted, Losada (Buenos Aires), 1952.
Cuentos de muerte y de sangre (title means "Stories of Death and Blood"; short stories; also see below), 1915, reprinted, Losada, 1958.
Raucho: Momentos de una juventud contemporánea (title means "Raucho: Moments in a the Life of a Contemporary Youth"; novel), 1917, Centro Editor de América Latina (Buenos Aires), 1968.
Rosaura (novel; also see below), 1922, reprinted with prologue by Victoria Ocampo, Sudamericana (Buenos Aires), 1960.
Xaimaca (title means "Jamaica"; novel written as prose poem), 1923, reprinted, Losada, 1967.
Don Segundo Sombra (novel), Proa (Buenos Aires), 1926, reprinted with preliminary note by wife, Adelina del Carril, Losada, 1940, reprinted, G. Kraft (Buenos Aires), 1960, translation by Harriet de Onis of original Spanish edition published as *Don Segundo Sombra: Shadows on the Pampas*, introduction by Waldo Frank, Farrar & Rinehart, 1935, abridged Spanish edition edited by Ethel W. Plimpton and María T. Fernández published under original title, Holt, 1945.
Poemas místicos (title means "Mystical Poems"), 1928, reprinted, Ricardo Güiraldes, 1969.

Poemas solitarios (title means "Solitary Poems"), edited by del Carril, Colón, 1928, reprinted, Ricardo Güiraldes, 1970.

Seis relatos con un poema de Alfonso Reyes y una fotografía (title means "Six Stories with a Poem by Alfonso Reyes and a Photograph"), Proa, 1929, reprinted, Perrot (Buenos Aires), 1957.

El sendero: Notas sobre mi evolución espiritualista en vista de un futuro (title means "The Path: Notes on My Sprititual Evolution in Light of the Future"), Maestricht (The Netherlands), 1932, reprinted, Ricardo Güiraldes, 1977.

Cuentos de muerte y de sangre, seguidos de Aventuras grotescas y una trilogía cristiana (title means "Stories of Death and Blood followed by Grotesque Adventures and a Christian Trilogy"), Espasa-Calpe (Madrid), 1933, reprinted, Losada, 1978.

Rosaura (novela corta) y siete cuentos (title means "Rosaura (Short Novel) and Seven Stories"), Losada, 1952.

Obras completas (title means "Complete Works"), Emecé, 1962.

Croquis, dibujos y poema de Ricardo Güiraldes: Obra inédita (title means "Sketches, Drawings and Poem by Ricardo Güiraldes: Unedited Works"), edited by del Carril, Ricardo Güiraldes (Buenos Aires), 1967.

El libro bravo, Ricardo Güiraldes, 1970.

Also author of *Pampa,* 1954. Contributor of short stories in English translation to numerous anthologies, including *Tales from the Argentine,* 1930, *The Golden Land,* edited by de Onis, 1948, and *Short Stories of Latin America,* edited by A. Torres-Ríoseco, 1963. Founding editor, with Jorge Luis Borges and Pablo Rojas Paz, of *Proa* (Buenos Aires literary review), 1924-25.

SIDELIGHTS: "He was a wealthy man, son of a ranchowner, and knew how to combine his enthusiasm for contemporary French and German literature with an authentic if slightly exalted love for his native country." This was how Argentine poet, short story writer, and novelist Ricardo Güiraldes was described by Emir Rodríguez Monegal in his biography of another Argentine author entitled *Jorge Luis Borges: A Literary Biography.* Borges was both Güiraldes's friend and his collaborator on the Buenos Aires literary review *Proa* but their friendship and collaboration came to an early end with Güiraldes's premature death at age forty-one. Shortly before he died, Güiraldes published what many consider his crowning achievement, *Don Segundo Sombra,* a novel that, according to Rodríguez Monegal's assessment, "was to make [Güiraldes] the most famous Argentine novelist of the first half of the century."

Güiraldes, like Borges and many of Argentina's most important authors of the early years of the twentieth century, felt a strong attraction for the new forms of literature being introduced in Europe at the time, but refused to abandon Argentine themes. Güiraldes was keenly aware of European ways and literature, having been taken on his first trip abroad when he was only two and having spoken fluent French and German along with his native Spanish since early childhood. In his early twenties, he took a two-year trip around the world, pausing to live in Europe for a while (Güiraldes is credited with introducing the Argentine tango to Parisian society). In between trips to Europe, Güiraldes spent most of his time on the family ranch, La Porteña, located in the province of Buenos Aires.

Both European and Argentine influences were to be important throughout Güiraldes's short literary career. In 1915, his first two books were published: *El cencerro de cristal* (title means "The Glass Cowbell") and *Cuentos de muerte y sangre* (title means "Tales of Death and Blood"). Each of the two works seemed to represent one side in the dual nature of Güiraldes's

background: the former, a book of poetry, showed a strong European influence, especially that of French symbolist poet Jules Laforgue; the latter was a collection of short stories of Argentine farm life. The same dichotomy can be seen unified in *Don Segundo Sombra:* although it is essentially a story of Argentine life (a fact that Güiraldes emphasized by using the rustic dialect of the gauchos to tell the story), it is written employing the techniques, including metaphors and synesthesia, Güiraldes learned from his avid reading of European literature.

In his *Spanish-American Literature: A History* Enrique Anderson-Imbert commented on how Güiraldes's choice of images converted the novel from being an expression of Argentine nationalism into an important work of Latin American fiction: "Even the most realistic details are doubly artistic: because they are chosen for their starkness and because of their evocative effect. Güiraldes combined the language spoken from birth by the Creoles with the language of the Creolist educated in European impressionism, expressionism, and ultraism. In spite of his realist dialogs, his folklore, his rural comparisons, his pampa dialect of cowhands and cattlemen, *Don Segundo Sombra* is an artistic novel." Ethel W. Plimpton and María T. Fernández explained in the introductory notes to their edition of *Don Segundo Sombra* some of the evocative power of the Argentine's prose, calling the book "one of the finest examples of how rudimentary and primitive literary material can be transformed in the hands of a conscious artist. In it the two planes of crude yet beautiful reality and of poetic fancy intersect in a way that inevitably recalls *Don Quijote.*"

Along with comparisons to Cervantes's seventeen-century masterpiece, *Don Segundo Sombra* has also been likened to a classic of U.S. literature, Mark Twain's *The Adventures of Huckleberry Finn.* In Waldo Frank's introduction to the English translation of Güiraldes's novel, the critic notes that both Güiraldes's and Twain's books concern the adventures of a young boy accompanied only by an older man from whom he learns a great deal. Frank also sees both books as dealing with the passing away of an era. *Don Segundo Sombra* is the tale of Fabio Cáceres, a boy who runs away from the Buenos Aires home of his aunts to live with a gaucho named Don Segundo Sombra. Fabio recounts episodes in their five years together. The adventures cease when the boy discovers he is the illegitimate son of a wealthy landowner who has died and left him his estate. At this point, no longer needed, Don Segundo Sombra says good-bye to his friend.

The gaucho life Güiraldes described in the book was much like that of the American cowboy of the Old West. Gauchos were horsemen, many of mixed Spanish and Indian blood, who lived on the pampas, the fertile grassy plains that make up the middle-section of Argentina, and made their living off the cattle they raised. Through Cáceres's commentary on gaucho life, Güiraldes is able to include a myriad of colorful details—including cockfights, dances, fairs, and knife duels—in his novel. As the *Don Segundo Sombra* was being published, the gauchos' picturesque form of life was starting to change, brought on by the laying of railroad tracks and the fencing of pasture land. Written in highly lyrical prose, the book became an evocation of the disappearing gaucho lifestyle. The reasons for the novel's popularity, according to Anderson-Imbert "were factors other than literary merits . . ., such as the nationalist feelings of the reader, the surprise of finding, in gaucho clothes, a metaphoric language fashionable in postwar literature, and a conception of the novel, also fashionable in those years, according to which the poetic tone was more important than the action and the characterization."

MEDIA ADAPTATIONS: Don Segundo Sombra was adapted by Augusto Roa Bastos for a film of the same title, 1968.

BIOGRAPHICAL/CRITICAL SOURCES:

BOOKS

Anderson-Imbert, Enrique, *Spanish-American Literature: A History,* Volume 2: *1910-1963,* 2nd edition revised and updated by Elaine Malley, Wayne State University Press, 1969.

Güiraldes, Ricardo, *Don Segundo Sombra: Shadows on the Pampas,* translation by Harriet de Onis, Farrar & Rinehart, 1935.

Plimpton, Ethel W. and María T. Fernández, editors, Ricardo Güiraldes, *Don Segundo Sombra,* Holt, 1945.

Rodríguez Monegal, Emir, *Jorge Luis Borges: A Literary Biography,* Dutton, 1978.

—*Sketch by Marian Gonsior*

*   *   *

GUTIERREZ, Gustavo
   See GUTIERREZ MERINO, Gustavo

*   *   *

GUTIERREZ M., Gustavo
   See GUTIERREZ MERINO, Gustavo

*   *   *

GUTIERREZ MERINO, Gustavo   1928-
   (Gustavo Gutiérrez, Gustavo Gutiérrez M.)

PERSONAL: Born June 8, 1928, in Lima, Peru; son of Gustavo O. and Raquel (Diaz) Gutiérrez Merino. *Education:* Received M.A. from University of Louvain; received M.Th. from Institut Catholique de Lyon.

ADDRESSES: Home—Inca 245, Lima, Peru. *Office*—Bentin 765, Lima, Peru.

CAREER: Ordained Roman Catholic priest; parish priest in Cristo Redentor, Peru; professor of theology at Universidad Católica de Lima, Lima, Peru; director of Instituto Bartolomé de las Casas; writer. Visiting professor at Union Theological Seminary, New York, N.Y.

AWARDS, HONORS: D.Th. from University of Nymegen.

WRITINGS:

La pastoral de la iglesia de América Latina, Centro de Estudios y Publicaciones (Lima, Peru), 1969.

(Under name Gustavo Gutiérrez M.) *Hacia una teología de la liberación* (title means "Toward a Theology of Liberation"), Indo-American Press Service (Bogotá, Colombia), 1971.

UNDER NAME GUSTAVO GUTIERREZ

Teología de la liberación prospectivos, Centro de Estudios y Publicaciones, 1971, translation by Caridad Inda and John Eagleson published as *A Theology of Liberation: History, Politics, and Salvation,* Orbis Books, 1973.

¿Religión, instrumento de liberación? (title means "Religion: Instrument of Liberation?"), Ediciones Marova (Madrid), 1973.

(Editor with Claude Geffre) *The Mystical and Political Dimension of the Christian Faith,* Herder & Herder, 1974.

Praxis of Liberation and Christian Faith, Mexican American Culture Center (San Antonio), 1974, revised edition, 1976.

La nueva frontera de la teología en América Latina (title means "The New Frontier of Theology in Latin America"), Sigueme (Salamanca, Mexico), 1977.

(With M. Richard Shaull) *Liberation and Change* (lectures and essays) edited with introduction by Ronald H. Stone, John Knox, 1977.

Teología desde el reverso de la historia, Centro de Estudios y Publicaciones, 1977.

Los pobres y la liberación en puebla, Indo-American Press Service, 1979.

(Editor with Guiseppe Alberigo) *Where Does the Church Stand?,* Seabury Press, 1981.

El Dios de la vida (Title means "The God of Life"), Centro de Estudios y Publicaciones, 1982.

(With others) *Sobre el trabajo humano: Comentarios a la encíclica "laborem exercens,"* Centro de Estudios y Publicaciones, 1982.

Entre las calandrias, published with Pedro Trigo's *Arguedas, mito, historia y religión,* Centro de Estudios y Publicaciones, 1982.

La fuerza histórica de los pobres, Centro de Estudios y Publicaciones, 1983, translation by Robert R. Barr published as *The Power of the Poor in History,* Orbis Books, 1983.

Beber en su propio pozo: En el itinerario espiritual de un pueblo, Centro de Estudios y Publicaciones, 1983, translation by Matthew J. O'Connell published as *We Drink From Our Own Wells: The Spiritual Journey of a People,* Orbis Books, 1983.

(Editor with others) *Different Theologies, Common Responsibility: Babel or Pentecost?,* T & T Clark, 1984.

(With José Luis Indigoras and others) *Reflexión sobre la teología de la liberación: Perspectivas desde el Perú,* Centro de Estudios Teologicos de la Amazonia (Iquitos, Peru), 1986.

La verdad los hará libres: Confrontaciones, Centro de Estudios y Publicaciones, 1986.

Hablar de Dios desde el sufrimiento del inocente: Una reflexión sobre el libro de Job, Centro de Estudios y Publicaciones, 1986, translation by O'Connell published as *On Job: God-Talk and the Suffering of the Innocent,* Orbis Books, 1987.

SIDELIGHTS: Gustavo Gutiérrez Merino is a Peruvian priest and theologian. Many of his books discuss Latin American social issues, some of which attempt to define theologically the Catholic church's role in resisting oppression. His best known work was translated as *A Theology of Liberation: History, Politics, and Salvation* in 1973.

BIOGRAPHICAL/CRITICAL SOURCES:

BOOKS

Brown, Robert McAffee, *Gustavo Gutiérrez,* John Knox, 1980.

PERIODICALS

America, March 31, 1973, May 5, 1973, October 15, 1983, September 15, 1984.

Christian Century, October 19, 1983, May 9, 1984.

Journal of Religion, July, 1983.

New York Review of Books, May 31, 1973.

New York Times, October 21, 1984.

Times Literary Supplement, June 14, 1974.

*   *   *

GUZMAN (FRANCO), Martín Luis   1887-1976

PERSONAL: Born October 6, 1887, in Chihuahua, Mexico; died in 1976; son of Martín L. Guzmán and Carmen Franco Terrazas;

married Anita West Villalobos, 1909; children: three sons. *Education:* Attended University of Mexico.

CAREER: Journalist and politician. Member of editorial staff, *El Imparcial,* 1908; took part in Mexican Revolution, 1913; cofounder, *El Honor Nacional,* 1913; counselor to minister of war, 1914; in exile, 1914-20; editor in chief, *El Heraldo de México,* 1920; founder, *El Mundo,* 1922; member, Chamber of Deputies, 1922-24; resided in Spain, 1924-30; founder, *Tiempo* (Mexico), 1942; ambassador to United Nations, 1951; president, Comisión Nacional de los Libros de Texto Gratuitos, 1964.

WRITINGS:

La querella de México (also see below), Imprenta Clásica Española, 1915.

A orillas del Hudson (also see below), Librería Editorial Andrés Boras e Hijo, 1920.

El águila y la serpiente, Compañía Ibero-americana de Publicaciones (Madrid), 1928, reprinted, Compañía General de Ediciones, 1974, published as *El águila y la serpiente: Memorias de la revolución mexicana,* edited by Ernest Richard Moore, Norton, 1943, translation by Harriet de Onís published as *The Eagle and the Serpent,* Knopf, 1930.

La sombra del caudillo (sequel to *El águila y la serpiente*), Espasa-Calpe, 1929, reprinted, Compañía General de Ediciones, 1974.

Mina el mozo, héroe de Navarra, Espasa-Calpe, 1932.

Memorias de Pancho Villa: Según el texto establecido y ordenado, Ediciones Botas, 1938, 2nd corrected edition, Compañía General de Ediciones, 1951, reprinted, 1971, translation by Virginia H. Taylor published as *Memoirs of Pancho Villa,* University of Texas Press, 1965.

Javier Mina: Héroe de España y de México, Compañía General de Ediciones, 1955, 4th revised edition, 1972.

Muertes históricas, Compañía General de Ediciones, 1958.

La querella de México, A orillas del Hudson, Otras páginas, Compañía General de Ediciones, 1958.

Academia: Tradición, independencia, libertad, Compañía General de Ediciones, 1959.

Islas Marías: Novela y drama; Guión para una película, Compañía General de Ediciones, 1959.

Filadelfia, paraíso de conspiradores y otras historias noveladas, Compañía General de Ediciones, 1960.

Obras completas, two volumes, Compañía General de Ediciones, 1961-63.

Febrero de 1913, Empresas Editoriales, 1963.

(With Alfonso Reyes and Federico de Onís) *Frente a la pantalla,* Dirección General de Difusión Cultural, UNAM, 1963.

Necesidad de cumplir las Leyes de Reforma, Empresas Editoriales, 1963.

Crónicas de mi destierro, Empresas Editoriales, 1964.

Antología de Martín Luis Guzmán, selected by Ermilo Abreu Gómez, Ediciones Oasis, 1970.

Martín Luis Guzmán, selected by Andrés de Luna, Senado de la República, 1987.

Martín Luis Guzmán: Iconografía, selected by Héctor Perea, Fondo de Cultura Económica, 1987.

Also author of *Aventuras democráticas,* 1929, *El hombre y sus armas,* 1938, *Campos de batalla,* 1939, *Panoramas políticos y la causa del pobre,* 1940, *Axkána González en las elecciones,* 1960, and *Maestros rurales y piratas y corsarios,* 1960.

SIDELIGHTS: Much of Martín Luis Guzmán's work focuses on the Mexican Revolution of 1913, in which Guzmán himself had an active role. His novel *El águila y la serpiente* reflects his revolutionary experiences, while his portrait of revolutionary leadership in *Memorias de Pancho Villa* has gained widespread critical acclaim. Guzmán returned to politics late in life, when he became Mexico's ambassador to the United Nations in 1951.

H

HAHN (GARCES), Oscar (Arturo) 1938-

PERSONAL: Born July 5, 1938, in Iquique, Chile; immigrated to United States, naturalized citizen; married Nancy Jorquera in 1971; children: one daughter. *Education:* Graduated from University of Chile, 1963; University of Iowa, M.A., 1972; University of Maryland at College Park, Ph.D., 1977.

ADDRESSES: Office—Department of Spanish, University of Iowa, Iowa City, Iowa 52240.

CAREER: University of Chile Arica, Santiago, professor of Hispanic literature, 1965-73; University of Maryland at College Park, instructor, 1974-77; University of Iowa, Iowa City, assistant professor, 1977-79, associate professor of Spanish-American literature, 1979—, honorary fellow of International Writing Program, 1972.

MEMBER: Instituto Internacional de Literatura Iberoamericana, Modern Language Association of America.

AWARDS, HONORS: Poetry Award from University of Chile, 1966.

WRITINGS:

Esta rosa negra (poems), Ediciones Alerce (Santiago), 1961.
Agua final (poems), Ediciones de la Rama Florida (Lima), 1967.
Arte de morir (poems), Hispamerica (Buenos Aires), 1977, 2nd edition, Editorial Nascimento (Santiago), 1979, translation by James Haggard published as *The Art of Dying,* Latin American Literary Review Press, 1987.
El cuento fantástico hispanoamericano en el siglo XIX, Premiá Editora (Mexico City), 1978.
Mal de amor, Ediciones Ganymedes (Santiago), 1981.
Imágenes nucleares, Ediciones América del Sur (Santiago), 1983.
Texto sobre texto, Coordinación de Humanidades, Universidad Nacional Autónoma de México, 1984.

Also author of *Flor de enamorados,* F. Zegers (Santiago). Contributing editor of *Handbook of Latin American Studies.* Contributor to literature journals.

BIOGRAPHICAL/CRITICAL SOURCES:

PERIODICALS

World Literature Today, autumn, 1982.

HAYASECA y EIZAGUIRRE, Jorge
See ECHEGARAY (y EIZAGUIRRE), José (María Waldo)

* * *

HEMEZE, Sebastian
See CABALLERO, Manuel

* * *

HERAUD, Javier 1942-1963

PERSONAL: Born in Miraflores, Lima, Peru, 1942; died in Puerto Maldonado, Peru, 1963, during a battle between guerrilla and Peruvian government forces. *Education:* Attended Roman Catholic University of San Marcos, Lima, Peru.

AWARDS, HONORS: First prize in El Poeta Joven del Perú competition, *Cuadernos Trimestrales de Poesía,* for *El viaje;* first prize in the Juegos Florales for *Estación reunida.*

WRITINGS:

El río (poetry), [Lima], 1960.
El viaje (poetry), [Lima], 1961.
Poesías completas, y homenaje (poetry), Ediciones de La Rama Florida (Lima), 1964, 2nd revised edition, Campodónico (Lima), 1973.
(With César Calvo) *Ensayo a dos voces,* [Lima], 1967.
Poemas, Casa de las Américas (Havana), 1967.
Poemas, Signo (Tucumán), c. 1968.
Palabra de guerrillero: Pequeña antología y homenaje, edited and with notes by Jesús Cabel, W. A. González (Lima), 1970.
Poesías completas y cartas, Peisa (Lima), 1976.

Also author of *Estación reunida,* 1963.

SIDELIGHTS: A promising young Peruvian poet, Javier Héraud was also a leftist whose involvement with revolutionary guerrillas led to his being killed by the Peruvian police at the early age of twenty-one. Because his promising poetic voice was silenced before it had the chance to fully mature, Héraud has become a symbol and cult hero for many members of Peru's younger generation. His verse is characterized by its confident tone and was influenced by such poets as Antonio Machado y Ruiz and Pablo Neruda.

HERNANDEZ AQUINO, Luis 1907-(?)

PERSONAL: Born in 1907, in Lares, Puerto Rico; deceased.

CAREER: Educator and writer. Professor of Puerto Rican literature at University of Puerto Rico, Río Piedras.

AWARDS, HONORS: Poetry Prize from Institute of Puerto Rican Literature, 1964.

WRITINGS:

Isla para angustia: Poemas integrales (poems), Insula (San Juan, Puerto Rico), 1943.
(Editor with Angel Valbuena Briones) *Nueva poesía de Puerto Rico* (anthology of Puerto Rican poetry), Cultura Hispánica (Madrid, Spain), 1952.
(Editor and author of introduction) *Poesía puertorriqueña* (anthology of Puerto Rican poetry), University of Puerto Rico, 1954.
Memoria de Castilla (poems), [Madrid], 1956.
La muerte anduvo por el guasío (novel), Areyto (Madrid), 1959.
(Editor and author of introduction) Antonio Nicolás Blanco, *Antología de Antonio Nicolás Blanco* (anthology), Ateneo Puertorriqueño (San Juan), 1959.
Del tiempo cotidiano (poems), [San Juan], 1961.
Nuestra aventura literaria: Los ismos en la poesía puertorriqueña, 1913-1948 (survey of early twentieth-century Puerto Rican poetry), 2nd edition, University of Puerto Rico, 1966.
(Editor and author of introduction) *Poetas de Lares* (anthology of Puerto Rican poetry), Instituto de Cultura Puertorriqueña-Centro Cultural de Lares, 1966.
(Editor) *Cantos a Puerto Rico* (anthology of Puerto Rican poetry), Instituto de Cultura Puertorriqueña (San Juan), 1967.
(Editor) *El modernismo en Puerto Rico: Poesía y prosa* (anthology of Puerto Rican modernist literature), University of Puerto Rico, 1967.
Entre la elegía y el réquiem (poems), Edil (Río Piedras), 1968.
Diccionario de voces indígenas de Puerto Rico (dictionary of words indigenous to Puerto Rico), Vasco Americana (Bilbao), 1969, 2nd edition, revised and enlarged, Cultural (Río Piedras), 1977.
(Editor) Ramón Emeterio Betances, *Betances, poeta* (poetry anthology), Sarobei (Bayamón, Puerto Rico), 1986.
Luis Hernández Aquino, Instituto de Cultura Puertorriqueña, 1988.

Also associated with the works "Niebla lírica," 1931, "Agua del remanso," 1939; "Poemas de la vida breve," 1940, "Movimientos literarios en el siglo XX en Puerto Rico," 1951, "Voz en el tiempo," 1952, and "Notas sobre la poesía puertorriqueña," 1956.

Contributor to periodicals, including *Alma Latina, El Día Estético, El Globo, El Mundo, El País,* and *Puerto Rico Ilustrado;* author of column "Lingüística borícua" for *El Mundo Dominical.* Editor of literary magazines *Bayoán, Insula,* and *Jaycoa.*

SIDELIGHTS: Luis Hernández Aquino was one of the most widely known Puerto Rican poets. His writings garnered many awards, perhaps most notably the 1964 Poetry Prize of the Institute of Puerto Rican Literature. In addition to several volumes of poetry, the author wrote a novel, *La muerte anduvo por el guasío,* about the United States seizure of his island in 1898. During the course of his career Hernández Aquino became increasingly interested in the unique features of Puerto Rican language, and accordingly he compiled a dictionary of words indigenous to his island—*Diccionario de voces indígenas de Puerto Rico*—and wrote a column on the subject, "Lingüística borícua," for *El*

Mundo Dominical. [Death confirmed by Biblioteca General de Puerto Rico, Instituto de Cultura Puertorriqueña]

* * *

HERRERA, Juan Felipe 1948-

PERSONAL: Born December, 1948, in Fowler, Calif. *Education:* Attended Stanford University.

CAREER: Artist and writer. Editor-in-chief of Citybender (applied arts publisher), San Diego, Calif.

AWARDS, HONORS: Mesoamerican research grant from the Chicano Cultural Center of the University of California, Los Angeles, 1970; Award of Merit from the San Diego Historical Society, 1975; California Arts Council grant, 1977.

WRITINGS:

Rebozos of Love / We Have Woven / Sudor de Pueblos / On Our Back (poems), illustrations by Gloria Amalia Flores, Toltecas en Aztlan (San Diego, Calif.), 1974.
(Editor with Charlotte Jaramillo and Pedro Ortiz Vásquez) Rodolfo E. Braceli, *The Last Testament: El último padre* (poem-novel), text in English and Spanish, translation by Fracisco A. Lomelí, preface by Gustavo V. Segade, Citybender (San Diego, Calif.), 1978.
Exiles of Desire, Lalo Press Publications (Fresno, Calif.), 1983, Arte Público, 1985.

Poems represented in anthologies, including *From the Belly of the Shark,* edited by Walter Lowenfels, Vintage, 1973; *Festival de Flor y Canto: An Anthology of Chicano Literature,* edited by Mary Ann Pacheco and others, University of Southern California Press, 1976; and *Calafia: An Anthology of California Poets,* edited by Ismael Reed, Yardbird Wing, 1978. Contributor of poems to periodicals, including *Aztlan, Mester, Vórtice,* and *Hispamérica.* Graphic design coordinator of *Vórtice,* the Chicano journal at Stanford University.

* * *

HERRERA-SOBEK, María

PERSONAL: Education: University of California, Los Angeles.

ADDRESSES: Office—c/o Mexico/Chicano Program, University of California, Irvine, Calif. 92664.

WRITINGS:

The Bracero Experience: Elitelore versus Folklore, UCLA Latin American Center Publications, University of California, 1979.
Beyond Stereotypes: The Critical Analysis of Chicana Literature, Bilingual Press, 1985.
(Editor with Helena M. Viramontes, and contributor) *Chicana Creativity and Criticism: Charting New Frontiers in American Literature,* Arte Público Press/University of California, Irvine, 1988.

SIDELIGHTS: María Herrera-Sobek's *The Bracero Experience: Elitelore versus Folklore* looks at the lives of the *braceros,* folk musicians who are as familiar in the United States as they are in the Latin American countries from which they have come. Interviews with the musicians, together with their original lyrics, combine to give this study an insider's view of the *braceros'* lives before and after coming to live in the United States.

HERRERA y REISSIG, Julio 1875-1910

PERSONAL: Born in 1875 in Montevideo, Uruguay; died in 1910.

CAREER: Poet. Founder, *La Revista,* 1899-1900, and *La Nueva Atlántida, 1907.*

WRITINGS:

Poesías, Imprenta Helénica, 1911.
La vida y otros poemas, O. M. Bertani (Montevideo, Uruguay), 1913.
Las lunas de oro (also see below), O. M. Bertani, 1913.
Las pascuas del tiempo, O. M. Bertani, 1913.
El teatro de los humildes (also see below), O. M. Bertani, 1913.
Los peregrinos de piedra (also see below), O. M. Bertani, 1913, reprinted, Salamandra, 1975, bound with *El teatro de los humildes* and *Las lunas de oro,* Garnier Hamanos (Paris), c. 1914.
Prosas: Crítica, cuentos, comentarios, M. García (Montevideo), 1918.
Páginas escogidas, Maucci (Barcelona), 1919.
Los parques abandonados, Ediciones Selectas América (Montevideo), 1919.
Antología lírica, Ediciones Ercilla (Santiago), 1939.
Poesías completas, Losada (Buenos Aires), 1942, reprinted, Aguilar (Madrid), 1965.
Los éxtasis de la montaña (also see below), Calomino (La Plata, Argentina), 1943, reprinted, Elite (Montevideo), c. 1965.
Epílogo wagneriano a 'La política de fusión,' C. García (Montevideo), c. 1946.
Obras poéticas, Ministerio de Instrucción Pública y Previsión Social (Montevideo), 1966.
Antología de Julio Herrera y Reissig, edited by Magda Olivieri, Centro Editor de América Latina (Montevideo), 1968.
Seis sonetos y un poema (transcriptions and facsimilies of selections from *Los peregrinos de piedra* and *Los éxtasis de la montaña*), Biblioteca Nacional, Departamento de Investigaciones (Montevideo), 1969.
Poemas, Horizonte (Medellín, Colombia), c. 1969.
Los cien mejores poemas, edited by Antonio Castro Leal, Aguilar (Mexico), 1970.
Poesías, Ediciones de la Banda Oriental (Montevideo), 1975.
Herrera y Reissig: Antología, estudio crítico y notas, edited by Rogelio Mirza, Arca (Montevideo), 1975.
Poesías, Porrúa (Mexico), 1977.
Poesía completa y prosa selecta, edited by Alicia Migdal, Biblioteca Ayacucho (Caracas), 1978.

Obras completas ("Complete Works") were published in five volumes, 1913-14.

SIDELIGHTS: Uruguayan poet Julio Herrera y Reissig was born into wealth. When his family fell into political disrepute in 1895, Herrera y Reissig earned a living as a civil servant. Emulating the French Symbolists, he eventually turned to modernism and later to *ultraísmo,* and was recognized especially for the innovative rhythms and rhymes in his poetry. "Like the majority of the Modernist poets in Spanish America, [he] was enchanted with the exotic," wrote George D. Schade in *Hispania,* adding that "along with other Modernist poets, Herrera y Reissig turned zealously to mythology for inspiration in order to lose himself in a world suffused with beauty, splendor and opulence, far removed from humdrum actualities."

BIOGRAPHICAL/CRITICAL SOURCES:

BOOKS

Bula Píriz, R., *Herrera y Reissig,* [New York], 1952.
Englekirk, John Eugene, *Edgar Allan Poe in Hispanic Literature,* Instituto de las Españas en los Estados Unidos (New York), 1934.
Gicovate, Bernard, *Julio Herrera y Reissig and the Symbolists,* University of California Press, 1957.
Seluja, Antonio, Magda Olivieri, and Diego Pérez Pintos, *Homenaje a Julio Herrera y Reissig,* Consejo Departamental de Montevideo, 1963.
Pino Saavedra, Y., *La poesía de Julio Herrera y Reissig,* [Santiago], 1932.

PERIODICALS

Hispania, Volume 42, March, 1959.
Revista Nacional, Number 63, 1943.

* * *

HIJUELOS, Oscar 1951-

PERSONAL: Surname is pronounced "E-way-los"; born August 24, 1951, in New York, N.Y.; son of Pascual (a hotel worker) and Magdalena (a homemaker; maiden name, Torrens) Hijuelos. *Education:* City College of the City University of New York, B.A., 1975, M.A., 1976. *Religion:* Catholic.

ADDRESSES: Home—211 West 106th St., New York, N.Y. 10025. *Agent*—Harriet Wasserman Literary Agency, 137 East 36th St., New York, N.Y. 10016.

CAREER: Transportation Display, Inc., Winston Network, New York, N.Y., advertising media traffic manager, 1977-84; writer, 1984—.

MEMBER: International P.E.N.

AWARDS, HONORS: Received "outstanding writer" citation from Pushcart Press, 1978, for the story "Columbus Discovering America"; Oscar Cintas fiction writing grant, 1978-79; Breadloaf Writers Conference scholarship, 1980; fiction writing grants from Creative Artists Programs Service, 1982, and Ingram Merrill Foundation, 1983; Fellowship for Creative Writers from National Endowment for the Arts, and American Academy in Rome Fellowship in Literature from American Academy and Institute of Arts and Letters, both 1985, for *Our House in the Last World;* nominated for National Book Award and National Book Critics Circle Award, 1989, for *The Mambo Kings Play Songs of Love;* Pulitzer Prize for fiction from Columbia University Graduate School of Journalism, 1990, for *The Mambo Kings Play Songs of Love;* Guggenheim fellowship in fiction, 1990.

WRITINGS:

Our House in the Last World (novel), Persea Books, 1983.
The Mambo Kings Play Songs of Love (novel), Farrar, Straus, 1989.

Work represented in anthology *Best of Pushcart Press III,* Pushcart, 1978.

WORK IN PROGRESS: A novel tentatively titled *Fourteen Sisters.*

SIDELIGHTS: Award-winning novelist Oscar Hijuelos told *CA:* "My novel *Our House in the Last World* traces the lives of a Cuban family who came to the United States in the 1940s and follows them to the death of the father and subsequent near collapse of the family. In many ways a realistic novel, *Our House in the Last World* also reflects certain Latin attributes that are usually termed 'surreal' or 'magical.' Although I am quite Americanized, my book focuses on many of my feelings about identity and my 'Cubanness.' I intended for my book to commemorate at least a few aspects of the Cuban psyche (as I know it)."

Reviewing *Our House in the Last World* in the *New York Times Book Review,* Edith Milton affirmed that Hijuelos is mainly concerned "with questions of identity and perspective" such as those affecting the Santinio family featured in his book. Hijuelos is "especially eloquent," lauded Cleveland *Plain Dealer* critic Bob Halliday, "in describing the emotional storms" that transform the Santinios as they "try to assimilate the rough realities of Spanish Harlem in terms of the values and personal identities they have inherited from their homeland." There is a "central tension," Milton explained, between the "lost, misremembered Eden [Cuba]" and the increasing squalor of the family's new life in their "last world"—New York. "Opportunity seems pure luck" to these well-intentioned immigrants, observed *Chicago Tribune Book World* reviewer Pat Aufderheide, and in the absence of hope, each ultimately succumbs to the pressures that "work against the [American] dream of upward mobility." Hijuelos's "elegantly accessible style," opined Aufderheide, "combines innocence and insight" in creating the individual voices of his characters. But beyond that and the infused elements of Cuban culture, noted the reviewer, there is a "feel for the way fear . . . pervades" the Santinios' lives. The characters and the "sheer energy" of the narrative are the book's strengths, determined Milton, adding that Hijuelos "never loses the syntax of magic, which transforms even the unspeakable into a sort of beauty." Critic Roy Hoffman in the *Philadelphia Inquirer* called *Our House in the Last World* a "vibrant, bitter and successful" story and compared Hijuelos to an "urban poet" who creates a "colorful clarity of life." Halliday likewise deemed the book a "wonderfully vivid and compassionate" first novel.

Hijuelos gained wide critical notice, a nomination for a National Book Award, and the prestigious Pulitzer Prize for fiction for his second novel, *The Mambo Kings Play Songs of Love.* The novel portrays César and Nestor Castillo, two brothers who leave their native Cuba and come to the United States, where they achieve a degree of fame playing in New York City's mambo clubs. They reach the pinnacle of their success by singing their romantic ballad and only hit song, "Beautiful María of My Soul" on the "I Love Lucy" television show. The song, which quiet, thoughtful Nestor rewrites twenty-two times, recalls his love affair in Cuba with a woman he can not forget—even throughout his marriage to another. César, on the other hand, is a hard-living womanizer who never achieves actual love. As an old man, César replays his music, his decisions, and his memories, becoming increasingly similar to his brother in his preoccupation with the past. Hijuelos portrays the brothers' vibrant music and sex lives as well as their wistful dreams, "alternat[ing] crisp narrative with opulent musings—the language of everyday and the language of longing," commented Margo Jefferson in the *New York Times Book Review.* Critic Michiko Kakutani in the *New York Times* described Hijuelos's "remarkable new novel" as "another kind of American story—an immigrant story of lost opportunities and squandered hopes. While it dwells in bawdy detail on César's sexual escapades, while it portrays the musical world of the 50s in bright, primary colors, the novel is essentially elegiac in tone—a Chekhovian lament for a life of missed connections and misplaced dreams."

Hijuelos added: "A lot of critics have gotten the thread of this story [*The Mambo Kings*], but the very best have seen beyond the social and cultural veneer of the book. Of course it's about Cubans and music, but I also wanted to do something about the way that memory works—like a spinning record, a TV rerun—that occurs again and again. In England, for the release of this book, I found that the reviewers, while recognizing the cultural sources of this book, had some real insight into my intentions. That is to say, these two brothers, clothed in flamboyant and elegiac prose, are ordinary human beings with complex inner lives—no stereotypes here, though they are sometimes 'read' that way."

AVOCATIONAL INTERESTS: Pen-and-ink drawing, old maps, turn-of-the-century books and graphics, playing musical instruments, jazz ("I absolutely despise modern rock and roll").

BIOGRAPHICAL/CRITICAL SOURCES:

BOOKS

Bestsellers 90, Issue 1, Gale, 1990.

PERIODICALS

Chicago Tribune, August 13, 1989.
Chicago Tribune Book World, July 17, 1983.
Detroit Free Press, August 20, 1989.
Detroit News, September 3, 1989.
Los Angeles Times Book Review, September 3, 1989.
New York Times, August 4, 1989, September 11, 1989.
New York Times Book Review, May 15, 1983, August 27, 1989.
Philadelphia Inquirer, July 17, 1983.
Plain Dealer (Cleveland), July 17, 1983.
Washington Post, August 20, 1989.

*   *   *

HINOJOSA(-SMITH), Rolando (R.) 1929-
(Rolando R. Hinojosa-S., Rolando Hinojosa-Smith; P. Galindo, a pseudonym)

PERSONAL: Born January 21, 1929, in Mercedes, Tex.; son of Manuel Guzman (a farmer) and Carrie Effie (a homemaker; maiden name, Smith) Hinojosa; married Patricia Mandley, September 1, 1963 (divorced, 1989); children: Clarissa Elizabeth, Karen Louise. *Education:* University of Texas at Austin, B.S., 1953; New Mexico Highlands University, M.A., 1963; University of Illinois, Ph.D., 1969. *Politics:* Democrat. *Religion:* Catholic.

ADDRESSES: Home—6201 Sneed Cove, #913, Austin, Tex. 78744. *Office*—Department of English, University of Texas at Austin, Austin, Tex. 78712.

CAREER: High school teacher in Brownsville, Tex., 1954-56; Trinity University, San Antonio, Tex., assistant professor of modern languages, 1968-70; Texas A & I University, Kingsville, Tex., associate professor of Spanish and chairman of modern language department, 1970-74, dean of College of Arts and Sciences, 1974-76, vice president for academic affairs, 1976-77; University of Minnesota—Minneapolis, chairman of department of Chicano studies, 1977-80, professor of Chicano studies and American studies, 1980-81; University of Texas at Austin, professor of English, 1981-85, E. C. Garwood Professor, 1985—. Consultant to Minneapolis Education Association, 1978-80, to U.S. Information Agency, 1980 and 1989, and to Texas Commission for the Arts and Humanities, 1981-82. *Military service:* U.S. Army Reserves, 1956-63; became second lieutenant.

MEMBER: Modern Language Association (chairman of commission on languages and literature in ethnic studies, 1978-80), PEN, Academia de la Lengua Española en Norteamérica, Hispanic Society, Fellow Society of Spanish and Spanish American Studies, Texas Institute of Letters.

AWARDS, HONORS: Best in West Award for foreign language radio programming, California, 1970-71; Quinto Sol Literary Award for best novel, 1972, for *Estampas del valle y otras obras;* Casa de las Américas award for best novel, 1976, for *Klail City y sus alrededores;* Southwest Studies on Latin America award for best writing in the humanities, 1981, for *Mi querido Rafa;* distinguished alumnus award, University of Illinois College of Liberal Arts, 1988.

WRITINGS:

NOVELS

Estampas del valle y otras obras (first novel in "Klail City Death Trip" series), Quinto Sol, 1972, bilingual edition with translation by Gustavo Valadez and José Reyna published as *Sketches of the Valley and Other Works,* Justa Publications, 1980, revised English language edition published as *The Valley,* Bilingual Press, 1983.

Klail City y sus alrededores (second novel in "Klail City Death Trip" series), bilingual edition with translation by Rosaura Sánchez, Casa de las Américas, 1976, published under name Rolando R. Hinojosa-S. as *Generaciones y semblanzas* (title means "Biographies and Lineages"), Justa Publications, 1977, translation by Hinojosa published as *Klail City,* Arte Público Press, 1987.

Korean Love Songs from Klail City Death Trip (novel in verse form; third in "Klail City Death Trip" series), illustrations by René Castro, Justa Publications, 1978.

Claros varones de Belken (fourth novel in "Klail City Death Trip" series), Justa Publications, 1981, bilingual edition with translation by Julia Cruz published as *Fair Gentlemen of Belken County,* Bilingual Press, 1987.

Mi querido Rafa (fifth novel in "Klail City Death Trip" series), Arte Público Press, 1981, translation by Hinojosa published as *Dear Rafe,* 1985.

Rites and Witnesses (sixth novel in "Klail City Death Trip" series), Arte Público Press, 1982.

Partners in Crime, Arte Público Press, 1985.

Los amigos de Becky, Arte Público Press, 1990, translation published as *Becky and Her Friends,* 1990.

OTHER

Generaciones, notas, y brechas/Generations, Notes, and Trails, (nonfiction; bilingual edition), translation by Fausto Avendaño, Casa, 1978.

(Author of introduction) Carmen Tafolla, *Curandera,* M & A Editions, 1983.

(Contributor under name Rolando Hinojosa-Smith) Alan Pogue, *Agricultural Workers of the Rio Grande and Rio Bravo Valleys,* Center for Mexican American Studies, University of Texas at Austin, 1984.

(Translator from the Spanish) Tomas Rivera, *This Migrant Earth,* Arte Público Press, 1985.

(Contributor) José David Saldívar, editor, *The Rolando Hinojosa Reader: Essays Historical and Critical,* Arte Público Press, 1985.

Also author, under pseudonym P. Galindo, of "Mexican American Devil's Dictionary." Work represented in anthologies, including *Festival de flor y canto: An Anthology of Chicano Literature,* edited by F. A. Cervantes, Juan Gomez-Quiñones, and others, University of Southern California Press, 1976. Contributor of short stories, articles, and reviews to periodicals, including *Texas Monthly, Texas Humanist, Los Angeles Times,* and *Dallas Morning News.*

SIDELIGHTS: The first Chicano author to receive a major international literary award, Rolando Hinojosa won the prestigious Premio Casa de las Américas for *Klail City y sus alrededores* (*Klail City*), part of a series of novels known to English-speaking readers as "The Klail City Death Trip." Hinojosa's fiction, often infused with satire or subtle humor, is widely praised for its multiple narratives that unite many characters' individual perspectives into the unique combined voice of the Chicano people. Hinojosa has also produced essays, poetry, and a detective novel titled *Partners in Crime.*

Hinojosa was born in Texas's Lower Rio Grande Valley to a family with strong Mexican and American roots: his father fought in the Mexican Revolution while his mother maintained the family north of the border. An avid reader during childhood, Hinojosa was raised speaking Spanish until he attended junior high, where English was the primary spoken language. Like his grandmother, mother, and three of his four siblings, Hinojosa became a teacher; he has held several professorial posts and has also been active in academic administration and consulting work. Although he prefers to write in Spanish, Hinojosa has also translated his own books and written others in English.

Hinojosa entered the literary scene with the 1973 *Estampas del valle y otras obras,* which was translated as *Sketches of the Valley and Other Works.* The four-part novel consists of loosely connected sketches, narratives, monologues, and dialogues, offering a composite picture of Chicano life in the fictitious Belken County town of Klail City, Texas. The first part of *Estampas* introduces Jehú Malacara, a nine-year-old boy who is left to live with exploitative relatives after the deaths of his parents. Hinojosa synthesizes the portrait of Jehú's life through comic and satiric sketches and narratives of incidents and characters surrounding him. The second section is a collection of pieces about a murder, presented through newspaper accounts, court documents, and testimonials from the defendant's relatives. A third segment, narrated by an omniscient storyteller, is a selection of sketches depicting people from various social groups in Klail City, while the fourth section introduces the series' other main character, Jehú's cousin Rafa Buenrostro. Also orphaned during childhood, Rafa narrates a succession of experiences and recollections of his life. Hinojosa later rewrote *Estampas del valle y otras obras* in English, publishing it as *The Valley* in 1983.

Hinojosa's aggregate portrait of the Spanish southwest continues in *Klail City y sus alrededores,* published in English as *Klail City.* Like its predecessor, *Klail City* is composed of interwoven narratives, conversations, and anecdotes illustrating the town's collective life spanning fifty years. Winner of the 1976 Premio Casa de las Américas, the book was cited for its "richness of imagery, the sensitive creation of dialogues, the collage-like structure based on a pattern of converging individual destinies, the masterful control of the temporal element and its testimonial value," according to Charles M. Tatum in *World Literature Today.* Introducing more than one hundred characters and developing further the portraits of Rafa and Jehú, *Klail City* prompts *Western American Literature* writer Lourdes Torres to praise Hinojosa for his "unusual talent for capturing the language and spirit of his subject matter."

Korean Love Songs from Klail City Death Trip and *Claros varones de Belken* are Hinojosa's third and fourth installments in the series. A novel comprised of several long poems originally written in English and published in 1978, *Korean Love Songs* presents protagonist Rafa Buenrostro's narration of his experiences as a soldier in the Korean War. In poems such as "Friendly Fire" and "Rafe," Hinojosa explores army life, grief, male friendships, discrimination, and the reality of death presented through dispassionate, often ironic descriptions of the atrocity of war. *Claros varones de Belken* (*Fair Gentlemen of Belken County*), released three years later, follows Jehú and Rafa as they narrate accounts of their experiences serving in the Korean War, attending the University of Texas at Austin, and beginning careers as high school teachers in Klail City. The book also includes the narratives of two more major characters, writer P. Galindo and local historian Esteban Echevarría, who comment on their own and others' circumstances. Writing about *Fair Gentlemen of Belken County*, *World Literature Today* contributor Tatum comments that Hinojosa's "creative strength and major characteristic is his ability to render this fictional reality utilizing a collective voice deeply rooted in the Hispanic tradition of the Texas-Mexico border." Also expressing a favorable opinion of the book was *Los Angeles Times Book Review* writer Alejandro Morales, who concludes that "the scores of names and multiple narrators at first pose a challenge, but quickly the imagery, language and subtle folk humor of Belken County win the reader's favor."

Hinojosa continued the "Klail City Death Trip" series with *Mi querido Rafa*. Translated as *Dear Rafe*, the novel is divided into two parts and consists of letters and interviews. The first half of the work is written in epistolary style, containing only letters from Jehú—now a successful bank officer—to his cousin Rafa. Between the novel's two parts, however, Jehú suddenly leaves his important position at the Klail City First National Bank, and in the second section Galindo interviews twenty-one community members about possible reasons for Jehú's resignation. The two major characters are depicted through dialogue going on around and about them; the reader obtains a glimpse of Rafa's personality through Jehú's letters, and Jehú's life is sketched through the opinions of the townspeople. *San Francisco Review of Books* writer Arnold Williams compares the power of Hinojosa's fictional milieu, striking even in translation, to that of twentieth-century Jewish writer Isaac Bashevis Singer, noting that "Hinojosa is such a master of English that he captures the same intimacy and idiomatic word play in his re-creations."

After writing *Rites and Witnesses*, the sixth novel in the "Klail City Death Trip" series, Hinojosa turned to a conventional form of the novel with the 1985 *Partners in Crime*, a detective thriller about the murder of a Belken County district attorney and several Mexican nationals in a local bar. Detective squads from both sides of the border are called to investigate the case; clues lead to an established and powerful cocaine smuggling ring. Jehú and Rafa reappear in the novel as minor characters who nevertheless play important parts in the mystery's development. "Those who might mourn the ending of the ['Klail City Death Trip' series] and their narrative experimentation and look askance at Hinojosa's attempting such a predictable and recipe-oriented genre as the murder mystery need not worry," concludes Williams. "He can weave a social fabric that is interesting, surprising, realistic and still entertaining."

Hinojosa told *CA:* "I enjoy writing, of course, but I enjoy the rewriting even more: four or five rewritings are not uncommon. Once finished, though, it's on to something else. At this date, every work done in Spanish has also been done in English with the exception of *Claros varones de Belken*, although I did work quite closely on the idiomatic expressions which I found to be at the heart of the telling of the story.

"I usually don't read reviews; articles by learned scholars, however, are something else. They've devoted much time and thought to their work, and it is only fair I read them and take them seriously. The articles come from France, Germany, Spain, and so on, as well as from the United States. I find them not only interesting but, at times, revelatory. I don't know how much I am influenced by them, but I'm sure I am, as much as I am influenced by a lifetime of reading. Scholars do keep one on one's toes, but not, obviously, at their mercy. Writing has allowed me to meet writers as diverse as Julio Cortázar, Ishmael Reed, Elena Poniatowski and George Lamming.

"My goal is to set down in fiction the history of the Lower Rio Grande Valley, and with *Becky and Her Friends*, due out in 1990, I am right on schedule. The Spanish version will also be out the same year. A German scholar, Wolfgang Karrer, from Osnabrueck University has a census of my characters; they number some one thousand. That makes me an Abraham of some sort.

"Personally and professionally, my life as a professor and as a writer inseparably combines vocation with avocation. My ability in both languages is most helpful, and thanks for this goes to my parents and to the place where I was raised."

BIOGRAPHICAL/CRITICAL SOURCES:

BOOKS

Bruce-Novoa, Juan, *Chicano Authors: Inquiry by Interview*, University of Texas Press, 1980.
Dictionary of Literary Biography, Volume 82: *Chicano Writers, First Series*, Gale, 1989.
Saldívar, José David, editor, *The Rolando Hinojosa Reader: Essays Historical and Critical*, Arte Público Press, 1985.

PERIODICALS

Hispania, September, 1986.
Los Angeles Times Book Review, April 12, 1987.
Publishers Weekly, November 28, 1986.
San Francisco Review of Books, spring, 1985, fall/winter, 1985.
Western American Literature, fall, 1988.
World Literature Today, summer, 1977, summer 1986.

—*Sketch by Emily J. McMurray*

* * *

HINOJOSA-S., Rolando R.
See HINOJOSA(-SMITH), Rolando (R.)

* * *

HINOJOSA-SMITH, Rolando
See HINOJOSA(-SMITH), Rolando (R.)

* * *

HOSTOS, Adolfo de 1887-

PERSONAL: Born January 8, 1887, in Santo Domingo, Dominican Republic; son of Eugenio María de Hostos (a philosopher, educator, and statesman).

ADDRESSES: Home—1859 Odette St., Santurce, P.R. 00912.

CAREER: Historian and archeologist. Member of Ibero-American Institute of University of Puerto Rico, Río Piedras. Director of the Caparra archeological excavations; research director of General Historical Index of Puerto Rico Project, 1937. Served on local board of Selective Service System, 1941-46; first director of Puerto Rican Lottery, 1934-35. Trustee of College of Sacred Heart, Santurce. *Military service:* U.S. Army, Infantry, 1909-1919; received Medal of Victory; became major.

MEMBER: American Anthropological Association, American Association for the Advancement of Science, Cuban Academy of History, Puerto Rico Atheneum (vice president of history section, 1929; vice president, 1931), Society of Americanists of Paris.

AWARDS, HONORS: Honorary degree from the Catholic University of Puerto Rico, 1971.

WRITINGS:

Ciudad murada, ensayo acerca del proceso de la civilización en la ciudad española de San Juan Bautista de Puerto Rico, 1521-1898, Lex, 1948, reprint published as *Historia de San Juan, ciudad murada; ensayo acerca del proceso de la civilización en la ciudad española de San Juan Bautista de Puerto Rico, 1521-1898,* Instituto de Cultura Puertorriqueña, 1966.

Tras las huellas de Hostos, Editorial de la Universidad de Puerto Rico, 1966.

Una colección arqueológica antillana, [San Juan, Puerto Rico], 1955.

Hombres representativos de Puerto Rico, Imprenta Venezuela, 1961.

Carribeans Born and Bred, Vantage Press, 1968.

Diccionario histórico bibliográfico comentado de Puerto Rico, Academia Puertorriqueña de la Historia, 1976.

(Editor) *Bibliography and Index of the Work of Eugenio María de Hostos,* Gordon Press, 1979.

Aplicaciones industriales de diseño indígena de Puerto Rico, Instituto de Cultura Puertorriqueña, 1981.

* * *

HOSTOS, E. M. de
    See HOSTOS (y BONILLA), Eugenio María de

* * *

HOSTOS, Eugenio M. de
    See HOSTOS (y BONILLA), Eugenio María de

* * *

HOSTOS, Eugenio María
    See HOSTOS (y BONILLA), Eugenio María de

* * *

HOSTOS (y BONILLA), Eugenio María de 1839-1903
(E. M. de Hostos, Eugenio M. de Hostos, Eugenio María Hostos)

PERSONAL: Born January 11, 1839, in Rio Cañas, Mayagüez, Puerto Rico; died August 11, 1903, in Santo Domingo, Dominican Republic; children: Eugenio Carlos. *Education:* Central University of Madrid Law School, J.D., c. 1860.

CAREER: Admitted to the Bar in Spain; became active in Spanish republican politics in the 1850s and 1860s; immigrated to United States, 1869; became active with the Cuban Revolutionary Junta of pro-independence Cuban exiles in New York City, c. 1869-70; traveled to South America to publicize the cause of Cuban independence and promote educational modernization, 1870-74; taught at the University of Santiago, Santiago, Chile, in the early 1870s; returned to New York, 1874-77; promoted education in Venezuela, 1877-80; founded and served as dean of the Santo Domingo Normal School, and became inspector general of public instruction, Santo Domingo, Dominican Republic, both 1880-88; headmaster of Miguel Luis Amunátequi secondary school, Santiago, c. 1888-90; professor of constitutional law at University of Chile, Santiago, c. 1890-98; active in movement for Puerto Rican independence, c. 1898-1900; founded League of Puerto Rican Patriots, 1899; worked in education in Santo Domingo, 1900-03.

WRITINGS:

La peregrinación de Bayoán (novel; title means "Bayoan's Pilgrimage"), 1863, revised and annotated, edited by Julio C. López, University of Puerto Rico Press, 1988.

Hamlet (criticism), originally published separately, 1873, published with a critical essay on *Romeo and Juliet,* Edil, 1972.

Lecciones de derecho constitucional (legal studies; title means "Lectures on Constitutional Law"), 1887, Publicaciones ONAP (Santo Domingo), 1982.

Moral social (moral philosophy; title means "Social Morality"), Imprenta de García Hermanos (Santo Domingo), 1888, reprinted, Vosgos (Barcelona), 1974.

Geografía evolutiva (geography; title means "Evolutionary Geography"), 1895, reprinted, Talleres Tipográficos "La Nación," (Santo Domingo), 1932.

Tratado de sociología (sociology, title means "Treatise on Sociology"), Imprenta de Bailly-Bailliere e Hijos (Madrid), 1904, reprinted, El Ateneo (Buenos Aires), 1942.

Meditando (criticism; title means "Meditating"), Ediciones Literarias y Artísticas (Paris), 1909.

Obras completas, twenty volumes, Cultural (Havana), 1939, reprinted, Editorial de la Universidad de Puerto Rico, 1988, translation published as *The Complete Works of Eugeno María de Hostos,* Gordon Press, 1979.

Páginas dominicanas, originally published in *Hostos en Santo Domingo,* [Dominican Republic], c. 1939, portions selected by E. Rodríguez Demorizi published separately, Librería Dominicana, 1963.

Antología, selected by son, Eugenio Carlos de Hostos, Litografía y Encuadernación (Madrid), 1952.

Páginas escogidas, A. Estrada (Buenos Aires), 1952.

Obras, compiled by Camila Henríquez Ureña, Casa de las Américas (Havana), 1976.

Eugenio María de Hostos: Sociólogo y maestro (selections; title means "Eugenio María de Hostos: Teacher and Sociologist") Antillana, 1981.

Hostos: Ensayos inéditos (title means "Hostos: Unpublished Essays"), Edil, 1987.

América, la lucha por la libertad (title means "America: The Struggle for Freedom") Siglo Vientiuno (Mexico), reprinted, Ediciones Compromiso, 1988.

Works also published in multititle volumes. Author of some works under name variations E. M. de Hostos, Eugenio M. de Hostos, and Eugenio María Hostos. Also author of *Reseña histórica de Puerto Rico* (title means "Historical Outline of Puerto Rico"), 1872; *La enseñanza científica de la mujer* (title means "Teaching Women Scientifically"), 1872; *Tres presidentes y tres repúblicas* [and] *Estudio de sociología americana* (titles mean "Three Presidents and Three Republics" and "A Study of American Sociology"), 1874; "To the Masters of the Normal School," 1884; and *Cartas públicas acerca de Cuba* (title means "Public Letters on Cuba"), 1895. Editor of periodicals, including Cuban Revolutionary Junta's newspaper, *La Revolución,* c. 1869-70; *La América Ilustrada,* 1874; and *Las Tres Antillas.*

SIDELIGHTS: The great Puerto Rican patriot and educator Eugenio María de Hostos wrote prolifically on a remarkably wide range of subjects in the course of his active and peripatetic life. Born in the town of Río Cañas, Mayagüez, Puerto Rico, in 1839, Hostos traveled to Spain at age thirteen to study law. As a young man, he was influenced by progressive political ideas and sought to enlist Spanish republican support for the independence movement in Spain's Antillean colonies, which included Cuba and Puerto Rico. But after coming to power in 1868, the republicans reneged on an earlier pledge to grant freedom to Cuba and Puerto Rico, prompting a disillusioned Hostos to migrate to New York City. He collaborated there with pro-independence political exiles in the Cuban Revolutionary Junta and edited their newspaper, *La Revolución.*

In 1870, Hostos began the first of his renowned series of extended journeys and residences in different Latin American countries, gathering support for the cause of Cuban and Puerto Rican independence and the broader goal of an independent Federated Antillean Republic of Cuba, Haiti, Santo Domingo, and Puerto Rico. In later years, feeling somewhat defeated in his political ideals, Hostos devoted himself to the promotion of education, a cause he considered vital to the social, political, and material development of Latin America. Hostos spread his ideas in newspaper articles, public lectures, classroom instruction, and a number of influential books.

Hostos's writings, collected in twenty volumes, include novels, plays, children's stories, arts criticism, biographical sketches, and essays on moral philosophy, sociology, history, politics, education, and constitutional law. The author's progressive political philosophy and positivistic social views (positivism is a philosophical approach which holds that true knowledge is logical and verifiable) inform much of this diverse work. His novel *La peregrinación de Bayoán,* for instance, is a political allegory about Antillean independence. Hostos's arts criticism reflects his understanding of social utility, and in them, he casts a suspicious eye on works judged morally deficient or untruthful. Among the author's outstanding critical essays is his study of *Hamlet,* which remains a leading Spanish-language interpretation of William Shakespeare's play.

The heart of Hostos's achievement as a writer and thinker is his work on politics, education, sociology, and moral philosophy. His political views, particularly expressed in his historical studies of the Americas, can be described as a kind of democratic liberalism, distinguished by an abiding confidence in the power of reason, education, and enlightened self-interest to guide social harmony. Although he rejected the politics of class struggle, Hostos was keenly aware of the difficulties in overcoming the vast social and economic disparities dividing the populations in many Latin American countries. In addition, he apparently mistrusted the regional imperial aspirations of the United States, a country he otherwise admired. As quoted by William Rex Crawford in *A Century of Latin-American Thought,* Hostos offered powerful commentary on U.S. policy in the Caribbean in the 1870s: "The United States has been almost as cruel and stupid with us as Spain. . . . We are sure [the strong] can possess us only after destroying us, but with our will never." Hostos understood the roots of the U.S.-Latin American conflict to lie partly in their different stages of national development, and he urged

the young Latin American nations on to greater progress with the slogan, "Civilization or death!"

Such virtues of civilization as social tolerance and respect for others are central to Hostos's moral philosophy. In his best-known work, *Moral social,* the author sees no necessary dichotomy between the concepts of individual good and social good; on the contrary, he indicates that they are almost always joined. Similarly, Hostos rejected the notion that man's instinctive or animal nature is something inherently evil and in need of suppression by reason and will; rather, the instinctive, rational, social, and individual aspects of human beings are, according to the author, indissolubly linked. Hostos also took issue with the common nineteenth-century understanding of nature as an alien force to be conquered, insisting rather that human beings learn to see themselves as part of the natural world. Though optimistic about humanity's potential for full individual and social development guided by reason and education, Hostos did not minimize the difficult and constant struggle necessary to overcome short-term passions and parochial interests. Pedro de Alba, writing in *Eugenio María de Hostos: Promoter of Pan Americanism,* noted that Hostos also warned about the danger of a "new barbarism" emerging in modern industrial society due to the breakdown of traditional social structures and a rapid accumulation of wealth.

Like his ethics, Hostos's writings on sociology and education reflect a fundamental confidence in the capacity for human progress. His *Tratado de sociología* ("Treatise on Sociology") offers a theoretical outline of social organization and methods of mediating social conflict. "To the Masters of the Normal School," Hostos's famous address to his first graduating class of secondary school instructors in Santo Domingo in 1884, outlines his progressive views on education, which include expanding educational opportunities for women and promoting social culture among the working class.

Recognized during his lifetime for his literary and pedagogical achievements, Hostos remained disappointed in his political goals. When Spain was defeated in the Spanish-American War and surrendered her Caribbean colonies, Hostos urged the United States to recognize Puerto Rican independence. But the United States occupied and annexed the island instead, prompting Hostos to organize the short-lived League of Puerto Rican Patriots to resist the new colonization. Not wishing to live under foreign domination, Hostos left his native island in 1900 for the Dominican Republic, where he died a few years later. The Puerto Rican thinker, educator, and patriot is honored throughout Latin America for his abiding humanism, love of freedom, and respect and tolerance for opposing belief systems and diverse cultures.

BIOGRAPHICAL/CRITICAL SOURCES:

BOOKS

Blanco-Fombona, Rufino, *Hostos,* C. García (Montevideo), 1945.

Bosch, J., *Hostos sembrador,* [Havana], 1939.

Bosch, J., *Eugenio María Hostos: Vida y obra,* [New York], 1940.

Crawford, William Rex, *A Century of Latin-American Thought,* Harvard University Press, 1944.

Henríquez-Ureña, Pedro, *Literary Currents in Hispanic America,* Harvard University Press, 1945.

Hostos, Eugenio Carlos de, editor, *Hostos, peregrino del ideal: Ideario y trabajos acerca de Eugenio María de Hostos,* Ediciones Literarias y Artísticas (Paris), 1954.

Hostos, Eugenio Carlos de, editor, *Eugenio María de Hostos: Promoter of Pan Americanism,* Juan Bravo, c. 1954.

Roig de Leuchsenring, Emilio, editor, *Hostos y Cuba,* Editorial de Ciencias Sociales (Havana), 1974.

Romeu y Fernández, Raquel, *E. M. de Hostos, antillano y ensayista,* [Madrid], 1959.

Twentieth-Century Literary Criticism, Volume 24, Gale, 1987.

PERIODICALS

Philosophical Abstracts, spring, 1940.

—*Sketch by Curtis Skinner*

*   *   *

HOYOS, Angela de 1940(?)-

PERSONAL: Born in Coahuila, Mexico; brought to the United States as a child.

ADDRESSES: Home—4946 Luz Ave., San Antonio, Tex. 78237.

AWARDS, HONORS: Avalon World Arts Academy, honorable mention in poetry, 1965; Centro Studi e Scambi Internazionale, Diploma di Benemerenza, 1967 and 1968, second prize in international poetry competition, 1974; Accademia L. Da Vinci, Diploma di Benemerenza, 1969 and 1970; World Poetry Society Intercontinental distinguished service citation, magna cum laude, 1970 and 1971.

WRITINGS:

Arise, Chicano! and Other Poems, Backstage Books, 1975.
Chicano Poems: For the Barrio, M & A Editions, 1976.
Selecciones, translation by Mireya Robles, Ediciones del Caballo Verde, Universidad Veracruzana, 1976.
Selected Poemas Selecciones, Arte Público, 1979.
Woman, Woman, Arte Público, 1986.

OTHER

Contributor of translations to *World Anthology of Living Poets.* Contributor to publications.

BIOGRAPHICAL/CRITICAL SOURCES:

BOOKS

Lomelí, Francisco A. and Donaldo W. Urioste, *Chicano Perspectives in Literature: A Critical and Annotated Bibliography,* Pajarito Publications, 1976.

Ramos, Luis Arturo, *Angela de Hoyos: A Critical Look,* Pajarito Publications, 1979.

Vásquez-Castro, Javier, *Acerca de literatura (Diálogo con tres autores chicanos).* M & A Editions, 1979.

*   *   *

HUERTA, Jorge
See HUERTA, Jorge A(lfonso)

*   *   *

HUERTA, Jorge A(lfonso) 1942-
(Jorge Huerta)

PERSONAL: Born November 20, 1942, in Los Angeles, Calif.; son of Jorge Rodriguez (a musician) and Elizabeth (a nurse; maiden name, Trevizo) Huerta; married Virginia Elizabeth De-Mirjian (a deli owner), February 5, 1966; children: Ronald, Gregory. *Education:* California State College at Los Angeles (now California State University), B.A., 1965, M.A., 1967; Uni-

versity of California, Santa Barbara, Ph.D., 1974. *Politics:* Democrat. *Religion:* Protestant.

ADDRESSES: Home—Cardiff, Calif. *Office*—Theater Department, University of California, San Diego, La Jolla, Calif. 92093.

CAREER: High school theater director, 1966-69; Pasadena City College, Pasadena, Calif., technical director and instructor in design, 1969-70; University of California, Santa Barbara, lecturer in Chicano studies, 1974-75; University of California, San Diego, La Jolla, assistant professor of drama, 1975-81, associate professor, 1981-88, professor of theater, 1988—, acting director of Chicano studies program, 1979-80, director of Chicano studies program, 1980-82, theater department chair, 1983-84, founder and head of master of fine arts program in Hispanic American theater, 1989—. Professional director of dozens of plays, 1971—; founder and artistic director of El Teatro de la Esperanza, 1971-74; El Teatro Nacional de Aztlan, founding director, 1971-80, treasurer, 1972-74; founding director of Teatro Mil Caras (now Teatro Nuevo Siglo), 1976—; co-founder of Teatro Meta of Old Globe Theatre, San Diego, 1982-86. Member of board of directors of La Casa de la Raza, 1971-74, TENAZ (national theatrical organization), 1971-81, California Confederation of the Arts, 1984-86, National Committee for the World Encyclopedia of Contemporary Theater, 1986-88, and Playwright's Foundation, 1989; member of theater program panels for National Endowment for the Arts, 1978-87, and California Arts Council, 1981 and 1984; national coordinator of National Coalition of Professional Hispanic-American Theaters, 1986-88. Lecturer on Chicano theater and workshop leader in improvisational theater, 1976—. Has appeared on radio and television programs in the United States, Mexico, Panama, Venezuela, and Spain.

MEMBER: Ephebian Society.

AWARDS, HONORS: Grants from National Endowment for the Humanities, 1970-72 and 1979, National Endowment for the Arts, 1972-74 and 1973, Ford Foundation, 1973-74, 1986, and 1987, University of California, San Diego, 1976 and 1977, National Chicano Council on Higher Education, 1978-79, and Chancellor's Advisory Committee, 1981-84.

WRITINGS:

(Editor) *A Bibliography of Chicano and Mexican Dance, Drama, and Music,* Colegio Quetzalcoatl, 1972.
(Editor) *El Teatro de la Esperanza: An Anthology of Chicano Drama,* El Teatro de la Esperanza, 1973.
Ritual to Rasquachi and Back (cassette), Center for Cassette Studies, 1974.
(Contributor) David Maciel, editor, *La otra cara de México: Los Chicanos,* Caballito, 1977.
(Editor with Nicolás Kanellos) *Nuevos pasos: Chicano and Puerto Rican Drama,* Arte Público, 1979.
(Contributor) Francisco Jiménez, editor, *The Identification and Analysis of Chicano Literature,* Bilingual Press, 1979.
Chicano Theater: Themes and Forms, Bilingual Press, 1982.
(Contributor) Phyllis Hartnoll, editor, *The Oxford Companion to the Theatre,* 4th edition, Oxford University Press, 1983.
(Contributor) Eugene E. García, Francisco A. Lomelí, and Isidro D. Ortiz, editors, *Chicano Studies: A Multidisciplinary Approach,* Teachers College Press, Columbia University, 1984.
(Editor and author of introduction, under name Jorge Huerta) *Necessary Theater: Six Plays About the Chicano Experience,* Arte Público, 1989.

Contributor to periodicals, including *Aztlan, Revista de la Universidad de México, La Luz,* and *Revista Chicano-Requeña.* Member of editorial board of *Americas Review,* 1980—, *Gestos,* 1986—, and *Latin American Theatre Review,* 1988—.

WORK IN PROGRESS: Chicano Theater: Themes and Forms, 2nd edition; critical essays and articles on Hispanic American theater.

SIDELIGHTS: Jorge A. Huerta told *Hispanic Writers:* "I am focusing my attention on our new graduate program, which I launched in 1989 as America's first master of fine arts program in Hispanic American theater. As a professional director, I have had to balance my writing, teaching, and practice of theater. But each of these activities informs the others. I believe I am a better teacher because I research and write and direct; and I am a better writer/director because I teach. These are all interrelated and I cannot imagine not doing any of them."

BIOGRAPHICAL/CRITICAL SOURCES:

PERIODICALS

La Luz, September, 1976.
Latin American Theatre Review, fall, 1985.
Theatre Journal, December, 1983.
Theatre Survey, May, 1984.

*   *   *

HUIDOBRO, Vicente
    See HUIDOBRO FERNANDEZ, Vicente García

*   *   *

HUIDOBRO FERNANDEZ, Vicente García   1893-1948
(Vicente Huidobro)

PERSONAL: Born January 10, 1893, in Santiago, Chile; died of stroke, January 2, 1948; married Manuela Portas Bello, 1912. *Education:* Attended Colegio San Ignacio (Jesuit College), Santiago, and Berthelot Lyceum.

CAREER: Poet, novelist, editor, and critic.

WRITINGS:

UNDER NAME VICENTE HUIDOBRO, UNLESS OTHERWISE INDICATED

POETRY

Ecos del alma (title means "Echoes of the Soul"), Imprenta Chile (Santiago, Chile), 1911.
(Under name Vicente García Huidobro Fernández) *La gruta del silencio* (title means "The Grotto of Silence"), Imprenta Universitaria (Santiago), 1913.
Canciones en la noche (title means "Songs in the Night"), Imprenta Chile, 1913.
Adán (title means "Adam"), Imprenta Universitaria, 1916.
El espejo de agua (title means "The Mirror of Water"), Orión (Buenos Aires), 1916.
Horizon carre (title means "Square Horizon"), Paul Birault (Paris), 1917.
Poemas árticos (title means "Arctic Poems"), Imprenta Pueyo (Madrid), 1918, reprinted with prologue by Hugo Montes, Nascimento (Santiago), 1972.
Ecuatorial (title means "Equatorial"), Imprenta Pueyo, 1918, reprinted with a prologue by Oscar Hahn, Nascimento, 1978.
Hallali, Jesús López (Madrid), 1918.

Tour Eiffel, illustrations by Robert Delaunay, [Madrid], 1918.
Automne regulier, Libraire de France (Paris), 1925.
Tout a coup (title means "Suddenly"), Au Sans Pareil (Paris), 1925.
Altazor, o el viaje en paracaídas, (originally published in various periodicals beginning in 1919), Compañía Iberoamericana de Publicaciones (Madrid), 1931, reprinted as *Altazor,* Visor (Madrid), 1981, translation by Eliot Weinberger published as *Altazor; or, A Voyage in a Parachute,* Graywolf, 1988.
Temblor de cielo (prose poem), Plutarco (Madrid), 1931, 4th edition, Pacífico (Santiago), 1960.
Ver y palpar (1923-1933), Ercilla (Santiago), 1941.
El ciudadano del olvido (1924-1934), Ercilla, 1941.
Antología, edited with prologue, translation, and notes by Eduardo Anguita, Zig-Zag, 1945.
Ultimos poemas, Talleres Gráficos Ahués (Santiago), 1948.
Obras poéticas selectas, edited with a prologue by Montes, translation of French poems by José Zañartu, Pacífico, 1957.
Poesías, edited with a prologue by Enrique Lihn, Casa de las Américas (Havana, Cuba), 1968.
Le Citoyen de l'oubli, preface by Pablo Neruda, translation by Fernand Verhesen, Librairie Saint-Germain-des-Prés (Paris), 1974.
Relativity of Spring: Thirteen Poems (bilingual edition), translation from French by Michael Palmer and Geoffrey Young, Sand Dollar (Berkeley), 1976.
Altazor [and] *Temblor de cielo,* Cátedra (Madrid), c. 1981.
The Selected Poetry of Vicente Huidobro, edited with an introduction by David M. Guss, translation by Guss and others, New Directions Publishing, 1981.

NOVELS

Mío Cid Campeador, hazaña, Compañía Iberoamericana de Publicaciones, 1929, reprinted, Andrés Bello (Santiago), 1983, translation by Warre B. Wells published as *Portrait of a Paladin,* H. Liveright, 1932.
The Mirror of a Mage (originally published in English), translation by Wells, Houghton, 1931, Spanish edition published as *Cagliostro,* Zig-Zag (Santiago), 1934, reprinted, Gordon Press, 1974 (also see below).
La próxima (title means "The Next One"), Walton (Santiago), 1934.
Papá, o el diario de Alicia Mir, Walton, 1934.
Sátiro, o el poder de las palabras (title means "Satyr, or the Power of Words"), Zig-Zag, 1939.

ESSAY COLLECTIONS

Pasando y pasando, Imprenta Chile, 1914.
Finis Britannia, J. Budry (Paris), 1923.
Manifestes, Revue Mondiale (Paris), 1925.
Vientos contrarios (title means "Contrary Winds"), Nascimento, 1926.

OTHER

"Cuando el amor se vaya" (play; title means "When Love Goes"), produced in Santiago at Palace Theater, 1913.
Las pagodas ocultas (title means "The Hidden Pagodas"; includes essays and prose poems), Imprenta Universitaria, 1914.
Saisons choisies (title means "Selected Seasons"; includes poetry and essays), La Cible (Paris), 1921.
Gilles de Raíz (play; portions produced in Paris at Theatre de l'Oeuvre, 1933), Totem (Paris), 1932.
En la luna (play; title means "On the Moon"; produced in Chile, c. 1964), Ercilla (Santiago), 1934.

Poesía y prosa: Antología, Aguilar (Madrid), 1957, 2nd edition, 1967.

Obras completas, edited with a prologue by Braulio Arenas, Zig-Zag, 1964, expanded edition published under same title, edited by Montes, Andrés Bello, 1976.

Antología de verso y prosa, edited with a prologue by Montes, Nacional Gabriela Mistral (Santiago), 1975.

Cagliostro y poemas, prologue by Carlos Ruiz-Tagle, Andrés Bello, 1978.

Founding or co-founding editor of literary reviews, including *Azul,* 1913, *Nord Sud,* 1916, *Creación,* 1921, *Acción,* 1925, *Ombligo,* 1934, *Vital,* 1934, *Total,* 1936, and *Actual,* 1944.

SIDELIGHTS: Chilean poet Vicente Huidobro was as much a controversial figure as he was a leading twentieth-century Latin American author. He was praised for his experimental poetry and prose and is recognized as one of the founders—he claimed to be *the* founder—of the literary school of *creacionismo,* or "creationism." His contentious personality, however, frequently led him into personal, political, and literary disputes that some critics say obscured his poetic genius. Some of the literary movements he publicly criticized were realism, futurism, and surrealism. Huidobro argued that the realists were wrong to insist that art should merely copy nature; that the futurists were mistaken to write about such technological wonders as skyscrapers and airplanes because these subjects would not appeal to future generations; and that the surrealists were wrong to diminish the role of the writer by asserting that artists are simply the medium of the unconscious. In response to these and other schools of thought, Huidobro introduced his view of creationism. He held that the artist's duty was to create something absolutely new, something that was added to rather than copied from nature. Consequently, his creationist poetry features unusual juxtapositions of words and ideas: "a bird's nest in a rainbow," for instance. As a creationist poet, though, Huidobro only practiced this approach for a few years, and he did not remain faithful to any movement for long, mainly because living in Chile, France, and Spain prevented him from fixing his allegiance to a single idea or culture. A few of the literary and political groups he identified with include the Spanish avant garde, European cubists, Communists, and the Loyalists of the Spanish Revolution.

Although Huidobro wrote essays, plays, and novels, he is best known for his poetry written in Spanish and French. While some detractors of his poetry insist that his experimental verse is often incomprehensible, other reviewers laud its inventiveness. H. R. Hays, whose *Twelve Spanish American Poets* is excerpted in *Modern Latin American Literature,* maintained that Huidobro's "work is extremely literary, elegant in design, and remarkable for humorous verbal legerdemain. Conservative critics disparage its value. They cannot forgive him for the picture poems, his disregard for punctuation, and his fantastic imagery."

One of Huidobro's most famous works is the poem *Altazor, o el viaje en paracaídas,* which was published in English in 1988 as *Altazor; or, A Voyage in a Parachute.* Appearing in various periodicals beginning in 1919 and published as a whole in 1931, *Altazor* is about the narrator's attempt to fill an otherwise empty universe with language, which becomes increasingly playful throughout the poem's seven cantos. According to Merlin H. Forster in his *Kentucky Romance Quarterly* article, the poem's subtitle indicates the primary thematic focus: "The image of a fall through space implied in the full title of the poem is used constantly in the development of this main theme: a fall from coherence to incoherence, from life to death, from verbal question to inarticulate wail." Forster concluded that he "sees *Altazor* in all its consciously brilliant verbosity and symphonic structure as a moving expression of the anguished artist-man coming to grips with the ultimate and insoluble problems of his existence." Forster's favorable opinion of *Altazor* is echoed by other modern reviewers who, in general, have been more sympathetic to Huidobro's work than have earlier critics.

BIOGRAPHICAL/CRITICAL SOURCES:

BOOKS

De Costa, René, *Vicente Huidobro: The Careers of a Poet,* Clarendon Press, 1984.

Foster, David William and Virginia Ramos Foster, editors, *Modern Latin American Literature,* Volume 1, Ungar, 1975.

Kunitz, Stanley J. and Howard Haycraft, editors, *Twentieth Century Authors: A Biographical Dictionary of Modern Literature,* H. W. Wilson, 1942.

Rodríguez Monegal, Emir, editor, *The Borzoi Anthology of Latin American Literature,* Volume 2: *The Twentieth Century—From Borges and Paz to Guimaraes Rosa and Donoso,* Knopf, 1977.

Twentieth-Century Literary Criticism, Volume 31, Gale, 1989.

Ward, Philip, editor, *The Oxford Companion to Spanish Literature,* Clarendon Press, 1978.

Wood, Cecil G., *The Creacionismo of Vicente Huidobro,* York Press, c. 1978.

PERIODICALS

Kentucky Romance Quarterly, Volume 17, number 4, 1970.
Voice Literary Supplement, October, 1988.

I

IBAÑEZ, Vicente Blasco
See BLASCO IBAÑEZ , Vicente

*   *   *

IBARBOUROU, Juana de 1895-1979

PERSONAL: Maiden name Juanita Fernández Morales; born 1895 in Melo, Cerro Largo, Uruguay; died, 1979; married Lucas Ibarbourou (a soldier). *Education:* Educated in a convent.

MEMBER: Uruguayan Society of Authors (president, 1950), Uruguayan Academy of Letters.

AWARDS, HONORS: Consecrated "Juana de América" by the Uruguayan government in August, 1929.

WRITINGS:

Las lenguas de diamante, Agencia General de Librerías y Publicaciones, 1919, new edition, Losada (Buenos Aires), 1969.
El cántaro fresco, La Uruguaya (Montevideo), 1920, new edition, Acacia (Montevideo), 1969.
Les mejores poesías (líricas) de los mejores poetas, Editorial Cervantes (Barcelona), 1921, 2nd edition, 1930.
Raíz salvaje, Maximino García, 1922, 3rd edition, 1930.
Ejemplario, A. Monteverde (Montevideo), 1925, 3rd edition, 1928.
(Editor) *Páginas de literatura contemporánea: obra adoptada como texto por el Consejo n. de enseñanza primaria y normal,* A. Monteverde, 1928.
La rosa de los vientos, Palacio del Libro, 1930.
Estampas de la Biblia, Barreiro y Ramos (Montevideo), 1934.
Loores de Nuestra Señora, Barreiro y Ramos, 1934.
San Francisco de Asís, Rosgal (Montevideo), 1935.
Los más bellos versos, Art (Los Angeles, Mexico City and Havana), 1936.
Antología poética, Zig-Zag (Santiago, Chile), 1940.
Poemas, Espasa-Calpe, 1942.
Chico Carlo, cuentos, Barreiro y Ramos, 1944, new edition, Kapelusz (Buenos Aires), 1953.
Los sueños de Natacha, cinco obras de teatro para niños, Liceo, 1945.
Perdida, Losada, 1950.
Azor, Losada, 1953.
Obras completas, Aguilar (Madrid), 1953, 3rd edition, 1968.

Romances del destino, Instituto de Cultura Hispánica (Madrid), 1955.
Oro y tormenta, Zig-Zag, 1956.
Tiempo, Plaza y Janés (Barcelona), 1962.
Angor Dei, Pan American Union, 1963.
El dulce milagro, Universitaria de Buenos Aires, 1964.
Elegía, Ayuntamiento de la Ciudad de Palma de Mallorca, 1967.
La pasajera, diario de una isleña: Elegía, Losada, 1967.
Verso y prosa, Kapelusz, 1968.
Los mejores poemas, Arca (Montevideo), 1968.
Antología poética, Cultura Hispánica (Madrid), 1970.
Juan Soldado, Losada, 1971.
Antología de poesía y prosa, 1919-1971, Losada, 1972.
Juana de Ibarbourou, edited by Jorge Arbeleche, Arca, 1978.
Antología de poemas y prosas, edited by Artura Sergio Visca and Julio C. da Rosa, Ministerio de Educación y Cultura del Uruguay, 1980.
Tres poetistas, Editores Mexicanos Unidos, 1982.

Also author of *Poemas de Juana de Ibarbourou,* Belo Horizonte (Medellín).

SIDELIGHTS: Juana de Ibarbourou was one of Uruguay's most beloved poets. The vast popularity of her work led the Uruguayan legislature in 1929 to consecrate Ibarbourou as "Juana of América." Her simple, rhythmic poems of nature and love, particularly those found in her first three collections, were known throughout the Spanish-speaking world.

BIOGRAPHICAL/CRITICAL SOURCES:

BOOKS

Puentes de Oyenard, Sylvia, *Juana de Ibarbourou,* Asociación Uruguaya de Literatura Infantil-Juvenil, 1988.
Queiroz, Maria José de, *A poesia de Juana de Ibarbourou,* Belo Horizonte, 1961.

*   *   *

IBARGÜENGOITIA, Jorge 1928-1983

PERSONAL: Born 1928 in Guanajuato, Mexico; married; died in airplane crash, November 27, 1983, near Madrid, Spain.

ADDRESSES: Home—Paris, France.

CAREER: Playwright, 1953-83; novelist, 1963-83. Columnist in Mexico for eight years with newspaper *Excélsior.* Teacher of Spanish literature at various universities.

AWARDS, HONORS: Casa de las Américas award, 1963, for *El atentado;* Guggenheim fellowship, 1969; National Prize for novel, Mexican National Institute of Fine Arts.

WRITINGS:

(With Osvaldo Dragún) *Milagro en el mercado viejo* [and] *El atentado* (plays; the former by Dragún, the latter by Ibargüengoitia; also see below), Casa de las Américas, 1963.

Clotilde, El viaje, y El pájaro (play collection; contains "Clotilde en su casa," three acts; "El viaje superficial," four acts; and "Pájaro en mano," three acts), Universidad Veracruzana, 1964.

Los relámpagos de agosto (novel), Casa de las Américas, 1964, published as *Los relámpagos de agosto: Memorias de un general mexicano,* Ediciones de la Flor, 1973, translation by Irene del Corral published as *The Lightning of August,* Avon Bard, 1986.

La ley de Herodes y otros cuentos (short stories; contains "El episodio cinematográfico," "La ley de Herodes," "La mujer que no," "What Became of Pampa Hash?" "Manos muertas," "Cuento del canario," "Las pinzas," "Los tres muertos," "Mis embargos," "La vela perpetua," "Conversaciones con Bloomsbury," "Falta de espíritu Scout," and ",Quién se lleva a Blanca?"), Mortiz, 1967.

Maten al león (novel), Mortiz, 1969.

(Author of introduction) Leopoldo Alas, *La regenta,* Porrúa, 1972.

Viajes en la América ignota (articles first published in *Excélsior*), Mortiz, 1972.

Estas ruinas que ves, Novaro, 1975.

Sálvese quien pueda (articles first published in *Excélsior*), Novaro, 1975.

Las muertas (novel), Mortiz, 1977, translation by Asa Zatz published as *The Dead Girls,* Avon, 1983.

El atentado (three-act play; also see above), Mortiz, 1978.

Dos crímenes (novel), Mortiz, 1979, translation by Zatz published as *Two Crimes,* David Godine, 1984.

Los conspiradores, Argas Vergara, 1981.

Los pasos de López, Ediciones Océano, 1982.

Also author of several other plays.

SIDELIGHTS: Jorge Ibargüengoitia, a prize-winning novelist and playwright, was known throughout his native Mexico for his satiric treatment of Mexican social behavior and government. In addition to publishing plays, novels, and short stories, he served as a columnist for the Mexican newspaper *Excélsior* for eight years. Praised as a "politically committed writer" by Michele Slung in the *Washington Book World,* Ibargüengoitia was on his way to attend a congress on Hispanic culture in Bogotá, Colombia, when the Avianca 747 aircraft in which he was traveling crashed in heavy fog. Three other Latin American writers, Marta Traba, Angel Rama, and Manuel Scorza, also perished in the crash. Reviewing Ibargüengoitia's third book in English translation, *The Lightning of August,* critic Ariel Dorfman mourned in the *New York Times Book Review,* "I wish it were possible to look forward to new works by this subtle, precise novelist."

El atentado, Ibargüengoitia's best-known play, is a "thinly disguised" dramatization of the 1928 assassination of Mexican President-elect Alvaro Obregón, according to Sam L. Slick in *World Literature Today.* The piece's action rises out of opposition between the Catholic church and the Mexican Government. Act one concerns the re-emergence of General Borges (Obregón's fictional counterpart) on the Mexican political scene and includes the Catholic bombing attempt on the Mexican Chamber of Deputies. Act two focuses on Pepe, a character based on José Toral, Obregón's assassin. Pepe's murder of Borges is depicted on stage, as is Pepe's capture and questioning. The assassin is also subjected to an interview with Vidal Sánchez, a likeness of then Mexican President Plutarco Elias Calles. Act three presents Pepe's trial, ending with Sánchez's reconciliation with the Catholic church as a result of Borges's death. Because of its controversial, political nature, *El atentado* was not performed in Mexico until thirteen years after its writing, in spite of its winning an award from Casa de las Américas in 1963. Slick concluded, "*El atentado . . .* is significant in Mexican letters, for it honestly and courageously scrutinizes the marrow of national consciousness."

Las muertas (translated as *The Dead Girls*), is also based on real events. Ibargüengoitia's first novel in English translation, *The Dead Girls* is "one of the best-written Mexican novels of recent vintage," in Slick's opinion, and builds on the foundation of the Poquianchi case. The two Poquianchi sisters ran a prostitution ring during the 1950s and 1960s. They were arrested in 1964, after the discovery of women's bodies buried on the grounds of one of their brothels. But, as Ibargüengoitia says of *The Dead Girls* in its preface, "Some of the events described herein are real. All of the characters are imaginary." "His treatment of the villains and victims," observed Slick, "add[s] a human dimension to an otherwise pathetic cast of assassins and child prostitutes." In the novel, brothel owners Serafina and Arcángela Baladro enjoy great success until a morals act is passed and surprisingly enforced by a provincial governor. The Baladros close two of their brothels "and retreat with their prize whores to the ostensibly padlocked [third, the] Casino del Danzo," related critic Laura Furman in the *Washington Post Book World.* Confined together with no opportunity to do business, the relationship between the Baladros and their prostitutes deteriorates. Some of the women rebel against their imprisonment within the casino; some are killed and secretly buried. As Furman explained, "the twists and turns of spiraling morality, presented without comment or judgment, form another plot line in this compelling book." Told from many different viewpoints and simulating police reports given by the principles in the case, "*The Dead Girls* is all the more effective for treating its grotesqueries in a cool and lucid tone," judged Nicholas Rankin of the *Times Literary Supplement.* The novel, lauded Furman, is "a beautifully wrought story" and "a brilliant, cool look at the forms and the tolls that power may take."

Dos crímenes (translated as *Two Crimes*) concerns Marcos González, described by John Sutherland in *Listener* as "a political radical in the evening, a minor civil servant by day," and by Jules Koslow in the *New York Times Book Review* as "a crafty antihero with a larcenous heart." Marcos gets into trouble with the Mexican authorities when he gives shelter to a terrorist—the government then suspects Marcos in the burning of a department store. He flees, heading for his family home in the small town of Muerdago. There he becomes embroiled in various plots by relatives to ingratiate themselves with a rich uncle, to be written into his will and then murder him. From the idealism of his former political activities, Marcos "soon reverts, without any great sense of irony, to the *macho* ethic and petit-bourgeois opportunism" of the "provincial" town, reviewer Savkar Altinel interpreted in the *Times Literary Supplement.* Employing what Altinel labeled "the conventions of bedroom farce," Ibargüengoitia further complicates Marcos's situation by having his protagonist seduce a mother and her daughter simultaneously. Called "a beautifully imagined and structured tale" by Slung, *Two Crimes* "seems a simple invitation to fun and frolic," declared Elizabeth Hanly, critiquing in the *Voice Literary Supplement,* but "prob[es] the dark side of experience, caressing it until secrets are delivered up." According to Slung, "Ibargüengoitia . . . lets no one off the hook, even though he seems to have some affection for even the rogues and deadbeats among his characters."

Los relámpagos de agosto: Memorias de un general mexicano's translation into English was heralded by Dorfman as making more accessible the "first satire" of the Mexican Revolution. Narrated by Major General Lupe Arroyo, *The Lightning of August* centers on a group of incompetent generals, Arroyo included, who are striving for power. In their efforts they execute the wrong people and shell the wrong villages. Arroyo stands out from his fellow power-grabbers, however, in that he does not pretend to be acting out of idealism and is honest with his audience. Commenting on the book's somewhat madcap tone, Dorfman cautioned that "it is only after the laughter has subsided that we realize with a chill that the humor has enticed us into accepting on their own terms the characters' cold, almost matter-of-fact violence."

Another of Ibargüengoitia's novels, *Maten al león,* was praised as "swift-moving" and "suspense-filled" by Edward M. Malinak in *Books Abroad. Maten al león* explores the nature of political dictatorship, featuring despot Don Manuel Belaunzaran of Arepa. Conspiracies to overthrow Belaunzaran are depicted, as are the consequences of these attempts on Arepa's people. Noting its "vivid picturesque detail," Malinak labeled *Maten al león* an "outstanding literary contribution."

BIOGRAPHICAL/CRITICAL SOURCES:

BOOKS

Contemporary Literary Criticism, Volume 37, Gale, 1986.
Ibargüengoitia, Jorge, *The Dead Girls,* translated by Asa Zatz, Avon, 1983.

PERIODICALS

Books Abroad, summer, 1970.
Listener, August 9, 1984.
Los Angeles Times Book Review, September 2, 1984.
New York Times Book Review, September 23, 1984, February 23, 1986.
Times Literary Supplement, March 8, 1984, August 10, 1984.
Voice Literary Supplement, December, 1984.
Washington Post Book World, February 25, 1983, September 16, 1984.
World Literature Today, winter, 1979, summer, 1979, winter, 1981.

OBITUARIES:

PERIODICALS

Review 32, January-May, 1984.

*   *   *

ICAZA (CORONEL), Jorge 1906-1979

PERSONAL: Born July 10, 1906, in Quito, Ecuador; died May 26, 1979, in Quito; son of José Icaza Manso (a landed farmer) and Carmen Coronel; married Marina Moncayo (an actress), July 16, 1936; children: Cristina Icaza Prado, Fenia Icaza Mon-

cayo. *Education:* Attended Universidad Central de Quito, 1924-27, and Conservatorio Nacional, 1927-28.

ADDRESSES: Home—Ave. República El Salvador #563, Quito, Ecuador.

CAREER: Playwright, 1929-36; writer, 1933-79. Actor in Compañía Dramática Nacional of Ecuador, 1928-31; Pagaduría General (government treasury), Pichincha, Ecuador, civil servant, 1932-37; bookstore proprietor, 1938-44; founder and titular member of Ecuadorian Cultural Council, 1944-63; National Library of Ecuador, Quito, director, 1963-73; ambassador to Soviet Union, Poland, and East Germany, 1973-77. Cultural attaché to Ecuadorian ambassador in Buenos Aires, 1949. Organizer of various acting companies, including "Compañía de Variedades," 1931, and "Marina Moncayo," 1932 and 1946. Organizer and secretary-general of Union of Artists and Writers, beginning 1936. Professor at University of New Mexico, Quito, beginning 1969. Guest lecturer in Mexico and Costa Rica, 1940, New York, 1942, Venezuela and Cuba, 1948, Puerto Rico, 1949, Buenos Aires, 1949-50, Bolivia, 1956, Lima, Peru, and University of San Marcos, 1957, People's Republic of China, 1960, Soviet Union, 1961, Cuba, 1962, Brazil, 1963, Mexico, 1967, and in thirty American universities, 1973.

AWARDS, HONORS: Primer Premio de Novela Hispanoamericana, 1935, for *Huasipungo;* Primer Premio de Novela Nacional de Ecuador, 1935, for *En las calles;* gold medal from city of Guayaquil, 1958, for literary merit.

WRITINGS:

Barro de la sierra (short stories), Labor, 1933.
Huasipungo (novel), Talleres Gráficos Nacionales, 1935, 9th edition, 1973, translation by Mervyn Savill published under same title, Dobson, 1962, authorized translation by Bernard M. Dulsey of expanded 1951 edition published as *The Villagers,* Southern Illinois University Press, 1973.
En las calles (novel; title means "In the Streets"), Talleres Gráficos Nacionales, 1935.
Cholos (novel), Editorial Sindicato de Escritores y Artistas, 1937.
Media vida deslumbrados (novel), Editorial Quito, 1942.
Huairapamushcas (novel), Editorial Casa de la Cultura Ecuatoriana, 1948, published as *Hijos del viento* (title means "Children of the Wind"), Plaza y Janés, 1973.
Seis relatos (title means "Six Tales"), Editorial Casa de la Cultura Ecuatoriana, 1952, 2nd edition published as *Seis veces la muerte.*
El chulla Romero y Flores (novel), Editorial Casa de la Cultura Ecuatoriana, 1958.
Viejos cuentos (title means "Old Stories"), Editorial Casa de la Cultura Ecuatoriana, 1960.
Obras escogidas, Aguilar, 1961.
Atrapados (novel), Volume 1: *El juramento* (title means "The Oath"), Volume 2: *En la ficción* (title means "In Fiction"), Volume 3: *En la realidad* (title means "In Reality"), Losada, 1972.

Also author of an unfinished novel, *Los jaúregui y la milagrosa.* Editor of *SEA* (Journal of Sindicato de Escritores y Artistas), 1938.

PLAYS

"El intruso" (title means "The Intruder"), produced in Quito, September 8, 1928.
"La comedia sin nombre" (three-act; title means "The Comedy Without a Name"), produced in Quito, May 23, 1929.

"Por el viejo" (title means "For the Old Man"), produced in Quito, August 3, 1929.

¿Cuál es? [and] *Como ellos quieren* ("¿Cuál es?" produced in Quito, May 23, 1931), Labor, 1931.

Sin sentido (title means "Without Meaning"), Labor, 1932.

Flagelo (title means "The Scourge"; produced in Buenos Aires, 1940), Imprenta Nacional, 1936.

Also author of "El amaño" (ballet), 1947, and an unfinished volume of plays.

SIDELIGHTS: Jorge Icaza is internationally renowned for his realistic depictions of life in Ecuador. He began his career as a playwright, but when his version of Jules Romains's *Le Dictateur* was banned by the Ecuador government, he started writing novels instead. His first novel, *Huasipungo* ("The Villagers"), was a tremendous success. It is his protest against the exploitation of Ecuadorian Indians by capitalists. José Yglesias observed that "the characters are sketchily drawn, the incidents rapidly developed; but the language of the Indians has an incantatory beauty, the horrors illustrate an undeniable logic, and its author's compassion and indignation are genuine." Icaza's books have been translated into Russian, French, German, and many other languages.

MEDIA ADAPTATIONS: El chulla Romero y Flores was staged in 1971.

BIOGRAPHICAL/CRITICAL SOURCES:

PERIODICALS

America, April 11, 1964.
Book Week, April 19, 1964.
Christian Science Monitor, December 29, 1964.
Nation, April 13, 1964.
Saturday Review, May 30, 1964.

*   *   *

IMBERT, Enrique Anderson
See ANDERSON IMBERT, Enrique

INFANTE, G(uillermo) Cabrera
See CABRERA INFANTE, G(uillermo)

*   *   *

ISLAS, Arturo   1938-

PERSONAL: Born May 24, 1938, in El Paso, Tex.; son of Arturo Islas and Jovita La Farga. *Education:* Stanford University, B.A. (with distinction), 1960; Stanford University, M.A., 1963, Ph.D., 1971.

ADDRESSES: Office—Department of English, Stanford University, Stanford, Calif. 94305.

CAREER: Stanford University, Stanford, Calif., assistant professor, 1971-76, associate professor, 1976-86, professor of American and Chicano literatures, 1986—.

MEMBER: Rocky Mountain Modern Language Association, Phi Beta Kappa.

AWARDS, HONORS: Woodrow Wilson fellow, 1963-64; fellow of Howard Foundation, 1973-74; Carnegie-Mellon faculty award, 1974; Dinkelspiel Award for Outstanding Service to Undergraduate Education from Stanford University, 1976; *The Rain God* was selected one of the three best novels of 1984 by the Bay Area Book Reviewers Association; best fiction prize from the Border Regional Library association, 1985, for *The Rain God.*

WRITINGS:

The Rain God (novel), Alexandrian Press, 1984.
Migrant Souls (novel), Morrow, 1990.

Editor of *Miquiztli,* 1974-75. Contributor to periodicals, including *ZYZZYVA.*

WORK IN PROGRESS: La Mollie and the King of Tears, a novel; a third novel about the Angel family who live on the Mexican-Texas border.

J-K

JACQUELINE
See CARPENTIER (y VALMONT), Alejo

* * *

JAIMES FREYRE, Ricardo 1868-1933

PERSONAL: Born in 1868 in Tacna, Bolivia; became Argentine citizen, 1916; died in 1933.

ADDRESSES: Home—Tucumán, Argentina.

CAREER: Teacher of philosophy and of Spanish language and literature in Tucumán, Argentina, c. 1900-1933. Co-founder, with Rubén Darío, of *Revista de América,* 1894.

WRITINGS:

Castalia bárbara (poems; title means "Primeval Fountain"), [Buenos Aires], 1899, recent edition, introduction by Juan Siles Guevara, Ministerio de Educación y Bellas Artes, Fondo Nacional de Cultura (La Paz, Bolivia), 1970.

Historia de la República de Tucumán (history), [Buenos Aires], 1911.

Leyes de la versificación castellana (literary study), Coni Hermanos (Buenos Aires), 1912 (also see below).

El Tucumán del siglo XVI, bajo el gobierno de Juan Ramírez de Velasco (history), Coni Hermanos, 1914.

(Author of introduction and notes) *El Tucumán colonial: Documentos y mapas del Archivo de Indias,* Coni Hermanos, 1915.

Historia del descubrimiento de Tucumán, seguida de investigaciones históricas (history), Coni Hermanos, 1916.

Los sueños son vida (poems; title means "Dreams Are Life") [and] *Anadiomena* [and] *Las víctimas,* Sociedad Cooperativa (Buenos Aires), 1917.

Tucumán en 1810 (history), [Tucumán, Argentina], 1919, recent edition, [Tucumán], 1985.

Poesías completas (title means "Complete Poems"), edited with an introduction by Eduardo Joubin Colombres, Claridad (Buenos Aires), 1944.

Poesías completas, edited by F. Díez de Medina, Ministerio de Educación y Bellas Artes (La Paz), 1957.

Poemas [and] *Leyes de la versificación castellana,* edited with an introduction and notes by Antonio Castro Leal, Aguilar (Madrid, Spain), 1974.

SIDELIGHTS: Ricardo Jaimes Freyre was a member Hispanic poetry's *modernista* movement, which valued artistic beauty over everyday reality. He was an associate of the great leader of *modernismo,* Rubén Darío, and the two men jointly founded the respected but short-lived periodical *Revista de América* in 1894. As a poet Jaimes Freyre differed notably from Darío through his preference for blank verse, a style that he championed in literary study *Leyes de la versificación castellana.* While Darío employed classical mythology in his work, Jaimes Freyre sought out the more exotic myths of ancient Germanic culture as a basis for his first and most notable volume of poetry, *Castalia bárbara* ("Primeval Fountain"). By the early 1900s Jaimes Freyre had moved to the university town of Tucumán, where he taught and produced several works on the history of the area, including *Historia de la República de Tucumán* and *Tucumán en 1810.*

* * *

JIMENEZ, Francisco 1943-

PERSONAL: Born June 29, 1943, in San Pedro, Tlaquepaque, Mexico; immigrated to United States, 1947, naturalized citizen, 1965; son of Francisco (a farm laborer) and María (a cannery worker; maiden name, Hernández) González Jiménez; married Laura Catherine Facchini (a teacher), 1968; children: Francisco Andres, Miguel Antonio, Tomas Roberto. *Education:* University of Santa Clara, B.A., 1966; Columbia University, M.A., 1969, Ph.D., 1972; attended Harvard University, 1989. *Politics:* Democrat. *Religion:* Roman Catholic.

ADDRESSES: Home—624 Enos Ct., Santa Clara, Calif. 95051. *Office*—Department of Modern Languages, Division of Arts and Humanities, University of Santa Clara, Santa Clara, Calif. 95053.

CAREER: Columbia University, New York, N.Y., instructor, 1971-72, assistant professor of Spanish, 1973; University of Santa Clara, Santa Clara, Calif., assistant professor, 1973-77, associate professor, 1977-81, professor of modern languages and literature, 1981—, Phil and Bobbie Sanfilippo Professor, 1986—, director of Division of Arts and Humanities, 1981—, director of Mexico Summer Study Program at Universidad Nacional Autónoma de México, 1984—, member of board of trustees of the university, 1981-87. Visiting professor at Universidad Nacional Autónoma de México, summer, 1987; lecturer at California State University, Bakersfield, San Diego State University, California State College (now University), Dominguez Hills, Stanford University, University of Texas at Austin, Harvard University, University of Notre Dame, Graduate Theological Union, and Wellesley College. Director of Institute of Poverty and Conscience, 1985; member of board of directors of Far West Laboratory for Educational Research and Development, 1988-94. California State Commission for Teacher Preparation and Licensing, vice-chairman, 1976-77, chairman, 1977-79; vice-chair of California State Humanities Council, 1987-91; member of Western Association Accrediting Commission for Senior Colleges and Universities, 1989-92; member of bilingual advisory board of California Student Aid Commission. Member of board of directors of Círculo Artístico y Literario, 1980—. Consultant to WNET-TV.

MEMBER: Modern Language Association of America (member of Delegate Assembly, 1989-92), American Association of Teachers of Spanish and Portuguese, Hispanic Institute of the United States, National Chicano Council on Higher Education, National Association on Chicano Studies, Institute of Latin American Studies, American Association for Higher Education, Asociación Latino Americana de Bellas Artes (member of board of directors, 1979—), Pacific Coast Council of Latin American Studies (member of board of governors, 1977-79), Association of California Teachers of Foreign Languages, Raza Administrators and Counselors in Higher Education.

AWARDS, HONORS: Woodrow Wilson fellow, 1966, faculty development grant, 1983; National Defense Foreign Language fellow, 1968-69, 1969-70, and 1970-71; Ford Foundation grant, 1969; annual award from Arizona Quarterly, 1973, for the short story "The Circuit"; Distinguished Leadership in Education Award from California Teachers Association, 1979; award for "dedicated and continuous service in education" from Association of Mexican American Educators, 1986; Resolution of Commendation from California State Legislature and California State Commission on Teacher Credentialing, both 1986.

WRITINGS:

Episodios nacionales de Victoriano Salado Alvarez (title means "National Episodes of Victoriano Salado Alvarez"), translated from the original English by Nicolás Pizarro Suárez, Editorial Diana (Mexico City), 1974.
(With Gary D. Keller) ¡Viva la lengua! A Contemporary Reader (title means "Long Live Language"), Harcourt, 1975, 2nd edition (with Keller and Rose Marie Beebe), 1987.
(With Keller and Nancy A. Sebastiani) Spanish Here and Now, Harcourt, 1978.
(Editor) Identification and Analysis of Chicano Literature, Bilingual Press, 1978.
(Editor with Keller) Hispanics in the United States: An Anthology of Creative Literature, Bilingual Press, Volume 1, 1980, Volume 2, 1982.
Mosaico de la vida: Prosa chicana, cubana y puertorriqueña (title means "Mosaic of Life: Chicano, Cuban, and Puerto Rican Prose"), Harcourt, 1981.
Poverty and Social Justice: Critical Perspectives, Bilingual Press, 1987.

Work represented in anthologies, including Perspectivas: Temas de hoy y de siempre, edited by Mary Ellen Kiddle and Brenda Wegmann, Holt, 1974, 2nd edition, 1978; Purpose in Literature, edited by Edmund J. Farrell, Ruth S. Cohen, and others, Scott, Foresman, 1979; Fronteras, edited by Nancy Levy-Konesky and others, Holt, 1989; and Mexican American Literature, edited by Charles Tatum, Harcourt, 1990. Contributor to Dictionary of Mexican American History. Contributor of articles, stories, and

reviews to periodicals, including Arizona Quarterly, American Hispanist, Owl, Bilingual Review, Tiempo, and Hispania. Member of editorial advisory board of the series "Studies in the Language and Literature of United States Hispanos," Bilingual Press. Co-founder and West Coast editor of Bilingual Review/La Revista Bilingüe.

WORK IN PROGRESS: Migrant Child, a collection of autobiographical short stories, publication expected in 1992; La correspondencia de Victoriano Salado Alvarez, publication by Fondo de Cultura Económica expected in 1993; research on the Mexican-American oral tradition.

SIDELIGHTS: Francisco Jiménez told HW: "My primary goal in writing both scholarly and creative works is to fill the need for cultural and human understanding, between the United States and Mexico in particular. I write in both English and Spanish. The language I use is determined by what period in my life I write about. Since Spanish was the dominant language during my childhood, I generally write about those experiences in Spanish. My scholarly research has been published in both English and Spanish. Because I am bilingual and bicultural, I can move in and out of both American and Mexican cultures with ease; therefore, I have been able to write stories in both languages. I consider that a privilege."

BIOGRAPHICAL/CRITICAL SOURCES:

BOOKS

Cassidy, Jack and other editors, Follow the Wind, Scribner, 1987.
Meier, Matt S., Mexican American Biographies, Greenwood Press, 1988.

PERIODICALS

California Today, October 19, 1980.
Hispano, December 26, 1977, February 19, 1979, October 8, 1986.
Semanario Azteca, November 3, 1986.
World Literature Today, winter, 1981, spring, 1983.

                              *   *   *

JIMENEZ (MANTECON), Juan Ramón 1881-1958
(Ramon Jiménez, Juan Jiménez Mantecón, Juan Ramón)

PERSONAL: Born December 24, 1881, in Moguer, Huelva, Spain; died May 29, 1958, in San Juan, P.R.; married Zenobia Camprubí Aymar, 1916 (deceased, 1956). Education: Studied painting and poetry at Universidad de Sevilla.

CAREER: Poet and educator. Protégé of Nicaraguan modernist poet Rubén Darío in Spain and lecturer in Spanish and French poetry, 1900-36; Residencia de Estudiantes, Madrid, Spain, resident editor, beginning 1912; lived in self-imposed exile after the outbreak of the Spanish civil war, beginning in 1936; traveled to Puerto Rico, Cuba, and the United States; lecturer in South America, 1948-49; faculty member, University of Puerto Rico, 1951-58.

AWARDS, HONORS: Nobel Prize for literature, 1956.

WRITINGS:

Almas de violeta (title means "Purple Souls"), [Madrid], 1900.
Ninfeas (title means "Water Lilies"), [Madrid], 1900.
Rimas, [Madrid], 1902, reprinted, Taurus, 1981.
Arias tristes, [Madrid], 1903, reprinted, Taurus, 1981.
Jardines lejanos, [Madrid], 1904, reprinted, Taurus, 1982.

Elejías puras (also see below), [Madrid], 1908, edited with prologue by Francisco Garfias, Losada (Buenos Aires), 1964.

Elejías intermedias (also see below), [Madrid], 1908.

Olvidanzas I: Las hojas verdes 1906, [Madrid], 1909, enlarged edition published as *Olvidanzas (1906-1907),* edited by Garfias, Aguilar, 1968.

Elejías lamentables (also see below), [Madrid], 1910.

Baladas de primavera, [Madrid], 1910, enlarged edition published as *Baladas de primavera (1907),* edited by Garfias, Losada, 1964, published with *Las hojas verdes (1906),* Taurus, 1982.

La soledad sonora, [Madrid], 1911, reprinted, Taurus, 1981.

Poemas májicos y dolientes, [Madrid], 1911, enlarged edition edited by Garfias, Losada, 1965.

Pastorales, [Madrid], 1911, enlarged edition edited by Garfias, Losada, 1965, new enlarged edition edited by A. Campoamor and R. Gullón, Taurus, 1982.

Melancolía, [Madrid], 1912, reprinted, Taurus, 1981.

Laberinto, [Madrid], 1913, reprinted, Taurus, 1982.

Platero y yo (also see below), partial edition, [Madrid], 1914, reprinted as *Platero y yo, elegía andaluza,* Losada, 1940, first complete edition, Calleja, 1917, reprinted as *Platero y yo; elegía andaluza, 1907-1916,* with fifty illustrations by Rafael Alvarez Ortega, Aguilar, 1953, published with a new introduction by the author and illustrations by Baltasar Lobo, Librairie des Editions Espagnoles, 1953, translation by William and Mary Roberts published as *Platero and I: An Andalusian Elegy,* with illustrations by Lobo, P.C. Duchenes (New York), 1956, reprinted, Paragon House, 1986.

Estío (also see below), Calleja, 1915, published as *Estío: A punta de espina,* Losada, 1959, reprinted, Taurus, 1982.

Diario de un poeta recién casado (title means "Diary of a Newly Married Poet"; also see below), [Madrid], 1916, enlarged edition edited by Sánchez Barbudo, Labor (Barcelona), 1970, reprinted, Taurus, 1982, published as *Diario de poeta y mar,* A. Aguado (Madrid), 1955, 3rd edition, Losada, 1972.

Sonetos espirituales (also see below), Calleja, 1917, reprinted, Taurus, 1982, published as *Sonetos espirituales (1914-1915),* A. Aguado, 1957, 3rd edition, Losada, 1970.

Obras de Juan Ramón Jiménez, Calleja (Madrid), 1917.

Poesías escojidas (1899-1917) de Juan Ramón Jiménez, Hispanic Society of America (New York), 1917.

Eternidades, verso 1916-1917 (also see below), [Madrid], 1918, reprinted, Losada, 1944, new edition, Taurus, 1982, published as *Obras: Eternidades, verso (1916-1917),* Renacimiento, 1931.

Piedra y cielo (also see below), [Madrid], 1919, published as *Piedra y cielo, 1917-1918,* Losada, 1948, reprinted, Taurus, 1981.

Antolojía poética, Losada, 1922, reprinted, 1966.

Segunda antolojía poética, [Madrid-Barcelona], 1922, published as *Segunda antología poética 1898-1918,* Espasa-Calpe (Madrid), 1956, reprinted, 1976.

Poesías escojidas, [Mexico], 1923.

Poesía en verso, privately printed (Madrid), 1923, reprinted, Taurus, 1981.

Belleza (also see below), privately printed (Madrid), 1923, reprinted, Taurus, 1981.

Poesías de Juan Ramón Jiménez, compiled by Pedro Henríquez Ureña, México Moderno, 1923.

Unidad (eight notebooks; also see below), [Madrid], 1925.

Poesía en prosa y verso (also see below), edited by his children and Z. C. Aymar, Signo, 1932, 2nd edition, 1933, reprinted, Aguilar, 1962.

Sucesión (also see below), [Madrid], 1932.

Presente (also see below), [Madrid], 1933.

Juan Ramón Jiménez: Canción, Signo, 1936, reprinted as *Canción,* with introduction by Agustín Caballero, Aguilar, 1961.

(Editor) *La poesía cubana en 1936,* Institución Hispanocubana de Cultura, 1937.

Ciego ante ciegos (poems), Publicaciones de la Secretaría de Educación, Dirección de Cultura (Cuba), 1938.

Españoles de tres mundos, viejo mundo, nuevo mundo, otro mundo: Caricatura lírica, 1914-1940 (poetry), Losada, 1942, reprinted, 1958, edited by Gullón, A. Aguado, 1960.

Voces de mi copla, Editorial Stylo, 1945, reprinted, Molinas de Agua, c. 1980, published with *Romances de Coral Gables,* Taurus, 1981.

La estación total (poetry; title means "The Total Season"; also see below), [Buenos Aires], 1946.

El zaratán, with etchings by Alberto Beltrán, Antigua Librería Robredo, 1946, commemorative edition published with illustrations by Gregorio Prieto, Dirección General de Archivos y Biblioteca, 1957.

Animal de fondo (poetry; title means "Animal of Depth"; also see below), [Buenos Aires], 1947, published with French translations by Galtier, Editorial Pleamar, 1949.

Romances de Coral Gables (1939-1942), Editorial Stylo (Mexico), 1948, reprinted as *La Florida en Juan Ramón Jiménez,* edited by Ana Rosa Núñez, 1968.

Fifty Spanish Poems, with English translations by J. B. Trend, Dolphin Book Co. (England), 1950, University of California Press, 1951.

Antología para niños y adolescentes, selected by Norah Borges and Guillermo de Torre, Losada, 1951.

Tres poemas: De "Dios deseado y deseante" (poems; title means "God Desired and Desiring"; also see below), Santander, 1953.

Los mejores versos de Juan Ramón Jiménez, [Buenos Aires], 1956.

Platero es pequeño, peludo, suave (excerpts from *Platero y yo*), Talleres Gráfico Octavio y Félez, 1956.

Libros de poesía: Sonetos spirituales, Estío, Diario de un poeta recién casado, Eternidades, Piedra y cielo, Belleza, Poesía, La estación total, Animal de fondo, edited with foreword by Caballero, Aguilar, 1957.

Tercera antolojía poética (1898-1953), Editorial Biblioteca Nueva, 1957, reprinted, 1971.

Antología poética (1898-1953), edited by Eugenio Florit, 1957, reprinted, Biblioteca Nueva, 1981, translation by H. R. Hays published as *Selected Writings,* Farrar, Straus and Cudahy, 1957.

Homenaje de la Revista la torre, University of Puerto Rico, 1957.

La estación total con las canciones de la nueva luz, 1923-1936, Losada, 1958.

Pájinas escojidas, prosa, compiled by Gullón, Editorial Gredos, (Madrid), 1958.

Pájinas escojidas, verso, compiled by Gullón, Editorial Gredos, 1958.

Moguer, illustrations by José R. Escassi, Dirección General de Archivos y Bibliotecas, 1958.

El romance, río de la lengua española, Universidad de Puerto Rico, 1959.

Primeros libros de poesía, compiled by Garfias, Aguilar, 1959.

Cuadernos (includes *Sucesión,* "Obra en marcha," *Unidad, Presente* and *Hojas*), edited by Garfias, Taurus, 1960.

Olvidos de Granada, 1924-1928, Universidad de Puerto Rico, 1960, facsimile edition, Gaballo Griego para la Poesía, 1979.

La corriente infinita; crítica y evocación, edited by Garfias, Aguilar, 1961.

Relaciones amistosas y literarias entre Juan Ramón Jiménez y los Martínez Sierra, compiled by Gullón, Ediciones de la Torre, 1961.

Por el cristal amarillo (also see below), compiled by Garfias, Aguilar, 1961.

El trabajo gustoso (lectures), compiled by Garfias, Aguilar, 1961.

Primeras prosas (also see below), compiled by Garfias, Aguilar, 1962.

El modernismo, edited by Gullón and E. F. Méndez, Aguilar, 1962.

Three Hundred Poems, 1903-1953, translations by Eloise Roach, University of Texas Press, 1962, published with poems in original Spanish as *Trecientos poemas,* Plaza & Janés, 1963, published with *Platero y yo,* Editorial Porrúa (Mexico), 1968.

Sevilla, edited by Garfias, [Sevilla], 1963.

La colina de los chopos (also see below), Círculo de Lectores, 1963, 2nd edition published as *La colina de los chopos: Madrid posible e imposible,* edited by Garfias, Taurus, 1971.

Poemas revividos del tiempo de Moguer, Ediciones Chapultepec, 1963.

Dios deseado y deseante: Animal de Fondo con numerosos poemas inéditos, with introduction and notes by A. Sánchez Barbudo, Aguilar, 1964, translation by Antonio T. de Nicolás published as *God Desired and Desiring,* Paragon House, 1987.

Libros inéditos de poesía (two volumes), compiled by Garfias, Aguilar, 1964-67.

Retratos líricos, R. Díaz-Casariego, 1965.

Antología poética, edited by Vicente Gaos, Anaya (Salamanca), 1965, 10th edition, Cátedra, 1984.

Estética y ética estética, crítica y complemento, edited by Garfias, Aguilar, 1967.

Libros de prosa, (includes *Primeras prosas, Platero y yo, La colina de los chopos,* and *Por el cristal amarillo*), Aguilar, 1969.

Nueva antolojía poética, Losada, 1969.

Fuego y sentimiento, 1918-1920, Artes Gráficas L. Pérez, 1969.

Juan Ramón y yo y Ríos que se van, selections by wife Zenobia Camprubí Jiménez, Gráficas L. Pérez, 1971.

Ellos, de mi propia sangre, 1918-1920, [Madrid], 1973.

Death of Death: Poems, translations by Renato J. Gonzalez, P. Lal (Calcutta, India), c. 1973.

Con el carbón del sol; antología de prosa lírica, edited by Garfias, EMESA, 1973.

Antología, compiled by A. González, Júcar, 1974, 3rd edition, EMESA, 1979.

En el otro costado, compiled by Aurora de Albornoz, Ediciones Júcar, 1974.

El andarín de su órbita: Selección de prosa crítica, edited by Garfias, EMESA, 1974.

Crítica paralela, selections and commentary by Arturo del Villar, Nárcea de Ediciones, 1975.

La obra desnuda, edited by del Villar, Aldebarán, 1976, translation by Dennis Maloney published as *The Naked Book! An Illustrated Poem of Juan Ramón Jiménez,* White Pine, 1984, 2nd edition published as *Naked Music: Poems of Juan Ramón Jiménez.*

Leyenda 1896-1958, edited by A. Sánchez Romeralo, CUSPA, 1978.

Don't Run: A Poem of Juan Ramón Jiménez, translation by Maloney, White Pine, 1980.

Edición del centenario: Juan Ramón Jiménez, twenty volumes, Taurus, 1981-82.

Prosas críticas, compiled by P. Gómez Bedate, Taurus, 1981.

Canta pájaro lejano, Espasa-Calpe, 1981.

Thirty-Five Poems del Mar, compiled by L. Jiménez Martos, Rialp, 1981.

Antolojía jeneral en prosa (1898-1954), edited by Crespo and Gómez Bedate, Biblioteca Nueva, 1981.

Baladas de amor: Selección de baladas para después y Odas líricas, Aro Artes Gráficas, 1981.

Juan Ramón Jiménez en Cuba, compiled by Cintio Vitier, Editorial Arte y Literatura, 1981.

Isla de la simpatía, Ediciones Huracán, 1981.

Poesía: Juan Ramón Jiménez, compiled by Emilio de Armas, Editorial Arte y Literatura, 1982.

Política poética, Alianza, 1982.

Poesías últimas escojidas (1918-1958), edited by Sánchez Romeralo, Espasa-Calpe, 1982.

Elegías (includes *Elejías puras, Elejías intermedias,* and *Elejías lamentables*), edited by Garfias, Taurus, 1982.

Espacio (also see below), edited by Albornoz, Editorial Nacional, 1982.

Flower Scene, translations by J. C. R. Green, Aquila, 1982.

Juan Ramón Jiménez: Antología poética, compiled by Germán Bleiberg, Alianza, 1983.

Alerta (essays), compiled by F. Javier Blasco, Universidad de Salamanca, 1983.

La realidad invisible, Támesis, 1983, translation by de Nicolás published as *Invisible Reality,* Pergamon, 1986.

Guerra en España, 1936-1953 (autobiography), edited by A. Crespo, Seix Barral, 1985.

Juan Ramón Jiménez para niños, Ediciones de la Torre, 1985.

Stories of Life and Death, translation by de Nicolás, Paragon House, 1986.

Tiempo y espacio, edited by Villar, 1986, translation by de Nicolás published as *Time and Space: A Poetic Autobiography,* Paragon House, 1988.

Hijo de la alegría, El Observatorio, 1986.

Antología comentada, compiled by Sánchez Barbudo, Ediciones de la Torre, 1986.

Light and Shadows: Selected Poems and Prose, translations by R. Bly and others, edited by Maloney, White Pine, 1987.

LETTERS

The Literary Collaboration and the Personal Correspondence of Rubén Darío and Juan Ramón Jiménez, edited by Donald F. Fogelquist, University of Miami Press, 1956.

Monumento de amor: Cartas de Zenobia Camprubí y Juan Ramón Jiménez, foreword by Gullón, Ediciones de la Torre, 1959.

Cartas de Antonio Machado a Juan Ramón Jiménez, Ediciones de la Torre, 1959.

Cartas; primera selección, compiled by Garfias, Aguilar, 1962.

Selección de cartas, 1899-1958, Ediciones Picazo, 1973.

Cartas literarias, Bruguera, 1977.

Cartas de Juan Ramón Jiménez al poeta malagueño José Sánchez Rodríguez, edited by A. Sánchez Trigueros, Editorial Don Quijote, 1984.

TRANSLATOR

Romain Rolland, *Vida de Beethoven,* [Madrid], 1915.

(With Aymar) John M. Synge, *Jinetes hacia el mar,* [Madrid], 1920.

(With Aymar) Rabindranath Tagore, *El cartero del rey; La luna nueva,* Losada, 1922, 10th edition, 1972.

(With Aymar) Tagore, *Verso y prosa para niños,* [Puerto Rico], 1936, 3rd edition, Editorial Orión, 1956, reprinted, 1976.

(With Aymar) Tagore, *El naufrajio* (title means "The Wreck"), Editorial Magisterio Español, 1974.

OTHER

Also author of *Aristocracia y democracia,* University of Miami, and *Poesía de siempre: Poemas,* Horizonte (Medellín). Works represented in numerous anthologies of Spanish poetry, such as *Antonio Machado, Juan Ramón Jiménez, Federico García Lorca,* edited by Aitana and Rafael Alberti, Ediciones Nauta, 1970. Contributor to newspapers and literary journals in Huelva, Seville, and Madrid, including *Helios, Indice, España, El Sol,* and *La Gaceta Literaria.*

SIDELIGHTS: Juan Ramón Jiménez is considered one of the best and most influential of Spanish poets. His early lyric poetry impressed the major modernist poets of his culture who enlisted him in their attempt to revitalize Spanish poetry. Accomplished in the poetic tradition he inherited, Jiménez went on to develop a new poetics that expanded the frontiers of Spanish literature. Critics divide his works into three periods or stages according to changes in his style. Works from the first period showed the influence of his modernist peers; in the second period he developed the personal aesthetic that became a spiritual discipline in the third. "In a nation where art is often associated with a kind of willful roughness, Jiménez will be remembered always for certain exceptionally 'perfect' compositions," Claudio Guillen noted in a *New Republic* review. *Platero y yo,* a collection of prose poems that record a man's conversations with his donkey, was tremendously popular during the author's lifetime and is still being enjoyed by children and adults around the world. His works have been translated into English, French, German, Italian, Swedish, Welsh, Finnish, Portuguese, Romanian, and the language of the East Indian people of Orissa. His achievement was rewarded by the Nobel Prize in 1956.

Jiménez was born in 1881 to a wealthy couple who lived in Moguer near Huelva on the southwestern coast of Spain. He studied at a Jesuit school and though he was often ill, he enjoyed life and took an early interest in literature. He was not yet twenty when his poems first appeared in literary journals in Huelva, Seville, and Madrid. These melodious lyrics are richly embellished with images of the natural beauty of the land near his family home. For Jiménez, the contemplation of natural beauty led to moments of epiphany, moments in which he experienced communion with God. Like the Greek philosopher Plato, Jiménez believed that every physical object is a copy of a pre-existing, conceptual prototype that exists in the world of ideas. As he caught glimpses of this perfect world in nature or art, the poet would experience "a flash of comprehension, a moment of ecstatic oneness with some natural beauty, a wave of emotion disclosing the essence of some thing," Walter T. Pattison wrote in *Hispania.* The beautiful or beloved objects, however, were subject to change or destruction so that the poet was always conscious of loss. His poems were his attempt to extend the life of the natural beauty and the mystical experiences he loved. Though "salvaging something enduring from the wreckage of time" has been a common theme among poets, "the whole of Juan Ramón Jiménez's poetic work may, indeed, be said to be devoted to the problem of this kind of 'salvation,'" Paul R. Olson observed in *Circle of Paradox: Time and Essence in the Poetry of Juan Ramón Jiménez.*

When his father died, the poet's fascination with the eternal as it revealed itself in nature became an obsession. Writing poetry was an essential component of this spiritual quest. In *The Religious Instinct of the Poetry of Juan Ramón Jiménez,* Leo R. Cole explained, "Juan Ramón was in search of a personal God who would reveal Himself through the poet's creative activity which makes the word part of the living consciousness." Between 1905 and 1912 Jiménez lived alone and worked as a lecturer in Spanish literature and French poetry. During this highly creative period he wrote many of the works he would spend the rest of his life perfecting. Poems he published before 1921 show his mastery of traditional poetic forms. Critics regard his sonnets (published in *Sonetos espirituales*) among the best ever written in Spanish.

During the second stage, Jiménez developed a personal aesthetic he called "la poesía desnuda" (naked poetry). While composing poems, he pruned away excess words formerly included for the sake of filling out patterns of rhyme or meter. Writing in free verse allowed him to zero in on the quintessential elements of his subject matter; the content—the perception he was trying to capture—would find its own best images arranged in their own best order. The resulting short poems, said Guillen, are held together by "the sensibility, the feeling, or the symbol" instead of the usual logic of speech, or the symmetry provided by forms of verse. "These poems seem to me . . . to represent not so much an attempt to create *things* as to seize an almost unseizable experience," Gerald Brenan wrote in *The Literature of the Spanish People From Roman Times to the Present Day.*

In poems from this period, it is clear that the poet's allegiance to his own purpose became so strong that his quest became his principle of composition. Two internal tensions infused the poems with an energy that critics call "mystery." Some tension was created while trying to communicate the eternal in the passing moment; another tension arose from the struggle to express a private inner world in terms of the surrounding reality. In addition, the strong emotions expressed in these shorter poems gave them a tone more urgent than the tone of previous works. Guillen observed, "If one virtue or one method may be considered characteristic of his poetry, it is that of concentration. Concentration on the indispensible effect, surrounded by silences, concentration above all on the single word, on the force and the magic of which language is capable."

Jiménez relished the symbolic capabilities of words in his 1916 work *Diario de un poeta recién casado.* Its poems expressed his meditations during his voyage to the United States for his wedding to Zenobia Camprubí Aymar. Throughout the *Diario,* Jiménez used the sea as the dominant metaphor, to express conflicting desires. He was accustomed to solitude, and the poet's inclination to remain insular fought with his desire to become more open, to share his personal world with his wife, to become vulnerable to intrusions from the outside world. Howard T. Young, writing in *The Victorious Expression: A Study of Four Contemporary Spanish Poets,* called *Diario* "one of the most remarkable books of Spanish poetry."

In *Diario* "a new practice of poetry achieves its maturity," Michael P. Predmore stated in *Contemporary Literature,* ". . . a new kind of ordering and structuring of poems within . . . a symbolic system." This "masterpiece," he explained, "is a highly complex structure of recurring clusters of images and recurring patterns of association. . . . Each recurring image acquires symbolic value and each poem is a symbolic poem" that contributes by means of its position in the sequence to the book's final effect. Because of the prominence of the sea as a symbol in this work, later editions were titled *Diario de un poeta y mar* ("Diary of a Poet and the Sea"). Roses, pine trees, and water images that recur in his poems also took on the significance of personal symbols.

In the poet's third stylistic period, his lifelong spiritual quest was most evident. Changes in his life in the late 1930s contributed a new urgency to his quest. After he broadened his sensibility through marriage, his sense of security was further challenged by the experience of loss. To escape pressures brought about by the Spanish Civil War, in 1936 Jiménez left his homeland, which remained fresh in his memory in the form of his poems. He traveled to Cuba, the United States, and Puerto Rico, where he became a lecturer at the university. While he coped with these challenges, the process of perfecting his poems—of recording his perceptions of the eternal as it revealed itself in nature—became for him a vital spiritual discipline. Guillen reported that Jiménez was a ruthless revisionist, burning manuscripts he felt were inferior and repeatedly going over earlier works to improve them. The process of seeking perfect articulation became a subject in many of these later poems, so that they became a study of poetics. About works from this period, Young commented that "much of his best final poetry is a metaphor of the creative human mind."

The spiritual longing that propelled Jiménez through earlier stages found its fulfillment in his final works. Published in 1946, *La estación total* includes poems Jiménez worked on between 1923 and 1936. In these poems, the opposite terms of several paradoxes are reconciled into a unified synthesis. For example, instead of perceiving the four seasons as signals of change and loss, Jiménez recognized them as a single unit or circle, a "total season." Carl W. Cobb observed in *Contemporary Spanish Poetry (1898-1963)* that the book's "title is of course meaningful: a *season* is a temporal period of growth and decay, but *total* suggests the poet's attempt to fuse all seasons into one, into a difficult eternity." In these poems, the poet also recognized that his spiritual quest could be satisfied. He came to see loss as a necessary experience, since beauty is not actually perfect until it has transcended its temporal being and become synonymous with its Platonic or spiritual ideal through memory. Though the prospect of death and non-being troubled Jiménez throughout his life, "as poet he struggled through to a position in which death does not negate the soul," related Cobb.

Animal de fondo ("Animal of Depth"), written on a voyage to Buenos Aires and published in 1946, celebrates the resolution of the poet's longing for eternity in a world of endless change. Young noted that its publication marked the poet's "joyful acclamation of mysticism as the final end of poetry." Informed by the teachings of both Christianity and Eastern religions, he affirmed that the traditional gulf between the flesh and the spirit, the temporal and the eternal, did not exist. He expressed this fusion in the word "*cuerpialma*—bodysoul—to describe the intimacy between matter and spirit, or, as he called it, the encounter of reality and its image," stated Young. Cobb explains, "He was to the end an 'Animal of depth,' a soul-and-body forever responsive to the colors, sounds, smells, and tastes of the earth. Yet with his symbols he sought to evoke the inner reality in, above, or beyond the senses. In the intensity of the lived moment he attempted to expand the limits of human consciousness and record it in permanent form in his *Obra*. . . . As a lyric poet this was his 'beautiful vocation,' his final 'ethics through aesthetics.' " Thus having overcome the melancholy that previously attended his sense of loss over the mutable world, in this "spiritual autobiography," Jiménez published a "shout of joy, the exultation that tugs at the reader," added Young. "At the pinnacle of his years, Jiménez saw the labor of a lifetime finally resolved, and wrote his first

book in which there is not a trace of despondency nor a touch of shadow."

Jiménez became a figure in the history of the Spanish literature he taught by making a number of important contributions to the art of poetry. Pattison suggested that his "first great contribution to the modern concept of poetry is precisely the idea of the poet as a mystic of nature. . . . In this century most Spanish poets have followed his lead." Jiménez also fostered a new critical and compositional perspective, the understanding that a single poem can best be understood when seen as a component part of a larger body of related symbols. Brenan remarked that because Jiménez found new forms and images to continue the self-examination central to lyric verse, "The whole of contemporary poetry comes out of him." Thus Jiménez is viewed as the essential link between his modernist predecessors and the generations of Spanish poets that came after him.

BIOGRAPHICAL/CRITICAL SOURCES:

BOOKS

Bell, Audrey F. G., *Contemporary Spanish Literature,* Knopf, 1925.

Brenan, Gerald, *The Literature of the Spanish People From Roman Times to the Present Day,* Cambridge University Press, 1951.

Cardwell, Richard, *Juan R. Jiménez: The Modernist Apprenticeship, 1895-1900,* Colloquium Verlag, 1977.

Cobb, Carl W., *Contemporary Spanish Poetry (1898-1963),* Twayne, 1976.

Cole, Leo R., *The Religious Instinct in the Poetry of Juan Ramón Jiménez,* Dolphin Book Co., 1967.

Diego, Gerardo, *Poesía española contemporánea (1901-1934),* Taurus, 1974.

Gullón, Ricardo, *Estudios sobre Juan Ramón Jiménez,* Losada, 1960.

Jiménez, Juan Ramón, *Guerra en España, 1936-1953* (autobiography), edited by A. Crespo, Seix Barral, 1985.

Olson, Paul R., *Circle of Paradox: Time and Essence in the Poetry of Juan Ramón Jiménez,* Johns Hopkins University Press, 1967.

Twentieth-Century Literary Criticism, Volume 4, Gale, 1981.

Young, Howard T., *The Victorious Expression: A Study of Four Contemporary Spanish Poets,* University of Wisconsin Press, 1964.

PERIODICALS

Books Abroad, autumn, 1961, summer, 1968.

Contemporary Literature, winter, 1972.

Hispania, February, 1950, September, 1971.

Modern Language Notes, June, 1960, November, 1961, January, 1963.

New Republic, December 16, 1957.

PMLA, January, 1970.

Poetry, July, 1953.

Revista Hispánica Moderna: Columbia University Hispanic Studies, Volume 34, number 4, 1970-71.

*　　*　　*

JIMENEZ, Ramón
　See JIMENEZ (MANTECON), Juan Ramón

JIMENEZ MANTECON, Juan
See JIMENEZ (MANTECON), Juan Ramón

* * *

JUARROZ, Roberto 1925-

PERSONAL: Born in 1925, in Coronel Dorrego, Argentina.

CAREER: Poet.

WRITINGS:

Poesía vertical, Equis, 1958, reprinted, Monte Avila Editores, 1976.
Segunda poesía vertical, Equis, 1963.
Tercera poesía vertical, Equis, 1965.
El curso audiovisual de bibliotecología para América Latina, UNESCO, 1969, published as *América Latina,* 1970.
Cuarta poesía vertical, Aditor, 1969.
Quinta poesía vertical, Equis, 1974.
Poesía vertical, antología mayor (contains selections from *Poesía vertical, Segunda poesía vertical, Tercera poesía vertical, Cuarta poesía vertical,* and *Quinta poesía vertical*), Carlos Lohlé, 1978, translation by W. S. Merwin published as *Vertical Poetry,* North Point Press, 1988.
Poesía y creación: Diálogos con Guillermo Boido, Carlos Lohlé, 1980.
Poesía vertical, nuevos poemas, Mano de Obra, 1981.
Séptima poesía vertical, Monte Avila Editores, 1982.
Octava poesía vertical, Carlos Lohlé, 1984.
Novena poesía vertical, décima poesía vertical, Carlos Lohlé, 1986.
Undécima poesía vertical, Pre-Textos, 1988.

SIDELIGHTS: In a review of Roberto Juarroz's *Vertical Poems* a critic for *Publishers Weekly* notes that the poetry in this book "convey the Argentine Juarroz's ideas about the continuity and infinity of human experience: once external factors are stripped away from one's life, what remains is abstract and primitive."

BIOGRAPHICAL/CRITICAL SOURCES:

PERIODICALS

Publishers Weekly, July 1, 1988.

* * *

KANELLOS, Nicolás 1945-

PERSONAL: Born January 31, 1945, in New York, N.Y.; son of Charles and Inés (de Choudens García) Kanellos; married Cristelia Pérez, 1983; children: Miguel José. *Education:* Fairleigh Dickinson University, Madison, B.A., 1966; University of Texas at Austin, M.A., 1968, Ph.D., 1973.

ADDRESSES: Office—c/o Arte Público Press, University of Houston, M. D. Anderson Library, Room 2, Houston, Tex. 77204-2090.

CAREER: Founder of *Revista Chicano-Riqueña* (now *Americas Review*), 1972, Gary, Ind., (now located in Houston, Tex.), publisher, 1979—; Indiana University Northwest, Gary, assistant professor, 1973-79; teacher at University of Houston, Houston; Arte Público Press, University of Houston, founder, 1979, publisher, 1979—.

MEMBER: American Association of Teachers of Spanish and Portuguese, National Association of Chicano Studies, Modern Language Association.

AWARDS, HONORS: Calouste Gulbenkian fellowship for study and research in Portugal, 1969-70; Eli Lilly Fellowship, 1976; Outstanding Editor Award from Coordinating Council of Literary Magazines, 1979; National Endowment for the Humanities Fellowship, 1979; induction into the Texas Institute of Letters, 1984; Ford Foundation/National research council fellowship, 1986-87; White House Hispanic Heritage Award for Literature, 1988; American Book Award, 1989.

WRITINGS:

(Editor) *Los Tejanos: A Texas-Mexican Anthology,* Arte Público, 1980.
(Editor) *A Decade of Hispanic Literature: An Anniversary Anthology,* Arte Público, 1982.
(Editor) *Mexican American Theater: Then and Now,* Arte Público, 1983.
(Editor) *Hispanic Theatre in the United States,* Arte Público, 1984.
Two Centuries of Hispanic Theatre in the Southwest, Arte Público, 1985.
Mexican American Theater: Legacy and Reality, Latin American Literary Review Press, 1987.
(Editor) *Biographical Dictionary of Hispanic Literature in the United States: The Literature of Puerto Ricans, Puerto Rican Americans, Cuban Americans, and Other Hispanic Writers,* Greenwood Press, 1989.
(Editor with Jorge A. Huerta) *Nuevos Pasos: Chicano and Puerto Rican Drama,* Arte Público, 1989.
A History of Hispanic Theatre in the United States, University of Texas Press, 1990.

Contributor of articles and play reviews to journals, including *Hispania, Theater, Journal of Popular Culture, Latin American Theatre Review, Bulletin of the Comediantes,* and *Vista.*

WORK IN PROGRESS: Reference works on U.S. Hispanic culture; a book on ethnic autobiography.

SIDELIGHTS: Nicolás Kanellos, a Puerto Rican-American publisher and educator, founded the magazine *Revista Chicano-Riqueña* (now *Americas Review*) and the Arte Público Press to promote works of Hispanic American writers and draw them into the mainstream of American fiction.

Kanellos told *CA:* "As a publisher of Hispanic literature in the United States, I feel like a missionary who has to convert people to their own religion and identity. Hispanic culture has always been a part of the United States and its identity. People do not realize this, because the publishing and intellectual establishment have kept it a secret while selling us on an old-world identity, purely white Anglo-Saxon simulacrum. Arte Público Press intends to give back to the United States its many varied peoples."

BIOGRAPHICAL/CRITICAL SOURCES:

PERIODICALS

American Bookseller, August, 1989.
Chronicle of Higher Education, May 17, 1989.
Lector, December, 1982.
Publishers Weekly, November 28, 1986, June 9, 1989.
Texas Journal, spring/summer, 1989.

KELLER, Gary D. 1943-
(El Huitlacoche)

PERSONAL: Born January 1, 1943, in San Diego, Calif.; son of Jack (a teacher) and Estela Cárdenas (an anthropologist) Keller; married Mary Lindemann (a publishing executive), 1967; children: Randall, Thomas and Shawn (twins). *Education:* University of the Americas, B.A. (philosophy), 1963; Columbia University, M.A. (Hispanic literature and linguistics), 1967, Ph.D. (Spanish), 1971; New School for Social Research, M.A. (psychology), 1971; graduate study at City University of New York, 1972-75.

ADDRESSES: Home—10330 East Jenan Dr., Scottsdale, Ariz. 85260. *Office*—Hispanic Research Center, Arizona State University, Tempe, Ariz. 85287.

CAREER: Spanish teacher in New York, 1963-67; Pace University, New York City, instructor in Spanish and French, 1967-69; Columbia University, New York City, instructor in department of Spanish and Portuguese, 1969-70; City College of the City University of New York, New York City, assistant professor of Spanish and supervisor of M.A. program in Hispanic linguistics, 1970-74; York College of the City University of New York, Jamaica, N.Y., associate professor, 1974-79, chairman of department of humanities, foreign languages, and English as a second language, 1974-76; Eastern Michigan University, Ypsilanti, graduate school dean and chief research officer, 1979-83; State University of New York at Binghamton, provost of graduate studies, 1983-86; Arizona State University, Hispanic Research Center, Tempe, Ariz., professor of Spanish, 1986—, Regents' Professor, 1988—. Visiting professor of Hispanic linguistics, New York University, 1973, 1978; adjunct professor of education, Columbia University, 1977-79; visiting professor of education, William Patterson State College of New Jersey, 1978-79. Consultant to the National Institute of Education, 1975, U.S. Information Service, 1978, Hispanic Higher Education Coalition, 1979—, National Endowment for the Humanities, 1981, Michigan Council for the Humanities, 1981, Michigan Council for the Arts, 1982, and numerous other organizations and institutions.

MEMBER: American Association of Higher Education, American Education Research Association, Modern Language Association of America, Linguistic Society of America, American Association of Teachers of Spanish and Portuguese, National Association for Chicano Studies, National Association for Bilingual Education, National Chicano Council of Higher Education.

AWARDS, HONORS: Awarded grants from Research Foundation of the City University of New York, 1972, Schiff Funds, City University of New York, 1973, New York University, 1975, New York State Council on the Arts, 1978, National Endowment for the Arts, 1978, 1980, 1982, Arizona State University, 1987, 1988, and numerous other grants; "Writer's Choice" award, National Endowment for the Arts, 1985, for *Tales of El Huitlacoche.*

WRITINGS:

(Editor with Antonio Regaldo and Susan Kerr) *España en el siglo veinte,* Harcourt, 1974.

(With Francisco Jiménez) *¡Viva la lengua!: A Contemporary Reader,* Harcourt, 1975, 2nd edition (with Jiménez and Rose Marie Beebe), 1987.

(With Gonzalo Sobejano) *Cuentos españoles concertados de Claría Benet,* Harcourt, 1975.

(Contributor) Luis Ortega, editor, *Introduction to Bilingual Education,* Las Américas-Anaya, 1975.

(Contributor) William G. Milán, J. Staczek, and J. Zamora, editors, *1974 Colloquium on Spanish and Portuguese Linguistics,* Georgetown University Press, 1975.

Mi escuela, Science Research Associates, 1976.

(Contributor with Karen S. Van Hooft) *The Analysis of Hispanic Texts: Current Trends in Methodology,* Mary A. Beck, Lisa Davis, José Hernández, and Isabel C. Tarán, editors, Volume 2, Bilingual Press, 1976.

(Contributor and editor with Richard V. Teschner and Silvia Viera) *Bilingualism in the Bicentennial and Beyond,* Bilingual Press, 1976.

The Significance and Impact of Gregorio Marañón: Literary Criticism, Biographies and Historiography, Bilingual Press, 1977.

(With Nancy A. Sebastiani and Jiménez) *Spanish Here and Now* (including, with Van Hooft, instructor's and student's manuals and cassettes), Harcourt, 1978.

(With Joshua A. Fishman, José Vázquez, and Milán) *The Bilingual Minimum Standards Committee Research Report and Policy Recommendations,* New Jersey State Department of Education, 1978.

(Contributor) Jiménez, editor, *The Identification and Analysis of Chicano Literature,* Bilingual Press, 1979.

(Editor with Jiménez) *Hispanics in the United States: An Anthology of Creative Literature,* Bilingual Press, Volume 1, 1980, Volume 2, 1982.

(Editor with Fishman, and contributor with Van Hooft) *Bilingual Education for Hispanic Students in the United States,* Teachers College Press of Columbia University, 1981.

(Contributor) Stanley S. Seider, *Issues of Language Assessment: Foundations and Research,* Illinois State Board of Education, 1982.

(Contributor) Juan Cobarrubias and Fishman, editors, *Progress in Language Planning: International Perspectives,* Mouton (The Hague), 1983.

Leo y entiendo (seven textbooks and four teacher's editions), Teachers College Press of Columbia University, 1984.

(Under pseudonym El Huitlacoche) *Tales of El Huitlacoche* (short story collection), edited by Alurista and Xelina, Maize, 1984.

(Contributor) Santiago Daydí-Tolson, editor, *Five Poets of Aztlán,* Bilingual Press, 1984.

(Editor) *Chicano Cinema: Research, Reviews and Resources,* Bilingual Press, 1985.

(With Vernon Lattin and Rolando Hinojosa) *Tomás Rivera, 1935-1984: The Man and His Work,* Bilingual Press, 1988.

Cine chicano, Cineteca Nacional, Secretaría de Gobernación, Dirección General de Radio, Televisión y Cinematografía, 1988.

Curricular Resources in Chicano Studies, Bilingual Press, 1989.

Contributor to *The Columbia Dictionary of Modern European Literature,* edited by Jean-Albert Bédé and William B. Edgerton, 2nd edition, Columbia University Press, 1980. Contributor of short stories and poetry, sometimes under pseudonym El Huitlacoche, to *Bilingual Review.* Contributor of reviews to *Literature and Psychology* and *Hispania.* General editor, *Bilingual Review/ Press,* 1974-82; consulting editor, *Journal of Higher Education,* 1985—, and Teachers College Press of Columbia University.

WORK IN PROGRESS: (With James Deneen and Rafael Magallán) *Assessment and Access: Hispanics in Higher Education;* a novel under pseudonym El Huitlacoche entitled *In This Interregnum.*

BIOGRAPHICAL/CRITICAL SOURCES:

PERIODICALS

Siempre, September 2, 1987.
Washington Post Book World, April 17, 1983.
World Literature Today, spring, 1983.

L

LAGUERRE, Enrique A(rturo)   1906-

PERSONAL: Born May 3, 1906, in Moca, P.R.; son of Juan N. Laguerre (in agriculture) and Atanasia Vélez Vargas; married Beatriz Saavedra, 1945 (deceased, 1948); married Luz V. Romero García (a professor), April, 1970; children: Beatriz. *Education:* University of Puerto Rico, B.A., 1938, M.A., 1941; doctoral studies at Columbia University, 1949.

ADDRESSES: Home—Centrum Plaza 7D, México esq. Uruguay, Hato Rey, P.R. 00918. *Office*—Box 22114, University of Puerto Rico, Río Piedras, P.R. 00931. *Agent*—Francisco Vázquez, Robles 51, Río Piedras, P.R. 00931.

CAREER: Writer. Worked as a rural teacher in Moca, P.R., beginning c. 1924; director, Rural Second Unit, 1938; high school teacher, 1939; Department of Education, San Juan, P.R., writer for School of the Air, 1939-41; University of Puerto Rico, Río Piedras, professor, 1941-88. Professor at universities in the United States, including visiting professor, City University of New York, 1969-70. Research adviser to Higher Council on Education; special consultant to Puerto Rico Department of Public Instruction. Cultural delegate to numerous congresses and meetings in North and South America.

MEMBER: National Endowment for the Arts, PEN, Institute of Iberoamerican Culture, Puerto Rican Institute of Culture (cofounder; member of board of directors), Sociedad de Autores (San Juan), Academia de Lengua (San Juan), Academia Artes y Ciencias (San Juan), Aleneo (San Juan), Phi Delta Kappa.

AWARDS, HONORS: Four awards from Institute of Literature, Puerto Rico; National Award, Institute of Culture, San Juan.

WRITINGS:

NOVELS

La llamarada, América Tipografía Ruiz (Aguadilla, Puerto Rico), 1935, 27th edition, Editorial Cultural (Río Piedras, Puerto Rico), 1987 (also see below).

Solar Montoya, Biblioteca de Autores Puertorriqueños (San Juan, Puerto Rico), 1941, 3rd edition, Editorial Cultural, 1978 (also see below).

El 30 de febrero: Vida de un hombre interino, Biblioteca de Autores Puertorriqueños, 1943, 3rd edition, Editorial Cultural, 1978 (also see below).

La resaca, first published, 1949, Editorial Cultural, 1967, 9th edition, 1971 (also see below).

Los dedos de la mano, Librería de M. Porrúa (Mexico), 1951, 3rd edition, Editorial Cultural, 1978 (also see below).

La ceiba en el tiesto, Biblioteca de Autores Puertorriqueños, 1956, 4th edition, Editorial Cultural, 1978 (also see below).

El laberinto, Las Américas Publishing (New York), 1959, translation by William Rose published as *The Labyrinth,* 1960, reprinted, Waterfront Press, 1984.

El fuego y su aire, Editorial Losada (Buenos Aires), 1970, 2nd edition, 1971.

Los amos benévolos, Editorial Universitaria, Universidad de Puerto Rico, 1976, translation by Gino Parisi published as *Benevolent Masters,* introduction and notes by Estelle Irizarry, Waterfront Press, 1986.

Infiernos privados, Editorial Cultural, 1986.

SHORT STORIES

(Editor) *Antología de cuentos puertorriqueños,* Orión (Mexico), 1954.

Cuentos españoles, Orión, 1956, recent edition, 1973.

Author of stories "El hombre caído," "El hombre que volvió," "Raíces," "El enemigo," "Pacholí," and "Naufragio."

OTHER

La resentida (three-act play), first published, 1944, Ediciones Rumbos (Barcelona, Spain), 1960.

Pulso de Puerto Rico, 1952-1954 (essays), Biblioteca de Autores Puertorriqueños, 1956.

Enrique Laguerre habla sobre nuestras bibliotecas, Departamento de Instrucción Pública, Servicio de Bibliotecas (San Juan), 1959.

Obras completas (collected works; contains *Semblanza, Prólogo, La llamarada, Solar Montoya, El 30 de febrero, Vocabulario, La resaca, Los dedos de la mano,* and *La ceiba en el tiesto*), Instituto de Cultura Puertorriqueña (San Juan), 1962.

Cauce sin río: Diario de mi generación, Nuevas Editoriales Unidas (Madrid), 1962, 9th edition, Editorial Cultural, 1978.

(Compiler with Esther M. Melón) *El jíbaro de Puerto Rico: Símbolo y figura,* Troutman Press (Sharon, Conn.), 1968, translation published as *The Jibaro in Puerto Rico: Symbol and Figure,* Gordon Press, 1979.

La poesía modernista en Puerto Rico (essays), Editorial Coquí (San Juan), 1969.

Polos de la cultura iberoamericana (essays), Florentia (Boston, Mass.), 1977.

Also author of two volumes of *Complete Works of Enrique Laguerre,* Gordon Press. Contributor to *Puerto Rico Ilustrado, La Democracia, El Mundo, Alma Latina, Isla, Ambito, Horizontes, El Diario de Puerto Rico,* and *Artes y Letras.* Co-founder of literary review *Paliques.*

WORK IN PROGRESS: Por boca de caracoles, a novel.

SIDELIGHTS: Enrique A. Laguerre is considered one of Puerto Rico's most important contemporary novelists. Also a prolific essayist and short story writer, he is acclaimed for infusing his works with a variety of social concerns. Laguerre first attracted literary attention with his 1935 novel *La llamarada.* Focusing on the conflicts between sugar cane workers and landowners, the novel is now considered a modern classic. Similar in theme is his 1941 work *Solar Montoya,* which depicts the problems faced by Puerto Rican coffee bean pickers. Other of Laguerre's novels portray political turmoil in Puerto Rico. *La resaca,* for example, concerns a group of Puerto Rican nationalists who conspire to free their island from Spanish rule; their rebellion is quashed, however, because of the apathy of Puerto Rico's citizens.

Laguerre has also written novels concerning the Puerto Rican experience in the United States. *El laberinto* deals with the complexities faced by Puerto Ricans living in New York City, and a later work titled *El fuego y su aire* also examines the difficulties Puerto Ricans find when they migrate to the U.S. mainland.

In addition to writing novels, Laguerre has pursued other literary efforts that have earned him wide recognition. The author's nonfiction *Cauce sin río: Diario de mi generación* conveys his thoughts on the conflict between contemporary social life and Puerto Rican tradition. And Laguerre's *Pulso de Puerto Rico* is a volume of essays discussing Puerto Rican education, journalism, folklore, and art.

BIOGRAPHICAL/CRITICAL SOURCES:

BOOKS

Irizarry, Estelle, *Enrique A. Laguerre,* Twayne, 1982.

*   *   *

LAINEZ, Manuel Mujica
    See MUJICA LAINEZ, Manuel

*   *   *

LEAL, Luis   1907-

PERSONAL: Born September 17, 1907, in Linares, Mexico; immigrated to United States, naturalized citizen; married wife in 1936; children: two. *Education:* Northwestern University, B.A., 1940; University of Chicago, A.M., 1941, Ph.D., 1950.

ADDRESSES: Home—542 Wessex Ct., Goleta, Calif. 93017.

CAREER: University of Chicago, Chicago, Ill., instructor, 1942-43 and 1946-48, assistant professor of Spanish, 1948-52; University of Mississippi, University, associate professor of modern languages, 1952-56; Emory University, Atlanta, Ga., associate professor of Spanish, 1956-59; University of Illinois at Urbana-Champaign, Urbana, associate professor, 1959-62, professor of Spanish, 1962-76, professor emeritus, 1976—. Visiting

professor at University of Arizona, 1955-56, University of California, Santa Barbara, 1976-77, and University of California, Los Angeles, 1977-78; acting director of Center for Chicano Studies at University of California, Santa Barbara, 1980—.

MEMBER: Instituto Internacional de Literatura Iberoamericana, Modern Language Association of America, American Association of Teachers of Spanish and Portuguese, Asociación de Escritores Mexicanos, Midwest Modern Language Association.

WRITINGS:

México: Civilizaciones y culturas, Houghton, 1955, revised edition, 1971.

Breve historia del cuento mexicano, Ediciones de Andrea (Mexico City), 1956.

(Editor) *Antología del cuento mexicano,* Ediciones de Andrea, 1957.

Bibliografía del cuento mexicano, Ediciones de Andrea, 1958.

(With Edmundo Valadés) *La revolución y las letras: Dos estudios sobre la novela y el cuento de la revolución mexicana,* Departamento de Literatura, Instituto Nacional de Bellas Artes, 1960.

(Editor with Carlos Castillo) Miguel de Cervantes Saavedra, *La ilustre fregona,* Heath, 1960.

Mariano Azuela: Vida y obra (title means "Mariano Azuela: Life and Work"), Ediciones de Andrea, 1961.

(Editor) *El cuento veracruzano: Antología,* Universidad Veracruzana, 1966.

Historia del cuento hispanoamericano, Ediciones de Andrea, 1966, 2nd edition, 1971.

(Editor) *El cuento mexicano de los orígenes al modernismo,* Editorial Universitaria de Buenos Aires, 1966.

El cuento hispanoamericano, Centro Editor de América Latina (Buenos Aires), 1967.

Mariano Azuela, Centro Editor de América Latina, 1967.

Panorama de la literatura mexicana actual, Unión Panamericana, 1968.

(With Joseph H. Silverman) *Siglo veinte* (title means "The Twentieth Century"), Holt, 1968.

(Editor) Juan Rulfo, *Pedro Páramo,* Appleton, 1970.

(With Frank Dauster) *Literatura de Hispanoamérica,* Harcourt, 1970.

Breve historia de la literatura hispanoamericana, Knopf, 1971.

Mariano Azuela, Twayne, 1971.

(Editor) *Cuentistas hispanoamericanos del siglo veinte,* Random House, 1972.

(Editor) *Mariano Azuela: Páginas escogidas,* Universidad Nacional Autónoma de México, 1973.

Cuentos de la revolución, Universidad Nacional Autónoma de México, 1977.

(Co-author) *A Decade of Chicano Literature, 1970-1979: Critical Essays and Bibliography,* Editorial La Causa, 1982.

Juan Rulfo, Twayne, 1983.

Aztlán y México: Perfiles literarios e históricos, Editorial Bilingüe, 1985.

(With Roberto G. Trujillo) *Literatura chicana,* Floricanto Press, 1985.

Contributor to literature journals.

BIOGRAPHICAL/CRITICAL SOURCES:

BOOKS

Bleznick, Donald W. and Juan O. Valencia, editors, *Homenaje a Luis Leal: Estudios sobre literatura hispanoamericana,* Insula (Madrid), 1978.

PERIODICALS

World Literature Today, winter, 1985.

* * *

LEON-PORTILLA, Miguel 1926-

PERSONAL: Born February 22, 1926, in Mexico City, Mexico; son of Miguel León-Ortiz and Luisa Portilla; married Ascensión Hernández Trivino (a historian), May 2, 1965. *Education:* Loyola University of Los Angeles (now Loyola Marymount University), B.A., 1948, M.A., 1952; National University of Mexico, Ph.D., 1956.

ADDRESSES: Home—Alberto Zamora 103, Coyoacán, Mexico City, District Federal 21, Mexico.

CAREER: Mexico City College (now University of the Americas), Mexico City, Mexico, professor of ancient Mexican history, 1954-57; National University of Mexico, Mexico City, professor of ancient Mexican history, 1957—, director of Institute of Historical Research, 1963—. Lecturer at universities in the United States, Israel, and Europe; distinguished lecturer at the seventy-fourth meeting of the American Anthropological Association, 1974. Member of council, Institute of Different Civilizations, Brussels, 1959—; Inter-American Indian Institute, secretary general, 1955-60, director, 1960-66; secretary general of thirty-fifth International Congress of Americanists, 1962.

MEMBER: Royal Spanish Academy of History, Royal Spanish Academy of the Language, Societe des Americanistes de Paris.

AWARDS, HONORS: Prize Elias Sourazky, bestowed by Mexican Secretary of Education, 1966; Guggenheim fellow, 1970; Fulbright fellow, 1976-77; Commendatore de la Republica Italiana, 1977; Serra Award, 1978; D.H.L. honoris causa, Southern Methodist University, 1980; Mexican National Prize in history and the social sciences, 1981.

WRITINGS:

(Compiler) *Indices de América indígena y Boletín indigenista,* fourteen volumes, Inter-American Indian Institute, 1954.

La filosofía náhuatl. Estudiada en sus fuentes, Inter-American Indian Institute, 1956, 4th edition, Institute of Historical Research, National University of Mexico, 1974, translation by Jack Emory Davis published as *Aztec Thought and Culture: A Study of the Ancient Nahuatl Mind,* University of Oklahoma Press, 1963.

(With Salvador Matéo) *Catálogo de los códices indígenas del México antiguo,* [Mexico City], 1957.

Siete ensayos sobre cultura náhuatl, National University of Mexico, 1958.

(Translator and author of introduction) Bernardino de Sahagún, *Ritos, sacerdotes y atavios de los dioses,* Institute of Historical Research, National University of Mexico, 1958.

(Editor and author of introduction and notes) *Visión de los vencidos: Relaciones indígenas de la conquista,* National University of Mexico, 1959, 5th edition, 1971, translation by Lysander Kemp published as *The Broken Spears: The Aztec Account of the Conquest of Mexico,* Beacon Press, 1962.

Los antiguos mexicanos a través de sus crónicas y cantares, Fondo de Cultura Económica, 1961, 3rd edition, 1970, translation published as *The Ancient Mexicans,* Rutgers University Press, 1968.

(Contributor) *Estudios de historia de la filosofía en México,* National University of Mexico, 1963, 2nd edition, 1973, translation by A. Robert Caponigri published as *Major Trends*

in Mexican Philosophy, University of Notre Dame Press, 1966.

Imagen del México antiguo, University of Buenos Aires Press, 1963.

Las literaturas precolombinas de México, Editorial Pormaca, 1964, translation by León-Portilla and Grace Lobanov published as *Pre-Columbian Literatures of Mexico,* University of Oklahoma Press, 1969.

Historia documental de México, Institute of Historical Research, National University of Mexico, 1964, 2nd edition, 1974.

El reverso de la conquista: Relaciones aztecas, mayas e incas, Editorial J. Mortiz, 1964, 2nd edition, 1970.

Trece poetas del mundo azteca, Institute of Historical Research, National University of Mexico, 1968, 2nd edition, 1975.

Quetzalcoatl, Fondo de Cultura Económica, 1968.

(Editor and author of introduction and notes) Jaime Bravo, Juan de Ugarte, and Clemente Guillen, *Nueva entra tablecimiento en el puerto de La Paz, 1720,* National University of Mexico, 1970.

(Compiler) *De Teotihuacan a los aztecas: Antología de fuentes e interpretaciones histúricas,* Institute of Historical Research, National University of Mexico, 1971.

(Author of introduction) Andrés de Olmos, *Arte para aprender la lengua mexicana,* Levy, 1972.

Nezahualcoyotl: Poesía y pensamiento, 1402-1472, Gobierno del Estado de México, 1972.

Religión de los nicaraos: Análisis y comparación de tradicionos culturales nahuas, Institute of Historical Research, National University of Mexico, 1972.

Tiempo y realidad en el pensamiento maya: Ensayo de acercamiento, foreword by Eric S. Thompson, Institute of Historical Research, University of Mexico, 1973, 2nd edition published as *Time and Reality in the Thought of the Maya,* translated by Charles L. Boiles and Fernando Horcasitas, University of Oklahoma Press, 1988.

Voyages of Francisco de Ortega: California 1632-1636, Dawson's Book Shop, 1973.

(Editor and author of introductory essay, notes, and appendices) Miguel del Barco, *Historia natural y crónica de la antigua California,* Institute of Historical Research, University of Mexico, 1973.

Microhistoria de la Ciudad de México, Secretary of Works and Services, Department of the Federal District (Mexico City), 1974.

(With Edward H. Spicer) *Aztecs and Navajos: A Reflection on the Right of Not Being Engulfed* [and] *Indian Identity versus Assimilation* (the former by León-Portilla, the latter by Spicer), Weatherhead Foundation, 1975.

Culturas en peligro, Alianza Editorial, 1976.

(With Fernando Pereznieto Castro) *Presencia azteca en la Ciudad de México: Presentación de Miguel León-Portilla,* J. Mortiz, 1977.

La minería en México: Estudios sobre su desarrollo histórico, National University of Mexico, 1978.

México-Tenochtitlán: Su espacio y tiempo sagrados, National Institute of Anthropology and History, 1978.

Los manifesto en náhuatl de Emiliano Zapata, Institute of Historical Research, National University of Mexico, 1978.

(Editor, translator, and author of introduction) *Literatura del México antiguo: Los textos en lengua náhuatl,* Biblioteca Ayacucho, 1978.

Datos para la historia demográfica de Baja California, Centro de Investigaciones Históricas, 1978.

Un catecismo náhuatl en imágenes, Edición Privada de Cartón y Papel de México, 1979.

(Editor and author of foreword, introduction, and notes) *Native Mesoamerican Spirituality: Ancient Myths, Discourses, Stories, Doctrines, Hymns, Poems from the Aztec, Yucatec, Quiche-Maya, and Other Sacred Traditions,* Paulist Press, 1980.

Los olmecas en Chalco-Amaquemecan: Un testimonio de Sahagún aprovechado por Chimalpahin, Centro de Estudios Bernardino de Sahagún, 1980.

Literatura maya, Biblioteca Ayacucho, 1980.

(Author of introductory essay) Horacio Carochi, *Arte de la lengua mexicana: Con la de declaración de los adverbios della; Edición facsimilar de la publicada por Juan Ruyz en la Ciudad de México,* Instituto de Investigaciones Filológicas, Universidad Nacional Autónoma de México, 1983.

Literatura de Mesoamérica, Secretaria de Educación Pública, 1984.

(Editor) Bernal Díaz del Castillo, *Historia verdadera de la conquista de la Nueva España,* 2 volumes, Historia 16 (Madrid), 1984.

(Editor with S. L. Cline) *The Testaments of Culhuacan,* UCLA Latin American Center Publications, 1984.

Los franciscanos vistos por el hombre náhuatl, Centro de Estudios Bernardino de Sahagún, 1985.

Hernán Cortés y la mar del sur, Ediciones Cultura Hispánica, 1985.

(With Clementina Díaz y de Ovando) *Vicente Riva Palacio y la identidad nacional: Discurso,* Dirección General de Publicaciones, Universidad Nacional Autonóma de México, 1985.

Also author of *El templo mayor de México,* 1982. Contributor to periodicals in Mexico, Belgium, France, and the United States, including *Evergreen Review, Current Anthropology, Américas,* and *América Indígena.*

WORK IN PROGRESS: A study "that includes indigenous testimonies on the sixteenth-century Spanish-Aztec confrontation; a work on the lives and productions of twenty pre-Columbian Aztec poets."

SIDELIGHTS: Miguel León-Portilla writes that his "main concern has been to present in a humanistic way the rich heritage of the history, art, and literature of ancient Mexico." *La filosofía náhuatl* was published in Moscow in 1961, and *Visión de los vencidos* has appeared in German, French, and Italian. León-Portilla is fluent in English, French, German, Italian, and Nahuatl; his travels cover most countries of the and many in Europe and the Far East.

BIOGRAPHICAL/CRITICAL SOURCES:

PERIODICALS

América Indígena, October, 1966.
Saturday Review, August 30, 1969.

*   *   *

LEZAMA LIMA, José   1910(?)-1976

PERSONAL: Born December 19, 1910 (some sources say 1912), in Campamento Militar de Columbia, Cuba; died August 9, 1976, in Havana, Cuba. *Education:* Earned law degree from University of Havana.

CAREER: In private law practice in Cuba, 1938-40; worked for various government agencies in Cuba, 1940-59; National Council of Culture, Havana, director of the department of literature and publications, 1959-76. Poet, essayist, and novelist.

WRITINGS:

La fijeza, Orígenes, 1949.
Analecta del reloj (essays), Orígenes, 1953.
El padre Gaztelu en la poesía, Orígenes, 1955.
La expresión americana (lectures), Ministerio de Educación, 1957.
Tratados en la Habana, Universidad Central de Las Villas, 1958.
Dador (poems), [Havana], 1960.
Antología de la poesía cubana, Consejo Nacional de Cultura, 1965.
Orbita de Lezama Lima, Unión Nacional de Escritores y Artistas, 1966.
Paradiso (novel), Unión Nacional de Escritores y Artistas, 1966, translation by Gregory Rabassa published under same title, Farrar, Straus, 1974, reprinted, University of Texas Press, 1988.
Lezama Lima (anthology), J. Alvarez, 1968.
Los grandes todos, ARCA, 1969.
Posible imagen de José Lezama Lima (poems), Llibres de Sinera, 1969.
Esferaimagen, Tusquets Editor, 1970.
La cantidad hechizada (essays), UNEAC, 1970.
Poesía completa (poems), Instituto del Libro, 1970.
Las eras imaginarias, Editorial Fundamentos, 1971.
Algunos tratados en La Habana, Editorial Anagrama, 1971.
Introducción a los vasos órficos, Barral Editores, 1971.
Coloquio con Juan Ramón Jiménez, Estudios Gráficos de CBA, 1973.
Obras completas, two volumes, Aguilar, 1975-77.
Cangrejos y golondrinas, Editorial Calicanto, 1977.
Oppiano Licario, Ediciones Era, 1977.
Fragmentos a su imán, Editorial Arte y Literatura, 1977.
Cartas (1939-1976): José Lezama Lima, compiled and edited by Eloísa Lezama Lima, Orígenes, 1979.
El reino de la imagen, Biblioteca Ayacucho, 1981.
Imagen y posibilidad, Editorial Letras Cubanas, 1981.
Juego de las decapitaciones, Montesinos, 1982.
Cuentos (short stories), Editorial Letras Cubanas, 1987.

Also author of *Muerte de Narciso,* 1937; *Enemigo rumor,* 1941; *Aventuras siglosas,* 1945; *Aristedes Fernández,* 1950. Co-founding editor, *Verbum,* 1937, *Nadie parecía, and* 1943, and *Orígenes,* 1945-56.

SIDELIGHTS: José Lezama Lima was a Cuban poet and novelist who gained an international reputation and a place in the history of Latin American literature with intricately-composed, highly original works. His controversial novel *Paradiso,* according to *Publishers Weekly,* "prompted critics to refer to him as 'the [Marcel] Proust of the Caribbean.' " The novel was released in the United States, France, Italy, and several Latin American countries, where it received important critical attention. Some critics took note particularly because the novel, which describes homosexual relationships, was published in Cuba during Castro's active campaign against homosexuality.

Paradiso records the journey of young José Cemí from childhood into sexual and intellectual maturity. Cemí's quest for a spiritual mentor is as well "a search for the lost father and for a literary vocation. And the journey is strictly homosexual," Enrique Fernández relates in a *Village Voice* review. The commitment to language, knowledge, and philosophy among Cemí's role models in his quest supercedes the sexual activity in the novel, which Fernández sees, by comparison, as "extreme male bonding." Though there is more thought than action in the long novel, he adds, "there is passion. Sexual passion but, most important, intellectual and aesthetic passion, passion for a key concept in Lezama: culture." *Nation* contributor Peter Moscoso-Gongora concurs, "Sensuality and intellectual puzzles, character and incident, the real and the imagined whirl away in the rush of a verbal storm that wishes to concentrate on itself."

Considered a "difficult" novel for its complex uses of language, *Paradiso* is as metaphysical as Lezama Lima's poetry, which also stretches the limits of language to create unorthodox possibilities of expression. For this author, writing was a creative act by which an alternative universe came into being. The culmination of the exaggerated pride and self-confidence characteristic of literary modernism, the novel aims "to defy the gods by fashioning a cosmos that is impregnable and humanistically divine," Fernández comments. Furthermore, Lezama Lima built his novel universe "while ignoring virtually all of modernism's tricks: cool narrative strategies, hip tones, jazzy dissonances, authorial detachment, alienation. And he roots his experiment in his native Cuban reality—including the famous dialectics of tobacco and sugar." Therefore, Fernández concludes, "Lezama's work is not only an artistic feat. It is a virtual proclamation of Latin American literary independence."

In *The Borzoi Anthology of Latin American Literature*, Volume two, edited by Emir Rodríguez Monegal, *Paradiso* is recognized as a masterpiece "of a totally unclassifiable literature." Commenting on the novel's unique range, the critic says, "Mixing the occult adroitly with a Rabelaisian sense of humor, highly convoluted prose with faulty scholarship, a wild imagination with the most ambitious rethinking of the West's greatest works of literature and philosophy, Lezama produced a truly encyclopedic novel. . . . It was a condensation and expansion simultaneously of everything he had attempted previously. It was, in a sense, monstrous . . . in the same way as a number of other landmark achievements in Latin American literature."

BIOGRAPHICAL/CRITICAL SOURCES:

BOOKS

Contemporary Literary Criticism, Volume 4, Gale, 1975.
Rodríguez Monegal, Emir, *The Borzoi Anthology of Latin American Literature*, Volume 2, Knopf, 1986.

PERIODICALS

Hispania, April, 1973, May, 1976.
Nation, May 11, 1974.
New Republic, June 15, 1974.
New York Review of Books, April 18, 1974.
New York Times Book Review, April 21, 1974.
Village Voice, April 25, 1974.
Washington Post, April 14, 1974.

OBITUARIES:

PERIODICALS

New York Times, August 10, 1976.
Publishers Weekly, August 23, 1976.

*   *   *

LIHN, Enrique   1929-1988

PERSONAL: Born September 3, 1929, in Santiago, Chile; died July 10, 1988, in Santiago; son of Enrique Lihn Döll and María Carrasco; married Yvette Mingram, November 10, 1957 (divorced January 14, 1960); children: Andrea. *Education:* Attended Liceo de los Padres Alemanes, Institute of Fine Arts (Santiago), and University of Chile.

ADDRESSES: Office—c/o Andrea Lihn, Marcel Duhaut 2935, Santiago, Chile.

CAREER: Poet and novelist, beginning 1949; University of Chile, Santiago, professor and researcher of literature, beginning 1973.

AWARDS, HONORS: Atenea Prize from Universidad de Concepción, 1964; municipal prize for narrative, 1965, for *Agua de arroz: Cuentos;* Casa de las Américas prize for poetry, 1966, for "Poesía de paso"; Pedro de Oña prize and municipal prize for poetry, both for "La musiquilla de las pobres esferas"; fellowships from UNESCO and Guggenheim.

WRITINGS:

Poemas de este tiempo y de otro, 1949-1954, Ediciones Renovación (Santiago), 1955.
La pieza oscura (title means "Dark Room"; also see below), Editorial Universitaria (Santiago), 1963.
Poesía de paso, Casa de las Américas (Havana), 1966.
Escrito en Cuba, Era (Mexico), 1969.
Agua de arroz: Cuentos (title means "Rice Water"; fiction), Centro Editor (Buenos Aires), 1969.
The Endless Malice: Twenty-five Poems of Enrique Lihn, translated by William Witherup and Serge Echeverria, Lillabulero, 1969.
La musiquilla de las pobres esferas, Editorial Universitaria (Santiago), 1969.
Algunos poemas, Ocnos (Barcelona), 1972.
La Chambre noire/La pieza oscura (bilingual edition), translated and presented by Michele Cohen and Jean-Michel Fossey, Pierre Jean Oswald Editeur, 1972.
(Editor and author of prologue) *Diez cuentos de bandidos* (fiction), Quimantu (Santiago), 1972.
Batman en Chile; o, El ocaso de un ídolo; o, Solo contra el desierto rojo (fiction), Ediciones de la Flor (Buenos Aires), 1973.
Por fuerza mayor, Ocnos, Barral Editores (Barcelona), 1975.
La orquesta de cristal (title means "The Crystal Orchestra"; novel), Editorial Sudamerica (Buenos Aires), 1976.
París, situación irregular, Ediciones Aconcagua (Santiago), 1977.
If Poetry Is to Be Written Right, translated by Dave Oliphant, Texas Portfolio, 1977.
The Dark Room and Other Poems (selections from *La pieza oscura*), edited and with an introduction by Patricio Lerzundi, translated by Jonathan Cohen, John Felstiner, and David Unger, New Directions, 1978.
A partir de Manhattan, Ediciones Ganymedes (Santiago), 1979.
El arte de la palabra (title means "The Art of Speaking"; novel), Pomaire (Barcelona), 1980.
Antología al azar (poetry), Ruray, 1981.
Derechos de autor, 1981/72, 69, etc., The Author, 1981.
Estación de los desamparados (poetry), Premiá Editora, 1982.
Al bello aparecer de este lucero (title means "At the Beautiful Arising of This Star"; poetry), Ediciones del Norte, 1983.
El paseo ahumada: Poema, Ediciones Minga, 1983.
(With Carmen Foxley, Cristián Huneeus, and Adriana Valdés) *Paradiso, Lectura de conjunto*, Coordinación de Humanidades, Universidad Nacional Autónoma de México, 1984.
Pena de extrañamiento, Sinfronteras (Santiago), 1986.
Mester de juglaría (poetry), Hiperión (Madrid), 1987.
(With Pedro Lastra) *Señales de ruta de Juan Luis Martínez*, Ediciones Archivo (Santiago), 1987.
La aparición de la Virgen (poem), [Santiago], 1987.
Eugenio Téllez, descubridor de invenciones, [Santiago], 1988.

La república independiente de Miranda (fiction), Editorial Sudamericana (Buenos Aires), 1988.

Diario de muerte (poetry), edited by Lastra and Valdés, Editorial Universitaria (Santiago), 1988.

(And author of prologue) *Album de toda especie de poemas* (poetry anthology), Editorial Lumen (Barcelona), 1989.

Also author of *Nada se escurre,* 1949.

SIDELIGHTS: Enrique Lihn was a popular poet in Chile for many years and is gaining recognition in the United States as his works are translated into English. His poetry often expresses sadness about death, loss of love, and other tragedies in life. Reviewing *La musiquilla de las pobres esferas,* F. A. Butler of *Books Abroad* writes, "This is poetry to be read with care and disquiet, for its beauty lies in its aberration." Hayden Carruth of *Nation* predicts, "Lihn's poems are certain to become better known in this country before long."

BIOGRAPHICAL/CRITICAL SOURCES:

BOOKS

Lastra, Pedro, *Conversaciones con Enrique Lihn,* Centro de Investigaciones Lingüistico-Literarias, Instituto de Investigaciones Humanísticas, Universidad Veracruzana. 1980.

Lihn, Enrique, *Derechos de autor, 1981/72, 69, etc.,* The Author, 1981.

PERIODICALS

Books Abroad, winter, 1971.
Nation, December 23, 1978.
World Literature Today, winter, 1985.

[Sketch reviewed by Andrea Lihn, Professor Felipe Alliende, and Adriana Valdés]

*   *   *

LIMA, José Lezama
  See LEZAMA LIMA, José

*   *   *

LIZARDI, Joseph   1941-

PERSONAL: Born February 12, 1941, in Caguas, P.R.; immigrated to United States, 1954, naturalized citizen; son of José (a factory worker) and Ana (a factory worker; maiden name, Medina) Lizardi; married wife, Linda (a secretary), July 14, 1972; children: Michael Joseph. *Education:* Bronx Community College, A.A.S., 1972; Bernard M. Baruch College of the City University of New York, M.B.A., 1977. *Politics:* Democrat. *Religion:* Roman Catholic.

ADDRESSES: Home—5 Ontario Ave., Plainview, N.Y. 11803. *Agent*—Bertha Klausner, 71 Park Ave., New York, N.Y. 10016.

CAREER: Daily News, New York City, guard, 1964-66; Seven-Up Bottling Co., New York City, filler operator, 1966—. Arena Players Repertory Theater, Farmingdale, N.Y., playwright in residence, 1980—. *Military service:* U.S. Marine Corps, 1960-64.

MEMBER: Dramatists Guild.

AWARDS, HONORS: "The Powderroom" was chosen as a finalist in the Actors Theater of Louisville's Great American Play Contest, 1980.

WRITINGS:

PLAYS

"The Agreement," first produced Off-Off Broadway at Carnegie Repertory Theater, 1970.

"The Contract," first produced Off-Off Broadway at Carnegie Repertory Theater, 1971.

"The Commitment," first produced Off-Off Broadway at Henry Street Playhouse, 1972.

"Summerville," first produced Off-Off Broadway at West Side Community Theater, 1972.

"The Block Party," first produced Off-Off Broadway at Henry Street Playhouse, 1974.

"El Macho," first produced Off-Off Broadway at Firehouse Theater, 1977.

"The Powderroom," first produced Off-Off Broadway at Arena Players Repertory Theater, 1980.

"Reunion," first produced Off-Off Broadway at Arena Players Repertory Theater, 1980.

"Blue Collars," first produced Off-Off Broadway at Arena Players Repertory Theater, 1980.

"Love's Comedy" (adapted from Henrik Ibsen's "La Comedia del Amor"), first produced Off-Off Broadway at Arena Players Repertory Theater, 1981.

"December in New York" (full-length), first produced Off-Off Broadway at Arena Players Repertory Theater, 1982.

"Blind Dates," first produced in Plainview, N.Y., at Old-Bethpage Library, 1982.

"Three on the Run," first produced Off-Off Broadway at Arena Players Repertory Theater, 1982.

Also author of "Joggers," "Love's Last Gasp," "The Family Room," "The Pretenders" (an adaptation of an Ibsen play), "The Runaway," "Save the Children," and "Couples."

OTHER

Author of screenplays "The Dope War" and "Spanish Harlem."

WORK IN PROGRESS: "Then Came the Stranger" and "A Place Along the Highway," two dramas.

SIDELIGHTS: Joseph Lizardi told *CA:* "It has always been my desire to learn and perfect my craft. Knowing that it was going to take a long time, I decided to hold a job which did not require my full devotion to it. That is the reason I have been a blue-collar worker for most of my working life. I do not regret the decision, for I have been able to compile a treasury of fascinating characters for all the plays I have written so far."

Born in Puerto Rico, Lizardi came to the United States at the age of fourteen, taught himself English, and became a notable New York playwright. His plays, such as "El Macho," "Block Party," and "Blue Collars," explore the lives of factory workers, the ambience of the Puerto Rican neighborhoods in which he has lived, and the ethnic experience in general. His writings, described by *Newsday* critic Leo Seligsohn as "a combination of naturalism and farce," are often compared to television situation comedies; yet reviewers have heard a somber echo behind the laughter. Critic Alvin Klein explained to readers of the *New York Times:* "Mr. Lizardi builds comic momentum right up to the point of tragedy." The playwright's characters spring from the crumbling world of his youth, wherein, as Klein wrote, "disasters . . . were a way of life and humor was the handiest survival mechanism."

BIOGRAPHICAL/CRITICAL SOURCES:

PERIODICALS

Daily News (New York), November 16, 1980.
Newsday, April 25, 1980, May 9, 1980, November 5, 1980, February 3, 1982.
New York Post, May 25, 1979.
New York Times, April 13, 1980, April 27, 1980, August 24, 1980, November 16, 1980, August 30, 1981, April 4, 1982.

* * *

LLORENS, Wáshington 1900-

PERSONAL: Born November 28, 1900, in Ponce, Puerto Rico.

CAREER: Pharmacist and writer; director of San Juan District Laboratory of the Alcohol Tax Unit, United States Internal Revenue Service, 1943—. Chairman of the Commonwealth's Board of Pharmacy Examiners, 1941; lecturer at the Interamerican University of Puerto Rico.

MEMBER: Puerto Rico Academy of Arts and Sciences (president), Puerto Rico Society of Journalists and Writers (vice-president), Puerto Rico Academy of the Spanish Language, Royal Spanish Academy of Language (corresponding member), Puerto Rico Institute of Hispanic Culture (president), Pharmaceutical Association of Puerto Rico (secretary-treasurer).

AWARDS, HONORS: Journalism prizes from Institute of Puerto Rican Literature, 1956 and 1964; honorary degree from Temple University for outstanding contributions to pharmacy.

WRITINGS:

El español de Puerto Rico y la décimoctava edición del Diccionario de la Real Academia Española, Club (San Juan Bautista, Puerto Rico), 1957.
Un intruso en la jardín de academo, Club, 1957.
Catorce pecados de humor y una vida descabellada, Club, 1959.
El humorismo, el epigrama y la sátira en la literatura puertorriqueña, Instituto de Cultura (San Juan, Puerto Rico), 1960.
El habla popular de Puerto Rico, Academia de Artes y Ciencias de Puerto Rico, 1968, revised edition, with introduction by Cesáreo Rosa-Nieves, Edil (Río Piedras), 1981.
Diez pecados de humor, Instituto de Cultura, 1977.
Humor, Epigram, and Satire in Puerto Rican Literature, Gordon Press, 1979.
La magia de la palabra, University of Puerto Rico, 1980.
Cazador de imposibles, Biblioteca de Autores Puertorriqueños (San Juan), 1981.

Editor of the literary publications *Alma Latina* and *Prensa Literaria;* editor of *Journal* of the Puerto Rico College of Pharmacy, and of *Revista Farmacéutica de Puerto Rico,* 1930-32.

* * *

LLOSA, (Jorge) Mario (Pedro) Vargas
See VARGAS LLOSA, (Jorge) Mario (Pedro)

* * *

LOPEZ, Diana 1948-
(Isabella Ríos)

PERSONAL: Born March 16, 1948, in Los Angeles, Calif.; daughter of Louis H. (a contracting business owner) and Valentine (a homemaker; maiden name, Ballesteros) López; children: Jason Ho. *Education:* San Francisco State University, B.A., 1967, M.A., 1969; Nova University, Ed.D., 1979.

ADDRESSES: Home—1066 Via Arroyo, Ventura, Calif. 93003. *Office*—Department of Language Arts, Moorpark College, 7075 Campus Rd., Moorpark, Calif. 93021.

CAREER: Moorpark College, Moorpark, Calif., English instructor, 1970—, assisted in establishing and taught in Bilingual Center and tutorial program for minority students; writer.

MEMBER: Ventura Writers' Club.

WRITINGS:

(Under pseudonym Isabella Ríos) *Victuum,* Diana-Etna (Ventura, Calif.), 1976.

Contributor of poems and short stories to periodicals.

WORK IN PROGRESS: A revision of *Victuum,* and a sequel; a book of poetry.

SIDELIGHTS: Diana López, who writes under the pseudonym Isabella Ríos, will be remembered in Hispanic literature as the author of the first Chicana bildungsroman, *Victuum.* The story of a Hispanic woman's coming of age and discovery of her psychic ability, *Victuum* also offers insight into the social and cultural changes Californian Chicano society underwent from the turn of the twentieth century to the present day. The book is based on the life and experiences of one of Ríos's female relatives, whom Ríos interviewed extensively for two years, but woven into it are bits of López's family history and Hispanic folklore.

Victuum begins with protagonist Valentina Ballesternos still in the womb, lamenting that once she is born she will not remember any of what she has learned in her past lives. As Ríos follows her through birth and adolescence to marriage and motherhood she writes of the Chicano experience during the Prohibition era, the Depression, and World War II as Valentina lived it. Valentina's psychic powers manifest themselves as she matures, and when describing her later years *Victuum* becomes her spiritual biography. Eventually Ríos relates Valentina's psychic experiences—such as visions and dreams peopled by such diverse figures as poet William Wordsworth, the prophet Isaiah, and Pope Eusebius—exclusively, and in the present tense. Thus Ríos recreates the mystical landscape of Valentina's mind, into which the reader is drawn and which forces him to question his own vision of reality and Hispanic spirituality.

BIOGRAPHICAL/CRITICAL SOURCES:

BOOKS

Dictionary of Literary Biography, Volume 82: *Chicano Writers, First Series,* Gale, 1989.

PERIODICALS

Minority Voices, spring, 1980.

* * *

LOPEZ PORTILLO (y PACHECO), José 1920-

PERSONAL: Born June 16, 1920, in Mexico City, Mexico; son of José López Portillo y Weber (a historian) and Sra. Pacheco de López Portillo (a schoolteacher); married Carmen Romano (a former concert pianist); children: José Ramón, Carmen, Paulina. *Education:* National Autonomous University of Mexico, LL.B., 1946; graduate study at the University of Chile.

LOPEZ PORTILLO (y PACHECO)   *HISPANIC WRITERS*

ADDRESSES: c/o Fernández Editores, Eje 1 Pte Mexico Coyoacán 321, Col Xoco 03330, Mexico. *Home*—Colina de Cuajimalpa, Mexico City, Mexico.

CAREER: Lawyer in private practice in Mexico City, Mexico; National Autonomous University of Mexico, Mexico City, instructor in government, 1954, associate professor of political science, 1956-58; joined Institutional Revolutionary Party (PRI), 1959; Ministry of National Patrimony, Mexico City, technical associate at local office, 1960; Federal Boards for National Improvements, Mexico City, general director, 1960-65; National Polytechnic Institute, Mexico City, professor of administrative sciences, 1961; border Urban Development Committee, coordinator, 1962; Ministry of the Presidency, Mexico City, director general of legal affairs and legislation, 1965-68, under secretary, 1968-70; Ministry of National Patrimony, Mexico City, under secretary, 1970-72; Federal Electricity Commission, Mexico City, general director, 1972-73, secretary of finances and public credit, 1973-75; president of Mexico, 1976-82; writer.

AWARDS, HONORS: Orden Nacional do Cruzeiro do Sul (Brazil), 1978; honorary doctorates from Hebrew University and Aix Marsella University.

WRITINGS:

Valoración de lo estatal (nonfiction; title means "Assessing the State"), UNAM, 1946.

Génesis y teoría general del estado moderno (nonfiction; title means "The Origin and General Theory of the Modern State"), Ediciones Botas, 1958.

La vida al través de la muerte (novel; title means "Life Across Death"), Ediciones de Andrea, 1964.

Quetzalcóatl (novel), Porrúa, 1965, reprinted with essays by Demetrio Sodi and Fernando Díaz Infante, Secretaria de Asentamientos Humanos y Obras Públicas, 1977, translation by Eliot Weinberger and Diana S. Goodrich published as *Quetzalcoatl: A Novel,* Seabury Press, 1976, translation also published as *Quetzalcoatl: In Myth, Archeology and Art,* Continuum, 1982.

Don Q: Conversaciones sobre la yoeidad y otras trascendentalidades (novel), Porrúa, 1969, translation by Weinberger and Wilfrido Corral published as *Don Q,* Seabury Press, 1976.

Mis tiempos: Biografía y testimonio político (autobiography; title means "My Times: Biography and Political Testament"), Fernández Editores, 1988.

Also author of numerous collections of speeches and short works on Mexican government and economic policy. Contributor of articles to newspapers and magazines.

SIDELIGHTS: Among the most intellectual and culturally sophisticated of modern Mexican political leaders, José López Portillo roused intense controversy as president of Mexico from 1976 to 1982. A successful lawyer, educator, and novelist, as well as a politician, López Portillo presided over Mexico's emergence as a major oil power, a period that saw both strong economic growth and unprecedented government corruption. López Portillo's ambitious and only partly successful schemes to develop Mexican industry and agriculture with the new oil revenues helped quadruple the country's foreign debt and set off an inflationary spiral that left workers and the poor in worse economic straits than before the oil boom began. At the same time, López Portillo brought Mexico new international stature by asserting a stronger role in regional political affairs and often opposing United States policy in strife-torn Central America. Breaking a long public silence after leaving office, the former president responded to his many critics in 1988 with a best-selling political

testament and defense of his administration titled *Mis tiempos* ("My Times").

López Portillo had never held elective office before becoming president; he ascended the political ranks instead through a succession of appointed technocratic posts. After taking a law degree and studying political science at the graduate level, he began his career teaching law, political science, and public administration at Mexico City's major public university. López Portillo wrote two scholarly works on the theory of the state during this period and became active in Mexico's quasi-official political party, the Institutional Revolutionary Party (PRI). He went on to earn a reputation as a talented and tough-minded administrator in a series of mid-level political posts with the Gustavo Díaz Ordaz administration and reached the upper echelons of appointed office when his friend Luis Echeverría Alvarez was elected Mexico's president in 1970. López Portillo served as Echeverría's under secretary for the National Patrimony (natural resources) and then reorganized the bureaucratically muddled Federal Electricity Commission before becoming finance secretary, where he gained prestige for improving tax collections and streamlining public works and welfare expenditures.

While pursuing his political career, López Portillo also found time to write two original and distinguished novels. *Quetzalcóatl* is a retelling of an old Mesoamerican Indian legend about a golden-haired man-god, also called the feathered serpent, who arrives in Mexico from the eastern ocean. Quetzalcóatl overthrows Tezcatlipoca, the blood-stained god of human sacrifice, and establishes a fifty-two-year reign of peace and scientific progress. Eventually, however, primitive human passions rise up again and restore Tezcatlipoca, sending the feathered serpent back to his mysterious land across the eastern waters. The Quetzalcóatl myth is said to have helped the Spanish conquistador Hernán Cortés conquer the Mexican Aztec empire in the sixteenth century when his troops were mistaken for emissaries from the feathered serpent; more recently, anthropologists have speculated that the fair-haired ruler Quetzalcóatl may have been a wandering Viking who landed on Mexican shores some time before the Spaniards. "In bringing together certain fragments of the myth, Mr. López Portillo has created a story of real dramatic power," observed *New York Times Book Review* critic D. J. R. Bruckner. *Quetzalcóatl* "is close to poetry in richness of imagery and force of emotion," added Edmund Fuller of the *Wall Street Journal.* "Its narrative style is swift and spare but at appropriate moments has a high incantatory tone. . . . This cryptic, poetic book will appeal to all who are interested in pre-Columbian Mexico."

López Portillo also earned critical praise for his comic philosophical novel *Don Q,* which was published in 1969. Described by its American publisher in *Spectator* as "a mordant exercise in rhetorical obfuscation . . . a novel wholly without action," this short work takes the form of a conversation between the mystic, paradox-loving old philosopher Don Q and his narrowly logical young companion, Pepe Seco ("Joe Dry"). "A wry, antic wit suffuses the book," noted Fuller, as this mismatched pair circles around the big philosophical questions, among them, Don Q's theory of "Ieity," or the self as God. Don Q is "an exuberantly singular Knight of Ideas, a somewhat Hegelian Quixote," remarked *Books and Bookmen* reviewer Derek Stanford, adding that the novel will "surprise and delight" those "choice spirits who find in ideas not a faith, a fortress or a strait-jacket, but an ever-renewable legerdemain [sleight of hand]."

In 1976, the PRI surprised political observers by selecting López Portillo as its candidate for the presidential election that year.

284

Although his relatively low public profile and inexperience in electoral office made him something of a dark horse, party leaders judged López Portillo's administrative skills and political moderation useful in taming the political passions roused by the outgoing, populist Echeverría administration. Under Mexico's de facto one-party political system, López Portillo's selection as the PRI candidate virtually guaranteed his election, and he ran opposed only by a write-in campaign for the Communist party's Valentín Campa. Taking office in December, 1976, the new president promised to fight government corruption, improve the business climate, promote industrialization, create jobs, and undertake a fiscal austerity program to counter rising inflation and the growing foreign debt.

Not long into his administration, however, the discovery of vast new Mexican hydrocarbon reserves prompted López Portillo to abandon any plans for fiscal austerity and launch a series of highly ambitious development projects. From 1976 to 1983, proven reserves of oil and natural gas jumped from eleven billion barrels to over seventy-two billion barrels, making Mexico one of the most energy-rich countries in the world. Determined to take advantage of the strong price for oil on the world market but wary of overheating the Mexican economy with excessively rapid development, López Portillo opted to gradually triple oil production over the course of this term, turning Mexico into the world's fourth largest producer. Above all, the new president wanted to avoid making Mexico overdependent on oil exports and use the country's newfound wealth instead to develop an industrialized economy and achieve national food self-sufficiency. To this end, López Portillo embarked on a series of ambitious infrastructure, transportation, and heavy industry projects funded with large government investments and foreign loans that helped turn Mexico into a minor industrial power by the early 1980s. López Portillo also inaugurated the Mexican Food System (SAM), a far-reaching attempt to encourage domestic self-sufficiency in basic grains by granting credit, input subsidies, and guaranteed prices to small-scale producers.

In other domestic policy, the Mexican president effectively promoted his country's first major birth control program, which succeeded in lowering the national population growth rate from a very rapid 3.5 percent per year to 2.9 percent per year by the end of his term. López Portillo also implemented some limited democratic reforms of Mexico's political system by legalizing three additional opposition parties (including the Communist party) and setting aside one-fourth of the total seats in the Chamber of Deputies (Mexico's lower legislative body) to represent the opposition. But the López Portillo administration also used repressive tactics to crush emerging grassroots social movements that sought to challenge the PRI's grip on Mexico's political and social institutions in the 1970s. With official connivance, trade union bureaucrats linked to the PRI violently purged dissident groups in their ranks, and the security forces harshly suppressed peaceful peasant and student movements in Oaxaca state along with a leftist guerrilla movement in the state of Guerrero. The Mexico City police forces were also accused of illegally detaining and sometimes killing leftist activists in the capital in addition to directing criminal enterprises and soliciting bribes from the citizenry.

Mexico's emergence as an oil power encouraged López Portillo to project a more assertive and independent political role for Mexico in Latin America. The Mexican president developed friendly relations with Cuba and became an early and outspoken supporter of the Sandinista insurgency against the United States-backed Nicaraguan dictator Anastasio Somoza. In early 1979, López Portillo broke normal diplomatic practice by severing Mexico's relations with Somoza even before the dictator had been overthrown; he then went on to provide substantial economic aid to the victorious Sandinistas. The Mexican president also clashed with United States policymakers in Central America when he recognized leftist insurgents in El Salvador as a representative political force. Finally, López Portillo was uncompromising in his dealings with the United States on a number of trade issues, including oil and gas pricing and supply. Seeking to avoid excessive dependence on the U.S. market, Mexico kept oil exports well below U.S. demand and chose to burn off the gas rather than sell at a price it considered too low.

The tables began to turn for Mexico when world oil overproduction and successful energy conservation among industrialized nations caused the international price for oil to fall precipitously in 1981 and 1982. López Portillo refused to cut Mexico's selling prices to defend its markets, and buyers responded by taking their business elsewhere. Anticipating a devaluation of the peso currency to boost exports and cut domestic consumption, rich Mexicans sent billions of dollars out of the country in 1981, putting pressure on Mexico's foreign exchange reserves. The value of López Portillo's belated devaluation in February 1982 was largely negated by substantial wage increases and continued high government deficit spending, which contributed to record inflation as the Mexican economy lurched into recession that year. Meanwhile, the loss of hundreds of millions of dollars in oil revenues left Mexico unable to service its swollen foreign debt and forced the United States government and creditor banks to arrange a $10 billion bail-out package of new credits in August of 1982. In the final months of his administration—Mexican presidents cannot be re-elected—López Portillo sought to gain control of the economy by imposing an austerity program and nationalizing private banks, but these measures were largely unsuccessful. The once-ebullient chief executive left office in November under a cloud of bitter national disappointment over the failure of Mexico's oil boom, which left many Mexicans poorer in real terms than they had been before.

Further trials awaited López Portillo after returning to private life. Shortly after taking office, his successor, Miguel de la Madrid Hurtado, initiated a highly publicized anticorruption campaign targeting scores of middle-ranking functionaries and several high former officials under the López Portillo administration. Among those arrested and subsequently jailed on charges of "inexplicable enrichment" and fraud were two of López Portillo's closest political associates, former Mexico City police chief Arturo Durazo Moreno and the former head of the Pemex state oil monopoly, Jorge Díaz Serrano. De la Madrid stopped short, however, at taking legal action against López Portillo himself, although surveys showed that many Mexicans favored such prosecution. Public contempt focused on a luxurious seaside house in the Pacific coastal resort of Acapulco that the former president received as a gift from Mexico's powerful oil workers' union and on a large family compound that López Portillo built for himself in Mexico City shortly before leaving office. The ex-president steadfastly refused to explain how he had financed his hilltop retreat, which included four opulently appointed houses for himself and his adult children and a five-story private library. Mexicans promptly dubbed the compound "Dog Hill" (la Colina del Perro)—a "sarcastic" allusion, noted *New York Times* contributor Larry Rohter, to López Portillo's presidential pledge to "defend the peso like a dog." The former president was also widely believed to have spirited billions of dollars out of the country and into Swiss bank accounts and to have known about and tolerated the creation of hundreds of thousands of questionable positions in his administration, which paid salaries for no work done to friends and relatives of the politically connected. As Mexicans endured harsh economic austerity under the de la Madrid government, resentment against López Portillo grew to the point that the former president could not leave his home without being jeered at and scolded by passers-by.

To counter this "extremely negative image I have in Mexican society," as López Portillo acknowledged to Rohter, the ex-president wrote a two-volume, thirteen-hundred-page history and defense of his administration titled *Mis tiempos.* Composed of excerpts from the detailed diaries he kept as president along with autobiographical notes and commentary on current national issues, *Mis tiempos* offers an unusual inside look at the normally veiled workings of the Mexican executive power. López Portillo's diary entries, for instance, candidly record his hand-picking of the PRI's candidates for powerful state governorships and his strong influence over the nominally independent legislature. Describing himself in his book as "half-intellectual, half-philosopher, half-writer, half-painter, half-sportsman, half-teacher, half-orator and half . . . vain," López Portillo acknowledges a sense of moral ambiguity over his luxurious houses, but insists that he never accepted gifts from political supporters in return for specific favors as president. He also vigorously defends his ambitious development projects, many of which were canceled or scaled back by his successor. Replete with reproductions of the author's paintings and photographs, *Mis tiempos* quickly became a best-seller in Mexico. "I wrote the book in anguish," López Portillo declared at a press conference to promote *Mis tiempos,* as quoted in the Mexican periodical *Proceso;* "History will judge whether it came out well or badly."

MEDIA ADAPTATIONS: Quetzalcóatl was adapted for a play of the same title by Mario Sevilla Mascarenas.

AVOCATIONAL INTERESTS: Painting, photography, sports.

BIOGRAPHICAL/CRITICAL SOURCES:

BOOKS

Bustamante Carmelo, Homero, *Sobre Quetzalcóatl de José López Portillo: Raíz y razón cultural del continente* (contains play version of *Quetzalcóatl* by Mario Sevilla Mascarenas), Aconcagua Ediciones, 1976.
Contemporary Literary Criticism, Volume 46, Gale, 1988.
López Portillo, José, *Mis tiempos: Biografía y testimonio político,* Fernández Editores, 1988.
Rudolph, James D., editor, *Mexico: A Country Study,* 3rd edition, Government Printing Office, 1985.

PERIODICALS

Books and Bookmen, August, 1978.
New Republic, February 7, 1981.
Newsweek, December 13, 1976, January 17, 1977, October 1, 1979.
New York Times, November 28, 1988.
New York Times Book Review, December 12, 1982.
Proceso, November 14, 1988, November 28, 1988.
Spectator, May 6, 1978.
Time, December 6, 1976, February 21, 1977, July 23, 1979, October 8, 1979, July 12, 1982, September 13, 1982.
Wall Street Journal, December 1, 1976.

—*Sketch by Curtis Skinner*

*   *   *

LOPEZ SURIA, Violeta 1926-

PERSONAL: Born May 19, 1926, in Santurce, Puerto Rico.

CAREER: Teacher, short story writer, and poet. Taught at the School of General Studies at the University of Puerto Rico, Río Piedras.

WRITINGS:

Sentimiento de un viaje (poems), [San Juan, Puerto Rico], 1955.
Unas cuantas estrellas en mi cuarto (poems), Juan Ponce de León, (San Juan), 1957.
Diluvio (poems), [San Juan], 1958.
Amorosamente (poems), Areyto (Madrid), 1961.
Hubo unos pinos claros (poems), [San Juan], 1961.
La piel pegada al alma (poems), [San Juan], 1962.
Resurrección de Eurídice (poems), Juan Ponce de León, 1963.
Poemas a la Cáncora, Juan Ponce de León, 1963.
Me va la vida (poems), [San Juan], 1965.
Las nubes dejan sombras (poems), [San Juan], 1965.
Obsesión de Heliotropo (essays and short stories), Edil (Río Piedras, Puerto Rico), 1969.
Antología poética, edited and with an introduction by Juan Martínez Capó, University of Puerto Rico, 1970.

Also author of the poetry collections *Gotas en mayo* and *Elegía,* both 1953; author of *En un trigal de ausencia,* 1954, *Riverside,* 1955, and *Poema de la yerma virgen,* 1956.

SIDELIGHTS: An intellectual, lyrical poet who emerged in the 1950s, Violeta López Suria often focuses on such spiritual subjects as love and mortality. The Puerto Rican author also published *Obsesión de Heliotropo,* a well-regarded collection of essays and short stories, in 1969, and a poetry anthology in 1970.

*   *   *

LOPEZ y FUENTES, Gregorio 1897(?)-1966
(Tulio F. Peseenz)

PERSONAL: Born November 17, 1897 (some sources say c. 1892 or 1895), in Hacienda El Mamey, Huasteca, Veracruz, Mexico; died December 11, 1966, in Mexico City, Mexico; son of a farmer, rancher, and store owner. *Education:* Attended school in the state of Veracruz and Escuela Normal teachers' college in Mexico City.

CAREER: Journalist and author. Professor of literature at Escuela Normal (teachers' college), Mexico City, Mexico; *El Universal Gráfico* (newspaper), Mexico City, beginning in early 1920s, author of daily column "La novela diaria de la vida real" under pseudonym Tulio F. Peseenz, beginning in 1923, director, beginning in 1937; *El Universal* (newspaper), Mexico City, director, 1945-52; director of Ediciones de Libros for Editorial Novaro. *Military service:* Fought against American troops who occupied the city of Veracruz, Mexico, in 1914; may have seen service elsewhere.

AWARDS, HONORS: National Prize for Literature from Mexico, 1935, for *El indio.*

WRITINGS:

La siringa de cristal (poems; title means "The Crystal Flute"), [Mexico], 1914.
Claros de selva (poems; title means "Forest Glades"), América Latina (Mexico), 1922.
El vagabundo (novel; title means "The Vagabond"), published in *El Universal Ilustrado,* 1922.
El alma del poblacho (novella), [Mexico], 1924.
Campamento: Novela mexicana (novel; title means "Bivouac"), Espasa-Calpe (Madrid), 1931.

Tierra: La revolución agraria en México (novel; title means "Land: The Agrarian Revolution in Mexico"), special edition, Talls. de *El Universal,* 1932, Editorial México, 1933, published in United States as *Tierra: A Novel of the Agrarian Revolution in Mexico,* introduction by Henry A. Holmes and Walter A. Bara, Ginn, 1949.

¡Mi general! Novela mexicana (novel; title means "My General"), Botas, 1934.

El indio: Novela mexicana (novel; title means "The Indian"), Botas, 1935, Porrúa, 1974, translation by Anita Brenner published as *El Indio,* illustrations by Diego Rivera, Bobbs-Merrill, 1937, reprinted, Ungar, 1972 (translation published in England as *They That Reap,* Harrap, 1937).

Arrieros: Novela mexicana (novel; title means "Muleteers"), Botas, 1937.

Huasteca: Novela del petróleo (novel), Botas, 1939.

Cuentos campesinos de México (short stories), Cima, 1940.

Acomodaticio: Novela de un político de convicciones (novel; title means "Accommodation: Novel of a Politician With Convictions"), Botas, 1943, Alacat (El Salvador), 1971.

Los peregrinos inmóviles, (novel; title means "The Immovable Pilgrims"), Botas, 1944.

Entresuelo (novel; title means "Mezzanine"), Botas, 1948.

Milpa, potrero y monte (novel; title means "Cornfield, Cattle Ranch, and Upland"), Botas, 1951.

Contributor of articles, stories, and poems to periodicals, including *El Universal Ilustrado, El Maestro,* and *Nosotros.*

SIDELIGHTS: Gregorio López y Fuentes was one of the most acclaimed novelists to emerge in Mexico during the 1930s. He wrote in the aftermath of Mexico's long and chaotic Revolution, which lasted from about 1910 to 1920 and produced a government pledged to fostering greater social and economic equality. By the 1930s López y Fuentes and his peers, often called the "novelists of the Revolution," were producing works of realistic fiction that measured Mexican society against its revolutionary ideals. These books—prompted by social concern and the growing sense that Mexico's reform movement might fail—attracted national and international attention. In 1935, López y Fuentes won Mexico's first National Prize for Literature for his novel *El indio* ("The Indian").

López y Fuentes was the son of a farmer and rancher who owned a small store patronized by Mexican Indians. By the early years of the Revolution, the author was a student at the Escuela Normal teachers' college in Mexico City. When U.S. troops attempted to intervene in the Revolution by occupying the port of Veracruz in 1914, he and many classmates went to the city and fought the Americans; he may also have fought on behalf of revolutionaries elsewhere in Mexico during this period. Then he began a teaching career, which included work as a professor of literature at the Escuela Normal. His first two books—*La siringa de cristal* ("The Crystal Flute") and *Claros de selva* ("Forest Glades")—were collections of poetry inspired by Hispanic modernist writers, who tended to avoid social reality in favor of lyrical verse and a detached appreciation of art. But by the early 1920s, when López y Fuentes had left teaching to become a journalist at Mexico City's *El Universal Gráfico,* the focus of his writing began to change. Under the pseudonym Tulio F. Peseenz, he developed a successful daily column titled "La novela diaria de la vida real" ("The Daily Novel of Real Life") that used newspaper stories as the basis for short fiction. As Ernest Herman Hespelt observed in his introduction to *El indio,* the author "c[a]me to realize how well this material was suited to his talents. He found that these assembled sketches of real events presented in the helter-skelter, planless fashion of daily reports have the effect of re-creating the composite life of the common people of a great city. When he began to write his more important novels he used the technique developed in the columns of 'La novela diaria' for more ambitious artistic ends."

Commentators suggest López y Fuentes based his first major novel, *Campamento* ("Bivouac"), on his military experiences in Veracruz. Set in the encampment of a revolutionary army, the book has neither a focused plot nor a set of main characters. Instead the author uses short vignettes, peopled with a wide variety of unnamed characters, to depict camp life over the course of a few days. Parts of the book, according to *Spanish Review*'s Ernest Moore, show the author's interest in social satire. An army officer, for example, thoughtlessly compels an Indian guide to run beside the horses of the general staff until the guide dies of exhaustion; and as the revolutionaries talk, the critic noted, some "frankly expose the miserable sources of their own 'revolutionary zeal.'" Much of the work consists of such minor incidents as preparing food or personal quarrels; the author's talent, declared Boyd Carter in *Prairie Schooner,* lies in giving these details "an animation that fixes them indelibly in the memory." López y Fuentes, Hespelt averred, is not portraying a particular historical event; his broad canvas creates a more general picture of "the Mexican people engaged in civil war." In *Mexico in Its Novel: A Nation's Search for Identity,* John Brushwood called the author's technique the "group protagonist." In such a work, Brushwood suggested, the social setting itself—not the individual—is the true main character. López y Fuentes continued to use the group protagonist in some of his most successful works.

Tierra ("Land") has been hailed as López y Fuentes's best novel by some commentators in Mexico. In this book, according to Brushwood, "the real protagonist . . . is the movement of the Revolution." The narrative begins in 1910 on a typical Mexican hacienda: on such large estates, landowners commonly treated peasants as slaves. As the story progresses, the hacienda's peasants gradually move from apathy to open revolt under the leadership of Emiliano Zapata, a historical figure who preached redistribution of the land to the poor who farmed it. By the novel's end in 1920, Zapata has died at the hands of political opponents; but many peasants insist that he is alive, for he has become a symbol of their rights to land. *Tierra* is "thoroughly readable," declared Moore, who called the book "*the* agrarian novel of the Revolution." Brushwood felt the work "contains perhaps an overdose" of Zapata's political ideology. Nonetheless, he considered the novel "one of the clearest pictures of what happened" during the turbulent era it surveys.

Some commentators pass lightly over López y Fuentes's third novel of the Revolution, *¡Mi general!* ("My General"). Brushwood, for instance, found that "the book adds very little to what the author has already said" about the conflict. Moore, however, valued the book as a work of social satire. Unlike the two novels that preceded it, *¡Mi general!* has a single main character, an obscure common man who briefly achieves fame as an army officer during the Revolution. This nameless soldier, Moore observed, is "obsessed by the idea of self-glorification, . . . a common ailment of the Mexican soldier patriot." As the general metamorphoses from officer to politician, counter-revolutionary, fugitive, and finally unemployed cowboy, López y Fuentes, according to Moore, "examine[s] the political corruption, the military 'racket', and the cynical side of revolution." The critic considered *¡Mi general!* equal in worth to *Tierra* and more accomplished in its use of detail.

In 1935 López y Fuentes produced *El indio,* one of the first Mexican novels to focus on the plight of the country's large Indian population. Highly successful in Mexico, where it has been reprinted regularly, the book was also translated into several foreign languages and was praised by prominent critics in the English-speaking world within a few years of its publication. Making use once more of a group protagonist, López y Fuentes offers a diverse portrait of life in an Indian village, marked by periodic intrusions of white society. As Charles Poore observed in the *New York Times Book Review, El indio* "begins and ends with episodes of invasion." At the opening, white traders arrive in the village, obtain an Indian guide, then torture and cripple him in an effort to find gold. By the end of the book, officials imbued with the spirit of the Revolution have brought a road and a Spanish-language school to the village, but these "improvements" appear to the Indians as trappings of a white civilization that they have no reason to accept. Though the characters "aren't even given names," Poore observed, "you come to know them with an ultimate thoroughness based on seeing how they live . . . what they do and what they fear and what they hate." Along with other reviewers, Poore praised López y Fuentes for his direct, uncluttered writing style and his well-rounded portrayal of Indian life. Brushwood questioned the use of a group protagonist in the novel, observing that "anonymity . . . emphasizes the primitive state of the people, perhaps more than the author intended. And it occasionally produces a 'wise-old-chief-has-spoken' effect that is dangerously close to the noble savage foolishness of a century earlier." Nevertheless, the critic acknowledged, *El indio* "became one of Mexico's best known and most influential novels." Writing just after the book was published, Moore predicted that "López y Fuentes . . . is likely to become Mexico's most prominent contemporary novelist."

But López y Fuentes never matched the acclaim he achieved for *El indio.* Some observers suggested that the very strength of his outrage over Mexico's enduring social problems—greed and dishonesty among the powerful, poverty among the common people—marred his effectiveness as a creator of fiction. For example, Brushwood complained that *Huasteca,* which records the corrupting effects of oil wealth on a rural Mexican family, resembles a series of "newspaper editorials." "The author sets forth his case," the critic observed, "but it is an explication of a problem, not a re-creation of life." The pain of observing a revolution unfulfilled, Brushwood acknowledged, "would hardly produce calm deliberation." As Hespelt wrote, López y Fuentes "is not only reporter; he is editor and headline writer as well." However, Hespelt concluded, "for an authentic introduction to life in Mexico . . . and a sympathetic understanding of the country's problems it would be hard to find a better guide."

BIOGRAPHICAL/CRITICAL SOURCES:

BOOKS

Brushwood, John S., *Mexico in Its Novel: A Nation's Search for Identity,* University of Texas Press, 1966.
Contemporary Literary Criticism, Volume 32, Gale, 1985.
Langford, Walter M., *The Mexican Novel Comes of Age,* University of Notre Dame Press, 1971.
López y Fuentes, Gregorio, *El indio: Novela mexicana,* introduction by Ernest Herman Hespelt, Norton, 1940.
López y Fuentes, Gregorio, *Tierra: A Novel of the Agrarian Revolution in Mexico,* introduction by Henry A. Holmes and Walter A. Bara, Ginn, 1949.

PERIODICALS

Mexican Life, November, 1940.
New York Times Book Review, February 21, 1937.
Prairie Schooner, summer, 1954.

Saturday Review of Literature, February 27, 1937.
Spanish Review, April, 1937.
Times Literary Supplement, September 18, 1937.

OBITUARIES:

PERIODICALS

New York Times, December 13, 1966.

—*Sketch by Thomas Kozikowski*

* * *

LORCA, Federico García
See GARCIA LORCA, Federico

* * *

LORENZO, Heberto Padilla
See PADILLA (LORENZO), Heberto

* * *

LUGONES, Leopoldo 1874-1938
(Gil Paz)

PERSONAL: Born June 13, 1874, in Río Seco, Córdoba, Argentina; committed suicide by ingesting cyanide, February 19, 1938, in Buenos Aires, Argentina; married; children: Leopoldo. *Education:* Attended Catholic secondary school in Córdoba, Argentina.

CAREER: Poet, novelist, essayist, and journalist. Co-founder of *La Revue Sudaméricaine,* 1914. Director of the library of the National Council of Education, 1914-1938; Argentine representative to the League of Nations' Committee on Intellectual Cooperation.

MEMBER: Centro Socialista de Estudios.

WRITINGS:

El imperio jesuítico (essays), Compañia Sudamericana de Billetes de Banco, 1904, reprinted with introduction by Roy Bartholomew, Editorial de Belgrano, 1981.
La guerra gaucha (novel; title means "The Gaucho War"), 1905, 10th edition, corrected and annotated by son, Leopoldo Lugones, Ediciones Centurión, 1962.
Los crepúsculos del jardín (poetry; title means "The Evening Shadows of the Garden"), 1905, reprinted, Editorial Babel, 1926, reprinted with prologue and notes by Ana María Amar Sánchez, Centro Editor de América Latina, 1980.
Las fuerzas extrañas (short stories and an essay; title means "Strange Forces"; includes "La lluvia de fuego"), 1906, 4th edition, with preliminary notes by son, Leopoldo Lugones, Huemul, 1966.
Lunario sentimental (poetry; title means "Sentimental Lunar Poems"), 1909, 3rd edition, Ediciones Centurión, 1961.
Odas seculares (poetry; title means "Secular Odes"), 1910, new corrected edition, Editorial Babel, 1923.
Prometeo, Talleres de Otero y Co., 1910.
Historia de Sarmiento (history), Otero and Co., 1911, revised edition, Editorial Babel, 1931, reprinted, Editorial Universitaria de Buenos Aires, 1960.
El ejército de la Iliada, Otero and Co., 1915.
Elogio de Ameghino, Otero and Co., 1915.
El payador, Otero Impresores, 1916, reprinted with sketches by Alberto Güiraldes, Ediciones Centurión, 1961, published as

El payador: Antología de poesía y prosa, prologue by Jorge Luis Borges, notes by Guillermo Ara, Biblioteca Ayacucho (Caracas), 1979.

El libro de los paisajes (poetry), Otero y García, 1917.

Mi beligerancia, Otero y García, 1917.

Las industrias de Atenas, Talleres Gráficos "Atlántida," 1919.

Selección (selected poetry), M. García (Montevideo, Uruguay), 1919.

La torre de Casandra, Talleres Gráficos "Atlántida," 1919.

Las horas doradas (poetry), Editorial Babel, 1922.

Cuentos fatales (short stories), Editorial Babel, 1924, 2nd edition, with preliminary notes by son, Leopoldo Lugones, Huemul, 1967.

Estudios helénicos (includes translations of selections from the *Iliad* and the *Odyssey*), four volumes, Editorial Babel, 1924, Volume 1: *La funesta Helena,* Volume 2: *Un paladín de la Iliada,* Volume 3: *La dama de la Odisea,* Volume 4: *Héctor el domador.*

Romancero (poetry), 1924, 2nd edition, Editorial Babel, 1925.

Filosofícula (poetry), Editorial Babel, 1924.

La organización de la paz, La Editora Argentina, 1925.

El ángel de la sombra (novel; title means "The Angel of the Shadow"), M. Gleizer, 1926.

Neuvos estudios helénicos, Biblioteca Argentina de Buenas Ediciones Literarias, 1928.

Poemas solariegos (poetry; title means "Ancestral Poems"), Biblioteca Argentina de Buenas Ediciones Literarias, 1928.

La patria fuerte (essays), Taller Gráfico de L. Bernard, 1930.

La grande Argentina, Editorial Babel, 1930, reprinted with prologue by son, Leopoldo Lugones, Huemul, 1962.

El estado equitativo: Ensayo sobre la realidad Argentina, La Editora Argentina, 1932.

Roca, prologue by Octavio R. Amadeo, "Coni," 1938, published as *Historia de Roca,* introduction by Tomás Alva Negri, Editorial de Belgrano, 1980.

Romancero del Río Seco (poetry), sketches by Alberto Güiraldes, Las Prensas de Francisco A. Colombo, 1938.

Antología poética (poetry), selected with an introduction by Carlos Obligado, Espasa-Calpe (Argentina), 1941.

Obras poéticas completas (poetry), prologue by Pedro Miguel Obligado, Aguilar (Madrid), 1948.

Antología de la prosa, selected with commentary by son, Leopoldo Lugones, Ediciones Centurión, 1949.

Obras en prosa, selected with prologue by son, Leopoldo Lugones, Aguilar, 1962.

Leopoldo Lugones: Selección de poesía y prosa, selected and edited by son, Leopoldo Lugones, Ediciones Culturales Argentinas, 1962.

Las primeras letras de Leopoldo Lugones, preliminary notes by son, Leopoldo Lugones, Ediciones Centurión, 1963.

La estatua de sal (short stories; includes "La lluvia de fuego" and "La estatua de sal"), selected with a prologue by Borges, Ediciones Siruela (Madrid), 1985.

Also author of *Las montañas del oro* (poetry; title means "The Mountains of Gold"), 1897, *El libro fiel* (poetry), 1912, and *El cariño de los tontos.* Author of series of *criollo* stories known as the "cuentos serranos" (mountain tales), left uncompleted at time of death. Works represented in anthologies, including *Argentine Anthology of Modern Verse, The Epic of Latin American Literature, Literature of Latin America,* and *The Modernist Trend in Latin American Poetry.*

Author of socialist articles under pseudonym Gil Paz. Contributor to periodicals, including *Stratford Journal, Inter-America, Christian Science Monitor, Commonweal,* and *Poetry.*

SIDELIGHTS: An innovative Argentine writer, Leopoldo Lugones figured prominently in the *modernista* movement that helped change the face of Spanish American literature in the early twentieth century. The author of fiction, essays, and a significant body of poetry, he is best known for his experimental verse forms, which blend unusual rhythms with nontraditional rhyming devices. Lugones is also credited with composing one of the first uniquely Hispanic works of science fiction, a short story collection titled *Las fuerzas extrañas* ("Strange Forces"). His writings are invariably characterized by a provocative use of imagery and reflect a persistent but ultimately unfulfilled need for stability.

Though praised by some for his experimental vision, Lugones has also been censured for his shifting artistic, political, and social beliefs; several critics have implied that the author was a literary mimic who merely duplicated radical stylistic writing trends introduced by his contemporaries. However, a majority of late-twentieth-century critics have speculated that the changing emphasis of Lugones's works mirrors the varying means he sought to attain a sense of balance and meaning in his life. Proponents of this view maintain that Lugones's arduous search for tranquility and psychic equilibrium is chronicled with striking lucidity in a canon of works that focuses in turn on social justice, emotional withdrawal, an intense nationalism, and a glorification of nature. In an article for *Modern Philology,* Dorothy McMahon called Lugones a "man in search of roots" and expounded: "Whenever he failed to achieve what he sought by one means [he] began casting about for another, until all had been exhausted. . . . It is this quest for a stabilizing force which provides the common element" in the writings of Lugones and other poets and "makes it possible for [him] to surpass at times his 'models.' "

Lugones was forced as a child to move with his family from his native village of Río Seco (in the Cordoban province) to the city of Córdoba, where he attended a Catholic secondary school. Opposed to school's dogmatic pedagogical approach, he abandoned both his studies and the Catholic church and, according to McMahon, "was left in early adolescence with the problem of attempting to fill the void left by his displaced beliefs." While still a teenager, Lugones moved to Buenos Aires, beginning his writing career as a journalist and developing a long-standing association with writer Rubén Darío, a founding member of the *modernista* movement.

Lugones's early articles and poems express socialist views. For instance, his first published volume of poetry, the 1897 collection *Las montañas del oro* ("The Mountains of Gold"), exalts the power of the poet as an adept leader in the revolt against social injustice. The free verse style of the collection is said to resemble the writings of American poet Walt Whitman, while the urgent and emotional call for the humane treatment of all people bears a likeness to that of French writer Victor Hugo's works. Ironically, Lugones later assumed a more conservative sociopolitical stance and attracted criticism from liberal intellectuals for his eventual advocation of fascism.

Lugones followed *Las montañas del oro* with the 1905 historical novel *La guerra gaucha* ("The Gaucho War"), about Argentina's struggle for independence, and *Los crepúsculos del jardín* ("The Evening Shadows of the Garden"), a poetry volume published the same year. In the latter, Lugones portrays the poet as a superior thinker detached from an emotionally alienating world. He continued to depict scenes of withdrawal in the last significant poetic work of his *modernista* phase, *Lunario senti-*

mental ("Sentimental Lunar Poems"), which is generally regarded as his literary masterpiece.

Lunario sentimental, published in 1909, is a technically innovative verse collection containing rhythmic, nontraditional forms of rhyme. Set under an omnipresent moon, the forty-two poems in this volume highlight Lugones's disdain for humanity and rejection of rationality. Infused with a sense of melancholia and lamentation, *Lunario sentimenal* has been compared to French writer Jules Laforgue's cynical classic *L'Imitation de Notre Dame la lune.* Several critics, including McMahon, have suggested that the dry, satiric nature of Lugones's collection parallels his continuing disillusionment and search for stability—a search characterized at this period in the poet's life by emotional detachment.

Lugones's next volume of poetry, *Odas seculares* ("Secular Odes"), marks a departure from the radical style of his earlier verse and a return to more traditional rhyming methods. The poems in this unusual volume eulogize the rural countryside of the poet's native Argentina. Jean Franco, writing in *An Introduction to Spanish-American Literature,* suggested that through the collection, Lugones sought to preserve the fading pastoral history of Argentina. Other critics expanded on this theme, implying that the writer's apparent identification with his country served as an indirect means of self-preservation.

Aside from his poetic innovations, Lugones contributed to the evolution of Hispanic fiction. He revealed a preoccupation with the fantastic in his highly acclaimed 1906 prose collection *Las fuerzas extrañas,* which is generally regarded as the exemplar of science fiction in Argentine literature. The most celebrated story in the volume, "La lluvia de fuego," evokes the horror that strikes an ancient city's inhabitants as a toxic copper rain falls to earth. The stories in *Las fuerzas extrañas* and *Cuentos fatales*—another collection of short fiction by Lugones which progresses from science fiction themes to an exploration of the occult—are noted for their provocative blend of reality and fantasy and have often been compared to the works of Edgar Allan Poe. In an article for *Inter-American Review of Bibliography,* Joan E. Ciruti theorized that in his short stories, Lugones "seems to suggest, by the attention . . . give[n] . . . to unpretentious, good people leading a pastoral existence, that happiness and contentment lie in an uncomplicated life where there is no consciousness of the limitations of man or his status in the universe."

Evaluating Lugones's significance as a writer, Manuel Ugarte, writing in *Escritores iberoamericanos de 1900,* surmised: "There can be no doubt that, from 1900 on, he was one of the fifteen or twenty main representatives of Latin American culture and that his work is linked unquestionably to the best of European literature." *Américas* contributor Manuel Belloni went even further, concluding that the linguistically brilliant Lugones was, essentially, "the first Argentine writer; that is, the first intellectual totally dedicated to letters, the first *homme des lettres* who as such heralded a step forward in Argentine culture." Unable to find solace in the scope of his writings, though, Lugones grew increasingly disillusioned and eventually succumbed to his despair, committing suicide on February 19, 1938.

BIOGRAPHICAL/CRITICAL SOURCES:

BOOKS

Blanco-Fombona, Rufino, *El modernismo y los poetas modernistas,* Editorial Mundo Latino (Madrid), 1929.
Foster, David William and Virginia Ramos Foster, editors, *Modern Latin American Literature,* Volume 1, Ungar, 1975.

Franco, Jean, *An Introduction to Spanish-American Literature,* Cambridge University Press, 1969.
Twentieth-Century Literary Criticism, Volume 15, Gale, 1985.
Ugarte, Manuel, *Escritores iberoamericanos de 1900,* Editorial Vértice, 1947.

PERIODICALS

Américas, January, 1969.
Inter-American Review of Bibliography, April-June, 1975.
Modern Philology, February, 1954.

—*Sketch by Barbara Carlisle Bigelow*

*   *   *

LUZMA
See UMPIERRE (HERRERA), Luz María

*   *   *

LYNCH, B. Suárez
See BIOY CASARES, Adolfo
and BORGES, Jorge Luis

*   *   *

LYNCH, Benito   1885-1951

PERSONAL: Born in 1885 (some sources say 1880) in Buenos Aires, Argentina; died in 1951.

CAREER: Novelist and short story writer.

WRITINGS:

Plata dorada (novel), [Argentina], 1909.
Los caranchos de la Florida (title means "The Vultures of Florida"), [Argentina], 1916, reprinted, Troquel (Buenos Aires), 1975.
La evasión (short stories; also see below), Cervantes (Barcelona, Spain), 1922.
Las mal calladas (novel), Babel (Buenos Aires), 1923.
El inglés de los güesos (novel; title means "The Englishman of the Bones"), Calpe (Madrid), 1924, reprinted, Troquel, 1974.
El antojo de la patrona (novel; also see below), [Argentina], 1925.
Palo verde (novel; also see below), [Argentina], 1925.
Raquela (novel; also see below), Ibérica, 1926.
. . . De los campos porteños (short stories), Librerías Anaconda (Buenos Aires), 1931, reprinted with introduction and notes by Leonidas de Vedia, Troquel, 1966.
El antojo de la patrona, y Palo verde, Librerías Anaconda, 1931, published as *Palo verde, El antojo de la patrona,* Prometeo (Santiago, Chile), c. 1940.
El romance de un gaucho (novel; title means "A Gaucho's Romance"), Librerías Anaconda, 1933, reprinted, G. Kraft (Buenos Aires), 1961.
Raquela, La evasión, El antojo de la patrona, Espasa-Calpe (Madrid), 1936.
Palo verde, y otras novelas cortas (contains *Palo verde, Locura de honor, El paquetitos, El casa su casa quiere*), Espasa-Calpe Argentina (Mexico), 1940, 2nd edition, Troquel, 1969.
Cuentos camperos (short stories), Troquel, 1964.
Cuentos (short stories), edited with an introduction and notes by Ana Bruzzone, Centro Editor de América Latina, 1980.

SIDELIGHTS: Some of the best known novels in Argentine writer Benito Lynch's sparse oeuvre include *Los caranchos de la*

Florida ("The Vultures of Florida"), *El inglés de los güesos* ("The Englishman of the Bones"), and *El romance de un gaucho* ("A Gaucho's Romance"). These books reveal their author's honesty in depicting the life of Argentina's lower classes. Lynch was especially noted for his accurate use of dialogue, as Edward E. Settgast commented in *Hispania:* "One of Lynch's greatest stylistic achievements was undoubtedly his ability to portray the personality and psychology of his characters by means of the rural dialect." In *El romance de un gaucho,* for example, the author captured his subject by writing the book entirely in gaucho slang.

Lynch grew up in the rural La Plata region of Argentina, and so was very familiar with the lifestyle of the gaucho, or South American cowboy. This lent an air of authenticity to his writing that a number of critics felt placed him above many of his contemporaries. "Indeed," *Crítica y polémica, tercera serie* author Roberto F. Giusti stated, "it would be impossible to name any Uruguayan or Argentine writer who has written about the man of the countryside with greater truth than has Lynch in *The Englishman of the Bones* and his earlier novels." Unlike other authors who idealized or romanticized the gaucho as a heroic, courageous figure, Lynch "did not commit the stupid error of believing that manliness was inextricably linked to courage," attested *Sur* contributor Estela Canto, who compared the psychological realism in Lynch's characters to that present in the works of Thomas Hardy and Alberto Moravia.

Also fascinated by Anglo-Saxon culture and language, Lynch often used English expressions in his books. But, as Marshall R. Nason observed in *Revista Iberoamericana,* the author was not fluent in English, which caused his use of the English language to sometimes border on "caricature." This flaw, however, did not detract from the writer's skill in describing life in rural Argentina. Carlos Horacio Magis concluded in *Cuadernos Hispanoamericanos:* "Among rural novelists, Benito Lynch . . . has been the most mature and the most nearly perfect."

BIOGRAPHICAL/CRITICAL SOURCES:

BOOKS

Giusti, Roberto F., *Crítica y polémica, tercera serie,* Agencia General de Librería y Publicaciones, 1927.
Salama, Roberto, *Benito Lynch,* "La Mandrágora," 1959.

PERIODICALS

Cuadernos hispanoamericanos, May, 1961.
Hispania, September, 1969.
Revista Iberoamericana, January-June, 1958.
Sur, September-October, 1952.

*   *   *

LYNCH DAVIS, B.
  See BIOY CASARES, Adolfo
  and BORGES, Jorge Luis

M

MACHADO, Eduardo 1953-

PERSONAL: Born June 11, 1953, in Havana, Cuba; immigrated to United States, 1961; son of Othon Eduardo and Gilda (Hernandez) Machado; divorced.

ADDRESSES: Agent—Annette Van Duren, 200 North Robertson Blvd., Suite 215, Beverly Hills, Calif. 90211.

CAREER: Playwright.

MEMBER: New Dramatists.

AWARDS, HONORS: Fellowships from National Endowment for the Arts, 1981, 1983, and 1986; fellowship from Rockefeller Foundation, 1985.

WRITINGS:

"FLOATING ISLANDS" SERIES

"The Modern Ladies of Guanabacoa" (two-act), produced in New York City at Ensemble Studio Theatre, 1983.
"Fabiola" (two-act), produced in New York City at Ensemble Studio Theatre, 1985.
"Broken Eggs" (two-act; produced in New York City at Ensemble Studio Theatre, 1984), published in On New Ground: Contemporary Hispanic American Plays, Theatre Communications Group, 1987; Spanish-language version produced as "Revoltillo" in New York City at Repertorio Española, 1989.

OTHER PLAYS

(With Rick Vartoreila) "Rosario and the Gypsies" (one-act musical; book and lyrics by Machado; music by Vartoreila), produced in New York City at Ensemble Studio Theatre, 1982.
(With Geraldine Sherman) "When It's Over" (two-act), produced in New Haven at Long Wharf Theatre, 1987.
"Why to Refuse" (one-act), produced in New York City at Theatre for a New City, 1987.
"A Burning Beach" (two-act), produced Off-Broadway at American Place Theatre, 1988.
"Don Juan in New York" (two-act musical), produced in New York City at Theatre for a New City, 1988.
"Once Removed" (two-act), produced in New Mexico, 1988.
"Wishing You Well" (one-act musical), produced in New York City, 1988.

"Cabaret Bambu" (one-act musical), produced in 1989.
(Translator) Jose Ignacio Cabrujas, "The Day You Love Me" (two-act), produced in Los Angeles at Mark Taper Forum, 1989.
"Stevie Wants to Play the Blues" (two-act musical), produced in Los Angeles, 1990.

Also author of unproduced works, including "Aliens in Their Own Planet" (two-act musical), "Fiances" (two-act musical), and, with Geraldine Sherman, "The Perfect Light."

WORK IN PROGRESS: "In the Eye of the Hurricane," a two-act play for the "Floating Islands" series.

SIDELIGHTS: Eduardo Machado is known for his stirring, frequently amusing depictions of Cuban life. Among his most important works is the "Floating Islands" cycle chronicling the bourgeois Marquez family from the late 1920s to the present. Los Angeles Times reviewer Sylvie Drake, who wrote that the series "has the earmarks of a life work," was particularly impressed with the second entry, "Fabiola," which is set during Fidel Castro's rise to power. "Nothing here is entirely logical, any more than it is in families or in life," Drake surmised. "It makes for a funny, sometimes absurd, often melodramatic, but always interesting veracity."

Aside from the "Floating Islands" cycle, Machado has earned acclaim for such plays as "A Burning Beach," which concerns, as Mel Gussow noted in the New York Times, "loyalty, patriotism and suppressed sexuality" in 1890s Cuba. In his positive appraisal, Gussow acknowledged the play's "provocative intensity" and its "air of intrigue."

BIOGRAPHICAL/CRITICAL SOURCES:

PERIODICALS

Los Angeles Times, October 12, 1985.
New York Times, June 5, 1982, January 27, 1983, February 23, 1984, September 6, 1985, October 19, 1986, November 5, 1988.

*   *   *

MADARIAGA (y ROJO), Salvador de 1886-1978

PERSONAL: Born July 23, 1886, in La Coruña, Galicia, Spain; died December 14, 1978, in Locarno, Switzerland; son of José (a colonel) and Ascensión (Rojo) de Madariaga; married Constance Helen Margaret Archibald, October 10, 1912 (died, 1970); married Emilie Szekely Rauman, November 18, 1970; children: (first marriage) Nieves and Isabel (daughters). *Education:* Graduated from College Chaptal, Paris, France, 1906; attended Ecole Polytechnique, Paris, 1906-08; graduated from Ecole Nationale Superieure des Mines, Paris, 1911. *Politics:* Liberal.

ADDRESSES: Home—L'Esplanade, 6600 Locarno, Switzerland.

CAREER: Employed by Railway Company of Northern Spain, Madrid, 1911-16, simultaneously wrote political articles for newspapers under a pseudonym; became a writer; spent 1916-21 in London as a journalist and critic; entered Secretariat of League of Nations, Geneva, Switzerland, 1921, member of press section, 1921-22, head of disarmament section, 1922-27; first occupant of King Alfonso XIII Chair of Spanish Studies at Oxford University, Oxford, England, 1927-30; Spanish Ambassador to United States, 1931, to France, 1932-34, and Spain's permanent delegate to League of Nations Assembly, 1931-36; served briefly as Spain's Minister of Education, 1934, then as Minister of Justice. Broadcaster to Latin America for British Broadcasting Corp. during war; broadcaster in Spanish, French, and German to European countries. Associated with various international organizations in postwar years, first president of Liberal International (became president of honor) and honorary president of Congress for Cultural Freedom. Honorary co-chairman of Spanish Refugee Aid, Inc.; Emory L. Ford Professor of Spanish at Princeton University, 1954; lecturer and speaker in many countries.

MEMBER: Spanish Academy of Letters and of Moral and Political Sciences, French Academy of Moral and Political Sciences, Academy of History of Caracas, and many other Spanish American learned societies; Reform Club (London), Ateneo (Madrid).

AWARDS, HONORS: M.A., Oxford University, 1928; gold medalist, Yale University; fellow, Exeter College, University of Pavia; honorary doctor of the Universities of Arequipa, Lima, Poitiers, Liege, and Lille, and of Oxford and Princeton Universities; Ere Nouvelle Prize, for *Englishmen, Frenchmen, Spaniards;* Knight Grand Cross of Order of the Republic (Spain), White Lion (Czechoslovakia), Order of Merit (Chile), Order of Jade in Gold (China), Order of Merit (Hungary), Boyaca (Colombia), Order of the White Rose (Finland), Grand Cross of Legion d'Honneur (France), Aztec Eagle (Mexico), and Order of the Sun (Peru); Europa Prize, Hans Deutsch Foundation, Bern University, 1963; Hanseatic Goethe Prize, 1967.

WRITINGS:

BIOGRAPHY AND HISTORY

Quatre Espagnols a Londres, Plon, 1928.
Spain (also see below), Scribner, 1930, 3rd edition, J. Cape, 1942, Creative Age, 1943.
Christopher Columbus: Being the Life of the Very Magnificent Lord Don Cristóbal Colón (first of the "New World" trilogy), Hodder & Stoughton, 1939, Macmillan, 1940, new edition, Hollis & Carter, 1949, Ungar, 1967.
Hernán Cortés: Conqueror of Mexico (second in the trilogy), Macmillan, 1941, 2nd edition, Regnery, 1955, reprinted, Greenwood Press, 1979.
Spain, two volumes (first volume based on previous book of same title), J. Cape, 1942, Creative Age, 1943.
Cuadro histórico de las Indias, Editorial Sudamericana, Volume 1: *El auge del Imperio Español en América,* 1945, 2nd edi-

tion, 1959, reprinted, Espasa-Calpe, 1977, translation published as *The Rise of the Spanish-American Empire,* Macmillan, 1947, reprinted, Greenwood Press, 1975, Volume 2: *El ocaso del Imperio Español en América,* 1945, 2nd edition, 1959, translation published as *The Fall of the Spanish-American Empire,* Hollis & Carter, 1947, Macmillan, 1948, revised edition, Collier, 1963, reprinted, Greenwood Press, 1975.
Bolívar (third in the trilogy), two volumes, Editorial Hermes (Mexico), 1951, 3rd edition, Editorial Sudamericana, 1959, translation by the author published in abridged edition with the same title, Hollis & Carter, 1951, reprinted, Greenwood Press, 1979.
De Colón a Bolívar, E.D.H.A.S.A. (Editorial y Distribuidora Hispano Americana, S.A.) (Barcelona), 1956.
El ciclo hispánico, two volumes, Editorial Sudamericana, 1958.
Spain: A Modern History, Praeger, 1958.
Españoles de mi tiempo, Editorial Planeta, 1974, 5th edition, 1976.
Memorias, 1921-1936: Amanecer sin mediodía, Espasa-Calpe, 1974.

POLITICAL BOOKS

La guerra desde Londres, Editorial Monclús (Tortosa), 1918.
Disarmament, Coward, 1929, reprinted, Kennikat Press, 1967.
Discursos internacionales, M. Aguilar (Madrid), 1934.
Anarquía o jerarquía, M. Aguilar, 1935, 3rd edition, 1970, translation by the author published as *Anarchy or Hierarchy,* Allen & Unwin, 1937, reprinted, 1970.
Theory and Practice in International Relations: William J. Cooper Foundation Lectures, 1937, Swarthmore College, University of Pennsylvania Press, 1937.
The World's Design, Allen & Unwin, 1938.
(With Edward Hallett Carr) *Future of International Government,* Universal Distributors, 1941.
(With others) *The British Commonwealth and the U.S.A. in the Postwar World,* National Peace Council, 1942.
¡Ojo, vencedores!, Editorial Sudamericana, 1945, translation by the author published as *Victors, Beware,* J. Cape, 1946.
De l'Angoisse a la liberte, Calmann-Levy (Paris), 1954, translation of second part by M. Marx published in England as *Democracy Versus Liberty?,* Pall Mall Press, 1958.
Rettet die Freiheit! (selected articles originally published in *Neue Zuercher Zeitung,* 1948-57), Francke (Bern), 1958.
¡General, márchese usted! (collection of lectures broadcast for the Spanish Service of the Radiodiffusion Francaise, 1954-57), Ediciones Ibérica, 1959.
The Blowing Up of the Parthenon; or, How to Lose the Cold War, Praeger, 1960, revised edition, 1961.
Latin America Between the Eagle and the Bear, Praeger, 1962.
Weltpolitisches Kaleidoskop (second collection of articles originally published in *Neue Zuercher Zeitung*), Fretz & Wasmuth Verlag (Zurich), 1965.

ESSAYS

Shelley and Calderón, and Other Essays on English and Spanish Poetry, Constable, 1920, reprinted, Kennikat Press, 1965.
The Genius of Spain, and Other Essays on Spanish Contemporary Literature, Clarendon Press, 1923, reprinted, Books for Libraries Press, 1968.
Arceval y los ingleses, Espasa-Calpe (Madrid), 1925, reprinted, 1973.
Guía del lector del "Quijote," Espasa-Calpe, 1926, reprinted, 1976, translation by the author published as *Don Quixote: An Introductory Essay in Psychology,* Gregynogg Press

(Wales), 1934, revised edition, Oxford University Press, 1961, reprinted, Greenwood Press, 1980.

Englishmen, Frenchmen, Spaniards: An Essay in Comparative Psychology, Oxford University Press, 1928, 2nd edition, Hill & Wang, 1969.

Americans, Oxford University Press, 1930, reprinted, Books for Libraries Press, 1968.

On Hamlet, Hollis & Carter, 1948, 2nd edition, Barnes & Noble, 1964.

Bosquejo de Europa (also see below), Editorial Hermes, 1951, reprinted, Editorial Sudamericana, 1969, translation by the author published as *Portrait of Europe,* Hollis & Carter, 1952, Roy, 1955, revised edition, University of Alabama Press, 1967.

Essays with a Purpose, Hollis & Carter, 1954.

Presente y porvenir de Hispanoamérica, y otros ensayos, Editorial Sudamericana, 1959, 2nd edition, 1974.

De Galdós a Lorca, Editorial Sudamericana, 1960.

El Quijote de Cervantes, Editorial Sudamericana, 1962.

Retrato de un hombre de pie, E.D.H.A.S.A., 1965, translation by the author published as *Portrait of a Man Standing,* University of Alabama Press, 1968.

Memorias de un federalista, Editorial Sudamericana, 1967.

(Contributor) Ivar Ivask and Juan Marichal, editors, *Luminous Reality: The Poetry of Jorge Guillén,* University of Oklahoma Press, 1969.

Selecciones de Madariaga (includes selections from *Bosquejo de Europa* [and] *El enemigo de Dios*), edited by Frank Sedwick and Elizabeth Van Orman, Prentice-Hall, 1969.

Mujeres españolas, Espasa-Calpe, 1972.

Obras escogidas: Ensayos, Editorial Sudamericana, 1972.

Mi respuesta: Artículos publicados en la revista Ibérica (1954-1974), selected with prologue by Victoria Kent, Espasa-Calpe, 1982.

NOVELS

The Sacred Giraffe: Being the Second Volume of the Posthumous Works of Julio Arceval (satire), Hopkinson, 1925.

Sir Bob (juvenile), Harcourt, 1930.

El enemigo de Dios (also see above), M. Aguilar, 1926, 2nd edition, Editorial Sudamericana, 1965.

Ramo de errores, Editorial Hermes, 1952, translation by the author published as *A Bunch of Errors,* J. Cape, 1954.

La camarada Ana, Editorial Hermes, 1954, 2nd edition, Editorial Sudamericana, 1956.

Sanco Panco, Latino-Americana (Mexico), 1963.

POETRY

Romances de ciego, Publicaciones Atenea (Madrid), 1922.

La fuente serena, Editorial Cervantes, 1927.

Elegía en la muerte de Unamuno, Oxford University Press, 1937.

Elegía en la muerte de Federico García Lorca, Oxford University Press, 1938.

The Home of Man (18 sonnets), privately printed, 1938.

Rosa de cieno y ceniza, Editorial Sudamericana, 1942.

El sol, la luna y las estrellas: Romances a Beatriz, Editorial Juventud (Barcelona), 1954, 3rd edition, 1974.

La que huele a tomillo y a romero, Editorial Sudamericana, 1959.

Poppy, bilingual Spanish and English edition, Imprenta Bernasconi (Lugano), 1965.

Obra poética, Plaza y Janés (Barcelona), 1977.

DRAMATIC WORKS

Elysian Fields, Allen & Unwin, 1937.

El toisón de oro, y tres obras más: La muerte de Carmen, Don Carlos y Mío Cid (the first a lyrical fantasy in three acts; the following three dramatic poems), Editorial Sudamericana, 1940, 2nd edition, 1945.

Don Juan y la Don-Juania (one-act verse play), Editorial Sudamericana, 1950.

Los tres estudiantes de Salamanca (includes "Los tres estudiantes de Salamanca," a three-act tragicomedy; "Viva la muerte," a three-act modern tragedy, produced in the Piccola Scala, Milan, Italy, 1966; and "El doce de octubre de Cervantes," a one-act historical fantasy), Editorial Sudamericana, 1962.

La Mappe-monde et le Pape-monde (three-act French verse play; broadcast by Radiodiffusion Francaise, 1948), Editions d'Art Jacques O'Hana (London), 1966.

La cruz y la bandera [y] Las tres carabelas (romances), Editorial Sudamericana, 1966.

Numance: Tragedie lyrique en un acte (opera; first produced in Paris, 1954), libretto by Henri Barraud, Boosey & Hawkes, 1970.

Diálogos famosos: Campos eliseos—Adán y Eva, Editorial Sudamericana, 1970.

RADIO PLAYS

"Campos eliseos" (Spanish version of "Elysian Fields"), broadcast by the British Broadcasting Corp. (BBC) for Spain, Radio Varsovia, updated version broadcast in German by Radio Berna, 1966.

"Cristóbal Colón," BBC, 1941.

"Las tres carabelas," BBC, 1942.

"Numancia" (English verse translation of Cervantes's tragedy), BBC, 1947.

"Christophe Colomb" (dramatization of the discovery of America in French), Radiodiffusion Francaise, 1954.

OTHER

(Author of introduction) Miguel de Unamuno, *The Tragic Sense of Life,* Macmillan, 1921.

(Contributor) *A League of Minds* (letters), International Institute of Intellectual Cooperation, League of Nations, 1933.

Europe: A Unit of Human Culture, European Movement, [Brussels], 1952.

Sobre mi Bolívar, Editorial Sudamericana, 1953.

Critique de l'Europe (originally published as preface to *European Annual*), Council of Europe, 1959.

(Author of introduction) *Echo de monde,* Metz Verlag (Zurich), 1960.

(Contributor) *Dauer im Wandel,* Verlag Georg D. W. Callwey (Munich), 1961.

(Editor) Miguel de Cervantes, *El ingenioso hidalgo don Quijote de la Mancha,* Editorial Sudamericana, 1962.

(Contributor) *Die Kraft zu leben,* Bertelsmann Verlag (Guetersloh), 1963.

Yo-yo y yo-el, Editorial Sudamericana, 1967.

(Compiler) *Charles Quint,* A. Michel, 1969.

(With others) *Freiheitliche Politik fuer eine freie Welt,* M. Hoch (Ludwigsburg), 1969.

(With others) *Ist die Marktwirtschaft noch gesichert?,* M. Hoch, 1971.

Morgen ohne Mittag (memoirs), Ullstein (Berlin), 1973, translation published as *Morning Without Noon,* Saxon House, 1974.

A la orilla del río de los sucesos, Ediciones Destino, 1975.

Dios y los españoles, Editorial Planeta, 1975.

"Esquiveles y Manriques" series; published by Editorial Sud-americana, except as indicated: *El corazón de piedra verde,* 1943, reprinted, Espasa-Calpe, 1975, translation by the author published as *The Heart of Jade,* Creative Age, 1944, reprinted, Hamilton, 1964, published in Spanish in three volumes, 1952, Volume 1: *Los fantasmas,* Volume 2: *Los dioses sanguinarios,* Volume 3: *Fe sin blasfemia.*

Guerra en la sangre, 1956, 4th edition, 1971, bound with *Una gota de tiempo,* Espasa-Calpe, 1977, translation by the author published as *War in the Blood,* Collins, 1957.

Una gota de tiempo, 1958, 3rd edition, 1971, bound with *Guerra en la sangre,* Espasa-Calpe, 1977.

El semental negro, 1961, 2nd edition, 1967, bound with *Satanael,* Espasa-Calpe, 1977.

Satanael, 1966, bound with *El semental negro,* Espasa-Calpe, 1977.

TRANSLATOR

Manojo de poesías ingleses puestas en verso castellano, William Lewis (Cardiff), 1919.

(And compiler) *Spanish Folk Songs,* Constable, 1922.

(And editor) William Shakespeare, *Hamlet,* bilingual edition, Editorial Sudamericana, 1949.

Assisted L. Araquistain in translating Rudyard Kipling's "The Fringes of the Fleet" and "Tales of 'The Trade'" (stories) into Spanish. Also author of numerous essays, studies, and commentaries on current affairs. Contributor to periodicals.

SIDELIGHTS: A European liberal, scholar, and statesman, Salvador de Madariaga was one of Spain's outstanding intellectuals. Aristide Briand described him as one of the ten best conversationalists in Europe. "Man's most precious possession is the gift of thinking freely," Madariaga once stated, "of adventuring in the realms of the mind and of nature, thus to discover his own existence and remain master of his fate."

In addition to his native Spanish, Madariaga wrote in English, German, and French. He occasionally prepared some of his books in all four languages. Many of Madariaga's writings, of both literary and political content, have stimulated heated discussion. The third book in the "New World" trilogy, *Bolívar,* proved to be "a literary bombshell that caused Spain and Latin America to go to war again, with plenty of ink spilled on both sides," said Marcelle Michelin of *Books Abroad.* Highly revered in Latin America as a key figure in the struggle for independence from Spain, Simón Bolívar, according to Madariaga, was "nothing but a vulgar imitator of Napoleon with dreams of reigning over a South American empire." Although very well received in North America and England, the book generated shock and outrage in Latin America and was banned in Argentina.

A severe critic of Francisco Franco's regime, Madariaga traveled to England in self-imposed exile at the outbreak of the Spanish Civil War in 1936 and did not return to Spain until after the country's military leader, Generalissimo Francisco Franco, died in 1975. Although he bore a passionate love for his homeland, he believed that Spain was caught in the grip of a totally destructive dictatorship. "Fascism hardly counts in Spain," he wrote. "It is the Army that keeps its boot on the neck of the Spanish people." In an August, 1969, article in the *New York Times,* he made the statement that Franco, "once an intelligent colonel, [has] turned insane by decades of unchecked power. We are told by his friends that he gave Spain thirty years of peace and ten of prosperity. Neither of these assertions is true. Outward quiet is not peace. Before it explodes, a bomb is quiet enough."

BIOGRAPHICAL/CRITICAL SOURCES:

PERIODICALS

Books Abroad, autumn, 1953.
Newsweek, June 9, 1958.
New York Herald Tribune Book Review, October 12, 1952.
New York Times, August 9, 1969.
Saturday Review, July 2, 1960.
Times Literary Supplement, February 22, 1968, February 8, 1974.
Washington Post, May 26, 1961.

OBITUARIES:

PERIODICALS

Chicago Tribune, December 15, 1978.
Time, December 25, 1978.
Washington Post, December 15, 1978.

* * *

MAGGIOLO, Marcio E. Veloz
See VELOZ MAGGIOLO, Marcio E.

* * *

MALDONADO-DENIS, Manuel 1933-

PERSONAL: Born in 1933 in Santurce, P.R. *Education:* Received B.A. from University of Puerto Rico; received M.A. and Ph.D. from University of Chicago.

ADDRESSES: Office—Department of Political Science, University of Puerto Rico, Río Piedras, POB N, Río Piedras, P.R. 00931.

CAREER: University of Puerto Rico, Río Piedras, 1959—, began as assistant professor, became professor of political science; Queens College of the City University of New York, New York, N.Y., professor of Puerto Rican studies, 1972-73.

MEMBER: Puerto Rican Sociological Association.

AWARDS, HONORS: Guggenheim fellowship, 1968; honorary doctorate from University of the Atlantic, 1972; prize from Casa de las Américas, 1976.

WRITINGS:

NONFICTION

Puerto Rico: Una interpretación histórico-social, Siglo Veintiuno (Mexico), 1969, translation by Elena Viálo published as *Puerto Rico: A Socio-Historic Interpretation.* Random House, 1972.

Puerto Rico: Mito y realidad (essays), Ediciones Península (Barcelona), 1973.

Semblanza de cuatro revolucionarios: Albizu, Martí, Ché Guevara y Camilo Torres (lectures), Ediciones Puerto, 1973.

En las entrañas: Un análisis sociohistórico de la emigración puertorriqueña, Casa de las Américas, 1976.

Puerto Rico y Estados Unidos: Emigración y colonialismo, un análisis sociohistórico de la emigración puertorriqueña, Siglo Veintiuno, 1976, translation published as *The Emigration Dialectic: Puerto Rico and the U.S.A.,* International Publishers, 1980.

La violencia en la obra de García Márquez (criticism), Ediciones Suramérica, 1977.

(Editor and author of introduction and notes) Pedro Albizu Campos, *La conciencia nacional puertorriqueña* (essays), Siglo Veintiuno, 1977.

Betances, revolucionario antillano y otros ensayos (essays), Antillana (Río Piedras, P.R.), 1978.

Contributor of articles and reviews to academic journals in Latin America, Europe, and the United States.

BIOGRAPHICAL/CRITICAL SOURCES:

PERIODICALS

Nation, January 8, 1973.

*   *   *

MALE, Belkis Cuza
    See CUZA MALE, Belkis

*   *   *

MALLEA, Eduardo   1903-1982(?)

PERSONAL: Born August 14, 1903, in Bahía Blanca, Argentina; died of leukemia c. 1982, in Buenos Aires, Argentina; son of Narciso Segundo (a physician and writer) and Manuela (Aztiria) Mallea; married Helena Muñoz Larreta, March 15, 1944. *Education:* Attended Colegio Nacional and Faculty of Law, Buenos Aires, beginning in 1920.

CAREER: Practiced law until 1927; *La Nación,* Argentina, correspondent, 1927-31, literary editor, 1931-55; UNESCO, Paris, France, ambassador-at-large for Argentina, 1955-58; writer, 1958-82. Lecturer in Italy, 1934. Former member of board of directors of *Sur* and *Realidad.*

MEMBER: Argentine Society of Writers (president, beginning 1940).

AWARDS, HONORS: Primer Premio Nacional de Letras, 1945; Gran Premio de Honor from Argentine Society of Writers, 1946; Premio Casavalle, 1955, for *La sala de espera;* Forti Glori prize, 1968; honorary doctorate from University of Michigan, 1968; Gran Premio in literature from Fondo Nacional de las Artes, 1970.

WRITINGS:

NOVELS AND NOVELLAS

Fiesta en noviembre (also see below), Club del Libro, 1938, translation by Alis de Sola published as *Fiesta in November,* Calder & Boyars, 1969.
La bahía de silencio (also see below), Sudamericana, 1940, translation by Stuart Edgar Grummon published as *The Bay of Silence,* Knopf, 1944.
Todo verdor perecerá (also see below), Espasa-Calpe, 1941, translation by John B. Hughes and others published as *All Green Shall Perish, and Other Novellas and Stories,* edited and introduced by Hughes, Knopf, 1966.
Las águilas (title means "The Eagles"; also see below), Sudamericana, 1943.
El vínculo, Los Rembrandts, [and] *La rosa de Cernobbio,* Emecé, 1946.
Los enemigos del alma (title means "The Enemies of the Soul"; also see below), Sudamericana, 1950.
La torre (title means "The Tower"; also see below), Sudamericana, 1951.
Chaves, Losada, 1953, translation by María Mercedes Aspiazu and others published as *Chaves, and Other Stories,* Calder & Boyars, 1970.
La sala de espera (title means "The Waiting Room"), Sudamericana, 1953.

Simbad (title means "Sinbad"), Sudamericana, 1957.
El resentimiento: Los ensimismados, El resentimiento, [and] *La falacia,* Sudamericana, 1966.
La penúltima puerta (title means "The Penultimate Door"), Sudamericana, 1969.
Gabriel Andaral, Sudamericana, 1971.
Triste piel del universo (title means "Sad Skin of the Universe"), Sudamericana, 1971.
En la creciente oscuridad, Sudamericana, 1973.

SHORT STORY COLLECTIONS

Cuentos para una inglesa desesperada (title means "Stories for a Desperate English Woman"; also see below), Gleizer, 1926, reprinted, Espasa-Calpe, 1969.
La ciudad junto al río inmóvil (title means "The City on the Motionless River"; also see below; includes "Sumersión," "Conversación," and "La causa de Jacobo Uber, perdida"), Sur, 1936.
Posesión (title means "Possession"), Sudamericana, 1958.
La barca de hielo (title means "The Ice Ship"), Sudamericana, 1967.
La red (title means "The Net"), Sudamericana, 1968.

Also author of *La mancha en el mármol.*

OTHER

Conocimiento y expresión de la Argentina (title means "Knowledge and Expression of Argentina"; also see below), Sur, 1935.
Nocturno europeo (title means "European Nocturne"; also see below), Sur, 1935.
Historia de una pasión argentina (title means "History of an Argentine Passion"; also see below), Sur, 1937, expanded edition, prologue by Francisco Romero, Espasa-Calpe, 1940.
Meditación en la costa (title means "Meditation at the Sea Shore"; essay collection; also see below), Imprenta Mercatali, 1939.
El sayal y la púrpura (essay collection; also see below), Losada, 1941.
Rodeada está de sueño (title means "Surrounded by Dreams"; also see below), two volumes, Espasa-Calpe, 1944.
El retorno (title means "The Return"; also see below), Espasa-Calpe, 1946.
Notas de un novelista (essay collection), Emecé, 1954.
El gajo de enebro: Tragedia en tres actos, Emecé, 1957.
La razón humana, Losada, 1959.
La vida blanca (title means "The Sterile Life"), Sur, 1960.
Las travesías (title means "The Crossings"), Sudamericana, Volume 1, 1961, Volume 2, 1962.
Obras completas, Emecé, Volume 1 (contains *Cuentos para una inglesa desesperada, Conocimiento y expresión de la Argentina, Nocturno europeo, La ciudad junto al río inmóvil, Historia de una pasión argentina, Fiesta en noviembre, Meditación en la costa, La bahía de silencio, Todo verdor perecerá,* and *El sayal y la púrpura*), 1961, Volume 2 (contains *Las águilas, Rodeada está de sueño, El retorno, El vínculo, Los enemigos del alma,* and *La torre*), 1965.
La representación de los aficionados: Un juego, Sudamericana, 1962.
La guerra interior (title means "The Inner War"), Sur, 1963.
Poderío de la novela (title means "The Power of the Novel"), Aguilar, 1965.
Los papeles privados, Sudamericana, 1974.

Co-founder of the magazine *Revista de América,* 1923. Contributor to periodicals, including *Revista de Occidente* and *Sur.*

SIDELIGHTS: During the 1930s and 1940s Eduardo Mallea was one of South America's leading writers. An essayist, short story writer, and novelist, Mallea was chiefly concerned with the absence of spirituality in the modern world, especially in his native Argentina. His fiction has been called existential because it often focuses on solitary figures who struggle amidst the materialism of twentieth-century life to find happiness and meaning, usually without success. In addition to writing dozens of fiction and nonfiction works, Mallea earned distinction between 1931 and 1955 as *La Nación*'s literary editor, a post that gave him considerable authority and influence in Argentine literary circles. His popularity, however, began to wane as early as 1943 when Colonel Juan Domingo Perón came to power in Argentina, bringing with him a populist autocracy that disdained the elite class of which Mallea was a member. Gradually social writers like David Viñas and magic realists like Gabriel García Márquez began to dominate the South American literary scene, leaving philosophical writers like Mallea out of vogue. Nonetheless, Mallea is considered significant for examining the important concerns of his day and for being an influential, prolific writer whose literary production spanned six decades.

Born into a prominent Argentine family descended from Spanish nobility, Mallea grew up under the shadow of his affectionate but authoritarian father, who was both a physician and a man of letters. His father's extensive library provided Mallea with an early exposure to such European writers as Charles Dickens, Leo Tolstoy, Friedrich Nietzsche, and Soeren Kierkegaard. The influence of European literature and culture played a prominent role not only in Mallea's early education but in his professional writings as well.

Beginning in 1914 Mallea lived and studied in Buenos Aires, a city that introduced him to many of his lifelong literary compatriots and served as the subject of some of his more important writings. It was during his years as a law student in the 1920s that Mallea first became associated with the "Florida" group of writers. Named after the street in the affluent section of Buenos Aires, the Florida group consisted of elitist writers whose cosmopolitan outlook stood in direct contrast to the socialist, proletarian writings of the so-called "Boedo" group. H. Ernest Lewald observed in his book *Eduardo Mallea* that "the mainstream of Argentine literature has been traveling in either one of these two channels since the original division took place [in the 1920s]." Against this backdrop Mallea began his own literary career by helping found the magazine *Revista de América* in 1923 and by publishing his first book, *Cuentos para una inglesa desesperada,* in 1926. The appearance of this collection of stories was considered important for two reasons: it encouraged Mallea to abandon his law career to pursue writing, and it gave him the requisite literary credentials to work as a correspondent for *La Nación,* the major Argentine newspaper for which he became literary editor.

After taking a hiatus from book writing between 1927 and 1934—during which time he made two trips to Europe—Mallea began publishing essays concerning the national character of Argentina. In 1935 he wrote *Conocimiento y expresión de la Argentina.* This collection of essays foreshadowed the author's ongoing interest in reconciling spiritual values of the Old World with the emerging materialistic values of South America. Through an expository blend of personal and Argentine history, Mallea's volume concludes that large, modern cities like Buenos Aires alienate rather than unify people. Mallea further developed this thesis in his 1937 essay collection, *Historia de una pasión argentina.* The collection, which includes autobiographical essays, posits a visible and invisible Argentina: the former refers to the majority of the population whose empty lives, according to Mallea, reflect the emptiness of modern city life; the latter refers to the few enlightened individuals in whom the hope for a better Argentina resides. Mallea believed that the invisible Argentina would one day bring about a new, rejuvenated Argentina. Critics generally agreed that the ideas laid out in these essay collections, though central to Mallea's thinking, were better expressed through his fiction, beginning with *La ciudad junto al río inmóvil.*

Published in 1936, *La ciudad junto al río inmóvil* is a collection of stories featuring individuals who grapple with the materialism and loneliness of modern life. The story "Sumersión" tells how Avesquin, a European, comes to Buenos Aires seeking a new life only to return home disappointed; "Conversación" is about an upper-middle-class couple's meaningless life of boredom and indecision; and "La causa de Jacobo Uber, perdida" recounts how a quiet desk clerk tries unsuccessfully to establish fulfilling relationships. Lewald felt "Sumersión" was especially reminiscent of the writings of Franz Kafka, citing in particular the story's "confrontation between the individual and an impersonal, all-pervasive entity that claims the mass-man and creates a deep feeling of anguish in those who, like Avesquin, are bearers of sensitivity and intelligence." Mallea's concern about the conflict between individual and state carried over into his novels as well.

La bahía de silencio, a novel later translated as *The Bay of Silence,* has been called autobiographical in that it details a Buenos Aires law student's quest to become a novelist. The story, told through the diary of Martín Tregau, is about the hero's journey towards self-knowledge and his interest in promoting the general welfare of his native Argentina. Some critics complained that the strictly sequential, first-person narrative grew wearisome after five hundred pages. Other reviewers, like William S. Lynch, whose *Saturday Review* article is quoted in *Modern Latin American Literature,* defended the novel's structure. While admitting the book was "talkative and disjointed" with "characters [who] are wooden," Lynch argued that the characters' dialogues are "pertinent to the intellectual biography of the man whose mental direction we follow. [The characters] are relevant, too, in their revelation of the winds of doctrine and opinion that blow with balm or blast not only across Argentina but wherever there are human beings assembled in what we call modern society."

Mallea's pessimistic view of modern civilization was most pronounced in his 1941 novel, *Todo verdor perecerá,* later published in English as *All Green Shall Perish.* Heroine Agate Cruz is surrounded by sterility: her husband is a farmer who cannot produce a crop, and the couple's conjugal relations fail to produce any children. Cruz makes one last attempt at happiness after the death of her husband by moving to the city and having an affair with a lawyer, but this too ends in disappointment and later madness. Once again Mallea's familiar themes of alienation and desperation are present. Critical opinion ranged between those who found the book too cold and lifeless to those who praised it as an important contribution to modern literature. Saying the narrative was told with "consummate skill," John A. Crow wrote in *Saturday Review,* as quoted in *Modern Latin American Literature,* that through the tragedy of the couple "we see the tragedy of modern man, rootless and sterile, making the wrong crucial decisions, already beyond the point of intelligent communication, doggedly plodding toward what seems an inevitable destruction." Moreover, Piers Brendon averred in *Books and Bookmen* that the "book is a classic, a jewel among the dross [of other foreign works], shining luminously even through the additional murk of translation."

Along with *The Bay of Silence* and *All Green Shall Perish,* *Chaves* is generally cited by critics as one of Mallea's best novels.

This 1953 work marked a transition for the Argentine author in that it is shorter and less overtly philosophical than previous books. The story is about a quiet, unambitious man whose modest way of life as a sawmill worker changes when he decides to marry and start a family. After taking a job as a salesman Chaves becomes interested in the power of words over people. The rest of the novel depicts Chaves's struggle to find meaning and eloquence in words when his business fails, his daughter dies at age four, and his wife dies. Dejected by his attempts to find purpose through words, Chaves retreats into silence and returns to the humbling work at the sawmill. Reviewers found *Chaves* more appealing than many of Mallea's earlier writings, and Lewald explained why: "Gone are the endless discussions on art, literature, history, or philosophy; gone also the repetitious descriptions of bourgeois behavior and milieu; and gone are the morose soliloquies by protagonists whose main occupation consists of eating, drinking, walking, and talking."

Mallea continued his literary output through the 1970s, though he never fully regained the popularity he lost during the Perón administration. After Perón was ousted in 1955, however, Mallea enjoyed renewed influence and prestige when he became an Argentinian representative at UNESCO in Paris. But his public approval declined again after 1958, when the Argentine author began writing full time only to discover that his country had become more interested in social rather than philosophical issues. Mallea remains nonetheless an important voice for a generation of Argentinians who were concerned with the deterioration of values and loss of spirituality in the New World.

BIOGRAPHICAL/CRITICAL SOURCES:

BOOKS

Foster, David William and Virginia Ramos Foster, editors, *Modern Latin American Literature,* Ungar, 1975.
Lewald, H. Ernest, *Eduardo Mallea,* Twayne, 1977.
Ocampo, Victoria, *Diálogo con Mallea,* Sur, 1969.
Polt, John H. R., *The Writings of Eduardo Mallea,* University of California Press, 1959.

PERIODICALS

Books Abroad, autumn, 1970, winter, 1970, spring, 1971.
Books and Bookmen, February, 1968.
Times Literary Supplement, December 28, 1967, March 13, 1969, September 18, 1970.

OBITUARIES:

PERIODICALS

Hispania, May, 1983.

—*Sketch by James F. Kamp*

*   *   *

MALTA, Demetrio Aguilera
See AGUILERA MALTA, Demetrio

*   *   *

MANGUEL, Alberto 1948-

PERSONAL: Born March 13, 1948, in Buenos Aires, Argentina; immigrated to Canada, 1982, naturalized citizen, 1988; son of Pablo and Rosalía (Finkelstein) Manguel; married Pauline Ann Brewer (a teacher), 1975 (divorced, 1986); children: Alice Emily, Rachel Claire, Rupert Tobias. *Education:* Attended Colegio Na-

cional de Buenos Aires, 1962-68. *Politics:* None. *Religion:* Agnostic.

ADDRESSES: Home and office—45 Geneva, Toronto, Ontario, Canada M5A 2J9. *Agent*—The Lucinda Vardey Agency Ltd., 228 Gerrard St. E., Toronto, Ontario, Canada M5A 2E8.

CAREER: Editor, translator, and writer. Broadcaster.

MEMBER: International PEN, Writer's Union of Canada, Association of Canadian Television and Radio Artists, Literary Translators Association.

AWARDS, HONORS: Premio de *La Nación* award from newspaper *La Nación,* 1972, for short story; honorable mention in Louis Gallantiére Prize for Excellence in Translation, 1986, for Marguerite Yourcenar's *Oriental Tales.*

WRITINGS:

(Editor and author of introduction) *Variaciones sobre un tema de Durero,* Galerna, 1968.
(Editor and author of introduction) *Variaciones sobre un tema policial: Cuentos,* Galerna, 1968.
(Editor) *Antología de literatura fantástica argentina,* Kapelusz, 1973.
(With Gianni Guadalupi) *The Dictionary of Imaginary Places,* illustrations by Graham Greenfield, maps and charts by James Cook, Macmillan, 1980, enlarged, Harcourt, 1987.
(Editor) *Black Water: The Book of Fantastic Literature,* C. N. Potter, 1983.
(Editor) *Dark Arrows: Chronicles of Revenge,* C. N. Potter, 1983.
(Translator) Marguerite Yourcenar, *Oriental Tales,* Farrar, Straus, 1985.
(Translator) Yourcenar, *Mishima: A Vision of the Void,* Farrar, Straus, 1986.
(Editor and author of introduction) *Other Fires: Short Fiction by Latin American Women,* C. N. Potter, 1986.
(Editor) *Evening Games: Tales of Parents and Children,* Penguin (Toronto), 1986, C. N. Potter, 1987.
(Editor) *The Oxford Book of Canadian Ghost Stories,* Oxford University Press, 1990.
(Editor) *Black Water II: The Next Book of Fantastic Literature,* C. N. Potter, 1990.
News From a Foreign Country Came (novel), Lester and Orpen Dennys (Toronto), in press.

Also author of short stories. Contributor to periodicals, including *Village Voice, Saturday Night,* and *Washington Post.*

SIDELIGHTS: Alberto Manguel is considered an astute and original editor of anthologies. While reviewers applauded his numerous works for their scholarship, they also cited Manguel's wide-ranging knowledge of the various genres in which he works. He has published and discussed fine examples of Latin American ghost stories, European classic tales, and American science fiction in such works as *The Dictionary of Imaginary Places, Black Water: The Book of Fantastic Literature,* and *Other Fires: Short Fiction by Latin American Women.*

The Dictionary of Imaginary Places, which Manguel wrote with Gianni Guadalupi, is a guidebook to more than twelve hundred villages, kingdoms, continents, and countries devised by authors from classical Greece to the present day. Illustrated with maps and drawings, entries on such places as Camelot, Oz, Jonathan Swift's Brobdingnag, and Franz Kafka's Penal Colony provide a brief history of the region, a description of its inhabitants and topography, and a reading list, in travel guide form. When visiting Dracula's Castle, for example, Manguel and Guadalupi advise bringing silver crosses and wooden stakes. "Presented with mock solemnity and written with grace and wit," Peter S. Prescott wrote in *Newsweek,* "[*The Dictionary of Imaginary Places*] is a work of genuine scholarship that is also a pleasure to read."

Manguel collected seventy-two tales of horror from several centuries and five continents in 1983's *Black Water.* Writers such as Vladimir Nabokov, Nathaniel Hawthorne, Herman Hesse, Julio Cortázar, Max Beerbohm, Jorge Luis Borges, and H. G. Wells are represented in what *New York Times Book Review* contributor Jack Sullivan called "an uncommonly satisfying collection." Two years later Manguel edited *Dark Arrows: Chronicles of Revenge,* a volume featuring tales of vengeance from writers as diverse as William Faulkner and Bram Stoker. This anthology also earned Manguel high praise. A *Book World* reviewer called him "an editor of real imagination," with an "expertise at discovering the unexpected."

In 1986 Manguel compiled *Other Fires,* possibly the first anthology dedicated to Latin American women writers. Comprised of stories from such prominent Hispanics as Liliana Heker, Elena Poniatowska, and Rosario Castellanos, the collection exhibits a wide range of artistic styles—from fables to science fiction to magic realism—and subject matter, including depictions of betrayal and murder, loneliness and suicide, and male-female relationships in a society where women are subjugated by men. Commenting on the lack of anthologies devoted to Latin American women writers, *New York Times Book Review* contributor Mary Morris noted that with the publication of *Other Fires,* "at last we can hear the voice that has been missing."

Manguel told *CA:* "I started compiling anthologies out of an urge to get my friends to read the stories I was crazy about, sometimes stories in other languages (which I had to translate), sometimes stories hidden in obscure collections. I see my anthologizing as a function of my reading—every reader is, in some measure, an anthologist, a collector of what he or she likes best.

"As a translator, I wish I had an extra life to devote to translating: there are so many authors I wish I had time to translate into English. Hector Bianciotti, Rodolfo Walsh, Liliana Heker, Juan José Hernández, Salvador Garmedia, Amparo Dávila . . . the list is endless.

"For the longest time, after having written a few forgotten short stories in Spanish, I decided I would not turn my hand to writing fiction because (using the oldest excuse in the book) I felt I would never be able to write as well as my favorite authors. But a story came to me, as these things will. I felt obliged to write it down in order to understand it. The result is *News From a Foreign Country Came,* which will appear in the spring of 1991."

BIOGRAPHICAL/CRITICAL SOURCES:

PERIODICALS

Book World, December 7, 1980, August 19, 1984, July 19, 1987.
Canadian Fiction Magazine, autumn, 1987.
Los Angeles Times Book Review, August 23, 1987.
Newsweek, February 19, 1981.
New York Times Book Review, August 26, 1984, May 4, 1986.
Times Literary Supplement, April 10, 1981.

*   *   *

MANTECON, Juan Jiménez
    See JIMENEZ (MANTECON), Juan Ramón

MARECHAL, Leopoldo 1900-1970

PERSONAL: Born June 11, 1900, in Buenos Aires, Argentina; died June 26, 1970, in Buenos Aires, Argentina; son of Alberto (a mechanic) and Lorenza (Beloqui) Marechal; married María Zoraida Barreiro (deceased); married Elbia Rosbaco, 1950; children: María de los Angeles, María Magdalena. *Education:* Graduated from Escuela Normal de Profesores "Mariano Austa" (Buenos Aires), 1922. *Politics:* Began as socialist; became Peronist. *Religion:* Roman Catholic.

ADDRESSES: Home—Buenos Aires, Argentina.

CAREER: Teacher and writer. President of general education board in Santa Fe province, Argentina, 1944; technical inspector general of schools in Buenos Aires, Argentina, 1944-46; section chief of ministry of justice and public education, beginning in 1944; president of national folklore commission, beginning in 1947; cultural director of ministry of education, c. 1950.

MEMBER: Sociedad Argentina de Escritores (vice president), Cursos de Cultura Católica.

AWARDS, HONORS: Municipal Poetry Prize from City of Buenos Aires, c. 1929, for *Odas para el hombre y la mujer;* National Poetry Prize from Argentina, 1941, for *Cinco poemas australes, El centauro,* and *Sonetos a Sophia;* Forti Glori Prize, 1966, for *El banquete de Severo Arcángelo.*

WRITINGS:

POETRY

Los aguiluchos (title means "The Eaglets"), Gleizer (Buenos Aires), 1922.
Días como flechas (title means "Days Like Arrows"), Gleizer, 1926.
Odas para el hombre y la mujer (title means "Odes for Man and Woman"), Libra (Buenos Aires), 1929.
Laberinto de amor (title means "Labyrinth of Love"), Sur (Buenos Aires), 1936.
Cinco poemas australes (title means "Five Southern Poems"), Cursos de Cultura Católica (Buenos Aires), 1937.
El centauro (title means "The Centaur"), Sol y Luna (Buenos Aires), 1940.
Sonetos a Sophia, y otros poemas (title means "Sonnets to Sophia, and Other Poems"), Sol y Luna, 1940.
El viaje de la primavera, Emecé (Buenos Aires), 1945.
La poética (canto of *Heptamerón* [also see below]), Hombre Nuevo (Buenos Aires), 1959.
La patria, [Buenos Aires], 1960.
La alegropeya: Primer día, Hombre Nuevo, 1962.
Heptamerón, Sudamericana (Buenos Aires), 1966.
El poema de robot, Américalee (Buenos Aires), 1966.
Poemas de Marechal (anthology), Universitaria de Buenos Aires, 1966.
Antología poética (anthology), edited by Oscar Grandov, Kapelusz (Buenos Aires), 1969.
Antología poética (anthology), edited by Alfredo Andrés, De La Flor (Buenos Aires), 1969.
Canto de San Martín, Castañeda (Buenos Aires), 1979.
Poemas de la creación, Castañeda, 1979.
(With Jorge Luis Borges and others) *La generación poética de 1922* (anthology), edited by María Raquel Llagostera, América Latina (Buenos Aires), 1980.
Poesía (1924-1950) (anthology), edited by Pedro Luis Barcia, Del 80, 1984.

Translations of poetry published in *Anthology of Contemporary Latin American Poetry,* 1942, and *Tri-Quarterly Anthology of Contemporary Latin American Literature,* 1969.

NOVELS

Adán Buenosayres (title means "Adam Buenosayres"), Sudamericana, 1948, recent edition, 1982.
El banquete de Severo Arcángelo (novel; title means "The Banquet of Severo Arcángelo"), Sudamericana, 1965.
Megafón; o, La guerra (title means "Megafón; or, The War"), Sudamericana, 1970.

PLAYS

Antígona Vélez, Citerea (Buenos Aires), 1965, recent edition, Colihue (Buenos Aires), 1981.
Las tres caras de Venus, Citerea, 1966.
La batalla de José Luna (title means "The Battle of José Luna"), Universitaria (Santiago, Chile), 1970.
Don Juan (three-act), Castañeda, 1978.

OTHER

Historia de la calle Corrientes, Municipalidad (Buenos Aires), 1937, recent edition, Paidós (Buenos Aires), 1967.
Descenso y ascenso del alma por la belleza (aesthetic commentary), Sol y Luna, 1939, recent edition, Salido (Buenos Aires), 1982.
El niño Dios (for children), Sudamericana, 1939.
Vida de santa Rosa de Lima (biography; title means "Life of St. Rose of Lima"), Emecé, 1943, recent edition, Castañeda, 1977.
Alejandro Bustillo, Peuser (Buenos Aires), 1944.
(Editor with wife, Elbia R. de Marechal) *Antología didáctica de la prosa argentina* (anthology of Argentine literature), Kapelusz, 1954.
Autopsia de Creso, El Barrilete (Buenos Aires), 1965.
(With Julio Cortázar, Adolfo Prieto, and Graciela de Sola) *Las claves de "Adán Buenosayres"* (commentary on his novel *Adán Buenosayres;* includes one article by each author), Azor (Mendoza, Argentina), 1966, 2nd edition published as *Interpretaciones y claves de "Adán Buenosayres,"* Acali (Montevideo, Uruguay), 1977.
Cuaderno de navegación, Sudamericana, 1966.
Palabras con Leopoldo Marechal (critical anthology), edited by Alfredo Andrés, C. Pérez (Buenos Aires), 1968.
El espía y otros relatos, Kiek (Buenos Aires), 1975.
"El beatle final" y otras páginas no recogidas en libro (previously uncollected writings), América Latina, 1981.

Contributor and editor for the periodicals *Martín Fierro* and *Proa,* during 1920s.

SIDELIGHTS: Little known in the English-speaking world and underappreciated in his native Argentina for many years, Leopoldo Marechal has increasingly been seen as an important forerunner of the "boom" in Spanish American fiction that began in the 1960s. In *Spanish American Writing Since 1941,* George R. McMurray ranked Marechal's achievement as a literary innovator beside that of his countryman Jorge Luis Borges.

Along with Borges, Marechal began his writing career as one of the iconoclastic young poets who flourished in Buenos Aires during the 1920s. He shared with his peers an enthusiasm for the linguistically innovative writing that was appearing in Europe at the time, and he helped to write and edit two influential new periodicals, *Martín Fierro* and *Proa,* that featured the work of such experimental writers as Irishman James Joyce and Spaniard Federico García Lorca. As a fledgling poet Marechal derived

from Borges an interest in ultraism, a Spanish movement which proclaimed that poetry should consist primarily of new and startling metaphors. The author's first major work, the 1926 poetry collection *Días como flechas* ("Days Like Arrows"), strongly reflects ultraist trends. Reviewer Francisco Luis Bernárdez, writing in the periodical *Sur* and quoted in *Modern Latin American Literature,* called the work "a masterpiece of sensory rejoicing."

Thereafter Marechal began to evolve a more idiosyncratic literary style, based on his personal religious concerns. As a visitor to Europe in the mid-1920s he had relished the antiestablishment lifestyle of its artists, but by 1929 he had returned to Argentina and become filled with religious turmoil, spurred by the grave illness of a friend. He turned to the writings of classical philosophers and Christian theologians, rejoining the Catholic church after many years of absence. The author's poetry reflected his newfound interest in traditional values. The 1936 collection *Laberinto de amor* ("Labyrinth of Love"), for instance, describes the differences between love as human emotion and as a spiritual need, and was written in the older style of rhymed couplets. Bernárdez said the book "represents the clearest synthesis of today's aesthetic of torture and the prodigious serenity of yesterday and eternity." Marechal continued to write traditional poetry about broad philosophical themes for the rest of his life. *Cinco poemas australes* ("Five Southern Poems"), perhaps his best work of this variety, helped him to win Argentina's National Poetry Prize in 1941.

Meanwhile, in 1930 Marechal began a lengthy work of fiction that further elaborated on his religious interests. A mixture of philosophical discussion and sharp urban realism, expressed in visionary and poetic prose, the seven-hundred-page novel appeared in 1948 as *Adán Buenosayres* ("Adam Buenosayres"). Though the work is highly indebted to Joyce's 1921 novel *Ulysses,* it represents a bold departure from traditional Spanish American fiction, which generally surveyed social problems in a straightforward, journalistic style. The first five of the seven parts of *Adán Buenosayres* bear the strongest resemblance to *Ulysses.* Here Marechal introduces the title character of Adán, a writer much like Marechal himself, and evokes the texture of urban life by showing Adán's excursions through Buenos Aires on two days in the 1920s. The novel contains thinly disguised portraits of everything from brothels to literary figures such as Borges. As if to underscore Adán's status as an outsider, the writer's best friend is an alienated Jewish philosopher named Tesler who rails at the teeming metropolis while enduring the jibes of anti-Semites. While Joyce's novel seems willing to accept life as it is—a mixture of comedy and pathos—Marechal's book conveys a growing sense of moral revulsion. Tesler and Adán both experience bouts of nausea, embodying, according to Ambrose Gordon in *Comparative Literature Studies,* their basic disgust with the city.

In the last two sections of *Adán Buenosayres,* Marechal departs from the model of *Ulysses* to depict Adán's search for human love and spiritual insight. Section six is a diary of Adán's love for a cold-hearted northern European woman, a futile affair that he resolves by imagining her death and funeral in great detail. Section seven is apparently Adán's dream, in which he plunges beneath Buenos Aires for a journey that resembles the poet Dante's voyage through hell in *The Inferno.* Here Adán views "sinners" who resemble the inhabitants of the city above, except that their moral failings have met with grotesque punishment. At his journey's end Adán is shown an ultimate monstrosity which is simple, formless chaos. Marechal does not say whether Adán finds redemption because of his unsettling vision. When *Adán Buenosayres* was first published, according to *Modern*

Latin American Literature, the respected Argentine fiction writer Julio Cortázar called it "an extraordinary event in Argentine literature."

The work went largely unpublicized, however, because of its author's increasingly conservative politics. By the time *Adán Buenosayres* appeared Marechal was identified with the administration of president Juan Perón, an Army officer whose authoritarianism made him an anathema to most of Argentina's intellectuals. Marechal's prominence in such posts as cultural director of Perón's ministry of education prompted fellow writers to shun him for years, and he retreated into obscurity after the president was deposed in 1955.

In 1965 Marechal released a second novel, *El banquete de Severo Arcángelo* ("The Banquet of Severo Arcángelo"), which discussed the emptiness of modern society by using the biblical imagery of Christ's Last Supper. Less intricate and sprawling than *Adán Buenosayres,* the book sold well and became an occasion for the Spanish American literary world to come to terms with Marechal's life and work. "I am not . . . about to defend the political and religious ideology of Leopoldo Marechal," wrote Manuel Pedro González in 1967 in *Cuadernos americanos,* quoted in *Modern Latin American Literature.* "One can, and even should, censure the . . . Peronist proclivity of the author and at the same time recognize the value of his writings." In particular González praised *Adán Buenosayres,* which over the next few years went through several new printings—including one by Casa de las Américas, the official publishing house of Marxist Cuba. Cortázar collaborated with Marechal and other writers on the book *Las claves de "Adán Buenosayres,"* a mixture of commentary and praise about the novel. The rediscovery of Marechal extended to Ernesto Sábato, an Argentine novelist who is often ranked beside Cortázar in prestige. Sábato, according to González, called Marechal "one of our most notable writers, unjustly and perversely forgotten by the official literature."

BIOGRAPHICAL/CRITICAL SOURCES:

BOOKS

Foster, David William and Virginia Ramos Foster, editors, *Modern Latin American Literature,* F. Ungar, 1975.
McMurray, George R., *Spanish American Writing Since 1941,* Ungar, 1987.

PERIODICALS

Comparative Literature Studies, Volume 19, 1982.
Latin American Theatre Review, Volume 9, number 1, 1975.
Hispania, March, 1972.

—*Sketch by Thomas Kozikowski*

* * *

MARIN, (José) Luis (Alberto) Muñoz
See MUÑOZ MARIN, (José) Luis (Alberto)

* * *

MARQUES, René 1919-1979

PERSONAL: Born October 4, 1919, in Arecibo, Puerto Rico; died March 22, 1979, in San Juan, Puerto Rico; son of Juan and Pura (García) Marqués; married Serena Velasco, 1942 (divorced c. 1957); children: Raúl Ferando, Brunhilda María, René Francisco. *Education:* College of Agriculture and Mechanical Arts, degree in agronomy, 1942; studied literature at University of Madrid, 1946; studied drama at Columbia University, 1949.

ADDRESSES: Home—Barrio Cubuy Buzón 792, Carretera 186 K8-H2, Canovanas, Puerto Rico 00629.

CAREER: Writer. Agronomist for Department of Agriculture, 1943-46; manager for Velasco Alonso, Inc. (department store), 1946-49; *Diario de Puerto Rico* (newspaper), San Juan, Puerto Rico, journalist, 1949-50; Puerto Rico Department of Public Education, Division of Community Education, San Juan, writer, beginning in 1950, director of editorial section, 1953-69. Visiting instructor at University of Puerto Rico. Founder and president of Pro Arte de Arecibo, beginning in 1947; Puerto Rican Ateneo, secretary of board of directors, 1951, founder and director of Experimental Theater, 1951-54; co-founder of Book Club of Puerto Rico, 1959. Member of Puerto Rican delegation to first Interamerican Biennial of Painting, 1958.

AWARDS, HONORS: Grant from Rockefeller Foundation, 1949; prize from Puerto Rican Atheneum, 1952, for story "The Fear"; Guggenheim grant, 1954; Ateneo first prizes, 1958, for the short story "La sala," the play "Un niño azul para esa sombra," a novel, and the essay "Pesimismo literario y optimismo político: Su coexistencia en el Puerto Rico actual"; first prize in Ateneo playwriting competition, 1960, for "La casa sin reloj"; prize for literature from Institute of Puerto Rico, 1961, for "Un niño azul para esa sombra"; Iberian-American prize for novel from William Faulkner Foundation, 1962, for *La víspera del hombre.*

WRITINGS:

PLAYS

Juan Bobo y la dama de occidente: Pantomima puertorriqueña para un ballet occidental (title means "Juan Bobo and the Lady of the Occident"), Los Presentes (Mexico), 1956, 2nd edition, Antillana (Río Piedras), 1971.
"Palm Sunday," first produced in San Juan at Municipal Theater Tapia, 1956.
"Los soles truncos" (two-act comedy; title means "The Truncated Suns"), first produced in San Juan at First Theater Festival, 1958; produced in Chicago at Festival of the Americas, 1959; produced Off-Broadway at Gramercy Arts Theater, 1976 (also see below).
Teatro (includes "Los soles truncos," "Un niño azul para esa sombra," and "La muerte no entrará en palacio"; also see below), Arrecife, 1959, 2nd edition, Editorial Cultural (Río Piedras, P.R.), 1974.
La carreta (three-act; produced in New York and San Juan, 1953; first published in *Asomante,* 1951-52), Editorial Cultural, 1961, 5th edition, 1969, translation by Charles Pilditch published as *The Oxcart* (produced in New York, c. 1968), Scribner, 1969.
La casa sin reloj (title means "The House Without a Clock"; first produced in Puerto Rico at Experimental Theater, 1961), Universidad Veracruzana, 1962.
El apartamiento (two-act; title means "The Apartment"; first produced at Puerto Rican Theater Festival, 1964), Rumbos (Barcelona), 1966.
Mariana; o, El alba (three-act; title means "Mariana; or, The Dawn"; first produced in San Juan at Eighth Puerto Rican Theater Festival, 1965), Rumbos, 1966.
Sacrificio en el Monte Moriah (title means "Sacrifice on Mount Moriah"; first produced at Puerto Rican Theater Festival, 1970), Antillana, 1969.
David y Jonatán, Tito y Berenice: Dos dramas de amor, poder y desamor (title means "David and Jonathan, Titus and Bernice: Two Dramas of Love, Power, and Hate"), Antillana, 1970.

Un niño azul para esa sombra (title means "A Blue Child for That Shadow"; produced in San Juan at Third Theater Festival, 1960), Editorial Cultural, 1970.

La muerte no entrará en palacio (two-act tragedy; title means "Death Shall Not Enter the Palace"), Editorial Cultural, 1970.

El hombre y sus sueños (title means "Man and His Dreams"; first published in *Asomante,* 1948), Editorial Cultural, 1971.

El sol y los MacDonald (title means "The Sun and the MacDonalds"; first produced at University of Puerto Rico, 1950; originally published in *Asomante,* 1957), Editorial Cultural, 1971.

Carnaval afuera, carnaval adentro (title means "Carnival Outside, Carnival Inside"; first produced in Havana, Cuba, at Festival of Latin American Theater, 1962), Antillana, 1971.

Vía Crucis del hombre puertorriqueño (oratorio), Antillana, 1971.

EDITOR

Los derechos del hombre, División de Educación de la Comunidad, 1957.

Ma mujer y sus derechos, División de Educación de la Comunidad, 1957.

Juventud, División de Educación de la Comunidad, 1958.

Cuatro cuentos de mujeres, División de Educación de la Comunidad, 1959.

(And contributor) *Cuentos puertorriqueños de hoy* (title means "Modern Puerto Rican Short Stories"), Club del Libro de Puerto Rico, 1959, reprinted, Editorial Cultural, 1985.

El cooperativismo y tu, División de Educación de la Comunidad, 1960.

Las manos y el ingenio del hombre, División de Educación de la Comunidad, 1966.

OTHER

Peregrinación (poems), Arecibo, 1944.

Otro día nuestro (short stories; title means "Another Day of Ours"), [San Juan, P.R.], 1955.

La víspera del hombre (novel; title means "The Eve of Manhood"), Club del Libro de Puerto Rico, 1959, reprinted, Editorial Cultural, 1981.

Pesimismo literario y optimismo político: Su coexistencia en el Puerto Rico actual (essay; title means "Literary Pessimism and Political Optimism in Present-Day Puerto Rico"), [Puerto Rico], 1959.

En una ciudad llamada San Juan (short stories; title means "In a City Called San Juan"), [Puerto Rico], 1960, reprinted, Editorial Cultural, 1983.

"Purificación en la Calle del Cristo" (cuento) y "Los soles truncos" (comedia dramática en dos actos) (short story and play; first title means "Purification on Cristo Street"), Editorial Cultural, 1963.

Ensayos, 1953-1966, Antillana, 1966, translation by Barbara B. Aponte published as *The Docile Puerto Rican: Essays,* Temple University Press, 1976, revised and enlarged edition published as *Ensayos (1953-1971),* 1972, published as *El puertorriqueño dócil y otros ensayos (1953-1971),* Antillana, 1977.

El puertorriqueño dócil: Literatura y realidad psicológica (essay), Antillana, 1967.

Ese mosaico fresco sobre aquel mosaico antiguo, Editorial Cultural, 1975.

La mirada (novel), Antillana, 1975, translation by Charles Pilditch published as *The Look,* Senda Nueva de Ediciones, 1983.

Inmersos en el silencio (short stories; title means "People Immersed in Silence"), Antillana, 1976.

(With Antonio Skármeta and Luis Britto García) *Tres cuentistas* (short stories), Casa de las Américas (Havana, Cuba), 1979.

Also author of short story "La sala." Contributor to periodicals, including *Alma Latina, Asomante, El Diario de Nueva York, El Imparcial, El Mundo, Puerto Rico Ilustrado,* and *Revista del Instituto de Cultura Puertorriqueña.*

BIOGRAPHICAL/CRITICAL SOURCES:

BOOKS

Martin, Eleanor J., *René Marqués,* Twayne, 1979.
Pilditch, C. R., *René Marqués: A Study of His Fiction,* Plus Ultra Educational, 1977.

PERIODICALS

New York Times, May 26, 1983.

OBITUARIES:

PERIODICALS

New York Times, March 25, 1979.

* * *

MARQUEZ, Gabriel (José) García
See GARCIA MARQUEZ, Gabriel (José)

* * *

MARTIN (MONTES), José L(uis) 1921-
(Ramar Yunkel)

PERSONAL: Born July 11, 1921, in Vega Baja, P.R.; son of Isidoro (an accountant) and Carmen (Montes) Martín; married Blanca Rodríguez (a teacher); children: five. *Education:* University of Puerto Rico, B.A., 1942, M.A., 1953; Columbia University, Ph.D., 1965.

ADDRESSES: Home—New York, N.Y. *Office*—Department of Spanish, Inter-American University of Puerto Rico, San German, P.R. 00753.

CAREER: University of Puerto Rico, Río Piedras, 1952-58, began as instructor, became assistant professor of Spanish and Spanish-American literature; Columbia University, New York City, 1958-60, began as lecturer, became instructor in Spanish and Spanish-American literature; Queens College of the City University of New York, Flushing, N.Y., instructor in Spanish, 1960-65; Inter-American University of Puerto Rico, San Juan, associate professor of stylistics and Spanish-American literature, 1965-68; Illinois State University, Normal, associate professor of Spanish-American literature, 1968-71; City College of the City University of New York, New York City, associate professor of Puerto Rican literature and stylistics, 1971-76; Inter-American University of Puerto Rico, San German, assistant professor of Spanish, 1976—. Visiting professor, New York University, summer, 1960; associate professor, Hofstra University, summer, 1964; member of board of directors, Institute of Puerto Rico, New York City, 1972—. Exhibitor of oil paintings in San Juan and New York. *Military service:* U.S. Army, 1943-46; became staff sergeant.

MEMBER: Instituto Internacional de Literatura Iberoamericana, Modern Language Association of America, Instituto de

Literatura Puertorriqueña, Asociación de Escritores de Puerto Rico, Sigma Delta Pi (honorary member).

AWARDS, HONORS: Diploma from Nueva Narrativa Hispanoamericana, 1971; literature award from Institute of Puerto Rico in New York, 1975; Order of Don Quixote from Sigma Delta Pi.

WRITINGS:

La poética de Oppenheimer (title means "The Poetry of Oppenheimer"), Asomante, 1952.

Agonía del silencio (title means "Agony of Silence"), Orfeo, 1953.

Análisis estilístico de "La Santaniada" de Tapia, Institute of Puerto Rican Culture, 1958.

Meditaciones puertorriqueñas: Una zambullida en la conciencia puertorriqueña (title means "Puerto Rican Meditations"), Departamento de Instrucción Pública, 1959.

Arco y flecha (title means "Bow and Arrow"), Club de la Prensa, 1961.

La poesía de José Eusebio Caro: Contribución estilística al estudio del romanticismo hispanoamericano (title means "The Poetry of José Eusebio Caro"), Instituto Caro y Cuervo (Bogotá), 1966.

Romancero del Cibuco (title means "Ballads From the Cibuco"), Orión, 1970.

(Under pseudonym Ramar Yunkel) *El retorno: Sueño* (title means "The Return"), Latinoamericana (Mexico), 1971.

Hostos: Escritor (title means "Hostos: Writer"), Institute of Puerto Rican Culture, 1971.

La crítica metódica de Anderson Imbert, Cuadernos Hispanoamericanos, 1972.

La yuxtaposición tiempo-espacial en El francotirador de P. L. Soto, Nueva Narrativa Hispanoamericana, 1972.

Cuentos municipales de Gata (1520-1524), Universidad de Salamanca, 1972.

El sabor de la carne, G. del Toro (Madrid), 1973.

Crítica estilística (title means "Stylistic Criticism"), Gredos (Madrid), 1973.

Literatura hispanoamericana contemporánea, Edil (San Juan), 1973.

La narrativa de Vargas Llosa, Gredos, 1974.

La península en la Edad Media, Teide, 1976.

Also author of *Psiquis,* 1938, *Sinopsis comparativa,* 1944, *La vida sale al encuentro,* 1959, and *El teatro de René Marqués,* Institute of Puerto Rican Culture. Contributor to periodicals, including *La Torre, Revista del Instituto de Cultura Puertorriqueña, Prensa Literaria, Cuadernos Hispanoamericanos,* and *Sin Nombre.* Founder and former editor, *Ateneo, Olimpo,* and *Aulas;* former editor, *Pegaso* and *Orfeo.*

WORK IN PROGRESS: A novel, *Bridge to Eternity,* under pseudonym Ramar Yunkel.

* * *

MARTIN, Luis 1927-

PERSONAL: Born October 6, 1927, in Seville, Spain; immigrated to the United States; naturalized U.S. citizen; married wife, 1967; children: one. *Education:* University of Seville, B.A., 1944; Recuerdo College, Madrid, Lit. in Ph., 1952; Boston College, S.T.L., 1960; Columbia University, Ph.D., 1966.

ADDRESSES: Office—Department of History, Southern Methodist University, Dallas, Tex. 75275.

CAREER: Sophia University, Tokyo, Japan, associate professor of history, 1966-67; University of Puerto Rico, Río Piedras, associate professor of history, 1967-68; Southern Methodist University, Dallas, Tex., 1968—, began as associate professor, Kahm Professor of Ibero-American History, 1973—, chairman of department and director of graduate studies, 1970-73, associate director of Ibero-American Center, 1968-70.

MEMBER: American Historical Association, Latin American Conference, American Association for the Advancement of the Humanities, Southwestern History Association.

WRITINGS:

The Intellectual Conquest of Peru: The Jesuit College of San Pablo, 1568-1767, Fordham University Press, 1968.

(Editor with Jo Ann Guerin Pettus) *Scholars and Schools in Colonial Peru,* School of Continuing Education, Southern Methodist University, 1973.

The Kingdom of the Sun: A Short History of Peru, Scribner, 1974.

Daughters of the Conquistadores, University of New Mexico Press, 1983.

Contributor to professional journals.

* * *

MARTINEZ, Enrique González
See GONZALEZ MARTINEZ, Enrique

* * *

MARTINEZ, Julio A(ntonio) 1931-

PERSONAL: Born October 4, 1931, in Santiago, Cuba; immigrated to United States, 1958, naturalized citizen, 1968; son of Julio Martínez (in business) and Maria M. Gandara (a homemaker). *Education:* Southern Illinois University, B.A., 1963; University of Michigan, M.A.L.S., 1967; University of Minnesota, M.A., 1970; University of California, Riverside, Ph.D., 1980.

ADDRESSES: Office—324-A University Library, San Diego State University, San Diego, Calif. 92182.

CAREER: San Diego State University Library, San Diego, Calif., assistant librarian, 1973-76, senior assistant librarian, 1976-80, associate librarian, 1980—, coordinator of Chicano collection, 1979—. Consultant to National Endowment of the Humanities and to California Council for the Humanities, both 1985—; consultant to American Philosophical Society, 1987—; consultant to and member of editorial board of Editorial Carike, 1989—.

MEMBER: National Librarians Association (former member of executive board; chair of professional concerns committee, 1984—; chair-elect of faculty status committee, 1989-90), Society for Iberian and Latin American Thought, Society of Interdisciplinary Latin American Thought, Reforma, Southern California Consortium for International Studies, Border State University Consortium for Latin America.

AWARDS, HONORS: Fulbright-Hays Inter-University Award, 1986.

WRITINGS:

A Bibliography of Writings on Plato, 1900-1967, Library, San Diego State University, 1978.

(Compiler) *Chicano Scholars and Writers: A Bio-Bibliographical Directory,* Scarecrow, 1979.

(Contributor) *The Utopian Vision: Dream and Reality,* San Diego State University Press, 1983.

(Compiler with Ada Burns) *Mexican Americans: An Annotated Bibliography of Bibliographies,* R&E Publishers, 1984.

(Editor with Francisco A. Lomelí) *Chicano Literature: A Reference Guide,* Greenwood Press, 1985.

(Editor) *Dictionary of Twentieth-Century Cuban Literature,* Greenwood Press, 1990.

Also author of *Estudio Español,* 1961. Contributor to journals. Associate editor of *Cognition and Brain Theory.*

SIDELIGHTS: Julio A. Martínez told *CA:* "As a professionally trained philosopher, my interests lie in the philosophy of mind, or what is commonly known in philosophical circles as the mind-body problem. I am also passionately interested in the philosophy of politics, with emphasis on the concepts of justice and right.

"My avocations are Chicano and Latin American literature, fields to which I have devoted considerable attention. My research, as a subject specialist for my library, has been concentrated on the preparation of research tools for undergraduate and graduate students."

* * *

MARTINEZ, Max(imiano) 1943-

PERSONAL: Born May 10, 1943, in Gonzales, Tex. *Education:* Received B.A. from St. Mary's University of San Antonio; East Texas State University, M.A., 1972; received Ph.D. from University of Denver.

CAREER: Writer. University of Houston, Houston, Tex., instructor in creative writing, 1977-82; affiliated with faculty of University of Denver, Denver, Colo. Worked as a laborer on farms and ranches. *Military service:* U.S. Navy.

WRITINGS:

Monologue of the Bolivian Major, M&A Editions, 1978.
The Adventures of the Chicano Kid and Other Stories, Arte Público, 1983.
Schoolland, Arte Público, 1988.

Work represented in anthologies, including *El quetzal emplumece,* edited by Carmela Montalvo, Leonardo Anguiano, and Cecilio Garcia Camarillo, Mexican American Cultural Center (San Antonio), 1976. Contributor of stories and reviews to magazines, including *De Colores, Rayas, Carta Abierta, Revista Chicano-Riqueña,* and *Caracol.* Founder of *Magazin.*

BIOGRAPHICAL/CRITICAL SOURCES:

BOOKS

Dictionary of Literary Biography, Volume 82: *Chicano Writers, First Series,* Gale, 1989.
Lomelí, Francisco A., and Donaldo W. Urioste, *Chicano Perspectives in Literature: A Critical and Annotated Bibliography,* Pajarito Publications, 1976.

* * *

MARTINEZ, Rafael Arévalo
See AREVALO MARTINEZ, Rafael

MARTINEZ, Tomás Eloy

PERSONAL: Born in Argentina; immigrated to United States, 1975.

ADDRESSES: Office—Department of Spanish and Portuguese, University of Maryland, College Park, Md. 20742.

CAREER: Professor of Latin American literature at University of Maryland, College Park; journalist; writer.

WRITINGS:

La obra de Ayala y Torre Nilsson en las estructuras del cine argentino, Culturales Argentinas, Ministerio de Educación y Justicia, Dirección General de Cultura, 1961.
Sagrado, Sudamericana, 1969.
La pasión según Trelew, Granica, 1973.
Los testigos de afuera, M. Neumann, 1978.
Lugar común la muerte, Monte Avila (Caracas), 1979.
(With Julio Aray and others) *Sadismo en la enseñanza,* Monte Avila, 1979.
La novela de Perón, translation by Asa Zatz published as *The Perón Novel,* Pantheon, 1987.

SIDELIGHTS: Argentine writer Tomás Eloy Martínez is the acclaimed author of *The Perón Novel,* a provocative blend of fact and fiction centering on Argentina's turbulent political history under the leadership of President Juan Domingo Perón. Perón rose to power in 1946, three years after the military overthrow of the Argentine government. But economic troubles led to his 1955 exile to Madrid and the restoration of civilian rule in Argentina. A decade later, however, the military government was reinstituted, and in 1973, Perón reassumed power. Through a series of flashbacks comprising *The Perón Novel,* Martínez offers three varying perspectives on Perón: the president's own cloudy memoirs, his secretary José López Rega's tainted version of events, and a journalist's report—based on interviews—spanning the president's childhood, his early career as an army officer, and his eventual fall from power. Furthermore, Martínez illuminates Perón's ambiguous nature: appealing to the conflicting political ideals of both right- and left-wing forces, the president fostered discord among his people and, after his death in 1974, left a legacy of violence and disorder in Argentina. Critics generally applauded *The Perón Novel* as a sharp and stunning portrait of an enigmatic man. Jay Cantor, writing in the *New York Times Book Review,* deemed the book "a brilliant image of a national psychosis."

BIOGRAPHICAL/CRITICAL SOURCES:

PERIODICALS

Hispania, March, 1971.
New York Times Book Review, April 15, 1988.
Village Voice, April 26, 1988.

* * *

MARTINEZ MORENO, Carlos 1917-1986

PERSONAL: Born in 1917 in Colonia del Sacramento, Uruguay; died in 1986. *Education:* Attended National University of Uruguay.

CAREER: Criminal lawyer; journalist in Bolivia and Cuba; writer.

AWARDS, HONORS: First prize in Nueva Imagen's "Militarism in Latin America" contest, 1981, and award from the Uruguayan government, 1986, both for *El color que el infierno me escondiera.*

WRITINGS:

Los días por vivir (short stories), Asir, 1960.

Cordelia (novel), Alfa, 1961.

El paredón (novel), Seix Barral (Barcelona), 1962.

Los aborígenes (short stories), Alfa, 1964.

(Editor) Carlos Reyles, *La raza de Caín,* Ministerio de Instrucción Pública y Previsión Social, 1965.

Con las primeras luces (novel), Seix Barral, 1966.

La otra mitad, J. Mortiz (Mexico), 1966.

Las cuatro, Alfa, 1967.

Los prados de la conciencia (short stories), Alfa, 1968.

"La Sirena," y otros relatos, Centro Editor de América Latina, 1968.

(Editor) *Color del novecientos* (essays), Centro Editor de América Latina, 1968.

Las bebidas azules, Monte Avila (Caracas), 1969.

Paritorio de un exceso vital, published with Leopoldo Muller's *De Viena a Macondo,* Fundacíon de Cultura Universitaria, 1969.

Coca (novel), Monte Avila, 1970.

De vida o muerte, Siglo Veintiuno Argentina Editores (Buenos Aires), 1971.

Montevideo en la literatura y en el arte, Nuestra Tierra, 1971.

(Contributor) *Temas para el socialismo democrático latinoamericano,* Centro de Estudios Democráticos de América Latina (San José), 1972.

Los días que vivimos (essays), Girón, 1973.

Tierra en la boca, Losada, 1974.

El color que el infierno me escondiera (novel), Nueva Imagen (Mexico), 1981, translation by Ann Wright published as *El infierno,* Readers International, 1988.

Animal de palabras, Arca, 1987.

Also author of civil and military legal papers. Works represented in anthologies, including *Short Stories in Spanish,* edited by Jean Franco, Penguin, 1966.

SIDELIGHTS: A prominent Uruguayan criminal lawyer and journalist, Carlos Martínez Moreno was also a prolific author of novels, short stories and essays. His stunningly realistic works examine the phenomenon of moral decay and often depict the political unrest and violence that ravaged Uruguay in the 1970s. Martínez Moreno was one of the first Uruguayan writers to relate the horrors of the *desaparecidos* or "disappeared ones" in his native land. The award-winning *El infierno,* the author's first book to be published in English, chronicles the military repression of the Tupamaros, a Uruguayan urban guerrilla organization that campaigned against dictatorship in the 1960s. The novel is generally considered an important and disturbing examination of the ways in which violence perpetuates violence and injustice gives rise to brutal revolutionary movements in many Latin American societies. In a review of *El infierno* for the *New York Times,* James Polk commented: "Martínez Moreno is clearly a moralist, and as such is . . . interested in exploring the subtleties of how individuals function in a moral vacuum. . . . That such people emerge from the inferno with some semblance of themselves intact is the most the author allows. . . . *El infierno* reminds us forcefully of a neglected corner of terror." Martínez Moreno also wrote on such diverse topics as the Cuban revolution, drug smuggling, life among derelicts, and human relationships. He died in exile in 1986.

BIOGRAPHICAL/CRITICAL SOURCES:

BOOKS

Rodríguez Monegal, Emir, editor, *The Borzoi Anthology of Latin American Literature,* Volume II: *The Twentieth Century From Borges and Paz to Guimaraes Rosa and Donoso,* Knopf, 1986.

PERIODICALS

New York Times Book Review, October 30, 1988.
World Literature Today, autumn, 1981.

* * *

MARTINEZ RUIZ, José 1873-1967
(Azorín)

PERSONAL: Born June 8, 1873, in Monóvar, Alicante, Spain; died March 2, 1967, in Madrid, Spain; son of Isidro Martínez (a lawyer) and Luisa Ruiz; married Julia Guinda Urzanqui, 1908. *Education:* Attended University of Valencia and University of Granada.

ADDRESSES: Home—Madrid, Spain.

CAREER: Writer. *El País* (newspaper), Madrid, Spain, staff member, beginning in 1896; *ABC* (Madrid newspaper), Paris, France, correspondent, 1917; *La Nación,* Buenos Aires, Argentina, columnist, 1930-67. Deputy of public instruction, 1907 and 1914; undersecretary of public instruction, 1917 and 1919.

MEMBER: Royal Spanish Academy.

WRITINGS:

IN ENGLISH TRANSLATION; UNDER PSEUDONYM AZORIN

Una hora de España (entre 1560 y 1590), Raggio, 1924, translation by Alice Raleigh published as *An Hour of Spain Between 1560 and 1590,* Routledge & Kegan Paul, 1930.

Don Juan, Raggio, 1927, reprinted, Espasa-Calpe (Madrid), 1940, translation by Catherine Alison Phillips published under same title, Chapman & Dodd, 1923.

Old Spain (play; also see below), edited with introduction, notes, and exercises by George Baer Fundenburg, Century, 1928.

The Syrens and Other Stories, translated by Warre B. Wells, Scholartis, 1931, reprinted as *The Sirens and Other Stories,* Richard West, 1978.

IN SPANISH; UNDER PSEUDONYM AZORIN

Buscapiés, F. Fé, 1893.

Moratín esboza por Candido (title means "Moratin's Outline by Candide"), F. Fé, 1893.

Literatura (title means "Literature"), F. Fé, 1896.

La intrusa: Drama en un acto (title means "The Intruder: A Play in One Act"), F. Vives Moro, 1896.

Bohemia, [Madrid], 1897.

La sociología criminal (title means "Criminal Sociology"), F. Fé, 1899.

La evolución de la crítica (title means "The Evolution of Criticism"), F. Fé, 1899.

Los hidalgos (title means "The Noblemen"), F. Fé, 1900.

El alma castellano (title means "The Castilian Soul"), [Madrid], 1900.

Diario de un enfermo (title means "Diary of a Patient"), F. Fé, 1901.

La fuerza del amor: Tragicomedia (title means "The Force of Love: A Tragicomedy"), [Madrid], 1901.

Los pueblos: Ensayos sobre la vida provinciana (title means "The Villages: Essays About Provincial Life"; also see below), 1905, Renacimiento, 1914.

La ruta de Don Quijote (title means "The Route of Don Quixote"), 1905, Renacimiento, 1915.

España: Hombres y paisajes (title means "Spain: Men and Landscape"), 1909, Espasa-Calpe, 1959.

Lecturas españolas (title means "Spanish Readings"), 1912, Espasa-Calpe (Buenos Aires), 1938.

Castilla (title means "Castile"; essays), 1912, Raggio, 1920.

Antonio Azorín: Pequeño libro en que se habla de la vida de este peregrino señor (title means "Antonio Azorin: A Little Book in Which the Life of This Wandering Man Is Told"), Renacimiento, 1913.

Clásicos y modernos (title means "Classics and Moderns"), 1913, Losada (Buenos Aires), 1939.

Los valores literarios (title means "Literary Values"), Renacimiento, 1913.

La voluntad (title means "The Will"), Renacimiento, 1913.

Al margen de los clásicos (title means "On the Fringes of the Classics"), Clásica Española, 1915.

Lecturas de Azorín (title means "Lectures of Azorin"), Grenas, 1915.

Parlamentarismo español (title means "Spanish Parliamentarism"), Calleja, 1916.

Entre España y Francia: Páginas de un francofilo (title means "Between Spain and France: Pages of a Francophile"), Bloud y Gay, 1917.

Páginas escogidas (title means "Selected Pages"), Calleja, 1917.

El paisaje de España visto por los españoles (title means "The Landscape of Spain Seen by the Spanish"), 1917, Espasa-Calpe, 1941.

Un pueblecito: Riofrío de Avila (title means "A Little Village, Riofrio of Avila"), Raggio, 1921.

París, bombardeado, y Madrid sentimental, mayo y junio 1918 (title means "Paris, Bombarded, and Sentimental Madrid, May and June, 1918"), Raggio, 1921.

El licenciado vidriero, Raggio, 1921, Oxford, 1939.

Los dos Luises, y otros ensayos (title means "The Two Louises, and Other Essays"), Raggio, 1921.

Un discurso de La Cierva (title means "A Lecture about La Cierva"), Raggio, 1921.

Rivas y Larra: Razón social del romanticismo en España (title means "Rivas and Larra: The Firm Name of Romanticism in Spain"), Raggio, 1921.

De Granada a Castelar (title means "From Granada to Castelar"), Raggio, 1922.

Las confesiones de un pequeño filósofo (title means "The Confessions of a Little Philosopher"), Heath, 1923.

El chirrión de los políticos: Fantasía moral (title means "The Squeak of the Politicians: A Moral Fantasy"), Raggio, 1923.

Racine y Moliere, [Madrid], 1924.

Discursos leídos ante la Real Academia Española en la recepción de don Joaquín Quintero el día 19 de abril de 1925 (title means "Discourses Read Before the Royal Spanish Academy at the Reception for Mr. Joaquin Quintero, April 19, 1925"), Clásica Española, 1925.

Los Quinteros, y otras páginas, Raggio, 1925.

Doña Inés, Raggio, 1926, text edition edited by Livingstone, Irvington, 1969.

Brandy, mucho brandy: Sainete sentimental en tres actos (title means "Brandy, Lots of Brandy: A Sentimental Farce in Three Acts"), Raggio, 1927.

Félix Vargas: Etopeya (novel), Biblioteca Nueva, 1928, published as *El caballero inactual* (title means "The Nonpresent Gentleman"), Espasa-Calpe, 1965.

(With Muñoz Seca) *El clamor: Farsa en tres actos* (title means "The Clamor: A Farce in Three Acts"), Artes Gráficos, 1928.

Lo invisible (title means "The Invisible One"), Prensa Moderna, 1928.

Comedia del arte: En tres actos (also see below), Prensa Moderna, 1928.

Doctor Fregoli; o, La comedia de la felicidad: Comedia en tres actos (title means "Doctor Fregoli; or, the Comedy of Happiness: A Comedy in Three Acts"), Prensa Moderna, 1928.

Leyendo a los poetas (title means "Reading the Poets"), Librería General, 1929.

Palabras al viento (title means "Words to the Wind"), Librería General, 1929.

Blanco en azul (title means "White on Blue"; short stories), Biblioteca Nueva, 1929.

Andando y pensando: Notas de un transeúnte (title means "Walking and Thinking: Notes of a Transient"), Páez, 1929.

Superrealismo, prenovela (title means "Surrealism, Prenovel"; novel), Biblioteca Nueva, 1929, published as *El libro de Levante* (title means "The Book of Levante"), Losada, 1952.

Pueblo: Novela de los que trabajan y sufren (title means "Village: A Novel of Those Who Work and Suffer"), Biblioteca Nueva, 1930.

Angelita: Auto sacramental (title means "Angelita: A One-Act Religious Play"), Biblioteca Nueva, 1930.

Nuevas obras (title means "New Works"), Biblioteca Nueva, 1930.

Lope en silueta (con aguja de navegar Lope), Arbol, 1935.

La guerilla: Comedia en tres actos (title means "The Skirmish: A Comedy in Three Acts"), Rivadeneyra, 1936.

Trasuntos de España (title means "Images of Spain"), Espasa-Calpe, 1938.

En torno a José Hernández (title means "Turning to Jose Hernandez"), Sudamericana (Buenos Aires), 1939.

Españoles en París (title means "Spaniards in Paris"), Espasa-Calpe, 1939.

Pensando en España (title means "Thinking about Spain"), Biblioteca Nueva, 1940.

Madrid, Biblioteca Nueva, 1941.

Visión de España (title means "Vision of Spain"), Espasa-Calpe, 1941.

Tomás Rueda, Espasa-Calpe, 1941.

Valencia, Biblioteca Nueva, 1941.

Sintiendo a España, Tartessos, 1942.

El escritor (title means "The Writer"), Espasa-Calpe, 1942.

Cavilar y contar, Destino, 1942.

Capricho (title means "Caprice"), Espasa-Calpe, 1943.

El enfermo (title means "The Patient"), Adán, 1943.

Veraneo sentimental (title means "Sentimental Summer Vacation"), Librería General (Zaragoza, Mexico), 1944.

Salvadora de Olbena, Cronos (Zaragoza), 1944.

María Fontán (novela rosa), Espasa-Calpe, 1944.

París, Biblioteca Nueva, 1945.

La farándula, Librería General, 1945.

Los clásicos redividos, los clásicos futuros, Espasa-Calpe, 1945.

El artista y el estilo (title means "The Artist and Style"), Aguilar, 1946.

Memorias inmemoriales (title means "Immemorial Memories"), B.N., 1946.

El político: Con un epílogo futurista (title means "The Politician: With a Futuristic Epilogue"), Espasa-Calpe, 1946.

Prosas selectas (title means "Selected Prose"), Secretaria de Educación Pública (Mexico), 1946.

Antes Baroja (title means "Before Baroja"), Librería General, 1946.

Ante las candilejas (title means "Before the Oil Lamps"), Librería General, 1947.

Con Cervantes (title means "With Cervantes"), Espasa-Calpe, 1947.

Escena y sala (title means "Scene and Parlor"), Librería General, 1947.

Obras completas (title means "Complete Works"), Aguilar, 1947, expanded edition, 1975.

Con permiso de los cervantistas (title means "With the Permission of the Cervantesites"), Biblioteca Nueva, 1948.

La cabeza de Castilla (title means "The Head of Castile"), Espasa-Calpe, 1950.

Con bandera de Francia (title means "With the Flag of France"), Biblioteca Nueva, 1950.

El oasis de los clásicos (title means "The Oasis of the Classics"), Biblioteca Nueva, 1952.

Dos comedias: Comedia del arte [and] *Old Spain* (title means "Two Comedies . . ."), Houghton, 1952.

Verano en Mallorca (title means "Summer in Majorca"), Palma, 1952.

El cine y el momento (title means "The Movies and the Moment"), Biblioteca Nueva, 1953.

Pintar como querer (title means "Painting as You Wish"), Biblioteca Nueva, 1954.

El buen Sancho (title means "The Good Sancho"), [Madrid], 1954.

El pasado (title means "The Past"), Biblioteca Nueva, 1955.

El efímero cine (title means "The Ephemeral Movies"), Aguado, 1955.

Cuentos de Azorín (title means "Stories of Azorin"), Aguado, 1956.

Escritores (title means "Writers"), Biblioteca Nueva, 1956.

Dicho y hecho (title means "No Sooner Said Than Done"), Destino, 1957.

De un transeúnte (title means "Concerning a Transient"), Aguado, 1958.

Sin perder los estribos (title means "Without Losing One's Balance"), Taurus, 1958.

La isla sin aurora (title means "The Island Without Dawn"), Destino, 1958.

Agenda (essays), Biblioteca Nueva, 1959.

De Valera a Miró (title means "From Valera to Miro"), Aguado, 1959.

Pasos quedos (title means "Quiet Passages"), Escelicer, 1959.

Posdata (title means "Postscript"), Biblioteca Nueva, 1959.

Ejercicios del castellano (title means "Exercises of a Castilian"), Biblioteca Nueva, 1960.

Mis mejores páginas (title means "My Best Pages"), Mateu, 1961.

La generación del 98 (title means "The Generation of '98"), Anaya (Salamanca), 1961.

Lo que pasó una vez (title means "That Which Once Happened"), Lumen, 1962.

Varios hombres y alguna mujer (title means "Various Men and Any Woman"), Aidos, 1962.

Historia y vida (title means "History and Life"), Espasa-Calpe, 1962.

En lontananza (title means "In the Background"), Bullon, 1963.

Los recuadros, Biblioteca Nueva, 1963.

Ni sí, ni no (title means "Neither Yes, Nor No"), Destino, 1965.

Los médicos (title means "The Doctors"), Prometco, 1965.

Ultramarinos (title means "Those From Overseas"), Hispano Americana, 1966.

España clara (title means "Clear Spain"), Doncel, 1966.

La amada España (title means "The Loved Spain"), Destino, 1967.

Azorín y los libros (title means "Azorin and Books"), Instituto Nacional del Libro Español, 1967.

Crítica de años cercanos (title means "Criticism of Neighboring Years"), Taurus, 1967.

Política y literatura: Fantasías y devaneos (title means "Politics and Literature: Fantasies and Frenzies"), Alianza, 1968.

Tiempo y paisaje: Visión de España (title means "Time and Landscape: Vision of Spain"), Cultura Hispánica, 1968.

Albacete, siempre (title means "Albacete, Always"), Ayuntamiento de Albacete, 1970.

Tiempos y cosas (title means "Times and Things"), Salvat, 1970.

Reflejos de España (title means "Reflections on Spain"), Moreno (Buenos Aires), 1971.

Rosalía de Castro y otros motivos gallegos (title means "Rosalia de Castro and Other Galician Motifs"), Celtia, 1973.

Cada cosa en su sitio (title means "Everything in Its Place"), Destino, 1973.

Los pueblos. La Andalucía trágica, y otros artículos, 1904-1905 (title means "The Towns. Tragic Andalusia, and Other Articles, 1904-1905"), Castalia, 1974.

SIDELIGHTS: Early in his career Jose Martínez Ruiz played with pseudonyms such as "Ahriman" and "Candido." But when he adopted the name "Azorín" for the protagonist of his autobiographical trilogy (the novels: *La Voluntad, Antonio Azorín,* and *Las confesiones de un pequeño filósofo*), the character gradually became an alter ego of the author, providing not only his literary identity, but his personal identification as well. As Azorín, he wrote in such diverse genres as plays, novels, and short stories, but came to be best known as one of Spain's leading essayists of the first half of the twentieth century.

Azorín was a member of the Spanish literary group called the *Generación del '98* (a term he first proposed in one of his essays). The name applied to those writers born roughly between 1880 and 1900 who were influenced by the stunning defeat suffered by Spain in 1898 when the Spanish-American War ended with Spain's loss of its colonies of Cuba, Puerto Rico, the Philippines, Guam, and the Marianas. The collapse of the Spanish empire that had endured for nearly four hundred years led many of Spain's intellectuals to pause and reflect on the essence of their country, hoping to find the reasons for what amounted to a national disaster. According to Beatrice P. Patt and Martin Nozick in their *Generation of 1898 and After,* "Azorín discovered the essence of Spain in the melancholy immobility of the Castilian landscape and in the minutiae of daily life he observed in small villages and cities." Azorín's most characteristic works, including *Castilla, Los pueblos: Ensayos sobre la vida provinciana,* and *La ruta de Don Quijote,* are filled with evocative descriptions of the Spanish countryside.

Patt and Nozick noted a relationship between the frequent landscapes in Azorín's work and one of his most important themes: time. They observed that the writer's emphasis on scenic descriptions "stemmed mainly from a desire to capture the fleeting moment of time and make it eternal." By describing Castile, the region in Spain's physical and historical center, Azorín hoped to capture the essence of his country—that which would outlast whatever political failures the future might hold. Azorín made use of time in a variety of ways in his work. In an *Hispania* essay Julian Palley listed a number of different aspects of the same theme in one of Azorín's novels and pointed out several European influences evident in the Spaniard's work: "In *Doña Inés* there is the Nietzschean Eternal Return; there is the Proustian evocation of the past through a physical sensation; there is an historical or demiurgic . . . vision of change and the passage of time; [and] there is time as duration, in the Bergsonian sense."

Azorín was a stylistic revolutionary, using the Spanish language in new and striking ways. He rejected the wordy, bombastic style favored by other writers of the time and used concise, short sentences almost exclusively. In *A History of Spanish Literature* Spanish literary historian Guillermo Díaz Plaja quoted from an essay in which Azorín described his technique of writing. "Style consists of writing in such a way," he observed, "that the reader thinks: 'There's nothing to this.' So that he thinks: 'I could write like that.' " In the same essay, Azorín admitted that although his style looks easy, it was "the most laborious" method of writing. Margarite Rand found in her *Castilla en Azorín* that the Spaniard's use of short sentences, coupled with his favored present tense and his tendency to repeat the same sentences several times in the same piece, gave a lyrical quality to his work.

Another aspect of Azorín's style is a tendency to accumulate details. He was so adept at minute descriptions of everyday objects that some critics called him a miniaturist. According to Rand, the Spanish philosopher and essayist José Ortega y Gasset described Azorín's art perfectly with the phrase, "Maximus in minimus." Azorín's love for details was guided by his desire to present the largest amount of meaning in the smallest amount of space, or as Ortega y Gasset observed, to find "the most in the least." His search for details led him often to use words with diminutive Spanish endings, such as "-ito," "-illo," or "-uelo." Azorín chose the tiniest detail for the emotion it lent to the narrative, since in an impressionist manner he interpreted objective reality through his own sensibility.

In 1947 the City of Madrid sponsored a public meeting in Azorín's honor, accompanied by a ten-day exposition of his works by the city's book dealers.

BIOGRAPHICAL/CRITICAL SOURCES:

BOOKS

Contemporary Literary Criticism, Volume 11, Gale, 1979.
Díaz Plaja, Guillermo, *A History of Spanish Literature,* translated and edited by Hugh A. Harter, New York University Press, 1971.
Patt, Beatrice P. and Martin Nozick, *The Generation of 1898 and After,* Harper, 1960.
Rand, Marguerite, *Castilla en Azorín,* Revista de Occidente, 1957.

PERIODICALS

Hispania, May, 1971.

OBITUARIES:

PERIODICALS

Antiquarian Bookman, March 27, 1967.
Books Abroad, spring, 1968.
New York Times, March 3, 1967.

*   *   *

MARZAN, Julio   1946-

PERSONAL: Born February 22, 1946, in Puerto Rico.

ADDRESSES: Home—175-20 Wexford Terrace, Jamaica Estates, N.Y. 11432.

CAREER: Teacher of Spanish language and literature at New York University; State University of New York, State University College at Old Westbury; and Fordham University. Writer.

WRITINGS:

(Editor and author of introduction) *Inventing a Word: An Anthology of Twentieth-Century Puerto Rican Poetry,* Columbia University Press, 1980.
Translations Without Originals, I. Reed Books, 1986.

Also author of a play titled "When Is a Pigeon a Dove?"

BIOGRAPHICAL/CRITICAL SOURCES:

PERIODICALS

World Literature Today, spring, 1981.

*   *   *

MATOS, Luis Palés
See PALES MATOS, Luis

*   *   *

MATOS PAOLI, Francisco   1915-

PERSONAL: Born in 1915 in Lares, P.R.

CAREER: Journalist, poet, literary critic, essayist, and politician. Professor of Puerto Rican literature at University of Puerto Rico, Río Piedras, P.R. Worked as secretary of Puerto Rican Nationalist Party.

WRITINGS:

Habitante del eco, 1937-1941 (poetry), Imprenta Soltero, 1944.
Teoría del olvido (poetry), University of Puerto Rico, 1944.
Luz de los héroes (poetry), [San Juan], 1954.
Criatura del rocío (poetry), prologue by Margot Arce de Vázquez, [San Juan], 1958.
Canto de la locura (poetry), Ediciones Juan Ponce de León, 1962, revised edition, Instituto de Cultura Puertorriqueña, 1976, bilingual English-Spanish edition with translation by Frances R. Aparicio published as *Song of Madness and Other Poems,* Latin American Literary Review Press, 1985.
El viento y la paloma, 1961-1963 (poetry), Ediciones Juan Ponce de León, 1969.
Cancionero (poetry), Ediciones Juan Ponce de León, 1970.
La marea sube (poetry), Ediciones Juan Ponce de León, 1971.
La semilla encendida (poetry), Ediciones Juan Ponce de León, 1971.
Antología poética (selected poetry), selected by José Emilio González, University of Puerto Rico, 1972.
Rostro en la estela (poetry), Ediciones Juan Ponce de León, 1973.
Variaciones del mar (poetry), Ediciones Juan Ponce de León, 1973.
Diario de un poeta, Ediciones Puerto Rico, 1973, two-volume edition published under the same title, Instituto de Cultura Puertorriqueña, División de Publicaciones y Grabaciones, 1987.
Testigo de la esperanza (poetry), University of Puerto Rico, 1974.
El engaño a los ojos (poetry), Ediciones Juan Ponce de León, 1974.
La orilla sitiada (poetry), Ediciones Juan Ponce de León, 1974.
Rielo del instante, Ediciones Juan Ponce de León, 1975.
Unción de la tierra, Ediciones Juan Ponce de León, 1975.
Dación y milagro, Ediciones Juan Ponce de León, 1976.
Antología minuto (poetry), Jardín de Espejos, 1977.
Ya se oye el cenit, Ediciones Juan Ponce de León, 1977.

Loor del espacio, Ramallo Bros., 1977.
Rapto en el tiempo (poetry), Ediciones Juan Ponce de León, 1978.
La caída del clavel (poetry), Ediciones Juan Ponce de León, 1979.
Jardín vedado, QESE, 1980.
Los crueles espejos (poetry), [San Juan], 1980.
Sombra verdadera (poetry), Orígenes, 1980.
Primeros libros poéticos (poetry), QESE, 1982.
Hacia el hondo vuelo (poetry), University of Puerto Rico, 1983.
Vestido para la desnudez, Mairena, 1984.
Romancillos para adolescentes (poetry), Mairena, 1985.
Francisco Matos Paoli: Poeta esencial (poetry), edited by Manuel de la Ruebla, Mairena, 1985.
Razón del humo, Mairena, 1986.
Las pausas blancas, Mairena, 1986.
La frontera y el mar, Mairena, 1987.
El acorde, Mairena, 1988.

Also author of *Signario de lágrimas* (poetry), 1931, *Cardo labriego* (poetry), 1932, and *Canto a Puerto Rico* (poetry), 1952. Contributor to periodicals, including *Asomante, Puerto Rico Ilustrado, Alma Latina, El Mundo, El Imparcial, Revista del Instituto de Cultura,* and *Puertorriqueña.*

* * *

MEDINA, Robert C.   1924-

PERSONAL: One source lists first name as Roberto; born February 11, 1924, in Las Cruces, N.M.; son of Jesús (a painter) and Petra (Cisneros) Medina; married Mary Louise Medina, January 5, 1948; children: Carol M. Maze, Agatha Rodriguez, Cathy Garcia, Mark, Pete, Rose S. Galgay. *Education:* Attended New Mexico State University. *Politics:* Democratic. *Religion:* Catholic.

ADDRESSES: Home—121 Ridgecrest Dr., Las Cruces, N.M. 88005. *Office*—Bilingüe Publications, P.O. Drawer H, Las Cruces, N.M. 88004.

CAREER: Federal Government Civil Service, White Sands Missile Range, N.M., worked thirty-two-and-a-half years as a photo-optical equipment operator; Bilingüe Publications, Las Cruces, N.M., owner, 1974—.

MEMBER: Knights of Columbus.

WRITINGS:

(Also editor) *Two Ranges* (novel), introduction by Patricio Quintana, Bilingüe Publications, 1974.
(Also editor) *Fabián no se muere: novela de amor* (novel; also see below), Bilingüe Publications, 1978.
(Also editor) *Fabian Doesn't Die* (condensed drama of *Fabián no se muere* in English), Bilingüe Publications, 1981.
(Editor, with Virginia Lark, of daughter Carol's book) Carol M. Maze, *Mexican Microwave Cookery,* Bilingüe Publications, 1984.

WORK IN PROGRESS: U.S. Spanish Thesaurus; English, Spanish, and bilingual play adaptations of *Fabian Doesn't Die.*

SIDELIGHTS: Robert C. Medina's second novel, *Fabián no se muere: novela de amor,* is the story of a young Chicano man (Fabián) who, after moving from the country to pursue a new life in the city, returns to operate his family's farm. A contributor to *Chicano Literature: A Reference Guide* notes Medina "establishes endearing images of Chicano culture" that "deal with the various levels of familial ties and cultural means by which they

are preserved: religion, language, and the work ethic." The contributor also describes Medina's use of *caló,* a mixture of Spanish, English, and Nahuatl (an Indian language), as Fabián's "way of identifying with big-city folk" that "establishes both an era and a locale—the 1940s in southern New Mexico and west Texas." Moreover, the contributor continues, "Medina's novels are telling examples of the view that *caló* is a vehicle of communication that must be recognized in fiction as an inescapable social datum. In this sense, . . . Medina's novels are in the tradition of promoting the Southwest as a pluralistic society that both affects and is affected by Chicanos in their efforts to find their unique place within it."

BIOGRAPHICAL/CRITICAL SOURCES:

BOOKS

Lomelí, Francisco A., and Donaldo W. Urioste, *Chicano Perspectives in Literature: A Critical and Annotated Bibliography,* Pajarito Publications, 1976.
Martínez, Julio A., and Francisco A. Lomelí, editors, *Chicano Literature: A Reference Guide,* Greenwood Press, 1985.

* * *

MELANTZON, Ricardo Aguilar
See AGUILAR MELANTZON, Ricardo

* * *

MELENDEZ (RAMIREZ), Concha   1892-
(Conchita Meléndez)

PERSONAL: Born November 23, 1892, in Caguas, Puerto Rico.

CAREER: University of Puerto Rico, Río Piedras, chairman of department of Hispanic studies, 1940-59, professor emeritus, 1959—. Consultant, Institute of Puerto Rican Culture.

AWARDS, HONORS: Institute of Puerto Rican Culture gold medal, 1965; named Puerto Rican Woman of the Year, Association of American Women, 1971; received citations of merit from Institute of Puerto Rican Literature, Puerto Rico Atheneum, Commonwealth of Puerto Rico, and Mexican Academy of Language.

WRITINGS:

Amado Nervo, Instituto de las Españas en los Estados Unidos (New York), 1926.
La novela indianista en Hispanoamérica (1832-1889), Imprenta de la Librería y casa editorial Hernando (Madrid), 1934, 2nd edition, Universidad de Puerto Rico (Río Piedras), 1961.
Signos de Iberoamérica, Manuel León Sánchez (Mexico), 1936.
Entrada en el Perú, La Verónica (Havana), 1941, 2nd edition, Editorial Cordillera (San Juan, P. R.), 1970.
Asomante: Estudios hispanoamericanos, Universidad de Puerto Rico, 1943, 2nd edition, Editorial Cordillera, 1970.
La inquietud sosegada poética de Evaristo Ribera Chevremont, Junta Editora, Universidad de Puerto Rico, 1946, 3rd edition, Editorial Cordillera, 1970.
(Editor and author of introduction and notes) *Cuentos hispanoamericanos,* Editorial Orión (Mexico), 1953.
Ficciones de Alfonso Reyes, Universidad Nacional (Mexico City), 1956.
(Editor) *El cuento,* Estado Libre Asociado de Puerto Rico (San Juan), 1957.
Figuración de Puerto Rico y otros estudios, Instituto de Cultura Puertorriqueña (San Juan), 1958.

El arte del cuento en Puerto Rico, Las Américas Publishing (New York), 1961, 4th edition, Editorial Cordillera, 1975.
(Author of prologue) Néstor A. Rodríguez Escudero, *Estampas de un peregrino: Crónicas de viaje,* Editorial Cordillera, 1964.
José de Diego en mi memoria, Instituto de Cultura Puerto-rriqueña, 1966, 2nd edition, Editorial Cordillera, 1970.
(Editor) Evaristo Ribera Chevremont, *Nueva antología,* Editorial Cordillera, 1966.
Literatura hispanoamericana, Editorial Cordillera, 1967, 2nd edition, 1972.
Obras completas, 15 volumes, Editorial Cordillera, 1967-71.
Literatura de ficción en Puerto Rico: Cuento y novela, Editorial Cordillera, 1971.
Palabras para oyentes: Conferencias, presentaciones de escritores, exposiciones de pintura, Editorial Cordillera, 1971.
Personas y libros, Editorial Cordillera, 1971.
Poetas hispanoamericanos diversos, Editorial Cordillera, 1971.
Moradas de poesía en Alfonso Reyes, Editorial Cordillera, 1973.
Complete Works of Concha Meléndez, 5 volumes, Gordon Press, 1979.

Also author of *Psiquis doliente,* 1926. Contributor to *Asomante, Alma Latina, Puerto Rico Ilustrado, El Mundo, Brújula, La Torre,* and other publications.

* * *

MELENDEZ, Conchita
See MELENDEZ (RAMIREZ), Concha

* * *

MELLIZO (CUADRADO), Carlos 1942-

PERSONAL: Surname is pronounced "Ma-*yee*-tho"; born October 2, 1942, in Madrid, Spain; immigrated to United States, 1969, naturalized citizen, 1977; son of Felipe (a civil engineer) and Asunción (a housewife; maiden name, Cuadrado) Mellizo; married Esther Vialpando (a teacher), July 24, 1970; children: Olga, Carlos, Marisa, Philip. *Education:* Universidad Complutense de Madrid, B.A., 1964, M.A., 1966, Ph.D. (with high honors), 1970.

ADDRESSES: Home—63 Corthell Rd., Laramie, Wyo. 82070. *Office*—Department of Modern Languages, University of Wyoming, Laramie, Wyo. 82071.

CAREER: High school Spanish teacher in Stoke-on-Trent, England, 1966; Universidad Complutense de Madrid, Madrid, Spain, lecturer in philosophy, 1967-68; University of Wyoming, Laramie, assistant professor, 1970-74, associate professor, 1974-77, professor of modern languages, 1977—, general editor of publications of the department, 1974-82. Translator for Alianza Editorial (Madrid publisher), 1985—.

MEMBER: American Association of Teachers of Spanish and Portuguese, Asociación Colegial de Escritores (Spain), Phi Sigma Iota (national vice-president, 1984-86).

AWARDS, HONORS: Teaching award from Amoco Foundation, 1974; Iberoamerican Writers Award from Iberoamerican Writers Guild, 1974, for short story "Un asunto para tres"; Hispanidad Literary Award from Office of Cultural Affairs of Spanish Embassy to Paraguay, 1975, for novella "Cerca del río"; second-place Cáceres Literary Award from University of Cáceres (Spain), 1975, for *Romero;* Hucha de Plata literary awards from Confederación Española de Cajas de Ahorros (Madrid, Spain), 1977, for short story "Historia de Caballos," and 1982, for short story "Viaje al Orinoco."

WRITINGS:

Los cocodrilos (stories; title means "The Crocodiles"), Indice, 1970.
(Editor) *Homenaje a Azorín: A Collection of Critical Essays,* University of Wyoming, 1974.
Romero (novel), La Encina, 1975.
(Translator into Spanish) David Hume, *Diálogos sobre la religión natural* (title means "Dialogues Concerning Natural Religion"), Aguilar, 1976.
(Translator into Spanish) David Hume, *Resumen* (title means "Abstract"), Aguilar, 1976.
(Editor with Richard Landeira) *Ignacio Aldecoa: A Collection of Critical Essays,* University of Wyoming, 1977.
(Translator into Spanish) Francisco Sánchez, *Que nada se sabe* (title means "That Nothing Is Known"), Aguilar, 1977.
En torno a David Hume (essays; title means "On David Hume"), Monte Casino, 1978.
Carmela (novella), Jelm Mountain Publications, 1978.
(Editor with Louise Salstad) *Blas de Otero: Study of a Poet,* University of Wyoming, 1979.
Nueva introducción a Francisco Sánchez "El Escéptico" (title means "A New Introduction to Francisco Sánchez's 'El Escéptico' "), Monte Casino, 1982.
(Translator into Spanish) Francisco Sánchez, *Sobre la duración y la brevedad de la vida* (title means "Of the Duration and Brevity of Life"), Archivo Histórico Diocesano (Tuy, Spain), 1982.
(Translator into Spanish and author of appendix) David Hume, *Mi vida: Carta de un caballero a su amigo de Edimburgo* (title means "My Life: A Letter From a Gentleman to His Friend in Edinburgh"), Alianza, 1985.
(Translator into Spanish) John Stuart Mill, *Autobiografía,* Alianza, 1986.
(Translator into Spanish) John Stuart Mill, *La utilidad de la religión* (title means "The Utility of Religion"), Alianza, 1986.
Historia de Sonia y otras historias (title means "The Story of Sonia and Other Stories"), Bilingual Press, 1987.
(Translator into Spanish) David Hume, *Sobre el suicidio y otros ensayos* (title means "Concerning Suicide and Other Essays"), Alianza, 1988.
(Translator into Spanish) Thomas Hobbes, *Leviatán,* Alianza, 1989.

Contributor of articles, stories, and reviews to periodicals.

WORK IN PROGRESS: El filólogo, a short novel, publication expected in 1991; *A Matter of Time,* a collection of stories, publication expected in 1991.

SIDELIGHTS: Carlos Mellizo told *HW:* "To me, as I suppose it is with most writers, literature is both a necessity and a luxury. I write with the hope of learning a few essential things about myself and others. I also write, as Pío Baroja used to say, to kill time in a reasonably dignified manner. The short story and the novella are the literary forms of expression I prefer, perhaps because they exclude all possibility of 'gossipy' writing—a practice I personally detest."

* * *

MENDEZ, Eugenio Fernández
See FERNANDEZ MENDEZ, Eugenio

MENDEZ M., Miguel   1930-

PERSONAL: Born June 15, 1930, in Bisbee, Ariz.; son of Francisco Méndez Cárdenas (a farmer and miner) and María Morales. *Education:* Attended schools in El Claro, Sonora, Mexico, for six years.

ADDRESSES: Office—Department of Language and Literature, Pima Community College, West Campus, 2202 West Anklam Rd., Tucson, Ariz. 85709.

CAREER: Writer. Went to work as an itinerant farm laborer along the Arizona-Sonora border at the age of fifteen; bricklayer and construction worker in Tucson, Ariz., 1946-70; Pima Community College, Tucson, Ariz., instructor in Spanish, Hispanic literature and creative writing, 1970—. Instructor in Chicano literature, University of Arizona.

MEMBER: Association of Teachers of Spanish and Portugese.

AWARDS, HONORS: Honorary Doctor of Humanities, University of Arizona, 1984.

WRITINGS:

(Contributor) Octavio I. Romano and Herminio Riós-C., editors, *El Espejo/The Mirror,* Quinto Sol, 1969.
Peregrinos de Aztlán (novel; title means "Pilgrims of Aztlán"), Editorial Peregrinos, 1974.
Los criaderos humanos y Sahuaros (poem; title means "The Human Breeding Grounds and Saguaros"), Editorial Peregrinos, 1975.
Cuentos para niños traviesos/Stories for Mischievous Children (short stories; bilingual edition), translations by Eva Price, Justa, 1979.
Tata Casehua y otros cuentos (short stories; bilingual edition; title means "Tata Casehua and Other Stories"), translations by Price, Leo Barrow, and Marco Portales, Justa, 1980.
De la vida y del folclore de la frontera (short stories; title means "From Life and Folklore along the Border"), Mexican American Studies and Research Center, University of Arizona, 1986.
El sueño de Santa María de las Piedras (novel; title means "The Dream of Santa Maria of the Stones"), Universidad de Guadalajara, 1986.
Cuentos y ensayos para reir y aprender (title means "Stories and Essays for Laughing and Learning"), Miguel Méndez M., 1988.

Contributor to periodicals, including *La Palabra* and *Revista Chicano-Riqueña.* The spring-fall 1981 issue of *La Palabra* is entirely devoted to his work.

SIDELIGHTS: "Chicano literature has in Miguel Méndez M. one of its finest and most sensitive writers," reports Salvador Rodríguez del Pino in *Chicano Writers.* Although not yet well known among English-speaking readers—much of his work, including his first novel, *Peregrinos de Aztlán,* remains untranslated—Méndez M. has attracted the admiration of many critics with his richly poetic prose, his erudite language, and his depictions of the poor members of an uprooted society at odds with the Anglo-American culture that threatens their heritage.

Much of Méndez M.'s work uses elements from his Spanish and Yaqui Indian heritages. The name Aztlán in *Peregrinos de Aztlán,* for instance, is taken from the mythic northern homeland of the Aztec Indians of Mexico, and is believed to have been somewhere in the southwestern United States. Loreto Maldonado, the main character of *Peregrinos de Aztlán,* who now wanders the streets of Laredo, Texas, making a living by washing cars, was once a revolutionary and served under Pancho Villa. The title character in "Tata Casehua," found in the short story collection *Tata Casehua y otros cuentos,* is actually the hero warrior Tetabiate, and the story details his search for an heir to whom he can pass on his tribe's history.

Méndez M. also draws upon his personal past, growing up in a Mexican government farming community and later working in agriculture and construction, for his stories. "During my childhood," he tells Juan Bruce-Novoa in *Chicano Authors: Inquiry by Interview,* "I heard many stories from those people who came from different places, and, like my family, were newcomers to El Claro. They would tell anecdotes about the [Mexican] Revolution, the Yaqui wars, and innumerable other themes, among which there was no lack of apparitions and superstitions. Those days were extremely dramatic. I learned about tragedy, at times in the flesh." When at the age of fifteen Méndez M. left Mexico to find work as an agricultural laborer in the United States, he met the exploited people who appear in his fiction—indigent workers, prostitutes, and Hispanics looking for jobs in the North, among others.

Another major component of the author's work is the oral tradition handed down by these poor people; indeed, Méndez M. sees their plight as one symptom of the loss of that tradition. "Familial, communal, ethnic, and national heritage, which once was preserved by word of mouth, is disappearing into silence," explains Bruce-Novoa. "At the same time, written history represents only the elite classes' vision of the past, ignoring the existence of the poor. Thus, as the poor abandon the oral preservation of their heritage and simultaneously embrace literacy, alienation and a sense of diaspora possess them. Méndez counterattacks through his writing, not only by revealing the threat to the oral tradition, but also by filling his written texts with oral tradition."

BIOGRAPHICAL/CRITICAL SOURCES:

BOOKS

Dictionary of Literary Biography, Volume 82: *Chicano Writers,* Gale, 1989
Bruce-Novoa, Juan D., *Chicano Authors: Inquiry by Interview,* University of Texas Press, 1980.

✦   ✦   ✦

MENENDEZ PIDAL, Ramón   1869-1968

PERSONAL: Born March 13, 1869, in La Coruña, Spain; died November 14, 1968, in Madrid, Spain; married María Goyri, 1900; children: Jimena, Gonzalo. *Education:* Ph.D., 1893; studied at Universities of Madrid and Toulouse.

CAREER: Ateneo, School for Higher Studies, Madrid, Spain, reader, 1896-1899; University of Madrid, Madrid, professor of Romance philology, 1899-1939. Founder of Center for Historical Studies, Madrid, 1907, and director, beginning 1910; president of Royal Spanish Academy, 1925-1939 and 1947-68. Minister in Spanish cabinet, 1912 and 1918. Visiting professor, University of Buenos Aires, 1914, and Columbia University, 1937-38. *Comisario regio* in settlement of border dispute between Ecuador and Peru, 1904-08.

AWARDS, HONORS: Special citations from Spanish History Academy, 1893, for *Cantar del Mío Cid: Texto, gramática y vocabulario,* and 1896, for *La leyenda de los Infantes de Lara;* honorary degrees from numerous universities, including the Universities of Toulouse, Oxford, Tuebingen, Paris, Louvain, and Brussels.

WRITINGS:

IN ENGLISH TRANSLATION

(Editor) *Poema del Cid,* annotated edition, [Madrid], 1900, abridged edition published with modern Spanish prose version by Alfonso Reyes as *Poema del Cid,* 1938, reprinted, 1967, abridged Spanish edition with translation by W. S. Merwin published as *Poema del Cid/Poem of the Cid* (bilingual edition), Las Américas (New York), 1960.

La España del Cid, two volumes, Plutarca (Madrid), 1929, revised edition, Espasa-Calpe, 1956, translation by Harold Sunderland of original Spanish edition published in one volume as *The Cid and his Spain,* J. Murray, 1934, reprinted, F. Cass, 1971.

(Editor and author of preface) *Historia de España,* seven volumes, [Madrid], 1947, translation by Walter Starkie of preface published as *The Spaniards in Their History: An Analysis of Spain's National Characteristics,* Norton, 1950.

IN SPANISH

(Editor) *La leyenda de los Infantes de Lara,* [Madrid], 1896, 2nd edition, [Madrid], 1934, revised edition, Espasa-Calpe, 1971.

(Editor) *Crónicas generales de España: Catálogo de la Real Biblioteca,* Sucesores de Rivadeneyra (Madrid), 1898, 3rd edition, corrected and enlarged, [Madrid], 1918.

Notas para el Romancero del Conde Fernán González, [Madrid], 1899.

(Editor) *Antología de prosistas castellanos,* [Madrid], 1899, 2nd edition, Clásica Español (Madrid), 1917, 5th edition published as *Antología de prosistas españoles,* Hernando (Madrid), 1928, reprinted, Espasa-Calpe, 1964.

(Editor) *"El condenado por desconfiado," por Tirso de Molina,* [Madrid], 1902.

La leyenda del Abad Don Juan de Montemayor, [Dresden], 1903.

Manual elemental de gramática histórica española, [Madrid], 1904, 3rd edition, V. Suárez, 1914, published as *Manual de gramática histórica española,* 1918, reprinted, Espasa-Calpe, 1977.

(Editor) Alfonso X, *Primera crónica general de España que mandó componer Alfonso el Sabio y se continuaba bajo Sancho IV en 1289,* [Madrid], 1906, 2nd edition, 1916, reprinted, Gredos, 1977.

(Editor) *Cantar del Mío Cid: Texto, gramática y vocabulario,* three volumes, [Madrid], 1908-11, 3rd edition with corrections, Espasa-Calpe (Madrid), 1954-56.

El romancero español: Conferencias dadas en la Columbia University de New York los días 5 y 7 de abril de 1909, bajo los auspicios de The Hispanic Society of America, Hispanic Society of America (New York), 1910.

(Editor and author of introduction and notes) *Poema del Mío Cid,* La Lectura (Madrid), 1913.

(Editor with wife, María Goyri) *La serrana de la vera, de Luis Vélez de Guevara,* [Madrid], 1916.

Documentos lingüísticos de España, Volume I: *Renio de Castilla,* Centro de Estudios Históricos, 1919, reprinted, Revista de Filología Española, 1966.

Estudios literarios, Ateneo (Madrid), 1920, reprinted, Espasa-Calpe, 1968.

Un aspecto en la elaboración del "Quijote," Ateneo, 1920.

(Contributor) *Cursos de metodología y alta cultura: Curso de lingüística,* [Barcelona], 1921.

El Cid y la historia, Jiménez y Molina (Madrid), 1921.

Poesía popular y poesía tradicional en la literatura española, Oxford University Press, 1922.

El rey Rodrigo en la literatura, Bulletin of the Royal Spanish Academy, 1924.

Poesía juglaresca y juglares: Aspectos de la historia literaria y cultural de España, Revista de Archivos (Madrid), 1924, 4th edition, corrected and enlarged, Instituto de Estudios Políticos (Madrid), 1957.

(Editor) *Rodrigo: El último godo,* Volume I: *La edad media,* La Lectura, 1925, reprinted, Espasa-Calpe, 1958.

Orígenes del español: Estudio lingüístico de la península ibérica hasta el siglo XI (also see below), Hernando, 1926, 4th edition, corrected and greatly enlarged, Espasa-Calpe, 1956.

El idioma español en sus primeros tiempos (previously published as part of *Orígenes del español: Estudio lingüístico de la península ibérica hasta el siglo XI*), Voluntad (Madrid), 1927, reprinted, Espasa-Calpe, 1968.

(Editor) *Flor nueva de romances viejos que recogió de la tradición antigua y moderna R. Menéndez Pidal,* Revista de Archivos, Bibliotecas y Museos, 1928, expanded edition, 1943, reprinted, Espasa-Calpe, 1968, original edition published as *Flor nueva de romances viejos,* Espasa-Calpe (Buenos Aires), 1939, reprinted, 1967.

El romancero: Teorías e investigaciones, Paez (Madrid), 1928.

Historia y epopeya (also see below), Hernando, 1934.

(Editor) *Epopeya y romancero: Pliegos impresos hasta julio de 1936 bajo los auspicios de la Hispanic Society of America* (also see below), Hernando, 1936.

Los romances de América y otros estudios, Espasa-Calpe (Buenos Aires), 1939, reprinted, Espasa-Calpe (Madrid), 1958.

De Cervantes y Lope de Vega, Espasa-Calpe, 1940, reprinted, 1973.

Idea imperial de Carlos V, La condesa traidora, El Romanz del infant García, Adefonsus, imperator toletanus (includes three essays previously published in *Historia y epopeya*), Espasa-Calpe (Buenos Aires), 1941, reprinted, Espasa-Calpe (Madrid), 1963.

Poesía árabe y poesía europea, con otros estudios de literatura medieval, Espasa-Calpe (Buenos Aires), 1941, reprinted, Espasa-Calpe (Madrid), 1963.

La lengua de Cristóbal Colón, El estilo de Santa Teresa, y otros estudios sobre el siglo XVI, Espasa-Calpe, 1942.

Mío Cid: El de Valencia, Universidad Literaria de Valencia, Facultad de Filosofía y Letras, 1943.

Castilla: La tradición, el idioma, Espasa-Calpe (Buenos Aires), 1945.

La epopeya castellana a través de la literatura española, Espasa-Calpe, 1945, (originally published in French translation by Henry Merimee from the original Spanish manuscript as *L'Epopee castillane a travers la litterature espagnole,* with preface by Ernest Merimee, [Paris], 1910), 2nd edition, Espasa-Calpe (Madrid), 1969.

(Author of introduction) *Cancionero de romances impreso en Amberes sin año,* facsimile edition, Consejo Superior de Investigaciones Científicas (Madrid), 1945.

Cómo vivió y cómo vive el romancero, E. López Mezquida (Valencia), 1947.

(Author of introduction) Guillermo Díaz Plaja, editor, *Historia general de las literaturas hispánicas,* five volumes, Barna (Barcelona), 1949-58.

El imperio hispánico y los cinco reinos: Dos épocas en la estructura política de España, Instituto de Estudios Políticos (Madrid), 1950.

De primitiva lírica española y antigua épica, Espasa-Calpe (Buenos Aires), 1951, reprinted, Espasa-Calpe (Madrid), 1977.

Los españoles en la historia y en la literatura: Dos ensayos (also see below), Espasa-Calpe (Buenos Aires), 1951.

Los orígenes de las literaturas románicas a la luz de un descubrimiento reciente, Publicaciones de la Universidad Internacional Menéndez Pelayo (Santander), 1951.

(Editor) *Reliquías de la poesía épica española* (also see below), Espasa-Calpe (Madrid), 1951.

Miscelánea histórica-literaria, Espasa-Calpe (Buenos Aires), 1952.

Los Reyes Católicos según Maquiavelo y Castiglione, with a biographical sketch by Dámaso Alonso, [Madrid], 1952.

Romancero hispánico (hispano-portugués, americano y sefardí): Teoría e historia, two volumes, Espasa-Calpe (Madrid), 1952.

(Contributor) Gonzalo Menéndez Pidal and Elisa Bernis, editors, *Antología de cuentos de la literatura universal,* Labor, 1953.

(Contributor) *Cómo vive un romance: Dos ensayos sobre tradicionalidad,* Revista de Filología Española (Madrid), 1954.

España: Eslabón entre la Cristianidad y el Islam, Espasa-Calpe (Madrid), 1956.

Los godos y la epopeya española, "chansons de geste" y baladas nórdicas, Espasa-Calpe, 1956.

(Editor with Goyri) *Romancero tradicional de las lenguas hispánicas (español, portugués, catalán, sefardí),* Gredos, 1957.

Mis páginas preferidas: Estudios lingüísticos e históricos, Gredos (Madrid), 1957.

Mis páginas preferidas: Temas literarios, Gredos, 1957.

España y su historia, two volumes, Minotauro (Madrid), 1957.

El padre las Casas y Victoria, con otros temas del siglo XVI y XVII, Espasa-Calpe, 1958.

Tres poetas primitivos: Elena y María, "Roncesvalles," Historia troyana polimétrica, Espasa-Calpe (Buenos Aires), 1958.

La épica francesa y el tradicionalismo, University of Barcelona, Facultad de Filosofía y Letras, 1958.

La Chanson de Roland y el neotradicionalismo (orígenes de la épica románica), Espasa-Calpe (Madrid), 1959.

(Author of prologue) *Pliegos poéticos españoles en la Universidad de Praga,* [Madrid], 1960.

Los españoles en la literatura, Espasa-Calpe (Buenos Aires), 1960.

(Contributor) *Seis temas peruanos,* Espasa-Calpe (Madrid), 1960.

Estudios de lingüística: Las leyes fonéticas, Menéndez, el diccionario ideal y otros, Espasa-Calpe, 1961.

(Contributor) Francisco Javier Sánchez Cantón, *La casa de Lope de Vega,* Real Academia Española (Madrid), 1962.

En torno a la lengua vasca, Espasa-Calpe (Buenos Aires), 1962.

El dialecto leonés, Instituto de Estudios Asturianos (Oviedo), 1962.

Los Reyes Católicos y otros estudios, Espasa-Calpe, 1962.

El padre las Casas: Su doble personalidad, Espasa-Calpe (Madrid), 1963.

En torno al poema del Cid, EDHASA (Barcelona), 1963, reprinted, 1983.

(Editor) *Crestomatía del español medieval* (manuscript completed and revised by Rafael Lapesa y María Soledad de Andrés), Gredos, 1965.

Toponimia prerrománica hispana, Gredos, 1968.

Textos medievales españoles: Ediciones críticas y estudios, Espasa-Calpe, 1977.

(Editor) *Reliquías de la poesía épica española; acompañadas de Epopeya y romancero* (Arabic, Latin, and Spanish text), Gredos, 1980.

Also editor of *Floresta de leyendas heroicas españolas.* Founder and editor of *Revista de Filología Española,* beginning 1914.

SIDELIGHTS: Called "the most profound and well informed scholar of the Spanish epic tradition" by Guillermo Díaz Plaja in his *A History of Spanish Literature,* Spanish literary historian and philologist Ramón Menéndez Pidal was the first scholar elected to the presidency of the prestigious Royal Spanish Academy who was not a member of the nobility or a politician. His election came after he had become well-known for his historical grammar of the Spanish language, *Manual de gramática histórica española,* and his most important work, an exhaustive study of Spain's twelfth-century epic poem, the *Cantar del Mío Cid.* His work on the *Cantar* spawned a renewed interest in Spain's rich medieval heritage which literary historians had previously neglected. A student of the great Spanish critic and historian Marcelino Menéndez y Pelayo, Menéndez Pidal in turn left a legacy of scholars who would make substantial contributions to Spanish literary studies, including essayist Alfonso Reyes, historian Américo Castro, and critic Dámaso Alonso.

Menéndez Pidal's scholarly approach to the ancient texts he worked with opened new avenues of research to Castilian philologists and provided fresh insights into the methodology of historical study. He became so enamored of the Cid legend that he named his chidren after characters from the story, naming his son Rodrigo after the Cid (whose real name was Rodrigo Díaz de Vivar) and his daughter Jimena after the Cid's wife. "His whole life [was] devoted to the Spanish Middle Ages," Walter Starkie commented in his biographical essay on the historian published as a preface to *The Spaniards in Their History,* "but so profound [was] his knowledge of the obscure workings of the human race in those centuries that he [became] universal, and his researches [were] no less significant to the Hispanists of England, France, Holland or Italy than they [were] to those of North and South America. For this reason his prestige . . . united the scholars of both hemispheres."

BIOGRAPHICAL/CRITICAL SOURCES:

BOOKS

Díaz Plaja, Guillermo, *A History of Spanish Literature,* New York University Press, 1971.

Menéndez Pidal, Ramón, *The Spaniards in Their History,* translated and with a prefatory essay by Walter Starkie, Norton, 1950.

OBITUARIES:

New York Times, November 16, 1968.

*   *   *

MERINO, Gustavo Gutiérrez
    See GUTIERREZ MERINO, Gustavo

*   *   *

MEYER, Doris (L.)   1942-

PERSONAL: Born January 2, 1942, in Summit, N.J.; daughter of Hans J. (an importer-exporter) and Maria L. (an editor and translator) Meyer. *Education:* Radcliffe College, B.A., (magna cum laude), 1963; University of Virginia, M.A., 1964, Ph.D., 1967.

ADDRESSES: Office—Department of Modern Languages, Brooklyn College of the City University of New York, Bedford Ave. and Ave. H., Brooklyn, N.Y. 11210. *Agent*—Sanford J. Greenburger Associates, Inc., 825 Third Ave., New York, N.Y. 10022.

CAREER: University of North Carolina, Wilmington, assistant professor of Spanish, 1967-69; Brooklyn College of the City University of New York, Brooklyn, N.Y., assistant professor, 1972-75, associate professor, 1976-79, professor of Spanish, 1980—.

MEMBER: Modern Language Association of America, American Association of Teachers of Spanish and Portuguese, PEN, Latin American Studies Association, American Literary Translators Association, National Women's Studies Association, Phi Beta Kappa.

AWARDS, HONORS: Woodrow Wilson fellowship, 1964-66; American Philosophical Society grant, 1976; National Endowment for the Humanities fellowship, 1977-78.

WRITINGS:

Traditionalism in the Works of Francisco de Quevedo, University of North Carolina Press, 1970.
Victoria Ocampo: Against the Wind and Tide, Braziller, 1979.
(Editor with Margarite Fernández Olmos) *Contemporary Women Authors of Latin America,* two volumes, Brooklyn College Press, Volume 1: *New Translations,* Volume 2: *Introductory Essays,* both 1983.
(Editor) *Lives on the Line: The Testimony of Contemporary Latin American Authors,* University of California Press, 1988.

Contributor of articles and translations to history and Spanish studies journals; contributor to *Nimrod.*

SIDELIGHTS: Regarding her 1979 work *Victoria Ocampo: Against the Wind and Tide,* Doris Meyer told *CA:* "I was motivated to write the book . . . through a combination of an Argentine background on my mother's side and an intense concern with bringing to the attention of North American readers the remarkable contributions of a much-overlooked South American woman, a legend in her own country, a social rebel and a feminist." Meyer knew Ocampo personally for nearly twenty years and, according to John Russell in the *New York Times,* provides an "unremittingly earnest" view of her life. "Books and the men who wrote them were what [Ocampo] most cared for in life," notes Russell. "She had the looks, the means and the gall to chase the writers of her choice, and for much of her life she did just that." The founder in 1931 of the influential literary review *Sur,* Ocampo also ran a publishing company that provided Spanish translations of such literary giants as James Joyce, Andre Malraux, William Faulkner, and Vladimir Nabokov. Russell praises Meyer's book as a "decent, serious, well-researched survey, and it is graced by a discretion now rare among biographers."

Since her book on Ocampo, Meyer has provided English-speaking readers with access to other Latin American authors, in particular women writers. In 1983, she co-edited the two-volume *Contemporary Women Authors of Latin America,* which collects previously unpublished translations by forty female writers and provides in-depth profiles of the lives and work of over a dozen. According to Sonja Karsen in *World Literature Today,* the volumes, which cover both established and little-known writers, "fill an important gap that has existed in our knowledge of Latin American literature." In 1988, Meyer edited *Lives on the Line: The Testimony of Contemporary Latin American Writers,* a collection of first-hand accounts by writers which, according to Alberto Ciria in the Toronto *Globe and Mail,* show "the artists' involvement (or lack of it) in social and political issues together with considerations about their literary experiences." Ciria comments that *Lives on the Line* is "helpful in suggesting some of the roots of [Latin American] literature, some of the

problems faced by those writers in their lives as well as in their crafts, and some of the painful consequences of repression, exile and 'interior exile' for Latin American intellectuals."

BIOGRAPHICAL/CRITICAL SOURCES:

PERIODICALS

Globe and Mail (Toronto), June 25, 1988.
Los Angeles Times Book Review, July 17, 1988.
New York Times, August 9, 1979.
World Literature Today, winter, 1985.

* * *

MIRANDA, Javier
 See BIOY CASARES, Adolfo

* * *

MIRON, Salvador Díaz
 See DIAZ MIRON, Salvador

* * *

MISTRAL, Gabriela
 See GODOY ALCAYAGA, Lucila

* * *

MOHR, Nicholasa 1935-

PERSONAL: Born November 1, 1935, in New York, N.Y.; daughter of Pedro and Nicholasa (Rivera) Golpe; married Irwin Mohr (a clinical child psychologist), October 5, 1957 (deceased); children: David, Jason. *Education:* Attended Art Students League, 1953-56, Brooklyn Museum of Art School, 1959-66, and Pratt Center for Contemporary Printmaking, 1966-69.

ADDRESSES: Home—727 President St., Brooklyn, N.Y. 11215.

CAREER: Fine arts painter in New York, California, Mexico, and Puerto Rico, 1952-62; printmaker in New York, Mexico, and Puerto Rico, 1963—; teacher in art schools in New York and New Jersey, 1967—; art instructor at Art Center of Northern New Jersey, 1971-73; MacDowell Colony, Peterborough, N.H., writer in residence, 1972, 1974, and 1976; artist in residence with New York City public schools, 1973-74; State University of New York at Stony Brook, lecturer in Puerto Rican studies, 1977. Visiting lecturer in creative writing for various educator, librarian, student, and community groups, including University of Illinois Educational Alliance Program (Chicago), 1977, Cedar Rapids community schools (Iowa), 1978, writers in residence seminar, University of Wisconsin—Oshkosh, 1978, and Bridgeport, Connecticut, public schools, 1978. Head creative writer and co-producer of television series "Aqui y Ahora" (title means "Here and Now"). Member of New Jersey State Council on the Arts; member of board of trustees, and consultant, of Young Filmmakers Foundation; consultant on bilingual media training for Young Filmmakers/Video Arts.

MEMBER: Authors Guild, Authors League of America.

AWARDS, HONORS: Outstanding book award in juvenile fiction from *New York Times,* 1973, Jane Addams Children's Book Award from Jane Addams Peace Association, 1974, and citation of merit for book jacket design from Society of Illustrators, 1974, all for *Nilda;* outstanding book award in teenage fiction from *New York Times,* 1975, best book award from *School Library*

Journal, 1975, and National Book Award finalist for "most distinguished book in children's literature," 1976, all for *El Bronx Remembered;* best book award from *School Library Journal,* best book award in young adult literature from American Library Association, and Notable Trade Book Award from joint committee of National Council for the Social Studies and Children's Book Council, all 1977, all for *In Nueva York; Nilda* selected as one of *School Library Journal's* "Best of the Best 1966-78"; Notable Trade Book Award from joint committee of National Council for the Social Studies and Children's Book Council, 1980, and American Book Award from Before Columbus Foundation, 1981, both for *Felita;* commendation from the Legislature of the State of New York, 1986, for *Rituals of Survival: A Woman's Portfolio;* distinguished visiting professor at Queens College of the City University of New York, 1988-90; honorary doctorate of letters from State University of New York at Albany, 1989.

WRITINGS:

JUVENILE

(And illustrator) *Nilda* (novel), Harper, 1973, 2nd edition, Arte Pblico, 1986.
(And illustrator) *El Bronx Remembered: A Novella and Stories,* Harper, 1975, 2nd edition, Arte Público, 1986.
In Nueva York (short story collection), Dial, 1977.
(And illustrator) *Felita* (novel), Dial, 1979.
Going Home (novel; sequel to *Felita*), Dial, 1986.

OTHER

Rituals of Survival: A Women's Portfolio (adult fiction), Arte Público, 1985.

Also author, with Ray Blanco, of "The Artist," a screenplay. Contributor of stories to textbooks and anthologies, including *The Ethnic American Woman: Problems, Protests, Lifestyles,* edited by Edith Blicksilver. Contributor of short stories to *Children's Digest, Scholastic Magazine,* and *Nuestro.* Member of board of contributing editors of *Nuestro.*

WORK IN PROGRESS: A novel; a screenplay.

SIDELIGHTS: Nicholasa Mohr is the author of young adult novels and short stories that offer what reviewers consider realistic and uncompromising portraits of life in New York's Puerto Rican barrio. In *Nilda,* Mohr's first novel, the author portrays a Puerto Rican girl as she grows from a child to a teenager, posing the question, "what does it feel like being poor and belonging to a despised minority?" according to *New York Times Book Review* contributor Marilyn Sachs, who found that although several books for young people have attempted to explore this condition, "few come up to 'Nilda' in describing the crushing humiliations of poverty and in peeling off the ethnic wrappings so that we can see the human child underneath." Another article in the *New York Times Book Review* notes that *Nilda* "provides a sharp, candid portrayal of what it means to be poor and to be called 'spics,' 'animals,' 'you people'—and worse."

Mohr's subsequent story collections, *El Bronx Remembered* and *In Nueva York,* have afforded similar insight into the lives of Hispanics in New York City. Sachs offers this assessment of *El Bronx Remembered:* "If there is any message . . . in these stories, any underlying theme, it is that life goes on. But Nicholasa Mohr is more interested in people than in messages." The reviewer notes that the stories are without "complicated symbolism . . . , trendy obscurity of meaning . . . hopeless despair or militant ethnicity. Her people endure because they are people."

Sachs adds: "Some of them suffer, some of them die, a few of them fail, but most of the time they endure."

BIOGRAPHICAL/CRITICAL SOURCES:

BOOKS

Contemporary Literary Criticism, Volume 12, Gale, 1980.

PERIODICALS

Newsweek, March 4, 1974.
New York Times Book Review, November 4, 1973, November 10, 1974, November 16, 1975, May 22, 1977.

*   *   *

MOLINA, Enrique 1910-

PERSONAL: Born 1910, near Buenos Aires, Argentina.

CAREER: Poet. Worked as a sailor in the Argentine merchant marine.

WRITINGS:

Las cosas y el delirio (con un dibujo del autor) (poetry), Editorial Sudamericana, 1941.
Pasiones terrestres, Emecé Editores, 1946.
Amantes antípodas (also see below), Losada, 1961.
Monzón Napalm: Ocho poemas, Ediciones Sunda, 1968.
Una sombra donde sueña Camila O'Gorman, Losada, 1973.
Amantes antípodas y otros poemas, selected by André Coyné, Editorial Llibres de Sinera, 1974.
Obra poética, Monte Avila, 1978.
Los últimos soles, Editorial Sudamericana, 1980.
Alta marea y otros poemas, Centro Editor de América Latina, 1983.
Hotel Pájaro, Centro Editor de América Latina, 1983.
Páginas de Enrique Molina, Celtica, 1983.
Una sombra donde sueña Camila O'Gorman y otros textos, Corregidor, 1984.
Obra completa, Corregidor, Volume 1: *Prosa,* 1984, Volume 2: *Obra poética,* 1987.
El ala de la gaviota, Dirección de Difusión Cultural, Departamento Editorial (Mexico), 1985.

Also author of *Costumbres errantes; o, La redondez de la tierra,* 1951, *Fuego libre,* 1962, and *Las bellas furias,* 1966.

*   *   *

MONCLOVA, Lidio Cruz
See CRUZ MONCLOVA, Lidio

*   *   *

MONEGAL, Emir Rodríguez
See RODRIGUEZ MONEGAL, Emir

*   *   *

MONTERROSO, Augusto 1921-

PERSONAL: Born in 1921 in Guatamala; immigrated to Mexico.

AWARDS, HONORS: El Aguila Azteca, 1989.

WRITINGS:

Monterroso (lectures and essays), compiled by Jorge Ruffinelli, Centro de Investigaciones Lingüístico-Literarias, Universidad Veracruzana, 1976.

La oveja negra y demás fábulas, Seix Barral, 1981.
Movimiento perpetuo, Seix Barral, 1981.
Obras completas (y otros cuentos) (short stories), Seix Barral, 1981.
Mr. Taylor and Co., Ciudad de la Habana, 1982.
Lo demás es silencio: La vida y la obra de Eduardo Torres, Seix Barral, 1982.
Viaje al centro de la fábula, M. Casillas, 1982.
La palabra mágica, Era, 1983.
Las ilusiones perdidas, Fondo de Cultura Económica, 1985.
Der Frosch, der ein richtiger Frosch ein Wollte, Reclam, 1986.
La letra e, Era, 1987.

Also author of *Estado religioso y la santidad,* 1967—.

*   *   *

MONTES de OCA, Marco Antonio 1932-

PERSONAL: Born August 3, 1932, in Mexico City, Mexico; son of David Montes de Oca (a general) and Mercedes Fernández Austri (a deputy); married Ana Luisa Vega Gleason (a translator), 1956; children: Mercedes, Alejandra, Gabriela, Ana Luisa. *Education:* Attended University of Mexico, 1950-54.

ADDRESSES: Home—Filosofía y Letras 52, Copilco Universidad, Mexico, 20 D.F., Mexico. *Office*—Coordinación de Humanidades, Torre 2 de Humandidades, Ciudad Universitaria, Mexico, 20 D.F., Mexico. *Agent*—Carmen Balcells, Diagonal 580, Barcelona 21, Spain.

MEMBER: Latin-American Community of Writers, PEN of Mexico (founder; secretary, 1968—), Association of Writers of Mexico (vice-president, 1974-75; president, 1975-78).

AWARDS, HONORS: Premio Xavier Villarrutia for *Delante de la luz cantan los pájaros,* 1959; grants from Fondo de Cultura Económica, 1963-64, and Guggenheim Foundation, 1967-68 and 1970-71; Premio Mazatlán, 1966.

WRITINGS:

POETRY, EXCEPT AS NOTED

Ruina de la infame Babilonia (title means "The Downfall of the Infamous Babylon"), Stylo (Mexico), 1953.
Contrapunto de la fe (title means "Faith Counterpoint"), Los Presentes (Mexico), 1955.
Pliego de testimonios (title means "List of Testimonies"), Metafora (Mexico), 1956.
Delante de la luz cantan los pájaros (title means "Before the Light, the Birds Sing"; includes, in Spanish, the poem later published in translation as "On the Ruins of Babylon With Teiresias"; also see below), Fondo de Cultura Económica (Mexico), 1959.
Cantos al sol que no se alcanza (title means "Songs to the Sun Out of Reach"), Fondo de Cultura Económica, 1961.
Fundación del entusiasmo (title means "Foundation of Enthusiasm"), Universidad Nacional Autónoma de México, 1963.
On the Ruins of Babylon With Teiresias, translation by Rolf Hennequel, Wattle Grove Press (Australia), 1964.
La parcela en el Edén (title means "A Parcel in Eden"), Ediciones Pájaro Cascabel, 1964.
Vendemia del juglar (title means "Minstrel's Vintage"), Ediciones Joaquín Mortiz (Mexico), 1965.
Las fuentes legendarias (title means "Legendary Fountains"), Ediciones Joaquín Mortiz, 1966.
Marco Antonio Montes de Oca (autobiographical essay), Empresas Editoriales (Mexico), 1967.

Pedir el fuego (title means "To Ask for Fire"), Ediciones Joaquín Mortiz, 1968.
Poesía reunida (title means "Selected Poetry"), Fondo de Cultura Económica, 1971.
Astillas (title means "Splinters"), Ediciones Villa Miseria (Mexico), 1973.
(Editor and author of introduction) *El surco y la brasa* (title means "The Furrow and the Live Coal"), Fondo de Cultura Económica, 1974.
Se llama como quieras (title means "It's Called As You Wish"), Universidad Nacional Autónoma de México, 1974.
Lugares donde el espacio cicatriza (title means "Places Where the Space Heals"), Ediciones Joaquín Mortiz, 1974.
(Compiler) *Poesía, crimen y prisión* (anthology; title means "Poetry, Crime, and Prison"), Ediciones de la Secretaria de Gobernación (Mexico), 1976.
Las constelaciones secretas (title means "Secret Constellations"), Fondo de Cultura Económica, 1976.
En honor de las palabras (title means "In Honor of Words"), Ediciones Joaquín Mortiz, 1979.
The Heart of the Flute (bilingual volume, including manuscript in original Spanish under title "El corazón de la flauta"), translation by Laura Villaseñor, with introduction by Octavio Paz, International Poetry Forum, 1978, reissued with introduction by the author, Ohio University Press, 1980.
Comparacencias, Seix-Barral (Barcelona), 1980.
Delante de la luz cantan los pájaros (collected poems, 1953-68), Plaza y Janés (Barcelona), 1980.
Twenty-one Poems, Latin American Literary Review Press, 1982.
Cuenta nueva y otros poemas (title means "New Account"), Ediciones Martin Casillas (Mexico), 1983.
Migraciones y vísperas, Oasis, 1983.
Tablero de orientaciones (title means "Director's Board"), Premiá (Mexico), 1984.
Antología de poemas breves, Joaquín Mortiz, 1986.
Vaivén, Joaquín Mortiz, 1986.
Pedir el fuego (collected poems), Joaquín Mortiz, 1987.

SIDELIGHTS: Marco Antonio Montes de Oca, according to Manuel Duran in a *World Literature Today* review, "has become by the sheer weight of his production . . . as well as for the high quality of his style, one of the leaders of the new generation in Mexico." His poetry is characterized by surrealistic techniques, including automatic writing, subconscious associations, complex symbols, metaphors, and, what Duran referred to in *Books Abroad* as "verbal fireworks."

Montes de Oca told *CA:* "In my poems, automatic writing is allied with directed writing in a technique of counterpoint to produce a double presence of chance and planned images, of freely formed and vigorously conceived concepts. Using this procedure, I have constructed—through my poetry—a testimony of gratitude, praise, and homage to the gods, to men, and to all things. Everything I have written is submerged in this univocal theme."

BIOGRAPHICAL/CRITICAL SOURCES:

PERIODICALS

Books Abroad, winter, 1972, autumn, 1975.
Times Literary Supplement, June 6, 1968.
World Literature Today, spring, 1981.

MONTOYA, José 1932-

PERSONAL: Born May 28, 1932, on a ranch near Escoboza, N.M.; parents employed as migrant and factory workers; married; children: six. *Education:* Attended City College in San Diego; California College of Arts and Crafts, B.A., 1962; received M.A.

ADDRESSES: Home—2119 D St., Sacramento, Calif. 95816. *Office*—California State University, Sacramento, Sacramento, Calif. 95819.

CAREER: High school teacher in Wheatland, Calif.; currently associate professor of art, California State University, Sacramento; painter. Art exhibited at California State University, Sacramento, 1972, Galeria de la Raza, San Francisco, University of New Mexico, Las Cruces, Yuba College, Three Seater Art Gallery, Berkeley, Calif., Beale Air Force Base Art Center, Mexican American Library, Oakland, Calif., Roseville Cultural Center, and Casa Hispana, San Francisco, all 1973. *Military service:* U.S. Navy; served as mine sweeper in Korea.

MEMBER: Central American Economics Association, National Art Education Association, Mexican American Art Liberation Front, Rebel Chicano Art Front (founder), California Concilios for the Spanish Speaking (member of state association, secretary), Sacramento Concilio (president of board, 1974), Mexican Concilio for Yuba-Sutter Counties, Marysville (founder).

AWARDS, HONORS: Best in Show Award, Marysville Mid-Valley Annual; honorable mention, Jack London Art Festival; second place in oils, Chico Northern California Annual; third prize in graphics, First Annual Casa Hispana, 1968; co-recipient of grant from California State University, Sacramento, to write article on Barrio Art.

WRITINGS:

El sol y los de abajo and Other RCAF Poems (bound with *Oración a la mano poderosa,* by Alejandro Murguía), Ediciones Pocho-Che (San Francisco), 1972.
Cultural and Ethnic Awareness Manual for Professionals Working with Mexican-American Migrant Families, The Council (Laredo, Tex.), 1980.

Poetry has been anthologized in *El Espejo: An Anthology of Mexican American Writers,* Quinto Sol, 1969, and *Festival de Flor y Canto: An Anthology of Chicano Literature,* edited by Alurista and others, University of Southern California Press, 1976. Contributor to *Nation, El Bonce,* and *Sacramento State Hornet.*

WORK IN PROGRESS: Fourth grade history book, edited by Duane Campbell, for Mexican American Project, Curriculum Library, California State University-Sacramento; volume of poetry with artist Esteban Villa, for La Causa.

SIDELIGHTS: A painter and poet who writes simultaneously in Spanish and English, José Montoya grew up in a barrio in Albuquerque, New Mexico, where few choices existed for its occupants. As he told Juan Bruce-Novoa for *Chicano Authors: Inquiry by Interview:* "In the barrio . . . the prison was about all you could look forward to. Peer pressure pushed you into activities that would eventually lead there. A lot of my partners either wound up in prison or O.D.'ed." He decided to try college and become an artist after serving with the Navy in the early 1950s. Montoya started as an evening student, then won a scholarship that allowed him to study full time. He became an associate professor and painter, and is now active with the Rebel Chicano Art Front in Sacramento, an artistic community that organizes readings and exhibitions.

Montoya feels prospects are bright for Chicano literature. He also told Bruce-Novoa: "I see the future as tremendously exciting, not just in terms of materials and technique, but in the fact there will be a place for Chicano literature. . . . We're not talking about Mexican literature or Mexican American literature; we're talking about something in the whole spectrum which is Chicano literature." Montoya continued, "Just like all the other major influences in literature, [it] will have an effect for all the other cultures. [Students are] going to have to study Chicano literature not because they're Chicanos but because it will be just as important to know the Chicano poets as it is for us to know the Russian short story writers or the French novelists. It's going to be there, distinctive and whole. It's happening."

BIOGRAPHICAL/CRITICAL SOURCES:

BOOKS

Bruce-Novoa, Juan, *Chicano Authors: Inquiry by Interview,* University of Texas Press, 1980.
Lomelí, Francisco A. and Donaldo W. Urioste, *Chicano Perspectives in Literature: A Critical and Annotated Bibliography,* Pajarito (Albuquerque, N.M.), 1976.

PERIODICALS

El Grito: Mexican American Journal of Contemporary Thought, summer, 1969.
Social Studies Review, summer, 1970.

* * *

MORA, Pat(ricia) 1942-

PERSONAL: Born January 19, 1942, in El Paso, Tex.; daughter of Raul Antonio (an optician) and Estella (a homemaker; maiden name, Delgado) Mora; married William H. Burnside, Jr., July 27, 1963 (divorced, 1981); married Vernon Lee Scarborough (an archaeologist), May 25, 1984; children: (first marriage) William, Elizabeth, Cecilia. *Education:* Texas Western College, B.A., 1963; University of Texas at El Paso, M.A., 1967. *Politics:* Democrat.

ADDRESSES: Home—6536 La Cadena, El Paso, Tex. 79912. *Office*—University of Texas at El Paso, El Paso, Tex. 79968-0500.

CAREER: El Paso Independent School District, El Paso, Tex., teacher, 1963-66; El Paso Community College, part-time instructor in English and communication, 1971-78; University of Texas at El Paso, part-time lecturer in English, 1979-81, assistant to vice president of academic affairs, 1981-88, director of University Museum, 1988—, assistant to president, 1988—. Member of literary advisory panel for Texas Commission on the Arts, 1987-88; poetry judge for Texas Institute of Letters, 1988. Host of radio show, "Voices: The Mexican-American in Perspective," on National Public Radio affiliate KTEP, 1983-84; gives presentations and poetry readings nationally and internationally.

MEMBER: Poetry Society of America, Academy of American Poets, Texas Institute of Letters.

AWARDS, HONORS: Creative writing award from National Association for Chicano Studies, 1983; *New America: Women Artists and Writers of the Southwest* poetry award, 1984; Harvey L. Johnson Book Award from Southwest Council of Latin American Studies, 1984; Southwest Book awards from Border Regional Library, 1985, for *Chants,* and 1987, for *Borders;* Kellogg National Fellowship, 1986-89; Leader in Education Award from El Paso Women's Employment and Education, Inc., 1987;

Chicano/Hispanic Faculty and Professional Staff Association Award, 1987, for outstanding contribution to the advancement of Hispanics at the University of Texas at El Paso; named to *El Paso Herald-Post* Writers Hall of Fame, 1988.

WRITINGS:

(Contributor) Sylvia Cavazos Peña, editor, *Revista Chicano-Riqueña: Kikiriki/Children's Literature Anthology,* Arte Público, 1981.
Chants (poems), Arte Público, 1984.
Borders (poems), Arte Público, 1986.
(Contributor) Peña, editor, *Tun-Ta-Ca-Tun* (children's literature anthology), Arte Público, 1986.

Also author of *Tomás and the Library Lady,* 1989. Work represented in anthologies, including *New Worlds of Literature,* Norton, and *Woman of Her Word: Hispanic Women Write.*

Contributor of articles and stories to periodicals, including *Hispanics in the United States: An Anthology of Creative Literature, New America: Women Artists and Writers of the Southwest, Kalliope: A Journal of Women's Art,* and *Calyx.*

WORK IN PROGRESS: Journeys, a book of poems; and *Angles,* a collection of essays.

SIDELIGHTS: Pat Mora told *CA:* "For a variety of complex reasons, anthologized American literature does not reflect the ethnic diversity of the United States. I write, in part, because Hispanic perspectives need to be part of our literary heritage; I want to be part of that validation process. I also write because I am fascinated by the pleasure and power of words."

* * *

MORAGA, Cherríe 1952-

PERSONAL: Born September 25, 1952, in Whittier, Calif.; daughter of Joseph Lawrence and Elvira Moraga. *Education:* Received B.A., 1974; San Francisco State University, M.A., 1980.

ADDRESSES: Home—c/o P.O. Box 3312, Santa Rosa, Calif. 95402-3312. *Office*—Chicano Studies Department, University of California, 3404 Dwinelle Hall, Berkeley, Calif. 94720.

CAREER: High school English teacher in Los Angeles, Calif., mid-1970s; Kitchen Table/Women of Color Press, New York, N.Y., co-founder and administrator, beginning in 1981; INTAR (Hispanic-American arts center), New York City, playwright in residence, 1984; University of California, Berkeley, part-time writing instructor, 1986—; writer.

AWARDS, HONORS: American Book Award from Before Columbus Foundation, 1986, for *This Bridge Called My Back: Writings by Radical Women of Color.*

WRITINGS:

(Editor with Gloria Anzaldúa, and contributor) *This Bridge Called My Back: Writings by Radical Women of Color,* Persephone Press, 1981, revised bilingual edition (edited with Ana Castillo) published as *Esta puente, mi espalda: Voces de mujeres tercermundistas en los Estados Unidos,* Spanish translation by Castillo and Norma Alarcón, ISM Press, 1988.
Loving in the War Years: Lo que nunca pasó por sus labios (poetry and essays; subtitle means "What Never Passed Her Lips"), South End Press, 1983.

(Editor with Alma Gómez and Mariana Romo-Carmona) *Cuentos: Stories by Latinas,* Kitchen Table/Women of Color Press, 1983.
Giving Up the Ghost: Teatro in Two Acts (two-act play; first produced as stage reading in Minneapolis at At the Foot of the Mountain theater, June 16, 1984; produced in Seattle at Front Room Theater, March 27, 1987; revised version produced in San Francisco at Mission Cultural Center, April 5, 1987), West End Press, 1986.
"Heroes and Saints" (two-act play), first produced in Los Angeles at Los Angeles Theatre Lab, 1989.

Also author of two-act plays "La extranjera," 1985, and "Shadow of a Man," 1988.

WORK IN PROGRESS: Dreaming of Other Planets, a collection of poems.

SIDELIGHTS: Through her writing, Cherríe Moraga explores her identity as a Chicana, a feminist, and a lesbian. By publicly addressing each of these aspects of herself, noted Yvonne Yarbro-Bejarano in her *Dictionary of Literary Biography* essay, Moraga speaks for feminists and lesbians within the Chicano culture, and for Chicanas within the larger American culture, who have not spoken or cannot speak for themselves; she "has given voice and visibility in Chicano writing to those who have been silenced." In addition to writing her own poetry, plays, and essays, Moraga has co-edited two collections of women's writings, and in 1981 she helped found Kitchen Table/Women of Color Press, which is devoted to publishing the works of minority women.

Moraga's first collection, *Loving in the War Years: Lo que nunca pasó por sus labios,* was published in 1983. It includes the poem "For the Color of My Mother," which explores the relationship between the light-skinned writer and her darker-skinned Chicana mother (the author's father is Anglo-American), and the essay "A Long Line of Vendidas," which interprets the sexuality of Chicanas in terms of their cultural identity. The essay describes women's subordination within Chicano culture and explains that women are raised to place men's needs before their own. Chicanas—whether heterosexual or homosexual—must resist this tendency, Moraga writes, and must instead emphasize their own needs. This assertion "is not separatist," according to Yarbro-Bejarano, "but woman-centered. Chicana feminism means putting women first." The reviewer called "A Long Line of Vendidas" "a cornerstone text in the development of a Chicana feminist analysis of sexuality and gender."

Moraga's plays, like her other writings, often illustrate Chicano themes from a feminist perspective. *Giving Up the Ghost,* for example, which was produced and published during the mid-1980s, consists of poetic monologues spoken by two women at different points in their lives. The characters, speaking a mixture of Spanish and English, recall the oppressive forces that have damaged their perceptions of themselves as women. One character, Marisa, has tried to cope with being raped—and with society's general disrespect for women—by assuming male attitudes and characteristics. The other woman, Amalia, has become emotionally lifeless from repressing her feelings, which she often finds too painful. For a time the women comfort each other by becoming lovers, but that relationship does not last. Each woman nonetheless gains something from the relationship, as Yarbro-Bejarano notes. Amalia once again allows herself to feel for another person, and Marisa learns to love and respect women after allowing herself to be loved.

Although Moraga has received considerable praise for her own writings, she probably remains best known for editing, with Gloria Anzaldúa, the 1981 anthology *This Bridge Called My Back: Writings by Radical Women of Color.* The collection of poetry, fiction, essays, letters, and other forms of writing addresses the differences as well as the similarities between feminist women, touching on such subjects as skin color, class, and sexual identity. "From this painful probing," observed Barbara Baracks in *Voice Literary Supplement,* "emerges mutual respect far firmer than bland generalizations of sisterhood." Sara Mandelbaum, writing in *Ms.,* praised the book for demonstrating that women can more truthfully communicate and more securely unite if they acknowledge, rather than ignore, their differences. "*This Bridge,*" she assessed, "marks a commitment of women of color to their *own* feminism—a movement based not on separatism but on coalition." Mandelbaum concluded, "*This Bridge* not only utterly challenged me, but it filled me with greater hope for feminism than I had felt in a long time."

BIOGRAPHICAL/CRITICAL SOURCES:

BOOKS

Dictionary of Literary Biography, Volume 82: *Chicano Writers, First Series,* Gale, 1989.

PERIODICALS

Ms., March, 1982.
Voice Literary Supplement, October, 1981.

* * *

MORALES, Alejandro 1944-

PERSONAL: Born October 14, 1944, in Montebello, Calif. *Education:* California State College, Los Angeles (now California State University), B.A.; Rutgers University, M.A., 1971, Ph.D., 1975.

ADDRESSES: Office—Department of Spanish and Portuguese, University of California, Irvine, Calif. 92715.

CAREER: Novelist. University of California, Irvine, professor of Latin American and Chicano literature, 1975—. Member, Yale Project of Chicano Writers.

AWARDS, HONORS: Ford Foundation fellowship, 1972-73; ITT International fellowship, 1973-74; first novel, *Caras viejas y vino nuevo,* was a finalist in a literary contest sponsored by Mexica Press, 1975.

WRITINGS:

Caras viejas y vino nuevo, Joaquín Mortiz (México), 1975 (translation by Max Martinez, edited and revised by J. Monleon-Alurista, published as *Old Faces and New Wine,* Maize Press [San Diego, Calif.], 1981).
La verdad sin voz, Joaquín Mortiz, 1979 (translation by Judith Ginsberg published as *Death of an Anglo,* Bilingual Press [Tempe, Ariz.], 1988).
Reto en el paraíso, Bilingual Press/Bilingüe (Ypsilanti, Mich.), 1982.
El proyecto del Código penal; Sus grandes lineamientos, sus detalles: Colección de artículos publicados en el diario "La Industria," Tip. Olaya (Trujillo, Dominican Republic), 1985.
The Brick People, Arte Público, 1988.

SIDELIGHTS: Novelist and educator Alejandro Morales grew up in the Chicano *barrios* of Los Angeles. Youngest of five children born to parents originally from Guanajato, Mexico, Mora-

les was educated in the public schools of California and was active in the sociopolitical movements of the 1960s. Concentrating his graduate studies at Rutgers University on Spanish language and literature, he has taught Latin American and Chicano literature at the University of California, Irvine, since 1975. And in structurally complex and stylistically innovative novels, he documents his Chicano culture from a variety of perspectives.

Morales's first novel, *Caras viejas y vino nuevo,* was a finalist in a literary contest sponsored by its publisher. Drawing heavily upon his early background in the *barrios,* Morales profiles both positive and negative aspects of that experience. Its protagonist and narrator, an intelligent and idealistic young man from a stable, extended family, provides a lens through which the reader is sympathetically introduced to the more volatile and destructive elements of *barrio* life. Morales's second novel, *La verdad sin voz,* employs a multitude of intersecting perspectives to reveal the Chicano experience outside the *barrio* with discrimination and governmental manipulation. And Morales's third novel, *Reto en el paraíso,* steps back for a larger, more historical perspective to present a story about the development of a Spanish-Mexican land grant in California and those associated with it.

BIOGRAPHICAL/CRITICAL SOURCES:

BOOKS

Dictionary of Literary Biography, Volume 82: *Chicano Writers,* Gale, 1989.
Lomelí, Francisco A., and Donaldo W. Urioste, *Chicano Perspectives in Literature: A Critical and Annotated Bibliography,* Pajarito Publications (Albuquerque, N.M.), 1976.
Rodríguez del Pino, Salvador, *La novela chicana escrita en español: Cinco autores comprometidos,* Bilingual Press/Bilingüe, 1982.
Tatum, Charles, *A Selected and Annotated Bibliography of Chicano Studies,* University of Kansas Press, 1976.

PERIODICALS

Bilingual Review/Revista Bilingüe, January-August, 1977, September-December, 1982.
Books Abroad, autumn, 1976.
Cambio, January-March, 1977.
Caracol, July, 1977.
Chasqui, November, 1976.
Cuadernos Americanos, Volume 39, number 4, 1980.
Cuadernos Hispanoamericanos, June, 1976.
La Palabra y el Hombre, Number 17, 1976.
Latin American Literary Review, Volume 7, number 10, 1977, Volume 7, number 14, 1979.
Los Angeles Times Book Review, September 18, 1988.
Maize, fall-winter, 1980-81.
Nation, November 14, 1988.
Revista Chicano-Riqueña, fall, 1980.
Siempre, March 31, 1976.

* * *

MORALES, Angel Luis 1919-

PERSONAL: Born January 13, 1919, in Culebra, Puerto Rico; son of Angel Pablo (a police officer) and Eulalia (Couvertier) Morales; married María Luisa Ortiz (an associate professor of Spanish), February 9, 1945; children: María de Lourdes (Mrs. Carlos Paralatici). *Education:* University of Puerto Rico, B.A. (education; cum laude), 1941, M.A., 1943; University of Madrid, Ph.D., 1951.

ADDRESSES: *Home*—Alda St., 1575, Urb. Caribe, Río Piedras, P.R. 00926. *Office*—Department of Hispanic Studies, University of Puerto Rico, Río Piedras, P.R. 00931.

CAREER: University of Puerto Rico, Río Piedras, instructor, 1943-47, assistant professor, 1947-53, associate professor, 1953-58, professor of Spanish-American literature, 1958-74, professor emeritus, 1974—, chairman of department of Hispanic studies, 1970-74.

MEMBER: Instituto Internacional de Literatura Iberoamericana, Modern Language Association of America, Asociación de Maestros de Puerto Rico, American Association of University Professors, Sociedad Bolivariana, Ateneo Puertorriqueño, Asociación de Profesores Universitarios (University of Puerto Rico).

AWARDS, HONORS: Medal of Honor, Fajardo High School (Puerto Rico), 1937; Martí Prize for outstanding work in the field of Spanish-American literature, 1941; scholarship from Ministerio de Relaciones Exteriores de España, 1950-51; Cervantes Prize for studies on Quijote.

WRITINGS:

(Editor and author of introduction) *Antología de Jesús María Lago* (title means "An Anthology of Jesús María Lago"), Ateneo Puertorriqueño, 1960.

(With José Ferrer Canales, James Willis Robb, Luis Leal, and Alfredo Roggiano) *Homenaje a Alfonso Reyes* (title means "In Homage of Alfonso Reyes"), Editorial Cultura, 1965.

Literatura hispanoamericana: Epocas y figuras (title means "Spanish American Literature: Epochs and Authors"), two volumes, Editorial del Departamento de Instrucción Pública, Estado Libre Asociado de Puerto Rico, 1967.

Dos ensayos rubendarianos (title means "Two Essays on Rubén Darío"), Biblioteca de Extramuros, Universidad de Puerto Rico, 1969.

La naturaleza venezolana en la obra de Rómulo Gallegos (title means "Venezuelan Nature in the Work of Romulo Gallegos"), Editorial del Departmento de Instrucción Pública, Estado Libre Asociado de Puerto Rico, 1969.

(Contributor) *El festival Rubén Darío en Puerto Rico* (title means "Rubén Darío Festival in Puerto Rico"), Recinto Universitario de Mayaguez, 1971.

Introducción a la literatura hispanoamericana, Edil (Río Piedras, P.R.), 1974.

Letras de Hispanoamérica (criticism), Edil, 1982.

Contributor to professional journals, including *Asomante, Pedagogía, Duquesne Review,* and *Extramuros.*

WORK IN PROGRESS: *Estudios literarios hispanoamericanos;* an anthology, *El cuento hispanoamericano.*

* * *

MORALES, Jorge Luis 1930-

PERSONAL: Born October 27, 1930 (one source says 1932), in Ciales, Puerto Rico; son of Rafael Morales Rubero (a writer) and Julia González González (a writer); married María Socorro Villalobos (an executive secretary), September 17, 1954; children: Jorge Luis, Rubén Shelley, Alga Solange. *Education:* University of Puerto Rico, B.A. (cum laude), 1951, M.A., 1963; University of Madrid, Ph.D., 1965.

ADDRESSES: *Office*—Department of Spanish Language and Literature, University of Puerto Rico, Río Piedras, Puerto Rico.

CAREER: Writer. Secondary school teacher, radio host, and school administrator in Puerto Rico, 1951-57; University of

Puerto Rico, Río Piedras, professor of Spanish language and literature, 1957-88, distinguished poet-in-residence, 1988—. Editor for Editorial Universitaria, 1959—; founder and president of Editorial ASOL. Founder and director of Instituto Nacional de Bellas Letras in Puerto Rico, beginning in 1981.

AWARDS, HONORS: First National Literature Awards from Puerto Rican Institute of Literature, 1960, for *La ventana y yo,* 1975, for *Nueva antología poética,* 1980, for *Alfonso Reyes y la literatura española,* and 1983, for *Salvado margen;* Gold Medal from Mexico's Cultural Olympiads, 1968, for "Los ríos redimidos"; Puerto Rican Award and Honor Medal, both from Arts and Sciences Academy of Puerto Rico; Manuel Alonso Award, 1980; numerous honorary degrees.

WRITINGS:

Metal y piedra: Poemas, 1949-1951 (poetry), Imprenta Soltero, 1952.

Mirada en el olvido, Orfeo, 1953.

Inspiración del viaje, Ediciones de Repertorio Americano, 1953.

Decir del propio ser (poetry), Las Américas, 1954.

La ventana y yo, Editorial Universitaria, Universidad de Puerto Rico, 1960, translation by Juan Duque published as *The Window and I,* Editorial ASOL, 1981.

Acto poético, Facultad de Estudios Generales, Universidad de Puerto Rico, 1961.

Journada precisa, Ediciones Rumbos, 1962, 2nd Edition, Ediciones Juan Ponce de León, 1963.

Discurso a los pájaros, Colección Moriviví, 1965, translation by Pedro Juan Duque published as *Address to the Birds,* Editorial ASOL, 1981.

Antología poética, Editorial Universidad de Puerto Rico, 1968, 2nd edition published as *Nuevo antología poética,* 1975.

Los ríos redimidos, Editorial Universitaria, Universidad de Puerto Rico, 1969.

(Editor) *Las cien mejores poesías líricas de Puerto Rico,* Editorial Edil, 1973.

España en Alfonso Reyes, Editorial Universitaria, Universidad de Puerto Rico, 1976.

(Editor) *Poesía afroantillana y negrista,* Editorial Universitaria, Universidad de Puerto Rico, 1976, revised edition, 1981.

Buho entre ruinas, Editorial ASOL, 1976.

Libertad por la poesía, Colegio Regional de Cayey, 1976.

Albores del pensamiento religioso en Grecia, Universidad de Puerto Rico, Revista La Torre, c. late 1970s.

Alfonso Reyes y la literatura española, Editorial Universitaria, Universidad de Puerto Rico, 1980.

Tiempo y fábula, Editorial ASOL, 1980.

Alto en ventana, Editorial ASOL, 1981.

Pura nieve, Editorial ASOL, 1981.

Estación del canto, Editorial ASOL, 1981.

Frente a las cosas, Editorial ASOL, 1981.

De la tormenta y el rayo, Editorial ASOL, 1981.

Sea de todos, Editorial ASOL, 1981.

La poesía salva y lecciones de teoría poética, Editorial ASOL, 1983.

Salvado margen, Editorial ASOL, 1983.

Estas en mí, Editorial ASOL, 1983.

Also author of *Constancia lírica de la mujer puertorriqueña,* Editorial Universitaria, Universidad de Puerto Rico, *Poetas extranjeros en la Universidad de Puerto Rico,* Editorial Universitaria, Universidad de Puerto Rico, *Teoría del poema,* Editorial ASOL, *Medida libertad,* Editorial ASOL, *Del sentir moriviví,* Editorial

ASOL, *Historia de mis libros,* Editorial ASOL, and *Marina arzola,* Editorial ASOL, all published in 1980s.

Author of columns, including "Alfabeto y abaco," 1970, and "Desde mi biblioteca" in *El Vocero,* 1979. Contributor to periodicals, including *Revista del Instituto de Cultura Puertorriqueña, Asomante,* and *El Mundo.* Editor for periodicals, including *La Torre* and *PLERUS.*

WORK IN PROGRESS: Manuel joglar cacho, for Editorial ASOL; *Jorge Luis Morales: Una jornada precisa; El río y los mares* (title means "The River and the Seas"), an eight-hundred-page poem; *Sartoria labor,* a one-thousand-page history of humankind; *Obelisco,* a poetry collection; *Poetría* (title means "Religion of Poetry"); *Ontiatría* (title means "Medicine of the Self Itself"), a treatise on medicine; two novels; a short story collection; various other volumes.

SIDELIGHTS: Jorge Luis Morales is widely regarded as Puerto Rico's greatest poet in the years since World War II, and his poetry, though frequently specific in its concerns with Puerto Rican life, is considered generally accessible in its depictions of modern life.

* * *

MORALES CARRION, Arturo 1913-1989

PERSONAL: Born November 16, 1913, in Havana, Cuba; died of cancer, June 28, 1989, in San Juan, P.R.; son of Arturo and Agripina (Carrión) Morales; married Inés Arandes; children: Arturo, Edgardo, Inés. *Education:* University of Puerto Rico, B.A., 1935; University of Texas, M.A., 1936; Columbia University, Ph.D., 1950. *Politics:* Democrat. *Religion:* Roman Catholic.

CAREER: University of Puerto Rico, Río Piedras, instructor in history, 1936-38, assistant professor of history, 1944-46, chairman of department, 1946-52, director of history research center and Latin American seminar, 1970-73, president of the university, 1973-79. U.S. Department of State, Washington, D.C., member of cultural affairs office staff, 1939-44, deputy assistant secretary of state for Latin American affairs, 1961-63; Commonwealth of Puerto Rico, San Juan, under secretary of state, 1953-60; special adviser to secretary general of Organization of American States, 1964-69. Visiting lecturer at Columbia University, 1947-49; affiliated with George Washington University's Center for International Studies. Member of U.S. delegation to inter-American conferences, 1954-63; member of Linowitz Commission of U.S.-Latin-American Relations, 1974-77; executive director of Puerto Rico Endowment for the Humanities, beginning in 1979.

MEMBER: Ateneo Puertorriqueño, American Council on Education (director beginning in 1977), National Association of State Universities and Land Grant Colleges (member of council of presidents, beginning in 1974), American History Association, American Academy of Political Science, Association of Caribbean Universities and Research Institutes, Peruvian Society of Geography and History, Franciscan Academy of History, Mexican Inter-American Academy, Puerto Rican Circle of Washington, D.C.

AWARDS, HONORS: Eugenio María de Hostos award from state of New York, 1962; awards from Institute of Puerto Rican Literature, 1968 and 1972; grant from National Foundation for the Humanities, 1972-73; LL.D. from Temple University, 1976.

WRITINGS:

(With Antonio Rivera) *La enseñanza de la historia en Puerto Rico,* [Mexico], 1953.

Historia del pueblo de Puerto Rico, desde sus orígenes hasta el siglo XVIII (juvenile), Departamento de Instrucción Pública, 1968.
Ojeada al proceso histórico y otros ensayos, Cordillera, 1971.
Puerto Rico and the Non-Hispanic Caribbean: A Study in the Decline of Spanish Exclusivism, 2nd edition, University of Puerto Rico Press, 1971.
Albores históricos del capitalismo en Puerto Rico, 2nd edition, University of Puerto Rico Press, 1972.
(With others) *Centenario de la abolición de la esclavitud,* University of Puerto Rico Press, 1973.
Testimonios de una gestión universitaria, University of Puerto Rico Press, 1978.
Auge y decadencia de la trata negrera en Puerto Rico, 1820-1860, Centro de Estudios Avanzados de Puerto Rico y el Caribe, Instituto de Cultura Puertorriqueña, 1978.
Puerto Rico: A Political and Cultural History, Norton, 1983.

Also author of *La revolución haitiana y el movimiento antiesclavista en Puerto Rico,* 1982; author of numerous published addresses and speeches. Member of editorial board of *Revista América.*

BIOGRAPHICAL/CRITICAL SOURCES:

PERIODICALS

New Republic, November 12, 1984.

OBITUARIES:

PERIODICALS

Chicago Tribune, July 2, 1989.
New York Times, June 30, 1989.

* * *

MORENO, Baldomero Fernández
See FERNANDEZ MORENO, Baldomero

* * *

MORENO, Carlos Martínez
See MARTINEZ MORENO, Carlos

* * *

MORENO, César Fernández
See FERNANDEZ MORENO, César

* * *

MORO, César 1903-1956
(Alfredo Quíspez Asín, César Quíspez Asín)

PERSONAL: Born in 1903 in Lima, Peru; died in 1956.

CAREER: Poet. Co-founder of Latin American surrealist journal *The Use of Words,* 1933.

WRITINGS:

Le chateau de grisou, Ediciones Tigrondine (Mexico), 1943.
Amor a mort, Le Cheval Marin (Paris), 1957, dual language edition, translation by Frances LeFevre, *Amor a mort/Love Till Death: Poems,* Vanishing Rotating Triangle Press (New York), 1973.
La tortuga ecuestre, y otros poemas, 1924-1949, Ediciones Tigrondine, 1957.
Los anteojos de asufre, [Lima], 1958.

Jesús-María, Calatrava, 1971.
Versiones del surrealismo, Tusquets, 1974.
The Scandalous Life of César Moro in His Own Words: Peruvian Surrealist Poetry, translated from the French and Spanish by Philip Ward, Oleander Press, 1976.
Antología esencial, Edocopmes Zendal (Lima), 1978.
(With André Breton and Wolfgang Paalen) *Exposición internacional del surrealismo, enero-febrero 1940,* Galería de Arte Mexicano, 1978.
Obra poética, Instituto Nacional de Cultura (Lima), 1980.

Also author of *Lettre d'amour,* 1944, *Trafalgar Square,* 1954, and *Pierre des soleils.*

BIOGRAPHICAL/CRITICAL SOURCES:

PERIODICALS

World Literature Today, summer, 1977.

*   *   *

MORTON, Carlos 1947-

PERSONAL: Born October 15, 1947, in Chicago, Ill.; son of Ciro (a non-commissioned army officer) and María Elena (López) Morton; married Azalea Marin, 1981; children: Seth Alexander Frack, Miguel Angel, Carlos Xuncú. *Education:* University of Texas, El Paso, B.A., 1975; University of California, San Diego, M.F.A., 1979; University of Texas at Austin, Ph.D., 1987.

ADDRESSES: Home—7931 Parral, El Paso, Tex. 79915. *Office*—Theatre Arts Department, University of California, Riverside, Calif. 92525.

CAREER: Essayist, poet, playwright, and actor, 1971—; *La Luz* magazine, Denver, Colo., associate editor, beginning 1975; University of California, Berkeley, lecturer, 1979-81; University of Texas at Austin, assistant instructor, 1981-85; University of California, Riverside, associate professor of theatre arts, 1990—. Instructor, Laredo Junior College, 1985-88. Playwright, San Francisco Mime Troupe, 1979-80. Artist-in-residence for California Arts Council and Texas Commission of the Arts.

WRITINGS:

White Heroin Winter (poetry), One Eye Press, 1971.
El Jardín (play), Quinto Sol, 1974.
Pancho Diablo (musical comedy), Tonatiuth International, 1976.
Las Many Muertes de Richard Morales, Tejidos, 1977.
The Many Deaths of Danny Rosales, and Other Plays, Arte Público Press, 1983.
Critical Responses to Zoot Suit and Corridos, University of Texas at El Paso, 1984.

Also author of unpublished plays, including: "The Foundling," "Desolation Car Lot," 1973, "Los Dorados," 1978, "Squash," 1979, "Rancho Hollywood," 1979, "Johnny Tenorio," 1983, "Malinche," 1985, "The Savior," 1986, (with Angel Vigil) "Cuentos," 1989, "The Miser of Mexico," 1989, and "At Risk," 1989. Contributor to *Drama Review, Nuestro, Caracol,* and other periodicals. Contributing editor, *Revista Chicano-Riqueña.*

SIDELIGHTS: Carlos Morton told *CA:* "I am working on recreating a viable reality for the colonized Chicano-Latino in the United States. Much of my work deals with stereotypes, both mythological and sociological, and my words are a mixture of English and Spanish.

"I am questioning stereotypes, especially in regards to the Latino here in the United States. For example, how could we explore the evolution of the infamous 'frito bandido' on stage? We would have to show the historical transition of the defeated soldier (Mexican) of the War of 1848 to that of the social Robin Hood bandits of the late 19th century (Juan Cortina and Jouquín Murieta) in Texas and California who carried on a type of guerrilla warfare against the Anglo colonizers in the Southwest. We would then have to switch to the Mexican Revolution (1910-1921) and the arrival of Pancho Villa and Emiliano Zapata who to the Mexican people are heros and standards of the Revolution, but who to the gringos were nothing more than 'bandits' and 'outlaws.' Throw in a dash of 'machismo' and a bit of the 'sleepy peon' and you got your modern day 'frito bandido.' "

*   *   *

MOYANO, Daniel 1930-

PERSONAL: Born in 1930 in Argentina.

CAREER: Writer.

AWARDS, HONORS: Sudamericana/*Primera plana* prize for fiction, 1968, for *El oscuro.*

WRITINGS:

Artistas de variedades (short stories), Assandri, 1960.
La lombriz (short stories), Nueve 64, 1964.
Una luz muy lejana (novel), Sudamericana, 1966.
El fuego interrumpido (short stories), Sudamericana, 1967.
El monstruo y otros cuentos (short stories), Centro Editor de América Latina, 1967.
El oscuro (novel), Sudamericana, 1968.
Mi música es para esta gente (short stories), Monte Avila (Caracas, Venezuela), 1970.
El estuche del cocodrilo (short stories), Ediciones del Sol, 1974.
El trino del diablo (novel), Sudamericana, 1974, translation by Giovanni Pontiero published as *The Devil's Trill,* Serpent's Tail (London), 1988.
El vuelo del tigre, Legasa, 1981.
La espera y otros cuentos (short stories), Centro Editor de América Latina, 1982.
Libro de navíos y borrascas, Legasa, 1983.

BIOGRAPHICAL/CRITICAL SOURCES:

PERIODICALS

Books Abroad, autumn, 1969.

*   *   *

MUJICA LAINEZ, Manuel 1910-1984

PERSONAL: Surname is pronounced "Moo-he-ka Ly-ness"; born September 11, 1910, in Buenos Aires, Argentina; died April 21, 1984, in Cruz Chica, Córdoba, Argentina; son of Manuel (a lawyer) and Lucía (Láinez) Mujica Farias; married Ana María de Alvear, November 5, 1936; children: Diego, Ana, Manuel Florencio. *Education:* Escuela Nacional de San Isidro, Buenos Aires, Argentina, B.A., 1928; studied law at University of Buenos Aires, 1928-30. *Politics:* Conservative. *Religion:* Roman Catholic.

ADDRESSES: Home—El Paraíso, 5178 Cruz Chica, Córdoba, Argentina; and O'Higgins 2150, Buenos Aires, Argentina.

CAREER: Novelist, short story writer, journalist, biographer, and art critic. *La Nación,* Buenos Aires, Argentina, staff member and critic, 1932-68; National Museum of Decorative Arts, Buenos Aires, secretary, 1935-45; Argentina Ministry of Foreign Relations, Buenos Aires, general director of cultural relations, 1955-58. *Military service:* Served in Argentine Navy; became commander.

MEMBER: Argentine Academy of Letters, National Academy of Fine Arts, Argentine Society of Writers (former vice-president).

AWARDS, HONORS: Argentine Society of Writers Grand Prize of Honor for Literature, 1955; Grand National Prize of Honor for Literature, 1962; First National Prize of Letters, 1963; John Kennedy Prize, 1964, for *Bomarzo;* Alberto Gerchunoff Prize; Forti Glori Prize.

WRITINGS:

NOVELS

Don Galaz de Buenos Aires (also see below), [Buenos Aires], 1938.
Los ídolos (also see below), Sudamericana (Buenos Aires), 1953.
La casa (also see below), Sudamericana, 1954, reprinted, 1984.
Los viajeros (also see below), Sudamericana, 1955, reprinted, 1984.
Invitados en El Paraíso (also see below), Sudamericana, 1957.
Bomarzo (also see below), Sudamericana, 1962, reprinted, 1979, English translation by Gregory Rabassa published under same title, Simon & Schuster, 1969.
El unicornio, Sudamericana, 1965, translation by Mary Fitton published as *The Wandering Unicorn,* Taplinger, 1982.
De milagros y de melancolías, Sudamericana, 1968.
Cecil (autobiographical), Sudamericana, 1972.
El laberinto, Sudamericana, 1974.
Sergio, Sudamericana, 1976.
Los cisnes, Sudamericana, 1977.
El escarabajo, Plaza & Janés, 1982.

Also author of *Hector Basaldúa,* 1956.

OTHER

Glosas castellanas (also see below), Librería y Editorial "La Facultad," Bernabé & Cia (Buenos Aires), 1936.
Miguel Cané (padre), C.E.P.A. (Buenos Aires), 1942.
Canto a Buenos Aires (long poem, also see below), Guillermo Kraft (Buenos Aires), 1943.
(Editor) *Poetas Argentinos en Montevideo,* Emecé (Buenos Aires), 1943.
Vida de Aniceto el Gallo (biography; also see below), Emecé, 1943, reprinted, Kapelusz (Buenos Aires), 1974.
(Author of introduction) Hilario Ascasubi, *Paulino Lucero,* Estrada (Buenos Aires), 1945.
Vida de Anastasio el Pollo (biography; also see below), Emecé, 1948.
(Author of introduction) Margarita Drago, *Figuras,* F. A. Colombo (Buenos Aires), 2nd edition, 1948.
Aquí vivieron: Historias de una quinta de San Isidro, 1583-1924 (short stories; also see below), Sudamericana, 1949, reprinted, 1979.
Misteriosa Buenos Aires (short stories; also see below), Sudamericana, 1951, reprinted, 1980.
(With Córdova Iturburu and Roger Pla) *Gambartes* (bilingual edition in Spanish and English), English translation by Patrick Orpen Dudgeon, Bonino's Gallery (Buenos Aires), 1954.
Victoria, 1884-1955, Bonino's Gallery, 1955.
Argentina, English translation by William McLeod Rivera, Pan American Union, 1961.
Russo (critical study), El Mangrullo (Buenos Aires), 1963.

(Compiler) *Lira romántica sudamericana,* new edition (Mujica Láinez was not associated with 1st edition), Emecé, 1964.
(Author of introduction) Oscar Hermes Villordo, *Oscar Hermes Villordo,* Culturales Argentinas (Buenos Aires), 1966.
Vidas del Gallo y el Pollo (biography), Centro Editor de América Latina, 1966.
"Bomarzo" (two-act opera; adapted by the author from his novel), music by Alberto Ginastera, first produced in Washington, D.C., May 19, 1967, published as *Cantata de Bomarzo: A Libretto,* with etchings by Luciano De Vita, Plain Wrapper Press (Verona), 1981.
Crónicas reales (short stories), Sudamericana, 1967.
(Contributor) *Cuentos recontados,* Tiempo Contemporáneo (Buenos Aires), 1968.
Cuentos de Buenos Aires (anthology), Huemul (Buenos Aires), 1972.
El viaje de los siete demonios, Sudamericana, 1974.
Antología general e introducción a la obra de Manuel Mujica Láinez, Felman (Madrid), 1976.
Letra e imagen de Buenos Aires, photographs by Aldo Sessa, Librería la Ciudad, 1977, reprinted as *Más letras e imágenes de Buenos Aires,* 1980.
Obras completas (title means "Complete Works"; contains *Glosas castellanas, Don Galaz de Buenos Aires, Miguel Cané (padre), Canto a Buenos Aires, Estampas de Buenos Aires, Cuatro poemas franceses, Vida de Aniceto el Gallo, Vida de Anastasio el Pollo, Cincuenta sonetos de Shakespeare, Aquí vivieron: Historias de una quinta de San Isidro, 1583-1924, Misteriosa Buenos Aires, Algunos poemas, 1940-1968, Los ídolos, La casa, Discurso en la Academia, Los viajeros, Miguel Carlos Victórica,* and *Invitados en El Paraíso*), Sudamericana, 1978.
El brazalete y otros cuentos (short stories), Sudamericana, 1978.
Los porteños (addresses, essays, and lectures), Librería la Ciudad, 1979.
El poeta perdido y otros relatos (short stories), edited and with an introduction by Jorge Cruz, Centro Editor de América Latina (Buenos Aires), 1981.
Jockey Club, un siglo, photographs by Sessa, Cosmogonías (Buenos Aires), 1982.
Páginas de Manuel Mujica Láinez, Celtia, 1982.
Nuestra Buenos Aires/Our Buenos Aires (bilingual edition in Spanish and English), photographs by Sessa, La Gaceta de Tucumán, 1982.
Placeres y fatigas de los viajes: Crónicas andariegas, Sudamericana, 1983.
Vida y gloria del Teatro Colón (in Spanish, with English, French, Italian, and German translations), photographs by Sessa, Cosmogonías (Buenos Aires), 1983.
Un novelista en el Museo del Prado, Sudamericana, 1984.
Cartas de Manuel Mujica Láinez (correspondences), collected by Oscar Monesterolo, Sudamericana, 1984.

SIDELIGHTS: During the 1960s and 1970s, a number of South American writers such as Gabriel García Márquez and Jorge Luis Borges came into international prominence. But another South American novelist, Manuel Mujica Láinez, remained a somewhat obscure author, despite his popularity in his native Argentina. Although critics recognized him for his skill as a writer, they also noticed that the works of Mujica Láinez were unique compared to other Hispanic writers of the time. As *New York Times Book Review* contributor David Gallagher remarked, Mujica Láinez's writing is "anachronistic" in that it is more reflective of "the modernist movement that flourished in the 1890's" than of more contemporary literature. John Walker also observed in *Queen's Quarterly* that "by style, temperament and cultural awareness, Mujica Láinez belongs to the European-ized, cosmopolitan aristocracy of the nineteenth century."

This is not to say, however, that the novelist's works completely ignore the contemporary problems of Argentina. Like García Márquez, one of Mujica Láinez's common themes was that of decay within his country's society. The four novels, *Los ídolos, La casa, Los viajeros,* and *Invitados en El Paraíso,* which together form the "Saga of Buenos Aires" tetralogy, concern the events in Argentina after World War II that led to the decline of the elite sector of the population. Decay is also the theme of *De mila-gros y de melancolías,* a novel about the deterioration of a fic-tional city. This novel was compared to García Márquez's *One Hundred Years of Solitude,* since both combine fantasy, reality, and satire to relate the history of a fictional city. Yet *De milagros y de melancolías* "received meager attention," according to George O. Schanzer, a *Latin America Literary Review* critic who surmised that this lack of notice occurred because Mujica Láinez's book was eclipsed by the enormous success of *One Hun-dred Years of Solitude.* But Schanzer asserted that *De milagros y de melancolías* "deserves to be better known" because it "lam-poons both foibles and traditions [of Latin America] . . . in a delightful, intelligently and artistically humorous way."

As Schanzer noted, *De milagros y de melancolías* was a "the-matic homecoming" for its author. The novels that proceeded it, *Bomarzo,* Mujica Láinez's best-known work, and *The Wander-ing Unicorn,* have European settings and concern broader themes such as love, art, and human values. These two novels, the only ones by Mujica Láinez as yet to be translated into En-glish, also share the device of immortal narrators who reflect back on the events of their lives centuries past with a contempo-rary perspective. In using this technique, the author's narrators have the advantage of employing modern interpretative tech-niques such as psychoanalysis to comment on the lives they led centuries before.

In *Bomarzo* Mujica Láinez's protagonist is a combination of the few known facts about Prince Pier Francesco Orsini, Duke of Bomarzo, who lived in sixteenth-century Italy, and the novelist's own imagination. Inspired by the bizarre stone statues of god-desses, demonic heads, and men being slain by elephants and gi-ants that Duke Orsini ordered constructed fifty miles north of Rome, Mujica Láinez reconstructed the duke as an immortal, but psychologically tortured hunchback. The story is thus told by a present day Duke Orsini, who tells the reader how, despite his intelligence and otherwise handsome features, he was re-jected by his family because of his hunchback. The stigmatiza-tion this deformity brings also leads to Duke Orsini's impotency. "Orsini's back is the burden of his genius," interpreted one *Time* critic. "It compels him to refine everything into art, including cruelty and murder." Developing this idea as the explanation for the statues at Bomarzo, Mujica Láinez "conveys not only the well-known creative energies of the Renaissance but its less un-derstood anxieties as well," the *Time* writer concluded.

Once a best-seller in Argentina, *Bomarzo* "is a skillful novel," in Gallagher's opinion. However, the reviewer also felt that the novel was a "slender" achievement because it catered too much to the sensationalist ingredients of a best-seller, such as exotic settings, larger-than-life characters, and sexual themes. David William Foster similarly believed that *Bomarzo* was "unlikely ever to be considered a great novel," although it is "one of the most memorable—and unusual—works of Argentine fiction in recent years."

Some critics also had doubts about the literary merit of Mujica Láinez's *The Wandering Unicorn.* A tale of fantasy, this novel

about the Middle Ages is filled with dragons, knights, fairies, and heroic battles woven into a tale told by the immortal fairy Melu-sine. She regales the reader with her story about the exploits of a knight named Aiol, with whom she is in love. However, be-cause she is an invisible spirit to him her love goes unreturned, and the narration ends tragically when Aiol dies and Melusine is unable to join him in Heaven. Although the novel "appears to be just a brilliant and imaginative exercise in the recreation of places and times of far away and long ago," said Walker, ac-knowledging the objections of some reviewers, "[the author's] treatment of the eternal themes of life and death, love and hate, mortality and immortality, and the search for values and ideals . . . transcends the geographical and chronological barriers to penetrate to the heart of the human condition."

Despite their merits, a number of critics doubted that *Bomarzo* and *The Wandering Unicorn* aspired to be anything more than popular fiction. *New York Times Book Review* contributor Ron-ald De Feo, for example, opined that in these works Mujica Láinez "comes across as an author who plays with history and myth rather than one who employs them to make a unique and personal statement. And 'The Wandering Unicorn,' for all of its remarkable scholarship and imagery, seems more an overelabor-ate entertainment than a serious work of literature." However, Anne Collins held that these books should not be judged harshly, even though they dwell on more fantastic than real subjects. "In Mujica Láinez's case," Collins asserted in *Maclean's,* "wishful thinking is not so much an evasion as a recognition of all those functional things that can make us happy." But because his writ-ing was meant more to entertain than provoke, even when set in contemporary Argentina, *Punch* reviewer Anthony Burgess cor-rectly (and somewhat ironically) predicted before the author's death that "Láinez will never get the Nobel: he writes too well and there is no political protest in him."

BIOGRAPHICAL/CRITICAL SOURCES:

BOOKS

Contemporary Literary Criticism, Volume 31, Gale, 1985.

PERIODICALS

America, February 7, 1970.
Américas, February, 1972.
Books, October, 1970.
Hispania, March, 1974.
Latin American Literary Review, spring, 1973.
Los Angeles Times Book Review, June 26, 1983.
Maclean's, March 29, 1982.
New Republic, June 10, 1967.
New York Times Book Review, January 11, 1970, March 25, 1984.
Punch, April 27, 1983.
Queen's Quarterly, winter, 1983.
Time, December 12, 1969.
Washington Post, December 31, 1969.
World Literature Today, autumn, 1977.

—*Sketch by Kevin S. Hile*

*   *   *

MUÑIZ, Angelina 1936-

PERSONAL: Born in 1936, in Mexico.

CAREER: Writer.

AWARDS, HONORS: Premio Xavier Villarrutia, 1986, for *Huerto sellado, huerto cerrado.*

WRITINGS:

Vilano al viento (poems), Universidad Nacional Autónoma de
    México, 1982.
La guerra del unicornio, Artifice Ediciones (Mexico City), 1983.
Huerto sellado, huerto cerrado (stories), 1986.
Enclosed Garden, translated by Lois P. Zamora, Latin American
    Literature Review Press, 1988.

Also author of *Tierra adentro,* 1978.

BIOGRAPHICAL/CRITICAL SOURCES:

PERIODICALS

World Literature Today, summer, 1978.

* * *

MUÑOZ MARIN, (José) Luis (Alberto)   1898-1980

PERSONAL: Born February 18, 1898, in San Juan, Puerto Rico;
died of a heart attack, April 30, 1980, in San Juan, Puerto Rico;
son of Luis Muñoz Rivera and Amalia Marín; married Muna
Lee (divorced); married Inés María Mendoza de Palacios; children: (first marriage) Luis, Muna (deceased); (second marriage)
Victoria, Viviana. *Education:* Attended Georgetown University
and Georgetown Law School.

CAREER: Journalist, orator, essayist, poet, and politician. Secretary to resident commissioner of Puerto Rico in Washington,
D.C., 1916-18; active in Pan American Labor movement; served
in secretariat of Pan American Union during Havana Conference, 1929; elected to Puerto Rico Senate as a Liberal, 1932, and
as the founder of the Popular Democratic Party, 1940 and 1944;
president of senate, 1941; Economic Commissioner of Puerto
Rico in United States; chairman of commission on political status of Puerto Rico, 1946; elected first Governor of Puerto Rico,
1949-65.

WRITINGS:

(Contributor) Félix Ojeda Reyes, editor, *Yo soy aquel que ayer
    no más decía; retrato de un colonizado,* Ediciones Puerto
    Rico (Río Piedras, Puerto Rico), 1972.
*Luis Muñoz Marín: Pensamiento político, económico, social y cul-
    tural, según expresado en los discursos oficiales,* Corpora-
    ción de Servicios Bibliotecarios (Río Piedras), 1973.
*Mensajes al Pueblo Puertorriqueño: Pronunciados ante las Cá-
    meras Legislativas, 1949-1964,* Inter American University
    Press, 1980.
Memorias: Autobiografía pública, 1898-1940, Universidad In-
    teramericana de Puerto Rico, 1982.
Historia del Partido Popular Democrático, El Batey (San Juan,
    Puerto Rico), 1984.
*Celebración del octogésimo octavo aniversario del natalicio de
    Don Luis Muñoz Marín,* Departamento de Instrucción
    Pública, Estado Libre Asociado de Puerto Rico, 1986.

Also author of *Borrones* and *Madre Haraposa,* 1917. Contributor
to *American Mercury, Nation, New Republic, New York Herald
Tribune,* and the *Baltimore Sun.* Editor and publisher of *La Democracia,* 1926-27. Editor of *El Imparcial, El Batey,* 1946, and
Revista de Indias, a journal about Pan American culture.

SIDELIGHTS: Government official, translator, and author,
Luis Muñoz Marín was the first elected governor of Puerto Rico.
Architect of the "Operation Bootstrap" program that encour-
aged the establishment of U.S. corporations in Puerto Rico,
Muñoz Marín witnessed improved economic conditions in his
country. Muñoz Marín's father, Luis Muñoz Rivera, had also

been active in politics and had worked for the country's auton-
omy from Spain; after the Spanish-American War of 1898 granting Puerto Rico to the United States, he held a non-voting seat
in the U.S. House of Representatives. Muñoz Marín accompanied his father to Washington, D.C., and studied briefly at
Georgetown University and Law School. Upon his father's death
in 1916, Muñoz Marín left school and began a literary career.
During the 1920s, he lived in New York City and contributed
articles to several periodicals. According to Manuel Suarez in a
New York Times' obituary, "He had the mind of a politician and
the soul of a poet. . . . He would write essays on United States
foreign policy one day and articles on the Broadway theatre the
next." When he returned to Puerto Rico, he favored socialism
and Puerto Rican independence. As founder of the Popular
Democratic Party, he assisted Puerto Rico in becoming a commonwealth in 1952 but campaigned against statehood during the
1970s. As Suarez observed, Muñoz Marín "firmly believed that
only commonwealth status safeguarded the island's Hispanic
culture while simultaneously giving it the security and economic
base it required."

BIOGRAPHICAL/CRITICAL SOURCES:

BOOKS

Aitken, Thomas, *Poet in the Fortress: The Story of Luis Muñoz
    Marín,* New American Library, 1964.
Alexander, Robert J., editor, *Biographical Dictionary of Latin
    American and Caribbean Political Leaders,* Greenwood
    Press, 1988.

PERIODICALS

Chicago Tribune, May 1, 1980.
Newsweek, May 12, 1980.
New York Times, May 1, 1980.
Time, May 12, 1980.
Times (London), May 2, 1980.
Washington Post, May 1, 1980.

* * *

MURENA, H. A.
   See ALVAREZ MURENA, Héctor Alberto

* * *

MURENA, Héctor Alberto Alvarez
   See ALVAREZ MURENA, Héctor Alberto

* * *

MURO, Amado (Jesús)
   See SELTZER, Chester E.

* * *

MUTIS, Alvaro   1923-

PERSONAL: Born in Bogotá, Colombia, 1923; resident of Mexico since 1956.

ADDRESSES: Home—Mexico.

AWARDS, HONORS: El Aquila Azteca, 1989.

WRITINGS:

Los elementos del desastre (poetry), Editorial Losada, 1953.
Diario de Lecumberri (fiction), Universidad Veracruzana, 1960,
    reprinted, Ediciones del Mall (Barcelona), 1986.

Los trabajos perdidos (prose and poetry), Era (Mexico), 1965.

La mansión de Araucaíma; relato gótico de tierra caliente (fiction), Editorial Sudamericana (Buenos Aires), 1973, Seix Barral (Barcelona), 1978.

Summa de Maqroll el Gaviero (Poesía 1947-1970) (poetry), Barral Editores, 1973, published as *Maqroll el Gaviero,* Instituto Colombiano de Cultura, Subdirección de Communicaciones Culturales, División de Publicaciones, 1975.

(Author of introduction) *El mar en la poesía,* Departmento de Pesca (Mexico), 1977.

Caravansary, Fondo de Cultura Económica, 1981.

Los emisarios (poetry; also see below), Fondo de Cultura Económica, 1984.

Obra literaria, Presidencia de la República, 1985.

Historia natural de las cosas, Fondo de Cultura Económica, 1985.

Crónica regia; y, Alabanza del reino (poetry; includes poems from *Los emisarios*), Ediciones Cátedra, 1985.

Sesenta cuerpos (selections), Comité de Publicaciones, U. de A. (Medellín, Colombia), 1985.

Ilona llega con la lluvia, Editorial Oveja Negra (Bogotá), 1987, Mondadori (Madrid), 1988.

La nieve del almirante, Alianza, 1986.

Un homenaje y siete nocturnos, Equilibrista (Mexico), 1986, Pamiela (Pamplona, Spain), 1988.

La muerte de estratega (selections), Fondo de Cultura Económica, 1988.

SIDELIGHTS: The poetry and fiction of Colombian-born writer Alvaro Mutis depicts the bleakness and futility of life in the late twentieth century. Colored by the terror and slaughter in Colombia he witnessed between 1947 and 1957, his works present characters who feel that their lives are fruitless. One such character, Maqroll el Gaviero, reacts to his frustrations by seeking dreams and visions induced by alcohol.

The author's interesting and skillful use of language "confer artistic validity to an otherwise dismal picture of humanity," Malva E. Filer remarks in *World Literature Today.* His poetry, for example, has the resonance of traditional meter without its constricting metrical patterns. In a *World Literature Today* review of *Los emisarios,* William Ferguson explains, "Mutis is clearly at home in free-verse lines of any length, but he seems especially successful as the measures approach Whitmanesque proportions."

BIOGRAPHICAL/CRITICAL SOURCES:

PERIODICALS

World Literature Today, autumn, 1986, winter, 1986, winter, 1988.

N

NAVA, Gregory 1949-

PERSONAL: Born in 1949; married Anna Thomas (a writer and filmmaker). *Education:* Attended University of California, Los Angeles.

ADDRESSES: Agent—International Creative Management, 40 West 57th St., New York, N.Y. 10010.

CAREER: Screenwriter and director.

AWARDS, HONORS: Academy Award nomination for best original screenplay, 1985, for "El Norte."

WRITINGS:

SCREENPLAYS

(With wife, Anna Thomas) "The Confessions of Amans," Bauer International, 1977.
(With Thomas) "El Norte," Cinecom International/Island Alive, 1984.

Also author, with Thomas, of the screenplay for the 1988 film "A Time of Destiny."

SIDELIGHTS: Screenwriter and director Gregory Nava earned accolades for the visually brilliant and moving 1984 film, "El Norte," which he wrote with his wife, Anna Thomas. The couple, who studied filmmaking at the University of California at Los Angeles, had earlier collaborated on "The Confessions of Amans," a tale of a tragic medieval love affair.

"El Norte," a film of "greater immediacy," according to *New York Times* critic Vincent Canby, portrays a Guatemalan brother and sister who flee their country and head for the North after their father, a spokesman for land reform, is murdered. Leaving lush but oppressive Guatemala, Enrique and Rosa encounter the poverty of Mexico and the glaring contrast of wealth on the U.S. side of the border. In a scene of the film that *Commonweal* critic Tom O'Brien claimed "sums up its rare strength," the characters cross into California by means of a rat-infested sewer tunnel and emerge to a view of San Diego. "The border is unique—the only place in the world where an industrialized first-world nation shares the border with a third-world country," Nava, who has relatives in Tijuana, told Annette Insdorf of the *New York Times.* "In California, it's just a fence: on one side are the Tijuana slums, on the other side—San Diego. It's so graphic! This was the germ of the story."

America does not immediately upset the newcomers' expectations of a better life, although they discover that the poverty they had "left behind" in Mexico also exists in California. The pair fares well; a new friend of Rosa's finds her a job as a maid, and Enrique becomes a waiter in a restaurant. Canby remarked, "The real and most poignant point of 'El Norte' is . . . the ease and eagerness with which, after their initial homesickness, they adapt themselves to the gringo world. . . . The plastic society enchants them." Several critics noted that "El Norte" critiques America more than Latin America, and considered the film more personal than political. O'Brien, for instance, declared that "there's no propaganda in the movie, just visual poetry, suspense and emotional force."

The film is unusual in portraying Hispanic characters directly—rather than through the eyes of Anglo-American characters. "Unlike many recent films about the struggles of third-world peoples," commented O'Brien, "[this film] actually concerns *them,* their viewpoints." *New York Times* critic Janet Maslin added, "This is one movie in which the white, English-speaking characters are strictly walk-ons. Mr. Nava thoroughly immerses the audience in the world of Hispanic exiles." In a *New York Times* interview Nava remarked that "in order to get films made about Latin America, you have to have Americans in the center of the story. . . . You don't get to know the people to whom things are really happening down there." It had been suggested to Nava and Thomas that they cast white American actors in the feature roles in order to draw audiences—an idea the filmmakers rejected in favor of employing Hispanic actors and operating on a small budget. The resulting film, according to the *Christian Science Monitor,* represents "clear, committed filmmaking in which talent and thoughtfulness easily compensate for budgetary limitations."

Reviewers mainly objected to what they considered the film's overly melodramatic conclusion. Canby asserted in the *New York Times* that the film "seems about to make one of the most boldly original and satirical . . . statements ever to be found in a film about the United States as a land of power as well as opportunity" until its "arbitrarily tragic ending." Critics faulted the couple's next project, "A Time of Destiny," on similar grounds. In this 1988 film, the daughter of an Italian-American immigrant elopes, infuriating her father. He interrupts the couple's wedding night and persuades the daughter to return home with him. The ensuing car chase by the newlywed husband results in the father's death, and the rest of the film concerns his son's obsession with avenging him. In a review of the film for *Maclean's,* Brian D. Johnson judged that Nava's talents better served "the deeply moving 'El Norte.'"

BIOGRAPHICAL/CRITICAL SOURCES:

PERIODICALS

Christian Science Monitor, March 1, 1984.
Commonweal, April 6, 1984.
Maclean's, April 25, 1988.
New Yorker, February 20, 1984.
New York Times, January 8, 1984, January 11, 1984, January 22, 1984.

* * *

NAVA, Julian 1927-

PERSONAL: Born June 19, 1927, in Los Angeles, Calif.; son of Julian and Refugio (Flores) Nava; married Patricia Lucas, June 30, 1962; children: Catherine and Carmen (twin daughters), Paul. *Education:* East Los Angeles Junior College, A.A., 1949; Pomona College, A.B., 1951; Harvard University, A.M., 1952, Ph.D., 1955. *Politics:* Democrat.

ADDRESSES: Home—18308 Septo, Northridge, Calif. 91235. *Office*—Department of History, California State University, Northridge, 18111 Nordhoff St., Northridge, Calif. 91330.

CAREER: U.S. Cultural Center, Caracas, Venezuela, instructor in English and U.S. history, 1953-54; University of Puerto Rico, Río Piedras, lecturer in humanities, 1955-57; California State University, Northridge, assistant professor, 1957-61, associate professor, 1961-65, professor of history, beginning in 1965; U.S. ambassador to Mexico, 1980-81; president of Lampman-Mexico (consulting firm), beginning in 1981. Fulbright lecturer at Universidad de Valladolid, 1962-63; founding director of Centro de Estudios Universitarios Colombo-Americanos, 1964-65. Member of Los Angeles board of education, 1965-80, president, 1971 and 1975. Chairman of founding committee to preserve the history of Los Angeles, 1961-62; founding director of Great Lakes Colleges Association Center in Bogotá, 1964-64; member of governing board of California State Colleges' Inter-America Institute, 1966; member of board of directors of Los Angeles World Affairs Council, 1970, Plaza del la Raza, 1970—, Hispanic Urban Center, 1971—, and National Hispanic Scholarship Foundation, 1975; member of advisory committee of Mexican American Legal Defense and Education Fund, National Urban Coalition, Bilingual Children's Television, La Raza Television, Educational Testing Service; member of Mexican advisory committee to California superintendent of public instruction. *Military service:* U.S. Navy, Air Force, 1945-46.

MEMBER: American Historical Association.

AWARDS, HONORS: Bravo Foundation fellowship, 1951-53; John Hay Whitney Foundation fellowship, 1951-54.

WRITINGS:

Mexican Americans: Past, Present and Future (high school textbook), American Book Co., 1969.
Mexican Americans: A Brief Look at Their History, Anti-Defamation League of B'nai B'rith, 1970.
(Author of foreword) Nathaniel Wagner and Maesha Haug, *Chicanos: Social and Psychological Perspectives,* Mosby, 1971.
(Editor) *The Mexican American in American History* (high school textbook), American Book Co., 1973.

(Editor) *Viva La Raza!: Readings on Mexican Americans,* Van Nostrand, 1973.
(Author of preface) Abraham Hoffman, *Unwanted Mexican Americans in the Great Depression,* University of Arizona Press, 1974.
(Contributor) Gus Tyler, editor, *Mexican-Americans Tomorrow,* University of New Mexico Press, 1975.
(With Robert Barger) *A General History of California* (college textbook), Benziger, 1976.
(With Barger) *California: Five Centuries of Cultural Contrasts,* Glencoe Press, 1979.

Also author children's educational series "Bilingual Stories of Today," Aardvark Media, 1973. Contributor to *Reader's Encyclopedia* and to professional journals.

* * *

NERUDA, Pablo 1904-1973

PERSONAL: Given name, Ricardo Eliezer Neftalí Reyes y Basoalto; adopted the pseudonym Pablo Neruda at the age of 14, name legally changed, 1946; born July 12, 1904, in Parral, Chile; died September 23, 1973, of heart failure following an operation for cancer of the prostate, in Santiago, Chile; son of José del Carmen Reyes Morales (a railroad worker) and Rosa de Basoalto (a schoolteacher); married Maruca Hagenaar Vogelzang, 1930 (marriage ended); married Matilde Urrutia, 1951; children (first marriage): Malva Marina, a daughter (died, 1942). *Education:* Attended local schools at Temuco, Chile; attended Instituto Pedagógico (Santiago, Chile) in the early 1920s, and University of Chile, 1926. *Politics:* Communist (member of central committee of Chilean party).

ADDRESSES: Home—Márquez de la Plata 0192, Santiago, Chile; and Isle Negra, near Valparaíso, Chile.

CAREER: Went to Rangoon, Burma, as Chilean consul, 1927; consul in Colombo, Ceylon, 1929, Batavia, Java, 1930 (visiting China, Japan, and Indo-China); during the early 1930s he was consul in Buenos Aires, Siam, Cambodia, Anam, and Madrid; helped Spanish refugees in Paris, 1939; sent to Chilean Embassy, Mexico City, Mexico, 1939-41, consul, 1941-44; when he returned to Chile in 1945, he was elected to the Senate as a Communist; he wrote letters from 1947-49, charging President González Videla with selling out to foreign investors and monopolists; threatened with arrest by the Chilean Supreme Court in 1948, he escaped to Mexico; also traveled in Italy, France, U.S.S.R., Red China; returned to Chile in 1953, after the victory of the anti-Videla forces; nominated for president on Chilean Communist Party ticket, 1970; Chilean ambassador to France, 1971-72. Came to New York for the PEN Congress, 1966. Member of World Peace Council, 1950-73.

MEMBER: Unión de Escritores Chilenos (president, 1959-73), Modern Language Association of America (honorary fellow), International PEN.

AWARDS, HONORS: Third prize, provincial Juegos Florales competition, 1919, for "Comunión ideal"; first prize for poetry in the Students' Federation spring festival, Instituto Pedagógico, 1921, for *La canción de la fiesta;* honorary doctorate, University of Michoacán (Mexico), 1941; Premio Municipal de Literatura (Chile), 1944; Premio Nacional de Literatura (Chile), 1945; International Peace Prize, 1950; Lenin and Stalin Peace Prize, 1953; Litt.D., Oxford University, 1965; awarded Czechoslovakia's highest decoration, 1966; Nobel Prize in literature, 1971.

WRITINGS:

La canción de la fiesta (poetry), Federación de Estudiantes de Chile (Santiago), 1921.

Crepusculario (poetry), Nascimento (Santiago), 1923, 4th edition, Losada (Buenos Aires), 1971.

Viente poemas de amor y una canción desesperada, Nascimento, 1924, definitive edition, 1932, 16th edition, Losada, 1972, translation by W. S. Merwin published as *Twenty Love Poems and a Song of Despair,* J. Cape, 1969.

El habitante y su esperanza (prose; also see below), Nascimento, 1925, 2nd edition, Ediciones Ercilla (Santiago), 1939.

(With Tomás Lago) *Anillos* (prose poems; also see below), Nascimento, 1926.

Tentativa del hombre infinito (poem; also see below), Nascimento, 1926, new edition, Editorial Orbe (Santiago), 1964.

Prosas de Pablo Neruda (prose), Nascimento, 1926.

El hondero entusiasta, 1923-1924 (poetry; also see below), Ediciones Ercilla, 1933, 3rd edition, 1938.

Residencia en la tierra (poetry and prose), Ediciones del Arbol (Madrid), Volume I (1925-31), 1933, Volume II (1931-35), 1935, published in one volume, Losada, 1944, 3rd edition, 1969.

Poesías de Yillamediana presentadas por Pablo Neruda, Cruz y Raya (Madrid), 1935.

Homenaje a Pablo Neruda de los poetas españoles: Tres cantos materiales (poetry), Plutarco (Madrid), 1935, translation by Angel Flores published as *Tres cantos materiales: Three Material Songs,* East River Editions, 1948.

Sonetos de la muerte de Quevedo, presentados por Pablo Neruda, Cruz y Raya, 1935.

España en el corazón: Himno a las glorias del pueblo en la guerra (poetry; first printed by Spanish Republican soldiers on the battlefront; also see below), Ediciones Ercilla, 1937, 2nd edition, 1938.

Las furias y las penas (poetry), Nascimento, 1939.

(With Emilio Oribe and Juan Marinello) *Neruda entre nosotros* (prose), A.I.A.P.E. (Montevideo), 1939.

Homenaje a García Lorca (prose), A.I.A.P.E., 1939.

Chile os acoge (prose), [Paris], 1939.

Un canto para Bolívar (poetry), Universidad Nacional Autónoma de México, 1941.

(Contributor of poetry) *Presencia de García Lorca,* Darro (Mexico), 1943.

Nuevo canto de amor a Stalingrado (poem), Comité de ayuda a Rusia en guerra (Mexico), 1943.

Canto general de Chile (poem), privately printed, 1943.

Cantos de Pablo Neruda (poetry), Hora del Hombre (Lima), 1943.

Cántico, La Gran Colombia (Bogota), 1943.

Pablo Neruda: Sus mejores versos, La Gran Colombia, 1943.

Saludo al norte y Stalingrado, privately printed, 1945.

Carta a México, Fondo de Cultura Popular (Mexico), 1947.

Tercera residencia, 1935-1945 (poetry; includes *España en el corazón*), Losada, 1947, 5th edition, 1971.

Viajes al corazón de Quevedo y por las costas del mundo (prose), Sociedad de Escritores de Chile (Santiago), 1947.

28 de Enero, Partido Comunista de Chile, 1947.

Los héroes de carcon encarnan los ideales de democracia e independencia nacional, El Tranviario (Santiago), 1947.

La verdad sobre las rupturas (prose), Principios (Santiago), 1947.

La crisis democrática de Chile, Hora del Hombre, 1947, translation published as *The Democratic Crisis of Chile,* Committee for Friendship in the Americas (New York), 1948.

Dura elegía, Cruz del Sur (Santiago), 1948.

Himno y regreso, Cruz del Sur, 1948.

¡Qué despierte el leñador! (poetry), Colección Yagruma (Havana), 1948, translation published as *Peace for Twilights to Come!,* Jayant Bhatt for People's Publishing House (Bombay, India), 1950.

Alturas de Macchu-Picchu (poetry), Librería Neira (Santiago), 1948, definitive edition, Nascimento, 1954, translation by Nathaniel Tarn published as *The Heights of Macchu Picchu,* J. Cape, 1966, Farrar, Straus, 1967.

Coral de año nuevo para mi patria en tinieblas, privately printed, 1948.

Pablo Neruda acusa, Ediciones Pueblos Unidos (Montevideo), 1948.

Y ha llegado el momento en que debemos elegir, privately printed, 1949.

González Videla, el Laval de América Latina: Breve biografía de un traidor, Fondo de Cultura Popular, 1949.

Dulce patria, Editorial del Pacífico (Santiago), 1949.

Neruda en Guatemala (prose), Saker-Ti (Guatemala), 1950.

Patria prisionera, Hora del Hombre, 1951.

A la memoria de Ricardo Fonseca, Amistad (Santiago), 1951.

Cuando de Chile, Austral (Santiago), 1952.

Poemas, Fundamentos (Buenos Aires), 1952.

Los versos del capitán: Poemas de amor (anonymously published until 3rd edition, 1963), privately printed in Naples, 1952, 7th edition, Losada, 1972, translation by Donald D. Walsh published as *The Captain's Verses,* New Directions, 1972.

Todo el amor (poetry), Nascimento, 1953.

En su muerte, Partido Comunista Argentino (Buenos Aires), 1953.

Poesía política: Discursos políticos, two volumes, Austral, 1953.

Las uvas y el viento (poetry), Nascimento, 1954.

Odas elementales (first volume of "Elementary Odes"; also see below), Losada, 1954, 3rd edition, 1970.

Discurso inauguración fundación Pablo Neruda, Universidad de Chile (Santiago), 1954.

Allí murió la muerte, Ediciones del Centro de Amigos de Polonia (Santiago), 1954.

Regreso la sirena (poetry), Ediciones del Centro de Amigos de Polonia, 1954.

Viajes (prose), Nascimento, 1955.

Nuevas odas elementales (second volume of "Elementary Odes"; also see below), Losada, 1956, 3rd edition, 1971.

Oda a la tipografía (poetry), Nascimento, 1956.

Dos odas elementales, Losada, 1957.

Estravagario (poetry), Losada, 1958, 3rd edition, 1971, translation by Alastair Reid published as *Extravagaria,* J. Cape, 1972, Farrar, Straus, 1974.

Tercer libro de las odas (third volume of "Elementary Odes"), Losada, 1959.

Algunas odas (poetry), Edición del 55 (Santiago), 1959.

Cien sonetos de amor (poetry), Losada, 1959, 6th edition, 1971, translation by Stephen J. Tapscott published as *100 Love Sonnets,* University of Texas Press, 1986.

Odas: Al libro, a las Américas, a la luz (poetry), Homenaje de la Asociación de Escritores Venezolanos (Caracas, Venezuela), 1959.

Todo lleva tu nombre (poetry), Ministerio de Educación (Caracas), 1959.

Navegaciones y regresos (poetry), Losada, 1959.

(With Federico García Lorca) *Discurso al Alimón sobre Rubén Darío,* Semana Dariana (Nicaragua), 1959.

(With Pablo Picasso) *Toros: 15 lavis inedits,* Au Vent d'Arles (Paris), 1960.

Canción de gesta (poetry), Imprenta Nacional de Cuba (Havana), 1960, 3rd edition, Siglo (Montevideo), 1968.

Oceana (poem), La Tertulia (Havana), 1960, 2nd edition, 1962.

Los primeros versos de amor (poetry), Austral, 1961.

Las piedras de Chile (poetry), Losada, 1961, translation by Dennis Maloney published as *The Stones of Chile,* White Pine, 1987.

Primer día de La Sebastiana, privately printed, 1961.

Cantos ceremoniales (poetry), Losada, 1961, 2nd edition 1972.

Plenos poderes (poetry), Losada, 1962, 2nd edition, 1971, translation by Reid published as *Fully Empowered: Plenos poderes,* Farrar, Straus, 1975.

(With Mario Toral) *Poema con grabado* (poetry), Ediciones Isla Negra (Santiago), 1962.

La insepulta de Paita (poetry), Losada, 1962.

Con los católicos hacia la paz, [Santiago], 1962, published as *Cuba: Los obispos,* Paz y Soberanía (Lima), 1962.

(With Nicanor Parra) *Discursos: Pablo Neruda y Nicanor Parra* (prose), Nascimento, 1962.

Mensaje de paz y unidad, Internacionalismo proletario, [and] *El poeta de la revolución* (addresses), Esclarecimiento (Lima), 1963.

(With Gustavo Hernán and Guillermo Atías) *Presencia de Ramón López Velarde en Chile,* Universitaria (Santiago), 1963.

Memorial de Isla Negra (poetry), Volume 1: *Donde nace la lluvia,* Volume 2: *La luna en el laberinto,* Volume 3: *El fuego cruel,* Volume 4: *El cazador de raíces,* Volume 5: *Sonata crítica,* Losada, 1964, translation by Reid published as *Isla Negra: A Notebook,* bilingual edition, Farrar, Straus, 1980.

Arte de pájaros, Sociedad de Amigos del Arte Contemporáneo (Santiago), 1966, translation by Jack Schmitt published as *The Art of Birds,* University of Texas Press, 1985.

Una casa en la arena (poetry and prose), Lumen (Barcelona), 1966, 2nd edition, 1969.

La barcarola (poem), Losada, 1967.

Fulgor y muerte de Joaquín Murieta: Bandido chileno injusticiado en California el 23 de julio de 1853 (play), Zig-Zag (Santiago), 1967, translation by Ben Belitt published as *Splendor and Death of Joaquin Murieta,* Farrar, Straus, 1972.

(With Miguel Angel Asturias) *Comiendo en Hungría* (poetry and prose), 1968.

Las manos del día (poetry), Losada, 1968, 2nd edition, 1970.

Aun: Poema, Nascimento, 1969.

Fin de mundo (poem), Losada, 1969.

La copa de sangre (poetry and prose), privately printed, 1969.

La espada encendida, Losada, 1970, 2nd edition, 1972.

Las piedras del cielo, Losada, 1970, translation by James Nolan published as *Stones of the Sky,* Copper Canyon, 1987.

Discurso pronunciado con ocasión de la entrega del premio Nobel de literatura, 1971, Centre de Recherches Hispaniques (Paris), 1972, translation published as *Toward the Splendid City: Nobel Lecture,* Farrar, Straus, 1974.

Cantos de amor y de combate (poetry), Austral, 1971.

Geografía infructuosa (poetry), Losada, 1972.

Cuatros poemas escritos en Francia, Nascimento, 1972.

Libro de las odas, Losada, 1972.

El mar y las campanas: Poemas, Losada, 1973, translation by William O'Daly published as *The Sea and the Bells,* Copper Canyon, 1988.

La rosa separada (poetry), Losada, 1973.

El corazón amarillo (poetry), Losada, 1974.

Elegía (poetry), Losada, 1974, published as *Elegía: Obra póstuma,* Seix Barral, 1976.

Incitación al Nixonicidio y alabanza de la revolución chilena (poetry), Grijalbo (Barcelona), 1974, translation by Steve Kowit published as *Incitement to Nixonicide and Praise for the Chilean Revolution,* Quixote, 1974, 2nd edition, 1980.

Defectos escogidos (poetry), Losada, 1974.

Oda a la lagartija (poem), P. R. Martorell (Camp Rico de Canovanas), 1974.

El mal y el malo (twenty fragments from *Canto general*), P. Alcantara y V. Amaya, 1974.

Jardín de invierno, Losada, 1974, published as *Jardín de invierno: Obras póstuma,* Seix Barral, 1977, translation by O'Daly published as *Winter Garden,* Copper Canyon, 1986.

Libro de las preguntas, Losada, 1974, published as *Libro de las preguntas,* Seix Barral, 1977.

Cartas de amor de Pablo Neruda (love correspondence), compiled by Sergio Lorrain, Ediciones Rodas (Madrid), 1974.

Confieso que he vivido: Memorias, Seix Barral (Barcelona), 1974, translation by Hardie St. Martin published as *Memoirs,* Farrar, Straus, 1977.

OMNIBUS VOLUMES

Selección (poetry), compiled by Arturo Aldunate, Nascimento, 1943.

Colección residencia en la tierra: Obra poética, ten volumes, Cruz del Sur, 1947-48.

Canto general (poetry), Comité Auspiciador (Mexico), 1950, 5th edition in two volumes, Losada, 1971.

Poesías completas, Losada, 1951.

Los versos más populares (poetry), Austral, 1954.

Los mejores versos de Pablo Neruda (poetry), [Buenos Aires], 1956.

Obras completas (complete works), Losada, 1957, 3rd updated edition in two volumes, 1968.

El habitante y su esperanza, El hondero entusiasta, Tentativa del hombre infinito, [and] *Anillos,* Losada, 1957, 4th edition, 1971.

Antología, Nascimento, 1957, 4th enlarged edition, 1970.

The Selected Poems of Pablo Neruda, edited and translated by Belitt, Grove, 1961.

Antología poética, selected by Pablo Luis Avila, Gheroni (Torino, Italy), 1962.

Poesías, selected by Roberto Retamar, Casa de las Américas (Havana), 1965.

Antología esencial, selected by Hernán Loyola, Losada, 1971.

Poemas imortales, selected by Jaime Concha, Quimantu (Santiago), 1971.

Obras escogidas (poetry), selected by Francisco Coloane, A. Bello (Santiago), 1972.

Antología popular 1972, [Santiago], 1972.

Pablo Neruda (includes poems, Nobel prize acceptance speech, interview, and chronologies), Noroeste (Buenos Aires), 1973.

Poesía, two volumes, Noguer (Barcelona), 1974.

OTHER ENGLISH TRANSLATIONS

Selected Poems (from *Residencia en la tierra*), translated by Flores, privately printed, 1944.

Residence on Earth and Other Poems (includes "Residence on Earth I and II," "Spain in the Heart," "General Song of Chile," and "Recent Poems"), translated by Flores, New Directions, 1946.

Let the Splitter Awake and Other Poems (selected from *¡Qué despierte el leñador!,* and *Canto general;* also see below), Masses & Mainstream, 1950.

Let the Rail-Splitter Awake (also see below), World Student News, 1951.

Twenty Love Poems; A Distaining Song, translated by W. S. Merwin, Grossman, 1961.

Elementary Odes (selections), translated by Carlos Lozano, G. Massa, 1961.

Residence on Earth (selections), translated by Clayton Eshleman, Amber House Press, 1962.

Bestiary/Bestiario: A Poem, translated by Elsa Neuberger, Harcourt, 1965.

Nocturnal Collection: A Poem, translated by Flores, [Madison, Wis.], 1966.

We Are Many (poem), translated by Reid, Cape Goliard Press, 1967, Grossman, 1968.

Twenty Poems (selected from *Residencia en la tierra, Canto general,* and *Odas elementales*) translated by James Wright and Robert Bly, Sixties Press, 1967.

A New Decade: Poems, 1958-1967, edited by Belitt, translated by Belitt and Reid, Grove, 1969.

Pablo Neruda: The Early Poems, translated by David Ossman and Carlos B. Hagen, New Rivers Press, 1969.

Selected Poems, edited by Nathaniel Tarn, translated by Anthony Kerrigan and others, J. Cape, 1970, Delacorte Press, 1972.

New Poems, 1968-1970, edited and translated by Belitt, Grove, 1972.

Residence on Earth (includes *Residencia en la tierra,* Volumes I and II, and *Tercera residencia*), translated by Donald D. Walsh, New Directions, 1973.

Five Decades: A Selection (Poems 1925-1970), edited and translated by Belitt, Grove, 1974.

Passions and Impressions, translated by Margaret S. Peden, Farrar, Straus, 1982.

Windows That Open Inward: Images of Chile, translated by Reid and others, White Pine, 1984.

Still Another Day, translated by O'Daly, Copper Canyon, 1984.

The House at Isla Negra, translated by Maloney and Clark Zlotchew, White Pine, 1988.

Let the Railsplitter Awake and Other Poems, translated by Waldeen, International Publishing, 1989.

Late and Posthumous Poems, 1968-1974, edited and translated by Belitt, Grove Press, 1989.

OTHER

(Translator into Spanish) William Blake, *Visiones de las hijas de Albión y el viajero mental,* Cruz y Raya, 1935.

(Translator into Spanish) William Shakespeare, *Romeo y Julieta,* Losada, 1964.

(Translator into Spanish) *Cuarenta y cuatro* (Rumanian poetry), Losada, 1967.

(Contributor) Robert Bly, compiler, *Neruda and Vallejo: Selected Poems,* translated by Bly and others, Beacon Press, 1971.

(Contributor) Walter Lowenfels, editor, *For Neruda, for Chile: An International Anthology,* Beacon Press, 1975.

(Contributor) Lloyd Mallan, editor, *Three Spanish American Poets: Pellicer, Neruda, Andrade,* translated by Mary Wicker, Gordon Press, 1977.

Also author of *Cartas de amor,* edited by Sergio Larrain, 1974, of *Cartas a Laura,* edited by Hugo Montes, 1978, of *Para nacer he nacido,* 1980, and, with Héctor Eandi, of *Correspondencia,* edited by Margarita Aguirre, 1980; also author of *Poemas,* for Horizonte. Also editor and translator of *Páginas escogidas de Anatole France,* 1924. Contributor of poems and articles to numerous periodicals worldwide, including *Selva austral, Poetry, Nation, Commonweal, Canadian Forum,* and *California Quarterly.* Work represented in many anthologies, including *Anthol-*

ogy of Contemporary Latin American Poetry, edited by Dudley Fitts, New Directions, 1942; *Three Spanish American Poets: Pellicer, Neruda, and Andrade,* Sage Books, 1942; *Modern European Po-etry,* edited by Willis Barnstone, Bantam, 1966. Founder and editor with Manuel Altolaguirre of *El caballo verde para la poesía* (poetry periodical), six issues, 1935-36, and *Aurora de Chile,* 1938.

SIDELIGHTS: "No writer of world renown is perhaps so little known to North Americans as the Chilean poet Pablo Neruda," observed *New York Times Book Review* critic Selden Rodman in 1966. "Yet on a recent visit to New York he held a capacity audience enthralled at the Y.M.H.A.'s Poetry Center as he read—in Spanish—from his works. Only Dylan Thomas and Robert Frost (reading in English, of course) had evoked a similar state of euphoria or aroused the standing ovation that was accorded Neruda on that memorable night." Numerous critics consider Neruda the greatest poet writing in the Spanish language during his lifetime, although many readers in the United States find it difficult to disassociate his poetry from his fervent commitment to Communism. An added difficulty lies in the fact that Neruda's poetry is very hard to translate; the volume of his work available in English is small compared to his total output. Nonetheless, declared John Leonard in the *New York Times,* Neruda "was, I think, one of the great ones, a Whitman of the South."

Born Ricardo Eliezer Neftalí Reyes y Basoalto, Neruda adopted the pseudonym under which he would become famous in his early teens. He grew up in the backwoods of southern Chile, in a frontier settlement called Temuco. The territory was harsh, a region where "vegetation covered a good part of the surroundings with thick foliage, and storms came from the sea," declared Salvadore Bizzarro in *Pablo Neruda: All Poets the Poet.* "Distant erupting volcanoes were a threat to the inhabitants. Outside of heavy rainfalls and frequent inundations, fires and earthquakes were the most feared calamities." Although his family, conditioned by the rugged atmosphere, did not themselves encourage Neruda's literary development, the budding writer received assistance from unexpected sources. Among his teachers "was the poet Gabriela Mistral, who would be a Nobel laureate years before Neruda," report Manuel Durán and Margery Safir in *Earth Tones: The Poetry of Pablo Neruda.* "It is almost inconceivable that two such gifted poets should find each other in such an unlikely spot. Mistral recognized the young Neftalí's talent and encouraged it by giving the boy books and the support he lacked at home."

It was in this atmosphere and under this encouragement that Neruda composed his first poetry. By the time he finished high school, he had published in local papers and Santiago magazines, and had won several literary competitions. In 1921, he left southern Chile for Santiago to attend school, with the intention of becoming a French teacher. He was a rather indifferent student, however, and, as Durán and Safir explained, "love affairs, books, classes at the Instituto Pedagógico, daydreams, long hours spent looking at the sunset from his window on Maruri Street occupied most of his time. And writing." While in Santiago, Neruda completed one of his most critically acclaimed and original works, the cycle of love poems called *Viente poemas de amor y una canción desesperada,* later published in English translation under the title *Twenty Love Poems and a Song of Despair*—a work that marked him as an important Chilean poet.

Viente poemas brought the author notoriety with its explicit celebration of sexuality, and, as Robert Clemens remarked in *Saturday Review,* "established him at the outset as a frank, sensuous spokesman for love." While other Latin American poets of the time used sexually explicit imagery, Neruda was the first to win popular acceptance for his presentation. Mixing memories of his love affairs with memories of the wilderness of southern Chile, he created a poetic sequence that not only describes a physical liaison, but also evokes the sense of displacement that Neruda felt in leaving the wilderness for the city. "Traditionally," stated René de Costa in *The Poetry of Pablo Neruda*, "love poetry has equated woman with nature. Neruda took this established mode of comparison and raised it to a cosmic level, making woman into a veritable force of the universe."

"In *20 poemas*," reported David P. Gallagher in *Modern Latin American Literature*, "Neruda journeys across the sea symbolically in search of an ideal port. In 1927, he embarked on a real journey, when he sailed from Buenos Aires for Lisbon, ultimately bound for Rangoon where he had been appointed honorary Chilean consul." Durán and Safir explained that "Chile had a long tradition, like most Latin American countries, of sending her poets abroad as consuls or even, when they became famous, as ambassadors." Neruda was not really qualified for such a post, Durán and Safir assert; his spoken English (Rangoon was the capital of the British colony of Burma) was sparse and he had no real knowledge of a consul's business. Above all, he was unprepared for the squalor, poverty, and loneliness to which the position would expose him. "Neruda travelled extensively in the Far East over the next few years," Gallagher continued, "and it was during this period that he wrote his first really splendid book of poems, *Residencia en la tierra*, a book ultimately published in two parts, in 1933 and 1935." Neruda added a third part, *Tercera residencia*, in 1947.

Residencia en la tierra, published in English as *Residence on Earth*, is widely celebrated as containing "some of Neruda's most extraordinary and powerful poetry," according to de Costa. Born of the poet's feelings of alienation, the work reflects a world which is largely chaotic and senseless, and which—in the first two volumes—offers no hope of understanding. De Costa quoted the Spanish poet García Lorca as calling Neruda "a poet closer to death than to philosophy, closer to pain than to insight, closer to blood than to ink. A poet filled with mysterious voices that fortunately he himself does not know how to decipher." With its emphasis on despair and the lack of adequate answers to mankind's problems, *Residencia en la tierra* in some ways foreshadowed the post-World War II philosophy of existentialism. "Neruda himself came to regard it very harshly," wrote Michael Wood in the *New York Review of Books*. "It helped people to die rather than to live, he said, and if he had the proper authority to do so he would ban it, and make sure it was never reprinted."

Residencia en la tierra also marked Neruda's emergence as an important international poet. By the time the second volume of the collection was published in 1935 the poet was serving as consul in Spain, where "for the first time," reported Durán and Safir, "he tasted international recognition, at the heart of the Spanish language and tradition. At the same time . . . poets like Rafael Alberti and Miguel Hernández, who had become closely involved in radical politics and the Communist movement, helped politicize Neruda." When the Spanish Civil War broke out in 1936, Neruda was among the first to espouse the Republican cause with the poem *España en el corazón*—a gesture that cost him his consular post. He later served in France and Mexico, where his politics caused less anxiety.

Communism rescued Neruda from the despair he expressed in the first parts of *Residencia en la tierra*, and led to a change in his approach to poetry. He came to believe "that the work of art

and the statement of thought—when these are responsible human actions, rooted in human need—are inseparable from historical and political context," reported Bizzarro. "He argued that there are books which are important at a certain moment in history, but once these books have resolved the problems they deal with they carry in them their own oblivion. Neruda felt that the belief that one could write solely for eternity was romantic posturing." This new attitude led the poet in new directions; for many years his work, both poetry and prose, advocated an active role in social change rather than simply describing his feelings, as his earlier oeuvre had done.

While some critics have felt that Neruda's devotion to Communist dogma was at times extreme—Leonard reported that "he drank Marxist slogans neat"—other have recognized the important impact his politics had on his poetry. Clayton Eshleman wrote in the introduction to César Vallejo's *Poemas humanos/Human Poems*, "Neruda found in the third book of *Residencia* the key to becoming *the* twentieth-century South American poet: the revolutionary stance which always changes with the tides of time." Gordon Brotherton, in *Latin American Poetry: Origins and Presence*, expanded on this idea, saying, "Neruda, so prolific, can be lax, a 'great bad poet' (to use the phrase Juan Ramón Jiménez used to revenge himself on Neruda). And his change of stance 'with the tides of time' may not always be be perfectly effected. But . . . his dramatic and rhetorical skills, better his ability to speak out of his circumstances, . . . was consummate. In his best poetry (of which there is much) he speaks on a scale and with an agility unrivalled in Latin America."

Neruda expanded on his political views in the poem *Canto general*, which, according to de Costa, is a "lengthy epic on man's struggle for justice in the New World." Although Neruda had begun the poem as early as 1935—when he had intended it to be limited in scope only to Chile—he completed some of the work while serving in the Chilean senate as a representative of the Communist Party. However, party leaders recognized that the poet needed time to work on his opus, and granted him a leave of absence in 1947. Later that year, however, Neruda returned to political activism, writing letters in support of striking workers and criticizing Chilean President Videla. Early in 1948 the Chilean Supreme Court issued an order for his arrest, and Neruda finished the *Canto General* while hiding from Videla's forces.

Although, as Bizzarro noted, "In [the *Canto General*], Neruda was to reflect some of the [Communist] party's basic ideological tenets," the work itself transcends propaganda. Looking back into American prehistory, the poet examined the land's rich natural heritage and described the long defeat of the native Americans by the Europeans. Instead of rehashing Marxist dogma, however, he concentrated on elements of people's lives common to all people at all times. Nancy Willard writes in *Testimony of the Invisible Man*, "Neruda makes it clear that our most intense experience of impermanence is not death but our own isolation among the living. . . . If Neruda is intolerant of despair, it is because he wants nothing to sully man's residence on earth." "In the *Canto*," explained Durán and Safir, "Neruda reached his peak as a public poet. He produced an ideological work that largely transcended contemporary events and became an epic of an entire continent and its people."

In *Poetry*, James Wright summed up the *Canto*'s argument: "Appalled by loneliness I sought my human brothers among the living; I do not really object to their death, as long as I can share with them the human death; but everywhere I go among the living I find them dying each by each a small petty death in the midst of their precious brief lives. So I ascended to the ancient ruins of the city of Macchu Picchu in the Andes; and there I found that, however the lives of my human brothers may have suffered, at least they are all now dead together. . . . I love the poor broken dead. They belong to me. I will not celebrate the past for its perfect power over the imperfect living. 'I come to speak for your dead mouths.' The silent and nameless persons who built Macchu Picchu are alive in Santiago de Chile. The living are the living, and the dead the dead must stay."

Neruda returned to Chile from exile in 1953, and, said Durán and Safir, spent the last twenty years of his life producing "some of the finest love poetry in *One Hundred Love Sonnets* and parts of *Extravagaria* and *Barcarole;* he produced Nature poetry that continued the movement toward close examination, almost still shots of every aspect of the external world, in the odes of *Voyages and Homecomings,* in *The Stones of Chile,* in *The Art of Birds,* in *A House by the Shore,* and in *Sky Stones.* He continued as well his role as public poet in *Chanson de Geste,* in parts of *Ceremonial Songs,* in the mythical *The Flaming Sword,* and the angry *A Call for Nixonicide and Glory to the Chilean Revolution.*"

However, at this time, Neruda's work began to move away from the highly political stance it had taken during the 1930s and toward a new type of poetry. Instead of concentrating on politicizing the common folk, Neruda began to try to speak to them simply and clearly, on a level that each could understand. He wrote poems on subjects ranging from rain to feet. By examining common, ordinary, everyday things very closely, according to Durán and Safir, Neruda gives us "time to examine a particular plant, a stone, a flower, a bird, an aspect of modern life, at leisure. We look at the object, handle it, turn it aroung, all the sides are examined with love, care, attention. This is, in many ways, Neruda . . . at his best."

In 1971, Neruda reached the peak of his political career when the Chilean Communist party nominated him for president. He withdrew his nomination, however, when he reached an accord with Socialist nominee Salvador Allende. After Allende won the election he reactivated Neruda's diplomatic credentials, making him ambassador to France. It was while Neruda was serving in Paris that he was awarded the Nobel Prize for literature, in recognition of his oeuvre. Poor health soon forced the poet to resign his post, however, and he returned to Chile, where he died in 1973—only days after a right-wing military coup had killed Allende and seized power. Many of his last poems—some of them published posthumously—indicate his awareness of his death's approach. Fernando Alegría wrote in *Modern Poetry Studies,* "I think Neruda confronted the final enigma with total consciousness and solved it in terms of love and surrender to the materialistic dynamic of the world as he conceived it. What I want to emphasize is something very simple: Neruda was, above all, a love poet and, more than anyone, an unwavering, powerful, joyous, conqueror of death."

MEDIA ADAPTATIONS: Some of Neruda's work has been recorded, including "Pablo Neruda Reads His Poems in Spanish," Spoken Arts, 1972, Rafael de Penagos reading "Poesías escogidas," Discos Aguilar, 1972, and "Loretta Pauker Reads Extended Excerpts of 'Let the Rail Splitter Awake' [and] 'The Dead in the Square,' " Khalan Records, 1973. Neruda has also been recorded by the Library of Congress. Christopher Logue's twenty poems *The Man Who Told His Love* [Middle Scorpion Press, 1958] are based on some of Neruda's poetry and Rudolph Holzmann's *Tres madrigales para canto y piano* [Editorial Argentina de Musica, 1946] sets Neruda's *Residencia en la tierra* to music.

AVOCATIONAL INTERESTS: Sailing.

BIOGRAPHICAL/CRITICAL SOURCES:

BOOKS

Benson, Rachel, translator, *Nine Latin American Poets,* Las Américas, 1968.
Bizzarro, Salvatore, *Pablo Neruda: All Poets the Poet,* Scarecrow Press, 1979.
Brotherton, Gordon, *Latin American Poetry: Origins and Presence,* Cambridge University Press, 1975.
Burnshaw, Stanley, editor, *The Poem Itself,* Holt, 1960.
Contemporary Literary Criticism, Gale, Volume 1, 1973, Volume 2, 1974, Volume 5, 1976, Volume 7, 1977, Volume 9, 1978, Volume 28, 1984.
de Costa, René, *The Poetry of Pablo Neruda,* Harvard University Press, 1979.
Durán, Manuel, and Margery Safir, *Earth Tones: The Poetry of Pablo Neruda,* Indiana University Press, 1981.
Eshleman, Clayton, translator and author of introduction, *Poemas humanos/Human Poems,* Grove Press, 1969.
Gallagher, David P., *Modern Latin American Literature,* Oxford University Press, 1973.
García Lorca, Federico, *Obras completas,* Aguilar, 1964.
Neruda, Pablo, *Confieso que he vivido: memorias,* Seix Barral (Barcelona), 1974, translation by Hardie St. Martin published as *Memoirs,* Farrar, Straus, 1977.
Reiss, Frank, *The Word and the Stone: Language and Imagery in Neruda's "Canto General,"* Oxford University Press, 1972.
Willard, Nancy, *Testimony of the Invisible Man: William Carlos Williams, Francis Ponge, Rainer Maria Rilke, Pablo Neruda,* University of Missouri Press, 1970.
Woodbridge, Hensley C., and David S. Zubatsky, compilers, *Pablo Neruda: An Annotated Bibliography of Biographical and Critical Studies,* Garland, 1988.

PERIODICALS

Book Week, May 28, 1967.
Books, June, 1966.
Encounter, September, 1965.
Evergreen Review, December, 1966.
Modern Poetry Studies, spring, 1974.
Nation, July 1, 1966.
New Leader, July 3, 1967.
New Statesman, June 4, 1965.
New York Review of Books, October 3, 1974.
New York Times, June 18, 1966, August 1, 1966, March 4, 1977.
New York Times Book Review, July 10, 1966, May 21, 1967.
Poetry, June, 1947, February, 1963, October, 1967, June, 1968.
Ramparts, September, 1974.
Saturday Review, July 9, 1966, November 13, 1971.

—Sketch by Kenneth R. Shepherd

*   *   *

NERVO, (José) Amado (Ruiz de) 1870-1919

PERSONAL: Born August 27, 1870, in Tepic, Mexico; died May 24, 1919, in Montevideo, Uruguay.

CAREER: Poet, novelist, short story writer, dramatist, and essayist. Worked as a journalist in Mazatlán, Mexico; *El Imparcial,* Mexico City, Mexico, journalist, beginning in 1894, European correspondent, 1900-01; served as secretary to the Mexican legation in Madrid, Spain, 1905-18, became minister to Argentina and Uruguay, 1919.

WRITINGS:

POETRY

Místicas, first published, 1898, published in *Perlas negras* (title means "Black Pearls"; also see below) [and] *Místicas,* 5th edition, Espasa-Calpe (Madrid), 1973.

Perlas negras, first published, 1898, published in *Perlas negras* [and] *Místicas,* 5th edition, Espasa-Calpe, 1973.

Poemas, first published, 1901, recent edition, Espasa-Calpe, 1973.

Los jardines interiores (title means "The Inner Gardens"), [Mexico], 1905.

En voz baja (title means "In a Low Voice"), first published, 1909, published in *En voz baja* [and] *La sombra del ala* [and] *Un libro amable* [and] *De "El éxodo y las flores del camino"* (also see below), Biblioteca "Las Grandes Obras," 1938.

Serenidad (title means "Serenity"), Renacimiento, 1914, 10th edition, Espasa-Calpe, 1973.

Elevación, Tipografía Artística (Madrid), 1917, 8th edition, introduction by Calixto Oyuela, Espasa-Calpe, 1973.

El estanque de los lotos (title means "The Lotus Pond"), 2nd edition, J. Menéndez (Buenos Aires), 1919.

La amada inmóvil (title means "The Motionless Lover"), first published, 1920, recent edition, introduction by Rafael Díaz Ycaza, Ariel, 1974.

Also author of *Lira heróica,* 1902. Poetry has been collected variously in such works as *Amado Nervo, sus mejores poemas, Poesías completas, Antología poética, Obras poéticas completas,* and *Los cien mejores poemas de Amado Nervo.* Translated selections of Nervo's poetry have appeared in *Some Spanish American Poets, The Modernist Trend in Spanish American Poetry, Anthology of Mexican Poets From the Earliest Times to the Present Day, Hispanic Anthology,* and *Anthology of Mexican Poetry.*

NOVELS

El donador de almas, first published, 1904, recent edition, B. Costa-Amic (Mexico), 1976 (also see below).

Otras vidas (includes *Pascual Aguilera* [also see below], *El bachiller* [also see below], and *El donador de almas*), J. Ballescá, 1909.

Also author of *El bachiller* (title means "The Bachelor"), 1895; *Pascual Aguilera,* 1896; *El diablo desinteresado,* 1916; *El diamante de la inquietud, Una mentira,* and *Un sueño,* all 1917; and *El sexto sentido* and *Amnesia,* both 1918.

SHORT STORIES

Almas que pasan, Tipografía de la Revista de Archivos (Madrid), 1906.

Ellos, Ediciones Literarias, c. 1912.

Amado Nervo, sus mejores cuentos, edited by Luis Leal, Houghton, 1951.

Cuentos y crónicas de Amado Nervo, prologue and selection by Manuel Durán, Universidad Nacional Autónoma de México, Dirección General de Publicaciones, Coordinación de Humanidades, 1971.

Also author of collection *Cuentos misteriosos* (title means "Mysterious Tales"), 1921. Author of "Leah and Rachel," published in *Spanish American Literature Since 1888.*

OTHER

Juana de Asbaje, Los Hijos de M. G. Hernández, 1910.

Plenitud (essays), first published, 1918, 11th edition, Espasa-Calpe (Mexico), 1963, translation by William F. Rice published as *Plenitude,* J. R. Miller (Los Angeles), 1928.

La mujer moderna y su papel en la evolución actual del mundo, Editorial Tor (Buenos Aires), 1919.

Obras completas de Amado Nervo, 28 volumes, edited by Alfonso Reyes, illustrations by Marco, Biblioteca Nueva (Madrid), 1920-22.

El arquero divino (poetry and prose), first published, 1922, published in *El arquero divino* [and] *Poesías varias* [and] *Pensando,* Biblioteca "Las Grandes Obras," 1938, 5th edition, Espasa-Calpe (Madrid), 1973.

Confessions of a Modern Poet, translated by Dorothy Kress, B. Humphries, 1935.

(Editor) *Lecturas literarias, tomadas de los mejores poetas y prosistas españoles hispanoamericanos* [and] *Seguidas de un breve juicio explicativo y crítico,* Editorial Patria (Mexico), 1939, 31st edition, 1972.

Fuegos fatuos y pimientos dulces, edited by Francisco González Guerrero, Porrúa (Mexico), 1951, 2nd edition, 1976.

Primavera y flor de su lírica, prologue and selection by Alfonso Méndez Plancarte, Aguilar (Madrid), 1952, 4th edition, 1971.

Semblanzas y crítica literaria, Universitaria (Mexico), 1952.

Obras completas, 2 volumes, 2nd edition, edited by González Guerrero and Méndez Plancarte, Aguilar, 1955-56, 4th edition, 1967.

Pensamientos de Amado Nervo, selection and notes by Antonia C. Gavaldá, Editorial Sintes (Barcelona), 1956.

Lecturas mexicanas, Editorial Patria, 1960.

Páginas de Amado Nervo, selection by Rafael Alberto Arrieta, Editorial Universitaria de Buenos Aires, 1964, 2nd edition, 1968.

Antología de Amado Nervo, prologue by Alfonso Reyes, Editorial Pax-México, 1969, 2nd edition, Oasis (Mexico), 1980.

Also author of poetry and prose collection *El éxodo y las flores del camino,* 1902, drama *Las voces,* 1904, and *Crónicas de Europa,* 1905-07. Author of essay "Let's Speak of Writers and Literature," published in *The Modern Mexican Essay.* Writer for literary journal *Revista Azul,* Mexico City; co-founder of *Revista Moderna.* Works have been collected variously in volumes.

SIDELIGHTS: Amado Nervo is widely regarded as one of Mexico's foremost modernist poets. Also a leading novelist, short story writer, and essayist, he is characterized by works imbued with religion, philosophy, and mysticism. Nervo, who embraced the "Modernismo" movement that emerged in Spanish-American literature near the turn of the twentieth century, was heavily influenced by French literary movements, in particular the French symbolist poets who sought to break from traditional poetic forms. While the author earned a reputation for his literary experimentation, he is perhaps most noted for his spiritual probes seeking to verify the existence of God. According to Roderick A. Molina writing in *The Americas,* "Nervo was, in every way, a religious temperament. He was one of those men so intent upon the divine that they can only find their happiness when they have solved for themselves, both theoretically and practically, the problem of God."

Born in Tepic, Mexico, Nervo was raised with religious training. He entered a seminary, but later opted against a career in the clergy and focused on writing. After working for a newspaper in Mazatlán, Nervo moved to Mexico City in 1894 to write for *El Imparcial.* One year later he realized his first literary success with the publication of *El bachiller.* A depiction of one man's struggle for spiritual wholeness, the novel concerns a seminarian who, awakened by sexual desire, castrates himself in order to successfully complete his religious pursuits.

Nervo wrote other novels concerning the importance of spiritual transcendence. His 1896 *Pascual Aguilera* depicts a protagonist whose uncontrollable passion and lack of spirituality ultimately destroy him. Similarly, Nervo's *El donador de almas* focuses on a man who, searching for a perfect relationship, becomes frustrated, torn between his desire for both worldly and spiritual love. Assessing Nervo's message in his novels, Dorothy Bratas wrote in *Romance Notes:* "Because of his intrinsic self-centeredness, man cannot love unselfishly. A perfect relationship must be completely reciprocal, and this condition can never exist because man is hindered by his physical desires. Nervo's ideal state is a sexless one. The best possible relationship is an intellectual marriage between individuals."

With his poetry, Nervo further searched for truth and the meaning of existence. Deeply involved in the modernist movement near the end of the nineteenth century (Nervo wrote for the modernist journals *Revista Azul* and *Revista Moderna*), the writer produced such verse collections as *Perlas negras* and *Poemas.* These early poems were heavily influenced by the symbolist poets and subsequently dwell in philosophy, mysticism, and melancholy. Nervo later turned to writing poetry influenced by the highly formalized French Parnassian poets of the early nineteenth century. "Enamored of the French poets," wrote Molina, "[Nervo's] poetry of that epoch is unforgettable; it was authentic; it was embellished, moreover, with expressive and musical forms, with graceful rhythms that combine with the turns of a dance, with a pleasant arrangement of metrical structures, and with an air of sadness, elegantly hidden and reserved."

Despite the acclaim he earned while writing under French influence, Nervo soon deviated from any fixed persuasion of literature and concentrated on his personal quest for spirituality. Questioning the tenets of Christianity, exploring the renunciation of the material world advocated by Hindu and Buddhist religions, and studying philosophy and mysticism, Nervo hoped to better understand both natural and supernatural existence. Such later volumes as *En voz baja, Serenidad, Elevación,* and his best-known *La amada inmóvil* reveal what critics recognized as an individual and mature style. "He had reached a stage where he recognized no arbitrary schools or rules in art," explained Isaac Goldberg in *Spanish-American Literature.* "[Nervo] had found himself and expressed his personality in poems that glow with a strange, new beauty. . . . A splendid independence, a wise ignorance, that may be purchased only at the price of so much slavery to the quest of beauty."

In addition to his novels and poems, Nervo wrote plays, short stories, and essays. Among the most celebrated of his nonfiction works are *Juana de Asbaje* and the 1918 essay collection *Plenitud.* The author died in 1919 in Uruguay after being named that country's diplomatic minister. *Obras completas,* twenty-eight volumes of Nervo's works, was published posthumously.

BIOGRAPHICAL/CRITICAL SOURCES:

BOOKS

Goldberg, Isaac, *Spanish-American Literature,* Brentano's Publishers, 1920.
Twentieth-Century Literary Criticism, Volume 11, Gale, 1983.

PERIODICALS

The Americas, Volume 6, number 2, October, 1949.
Romance Notes, Volume 9, number 2, spring, 1968.

NIGGLI, Josefina (Maria)   1910-

PERSONAL: Born July 13, 1910, in Monterrey, Neuvo León, Mexico; United States citizen; daughter of Frederick Ferdinand (a cement manufacturer) and Goldie (Morgan) Niggli. *Education:* Incarnate World College, B.A., 1931; University of North Carolina, M.A., 1937; attended Old Vic Theatre School, 1955.

ADDRESSES: Office—Department of Speech and Theatre Arts, Western Carolina University, Cullowhee, N.C. 28723. *Agent*—Ashley Famous Agency, Inc., 1301 Avenue of the Americas, New York, N.Y. 10019.

CAREER: University of North Carolina, Chapel Hill, instructor in radio, 1942-44; Metro-Goldwyn-Mayer Studios, Culver City, Calif., writer, 1951-52; University of North Carolina, Woman's College, Greensboro, assistant professor of drama, 1955-56; Western Carolina University, Cullowhee, N.C., associate professor, 1956-76, emeritus professor of speech and theatre arts, 1976—. Broadcaster of Latin American material for U.S. Department of State, 1942; guest instructor in playwriting at Bristol University, 1955-56.

MEMBER: American Theatre Association, American Educational Theatre Association, Dramatists Guild, Authors Guild, Photographic Society of America, Carolina Dramatic Association (past president).

AWARDS, HONORS: Rockefeller fellowships in playwriting, 1935-36 and 1937-38; Theatre Guild Bureau of New Plays fellowship, 1938-39; Rockefeller fellowship in Europe, 1950-51; Mayflower Cup for best work by a North Carolinian, 1946, for *Mexican Village;* Alumnia Award from University of North Carolina for work in drama.

WRITINGS:

Mexican Silhouettes (verse), privately printed, 1928, revised edition, Silhouette Press (San Antonio), 1931.
"Tooth or Shave" (play), first produced in 1935.
"The Cry of Dolores" (play), first produced in 1935.
"Soladadera" (play), first produced in 1936, published in *The Best One-Act Plays of 1937,* edited by Margaret Mayorga, Dodd, 1938.
"Azteca" (play), first produced in 1936.
"The Fair God" (play), first produced in 1936.
"Singing Valley" (play), first produced in 1936.
(Editor) *Mexican Folk Plays,* University of North Carolina Press, 1938, reprinted, Arno, 1976.
"This Is Villa" (one-act play), first produced in 1938, published in *The Best One-Act Plays of 1938,* edited by Mayorga, Dodd, 1939.
Red Velvet Goat (one-act play; first produced in 1936), Samuel French, c. 1938.
Sunday Costs Five Pesos (one-act play; first produced in 1936), Samuel French, 1939.
Miracle at Blaise (play), Samuel French, c. 1940, published in *Non-Royalty One-Act Plays for All-Girl Casts,* edited by Betty Smith, Greenburg, 1942.
"The Ring of General Macias" (play), published in *Twenty Prize-Winning Non-Royalty One-Act Plays,* edited by Smith, Greenburg, 1943.
"This Bull Ate Nutmeg" (play), in *Plays Without Footlights,* edited by Esther E. Galbraith, Harcourt, 1945.
Mexican Village (novel), University of North Carolina Press, 1945.
Pointers on Playwriting, The Writer (Boston), 1945, revised and enlarged edition published as *New Pointers on Playwriting,* 1967.

Pointers on Radio Writing, The Writer, 1946.
Step Down, Elder Brother (novel; Book-of-the-Month Club selection), Rinehart, 1947.
(With Norman Foster) "Sombrero" (screenplay), Metro-Goldwyn-Mayer, 1953.
A Miracle for Mexico (juvenile), New York Graphic Society, 1964.

Author of screenplays and television scripts. Work represented in anthologies. Contributor to periodicals, including *Collier's, Mexican Life, Ladies Home Journal, Vogue,* and *Writer.*

WORK IN PROGRESS: Red Amapola, a novel.

SIDELIGHTS: Josefina Niggli has distinguished herself in a variety of media and literary genres. As a playwright she has won particular acclaim for her one-act works, and as a novelist she has been recognized as a formidable colorist. In addition, she has written for film and has published a book offering advise to aspiring playwrights. Altogether, her writings constitute what Paula W. Shirley described in the *Dictionary of Literary Biography Yearbook: 1980* as "a notable contribution to American drama and prose."

Niggli is probably best known for her first novel, *Mexican Village.* In this episodic work Niggli conveys the rich and varied aspects of life in small-town Mexico. Ostensibly, the novel's hero is Bob Webster, a half-Mexican, half-American who arrives in the village of Hidalgo with intentions of only a brief stay. In ensuing episodes, village life is extensively revealed, with Niggli relying on folktales and related lore to enhance the account. Tradition is seen as an immensely important aspect of Hidalgo life, and social customs are emphasized as key elements in day-to-day activities. Webster, skeptical and aloof, initially resists the appeal of village traditions and thus gains respect as a relatively independent thinker. By novel's end, however, he has undergone complete integration into Hidalgo life. He abandons the Anglo surname acquired from his father, who never acknowledged the illegitimate Webster as his own son, and assumes his mother's family name, Ortega.

Upon publication in 1945, *Mexican Village* was hailed as a classic portrait of small-town Mexico. Orville Prescott, in *Yale Review,* declared that Niggli "is steeped in Mexican atmosphere" and added that *Mexican Village* is "an utterly engaging book by a richly gifted writer." Similarly, J. H. Jackson wrote in the *Weekly Book Review* that Niggli's novel is "without a peer in its field." "The American reader," Jackson continued, "will understand this particular Mexico . . . better, after he has read *Mexican Village,* than ever before."

Reviewers of *Mexican Village* also praised Niggli's narrative sensibility and her skill in creating believable characters. *New York Times* critic Mildred Adams noted the work's "pace and charm," while Prescott wrote in *Yale Review* that Niggli "is a strong advocate of the old-fashioned story-telling virtues." And *Book Week* reviewer J. T. Frederick noted that the book's "characters and incidents are warm with human reality."

Step Down, Elder Brother, Niggli's second novel, also features vivid descriptions and memorable characters. In this ambitious work Niggli addresses issues pertinent to both Mexico's upper and lower-middle classes in Monterrey: Domingo Vázquez de Anda, the oldest son in a distinquished family, finds himself torn between adherence to traditional values and pursuit of his own beliefs; Mateo Chapa, a budding businessman from a less prosperous family, aspires to the status of the Vázquez de Anda clan, and eventually marries into the family.

Like *Mexican Village,* Niggli's *Step Down, Elder Brother* impressed reviewers with its vivid, authentic depiction of Mexican life. Mildred Adams wrote in the *New York Times* that "the skill with people, the sense of place and dialogue, the ability to make the reader smell and taste and feel . . . are here," and B. D. Wolfe, in his assessment for the *New York Herald Tribune Weekly Book Review,* noted that "every page of [*Step Down, Elder Brother*] pulses with the pulsing life of Monterrey." For Wolfe, Niggli succeeded in evoking "the sense of being of an entire community." Likewise, *Commonweal* reviewer Bonaventure Schwinn declared that Niggli's "love for [Monterrey's] local color and her sympathetic understanding of the Mexican mind shine on every page."

Aside from her two novels, Niggli has published the children's book *A Miracle for Mexico,* which details a Spanish-Indian boy's adventures during the sixteenth-century. She also produced a how-to volume, *Pointers on Playwriting* (revised as *New Pointers on Playwriting*), that *New York Times* reviewer C. V. Terry hailed as "pure gold for anyone interested in the mysteries of dramaturgy."

Niggli has also written many plays, including various one-act works presented by the Carolina Players while she attended the University of North Carolina in the 1930s. In such plays as "Tooth or Shave," "The Red Velvet Goat," and "Sunday Costs Five Pesos," she presented humorous depictions of Mexican village life. "Tooth or Shave," for instance, provides a comedic perspective on the importance of possessions in determining status. In this play, one woman plans for her elaborate funeral, while another woman covets a record player. Ludicrous behavior is also manifest in this work—one character fears that he is too cowardly because he resists having his head removed. The more curious aspects of human nature are also explored in "Sunday Costs Five Pesos," in which a wood-carver becomes convinced that his lover has jumped down a well.

Among Niggli's other plays are historical works such as "The Fair God," "The Cry of Dolores," and "Azteca," which depicts Mexican life a century before the arrival of Spanish conquistadors. Another historical play, "Soldadera," is set during the Mexican revolution of 1910, as is "This Is Villa," which details the exploits of the controversial revolutionary.

Since the 1940s Niggli has published few works. But she is known to be working on another novel, *The Red Amapola,* which is concerned with leftist politics in Mexico in the later nineteenth century. Perhaps this work will lead to further recognition for Niggli as one whose writings afford readers an unmatched perspective on Mexican life.

AVOCATIONAL INTERESTS: Color photography.

BIOGRAPHICAL/CRITICAL SOURCES:

BOOKS

Dictionary of Literary Biography Yearbook: 1980, Gale, 1981.
Spearman, Walter, *The Carolina Playmakers: The First Fifty Years,* University of North Carolina Press, 1970.

PERIODICALS

Chicago Sun, January 29, 1948.
Christian Science Monitor, November 3, 1945.
Cleveland Open Shelf, January, 1948.
Commonweal, December 14, 1945, December 19, 1947, May 22, 1964.
MELUS, summer, 1978.

New York Herald Tribune Weekly Book Review, February 22, 1948.
New York Times, December 16, 1945, February 8, 1948.
New York Times Book Review, July 12, 1964.
San Francisco Chronicle, February 9, 1948.
Saturday Review of Literature, October 13, 1945, January 24, 1948.
Times Literary Supplement, September 7, 1967.
Weekly Book Review, October 7, 1945.
Yale Review, winter, 1946, spring, 1948.

—*Sketch by Les Stone*

* * *

NIOSI, Jorge 1945-

PERSONAL: Born December 8, 1945, in Buenos Aires, Argentina; son of Salvador (in business) and Emilia (Farina) Niosi; married Graciela Ducatenzeiler (a university professor), November, 1971; children: Marianne, Laurence. *Education:* National University of Buenos Aires, license in sociology, 1967; Institut d'Etudes du Developpement Economique et Social, Paris, France, certificate in advanced studies in economics, 1970; Ecole Pratique, Paris, Ph.D., 1973.

ADDRESSES: Home—4052 Marlowe, Montreal, Quebec, Canada H4A 3M2. *Office*—Center for Research on the Development of Industry and Technology, University of Quebec at Montreal, Annexe Garneau, 1750 rue Saint-Andre, Montreal, Quebec, Canada H3C 3P8.

CAREER: University of Quebec at Montreal, associate professor, 1970-74, aggregate professor, 1974-81, professor of sociology, 1981—, director of Center for Research on the Development of Industry and Technology, 1986—. Researcher at Statistics Canada, 1987-90.

MEMBER: International Sociological Association, Canadian Sociology and Anthropology Association.

AWARDS, HONORS: John Porter Award from Canadian Sociological Association, 1983, for *Canadian Capitalism.*

WRITINGS:

Los empresarios y el estado Argentino (title means "Business and the Argentine State"), Siglo XXI, 1974.
Le Controle financier du capitalisme canadien, Presses de l'Universite du Quebec, 1978, translation by Hugh Ballem and Penelope Williams published as *The Economy of Canada: Who Controls It?,* Black Rose Books, 1978.
Canadian Capitalism, Lorimer, 1981.
Canadian Multinationals, Garamond, 1985.
(With Bertrand Bellon) *L'Industrie americaine: Fin de siecle,* Boreal, 1987, translation published as *Industrial Decline: The End of the American Century,* Lexington Books, 1988.
The Decline of the American Economy, translation from the French by Robert Chodos, Black Rose Books, 1988.

WORK IN PROGRESS: Research on Canadian technology transfer abroad.

SIDELIGHTS: Jorge Niosi told *CA:* "I started working on Canada with the idea of comparing it to Argentina. Both countries were similarly rich and successful fifty years ago. Why did Argentina fail when Canada succeeded? The comparison, however, never materialized.

"In Canada, I discovered that Canadian-owned large firms were much stronger and numerous than generally believed, that many of them were multinational corporations, and that their industrial base was much healthier than most of the literature had previously stated. The relative decline of American industry is not strongly affecting Canada's manufacturing industry, which is mostly based on energy- and resource-intensive strongholds like pulp and paper, metal refining, and petrochemicals."

* * *

NOVAS CALVO, Lino 1905-1983

PERSONAL: Born September 22, 1905, in Granas del Sor, Spain; died in April, 1983, in New York.

CAREER: Short story writer, novelist, poet, playwright, essayist, translator, and journalist. Correspondent for journal *Orbe,* Spain, beginning in 1931; writer for various newspapers and journals in Europe, 1931-39; editor for magazine *Ultra,* Cuba, beginning in 1940; teacher of French at Havana Teachers College, 1947-60; self-imposed exile to New York, 1960; staff member of magazines *Bohemia Libre* and *Vanidades,* New York; Syracuse University, Syracuse, N.Y., visiting professor of Spanish, 1967-74.

AWARDS, HONORS: Hernández-Catá Prize, 1942, for short story "Un dedo encima"; honorary degree in journalism from National School of Journalism, Havana, 1943; National Short Story Prize, 1944, for *La luna nona y otros cuentos.*

WRITINGS:

El negrero: Vida novelada de Pedro Blanco Fernández de Trava (novel), Espasa-Calpe (Madrid), 1933, 2nd edition, Espasa-Calpe Argentina (Buenos Aires), 1944.
La luna nona y otros cuentos (stories; contains "La luna nona," "Aquella noche salieron los muertos," "La noche de Ramón Yendía," "Long Island," "En el Cayo," "En las afueras," "La primera lección," and "Hombre malo"), Ediciones Nuevo Romance (Buenos Aires), 1942.
No sé quién soy (novel), Viñetas de Rigol (Mexico), 1945.
En los traspatios (novel), Editorial Páginas (Havana), 1946.
Cayo Canas (stories; contains "Cayo Canas," "El otro cayo" [also see below], "La visión de Tamaría," "Un dedo encima," "No le sé desil," ".Trínquenme ahí a ese hombre!," and " 'Aliados' y 'alemanes' "), Espasa-Calpe Argentina, 1946.
El otro cayo, 2nd edition, Cruzada Latino-Americana de Difusión Cultural (Havana), 1959.
Maneras de contar, Las Américas Publishing (New York), 1970.

Also author of poetry, published in *Revista de Avance,* 1928-29. Author of plays and essays. Translated into Spanish works by William Faulkner, Robert Graves, Aldous Huxley, D. H. Lawrence, Ernest Hemingway, and Honoré de Balzac. Contributor to periodicals, including *Revista de Occidente, Gaceta Literaria, El Sol, La Voz,* and *Diario de Madrid.*

SIDELIGHTS: A Spanish-born writer who moved to Cuba at an early age, Lino Novás Calvo is perhaps most noted for his 1933 novel *El negrero,* a novelized biography of slave-trader Pedro Blanco Fernández de Trava. He also earned literary recognition for his award-winning short stories that concern Cuba's lower class; these stories were published in the collections *La luna nona y otros cuentos* and *Cayo Canas.*

BIOGRAPHICAL/CRITICAL SOURCES:

BOOKS

Souza, Raymond D., *Lino Novás Calvo,* Twayne, 1981.

NOVO, Salvador 1904-1974

PERSONAL: Born July 30, 1904, in Mexico City, Mexico; died of a heart attack in 1974 in Mexico City, Mexico; son of Andrés Novo and Amelia López (Espino) Blanco. *Education:* Attended Universidad Nacional, Mexico, 1917-24.

CAREER: Poet and playwright. Professor of drama, National Conservatory, 1930-33; director of public relations, Foreign Relations Ministry, 1930-34; Instituto Nacional de Bellas Artes, Chapultepec Park, Mexico, director of School of Drama and head of theatrical productions, 1946-56; Universidad Nacional, Mexico City, Mexico, professor of literature and theater, 1955-74; official chronicler of Mexico City, 1965-74. Play director and owner, Teatro de la Capilla, Coyoacán, Mexico; owner, La Capilla Restaurant; script writer for Light and Sound show, Teotihuacán Pyramids.

MEMBER: Mexican Academy of Languages, Spanish Academy (corresponding member).

AWARDS, HONORS: National Letters prize (Mexico), 1967; Mexico City Prize.

WRITINGS:

POEMS

Espejo, poemas antiguos (also see below), Taller de la Mundial, 1933.
Nuevo amor (also see below), translated by Edna Worthley Underwood, Mosher Press, 1935, reprinted, Gordon Press, 1977.
Poesías escogidas, Nandino (Mexico City), 1938.
Poesía, 1915-1955, Impresiones Modernas, 1955.
Poesía: Veinte poemas. Espejo. Nuevo amor, y poesías no coleccionadas (anthology), Fondo de Cultura Económica, 1961, reprinted, 1977.
Dieciocho sonetos, [Mexico], 1963.
Antología, 1925-1965, prologue by Antonio Castro Leal, Porrúa, 1966.
Catorce sonetos de Navidad y Año Nuevo, 1955-1968, [Mexico], 1968, published with English translation by Laura Villaseñor, 1969.
Sátira, Alberto Dallal, 1970.
Nuevo amor y otras poesías, Fondo de Cultura Económica, 1984.

PLAYS

"Divorcio" (title means "Divorce"), produced in Mexico, 1924.
"La señorita Remington," produced in Mexico, 1924.
El coronel Astucia y los Hermanos de la Hoja; o, Los Charros Contrabandistas (adapted from the novel by Luis G. Inclán), Instituto Nacional de Bellas Artes, 1948.
Don Quijote; farsa en tres actos y dos entremeses, Instituto Nacional de Bellas Artes, 1948.
La dama culta, comedia en tres actos, [Mexico], 1951, reprinted (with *Hoy invita a Güera* by Federico S. Inclán), Secretaría de Educación Pública, Cultura, 1984.
El joven II; un monólogo (also see below), [Mexico], 1951.
A ocho columnas; pieza en tres actos, [Mexico], 1956, Novaro, 1970.
Diálogos: El joven II. Adán y Eva. El tercer Fausto. La güera y la estrella. Sor Juana y Pita. Malinche y Carlota. Diego y Betty. Cuauhtémoc y Eulalia (anthology), [Mexico], 1956.
Yocasta, o casi; pieza en tres actos, (also see below), [Mexico], 1961, Novaro, 1970.
Ha vuelto Ulises; un acto, Alacena, 1962.
Cuauhtémoc, pieza en un acto (also see below), [Mexico], 1962.

La guerra de las gordas (also see below; title means "The War of the Fat Ladies"), Fondo de Cultura Económica, 1963.
In Ticitezcatl; or, El espejo encantado. Cuauhtémoc. El sofá. Diálogo de ilustres en la Rotonda (anthology), Universidad Veracruzana, 1966.
Diálogos (anthology), Novaro, 1970.
Yocasta o casi; La guerra de las gordas, Mexicanos Unidos, 1985.

ESSAYS

En defensa de lo usado, y otros ensayos, Polis, 1938.
Las aves en la poesía castellana, Fondo de Cultura Económica, 1953.
El teatro inglés, Instituto Nacional de Bellas Artes, 1960.
(With Celestino Gorostiza) *Los paradojas del teatro,* [Mexico], 1960.
Don Quijote en la escena, Universidad de Nuevo León, 1961.
Letras vencidas, Universidad Veracruzana, 1962, reprinted, 1981.
Las locas, el sexo, los burdeles, Novaro, 1972.

HISTORY

Breve historia de Coyoacán, Era, 1962.
La vida en México en el período presidencial de Lázaro Cárdenas, Empresas Editoriales, 1964.
Breve historia y antología sobre la fiebre amarilla, edited by the Secretary of Health and Assistance, Prensa Médica Mexicana, 1964.
La vida en México en el período presidencial de Manuel Avila Camacho, Empresas Editoriales, 1965.
La ciudad de México, del 9 de junio al 15 de julio de 1867 (also see below), Porrúa, 1967.
Cocina mexicana; o, Historia gastronómica de la ciudad de México, Porrúa, 1967.
La vida en México en el período presidencial de Miguel Alemán, Empresas Editoriales, 1967.
Apuntes para una historia de la publicidad en la ciudad de México, Organización Editorial Novaro, 1968.
(With others) *La vida y la cultura en México al triunfo de la República en 1867* (includes *La ciudad de México, del 9 de junio al 15 de julio de 1867*), Instituto Nacional de Bellas Artes, 1968.
(With Edmundo O'Gorman) *Guía de las actas de Cabildo de la ciudad de México, siglo XVI,* Fondo de Cultura Económica, 1970.
Historia y leyenda de Coyoacán, Novaro, 1971.
Un año, hace ciento; la ciudad de México en 1873, Porrúa, 1973.
Historia de la aviación en México, Compañía Mexicana de Aviación, 1974.
Los paseos de la ciudad de México, Fondo de Cultura Económica, 1974.
(With Miguel Capistrán) *La vida en la ciudad de México en 1824,* Novaro, 1974.
Una visita a la sala México, Instituto Nacional de Antropología e Historia, 1977.

OTHER

(Editor) *Antología de cuentos mexicanos e hispanoamericanos* (short stories), "Cvltvra", 1923.
Continente vacío (viaje a Sudamérica) (travel), Espasa-Calpe (Madrid), 1935.
Nueva grandeza mexicana; ensayo sobre la ciudad de México y sus alrededores, Hermes, 1946, translation by Noel Lindsay published as *New Mexico Grandeur,* Era, 1967.
Este y otros viajes (travel), Stylo, 1951.

(Author of prologue) Enrique de Olavarría y Ferrari, *Reseña histórica del teatro en México, 1538-1911,* Porrúa, 1961.

(Editor and author of introduction) *Mil y un sonetos mexicanos del siglo XVI al XX* (sonnets), Porrúa, 1963.

Toda la prosa (anthology of prose writings), Empresas Editoriales, 1964.

(Editor) *Joyas de la amistad, engarzada en una antología,* Porrúa, 1964.

(Editor) *101 poemas; antología bilingüe de la poesía norteamericana/101 Poems; Bilingual Anthology of Modern American Poetry,* Letras, 1965.

(Author of prologue) José Zorrilla y Moral, *Don Juan Tenorio y El puñal del godo,* Porrúa, 1966.

México, imagen de una ciudad (guidebook), Fondo de Cultura Económica, 1967.

(Author of text with Carlos Pellicer) Fulvio Roiter, *Mexico,* Atlantis (Zurich), 1968.

(With Francis Stoppelman) *México en movimiento/Mexico on the Move* (travel), bilingual edition with English translation by Flora van Os-Gammon, Nederlandse Rotogravure Maatschappij (Netherlands), 1970.

(Editor) *Seis siglos de la ciudad de México: Antología,* Fondo de Cultura Económica, 1974.

(Editor) María del Carmen Ruiz Castañeda, Luis Reed Torres, and Enrique Cordero y Torres, *El periodismo en México: 450 años de historia,* Tradición, 1974.

(Author of prologue) Federico García Lorca, *Selecciones,* Porrúa, 1982.

Also author of children's plays and Spanish translations of plays. Editor and writer, *Contemporáneos,* 1928-33; founder, *Ulises.*

SIDELIGHTS: "After almost half a century of literary production, which encompasses all genres, the impact of Salvador Novo's works on Mexican literature is incalculable," Michele Muncy asserted in *Salvador Novo y su teatro.* "A poet of great talent," as the critic described him, Novo was a member of the *Contemporáneos* circle which included such notable Mexican writers as Xavier Villaurrutia; nevertheless, Novo "stands apart from the rest of the Contemporáneos group because of his note of irony," Frank Dauster wrote in *Ensayos sobre poesía mexicana: Asedio a los "Contemporáneos."* The critic explained that like T. S. Eliot, Novo is "desolate; therefore, one sees more clearly in his poetry the terrible dichotomy that characterizes the true ironist, the open wound of lacerated feeling hidden behind the ironic face." Raúl Leiva similarly noted in *Imagen de la poesía mexicana contemporánea* that the author's poetry "is surprising in the complexity of its tones, for Novo has made his lyre vibrate with multiple accents that offer to us the intimate story of his soul." He is, the critic concluded, "one of only a few who have known how to use his lyre to play the exemplary sounds of true poetry."

"Salvador Novo is one of the most understanding poets of Mexico, and he has contributed something uncommon in Mexican poetry—irony," an *Insula* critic claimed. "Therefore, it is no surprise that [Novo] now gives us in *The War of the Fat Ladies* a theatrical farce based on historical episodes prior to the Spanish Conquest." Novo was also a prolific dramatist who helped found Mexico's first experimental theater, Teatro Ulises, and as Muncy observed, "his dramatic oeuvre makes him one of the writers of the Mexican theater who most deserves fame. His development

has paralleled that of the Mexican theater, which moved from a period of social criticism to a theater that exalted the Indian." With works such as "La dama culta" ("The Cultured Lady") and "Yocasta o casi" ("Jocasta, or Almost"), Novo created a "social theater [which] enabled him to get close to the public, which recognized his virtues as a dramatist."

As well as his ventures into poetry and drama, Novo excelled in novels, criticism, and nonfiction; he penned several travelogues in addition to the numerous histories he wrote in his capacity as official chronicler of Mexico City. "Among the essayists born in this century, Novo has no equals," Emmanuel Carballo remarked in *Diecinueve protagonistas de la literatura mexicana del siglo XX.* "He has created successive rhetorical modes, abandoning each as it became part of the public domain." Despite Novo's influence as a creative writer, Merlin H. Forster believed that "to achieve an overall understanding of Salvador Novo's work, one must know his prose writings," as he stated in *Los contemporáneos, 1920-1932: Perfil de un experimento vanguardista mexicano.* "The development of what Guillermo Jiménez has called a 'deserved reputation as an agile and sardonic genius' is due in great part to the numerous articles, essays, descriptive narratives, and travel commentaries Novo has written. This work," the critic concludes, "is extremely varied and not easily separable . . . into categories like creative narrative prose and critical prose," for many of Novo's essays were "unique within the [Contemporáneos] group."

BIOGRAPHICAL/CRITICAL SOURCES:

BOOKS

Carballo, Emmanuel, *Diecinueve protagonistas de la literatura mexicana del siglo XX,* Empresas, 1965.

Dauster, Frank, *Ensayos sobre poesía mexicana: Asedio a los "Contemporáneos,"* De Andrea, 1963.

Forster, Merlin H., *Los contemporáneos, 1920-1932: Perfil de un experimento vanguardista mexicano,* De Andrea, 1964.

Foster, David William and Virginia Ramos Foster, editors, *Modern Latin American Literature,* Ungar, 1975.

Leiva, Raúl, *Imagen de la poesía mexicana contemporánea,* Universitaria, 1959.

Muncy, Michele, *Salvador Novo y su teatro,* Atlas, 1971.

PERIODICALS

Insula, October, 1964.

OBITUARIES:

PERIODICALS

Hispania, September, 1974.

*   *   *

NOVOA, John David Bruce
  See BRUCE-NOVOA, Juan D.

*   *   *

NOVOA, Juan Bruce
  See BRUCE-NOVOA, Juan D.

O

OCA, Marco Antonio Montes de
   See MONTES de OCA, Marco Antonio

*   *   *

OCAMPO, Silvina 1906-

PERSONAL: Born in 1906, in Buenos Aires, Argentina; married Adolfo Bioy Casares (a writer), 1940; children: Marta. *Education:* Studied painting in Paris.

ADDRESSES: Home—Posadas 1650, 1112 Buenos Aires, Argentina.

CAREER: Writer. Has exhibited her paintings.

AWARDS, HONORS: Second prize, National Poetry Competition (Argentina), 1953, for *Los nombres;* first prize, National Poetry Competition (Argentina), 1962, for *Lo amargo por dulce;* Premio Club de los XIII (Argentina), 1988.

WRITINGS:

IN ENGLISH TRANSLATION

(Editor with Jorge Luis Borges and husband, Adolfo Bioy Casares) *Antología de la literatura fantástica* (title means "Anthology of Fantastic Literature"), with foreword by Bioy Casares, Sudamericana, 1940, enlarged edition with postscript by Bioy Casares, 1965, translation of revised version published as *The Book of Fantasy,* with an introduction by Ursula K. Le Guin, Viking, 1988.

(Contributor) Bioy Casares and Borges, editors, *Cuentos breves y extraordinarios: Antología,* Raigal (Buenos Aires), 1955, revised and enlarged edition, Losada, 1973, translation by Anthony Kerrigan published as *Extraordinary Tales,* Souvenir Press, 1973.

Leopoldina's Dream (short story anthology), translated by Daniel Balderston, Penguin, 1988.

IN SPANISH

Viaje olvidado (short stories), Sur, 1937.

(Editor with Bioy Casares and Borges) *Antología poética argentina* (title means "Anthology of Argentine Poetry"), Sudamericana, 1941.

Enumeración de la patria y otros poemas (also see below), Sur, 1942.

Espacios métricos (also see below; title means "Metric Spaces"; poetry), Sur, 1945.

(With Bioy Casares) *Los que aman, odian* (title means "Those Who Love, Hate"; novel), Emecé, 1946.

Sonetos del jardín (title means "Garden Sonnets"; poetry; contains selections from *Enumeración de la patria* and *Espacios métricos*), Colección La Perdiz, 1948.

Poemas de amor desesperado (also see below; title means "Poems of Hopeless Love"), Sudamericana, 1949.

Los nombres (title means "The Names"; poetry), Emecé, 1953.

Pequeña antología (title means "Small Anthology"; poetry; includes selections from *Poemas de amor desesperado, Espacios métricos,* and *Enumeración de la patria*), Ene (Buenos Aires), 1954.

(With J. R. Wilcock) *Los traidores* (title means "The Traitors"; drama in verse), Losada, 1956.

La furia y otros cuentos (also see below; title means "The Storm and Other Stories"), Sur, 1959.

(Contributor) Bioy Casares and Borges, editors, *Libro del cielo y del infierno* (title means "Book of Heaven and Hell"), Sur, 1960.

Las invitadas (also see below; title means "The Guests"; short stories), Losada, 1961.

Lo amargo por dulce, Emecé, 1962.

El pecado mortal (title means "The Mortal Sin"; short stories; contains stories from *Las invitadas* and *La furia y otros cuentos*), Universitaria, 1966.

Informe del cielo y del infierno (title means "Report on Heaven and Hell"; short stories; includes stories from *La furia y otros cuentos* and *Las invitadas*), Monte Avila (Caracas), 1970.

Los días de la noche (title means "The Days of the Night"; short stories), Sudamericana, 1970.

Amarillo celeste (title means "Sky Yellow"; poems), Losada, 1972.

El caballo alado (title means "The Winged Horse"; juvenile fiction), Ediciones de la Flor, 1972.

El cofre volante (also see below; title means "The Flying Trunk"; juvenile fiction), Estrada (Buenos Aires), 1974.

Autobiografía de Irene (title means "Irene's Autobiography"; short stories and a novella), Sudamericana, 1975.

El tobogán (title means "The Toboggan"; juvenile fiction; sequel to *El cofre volante*), Estrada, 1975.

La naranja maravillosa: Cuentos juveniles (title means "The Magical Orange: Juvenile Stories"), Orión, 1977.

(With Aldo Sesso) *Arboles de Buenos Aires* (title means "Trees of Buenos Aires"; poetry), Librería de la Ciudad (Buenos Aires), 1980.

La continuación y otras páginas (anthology), Centro Editor de América Latina, 1981.

Breve santoral (title means "Short Book of Saints"), illustrations by Norah Borges, Ediciones de Arte Gaglianone (Buenos Aires), 1984.

Así sucesivamente (short stories and a poem), Tusquets (Barcelona), 1987.

Also author of *Canto escolar,* a book of poetry.

SIDELIGHTS: Although not well-known outside her native Argentina, Silvina Ocampo enjoys a reputation as an established poet and short story writer in her homeland. Active in Argentine literary life since the late 1930s, Ocampo, the younger sister of *Sur* editor Victoria Ocampo, is married to Argentine novelist Adolfo Bioy Casares and is also a lifelong friend of Argentine short story writer and poet Jorge Luis Borges. According to a *World Literature Today* contributor, Borges was enthusiastic about Ocampo's writing and once referred to her as "one of the best poets in Spanish." An artist as well as a writer, among Ocampo's first creative works to be published were drawings based on a couple of Borges's earliest poems. After her 1940 marriage to Adolfo Bioy Casares, who collaborated with Borges on several fictional works, she and her husband hosted a weekly literary open house for Borges and other writers of their acquaintance, including Chilean novelist María Luisa Bombal and Argentine poet Ezequiel Martínez Estrada.

English-speaking readers will be most familiar with Ocampo's collaborations with Bioy Casares and Borges, especially their work as editors on *The Book of Fantasy* (*Antología de literatura fantástica*), an anthology of fantastic tales. *Los Angeles Times Book Review* contributor Laurence Coven notes that the work "provides a woodshed of tales, parables and fragments to rekindle the fire of our imagination." First appearing in English more than forty years after its original Spanish edition, the volume is an early look at the fantastic element evident in many of the works of Latin American writers of recent years. Its importance in literary history is commented on by Alberto Manguel in the *Ottawa Citizen:* "The *Antologia* was an extraordinary success, not as much in the actual number of copies sold . . . but in the influence it had on its select public. It provided readers with a guide to realms that had until then belonged to either campfire tales or to the psychological novel, and it showed to writers vast areas of fiction that demanded neither the journalistic constraints of a Sinclair Lewis nor the fancies of children's fairy tales."

BIOGRAPHICAL/CRITICAL SOURCES:

PERIODICALS

Los Angeles Times Book Review, March 26, 1989.
Ottawa Citizen, July 8, 1989.
World Literature Today, spring, 1988.

*   *   *

OCAMPO (de ESTRADA), Victoria 1890-1979

PERSONAL: Born in 1890 in Argentina; died January 27, 1979, in San Isidro, Argentina; married, c. 1912 (separated, c. 1923).

ADDRESSES: Home—San Isidro, Argentina.

CAREER: Writer. Founding editor of *Sur,* 1931; founder of Sur publishing company. Head of management of Teatro Colón, Buenos Aires, Argentina, 1933; co-founder of Argentine Women's Union, 1936 (president, 1936 and 1938); president of Commission of Letters of National Foundation for the Arts in Argentina.

MEMBER: International PEN, Argentine Academy of Letters.

AWARDS, HONORS: Grand prize of honor from Argentine Society of Writers, 1950; Vaccaro Prize (Argentina), 1966; Premio Alberti y Sarmiento, 1967; decorated Palmes Academiques; officer of French Legion of Honor; Commander of Order of the British Empire.

WRITINGS:

IN ENGLISH TRANSLATION

338171 T. E. (Lawrence de Arabia) (biography of T. E. Lawrence), Sur, 1942, enlarged edition, Sur, 1963, translation by David Garnett published as *338171 T. E. (Lawrence of Arabia),* Dutton, 1963.

(Contributor) Doris Meyer, *Victoria Ocampo: Against the Wind and the Tide* (includes fifteen essays by Ocampo), Braziller, 1980.

IN SPANISH

De Francesca a Beatrice: A través de La Divina Comedia (title means "From Francesca to Beatrice: Across The Divine Comedy"), 1924, Revista de Occidente (Madrid), 1928, Sur, 1963.

Supremacía del alma y de la sangre, Sur, 1935.

La mujer y su expresión (title means "Woman and Her Expression"), Sur, 1936.

Domingos en Hyde Park (title means "Sundays in Hyde Park"), Sur, 1936.

Viaje olvidado, Sur, 1937.

Emily Bronte (Terra incognita), Sur, 1938.

Virginia Woolf: Orlando y cia (title means "Virginia Woolf: Orlando and Company"), Sur, 1938.

San Isidro: Con un poema de Silvina Ocampo y 68 fotos de Gustav Thorlichen (title means "San Isidro: With a Poem by Silvina Ocampo and 68 Photographs by Gustav Thorlichen"), Sur, 1941.

Henry V y Laurence Olivier, con los principales pasajes de la obra (title means "Henry V and Laurence Olivier, with Principle Passages from the Work"), Sur, 1947.

Lawrence de Arabia, y otros ensayos (title means "Lawrence of Arabia, and Other Essays"), Aguilar, 1951.

Habla el algarrobo, Sur, 1959.

(Author of prologue) Ricardo Güiraldes, *Rosaura,* Sudamericana, 1960.

Tagore en las barrancas de San Isidro, Isidro, Sur, 1961.

Fryda Schultz, *Victoria Ocampo* (contains anthology of works by Ocampo), Ediciones Culturales Argentinas, 1963.

La belle y sus enamorados (title means "Beauty and Her Lovers"), Sur, 1964.

Also author of *La laguna de los nenufares,* 1926; *Testimonios* (memoirs, personal essays, and criticism), ten volumes, c. 1935-75; *Soledad sonora,* 1950; *El viajero y una de sus sombras,* 1951; *Antología de Jawaharlal Nehru: Selección y prólogo,* 1966; *Diálogos con Borges,* 1969; *Diálogos con Mallea,* 1969. Translator of works by various authors, including William Faulkner, Graham Greene, D. H. Lawrence, Albert Camus, Collette, Dylan Thomas, John Osborne, and Lanza del Vasto. Contributor to *La Nación.*

SIDELIGHTS: Although Victoria Ocampo's writings are extensive, they stand in the background of her work as editor of the influential Argentine literary magazine *Sur.* For more than forty years her publication served as a forum for both Latin and North American authors and earned Ocampo the distinction as the "grande dame" of Argentine letters. Besides her work as an editor and writer, Ocampo is also remembered for her efforts in support of women's rights and her strong stand against the Perón dictatorship which led to a one-month prison stay in the 1950s.

Ocampo was born the eldest of six daughters in a family that stood "at the center of artistic, financial, and social aristocracy" in her country, reported Eleanor Munro in *Ms.* At the age of six Ocampo lived in London and Paris, and she learned English, French, and Italian as a child. Her first literary interests were the works of French and English authors; it was not until she was in her thirties, when she read the writings of José Ortega y Gasset, that she developed an appreciation of her native Spanish language.

The same aristocratic upbringing that provided her an education also restricted her. Women were not expected to achieve outside the home, and her father reinforced that notion: he once lamented that Victoria was born a girl, for she would otherwise have been a brilliant student. The limits of her class also confined Ocampo, whose love of Shakespeare and Racine had made her want to pursue an acting career. As Munro noted, the possibility of becoming an actress "was out of the question for a girl of her class." Ocampo would likely have taken up writing sooner, too, if it were not for her society's belief that "women didn't write."

Despite familial and cultural restrictions, Ocampo managed to establish herself in the Buenos Aires literary world. She befriended Indian poet Rabindranath Tagore on his visit to Argentina in 1923, and a year later her first book, a guide to Dante's *Divine Comedy,* was published. In 1929 novelist and critic Waldo Frank urged Ocampo to begin an avant-garde literary magazine of her own. With that advice and additional encouragement from Ortega y Gasset, Ocampo published the first edition of *Sur* in 1931. According to Munro, *Sur* was Ocampo's "bridge of human understanding between artists of the world." The magazine held a dual function for its readers: it introduced new Latin American talent while offering Spanish translations of the works of North American and European artists. Ocampo is credited with being the first to publish a number of Argentine writers, most notably Jorge Luis Borges. At the same time she brought the works of D. H. Lawrence, William Faulkner, Richard Wright, James Joyce, Carl Jung, and Virginia Woolf, among others, to Latin American readers. Through her efforts with *Sur,* Ocampo "put her personal and financial resources at the disposition of Argentine letters," observed H. Ernest Lewald of *Books Abroad* in 1968. "*Sur* has been the finest literary outlet in Latin America for almost forty years."

Ocampo's only book to appear in English was her 1963 biography of T. E. Lawrence (Lawrence of Arabia), *338171 T.E.* The bulk of her effort went towards *Sur,* and because of it, declared Munro, Ocampo "is still a legend in the international literary world." Doris Meyer wrote in her *Review* tribute to the Argentine, "Whether defending democratic principles under the Peronist dictatorship, speaking out for women's rights or for international dialogues in the pursuit of excellence in the arts, she never shied away from controversy. As she once put it, 'Tranquility was never my ideal as a goal in life.'"

BIOGRAPHICAL/CRITICAL SOURCES:

BOOKS

Meyer, Doris, *Victoria Ocampo: Against the Wind and the Tide,* Braziller, 1980.

PERIODICALS

Américas, May, 1976.
Books Abroad, spring, 1969.
Ms., January, 1975.
Review, number 24, 1979.
Time, April 8, 1946.
UNESCO Courier, August, 1977.

OBITUARIES:

PERIODICALS

Publishers Weekly, February 26, 1979.
Time, February 12, 1979.

* * *

OLIVELLA, Manuel Zapata
See ZAPATA OLIVELLA, Manuel

* * *

ONETTI, Juan Carlos 1909-

PERSONAL: Born July 1, 1909, in Montevideo, Uruguay; son of Carlos and Honoria (Borges) Onetti; married Dolly Muhr, November, 1955; children: Jorge, Isabel.

ADDRESSES: Home—Gonzalo Ramfrez 1497, Montevideo, Uruguay.

CAREER: Writer of novels and short stories. Worked as editor for Reuter Agency in Montevideo, Uruguay, 1942-43, and in Buenos Aires, Argentina, 1943-46; manager of advertising firm in Montevideo, 1955-57; director of municipal libraries in Montevideo, beginning 1957.

AWARDS, HONORS: National Literature Prize of Uruguay, 1963; Ibera-American Award from William Faulkner Foundation, 1963; Casa de las Américas Prize, 1965; Italian-Latin American Institute Prize, 1972.

WRITINGS:

El pozo (also see below), Signo, 1939, enlarged and revised edition bound with *Origen de un novelista y de una generación literaria* by Angel Rama, Editorial Alfa, 1965, 2nd revised edition, Arca, 1973.
Tierra de nadie (novel), Editorial Losada, 1941, reprinted, Editorial Seix Barral, 1979.
Para esta noche, Editorial Poseidon, 1943.
La vida breve (novel), Editorial Sudamericana, 1950, reprinted, Edhasa, 1980, translation by Hortense Carpentier published as *A Brief Life,* Grossman, 1976.
Un sueño realizado y otros cuentos (also see below), Número, 1951.
Los adioses (novel; also see below), Sur, 1954, reprinted, Bruguera, 1981.
Una tumba sin nombre, Marcha, 1959, published as *Para una tumba sin nombre* (also see below), Arca, 1959, reprinted, Editorial Seix Barral, 1982.
La cara de la desgracia (novella; also see below), Editorial Alfa, 1960.

El astillero (novel), Compañía General Fabril Editora, 1961, reprinted, Cátedra, 1983, translation by Rachel Caffyn published as *The Shipyard,* Scribner, 1968.

El infierno tan temido, Editorial Asir, 1962.

Tan triste como ella (also see below), Editorial Alfa, 1963, reprinted, Lumen, 1982.

Juntacadáveres (novel), Editorial Alfa, 1964, revised edition, Arca, 1973.

Jacob y el otro (also see below) [and] *Un sueño realizado y otros cuentos,* Ediciones de la Banda Oriental, 1965.

Cuentos completos, Centro Editor de América Latina, 1967, revised edition, Corregidor, 1974.

Tres novelas (contains *La cara de la desgracia, Tan triste como ella,* and *Jacob y el otro*), Editorial Alfa, 1967.

Novelas cortas completas (contains *El pozo, Los adioses, La cara de la desgracia, Tan triste como ella,* and *Para una tumba sin nombre*), Monte Avila Editores, 1968.

La novia robada y otros cuentos (short stories including "La novia robada"; also see below), Centro Editor de América Latina, 1968, reprinted, Siglo Veintiuno Editores, 1983.

Los rostros del amor, Centro Editor de América Latina, 1968.

Obras completas, Aguilar, 1970.

La muerte y la niña (also see below), Corregidor, 1973.

Onetti (collection of articles and interviews), Troisi y Vaccaro, 1974.

Tiempo de abrazar y los cuentos de 1933 a 1950 (short stories), Arca, 1974.

(With Joacquin Torres-García and others) *Testamento artístico,* Biblioteca de Marcha, 1974.

Réquiem por Faulkner, Arca, 1975.

Tan triste como ella y otros cuentos (short stories), Lumen, 1976.

El pozo [and] *Para una tumba sin nombre,* Editorial Calicanto/ Arca, 1977, 2nd edition, Seix Barral, 1980.

Dejemos hablar al viento, Bruguera Alfaguara, 1979.

La muerte y la niña [and] *La novia robada,* Bruguera, 1980.

Cuentos secretos, Biblioteca de Marcha, 1986.

Presencia y otros cuentos, Almarabu, 1986.

Cuando entonces, Editorial Sudamericana, 1988.

Editor of *Marcha,* 1939-42, and *Vea y Lea,* 1946-55.

SIDELIGHTS: Although considered by a number of critics to be among the finest and most innovative novelists in South America, Juan Carlos Onetti is generally not well known outside of his homeland of Latin America. While praised and admired for their richness in imagination, creativity, and unique vision, Onetti's writings have also been described as fundamentally ambiguous, quite fragmentated, and often complex. As M. Ian Adams confirms in his book, *Three Authors of Alienation: Bombal, Onetti, Carpentier,* "Complexity and ambiguity are the major characteristics of Onetti's novels."

"Onetti's art is a strange aggregate of cultural characteristics and personal circumstances (some elusive, many contradictory and a few truly illuminating) none of which would really endear his writings to us were it not for the extraordinary nature of his style," states Luys A. Diez in *Nation.* Diez continues, "His prose has a genuinely hypnotic force, digressive and meandering, but quite without apparent *longueurs,* studded with linguistic quirks and poetic flights, economically terse and playfully serious; he teases the reader with alternate scenarios for a given situation to concentrate afterwards on a passing thought or a seemingly unimportant gesture."

Only two of Onetti's books have been translated into English. *The Shipyard,* though written after *A Brief Life,* was published first. It tells the story of Larsen, a shipyard worker who seeks to improve his social status by attaching himself to the shipyard owner's daughter. But he is unable to see that the society he aspires to has disintegrated, and the novel ends with his death. "Larsen moves through Onetti's pages as a figure virtually doomed to disaster," declares James Nelson Goodsell in the *Christian Science Monitor.* "Onetti is trying to evoke a picture of futility and hopelessness—a task which he performs very ably. . . . Onetti's purpose is to keep the reader absorbed, but to remain enigmatic. He succeeds admirably. [He] is a skillful writer whose prose is absorbing and demanding." And David Gallagher endorses *The Shipyard* in the *New York Times Book Review* as "a book which, for all its portentousness, few Latin American novelists have equaled."

The plot of *A Brief Life* is much more fantastical than that of *The Shipyard.* It concerns Juan Carlos Brausen, referred to as a "sort of Argentine Walter Mitty" by Emir Rodríguez Monegal in the *New York Times Book Review.* Brausen escapes from his many burdens by retreating from reality into a series of complex and often bizarre fantasy adventures. In *Review 75,* Hugo J. Verani calls *A Brief Life* "one of the richest and most complex novelistic expressions in Spanish-American fiction."

In a *Newsweek* review, Margo Jefferson writes that *A Brief Life* "is a virtuosic blend and balance of opposites: melodrama and meditation, eroticism and austerity, naturalism and artifice. . . . In Onetti's hands, the novel becomes an excursion into a labyrinth where the real and the imagined are mirror images. . . . Behind his sleight of hand is a melancholy irony—for all our efforts to escape a single life, we remain prisoners of a pattern, 'condemned to a soul, to a manner of being.' "

Because of its unique unfolding of plot, *A Brief Life* has received inevitable comparisons with the work of William Faulkner. Luys A. Diez notes in the *Nation* that "much of Faulkner's rich, dark sap flows through the meandering narrative." Diez also contends that "Onetti's novelistic magic, like Faulkner's, requires a certain amount of perseverance on the reader's part." And Rodríguez Monegal remarks that "in *A Brief Life,* Onetti's love for Faulknerian narrative is already evident."

Several critics have expressed their high regard for Onetti's skillful use of experimental narration. Zunilda Gertel writes in *Review 75* that "Onetti's narrative does not postulate an ideology or an intellectual analysis of the ontological. Instead, the existential projection of the 'I' is shown as a revelation within the signs imposed on him by literary tradition considered as ritual, not as reconciliation." Also writing in *Review 75,* John Deredita claims that *A Brief Life* "exhaustively tests the power of fantasy and fictional imagination as a counter to the flow of time. . . ." And Verani concludes that "Onetti does not emphasis the mimetic quality of narrative. The aim of his fiction is not to reflect an existent reality, a factual order, but . . . to create an essentially fabulated reality invested with mythic significance."

BIOGRAPHICAL/CRITICAL SOURCES:

BOOKS

Adams, M. Ian, *Three Authors of Alienation: Bombal, Onetti, Carpentier,* University of Texas Press, 1975.

Contemporary Literary Criticism, Gale, Volume 7, 1977, Volume 10, 1979.

Harss, Luis and Barbara Dohmann, *Into the Mainstream: Conversations with Latin-American Writers,* Harper, 1967.

Kadir, Djelal, *Juan Carlos Onetti,* Twayne, 1977.

Milián-Silveira, María C., *El primer Onetti y sus contextos,* Editorial Pliegos, 1986.

`PERIODICALS`

Christian Science Monitor, October 8, 1968.
Hispania 71, May, 1988.
Library Journal, March 1, 1976.
Nation, April 3, 1976.
Newsweek, February 16, 1976.
New Yorker, February 9, 1976.
New York Times Book Review, June 16, 1968, January 11, 1976.
Review 75, winter, 1975.
Saturday Review, January 24, 1976.

* * *

ORJUELA, Héctor H(ugo)   1930-

PERSONAL: Born July 6, 1930, in Bogotá, Colombia; son of Reynaldo (a broker) and Carmen (Gómez) Orjuela; married Helena Aguirre, June 25, 1965; children: Héctor H., Jr., Luis-Reynaldo, Andres-Felipe, Ximena del Pilar, Rodrigo. *Education:* North Texas State University, B.A., M.A., 1952; Indiana University, graduate study, 1952-53; University of Kansas, Ph.D., 1960; Universidad Central (Madrid), postdoctoral study, 1962.

ADDRESSES: Home—Transv. 31, No. 136-14, Bogotá, Colombia. *Office*—Ediciones El Dorado, Bogotá, Colombia.

CAREER: Virginia Military Institute, Lexington, assistant professor of Spanish, 1957-60; University of Southern California, Los Angeles, associate professor of Spanish, 1960-69; University of California, Irvine, professor of Spanish, 1969-73; Ediciones El Dorado, Bogotá, Colombia, director-editor, 1973—. Visiting professor, Texas Tech University, summer, 1963. Consultant, Instituto Caro y Cuervo (Colombia), 1972—.

MEMBER: Academia Colombiana de la Lengua, Instituto de Literatura Iberoamericana, Sigma Delta Pi (adviser, Eta Chapter, 1960-64).

AWARDS, HONORS: First International Literary Prize, Laureano Carus Pando, 1978, for *La imagen de los Estados Unidos en la poesía de Hispanoamérica;* Legión de Honor Nacional y Academia de Bellas Artes, 1979; Diploma de Honor, Comité Hernandiano de California, 1979.

WRITINGS:

(Author of introduction) José Joaquín Ortega Torres, *Indice del "Papel periódico ilustrado" y de "Colombia ilustrada,"* Instituto Caro y Cuervo, 1961.
(With E. W. Hesse) *Spanish Conversational Review Grammar,* 2nd edition (Orjuela was not associated with earlier edition), American Book Co., 1964, 5th edition published as *Spanish Review,* Van Nostrand, 1980.
Biografía y bibliografía de Raphael Pombo (title means "Biography and Bibliography of Rafael Pombo"), Instituto Caro y Cuervo, 1965.
Las antologías poéticas de Colombia (title means "The Poetic Anthologies of Colombia"), Instituto Caro y Cuervo, 1966.
(Editor) José A. Silva, *Obras completas* (title means "Complete Works"), two volumes, Plus Ultra (Buenos Aires), 1967.
Fuentes generales para el estudio de la literatura colombiana: Guía bibliográfica, (title means "General Sources for the Study of Colombian Literature"), Instituto Caro y Cuervo, 1968.
(Editor) Rafael Pombo, *Poesía inédita y olvidada* (title means "Unpublished and Forgotten Poetry"), two volumes, Instituto Caro y Cuervo, 1970.
Bibliografía de la poesía colombiana (title means "Bibliography of Colombian Poetry"), Instituto Caro y Cuervo, 1971.

Poemas de encrucijada (title means "Crossroads Poems"), Editorial Cosmos (Bogotá), 1972.
(Editor) *José A. Silva: Poesías* (title means "José A. Silva: Poems"), Editorial Cosmos, 1973, critical edition, Instituto Caro y Cuervo, 1979.
(Editor) *Ficciones de "El Carnero,"* Editorial Cosmos, 1974.
Bibliografía del teatro colombiano, Instituto Caro y Cuervo, 1974.
Relatos y ficciones, Ediciones El Dorado, 1975.
(Editor) Pombo, *Antología poética,* Ediciones La Candelaria, 1975.
La obra poética de Raphael Pombo, Instituto Caro y Cuervo, 1975.
"De sobremesa" y otros estudios sobre José Asunción Silva, Instituto Caro y Cuervo, 1976.
(Editor and author of introduction) *José Asunción Silva: Intimidades,* Instituto Caro y Cuervo, 1977, reprint with introduction by Germán Arciniegas published as *Intimidades: José Asunción Silva,* Instituto Caro y Cuervo, 1977.
El primer Silva, Editorial Kelly, 1978.
La imagen de los Estados Unidos en la poesía de Hispanoamérica, Universidad Nacional Autónoma de México, 1980.
Los hijos de la salamandra (novel), Ediciones Tercer Mundo, 1980.
Literatura hispanoamericana, Instituto Caro y Cuervo, 1980.
Yurupary, Instituto Caro y Cuervo, 1983.
"El desierto prodigioso y prodigio del desierto," de Pedro de Solis y Valenzuelá, Instituto Caro y Cuervo, 1984.
Estudios sobre literatura indígena y colonial, Instituto Caro y Cuervo, 1986.
Mitopoemas, Instituto Caro y Cuervo, 1987.

WORK IN PROGRESS: Historia de la poesía hispanoamericana, Volume I: *Poesía indígena de Hispanoamérica: Azteca, maya, quechua.*

BIOGRAPHICAL/CRITICAL SOURCES:

PERIODICALS

Hispaña, March, 1967, September, 1968, September, 1969, September, 1976, May, 1977, December, 1977, March, 1978, May, 1982, December, 1982, March, 1984.

* * *

OROPEZA, Renato Prada
See PRADA OROPEZA, Renato

* * *

OROZCO, Olga   1920-

PERSONAL: Born in 1920 in Argentina.

CAREER: Writer.

AWARDS, HONORS: Premio Fundación Alfredo Fortabat, 1987.

WRITINGS:

Las muertes (poetry), Losada, 1951.
Los juegos peligrosos (poetry), Losada, 1962.
La oscuridad es otro sol (poetry), Losada, 1967.
Cantos a Berenice (poetry), Sudamericana, 1977.
Obra poética (poetry), Corregidor, 1979.
Mutaciones de la realidad (poetry), Sudamericana, 1979.
Poesía: Antología (poetry), edited by Telma Luzzani Bystrowicz, Centro Editor de América Latina, 1982.

(Editor with Ana Becciu) Alejandra Pizarnik, *Textos de sombra y últimos poemas,* Sudamericana, 1982.

La noche a la deriva (poetry), Fondo de Cultura Económica, 1983.

Páginas de Olga Orozco: Seleccionadas por la autora (poetry), edited by Christina Piña, Celtia, 1984.

Poemas (poetry), Departamento de Bibliotecas, Universidad de Antioquía, 1984.

En el revés del cielo (poetry), Sudamericana, 1987.

Also author of volumes of poetry *Desde lejos* and *Museo salvaje.*

*   *   *

ORTEGA y GASSET, José   1883-1955

PERSONAL: Born May 9, 1883, in Madrid, Spain; died October 18, 1955, in Madrid; son of José Ortega y Munilla (a journalist and novelist) and María Dolores Gasset Chinchilla; married Rosa Spottorno y Topete, April 7, 1910; children: Miguel Germán, José, Soledad. *Education:* University of Madrid, licenciatura en filosofía y letras (M.A.), 1902, Ph.D., 1904; postgraduate study at universities of Leipzig, 1905, Berlin, 1906, and Marburg, 1906-07, 1911.

ADDRESSES: Home—Monte Esguinza 28, Madrid, Spain.

CAREER: Escuela Superior del Magisterio (normal school), Madrid, Spain, professor of psychology, logic, and ethics, 1908-10; University of Madrid, Madrid, professor of metaphysics, 1910-29 (resigned in protest against Spanish government), and 1930-36; representative of Province of León to Constitutional Parliament of Second Spanish Republic, 1931. Writer in exile in France, Netherlands, Argentina, and Portugal, beginning in 1936; University of San Marcos, Lima, Peru, professor of philosophy, beginning in 1941. Founder of Instituto de Humanidades (Madrid), 1948. Founder or co-founder of several publications, including *Faro* (title means "Beacon"); *Europa,* 1911; monthly journal *España* (organ of League for Political Education), c. 1914; newspaper *El Sol,* 1917; founder and co-editor of literary monthly *La Revista de Occidente,* 1923-35.

MEMBER: League for Political Education (founder, c. 1914), Group at the Service of the Republic (co-founder, 1931), Pen Club (president).

AWARDS, HONORS: Scholarship from Spanish government for postgraduate study in Germany, 1906; elected to Royal Academy of Moral and Political Sciences, 1914; Gold Medal of City of Madrid, 1936; named to Bavarian Academy of Fine Arts, 1949; honorary doctorates from universities of Marburg and Glasgow, 1951.

WRITINGS:

Meditaciones del Quijote, Residencia de Estudiantes (Madrid), 1914, reprinted, Revista de Occidente en Alianza (Madrid), 1981, translation by Evelyn Rugg and Diego Marín published as *Meditations on Quixote,* Norton, 1961.

El Espectador (title means "The Spectator"), Volumes 1 and 2, Renacimiento (Madrid), 1916, 1917, Volume 3, Calpe (Madrid), 1921, Volumes 4-8, Revista de Occidente, 1925-34, reprinted as one volume, Biblioteca Nueva (Madrid), 1950.

Personas, obras, cosas (title means "Persons, Works, Things"), Renacimiento, 1916, published as *Mocedades* (title means "Juvenilia"), Revista de Occidente, 1973.

España invertebrada (title means "Invertebrate Spain"), Calpe, c. 1921, reprinted, Revista de Occidente en Alianza, 1981,

translation of selections by Mildred Adams published by Norton, 1937.

El tema de nuestro tiempo, Calpe, 1923, reprinted, Revista de Occidente en Alianza, 1981, translation by James Cleugh published as *The Modern Theme,* Harper, 1931.

La deshumanización del arte e ideas de la novela, Revista de Occidente, 1925, reprinted, Revista de Occidente en Alianza, 1984, translation by Helene Weyl published as *The Dehumanization of Art: Ideas on the Novel,* Princeton University Press, 1948.

La rebelión de las masas, Revista de Occidente, 1930, reprinted, Revista de Occidente en Alianza, 1981, translation by J. R. Carey published as *The Revolt of the Masses,* 1932, translation by Anthony Kerrigan published under the same title, with foreword by Saul Bellow, University of Notre Dame Press, 1986.

La misión de la universidad, Revista de Occidente, 1930, reprinted, Revista de Occidente en Alianza, 1982, translation by Howard Lee Nostrand published as *Mission of the University,* Norton, 1946.

La redención de las provincias y de la decencia nacional (title means "The Redemption of the Provinces and National Decency"), Revista de Occidente, 1931, reprinted, Revista de Occidente Alianza, 1966.

Rectificación de la República (title means "Rectification of the Republic"), Revista de Occidente, 1931.

Obras (title means "Works"), Espasa-Calpe (Madrid), 1932, reprinted with additions, 1943.

Pidiendo un Goethe desde dentro, Revista de Occidente, 1932, title essay translated by Willard R. Trask as "In Search of Goethe from Within" and included in *The Dehumanization of Art and Other Essays on Art, Culture, and Literature,* Princeton University Press, 1968.

Notas (title means "Notes"), Espasa-Calpe, 1938, reprinted with introduction by Julián Marías, Anaya (Salamanca), 1967.

Ensimismamiento y alteración [and] *Meditación de la técnica* (title means "Self Contemplation and Alteration" [and] "Meditation on the Technical"), Espasa-Calpe Argentina, 1939, translation of *Ensimismamiento y alteración* by Willard R. Trask published as "The Self and the Other" in *Partisan Review,* July, 1952, translation of *Meditación de la técnica* by W. Atkinson published as "Man the Technician" in *History as a System and Other Essays toward a Philosophy of History,* Greenwood Press, 1961 (also see below).

Ideas y creencias (title means "Ideas and Beliefs"), Espasa-Calpe Argentina, 1940, reprinted, Revista de Occidente, 1942.

El libro de las misiones (title means "The Book of Missions"), Espasa-Calpe Argentina, 1940, reprinted, Espasa-Calpe (Madrid), 1959.

Historia como sistema [and] *Concordia y libertad,* Revista de Occidente, 1941; *Historia como sistema* reprinted in *Historia como sistema y otros ensayos de filosofía,* Revista de Occidente en Aliaza, 1981; translation of *Historia como sistema* by W. Atkinson published in *History as a System and Other Essays toward a Philosophy of History,* Greenwood Press, 1961; translation of *Concordia y libertad* by Helene Wehl published as *Concord and Liberty,* Norton, 1946.

Castilla y sus castillos (title means "Castile and Her Castles"), Afrodisio Aguado (Madrid), 1942, reprinted, 1952.

Teoría de Andalucía (title means "Theory of Andalucia"), Revista de Occidente, 1942.

Man and Crisis, Revista de Occidente, 1942, translation by Mildred Adams published as *Man and Crisis,* Norton, 1958, published as *Entorno a Galileo* (title means "Concerning Galileo"), Revista de Occidente en Alianza, 1982.

Two Prologues, Revista de Occidente, 1944, first prologue reprinted in *Veinte años de caza mayor* (title means "Twenty Years of Big-Game Hunting") by Eduardo Figueroa, Plus Altra (Madrid), 1948, translation of *Veinte años* by Howard B. Wescott published as *Meditations on Hunting,* Scribner, 1986.

Obras completas, Revista de Occidente, volumes 1 and 2, 1946, volumes 3-6, 1947, Volume 7, 1961, volumes 8 and 9, 1962, volumes 10 and 11, 1969; volumes 1-11 reprinted, and Volume 12 published, by Alianza Editorial, Revista de Occidente, 1983.

Sobre la aventura y la caza (title means "On Adventure and the Hunt"), Afrodisio Aguado, 1949.

Papeles sobre Velázquez y Goya, Revista de Occidente, 1950, translation by Alexis Brown published in *Velázquez, Goya, and the Dehumanization of Art,* Studio Vista (London), 1972.

Estudios sobre el amor (title means "Studies on Love"), Aguilar (Madrid), 1950, reprinted, Revista de Occidente en Alianza, 1981, translation by Toby Talbot published in *On Love: Aspects of a Single Theme,* Meridian Books, 1960.

El hombre y la gente, Revista de Occidente, 1957, reprinted, Revista de Occidente an Alianza, 1981, translation by Willard R. Trask published as *Man and People,* Norton, 1963.

Meditación de un pueblo joven (title means "Meditation on a Young Nation"), Revista de Occidente, 1958.

La idea de principio en Leibniz y la evolución de la teoría deductiva, Revista de Occidente, 1958, reprinted by Revista de Occidente en Alianza, 1981, translation by Mildred Adams published as *The Idea of Principle in Leibniz and the Evolution of Deductive Theory,* Norton, 1971.

Prólogo para alemanes (title means "Prologue for Germans"), Taurus (Madrid), 1958, reprinted, 1974, translation by Philip W. Silver published in *Phenomenology and Art,* Norton, 1975.

Idea del teatro (title means "Idea of Theatre"), Revista de Occidente, 1958, reprinted in *Ideas del teatro y de la novela,* Alianza, 1982, translation of *Idea del teatro* by Philip W. Silver published in *Phenomenology and Art* (see above).

Kant, Hegel, Dilthey, Revista de Occidente, 1958, reprinted, 1973.

¿Qué es filosofía?, Revista de Occidente, 1958, reprinted, Revista de Occidente en Alianza, 1982, translation by Mildred Adams published as *What Is Philosophy?,* Norton, 1960.

Apuntes sobre el pensamiento: su teurgia y su demiurgia (title means "Notes on Thinking: Its Creation of the World and Its Creation of God"), Revista de Occidente, 1959, reprinted, Revista de Occidente en Alianza, 1980, translation by Helene Weyl published in *Concord and Liberty* (see above).

Una interpretación de la historia universal, Revista de Occidente, 1960, reprinted, Revista de Occidente en Alianza, 1980, translation by Mildred Adams published as *An Interpretation of Universal History,* Norton, 1973.

Meditación de Europa (reprinted from *Obras completas,* Volume 9), Revista de Occidente, 1960.

Vives-Goethe, Revista de Occidente, 1961, reprinted, 1973.

Pasado y porvenir para el hombre actual (title means "Past and Future for Man Today"; reprinted from *Obras completas,* Volume 9), Revista de Occidente, 1962, portions translated and published as "The Past and Future of Western Thought" in *Modern Age,* summer, 1958.

Misión del bibliotecario (y otros escritos afines) (title means "Mission of the Librarian [and Other Related Writings]"; reprinted from *Obras completas,* Volume 5), Revista de Occi-

dente, 1962, portions translated by H. Muller and published as "Man Must Tame the Book" in *Wilson Library Bulletin,* 1936.

Unas lecciónes de metafísica, Alianza, 1966, reprinted, Revista de Occidente en Alianza, translation by Mildred Adams published as *Some Lessons in Metaphysics,* Norton, 1969.

Origen de la filosofía, Revista de Occidente, 1967, reprinted, Revista de Occidente en Alianza, 1981, translation by Toby Talbot published as *Some Lessons in Metaphysics,* Norton, 1967.

Sobre la razón histórica, Revista de Occidente, 1979, reprinted, Revista de Occidente en Alianza, 1983, translation by Philip W. Silver published as *Historical Reason,* Norton, 1984.

Investigaciónes psicológicas, Revista de Occidente Alianza, 1982, translation by Jorge Garcia-Gomez published as *Psychological Investigations,* Norton, 1987.

¿Qué es conocimiento? (title means "What Is Knowledge?"), Revista de Occidente en Alianza, 1984.

Contributor to numerous periodicals.

SIDELIGHTS: The significance of José Ortega y Gasset, whose world fame mainly stems from his controversial book *La rebelión de las masas* (*The Revolt of the Masses;* 1930) has always sparked debate. His most enthusiastic students believe that his philosophy is on a level "beyond which nothing has yet been achieved," as Julián Marías declares in *Ortega y Gasset,* while his critics see him as imprecise, inconsistent, literary rather than philosophical, and overly metaphorical in handling serious intellectual problems. Despite this critical split, Ortega y Gasset merits a place in history as both a major transitional figure between phenomenology and existentialism and as a key figure in Spanish culture. He aspired to elevate Spanish culture to match that of the rest of Western Europe, and in the first three decades of the twentieth century he indeed accomplished much toward achieving that goal.

During Ortega y Gasset's adolescence, Spain still reeled from losing its brief 1898 war with the United States. A group of writers, today known as the Generation of 1898, found that Spain's humiliation could be viewed as the symptom of a deeper national disease—demoralization—and that this sense of defeatism had actually preceded colonial defeat. As a young man Ortega y Gasset considered himself a member of the Generation of 1898, and he joined forces with such leading lights as Miguel de Unamuno and Antonio Machado in promoting the Europeanization of Spanish culture.

The Generation of 1898 was fortunate to have found a sympathizer in Ortega y Gasset. Breaking into print at an early age, he gave the group's writings ample publicity in his own articles, and he encouraged members to publish in the many magazines he founded to promote the moral and mental reform of Spanish society. Ortega y Gasset's writing style was so effective, his mode of presenting his ideas so attractive and persuasive, that, had he desired, he could have developed like his father into a brilliant journalist. Instead, in 1905 he decided to pursue postgraduate philosophy studies in Germany.

In his adolescence Ortega y Gasset had developed a passion for the works of German philosopher Friedrich Wilhelm Nietzsche, and he carried this enthusiasm with him to Germany when he went there at age twenty-two. At the University of Leipzig, where he was unable to secure admittance into classes of philology, he spent his days reading in the university library. He then went to Berlin, where he attended the public lectures of philosopher Georg Simmel. As a neo-Kantian, Simmel applied Immanuel Kant's philosophy—that knowledge is limited by perception—to an understanding of man and his relation to culture. Influenced by Nietzsche, Simmel enthralled Ortega y Gasset with his subtle ideas on life as a conflict between man—the creator of culture—and his own cultural products.

Late in 1906, Ortega y Gasset began studying at the University of Marburg under such Neo-Kantians as Hermann Cohen and Paul Natorp. From Cohen, Ortega y Gasset learned a sense of the drama associated with problems in philosophy along with the will to solve them with a system of disciplined ideas. Cohen based his own system on the discipline of modern physics, and he applied the logic of mathematics in solving philosophical problems. He believed that the mind could establish laws of conduct that would prove as valid for sciences of the spirit as Newton's laws are for the sciences of nature. Moreover, Cohen contended that the laws of nature and the laws of the spirit, when expressed in art, aroused a feeling for beauty, a sentiment valid as a law for all mankind. Cohen regarded individual life as an awareness and pursuit of the personal ideal, and he saw culture (logic, ethics, aesthetics) as the solution to the problem. But Ortega y Gasset, in considering culture, always returned to the problem of life, a self-conscious search for identity.

Through Natorp, a psychologist, Ortega y Gasset discovered the means of extending philosophy beyond neo-Kantian thought. Following the blueprint of Cohen, who intended to crown his own structure of ideas with psychology, Natorp built a two-part psychological system, one both descriptive and genetic. The first part described psychic experience; the second traced its causes.

After studying Natorp's ideas in 1912, Ortega y Gasset turned to the writings of one of Natorp's inspirations, Edmund Husserl, whose concept of psychic experience, particularly as explicated in *Logische Untersuchungen* (*Logical Investigations*), differed somewhat from Natorp's, and—as Julián Marías noted—provided the cornerstone for Ortega y Gasset's own philosophy. To the question, Who is the thinker of mathematical logic, the willer of logical ethics, the feeler of logical aesthetics?, Natorp responded, Spirit (or mind-in-general), thinking, willing, and feeling throughout history; and he added that psychology has the task of studying the mind-in-general. But Husserl held that the mind could be studied not only externally by psychology, but internally by phenomenology. Ortega y Gasset argued that what was real was the mind conceived as a natural object situated among other natural objects; toward these objects the mind constantly focused its attention, and from them it received endless stimuli. Thus Husserl's notion of the life-world was reflected in Ortega y Gasset's "I am myself and my circumstance," a statement that comprised both the first principle and summary of Ortega y Gasset's entire philosophy.

Ortega y Gasset reached this conclusion in 1914, the same year that he reconciled his enthusiasm for Germanic culture with his loyalty to native Spain. Inspired by the writings of Generation of 1898 leader Unamuno, Ortega y Gasset published *Meditaciones del Quijote* (*Meditations on Quixote,* 1914), which he intended as the first in a series of works noting universal values to be found in specific aspects of Spanish culture—Cervantes's view of life, the writings of Baroja and Azorín, and bullfighting, as examples. The book contained many philosophical insights, including the notion of human life as the frame of reference for all other realities; the idea of life as having nothing given to it except the problem of clarifying its own destiny; and the imperative to address this problem in view of concrete possibilities or circumstances.

Both Ortega y Gasset's conciliatory mood and the incomplete state of *Meditations* derived from his increased involvement in politics. In the fall of 1913 he founded a new political party, the League for Political Education, which he launched in a public lecture, "Vieja y nueva política" ("Old and New Politics"). In his speech he claimed to live in a country of two Spains: Official Spain which was comprised of outworn institutions, the corrupt Parliament, the established political parties, the conservative press, and the ministries, and Vital Spain, which included the creative forces in the country, especially select minorities of intellectuals and the Spanish people. Old Spain, he declared, had crippled the country. New Spain, he added, might restore it. He attributed much of Spain's cultural deficiency to its lack of outstanding individuals and inspiring projects, and he defined a healthy society as one in which select minorities encourage the masses to willingly ignore their own private interests and enthusiastically collaborate. As the League's first priority Ortega y Gasset set the formation of an elite to educate the people in creative politics. But because he offered no concrete platform or program for the League, it dissolved in less than two years.

During the 1923 to 1930 military dictatorship of Miguel Primo de Rivera, Ortega y Gasset's intellectual creativity reached its peak. Unable to partake in politics, he wrote his most famous works. In 1925 he published a five-part series of articles titled "Hacia una antropología filosófica" ("Toward a Philosophical Anthropology") in which he applied phenomenologist Max Scheler's idea of a basic science centered on man and his relationship to all other beings, and completed *Les deshumanización del arte e ideas de la novela* (*The Dehumanization of Art*) which is respected by critics for its insights into the experimental—what Ortega y Gasset called "dehumanizing"—art of the early twentieth century. During that same period of inspiration, he also borrowed from such thinkers as Martin Heidegger and Wilhelm Dilthey to further develop his own philosophy. The result was the explication of four basic principles, repeated in nearly every major work written by Ortega y Gasset after 1929: First, individual human life is the "root reality" to which all other realities must be referred and in which all others appear as in a framework; second, life is given to each human being as a problem to solve, as a "task" not finished beforehand, but needing to be done; third, life is a "decision" about what to do to be oneself; and fourth, life is a series of concrete possibilities from which to decide, and the possibilities, plural but not infinite in number, make up each individual's "circumstances."

The circumstances in which Ortega y Gasset unveiled his mature principles to the public represented a crowning moment of his life. This moment occurred in 1929, the year before the fall of the dictator Rivera, whose power diminished as a result of economic depression. When Rivera closed the University of Madrid, Ortega y Gasset protested by resigning as professor of metaphysics there, then rented a theater and sold tickets of admission to "What Is Philosophy?," the very course interrupted by the closure. In these lectures Ortega y Gasset expressed his four mature principles of human life and defined philosophy as universal knowledge, free of forejudgments. Because this knowledge relied on concepts, he saw philosophy as more akin to theology than to mysticism, which was unable to conceptualize union with God. He likened philosophy to sports—disciplined in accordance with internal rules requiring direct proof of every philosophical statement—and declared that life, with its four principles, is self-evident.

While teaching "What Is Philosophy?" Ortega y Gasset published parts of *The Revolt of the Masses* as separate articles. Like *¿Qué es filosofía?* (*What Is Philosophy?*), a collection of the course lectures published in 1958, *The Revolt of the Masses* is a transitional work between anthropology and existentialism. Here Ortega y Gasset studied the character-type of the average European of his day. With every trait described, he passed judgment from the standpoint of his metaphysical principles of human life. Life was a task, a decision, and a repertory of possibilities, he declared, but the mass man was any person, whatever his social class, who performed no task and never innovated. His counter-type was the select individual, ever pioneering and perfectionistic.

The Revolt of the Masses is significant for its dire prophecies, made in the late 1920s, of what actually took place in the 1930s and 1940s. In retrospect, writes José Gaos in *Sobre Ortega y Gasset y otros trabajos de historia de las ideas en España y la América española,* "the prediction seems to have come true of the seriousness of the crisis, socialization, the reign of the masses—although in the face of facts like those represented by the *Duce* and the *Führer,* there may be room for discussion about their susceptibility to direction from without, denied by Ortega y Gasset."

As if unmindful of his pessimism about the masses, Ortega y Gasset plunged back into politics after the fall of Primo de Rivera in January 1930. In February of 1931, Ortega y Gasset and writers Gregorio Marañón and Ramón Pérez de Ayala founded the Group at the Service of the Republic, which resembled the earlier League for Political Education. The Group wanted Spain divided into ten large regions, each with its own local government, but all recognizing the sovereignty of the nation as a whole; it desired a strong central Parliament with as much authority as the executive to provide a system of checks and balances; it advocated a planned economy, designed to bring about agrarian reform; it supported a gradual but complete separation of Church and State; and it argued for a balanced budget as a first step to energetic public and private investment. On April 14, 1931, municipal elections in Madrid brought in the Second Spanish Republic, while voting out the monarchy. Surprised by the speed and peacefulness of the transition, Ortega y Gasset privately expressed uneasiness, though in his articles he hailed the simplicity with which the Republic had come into being.

Less than a year later, Ortega y Gasset's political aspirations ended as the result of an escalating disagreement. Minister of Labor Gabriel Maura questioned Ortega y Gasset's elitism, which was seen as incompatible with concern for the interests of workers. As recorded in his 1931 essay "Siguen los 'problemas concretas' " ("More on 'Concrete Problems' ") Ortega y Gasset merely responded with a sportive metaphor, suggesting that his service to the Republic was a form of aristocracy, which meant "fair play." In parliamentary debate over the emerging Constitution of the Republic, when his metaphorical style of speaking was attacked as false and affected, he defended its authenticity and claimed an unalienable right to practice, as he declared in *Rectificación de la República* ("Rectification of the Republic"), "a poetic, philosophical, heart-felt, and merry politics." But Parliament was unresponsive to his wit and keen thought. As partisanship and extremism divided the Republic, Ortega y Gasset left politics in August 1932, and he dissolved the Group at the Service of the Republic the following October.

After leaving politics, Ortega y Gasset resumed his studies of Heidegger and Dilthey. History, Dilthey's favorite area of interest, dominated the last twenty years of Ortega y Gasset's thought. He attempted to make history a scientific discipline. Ortega y Gasset's justification for treating history as a science appeared in *Historia como sistema* (*History as a System;* 1941).

Here Ortega y Gasset posed a historical problem, as always: humanity by the early twentieth century had lost confidence in natural science, once a replacement for religious faith. Now he wondered what life meant. Physics could not provide an answer; neither could any sciences that used its methods. Ortega y Gasset, following Dilthey, believed that the science of history could cure this crisis of faith, for history discovered the system of beliefs that guided man in deciding among possibilities for being himself—a process that was, after all, the task of life. For Ortega y Gasset, beliefs differed from mere ideas, or views of the world that man himself manipulated with full awareness. To understand the impact of subconscious beliefs on men's lives, it was only necessary to tell the story of their lives. Thus, Ortega y Gasset maintained, the science of history was the new science on which man must pin his faith. History told man what he was and clarified the meaning of his life. History could also guide his future: Once he learned the mistakes of the past, he would avoid them afterwards in the trial-and-error process that is living.

The year after publishing *History as a System,* Ortega y Gasset made an unpopular decision, one that prompted criticism from many Spaniards, for he fled Spain shortly after the outset of civil war there. Some critics, such as Pedro Cerezo Galán, feel that when Ortega y Gasset went into exile, he lost the power to speak as he had before. The books he wrote afterwards, declared Cerezo Galán in *La voluntad de aventura,* "lacked . . . the feel and breath of that circumstantial reality which blew like a clean wind throughout his best works."

From 1936 to 1945 Ortega y Gasset remained outside Spain. In France, the Netherlands, Argentina, and Portugal, he endured great hardships while desiring to write two long books, *Aurora de la razón histórica* ("Dawn of Historical Reason") and *El hombre y la gente* (*Man and People,* 1957). In a prologue to *Ideas y creencias* ("Ideas and Beliefs"; 1940), he declared, "I have suffered misery, I have suffered long sicknesses of the kind in which death is breathing down your neck, and I should say that if I have not succumbed among so much commotion, it has been because the hope of finishing those two books has sustained me when nothing else would." Ortega y Gasset wrote merely a few pages of *The Dawn of Historical Reason,* mostly repeating ideas from *History as a System.* As for *Man and People,* in its final form was a lengthy course in sociology given in 1949 and 1950.

Far more revealing about Ortega y Gasset's life and times is *La idea de principio en Leibniz y la evolución de la teoría deductiva* (*The Idea of Principle in Leibniz and the Evolution of Deductive Theory;* 1958), the book praised by Marías in *Ortega y Gasset* as the writer's best. The longest work he ever wrote, *The Idea of Principle in Leibniz* was left incomplete among his papers to be published after his death. Compared with its German sources—chiefly Husserl, Dilthey, and Heidegger—it is stimulating, often entertaining reading, filled with wordplay and jokes, and it shows Ortega y Gasset at his sharpest as an intellectual sportsman. Its theme is the history of the idea of principle. Ortega y Gasset began the work by translating into Spanish many notions from Heidegger's 1929 essay "Vom Weser des Grundes" ("On the Essence of Ground"), which explained how the philosophers Gottfried Wilhelm Leibniz, Kant, and Aristotle dealt with the idea of principle. Next Ortega y Gasset used his science of history to show that Aristotle, in handling principles, was inexact and "unprincipled," and he implied that Heidegger was similarly imprecise.

In *The Idea of Principle in Leibniz* Ortega y Gasset also objected to Heidegger's general tone, which he found too somber and anguished for philosophy. Among the Greeks, noted Ortega y Gasset, philosophy was a game of riddle-solving. Plato, for instance, often compared philosophy to sports and games. But Heidegger, when philosophizing about anguish and nothingness, seemed to make a sport of wallowing in despair, and his gloomy view of the world struck Ortega y Gasset as too narrow. "For that reason," wrote Ortega y Gasset in *The Idea of Principle in Leibniz,* "since my first writings, against the narrowness of a 'tragic sense of life' . . . I have counterposed a 'sportive and festive sense of existence,' which my readers—naturally!—read as a mere literary phrase."

Ortega y Gasset wanted to spend his final years in Madrid, the city of his birth and of his greatest triumphs, but on his return in 1945, according to Victor Ouimette in *José Ortega y Gasset,* he had to face "the hostility of the Church and the mistrust felt by the government of General Franco." He did extensive lecturing abroad in Germany and made appearances in Britain and Italy, with one visit, in addition, to the United States. Operated on for cancer on October 12, 1955, he died six days later. Controversy surrounded his death as it had so many aspects of his life. The Spanish press reported the visit to his home of the Jesuit Father Félix García and the Archbishop of Saragossa. Had he converted to Catholicism at the last moment? Conservative factions contended that he had. But intimates of the philosopher, according to Guillermo Morón in *Historia política de José Ortega y Gasset,* reported that he said, when the priests wanted to be admitted to confess him, "Let them allow me to die in peace."

BIOGRAPHICAL/CRITICAL SOURCES:

BOOKS

Abellán, José Luis, *Ortega y Gasset en la filosofía española: Ensayos de apreciación,* Tecnos (Madrid), 1966.

Bayón, J., *Razón vital y dialéctica en Ortega y Gasset,* Revista de Occidente, 1972.

Benítez, Jaime, *Political and Philosophical Theories of José Ortega y Gasset,* University of Chicago Press, 1939.

Brenan, Gerald, *The Spanish Labyrinth,* Cambridge University Press, 1960.

Cepeda Calzada, Pablo, *Las ideas políticas de Ortega y Gasset,* Alcalá (Madrid), 1968.

Cerezo Galán, Pedro, *La voluntad de aventura: Aproximamiento crítico al pensamiento de Ortega y Gasset,* Ariel (Barcelona), 1984.

Chamizo Domínguez, Pedro J., *Ortega y Gasset y la cultura española,* Cincel (Madrid), 1985.

Dilthey, Wilhelm, *Introducción a las ciencias del espíritu,* translated by Julián Marías, 2nd edition, Revista de Occidente, 1966.

Durán, Manuel, editor and author of prologue, *Ortega y Gasset hoy,* Biblioteca Universitaria Veracruzana (Mexico), 1985.

Fernández, Pelayo H., *La paradoja en Ortega y Gasset,* José Porrúa Turanzas (Madrid), 1985.

Ferrater Mora, José, *Ortega y Gasset: An Outline of His Philosophy,* Yale University Press, 1963.

Gaete, Arturo, *El sistema maduro de Ortega y Gasset,* Compañía General Fabril Editora (Buenos Aires), 1962.

Gaos, José, *Sobre Ortega y Gasset y otros trabajos de historia de las ideas en España y la América española,* Imprenta Universitaria (Mexico), 1957.

Garagorri, Paulino, *Introducción a Ortega y Gasset,* Alianza (Madrid), 1970.

García Astrada, Arturo, *El pensamiento de Ortega y Gasset,* Torquel (Buenos Aires), 1961.

Hanneman, Bruno, contributor, *Ortega y Gasset Centennial/Centenario Ortega y Gasset,* José Porrúa Turanzas (Madrid), 1985.

Holmes, Oliver W., *Human Reality and the Social World: Ortega y Gasset's Philosophy of History,* University of Massachusetts Press, 1975.

Kern, Iso, *Husserl und Kant,* Nijhoff (The Hague), 1964.

L. Aranguren, José Luis, *La ética de Ortega y Gasset,* 2nd edition, Taurus (Madrid), 1959.

Lalcona, Javier F., *El idealismo político de Ortega y Gasset,* Cuadernos para el Diálogo (Madrid), 1974.

Larraín Acuña, Hernán, *La génesis del pensamiento de Ortega y Gasset,* Compañía General Fabril Editora (Buenos Aires), 1962.

López Campillo, Evelyn, *La Revista de Occidente y la formación de minorías, 1923-1936,* Taurus (Madrid), 1972.

López-Morillas, Juan, contributor, *Intelectuales y espirituales,* Revista de Occidente (Madrid), 1961.

Marías, Julián, *El lugar del peligro; Una cuestión disputada en torno a Ortega y Gasset,* Taurus (Madrid), 1958.

Marías, Julián, *Ortega y Gasset,* 2 volumes, Alianza (Madrid), 1983.

Marrero, Domingo, *El centauro: Persona y pensamiento de Ortega y Gasset,* Imprenta Soltero (Puerto Rico), 1961.

Marrero, Vicente, *Ortega y Gasset, filósofo "mondain,"* Rialp (Madrid), 1961.

McClintock, Robert, *Man and His Circumstances: Ortega y Gasset as Educator,* Teachers College Press, 1971.

Menéndez Pidal, Ramón, *La España del Cid,* Espasa-Calpe, 1967.

Molinuevo, José Luis, *El idealismo de Ortega y Gasset,* Narcea (Madrid), 1984.

Morón, Guillermo, *Historia política de José Ortega y Gasset,* Ediciones Oasis (Mexico), 1960.

Morón Arroyo, Ciriaco, *El sistema de Ortega y Gasset,* Alcalá (Madrid), 1968.

Niedermayer, Franz, *José Ortega y Gasset,* Colloquium Verlag (Berlin), 1959.

Orringer, Nelson R., *Ortega y Gasset y sus fuentes germánicas,* Gredos (Madrid), 1979.

Orringer, Nelson R., *Nuevas fuentes germánicas de ¿Qué es filosofía? de Ortega y Gasset,* Consejo Superior de Investigaciones Científicas (Madrid), 1984.

Ortega y Gasset, José, *Ideas y creencias,* Espasa-Calpe Argentina, 1940.

Ortega y Gasset, José, *The Idea of Principle in Leibniz and the Evolution of Deductive Theory,* Norton, 1971.

Ortega y Gasset, José, *The Modern Theme,* introduction by José Ferrater Mora, translated by James Cleugh, Harper, 1961.

Ortega y Gasset, Manuel, *Niñez y mocedad de Ortega y Gasset,* C.L.A.V.E. (Madrid), 1964.

Ouimette, Victor, *José Ortega y Gasset,* Twayne, 1982.

Paine, Stanley G., *The Spanish Revolution,* Norton, 1970.

Raley, Harold C., *José Ortega y Gasset: Philosopher of European Unity,* University of Alabama Press, 1971.

Rama, Carlos, *La crisis de la España del siglo XX,* Fondo de Cultura Económica (Mexico), 1960.

Rodríguez Huéscar, Antonio, *Con Ortega y Gasset y otros escritos,* Taurus (Madrid), 1964.

Romero, Francisco, *Ortega y Gasset y el problema de la jefetura espiritual,* Losada (Buenos Aires), 1960.

Rukser, Udo, *Bibliografía de Ortega y Gasset,* Revista de Occidente (Madrid), 1971.

Salmerón, Fernando, *Las mocedades de Ortega y Gasset,* Colegio de Mexico, 1959.

Sánchez Villaseñor, José, *Ortega y Gasset, Existentialist: A Critical Study of His Thought and His Sources,* translated by Joseph Small, Regnery, 1949.

Silver, Philip W., *Ortega y Gasset as Phenomenologist: The Genesis of "Meditations on Quixote,"* Columbia University Press, 1978.

Spiegelberg, Herbert, *The Phenomenological Movement: A Historical Introduction,* 2nd edition, 2 volumes, Nijhoff (The Hague), 1971.

Thomas, Hugh, *The Spanish Civil War,* Harper, 1961.

Twentieth-Century Literary Criticism, Volume 9, Gale, 1983.

Unamuno, Miguel de, *Obras completas,* 9 volumes, Escelicer (Madrid), 1966-71.

PERIODICALS

Aporía, number 3, 1981.
Azafea, number 1, 1985.
Comparative Criticism, number 6, 1984.
Cuadernos Salmantinos de Filosofía, number 8, 1981.
Cuenta y Razón, number 3, 1981.
Estudios, number 29, 2973.
Hispanic Review, number 47, 1979.
Journal of Aesthetics and Art Criticism, number 23, 1964.
Modern Language Notes, number 85, 1970, number 88, 1973, number 92, 1977.
Razón y Fe, June, 1941.
Revista de Occidente, number 140, 1974.
Romance Notes, number 17, 1976.

—*Sketch by Nelson R. Orringer*

* * *

ORTEGO, Philip D.
See ORTEGO y GASCA, Philip D.

* * *

ORTEGO y GASCA, Philip D. 1926-
(Philip D. Ortego)

PERSONAL: Born August 23, 1926, in Blue Island, Ill. *Education:* Texas Western College (now University of Texas at El Paso), B.A., 1959, M.A., 1966; University of New Mexico, Albuquerque, Ph.D., 1971; Columbia University, certificate in management planning, 1973.

ADDRESSES: Office—Department of English, University of Houston, Houston, Tex. 77004.

CAREER: Teacher of Spanish and French in schools in Pennsylvania and Texas, 1952-65; New Mexico State University, Las Cruces, instructor, 1965-69; University of New Mexico, Albuquerque, instructor, 1969-70; University of Texas at El Paso, assistant professor of English and director of Chicano affairs, 1970-72; Metropolitan State College, Denver, Colo., professor of urban studies and assistant to president, 1972-73; San Jose State University, lecturer in English, beginning in 1973; member of staff of Department of English, University of Houston, Houston, Tex. Fulbright lecturer in American studies, University of Rosario, Argentina, 1971. *Military service:* U.S. Marine Corps, 1944-47; U.S. Marine Corps Reserves, 1947-50. U.S. Air Force, 1953-62; U.S. Air Force Reserves, 1952-53; retired as captain.

MEMBER: International Reading Association, International Platform Association, Linguistic Society of America, American Dialect Society, National Education Association, Modern Language Association of America, Association for Higher Education, American Association of University Professors, National Council of Teachers of English, Teachers of English to Speakers of Other Languages, College Language Association, Chicano Teachers of English, Southwest Council for Bilingual Education, Rocky Mountain Modern Language Association, Colorado Civil Liberties Union.

WRITINGS:

(Contributor) *Shakespeare in the Southwest,* Texas Western Press, 1969.

(Contributor) Edward Ludwig and James Santibañez, editors, *The Chicanos: Mexican-American Voices,* Penguin, 1971.

(Contributor) Edward Simmen, editor, *The Chicano: From Caricature to Self-Portrait,* New American Library, 1971.

(Under name Philip D. Ortego) *Selective Mexican-American Bibliography,* Border Regional Library Association, 1972.

(Contributor) Simmen, editor, *Pain and Promise: The Chicano Today,* New American Library, 1972.

(Contributor) Leslie Wilbur and others, editors, *Improving College English Skills,* Scott, Foresman, 1972.

(Editor, under name Philip D. Ortego) *We Are Chicanos: An Anthology of Mexican-American Literature,* Washington Square Press, 1973.

(With Marta Sotomayor, under name Philip D. Ortego) *A medio grito: Chicanos and American Education,* Marfel Associates, 1974.

(Editor and compiler with Arnoldo de León, under name Philip Ortego y Gasca) *The Tejano Yearbook, 1519-1978: A Selective Chronicle of the Hispanic Presence in Texas,* Caravel, 1978.

* * *

ORTIZ, Adalberto 1914-

PERSONAL: Born 1914 in Esmeraldas, Ecuador.

CAREER: Poet, novelist, short story writer, and diplomat. Served as secretary of Casa de la Cultura Ecuatoriana.

AWARDS, HONORS: Premio Nacional de Novela, 1942, for *Juyungo: Historia de un negro, una isla y otros negros;* National Prize for Literature, 1964, for *El espejo y la ventana.*

WRITINGS:

Juyungo: Historia de un negro, una isla y otros negros (novel), Editorial Américalee (Buenos Aires), 1943, reprinted, with prologue by José-Carlos Mainer, Seix Barral (Barcelona), 1976, translation by Jonathan Tittler and Susan Hill published as *Juyungo: The First Black Ecuadorian Novel,* Three Continents, 1982.

Tierra, son y tambor: Cantares negros y mulatos (also see below; poems; main title means "Land, Sound, and Drum"), prologue by Joaquín Gallegos Lara, Ediciones la Cigarra (Mexico City), 1945.

Camino y puerto de la angustia: Poemas (poems), Isla (Mexico City), 1945.

Los contrabandistas, viñetas del autor, [Mexico], 1945.

La mala espalda: Once relatos de aquí y de allá (stories; main title means "The Bad Back"), Casa de la Cultura Ecuatoriana, Núcleo del Guayas, (Guayaquil, Ecuador), 1952.

El animal herido: Antología poética (poems; contains *Tierra, son y tambor* and *El vigilante insepulto;* also see below), Casa de la Cultura Ecuatoriana (Quito), 1959, reprinted as *El animal herido: Poesía completa,* Kraus Reprint, 1970.

Cuentos, Ediciones Populares (Guayaquil), 1966.

El espejo y la ventana: Novela a dos voces (novel), Casa de la Cultura Ecuatoriana, 1967, reprinted, Editorial El Conejo (Quito), 1983.
La entundada y cuentos variados (stories), Casa de la Cultura Ecuatoriana, 1971.
Fórmulas: Poemario "sin poesía" [and] *El vigilante insepulto* [and] *Tierra, son y tambor,* Casa de la Cultura Ecuatoriana, 1973.
La envoltura del sueño: Novela (novel), Casa de la Cultura, Núcleo del Guayas (Quito), 1982.
La niebla encendida, Casa de la Cultura Ecuatoriana, 1984.

Early writings appeared in *El Telégrafo* (Guayaquil), c. 1940.

SIDELIGHTS: Ecuadorian poet, novelist, and short story writer Adalberto Ortiz is considered one of the leading Afro-Hispanic authors of South America. Ortiz writes of specific problems concerning blacks in the New World, such as racial prejudice and social injustice, yet he is also noted for presenting the universal scope of such problems. Primarily a poet and novelist, the mulatto Ortiz weaves elements of Afro-Hispanic and African culture into his work—particularly folklore, music, and vernacular—and voices a wide admiration and respect for black people all over the world.

Among Ortiz's best known works is his first novel *Juyungo: Historia de un negro, una isla y otros negros* (translated as *Juyungo: The First Black Ecuadorian Novel*). Winner of Ecuador's Premio Nacional de Novela in 1942, when Ortiz was only twenty-eight, *Juyungo* is considered by Enrique Anderson Imbert in *Spanish-American Literature: A History* to be "one of the best Hispanic-American novels." Described by Richard L. Jackson in *The Black Image in Latin American Literature* as "one of the best expressions of the black experience and the negritude of synthesis in Latin America," *Juyungo* is the story of a black man named Asención who devotes his life to fighting racism, exploitation, and injustice. "Characterized by black pride and traditional hatred for white people, [*Juyungo*] is concerned, nevertheless, with the larger question of universal justice for all men and the suffering of all mankind, regardless of color," notes Jackson, while Anderson Imbert remarks that Ortiz's "purpose . . . is to superimpose upon the concern for the sufferings of his race the more universal sufferings caused by social injustice and war." Set a few miles north of the equator in the Esmeraldas region of Ecuador, *Juyungo* also "merits accolades," according to Jackson, "because of its artistic worth and because of the stylistic beauty of some of the passages depicting national scenery and the customs of black people in Ecuador."

BIOGRAPHICAL/CRITICAL SOURCES:

BOOKS

Anderson Imbert, Enrique, *Spanish-American Literature: A History,* 2nd edition, Wayne State University Press, 1969.
Foster, David William, and Virginia Ramos Foster, editors, *Modern Latin American Literature,* Ungar, 1975.
Jackson, Richard L., *The Black Image in Latin American Literature,* University of New Mexico Press, 1976.

PERIODICALS

Américas, March, 1978.

* * *

OTERO, Miguel Antonio (II) 1859-1944

PERSONAL: Born October 17, 1859, in St. Louis, Mo.; died August 7, 1944, in Santa Fe, N.M.; son of Miguel Antonio (a banker, businessman, and lawyer) and Mary Josephine (Blackwood) Otero; married Caroline Virginia Emmett, December 19, 1888; married Maud Paine Frost, October 1, 1913; children: (first marriage) Miguel A. III (died in infancy), Miguel A. IV, Elizabeth Emmett. *Education:* Attended St. Louis University and University of Notre Dame. *Politics:* Democrat.

CAREER: Bookkeeper for Otero, Sellar, & Co., late 1870s; San Miguel National Bank, Las Vegas, N.M., cashier, 1880-85; City of Las Vegas, N.M., treasurer, 1883-84; San Miguel County, N.M., probate clerk, 1886-90; clerk, U.S. District Court, Fourth Judicial District (N.M.), 1890-93; Territory of New Mexico, governor, 1897-1906, treasurer, 1910-1911; president, New Mexico Board of Penitentiary Commissioners and Parole Board, 1913-17; Panama Canal Zone, Isthmus of Panama, U.S. marshal, 1917-1921. President of board of regents, New Mexico Normal University, 1923-25, 1933-34; chairman of state advisory board, Federal Emergency Administration of Public Works, 1933. Officer or director of several business enterprises. Republican Party national delegate, 1892, 1900, 1904, 1908; Progressive Party national delegate, 1912, 1916; member of Democratic National Committee, and national delegate, 1920, 1924.

MEMBER: Masons, Elks, Santa Fe Club.

WRITINGS:

(Editor with Paul A. F. Walter and Frank W. Clancy, and contributor) *Colonel José Francisco Chaves, 1833-1924,* Historical Society of New Mexico, 1926.
My Life on the Frontier (also see below), Volume 1: *1864-1882,* Press of the Pioneers, 1935, reprinted, University of New Mexico Press, 1987, Volume 2: *1882-1897,* University of New Mexico Press, 1939.
The Real Billy the Kid: With New Light on the Lincoln County War, R. F. Wilson, 1936.
My Nine Years as Governor of the Territory of New Mexico, 1897-1906 (also see below), edited and with a foreword by Marion Dargan, University of New Mexico Press, 1940.
Otero: An Autobiographical Trilogy (contains *My Life on the Frontier,* Volumes 1-2, and *My Nine Years as Governor of the Territory of New Mexico, 1897-1906*), Arno Press, 1974.

Also author of *Conquistadores of Spain and Buccaneers of England, France and Holland,* 1925. The University of New Mexico has compiled papers and photographs of Otero in the Miguel A. Otero Collection.

SIDELIGHTS: "Miguel Antonio Otero's three-volume autobiography is one of the best documentations of life on the American frontier during the last half of the nineteenth century," Luis Leal asserted in a *Dictionary of Literary Biography* essay. The son of a prominent businessman and former congressional delegate, Otero grew up in the frontier Midwest and Southwest, and there he met such legendary figures as "Wild Bill" Hickok, "Buffalo Bill" Cody, and William H. Bonney, who became infamous as "Billy the Kid." The first volume of *My Life on the Frontier* contains tales of these men, as well as stories of the Old West that Otero learned from his mother. In making "observations about life on the frontier as seen first through the eyes of a boy and then of a young man," Leal reported, the author "made use of his early impressions to elaborate the early part of his memoirs." The result, the critic continued, is that "the reader . . . is impressed with the vividness of the narration and receives the impression that it was written shortly after the mentioned events took place," even though Otero did not begin to write until after his retirement.

The second volume of Otero's autobiography relates his growing involvement in the development of the Southwest; making "greater use of quotations from newspapers and even books . . . to document his studies," summarized Leal, Otero gave "less emphasis to personal experiences and more to territorial matters." But Otero's work in local government and with the Republican Party was leading to a position in which he would directly affect political concerns; in 1897, President William McKinley appointed his friend to the governorship of New Mexico, making Otero the first Hispanic governor of a southwestern territory. Despite his disregard for the existing political machinery, Otero forged a strong alliance with the Legislature and led his territory to a stronger economy and eventually, application for statehood.

This period of Otero's life is recalled in *My Nine Years as Governor of the Territory of New Mexico, 1897-1906,* and includes the governor's stormy relationship with President Theodore Roosevelt. Although the two men collaborated on the creation of the Rough Riders regiment, their disagreement over the conditions for New Mexico's statehood led Roosevelt to replace Otero as governor in 1906. Otero remained politically active well into his seventies, however, and eventually switched his allegiance to the Democratic Party. "Not an intellectual but rather a politician and a man of action, Otero was able to leave an autobiography that is vigorous, warm, and full of life," observed Leal. "His writings reflect his personality, which was that of a man of strong convictions who did not hesitate to fight those who opposed him, nor to help his friends." The trilogy consisting of *My Life on the Frontier*'s two volumes and *My Nine Years as Governor* "remains one of the most important sources of information about life in the Southwest during a critical period," the critic concluded. "Otero's autobiography is one of the most important and worthy antecedents of a genre that has been a favorite among contemporary Chicano writers."

BIOGRAPHICAL/CRITICAL SOURCES:

BOOKS

Crocchiola, F. L. Stanley, *The Otero, New Mexico, Story,* [Pantex, Tex.], 1962.
Dictionary of Literary Biography, Volume 82: *Chicano Authors, First Series,* Gale, 1989.
Otero, Miguel Antonio, *My Life on the Frontier,* Volume 1: *1864-1882,* Press of the Pioneers, 1935, reprinted, University of New Mexico Press, 1987, Volume 2: *1882-1897,* University of New Mexico Press, 1939.
Otero, Miguel Antonio, *My Nine Years as Governor of the Territory of New Mexico, 1897-1906,* edited and with a foreword by Marion Dargan, University of New Mexico Press, 1940.

OBITUARIES:

PERIODICALS

New York Times, August 8, 1944.

P

PACHECO, Henrícus Luis 1947-
(Henry L. Pacheco)

PERSONAL: Surname pronounced Patch-*echo;* born July 27, 1947, in Holman, N.M.; son of Henry Benjamin Pacheco and Resauda (Martinez) Pacheco Cordova; married Lynda DeCroo (a high school guidance counselor), August 9, 1969; children: Joseph. *Education:* Highlands University, summer study, 1965-67; University of Wyoming, B.A., 1970, M.A., 1973. *Politics:* Democrat. *Religion:* Roman Catholic.

CAREER: Fleetwood Corp., Cheyenne, Wyo., manager of editorial services, 1973; free-lance writer; journalist; copywriter. Director, University of Wyoming Ethnic Cultural Media Center, 1972. *Military service:* U.S. Marine Corps, 1970-72.

MEMBER: Marine Corps Combat Correspondents Association, Chicano Teachers of English, Sigma Delta Chi.

AWARDS, HONORS: Poetry fellowship from Harcourt, World & Brace, 1968, for University of Colorado Writer's Conference.

WRITINGS:

The Kindred/La Familia (poems) Totinem (Denver, Colo.), 1972.
(Contributor) Alurista, editor, *Festival de flor y canto: An Anthology of Chicano Literature,* Centro Chicano, University of Southern California, 1974.

Translator, Rose Cordoba, *Secretos de los árboles de piñón.* Contributor to "Chicano Renaissance," produced by KOA-TV, Denver. Contributor of poems to periodicals, including *Alkahest, New Mexico Magazine, Poetry West, Pembroke,* and *Rocky Mountain Creative Arts Journal.*

WORK IN PROGRESS: A book of poetry, *The Mexican Relic;* an anthology, *Testudo.*

SIDELIGHTS: "In order for poetry to grow in America," Henrícus Luis Pacheco wrote, "it has had to draw from the spirits of all its peoples. The Chicano experience will be one of American poetry's most valuable works and unlike American Indian poetry, most writers will be native to the culture and experience—Chicanos and Hispanos."

BIOGRAPHICAL/CRITICAL SOURCES:

BOOKS

Alurista, editor, *Festival de flor y canto: An Anthology of Chicano Literature,* Centro Chicano, University of Southern California, 1974.*

*   *   *

PACHECO, Henry L.
See PACHECO, Henrícus (Luis)

*   *   *

PACHECO, José Emilio 1939-

PERSONAL: Born June 30, 1939, in Mexico City, Mexico. *Education:* Attended National Autonomous University of Mexico.

ADDRESSES: c/o New Directions, 80 Eighth Ave., New York, N.Y. 10011; and Reynosa 63, Mexico City Z.P. 11, Mexico.

CAREER: Writer, 1958—. Lecturer at the University of Maryland and other universities in Mexico, the United States, Canada, and Great Britain; editorial collaborator on literary journals.

AWARDS, HONORS: National Poetry Prize (Mexico), 1969, for poetry collection *No me preguntes cómo pasa el tiempo (Poemas, 1964-1968);* elected to the Colegio Nacional, 1986.

WRITINGS:

POETRY

Los elementos de la noche (title means "The Elements of the Night"), Universidad Nacional Autónoma de México, 1963.
El reposo del fuego (title means "The Repose of Fire"), Fondo de Cultura Económica, 1966.
No me preguntes cómo pasa el tiempo (Poemas, 1964-1968), J. Mortiz, 1969, translation by Alastair Reid published as *Don't Ask Me How the Time Goes By: Poems, 1964-1968,* Columbia University Press, 1978.
Arbol entre dos muros/Tree Between Two Walls, bilingual Spanish-English edition with translation by Edward Dory and Gordon Brotherston, Black Sparrow Press, 1969.
Irás y no volverás (title means "You'll Go and You Won't Return"), Fondo de Cultura Económica, 1973.

Islas a la deriva (title means "Islands Adrift"), Siglo Veintiuno, 1976.

Ayer es nunca jamás (anthology; title means "Yesterday Is Never Again"), Monte Avila (Caracas), 1978.

Desde entonces: Poemas 1975-1978 (title means "Since Then: Poems, 1975-1978"; includes "Jardín de niños"), Ediciones Era, 1980.

Tarde o temprano (anthology; title means "Sooner or Later"), Fondo de Cultura Económica, 1980.

Signals from the Flames (anthology), translated by Thomas Hoeksema, edited by Yvette Miller, Latin American Literary Review Press, 1980.

Los trabajos del mar (title means "Labors of the Sea") Ediciones Era, 1983.

Fin de siglo (anthology; title means "End of the Century"), Cultura SEP, 1984.

Alta traición (anthology; title means "High Treason"), Alianza (Madrid), 1985.

Miro la tierra (title means "I Look at the Earth"; includes "Las ruinas de México [Elegía del retorno]" and "Lamentaciones y alabanzas"), Ediciones Era, 1986.

José Emilio Pacheco: Selecciones (anthology), edited by Luis Antonio de Villena, Ediciones Júcar (Madrid), 1986.

Selected Poems (anthology), bilingual English/Spanish edition with translations by Hoeksema and others, edited by George McWhirter, New Directions, 1987.

NOVELS AND SHORT STORIES

El viento distante (short stories; title means "The Distant Wind"), Ediciones Era, 1963.

Morirás lejos (novel; title means "You'll Die Far Away"), J. Mortiz, 1967.

El principio del placer (short stories; title means "The Pleasure Principle"), J. Mortiz, 1972.

Las batallas en el desierto (short stories), Ediciones Era, 1981, translation by Katherine Silver published as *Battles in the Desert and Other Stories,* New Directions, 1987.

EDITOR

La poesía mexicana del siglo XIX: Antología (title means "Nineteenth-Century Mexican Poetry: An Anthology"), Empresas, 1965.

Universidad, política y pueblo (title means "University, Politics, and the People"), Universidad Nacional Autónoma de México, 1967.

Antología del modernismo (1884-1921) (title means "Anthology of Modernism"), Universidad Nacional Autónoma de México, 1970.

(Editor with Gabriel Zaid) José Carlos Becerra, *El otoño recorre las islas (Obra poética, 1961-1970),* Ediciones Era, 1973.

Diario de Federico Gamboa, 1892-1939 (title means "The Diary of Federico Gamboa, 1892-1939"), Siglo Veintiuno, 1977.

OTHER

(Author of prologue) *Giménez Botey: Escultura* (title means "Giménez Botey: Sculpture"; text in Spanish, French, and English), Fournier, 1964.

(Contributor) *Ensayos contemporáneos sobre Jaime Torres Bodet* (title means "Contemporary Essays on Jaime Torres Bodet"), edited by Beth Miller, Universidad Nacional Autónoma de México, 1976.

(Contributor) *Inframundo, the Mexico of Juan Rulfo,* Ediciones del Norte (Hanover, N.H.), 1983.

Album de zoología (title means "Zoology Album"), Cuarto Menguante, 1985.

Contributor of essays, articles, and criticism to literary journals.

SIDELIGHTS: José Emilio Pacheco is one of Mexico's most prominent poets. His earliest verse collections, *Los elementos de la noche* ("The Elements of the Night") and *El reposo del fuego* ("The Repose of Fire") plumb metaphysical questions of time and human destruction with surrealist and symbolist imagery. In both volumes Pacheco's language is hermetic and his poetic voice bleakly prophetic as it presents a doomed world of ceaseless flux, in which man is represented as both victim and perpetrator of disaster.

Pacheco's third collection, *No me preguntes cómo pasa el tiempo* (*Don't Ask Me How the Time Goes By*), marks a shift to simpler, more direct writing and broader thematic concerns. But a dark underlying mood centered on the futility of experience in time still permeates the volume. The poet's precision, restraint, and balance, a *Times Literary Supplement* critic pointed out, "makes the sense of evil and disaster in his poems the more striking." Pacheco's diverse subjects include travel impressions and such political events as the death of South American revolutionary leader Che Guevara and the 1968 Tlatelolco student massacre in Mexico City. The poet also introduces whimsical verse meditations on animal life that reveal human foibles. Some translated verses from other poets—or "approximations," as Pacheco prefers to call them—complete the volume, which won Mexico's prestigious National Poetry Prize in 1969.

Pacheco's succeeding volumes of poetry are similarly structured. Free verse and prose poem forms predominate as the poet's technical mastery allows him to experiment with a wide variety of styles, particularly in his "approximations." Metaphysical concerns are always present, but they lie beneath reflections on social life, the natural environment, and the nature of artistic creation. For example, in "Jardín de niños" ("Children's Garden"), a cycle of twenty poems in the collection *Desde entonces* ("Since Then"), Pacheco uses the metaphor of a child's development from the womb to adulthood to illuminate ethical and epistemological questions in the modern world. "The poems seem . . . extraordinarily powerful and effective, a remarkable statement of a generation's conscience and temper," remarked Michael J. Doudoroff in *Hispania.*

The devastating Mexico City earthquake of 1985 is Pacheco's central metaphor in *Miro la tierra* ("I Look at the Earth"). The longest work in this volume is "Las ruinas de México (Elegía del retorno)" (title means "The Ruins of Mexico [Elegy of Return]"). Each of its five sections begins with an abstract meditation and progresses through twelve short poems to a detailed portrait of the ruined city's human suffering. "Pacheco transforms this harrowing experience into a major elegy, perhaps his most important single poem since *El reposo del fuego,*" opined Doudoroff. *Miro la tierra* also includes a group of twenty short verses titled "Lamentaciones y alabanzas" ("Laments and Praises") that mourn humankind's seemingly insoluble social and metaphysical problems but celebrate the fleeting small pleasures in life.

Intertextuality and a broad interpretation of the poetic are key features of Pacheco's work. His original poems are often replete with allusions to the work of others, and he sometimes includes "found" poems—fragments of prose texts from many sources—in his verse collections. The "approximations" that appear in Pacheco's books range from very precise and formally exact translations to extensively rewritten interpretations. Pacheco's poetic quotes, translations, and rewritings reflect his view of poetry as essentially social and transient, with no single meaning enduring through all ages and cultures and, in a sense, no single author. Thus, one of his "approximations" in *Miro la tierra* is a translation of American poet Ezra Pound's translation of a Japanese version of an ancient Chinese poem.

In addition to his poetry, Pacheco has published a well-received historical novel, *Morirás lejos* ("You'll Die Far Away"), and several short story collections. A principal theme in these prose works is the interplay of historical myth, social injustice, and personal alienation in contemporary Mexico City.

BIOGRAPHICAL/CRITICAL SOURCES:

BOOKS

Forster, Merlin H., *Four Contemporary Mexican Poets: Tradition and Renewal,* Illinois University Press, 1975.

PERIODICALS

Hispamerica, May 15, 1976, July 20, 1978.
Hispania, May, 1989.
New York Times Book Review, May 24, 1987.
Times Literary Supplement, June 18, 1970, October 12, 1973.
Virginia Quarterly Review, winter, 1979.
World Literature Today, spring, 1979.

* * *

PADILLA (LORENZO), Heberto 1932-

PERSONAL: Born January 20, 1932, in Puerta de Golpe, Pinar del Río, Cuba; immigrated to United States, 1980; Cuban citizen; son of Francisco Padilla (a lawyer) and Dolores Lorenzo (a housewife); married first wife, Berta Hernández (a teacher), 1956 (divorced, 1968); married Belkis Cuza Malé (a writer), 1968; children: (first marriage) Giselle, María, Carlitos, (second marriage) Ernesto. *Education:* Attended University of Havana, 1952-56. *Religion:* Catholic.

ADDRESSES: Home and office—103 Cuyler Rd., Princeton, N.J. 08540.

CAREER: Writer and journalist. WMIE-Radio, Miami, Fla., commentator, 1957; Berlitz School, New York, N.Y., teacher of Spanish and French, 1958; Prensa Latina (government press agency), Havana, Cuba, journalist in New York City, 1959, in London, England, 1960-61, in Moscow, U.S.S.R., 1962-63; *Lunes de Revolución* (literary supplement to newspaper *Revolución*), Havana, contributing editor, 1959-63; Cubartimpex (cultural import-export agency of Cuban government), Havana, director with assignments in Eastern Europe, 1964-66; University of Havana, Havana, lecturer in literature, 1969-70; imprisoned and compelled to make political confession, 1971; citrus farmer in government agricultural project near Cumanayagua, Las Villas, Cuba, 1971; translator in Cumanayagua, 1971-80; New York University, New York City, fellow at New York Institute for the Humanities, 1980-83; *Linden Lane* (literary journal), Princeton, N.J., publisher and editor, 1982—. Cuban Union of Writers and Artists, co-founder, 1960, director of literature section, 1966. Executive director of Center for Hemispheric Affairs of Institute for Contemporary Studies (San Francisco), 1986-87.

MEMBER: PEN American Center.

AWARDS, HONORS: Honorable mention from Casa de las Américas, 1962, for *El justo tiempo humano;* Julián del Casal Poetry Prize from Cuban Union of Writers and Artists, 1968, for *Fuera del juego.*

WRITINGS:

POETRY

El justo tiempo humano (title means "Just, Human Time"), Cuban Union of Writers and Artists, 1962.
Fuera del juego (title means "Out of the Game"), Cuban Union of Writers and Artists, 1968.
Sent Off the Field: A Selection From the Poetry of Heberto Padilla, translation and introduction by J. M. Cohen, Deutsch, 1972.
Provocaciones (title means "Provocations"), introduction by José Mario, La Gota de Agua (Madrid), 1973.
Poesía y política: Poemas escogidos de Heberto Padilla/ Poetry and Politics: Selected Poems of Heberto Padilla, translation by Frank Calzón, Playor (Madrid), 1974.
El hombre junto al mar (collection; title means "The Man by the Sea"), Barral, 1981, published in bilingual edition with English translation by Alastair Reid and Andrew Hurley as *Legacies: Selected Poems,* Farrar, Straus, 1982.

Also author of *Un cielo perdido* (title means "A Lost Sky"), 1987. Contributor of poems to periodicals, including *New York Review of Books.*

TRANSLATOR

René Dépestre, *Un arcoiris para el occidente cristiano: Poema, misterio, vodú,* Casa de las Américas, 1967.
Hans Magnus Enzensberger, *Poesías para los que no leen poesías* (title means "Poems for People Who Don't Read Poems"), Barral (Barcelona), 1972.
Poesía romántica inglesa (anthology of English Romantic poetry), Arte y Literatura (Havana), 1979.

OTHER

(Editor and author of introductions with Luis Suardíaz, and contributor) *Cuban Poetry, 1959-1966,* Book Institute (Havana), 1967.
En mi jardín pastan los héroes (novel), Argos Veraga, 1981, translation by Andrew Hurley published as *Heroes Are Grazing in My Garden,* Farrar, Straus, 1984.
Autoretrato del otro: La mala memoria (memoir), Plaza y Janés (Madrid), 1988, translation by Alexander Coleman published as *Self-Portrait of the Other,* Farrar, Straus, 1990.

Also author of the unpublished novel *Prohibido el gato* (title means "No Cats Allowed"). Contributor of articles to periodicals, including *New York Times.* Columnist for Spanish-language periodicals, including *Miami Herald* (Spanish section), 1983—. Member of editorial board of *Unión* (Cuban Union of Writers and Artists), 1966.

SIDELIGHTS: "The last thing I want to be is the Rebel Poet in a socialist society," Heberto Padilla once said, according to Lewis Hyde of *Nation.* "But," Hyde observed, "that is what he became." After Cuba gained a Marxist government in the revolution of 1959, Padilla was hailed as one of the finest poets to emerge under the new regime; within a dozen years he was in political disgrace, forced to recant his work in a public "confession" that drew the outrage of writers around the world.

Born in Cuba in 1932, Padilla grew to adulthood while his homeland endured varying degrees of repression, chaos, and corruption under a series of governments, most of them controlled by military strongman Fulgencio Batista. Padilla spent most of the 1950s working in the United States, but after Batista fell to Marxist rebel Fidel Castro in 1959, the poet returned enthusiastically to his native land. As with many Latin American intellectuals at the time, he apparently saw the new regime as a harbinger of freedom and self-respect, both for Cubans and for the rest of the Hispanic world. Padilla, surmised the *Miami Herald*'s Frank Soler, "anticipated an era of enlightenment where the individual Cuban might be allowed to express himself as he never had done before."

For the next several years Padilla held a variety of important posts with the new regime. With novelist Guillermo Cabrera Infante he edited a literary weekly, *Lunes de Revolución,* that was distributed as part of a state-controlled newspaper; he reported from London and Moscow as a correspondent for Prensa Latina, the government press agency; and he journeyed through Eastern Europe as director of Cubartimpex, facilitating Cuba's trade in books and artwork. But as the author traveled the Communist world and met with Cuban leaders, he was increasingly filled with doubt about his country's new course. In several autobiographical writings, including the memoir *Autoretrato del otro* (*Self-Portrait of the Other*) and the afterword to his novel *En mi jardín pastan los héroes* (*Heroes Are Grazing in My Garden*), he describes his gradual disillusionment. While some outsiders lavished uncritical praise on the Castro regime, Padilla met others—including a Soviet intelligence agent—who warned him to expect oppression. He realized that some of Castro's top officials were fiercely hostile to intellectuals. The author found, for instance, that Che Guevara, a famed guerrilla leader who was also Castro's minister of industry, despised Latin America's leading writers in spite of their support for Cuba. "I've been to almost all the socialist countries," Padilla finally concluded, "and in every one of them I saw very clearly that the political apparatus in the end becomes a force of unquestioning authority, political leadership unfailingly becomes alienated from its popular base."

Padilla's poetry soon reflected his doubts—a natural development, admirers suggest, since he excels at straightforward, unpretentious statements of his personal concerns. "Spanish and Latin American poetry is full of bombast and easy rhythms and alliterations," wrote José Yglesias in *New York Review of Books,* but "Padilla's has none of that." Nor does the author hide his meanings in symbols and dreamlike imagery. Instead, Yglesias averred, he "insist[s] on the facts of experience and . . . refus[es] to comfort us when the experience is harsh." "Padilla's great ability," declared Elizabeth Macklin in *Parnassus,* "is to put pure emotion into words, lines, stanzas, building a frame for an impression that shocks with immediacy: he feels — you feel." "In this," Macklin continued, "he's somewhat akin to the English Romantic [poets of the early nineteenth century], whom he's translated, and whom he adores."

According to translator J. M. Cohen, Padilla's misgivings about Cuba appear even in his first major collection, *El justo tiempo humano* ("Just, Human Time"), published in 1962. Cohen, who introduced Padilla to English-speaking readers in the 1972 anthology *Sent Off the Field,* observed in his preface that "*El justo tiempo humano* ends with a number of poems that accept the Cuban revolution naively and perhaps rather crudely." However, Cohen continued, "in its outstanding poem, 'The Childhood of William Blake,' Padilla stands for the poet against the petty agents of society, the 'inspectors of heresies.' " William Blake, a precursor of the Romantic poets, insisted on writing visionary, idiosyncratic poems and books even though English society failed to understand or appreciate his talents. Padilla imagines Blake as a child, then contrasts Blake's childish innocence with the disappointments that would haunt his adulthood. The poem, Cohen averred in *New York Review of Books,* "voices [Padilla's] fear that terror will eventually overcome the new [society] that seemed to be coming to birth in Cuba."

By the mid-1960s *Lunes de Revolución* had been disbanded by government officials, some of whom began to suggest that its writers were intellectual elitists. *Lunes* staffer Cabrera Infante exiled himself from Cuba, saw his work shunned by the government printing house, and prepared to denounce the regime. Padilla defended his colleague's writing and questioned the integrity of state-controlled publishers; soon thereafter, he was stripped of his prestigious foreign posts and found himself back in his homeland, unable to obtain steady work. Only a personal appeal to Castro brought him a teaching job at the University of Havana.

Meanwhile the author's 1968 volume of poetry, *Fuera del juego* ("Out of the Game"), became the focus of a literary scandal. Padilla had entered the book in competition for the Julián del Casal Poetry Prize, one of several Cuban-sponsored literary awards that had gained international stature during the 1960s. But the award's judges, who included Cohen and other respected literary figures from inside and outside of Cuba, faced unaccustomed state pressure to deny Padilla the prize. In the end, even the most orthodox Communist on the panel concluded that *Fuera del juego* was far superior to any other entry. The Cuban Union of Writers and Artists reluctantly published Padilla's winning volume, adding a preface that denounced the author on political grounds.

"The prevailing mood of *Fuera del juego,*" Cohen wrote, "is one of anger and disillusion reinforced by the romantic feeling that in the new society there is no place for the poet." As Luis Quesada suggested in *Latin American Literature Review,* Padilla does not question the need for a revolution, but he does claim the right to question its effects. The volume's first poem, "In Hard Times," describes a citizen who gradually surrenders his time, hands, legs, and tongue for the sake of the revolution, and then is asked to move on without complaint. Some poems, such as "Discourse on the Method" and "Years Later," evoke pity for members of the old ruling class that the revolution overthrew; Padilla does not sympathize with their politics, but rather with their pain as individual human beings. In "Prayer for the End of the Century," one of several poems that Quesada translated, Padilla writes that "We, who have seen the collapse of the parliaments/ . . . [and] learned to distrust glorified myths/ . . . know that today we have the error/ which someone will condemn tomorrow." The volume ends with the title poem, "Out of the Game," which satirically declares: "Fire the poet!/ . . . He always raises objections." "Padilla," Quesada explained, "firmly believes that the true revolutionary is not the one who bows and obeys blindly, a 'yes man' who always agrees."

Accordingly Padilla continued to air his doubts despite his tenuous situation. He worked on a novel, published years later as *Heroes Are Grazing in My Garden,* in which the lagging spirit of Castro's revolution is symbolized by the middle-aged despair of two Cuban intellectuals. He wrote satirical poems, praised by Cohen for their "wit and conciseness," and mailed them to friends overseas. At a 1971 meeting of the Union of Writers and Artists he read from a new poetry collection, titled *Provocaciones* ("Provocations"), and soon thereafter he was arrested, beaten, and terrorized by state officials. Castro visited his prison cell to denounce the literary world; Padilla's wife, writer Belkis Cuza Malé, was jailed without cause; authors from throughout the world, including Latin Americans Carlos Fuentes and Mario Vargas Llosa, protested to no avail. In a stunning reversal, Padilla appeared before another meeting of the Union of Writers and Artists to repent his previous conduct. His new statements, including "confessions" of psychological maladjustment and of lending comfort to Cuba's enemies, were quickly discounted by outside observers as the product of duress. Years later, in his afterword to *Heroes Are Grazing in My Garden,* Padilla observed: "Standing up to a perfectly orchestrated, unscrupulous maneuver is utterly futile. There is no courage more impotent and unrecognized than a Cuban's as he tries to shout his truths at a police squad." The author's humiliation deeply affected talented young writers throughout Latin America, as Chilean novelist José Donoso recalled in *The Boom in Spanish American Literature: A Personal History.* Many of the writers felt bound together by their "faith in the cause of the Cuban Revolution," Donoso wrote, adding, "I think the disillusionment produced by the Padilla case destroyed that faith and destroyed [their sense of] unity."

Padilla dwelled in obscurity for the rest of the 1970s. After submitting to several months of forced labor on a farm, the poet was allowed a modest living as a translator, but both he and his wife remained social pariahs. He was not allowed to leave Cuba or to publish new writings. A few of his new poems reached the United States, where they were published in the *New York Review of Books;* more eventually appeared in the 1982 volume *Legacies.* According to Cohen, much of the work from Padilla's years as an outcast falls into three categories. Some poems, including the title poem of *Legacies,* are "devoted to the theme of childhood and ancestry," the critic wrote. "In these Padilla seems to demolish the time sequence and see himself as the contemporary of his grandparents who first landed in Cuba." In other verses Padilla speaks to his wife, celebrating their marriage while noting the presence around them of a "hostile and unpitying world." Still other poems, Cohen noted, focus on "characters in the past with whom [Padilla] can identify." Several critics made special mention of a poem about Sir Walter Raleigh, a talented Elizabethan explorer, courtier, and writer who was imprisoned as the result of political intrigue. Citing the virtues of Raleigh and other such historical figures, *Review*'s Nereo Condini wrote: "These are our legacies, and together with our land and the memory of our ancestors and parents, they bring relief to our isolation."

In an unexpected move in 1980, Castro allowed many dissidents to flee Cuba, one was Padilla, who was freed after pleas from such notable Americans as novelist Bernard Malamud and Senator Edward Kennedy. With his wife Padilla established *Linden Lane* magazine, devoted to the writings of Cuban-Americans, and he found publishers for his own long-suppressed works. *Legacies,* which surveys poems from throughout Padilla's career, received widespread praise: Cohen compared the author's work to that of Robert Lowell, one of America's most respected modern poets. The novel *Heroes Are Grazing in My Garden,* however, garnered mixed reviews. "*Heroes* . . . hauntingly evokes a revolution in the throes of a wasting mid-life crisis," wrote a reviewer for *Time.* By contrast, Alma Guillermoprieto of *Washington Post Book World* called the novel "pointless and unfocused." "The revolution is Padilla's overwhelming concern," the *Post* reviewer continued, "and he has no esthetic distance from it." In his afterword to the novel, Padilla comments on the problem of writing about one's own political oppression. "Everything written in a suffocating political atmosphere is inconclusive and fragmentary," he declares; such a climate "stamps books with a feeling of desperation or neurosis." He concludes: "Those books require an impossible reading by an impossible reader, since no reader will have the kind of knowledge required for their understanding. It's a kind of writing for the blind."

"This is sad stuff, really," wrote Lewis Hyde in *Nation,* while discussing the themes of Padilla's poems. Hyde considered *Legacies* nearly flawless, the product of an author who was at his best in depicting fragile human emotions; the reviewer lamented the injustice that had forced Padilla to wrestle with politics. "In Padilla," Hyde averred, "we have . . . a poet who has not been able to mine the richest veins of his sensibility because of the situation of his birth." As Padilla experienced new freedom in the United States, he struggled to come to terms with his past while retaining hope for the future. "I do not admire people who suffer professionally," he declared in *Time.* "I want to be a new man. I am eager to be alive. My duty is to write."

Padilla told *HW* that the world—fortunately—has changed, and anxieties and anguishes are beginning to be the same for all people. Writers that lived and suffered under communist totalitarian regimes, he continued, now have a single mission in front of them: to write. No one should expect the impossible, but people should expect that, through writing, intellectuals will participate in society by doing what they do best. Padilla observed that ideology has preoccupied literature in preceding years, to the point of supplanting sentiment. He hailed the return of romanticism, a style that he felt could best express the anxieties of all.

BIOGRAPHICAL/CRITICAL SOURCES:

BOOKS

Authors in the News, Volume 1, Gale, 1976.
Contemporary Literary Criticism, Volume 38, Gale, 1986.
Donoso, José, *The Boom in Spanish American Literature: A Personal History,* Columbia University Press, 1977.
Johnson, Scott, *Case of the Cuban Poet Heberto Padilla,* Gordon Press, 1978.
Padilla, Heberto, *Sent Off the Field: A Selection From the Poetry of Heberto Padilla,* translation and introduction by J. M. Cohen, Deutsch, 1972.
Padilla, Heberto, *Heroes Are Grazing in My Garden,* translation by Andrew Hurley, Farrar, Straus, 1984.
Padilla, Heberto, *Self-Portrait of the Other,* translation by Alexander Coleman, Farrar, Straus, 1990.

PERIODICALS

Américas, May-June, 1982.
Best Sellers, May, 1982, December, 1984.
Latin American Literary Review, spring-summer, 1975.
Los Angeles Times, August 16, 1984.
Miami Herald, March 10, 1974.
Nation, January 23, 1982.
New York Review of Books, June 3, 1971, June 30, 1983, July 18, 1985.
New York Times, November 17, 1968, May 2, 1971, May 9, 1971, May 22, 1971, May 26, 1971, June 8, 1971, March 17, 1980, September 17, 1981. March 3, 1990.
New York Times Book Review, April 11, 1982.
Parnassus, spring, 1982.
Review, January-April, 1982, January-June, 1985.
Time, May 24, 1971, September 24, 1984, July 8, 1985.
Washington Post Book World, September 23, 1984.
Wilson Quarterly, Number 1, 1985.

—*Sketch by Thomas Kozikowski*

*   *   *

PADILLA, Raymond V. 1944-

PERSONAL: Surname is pronounced "Pa-*dee*-ya"; born December 22, 1944, in Mexico; immigrated to United States; son of Pedro Padilla (a farm worker) and Andrea Varela (a homemaker); married Mary Joan Morrow (in public relations), January 2, 1971; children: Brianda. *Education:* Attended Universidad de Guanajuato, 1965; University of Michigan, B.A. (magna cum laude), 1970; University of California, Berkeley, M.A., 1972, Ph.D., 1975.

ADDRESSES: Home—3327 North Dakota, Chandler, Ariz. 85224. *Office*—Hispanic Research Center, Arizona State University, Tempe, Ariz. 85287-2702.

CAREER: University of California, Berkeley, research assistant and acting project director at Survey Research Center, 1972, researcher in Chicano studies program, 1973; higher education consultant and coordinator of Latino education with Michigan Department of Education, 1975-77; Eastern Michigan University, Ypsilanti, assistant professor of social foundations, 1977-80, associate professor of foreign languages and bilingual studies, 1981; Arizona State University, Tempe, associate professor of educational leadership and policy studies, 1982—, director of Hispanic Research Center, 1986—. Visiting scholar at University of Michigan's Survey Research Center, 1982.

WRITINGS:

(Editor) *Ethnoperspectives in Bilingual Education Research,* Bilingual Programs, Department of Foreign Languages and Bilingual Studies, Eastern Michigan University, Volume I: *Bilingual Education and Public Policy in the United States,* 1979, Volume II: *Theory in Bilingual Education,* 1980, *Bilingual Education Technology,* 1981.
(Editor and contributor) *Theory, Technology, and Public Policy in Bilingual Education,* National Clearinghouse for Bilingual Education, 1983.
(Contributor) National Association for Chicano Studies, editors, *The Chicano Struggle: Analyses of Past and Present Efforts,* Bilingual Press, 1984.
(Editor with M. Montiel, and contributor) *Chicanos and the Higher Learning,* AACHE, 1985.
(Editor with Eugene E. Garcia) *Advances in Bilingual Education Research,* University of Arizona Press, 1985.
(Contributor) Rodolfo Jacobson and Christian Faltis, editors, *Language Distribution Issues in Bilingual Schooling,* Multilingual Matters, 1989.

Contributor to periodicals.

*   *   *

PAGAN FERRER, Gloria M. 1921-
  (Marigloria Palma)

PERSONAL: Born September 6, 1921, in Canóvanas, P.R.; daughter of José Pagán Carrasquillo and María Filomena Ferrer; married Alfred Stern, 1944 (deceased). *Education:* Studied art for two years in Los Angeles, Calif.; studied French for two years. *Politics:* None. *Religion:* "Catholic (very little)."

ADDRESSES: Home—Calle de la Luna 270, San Juan, P.R. 00901.

CAREER: Writer. Spanish instructor, 1946-55.

AWARDS, HONORS: Premio del Instituto de Literatura, 1941, for poetry volume *Agua suelta,* and 1966, for poetry volume *San Juan entre dos azules.*

WRITINGS:

UNDER PSEUDONYM MARIGLORIA PALMA

POETRY

Agua suelta, Biblioteca de Autores Puertorriqueños (San Juan), 1940.
Voz de lo transparente, Ateneo Puertorriqueño (San Juan), 1965.
San Juan entre dos azules, Rumbos (Barcelona), 1965.
Arboles míos, Rumbos, 1965.
Canto de los olvidos, Rumbos, 1965.
Palomas frente al eco, Rumbos, 1968.
La razón del cuadrante, Rumbos, 1968.
Los cuarenta silencios, El Toro de Barro (Cuenca), 1973.
La noche y otras flores eléctricas, Instituto de Cultura Puertorriqueña (San Juan), 1976.
Versos de cada día, Universidad de Puerto Rico (Río Piedras), 1980.
Aire habitado, Mairena (San Juan), 1981.

OTHER

Saludando la noche (play), Rumbos, 1968.
Entre Francia y Suiza (play), Rumbos, 1968.
La herencia (play), Rumbos, 1968.
Amy Kootsky (novel), Edil (Río Piedras), 1973.
Cuentos de la abeja encinta (short stories), Universidad de Puerto Rico, 1976.
Don Güi-Güi y otros cuentos (short stories for children), Instituto de Cultura Puertorriqueña, 1979.
Viento salado (novel), Instituto de Cultura Puertorriqueña, 1981.
Muestras del folklore Puertorriqueño (folklore), Edil, 1981.
Cuentos de mamita chepa (short stories for children), Edil, 1984.
Teatro para niños (collection of plays for children), Instituto de Cultura Puertorriqueña, 1985.
Teatro infantil (collection of plays for children), Instituto de Cultura Puertorriqueña, 1985.
Bolitas de mármol (essay collection), Instituto de Cultura Puertorriqueña, in press.
Julia de Burgos y yo (essay collection), Instituto de Cultura Puertorriqueña, in press.
Cuentos para mirar (short stories), Universidad de Puerto Rico, in press.

*   *   *

PALES MATOS, Luis 1898-1959

PERSONAL: Born March 20, 1898, in Guayama, Puerto Rico; died February 23, 1959, in Santurce, Puerto Rico; son of Vicente Palés Anés (a poet).

CAREER: Poet. Founder, with José de Diego Padró, of postmodernist literary movement, "Diepalismo," which featured the use of onomatopoeisms.

WRITINGS:

Tuntún de pasa y grifería: Poemas afroantillanos, Biblioteca de Autores Puertorriqueños, 1950.
Poesía, 1915-1956, Ediciones de la Universidad de Puerto Rico, 1957, 4th revised edition, 1971.
Luis Palés Matos: Vida y obra, bibliografía, antología, compiled by Federico de Onís, Universidad Central de las Villas, 1959.
Luis Palés Matos (1898-1959): Vida y obra, bibliografía, antología, poesías inéditas, compiled by de Onís, Ediciones Atenco Puertorriqueños, 1960.
Poesía completa y prosa selecta, edited by Margot Arce de Vázquez, Biblioteca Ayacucho, 1978.

Obras (1914-1959), two volumes, edited by Arce de Vázquez, Editorial de la Universidad de Puerto Rico, 1984.

Also author of *Azaleas,* 1915, and *Pueblo negro,* 1925.

SIDELIGHTS: "Luis Palés Matos's place in the history of Puerto Rican poetry is clear," wrote Ricardo Gullón in *La torre:* "He is the most important poet of Puerto Rico, the one who has best expressed the special qualities of his land, its own passionately Puerto Rican self." Scion of a prominent Puerto Rican family, Palés Matos grew up in a literary household. His father, Vicente Palés Anés, and his brothers, Vicente and Gustavo Palés Matos, all were poets laureate of Puerto Rico. Although Luis Palés Matos celebrated many themes in his work—James Hilary Ward II listed six of them in *DA*—he is perhaps best known for his poetic celebration of Negros and use of African rhythms. "The poet presents us with a profound, radical vision of the Puerto Rican Negro," wrote Miguel Enguídanos in his study *La poesía de Luis Palés Matos.* "He sees himself not as the defender of an oppressed race but as a poet or a prophet of the qualities the Negro has that are superior to those of the white man. And he communicates, above all, the Negro's sense of rhythm his overly developed sensuality, and his majesty—his strength in the face of suffering."

BIOGRAPHICAL/CRITICAL SOURCES:

BOOKS

Coulthard, G. R., *Race and Colour in Caribbean Literature,* Oxford University Press, 1962.
Enguídanos, Miguel, *La poesía de Luis Palés Matos,* Editorial de la Universidad de Puerto Rico, 1962.

PERIODICALS

DA, Volume 28, 1968.

Hispania, February, 1948.
La torre, January-June, 1960.

*   *   *

PALMA, Marigloria
See PAGAN FERRER, Gloria M.

*   *   *

PAOLI, Francisco Matos
See MATOS PAOLI, Francisco

*   *   *

PAREDES, Américo 1915-

PERSONAL: Born September 3, 1915, in Brownsville, Tex.; son of Justo (a rancher) and Clotilde (Manzano-Vidal) Paredes; married Consuelo Silva, August 13, 1939 (marriage ended); married Amelia Sidzu Nagamine, May 28, 1948; children: Américo, Jr., Alan, Vicente, Julia. *Education:* University of Texas, B.A. (summa cum laude), 1951, M.A., 1953, Ph.D., 1956. *Politics:* Independent. *Religion:* No denomination.

ADDRESSES: Home—3106 Pinecrest Dr., Austin, Tex. 78757. *Office*—Department of English, University of Texas, Austin, Tex. 78712.

CAREER: Worked as journalist, 1936-50; University of Texas at Austin, member of faculty, beginning in 1951, director of Folklore Center, 1957-70, director of Mexican-American Studies Program, beginning in 1970, Ashbell Smith Professor of English and Anthropology, 1981-83, Dickson, Allen, and Anderson Centennial Professor, 1983-85, Dickson, Allen, and Anderson Centennial Professor Emeritus, 1985—. *Military service:* U.S. Army, 1944-46; served in infantry.

MEMBER: International Committee on Comparative Folklore Research, American Anthropological Association, American Folklore Society, Societé Internationale d'Ethnologie et de Folklore, Mexican Academy of History, Sociedad Folklórica de México, Comisión de Historia, Comité de Folklore, Academy Norteamericana de la Lengua Española, South Atlantic Modern Language Association, Texas Folklore Society, California Folklore Society, Phi Theta Kappa.

AWARDS, HONORS: First prize in poetry from Trinity University, 1934; first prize in short story from *Dallas Times-Herald,* 1952; first prize from D. A. Frank novel-writing contest, 1955; Guggenheim fellow, 1962; Charles Frankel Prize from National Endowment for the Humanities, 1989.

WRITINGS:

With His Pistol in His Hand: A Border Ballad and Its Hero, University of Texas Press, 1958.
(Translator and author of notes) Edward Larocque Tinker, editor, *Corridos and Calaveras,* University of Texas Press, 1961.
(Translator) Daniel Cosio Villegas, *American Extremes,* University of Texas Press, 1964.
(Editor with Richard M. Dorson) *Folktales of Mexico,* University of Chicago Press, 1970.
(Editor with Ellen Stekert) *The Urban Experience and Folk Tradition,* University of Texas Press, 1971.
(Editor with Raymund Paredes) *Mexican-American Authors,* Houghton, 1972.
(Editor with Richard Bauman) *Toward New Perspectives in Folklore,* University of Texas Press, 1972.
A Texas-Mexican Cancionero, University of Illinois Press, 1976.
(Editor) *Humanidad: Essays in Honor of George I. Sánchez,* University of California Press, 1977.
(Editor) *Folktales of Mexico,* University of Chicago Press, 1979.

Also author of *Cantos de adolescencia* (verse), 1937. Contributor to periodicals, including *Journal of American Folklore* and *University of Texas Studies in Literature.* Editor of *Journal of American Folklore,* 1968-73.

WORK IN PROGRESS: Editing a glossary and study of derogative names for Anglos and Mexican-Americans.

SIDELIGHTS: Américo Paredes is an authority on Chicano folklore. He has devoted himself to tracing, analyzing, and elucidating the legends, tales, and ballads of Mexican-American culture, and in his many books and articles he has addressed subjects ranging from word origins to social phenomena.

BIOGRAPHICAL/CRITICAL SOURCES:

BOOKS

Bauman, Richard, and Roger D. Abrahams, *"And Other Neighborly Names": Social Process and Cultural Image in Texas Folklore,* University of Texas Press, 1981.
Simmen, Edward, editor, *New Voices in Literature: The Mexican American,* Pan American University, 1971.

PERIODICALS

Revista Chicano-Riqueña, summer, 1980.

PARRA, Nicanor 1914-

PERSONAL: Born September 5, 1914, in Chillán, Chile; son of Nicanor P. (a teacher) and Clara S. (Navarette) Parra; married Ana Troncoso, 1948 (marriage ended); married Inga Palmen; children: seven. *Education:* University of Chile, degree in mathematics and physics, 1938; attended Brown University, 1943-45; studied cosmology at Oxford University, 1949-51.

ADDRESSES: Home—c/o Julia Bernstein, Parcela 272, Lareina, Santiago, Chile. *Office*—Instituto Pedagógico, Avenida Macul 774, Santiago, Chile.

CAREER: Poet and scientist. Secondary school teacher, 1938-43; University of Chile, Santiago, professor, 1947-52, director of school of engineering, 1948—, professor of theoretical physics, 1952—. Visiting professor at Louisiana State University, 1966-67, and New York University, Columbia University, and Yale University, 1971; has given poetry readings in many countries, including the United States, Russia, Venezuela, Cuba, Peru, and Argentina.

AWARDS, HONORS: Premio municipal de poesía, Santiago, Chile, 1937, for *Cancionero sin nombre,* and 1954, for *Poemas y antipoemas;* Writers Union Prize, 1954; Premio Nacional de Literatura (national prize for literature), Chile, 1969, for *Obra gruesa;* Guggenheim fellowship, 1972; first Richard Wilbur prize for poetry, American Literary Translators Association and University of Missouri Press, 1984, for *Sermons and Homilies of the Christ of Elqui.*

WRITINGS:

IN ENGLISH TRANSLATION

Poemas y antipoemas, Nascimento, 1954, Cátedra (Madrid), 1988, translation of selected poems by Jorge Elliot published as *Anti-poems,* City Lights, 1960.
Poems and Antipoems (bilingual selection of poems from other works), edited by Miller Williams, New Directions, 1967.
Obra gruesa, Editorial Universitaria, 1969, Editorial Andrés Bello, 1983, translation by Williams of selected poems published as *Emergency Poems,* New Directions, 1972.
Sermones y prédicas del Cristo de Elqui, Universidad de Chile Estudios Humanísticos, 1977, translation by Sandra Reyes published as *Sermons and Homilies of the Christ of Elqui* (bilingual edition; also see below), University of Missouri Press, 1984.
Nuevos sermones y prédicas del Cristo de Elqui, Ganymedes, 1979, translation by Reyes published in *Sermons and Homilies of the Christ of Elqui,* University of Missouri Press, 1984.
Antipoems: New and Selected, edited by David Unger, translation by Lawrence Ferlinghetti and others, New Directions, 1985.

OTHER

Cancionero sin nombre (title means "Untitled Book of Ballads"), Nascimento, 1937.
La cueca larga (also see below), Editorial Universitaria, 1958, 2nd edition, 1966.
Versos de salón, Nascimento, 1962.
(With Pablo Neruda) *Discursos,* Nascimento, 1962.
La cueca larga y otros poemas, edited by Margarita Aguirre, Editorial Universitaria de Buenos Aires, 1964.
(Editor) *Poesía soviética rusa,* Editorial Progreso, 1965.
Canciones rusas, Editorial Universitaria, 1967.
Poemas, Casa de las Américas, 1969.

Poesía rusa contemporánea, Ediciones Nueva Universidad, Universidad Católica de Chile, 1971.
Los profesores, Antiediciones Villa Miseria (New York), 1971.
Antipoemas: Antología (1944-1969), Seix Barral, 1972.
Artefactos/Nicanor Parra, Ediciones Nueva Universidad, Universidad Católica de Chile, 1972, enlarged edition, 1972.
Poema y antipoema a Eduardo Frei, Editorial América del Sur, 1982.
Coplas de Navidad, Ediciones del Camaleón, 1983.
Poesía política, Bruguera, 1983.
Nicanor Parra: Biografía emotiva (selected poems), compiled by Efrain Szmulewicz, Ediciones Rumbos, 1988.

Also author of *La evolución del concepto de masa,* 1958; *Deux poemas,* 1964; *Tres poemas,* 1965; *Defensa de Violeta Parra,* 1967; (translator from the English) R. D. Lindsay and Henry Margenau, *Fundamentos de la física* (title means "Foundations of Physics"), 1967; *Muyeres,* 1969; and *Ejercicios respiratorios.*

SIDELIGHTS: Chilean poet Nicanor Parra, a contemporary of Pablo Neruda, inherited a poetic tradition that ensconced lofty themes in grandiose language. "Parra," declared *New York Times Book Review* contributor Alexander Coleman, "is an antipoet. Antipoets . . . dread the very idea of Poetry and its attendant metaphors, inflated diction, romantic yearning, obscurity and empty nobility." Poetry is not an elite pastime, but belongs to the less-privileged majority, he believes. Its proper subject matter is not truth and beauty, but the vulgar surprises of life that more often than not amount to a bad joke. His antipoems relate the ironies of life in ordinary speech made colorful by witty insights into the unpretentious characters he presents. Coleman describes Parra's tools as "irony, burlesque, an astringent barrage of cliches and found phrases, all juxtaposed in a welter of dictions that come out in a wholly original way, laying open everybody's despair." With these methods, says a *Publishers Weekly* reviewer, "Parra bids to break the barrier between the poem and the public." As a champion of accessible poetry, Parra has exerted a major influence on Hispanic literature.

Parra was born in southern Chile near the small town of Chillán in 1914. Having an interest in science and an aptitude for mathematics, he studied mathematics and physics at the University of Chile, advanced mechanics at Brown University in Rhode Island, and, with the aid of a British Council grant, cosmology at Oxford. Since 1948, he has been a professor of theoretical physics at the University of Chile. In addition to his professional activities, he has maintained an interest in American and British poetry, both of which have influenced his work. The factor which perhaps shaped his personal aesthetic the most, however, was having to write in the shadow of the Nobel Prize winner Neruda. Parra became an antipoet, says Emir Rodríguez Monegal in *The Borzoi Anthology of Latin American Literature,* "in order to negate the exalted conception of the poet that Neruda represented so grandly. The fact that he finally succeeded in creating a viable alternative confirms his unique gifts." Parra's antipoetry "is a prime example of a generational reaction to the styles and concerns of earlier poets: it negates the highly metaphorical, surrealistic style of the 1930s," Edith Grossman suggests in *Contemporary Foreign Language Writers.*

Though Parra's early books contain some surreal imagery, later books rely on manipulation of narrative structure to achieve their effects. "Using narrative devices but deflecting the normal expectations of the reader by interrupting and even cutting short the anecdotal flow, Parra 'deconstructs' the poem and finally achieves an almost epigrammatic structure that moves from one intense fragment of verbal reality to the next," Rodríguez Monegal suggests. In addition, the antipoet feels that poetry need not be musical to be good. He maintains that since man talks more than he sings, man should leave the singing to the birds. Another feature the antipoems borrow from prose is the presence of characters found in contemporary urban settings. Mobsters and nymphomaniacs, ragged and rough-talking bag ladies, pugilistic youth and frustrated office workers alike have their say in Parra's antipoems.

Another character that caught Parra's sustained attention was Domingo Zarate Vega, a construction worker who became a self-styled prophet in the 1920s. Parra borrows the folk legend's voice for all the poems in *Sermons and Homilies of the Christ of Elqui.* The result, says a *Georgia Review* contributor, "makes for a powerful, entertaining, and often quirky reading experience." Doing for the figure of Christ what he has always done for Hispanic poetry, Parra demythologizes the Chilean prophet (and, by implication, other religious figures) by describing the profane conditions of their lives. Parra's Christ matter-of-factly jokes about his sackcloth robe and his breakfast of hot water. Later, he chides followers for giving the pages of the Bible and the Chilean flag a reverence that is inappropriate and impractical. Here, as in his other books, Parra shows the humor (and fury) to be gained from recognizing that people or objects traditionally considered sacred are not.

Parra's iconoclasm is so thoroughgoing that after poetry readings, he says "Me retracto de todo lo dicho" ("I take back everything I told you"). He also refuses to formulate a firm definition of antipoetry. He turns interviews into anti-interviews, frustrating most inquiries into his personal life and writing process, which he calls "a professional secret," Grossman reports. He has written that the thanks he gets for his freedom from tradition is to be declared *persona non grata* in literary circles. Yet many critics offer generally favorable impressions of Parra's work. In his *New York Times Book Review* piece about *Poems and Antipoems,* Mark Strand comments: "Parra's poems are hallucinatory and violent, and at the same time factual. The well-timed disclosure of events—personal or political—gives his poems a cumulative, mounting energy and power that we have come to expect from only the best fiction." In a *Poetry* review, Hayden Carruth adds: "Free, witty, satirical, intelligent, often unexpected (without quite being surrealistic), mordant and comic by turns, always rebellious, always irreverent—it is all these and an ingratiating poetry too."

Partisan Review contributor G. S. Fraser observes that among Hispanic writers, Parra possesses the liveliest wit. "I think that being a professor of mathematics may have given him the logical quickness which lies at the essence of wit," Fraser suggests. Grossman concurs that Parra "has brought to Hispanic literature a new vision of the expressive possibilities of colloquial Spanish." Strand points out, "It is the difference between Parra's antipoems and anybody else's that is significant. . . . To many readers Parra will be a new poet, but a poet with all the authority of a master."

BIOGRAPHICAL/CRITICAL SOURCES:

BOOKS

Contemporary Foreign Language Writers, St. Martin's, 1984.
Contemporary Literary Criticism, Volume 2, Gale, 1974.
Gottlieb, Marlene, *No se termina nunca de nacer: La poesía de Parra,* Playor, 1977.
Grossman, Edith, *The Antipoetry of Parra,* New York University Press, 1975.
Montes, Hugo, *Parra y la poesía de lo cotidiano,* Pacifico, 2nd edition, 1974.
Rodríguez Monegal, Emir, editor, *The Borzoi Anthology of Latin American Literature,* Volume 2: *The Twentieth Century—From Borges and Paz to Guimaraes Rosa and Donoso,* Knopf, 1986.

PERIODICALS

Arizona Quarterly, summer, 1967.
Books Abroad, summer, 1968.
Carleton Miscellany, spring, 1968.
Hudson Review, autumn, 1968, winter, 1972-73.
Nation, August 7, 1972.
National Observer, March 24, 1973.
New Statesman, November 8, 1968.
New York Times Book Review, December 10, 1967, May 7, 1972.
Partisan Review, summer, 1974.
Poetry, September, 1968.
Review, winter, 1971, spring, 1972.

—*Sketch by Marilyn K. Basel*

* * *

PASARELL, Emilio J(ulio) 1891-?

PERSONAL: Born in 1891 in Ponce, Puerto Rico.

CAREER: Writer. Worked as a U.S. Federal customs officer.

AWARDS, HONORS: Received several awards from the Puerto Rico Atheneum.

WRITINGS:

Orígenes y desarrollo de la afición teatral en Puerto Rico (title means "Origins and Development of the Love of the Theatre in Puerto Rico"), Editorial Universitaria de la Universidad de Puerto Rico, Volume 1: *Hasta el siglo XIX,* 1951, Volume 2: *Siglo XX,* 1967, 2nd edition published in one volume, 1970.

Panorama teatral de Puerto Rico en el siglo XIX (title means "Panorama of the Puerto Rican Theatre in the Nineteenth Century"), Instituto de Cultura Puertorriqueña, 1960.

Conjunto literario (title means "Collected Works"), Rumbos (Barcelona), 1963.

De la pluma al papel (title means "From the Pen to the Paper", newspaper articles), Rumbos, 1967.

Esculcando el siglo XIX en Puerto Rico (title means "Investigating the Nineteenth Century in Puerto Rico"), Rumbos, 1967.

Ensayos y artículos (title means "Essays and Articles"), Cordillera (San Juan, Puerto Rico), 1968.

Also author of *Trío incoherente-del ambiente.* Frequent contributor to *The Review of Reviews, Revista del Instituto de Cultura Puertorriqueña, El Mundo, Almanaque Asenjo,* and other periodicals.

* * *

PAU-LLOSA, Ricardo 1954-

PERSONAL: Born May 17, 1954, in Havana, Cuba; came to the United States in 1960, naturalized citizen, 1976. *Education:* Miami Dade Community College, A.A., 1972; attended Concordia University, 1972-73; Florida International University, B.A., 1974; Florida Atlantic University, M.A., 1976; attended University of Florida, 1978-86.

ADDRESSES: Home—3225 Southwest 58th Ave., Miami, Fla. 33155.

CAREER: University of Miami, Coral Gables, Fla., and Miami Dade Community College, New World Center Campus, instructor in English, 1976-77; Nova University, Fort Lauderdale, Fla., instructor in English as a second language, 1977-78; Florida International University, Miami, adjunct professor of Latin American art history, 1980-84; St. Thomas University, Miami, Fla., instructor in English, 1984-85; Miami Dade Community College, South Campus, associate professor of English, 1985—. Cocurator of touring art exhibits "Outside Cuba/Fuera de Cuba," 1987-89, ".Mira! The Canadian Club Hispanic Art Tour III," 1988-89, and an exposition of Costa Rican art, 1989. Lecturer in Latin American art, poetry, and folk traditions in the United States, Canada, Puerto Rico, Dominican Republic, Venezuela, and Argentina. Member, Chancelor's Council, University of Texas System.

MEMBER: International PEN, International Association of Art Critics.

AWARDS, HONORS: Anhinga Poetry Prize, Florida State University, 1983, for *Sorting Metaphors;* Cintas fellowship, Oscar B. Cintas Foundation, Institute of International Education, United Nations, 1984-85; English Language Poetry Prize, *Linden Lane Magazine,* 1987.

WRITINGS:

Veinticinco poemas (title means "Twenty-Five Poems"), privately printed, 1973.
Dirube (nonfiction; bilingual text in Spanish and English), Editorial Playor, 1979.
(Contributor) Gary Keller and Francisco Jiménez, *Hispanics in the United States: An Anthology of Creative Literature,* Bilingual Review Press, 1980.
(Contributor) Ivonne Nichols, editor, *David Manzur* (monograph in Spanish), Seguros Bolívar, 1981.
Sorting Metaphors (poems), Anhinga Press, 1983.
Rogelio Polesello (monograph in Spanish), Ediciones Gaglianone, 1984.
(Contributor) Robert J. Phelan, *New Traditions: Thirteen Hispanic Photographers,* New York State Museum, State Education Department, 1986.
(Contributor) *Clarence Holbrook Carter* (monograph), Rizzoli, 1988.
Bread of the Imagined (poems), Bilingual Press, Arizona State University, 1991.

Author of texts of many art exhibition catalogues. Adviser on Cuban and Latin American art and contributor to *Dictionary of Art,* Macmillan, 1991. Works represented in anthologies, including *Cuban-American Writers: Los Atrevidos,* edited by Carolina Hospital, 1989, and *Anthology of Magazine Verse and Yearbook of American Poetry,* edited by Alan Pater, 1981 and 1983. Art critic for *Vanidades Continental,* 1982-83. Contributor of articles and art criticism to magazines and newspapers, including *Art International, Arts, Terzo Occhio, Dreamworks, New Orleans Review,* and *Caribbean Review.* Contributor of poems to *American Poetry Review, Partisan Review, Black Warrior Review, Denver Quarterly, Agni Review,* and other literary journals. Guest editor and translator, *Beloit Poetry Journal,* summer, 1982; senior editor for Latin America, *Art International,* 1983-85, contributing editor, 1987—; guest editor with others, *Palmetto Review,* Number 4, 1986; art and film editor, *Caribbean Review,* 1987-88.

WORK IN PROGRESS: Monographs on contemporary artists; a book on twentieth-century Latin American art; a novel; a third collection of poems.

SIDELIGHTS: Cuban-born poet Ricardo Pau-Llosa is a specialist in contemporary Latin American Art. He served as co-curator of two major exhibits that toured the United States. "Outside Cuba/Fuera de Cuba" featured the works of forty-eight Cuban artists now living outside Cuba. ".Mira! The Canadian Club Hispanic Art Tour III," which opened in Los Angeles, California, in 1988, featured the works of Chicano, Cuban-American, Puerto-Rican, and Latin-American artists in the United States. Pau-Llosa has contributed text to more than thirty exhibition catalogues, and he is the author of monographs on the Latin American artists Rolando Lopez Dirube, David Manzur, and Rogelio Polesello.

Pau-Llosa's constant interaction with the visual arts puts him in touch with images that serve as catalysts when he is writing poetry, he told Carolina Hospital in a *Linden Lane Magazine* interview. It "has affected the way I process intellectually and experientially everyday events as well as images from my dreams," he added. Speaking of his early poetry, which highlights figures of speech, he told Hospital that he arranged sequences of metaphors, similes, and other tropes in order to "penetrate the way the mind organizes perceptions of events and objects" based on resemblances or features they share in common. Figurative language is founded on the same comparisons and contrasts that allow the mind to "synthesize sense impressions and turn them into thoughts, memories, and ideas," he told Hospital. "That is, tropes are the software of consciousness. Without them, perception would be a jumble of sense impressions."

Pau-Llosa told *CA:* "My interest in theories of metaphor, especially those of phenomenologists and deconstructionist critics, has motivated me to write poems that reduce the importance of syntax, or suspend it entirely, and draw on sequences of metaphors to move the reader through the text. This movement is anything but linear. I have been pursuing a kind of poem that generates a cognitive time that is different from the temporality involved in understanding the usual 'spoken chain' of language. When I write poems that use syntax in traditional ways, I also aim toward generating a sense of time that coalesces past and present, or that discloses the fact that the 'present' is but a confluence of multiple pasts. Whether my poems involve sequences of metaphors or discursive, if oneiric [i.e., dream-like], expressions, I aim to evoke a cognitive temporality that is based on simultaneity. My poetry draws a great deal from Latin American traditions—literary, philosophical and pictorial—although I write solely in English. The work of various Latin American visual artists has helped me see the need to engage a new kind of temporality in the ways we write and read poetry." As a result, *Sorting Metaphors,* which won the Anhinga Poetry Prize in 1983, "is a book of imagination, of surprising connections," Deno Trakas comments in the *Georgia Review.*

Since 1985, Pau-Llosa's poetry has taken on narrative dimensions. Of his novel in progress, he told Hospital, "It deals with poets in a position of political power. . . . It is a political fantasy, and I am thoroughly enjoying it."

BIOGRAPHICAL/CRITICAL SOURCES:

BOOKS

Hospital, Carolina, editor, *Cuban-American Writers: Los Atrevidos,* Ediciones Ellas/Linden Lane Press, 1989.

PERIODICALS

Atlanta Constitution, March 23, 1988.
Dallas Times Herald, June 9, 1988.
Georgia Review, summer, 1984.

Linden Lane Magazine, Volume 6, number 4, 1987, Volume 7, number 1, 1988.
Los Angeles Times, April 20, 1988.
Miami Herald, October 9, 1988.
New York Times, April 19, 1987.
Palmetto Review, Volume 1, number 3, 1984.
Sun Dog, Volume 5, number 2-3, 1984.

* * *

PAYRO, Roberto J(orge)   1867-1928

PERSONAL: Born in 1867 in Mercedes, Buenos Aires, Argentina; died in 1928.

CAREER: La Nación, Buenos Aires, Argentina, journalist, beginning in 1894; writer.

WRITINGS:

FICTION

Scripta, J. Peuser, 1887.
El casamiento de Laucha, Chamijo [and] *El falso inca,* Losada (Buenos Aires), 1940, reprinted, 1974, first title reprinted, Colihué/Hachette (Buenos Aires), 1979.
Veinte cuentos, Poseidón (Buenos Aires), 1943.
Sobre las ruinas (four-act play), edited by C. K. Jones and Antonio Alonso, D.C. Heath (Boston), 1943.
El mar dulce: Crónica novelesca del descubrimiento del Río de la Plata, Losada, 1944.
Marco Severi (play), Instituto Nacional de Estudios de Teatro (Buenos Aires), 1946.
Divertidas aventuras del nieto de Juan Moreira [and] *Los tesoros del Rey Blanco,* M. Aguilar (Madrid), 1948, first title reprinted as *Divertidas aventuras de un nieto de Juan Moreira,* Colihué (Buenos Aires), 1981.
Evocaciones de un porteña viejo, Quetzal, 1952.
Pago Chico y Nuevos cuentos de Pago Chico, Losada, 1953, reprinted, Colihué/Hachette, 1980.
El diablo en Bélgica, Quetzal (Buenos Aires), 1953.
Teatro completo, Hachette (Buenos Aires), 1956.
Violines y toneles, Centro Editor de América Latina (Buenos Aires), 1968.
(With others) *El escritor y la industria cultural: El camino hacia la profesionalización, 1810-1900,* edited by Jorge B. Rivera, Centro Editor de América Latina, 1980.
Obras, edited by Beatriz Sarlo, Biblioteca Ayacucho (Caracas), 1984.

NONFICTION

La Australia Argentina: Excursión periodística a las costas patagónicas, Tierra del Fuego e Isla de los Estados, La Nación (Buenos Aires), 1898, reprinted, Centro Editor de América Latina, 1982.
En las tierras de Inti, Universitaria de Buenos Aires, 1960.
Crónica de la revolución oriental de 1903, La Banda Oriental (Montevideo), 1967.
Al azar de las lecturas (articles originally published in periodical *La Nación*), Facultad de Humanidades y Ciencias de la Educación, Universidad Nacional de La Plata (La Plata), 1968.

Also author of nonfiction book *Cartas chilenas,* of play "Canción trágica," and of historical novel, the title of which means "Captain Vergara." Work represented in anthologies, including *El cuento argentino, 1900-1930: Antología,* Centro Editor de América Latina, 1980.

BIOGRAPHICAL/CRITICAL SOURCES:

BOOKS

Cuatro escritores argentinos: Roberto Arlt, Ricardo Güiraldes, Benito Lynch y Roberto J. Payró, [Buenos Aires], 1965.

* * *

PAZ, Gil
See LUGONES, Leopoldo

* * *

PAZ, Octavio   1914-

PERSONAL: Born March 31, 1914, in Mexico City, Mexico; son of Octavio Paz (a lawyer) and Josephina Lozano; married Marie José Tramini, 1964; children: one daughter. *Education:* Attended National Autonomous University of Mexico, 1932-37. *Politics:* "Disillusioned leftist." *Religion:* Atheist.

ADDRESSES: Home—Lerma 143-601, México 5, D.F., México. *Office*—c/o *Vuelta,* Avenida Contreras 516, Tercer Piso, San Jerónimo 10200 DF, México City, México.

CAREER: Writer. Government of Mexico, Mexican Foreign Service, posted to San Francisco, Calif., and New York, N.Y., secretary at Mexican Embassy in Paris, beginning 1945, charge d'affaires at Mexican Embassy in Japan, beginning 1951, posted to Mexican Secretariat for External Affairs, 1953-58, Extraordinary and Plenipotentiary Minister to Mexican embassy, 1959-62, ambassador to India, 1962-68. Visiting professor of Spanish American literature, University of Texas at Austin and Pittsburgh University, 1968-70; Simón Bolívar Professor of Latin American Studies, 1970, and fellow of Churchill College, Cambridge University, 1970-71; Charles Eliot Norton Professor of Poetry, Harvard University, 1971-72. Regent's fellow at University of California, San Diego.

MEMBER: American Academy and Institute of Arts and Letters (honorary).

AWARDS, HONORS: Guggenheim fellowship, 1944; Grand Prix International de Poésie (Belgium), 1963; Jerusalem Prize, Critics Prize (Spain), and National Prize for Letters (Mexico), all 1977; Grand Aigle d'Or (Nice), 1979; Premio Ollin Yoliztli (Mexico), 1980; Miguel de Cervantes Prize (Spain), 1982; Neustadt International Prize for Literature, 1982; Wilhelm Heinse Medal (West Germany), 1984; T S Eliot Award for Creative Writing, Ingersoll Foundation, 1987; Tocqueville Prize, 1989.

WRITINGS:

POETRY

Luna silvestre (title means "Sylvan Moon"), Fábula (Mexico City), 1933.
¡No pasarán!, Simbad (Mexico City), 1936.
Raíz del hombre (title means "Root of Man"; also see below), Simbad, 1937.
Bajo tu clara sombra y otros poemas sobre España (title means "Under Your Clear Shadow and Other Poems about Spain"; also see below), Españolas (Valencia), 1937, revised edition, Tierra Nueva (Valencia), 1941.
Entre la piedra y la flor (title means "Between the Stone and the Flower"; Nueva Voz (Mexico City), 1938, 2nd edition, Asociación Cívica Yucatán (Mexico City), 1956.
A la orilla del mundo y Primer día; Bajo tu clara sombra; Raíz del hombre; Noche de resurrecciones, Ars (Mexico City), 1942.
Libertad bajo palabra (title means "Freedom on Parole"), Tezontle (Mexico City), 1949.

¿Aguila o sol? (prose poems), Tezontle, 1951, 2nd edition, 1973, translation by Eliot Weinberger published as *¿Aguila o sol?/Eagle or Sun?* (bilingual edition), October House, 1970, revised translation by Weinberger published under same title, New Directions, 1976.

Semillas para un himno, Tezontle, 1954.

Piedra de sol, Tezontle, 1957, translation by Muriel Rukeyser published as *Sun Stone/Piedra de sol* (bilingual edition; also see below), New Directions, 1963, translation by Peter Miller published as *Sun-Stone,* Contact (Toronto), 1963, translation by Donald Gardner published as *Sun Stone,* Cosmos (New York), 1969.

La estación violenta, Fondo de Cultura Económica (Mexico City), 1958, reprinted, 1978.

Agua y viento, Ediciones Mito (Bogotá), 1959.

Libertad bajo palabra: Obra poética, 1935-1958, Fondo de Cultura Económica, 1960, revised edition, 1968.

Salamandra (1958-1961) (also see below), J. Mortiz (Mexico City), 1962, 3rd edition, 1975.

Selected Poems of Octavio Paz (bilingual edition), translation by Rukeyser, Indiana University Press, 1963.

Viento entero, Caxton (Delhi), 1965.

Blanco (also see below) J. Mortiz, 1967, 2nd edition, 1972, translation by Weinberger published under same title, The Press (New York), 1974.

Disco visuales (four spatial poems), Era (Mexico City), 1968.

Ladera este (1962-1968) (title means "Eastern Slope (1962-1968)"; also see below) J. Mortiz, 1969, 3rd edition, 1975.

La centena (Poemas: 1935-1968), Seix Barral (Barcelona), 1969, 2nd edition, 1972.

Topoemas (six spatial poems), Era, 1971.

Vuelta (long poem), El Mendrugo (Mexico City), 1971.

Configurations (contains *Piedra de sol/Sun Stone, Blanco,* and selections from *Salamandra* and *Ladera este*), translations by G. Aroul and others, New Directions, 1971.

(With Jacques Roubaud, Edoardo Sanguinetti, and Charles Tomlinson; also author of prologue) *Renga* (collective poem written in French, Italian, English, and Spanish), J. Mortiz, 1972, translation by Tomlinson published as *Renga: A Chain of Poems,* Braziller, 1972.

Early Poems: 1935-1955, translations by Rukeyser and others, New Directions, 1973.

3 Notations/3 Rotations (contains fragments of poems by Paz), Carpenter Center for the Visual Arts, Harvard University, 1974.

Pasado en claro (long poem), Fondo de Cultura Económica, 1975, revised edition, 1978, tranlation included as title poem in *A Draft of Shadows and Other Poems* (also see below), New Directions, 1979.

Vuelta, Seix Barral, 1976.

(With Tomlinson; sonnets written by Paz and Tomlinson in Spanish and English) *Air Born/Hijos del aire,* Pescador (Mexico City), 1979.

Poemas (1935-1975), Seix Barral, 1979.

A Draft of Shadows and Other Poems, edited and translated by Weinberger, with additional translations by Elizabeth Bishop and Mark Strand, New Directions, 1979.

Selected Poems (biligual edition), translations by Tomlinson and others, Penguin, 1979.

Octavio Paz: Poemas recientes, Institución Cultural de Cantabria de la Diputación Provincial de Santander, 1981.

Selected Poems, edited by Weinberger, translations by G. Aroul and others, New Directions, 1984.

Cuatro chopos/The Four Poplars (bilingual edition), translation by Weinberger, Center for Edition Works (New York), 1985.

The Collected Poems, 1957-1987: Bilingual Edition, New Editions, 1987.

PROSE

El laberinto de la soledad (also see below), Cuadernos Americanos, 1950, revised edition, Fondo de Cultura Económica, 1959, reprinted, 1980, translation by Lysander Kemp published as *The Labyrinth of Solitude: Life and Thought in Mexico,* Grove, 1961.

El arco y la lira: El poema; La revelación poética; Poesía e historia, Fondo de Cultura Económica, 1956, 2nd edition includes text of *Los signos en rotación* (also see below), 1967, 3rd edition, 1972, translation by Ruth L. C. Simms published as *The Bow and the Lyre: The Poem, the Poetic Revelation, Poetry and History,* University of Texas Press, 1973, reprinted, 1977, 2nd edition, McGraw-Hill, 1975.

Las peras del olmo, Universidad Nacional Autónoma de México, 1957, revised edition, Seix Barral, 1971, 3rd edition, 1978.

Tamayo en la pintura mexicana, Universidad Nacional Autónoma de México, 1959.

Cuadrivio: Darío, López Velarde, Pessoa, Cernuda, J. Mortiz, 1965.

Los signos en rotación, Sur (Buenos Aires), 1965.

Puertas al campo (also see below), Universidad Nacional Autónoma de México, 1966.

Claude Lévi-Strauss; o, El nuevo festín de Esopo, J. Mortiz, 1967, translation by J. S. Bernstein and Maxine Bernstein published as *Claude Lévi-Strauss: An Introduction,* Cornell University Press, 1970 (published in England as *On Lévi-Strauss,* Cape, 1970).

Corriente alterna, Siglo Veintiuno Editores (Mexico City), 1967, reprinted, 1980, translation by Helen R. Lane published as *Alternating Current,* Viking, 1973.

Marcel Duchamp; o, El castillo de la pureza, Era, 1968, translation by Gardner published as *Marcel Duchamp; or, The Castle of Purity,* Grossman, 1970.

Conjunciones y disyunciones, J. Mortiz, 1969, 2nd edition, 1978, translation by Lane published as *Conjunctions and Disjunctions,* Viking, 1974.

México: La última década, Institute of Latin American Studies, University of Texas, 1969.

Posdata (also see below) Siglo Veintiuno, 1970, translation by Kemp published as *The Other Mexico: Critique of the Pyramid,* Grove, 1972.

(With Juan Marichal) *Las cosas en su sitio: Sobre la literatura española del siglo XX,* Finisterre (Mexico City), 1971.

Los signos en rotación y otros ensayos, edited and with a prologue by Carlos Fuentes, Alianza (Madrid), 1971.

Traducción: Literatura y literalidad, Tusquets (Barcelona), 1971.

Aparencia desnuda: La obra de Marcel Duchamp, Era, 1973, new enlarged edition, 1979, translation by Rachel Phillips and Gardner published as *Marcel Duchamp: Appearance Stripped Bare,* Viking, 1978.

El signo y el garabato (contains *Puertas al campo*), J. Mortiz, 1973.

(With Julián Ríos) *Solo a dos voces,* Lumen (Barcelona), 1973.

Teatro de signos/Transparencias, selection and montage by Ríos, Fundamentos (Madrid), 1974.

La búsqueda del comienzo: Escritos sobre el surrealismo, Fundamentos, 1974, 2nd edition, 1980.

El mono gramático, Seix Barral, 1974, translation from the original Spanish manuscript published as *Le singe grammarien,* Skira (Geneva), 1972, translation by Lane of Spanish original published as *The Monkey Grammarian,* Seaver, 1981.

Los hijos del limo: Del romanticismo a la vanguardia, Seix Barral, 1974, translation by Phillips published as *Children of the Mire: Modern Poetry from Romanticism to the Avant-Garde,* Harvard University Press, 1974.

The Siren and the Seashell, and Other Essays on Poets and Poetry, translations by Kemp and Margaret Sayers Peden, University of Texas Press, 1976.

Xavier Villaurrutia en persona y en obra, Fondo de Cultura Económica, 1978.

El ogro filantrópico: Historia y política, 1971-1978 (also see below), J. Mortiz, 1979.

In/mediaciones, Seix Barral, 1979.

México en la obra de Octavio Paz, edited by Luis Mario Schneider, Promexa (Mexico City), 1979.

El laberinto de la soledad; Posdata; Vuelta a El laberinto de la soledad, Fondo de Cultura Económica, 1981.

Sor Juana Inés de la Cruz; o, Las trampas de la fe, Seix Barral, 1982, translation by Peden published as *Sor Juana; or, The Traps of Faith,* Harvard University Press, 1988.

(With Jacques Lassaigne) *Rufino Tamayo,* Ediciones Poligrafia (Barcelona), 1982, translation by Kenneth Lyons published under same title, Rizzoli, 1982.

(With John Golding) *Guenther Gerzo* (Spanish, English and French texts), Editions du Griffon (Switzerland), 1983.

Sombras de obras: Arte y literatura, Seix Barral, 1983.

Hombres en su siglo y otros ensayos, Seix Barral, 1984, translation by Michael Schmidt published as *On Poets and Others,* Seaver Books, 1987.

Tiempo nublado, Seix Barral, 1984, translation by Lane with three additional essays published as *On Earth, Four or Five Worlds: Reflections on Contemporary History,* Harcourt, 1985.

The Labyrinth of Solitude, The Other Mexico, Return to the Labyrinth of Solitude, Mexico and the United States, The Philanthropic Ogre, translated by Kemp, Yara Milos, and Rachel Phillips Belash, Grove, 1985.

Arbol adentro, Seix Barral, 1987, translation published as *A Tree Within,* New Directions, 1988.

Convergences: Essays on Art and Literature, translation by Lane, Harcourt, 1987.

EDITOR

Voces de España, Letras de México (Mexico City), 1938.

(With others) *Laurel: Antología de la poesía moderna en lengua española,* Séneca, 1941.

Antologie de la poesie mexicaine, Nagel, 1952.

Antología poética, Revista Panoramas (Mexico City), 1956.

(And translator with Eikichi Hayashiya) Matsuo Basho, *Sendas de Oku,* Universidad Nacional Autónoma de México, 1957, 2nd edition, Seix Barral, 1970.

Anthology of Mexican Poetry, translation of Spanish manuscript by Samuel Beckett, Indiana University Press, 1958, reprinted as *Mexican Poetry: An Anthology,* Grove, 1985.

Tamayo en la pintura mexicana, Imprenta Universitaria (Mexico City), 1958.

Magia de la risa, Universidad Veracruzana, 1962.

Fernando Pessoa, *Antología,* Universidad Nacional Autónoma de México, 1962.

(With Pedro Zekeli) *Cuatro poetas contemporáneos de Suecia: Martinson, Lundkvist, Ekeloef, y Lindegren,* Universidad Nacional Autónoma de México, 1963.

(With others and author of prologue) *Poesía en movimiento: México, 1915-1966,* Siglo Veintiuno, 1966, translation edited by Mark Strand and published as *New Poetry of Mexico,* Dutton, 1970.

(With Roger Caillois) *Remedios Varo,* Era, 1966.

(And author of prologue) Xavier Villaurrutia, *Antología,* Fondo de Cultura Económica, 1980.

CONTRIBUTOR

In Praise of Hands: Contemporary Crafts of the World, New York Graphic Society, 1974.

Avances, Fundamentos, 1978.

Democracy and Dictatorship in Latin America: A Special Publication Devoted Entirely to the Voices and Opinions of Writers from Latin America, Foundation for the Independent Study of Social Ideas (New York), 1982.

Instante y revelación, Fondo Nacional para Actividades Sociales, 1982.

Frustraciones de un destino: La democracia en América Latina, Libro Libre, 1985.

Weinberger, editor, *Nineteen Ways of Looking at Wang Wei: How a Chinese Poem Is Translated,* Moyer Bell, 1987.

TRANSLATOR

(And author of introduction) William Carlos Williams, *Veinte Poemas,* Era, 1973.

Versiones y diversiones (translations of poems from English, French, Portuguese, Swedish, Chinese, and Japanese), J. Mortiz, 1974.

Apollinaire, *15 Poemas,* Latitudes (Mexico City), 1979.

OTHER

"La hija de Rappaccini" (one-act play; based on a short story by Nathaniel Hawthorne; first produced in Mexico, 1956), translation by Harry Haskell published as "Rappaccini's Daughter" in *Octavio Paz: Homage to the Poet,* Kosmos (San Francisco), 1980.

(Author of introduction) Carlos Fuentes, *Cuerpos y ofrendas,* Alianza, 1972.

(Author of introduction) *Antonio Peláez: Pintor,* Secretaría de Educación Pública (Mexico), 1975.

(Author of foreword) *A Sor Juana Anthology,* translation by Alan S. Trueblood, Harvard University Press, 1988.

One Word to the Other, Latitudes, 1989.

Contributor to numerous anthologies. Founder of literary review, *Barandal,* 1931; member of editorial board and columnist, *El Popular,* late 1930s; co-founder of *Taller,* 1938; co-founder and editor, *El Hijo Pródigo,* 1943-46; editor of *Plural,* 1971-75; founder and editor, *Vuelta,* 1976—.

SIDELIGHTS: Often nominated for the Nobel Prize, Mexican author Octavio Paz has a world-wide reputation as a master poet and essayist. Although Mexico figures prominently in Paz's work—one of his best-known books, *The Labyrinth of Solitude,* for example, is an comprehensive portrait of Mexican society— *Los Angeles Times* contributor Jascha Kessler calls Paz "truly international." *World Literature Today*'s Manuel Durán feels that Paz's "exploration of Mexican existential values permits him to open a door to an understanding of other countries and other cultures" and thus appeal to readers of diverse backgrounds. "What began as a slow, almost microscopic examination of self and of a single cultural tradition widens unexpectedly," Durán continues, "becoming universal without sacrificing its unique characteristic."

One aspect of Paz's work often mentioned by critics is his tendency to maintain elements of prose—most commonly philosophical thought—in his poetry and poetic elements in his prose. Perhaps the best example to support this claim can be found in Paz's exploration of India entitled *The Monkey Grammarian,* a work which *New York Times Book Review* contributor Keith Botsford calls "exceedingly curious" and describes as "an extended meditation on the nature of language." In separate *World Literature Today* essays critics Jaime Alazraki and José Miguel Oviedo discuss the difficulty they would have assigning the book to a literary genre. "It is apparent," Alazraki notes, "that *The Monkey Grammarian* is not an essay. It is also apparent that it is not a poem, at least not in the conventional sense. It is both an essay and a poem, or perhaps neither." Oviedo similarly states that the book "does not belong to any specific genre—although it has a bit of all of them—because it is deliberately written at the edge of genres."

According to Oviedo, *The Monkey Grammarian* is the product of Paz's long-stated quest "to produce a text which would be an intersection of poetry, narrative and essay." The fusion of opposites found in this work is an important element in nearly all Paz's literary production. In many instances both the work's structure and its content represent a blending of contradictory forces: *Renga,* for example, is written in four languages, while *Air Born/Hijos del Aire,* is written in two. According to *World Literature Today* contributor Frances Chiles, Paz strives to create in his writing "a sense of community or communion" which he finds lacking in contemporary society. In his Neustadt Prize acceptance speech reprinted in *World Literature Today,* Paz attempts to explain his emphasis on contrasting thoughts: "Plurality is Universality, and Universality is the acknowledging of the admirable diversity of man and his works. . . . To acknowledge the variety of visions and sensibilities is to preserve the richness of life and thus to ensure its continuity."

Through juxtapostion of contrasting thoughts or objects Paz creates a more harmonious world, one based on complementary association of opposites found in the Eastern concept of yin and yang. This aspect of Paz's thinking reveals the influence of his six-year stay in India as Mexican ambassador to that country. Grace Schulman explains Paz's proclivity for Eastern philosophy in her *Hudson Review* essay: "Although he had embraced contraries from the beginning of his writing career, [as] Mexican ambassador to India [he] found in Tantric thought and in Hindu religious life dualities that enforced his conviction that history turns on reciprocal rhythms. In *Alternating Current,* he writes that the Hindu gods, creators or destroyers according to their names and region, manifest contradiction. 'Duality,' he says, 'a basic feature of Tantrism, permeates all Hindu religious life: male and female, pure and impure, left and right. . . . In Eastern thought, these opposites can co-exist; in Western philosophy, they disappear for the worst reasons: far from being resolved into a higher synthesis, they cancel each other out.'"

Critics point to several repeated contrasting images that dramatically capture the essence of Paz's work. Ronald Christ, for example, comments in his *Nation* review of *¿Aguila o sol?/Eagle or Sun?* (the Spanish portion of which is the equivalent of the English expression "heads or tails?"): "The dual image of the Mexican coin which gives *Eagle or Sun?* its title epitomizes Paz's technique and credo, for we see that there is no question of eagle *or* sun rather of eagle *and* sun which together in their oppositeness are the same coin." Another of the poet's images which reviewers frequently mention is "burnt water," an ancient Mexican concept which appears in Paz's work in both Spanish and in the Aztec original, "atl tlachinolli." Schulman maintains that

"burnt water" is "the dominant image of [Paz's] poetry" and finds that the image fulfills a role similar to that of the two sides of the coin in *Eagle and Sun?* She notes: "Paz sees the world burning, and knows with visionary clarity that opposites are resolved in a place beyond contraries, in a moment of pure vision: in that place, there are no frontiers between men and women, life and death." Chiles calls the Aztec combination of fire and water "particularly apt in its multiple connotations as a symbol of the union of all warring contraries."

Critics agree that Paz's great theme of a blended reality situates his work in the forefront of modern literature. As Christ notes: "By contraries then, by polarities and divergences converging in a rhetoric of opposites, Paz [has] established himself as a brilliant stylist balancing the tension of East and West, art and criticism, the many and the one in the figures of his writing. Paz is thus not only a great writer: he is also an indispensable corrective to our cultural tradition and a critic in the highest sense in which he himself uses the word." Enrique Fernández similarly sees Octavio Paz as a writer of enormous influence. "Not only has he left his mark on world poetry, with a multilingual cortege of acolytes," Fernández writes in a *Village Voice* essay, "he is a force to be reckoned with by anyone who chooses that modernist *imitaio Christi,* the Life of the Mind."

BIOGRAPHICAL/CRITICAL SOURCES:

BOOKS

Contemporary Literary Criticism, Gale, Volume 3, 1975, Volume 4, 1975, Volume 6, 1976, Volume 10, 1979, Volume 19, 1981, Volume 51, 1989.
Wilson, Jason, *Octavio Paz,* Twayne, 1986.

PERIODICALS

Hudson Review, autumn, 1974.
Interview, October, 1989.
Los Angeles Times, November 28, 1971.
Nation, August 2, 1975.
New York Times Book Review, December 27, 1981, December 25, 1988.
Times (London), June 8, 1989.
Village Voice, March 19, 1985.
World Literature Today, autumn, 1982.

—*Sketch by Marian Gonsior*

* * *

PELLICER, Carlos 1899-1977

PERSONAL: Born November 4, 1899, in Villahermosa, Tabasco, Mexico; died February 15, 1977, in Mexico City, Mexico; son of Carlos (an army colonel) and Deifilia Cámara de Pellicer. *Education:* Escuela Nacional Preparatoria, graduate.

CAREER: Served in Mexican diplomatic corps in Columbia and other countries; university professor of modern poetry; director of the Ministry of Fine Arts; founding curator, Museo-Parque de la Venta, Villahermosa, Mexico; director, Palacio de Bellas Artes.

MEMBER: Congress of Latin American Writers (president, 1965).

AWARDS, HONORS: National Literature Prize, Mexico, 1964.

WRITINGS:

Colores en el mar y otros poemas, Librería Cultura, 1921.
Piedra de sacrificios, Poema iberoamericano, Editorial Nayarit, 1924.

Seis, siete poemas, Aztlán-Editores, 1924.

Bolívar, Secretaría de Educación Pública, 1925.

Hora y Veinte, Editorial París-América (Paris), 1927.

Camino, Talleres de Tipografía Solsona (Paris), 1929.

Esquemas para una oda tropical, Secretaría de Relaciones Exteriores, 1933, reprinted, Fondo de Cultura Económica, 1976.

Estrofas del mar marino, Imprenta Mundial, 1934.

Hora de junio, Ediciones Hipocampo, 1937, reprinted, Fondo de Cultura Económica, 1979.

Recinto y otras imágenes, Edición Tezontle, 1941, reprinted, Fondo de Cultura Económica, 1979.

Exágonos, Nueva Voz, 1941.

(Contributor) *Three Spanish American Poets: Pellicer, Neruda, and Andrade,* Swallow & Critchlow (Albuquerque), 1942.

Subordinaciones: Poemas, Editorial Jus, 1949.

Sonetos, [Mexico], 1950.

(With Salvador Toscano) *Julio Castellanos, 1905-1947,* Editorial Netzahualcoyotl, 1953.

Práctica de vuela, Edición Tezontle, 1956.

Museo de Tabasco: Guía oficial, Instituto Nacional de Antropología e Historia, 1961.

Material poético, 1918-1961, Universidad Nacional Autónoma de México, 1962.

Con palabras y fuego, Fondo de Cultura Económica, 1962.

Teotihuacán, y 13 de agosto: Ruina de Tenochtitlán, Ediciones Ecuador 000'0, 1964.

Simón Bolívar, Secretaría de Educación Pública, Subsecretaría de Asuntos Culturales, 1965.

(With José Vasconcelos and Manuel R. Mora) *Geopolítica de Tabasco,* Editorial Política Nueva, 1965.

(With Ruth Rivera and Dolores Olmedo de Olvera) *Anahuacalli: Museo Diego Rivera,* Artes de México, 1965.

Leonardo Nierman, Artes de México, 1967.

(Author of text with Max Mittler) *Mexiko,* Atlantis Verlag (Zurich), 1968.

(Editor with others) *Primera antología poética: Poemas líricos, heroicos, en el paisaje y religiosos,* Fondo de Cultura Económica, 1969.

(Author of prologue and three poems) *José Mariá Velasco: Pinturas, dibujos, acuarelas,* Fondo Editorial de la Plástica Mexicana, 1970.

Noticias sobre Nezahualcoyotl y algunos sentimientos, Gobierno del Estado de México, 1972.

(With Justino Fernández and Gonzalo Obregón) *Las manos del mexicano,* Grupo Financiero Comermex, 1975.

Reincidencias, Fondo de Cultura Económica, 1978.

Cosillas para el nacimiento, Editorial Latitudes, 1978.

Práctica de vuela, Fondo de Cultura Económica, 1979.

Cuaderno de viaje, Ediciones del Equilibrista, 1987.

Also author, with Martínez Negrete, of *Es un país lejano,* Impreso por Foto-Ilustradores.

SIDELIGHTS: Carlos Pellicer was a Mexican poet known for a "dazzling and sensuous tropicalism," according to Edward J. Mullen in his book-length study *Carlos Pellicer.* The poet's place in contemporary Mexican literature is secure. As Mullen stated, "Pellicer's celebration of the physical and cosmic splendors of the New World, his constant identification with the immediate world of the senses, and pervasive concern for social justice, clearly place him in the mainstream of twentieth-century Spanish-American literature."

BIOGRAPHICAL/CRITICAL SOURCES:

BOOKS

Mullen, Edward J., *Carlos Pellicer,* Twayne, 1977.

OBITUARIES:

New York Times, February 18, 1977.

* * *

PEPECE
  See PRADO (CALVO), Pedro

* * *

PEREZ GALDOS, Benito   1843-1920

PERSONAL: Born May 10, 1843, in Las Palmas, Grand Canary Island, Canary Islands, Spain; died in Madrid, Spain, January 4, 1920; buried in Madrid's Almudena Cemetery; son of Sebastián Pérez (lieutenant colonel in the army) and María de los Dolores Galdós; children: (with Lorenza Cobián) María. *Education:* Studied law at University of Madrid, Spain, 1862-65.

CAREER: Writer. Partner, with Miguel Honorio de Cámara y Cruz, in publishing business, 1874-96; founder of publishing company, 1898. Elected to Spanish parliament as Liberal representative for the Guayama district of Puerto Rico, 1886, as Republican representative for Madrid, 1907, and as Republican representative for Las Palmas, 1914.

WRITINGS:

NOVELS; "NOVELAS ESPAÑOLAS CONTEMPORANEAS" SERIES

La desheredada, [Madrid], 1881, reprinted, La Guirnalda, 1890, translation by Guy E. Smith published as *The Disinherited Lady: A Novel,* Exposition Press (New York), 1957, translation by Lester Clark published as *The Disinherited,* Folio Society (London), 1976.

El amigo Manso (title means "Friend Manso"), [Madrid], 1882, reprinted, Losada (Buenos Aires), 1939, edited with an introductory note by Federico Carlos Sáinz de Robles, Aguilar, 1969, translation by Robert Russell published as *Our Friend Manso,* Columbia University Press, 1987.

El Doctor Centeno, [Madrid], two volumes, 1883, published in one volume, La Guirnalda, 1896.

Tormento, [Madrid], 1884, translation by J. M. Cohen published as *Torment,* Weidenfeld & Nicolson, 1952, Farrar, Straus, 1953.

La de Bringas, La Guirnalda, 1884, translation by Gamel Woolsey published as *The Spendthrifts,* introduction by Gerald Brenan, Farrar, Straus, 1952, reprinted, Arden Library, 1978.

Lo prohibido (title means "The Prohibited"), two volumes, La Guirnalda, 1884-85, edited with introduction and notes by José F. Montesinos, Castalia, 1971.

Fortunata y Jacinta (dos historias de casadas), four volumes, [Madrid], 1886-87, reprinted, Hernando, 1979, translation by Clark of original Spanish edition published as *Fortunata and Jacinta: Two Stories of Married Women,* Penguin, 1973, translation by Agnes Moncy Gullón published under same title, University of Georgia Press, 1986.

Miau (title means "Meow"), La Guirnalda, 1888, edited with introduction by Ricardo Gullón, Ediciones de la Universidad de Puerto Rico, 1957, translation by J. M. Cohen published under same title, Methuen, 1963, Dufour, 1965.

La incógnita, La Guirnalda, 1889, edited by R. Gullón, Taurus, 1976.

Torquemada en la hoguera (also see below), [Madrid], 1889, reprinted, Tello (Madrid), 1898, edited with introduction and notes by Angel del Río, Instituto de las Españas en los Estados Unidos (New York), 1932, edited with an introduction by J. L. Brooks, Pergamon, 1973, translation by N. Round of original Spanish edition published as *Torquemada in the Fire,* University of Glasgow, Department of English Literature, 1985.

Realidad: Novela en cinco jornadas (also see below), La Guirnalda, 1890, edited by R. Gullón, Taurus, 1977.

Angel Guerra, three volumes, La Guirnalda, 1890-91, reprinted, Hernando, 1970.

Tristana, La Guirnalda, 1892, translation by R. Selden Rose published under same title, R. R. Smith (Peterborough, N.H.), 1961.

La loca de la casa (title means "The Mad Woman of the House"; also see below), [Madrid], 1892, reprinted, Revista Literaria—Novelas y Cuentos (Madrid), 1963.

Torquemada en la Cruz (title means "Torquemada on the Cross"; also see below), La Guirnalda, 1893.

Torquemada en el purgatorio (title means "Torquemada in Purgatory"; also see below), La Guirnalda, 1894.

Torquemada y San Pedro (title means "Torquemada and Saint Peter"; also see below), La Guirnalda, 1895.

Nazarín, La Guirnalda, 1895, reprinted, Hernando, 1969.

Halma, La Guirnalda, 1895.

Misericordia, [Madrid], 1897, published with a special preface by the author, Nelson, 1913, edited with notes by José Padín and prologue by Federico de Onís, Heath, 1928, college edition edited with introduction, notes, vocabulary and questions by Angel del Río and McKendree Petty, Dryden Press (New York), 1946, translation by Tony Talbot of original Spanish edition published as *Compassion: A Novel,* Ungar, 1962, translation by Joan MacLean of original Spanish edition published as *Compassion,* American R. D. M. Corp., 1966.

El abuelo (novela en cinco jornadas) (title means "The Grandfather [Five-Act Novel]"; also see below), Tello, 1897, reprinted, Hernando, 1956.

Casandra (novela en cinco jornadas) (title means "Casandra [Five-Act Novel]"; also see below), [Madrid], 1905, with prologue by Sáinz de Robles, Aguilar, 1961.

El caballero encantado (cuento real . . . inverosímil), Perlado, Páez, 1909, edited by Julio Rodríguez-Puértolas, Cátedra, 1977.

La razón de la sinrazón: Fábula teatral absolutamente inverosímil, [Madrid], 1915.

Torquemada (translation by Frances M. López-Morillas of *Torquemada en la hoguera, Torquemada en la Cruz, Torquemada en el purgatorio, and Torquemada y San Pedro*), Colombia University Press, 1986.

NOVELS; EPISODIOS NACIONALES: FIRST SERIES

Trafalgar, [Madrid], 1873, corrected edition, Tello, 1901, reprinted, Losada, 1939, translation by Clara Bell of original Spanish edition published as *Trafalgar: A Tale,* W. S. Gottsberger (New York), 1884, abridged edition adapted and edited by Ramón Espinosa and Alden R. Hefler, Oxford University Press (New York), 1941.

La corte de Carlos IV, [Madrid], 1873, corrected edition, Tello, 1900, translation by Bell of original Spanish edition published as *The Court of Charles IV: A Romance of the Escorial,* W. S. Gottsberger (New York), 1888, corrected Spanish edition reprinted, Hernando, 1970.

El 19 de marzo y el 2 de mayo (title means "March Nineteenth and May Second"), [Madrid], 1873, reprinted, Obras de Pérez Galdós, 1898.

Bailén, [Madrid], 1873, corrected edition, Obras de Pérez Galdós (Madrid), 1900, reprinted, Alianza Hernando, 1976.

Napoleón en Chamartín (title means "Napoleon in Chamartin"), [Madrid], 1874, corrected edition, Tello, 1899, reprinted, Alianza, 1976.

Zaragoza, [Madrid], 1874, corrected edition, Tello, 1901, edited with introduction, notes, and vocabulary by John Van Horne, Ginn, 1926, translation of original Spanish edition by Minna Caroline Smith published as *Saragossa: A Story of Spanish Valor,* Little, Brown, 1899.

Gerona (also see below), [Madrid], 1874, corrected edition, Obras de Pérez Galdós, c. 1897, reprinted, Alianza, 1976.

Cádiz, [Madrid], 1874, corrected edition, Obras de Pérez Galdós, 1901.

Juan Martín, el Empecinado, [Madrid], 1874, corrected edition, Obras de Pérez Galdós, 1898, edited with introduction, notes and vocabulary by Paul Patrick Rogers, Stanford University Press, 1929, corrected Spanish edition reprinted, Alianza, 1976.

La batalla de los Arapiles, [Madrid], 1875, corrected edition, Obras de Pérez Galdós, c. 1898, abridged edition, edited by Juan B. Rael, Odyssey Press (New York), 1941.

NOVELS; EPISODIOS NACIONALES: SECOND SERIES

El equipaje del rey José, [Madrid], 1875, corrected edition, Obras de Pérez Galdós, 1899, reprinted, Alianza/Hernando, 1976.

Memorias de un cortesano de 1815 (title means "Memoirs of a Cortesan of 1815"), [Madrid], 1875, corrected edition, Obras de Pérez Galdós, 1897.

La segunda casaca, [Madrid], 1876, corrected edition, Obras de Pérez Galdós, 1899, reprinted, Alianza, 1976.

El Grande Oriente, [Madrid], 1876, corrected edition, Obras de Pérez Galdós, 1898, reprinted, Alianza, 1976.

7 de julio (title means "July Seventh"), [Madrid], 1876, corrected edition, Obras de Pérez Galdós, 1899, reprinted, Alianza, 1976.

Los cien mil hijos de San Luis, [Madrid], 1877, corrected edition, Obras de Pérez Galdós, 1899, reprinted, Alianza, 1976.

El terror de 1824 (title means "The Terror of 1824"), [Madrid], 1877, corrected edition, Obras de Pérez Galdós, 1899, reprinted, Alianza, 1976.

Un voluntario realista, [Madrid], 1878, corrected edition, Obras de Pérez Galdós, 1900, reprinted, Alianza, 1976.

Los apostólicos, [Madrid], 1879, corrected edition, Obras de Pérez Galdós, 1899, reprinted, Hernando, 1932.

Un faccioso más y algunos frailes menos, [Madrid], 1879, corrected edition, Tello, 1898.

NOVELS; EPISODIOS NACIONALES: THIRD SERIES

Zumalacárregui, [Madrid], 1898, reprinted, Perlado, Páez, 1906.

Mendizábal, [Madrid], 1898, Obras de Pérez Galdós, 1900.

De Oñate a la Granja, [Madrid], 1898, reprinted, Hernando, 1930, reprinted, Alianza, 1977.

Luchana, [Madrid], 1899, reprinted, Perlado, Páez, 1906, reprinted, Alianza/Hernando, 1976.

La campaña del Maestrazgo, Obras de Pérez Galdós, 1899, reprinted, Hernando, 1953.

La estafeta romántica, [Madrid], 1899, reprinted, Obras de Pérez Galdós, 1900, reprinted, Alianza, 1978.

Vergara, [Madrid], 1899, reprinted, Perlado, Páez, 1906, reprinted, Alianza, 1978.

Montes de Oca, [Madrid], 1900, reprinted, Hernando, 1930, reprinted, Alianza, 1978.

Los Ayacuchos, [Madrid], 1900, reprinted, Alianza/Hernando, 1978.

Bodas reales (title means "Royal Wedding"), [Madrid], 1900, corrected edition, Obras de Pérez Galdós, 1903, reprinted, Alianza, 1978.

NOVELS; EPISODIOS NACIONALES: FOURTH SERIES

Las tormentas del 48 (title means "The Storms of '48"), Tello, 1902, reprinted, Alianza/Hernando, 1978.
Narváez, Obras de Pérez Galdós, 1902, reprinted, Alianza, 1979.
Los duendes de la camarilla, Obras de Pérez Galdós, 1903.
La revolución de julio, Obras de Pérez Galdós, 1903.
O'Donnell, Obras de Pérez Galdós, 1904, reprinted, Alianza, 1979.
Aita Tettauen, Obras de Pérez Galdós, 1905, reprinted, Alianza, 1979.
Carlos VI en la Rápita, Obras de Pérez Galdós, 1905, reprinted, Alianza/Hernando, 1979.
La vuelta al mundo en la Numancia, Perlado, Páez, 1906, reprinted, Alianza/Hernando, 1980.
Prim, Perlado, Páez, 1906, reprinted, Alianza, 1980.
La de los tristes destinos, Perlado, Páez, 1907, reprinted, Alianza/Hernando, 1980.

NOVELS; EPISODIOS NACIONALES: FINAL SERIES

España sin rey (title means "Spain without a King"), Perlado, Páez, 1908.
España trágica (title means "Tragic Spain"), Perlado, Páez, 1909.
Amadeo I, Perlado, Páez (Madrid), 1910.
La primera República (title means "The First Republic"), Perlado, Páez, 1911, reprinted, Alianza, 1980.
De Cartago a Sagunto, Perlado, Páez, 1911, reprinted, Alianza, 1980.
Cánovas, Perlado, Páez, 1912, reprinted, Alianza, 1980.

PLAYS

Realidad: Drama en cinco actos (title means "Reality: Five-Act Drama"; adapted from his novel; first produced in Madrid at Teatro de la Comedia, March 15, 1892), [Madrid], 1892.
La loca de la casa: Comedia en cuatro actos (four-act, adapted from his novel), first produced in Madrid at Teatro de la Comedia, January 16, 1893), La Guirnalda, 1893, edited with introduction, notes, exercises, and vocabulary by J. Warshaw, Holt, 1924.
"Gerona" (four-act drama; adapted from his novel), first produced in Madrid, February 3, 1893.
La de San Quintín: Comedia en tres actos (three-act; first produced in Madrid at Teatro de la Comedia, January 27, 1894), La Guirnalda, 1894, translation by Philip M. Hayden published as "The Duchess of San Quintín—La de San Quintín" in *Masterpieces of Modern Spanish Drama,* [New York], 1917.
"Los condenados" (three-act drama with prologue), first produced in Madrid at Teatro de la Comedia, December 11, 1894.
Voluntad: Comedia en tres actos (title means "Will Power: Three-Act Play"; first produced in Madrid at Teatro Español, December 20, 1895), [Madrid], 1907.
Doña Perfecta: Drama en cuatro actos (four-act drama; based on his novel; first produced in Madrid at Teatro de la Comedia, January 28, 1896; also see below), [Madrid], 1896.
"La fiera" (three-act drama), first produced in Madrid at Teatro de la Comedia, December 23, 1896.
Electra: Drama en cinco actos (first produced in Madrid at Teatro Español, January 30, 1901), Obras de Pérez Galdós, 1901, published in English translation by C. A. Turrell

under same title in *Contemporary Spanish Dramatists,* [Boston], 1919.
Alma y vida: Drama en cuatro actos precedido de un prólogo (title means "Soul and Life: Four-Act Drama Preceded by a Prologue"; first produced in Madrid at Teatro Español, April 9, 1902), Obras de Pérez Galdós, 1902.
Mariucha: Comedia en cinco actos (five-act comedy; first produced in Barcelona at Teatro Eldorado, July 16, 1903), [Madrid], 1903, edited with an introduction, notes, and vocabulary by S. Griswold Morley, Heath, 1921.
El abuelo: Drama en cinco actos (adapted from his novel; first produced in Madrid at Teatro Español, February 14, 1904; also see below), [Madrid], 1904, edited by H. Chonon Berkowitz, Century, 1929, translation by Elizabeth Wallace published as *The Grandfather (Drama in Five Acts),* R.G. Badger, 1910.
"Bárbara: Tragicomedia en cuatro actos" (four-act tragicomedy), first produced in Madrid at Teatro Español, March 28, 1905.
Amor y ciencia: Comedia en cuatro actos (four-act tragicomedy; first produced in Madrid at Teatro de la Comedia, November 17, 1905), [Madrid], 1905.
"Pedro Minio" (two-act comedy), first produced in Madrid at Teatro de Lara, December 15, 1908.
"Casandra" (four-act drama; adapted from his novel), first produced in Madrid at Teatro Español, February 28, 1910.
Celia en los infiernos: Comedia en cuatro actos (four-act comedy; first produced in Madrid at Teatro Español, December 9, 1913), [Madrid], 1913.
Alceste: Tragicomedia en tres actos (three-act tragicomedy; first produced in Madrid at Teatro de la Princesa, April 21, 1914), [Madrid], 1914.
Sor Simona: Drama en tres actos y cuatro cuadros (title means "Sister Simone: Drama in Three Acts and Four Scenes"; first produced in Madrid at Teatro de la Infanta Isabel, December 1, 1915), [Madrid], 1916.
El tacaño Salomón: Comedia en dos actos (two-act comedy; first produced in Madrid at Teatro de Lara, February 2, 1916), [Madrid], 1916.
Santa Juana de Castilla: Tragicomedia en tres actos (three-act tragicomedy; first produced in Madrid at Teatro de la Princesa, May 8, 1918), [Madrid], 1918.
Antón Caballero: Comedia en tres actos (three-act; posthumous work adapted by Serafín and Joaquín Alvarez Quintero; first produced in Madrid at Teatro del Centro on December 16, 1921), Hernando, 1922.
Teatro selecto (collection), Escelicer (Madrid), 1972.

Also author of "Un joven de provecho" (four-act comedy; written c. 1867), published in *PMLA,* 1935, and "Quien mal hace, bien no espere" (one-act dramatic experiment; written 1861), 1974.

OTHER

La fontana de oro: Novela histórica (title means "The Golden Fountain: Historical Novel"), privately printed (Madrid), 1870, reprinted, Brockhaus, 1883, special commemorative edition celebrating the centenary of the author's birth, Losada, 1943.
La sombra, [Madrid], 1871, reprinted, La Guirnalda, 1890, Spanish text edited with English introduction by Rodolfo Cardona, Norton, 1964, translation of original Spanish edition by Karen O. Austin, published as *The Shadow,* Ohio University Press, 1980.

El audaz: Historia de un radical de antaño (novel), [Madrid], 1871, reprinted, La Guirnalda, 1891, edited with a prologue by Elías Lynch Rivers, Geminis (Montevideo), 1975.

Doña Perfecta (novel), [Madrid], 1876, reprinted, Hernando, 1969, translation by D. P. W. published as *Doña Perfecta: A Tale of Modern Spain,* Tinsley (London), 1880, translation by Mary Wharton published as *Lady Perfecta,* Independent Novel Series, 1894, translation by Mary Jane Serrano published as *Doña Perfecta,* Harper, 1896, Serrano's translation reprinted, Arden Library, 1979, translation by Harriet de Onís with her introduction published under same title, Barron's, 1960.

Gloria, two volumes, [Madrid], 1876-77, translation by N. Wetherell published under same title, two volumes, [London], 1879, translation by Bell published under same title, two volumes, W. S. Gottsberger (New York), 1882, Bell's translation reprinted, Fertig, 1974, corrected Spanish edition, Obras de Pérez Galdós, 1900-01, published as *Gloria: Novela de costumbres,* edited with notes, exercises and vocabulary by Alexander H. Krappe and Lawrence M. Levin, Century (New York), 1927.

Marianela (novel), [Madrid], 1878, corrected edition, Obras de Pérez Galdós, 1899, translation by Bell published under same title, W. S. Gottsberger, 1883, translation by Helen W. Lester published as *Marianela: A Story of Spanish Love,* A. C. McClurg and Co. (Chicago), 1892, Lester's translation reprinted, Arden Library, 1979, translation by Wharton published as *Marianela,* Digby & Long (London), 1893, corrected Spanish edition edited by Nicholson B. Adams, reprinted, Ginn, 1951.

La familia de León Roch (title means "The Family of Leon Roch"; novel), [Madrid], three volumes, 1878-79, reprinted with prologue by Sáinz de Robles, Aguilar, 1960, translation by Bell of original Spanish edition published as *Leon Roch: A Romance,* W. S. Gottsberger, 1888, reprinted, Fertig, 1974.

Guerra de la independencia: Extractada para uso de los niños (title means "War of Independence: Extracts for Use by Children"; abridged juvenile edition of novels of "Episodios nacionales: First Series"), Hernando, c. 1906.

Memoranda, Perlado, Páez, 1906.

Casa de Shakespeare. Portugal. De vuelta de Italia., A. López (Barcelona), c. 1920.

Obras inéditas (title means "Unpublished Works"), Volume 1: *Fisonomías sociales,* Renacimiento, 1923, Volume 2: *Arte y crítica* (title means "Art and Criticism"), Renacimiento, 1923, Volumes 3 and 4: *Política española* (title means "Spanish Politics"), Renacimiento, 1923, Volume 5: *Nuestro teatro,* Renacimiento, 1923, Volumes 6 and 7: *Cronicón,* Renacimiento, 1924, Volume 8: *Toledo (su historia y su leyenda)* (title means "Toledo [Her History and Her Legend]"), Renacimiento, 1924, Volume 9: *Viajes y fantasías* (title means "Travels and Fantasies"), Compañía Ibero-Americana de Publicaciones (Madrid), 1928, Volume 10: *Memorias,* Renacimiento, 1930, Volume 11: *Crónica de Madrid (1865-1866),* Castro (Madrid), 1933.

La novela en el tranvía: Obra inédita, Ercilla, 1936.

Obras completas, edited by Sáinz de Robles, six volumes, Aguilar, 1941-42.

Cartas de Pérez Galdós a Mesonero Romanos (correspondence), Sección de Cultura e Información (Madrid), 1943.

Crónica de la quincena, edited with a preliminary study by William H. Shoemaker, Princeton University Press, 1948.

Episodios nacionales: Narrados a los niños (title means "National Episodes: Told to Children"), school edition edited by daughter, María Pérez Galdós, Hernando, 1948.

Antología (title means "Anthology"), edited by Amando de Miguel, Doncel (Madrid), 1960.

Benito Pérez Galdós y la Revista del Movimiento Intelectual de Europa, Madrid, 1865-1867 (collection of journalistic pieces), compiled by Leo J. Hoar, Jr., Insula, 1968.

Los artículos de Galdós en "La Nación," 1865-1866, 1868, edited with a preliminary study by Shoemaker, Insula, 1972.

Las cartas desconocidas de Galdós en "La Prensa" de Buenos Aires (title means "The Undiscovered Letters of Galdos in 'La Prensa' of Buenos Aires"), edited by Shoemaker, Cultura Hispánica, 1973.

Rosalía, Cátedra, 1984.

Author of numerous prologues. Translator of Charles Dickens's *Pickwick Papers,* 1868. Contributor of "The Battle of Salamanca: A Tale of the Napoleonic War," translated by Rollo Ogden, to *Lippincott's Monthly Magazine,* Philadelphia, Pa., 1895. Contributor to periodicals, including *La Nación* (newspaper), *El Debate* (newspaper), *La Guiralda* (magazine), *El Océano* (magazine) and *La Prensa* (Buenos Aires newspaper). Contributor to and editor of *Revista de España* (magazine), 1872-73.

SIDELIGHTS: Benito Pérez Galdós (usually referred to by his maternal surname) is regarded as the most important Spanish novelist since Cervantes. Many critics, such as noted Spanish scholar Salvador de Madariaga, assign him a position among the giants of nineteenth-century European letters. In *The Genius of Spain and Other Essays on Spanish Contemporary Literature,* Madariaga noted, "In European literature Galdós undoubtedly deserves to rank with the great novelists of the century, in line with Dickens, Balzac, and Dostoievsky." Although Galdós's works are intimately linked with nineteenth-century Spain, his ability to appeal to audiences outside his own time and culture appeared to be confirmed when several of his most important novels were released in English translation in the 1980s to general critical approval.

Galdós showed his inclination toward the writing profession at an early age when he began contributing articles to local papers while still a secondary-school student living in his native Canary Islands, an archipelago under Spanish jurisdiction off the coast of Africa. While he had considered continuing his education with university studies in architecture, his mother was insistent that her youngest child become a lawyer. Duly enrolled at the University of Madrid's Law School, Galdós soon found his interests lay elsewhere and rarely attended classes after the first year. He preferred to study the city which was to become the backdrop for most of his novels on innumerable walks through its picturesque lower-class neighborhoods. He established himself as a regular at several of the capital's popular cafes where he could spend hours observing its colorful types and colloquial language. He also tried to learn as much as he could about Madrilenian customs by reading the works of authors such as Ramón de la Cruz, who produced many short plays depicting the customs of eighteenth-century Madrid.

During Galdós's first decade in the Spanish capital he concentrated on his journalistic endeavors, including contributing to a variety of periodicals and working as an editor. Eventually, finding himself drawn to the theater, he wrote several plays for which he was unable to find a producer or publisher. A trip to Paris in May, 1867—which strengthened his recently awakened interest in the French novelist Honore de Balzac—seemed to be the catalyst the young writer needed to finally attempt to write in the genre which would become his life's work: the novel. The following summer he wrote *La fontana de oro,* his first published novel, while once again in France, and in 1871 two of his novels, *La sombra* and *El audaz,* were published in serial form by two of Madrid's leading periodicals. Two years later, encouraged by the success of these early writings, Galdós abandoned most of his journalistic activities and began to write a series of novels he called "Episodios nacionales" ("National Episodes"), which established his reputation as Spain's foremost novelist.

The novels were written at an incomparable speed; the first series of ten were completed by 1875. At that time, Galdós immediately began a new series which he finished writing before the end of the decade. The first series was an account of Spanish history beginning at the Battle of Trafalgar in 1805, concluding with the end of the Napoleonic invasion of Spain at the Battle of Los Arapiles in 1812. The second series dealt with the struggle of the Spanish people to gain independence from the oppressive reign of King Ferdinand VII and ended with the monarch's death in 1834. Eventually, the series included forty-six volumes in five separate series spanning the first three quarters of the nineteenth century.

The interconnectedness between volumes in each series, through repetition of characters and related events, led to a comparison with the similarly constructed *Comedie humaine* of Balzac and the "Rougon-Macquart" novels of Emile Zola. Despite these foreign influences, Galdós's focus in the "Episodes" was fixed on his native country. "The aim of the novels was nothing less," wrote Lester Clark in his introduction to his English translation of Galdós's *Fortunata y Jacinta,* "than the regeneration of Spain through the awakening of a new national conscience." Using newspaper accounts and eyewitness testimonies, weaving historical fact with vibrant fiction, Galdós was áble to paint a grand portrait of Spain's history. In *Hispania* Hayward Keniston called the series "the great national epic of the first half of the past century."

Although some critics find the novels of the later series less appealing than those of the first two, together the "Episodes" are considered to form an unequalled literary achievement. "In these stories," observed Clyde Chew Glascock in the *Texas Review,* "historical personages live again whose names were indistinctly engraven on the memory of Spaniards. [Galdós] gave them precision and personality, a body and a soul. These books are indeed a faithful reproduction of the national incidents and characters of the epoch, of the inner and outer life of Spaniards during the nineteenth century." Madariaga similarly commented, "In these forty-six volumes, many of which are admirable, and none of which can be passed over, Galdós gave us the history of Spain as seen from the drawing-room of contemporaries, not from the study of the historian. It is . . . a vivid and dramatic interpretation of the life of the people through the events of the century, their hopes, feelings, thoughts, and disappointments." In L. B. Walton's *Pérez Galdós and the Spanish Novel of the Nineteenth Century,* the critic proclaimed, "The ['Episodes'] are not . . . historical romances, in the orthodox sense of the term; but, inasmuch as they are an endeavour to interpret history in terms of the human spirit, they belong to the historical genre—of which, in modern Spanish literature, Galdós is, indisputably, the creator."

While the "Episodes" were extremely popular, Galdós felt confined by their historical outline. While he was writing the ten volumes of the second series he also composed four non-series novels: *Doña Perfecta, Gloria, La familia de León Roch,* and *Marianela.* Galdós used the first three works to express his vehement

anti-clericalism. While not anti-Catholic, he felt that the heavy influence of the Roman Catholic church in Spain was a hindering block to Spain's intellectual and cultural growth. Of the three volumes, *Doña Perfecta* was, by far, the most popular and through several translations introduced Galdós to an enthusiastic international audience. The work was first published in 1876 in serial form in the prestigious Spanish magazine, *Revista de España,* for which Galdós had served as editor a few years earlier.

The novel takes place in the fictional provincial Spanish town of Orbajosa which W. D. Howells referred to in *Criticism and Fiction and Other Essays* as "the microcosm of bigoted and reactionary Spain." The story revolves around the monstrous figure of Doña Perfecta who permits her nephew, Pepe Rey, a liberal intellectual from Madrid, to be murdered rather than have her daughter marry him. Although the novel could be read as the struggle between an aunt and her nephew, critics noted that the characters are essentially symbols for the conflict Galdós saw in Spanish society at large. "The confrontation of Perfecta and Pepe," wrote John Devlin in *Spanish Anticlericalism: A Study in Modern Alienation,* "has all the tell-tale signs of the larger confrontation of clericalism and sincere liberalism that was taking place in Spain, and that was to culminate eventually in the murder and bloodshed of the Civil War." While some critics, such as Sherman H. Eoff, fault the novel for Galdós's obvious manipulation of the storyline to further his didactic purpose, they find in his portrait of Doña Perfecta the novel's redeeming quality. In *The Novels of Pérez Galdós: The Concept of Life as Dynamic Process,* Eoff wrote, "The characterization of Doña Perfecta, nevertheless, more than counterbalances the novel's technical flaws. The portrait of her personality overshadows all else in the story and bears strong testimony to the assertion that Galdós' fundamental strength as a novelist is psychological."

Rodolfo Cardona praised Galdós's skill as a novelist in the introduction to his edition of *Doña Perfecta,* noting that only an author of Galdós's stature could keep the emotionally-charged atmosphere of the novel from becoming excessively melodramatic. In particular, he pointed out how Galdós used name symbolism (a technique found in other Galdosian works as well) to highlight at every opportunity the issue that Cardona saw as the novel's theme: hypocrisy. As Pepe Rey travels toward Orbajosa he notices that the names of some of the ugliest areas through which he must pass carry the most poetic names and he gives the examples of Valleameno ("Pleasant Valley") and Valdeflores ("Valley of the Flowers"). The litany of characters and places with fraudulent names continues throughout the novel: Doña Perfecta is not perfect, the town's conniving cleric, Don Inocencio, is not innocent, and Orbajosa, which Orbajosans fancy an "Urbs Augusta", is revealed as an "Orbajosa" or dunghill. "It is . . .," Cardosa commented, "the contact of these two perspectives [inherent in the duality of each of the names] that causes the violent collision of the characters, which, in the context of the entire novel, is also seen as the collision between Orbajosa—the Spanish province—and Madrid—the metropolis—and what these places represent."

According to Cardosa, Galdós's ability to raise this story of familial strife to the height of a classical confrontation between good and evil endows the work with an universal appeal. Glascock also observed the timeless quality of the tale, noting, "The backwardness of country people in conforming to new conditions produced by the advance of education is found in every land. . . . The ill-feeling aroused in a little Spanish town because of difference in religious opinion due to differences of education and rearing might have been intense in almost any place if brought about by similar circumstances." And for this reason

Doña Perfecta excited universal interest. Cardosa concluded: "The reason that Galdós's successful thesis novels, like *Doña Perfecta,* can continue to be read today is that they embody not doctrines but specific insights."

Although his "National Episodes" and his novels like *Doña Perfecta* were very popular, in 1879 Galdós announced that he would never write another historical novel (a promise he was later to break for financial reasons) and began work on a series of novels which he called his "Novelas contemporáneas españolas" ("Contemporary Spanish Novels"). Although this series did not sell as well as his previously published works, it represents his most critically acclaimed writing. These "Contemporary Spanish Novels" show Galdós as a keen observer of daily life and a master of character delineation. Comparing these newer novels to Galdós's earlier production, Gerald Brenan wrote in *The Literature of the Spanish People: From Roman Times to the Present:* "There is a change of accent from the earlier works. In them the principal characters personified ideas, now he draws individuals." Glascock offered his comparison of the new series of novels to the old with the observation: "After passing through a didactic, anticlerical stage . . . Galdós began a series of more realistic novels in which he aimed to present truth as he saw it and let the reader draw conclusions. The purpose does not obtrude, or is supposed not to do so, and interfere with art."

General critical consensus names *Fortunata y Jacinta (dos historias de casadas)* (*Fortunata y Jacinta: Two Stories of Married Women*), one of the "Contemporary Spanish Novels" and the longest the novelist ever wrote, as Galdós's masterpiece. Eoff called the novel, "one of the richest and most elaborate examples of nineteenth-century realism." Amongst its pages are found the characteristics of Galdós's work that align him with the great novelists of his day. "Sharing the determination of Balzac, Dickens, and Zola to present a faithful record of bourgeois society," wrote *Village Voice* contributor William Grimes, "he takes the reader down unfamiliar streets and peers behind the city's anonymous facades. He is a prolific creator of characters and types. Like Dostoyevski and Tolstoy, he regards his creations as spiritual beings, wrestling with questions that will determine the fate of their immortal souls." Critics also noted in this and in *La desheredada* and *Lo prohibido,* two other novels from the series, Galdós's growing affinity for the naturalism of Zola, with its emphasis on the debased side of human life.

Although influenced by Zola's ideas, Galdós never completely adopted the naturalist's tendencies, even though many of the twenty-four volumes of the "Contemporary Spanish Novels," including *Fortunata and Jacinta,* depict Madrid's lower classes in great detail. Galdós believed that in order to engender change in his society, the novelist had to depict every part of that society without exception. His descriptions of Madrid in *Fortunata and Jacinta,* in particular, are so accurate that one can trace the footsteps of the novel's characters on a map of modern day Madrid without difficulty. Galdós offers a social panorama of Madrid as well as a geographical one: By choosing one of his title characters, Jacinta, from Madrid's middle class, and the other, Fortunata, from Madrid's slum area, he was able to present a complete cross-section of Madrid's society in the 1870s. The novel explores the interactions of the childless Jacinta with her husband, Juanito, and his mistress, Fortunata, who bears him a child. The highlight of the work is found in Galdós's psychological portrait of the two women mentioned in the title. Commenting on this aspect of the novel, Brenan maintained: "His two women—Jacinta especially—are drawn with marvelous skill and delicacy. No writer, except perhaps Tolstoy, has shown such a deep and intimate understanding of women's characters and feelings."

Because the "Contemporary Spanish Novels" did not draw as many readers as his historical novels, Galdós found himself facing mounting debts and in 1898 returned to writing his "National Episodes." During this last period of his life, he also wrote nearly two dozen plays, including several adapted from his novels, and attempted to enact the reforms indicated in his fiction by re-entering politics as a member of the Spanish parliament (he had served one term in parliament nearly twenty years earlier). In 1905, he suffered a stroke that left him partially paralyzed, and in 1912 became blind. That same year, the Spanish Royal Academy answered those who had been attempting to gain the Noble prize for the aging author by refusing to sponsor his candidacy for the award, largely due to his liberal, anticlerical philosophy. By October 1919 he was confined to his bed after an attack of uremia. The novelist died three months later, on January 4, 1920, and, the following day, was laid in state in Madrid's City Hall where tens of thousands of Madrileños thronged to pay their last respects.

According to many critics Galdós was the father of the modern Spanish novel, for the genre was nearly nonexistent in Spain when he began his literary career. His sweeping portrait of Spanish history, his fierce criticism of Spanish society, and his skill at drawing memorable individuals has led commentators to universally acknowledge Galdós as the premier novelist of nineteenth-century Spain. "Superior to all others in Spain in writing historical novels, in characterizing contemporary Spaniards of the middle class, in fertility of invention and in versatility of production," Glascock concluded, "his fame appears secure, not merely for our day, but as well for time to come."

MEDIA ADAPTATIONS: El audaz was adapted by Jacinto Benavente for a play of the same title, 1919; *Marianela* was adapted by Serafín and Joaquín Quintero for a play of the same title, 1916; *Tristana* was adapted for a film of the same title by Luis Buñuel, 1970.

BIOGRAPHICAL/CRITICAL SOURCES:

BOOKS

Bell, Aubrey F. G., *Contemporary Spanish Literature,* Knopf, 1925.
Brenan, Gerald, *The Literature of the Spanish People: From Roman Times to the Present,* 2nd edition, Cambridge University Press, 1953, reprinted, 1976.
Devlin, John, *Spanish Anticlericalism: A Study in Modern Alienation,* Las Américas, 1966.
Eoff, Sherman H., *The Novels of Pérez Galdós: The Concept of Life as Dynamic Process,* Washington University Studies, 1954.
Eoff, Sherman H., *The Modern Spanish Novel: Comparative Essays Examining the Philosophical Impact of Science on Fiction,* New York University Press, 1961.
Ford, J. D. M., *Main Currents of Spanish Literature,* Holt, 1919.
Kirk, Clara Marburg and Rudolf Kirk, editors, *Criticism and Fiction and Other Essays,* New York University Press, 1959.
Madariaga, Salvador de, *The Genius of Spain and Other Essays on Spanish Contemporary Literature,* Oxford at the Clarendon Press, 1923.
Pattison, Walter T., *Benito Pérez Galdós,* Twayne, 1975.
Pérez Galdós, Benito, *Doña Perfecta,* edited with notes and introduction by Rodolfo Cardona, Anaya, 1974.
Pérez Galdós, Benito, *Fortunata and Jacinta: Two Stories of Married Women,* translated by Lester Clark, Penguin, 1973.

Twentieth-Century Literary Criticism, Volume 27, Gale, 1988.

Walton, L. B., *Pérez Galdós and the Spanish Novel of the Nineteenth Century,* Dent, 1927.

PERIODICALS

Hispania, October, 1920.
Los Angeles Times Book Review, July 13, 1986.
New York Times Book Review, February 22, 1987.
Texas Review, January, 1923.
Times Literary Supplement, October 12, 1973, August 28, 1987.
Village Voice, November 4, 1986.

—*Sketch by Marian Gonsior*

* * *

PEREZ-GOMEZ, Alberto 1949-

PERSONAL: Born December 24, 1949, in Mexico City, Mexico; son of Jorge (an aeronautical engineer) and Angela (a housewife; maiden name, Gómez) Pérez; children: Alejandra. *Education:* National University of Mexico, diploma in theory of architecture, 1970; Instituto Politécnico Nacional, Mexico, Dipl. Eng. Arch. (with honors), 1971; Cornell University, diploma in urban development and history of architecture, 1972; University of Essex, M.A., 1975, Ph.D., 1979.

ADDRESSES: Office—School of Architecture, Macdonald-Harrington Building, McGill University, 815 Sherbrooke St. West, Montreal, Quebec, Canada H3A 2K6.

CAREER: Instituto Politécnico Nacional, Mexico City, Mexico, lecturer in vocational education, 1969-71, lecturer in architecture, 1972-73; Architectural Association School of Architecture, London, England, instructor in design, 1975-77; University of Toronto, Toronto, Ontario, lecturer, 1977-78, assistant professor of architecture, 1978-79; Syracuse University, Syracuse, N.Y., assistant professor, 1979-80, associate professor of architecture, 1980-81; University of Houston, Houston, Tex., associate professor of architecture, 1981-83; Carleton University, Ottawa, Ontario, associate professor of architecture and director of School of Architecture, 1983-86; McGill University, Montreal, Quebec, visiting professor, 1986, Saidye Rosner Bronfman Professor of the History of Architecture and director of School of Architecture, 1987—. Part-time lecturer at Universidad Anáhuac, Mexico City, 1972-73; instructor at Polytechnic of Central London, 1976-77; lecturer at University of Essex, 1977; visiting lecturer at universities and colleges in the United States, Canada, Mexico, and Europe, including University of Waterloo, School of Architecture at Mérida, Yucatán, and Princeton, Harvard, and Yale Universities. Administrative assistant of Organizing Committee for the Nineteenth Olympiad, Mexico City, 1968; academic representative in charge of exchange programs for Universidad Anáhuac in the United Kingdom, 1976-77; academic representative of Instituto Politécnico Nacional in the United States and Canada, 1977-81. Member of Canadian Commonwealth Scholarship and Fellowship Committee, 1986-88; member of advisory board of Canadian Center for Architecture, 1986—.

MEMBER: American Society for Eighteenth Century Studies, Society of Architectural Historians, Royal Architectural Institute of Canada, Ottawa Society of Architects, Mexican Academy of Architecture (fellow), Sociedad de Arquitectos Mexicanos, Sociedad de Ingenieros Arquitectos del Estado de México.

AWARDS, HONORS: Alice Davies Hitchcock Book Award from Society of Architectural Historians, 1983, for *Architecture and the Crisis of Modern Science.*

WRITINGS:

Eclosión (poems; title means "Blooming"), privately printed, 1967.
Iber (prose poem), privately printed, 1968.
La teoría de la arquitectura (title means "The Theory of Architecture"), National Polytechnic Institute Press (Mexico City), 1969.
La génesis y superación del funcionalismo en arquitectura (title means "The Origins and Limitations of Functionalism in Architecture"), Limusa-Wiley, 1980.
Architecture and the Crisis of Modern Science, MIT Press, 1983.
(Translator from English) Joseph Rykwert, *La idea de la ciudad* (title means "The Idea of a Town"), Ediciones Blume, 1983.

Also author of *Polyphilo of the Dark Forest Revisited,* 1990; contributor to Claude Perrault's *Ordonnance des Cinq Especes de Colonnes,* translation published by Chicago University Press, 1990.

Contributor of articles and reviews to architecture journals and newspapers, including *The Fifth Column, Modernity and Popular Culture,* and *Urban Design and Preservation Quarterly.* Member of editorial board of *Journal of Architectural Education.*

SIDELIGHTS: Alberto Pérez-Gómez told *CA:* "My current focus is on the nature of architectural theory and its history, the problem of the city as urban stage and its modern deterioration, and issues concerning theoretical projects in architecture. Particularly crucial is the understanding of architecture in relation to contemporary art and philosophy and to the problems of modern culture at large."

BIOGRAPHICAL/CRITICAL SOURCES:

PERIODICALS

Annals of the Architectural Association School of Architecture, September, 1984.
Architectural Journal, May 30, 1984.
Architecture, September, 1984.
Ottawa, September, 1984.
Times Literary Supplement, August 3, 1984.

* * *

PEREZ-MARCHAND, Monelisa L(ina) 1918-

PERSONAL: Born January 7, 1918, in Ponce, Puerto Rico.

CAREER: Professor at University of Puerto Rico, Río Piedras; chairman, Puerto Rican Commission to study the history of ideas.

WRITINGS:

Dos etapas ideológicas del siglo XVIII en México a través de los papeles de la Inquisición, El Colegio de México, 1945.
Historia de las ideas en Puerto Rico, Instituto de Cultura Puertorriqueña, 1960, translation published as *History of Ideas in Puerto Rico,* Gordon Press, 1979.

Also author of monographs and essays. Assistant editor, *Asomante* (literary review).

* * *

PERI ROSSI, Cristina 1941-

PERSONAL: Born in 1941 in Uruguay; immigrated to Barcelona, Spain, 1972. *Politics:* Leftist.

CAREER: Writer, 1963—. Teacher of literature in Montevideo, Uruguay; writer for newspapers and magazines, including *Marcha;* exiled from Uruguay, settled in Barcelona, Spain, 1972.

AWARDS, HONORS: Inventarios Provisionales Prize, 1973, for *Diáspora.*

WRITINGS:

Viviendo (short stories), Alfa (Montevideo), 1963.
El libro de mis primos (novel), Biblioteca de Marcha (Montevideo), 1969.
Los museos abandonados (short prose), Arca (Montevideo), 1969.
Indicios pánicos (poetry and short prose), Nuestra América (Montevideo), 1970.
Descripción de un naufragio (poetry), Lumen (Barcelona), 1975.
Diáspora (poetry), Lumen, 1976.
La tarde del dinosaurio (short stories), Planeta (Barcelona), 1976.
Lingüística general (poetry), Prometeo (Valencia, Spain), 1979.
La rebelión de los niños (short stories), Monte Avila (Caracas), 1980.
El museo de los esfuerzos inútiles (short stories and essays), Seix Barral (Barcelona), 1983.
La nave de los locos, Seix Barral, 1984, translation by Psiche Hughes published as *The Ship of Fools,* Readers International, 1989.
Una pasión prohibida, Seix Barral, 1986.

Also author of *Evohé: Poemas eróticos.*

SIDELIGHTS: An Uruguayan writer living in exile in Spain, Cristina Peri Rossi is the author of revolutionary poetry and prose. Her darkly humorous writings reflect a strong opposition to the inequities of class division and to the social and political repression that exists within dictatorial states. Themes of alienation, eroticism, and uncontrolled power dominate Peri Rossi's works. Her 1984 novel, *La nave de los locos,* translated as *The Ship of Fools,* is an unusual narrative which follows the exiled Ecks (pronounced "X") on a never-ending journey, tracing the character's numerous encounters with women and his revelations about the lack of communication in the world. Dan Bellm, writing in the *Voice Literary Supplement,* commented, "*The Ship of Fools* is a mess in the finest sense—a glorious mess, baffling and alluring." Quoting from Peri Rossi's prose, the critic continued, " 'We value in art the exercise of mind and emotion that can make sense of the universe without reducing its complexity.' That's hard to do, and that's what she's done."

BIOGRAPHICAL/CRITICAL SOURCES:

BOOKS

The Ship of Fools, translated by Psiche Hughes, Readers International, 1989.

PERIODICALS

Voice Literary Supplement, May, 1989.

*   *   *

PESEENZ, Tulio F.
  See LOPEZ y FUENTES, Gregorio

*   *   *

PIDAL, Ramón Menéndez
  See MENENDEZ PIDAL, Ramón

PIETRI, Arturo Uslar
  See USLAR PIETRI, Arturo

*   *   *

PIETRI, Pedro (Juan)   1943-

PERSONAL: Born March 21, 1943, in Ponce, Puerto Rico; immigrated to United States, 1945; son of Francisco and Petra (Aponte) Pietri; married Phyllis Nancy Wallach (a teacher and translator), March 3, 1978. *Education:* Attended public schools in New York, N.Y.

ADDRESSES: Home—New York, N.Y. *Office*—Cultural Council Foundation, 175 Fifth Ave., New York, N.Y. 10010; and 400 West 43rd St., 38E, New York, N.Y. 10036.

CAREER: State University of New York at Buffalo, instructor in creative writing, 1969-70; poet and playwright, 1970-78; Cultural Council Foundation, New York, N.Y., literary artist, 1978—. Conducted children's poetry workshops, 1970-72; member of bilingual and bicultural early childhood project of Puerto Rican Association for Community Affairs, 1974; consultant to El Museo del Barrio. *Military service:* U.S. Army, 1966-68.

MEMBER: Latin Insomniacs Motorcycle Club.

AWARDS, HONORS: New York State Creative Arts in Public Service Grant, 1974-75.

WRITINGS:

Puerto Rican Obituary (poems), c. 1971, reprinted, Monthly Review Press, 1974.
The Blue and the Gray, Cherry Valley, 1975.
Invisible Poetry, Downtown Train Publishers, 1979.
Loose Joints (sound recording), Folkways Records, 1979.
Lost in the Museum of Natural History (short story), Ediciones Huracán, 1980.
Out of Order (poems), Downtown Train Publishers, 1980.
Uptown Train (poems), Downtown Train Publishers, 1980.
An Alternate, Hayden Book, 1980.
Traffic Violations (poems), Waterfront Press (Maplewood, N.J.), 1983.
Missing Out of Action, Waterfront Press, in press.

Work represented in *Inventing a Word: An Anthology of Twentieth-Century Puerto Rican Poetry,* edited by Julio Marzán, Columbia University Press, in association with the Center for Inter-American Relations, 1980.

PLAYS

"Lewlulu" (one-act), first produced in New York City at Harlem Performance Center, April 23, 1976.
"What Goes Up Must Come Down" (one-act), first produced in New York City at El Porton, May 7, 1976.
"The Living-room" (one-act), first produced in New York City at H. B. Studio, March 15, 1978.
"Dead Heroes Have No Feelings" (one-act), first produced in New York City at Manhattan Plaza, October 8, 1978.
"Appearing in Person Tonight—Your Mother" (one-act), first produced in New York City at La Mama, November 8, 1978.
"Jesus Is Leaving" (one-act), first produced in New York City at Nuyorican Poets' Cafe, December 13, 1978.
(Translator) Luis Rochani Agrait, "The Company" (one-act), first produced in New York City by Puerto Rican Traveling Theater, 1978.
The Masses Are Asses (produced by Puerto Rican Traveling Theater, 1984), Waterfront Press, 1984.

Also author of the plays "No More Bingo at the Wake," "Eat Rocks!," and an unproduced play, "I Dare You to Resist Me."

* * *

PIÑERA, Virgilio 1912-

PERSONAL: Born in 1912 in Cuba.

CAREER: Writer, 1956—, and playwright, 1959—.

WRITINGS:

Cuentos fríos, Editorial Losada, 1956, translation by Mark Schaffer published as *Cold Tales,* Eridanos Press, 1988.

Aire frío (three-act play), Editorial Pagrán, 1959, translation published as *Cold Air,* Theatre Communications Group, 1985.

Teatro completo (contains "Electra Garrigó," "Jesús," "Falsa alarma," "La boda," "El flaco y el gordo," "Aire frío," and "El filántropo"), Ediciones Revolución, 1960.

(Translator) René Dépestre, *Mineral negro: Poemas,* Ediciones Revolución, 1962.

Pequeñas maniobras (novel), Ediciones Revolución, 1963.

Cuentos, Bolsilibros Unión, 1964.

Presiones y diamantes, Ediciones Unión (Havana), 1967.

(Editor) *Teatro del absurdo,* Instituto del Libro (Havana), 1967.

(Editor) *Teatro de la crueldad,* Instituto del Libro, 1967.

Dos viejos pánicos, Centro Editor de América Latina (Buenos Aires), 1968.

(Translator) Jean Price Mars, *Así habló el tío,* Casa de las Américas, 1968.

La vida entera (poems), UNEAC, 1969.

(Editor) Antonin Artaud, *El teatro y su doble,* Instituto del Libro, 1969.

El que vino a salvarme, Editorial Sudamericana, 1970.

Cuentos (stories), Ediciones Alfaguara, 1983.

(With Luis F. González-Cruz) *Una caja de zapatos vacía,* Ediciones Universal (Miami), 1986.

Un fogonazo, Editorial Letras Cubanas, 1987.

Contributor to periodicals, including *Orígines* and *Ciclón.*

* * *

PIÑERO, Miguel (Antonio Gómez) 1946-1988

PERSONAL: Born December 19, 1946, in Gurabo, Puerto Rico; died of cirrhosis of the liver, June 16 (some sources say June 17), 1988, in New York, N.Y.; son of Miguel Angel Gómez Ramos and Adelina Piñero; married Juanita Lovette Rameize, 1977 (divorced, 1979); children: Ismael Castro (adopted). *Education:* Attended public schools in New York City; received high school equivalency diploma.

ADDRESSES: Agent—Neil I. Gantcher, Cohn, Glickstein, Lurie, 1370 Avenue of the Americas, New York, N.Y. 10019.

CAREER: Writer and actor. Founder of NuYorican Poets' Theatre, New York, N.Y., 1974.

AWARDS, HONORS: New York Drama Critics Circle Award, Obie Award, and Drama Desk Award, all 1974, all for *Short Eyes: The Killing of a Sex Offender by the Inmates of the House of Detention Awaiting Trial.*

WRITINGS:

PUBLISHED PLAYS

Short Eyes: The Killing of a Sex Offender by the Inmates of the House of Detention Awaiting Trial (first produced in New York City at Theater of Riverside Church, January, 1974; produced on Broadway at Vivian Beaumont Theatre, May, 1974), Hill & Wang, 1975 (also see below).

The Sun Always Shines for the Cool, A Midnight Moon at the Greasy Spoon, Eulogy for a Small-Time Thief, Arte Público (Houston), 1983 (also see below).

Outrageous: One-Act Plays, Arte Público, 1986.

PRODUCED PLAYS

"All Junkies," first produced in New York City, 1973.

"Sideshow," first produced in New York City at Space Theatre, 1975.

"The Gun Tower," first produced in New York City, 1976.

"The Sun Always Shines for the Cool," first produced in New York City at Booth Theatre, 1976.

"Eulogy for a Small-Time Thief," first produced Off-Off-Broadway at Ensemble Studio Theatre, 1977.

(With Neil Harris) "Straight from the Ghetto," first produced in New York City, 1977.

"Paper Toilet," first produced in Los Angeles, c. 1979.

"Cold Beer," first produced in New York City, 1979.

"NuYorican Nights at the Stanton Street Social Club," first produced in New York City at NuYorican Poets' Cafe, 1980.

"Playland Blues," first produced in New York City at Henry Street Settlement Theatre, 1980.

"A Midnight Moon at the Greasy Spoon" (two-act), first produced in New York City at Theater for the New City, 1981.

OTHER

(Editor with Miguel Algarin) *NuYorican Poets: An Anthology of Puerto Rican Words and Feelings,* Morrow, 1975.

"Short Eyes" (screenplay; adapted from Piñero's play "Short Eyes: The Killing of a Sex Offender by the Inmates of the House of Detention Awaiting Trial"), Film League, Inc., 1977.

La Bodega Sold Dreams (poetry), Arte Público, 1979.

Also author of scripts for television series "Baretta," and of unproduced and unpublished play "The Cinderella Ballroom."

WORK IN PROGRESS: "Every Form of Refuge Has Its Price," a play set in the intensive-care unit of a hospital, to be produced at the New York Shakespeare Public Theater.

SIDELIGHTS: Joseph Papp, head of the New York Shakespeare Festival Public Theater, hailed Miguel Piñero in the *New York Times* as "the first Puerto Rican playwright to really break through and be accepted as a major writer for the stage" and as "an extraordinarily original talent." During Piñero's short life, however, the playwright probably heard more condemnation than praise. Born in Puerto Rico, he and his family moved to New York City when he was four years old. A few years later, his father abandoned the family of four children, who were forced to live on the streets of Manhattan for several months until their mother (who was pregnant) could find a source of income. Piñero began a life punctuated by brushes with the law, spending time in juvenile detention centers and, eventually, serving two prison terms for robbery and drug possession convictions. In 1971, he was incarcerated in the New York State prison at Ossining, known as Sing Sing, for armed robbery. His life seemed to turn around during this last term in prison, when he happened upon a playwright's workshop and wrote the first draft of what was to be his best-known play, "Short Eyes: The Killing of a Sex Offender by the Inmates of the House of Detention Awaiting Trial." "I really got hooked on theatre," Piñero told the *New York Times*'s Mel Gussow. "It was like a shot of dope."

The play, which deals with the murder of a "short eyes" (prison slang for a child molester) at the hands of his fellow inmates, was produced after Piñero was paroled from prison. It received such favorable reviews that the production was soon moved to Broadway from the small church theater where it had opened. Critics hailed Piñero as a bright new face on the theatrical scene and saw the play as brutally realistic. In *Newsweek* Jack Kroll, for example, wrote: " 'Short Eyes' needs absolutely no apology—it isn't occupational therapy and it isn't a freak show; it's an authentic, powerful theatrical piece that tells you more about the anti-universe of prison life than any play outside the work of Jean Genet." *People* contributor Leroy Aarons noted: "It was a smash. Pinero's unsentimental drama in which black, Puerto Rican and white prisoners systematically destroy a fellow inmate accused of molesting a child . . . sizzled like a dynamite fuse to an explosive conclusion." In a *Contemporary Dramatists* essay, Gaynor F. Bradish called the play "the most ruthlessly exciting drama with a prison setting so far produced by the American theater. Harrowing, brutal, yet suffused with a transforming, unsettling sensuality, it succeeds in imparting a special kind of understated, deliberately minimal poetic beauty and compassion to the rather terrifying events it dramatizes."

Piñero was surprised by his rapid success. "Here I was with $60 one day and all of a sudden somebody was giving me $15,000," he told Aarons. "I was being asked to lecture at Princeton, at Rutgers, at Pratt Institute. Here I have no education whatsoever and I am working as a mentor to the top students at Pratt Institute. What the hell am I doin' here?"

BIOGRAPHICAL/CRITICAL SOURCES:

BOOKS

Contemporary Dramatists, 4th edition, St. James Press, 1988.
Contemporary Literary Criticism, Gale, Volume 4, 1974, Volume 55, 1989.

PERIODICALS

New Republic, April 20, 1974.
Newsweek, April 8, 1974.
New York Times, March 27, 1974, May 5, 1974, January 23, 1977, September 28, 1977, September 28, 1979, April 27, 1981.
People, November 14, 1977.
Times (London), June 27, 1987.
Village Voice, March 28, 1974.

OBITUARIES:

PERIODICALS

Chicago Tribune, June 19, 1988.
Los Angeles Times, June 18, 1988.
New York Times, June 18, 1988.
Times (London), June 17, 1988.
Washington Post, June 16, 1988.*

* * *

PIZARRO, Agueda 1941-

PERSONAL: Born in 1941; married Omar Rayo (an artist). *Education:* Columbia University, Ph.D., 1974.

ADDRESSES: Home—Roldanillo, Colombia; and New York, N.Y. *Office*—Barnard College, 606 West 120th St., New York, N.Y. 10027.

CAREER: Poet, 1969—. Affiliated with Brooklyn College, Brooklyn, N.Y., and Barnard College, New York, N.Y.

WRITINGS:

Aquí beso yo (poems), Tercer, 1969.
Labio adicto (poems), Tercer, 1972.
Sombraventadora: Shadowinnower (poems; bilingual edition), English translation by Barbara Stoler Miller and Pizarro, Columbia University Press, 1979.

Also author of introduction to Omar Rayo's *Blind Knot: Nudo ciego* (bilingual edition), 1972.

BIOGRAPHICAL/CRITICAL SOURCES:

PERIODICALS

World Literature Today, winter, 1981.

* * *

PLAJA, Guillermo Díaz
See DIAZ PLAJA, Guillermo

* * *

POLANCO, Vincente Géigel
See GEIGEL POLANCO, Vincente

* * *

PONCE, Juan García
See GARCIA PONCE, Juan

* * *

PONIATOWSKA, Elena 1933-

PERSONAL: Born May 19, 1933, in Paris, France; daughter of John E. and Paula (Amor) Poniatowska; married Guillermo Haro (an astronomer); children: Emmanuel, Felipe, Paula. *Education:* Educated in Philadelphia, Pa. *Religion:* Roman Catholic.

ADDRESSES: Home—Cerrada del Pedregal 79, Coyoacán, Z.P. 21, Mexico City, Mexico. *Office*—*Novedades,* Balderras 87, Mexico City 1, Mexico.

CAREER: Member of writing staff of *Excelsior,* 1954-55; *Novedades,* Mexico City, Mexico, staff member, 1955—. Instructor at Injuve. Founder of Editorial Siglo Veinto Uno, Cineteca Nacional, and Taller Literario. Speaker at schools and conferences; guest on radio and television programs.

MEMBER: International P.E.N.

AWARDS, HONORS: D.H.C. from University of Sinaloa; fellowship from Centro de Escritores, 1957; Premio de Periodismo from Turismo Frances, 1965; Premio Mazatlan, 1970, for *Hasta no verte Jesús mío;* Premio Villaurrutia, 1970, for *La noche de Tlatelolco: Testimonios de historia oral;* Premio de Periodismo from *Revista Siempre,* 1973; Premio Nacional de Periodismo, 1978.

WRITINGS:

IN ENGLISH TRANSLATION

La noche de Tlatelolco: Testimonios de historia oral, Ediciones Era, 1971, translation by Helen R. Lane published as *Massacre in Mexico,* introduction by Octavio Paz, Viking, 1975.
Querido Diego, te abraza Quiela, Ediciones Era, 1978, translation by Katherine Silver published as *Dear Diego,* Pantheon, 1986.
Until We Meet Again, translation by Magda Bogin, Pantheon, 1987.

IN SPANISH

Lilus Kikus, Los Presentes, 1954.

Melés y teleo: A puntes para una comedia, Panoramas, 1956.

Palabras cruzadas: Crónicas, Ediciones Era, 1961.

Todo empezó el domingo, Fondo de Cultura Económica, 1963.

Los cuentos de Lilus Kikus (title means "The Stories of Lilus Kikus"), Universidad Veracruzana, 1967.

Hasta no verte, Jesús mío (novel; title means "See You Never, Sweet Jesus"), Ediciones Era, 1969, reprinted, 1983.

(Contributor) *El Primer Primero de Mayo,* Centro de Estudios Históricos del Movimiento Obrero Mexicano, 1976.

Gaby brimmer, Grijalbo, 1979.

De noche vienes (stories), Grijalbo, 1979.

Fuerte es el silencio, Eras Crónicas, 1980.

Domingo 7, Océano, 1982.

El último guajolote, Cultura, 1982.

¡Ay vida, no me mereces!, J. Mortiz, 1985.

Serena y alta figura, Océano, 1986.

Author of screenplay "Hasta no verte, Jesús mío," released by Producciones Barbachano Ponce.

OTHER

Work represented in anthologies, including *Antología de cuentistas mexicanos,* Emmanuel Carballo, 1956; *Rojo de vida, y negro de muerte,* edited by Carlos Coccoli. Contributor to magazines, including *Revista Mexicana de Literatura, Siempre!, Estaciones, Abside,* and *Evergreen Review.*

SIDELIGHTS: Elena Poniatowska is a respected and well-known journalist contributing to several of Mexico's finest newspapers and periodicals as well as an author of many books of fiction and nonfiction. Born in Paris, the daughter of a Polish father and Mexican mother, Poniatowska immigrated with her family to Mexico when she was ten years old. A few years later, Poniatowska was sent to Philadelphia to attend the Convent of the Sacred Heart.

Poniatowska writes almost exclusively in Spanish—to date only a few of her books have been translated into English. *La noche de Tlatelolco: Testimonios de historia oral* later translated as *Massacre in Mexico* recounts Poniatowska's experiences in Mexico City during the 1968 student riots. J. A. Ellis explains in the *Library Journal* that Poniatowska's *Massacre in Mexico* is "the story of the continuing tragedy of Mexico. . . . The mood ranges from the early heady optimism of the students . . . to shock and despair. In a *Commonweal* review, Ronald Christ states that *Massacre in Mexico* is a "shatteringly beautiful book. . . . Recording everything she could about the incident and the events that led up to it, Poniatowska has assembled what she calls 'a collage of voices,' a brilliantly edited text whose texture is the weaving of anecdote, official history, gossip, placards, graffiti, journalism, eye-witness accounts, agonized interpretation."

Dear Diego, the translation of Poniatowska's *Querido Diego, te abraza Quiela,* is a fictionalized reconstruction of the correspondence between the internationally famed artist, Diego Rivera, and his common-law wife of seven years, Russian painter Angelina Beloff. Written in the voice of Beloff, *Dear Diego* is a series of twelve imaginary letters describing the emotions and thoughts the young woman must have experienced after her lover leaves their home in Paris to return to his native Mexico. Although hopeful at first that Rivera will send for her and they will be reunited, Beloff eventually realizes that they will never be together again.

Barbara Probst Solomon explains the premise of this book in the *Nation:* "Elena Poniatowska's *Dear Diego* . . . is about a heated *ménage á trois* between Diego Rivera, his Russian émigré common-law wife, Angelina Beloff, and the jealous third lover, art itself. Poniatowska's narrative . . . blends real documents with her own imaginative reconstruction of Angelina Beloff 's relation to Diego Rivera. Exactly how much of this is Poniatowska and how much is drawn from actual documents is not made clear, and since Rivera was a real person, the reader can't help filling the gaps in this impressionistic novella with what is already known about him."

"The novella's subject is longing," writes Hayden Herrera in the *New York Times Book Review.* Herrera continues: "Angelina tries to span the ocean separating her from Diego with a bridge of words. Her mood shifts from despair to anger to nostalgic affection. We feel her growing apprehension that his absence is permanent. As we share her struggle with loneliness, poverty, and illness, we come to admire her determination to survive. . . . Although she was abandoned, she was not a loser. To be able to love as she did was a gift."

BIOGRAPHICAL/CRITICAL SOURCES:

PERIODICALS

Best Sellers, November, 1975.
Commonweal, January 16, 1976.
Library Journal, June 1, 1975.
Nation, August 2-9, 1986.
New York Times Book Review, July 20, 1986.

*   *   *

PORTILLO, Estela
    See PROTILLO TRAMBLEY, Estela

*   *   *

PORTILLO (y PACHECO), José López
    See LOPEZ PORTILLO (y PACHECO), José

*   *   *

PORTILLO TRAMBLEY, Estela 1936-
(Estela Portillo)

PERSONAL: Born January 16, 1936, in El Paso, Tex.; daughter of Frank (a diesel mechanic) and Delfina (Fierro) Portillo; married Robert D. Trambley (in the automobile business), 1953; children: Naurene (Mrs. Karl Klements), Joyce, Tina, Robbie, Tracey (Mrs. Kenneth Nance). *Education:* University of Texas, El Paso, B.A., 1957, M.A., 1977.

ADDRESSES: Home—131 Clairemont, El Paso, Tex. 79912. *Office*—Department of Drama, Community College, 6601 Dyer, El Paso, Tex. 79904.

CAREER: High School English teacher in El Paso, Tex., 1957-64; El Paso Technical Institute, El Paso, chairman of department, 1965-69; Community College, El Paso, resident dramatist, 1970-75; affiliated with Department of Special Services, El Paso Public Schools, 1979—. Hostess of "Estela Sezs," a talk show on Radio KIZZ, 1969-70, and "Cumbres," a cultural show on KROD-TV, 1971-72.

AWARDS, HONORS: Quinto Sol Award from Quinto Sol Publications Bilingual League of the San Francisco Bay Area, 1973.

WRITINGS:

Impressions (haiku poetry), El Espejo Quinto Sol, 1971.
(Editor) *Chicanas en literatura y Arte* (title means "Chicana Women in Literature and Art"), Quinto Sol, 1974.
Rain of Scorpions and Other Writings (short stories), Tonatiuh International, 1976.
Trini, Bilingual Press, 1986.

PLAYS

The Day of the Swallows (also see below), El Espejo Quinto Sol, 1971.
"Morality Play" (three-act musical), first produced in El Paso, Tex., at Chamizal National Theatre, 1974.
(Contributor) *We Are Chicano,* Washington Square Press, 1974.
"Black Light" (three-act), first produced in El Paso at Chamizal National Theatre, 1975.
"El hombre cósmico" (title means "The Cosmic Man"), first produced at Chamizal National Theatre, 1975.
"Sun Images" (musical), first produced at Chamizal National Theatre, 1976.
(Contributor) Roberto Garza, editor, *Chicano Theatre* (includes "the Day of the Swallows"), Notre Dame University Press, 1976.
"Isabel and the Dancing Bear" (three-act), first produced at Chamizal National Theatre, 1977.
Sor Juana and Other Plays, Bilingual Press, 1983.

Also author of "Autumn Gold" (three-act comedy), "Broken Moon" (three-act play), and "Los amores de Don Estafa" (three-act comedy in English).

OTHER

Author of unpublished novel, *Women of the Earth.* Contributor of poems and plays to *El Grito* and *Grito del Sol.*

WORK IN PROGRESS: Perla, a novel; producing and directing a video film, "Por la Calle" (title means "Along the Street").

SIDELIGHTS: Estela Portillo Trambley is the first Chicana to publish a book of short stories and first to write a musical comedy. Her work examines the quest for self-determination of women and Chicanos in societies that assign them to subservient roles. Critics relate that her acclaimed work tends to use powerful images. For example, in *Rain of Scorpions and Other Stories,* young boys trapped in a smelting town barrio enter a cave looking for a mythical underground paradise; meanwhile, a rainstorm starts an avalanche of mud above them. "The thousands of scorpions unearthed by the avalanche rumble down the main street of Smelterstown like a sea of filth and death, a symbol of the Anglo city's dumping its waste and poison into the ghetto," Vernon E. Lattin observes in *Studies in American Literature.* Some readers find these images overwhelming, while others appreciate her ability to give topics familiar to Chicano literature new life.

While other fiction cries out against the destructive forces of the ghetto, Portillo Trambley's stories present the barrio as the site of spiritual growth and comfort despite its squalor. The triumph of the human spirit over oppression and natural catastrophe makes the ghetto a place that, her characters decide, finally, is difficult to leave behind. In "Duende," Lattin notes, "although [Portillo] Trambley realistically represents the poverty and suffering of the ghetto, the final impression is of a spirit which transcends this misery. It is the spirit of [the young man] Triano, a mountain freedom brought from Duende, that the author sees as more powerful. The reader is left with the expectation that

even Marusha [a woman who longs to escape the ghetto] will find warmth and freedom in the barrio."

Portillo Trambley found these qualities in her childhood home. As she told Juan Bruce-Novoa for an interview collected in *Chicano Authors: Inquiry by Interview,* "I would watch sunlight continuing itself on adobe walls; the silences in early afternoon had a mysterious splendor. We were poor. I am still poor, pero la pobreza nunca derriba el espíritu [but poverty never defeats the spirit]. When I was a child, poverty was a common suffering for everybody around me. A common suffering is a richness in itself." Her view that the human spirit is more powerful than its environment is rooted in ancient Náhuatl cosmology, notes Thomas Vallejos in *Frontiers: A Journal of Women Studies.*

Portillo Trambley's plays express feminist, ethnic, and nonpolitical themes. *The Day of the Swallows,* considered her best work in this genre, follows the lesbian protagonist Josefa through stages of secrecy, violence against a boy who accidentally discovers her secret, despair when her affair ends, and suicide by drowning while dressed in a wedding gown. Phyllis Mael, writing in *Frontiers,* suggests that Josefa's desperate actions are not actions of free choice, but reactions against a male-dominated society. Portillo Trambley's other plays carry images from the past forward to express the reality of life for Chicanos in the United States, the conflict between traditional values and contemporary institutions. "Black Light" includes a Mayan dance as one of many contrasts between the Chicano past and the urban present. "Morality Play," also unpublished, borrows the fifteenth-century drama form to show the victory of human faith, hope, and charity over the dehumanizing influences of power-brokers. Perhaps the least political of her plays is "Sun Images," a musical comedy in which viewers are allowed to draw their own conclusions about the long-standing conflict between Chicanos and immigration officers.

Portillo Trambley appreciates Chicano literature that stresses what it means to be human anywhere in the world. She told Bruce-Novoa, "There are so many features of the Chicano experience that are 100 percent eternal, that any people in the world can identify with. The strengths, our hopes, our family structure, our capacity to love, all the results of the closure of our society and what it has made of us. This vital and human experience could actually find readers, aside from the Americans, readers in Italy, Spain and . . . because it is a universal one. They have all been through the same thing historically."

When asked if her work has a political focus, she told Bruce-Novoa, "I separate politics from literature because I believe that when you inject politics into it you limit its life, as I said before. All good literature is based on the human experience which is nonpolitical. Use literature as a political tool and it becomes provincial, time-bound. . . . There is a place for the powerful force literature can be; it's needed in our Movement to give it cohesion. But literature itself is very impersonal, nonpolitical. There is a tenacity about it, to stay alive, to believe in love, to cope, to pick ourselves up, to fly. Political literature, no matter how clever it might be, tends to make stereotypes of the evil exploiter and the poor, innocent victim. That is not life. The exploiter is a human being too. He might be violent and selfish and greedy and mean, but down deep, despite having mutated into a Machiavellian oddity, he is still human. Once you take this away from your character in literature, you've taken away his life. Political literature assassinates characters."

The former resident dramatist of Community College in El Paso once told *CA:* "I would like to write and produce plays that are structured in traditional form. It is another direction from the 'acto' and the socio-political products which, innovative though they may be, still fail to meet the standards of good theatre. My own work in drama must undergo a lot of rewriting and change to meet those standards too. Having the opportunity to experiment with live productions of my own work focuses the flaws and the strong points in my work.

"The writing of the novel is another kind of challenge, lonely, retrospective, an inward drama of evolutionary growth and change. A novel is 'all up to me' if it has any worth or success. Drama involves the players, the audience outside of myself. It is a more precarious challenge, more joyous than the writing of a novel because one works with people—energy outside of oneself as a writer. But the 'power of myself,' the lonely and creative elation of novel-writing is winning over. The energy is from within."

BIOGRAPHICAL/CRITICAL SOURCES:

BOOKS

Bruce-Novoa, Juan, *Chicano Authors: Inquiry by Interview,* University of Texas Press, 1980.
Meier, Matt S., *Mexican American Biographies: A Historical Dictionary, 1836-1987,* Greenwood Press, 1988.

PERIODICALS

Belles Lettres, May, 1988.
Critique, Volume 21, number 1, 1979.
De Colores, Volume 3, number 3, 1977.
Drama, winter, 1983.
Frontiers: A Journal of Women Studies, summer, 1980.
MELUS, Volume 7, number 4, 1980, Volume 9, winter, 1981.
Revista Chicano-Riqueña, summer, 1977, winter, 1979.
Studies in American Fiction, spring, 1978.

* * *

PRADA, Manuel González
See GONZALEZ PRADA, Manuel

* * *

PRADA OROPEZA, Renato   1937-

PERSONAL: Born October 17, 1937, in Potosí, Bolivia; son of Augusto (an advocate) and Bertha (Oropeza) Prada; married Elda Rojas, December 17, 1956; children: Ingmar, Fabrizio. *Education:* Calatayud High School, bachelor of humanities, 1961; Normal Superior Católica, high school teacher certification, 1964; Universita degli Studi di Roma, Ph.D. (philosophy), 1972. *Religion:* Roman Catholic.

ADDRESSES: Home—Fochplein 19, Louvain, Belgium 3000. *Agent*—Carmen Ballcels, Urgel 241, Barcelona 11, Spain.

CAREER: High school teacher of Spanish and philosophy in Cochabamba, Bolivia, 1965-67; Normal Superior Católica, Cochabamba, professor of philosophy, 1967-70. Subdirector and professor of philosophy, Maryknoll Institute, 1963-67; professor of philosophy, Universidad Católica, 1969-70. *Military service:* Bolivian Army, 1956.

AWARDS, HONORS: Premio Municipal de Cuento, 1967, for *Argal;* Premio Nacional de Cuento, 1968, for short story "El combate"; Concurso Nacional del Novela Erich Guttentag, Los Amigos del Libro, and Premio de Novela, Casa de las Américas (Cuba), both 1969, both for *Los fundadores del alba.*

WRITINGS:

Argal (short stories), Los Amigos del Libro, 1967.
Ya nadie espera al hombre (short stories), Don Bosco, 1969.
Al borde del silencio (short stories), ALFA, 1969.
Los fundadores del alba (novel), Los Amigos del Libro, 1969, translation by Walter Redmond published as *The Breach,* Doubleday, 1971.
El último filo, Planeta (Barcelona), 1975.
La autonomía literaria: sistema y función, Los Amigos del Libro, 1976.
La autonomía literaria: formalismo ruso y Círculo de Praga, Centro de Investigaciones Lingüístico-Literarias, Universidad Veracruzana (Jalapa, Mexico), 1977.
(Editor and author of prologue) Roland Barthes and others, *Lingüística y literatura,* Centro de Investigaciones Lingüísticas-Literarias, Instituto de Investigaciones Humanísticas, Universidad Veracruzana, 1978.
El lenguaje narrativo: prolegómenos para una semiótica narrativa, EDUCA (Costa Rica), 1979.
Larga hora, la vigilia, Premia Editora (Mexico), 1979.
La ofrenda y otros relatos, Premia Editora, 1981.
Los nombres del infierno, Universidad Autónoma de Chiapas (Mexico), 1985.

SIDELIGHTS: Renato Prada Oropeza's award-winning short novel, *Los fundadores del alba* (*The Breach*), helped to introduce the theme of the guerrilla to literature by telling the story of a group of rebels who are exterminated by the Bolivian Army. Prada Oropeza does not take sides in this narrative, however, and offers a sympathetic eye to both factions while attempting to show the need for compassion for all of humanity.

The author's short stories address the themes of the isolation of modern man and his inability to affect changes in his life.

BIOGRAPHICAL/CRITICAL SOURCES:

PERIODICALS

Times Literary Supplement, July 3, 1969.

* * *

PRADO (CALVO), Pedro   1886-1952
(Androvar, Alvaro J. de Credo, PEPECE)

PERSONAL: Born October 8, 1886, in Santiago, Chile; died of a cerebral hemorrhage, January 31, 1952, in Viña del Mar, Chile; son of Absalón (a doctor) and Laura (Calvo) Prado; married Adriana Jaramillo Bruce, January 1, 1910; children: Pedro, Inés, Teresa; six other children. *Education:* Attended Instituto Nacional and School of Engineering, Chile. *Religion:* Roman Catholic.

CAREER: Poet, novelist, and essayist. Museo de Bellas Artes, Santiago, Chile, director, 1921-25; delegate in Chilean cultural mission to Bolivia, 1925; Chilean ambassador to Colombia, 1926-27. Also worked as a painter, architect, district judge, and lecturer of aesthetics and art history.

MEMBER: Society of Writers (Chile; president), Los Diez (literary society; founder).

AWARDS, HONORS: Premio Roma poetry prize, Italian Embassy, 1935; National Literary Prize, Chile, 1949.

WRITINGS:

POETRY

Flores de cardo (free verse; also see below), 1908, Imprenta Universitaria (Santiago), reprinted, 1968.

La casa abandonada: Parábolas y pequeños ensayos (prose poems), Imprenta Universitaria, 1912.

El llamado del mundo (free verse; also see below), Imprenta Universitaria, 1913.

Los Diez: El claustro, La barca, Imprenta Universitaria, 1915.

Los pájaros errantes: Poemas menores y breves divagaciones (prose poems), Imprenta Universitaria, 1915, reprinted, Nascimento, 1960.

Las copas (prose poems), Glusberg (Buenos Aires), 1921.

Androvar, poema dramático (poem in drama form), Nascimento, 1925.

Camino de las horas, Nascimento, 1934, reprinted, 1965.

Otoño en las dunas (sonnets), Nascimento, 1940.

Esta bella ciudad envenenada (sonnets), Imprenta Universitaria, 1945.

No más que una rosa (sonnets), Losada (Buenos Aires), 1946.

Viejos poemas inéditos (poems and autobiography), Escuela Nacional de Artes Gráficas (Santiago), 1949.

Antología: Las estancias del amor, edited with an introduction by Raúl Silva Castro, Pacífico (Santiago), 1949.

La roja torre de los Diez: Antología de Pedro Prado, edited with a prologue by Enrique Espinoza, Zig-Zag (Santiago), 1961.

Pedro Prado: Antología, edited with a prologue by Enrique Pascal G. H., Nacional Gabriela Mistral (Santiago), 1975.

OTHER

La reina de Rapa Nui (novel), Nascimento, 1914, reprinted, Andrés Bello (Santiago), 1983.

Ensayos sobre la arquitectura y la poesía (essays), Imprenta Universitaria, 1916, reprinted, Nascimento, 1981.

Alsino (novel), Nascimento, 1920, reprinted, 1983.

(With Antonio Castro Leal) *Karez-I-Roshan* (also see below), Imprenta de Silva (Santiago), 1922.

Un juez rural (novel), Nascimento, 1924, reprinted, Andrés Bello, 1983, translation by Lesley Byrd Simpson published as *Country Judge: A Novel of Chile,* University of California Press, 1968.

El llamado del mundo . . . Flores de cardo, Karez-I-Roshan y textos inéditos (includes previously unpublished work), edited and with prologue and notes by René de Costa, Editorial Universitaria, 1971.

Cartas a Manuel Magallanes Moure (letters), Academia Chilena de la Lengua (Santiago), 1986.

Also author of *Bases para un nuevo gobierno y un nuevo parlamento* (political essay), 1924. Contributor, sometimes under pseudonyms Alvaro J. de Credo and PEPECE, to periodicals, including *Zig-Zag* and *Juventud.* Author of column, under pseudonym Androvar, for *Claridad.* Founder, *Revista Contemporánea,* 1910.

SIDELIGHTS: "Pedro Prado was the first important poetic voice heard in Chile in the twentieth century," John R. Kelly asserted in his study *Pedro Prado.* An author whose poetry ranged from prose and dramatic poems to free verse, Prado influenced such Chilean luminaries as Gabriela Mistral and Pablo Neruda through his example, demonstrating that a poem "need not adhere to any pre-established systems of rhythm and rhyme," Kelly continued. "This stance opened the way for later poetic experimentation by others." In addition, Prado wrote fiction and essays, and a common feature of his work was his attempt "to erase and blend genres and forms . . . reject[ing] the conventional formal bounds of literature and work[ing] in whatever genre or combination best suited his ideas and themes," the critic related.

For example, *Country Judge,* one of Prado's only works published in English, is "not at all a novel," *New York Times Book Review* contributor Alexander Coleman averred, but rather "a collection of stock encounters of a recently appointed judge with the chicanery and obfuscation of the locals in his district." Prado's most notable work, *Alsino,* has been alternately described as a novel and a prose poem; it presents in allegorical form the story of "a hunchback hero who is miraculously transformed into a winged being . . . [who] emits prose poems while in flight," Coleman summarized. "*Alsino* represented a break with the conventional novel," Kelly remarked, and with the figure of the winged youth Prado "became an early practitioner of fantastic literature which . . . has produced some of Latin America's best fiction." The critic concludes that "even though most of Prado's works and reputation have been confined to Chile, his novels and [his] original, unique prose poems .. have earned him a place of honor in the evolution of Latin American literature. No writer of his time, and possibly no writer since, at least in Chile, has more successfully combined philosophy, esthetic good sense, fiction, and poetry."

BIOGRAPHICAL/CRITICAL SOURCES:

BOOKS

Kelly, John R., *Pedro Prado,* Twayne, 1974.
Silva Castro, Raúl, *Pedro Prado: Vida y obra,* Hispanic Institute (New York), 1965, expanded edition published as *Pedro Prado,* Andrés Bello, 1965.

PERIODICALS

New York Times Book Review, June 9, 1968.
Revista Hispánica Moderna, January-April, 1960.

*   *   *

PUIG, Manuel 1932-1990

PERSONAL: Born December 28, 1932, in General Villegas, Argentina; son of Baldomero (a businessman) and Maria Elena (a chemist; maiden name, Delledonne) Puig. *Education:* Attended University of Buenos Aires, beginning 1950, and Centro Sperimentale di Cinematografia, beginning 1955; studied languages and literature at private institutes. *Religion:* None.

ADDRESSES: Home—Rio de Janiero, Brazil. *Office*—c/o Erroll McDonald, Vintage Books, 201 East 50th St., New York, N.Y. 10022.

CAREER: Translator and Spanish and Italian teacher in London, England, and Rome, Italy, 1956-57; assistant film director in Rome and Paris, France, 1957-58; worked as a dishwasher in London and in Stockholm, Sweden, 1958-59; assistant film director in Buenos Aires, Argentina, 1960; translator of film subtitles in Rome, 1961-62; Air France, New York, N.Y., clerk, 1963-67; writer, 1967—. *Military service:* Argentina Air Force, 1953; served as translator.

AWARDS, HONORS: La traición de Rita Hayworth was named one of the best foreign novels of 1968-69 by *Le Monde* (France); best script award, 1974, for "Boquitas pintadas," and jury prize, 1978, for "El lugar sin límites," both from San Sebastian Festival; American Library Association (ALA) Notable Book, 1979, for *The Kiss of the Spider Woman; Plays & Players* Award for most promising playwright, 1985, for "Kiss of the Spider Woman."

WRITINGS:

La traición de Rita Hayworth, Sudamericana (Buenos Aires), 1968, reprinted, Casa de las Américas, 1983, translation by Suzanne Jill Levine published as *Betrayed by Rita Hayworth,* Dutton, 1971, reprinted, 1987.

Boquitas pintadas (also see below), Sudamericana, 1969, translation by Levine published as *Heartbreak Tango: A Serial,* Dutton, 1973.

The Buenos Aires Affair: Novela policial, Sudamericana, 1973, translation by Levine published as *The Buenos Aires Affair: A Detective Novel,* Dutton, 1976.

El beso de la mujer araña (also see below), Seix-Barral (Barcelona), 1976, translation by Thomas Colchie published as *The Kiss of the Spider Woman,* Knopf, 1979.

Pubis angelical (also see below), Seix-Barral, 1979, translation by Elena Brunet published under same title, Vintage, 1986.

"El beso de la mujer araña" (play; adapted from his novel; also see below), first produced in Spain, 1981, translation by Allan Baker titled "Kiss of the Spider Woman," first produced in London at the Bush Theatre, 1985, produced in Los Angeles at the Cast Theatre, 1987.

Eternal Curse upon the Reader of These Pages, Random House, 1982, Spanish translation by the author published as *Maldición eterna a quien lea estas páginas,* Seix Barral, 1982.

Sangre de amor correspondido, Seix Barral, 1982, translation by Jan L. Grayson published as *Blood of Requited Love,* Vintage, 1984.

Bajo un manto de estrellas: Pieza en dos actos [and] *El beso de la mujer araña: Adaptación escénica realizada por el autor* (plays; also see below), Seix Barral, 1983.

Under a Mantle of Stars: A Play in Two Acts, translation by Ronald Christ, Lumen Books, 1985 (produced in the original Spanish as "Bajo un manto de estrellas").

(Contributor) G. W. Woodyard and Marion P. Holt, editors, *Drama Contemporary: Latin America,* PAJ Publications, 1986.

Mystery of the Rose Bouquet (play; produced at the Bush Theatre, 1987, produced in Los Angeles, Calif., at Mark Taper Forum, November 16, 1989), translation by Baker, Faber, 1988 (produced in the original Spanish as "Misterio del ramo de rosas").

Also author of screenplays for "Boquitas Pintadas," adapted from his novel, 1974, "El lugar sin límites," adapted from José Donoso's novel, 1978, and "Pubis angelical." Contributor to various periodicals, including *Omni.*

WORK IN PROGRESS: Production of his screenplay "Seven Tropical Sins" by David Weisman's Sugarloaf Films company; developing a musical comedy with Weisman, "Chica Boom!"; the book for a musical version of *The Kiss of the Spider Woman.*

SIDELIGHTS: As a boy growing up in rural Argentina, novelist Manuel Puig spent countless hours in the local movie house viewing screen classics from the United States and Europe. His enchantment with films led him to spend several years pursuing a career as a director and screenwriter until he discovered that what he wanted to write was better suited to fiction; nevertheless, Puig's work is saturated with references to films and other popular phenomena. "[But] if Puig's novels are 'pop,' " observes Jonathan Tittler in his *Narrative Irony in the Contemporary Spanish-American Novel,* it is because "he incorporates into his fiction elements of mass culture—radionovelas, comic books, glamour magazines, and in *Betrayed by Rita Hayworth,* commercial mov-

ies—in order to unveil their delightfully insidious role in shaping contemporary life." Puig echoes the design of these media, "us[ing] those forms as molds to cast his corny, bathetic material in a form displaying a witty, ironic attitude toward that material," notes Ronald Christ in *Commonweal.* Ronald Schwartz concurs with this assessment; writing in his study *Nomads, Exiles, and Emigres: The Rebirth of the Latin American Narrative, 1960-80,* the critic contends that Puig employs "the techniques of pop art to communicate a complex vision of his own world. It is [the] cinematic influence that makes *Betrayed by Rita Hayworth* and Puig's subsequent novels some of the most original contemporary Latin American narratives."

In *Betrayed by Rita Hayworth,* "the idea of the novel is simple: the drama and pathos of moviegoing as a way of life in the provinces, where often people get to respond to life itself with gestures and mock programs taken over from film," describes *New York Times Book Review* contributor Alexander Coleman. The story is narrated primarily through the eyes of Toto, a young boy born in the Argentinian pampas, and recounts the everyday life of his family and friends. "The novel's charm," claims *Newsweek* writer Walter Clemons, "is in the tender gravity with which Puig records the chatter of Toto's family and neighbors. Kitchen conversations, awkwardly written letters and flowery schoolgirl diary entries . . . combine to evoke lives of humblest possibility and uncomplaining disappointment."

While this description may sound gloomy, states Coleman, nevertheless *Betrayed by Rita Hayworth* "is a screamingly funny book, with scenes of such utter bathos that only a student of final reels such as Puig could possibly have verbally re-created [it] for us." "Above all, Puig has captured the language of his characters," D. P. Gallagher reports in his *Modern Latin American Literature,* and explains: "There is no distance separating him from the voices he records, moreover, for they are the voices that he was brought up with himself, and he is able to reproduce them with perfect naturalness, and without distortion or parodic exaggeration. That is not to say that his novels are not very polished and very professional," the critic continues. "Like all the best Latin American novels . . . , they are structured deliberately as fictions. But the authenticity with which they reflect a very real environment cannot be questioned."

Puig's next novel, *Heartbreak Tango,* "in addition to doing everything that *Rita Hayworth* did (and doing it better, too) actually proclaims Puig not only a major writer but a major stylist whose medium brings you both the heartbreak *and* the tango," Christ declares in *Review 73.* Bringing together letters, diaries, newspapers, conversations, and other literary artifices, *Heartbreak Tango,* as *New York Times* reviewer Christopher Lehmann-Haupt relates, "reconstructs the lives of several Argentine women, most of whom have in common the experience of having once passionately loved a handsome, ne'er-do-well and doomed young man who died of tuberculosis." Mark Jay Mirsky comments in the *Washington Post Book World* that at first "I missed the bustle, noise and grotesque power of *Betrayed by Rita Hayworth.* The narrative of *Heartbreak Tango* seemed much thinner, picking out the objects and voices of its hero [and] heroines with too obvious a precision." Nevertheless, the critic admits, "as we are caught up in the story, this taut line begins to spin us around."

Michael Wood, however, believes that it is this "precision" which makes *Heartbreak Tango* the better novel, as he details in a *New York Review of Books* article: "*Heartbreak Tango* seems to me even better than Puig's earlier *Betrayed by Rita Hayworth* because its characters' moments are clearer, and because the general implication of the montage of cliché and cheap romance and gossip is firmer." The critic adds that "the balance of the new book," between irony and sentimentalism, "is virtually perfect." Gallagher presents a similar opinion in the *New York Times Book Review,* noting that "it has been said that [*Heartbreak Tango*] is a parody, but that underestimates the balance between distance and compassion that Puig achieves. His characters are camp, but they are not camped up, and their fundamental humanity cannot be denied." Despite this serious aspect, the critic remarks that *Heartbreak Tango* "is a more accessible book than its predecessor without being less significant. It is compelling, moving, instructive and very funny." "At the same time," concludes David William Foster in *Latin American Literary Review,* "no matter how 'popular' or 'proletarian' the novel may appear to be on the surface, the essential and significant inner complexity of [*Heartbreak Tango*], like that of *Betrayed by Rita Hayworth,* bespeaks the true artistic dimensions of Puig's novel."

"The appearance of Manuel Puig's new novel, *The Buenos Aires Affair,* is especial cause for celebration," Ronald De Feo asserts in the *National Review,* "not only because the book makes for fascinating reading, but also because it demonstrates that its already highly accomplished author continues to take chances and to grow as an artist." Subtitled *A Detective Novel,* the story takes place in the city and investigates a kidnapping involving two sexually deviant people. "It is not devoid of the lucid and witty observation of absurd behaviour that characterized" *Heartbreak Tango,* maintains a *Times Literary Supplement,* "but it is altogether more anguished." As Toby Moore elaborates in another *Times Literary Supplement* review, "Puig's subject is the tangle made up of love and sexual desire. . . . In *The Buenos Aires Affair* the anxieties and inhibitions of the two characters are so great that they never get to a point of love; all they have is the dream of sex which obsesses and torments them."

The author sets this psychological drama within the framework of a traditional thriller; "what makes Puig so fascinating," writes *New York Times Book Review* contributor Robert Alter, is "the extraordinary inventiveness he exhibits in devising new ways to render familiar material." De Feo, however, faults the author for being "a shade too inventive, [for] we are not always convinced that [these methods] are necessary. But," the critic adds, "the book is more intense, serious, and disturbing than the other novels, and it is a welcome departure for this searching, gifted writer." And the *Times Literary Supplement* writer claims that *The Buenos Aires Affair* "is technically even more accomplished than the previous novels, and Sr Puig is able to handle a wide variety of narrative devices in it without ever making them seem gratuitous."

Shortly after the publication of *The Buenos Aires Affair* in 1973, Puig found it more difficult to remain in Argentina; *Affair* had been banned (presumably because of its sexual content), and the political situation was becoming more restrictive. This increasingly antagonistic climate led Puig to a self-imposed exile, and is reflected in what is probably his best-known work, *The Kiss of the Spider Woman.* Set almost entirely in an Argentinian jail cell, the novel focuses on Valentín, a radical student imprisoned for political reasons, and Molina, a gay window dresser in on a "morals" charge, who recounts his favorite 1930s and '40s movies as a means of passing time. "In telling the story of two cellmates, Puig strips down the narrative to a nearly filmic level— dialogue unbroken even to identify the speakers, assuming we can project them onto our own interior screens," relates Carol Anshaw in the *Voice Literary Supplement.* "If this insistent use of unedited dialogue tends to make the book read a bit like a radio script, however," observes *New York Times Book Review*

contributor Robert Coover, "it is Mr. Puig's fascination with old movies that largely provides [the novel's] substance and ultimately defines its plot, its shape. What we hear," the critic continues, "are the voices of two suffering men, alone and often in the dark, but what we see . . . [is] all the iconographic imagery, magic and romance of the movies." The contrast between the two men, who gradually build a friendship "makes this Argentinian odd couple both funny and affecting," Larry Rohter states in the *Washington Post Book World.* But when Molina is released in hopes that he will lead officials to Valentín's confederates, "the plot turns from comedy to farce and Puig's wit turns mordant."

In addition to the continuous dialogue of the jail cell and surveillance report after Molina's release, *The Kiss of the Spider Woman* contains several footnotes on homosexuality whose "clumsy academic style serves to emphasize by contrast that the two prisoners' dialogue is a highly contrived storytelling device, and not the simulation of reality you may take it to be at first," comments Lehmann-Haupt. Because of this, the critic explains, the book becomes "a little too tricky, like a well-made, 19th-century play." Other reviewers, however, find *The Kiss of the Spider Woman* "far and away [Puig's] most impressive book," as Anshaw says. "It is not easy to write a book which says something hopeful about human nature and yet remains precise and unsentimental," Maggie Gee remarks in the *Times Literary Supplement.* "Puig succeeds, partly because his bleak vision of the outside world throws into relief the small private moments of hope and dignifies them, partly through his deft manipulation of form." Schwartz similarly concludes that *The Kiss of the Spider Woman* "is not the usual jumble of truncated structures from which a plot emerges but, rather, a beautifully controlled narrative that skillfully conveys basic human values, a vivid demonstration of the continuing of the genre itself."

Inspired by a stay in New York, *Eternal Curse on the Reader of These Pages* was written directly in English and, similar to *The Kiss of the Spider Woman,* is mainly comprised of an extended dialogue. Juan José Ramírez is an elderly Argentinian living in exile in New York and Lawrence John is the irritable, taciturn American who works part-time caring for him. But as their dialogues progress, Lehmann-Haupt notes, "it becomes increasingly difficult to tell how much is real and how much the two characters have become objects of each other's fantasy life." *Los Angeles Times Book Review* critic Charles Champlin, although he believes these dialogues constitute a technical "tour de force," questions "whether a technical exercise, however clever, [is] the best way to get at this study of conflicting cultures and the ambiguities in the relationship."

Gilbert Sorrentino similarly feels that *Eternal Curse* is "a structural failure, . . . for the conclusion, disastrously, comments on and 'explains' an otherwise richly ambivalent and mysterious text." The critic continues in the *Washington Post Book World:* "It's too bad, because Puig *has* something, most obviously a sense that the essential elements of life, life's serious 'things,' are precisely the elements of soap opera, sit-coms, and B-movies." But Lehmann-Haupt thinks *Eternal Curse* is "more austere and intellectually brittle than any of [Puig's] previous books, [and] less playful and dependent on the artifacts of American pop culture," and calls the novel a "fascinating tour de force." "Puig is an artist, . . . and his portrait of two men grappling with their suffering is exceedingly moving and brilliantly done," declares William Herrick in the *New Leader.* "Strangely, the more space I put between the book and myself, the more tragic I find it. It sticks to the mind. Like one cursed, I cannot find peace, cannot escape from its pain."

Echoing themes of Puig's previous work, maintains *Nation* contributor Jean Franco, "politics and sexuality are inseparable in *Pubis Angelical*," the latest of Puig's novels to be published in the United States. Alternating the story of Ana, an Argentinian exile dying of cancer in Mexico, with her fantasies of a 1930s movie star and a futuristic "sexual soldier," *Pubis Angelical* speaks "of the political nightmares of exile, disappearance, torture and persecution," describes Franco, "though as always in Puig's novels, the horror is tempered by the humor of his crazy plots and kitsch stage props." "Puig is both ruthless and touching in his presentation of Ana's muddled but sincere life," states Jason Wilson in the *Times Literary Supplement;* "and if he is sometimes too camp, he can also be very funny." The critic elaborates: "His humour works because he refuses to settle for any single definition of woman; Ana is all feeling and intuition . . . although she is also calculating, and unfeeling about her daughter." But while Ana's advancing cancer and the problems of her dream counterparts are severe, "however seriously Puig is questioning gender assumptions and behavior his voice is never a solemn one," Nick Caistor claims in the *New Statesman.* "The work as a whole fairly bristles with ingenuity and energy," Robert Towers writes in the *New York Review of Books;* "the thematic parallels between the three texts seem almost inexhaustible, and one finishes the novel with a sense of having grasped only a portion of them." Nevertheless, the critic faults *Pubis Angelical* for being "an impressive artifact rather than a fully engrossing work of fictional art."

Steve Erickson likewise criticizes the novel, commenting in the *New York Times Book Review* that "what's amazing about 'Pubis Angelical' is how utterly in love it is with its own artificiality." The critic adds that "the novel fails most devastatingly" in the portrayals of Ana's fantasies: "There's nothing about their lives to suggest that . . . they have a reality for her." While Jay Cantor similarly believes that "it isn't till the last quarter of the book that the fantasies have sufficient, involving interest," he acknowledges in the *Los Angeles Times Book Review* that "there is an audacity to Puig's method, and an intellectual fire to Puig's marshaling of motifs that did then engage me." "In any case, whatever the whole [of the novel] amounts to, each individual part of 'Pubis Angelical' develops its own irresistible drama," counters Lehmann-Haupt. "Though it takes an exercise of the intellect to add them together, they finally contribute to what is the most richly textured and extravagant fiction [Puig] has produced so far."

"Less interested in depicting things as they might be, and concerned with things as they are, Puig does not resort to make-believe," Alfred J. MacAdam asserts in *Modern Latin American Narratives: The Dreams of Reason.* "His characters are all too plausible, . . . [and their lives] simply unfold over days and years until they run their meaningless course." It is this ordinary, commonplace quality of life, however, that the author prefers to investigate, as he told the *Washington Post*'s Desson Howe: "I find literature the ideal medium to tell certain stories that are of special interest to me. Everyday stories with no heroics, the everyday life of the gray people." And films play such a large role in his work because of the contrast they provide to this mundane world: "I think I can understand the reality of the 1930s by means of the unreality of their films," Puig remarked in a *Los Angeles Times* interview with Ann Marie Cunningham. "The films reflect exactly what people dreamed life could be. The relationships between people in these films are like the negative of a photograph of real life." "I can only understand realism," the author further explained to *New York Times* writer Samuel G. Freedman. "I can only approach my writing with an analytical sense. . . . I can write dreams, but I use them as part of the accumulation of detail, as counterpoint." Because of his realistic yet inventive portrayals, contends Schwartz, "Manuel Puig is a novelist moving in the direction of political commitment in his depiction of the provincial and urban middle class of Argentina, something that has never before been attempted so successfully in Latin American letters." The critic concludes: "Clearly, Puig, thriving self-exiled from his native country, is an eclectic stylist, a consummate artist."

MEDIA ADAPTATIONS: The Kiss of the Spider Woman was made into a film by Brazilian director Hector Babenco in 1985 and starred Raul Julia, William Hurt (in an Oscar-winning performance), and Sonia Braga.

BIOGRAPHICAL/CRITICAL SOURCES:

BOOKS

Contemporary Literary Criticism, Gale, Volume 3, 1975, Volume 5, 1976, Volume 10, 1979, Volume 28, 1984.
Gallagher, D. P., *Modern Latin American Literature,* Oxford University Press, 1973.
MacAdam, Alfred J., *Modern Latin American Narratives: The Dreams of Reason,* University of Chicago Press, 1977.
Schwartz, Ronald, *Nomads, Exiles, and Emigres: The Rebirth of the Latin American Narrative, 1960-80,* Scarecrow, 1980.
Tittler, Jonathan, *Narrative Irony in the Contemporary Spanish-American Novel,* Cornell University Press, 1984.

PERIODICALS

Chicago Tribune Book World, April 15, 1979.
Commonweal, June 24, 1977.
Latin American Literary Review, fall, 1972.
Los Angeles Times, January 30, 1987, February 3, 1987, November 16, 1989, November 17, 1989.
Los Angeles Times Book Review, June 20, 1982, December 28, 1986.
Nation, April 18, 1987.
National Review, October 29, 1976.
New Leader, June 28, 1982.
New Statesman, October 2, 1987.
Newsweek, October 25, 1971, June 28, 1982.
New York Review of Books, December 13, 1973, January 24, 1980, December 18, 1986.
New York Times, November 28, 1973, April 23, 1979, June 4, 1982, September 25, 1984, August 5, 1985, December 22, 1986, October 25, 1988.
New York Times Book Review, September 26, 1971, December 16, 1973, September 5, 1976, April 22, 1979, July 4, 1982, September 23, 1984, December 28, 1986.
Review 73, fall, 1973.
Times (London), August 23, 1985.
Times Literary Supplement, November 6, 1970, August 31, 1973, September 21, 1984, October 16, 1987, August 11-17, 1989.
Voice Literary Supplement, April, 1989.
Washington Post, November 16, 1985.
Washington Post Book World, November 25, 1973, April 22, 1979, August 1, 1982.
World Literature Today, winter, 1981.

—*Sketch by Diane Telgen*

Q

QUINN, Anthony (Rudolph Oaxaca) 1915-

PERSONAL: Born April 21, 1915, in Chihuahua, Mexico; son of Frank and Manuela (Oaxaca) Quinn; brought to United States as an infant; naturalized citizen, 1947; married Katherine de Mille (adopted daughter of Cecil B. de Mille; divorced); married Yolanda Addolari (January, 1966); children: (first marriage) Christopher (deceased), Christina, Kathleen, Duncan, Valentina; (second marriage) Francesco, Daniele, Lorenzo. *Education:* Attended Polytechnic High School, Los Angeles, Calif.

ADDRESSES: Office—Anthony Quinn Studios, 402 East 90th St., New York, N.Y. 10128. *Agent*—McCartt Oreck Barrett, 402 East 90th St., New York, N.Y. 10128.

CAREER: Actor, artist, and writer. Worked as fruit picker, boxer, and taxi driver before securing his first job as an actor in a federal theatre project. Film appearances include "Parole," 1936, "The Plainsman," "Daughter of Shanghai," "Last Train from Madrid," and "The Buccaneer," 1937, "Dangerous to Know" and "King of Alcatraz," 1938, "Union Pacific" and "Television Spy," 1939, "Emergency Squad," "Road to Singapore," "Parole Fixer," "City for Conquest," and "The Ghost Breakers," 1940, "Blood and Sand," 1941, "The Black Swan," "Larceny, Inc.," and "Road to Morocco," 1942, "Ox Bow Incident," 1943, "Roger Touhy, Gangster," "Guadalcanal Diary," "Buffalo Bill," and "Irish Eyes Are Smiling," 1944, "China Sky," "Back to Bataan," and "Where Do We Go from Here?," 1945, "Black Gold" and "California," 1947, "Tycoon," 1948, "The Brave Bulls," "Mask of the Avenger," "They Died with Their Boots On," "The Brigand," "World in His Arms," 1951, "Viva Zapata" and "Against All Flags," 1952, "Ride, Vaquero," "City Beneath the Sea," "Seminole," "Blowing Wild," "East of Sumatra," 1953, "Long Wait" and "Attila the Hun," 1954, "Magnificent Matador," "Ulysses," "Naked Street," and "Seven Cities of Gold," 1955, "La Strada," "Lust for Life," "Wild Party," "Hunchback of Notre Dame," and "Man from Del Rio," 1956, "Ride Back," "The River's Edge," "Last Train from Gun Hill," and "Wild Is the Wind," 1957, "Hot Spell," 1958, "Black Orchid" and "Warlock," 1959, "Savage Innocents," "Heller With a Gun," and "Heller in Pink Tights," 1960, "Guns of Navarone," 1961, "Barabbas" and "Lawrence of Arabia," 1962, "Requiem for a Heavyweight," 1963, "The Visit" and "Behold a Pale Horse," 1964, "Zorba the Greek" and "High Wind in Jamaica," 1965, "Lost Command," 1966, "The Happening," "The Rover," and "The Twenty-fifth Hour," 1967,

"Guns for San Sebastian," "The Magus," and "The Shoes of the Fisherman," 1968, "Secret of Santa Vittoria" and "Dream of Kings," 1969, "Flap," "The Last Warrior," "Walk in the Spring Rain," and "R.P.M.," 1970, "Across 110th Street," 1972, "Deaf Smith and Johnny Ears," "The Don Is Dead," and "Los Amigos," 1973, "The Marseilles Contract," 1974, "Mohammed: Messenger of God," and "Tigers Don't Cry," 1977, "The Inheritance," "The Greek Tycoon," "Caravans," and "Children of Sanchez," 1978, "The Passage," 1979, "Lion in the Desert," 1981. Has appeared on stage in "A Streetcar Named Desire," 1948-49, "Let Me Hear the Melody," 1951, "Becket," 1960, "Tchin-Tchin," 1962, "The Red Devil Battery Sign," 1975, and "Zorba, *Zorba!*," 1983. Has also appeared in television films, "Jesus of Nazareth" and "Onassis: The Richest Man in the World," and in television series, "The Man and the City." Has exhibited his oil paintings, sculptures, and serigraphs in Hawaii, 1982 and 1987, San Francisco, 1983, San Antonio and Houston, 1984, New York City, 1984 and 1989, Washington, 1985, and Beverly Hills, Calif., 1986.

AWARDS, HONORS: Academy Award for best supporting actor, 1952, for "Viva Zapata!," and 1956, for "Lust for Life."

WRITINGS:

The Original Sin: A Self-Portrait, Little, Brown, 1972.

Also author of play, "Thirty-three Men," 1937, and a short story later filmed by Metro-Goldwyn-Mayer as "The Farm."

SIDELIGHTS: Anthony Quinn, son of an Indian mother and an Irish father, found himself head of the household at the age of nine when his father was killed in an automobile accident. Supporting himself, his younger sister, and his mother through several menial jobs, Quinn was unable to finish his education but realized his dreams to become an actor in the midst of the Depression by participating in the Federal Theatre Project. *The Original Sin: A Self-Portrait,* Quinn's autobiography, which has been translated into Greek, Spanish, and Slovenian, details the author's life experiences, his religious and cultural beliefs, and his drive to succeed. Calling it "a gripping portrayal of a many faceted character," Barbara Emigh states in a *Catholic Library World* review: "The manner in which he reveals his self-doubts, his failures and his triumphs is disarmingly and brutally frank. . . . His Mexican mother and his Irish father are skillfully revealed, as are their contrasting influences on the boy. Poverty in childhood, humiliation as a Chicano youth growing up in a disdainful Los Angeles, eventual success in films combine to form the man."

Quinn made his film debut in "Parole" in 1936; and, in the more than fifty years since, has performed in scores of motion pictures. Known for his supporting and ethnic roles, Quinn has portrayed dozens of ethnic types and nationalities. "But for all that," states Richard Christiansen in a *Chicago Tribune Book World* interview, "and despite his supporting actor Academy Awards for 'Lust for Life' and 'Viva Zapata,' to many moviegoers he was, is and forever will be Zorba, the vigorous embodiment of the life force." Noting that Quinn's identification with Zorba, the title character from Nikos Kazantzakis' novel, is so profound that occasionally, during a stage revival of the role, "he doesn't know if Anthony Quinn is playing Zorba or Zorba is playing Anthony Quinn," Christiansen quotes the actor as saying, "I am perhaps a little more well read and more traveled than Zorba, but I would say that I agree with 80 percent of his philosophy. I understand him. He is my man."

BIOGRAPHICAL/CRITICAL SOURCES:

PERIODICALS

Atlantic, November, 1972.
Catholic Library World, Volume 44, 1973.
Chicago Tribune Book World, March 13, 1983.
Newsweek, May 6, 1957, January 16, 1978.
New York Times Book Review, October 8, 1972.
Saturday Review, October 21, 1972.
Times Literary Supplement, May 18, 1973.

* * *

QUINTANA, Leroy V. 1944-

PERSONAL: Born June 10, 1944, in Albuquerque, N.M.; married Yolanda Holguín (a registered nurse), 1969; children: Sandra, Elisa, Jose. *Education:* University of New Mexico, B.A., 1971; graduate study at University of Denver; New Mexico State University, M.A. (English), 1974; Western New Mexico University, M.A. (counseling), 1984. *Politics:* Democrat. *Religion:* Roman Catholic.

ADDRESSES: Home—9230-C Lake Murray, San Diego, Calif. 92119. *Office*—San Diego Mesa College, 7250 Mesa College Dr., San Diego, Calif. 92111.

CAREER: New Mexico State University, Las Cruces, instructor in English, beginning in 1975; El Paso Community College, El Paso, Texas, instructor in English, 1975-80, coordinator of poetry series; University of New Mexico, Albuquerque, instructor in English, beginning in 1980; *Albuquerque Tribune,* Albuquerque, feature writer and sportswriter, 1981-82; National City Family Clinic, San Diego, counselor, 1984—; San Diego Mesa College, San Diego, Calif., associate professor of English, 1988—; writer. Worked as a roofer, and as an alcoholism counselor in Albuquerque. *Military service:* U.S. Army, Airborne, 1967-69, served in Vietnam.

MEMBER: Modern Language Association.

AWARDS, HONORS: National Endowment for the Arts creative writing fellow, 1978; American Book Award for poetry from Before Columbus Foundation and El Paso Border Regional Library Association award, both 1982, both for *Sangre.*

WRITINGS:

Hijo del Pueblo: New Mexico Poems (title means "Son of the People"), illustrations by Trini López, Puerto Del Sol Press, 1976.

Sangre (title means "Blood"), Prima Agua Press, 1981.
The Reason People Don't Like Mexicans, Bilingual Review/Press, 1984.

Also editor of *Metaforas Verdes: Anthology of Spanish/English Poetry.* Works represented in anthologies, including *Shore Anthology of Poetry, Chicano Voices, Hispanics in the United States: An Anthology of Creative Literature,* edited by Gary D. Keller and Francisco Jiménez, Bilingual/Editorial Bilingüe, 1980, and *Five Poets of Aztlán,* edited by Santiago Daydí-Tolson, Bilingual/Editorial Bilingüe, 1985.

Contributor to periodicals, including *Contact/II, Latin America Literary Review, New Mexico Magazine, Poetry Texas, Revista Chicano-Riqueña, Rocky Mountain Review, Southwest Heritage,* and *Voices International.* Poetry editor of *Thunderbird,* University of New Mexico literary magazine, 1970, and of *Puerto del Sol,* New Mexico State University literary magazine, 1973-74. Contributing editor to the Baleen Press, Phoenix, Ariz., 1974.

WORK IN PROGRESS: Why, or Me, a Thousand Lives, poetry about grade school chums; *Interrogations,* poetry about Vietnam; *My Hair Turning Gray Among Strangers,* poetry about a New Mexican in California; a collection of short stories; a novel; research on the image of the Chicano in American detective fiction.

SIDELIGHTS: "In many ways, I'm still basically a small-town New Mexico boy carrying on the oral tradition," American Book Award-winning poet Leroy V. Quintana was quoted as saying in an article in *Dictionary of Literary Biography.* Author of the collections *Hijo del Pueblo* ("Son of the People") and *Sangre* ("Blood"), Quintana was born in Albuquerque and raised by his grandparents, who told him *cuentos,* or traditional Mexican folk tales, and stories of life in the Old West. For his poems Quintana draws on Hispanic folklore for subject matter as well as spirit, and he includes many ancient storytelling devices—such as conversational structure and unreliable narrators—in his contemporary poetic form.

After high school and a tour in Vietnam, Quintana enrolled in the University of New Mexico, where he first wrote poems and edited *Thunderbird,* the school's literary journal. In 1976 he published his first poetry collection, *Hijo del Pueblo,* a celebration of small-town New Mexican life as seen through the eyes of a young boy. Using phrases borrowed from the storytellers—"I have been told" and "Grandfather used to say"—Quintana effectively draws the reader into his writings, which bring modern expression to such Mexican and Indian traditions as undertaking pilgrimages to the shrine of the Virgin Mary of Guadalupe and performing ritual dances. He also addresses new phenomena, including the return home of Mexican-American soldiers from foreign wars and the effects of Anglos on Hispanic culture and society. And in "Sterling, Colorado," quoted by Douglas K. Benson in an article in the *Dictionary of Literary Biography,* Quintana discusses the prejudice many Hispanics suffer: "On Saturdays we would go into town / after picking potatoes all week / and the Anglos would laugh at us / and call us dirty Mexicans." But Quintana also recalls that as her way of overcoming her consequent frustration his mother "loops and loops the laughter" into "yet another doilie."

Quintana's subsequent collection, *Sangre,* follows in the same grassroots tradition and was honored with an American Book Award. In the five years since *Hijo del Pueblo* was published Quintana's poetic style matured, and the poems of *Sangre* express this greater range and vision. The New Mexican experience—particularly village life—is portrayed colorfully and effectively, and Quintana addresses contemporary issues as well: the Vietnam War, the fallibility of television heroes, the realization that the simple life of the past is gone. Indeed, in the final poem of the collection, "A Legacy," the narrator, who was educated among Anglos, longs to return to the innocence and security of the time when his grandfather told *cuentos*.

Quintana told *HW:* "My major areas of interest are Vietnam and New Mexico. I was raised by my grandparents and my major form of entertainment was the old *cuentos* (stories) I was told. I have always enjoyed stories—I read comic books by the hundreds, went to the movies, and recited the stanzas in the back of the catechism religiously. I am a licensed marriage, family, and child counselor and my foray into psychology helped me to understand human motivation and has helped me tremendously in my writing.

"I seem to be tied to a sense of the past; my work reflects the 'sense of place' evoked by New Mexico. I hope I am worthy of portraying the land and its people well."

BIOGRAPHICAL/CRITICAL SOURCES:

BOOKS

Dictionary of Literary Biography, Volume 82: *Chicano Writers,* Gale, 1989.
Lomelí, Francisco A. and Donaldo W. Urioste, *Chicano Perspectives in Literature: A Critical and Annotated Bibliography,* Pajarito Publications, 1976.
Quintana, Leroy V., *Hijo del pueblo: New Mexico Poems,* Puerto del Sol Press, 1976.
Quintana, Leroy V., *Sangre,* Prima Agua Press, 1981.

PERIODICALS

American Book Review, December, 1977.
Bilingual Review/La Revista Bilingüe, Number 12, 1987.
Contact/II, winter/spring, 1984-85.
New Mexico Humanities Review, spring, 1982.
Perspectives on Contemporary Literature, Number 12, 1986.

* * *

QUINTERO, José (Benjamin) 1924-

PERSONAL: Born October 15, 1924, in Panama City, Panama; son of Carlos Rivira and Consuelo (Palmorala) Quintero. *Education:* University of Southern California, B.A., 1948; attended Goodman Theatre Dramatic School, c. 1948-49.

CAREER: Theater director, producer, and actor. Circle in the Square (theater), New York, N.Y., director and producer of plays, 1951-c. 1963; Brandeis University, Waltham, Mass., artistic director of Spingold Theater, beginning in 1983; affiliated with Chaplin-O'Neill Theater, Los Angeles, Calif. Director of numerous plays, including "The Glass Menagerie" and "Riders to the Sea," 1949, "Dark of the Moon," 1950, "Bonds of Interest," "The Enchanted," "Yerma," and "Burning Bright," 1951, "Summer and Smoke," 1952, "In the Summer House," "The Grass Harp," and "American Gothic," 1953, "The Girl on the Via Flaminia" and "Portrait of a Lady," 1954, "La Ronde" and "Cradle Song," 1955, "The Innkeepers," "Long Day's Journey Into Night," and "The Iceman Cometh," 1956, "Lost in the Stars," "Children of Darkness," and "The Quare Fellow," 1958, "The Triumph of St. Joan," "Macbeth," and "Our Town," 1959, "Camino Real," "Laurette," and "The Balcony," 1960, "Look, We've Come Through" and "Under Milkwood," 1961, "Great Day in the Morning," "Pullman Car Hiawatha," and "Plays for Bleecker Street," 1962, "Strange Interlude" and "Desire Under

the Elms," 1963, "Marco Millions" and "Hughie," 1964, "Diamond Orchid" and "Matty and the Moron and the Madonna," 1965, "More Stately Mansions," 1967, "The Seven Descents of Myrtle," 1968, "Gandhi," 1970, "Johnny Johnson" and "The Big Coca-Cola Swamp in the Sky," 1971, "A Moon for the Misbegotten," 1973, "Gabrielle," 1974, "The Skin of Our Teeth," 1975, "Knock Knock," 1976, "Anna Christie" and "A Touch of the Poet," 1977, "The Human Voice," 1978, "Faith Healer," 1979, "Clothes for a Summer Hotel," "Welded," and "Ah! Wilderness," 1980, "Cat on a Hot Tin Roof," 1982. Director of the television productions "Medea" and "Our Town," 1959, and the film "The Roman Spring of Mrs. Stone," 1961. Producer or co-producer of plays, including "Long Day's Journey Into Night," c. 1956.

MEMBER: Directors Guild of America, Society of Stage Directors and Choreographers.

AWARDS, HONORS: Obie Award for best director from *Village Voice,* 1956, for "The Iceman Cometh"; Antoinette Perry (Tony) awards from League of American Theatres and Producers, 1957, as co-producer of "Long Day's Journey Into Night," and 1974, as director of "A Moon for the Misbegotten"; Drama League Unique Contributions to the Theatre Award, 1987, for directing plays by Eugene O'Neill; Caballero de la Orden de Vasco Núñez de Balboa; special citation from Asamblea Nacional de Panama.

WRITINGS:

If You Don't Dance They Beat You (memoir), Little, Brown, 1974.
"Gabrielle" (play), produced in Buffalo, N.Y., at Studio Arena, 1974.

Contributor to periodicals, including *New York Times.*

SIDELIGHTS: Panamanian-born José Quintero is an acclaimed director of plays by Eugene O'Neill, a Nobel Prize-winning American author whose work is renowned for its pessimism and dramatic power. "Other directors have staged O'Neill," wrote Barbara Gelb in the *New York Times,* "but—even during the dramatist's lifetime—none with anything like Quintero's mastery." After growing up in Panama, Quintero went to the United States in the 1940s and studied acting. By 1949 he had joined a group of young actors in founding a short-lived theater in Woodstock, New York, where he realized that he preferred directing plays to performing in them. He accompanied his friends to New York City, where they turned a cramped and disused nightclub into Circle in the Square, one of most acclaimed small theaters of the 1950s. Here Quintero directed a variety of up-and-coming young actors, including Geraldine Page and, most notably for Quintero's career, Jason Robards. Quintero and Robards joined forces to restore the sagging reputation of O'Neill, beginning with their Obie Award-winning revival of "The Iceman Cometh" in 1956. The production so impressed O'Neill's widow Carlotta that she chose the young director to stage the American premiere of O'Neill's autobiographical masterpiece, "Long Day's Journey Into Night." The success of the ensuing production secured Quintero's status as a major director. Though Quintero left Circle in the Square in the early 1960s due to artistic differences, he has continued to direct well-received productions of O'Neill plays in succeeding years, often working with Robards.

In 1974 Quintero released a memoir of his years in the theater, *If You Don't Dance They Beat You.* The book focuses on the people Quintero has encountered during his career, including the Circle in the Square troupe, O'Neill's widow and children, and many others, such as an unhappy child dancer whose "stage mother" beat her to make her perform. In the *New York Times Book Review* drama critic Brooks Atkinson praised the work, saying it contains "the essence of theater." "The reader soon understands why Mr. Quintero is so able," Atkinson observed. "He is a free spirit and he draws his knowledge of directing out of his knowledge of people."

BIOGRAPHICAL/CRITICAL SOURCES:

BOOKS

Martinez, Al, *Rising Voices,* New American Library, 1974.
Quintero, José, *If You Don't Dance They Beat You,* Little, Brown, 1974.
Van Italie, J. C., *Behind the Scenes,* Holt, 1971.

PERIODICALS

Américas, September, 1955, November, 1958.
Cue, January 23, 1954.
Horizon, January, 1978.
New York Times, January 28, 1974, November 18, 1974, December 11, 1977, February 18, 1983, June 16, 1988.
New York Times Book Review, November 24, 1974.
Theatre Arts, May, 1960.

* * *

QUIRARTE, Jacinto 1931-

PERSONAL: Surname is pronounced Key-*ar*-tay; born August 17, 1931, in Jerome, Ariz.; son of Francisco (a teamster) and Frutosa (Jimenez) Quirarte; married Sara Bel Farmer, December 18, 1954; children: Sabrina Pilar. *Education:* San Francisco State College (now San Francisco State University), B.A., 1954, M.A., 1958; National University of Mexico, Ph.D., 1964. *Politics:* Democrat. *Religion:* Roman Catholic.

ADDRESSES: Home—10902 Bar X Trail, San Antonio, Tex. 78228. *Office*—Research Center for the Arts, University of Texas at San Antonio, San Antonio, Tex. 78285.

CAREER: Colegio Americano, Mexico City, Mexico, art teacher, 1959-61; National University of Mexico, Mexico City, assistant to Alberto Ruz Lhuillier, 1961-62; University of the Americas, Mexico City, Mexico, professor of art history and dean of men, 1962-64; Centro Venezolano-Americano, Caracas, Venezuela, director of Asuntos Culturales, 1964-66; University of Texas at Austin, Austin, professor of art history, 1967-72; University of Texas at San Antonio, San Antonio, professor of art history and dean of College of Fine and Applied Arts, 1972-1978, director of Research Center for the Arts, 1979—. Visiting professor at Universidad Central de Venezuela, spring, 1966, Yale University, spring, 1967, and University of New Mexico, spring, 1971. *Military service:* U.S. Air Force, flight office, navigator, and radar-bombardier for Strategic Air Command (SAC), 1954-57; became captain. U.S. Air Force Reserve, 1957-62.

MEMBER: International Congress of Anthropology and Ethnology, International Congress of the History of Art, International Congress of Americanists, Society for American Archaeology, Mid-America College Art Association, Texas Council of the Arts in Education (member of visual arts and humanities panel), San Antonio Arts Council (vice president and member of board, 1973-77).

WRITINGS:

(Translator) Alfonso Caso, *El Códice Selden* (title means "The Selden Codex"), Sociedad Mexicana de Antropología, 1964.
Mexican American Artists, University of Texas Press, 1973.

Izapan Style Art: A Study of Its Form and Meaning (monograph), Harvard University Press, 1973.
(Contributor) Philip D. Ortego, editor, *We Are Chicanos: An Anthology of Mexican American Literature,* Washington Square Press, 1973.
(Contributor) Henry Nicholson, editor, *Origins of Religious Art and Iconography in Preclassic Mesoamerica,* Latin American Center, University of California, Los Angeles, 1976.
(Contributor) David L. Browman, editor, *Cultural Continuity in Mesoamerica,* Mouton, 1978.
(Contributor) Gordon Willey and R. E. W. Adams, editors, *Origins of Maya Civilization,* University of New Mexico Press, 1977.
(Contributor) Norman Hammond and Willey, editors, *Maya Archaeology and Ethnohistory,* University of Texas Press, 1979.
(Contributor) Merle Greene Robertson and Connan Call Jeffers, *Tercera Mesa Redonda de Palenque,* Pre-Columbian Art Research, 1979.
(Editor with Maria Elena Gonzalez-Rich) *Directory of Hispanic American Arts Organizations,* Research Center for the Arts and Humanities, University of Texas at San Antonio, 1982.
(Editor) *The Hispanic American Aesthetic,* Research Center for the Arts and Humanities, University of Texas at San Antonio, 1983.
(Editor and author of introductory notes) *Chicano Art History: A Book of Selected Readings,* Research Center for the Arts and Humanities, University of Texas at San Antonio, 1984.

Contributor to proceedings and to journals.

* * *

QUIROGA, Horacio (Sylvestre) 1878-1937
(Guillermo Eynhardt)

PERSONAL: Born December 31, 1878, in Salto, Uruguay; committed suicide by taking poison while suffering from cancer, February 19, 1937, in Buenos Aires, Argentina; interred in Salto, Uruguay; son of an Argentine vice consul; married Ana María Cires, December 30, 1909 (committed suicide, December, 1915); married second wife, María Elena, July, 1927 (separated); children: (first marriage) Eglé (daughter), Darío; (second marriage) one child. *Education:* Attended University of Montevideo.

CAREER: Writer. Colegio Nacional, Buenos Aires, Argentina, Spanish teacher, 1903; member of Argentine Government commission studying Jesuit ruins in Misiones, Argentina, in early 1900s; cotton farmer in Chaco, Argentina; Escuela Normal, Buenos Aires, professor of Spanish language and literature, 1906-11; justice of the peace and official recorder, San Ignacio, Argentina; farmer, charcoal maker, and distiller in Misiones; employed at Uruguayan consulates in Buenos Aires, beginning c. 1917, and San Ignacio, 1932.

MEMBER: El Consistorio de Gay Saber.

WRITINGS:

Los arrecifes de coral (poems and stories; title means "Coral Reefs"), originally published in 1901, published with essays by Carlos A. Herrera MacLean and Antonio M. Grompone, C. García & cía (Montevideo, Uruguay), 1943.
Las sacrificadas, cuento excénico en cuatro actos (four-act play; title means "The Sacrificed"), "Buenos Aires" Cooperativa Editorial Limitada, 1920.
Diario de viaje a París, introduction and notes by Emir Rodríguez Monegal, Número (Montevideo), 1950.

La vida en Misiones, prologue and notes by Jorge Ruffinelli, Arca (Montevideo), 1969.

Sobre literatura, prologue by Roberto Ibáñez, notes by Ruffinelli, Arca, 1970.

Epoca modernista, prologue by Arturo Sergio Visca, notes by Ruffinelli, Arca, 1973.

FICTION

Historia de un amor turbio (title means "The Story of a Troubled Courtship"), originally published in 1908, Babel (Buenos Aires, Argentina), 1923, reprinted, Barreiro y Ramos (Montevideo), 1968.

Cuentos de amor, de locura y de muerte (title means "Stories of Love, Madness, and Death"; includes "Nuestro primer cigarro," "El meningitis y su sombra," "Una estación de amor," "La muerte de Isolda," "Buques suicidantes," "El almohadón de pluma," "El solitario," and "La gallina degollada"), originally published in 1917, Babel, 1925, reprinted, Bello (Santiago, Chile), 1984.

Cuentos de la selva, originally published in 1918, C. García y cía, 1940, reprinted, Juventud (La Paz, Bolivia), 1982, translation by Arthur Livingston published as *South American Jungle Tales,* illustrations by A. L. Ripley, Duffield, 1922.

"El salvaje" y otros cuentos (title means " 'The Savage' and Other Stories"; includes "El salvaje," "La realidad," "Reyes," "La navidad," "La pasión," "Corpus," "La reina italiana," "Los cementerios belgas," "Estefanía," "La llama," "Fanny," "Lucila Strinberg," "Un idilio," "Tres cartas y un pie," and "Cuento para novios"), Biblioteca Argentina de Buenas Ediciones Literarias (Buenos Aires), 1920, reprinted, Alianza (Madrid, Spain), 1982.

Anaconda (contains "Anaconda," "El simún," "Gloria tropical," "El yaciyateré," "Los fabricantes de carbón," "El monte negro," "En la noche," "Polea loca," "Dieta de amor," and "Miss Dorothy Phillips, mi esposa"), originally published in 1921, reprinted, Biblioteca Argentina de Buenas Ediciones Literarias, 1930, reprinted, Alianza, 1981.

El desierto (title means "The Wilderness"; contains "El desierto," "Un peón," "Una conquista," "Silvina y Montt," "El espectro," "El sincope blanco," "Los tres besos," "El potro salvaje," "El león," "La patria," and "Juan Darién"), Babel, 1924, reprinted, Losada (Buenos Aires), 1974.

"La gallina degollada," y otros cuentos, Calpe (Madrid), 1925, reprinted, Centro Editor de America Latina (Buenos Aires), 1967, translation by Margaret Sayers Peden published as *"The Decapitated Chicken," and Other Stories,* introduction by George D. Schade, illustrations by Ed Lindlof, University of Texas Press, 1976.

Los desterrados: Tipos de ambiente (title means "The Exiled"; contains "El ambiente: El regreso de Anaconda," "Los tipos: Los desterrados," "Van-Houten," "Tacuaramansión," "El hombre muerto," "El techo de incienso," "La cámara oscura," and "Los destiladores de naranja"), originally published in 1926, Biblioteca Argentina de Buenas Ediciones Literarias, 1927, reprinted, Losada, 1983, translation by J. David Danielson and Elsa K. Gambarini published as *"The Exiles" and Other Stories,* University of Texas Press, 1987.

Pasado amor (title means "Bygone Love"), Biblioteca Argentina de Buenas Ediciones Literarias, 1929, reprinted, Losada, 1981.

Más allá (title means "The Great Beyond"; contains "Más allá," "El vampiro," "Las moscas," "El conductor del rápido," "El llamado," "El hijo," "La señorita Leona," "El puritano," "Su ausencia," "La bella y la bestia," and "El ocaso"), originally published in 1934, [Buenos Aires], 1935, reprinted as *El más allá,* Losada, 1964.

Our First Smoke, translated from the Spanish "Nuestra primer cigarro" by Annmarie Colbin, Vanishing Rotating Triangle, 1972.

"The Flies," in *Review 76,* 1976.

Also author of *El crimen del otro* (title means "Another's Crime"; includes "El crimen del otro," "La justa proporción de las cosas," "La princesa bizantina," and "Hashish"), 1904, and *Los perseguidos* (title means "The Pursued"), 1905.

LETTERS

Cartas inéditas de Horacio Quiroga, [Montevideo], 1959.

Cartas inéditas, edited with notes by Arturo Sergio Visca, Biblioteca Nacional, Departamento de Investigaciones (Montevideo), 1970.

El mundo ideal de Horacio Quiroga [y cartas inéditas de Quiroga a Isidoro Escalera], edited by Antonio Hernán Rodríguez, Centro de Investigación y Promoción Científico-Cultural, Instituto Superior del Profesorado Antonio Ruiz de Montoya (Posadas, Argentina), 1971.

Cartas desde la selva, Gente Nueva (Havana, Cuba), 1971.

Cartas de un cazador, Arca, 1986.

OMNIBUS VOLUMES

Cuentos (stories), C. García y cía, 1937.

Horacio Quiroga: Sus mejores cuentos (stories), edited with introduction and notes by John A. Crow, Cultura (Mexico), 1943, reprinted with prologue by Mario Rodríguez Fernández, Nascimento (Santiago), 1971.

Cuentos escogidos (stories; contains "Nuestro primer cigarro," "La insolación," "El alambre de púa," "Yaguai," "Anaconda," "Los fabricantes de carbón," "En la noche," "Los pescadores de vigas," "La voluntad," "El simún," "A la deriva," "El hombre muerto," "El yaciyateré," and "Tacuara-Mansión"), prologue by Guillermo de Torre, [Madrid], 1950.

"El regreso de Anaconda," y otros cuentos (stories; title means " 'The Return of Anaconda,' and Other Stories"), Universitaria de Buenos Aires, 1960.

Anaconda. El salvaje. Pasado amor, Sur (Buenos Aires), 1960.

Cuentos (stories; contains "El potro salvaje," "Juan Darién," "El regreso de Anaconda," "El desierto," "Los desterrados," "El hombre muerto," "Los destiladores de naranja," "Las moscas," "El hijo," "El conductor del rápido," "El almohadón de plumas," "Los inmigrantes," and "Una bofetada"), edited with introduction by Ezequiel Martínez Estrada, Casa de las Américas (Havana), 1964.

Selección de cuentos (stories), two volumes, edited by Emir Rodríguez Monegal, [Montevideo], 1966.

Obras inéditas y desconocidas, edited by Angel Rama, Arca, 1967—.

De la vida de nuestros animales (stories), prologue by Mercedes Ramírez de Rossiello, notes by Jorge Ruffinelli, Arca, 1967.

Novelas cortas, two volumes, Arca, 1967.

"A la deriva" y otros cuentos (stories; title means " 'Drifting' and Other Stories"), Centro Editor de América Latina (Montevideo), 1968.

Cuentos, 1905-1935 (stories), prologue by Rama, notes by Ruffinelli, Arca, 1968.

Los cuentos de mis hijos (stories), Arca, 1970.

El desafío de las Misiones (stories; contains "A la deriva," "Anaconda," and "Los desterrados"), introduction by Angel L. Grenes, Casa del Estudiante (Montevideo), 1977.

Novelas completas (contains "Historia de un amor turbio," "Las fieras cómplices," "El mono que asesinó," "El hombre artificial," "El devorador de hombres," "El remate del imperio romano," "Una cacería humana en Africa," and "Pasado amor"), Ediciones del Atlántico (Montevideo), 1979.

Cuentos completas (stories), two volumes, Ediciones la Plaza, 1979.

Más cuentos (stories), introduction by Arturo Souto Alabarce, Porrúa, 1980.

"El síncope blanco" y otros cuentos de horror (horror stories), Valdemar Ediciones (Madrid), 1987.

OTHER

Work represented in anthologies, including *A World of Great Stories,* edited by Hiram Haydn and John Cournos, Crown, 1947; *Classic Tales From Spanish America,* edited and translated by William E. Colford, Barron's, 1962; and *Spanish American Literature Since 1888 in Translation,* edited by Willis Knapp Jones, Ungar, 1963. Contributor to Salto periodicals under pseudonym Guillermo Eynhardt, 1897-98. Founder and editor of journal *Revista del Salto,* 1899.

SIDELIGHTS: Known for his preoccupation with the themes of madness and death and his vivid depictions of the jungle, Horacio Quiroga won acclaim as one of the greatest short story writers of Latin America. His fiction was considered closely linked to the violence and tragedy that punctuated his life. Several of his relatives and friends died in accidents—one at Quiroga's hands—or committed suicide; Quiroga himself experienced recurring bouts of illness, which led to his own suicide at the age of fifty-eight, and both his marriages failed. The personal element deemed strongest in his work, however, was his jungle experience. Born in Uruguay, Quiroga spent much of his life in Argentina's wild Misiones region, which became the foundation of some of his best-known writings. Observed Jefferson Rea Spell in *Contemporary Spanish-American Fiction,* "It is [Quiroga's] ability to transfer to his pages the atmosphere of Misiones, the scene of so many of his joys and sorrows, that catches the attention of his readers and gives him distinction as a writer." Critics such as Jean Franco, writing in *An Introduction to Spanish-American Literature,* recognized Quiroga's contribution to "the art of the short story" also. Assessed Franco, "He can certainly be counted one of the Latin-American masters of the genre."

Quiroga began his writing career as part of the *modernista* school of Spanish-American literature at the turn of the century. The movement was characterized by its rejection of naturalism in favor of innovative language, meter, and rhyme. Quiroga's involvement included founding a short-lived modernist journal, *Revista del Salto,* writing a volume of modernist stories and verse, *Los arrecifes de coral,* and founding the school's first Uruguayan group, El Consistorio de Gay Saber. He had become interested in modernism through acquaintance with Argentine poet Leopoldo Lugones, and it was through Lugones that Quiroga ultimately found his own literary niche—Lugones headed the historical commission with which Quiroga first visited Misiones to study Jesuit ruins in 1903.

With his second book, the 1904 collection *El crimen del otro,* Quiroga began to move away from modernism. He adopted a more realistic, detail-oriented prose and revealed his lifelong fascination with madness, horror, and death—macabre concerns that suggested a literary kinship with Gothic writer Edgar Allan Poe. In addition to modernistic tales such as "La princesa bizantina," the volume contains stories powerfully influenced by Poe. For instance, Poe's "Cask of Amontillado" provides the framework for the title story: Quiroga's mentally unbalanced charac-

ters discuss the classic tale and eventually enact its climactic scene, one character interring the other alive. Reflected Ernesto Montenegro in the *New York Times Book Review,* Quiroga "seems to hold a strong predilection for those states of mind not yet out of the twilight of reason or already drifting beyond the world of consciousness. . . . Still, his stories are seldom gruesome and never lugubrious. Almost always a sardonic humor plays a light accompaniment to his more fearsome imaginings." Like Poe, Quiroga earned a reputation as a craftsman of the short story, creating vivid images and skillfully evoking atmosphere with a few carefully chosen words. Remarked John Eugene Englekirk in his book *Edgar Allan Poe in Hispanic Literature:* "No other Hispanic prose writer has so vividly expressed the spirit of Poe's tales as has Horacio Quiroga. . . . [He] has fortified himself with Poe's magic art of availing himself of every possible means for creating the effect desired. . . . That is why Quiroga, like Poe, can hold his reader's interest in tales that under another's pen would fail utterly."

Quiroga earned his first widespread popularity with *Cuentos de amor, de locura y de muerte,* published in 1917, which was also his first book to feature Misiones. Noted Spell, "The stories [Quiroga] wrote in Misiones . . . brought him a very enviable reputation as a *cuentista,*" or storyteller. *Cuentos de amor* contains "fifteen of the most representative," including stories closely identified with events from Quiroga's life, dark stories demonstrating the continued influence of Poe, and the first jungle stories, in which Quiroga's depiction of the conflict between man and nature is considered central. Poisonous and nonpoisonous snakes, rabid dogs, tropical rain and heat, and the Paraná River are among the jungle elements on which the plots hinge. In the setting of Misiones, Franco suggested, "an accident or a moment of carelessness can change a normal working day into a fierce struggle for life. It was this that fascinated Quiroga." In the jungle, Englekirk asserted, Quiroga "uncovered untold treasures with which to bring into original and masterful display those characteristics that had, up to this time, been employed on imaginary themes of a decidedly Poesque trend."

Two of the stories without a specific Misiones slant also impressed critics: "El solitario" ("The Solitaire") and "La gallina degollada" ("The Decapitated Chicken"). According to Spell, they "come as near meeting the requirements of an artistic short story as anything that Quiroga wrote." The first describes a jeweler who suffers with a vain and unfaithful wife, until he kills her with a scarf pin she had coveted; the second, "the most tragic story that Quiroga wrote," relates how several mentally deficient children, after seeing a cook behead a chicken, kill their sister. Wrote Spell, "Both are told in a very direct and straightforward manner; each creates a very definite mood; the plots, though simple, are well constructed . . . and the characters . . . are well delineated." With such stories, judged Englekirk, Quiroga "emerged, at last, as a master of the short story and as a truly original writer."

Quiroga frequently featured animal protagonists in his fiction, notably in the jungle fables of *Cuentos de la selva* and *Anaconda,* which were aimed at children and adults, respectively. Stories such as "Anaconda," in which a group of snakes, disagreeing among themselves, try to prevent scientists from making an antivenin that will render their sole weapon useless, dramatize "the struggle . . . between the undisciplined, bold forces of savagery and the snares of civilization," assessed Montenegro. Spell deemed "Anaconda" Quiroga's masterpiece. "In nothing else that he has written can there be found such a large number of excellent qualities," the critic maintained, lauding the "intensely individual" setting, precise characterization, simple and effective style, and sympathy Quiroga evokes in the reader. Celebrated as among Quiroga's best writing, the collections prompted favorable comparisons to the works of British writer Rudyard Kipling. Montenegro, for example, likened Quiroga's social satire to Kipling's while commending Quiroga's "superior learning in natural history and more direct contact with his subject." *Cuentos de la selva* was Quiroga's first book to be translated into English, appearing as *South American Jungle Tales* in 1922.

In his 1926 collection, *Los desterrados: Tipos de ambiente,* Quiroga depicted the "exiles" of the jungle—frontiersmen, drunkards, laborers, and eccentrics who made the wilderness their home. Notable is "El hombre muerto" ("The Dead Man"), judged one of Quiroga's best stories and singled out by George D. Schade, in his introduction to *The Decapitated Chicken, and Other Stories,* for its tight structure, precise diction, and skillful use of "suggestion and implication, rather than outright telling." The story focuses on the thoughts of a farmer dying because he accidentally wounded himself with a machete; unable to accept his fate, he continues to make plans for his farm until, ultimately, his self-awareness is vanquished by death. According to Schade, "El hombre muerto" exemplifies Quiroga's "magnificent treatment of death"—it is told in a "natural and matter-of-fact" manner and achieves "a high degree of emotional intensity." Other stories in the collection feature the widow of a drunken judge who had a photograph made of her husband's corpse, the boa constrictor from the earlier "Anaconda," and a delirious, drunken father who mistakes his daughter for a rat and kills her.

Published in 1934, Quiroga's final story collection was the somber and, to some reviewers, even morbid *Más allá.* One story, reminiscent of "El hombre muerte," describes a man who awaits death after falling and breaking his back; another shows a father who, though hallucinating, has an accurate precognition of his son's death. In the title story, two lovers commit suicide and are reunited after death, only to be separated without knowing what awaits them. Other tales describe a train engineer going insane; a man who, obsessed by a deceased actress, commits suicide to be with her; and a woman in an insane asylum. In Spell's opinion, the book was strongly shaped by "the troubles that marred the last years of [Quiroga's] life—domestic dissensions, financial difficulties, and ill health." The critic felt that Quiroga's preoccupation with death and suicide and his return to the theme of insanity seemed "not only to indicate an unhealthy state of mind but to presage his own tragic end."

Critics have expressed a range of opinions regarding Quiroga's literary talent. Although some criticized his work for being undisciplined and uneven in quality, many agreed with William Peden, who stated in *Review,* "At their best, Quiroga's stories succeed as entertainment, as art, as commentary on the human situation." Spell, who found the total impact of Quiroga's work "slight," nonetheless acknowledged that the handful of outstanding stories was "enough to entitle him to international fame." Praise for Quiroga's technical skills came from various sources, including Schade, who found Quiroga "a master craftsman," and Franco, who acknowledged him as a significant regional writer and short story master. And if Quiroga's writing seemed narrowly focused on the bizarre and macabre, it also proved memorable. Commented Peden: "Quiroga's stories pass what to me is perhaps the ultimate test of a work of fiction, that of memorableness. Quiroga is a master of the stunning effect, the vivid detail, the unforgettable scene that linger painfully in the reader's consciousness, as real as remembrances of past injustices or unhealed wounds."

BIOGRAPHICAL/CRITICAL SOURCES:

BOOKS

Englekirk, John Eugene, *Edgar Allan Poe in Hispanic Literature,* Instituto de las Españas, 1934.
Franco, Jean, *An Introduction to Spanish-American Literature,* Cambridge University Press, 1969.
Peden, Margaret Sayers, editor, *The Latin American Short Story: A Critical History,* Twayne, 1983.
Quiroga, Horacio, *"The Decapitated Chicken," and Other Stories,* University of Texas Press, 1976.
Rodés de Clérico, María E. and Ramón Bordoli Dolci, *Horacio Quiroga: Antología, estudio crítico y notas,* Arca, 1977.
Spell, Jefferson Rea, *Contemporary Spanish-American Fiction,* University of North Carolina Press, 1944.
Twentieth-Century Literary Criticism, Volume 20, Gale, 1986.

PERIODICALS

Hispania, September, 1972.
New York Times Book Review, October 25, 1925.
Review, winter, 1976.

—*Sketch by Polly A. Vedder*

R

RABASSA, Gregory 1922-

PERSONAL: Born March 9, 1922, in Yonkers, N.Y.; son of Miguel and Clara (Macfarland) Rabassa; married Roney Edelstein, July 14, 1956 (marriage ended, 1966); married Clementine C. Christos (a teacher and critic), May 29, 1966; children: Catherine, Clara. *Education:* Dartmouth College, A.B., 1945; Columbia University, M.A., 1947, Ph.D., 1954. *Politics:* Democrat. *Religion:* None.

ADDRESSES: Home—136 East 76th St., New York, N.Y. 10021. *Office*—Department of Romance Languages, Queens College of the City University of New York, 65-30 Kissena Blvd., Flushing, N.Y., 11367.

CAREER: Columbia University, New York City, assistant professor, 1948-64, associate professor of Spanish and Portuguese, 1964-68; City University of New York, Queens College, Flushing, N.Y., and Graduate School and University Center, New York City, professor, 1968-85, distinguished professor of Romance languages and comparative literature, 1985—. Democratic committeeman, New York County, 1956-60. *Military service:* U.S. Army, Office of Strategic Services, 1942-45; became staff sergeant; received Croce al Merito di Guerra (Italy), and special citation from Allied Forces Headquarters, both 1945.

MEMBER: Modern Language Association of America, PEN American Center (member of executive board, 1972-77), American Association of Teachers of Spanish and Portuguese, American Association of University Professors, Latin American Studies Association, American Literature Translators Association, Hispanic Society of America, Renaissance Society of America, Modern Language Association, Congreso Internacional de Literatura Iberoamérica, Phi Beta Kappa.

AWARDS, HONORS: Fulbright-Hays fellow, Brazil, 1965-66; National Book Award for translation, 1967, for *Hopscotch;* National Book Award nominations for translations, 1971, for *One Hundred Years of Solitude,* and 1977, for *The Autumn of the Patriarch;* American PEN translation prize, 1977, for *The Autumn of the Patriarch;* National Endowment for the Humanities grant, 1980; Alexander Gode Medal, American Translators Association, 1980; Gulbenkian Award, 1981, for translation of *Avalovara;* PEN Medal for Translation, 1982; Litt.D., Dartmouth College, 1982; Professional Staff Congress/City University of New York grant, 1983; New York Governor's Arts Award, 1985; Guggenheim fellow, 1988-89; Wheatland Prize for Translation, 1988; Decorated Order of San Carlos (Colombia).

WRITINGS:

O Negro na ficcao brasileira (title means "The Negro in Brazilian Fiction"), Tempo Brasileiro, 1965.
(Author of introduction) *The World of Translation,* PEN American Center, 1987.

TRANSLATOR

Julio Cortázar, *Hopscotch,* Pantheon, 1966.
Clarice Lispector, *The Apple in the Dark,* Knopf, 1967, University of Texas Press, 1986.
Miguel Asturias, *Mulata,* Delacorte, 1967 (published in England as *The Mulatta and Mr. Fly,* P. Owen, 1967).
Mario Vargas Llosa, *The Green House,* Harper, 1969.
Juan Goytisolo, *Marks of Identity,* Grove, 1969.
Afranio Coutinho, *An Introduction to Literature in Brazil,* Columbia University Press, 1969.
Asturias, *Strong Wind,* Delacorte, 1969.
Manuel Mujica-Lainez, *Bomarzo,* Simon & Schuster, 1969.
Gabriel García Márquez, *One Hundred Years of Solitude,* Harper, 1970.
Asturias, *The Green Pope,* Delacorte, 1969.
García Márquez, *Leaf Storm and Other Stories,* Harper, 1972.
Cortázar, *Sixty-Two: A Model Kit,* Pantheon, 1973.
Dalton Trevisan, *The Vampire of Curitiba,* Knopf, 1973.
Asturias, *The Eyes of the Interred,* Delacorte, 1973.
José Lezama Lima, *Paradiso,* Farrar, Straus, 1974.
Vargas Llosa, *Conversations in the Cathedral,* Harper, 1975.
García Márquez, *The Autumn of the Patriarch,* Harper, 1976.
García Márquez, *Innocent Erendira and Other Stories,* Harper, 1978.
Cortázar, *A Manual for Manuel,* Pantheon, 1978.
Demetrio Aguilera-Malta, *Seven Serpents and Seven Moons,* University of Texas Press, 1979.
García Márquez, *In Evil Hour,* Harper, 1979.
Osman Lins, *Alvalovara,* Knopf, 1980.
Cortázar, *A Change of Light and Other Stories,* Knopf, 1980.
Luis Rafael Sanchez, *Macho Camacho's Beat,* Pantheon, 1981.
Vinicus de Moraes, *The Girl from Ipanema,* Cross-Cultural Communications, 1982.
Juan Benet, *A Meditation,* Persea Books, 1983.

Cortázar, *We Love Glenda So Much and Other Tales,* Knopf, 1983.

García Márquez, *Chronicle of a Death Foretold,* Knopf, 1983.

Luisa Valenzuela, *The Lizard's Tail,* Farrar, Straus, 1983.

Jorge Amado, *Sea of Death,* Avon, 1984.

Cortázar, *A Certain Lucas,* Knopf, 1984.

(With B. J. Bernstein) García Márquez, *Collected Stories,* Harper, 1984.

Benet, *Return to Región,* Columbia University Press, 1985.

Oswald Franca, Jr., *The Man in the Monkey Suit,* Ballantine, 1986.

Amado, *Captains of the Sand,* Ballantine, 1988.

Amado, *Showdown,* Bantam, 1988.

Contributor of translations, articles, and reviews to *Playboy, Esquire, Nation, New York Times Book Review, New Yorker, Atlantic, Saturday Review,* and other periodicals, and to professional journals. Associate editor, *Odyssey Review,* 1961-63. Latin American editor, *Kenyon Review,* 1978—.

WORK IN PROGRESS: An anthology of Antonio Vieira; a book on the craft of translation for Yale University Press; a tanslation of Volodia Teitelboim's *Internal War.*

SIDELIGHTS: Translator of over thirty works, Gregory Rabassa is "a one-man conveyor belt" bringing Latin American fiction to the English-speaking world, according to Patrick Breslin in the *Washington Post Book World.* A professor of Romance languages with the City University of New York, Rabassa never had the intention of becoming a professional translator. In the early 1960s, however, Rabassa began translating short fiction as part of his work with *Odyssey Review,* a literary quarterly. Shortly after the magazine folded, Rabassa was contacted about writing an English version of Julio Cortázar's *Hopscotch.* "An editor called me up and we had lunch," Rabassa recalled to Edwin McDowell in *Americas.* "I looked through the novel, liked it and gave her a couple of sample chapters. . . . She chose me, and I went to work on it immediately in my spare time. It took about a year working in spurts, and I've been translating ever since."

Cortázar so approved of Rabassa's manuscript that he recommended the translator to Gabriel García Márquez, a Colombian writer. Rabassa's rendition of *One Hundred Years of Solitude,* published in 1970, gained widespread attention in the U.S. for both García Márquez's work and that of other Latin American writers. The work also gained attention for Rabassa when García Márquez, the 1982 Nobel laureate, remarked that he preferred the translation to his own work; "Rabassa's *One Hundred Years of Solitude* improved the original," the author remarked to *Time* contributor R. Z. Sheppard. Rabassa comments, however, that the work lent itself to translation because of its quality: "A very good book in its own language goes over more easily into another language than a book that's not so good," he told Jason Weiss in the *Los Angeles Times.* "Part of the quality of the well-written book is that it's easy to translate."

Rabassa takes a reader's approach to his writing, almost always choosing to work with manuscripts that interest him. His translating methods also reflect this interest; in working with *Hopscotch,* "I read it as I translated it," Rabassa remarked to McDowell. "I do that with many books because it's more fun that way, and because translation should be the closest possible reading of the book." Although he commented to Weiss that translation is "lazy man's writing," he sees it as creative work in its own right. "One of the great advantages of translation," he told McDowell, "is that your plots and characters are already written, all you have to do is breathe life into them."

BIOGRAPHICAL/CRITICAL SOURCES:

BOOKS

Contemporary Authors Autobiography Series, Volume 9, Gale, 1989.

PERIODICALS

Américas, July-August, 1986.

Hispania, March, 1967.

Los Angeles Times, August 12, 1982.

New York Times, March 25, 1983.

Time, March 7, 1983, July 11, 1988.

Washington Post Book World, December 19, 1984.

World Literature Today, winter, 1976.

* * *

RAMIREZ, Susan E(lizabeth) 1946-

PERSONAL: Born October 11, 1946, in Ohio; daughter of Eduardo (in sales) and Helen (an account manager; maiden name, McCartney) Ramirez; married Douglas Earl Horton, 1966 (divorced, 1974). *Education:* University of Illinois at Urbana-Champaign, B.A. (with high honors), 1968; attended Cornell University, 1967-70, and Centro Intercultural de Documentación, Cuernavaca, Mexico, 1968; University of Wisconsin—Madison, M.A., 1973, Ph.D., 1977; University of Pennsylvania, certificate in business administration, 1982.

ADDRESSES: Home—2243 North Bissell, Chicago, Ill. 60614. *Office*—Department of History, DePaul University, 804 West Belden, Chicago, Ill. 60614.

CAREER: Ohio University, Athens, assistant professor of history, 1977-82, associate director of Latin American Studies Program, 1979-80; DePaul University, Chicago, Ill., assistant professor, 1982-84, associate professor, 1984-89, professor of history, 1989—. Research fellow at Field Museum of Natural History, 1982-86; consultant to Royal Ontario Museum and Princeton University's Projecto Arqueologico Batan Grande-La Leche.

MEMBER: American Historical Association, Latin American Studies Association, Conference on Latin American History (member of board of directors), Illinois Congress on Latin America (president).

AWARDS, HONORS: Fellow of Social Science Research Council in Spain and Peru, 1974-76; grants from Rockefeller Foundation and National Endowment for the Humanities, 1977, and Sigma Xi, 1978; Fulbright fellow in Peru, 1978-79; grants from National Endowment for the Humanities, 1984, 1986, and 1987; grants from DePaul University for Spain, 1986, and Peru, 1987; fellow of Ford Foundation and National Research Council, 1987-88; Outstanding Academic Book Award from *Choice,* 1987, for *Provincial Patriarchs: Land Tenure and the Economics of Power in Colonial Peru.*

WRITINGS:

Provincial Patriarchs: Land Tenure and the Economics of Power in Colonial Peru, University of New Mexico Press, 1986.

(Editor and author of introduction) *Indian-Religious Relations in Colonial Spanish America,* Syracuse University Press, 1989.

Contributor to books, including *Nicaragua in Revolution,* edited by Thomas W. Walker, Praeger, 1982; *Andean Ecology and Civilization,* edited by Shozo Mazuda, Izumi Shimada, and Craig

Morris, University of Tokyo Press, 1985; *Andean Archaeology,* edited by Ramiro Matos, Solveig Turpin, and Herbert Eling, Jr., Institute of Archaeology, University of California, Los Angeles, 1986; *Cities and Society in Colonial Latin America,* edited by Susan M. Socolow and Louisa Hoberman, University of New Mexico Press, 1986; *Common Studies: A World History Text,* edited by J. Krokar, two volumes, Ginn, 1987; and *Sican Metallurgy: Cultural and Technological Dimensions of Ancient Andean Metallurgy,* edited by Izumi Shimada, Cambridge University Press, 1989.

Contributor of articles and reviews to scholarly journals.

WORK IN PROGRESS: The World Upside Down: Cross Cultural Contact and Conflict in Peru; research on Peru in the 1780s.

* * *

RAMIREZ de ARELLANO, Diana (T. Clotilde) 1919-

PERSONAL: Born June 3, 1919, in New York, N.Y.; daughter of Enrique Ramírez Brau (a writer and journalist) and Maria Teresa (Rechani) Ramírez de Arellano. *Education:* University of Puerto Rico, B.A., 1941; Columbia University, M.A., 1946; University of Madrid, Ph.D., 1952, licenciada en filosofía y letras, 1959, doctora en filosofía y letras, 1962. *Religion:* Roman Catholic.

ADDRESSES: Home—23 Harbour Circle, Centerport, Long Island, N.Y. 11721; and, de la Marina Española, 22 Benidorm Ave., Alicante, Spain. *Office*—Department of Romance Languages, City College of the City University of New York, 138th St. and Convent Ave., New York, N.Y. 10031.

CAREER: University of North Carolina, Greensboro, instructor in Spanish, 1946-48; Douglass College, Rutgers University, New Brunswick, N.J., instructor, 1948-52, assistant professor of Romance languages, 1953-58; City College of the City University of New York, New York City, assistant professor, 1958-68, associate professor, 1968-71, professor of Romance languages, 1971-84, professor emeritus, 1984— . Lecturer at colleges and organizations in Spain, Puerto Rico, and the United States. Consultant to Ford Foundation, Canadian Council of the Arts.

MEMBER: International PEN, American Association of Teachers of Spanish and Portuguese, American Association of University Professors, Modern Language Association of America, Hispanic Society of America, Puerto Rican Writers' Association, Society of Puerto Rican Authors (San Juan), Ateneo Puertorriqueño de Nueva York (honorary president), Academy of Doctors of Madrid.

AWARDS, HONORS: Poet laureate of Puerto Rico, 1958; first prize in literature from University of Puerto Rico Institute of Puerto Rican Literature, citation from Club Civico de Damas (San Juan), and diploma de honor from Ateneo Puertorriqueño de San Juan, all in 1958, all for *Angeles de ceniza;* award for literary criticism from University of Puerto Rico, and honorary diploma from Ateneo Puertorriqueño de San Juan, both 1961, both for *Poesía contemporánea en lengua española;* poetry prize, Ministry of Bolivia, 1961; citation from Puerto Rican Writers Society of New York, 1963, for contribution to Puerto Rican literature and to the Spanish community of New York; Silver Medal for literature from Republic of Bolivia, 1963; Gold Medal for poetry from Institute of Ecuadorian Culture (New York), 1966; Gold Trophy from Riveroeste Club of Ecuador, 1966; Order of Merit, Ecuador, 1967; literature prize from Instituto de

Puerto Rico en Nueva York, 1969; Laurel Clara Lair, APE Poets and Writers Association, 1985; poetry prize Lola Rodriguez de Tió, 1985; Rev Al Marger Agosto, 1985; Medal Dr. Gregorio Marañón, 1985; certificate of honor, Soc. Autores Puerto Rico; Medal Beaux Arts, Institute of Puerto Rican Culture.

WRITINGS:

Yo soy Ariel (poetry; title means "I Am Ariel"), Casa Unida de Publicaciones (Mexico), 1947.

Los Ramírez de Arellano de Lope de Vega (title means "Lope de Vega's Comedy, *The Ramírez de Arellano*"), Consejo Superior de Investigaciones Cientificas (Madrid), 1954.

Albatros sobre el alma (poetry; title means "Albatross Over the Soul"), Colección de Poesía para Bibliofilos (Madrid), 1955.

Angeles de ceniza (poetry; title means "Angels of Ashes"), Colección de Poesía para Bibliofilos, 1958.

Un vuelo casi humano (poetry; title means "An Almost Human Flight"), Colección de Poesía para Bibliofilos, 1960.

Caminos de la creación poética en Pedro Salinas (title means "Roads to Pedro Salinas' Poetic Creation"), Biblioteca Aristarco de Erudición y Crítica, 1961.

Poesía contemporánea en lengua española (title means "Contemporary Poetry in the Spanish Language"), Biblioteca Aristarco de Erudición y Crítica, 1961.

La cultura en el panorama puertorriqueño de Nueva York, El Ateneo, 1964.

Privilegio (poetry; title means "Privilege"), Colección Ateneo de Poetas Hispánicos (New York), 1965.

Del señalado oficio de la muerte (title means "Of the Assigned Task of Death"), Ateneo Puertorriqueño de Nueva York, 1974.

El himno deseado (title means "The Desired Hymn"), Editorial Romo (Madrid), 1979.

(Contributor) Josefina Romo Arregui, *Poetas románticos desconocidos: Concepción de Estevarena, 1854-1876,* Librería Internacional de Romo, 1979.

Arbol en vísperas (title means "Tree in Vespers"), Torremozas, 1987.

AUTHOR OF INTRODUCTION

Vicente Geigel Polanco, *Canto de la tierra adentro,* Ateneo Puertorriqueño de Nueva York, 1965.

Moises Ledesma, *Ensayos y fábulas,* Ateneo Puertorriqueño de Nueva York, 1966.

Isabel Hernandez de Norman, *La novela romántica en las Antillas,* Ateneo Puertorriqueño de Nueva York, 1969.

Jaime Montesinos, *Viaje al punto de partida,* [Ecuador], 1969.

Taller de poesía diacunista (anthology), Academia de la Lengua en Nueva York, 1973.

OTHER

Also author of *Josefina Romo-Arregui: Homenaje,* 1988. Poetry is represented in anthologies, including *Aguinaldo lírico de la poesía,* edited by Hernandez Aquino, Instituto de Cultura Puertorriquena, 1967. Contributor of articles, poetry, and reviews to Spanish-language journals in Spain, Mexico, Puerto Rico, and the United States.

WORK IN PROGRESS: A book of poems, critical edition and catalogue of Lope de Vega's genealogical comedies; a book of criticism.

BIOGRAPHICAL/CRITICAL SOURCES:

BOOKS

Arce, Margot, *Poesía de Puerto Rico,* Troutman Press, 1969.

López, Julio César, *Pasión de poesía,* Ediciones Rumbos (Barcelona), 1968.

Rosa-Nievos, Cesareo, *Biografías puertorriqueñas,* [Puerto Rico], 1970.

Revilla, Andres, *Estudios segovianos,* Consejo Superior de Investigaciones Científicas, 1962.

Rivera-Alvarez, Josefina, *Historia de la literatura puertorriqueña,* Volume 3, University of Puerto Rico, 1971.

PERIODICALS

Bulletin of Hispanic Studies (Liverpool University), Volume 35, number 2, 1958.

El Mundo (San Juan), October 28, 1954, October 22, 1955, January 23, 1957, May 21, 1959.

Modern Language Notes, February, 1959.

Ya (Madrid), December 5, 1954, March 20, 1955, September 7, 1956.

*   *   *

RAMIREZ de ARELLANO, Rafael W(illiam) 1884-

PERSONAL: Born 1884 in Puerto Rico.

ADDRESSES: Office—c/o AMS Press, 56 E. 13th St., New York, N.Y. 10003.

CAREER: Historian and educator. Teacher and superintendent of schools, 1900-1912. University of Puerto Rico, Mayagüez campus, professor, and School of Humanites at Río Pedras, professor of Puerto Rican history, for thirty years, professor emeritus, 1950—. Founder, University of Puerto Rico Historical Museum. Chairman of Spanish Department, University of Georgia. Chief of Protocol for the City of San Juan, Puerto Rico, 1962.

WRITINGS:

Junta para amplicación de estudios e investigaciones científicas: Folklore puertorriqueño, Tipografia y Encuadernación de S. Martín (Madrid), 1926, reprint published as *Folklore puertorriqueño,* AMS Press, 1989.

Los huracanes de Puerto Rico, Universidad de Puerto Rico, 1932.

La capital a través de los siglos, [San Juan, Puerto Rico], 1950.

Como vivían nuestros abuelos (history), Instituto de Cultura Puertorriqueña, 1957.

La calle museo, Ediciones Rumbos, 1967.

Editor, *Fuentes históricas sobre Puerto Rico,* 1929.

*   *   *

RAMON, Juan
See JIMENEZ (MANTECON), Juan Ramón

*   *   *

RECHY, John (Francisco) 1934-

PERSONAL: Born in 1934, in El Paso, Tex.; son of Roberto Sixto and Guadalupe (Flores) Rechy. *Education:* Texas Western College (now University of Texas at El Paso), B.A.; attended New School for Social Research.

ADDRESSES: Home—Los Angeles, Calif.; and New York, N.Y. *Office*—c/o Georges Borchardt Inc., 136 East 57th St., New York, N.Y. 10022.

CAREER: Writer. Conducted writing seminars at Occidental College and University of California; presently teaches in the graduate school of the University of Southern California. *Military service:* U.S. Army; served in Germany.

MEMBER: Authors Guild, Authors League of America, PEN, Texas Institute of Letters.

AWARDS, HONORS: Longview Foundation fiction prize, 1961, for short story "The Fabulous Wedding of Miss Destiny"; International Prix Formentor nominee, for *City of Night;* National Endowment for the Arts grant, 1976; *Los Angeles Times* Book Award nomination, 1984, for body of work.

WRITINGS:

City of Night (novel), Grove, 1963.
Numbers (novel), Grove, 1967.
This Day's Death (novel), Grove, 1969.
The Vampires (novel), Grove, 1971.
The Fourth Angel (novel), Viking, 1973.
The Sexual Outlaw: A Documentary (nonfiction), Grove, 1977.
"Momma as She Was—Not as She Became" (play), produced in New York, N.Y., 1978.
Rushes (novel), Grove, 1979.
Bodies and Souls (novel), Carroll & Graf, 1983.
"Tigers Wild" (play), first produced in New York, N.Y., at Playhouse 91, October 21, 1986.
Marilyn's Daughter (novel), Carroll & Graf, 1988.

Also author of a screenplay based on his novel *City of Night* and a play based on *Rushes.*

CONTRIBUTOR

LeRoi Jones, editor, *The Moderns,* Corinth, 1963.
Robert Rubens, editor, *Voices,* M. Joseph, 1963.
Bruce Jay Friedman, editor, *Black Humor,* Bantam, 1965.
Donald M. Allen and Robert Creeley, editors, *New American Story,* Grove, 1965.
Collision Course, Random House, 1968.
Floren Harper, editor, *Scripts,* Houghton, 1973.
W. Burns Taylor, Richard Santelli, and Kathleen McGary, editors, *Passing Through,* Santay Publishers, 1974.
Susan Cahill and Michele F. Couper, editors, *Urban Reader,* Prentice-Hall, 1979.
David Madden and Peggy Bach, editors, *Rediscoveries II,* Carroll & Graf, 1988.

Also contributor to Edmundo García Girón, editor, *Literatura Chicana,* Prentice-Hall, and to Carlota Cardeneste Dwyer, editor, *Chicano Voices,* 1975. Contributor of short stories, articles, and reviews to periodicals, including *Evergreen Review, Nugget, Big Table, Mother Jones, London Magazine, Los Angeles Times Book Review, New York Times Book Review, Saturday Review, Washington Post Book World, Village Voice,* and *Nation;* contributor of translations from Spanish to periodicals.

WORK IN PROGRESS: Three novels, *The Miraculous Day of Amalia Gómez, Our Lady of Babylon,* and "*Autobiography: A Novel.*"

SIDELIGHTS: John Rechy's first book, *City of Night,* was "hailed as the advent of a unique voice by critics and writers as diverse as Larry McMurtry, James Baldwin, Herbert Gold, and Christopher Isherwood," declares Gregg Barrios in *Newsday.* It became a best seller in 1963, a rare accomplishment for a first novel, and it is now regarded as a modern classic and is taught in modern literature courses. However, the book's controversial subject matter—it traced the journey of a sexual adventurer through the night life of urban America—has drawn attention away from what Rechy considers a more important aspect of his work: the structure of the novel and the craftsmanship of Rechy's art, aspects the author continues to emphasize in his more recent fiction.

Rechy draws on many aspects of his Mexican-American heritage, as well as his past, to create his own vision of art. His novels, declare Julio A. Martínez and Francisco A. Lomelí in *Chicano Literature: A Reference Guide,* "reveal the underlying power that Chicano culture can exert even on those Mexican-American writers generally considered outside the mainstream of Chicano literature." One recurring symbol Rechy uses in his novel *Rushes* is drawn from the Catholic faith he practiced in childhood; as the protagonist advances further into despair, his trip reflects the stations of the cross, the route that Jesus took through Jerusalem on his way to Calvary. "Whether Chicano literature is defined as literary work produced about Mexican-Americans or by them," state Martínez and Lomelí, "his works can be included in that category, especially since their plots usually contain some Mexican details and their themes frequently derive, at least in part, from Chicano culture." "Still, beyond these restrictive labels," Rechy told *CA,* "I am and always have been a LITERARY WRITER, a novelist, a creative writer who has experimented with various forms."

Much of Rechy's work concerns finding patterns in life, and reflecting those patterns in his fiction. His first novel, he tells John Farrell in the University of Southern California's faculty newsletter *Transcript,* grew out of his "desperate need to try to give order to the anarchy I had experienced." In later books, such as *Numbers, The Vampires, The Fourth Angel, The Sexual Outlaw,* and *Bodies and Souls,* Rechy has experimented not only with content, but also with the form of storytelling itself. *The Sexual Outlaw,* he told *CA,* is an experiment "with a form I called a 'documentary,' " while *Bodies and Souls* "is, I believe," writes Rechy in his *Contemporary Authors Autobiography Series* entry, "a daring novel in content and form; a grand and lasting artistic achievement."

Bodies and Souls relates the story of three runaways who have come to Los Angeles looking for answers and the realization of their dreams. However, Rechy intersperses their tale with vignettes of Los Angeles residents whose lives are as empty as those of the three young people. "The all-pervading isolation and loneliness that Mr. Rechy dramatized so effectively in his novels about homosexual night life," declares Alan Cheuse in the *New York Times Book Review,* "becomes in this . . . book a commonplace about daily life in California." Rechy tells Jean Ross in *Dictionary of Literary Biography Yearbook: 1982,* "I think of it as an epic novel of Los Angeles today—an 'apocalyptic' novel. In it, through the many lives I depict, I explore what I call 'the perfection of what is called accident'—the seemingly random components that come together perfectly to create what in retrospect we name 'fate.' "

Rechy told *CA* that he considers *Marilyn's Daughter* his "most complex and literary novel, dealing with artifice as art, the power of legend over truth." Richard Hall, writing in the *San Francisco Chronicle,* terms the novel "a marvel of literary engineering," praising its "complex plot . . . which loops and doubles back in time." Normalyn Morgan, who may or may not be Marilyn Monroe's daughter by Robert Kennedy, travels to Los Angeles after her foster mother's suicide to find out if Monroe was, in fact, her mother. Normalyn's journey of discovery leads her through a many-layered maze of deception and ambiguity—some of it laid down by Monroe herself, other parts hidden or forgotten by people whose lives intersected at one time with hers. "In her search for Monroe," explains Hall, "Normalyn comes up against one of the great, overarching symbols of American confusion." "Rechy notes that, whether [the book] succeeds on its own terms or not," states Farrell, "what the novelist intended was a truly innovative approach to narrative and a serious exploration into the origin of legends and their power over truth."

Marilyn's Daughter, says its author in *Newsday,* is "an extravagant literary creation. It deals with how one finally cannot run away from one's self." "Marilyn Monroe was a monument to self-creation, to self-consciousness," Rechy explains to Farrell. "She was artifice as art." Farrell continues: "Art, he insists, signifies only secondarily. Primarily and permanently—in all its potency to move us to exquisite vicarious experience—art *is.*"

For an interview with this author, see *Contemporary Authors New Revisions Series,* Volume 6.

BIOGRAPHICAL/CRITICAL SOURCES:

BOOKS

Contemporary Authors Autobiography Series, Volume 4, Gale, 1986.
Contemporary Literary Criticism, Gale, Volume 1, 1973, Volume 7, 1977, Volume 14, 1980, Volume 18, 1981.
Dictionary of Literary Biography Yearbook: 1982, Gale, 1983.
Gilman, Richard, *The Confusion of Realms,* Random House, 1963, 5th edition, 1969.
Martínez, Julio A., and Francisco A. Lomelí, editors, *Chicano Literature: A Reference Guide,* Greenwood Press, 1985.

PERIODICALS

Chicago Review, 1973.
Library Journal, February 1, 1963.
London Magazine, June, 1968.
Los Angeles Times, September 7, 1988.
Los Angeles Times Book Review, July 17, 1982, January 27, 1985, October 2, 1988.
Nation, January 5, 1974.
Newsday, September 10, 1988.
New York Times Book Review, June 30, 1963, January 14, 1968, April 3, 1977, July 17, 1977, February 17, 1980, July 10, 1983.
New York Times, December 27, 1967.
People, May 22, 1978.
Prairie Schooner, fall, 1971.
San Francisco Chronicle, August 7, 1988.
Saturday Review, June 8, 1963.
Times Literary Supplement, September 11, 1970.
Transcript, November 28, 1988.
Village Voice, August 22, 1977, October 3, 1977, March 3, 1980.
Washington Post Book World, August 12, 1973.

—*Sketch by Kenneth R. Shepherd*

*   *   *

REIN, Mercedes

PERSONAL: Born in Uruguay.

AWARDS, HONORS: Premio de Narrativa "Antonio y María Foglia," 1986, for *Casa vacía.*

WRITINGS:

Zoologismos, Arca, 1967.
Julio Cortázar: El escritor y sus máscaras, Diaco, 1969.
Nicano Parra y la antipoesía, Universidad de la República, Facultad de Humanidades y Ciencias, 1970.

(Editor and author of introduction) Alejo Carpentier, *El acoso,* Biblioteca de Marcha, 1972.
Cortázar y Carpentier, Ediciones de Crises (Buenos Aires), 1974.
Introducción a la poesía de Antonio Machado, Técnica, 1974.
Información general sobre la literatura del siglo veinte, Casa del Estudiante, 1976.
Casa vacía (novel), Arca, 1983.
Bocas de tormenta, Arca, 1987.

* * *

REISSIG, Julio Herrera y
 See HERRERA y REISSIG

* * *

RETAMAR, Roberto Fernández
 See FERNANDEZ RETAMAR, Roberto

* * *

REYES, Alfonso 1889-1959

PERSONAL: Born May 17, 1889, in Monterrey, Nuevo León, Mexico; died December 12 (one source says December 27), 1959, in Mexico City, Mexico; buried in Rotonda de Hombres Ilustres, Mexico; married. *Education:* Earned law degree from University of Mexico, 1913.

CAREER: Writer. Worked as a teacher, 1913; Government of Mexico, second secretary of Mexican legation in Paris, France, 1913, second secretary of Mexican legation in Madrid, 1920-22, chargé d'affairs in Madrid, Spain, 1922-24, minister to France, 1924-27, ambassador to Argentina, 1927-30, ambassador to Brazil, 1930-36, ambassador to Argentina, 1936-37; president of Casa de España (became Colegio de México), beginning c. 1939. Worked in Madrid as translator, secretary of Madrid Ateneo, and member of Centro de Estudios Históricos (research group) in late 1910s.

MEMBER: Academia Mexicana de la Lengua (director, 1957-59).

AWARDS, HONORS: National Prize in Literature (Mexico), 1945.

WRITINGS:

Cuestiones estéticas (essays), P. Ollendorff, 1911.
Cartones de Madrid (essays), Cultura, 1917.
El suicida (essays; title means "The Suicide"), 1917, reprinted as *El suicida: Libro de ensayos,* Tezontle, 1954.
El plano oblicuo (fiction; title means "The Oblique Plane"), Tipográfica "Europa," 1920.
Retratos reales e imaginarios (essays; title means "Real and Imaginary Portraits"), Lectura Selecta, 1920.
El cazador: Ensayos y divagaciones, 1911-1920 (essays), Biblioteca Nueva, 1921.
Simpatías y diferencias (essays; title means "Sympathies and Differences"), five volumes, Talleres Tipográficos del Suc. de E. Teodora, 1921-26.
Ifigenia cruel (verse; title means "Cruel Iphigenia"), 1924, reprinted, Nuevo Mundo, 1961.
Calendario (essays), [Madrid], 1924.
Pausa, [Paris], 1926.
Cuestiones gongorinas (essays), Talleres Espasa-Calpe, 1927.
Horas de Burgos, Officinas Graphicas de Villas Boas and Co., 1932.
A la memoria de Ricardo Güiraldes (verse), [Rio de Janeiro], 1934.

Las vísperas de España (title means "The Eves of Spain"), Sur, 1937.
Capítulos de literatura española (essays), Volume 1, La Casa de España en México, 1939, Volume 2, El Colegio de México, 1945.
La crítica en la edad ateniense (criticism), El Colegio de México, 1941.
Algunos poemas: 1925-1939 (verse), Nueva Vox, 1941.
Pasado inmediato, y otros ensayos (essays), El Colegio de México, 1941.
La antigua retórica (criticism), Fondo de Cultura Económica, 1942.
Ultima tule, Imprenta Universitaria, 1942.
La experiencia literaria (criticism; title means "The Literary Experience"), Editorial Losada, 1942.
El deslinde: Prolegómenos a la teoría literaria (criticism), [Mexico], 1944.
Norte y sur (essays), Editorial Leyenda, 1944.
Romances (y afines) (verse), Editorial Stylo, 1945.
Los trabajos y los días: 1934-1944, Ediciones "Occidente," 1945.
Momentos de España: Memorias políticas, 1920-1923, [Mexico], 1947.
A lápiz: 1923-1946, Editorial Stylo, 1947.
Burlas literarias: 1919-1922, [Mexico], 1947.
Entre libros: 1912-1923, El Colegio de México, 1948.
Letras de la Nueva España (criticism), Fondo de Cultura Económica, 1948.
Grata compaña, Tezontle, 1948.
Homero en Cuernavaca, recreo en varias voces (verse), Bajo el Signo de "Abside," 1949.
Sirtes: 1932-1944, Tezontle, 1949.
Tertulia de Madrid, Espasa-Calpe, 1949.
The Position of America, and Other Essays (includes "Vision of Anáhuac," "Thoughts on the American Mind," "Social Science and Social Responsibility," "Native Poetry of New Spain," "The Tenth Muse of America," and "Virgil in Mexico"), foreword by Federico de Onís, edited and translated by Harriet de Onís, Knopf, 1950.
Ancorajes, Tezontle, 1951.
Trazos de historia literaria, Espasa-Calpe, 1951.
Medallones, Espasa-Calpe, 1951.
Obra poética, Fondo de Cultura Económica, 1952.
Arbol de pólvora, [Mexico], 1953.
Memorias de cocina y bodega, Tezontle, 1953.
Trayectoria de Goethe (criticism), Fondo de Cultura Económica, 1954.
Parentalia, primer capítulo de mis recuerdos, Los Presentes, 1954.
Quince presencias (fiction), Obregón, 1955.
Mallarmé entre nosotros, Tezontle, 1955.
Obras completas (title means "Complete Works"), fifteen volumes, Fondo de Cultura Económica, 1955-63.
Estudios helénicos, Edición de El Colegio Nacional, 1957.
Los sacros lugares de los griegos, [Mexico], 1957.
Resumen de la literatura mexicana, [Mexico], 1957.
Génesis de la crítica, [Mexico], 1958.
Las burlas veras, Tezontle, 1959.
La filosofía helenística, Fondo de Cultura Económica, 1959.
Cartilla moral, Instituto Nacional Indigenista, 1959.
Al yunque, 1944-1958 (essays), Tezontle, 1960.
Albores, segundo libro de recuerdos (nonfiction), El Cerro de la Silla, 1960.
A campo traviesa (essays), El Cerro de la Silla, 1960.

Mexico in a Nutshell, and Other Essays, introduction by Arturo Torres-Rioseco, translated by Charles Ramsdell, University of California Press, 1964.

Antología: Prosa, teatro, poesía, Fondo de Cultura Económica, 1965.

Dante y la ciencia de su época, Instituto Francisco Bauzá, 1965.

Universidad, política y pueblo, edited by José Emilio Pacheco, Universidad Nacional Autónoma de México, 1967.

Anecdotario, Ediciones Era, 1968.

Ensayos, edited by Roberto Fernández Retamar, Casa de las Américas, 1968.

Diario, prologue by Alicia Reyes, Universidad de Guanajuato, 1969.

Cuatro poemas en torno a Monterrey (verse), Ediciones Sierra Madre, 1971.

Prosa y poesía, edited by James Willis Robb, Ediciones Cátedra, 1975.

(With José M. a Chacón and Zenaida Guitiérrez-Vega) *Epistolario Alfonso Reyes, José M. a Chacón, Zenaida Gutiérrez-Vega* (correspondence), Fundación Universitaria Española, 1976.

Antología personal, Martin Casillas Editores, 1983.

La cena y otras historias, Fonda de Cultura Económica, 1984.

(With Antonio Castro Leal) *Recados entre Alfonso Reyes y Antonio Castro Leal* (correspondence), Colegio Nacional, 1987.

Also author of *Visión de Anáhuac* (essays), 1917, *Huellas* (verse), 1922, *El testimonio de Juan Peña* (novel), 1930, *Tren de ondas* (essays), 1932, and *Los tres tesoros* (novel), 1955.

Also editor and translator of various works, including a Spanish-language edition of Homer's *Iliad.* Works represented in various anthologies, including *Anthology of Contemporary Latin American Poetry,* 1942, and *An Anthology of Mexican Poetry,* 1958. Contributor to periodicals, including *Revista de Filología Española.*

SIDELIGHTS: Alfonso Reyes was a distinguished figure in Hispanic literature. In his verse he displayed a wide range of styles and proved equally adept in both expression and description, and in his essays he showed himself a provocative thinker whether writing about literary theory or politics or Hispanic culture. Noting Reyes's extraordinary versatility, Antonio Castro Leal described him in *Books Abroad* as "this superman of letters" and hailed him as the literary equivalent of the Renaissance artists. Likewise impressed was Tomas Navarro, who called particular attention to Reyes's fluid, precise style. "The great Mexican writer," Navarro wrote in *Books Abroad,* "has constantly and steadily perfected the clarity of expression, rich in nuances and reflections, of which he is . . . an acknowledged master."

Reyes began his literary career in 1911 with the essay collection *Cuestiones estéticas,* which he published while he was still a student. After completing this volume, which Castro deemed "beautiful" in his *Books Abroad* piece, Reyes worked briefly as a teacher, then began a diplomatic career that—aside from interruptions caused by the Mexican civil war and World War I—lasted until 1939. He first worked for the Mexican government as an under-secretary in Paris, but when World War I erupted he fled with his family to Madrid, where he eventually found work as a translator, researcher, and secretary.

During this period Reyes continued to write, and in 1917 he produced one of his most important works, the essay *Visión de Anáhuac* (published in English in the collection *The Position of America*). In this volume Reyes presents a poetic account of Mexican history from Aztec times. Among the essay's many champions was Federico de Onís, who described it—in his intro-

duction to *The Position of America*—as "a beautiful example of Reyes's ability to fuse historic reality and poetry as he reconstructs the dawn of modern Mexico." Some critics were particularly impressed with the style in which *Anáhuac* unfolds. Leal, in his *Books Abroad* assessment, declared that the essay "attains perfection in the purity and precision of its lines, in its balanced power of evocation and synthesis." Among the work's other enthusiasts were Bertram D. Wolfe, who wrote in the *New York Herald Tribune Book Review* that it constitutes "a veritable poet's vision," and Walter Bara, who wrote in the periodical *Hispania* that Reyes's account "is not very far removed from poetry itself."

In 1920 Reyes resumed his diplomatic career, and in 1924 he was named head of Mexico's diplomatic corps in Paris. By this time Reyes had published many of his most respected volumes. In addition to *Anáhuac,* he completed such works as *Cartones de Madrid,* a collection of poetically rendered descriptive sketches; *El suicida,* an evocative philosophical inquiry; and *Ifigenia cruel,* a verse epic that Octavio Paz hailed in *The Siren and the Seashell* as "one of the most complete and perfect works in modern Spanish American poetry."

As a poet, Reyes embraced an impressive range of subjects and styles, and his 1922 collection *Huellas* reveals both his versatility and his extraordinary flair for language. In *Spanish-American Literature: A History,* Enrique Anderson-Imbert noted that Reyes's poetry could be topical, Parnassian, Modernist, symbolist, or even prosaic, while his subjects and themes "were as varied as the turns of his own life: autobiographical evocations, the homeland, friends and loves, works, and death." Anderson-Imbert added that Reyes "gives only essences" and averred, "His poetry is concise, sober, insinuating."

Still another literary genre in which Reyes proved a master was criticism. He was especially interested in Spanish literature, and in studies such as *Cuestiones gongorinas, Capítulos de literatura española,* and *El deslinde,* he addressed both practical and theoretical subjects. Arturo Torres-Rioseco, in his introduction to Reyes's *Mexico in a Nutshell,* wrote that *El deslinde* "is considered the masterpiece of Reyes." The critic noted that the work "marks the most ambitious attempt to systematize literary theory," one he defined as both "a philosophic and aesthetic study of literature." For Torres-Rioseco, Reyes was "one of the most logical thinkers of his time" and "the outstanding cultivator of the artistic style in modern Mexican literature."

Although he wrote prolifically throughout the 1920s and 1930s, Reyes continued working as a diplomat until 1939, when he returned to Mexico and became a teacher and administrator at the Casa de España (which became the Colegio de México). In the remaining decades of his life Reyes still produced important writings. In *Letras de la Nueva España* he provided readers with what Walter Bara, in *Hispania,* called "a truly exquisite literary panorama of Mexican literature in its three centuries of colonial times," and in *La experiencia literaria* Reyes afforded readers an ample overview of his own literary concerns. Bara noted that this work, with its impressive array of subjects and themes, "may in many respects be considered Reyes' literary biography."

Although Reyes wrote in many genres, it is probably as an essayist that he is most remembered. In subjects ranging from literary theory to ethics, and from history to sociology and politics, he proved himself a provocative, fluent thinker, one capable of shaping opinion through analysis and self-expression. Notably impressed by Reyes's achievement in the essay form is Anderson-Imbert, who contended in *Spanish-American Literature* that

"Reyes is without any doubt the keenest, most brilliant, versatile, cultured and profound essayist in [Spanish] today."

Reyes is probably best known to English-language readers for the essay collections *The Position of America* and *Mexico in a Nutshell,* both of which deal largely with socio-political issues, though literature is often appraised as well. Critics have noted, however, that his literary achievement—in its entirety—shows a range of knowledge and experience surpassing even the impressive scope of the English volumes. "From Aristotle to Zola," Bara wrote in *Hispania,* "from Chaucer to Chaplin, the literary experience of Reyes is so broad that it defies comparison with the personal culture of any living writer."

BIOGRAPHICAL/CRITICAL SOURCES:

BOOKS

Anderson-Imbert, Enrique, *Spanish-American Literature: A History,* translated by John V. Falconieri, Wayne State University Press, 1963.

Aponte, Barbara Bockus, *Alfonso Reyes and Spain: His Dialogue With Unamuno, Valle-Inclán, Ortega y Gasset, Jiménez, and Gómez de la Serna,* University of Texas Press, 1972.

Bhalla, Alok, *Latin American Writers: A Bibliography With Critical Biographical Introductions,* Envoy Press, 1987.

Paz, Octavio, *The Siren and the Seashell, and Other Essays on Poets and Poetry,* translated by Lysander Kemp and Margaret Sayers Peden, University of Texas Press, 1976.

Peña, Carlos Gonzáles, *History of Mexican Literature,* translated by Gusta Barfield Nance and Florene Johnson Dunstan, revised edition, University Press, 1943.

Reyes, Alfonso, *The Position of America, and Other Essays,* foreword by Federico de Onís, translated by Harriet de Onís, Knopf, 1950.

Robb, James Willis, *Patterns of Image and Structure in the Essays of Alfonso Reyes,* Catholic University of America, 1958.

Stabb, Martin S., *In Quest of Identity: Patterns in the Spanish American Essay of Ideas, 1890-1960,* University of North Carolina Press, 1967.

Twentieth-Century Literary Criticism, Volume 33, Gale, 1989.

PERIODICALS

America, April, 1966.
Books Abroad, spring, 1945.
Hispania, November, 1951, September, 1987.
New York Herald Tribune Book World, December 24, 1950.
New York Times Book Review, October 22, 1950.
Romance Notes, autumn, 1970.
Texas Quarterly, spring, 1959.

—*Sketch by Les Stone*

*   *   *

REYES, Carlos José 1941-

PERSONAL: Born in 1941 in Bogotá, Colombia. *Education:* Attended Club de Teatro Independiente.

CAREER: Playwright and author. Director of theater group at Universidad Externada de Colombia, 1966—.

AWARDS, HONORS: Award from Casa de las Américas, 1975, for children's literature.

WRITINGS:

PLAYS

Soldados (adapted from Alvaro Cepeda Zamudio's novel *La casa grande;* first produced in 1967), Ediciones de Marcha Colombia (Bogota), 1971.

Teatro para niños (for children; contains *La piedra de la felicidad, La fiesta de los muñecos,* and *Dulcita y el burrito* [first produced in 1964]), Instituto Colombiano de Cultura, 1972.

Los viejos baúles empolvados que nuestros padres nos prohibieron abrir (Melodrama y crónica de las desventuras de una familia), Instituto Colombiano de Cultura, 1973.

Globito manual [and] *El hombre que escondió el sol y la luna,* illustrations by Armando Millares and Justo Luis, Casa de las Américas (Havana), 1977.

Also author of the plays *Bandidos,* 1962, *La antesala,* 1965, and *Variaciones sobre la metamorfosis,* 1966, and of plays adapted from works by Franz Kafka, Julio Cortázar, and Gabriel García Márquez.

*   *   *

REYLES, Carlos 1868-1938

PERSONAL: Born in 1868 in Uruguay; died in 1938.

CAREER: Wealthy landowner and writer.

WRITINGS:

El embrujo de Sevilla (novel), first published in 1922, translation by Jacques Le Clercq published as *Castanets,* [New York], 1929, recent edition, Gordon Press, 1977.
Cuentos completos, Arca, 1968.
Diario, Arca, 1970.

Also author of *Por la vida,* 1888; and the novels *Beba,* 1894, *La raza de Caín,* 1900, *El terruño,* 1916, and *El gaucho Florido,* 1932.

SIDELIGHTS: A regional writer influenced by French naturalists such as Emile Zola, Carlos Reyles is best known for his novel *La raza de Caín,* in which he offers a psychological and sociological analysis of characters from the ranches and cities of Uruguay.

BIOGRAPHICAL/CRITICAL SOURCES:

BOOKS

Torres Ríoseco, Arturo, *Grandes novelistas de la América Hispana,* University of California Press, 1947.

PERIODICALS

Hispania, May, 1968.

*   *   *

RIBERA CHEVREMONT, Evaristo 1896-1976

PERSONAL: Born 1896, in San Juan, Puerto Rico; died 1976.

CAREER: Writer. Reporter for *El Imparcial* (news daily), beginning 1918.

WRITINGS:

Color (poetry), Romero (San Juan, Puerto Rico), 1938.
Tonos y formas, Biblioteca de Autores Puertorriqueños, 1943.
La naturaleza en "Color" (criticism), Venezuela (San Juan), 1943.
Barro (poetry), [San Juan], 1945.

Anclas de oro (poetry), [San Juan], 1945.

Tú, mar, y yo y ella (poetry), Universidad de Puerto Rico, 1946.

Verbo (poetry), [San Juan], 1947.

El niño de Arcilla: Novela (novel), Biblioteca de Autores Puertorriqueños (San Juan), 1950.

Creación (poetry), Venezuela, 1951.

Antología poética (1924-1950) y La llama pensativa, sonetos inéditos (1950) (also see below), Ediciones Cultura Hispánica (Madrid), 1954.

La llama pensativa: Los sonetos de Dios, del amor, y de la muerte, [San Juan], 1955.

Antología poética, 1924-1950, Universidad de Puerto Rico, 1957.

Evaristo Ribera Chevremont: Poesías, Instituto de Cultura Puertorriqueña, 1960.

Inefable orilla (poetry), Venezuela, 1961.

Punto final: Poemas del sueño y de la muerte, [San Juan], 1963.

El semblante (poems), Universidad de Puerto Rico, 1964.

Guía al Archivo General de Puerto Rico, Instituto de Cultura Puertorriqueña, 1964.

Principio de canto, [Puerto Rico], 1965.

Nueva antología, Cordillera (San Juan), 1966.

Antología poética, 1929-1965, Editorial del Departamento de Instrucción Pública, Estado Libre Asociado de Puerto Rico, 1967.

Río volcado, Universidad de Puerto Rico, 1968.

Canto de mi tierra, Universidad de Puerto Rico, 1971.

El caos de los sueños, Cordillera, 1974.

El hondero lanzó la piedra, Cordillera, 1975.

El libro de las apologías, Cordillera, 1976.

Obra poética, two volumes, Universidad de Puerto Rico, 1976.

Jinetes de la inmortalidad, Instituto de Cultura Puertorriqueña, 1977.

Elegías de San Juan, Instituto de Cultura Puertorriqueña, 1980.

Also author of *Desfile romántico*, 1912, *El templo de los alabastros*, 1919, *La copa de Hebe*, 1922, *Los alemendros del paseo de Covadonga*, 1928, *Pajarera*, 1929, *Tierra y sombra*, 1930, and *Memorial de arena*, 1962. Contributor of numerous articles and poems to periodicals, including *El Carnaval, El Mundo, Poliedro*, and *Revista del Instituto de Cultura Puertorriqueña*. Editor of newspaper section, "Páginas de Vanguardia," for *La Democracia*, for ten years.

SIDELIGHTS: Evaristo Ribera Chevremont's return in 1924 to his native Puerto Rico after a five-year stay in Spain was the catalyst for an upheaval in Puerto Rican poetry. The years the young poet had spent in Spain were marked with important developments in Hispanic literature, including the birth of many schools of thought that promoted the departure from traditional modes of artistic expression. Influenced by the ideas he had come into contact with during his stay abroad, Ribera Chevremont rejected the somber and eloquent forms of modernism and founded his own literary movement called *Girandulismo* to promote his beliefs. He also spread his enthusiasm for the new poetic forms through the pages of *La Democracia*, for which he edited a special literary section, and through numerous articles he contributed to other Puerto Rican newspapers and magazines. Eventually, his own poetic experiments were replaced by a return to the more traditional style he once scorned, but he had successfully introduced European post-modernist thought into Puerto Rican poetry.

BIOGRAPHICAL/CRITICAL SOURCES:

BOOKS

Anderson-Imbert, Enrique, *Spanish-American Literature: A History*, Volume 2: *1910-1963*, 2nd edition, Wayne State University Press, 1969.

*   *   *

RIOS, Isabella
  See LOPEZ, Diana

*   *   *

RIVERA, Geraldo (Miguel)   1943-

PERSONAL: First name pronounced Hare-*al*-doe; born July 4 (some sources say July 3), 1943, in New York, N.Y.; son of Cruz Allen (a cab driver and restaurant worker) and Lillian (a waitress; maiden name, Friedman) Rivera; married first wife, Linda (divorced after one year); married Edith Bucket Vonnegut (an artist and fashion designer), December 14, 1971 (divorced); married Sherryl Raymond (a television producer), December 31, 1976 (divorced); married C. C. Dyer (a television producer), 1987; children: (third marriage) Gabriel Miguel. *Education:* Attended New York City Community College of Applied Arts and Sciences and State University of New York Maritime College; University of Arizona, B.S., 1965; Brooklyn Law School, J.D., 1969; graduate study at University of Pennsylvania, 1969, and Graduate School of Journalism, Columbia University, 1970. *Religion:* Jewish.

ADDRESSES: Home—New York, N.Y.; and Cape Cod, Mass. *Office*—Investigative News Group, 311 West 43rd St., New York, N.Y. 10036. *Agent*—William Morris Agency, 1350 Avenue of the Americas, New York, N.Y. 10019.

CAREER: Broadcast journalist. Worked as a salesman and merchant seaman before attending college; Harlem Assertion of Rights and Community Action for Legal Services (anti-poverty neighborhood law firms), New York City, clerk, 1968-70; admitted to the Bar of New York State, 1970; American Broadcasting Co. (ABC), New York City, member of "Eye Witness News" team for WABC-TV, 1970-75, host of late-night program, "Good Night America," 1974-78, contributor to "Good Morning America," 1974-78, special correspondent and producer for "20/20," 1978-85; special correspondent for "Entertainment Tonight," 1985-87; host of syndicated program, "Geraldo," 1987—. Founder and owner of production company, Investigative News Group, 1985—. Host of documentaries and specials aired on network television, including "Willowbrook: The Last Disgrace," "The Littlest Junkie: A Children's Story," "Migrants: Dirt Cheap," "Tell Me Where I Can Go," "Marching Home Again," "Barriers: The View from a Wheelchair," "Working Class Heroes," "Devil Worship: Exposing Satan's Underground," "Whatta Year . . . '86," and "Our Kids and the Best of Everything." Host and executive producer of documentaries and specials aired on network television, including "The Opening of Al Capone's Vault," "American Vice: The Doping of America," "Innocence Lost: The Erosion of American Childhood," "Modern Love," "Sons of Scarface: The New Mafia," and "Murder: Live from Death Row." *Military service:* Served in the U.S. Merchant Marine Corps for two years.

MEMBER: One-to-One (chairman of board).

AWARDS, HONORS: Award from New York State Associated Press Broadcasters Association, 1971, for "Drug Crisis in East

Harlem," and named Broadcaster of the Year, 1971, 1972, and 1974; George Foster Peabody Award for distinguished achievement in broadcast journalism, 1972, for "Willowbrook: The Last Disgrace"; Robert F. Kennedy Journalism awards, 1973 and 1975; two Alfred I. du Pont-Columbia University citations; ten Emmy awards for local and national broadcast journalism from the National Academy of Television Arts and Sciences; three honorary doctorates; and has received more than 150 additional awards for achievement in broadcast journalism.

WRITINGS:

Willowbrook: A Report on How It Is and Why It Doesn't Have to Be That Way (based on his television special of the same title), Random House, 1972.

BOOKS FOR YOUNG PEOPLE

(With second wife, Edith Rivera) *Miguel Robles—So Far,* illustrated by E. Rivera, Harcourt, 1973.
Puerto Rico: Island of Contrasts, illustrated by William Negron, Parents Magazine Press, 1973.
A Special Kind of Courage: Profiles of Young Americans, illustrated by E. Rivera, Simon & Schuster, 1976.

TELEVISION SPECIALS

"The Opening of Al Capone's Vault," broadcast on ABC-TV, 1986.
"American Vice: The Doping of America," broadcast on ABC-TV, 1986.

SIDELIGHTS: Geraldo Rivera has become a phenomenon in modern broadcast journalism. Born the son of working class parents, he is now considered by many to be one of the most controversial television journalists in history. Rivera currently hosts the enormously popular program "Geraldo," the third most popular syndicated talk show produced in the United States. While reviewers such as Jeff Jarvis of *People* have described Rivera as "the Robin Leach of TV news," others such as the New York State Associated Press Broadcasters Association have given him a number of awards, hailing him as "a special kind of individualist in a medium which too often breeds the plastic newsman."

Rivera grew up in the Williamsburg section of Brooklyn, N.Y., the son of a Puerto Rican father and a Jewish mother. Well-aware that ethnic prejudices would adversely affect their children, the family often used the surname, "Riviera." In a *Christian Science Monitor* interview Rivera spoke of his mixed ethnic background in this manner: "If you add them together, I'm actually a one man majority . . . in New York. But, there are two distinctive identities and it was very difficult for me as a kid to handle them both. So, I guess I compromised by being one or the other at various times in my life."

His ethnicity was especially difficult for Rivera to deal with during his years as an undergraduate at the University of Arizona. As he explains in the *New York Sunday News:* "Here I was, this little hood from New York with the Brooklyn Spanish-American accent. I wanted to be like them, to belong. So I said my name was Jerry Rivers and I did everything I could to please them. But they never accepted me."

A less than model student in high school (he was more interested in sports and street gangs), Rivera completed a two-year stint in the U.S. Merchant Marine Corps before attending the New York City Community College of Applied Arts and Sciences and New York Maritime College. He earned a B.S. from University of Ar-izona, and a law degree from Brooklyn Law School. And in 1970, Rivera was admitted to the Bar of New York State.

Poverty law was the focus of Rivera's legal career. He was a law clerk for the Harlem Assertion of Rights and for the Community Action for Legal Services before receiving his J.D. After completing graduate work, Rivera worked as a lawyer for the Legal Service Program of the Office of Economic Opportunity. For a short while he represented a gang of Spanish-speaking youths called the Young Lords, whose energies with Rivera's help were eventually redirected from revolutionary action to such things as organizing day care centers. However, Rivera grew restless with his law career. "I couldn't change the world defending gangs and poverty cases," he explained to a writer for *Esquire.* "Besides, all I ever earned in law was maybe three months' rent."

Around the time Rivera was rethinking his career in law, the Federal Communications Commission (FCC) expressed their intent to increase the number of opportunities for minorities in broadcasting. Despite his lack of journalistic experience, Rivera applied for a job as newscaster with WABC-TV in New York City and was hired. In September of 1970, after three months of intensive study at Columbia University's Graduate School of Journalism, Rivera made his debut on the station's "Eyewitness News" program. As a rookie reporter, Rivera was assigned to report such features as fashion shows, charity functions, parties, and conduct celebrity interviews. One day, while en route to cover a story, he encountered a junkie who was threatening to jump from a rooftop. Rivera tape-recorded a dramatic and emotional plea for help from the junkie's brother—also a drug addict—while the camera crew filmed the entire event. This story was shown on the evening news and Rivera was allowed to enlarge the story into a three-part series entitled "Drug Crisis in East Harlem."

Impressed with his aggressive search for a good story, energetic approach to reporting, and flair for dramatically presenting a news item, the "Eyewitness News" management people assigned Rivera more and more hard news stories to cover. Rivera's popularity grew quickly, especially among younger viewers, and his work was being rewarded with honors such as the New York State Associated Press Broadcasters Association Award.

In a 1971 *New York Times* article, John J. O'Connor attempts to sum up Rivera's appeal: "The secret of Rivera's rapid success? He knows what he is talking about. Unlike many newsmen who have difficulty telling the difference between a drunk and a heroin mainliner, he is knowledgeable about all aspects of the city jungle. He is not an outsider relying on 'official sources' for a story; he sees the story 'at the level that it happens.'. . . He is convinced that the television viewer has become immune to statistics—on drug addicts or welfare rolls or moon shots. The people count, he says, and it is the people who must be shown, be given access, on television."

Although well-known locally, Rivera gained extraordinary national publicity after his story "Willowbrook: A Report on How It Is and Why It Doesn't Have To Be That Way" aired. With the help of an employee recently fired from the Willowbrook State School for the Mentally Retarded on Staten Island, Rivera smuggled a camera crew into the school to film the vile conditions in which the patients lived. During the taping, an emotional Rivera declared: "This is what it looked like, this is what it sounded like. But how can I tell you how it smelled? It smelled of filth, it smelled of disease, and it smelled of death." The airing of the heartrending story catapulted Rivera to celebrity status and earned him additional awards. Scores of television and movie offers poured in.

In 1972, Rivera wrote *Willowbrook: A Report on How It Is and Why It Doesn't Have to Be That Way*, revealing the details behind the making of the news series. The book did not meet with the same enthusiasm as the television documentary. I. S. Land remarks in *Library Journal* that "On the air Rivera was obviously touched, upset, and outraged at what he found. And he was able to move the public to action. . . . The written words are as cold and as empty as the tile floors and unlived lives of the children of Willowbrook."

Due in part to the public reaction, support, and donations that poured in following his television report on Willowbrook, Rivera and actress Geraldine Fitzgerald created "One-to-One," a fundraising project to benefit mentally disabled people. As cochairperson, Rivera volunteered many hours working for the group—organizing festivals, participating in telethons and concerts, and anything else to aid the charity. Today he is chairman of the board of the association. Rivera also initiated a consumer action bureau called "Help 7," which is staffed by Fordham University law students and trained volunteers who answer hundred of calls for assistance daily.

Rivera explains his reasons for donating his time and effort to helping others in an article he wrote for *Esquire:* "I love being a newsman. Given enormous power and responsibility by the network, I have tried to use my position to make the world a slightly better place. Questions of style aside, this is where I differ substantively from conventional news-industry wisdom. Sometimes the reporter has to become involved in helping society change the thing he is complaining about."

Along with his meteoric rise in popularity among television viewers, criticism of Rivera's unorthodox reporting methods also rose significantly. A number of reviewers questioned his objectivity, disapproved of his tendency to sensationalize facts, and wondered if some of the truth might be sacrificed in favor of high drama. Alan Richman writes in *People:* "Almost from his beginning in 1970 as a local news reporter, Rivera has been unable to shake unrelenting criticism that he either exaggerates or distorts the news. Years ago he punched out a colleague who spread rumors that footage of Rivera dodging bullets in the Middle East had been faked."

Answering these critics, Rivera remarked to Richman: "Perhaps some critics are sincerely offended by me. Maybe there is professional jealousy involved. Maybe they are judging me by their own inner cynicism. Maybe there is a racial component."

While some critics have questioned his sincerity on some of the issues that he has reported on, Rivera has frequently stood up against convention and the establishment for his convictions, as in the 1972 president campaign. Disregarding WABC-TV's policy of station reporters being neutral, Rivera very vocally and openly supported Senator George S. McGovern for president that year. Eventually, Rivera took a leave of absence without pay from his reporting duties at the station until after the election. Rivera has also been known to refuse assignments he did not believe in and fight for others that he felt were important and needed coverage.

Despite the criticism of some but with the loyal support of fans, Rivera continued to develop and host a number of intriguing and discussion-provoking documentaries that continued to grab a huge share of the television viewers in its time slot. Huge audiences watched such documentary-styled specials as "The Littlest Junkie: A Children's Story," "Migrants: Dirt Cheap," "Tell Me Where I Can Go," "Marching Home, Again," and other extremely popular investigative reports exploring such social problems as drug addition, exploitation of migrant workers, the plight of Vietnam veterans, and discrimination against the physical handicapped.

In 1973, ABC developed "Good Night, America," a ninety-minute news magazine, and signed Rivera to host the program. The format of the show, designed by the network with a great deal of input from Rivera, consisted of various entertainment segments mixed carefully with controversial news reports into which Rivera injected his own opinions. According to a reviewer for *Time,* on his late-night programs Rivera took "stands in favor of decriminalization of marijuana, granting amnesty for draft evaders, and setting up quasi-legal redlight districts as a solution to the prostitution problems." For four years this program drew in a very large share of the audience in the large cities in which it aired—such as New York and Los Angeles.

From 1978 to 1985, Rivera worked as a special correspondent and producer for ABC's successful program, "20/20." During this time Rivera traveled the world aggressively and relentlessly covering many of the political and social events that have forever shaped our world. After a brief respite during which he concentrated on "20/20" duties, Rivera returned to the documentary/investigative format to produce and host another series of specials, including "The Opening of Al Capone's Vault," "American Vice: The Doping of America," "Innocence Lost: The Erosion of American Childhood," "Modern Love," "Sons of Scarface: The New Mafia," and "Murder: Live from Death Row." As usual, while all of these shows proved extremely popular and well-watched by the general public, they continued to draw criticism from reviewers for their sensationalized and exploitive treatment of the chosen subject matter.

In 1987, Rivera's syndicated, hour-long talk show, "Geraldo" premiered, establishing the host as a true celebrity in his own right and making his first name a household word. Competing against the great talk show hosts, Phil Donahue, Oprah Winfrey, and Sally Jessy Raphael, Rivera's "Geraldo" is carried daily by over 170 stations, representing about 96 percent of the nation. Rivera takes pride in the fact that he continues to apply as much energy, action, preparation, and dedication to presenting the social and political news of the day on his show as he did when he first started in television. "Take the last twelve months," he told a writer for *Playgirl* in September, 1988. "I've been threatened by the mob. . . . I've had an AIDS-infected needle stuck at me by junkies in a shooting gallery. I've put my ass on the line probably a half a dozen times in the last year. And I bet if you went through the core of network newspeople, you wouldn't find that."

One very public example of Rivera's tendency to find himself in the center of volatile situations is the event that took place during the taping of a "Geraldo" show entitled "Teen Hatemongers." A violent brawl broke out between the guests—white supremacists and black activist, Roy Innis. Fists, bodies, and chairs flew across the stage after Innis, provoked by a racial slur, attacked a member of the White Aryan Resistance Youth Group. Members of the audience jumped on stage and bedlam reigned. Rivera's attempts to calm the group met with more violence. A chair hurled toward him, broke his nose, and a bloody Rivera called for a commercial break. Police were brought in and they got the situation under control. A bandaged Rivera concluded the segment and went on to tape two more episodes of "Geraldo."

As Rivera explains to Charles Leerhsen in *Newsweek:* "It happens. In the course of doing stories in Missouri, Montana, the shooting galleries of New York and Central America, my style of street-level journalism is up close and personal, and people tend to act in a very negative way."

Many television critics have called shows such as these "tabloid tv" or even "trash tv." A writer for *Newsweek* remarks: "Battered by dwindling audience shares and the encroachments of cable and home video, the television industry is fervently embracing a radical survival tactic: anything goes as long as it gets an audience. Shock 'em to attention. Hammer their ideological hot buttons. Inflame their libidos. Deliver a visceral rush by playing to their most primitive fascinations." "Shows like 'Geraldo,'" comments Richard Salant, former president of CBS-TV News, are "supermarket checkout-counter journalism." He continues in *Newsweek*: "Nothing on television surprises me anymore. . . . There would be none of this stuff if it did not have an audience."

MEDIA ADAPTATIONS: Miguel Robles—So Far and *Puerto Rico: Island of Contrasts* have been produced on audio cassette.

BIOGRAPHICAL/CRITICAL SOURCES:

PERIODICALS

Best Sellers, June, 1976.
Business Week, November 21, 1988.
Christian Science Monitor, April 3, 1974.
Esquire, April, 1975, April, 1986.
Harper's Bazaar, November, 1972, August, 1974.
Library Journal, June 15, 1972.
Life, June 9, 1972.
Mademoiselle, August, 1974.
Nation, July 19, 1975.
Newsday, March 31, 1974.
Newsweek, July 17, 1972, November 6, 1972, November 14, 1988.
New York Daily News, November 4, 1988.
New York Magazine, August 7, 1972.
New York Post, November 5, 1988.
New York Times, November 21, 1971, October 27, 1988.
New York Sunday News, September 10, 1972.
People, December 7, 1987, May 2, 1988, September 19, 1988, November 21, 1988.
Playgirl, September, 1988.
Time, May 13, 1974, December 22, 1986, October 31, 1988.
Vogue, May, 1988.

—*Sketch by Margaret Mazurkiewicz*

* * *

RIVERA, José Eustasio 1889-1928

PERSONAL: One source spells middle name Eustacio; born in 1889 in Neiva, Colombia; died in 1928. *Education:* Studied as a teacher and lawyer in Bogotá, Colombia.

CAREER: Lawyer, poet, and novelist. Served on government commission tracing boundary between Colombia and Venezuela.

WRITINGS:

Tierra de promisión (poetry), originally published in 1921, reprinted, Ancora (Bogotá, Colombia), 1985.
La vorágine (novel), originally published in 1924, reprinted, Distribuidora Cultural (Managua, Nicaragua), 1983, translation by Earle K. James published as *The Vortex,* Putnam, 1935.
Obras completas (complete works), Montoya (Medellín, Colombia), 1963.

Work represented in anthologies, including *José Eustasio Rivera, Eduardo Castillo, Miguel Rasch Isla: Sus mejores versos,* La Gran Colombia (Bogotá), 1944.

BIOGRAPHICAL/CRITICAL SOURCES:

BOOKS

Neale-Silva, Eduardo, *Estudios sobre José Eustasio Rivera,* Volume 1: *El arte poético ("Tierra de promisión"),* Hispanic Institute in the United States, 1951.
Neale-Silva, Eduardo, *Horizonte humano: Vida de José Eustasio Rivera,* University of Wisconsin Press, 1960.

* * *

RIVERA, Tomás 1935-1984

PERSONAL: Born December 22, 1935, in Crystal City, Tex.; died in Fontana, Calif., May 16, 1984; son of Florencio M. (a laborer and cook) and Josefa (Hernández) Rivera; married Concepción Garza, November 27, 1958; children: Ileana, Irasema, Florencio Javier. *Education:* Southwest Texas Junior College, A.A., 1956; Southwest Texas State College (now University), B.A., 1958, M.Ed., 1964; University of Oklahoma, M.A., 1969, Ph.D., 1969.

ADDRESSES: Home—5912 Trone Tr., San Antonio, Tex. 78238. *Office*—College of Multidisciplinary Studies, University of Texas at San Antonio, 4242 Piedras Dr., San Antonio, Tex. 78284.

CAREER: Teacher of English and Spanish in public schools of San Antonio, Tex., 1957-58, Crystal City, Tex., 1958-60, and League City, Tex., 1960-65; Southwest Texas Junior College, Uvalde, instructor in English, French, and Spanish, 1965-66; University of Oklahoma, Norman, instructor in Spanish, 1968-69; Sam Houston State University, Huntsville, Tex., associate professor, 1969-71; University of Texas at San Antonio, professor of Spanish, beginning 1971, associate dean of College of Multidisciplinary Studies, beginning 1973, became vice-president for administration; University of Texas at El Paso, executive vice-president. Chancellor, University of California, Riverside. Visiting professor at Trinity University, San Antonio, Tex., 1973. Member, American Council on Teaching of Foreign Languages.

MEMBER: Pan American Student Forum (member of board of directors, 1965); American Association of Teachers of Spanish and Portuguese; National Association of Bilingual Educators; South Central Modern Language Association; Texas Foreign Language Association; San Antonio Bilingual Educators/Texas Association of Bilingual Educators; Phi Theta Kappa, Sigma Delta Pi (president of University of Oklahoma chapter, 1968).

AWARDS, HONORS: Premio Quinto Sol National Literary Award, 1970, for *. . .y no se lo tragó la tierra/And the Earth Did Not Part;* appointed chancellor, University of California at Riverside, 1979.

WRITINGS:

. . .y no se lo tragó la tierra/And the Earth Did Not Part (bilingual edition of short stories), Quinto Sol Publications, 1971, reprinted, Arte Público Press, 1987, English-language edition published as *The Earth Did Not Part,* Quinto Sol Publications, 1971, English-language edition published as *This Migrant Earth,* Arte Público Press, 1985.
(Contributor) Joseph Flores, editor, *Songs and Dreams,* Pendulum Press, 1972.

(With Ed Simmen) *New Voices in Literature: The Mexican Americans,* Pan American University, 1972.

Always and Other Poems, Sisterdale Press, 1973.

(Author of preface) Ron Arias, *The Road to Tamanzuchale,* West Coast Poetry Review, 1975.

(Contributor of poems) Leonardo Anguiano and Cecilio Garcia, editors, *El Quetzal Emplumece,* Carmela Notalvo, Mexican American Cultural Center, 1976.

(Contributor) Francisco Jiménez, editor, *The Identification and Analysis of Chicano Literature,* Bilingual Press, 1979.

The Harvest-La Cosecha, Arte Público, 1989.

Also author of *Chicano Literature: A Dynamic Intimacy* (nomograph), Pan American University, and *La Casa Grande* (novel). Also contributor to *Proceedings; Conference on Challenge of the Spanish Speaking American,* Brigham Young University, and to *Café Solo,* edited by Ernest Padilla, 1974. Contributor to journals, including *Southwestern American Literature Journal,* and *Foreign Language Quarterly.* Work represented in anthologies, including *Aztlan: An Anthology of La Raza Literature,* Knopf, 1972; *El Espejo/The Mirror: Selected Mexican-American Literature,* Quinto Sol Publications, revised edition, 1972; *Chicano Literature: An Anthology,* Simon & Schuster, 1973; *We Are Chicanos: An Anthology of Mexican-American Literature,* Washington Square Press, 1973; *Anthology of Texas Poets,* Prickly Pear, 1974; *The Chicano Short Story,* University of Indiana Press, 1974; *Cuento: Revista de Imaginación,* Verano, 1975; *Voices of Aztlan,* New American Library, 1974; *The New Breed: Anthology of Texas Poets,* Prickly Pear, 1974; *An Anthology of Mexican Literature,* Mexican American Cultural Center; and *Floricanto II,* Aztlan Publications. Member of editorial board of MICTLA Publications, beginning 1971, and *El Magazin,* beginning 1972; contributing editor of *El Grito,* beginning 1971, and *Revista Chicano-Riqueña,* beginning 1973.

WORK IN PROGRESS: A large volume of poetry.

SIDELIGHTS: Poet and novelist Tomás Rivera's "prose style is concise, even pithy . . ., held carefully within the world of the migrant worker which Rivera has chosen as his subject," writes Juan Bruce-Novoa in *Chicano Authors: Inquiry by Interview.* Rivera once told *Contemporary Authors:* "Up to the time I started teaching, I was part of the migrant labor stream that went from Texas to the Midwest. I lived and worked in Iowa, Minnesota, Wisconsin, Michigan, and North Dakota." Despite the constant travelling required by the migrant's life, Rivera managed to attend school and eventually attended Southwest Texas State College in San Marcos, where he studied English. When Bruce-Novoa asked him how his formal education has affected him as a writer, Rivera responded: "I think it has helped me in several ways. First of all, it allowed me to see better the context of what I write and of the literature emerging from the Chicano Movement within the whole idea of literature itself. Because of the training I have a more total picture. . . . I prefer to see Chicano literature within the context of all these other literatures."

Rivera's collection . . .*y no se lo tragó la tierra,* which *Modern Chicano Writers* contributor Daniel P. Testa calls "a fascinating composite of stories and anecdotes of personal and collective true-to-life situations," parallels Rivera's childhood in that it is a family of migrant workers and their son. According to Testa, "With a free and flexible narrative technique, the author blends abrupt exchanges of dialogue, shifts of perspective, and internal monologue into the account of an external action or series of actions. . . . [Rivera] is at his very best in those well-sustained individual perspectives in which the language expresses the character's intimate thoughts and feelings with true-to-life natural-

ness and vitality. He has also discovered, in evoking the events of his Chicano past, a joyful cohesiveness." Bruce-Novoa continues: "Though narrative, [his work] is not expository, but, rather, strangely impressionistic. It is a measure of Rivera's talent that the reader thinks that s/he has read a detailed depiction of reality, so much so that many have used the book as an accurate sociological statement of the migrants condition. What Rivera achieves is the evocation of an environment with a minimum of words, and within that environment the migratory farmworkers move with dignity, strength, and resilience."

Ralph F. Grajeda notes in the same book how different generations in the community portrayed in . . .*y no se lo tragó la tierra* respond to their difficult lives: "Throughout the book tension is created between the opposing values of resignation and rebellion as the people are shown enduring the repetitive hardships of the present, and as they anticipate their future." Grajeda also praises Rivera's portrayals of the migrant's existence: "Rivera has a clear eye for the cruel ironies of life. In the world his characters inhabit, people are often victimized by the very hopes they nurture, hopes that spring from the positions in life which they endure." But Rivera does not see his work as political. He told Bruce-Novoa: "I have no distinct political purpose when I write. I do not write a creative piece to prove a political point." He added: "I just feel that there is a separation. I want to have in literature that one point where I can really be creative and totally human, where I can really try to see things apart from any gain or loss aspects, as you must in politics. . . . Literature is a much more complete game than politics, which is kind of mundane and of this world."

BIOGRAPHICAL/CRITICAL SOURCES:

BOOKS

Bruce-Novoa, Juan, *Chicano Authors: Inquiry by Interview,* University of Texas Press, 1980.

Davila, Luis, editor, *Chicano Literature and Tomás Rivera,* University of Indiana Press, 1974.

Sommers, Joseph and Tomás Ybarra-Frausto, editors, *Modern Chicano Writers: A Collection of Critical Essays,* Prentice-Hall, 1979.

*   *   *

ROA BASTOS, Augusto (Antonio) 1917-

PERSONAL: Born June 13, 1917, in Iturbe, Guairá, Paraguay. *Education:* Attended school in Asunción, Paraguay.

CAREER: Writer and journalist. Reporter for newspapers in Asunción, Paraguay, c. early 1940s; newspaper correspondent in Europe and North Africa, c. mid-1940s; lived in exile in Argentina and France, 1947-1989; University of Toulouse, Toulouse, France, professor of Guaraní (Indian language of Paraguay) and Spanish American studies, through 1985; returned to Paraguay, 1989. Lecturer and director of writing workshops. Served as Paraguay's cultural attaché in Buenos Aires, Argentina, 1946. *Military service:* Served in Paraguayan military during Chaco War.

AWARDS, HONORS: Fellow of British Council, 1944, and John Simon Guggenheim Memorial Foundation, 1970; Concurso Internacional de Narrativa from Editorial Losada, 1959, for *Hijo de hombre;* Premio Cervantes de Literatura, 1989.

WRITINGS:

El ruiseñor de la aurora, y otros poemas (poetry), Imprenta Nacional, 1942.

El trueno entre las hojas (short stories; title means "Thunder among the Leaves"), Losada (Buenos Aires), 1953.

El naranjal ardiente, nocturno paraguayo: 1947-1949 (poetry), Diálogo, 1960, reprinted, Alcándara, 1983.

Hijo de hombre (novel), Losada, 1960, reprinted, Lector, 1983, translation by Rachel Caffyn published as *Son of Man,* Gollancz, 1965, reprinted, Monthly Review Press, 1989.

El baldío (short stories; title means "The Empty Field"), Losada, 1966.

Madera quemada (short stories), Universitaria (Santiago), 1967, Lector, 1983.

Los pies sobre el agua (short stories), Centro Editor de America Latina (Buenos Aires), 1967.

Moriencia (short stories; title means "Slaughter"), Monte Avila (Caracas), 1969.

Cuerpo presente, y otros textos (short stories), Centro Editor de America Latina, 1972.

El pollito de fuego, Ediciones de la Flor (Buenos Aires), 1974.

Yo el supremo (novel), Siglo Veintiuno Argentina Editores (Buenos Aires), 1974, translation by Helen Lane published as *I the Supreme,* Knopf, 1986.

Antología personal (short stories), Nueva Imagen (Mexico), 1980.

Contar un cuento, y otros relatos (short stories), selected with preliminary notes by Ana Becciú, Kapelusz (Buenos Aires), 1984.

Carta abierta a mi pueblo (letters), Frente Paraguayo en Argentina (Buenos Aires), 1986.

On Modern Latin American Fiction, edited by John King, Noonday Press, 1989.

Also author of *Los congresos,* 1974, *El somnámbulo,* 1976, *Los juegos,* 1979, and *Lucha hasta el alba,* 1979. Author of screenplays, including "El trueno entre las hojas," 1955; "Hijo de hombre," 1960; "Shunko," 1960; "Alias Gardelito," 1963; "Castigo al traidor," 1966; "El señor presidente," 1966; and "Don Segundo Sombra," 1968. Works represented in anthologies, including *Cuentos con gorilas,* Extemporáneos, 1973, and *Así escriben los latinoamericanos,* Ediciones Orión, 1974. Contributor to periodicals, including *El País.*

WORK IN PROGRESS: El Fiscal.

SIDELIGHTS: Augusto Roa Bastos is generally regarded as the finest Paraguayan author of the twentieth century. Although his first work, a volume of poetry titled *El ruiseñor de la aurora, y otros poemas,* was published in 1942, he did not gain international acclaim until the late stages of the Latin American "boom," a period in the 1960s of unprecedented worldwide interest in Latin American literature. Finding poetry an inappropriate medium for conveying his ideas, Roa Bastos published only a small fraction of his verse before assuming a prosaic voice to render his social concerns. A distinctive blend of myth, fantasy, and realism, his long and short works of fiction mirror his native country's tumultuous political and military history while emphasizing the redemptive power of human suffering.

Roa Bastos worked as a journalist in Paraguay after the Chaco War—a long conflict with Bolivia over the Chaco region of central South America—had drawn to a close in 1935. Almost a decade later, he traveled to Europe to pursue a study of journalism. In 1947, Roa Bastos returned to a war-ravaged Paraguay: a popular revolt against the oppressive political regime of Higinio Morínigno had led to civil war within the country. That same year, Roa Bastos was forced into an exile that would last for more than forty years.

El trueno entre las hojas ("Thunder among the Leaves"), the author's first collection of short stories, deals with the social, political, and economic injustices plaguing Paraguayans. In *Augusto Roa Bastos,* David William Foster theorized that the stories in the volume prefigure the author's later works of long fiction: "A good number of the stories are technically and artistically defective because Roa [Bastos] had yet to find a balanced literary voice," noted the critic. Foster went on to suggest that among the stories in the collection, "The Excavation" enunciates with particular power and clarity the author's views of the Paraguayan experience. The story centers on the thwarted attempts by a group of political prisoners to excavate an underground escape tunnel from their cell. Those prisoners who survive the dangerous excavation process are discovered by officials and executed.

Upon *El trueno entre las hojas*'s publication in 1953, Paraguay was the scene of considerable civil strife, having witnessed six more revolts in the late 1940s. Some critics have suggested that the dismal conclusions of works like "The Excavation" reflect Roa Bastos's belief at the time that rampant oppression would continue to dominate life in Paraguay indefinitely. Foster termed "The Excavation" a "harsh, unrelenting portrayal of tyrannical oppression in all of its boundless cruelty" and alluded to the symbolic value of the narrative, noting that "the story is metaphoric of man's spiritual imprisonment by social injustice and of his strivings for self-liberation; . . . those strivings are frustrated with his annihilation by the forces that oppress him."

Roa Bastos's first novel, the award-winning *Hijo de hombre (Son of Man),* is seen as an outgrowth of his early short stories. First published in 1960, *Son of Man* is generally considered an important work of regionalism and a stunning exemplification of the growth and refinement of the author's writing style. The novel is essentially a series of interwoven stories and legends tracing Paraguay's history from the beginning of José Gaspar Rodríguez de Francia's dictatorship in 1814 through the end of the Chaco War. *Modern Language Journal* contributor Tamara Holzapfel echoed Williams's theory that the sober tone of Roa Bastos's fiction parallels the true nature of the Paraguayan condition: "[In *Son of Man,*] the life of the Paraguayan poor is presented as a vicious cycle. During times of revolution and war these people rise to heroism but afterwards return to the hopelessness of their former existence. Roa Bastos, by exploring Paraguay's myths, discovers its reality."

Roa Bastos published his masterwork, *Yo el supremo,* in 1974. Available in English translation as *I the Supreme,* the complex and unusual novel is a fictionalization of the final days of Paraguayan despot Francia, alias "El Supremo," a former revolutionary who was declared dictator for life in 1814 and exercised near-absolute power over the country until his death in 1840. After assuming leadership of the country, Francia effectively suppressed the powers of the church and the aristocracy in Paraguay and—fearing domination by Brazil and Argentina—isolated his country from the rest of the world.

I the Supreme has been compared favorably to Gabriel García Márquez's *Autumn of the Patriarch,* a fantasy about a Latin American dictator. A compilation of fragmented dreams and ramblings, extended soliloquies, and alternatively lucid and irrational declamations, *I the Supreme* offers a hypothetical account of a dying tyrant's attempt to justify his obsessive use of power. The novel begins with the erroneous announcement of Francia's death and then proceeds to recant the declaration, providing instead an imagined look at the final days in the life of the despot. Francia dictates his thoughts to a "Compiler" in an effort to establish his own untarnished place in history: "I can remake [history] as I please, adjusting, stressing, enriching it's meaning and truth."

Commenting on *I the Supreme* in an article for the *New York Times Book Review,* esteemed Mexican novelist Carlos Fuentes called the book "one of the milestones of the Latin American novel" and deemed Roa Bastos "his country's most eminent writer." *Washington Post Book World* contributor Paul West concurred, proclaiming: "Augusto Roa Bastos is himself a supreme find, maybe the most complex and brilliant . . . Latin American novelist of all."

In a *New York Times Book Review* interview, Roa Bastos revealed his thoughts on life as an exile: "I try to see exile not as a political sanction, as a punishment or restriction, but as something that has forced me to open to the world, to look at it in all of its complexity and breadth. The exile exists in a state of limbo, but he is also a privileged observer." The toppling of Paraguayan president Alfredo Stroessner's oppressive regime in 1989 brought an end to Roa Bastos's forty-two-year exile. At the request of André Rodríguez, the country's new political leader, the distinguished literary figure returned to a freer Paraguay in May of 1989.

BIOGRAPHICAL/CRITICAL SOURCES:

BOOKS

Contemporary Literary Criticism, Volume 45, Gale, 1987.
Foster, David William, *Augusto Roa Bastos,* Twayne, 1978.
Meyer, Doris, editor, *Lives on the Line: The Testimony of Contemporary Latin American Authors,* University of California Press, 1988.
Roa Bastos, Augusto, *I the Supreme,* translated by Helen Lane, Knopf, 1986.

PERIODICALS

Commonweal, May 23, 1986.
Globe and Mail (Toronto), June 21, 1986.
Los Angeles Times Book Review, July 13, 1986.
Modern Language Journal, November, 1971.
New Republic, June 15, 1987.
New Yorker, September 22, 1986.
New York Times, April 2, 1986, May 14, 1989.
New York Times Book Review, April 6, 1986.
Observer, August 8, 1965.
Times Literary Supplement, August 15, 1975.
Tribune Books, June 1, 1986.
Washington Post Book World, May 11, 1986.

—*Sketch by Barbara Carlisle Bigelow*

* * *

ROBLES, Mireya 1934-

PERSONAL: Born March 12, 1934, in Guantanamo, Cuba; came to the United States in 1957, naturalized citizen, 1962; daughter of Antonio and Adelaida (Puertas) Robles. *Education:* Russell Sage College, B.A., 1966; State University of New York at Albany, M.A., 1968; State University of New York at Stony Brook, Ph.D., 1975.

ADDRESSES: Home—87 South Highland Ave., No. B25, Ossinning, N.Y. 10562.

CAREER: Russell Sage College, Troy, N.Y., instructor in Spanish, 1963-73; Briarcliff College, Briarcliff Manor, N.Y., assistant professor, 1973-74, associate professor of Spanish, 1974-77; poet and writer, 1977—. Guest on television and radio programs in Spain and the United States; has given poetry readings and a book exhibition in New York City. Panel member of First Con-

gress of Cuban Literature, 1973, Conference on Women Writers from Latin America, 1975, Congress of Inter-American Women Writers, 1976, and Conference of Inter-American Women Writers, 1978.

MEMBER: Centro Cultural Literario e Artístico (Portugal; honorary member).

AWARDS, HONORS: First prize from Iberoamerican Poets and Writers Guild of New York, 1971, for *Tiempo artesano;* gold medal from L'Academie Internationale de Lutece, 1974, for essays, stories, and poems; first prize from Círculo de Escritores y Poetas Iberoamericanos de New York, 1974, for "La relatividad de la realidad"; second prize from *Silarius Literary Review,* 1973, for short story "Hidra," and University of Maine at Orono, 1973, for short story "Trisagio de la muerte"; prize from *Xilote* magazine, for poetry and essay.

WRITINGS:

Petits Poèmes (title means "Little Poems"), translated into French by Henri de Lescoet, Profils Poetiques, 1969.
(Contributor) *Voces de mañana* (title means "Voices of Tomorrow"), edited by Zenia S. da Silva, Harper, 1973.
(Contributor) *La última poesía cubana* (anthology), Hispanova de Ediciones, 1973.
Tiempo artesano (poems), Editorial Campos, 1973, bilingual edition, *Time the Artesan/Tiempo artesano,* translated by Angela de Hoyos, Dissemination Center for Bilingual Bicultural Education, 1975.
(Translator from the English) de Hoyos, *Levantate Chicano/Arise Chicano and Other Poems* (bilingual text), Backstage Books, 1975.
(Author of prologue) de Hoyos, *Chicano Poems,* Backstage Books, 1975.
(Contributor) *Narradores cubanos de hoy* (anthology), Librería Universal, 1975.
En esta aurora (poems; title means "In This Dawn"), Cuadernos del Caballo Verde, Universidad Veracruzana, 1976.
(Translator from the English) *Selecciones* (title means "Selections"), Universidad Veracruzana, 1976.
Hagiografía de narcisa la bella, Ediciones del Norte, 1985.

Work represented in anthologies. Contributor of more than one hundred seventy-five articles, stories, poems, translations, and reviews to journals all over the world, including *Opinion, Poet, Star West, International Poetry Review,* and *Thesaurus,* and to newspapers.

WORK IN PROGRESS: A novel.

SIDELIGHTS: Mireya Robles comments: "I write because I have to. My main aspiration: not to have to waste my time in stupid jobs that have nothing to do with my only vocation, writing."

Robles's work has been published all over Europe, Latin America, and India. She has visited Spain, Portugal, Italy, France, Switzerland, Morocco, Greece, Argentina, and Mexico.

BIOGRAPHICAL/CRITICAL SOURCES:

BOOKS

Miller, Yvette E. and Charles M. Tatum, editors, *Latin American Women Writers: Yesterday and Today,* Latin American Literary Review, 1977.

PERIODICALS

Diario las Américas, February 13, 1971, February 10, 1973.
El Diario la Prensa, September 9, 1974, June 16, 1975.
Envíos, Number 5, 1973.

Explicación de Textos Literarios, Volume 4, number 2, 1975-76.
Hispania, December, 1976.
Opinion, August-September, 1976.

* * *

ROCHA, Rina García
See GARCIA ROCHA, Rina

* * *

RODRIGUEZ, Richard 1944-

PERSONAL: Born July 31, 1944, in San Francisco, Calif.; son of Leopoldo (a dental technician) and Victoria (a clerk-typist; maiden name, Moran) Rodriguez. *Education:* Stanford University, B.A., 1967; Columbia University, M.A., 1969; graduate study at University of California, Berkeley, 1969-72, 1974-75, and Warburg Institute, London, 1972-73. *Religion:* Roman Catholic.

ADDRESSES: Home—San Francisco, Calif. *Agent*—Georges Borchardt, Inc., 136 East 57th St., New York, N.Y. 10022.

CAREER: Held a variety of jobs, including janitorial work and free-lance writing, 1977-81; full-time writer, 1981—.

AWARDS, HONORS: Fulbright fellowship, 1972-73; National Endowment for the Humanities fellowship, 1976-77; Gold Medal from the Commonwealth Club, 1982; Christopher Award, 1982, for *Hunger of Memory: The Education of Richard Rodriguez;* Anisfield-Wolf Award for Race Relations, 1982.

WRITINGS:

Hunger of Memory: The Education of Richard Rodriguez (autobiography), David R. Godine, 1982.

WORK IN PROGRESS: Mexico's Children, a book about Mexico and California, for Viking; a book about migrant workers.

SIDELIGHTS: In the opinion of *New York Times* critic Le Anne Schreiber, Richard Rodriguez's autobiography, *Hunger of Memory: The Education of Richard Rodriguez,* is an "honest and intelligent account of how education can alter a life." Through its detailing of Rodriguez's journey through the American educational system and his resultant loss of ethnicity, *Hunger of Memory* also offers a negative view of bilingual education and affirmative action policies that some readers have applauded and others have decried. The son of Mexican-American immigrants, Rodriguez was unable to speak English when he entered a Sacramento, California, elementary school; nevertheless, he went on to earn a master's degree and was a Fulbright scholar studying English Renaissance literature in London when he abruptly decided to leave academic life. The choice was prompted by the feeling that he was "the beneficiary of truly disadvantaged Mexican-Americans"; as the author told *Publishers Weekly* interviewer Patricia Holt, the grants he was awarded as a minority student made him feel as if "I benefited on their backs."

The alienation from his culture began early in Rodriguez's life; as soon, in fact, as he learned the "public" language that would separate him from his family. Catholic nuns who taught Rodriguez asked that his parents speak English to him at home; when they complied, related the author in a *Newsweek* article by Jean Strouse, the sound of his "private" language, Spanish, and its "pleasing, soothing, consoling reminder of being at home," were gone. Paul Zweig similarly observes in a *New York Times Book Review* article that as Rodriguez became acculturated, "son and

parents alike knew that an unnameable distance had come between them." Rodriguez's parents were eventually "intimidated by what they had worked so diligently to bring about: the integration of their son into the larger world of gringo life so that he, unlike they themselves, could go far, become, one day, powerful, educated," the reviewer notes.

Rodriguez reached the goals his parents had sought for him but eventually began to fight the very policies that helped him to attain them. In ten years of college and postgraduate education, Rodriguez received assistance grounded in merit but based in part on his minority status. His revolt against affirmative action began when he turned down several university-level teaching jobs. As Schreiber explains: "He wrote letters to all the chairmen of English departments who thought they had found the perfect answer to affirmative action in Richard Rodriguez. He declined their offers of jobs, because he could not withstand the irony of being counted a 'minority' when in fact the irreversibly successful effort of his life had been to become a fully assimilated member of the majority." Rodriguez spent the next six years writing *Hunger of Memory,* parts of which appeared in magazines before being brought together in book form.

Rodriguez's arguments against affirmative action stem from his belief, as he told *Detroit Free Press* reporter Suzanne Dolezal, that "the program has primarily benefited people who are no longer disadvantaged, as I no longer was when I was at Stanford, [by] ignoring the educational problems of people who are genuinely disadvantaged, people who cannot read or write." His opposition to bilingual education is just as vocal. "To me," he declared in the *Publishers Weekly* interview, "public educators in a public schoolroom have an obligation to teach a public language. Public language isn't just English or Spanish or any other formal language. It is the language of public society, the language that people outside that public sector resist. For Mexican-Americans it is the language of los gringos. For Appalachian children who speak a fractured English or Black children in a ghetto, the problem is the same it seems to me." The author further stated that "my argument has always been that the imperative is to get children away from those languages that increase their sense of alienation from the public society."

Hunger of Memory has been praised by several critics, especially for its discussion of the impact of language on life. Schreiber believes that "what matters most about this intensely thoughtful book is that Richard Rodriguez has given us the fruit of his long meditation upon language—his intimate understanding of how we use language to create private and public selves, his painful awareness of what we gain and lose when we gain and lose languages." Zweig likewise claims that "the chapters Mr. Rodriguez devotes to his early experiences of language are uncannily sensitive to the nuances of language learning, the childhood drama of voices, intonations." In addition, the author brings a literary sensibility to his autobiographical account; a *New Yorker* reviewer, for instance, commends Rodriguez as "a writer of unusual grace and clarity, eloquent in all his reflections."

Rodriguez told *CA:* "I see myself straddling two worlds of writing: journalism and literature. There is Richard Rodriguez, the journalist—every day I spend more time reading newspapers and magazines than I do reading novels and poetry. I wander away from my desk for hours, for weeks. I want to ask questions of the stranger on the bus. I want to consider the political and social issues of the day.

"Then there is Richard Rodriguez, the writer. It takes me a very long time to write. What I try to do when I write is break down the line separating the prosaic world from the poetic word. I try to write about everyday concerns—an educational issue, say, or the problems of the unemployed—but to write about them as powerfully, as richly, as well as I can.

"My model in this marriage of journalism and literature is, of course, George Orwell. Orwell is the great modern example. He embarrasses other journalists by being more. He never let the urgency of the moment overwhelm his concern for literary art. But, in like measure, he embarrasses other writers because he had the courage to attend to voices outside the window, he was not afraid to look up from his papers. I hope I can be as brave in my life."

BIOGRAPHICAL/CRITICAL SOURCES:

BOOKS

Dictionary of Literary Biography, Volume 82: *Chicano Writers, First Series,* Gale, 1989.
Rodriguez, Richard, *Hunger of Memory: The Education of Richard Rodriguez,* David R. Godine, 1982.

PERIODICALS

Detroit Free Press, January 20, 1982.
Nation, May 15, 1982.
Newsweek, March 15, 1982.
New Yorker, April 5, 1982.
New York Times, March 1, 1982.
New York Times Book Review, February 28, 1982.
People, August 16, 1982.
Publishers Weekly, March 26, 1982, September 30, 1983.
Village Voice, April 27, 1982.
Washington Post, March 21, 1983.
Washington Post Book World, February 14, 1982.

*   *   *

RODRIGUEZ-ALCALA, Hugo (Rosendo) 1917-

PERSONAL: Born November 25, 1917, in Asunción, Paraguay; U.S. citizen; children: Hugo Luis, Ramiro Antonio, Marina Renee, Kimberly, Christopher José. *Education:* University of Asunción, J.D., 1943; Washington State University, M.A., 1950; University of Wisconsin, Ph.D., 1963. *Religion:* Catholic.

ADDRESSES: Home— Nicanor Torales, esquina Sucre, Barrio Herrera, Asunción, Paraguay.

CAREER: Secretary to supreme court justice in Paraguay, 1943-47; Rutgers University, New Brunswick, N.J., assistant professor, 1956-58; University of Washington, Seattle, 1958-63, began as associate professor, became professor; University of California, Riverside, professor of Spanish, beginning in 1963, became professor emeritus, chairman of department, 1965-67. *Military service:* Paraguayan Army, 1934-35.

MEMBER: International Association of Hispanists, Institute of Latin-American Literature, Modern Language Association of America, Paraguayan Academy of the Spanish Language (president, 1989—).

AWARDS, HONORS: First prize from Paraguayan Ministry of Education, 1939, for *Horas líricas.*

WRITINGS:

La danza de la muerte, [Asunción], 1937.
Estampas de la guerra, Zampiropolos, 1939.
Horas líricas (poems), Imprenta Nacional, 1939.
Francisco Romera: Vida y obra, Columbia University Press, 1951.
(With Everett W. Hesse) *Cinco yanquis en España,* Ronald, 1955.

(Contributor) *La cultura y la literatura iberoamericana,* de Andrea, 1957.
Korn, Romero, Güiraldes, Unamuno, Ortega, de Andrea, 1958.
Misión y pensamiento de Francisco Romero, National University of Mexico Press, 1959.
Abril que cruza el mundo (poems), Estaciones, 1960.
Ensayos de norte a sur, University of Washington Press, 1960.
(Contributor) *Homenaje a Alejandro Korn (1860-1960),* Universidad Nacional de la Plata, 1960.
(With William Wilson) *Por tierras de sol y de español,* Ronald, 1963.
(With Sally Rodríguez-Alcalá) *Un país hispánico visto por dentro,* Prentice-Hall, 1965.
El arte de Juan Rulfo, Instituto Nacional de Bellas Artes, 1965.
(Editor with S. Rodríguez-Alcalá) *Cuentos nuevos del sur,* Prentice-Hall, 1967.
Literatura paraquaya, Centro Editor de América Latina, 1968.
Historia de la literatura paraguaya, de Andrea, 1970.
Palabras de los días: Poemas, Facultad de Humanidades y Educación, Universidad de Zulia, 1972.
Narrativa hispanoamericana, Gredos, 1973.
El canto del aljibe, National University of Mexico, 1973.
(Editor and author of introduction) *Nine Essays on Rómulo Gallegos,* Latin American Studies Program, University of California, 1979.
Literatura de la Ilustración, La Muralla, 1979.
Literatura de la Independencia, La Muralla, 1980.
El portón invisible, Alcandara, 1983.
Relatos de norte y sur, Napa, 1983.

Also author of *La incógnita del Paraguay y otros ensayos,* 1987; *Quince ensayos,* 1987; *Poetas y prosistas paraguayos,* 1988; and *Terror bajo la luna,* 1988.

Contributor of more than one hundred articles, translations, short stories, poems, and reviews to yearbooks, journals, and newspapers in North and South America, Mexico, and Europe; articles include a series of twenty-two about Brazil published in *El País,* 1940.

*   *   *

RODRIGUEZ MONEGAL, Emir 1921-1985

PERSONAL: Born July 28, 1921 (one source says 1927), in Melo, Uruguay; died November 14, 1985, in New Haven, Conn. *Education:* Attended University of Montevideo.

ADDRESSES: Home—New Haven, Conn.

CAREER: Worked as secondary school teacher in Montevideo, Uruguay, 1945-52; Instituto de Profesores, Montevideo, professor of English literature, 1952-62; Yale University, New Haven, Conn., professor of Latin American and comparative literature, 1969-85, director of Latin American Studies Council and chairman of department of Spanish and Portuguese; writer. Visiting professor at El Colegio de México, 1964, Harvard University, 1965, and other schools; visiting scholar at Liverpool University's Center for Latin American Studies.

WRITINGS:

José Enrique Rodó en el novecientos, Número, 1950.
Objetividad de Horacio Quiroga, Número, 1950.
(Editor) Horacio Quiroga, *Diario de viaje a París,* Número, 1950.
El juicio de los parricidas: La nueva generación argentina y sus maestros, Deucalión, 1956.
Las raíces de Horacio Quiroga, Alfa, 1961.
Narradores de ésta América: Ensayos, Alfa, 1962, reprinted, Volume 1, 1969, Volume 2, 1974.

Páginas de José Enrique Rodó, Editorial Universitaria de Buenos Aires, 1963.

Eduardo Acevedo Díaz: Dos versiones de un tema, Ediciones del Río de la Plata, 1963.

(Editor) *Eduardo Acevedo Díaz, Grito de gloria,* Ministerio de Instrucción Pública y Previsión Social, 1964.

(With Alsina Thevenet) *Ingmar Bergman: Un dramaturgo cinematográfico,* Renacimiento, 1964.

(Editor) *El cuento uruguayo: De los orígenes al modernismo,* Universitaria de Buenos Aires, 1965.

(Editor) *Díaz, Lanza y sable,* Ministerio de Instrucción Pública y Previsión Social, 1965.

El viajero inmóvil: Introducción a Pablo Neruda, Losada, 1966, published as *Neruda, el viajero inmóvil,* Monte Avila, 1977.

Literatura uruguaya del medio siglo, Alfa, 1966.

(Editor) *José Enrique Rodó: Obras completas* (title means "José Enrique Rodó: Complete Works"), Aguilar, 1967.

Rodó en el novecientos: Ensayos, La Casa del Estudiante, 1967.

Genio y figura de Horacio Quiroga, Editorial Universitaria de Buenos Aires, 1967.

El arte de narrar: Diálogos, Monte Avila, 1968.

Vínculo de sangre: Crítica, Alfa, 1968.

El desterrado: Vida y obra de Horacio Quiroga, Losada, 1968.

Sexo y poesía en el 900 uruguayo; los extraños destinos de Roberto y Delmira: Ensayo, Alfa, 1969.

El otro Andrés Bello, Monte Avila, 1969.

Tres testigos españoles de la guerra civil, Monte Avila, 1971.

El boom de la novela latinoamericana: Ensayo, Tiempo Nuevo, 1972.

Borges y la nouvelle critique, Revista Iberoamericana, 1972.

Borges: Hacia una lectura poética, Guadarrama, 1976.

(Editor) *The Borzoi Anthology of Latin American Literature,* Knopf, 1977.

Jorge Luis Borges: A Literary Biography, Dutton, 1978.

(Editor with Jill Levine) *Maestros hispánicos del siglo veinte,* Harcourt, 1979.

Borges por él mismo, Monte Avila, 1980.

(Editor with Mario Santí) *Pablo Neruda: El escritor y la crítica,* Taurus, 1980.

(Editor) *Horacio Quiroga, Cuentos* (short stories), Biblioteca Ayacucho, 1981.

(Editor with Alastair Reid) *Borges, a Reader: A Selection From the Writings of Jorge Luis Borges,* Dutton, 1982.

Also editor of *José Enrique Rodó, 1871-1917,* 1963. Literary editor of *Marcha,* 1945; co-editor of *Número,* 1949-55; editor of *Mundo Nuevo,* c. 1966-69.

SIDELIGHTS: Emir Rodríguez Monegal was a distinguished critic and biographer. Among his many publications are volumes on such noted Hispanic authors as Horacio Quiroga, Pablo Neruda, and Jorge Luis Borges. Rodríguez Monegal earned praise in English-language periodicals for many of his biographical-critical writings. *El viajero inmóvil,* an account of Neruda's life and work, was recommended in a 1970 *Times Literary Supplement* as "by far the best book yet written on Neruda," while *Pablo Neruda: El escritor y la crítica,* which Rodríguez Monegal edited with Mario Santí, was lauded in *World Literature Today* as "an excellent volume of essays."

Although extremely prolific, Rodríguez Monegal has few works in English translation. A notable exception is his *Jorge Luis Borges: A Literary Biography,* which explores the life and work of the celebrated Argentine writer. This work, widely reviewed in America, enjoyed substantial acclaim. J. D. O'Hara, reviewing *Jorge Luis Borges* in the *Washington Post Book World,* described it as "fascinating" and declared that "all [Borges's] readers will

profit from this study." *New Republic* reviewer Jay Parini was also impressed, writing that Rodríguez Monegal's book was "absorbing from start to finish." Another laudatory appraisal came from V. S. Pritchett in *New Yorker:* he called Rodríguez Monegal's book "an absorbing, even exciting work of discreet detection, written with verve" and added that it is "often very moving."

BIOGRAPHICAL/CRITICAL SOURCES:

PERIODICALS

Atlantic Monthly, December, 1978.
Hispania, December, 1986.
New Republic, February 3, 1979.
New Yorker, February 19, 1979, May 24, 1982.
New York Review of Books, January 25, 1979.
New York Times Book Review, November 25, 1979, October 25, 1981.
Times Literary Supplement, April 16, 1970.
Washington Post Book World, November 26, 1978.
World Literature Today, winter, 1978, winter, 1982.

*   *   *

RODRIGUEZ O(RDONEZ), Jaime E(dmundo)   1940-

PERSONAL: Born April 12, 1940, in Guayaquil, Ecuador; came to the United States in 1948, naturalized citizen, 1973; son of Luis A. (an Ecuadorean army officer and military writer) and Beatriz (Ordonez) Rodríguez; married Linda G. Alexander (an historian), November 24, 1965. *Education:* University of Houston, B.A., 1965, M.A., 1966; University of Texas, Ph.D., 1970. *Politics:* Democrat.

ADDRESSES: Office—Department of History, University of California, Irvine, Calif. 92717.

CAREER: California State University, Long Beach, assistant professor of history, 1963-73; University of California, Irvine, assistant professor, 1973-75, associate professor, 1975-81, professor of history, 1981—, distinguished faculty lecturer, 1979-80, dean of graduate studies and research, 1980-86. Honorary fellow at National University of Mexico's Institute for Historical Research, 1979—. Member of Conference on Latin American History (chairman of Andean studies committee, 1976; chairman of Mexican studies committee, 1979-80); member of council of Smithsonian Institution, 1988. *Military service:* U.S. Army, Medical Corps, 1959-62.

MEMBER: Congress of Mexican and United States Historians (member of U.S. organizing committee, 1981-91), American Historical Association, Latin American Studies Association, National Chicano Council on Higher Education, American Academy of Franciscan History (associate member), Council of Graduate Schools of the United States, National Association of State Universities and Land-Grant Colleges, National Council of University Research Administrators, National Academy of History of Ecuador (corresponding member), Centro de Estudios Historicos del Guayas (corresponding member), Pacific Coast Council on Latin American Studies (vice-president, 1979; president, 1980).

AWARDS, HONORS: Organization of American States fellowship for Mexico, summer, 1968; Social Science Research Council fellowship for Ecuador, 1971-72; University of California faculty fellowships for Ecuador, summers, 1975 and 1978, fellowships for Mexico, summers, 1976, 1977, 1979, 1986, 1987, and 1988; Mellon Foundation fellowship, 1980-81; Hubert Herring Memorial Award from Pacific Coast Council on Latin American Studies, 1980, for *The Forging of the Cosmic Race;* Fulbright grant for Mexico, 1982.

WRITINGS:

(Contributor) Richard Greenleaf and Michael Meyer, editors, *Research in Mexican History,* University of Nebraska Press, 1973.
(Translator) Romeo Flores Caballero, *Counterrevolution,* University of Nebraska Press, 1974.
The Emergence of Spanish America: Vicente Rocafuerte and Spanish Americanism, 1808-1832, University of California Press, 1975.
Estudios sobre Vicente Rocafuerte (title means "Studies About Vicente Rocafuerte"), Archivo Historico del Guayas, 1975.
(Editor) *Andean Field Research Guide,* Duke University Press, 1977.
El nacimiento de Hispanoamérica (title means "The Birth of Spanish America"), Fondo de Cultura Económica, 1980.
(With Colin M. MacLachlan) *The Forging of the Cosmic Race: A Reinterpretation of Colonial Mexico,* University of California Press, 1980.
(Editor with John Te Paske, William Sater, and Leon Campbell) *Research Guide to Andean History,* Duke University Press, 1981.
Down From Colonialism: Mexico's Nineteenth-Century Crisis, Chicano Studies Research Center, University of California, Los Angeles, 1983.
(Editor and contributor) *The Mexican and the Mexican Experience in the Nineteenth Century,* Bilingual Press, 1988.
(Editor) *La formación de un Republicano* (title means "The Making of a Republican"), Volume IV: *Obras completas de Servando Teresa de Mier* (title means "The Complete Works of Servando Teresa de Mier"), Universidad Nacional Autonoma de Mexico, 1988.
(Editor and contributor) *The Independence of Mexico and the Creation of the New Nation,* Latin American Center, University of California, Los Angeles, 1989.

Contributor to Latin American studies journals. Editor of *Mexican Studies/Estudios Mexicanos;* Mexico-area editor for *Américas,* 1978-86; member of editorial board of *New Scholar,* 1978-86, and *Journal of Interamerican Studies and World Affairs,* 1982-88.

WORK IN PROGRESS: A Socioeconomic History of the First Federal Republic of Mexico, 1824-1834; A Study of the Ideological Process of Mexican Independence; A Socioeconomic History of Quito, Ecuador, 1750-1850.

SIDELIGHTS: Jaime E. Rodríguez O. told *CA:* "My work seeks to explain Spanish America's failure to modernize in the early nineteenth century. At the time Western Europe and the United States were being transformed into modern industrial societies, the newly independent nations of Spanish America were crippled by economic depression and extreme political instability. Scholars have generally argued that this failure to modernize stemmed from the feudal Spanish colonial structure which did not prepare Spanish Americans for self-government. According to this view, after independence Spanish American leaders rejected colonial traditions and adopted foreign systems of government unsuited to their nations' needs, causing Spanish America's nineteenth-century crisis.

"I examined some of the problems of nation-building in Spanish America in a series of studies and concluded that independence was not a sharp break with the past and that Spanish American leaders had not blindly accepted alien forms of government. Instead, I demonstrated the continuity of the Spanish and Spanish American reform tradition and its influence upon the leaders of the new countries. With Professor Colin M. MacLachlan of Tulane University, I examined Mexico's colonial epoch to test the validity of the neo-feudal thesis. We concluded that colonial Mexico had not been a feudal but a capitalist society; that the region developed a complex, balanced, and integrated economy which transformed the area into the most dynamic part of the Spanish empire; and that it was one of the few regions in the world where racial and cultural intermingling created a new society.

"I am presently engaged in two studies to explain the post-independence period: an analysis of Mexico's early nineteenth-century economy to explain why one of the Western Hemisphere's most prosperous areas plunged into a prolonged economic depression in the first half of the nineteenth century; and a second work, a study of Quito, Ecuador, during the years 1750-1850, to examine the way in which a peripheral area of Spanish America made the transition from colony to independent nation."

* * *

ROJAS, A. R.
See ROJAS, Arnold R.

* * *

ROJAS, Arnold R. 1896(?)-1988
(A. R. Rojas)

PERSONAL: Born September 25, 1896 (one source says 1899), in Pasadena, Calif.; died September 8, 1988. *Education:* Attended elementary school; subsequently self-educated.

CAREER: Vaquero at V7 Ranch, San Luis Obispo, Calif., San Emideo Ranch, and Rancho Tejon until 1935; Bar-O Stable, Bakersfield, Calif., owner, 1935-50; equine dentist and horse trainer, beginning in 1950; writer. Rodeo chairman in Bakersfield, c. late 1940s.

WRITINGS:

California Vaquero, Academy Library Guild, 1953.
Lore of the California Vaquero, Academy Library Guild, 1958.
Last of the Vaqueros, Academy Library Guild, 1960.
The Vaquero, illustrations by Nicholas S. Firfires, McNally & Loftin, 1964.
(Under name A. R. Rojas) *Bits, Bitting and Spanish Horses: The Chief Rojas Fact Book About Successful Horse Training and the Proper Use of Equipment,* Kimberly Press, 1970.
These Were the Vaqueros: Collected Works of Arnold R. Rojas, illustrations by Rich Rudish, privately printed, 1974.
Vaqueros and Buckeroos, privately printed, 1979.

Contributor to *Bakersfield Californian.*

SIDELIGHTS: Grounded in personal experience, Arnold R. Rojas's books about the life of California's vaqueros—Mexican cowboys—are regarded as regional classics. A vaquero himself, he heard many anecdotes and legends around campfires and in bunkhouses and set them down, along with his own observations of cowboys, horses, Indians, and cattle, in "brief tales that hover on the line between fiction and history," according to Gerald Haslam in *Dictionary of Literary Biography.* Rojas, whose formal schooling ended at third grade, learned to write through the tradition of oral story-telling and the example of authors such as Alexandre Dumas, Miguel de Cervantes, Rudyard Kipling, Robert Louis Stevenson, Emile Zola, and Jack London. His first writings were thumbnail sketches of several vaqueros written for the *Bakersfield Californian* as publicity for a rodeo Rojas was organizing. These led to regular contributions to the paper and the Academy Library Guild's offer to publish his work in book form. Observed Haslam: "It is the unexpected and magical that readers find in Rojas's work. He captured in print a time and a culture whose human qualities would otherwise have been forgotten."

BIOGRAPHICAL/CRITICAL SOURCES:

BOOKS

Dictionary of Literary Biography, Volume 82: *Chicano Writers, First Series,* Gale, 1989.

*   *   *

ROJAS, Guillermo 1938-

PERSONAL: Born January 18, 1938, in Victoria, Tex. *Education:* North Texas State University, B.A., 1963, M.A., 1965; University of Illinois at Urbana-Champaign, Ph.D., 1970.

ADDRESSES: Office—Department of Mexican-American Studies, University of California, Davis, Calif. 95616.

CAREER: Southern University, Baton Rouge, La., assistant professor of Spanish and German, 1966-67; University of California, Davis, assistant professor of Spanish, 1970—.

MEMBER: American Association of Teachers of Spanish and Portuguese, Modern Language Association.

AWARDS, HONORS: National Endowment for the Humanities fellowship, 1972-73.

WRITINGS:

Characterization of Pancho Villa and Other Historical Figures in the Major Works of Martín Luis Gazmán, University of Illinois at Urbana-Champaign, 1971.
Camino abierto, Ediciones ECLCA, 1986.
(Editor) *Chicano Studies: Nuevos Horizontes,* Prisma Books, 1988.

Contributor to numerous periodicals. Associate editor of *Anuario de Letras Chicanas,* 1977—.

*   *   *

ROJAS (SEPULVEDA), Manuel 1896-1973

PERSONAL: Born January 8, 1896, in Buenos Aires, Argentina; died in 1973.

CAREER: Writer.

AWARDS, HONORS: Premio Nacional de Literatura, 1957.

WRITINGS:

Hombres del sur (short stories), prologue by Raul Silva Castro, Nascimento, 1927.
Tonada del transeunte (poems), Nascimento, 1927.
El delincuente (short stories), Sociedad Chilena de Ediciones, 1929, reprinted, Zig-Zag, 1963.
Lanchas en la bahía (novel), Empresa Letras, 1932, reprinted, Zig-Zag, 1959.
Travesía (short stories), Nascimento, 1934, reprinted, 1973.
La ciudad de las césares (novel), Ediciones Ercilla, 1936, reprinted, Zig-Zag, 1972.

De la poesía a la revolución, Ediciones Ercilla, 1938.
El bonete maulino, Cruz del Sur, 1943.
Hijo de ladrón (novel), Nascimento, 1951, translation by Frank Gaynor published as *Born Guilty,* Library Publishers, 1955.
Deshecha rosa (poems), 2nd edition, Babel, 1954.
(Editor) *Chile: 5 navegantes y 1 astrónomo,* Zig-Zag, 1956.
Imágenes de infancia y adolescencia, Babel, c. 1956, reprinted, Zig-Zag, 1983.
Antología de cuentos, prologue by Enrique Espinoza, Zig-Zag, 1957.
(With Mary Canizzo) *Los costumbristas chilenos,* Zig-Zag, 1957.
Mejor que el vino (novel), Zig-Zag, 1958.
El vasa de leche y sus mejores cuentos, Nascimento, 1959.
Punta de rieles, Zig-Zag, 1960.
(Editor) Alberto Blest Gana, *Blest Gana: Sus mejores páginas,* Ercilla, 1960.
El árbol siempre verde, Zig-Zag, 1960.
Obras completas, Zig-Zag, 1961.
Apuntes sobre la expresión escrita, [Caracas], c. 1961.
Antología autobiográfica, Ercilla, 1962.
Cuentos del sur y diario de México, Ediciones Era, 1963.
(Editor) *Esencias del país chileno: Poesías,* Universidad Nacional Autónoma de México, 1963.
El hombre de la rosa, Editorial Losada, 1963.
Sombras contra el muro (novel), Zig-Zag, 1963.
Pasé por México un día, Zig-Zag, 1964.
Manual de literatura chilena, Dirección de Cursos Temporales, 1964.
Historia breve de la literatura chilena, Zig-Zag, 1965.
A pie por Chile, Editora Santiago, 1967.
El bonete maulino, y otros cuentos, Editorial Universitaria, 1968.
Viaje al país de los profetas, Ediciones Zlotopioro, 1969.
Cuentos, Editorial Sudamericana, 1970.
La oscura vida radiante, Editorial Sudamericana, 1971.
Obras, prologue by Jorge Campos, Aguilar, 1973.
Mares libres, edited by Norman Cortés L., Ediciones Universitarias de Valparaíso, Universidad Católica de Valparaíso, 1975.
El colocolo y otros cuentos, Ediciones Huracán, Editorial Arte y Literatura, 1977.

BIOGRAPHICAL/CRITICAL SOURCES:

BOOKS

Yates, Donald A., editor, *Tres cuentistas hispanoamericanos,* Macmillan, 1969.

PERIODICALS

World Literature Today, spring, 1965, winter, 1965.

*   *   *

ROMANO, Octavio I. 1932-

PERSONAL: Born in 1932. *Education:* Received B.A. and M.A. from University of New Mexico; University of California, Berkeley, Ph.D., 1964.

ADDRESSES: Office—Tonatiuh/Quinto Sol International, Inc., P.O. Box 9275, Berkeley, Calif. 94709; and Department of Public Health, University of California, Berkeley, Berkeley, Calif. 94720.

CAREER: Associate professor of behavioral science at University of California, Berkeley; president of Tonatiuh-Quinto Sol International, Inc., Berkeley. Member of California State Advisory Commission on Compensatory Education, 1967-68; former chairman of Spanish Speaking People's Institute for Education.

WRITINGS:

(Editor) *El Espejo—The Mirror: Selected Mexican-American Literature,* Tonatiuh/Quinto Sol International, 1969.
(Editor) *The Grito del Sol Collection: Anthology, Winter, 1984,* Tonatiuh/Quinto Sol International, 1985.
Geriatric Fu, Tonatiuh/Quinto Sol International, 1989.

Contributor of articles and short stories to periodicals, including *El Grito* and *Grito del Sol.* Editor of *Grito del Sol: A Chicano Quarterly.*

* * *

ROMERO, José Rubén 1890-1952

PERSONAL: Born September 25, 1890, in Cotija de la Paz, Michoacán, Mexico; died of a heart attack, July 4, 1952, in Mexico City, Mexico.

CAREER: Government official, university president, lawyer, author. Proprietor of grocery store in 1900s; helped draft the 1911 Mexican constitution; appointed tax collector for Michoacán, Mexico, 1912; served in federal posts during the 1920s; appointed Consul General to Barcelona, Spain, 1931; Mexican ambassador to Brazil, 1937-38, and to Cuba, 1939-44; lecturer, and president, beginning 1944, University of Michoacán; former Inspector General of Communications and head of Foreign Office administrative department; advisor to President Miguel Alemán. Owner and manager of publishing company. *Military service:* Fought in Mexican Revolution against Porfirio Díaz, 1911.

MEMBER: Mexican Academy of Letters.

WRITINGS:

NOVELS

Apuntes de un lugareño, A. Núñez, 1932, translation by John Mitchell and Ruth M. De Aguilar published as *Notes of a Villager: A Mexican Poet's Youth and Revolution,* Plover Press, 1988.
El pueblo inocente, Imprenta Mundial, 1934.
Desbandada, [Mexico], 1934, A. Núñez, 1936.
Mi caballo, mi perro y mi rifle, A. Núñez, 1936.
La vida inútil de Pito Pérez, México Nuevo, 1938, translation by William O. Cord published as *The Futile Life of Pito Pérez,* Prentice-Hall, 1966.
Anticipación de la muerte, J. R. Romero, 1939.
Una vez fui rico, Imprenta Aldina, 1942.
Rosenda, Porrúa, 1946.

OTHER

Sentimental (poems), Talleres Gráficos de Herrero Hermanos, 1919.
Semblanza de una mujer, J. R. Romero, 1941.
Rostros, Imprenta Aldina, 1942.
Algunas cosillas de Pito Pérez que se me quedaron en el tinero (aphorisms), Viñetas de Oscar Frías, 1945.
Como leemos el "Quijote" (essay), [Mexico], 1947.
Obras completas, prologue by Antonio Castro Leal, Oasis, 1957.
Cuentos y poesías inéditos (stories and poems), edited by Cord, Ediciones de Andrea, 1963.
(With others) *Cervantes y Don Quijote,* Secretaria de Educación Pública, 1972.
Alvaro Obregón, Cultura, 1976.

Also author of poetry volumes *Fantasías,* 1908, *Rimas bohemias,* 1908, *La musa heroica,* 1915, *La musa loca,* 1917, *Tacámbaro,* 1922, and *Versos viejos,* 1930; author of *Cuentos rurales* (stories),

1915, and *Mis amigos, mis enemigos,* 1921. Author of political columns and articles.

SIDELIGHTS: "When José Rubén Romero appeared in the national field of Mexican letters in 1932, he easily obtained one of the first places among the novelists because he brought with him those much-desired traits of humor, graceful picturesqueness, and love for the people of his state of Michoacán, which combined to make him an excellent [novelist of manners]," Ruth Stanton related in *Hispania.* His best-known work was *La vida inútil de Pito Pérez,* which was a best-seller in Mexico for over twenty-five years. Translated as *The Futile Life of Pito Pérez,* the novel "stems from the long tradition of picaresque novels that began in 16th-century Spain," Lois Hobart stated in the *New York Times Book Review.* "Like his predecessors, Pito Pérez is an anti-hero, a rascal dedicated to the proposition that his welfare, dependent on his wits, takes precedence over the convenience and well-being of others and the morals, whatever they may be, of his time and environment." Travelling from town to town, Pito engages in a series of adventures, which, in the picaresque tradition, become "a vehicle for satire at the expense of the clergy, physicians, romance, and pretensions in general," Hobart noted.

A typical *pícaro* of humble birth, Pito turns to an antisocial lifestyle through a series of mishaps. Pito's troubles begin in his infancy, when he is denied his share of his mother's milk, which she donates to an orphaned child. His older brothers use all the family's money for their own education, leaving Pito to become an altar boy. Persuaded by another to steal from the collection box, Pito loses his position and soon runs away from home. He is then employed by a pharmacist—until the man discovers his wife is having an affair with Pito. He travels on, his fortunes continuing to decline, until he is reduced to stealing a skeleton to be his companion, and eventually "ends up in death on a pile of rubbish, leaving a legacy of bitterness but unrepentant," Hobart summarized.

While Pito's adventures are amusing and even risqué, "in addition to the obvious humor, there is a much more subtle current that rides the line between tragedy and comedy in a wonderful fashion," John S. Brushwood commented in *Mexico in Its Novel: A Nation's Search for Identity.* As Stanton observed, the protagonist's "social ostracism gives Pito Pérez opportunity for meditation and an angle from which to observe certain social problems." Nevertheless, *Nation* contributor John A. Crow remarked, "Pito is not interested in social reform; his entire life is an attempt to integrate his own battered, disjointed, embittered personality. He finds all social standards and institutions to be rooted in pretense." As Brushwood noted, "[Pito's] life is active only when it is a negation of society, so the end result of his nonconformism is that his role is essentially passive. He cannot be what he would be, what his inner self would have him be."

While *The Futile Life of Pito Pérez* is a picaresque satire, it is also symbolic of the social upheaval brought about by the Mexican Revolution. *The Mexican Novel Comes of Age* author Walter M. Langford, for instance, maintained that "in the final parts of the novel when we see Pito Pérez embittered by the futility of his continuing one-man campaign against dehumanizing forces, we have to interpret it as Romero's backhanded slap at the Revolution, which has largely failed to change life in the rural villages." Calling Romero one of the "novelists of the Mexican Revolution," *Hispania* contributor R. Anthony Castagnaro likewise observed that the author "has used the Mexican rogue to make articulate all his anger at the injustices of the world. . . . Like Cervantes' greater character projection, Pito Pérez expresses his author's complaint against the world's wrongs."

Many critics believed that it was Romero's portrayal of village life, such as that in *Pito Pérez,* that comprised the strength of his works. Brushwood stated that Romero's "intense regionalism . . . [was] probably the outstanding characteristic of his works," while Hobart found *Pito Pérez* "compounded of the idiom and mythology of the villages, . . . roguish, peppery, and thoroughly Mexican in flavor." "His novels show a wide and humorous understanding of the provincial proprieties," Stanton similarly asserted, "and this has contributed greatly to his position as one of the outstanding painters of Mexican village life. He is also an indefatigable narrator of popular stories, and the maze of Mexican folklore holds no secrets from him." In general, the critic concluded, "[José] Rubén Romero's novels represent a decisive advance in simplicity and reality over the nineteenth-century Mexican novels. . . . His novels are faithful to Mexican life, at least to those phases which he has chosen to record."

BIOGRAPHICAL/CRITICAL SOURCES:

BOOKS

Brushwood, John S., *Mexico in Its Novel: A Nation's Search for Identity,* University of Texas Press, 1966.
Langford, Walter M., *The Mexican Novel Comes of Age,* University of Notre Dame Press, 1971.
Torres-Ríoseco, Arturo, *Aspects of Spanish-American Literature,* University of Washington Press, 1963.
Twentieth-Century Literary Criticism, Volume 14, Gale, 1984.

PERIODICALS

America, March 11, 1967.
Hispania, December, 1941, August, 1953, May, 1956, September, 1961, December, 1962, December, 1964, April, 1973.
Modern Language Journal, November, 1953.
New York Times Book Review, January 29, 1967.
Saturday Review, May 27, 1967.
Time, February 17, 1967.

OBITUARIES:

PERIODICALS

Américas, November, 1952.
New York Times, July 6, 1952.

*   *   *

ROMERO, Orlando 1945-

PERSONAL: Born September 24, 1945, in Santa Fe, N.M.; son of José (a machinist) and Ruby Anne (Romero) Romero; married Rebecca López (a journalist), February 10, 1968; children: Carlota Bernarda, Orlando Cervantes, Enrique Alvaro. *Education:* College of Santa Fe, B.A., 1974; University of Arizona, M.L.S., 1976. *Politics:* "A determination to save blue corn, blue sky, and New Mexico's earth." *Religion:* "Humanity revealed through the contemplative mysteries of God and Nature."

ADDRESSES: Home—Rt. 1, Box 103, Santa Fe, N.M. 87501. *Office*—History Library, P.O. Box 2087, Santa Fe, N.M. 87504-2087.

CAREER: Office of the New Mexico Secretary of State, Santa Fe, aide, 1964-67; New Mexico State Library, Santa Fe, library assistant, 1967-69, librarian for Southwest and special collections, 1977-83; New Mexico State Supreme Court Law Library, Santa Fe, library assistant, 1969-74; New Mexico History Library, Palace of the Governors, Santa Fe, director, 1983—. Guest lecturer. Sculptor; work on permanent exhibit at Folk Art Museum, Santa Fe. Former chairman, Santa Fe Council for the Arts. Consultant.

MEMBER: New Mexico Preservation Coalition (board member), New Mexico Historical Society (former board member), Santa Fe Historical Society (board member).

AWARDS, HONORS: Fellowship in creative writing, National Endowment for the Arts, 1979; member, New Mexico Eminent Scholars Program, 1989.

WRITINGS:

Nambé—Year One (novel; excerpts first appeared in *Puerto del Sol,* 1974, and *El Grito del Sol,* January-March, 1976), Tonatiuh International, 1976.
(Contributor) Karl and Jane Kopp, editors, *Southwest,* Red Earth (Albuquerque, N.M.), 1977.
(Contributor) Rudolfo A. Anaya and Simon J. Ortiz, editors, *A Ceremony of Brotherhood: 1680-1980,* Academia (Albuquerque), 1981.

Also author of *The Day of the Wind* (short stories). Contributor of weekly column for *Santa Fe Reporter,* 1988—. Contributor of about 150 articles, short stories and poems relating to people and history of New Mexico and the Southwest. Romero's papers are held by the Special Collections Department at the University of New Mexico, Albuquerque, and the New Mexico History Library, Santa Fe.

SIDELIGHTS: "Through his writings, Orlando Romero recreates an image of a people whose values and customs may soon be erased, or significantly altered, by forces dedicated to progress," writes J. Allan Englekirk in the *Dictionary of Literary Biography.* Englekirk continues that Romero's literary efforts "attempt to preserve the past for the future, so that succeeding generations may be exposed to those beliefs most basic to traditional Hispanic culture in the southwestern United States." Englekirk sees Romero's grandfather, Enrique, as a primary influence in the writer's approach to man and nature: "A man tied to 'los tiempos de antes' (the bygone days), [Romero's] grandfather preferred traditional methods of irrigation, cultivation, and harvest and taught Orlando the value of a slower, more philosophical pace."

Critics have identified Romero as a Chicano author, a tag which does not please him. According to Englekirk, Romero "believes that the culture of the Southwest and West is too diverse to be identified by a single phrase: 'Chicano culture—you cannot mix together people from California, Arizona, southern Colorado . . . into a homogeneous bottle of milk. Our food is different, our thinking is different—we are united politically under *chicanismo*'. . . . When asked to define his literature, he prefers to consider it 'New Mexican literature.' "

Orlando Romero once wrote *CA:* "What motivates my writing? Primarily, *Nambé—Year One* was the beginning of self-realization, more precisely, an autobiographical way to state the Hispano's relationship to the earth. Ritual motivates me. Ritual as in the seasons, the menstrual cycles of streams and all the life therein. Wild dogs howling at the moon and barren wombs whispering the decay of autumn. Which in essence means redefining ritual.

"What motivates my writing? Hope for mankind and the eternal dream that we can live in peace with ourselves and the earth that sustains us. It is not concrete that inspires it, or cities like Albuquerque or Phoenix or Los Angeles, but ancient people against the background of eternally blue skies and their determination to remain self-sufficient despite the cost.

"My work is regional only in the sense that spawning salmon return to their place of birth, only in the sense that all of us are part of dark, brown earth and only in the sense that I am nourished by blue corn meal and blue skies."

AVOCATIONAL INTERESTS: "I am a voracious reader. I sculpt in wood. I tie flies and I can squander my life away in the midst of a trout stream or in a field of ripening blue corn. I also like to build with adobe bricks. And conversation, be it with a philosophical hobo or a great man of letters."

BIOGRAPHICAL/CRITICAL SOURCES:

BOOKS

Dictionary of Literary Biography, Volume 82: *Chicano Writers, First Series,* Gale, 1989.

* * *

ROSA, Alexis Gómez
See GOMEZ ROSA, Alexis

* * *

ROSALES, Francisco A(rturo) 1942-

PERSONAL: Born July 19, 1942, in Fresno, Calif. *Education:* Arizona State University, B.A., 1969; Stanford University, M.A., 1972; received Ph.D. from Indiana University—Bloomington.

ADDRESSES: Office—Department of History, University of Houston, Houston, Tex. 77004.

CAREER: Assistant professor of history at University of Houston, Houston, Tex. Member of Texas Farmworkers Organizing Committee and Centro de Servicios Sociales.

MEMBER: Organization of American Historians, National Association of Chicano Scholars.

AWARDS, HONORS: Ford Foundation fellow, 1972-73.

WRITINGS:

(With David W. Foster) *Hispanics and the Humanities in the Southwest: A Directory of Resources,* Center for Latin American Studies, Arizona State University, 1983.
(Editor with Barry J. Kaplan) *Houston: A Twentieth-Century Urban Frontier,* Associated Faculty Press, 1983.

Contributor to magazines, including *Aztlán: Chicano Journal of the Social Sciences and Art* and *Revista Chicano-Riqueña.*

* * *

ROSA-NIEVES, Cesáreo 1901-1974

PERSONAL: Born July 17, 1901, in Juana Díaz, Puerto Rico; died October 3, 1974; son of Cesáreo Rosa-Solivan (a merchant) and Evangelina Nieves; married Emilia Perez Carrasquillo (a teacher), September 1, 1928; children: Cesar E. Rosa-Perez. *Education:* University of Puerto Rico, teacher's certificate, 1925, B.A., 1927, M.A., 1936; University of Mexico, Ph.D., 1944. *Religion:* Roman Catholic.

CAREER: Teacher of Spanish language and literature in secondary schools in Humacao, Carolina, and Caguas, all Puerto Rico;

University of Puerto Rico, Río Piedras, instructor, 1936-43, assistant professor, 1943-45, associate professor, 1945-47, professor of Spanish language and literature, beginning 1947. Directed conferences in secondary schools, universities, and at the Ateneo de Puerto Rico. Named life secretary of Academy of Arts and Sciences of Puerto Rico, 1969.

MEMBER: National Education Association, Asociación de Maestros de Puerto Rico, Sociedad de Autores Puertorriqueños, Sociedad Puertorriqueña de Escritores, Masons.

AWARDS, HONORS: Cervantes Medal, 1924; Morel Campos Prize, 1930, for poem "La danza puertorriqueña"; Roosevelt Medal, Puerto Rico Atheneum, 1930, for poem "Estampas sinfónicas"; Carnaval Award, 1931, for poem "Carta a Momo"; diploma of honor from Institute of Puerto Rican Literature, 1958, for *La poesía en Puerto Rico,* and 1963, for *Historia panorámica de la literatura puertorriqueña;* diploma of honor from Spanish journal *Rumbos,* 1958, for *Los nísperos del alba maduraron;* Gold Medal and diploma of honor from Academy of Arts and Sciences of Puerto Rico, 1967; Award of the Society of Puerto Rican Authors, 1967; Gran Premio de Crítica Literaria.

WRITINGS:

PLAYS

Román Baldorioty de Castro (three-act play in verse), Imprenta Soltero, 1948.

Also author of "El huésped del mar," 1945, "Flor de areyto," 1945, "Brazo de oro," 1948, "Pachín Marín," 1948, "Nuestra enemiga la piedra," 1948, "La otra," 1948, "Campesina en palacio," 1949, and "Norka," 1957.

POEMS

Siete caminos en luna de sueños, Biblioteca de Autores Puertorriqueños, 1957.
Los nísperos del alba maduraron, Editorial Campos, 1959.
Diapasón negro, Editorial Campos, 1960.
Girasol, Editorial Campos, 1960.
El plenamar de las garzas de ámbar, Editorial Campos, 1964.
Estrellas y caramelos, Editorial Partenon (Madrid), 1972.

Also author of *Las veredas olvidadas,* 1922, *La feria de las burbujas,* 1930, *Paracaídas,* 1933, *Tu en los pinos,* 1938, *Undumbre,* 1953, and *La emoción divertida,* 1967.

NOVELS

El mar bajo de la montaña, Editorial Yaurel, 1963.
La canción de los luceros, Tipografía Miguza (Barcelona), 1972.
Los espejos de sal bajo la luna, Tipografía Miguza, 1972.

OTHER

Francisco de Ayerra Santa María: Poeta puertorriqueño, 1630-1708, Editorial Universitaria, University of Puerto Rico, 1948.
(Editor and author of introduction and notes) *Aguinaldo lírico de la poesía puertorriqueña,* Volume 1: *1843-1907,* Volume 2: *1907-1921,* Volume 3: *1921-1956,* Librería Campos, 1957, revised edition, Editorial Edil, 1971.
La lámpara del faro: Variaciones críticas sobre temas puertorriqueños, Editorial Club de la Prensa, Volume 1, 1957, Volume 2, 1960.
Tierra y lamento: Rodeos de contorno para una telúrica interpretación poética de lo puertorriqueño, Editorial Club de la Prensa, 1958.
La poesía en Puerto Rico (doctoral thesis), Editorial Campos, 1958, 3rd edition, Editorial Edil, 1969.

(Editor with Felix Franco Oppenheimer) *Antología general del cuento puertorriqueño* (short fiction anthology), two volumes, Editorial Campos, 1959, 2nd edition, Editorial Edil, 1970.

Historia panorámica de la literatura puertorriqueña (1589-1959), two volumes, Editorial Campos, 1963.

Calambreñas, decimario boricua, Editorial Cordillera, 1964.

Mi vocación por el víspero (short stories), Editorial Rumbos (Barcelona), 1965.

El sol pintó de oro los bohíos, Editorial Rumbos, 1965.

Plumas estelares en las letras a Puerto Rico, Volume 1, Ediciones de la Torre, University of Puerto Rico, 1967, Volume 2, [Barcelona], 1972.

Vox folklórica de Puerto Rico, Troutman Press (Sharon, Conn.), 1967.

Ensayos escogidos, Academy of Arts and Sciences of Puerto Rico, 1970.

(With Esther M. Melon) *Biografías puertorriqueñas,* Troutman Press, 1970.

(Editor) *Antología de décimas cultas de Puerto Rico,* Editorial Cordillera, 1971.

El costumbrismo literario en la prosa de Puerto Rico, two volumes, Editorial Cordillera, 1971.

Romanticism in Puerto Rican Literature, Gordon Press, 1979.

Also author of booklets. Contributor to *El Mundo, Alma Latina, Puerto Rico Ilustrado, Brújula, Prensa, Revista del Instituto de Cultura Puertorriqueña,* and *Revista Internacional de Literatura Iberoamericana.* Co-founder, *Noísmo,* 1926-27; editor, *Brújula,* 1940.

SIDELIGHTS: A versatile Puerto Rican writer, Cesáreo Rosa-Nieves wrote in a number of different genres and participated in such literary movements as Noísmo, Vanguardismo, Criollismo, and Ensueñismo. His historical play *Román Baldorioty de Castro* is often ranked as his most important work, while the anthology *Antología general del cuento puertorriqueño* is considered a standard source on Puerto Rican literature.

BIOGRAPHICAL/CRITICAL SOURCES:

BOOKS

Figueroa de Cifredo, Patria, *Apuntes biográficos en torno a la vida obra de Cesáreo Rosa-Nieves,* Editorial Cordillera, 1965.

Figueroa de Cifredo, Patria, *Nuevo encuentro con la estética de Rosa-Nieves,* [San Juan], 1969.

*   *   *

ROSARIO GREEN (de HELLER), María del 1941-

PERSONAL: Born March 31, 1941, in Mexico City, Mexico. *Education:* National University of Mexico, B.A., 1963, licenciada en ciencias diplomáticas, 1966; El Colegio de México, M.A. (economics), 1966; Columbia University, M.A. (economics) and certificate in Latin American studies, both 1968; Instituto para la Integración de América Latina, Buenos Aires, Argentina, diploma, 1969.

ADDRESSES: Home—San Marcos 11, Edif. Atenas, Depto. 401, Pedregal 2, Santa Teresa Contreras, Mexico 20, D.F., Mexico. *Office*—El Colegio de Mexico, Camino al Ajusco No. 20, Mexico 20, D.F. 10001, México.

CAREER: El Colegio de México, Mexico City, professor of economics and social studies, 1968-72, member of Publications Commission, 1970-72; Mexican Foreign Service, Mexico City,

first secretary in Geneva, Switzerland, 1972-74; El Colegio de México, professor of economics and social studies, 1974—, member of Publications Commission, 1979-80. Visiting professor at National University of Mexico, 1969 and 1975-82, and Universidad Iberoamericana, 1970-71; associate professor at Center for Economic and Social Studies of the Third World, 1980—. Assistant to the executive director of the World Bank, 1982. Member of International Relations Commission of Partido Revolucionario Institucional, 1982—.

WRITINGS:

(Editor with Bernardo Sepúlveda A.) *La ONU: Dilema a los veinte cinco años,* El Colegio de México, 1970.

El endeudamiento público externo de México, 1940-1973, El Colegio de México, 1976.

La economía, ANUIES, 1976.

(With Jorge Alberto Lozoya and Jaime Estevez) *Alternativas para un nuevo orden internacional,* Centro de Estudios Económicos y Sociales del Tercer Mundo, 1978, translation published as *Alternative Views to a New International Order,* Pergamon, 1979.

(Contributor) L. Gonzales Sosa and R. Méndez Silva, editors, *Los problemas en un mundo en proceso de cambio,* National University of Mexico, 1978.

(Contributor) Nora Lusting, editor, *Panorama y perspectivas de la economía mexicana,* El Colegio de México, 1979.

(Contributor) Jorge Alberto Lozoya and A. Bhattacharya, editors, *The Financial Issues of the New International Economic Order,* Pergamon, 1980.

(With E. Laszlo, Jorge Alberto Lozoya, Jaime Estevez, and others) *Obstacles to a New International Economic Order,* Pergamon, 1980.

(Editor with Jorge Alberto Lozoya) *International Trade, Industrialization, and the New International Economic Order,* Pergamon, 1981.

(Contributor) Susan Kaufan-Purcell, editor, *Mexico,* New York Academy of Political Science, 1981.

(Contributor) Jaime Estevez and Samuel Lichtensztejn, editors, *Nueva fase del capital financiero,* Nueva Imagen, 1981.

(Contributor) Jorge Alberto Lozoya and A. Bhattacharya, editors, *Finanzas y el nuevo orden económico internacional,* Nueva Imagen, 1981.

(Contributor) Eugenio Anguiano Roch, editor, *Cooperación económica internacional: Diálogo o confrontación,* Nueva Imagen, 1981.

Estado y banca transnacional en México, Centro de Estudios Económicos y Sociales del Tercer Mundo, 1981.

(Contributor) Hector Aguilar Camín, editor, *El desafío Mexicano,* Nexos, 1982.

El pensamiento de Cardoso y Prebisch en torno al desarrollo, Nueva Imagen, 1982.

(Editor) *Los mitos de Milton Friedman,* Grijalbo, 1983.

Author of "Panorama Económico Latinoamericano," a column in *El Universal,* 1980-81. Contributor of more than thirty articles to economic journals. Member of editorial board of *Foro Internacional,* 1974—, and *Journal of Inter-American Studies and World Affairs,* 1979—.

*   *   *

ROSSI, Cristina Peri
See PERI ROSSI, Cristina

RUIZ, José Martínez
   See MARTINEZ RUIZ, José

*   *   *

RUIZ, Ramon Eduardo 1921-

PERSONAL: Born September 9, 1921, in Pacific Beach, Calif.; son of Ramon and Dolores (Urueta) Ruiz; married Natalia Marrujo (a teacher), October 14, 1944; children: Olivia Teresa, Maura Natalia. *Education:* San Diego State College (now University), B.A., 1947; Claremont Graduate School, M.A., 1948; University of California, Berkeley, Ph.D., 1954. *Politics:* Independent.

ADDRESSES: P.O. Box 1775, Rancho Santa Fe, Calif. 92067. *Office*—Department of History, University of California, San Diego, Calif. 92037.

CAREER: University of Oregon, Eugene, instructor, 1955-56, assistant professor of history, 1956-57; Southern Methodist University, Dallas, Tex., assistant professor of Spanish, 1957-58; Smith College, Northampton, Mass., assistant professor, 1958-60, associate professor, 1960-63, professor of history, 1963-69; University of California, San Diego, professor of history, 1970—. *Military service:* U.S. Army Air Forces, 1943-46; served in Pacific theater; became second lieutenant.

MEMBER: American Historical Association, Conference on Latin American History, Phi Beta Kappa.

AWARDS, HONORS: Huntington Library fellow, 1958; American Philosophical Society fellow, 1959; Fulbright scholar in Mexico, 1965-66; *Cuba: The Making of a Revolution* was named one of the twenty-one best history books of 1968 by *Washington Post Book World* and *Chicago Tribune;* Hubert C. Herring Best Book prize, Pacific Coast Council on Latin American Studies, 1981, for *The Great Rebellion: Mexico, 1905-1924;* Center for Advanced Study in the Behavioral Sciences, Stanford, Calif., 1984-85.

WRITINGS:

(Editor) *An American in Maximilian's Mexico, 1865-1866: The Diaries of William Marshall Anderson,* Huntington Library, 1959.
Mexico, the Challenge of Poverty and Illiteracy, Huntington Library, 1963.
(Editor) *The Mexican War—Was it Manifest Destiny?,* Holt, 1963.
Cuba: The Making of a Revolution, University of Massachusetts Press, 1968.
(With John William Tebbel) *South by Southwest: The Mexican-American and His Heritage* (juvenile), Doubleday, 1969.
(With James David Atwater) *Out From Under: Benito Juárez and the Struggle for Mexican Independence* (juvenile), Doubleday, 1969.
(Editor) *Interpreting Latin American History,* Holt, 1970.
Labor and the Ambivalent Revolutionaries: Mexico, 1911-1923, Johns Hopkins Press, 1976.
(Editor, with Robert Detweiler) *Liberation in the Americas,* Campile Press, 1978.
The Great Rebellion: Mexico, 1905-1924, Norton, 1980.
The People of Sonora and Yankee Capitalists, University of Arizona Press, 1988.
A History of the Mexican People, Norton, 1990.

SIDELIGHTS: "The prevailing American view of the Mexican Revolution is of an oppressed people rising up against foreign

bosses, military dictatorship, and feudalism, recovering national pride, establishing popular rule, . . . and providing justice for the worker; in short, 'the first of the 20th-century social revolutions,' " writes John Womack, Jr., in his *New Republic* review of Ramon Eduardo Ruiz's *The Great Rebellion: Mexico, 1905-1924.* The "chief merit [of the book]," Womack says, "is its central thesis, that far from a 'radical change' of Mexican society the revolution was 'essentially a face-lifting of Mexican capitalism, . . . one of the last bourgeois protests of the 19th century, and not . . . the precursor of the socialist explosions of the 20th century.' "

While the critic finds that Ruiz's "thesis is not original," he states that *The Great Rebellion* "is the first major statement by an eminent American historian of Mexico that the real revolution was not a triumph of 'the people' at large, but a long, violent, specifically bourgeois reform, which crushed other popular uprisings for the sake of better business." And although Womack cites "several faults" in the book, including the author's discussion of the difference between "a rebellion" and a "revolution" and his omission of Mexico's financial history during the conflict, the reviewer concludes that the work "deserves wide circulation. More than a reinterpretation of the Mexican Revolution, Ruiz implicitly offers important wisdom on contemporary Mexico."

BIOGRAPHICAL/CRITICAL SOURCES:

BOOKS

Ruiz, Ramon Eduardo, *The Great Rebellion: Mexico, 1905-1924,* Norton, 1980.

PERIODICALS

Nation, July 22, 1968.
New Republic, July 20, 1968, February 14, 1981.
New York Times Book Review, November 16, 1980.
Washington Post Book World, August 18, 1968.

*   *   *

RULFO, Juan 1918-1986

PERSONAL: Born May 16, 1918, in Sayula, Jalisco, Mexico; died of a heart attack, January 7, 1986, in Mexico City, Mexico; married in 1948; wife's name, Clara; children: four.

ADDRESSES: Home—Mexico City, Mexico. *Office*—Centro Mexicano de Escritores, Luis G. Inclán, no. 2709, Col Villa de Cortes, 03130 México 13, D.F., México.

CAREER: Worked as an accountant and in several clerical positions; on staff of Mexican Immigration Department, beginning 1935, processed the crews of impounded German ships during World War II; member of sales staff, B. F. Goodrich Rubber Co., 1947-54; member of Papaloapan Commission, 1955; National Institute for Indigenous Studies, Mexico City, Mexico, beginning 1962, became director of editorial department. Adviser to writers at Centro Mexicano de Escritores.

MEMBER: Centro Mexicano de Escritores (fellow).

AWARDS, HONORS: Rockefeller grants, 1953 and 1954; Guggenheim fellowship, 1968; National Prize for Letters (Mexico), 1970; Príncipe de Asturias award (Spain), 1983.

WRITINGS:

FICTION

El llano en llamas y otros cuentos, Fondo de Cultura Económica, 1953, translation by George D. Schade published as *The*

Burning Plain and Other Stories, University of Texas Press, 1967, 2nd Spanish edition, corrected and enlarged, Fondo de Cultura Económica, 1970.
Pedro Páramo (novel), Fondo de Cultura Económica, 1955, translation by Lysander Kemp published as *Pedro Páramo: A Novel of Mexico,* Grove, 1959.
El gallo de oro y otros textos para cine, Ediciones Era, 1980.

OMNIBUS VOLUMES

Obra completa, Biblioteca Ayacucho, 1977.
Antología personal, Nueva Imagen, 1978.

CONTRIBUTOR

Aberlardo Gómez Benoit, editor, *Antología contemporánea del cuento hispano-americano* (title means "A Contemporary Anthology of the Hispanic-American Story"), Instituto Latinoamericano de Vinculación Cultural, 1964.
Crónicas de Latinoamericano, Editorial Jorge Alvarez, 1968.

OTHER

Juan Rulfo: Autobiografía armada, compiled by Reina Roffé, Ediciones Corregidor, 1973.
(With others) *Juan Rulfo: Homenaje nacional,* with photographs by Rulfo, Instituto Nacional de Bellas Artes (Mexico City), 1980, 2nd edition published as *Inframundo: El México de Juan Rulfo,* edited by Juan J. Bremer, Ediciones del Norte (Hanover, N.H.), 1983, translation by Jo Anne Engelbert published as *Inframundo: The Mexico of Juan Rulfo,* Ediciones del Norte, 1983.

Also author of television scripts and film adaptations, beginning 1954. Collaborator with Juan José Arreola on the review *Pan.*

WORK IN PROGRESS: La cordillera (title means "The Mountain Range"), a novel.

SIDELIGHTS: The late Mexican novelist Juan Rulfo is included in what Alan Riding called in the *New York Times Magazine* "the contemporary Latin American literary boom." Rulfo and such writers as Jorge Luis Borges, Julio Cortázar, and Carlos Fuentes wrote imaginative fiction that was made available through translation to readers in the United States during the fifties, sixties, and early seventies. Unlike the other writers, who prolifically turned out stories and novels, Rulfo established his reputation with a solitary collection of stories, *El llano en llamas y otros cuentos*—translated as *The Burning Plain and Other Stories*—and one novel, *Pedro Páramo.*

Two characteristics of these Latin American writers were their special affinity for innovative narrative techniques and their style of interweaving the historical with the marvelous, called magic realism; both qualities are often mentioned by reviewers of Rulfo's work. In his introduction to *The Burning Plain and Other Stories,* George D. Schade used the story "Macario"—included in the collection—as an example of Rulfo's narrative style. "In 'Macario,' " Schade observed, "the past and present mingle chaotically, and frequently the most startling associations of ideas are juxtaposed, strung together by conjunctions which help to paralyze the action and stop the flow of time in the present." In *Into the Mainstream: Conversations with Latin-American Writers,* Luis Harss and Barbara Dohmann comment on the story "The Man," noting the multiple points of view and foreshadowing used to heighten the reader's identification with the protagonist.

The narrative devices mentioned by Schade, Harss and Dohmann are also found in Rulfo's *Pedro Páramo,* a novel which Schade called "a bold excursion into modern techniques of writ-

ing." Using flashbacks, interior monologues and dialogues, and atemporal time sequences, Rulfo creates what Enrique Anderson-Imbert claimed in *Spanish-American Literature: A History* is a "story . . . told in loops, forward, backward, [and] to the sides." The narrative technique demands a lot of the reader, and the story in itself is also difficult. Halfway through the novel, for example, the reader realizes that all the characters are dead; the story all along has been the remembered history of ghosts conversing from their graves.

Startling as this revelation is, the mingling of death and life is typical of Mexican culture. Commenting in a *Nation* essay, Earl Shorris noted: "Everywhere in the novel, death is present: not the hidden, feared death we know in the Unites States but Mexican death, the death that is neither the beginning nor the end, the death that comes and goes in the round of time." Shorris observed that the constant reminders of death in Mexican life destroy "the distinction between [this] life" and the next. This hazy line between life and death accentuates that author's deliberately ambiguous delineation of scenes, narrators, and past and present time. The technical difficulties with which Rulfo confronts the reader become the framework for what Kessel Schwartz called in *A New History of Spanish-American Fiction* "an ambiguous and magical world, a kind of timeless fable of life and death" where historical facts—references to actual events in Mexican history—and fictive details are fused.

In his analysis of *Pedro Páramo* appearing in *Tradition and Renewal: Essays on Twentieth-Century Latin American Literature and Culture,* Luis Leal observed that while Rulfo's style was experimental, it was also firmly rooted in the historical reality of Mexico. Leal wrote: "The scenes are juxtaposed, united only by the central theme and lyrical motifs. . . . The novel, a mixture of realism and fantasy . . . has been created through the use of images, which, although poetic, are structured in a language that is characteristic of the countryside."

Rulfo's sparse, dry prose reflects the parched, stark Mexican landscape. Harss and Dohmann remarked: "His language is as frugal as his world, reduced almost to pure heartbeat. . . . He sings the swan song of blighted regions gangrened by age, where misery has opened wounds that burn under an eternal midday sun, where a pestilent fate has turned areas that were once rolling meadows and grasslands into fetid open graves. . . . He writes with a sharp edge, carving each word out of hard rock, like an inscription on a tombstone." According to Irving A. Leonard in the *Saturday Review,* "the bleak, harsh surroundings" Rulfo described with his "bare phrases" reflected his "pessimistic view of man's condition. Murder, incest, adultery, death overpowering life, violence in varied forms are predominant themes, unrelieved by humor or love."

Although Rulfo published a collection of film scripts and worked on the manuscript for another novel, *La cordillera,* for the rest of his life, further success as a writer eluded him. While a London *Times* reporter noted that *Pedro Páramo* "will be remembered as a unique achievement," the same writer believed that Rulfo himself seemed content to be known merely as "the master who could not write a second masterpiece."

MEDIA ADAPTATIONS: Pedro Páramo was made into a film in the 1960s.

BIOGRAPHICAL/CRITICAL SOURCES:

BOOKS

Anderson-Imbert, Enrique, *Spanish-American Literature: A History,* Volume II: *1910-1961,* 2nd edition, revised and updated by Elaine Malley, Wayne State University Press, 1969.

Contemporary Literary Criticism, Volume 8, Gale, 1978.

Forster, Merlin H., editor, *Tradition and Renewal: Essays on Twentieth-Century Latin American Literature and Culture,* University of Illinois Press, 1975.

Harss, Luis, and Barbara Dohmann, *Into the Mainstream: Conversations with Latin-American Writers,* Harper, 1967.

Rulfo, Juan, *The Burning Plain and Other Stories,* translation by George D. Schade, University of Texas Press, 1967.

Schwartz, Kessel, *A New History of Spanish-American Fiction,* Volume II, University of Miami Press, 1971.

PERIODICALS

Christian Science Monitor, January 4, 1968.
English Journal, January, 1974.
Hispania, December, 1971, September, 1974, March, 1975.
Nation, May 15, 1982.

National Observer, March 24, 1973.
New York Herald Tribune Book Review, August 2, 1959.
New York Times Book Review, June 7, 1959.
New York Times Magazine, March 13, 1983.
San Francisco Chronicle, August 30, 1959.
Saturday Review, June 22, 1968.
Times (London), January 10, 1986.
Times Literary Supplement, February 5, 1960.

OBITUARIES:

PERIODICALS

AB Bookman's Weekly, February 17, 1986.
Los Angeles Times, January 9, 1986.
New York Times, January 9, 1986.
Times (London), January 10, 1986.
Washington Post, January 11, 1986.

—Sketch by Marian Gonsior

S

SABATO, Ernesto (R.) 1911-

PERSONAL: Born June 24, 1911, in Rojas, Argentina; son of Francisco Sábato (a mill owner) and Juana Ferrari; married Matilde Kusminsky-Richter, 1934; children: Jorge Federico, Mario. *Education:* National University of La Plata, Ph.D., 1937; additional study at Joliot-Curie Laboratory (Paris), 1938, and Massachusetts Institute of Technology, 1939.

ADDRESSES: Home—1676 Santos Lugares, Buenos Aires, Argentina.

CAREER: National University of La Plata, La Plata, Argentina, professor of theoretical physics, 1940-43; novelist and essayist, 1943—. Guest lecturer at universities throughout the United States and Europe. Chairman of National Commission on the Disappearance of Persons (Argentina), 1983.

AWARDS, HONORS: Argentine Association for the Progress of Science fellowship in Paris, 1937; sash of honor from Argentine Writers Society and Municipal Prose prize from the City of Buenos Aires, both 1945, both for *Uno y el universo;* prize from the Institute of Foreign Relations (West Germany), 1973; Grand Prize of Honor from the Argentine Writers Society, Premio Consagración Nacional (Argentina), and Chevalier des Arts et des Lettres (France), all 1974; Prix au Meilleur Livre Etranger (Paris), 1977, for *Abaddón, el Exterminador;* Gran Cruz al Mérito Civil (Spain) and Chevalier de la Legion D'Honneur (France), both 1979; Gabriela Mistral Prize from Organization of American States, 1984; Miguel de Cervantes Prize from the Spanish Ministry of Culture, 1985; Commandeur de la Legion d'Honneur (France), 1987; Jerusalem Prize, 1989.

WRITINGS:

NOVELS

El túnel, Sur, 1948, translation by Harriet de Onis published as *The Outsider,* Knopf, 1950, translation by Margaret Sayers Peden published as *The Tunnel,* Ballantine, 1988.
Sobre héroes y tumbas, Fabril, 1961, reprinted, Seix Barral, 1981, excerpt published as *Un dios desconocido: Romance de la muerte de Juan Lavalle (de "Sobre héroes y tumbas"),* A. S. Dabini, 1980, translation by Stuart M. Gross of another excerpt published as "Report on the Blind" in *TriQuarterly,* fall-winter, 1968-69, translation by Helen Lane of entire novel published as *On Heroes and Tombs,* David Godine, 1981.

Abaddón, el Exterminador (title means "Abaddón: The Exterminator"; novel), Sudamericana, 1974.

ESSAYS

Uno y el universo (title means "One and the Universe"), Sudamericana, 1945.
Hombres y engranajes (title means "Men and Gears"), Emecé, 1951, reprinted, 1985.
Heterodoxia (title means "Heterodoxy"), Emecé, 1953.
El otro rostro del peronismo: Carta abierta a Mario Amadeo (title means "The Other Face of Peronism: Open Letter to Mario Amadeo"), López, 1956.
El caso Sábato: Torturas y libertad de prensa—Carta abierta al Gral. Aramburu (title means "Sábato's Case: Torture and Freedom of the Press—Open Letter to General Aramburu"), privately printed, 1956.
Tango: Discusión y clave (title means "Tango: Discussion and Key"), Losada, 1963.
El escritor y sus fantasmas (title means "The Writer and His Ghosts"), Aguilar, 1963.
Tres aproximaciones a la literatura de nuestro tiempo: Robbe-Grillet, Borges, Sartre (title means "Approaches to the Literature of Our Time . . ."; essays), Universitaria (Chile), 1968.
La convulsión política y social de nuestro tiempo (title means "The Political and Social Upheaval of Our Time"), Edicom, 1969.
Ernesto Sábato: Claves políticas (title means "Ernesto Sábato: Political Clues"), Alonso, 1971.
La cultura en la encrucijada nacional (title means "Culture in the National Crossroads"), Ediciones de Crisis, 1973.
(With Jorge Luis Borges) *Diálogos* (title means "Dialogues"), Emecé, 1976.
Apologías y rechazos (title means "Apologies and Rejections"), Seix Barral, 1979.
La robotización del hombre y otras páginas de ficción y reflexión (title means "The Robotization of Man and Other Pages of Fiction and Reflection"), Centro Editorial del América Latina, 1981.

COLLECTIONS

Obras de ficción (title means "Works of Fiction"; contains *El túnel* and *Sobre héroes y tumbas*), Losada, 1966.

Itinerario (title means "Itinerary"; selections from Sábato's novels and essays), Sur, 1969.

Obras: Ensayos (title means "Works: Essays"), Losada, 1970.

Páginas vivas (title means "Living Pages"), Kapelusz, 1974.

Antología (title means "Anthology"), Librería del Colegio, 1975.

Narrativa completa (title means "Complete Narrative"), Seix Barral, 1982.

Páginas de Ernesto Sábato (title means "Pages from Ernesto Sábato"), Celtia (Buenos Aires), 1983.

OTHER

(Editor) *Mitomagia: Los temas del misterio* (title means "Mitomagia: Themes of the Mysterious"), Ediciones Latinoamericanas, 1969.

(Author of introduction) *Testimonios: Chile, septiembre, 1973* (title means "Eyewitness Accounts: Chile, September, 1973"), Jus, 1973.

(With Antonio Berni) *Cuatro hombres de pueblo,* Librería de la Ciudad, 1979.

(Editor with Anneliese von der Lipper) *Viaje a los mundos imaginarios,* Legasa, 1983.

Contributor to *Sur* and other periodicals.

SIDELIGHTS: When one considers that Argentine novelist and essayist Ernesto Sábato has published only three novels, the impact he has had on Hispanic literature is remarkable: His first novel, *The Tunnel,* was a best-seller in his native land; his second work of fiction, *On Heroes and Tombs,* according to Emir Rodríguez Monegal in the *Borzoi Anthology of Latin American Literature,* "is one of the most popular contemporary novels in Latin America." *Abaddón, the Exterminator,* his third novel, was similarly acclaimed and was granted France's highest literary award—the Prix au Meilleur Livre Etranger. Sábato's importance was officially recognized in 1985 when he received the first Miguel de Cervantes Prize (considered the equivalent of the Nobel in the Hispanic world) from Spain's King Juan Carlos. Harley Dean Oberhelman, in his study of the author titled *Ernest Sábato,* calls Sábato "Argentina's most discussed contemporary novelist." His appeal rests largely in his portrayals of Argentine society under the domination of military strongmen such as Juan Perón and others, with his recurrent themes of incest, blindness, insanity, and abnormal psychology reflecting the distress of the Argentine people.

Born into a large, prosperous family of Italian origin, at age thirteen Sábato left the rural community where he had grown up to attend school in the city of La Plata. The transition from familial life to life alone in a unfamiliar urban area was a disturbing one for the future writer, and Sábato found order in his otherwise turbulent world in the study of mathematics. His academic studies were briefly interrupted for a five year period, however, when he became involved in the Argentine communist movement. Soon, upon learning of Stalinist atrocities, he lost faith in the communist cause and decided to retreat again to his academic work.

Sábato's success as a student earned him a research fellowship for study in Paris, and, while there his interest in writing was born. Deeply impressed by the surrealist movement, he secretly began writing a novel. Although his writing started to play an increasingly important role in his life, Sábato continued his scientific research and accepted a teaching position upon his return to Argentina. Nonetheless, his literary efforts continued and he became a regular contributor to the popular Argentine magazine, *Sur.* Teaching was to remain his livelihood until 1943 when a conflict with the Juan Perón government resulted in his dismissal from his posts.

Commenting on his departure from the scientific world, Sábato wrote in an autobiographical essay appearing in English translation in *Salmagundi,* "The open, public transition from physics to literature was not an easy one for me; on the contrary, it was painfully complicated. I wrestled with my demons a long time before I came to a decision in 1943—when I resolved to sequester myself, with wife and son, in a cabin in the sierras of Córdoba, far from the civilized world. It was not a rational decision. . . . But in crucial moments of my existence I have always trusted more in instinct than in ideas and have constantly been tempted to venture where reasonable people fear to tread."

While living in the cabin for a year Sábato wrote an award-winning book of essays, *Uno y el universo,* in which he condemned the moral neutrality of science. Two years later his first novel, *The Tunnel,* appeared. Profoundly influenced by psychological thought and existential in tone, the work evoked comparison to the writings of French authors Albert Camus and Jean-Paul Sartre. It is the story of an Argentine painter who recounts the events leading up to his murder of his mistress. As an exercise in self-analysis for the lonely painter, unable to communicate his thoughts and feelings, *The Tunnel* contains many of the themes found in Sábato's later work. "The almost total isolation of a man in a world dominated by science and reason," notes Oberhelman, "is the most important of these themes, but at the same time the reader sees the inability of man to communicate with others, an almost pathological obsession with blindness, and a great concern for Oedipal involvement as important secondary themes."

The landmark of Sábato's work stands to be his 1961 novel, *On Heroes and Tombs,* which appeared in an English edition in 1982. It tells the story of Martín del Castillo and his love for Alejandra Vidal Olmos. Alejandra's father, Fernando Vidal Olmos, apparently involved in an incestuous relationship with his daughter, is another important figure in the book along with Bruno Bassán, a childhood friend of Fernando. The work is lengthy and complex and has spawned numerous critical interpretations. "When it first appeared twenty years ago," writes *Newsweek* contributor Jim Miller, "Ernesto Sábato's Argentine epic was widely praised. This belated translation finally lets Americans see why. Bewitched, baroque, monumental, his novel is a stunning symphony of dissonant themes—a Gothic dirge, a hymn to hope, a tango in hell." Commenting on the novel's intricacy, John Butt observes in the *Times Literary Supplement,* "This monster novel . . . works on so many levels, leads down so many strange paths to worlds of madness, surrealistic self-analysis and self-repudiation, and overloads language so magnificently and outrageously, that the reader comes out of it with his critical nerve shot, tempted to judge it as 'great' without knowing why." Also noting the novel's multi-faceted contents, Ronald Christ in his *Commonweal* review referred to it as "wild, hypnotizing, and disturbing."

On Heroes and Tombs is divided into four parts, the third being a novel-within-a-novel called "Report on the Blind." *Review* contributor William Kennedy characterizes this portion of the novel—a first person exploration of Fernando's theories about a conspiracy of blind people who rule the world—as "a tour de force, a document which is brilliant in its excesses, a surreal journey into the depths of Fernando's personal, Boschian hells, which in their ultimate landscapes are the provinces of a 'terrible nocturnal divinity, a demoniacal specter that surely held supreme power over life and death.' " In his *Washington Post Book*

World review Salman Rushdie calls the section "the book's magnificent high point and its metaphysical heart." In Sábato's hands Fernando's paranoidal ravings fuse with the rest of the novel making the work at once a cultural, philosophical, theological, and sociological study of man and his struggle with the dark side of his being. According to Oberhelman, *On Heroes and Tombs* "without a doubt is the most representative national novel of Argentina written in the twentieth century." Kennedy describes the impact of the work when he concludes: "We read Sábato and we shudder, we are endlessly surprised, we exult, we are bewildered, fearful, mesmerized. He is a writer of great talent and imagination."

BIOGRAPHICAL/CRITICAL SOURCES:

BOOKS

Contemporary Literary Criticism, Gale, Volume 10, 1979, Volume 23, 1983.
Oberhelman, Harley Dean, *Ernesto Sábato,* Twayne, 1970.
Rodríguez Monegal, Emir, *The Borzoi Anthology of Latin American Literature,* Knopf, 1986.

PERIODICALS

Commonweal, June 18, 1982.
Newsweek, September 21, 1981.
Review, May-August, 1981.
Salmagundi, spring-summer, 1989.
Times Literary Supplement, August 13, 1982.
Washington Post Book World, August 16, 1981.

—*Sketch by Marian Gonsior*

* * *

SABINES, Jaime 1925(?)-

PERSONAL: Born in 1925 (one source says 1926) in Tuxtla Gutiérrez, Chiapas, Mexico. *Education:* Attended school in Mexico City, Mexico.

CAREER: Writer.

WRITINGS:

Horal, Departamento de Prensa y Turismo (Tuxtla Gutiérrez, Mexico), 1950 (also see below).
Tarumba, Colección Metáfora, 1956 (also see below), translation by Philip Levine and Ernesto Trejo published as *Tarumba: The Selected Poems of Jaime Sabines* (bilingual edition), Twin Peaks Press, 1979.
Poesía de la sinceridad (anthology), [Tlaxcala, Mexico], 1959.
Diario semanario y poemas en prosa, Universidad Veracruzana (Xalapa, Mexico), 1961 (also see below).
Recuento de poemas (includes poems previously published in other volumes), Universidad Nacional Autónoma de México, 1962.
Yuria, J. Mortiz, 1967 (also see below).
Maltiempo, J. Mortiz, 1972 (also see below).
Algo sobre la muerte del mayor Sabines, J. Mortiz, 1973 (also see below).
Nuevo recuento de poemas (includes *Horal, Tarumba, Diario semanario y poemas en prosa, Yuria, Algo sobre la muerte del mayor Sabines,* and *Maltiempo*), J. Mortiz, 1977.
Poemas sueltos, Papeles Privados, 1981.
Poesía, Casa de las Américas, 1987.

Also author of *La señal,* 1951, and *Doña Luz,* 1969. Contributor to literary reviews, including *Pájaro Cascabel.*

BIOGRAPHICAL/CRITICAL SOURCES:

BOOKS

Hernández Palacios, Esther, editor, *La poesía de Jaime Sabines: Análisis poético estrutural de "Algo sobre la muerte del mayor Sabines,"* Centro de Investigaciones Lingüístico-Literarias, Instituto de Investigaciones Humanísticas, Universidad Veracruzana, 1984.
Rodríguez Monegal, Emir, editor, *The Borzoi Anthology of Latin American Literature,* Volume II: *The Twentieth Century—From Borges and Paz to Guimaraes Rosa and Donoso,* Knopf, 1986.

PERIODICALS

Times Literary Supplement, May 18, 1973.

* * *

SACASTRU, Martín
See BIOY CASARES, Adolfo

* * *

SAENZ, Dalmiro
See SAENZ, Dalmiro A.

* * *

SAENZ, Dalmiro A. 1926-
(Dalmiro Sáenz)

PERSONAL: Born in 1926 in Argentina.

CAREER: Writer.

WRITINGS:

Setenta veces siete (short stories), Emecé (Buenos Aires), 1957.
No (short stories), Goyanarte (Buenos Aires), 1961.
Qwertyuiop (one-act play), Goyanarte, 1961.
Treinta treinta (short stories), Emecé, 1963.
El pecado necesario (novel), Emecé, 1964.
Dos guiones: Treinta treinta, el sexto día, Goyanarte, 1966.
El oficio de escribir cuentos (short stories), Emecé, 1968.
Carta abierta a mi futura ex mujer, Torres Agüero (Buenos Aires), 1982.
Cuentos para niños pornográficos (short stories), Torres Agüero, 1983.

UNDER NAME DALMIRO SAENZ

Hay hambre dentro de tu pan, J. Alvarez (Buenos Aires), 1963.
¿Quién, yo? (play), Goyanarte, 1965.
¡Hip . . . hip . . . ufa! (play), Sudamericana (Buenos Aires), 1967.
Yo también fui un espermatozoide, Merlín (Buenos Aires), 1968.
Vagabundia, Merlín, 1969.
(With Carlos Marcucci) *Vida sexual de Robinson Crusoe* (play), Ediciones L.H. (Buenos Aires), 1969.
El que se muere pierde, Merlín, 1970.
Diálogo con un homosexual, Merlín, 1974.
Charla sobre sexo, política y vida, Merlín, 1974.
El ladrón de tiempo, Castor y Pollux (Buenos Aires), 1977.
¡Esto es cultura animal!, Goyanarte, 1977.
Acordate de olvidar, Goyanarte, 1978.
Ese, Pomaire (Buenos Aires), 1981.
El argentinazo: Novela (novel), Nueva Editorial Latinoamericana (Buenos Aires), 1983.
Un vagabundo llamado Dalmiro, Torres Agüero, 1985.

(With Sergio Joselovsky) *El día que mataron a Alfonsín,* Ediciones Tarso (Buenos Aires), 1986.

Sobre sus párpados abiertos caminaba una mosca, Torres Agüero, 1986, adapted by the author into a play, *Las boludas,* Torres Agüero, 1988.

(With Sergio Josevovshy) *El día que mataron a cafiero,* Puntosur (Montevideo), 1987.

Cristo de pie, Puntosur (Buenos Aires), 1988.

* * *

SAGEL, Jim 1947-

PERSONAL: Born June 19, 1947, in Fort Morgan, Colo.; married Teresa Archuleta, 1970. *Education:* University of Colorado, B.A., 1969; received M.A. from University of New Mexico.

ADDRESSES: P.O. Box 942, Espanola, N.M. 87532.

CAREER: High school teacher in New Mexico, 1970-76; Northern New Mexico Community College, El Rito, teacher, 1976-81; became professor of creative writing at University of New Mexico at Los Alamos and Institute of Creative Indian Arts, Santa Fe, N.M.

WRITINGS:

Hablando de brujas y la gente de antes: Poemas del río chama, Place of Herons, 1981.

Foreplay and French Fries: Poems, Mango, 1981.

(With Nila Northsun) *Small Bones, Little Eyes,* Duck Down Press, 1981.

Tunomás Honey, Casa de las Américas (Havana), 1981, bilingual edition, Bilingual Press/Editorial Bilingüe, 1983.

Los cumpleaños de doña Agueda, Place of Herons, 1984.

Sábelotodo Entiendelonada and Other Stories, Bilingual Press/Editorial Bilingüe, 1988.

Otra vez en la movida/On the Make Again: New and Collected Poems, West End Press, 1990.

Contributor to *Puerto del Sol* and other publications.

SIDELIGHTS: Although descended from a Russian family, Jim Sagel writes about the Chicanos of northern New Mexico, an area he has made his home since 1969. Sagel "sees his writing," Lawrence Benton explains in the *Dictionary of Literary Biography,* "as an attempt to portray their lives—particularly their language—with realistic accuracy." In books of short stories and poetry, written in both English and Spanish, Sagel depicts his characters and their relationship with the dominant Anglo culture. He covers such subjects as the New Right, the Vietnam War, and struggles between land developers and Chicano farmers. In perhaps his best-known work, *Tunomás Honey,* first published in Cuba, Sagel presents character studies of the elderly, handicapped, or eccentric. Writing in the *Santa Fe New Mexican,* Michael R. J. Roth calls the collection "as wry and sharp as the people it portrays."

BIOGRAPHICAL/CRITICAL SOURCES:

BOOKS

Dictionary of Literary Biography, Volume 82: *Chicano Writers, First Series* Gale, 1989.

PERIODICALS

Santa Fe New Mexican, April 12, 1985.

SAINZ, Gustavo 1940-

PERSONAL: Born July 13, 1940, in Mexico City, Mexico. *Education:* Attended National Autonomous University of Mexico.

ADDRESSES: Río Nazas 77-6, Mexico 5, D.F., Mexico.

CAREER: Writer, 1965—; editor for *Siete* magazine in Mexico City, Mexico; teacher of literature courses at the National Autonomous University of Mexico and at the University of New Mexico.

WRITINGS:

Gazapo (novel), J. Mortiz, 1965, translation by Hardie St. Martin published under the same title, Farrar, Straus, 1968.

Gustavo Sáinz (autobiography), Empresas, 1966.

Obsesivos días circulares (novel; title means "Obsessive Circular Days"), J. Mortiz, 1969.

(Editor) *Antología de poesía erótica* (poetry; title means "Anthology of Erotic Poetry"), Orientación, 1972.

La princesa del Palacio de Hierro (novel), J. Mortiz, 1974, translation by Andrew Hurley published as *The Princess of the Iron Palace,* Grove, 1987.

(Contributor) *Conversaciones con José Revueltas* (biography; title means "Conversations with José Revueltas"), Centro de Investigaciones Lingüístico-Literarias, Universidad Veracruzana, 1977.

Compadre lobo (novel; title means "Friend Wolf"), Grijalbo, 1979.

(Editor) *Jaula de palabras: Una antología de la nueva narrativa mexicana* (fiction; title means "Cage of Words: An Anthology of the New Mexican Narrative"), Grijalbo, 1981.

Fantasmas aztecas: Un pre-texto (novel; title means "Aztec Phantoms: A Pre-Text"), Grijalbo, 1982.

(Editor) *Los mejores cuentos mexicanos* (short stories; title means "The Best Mexican Short Stories"), Océano (Barcelona), 1982.

Ojalá te mueras y otras novelas clandestinas mexicanas (title means "I Hope You Die and Other Underground Mexican Novels"), Océano, 1982.

Ritos de iniciación (title means "Initiation Rites"), Océano, 1982.

Paseo en trapecio (title means "Trapeze Ride"), Edivisión, 1985.

Muchacho en llamas (title means "Boy in Flames"), Grijalbo, 1988.

SIDELIGHTS: Mexican novelist Gustavo Sáinz is celebrated for his keen eye and ear for the culture and language of bohemian youth in Mexico City. *Gazapo,* Sáinz's first novel, depicts a week in the lives of a group of teenagers, focusing on how the young people communicate with one another. The protagonist Menelao has left home after a spat with his stepmother and takes refuge in his mother's empty apartment, where he talks compulsively to his friends and clumsily plots how to coax his girlfriend into bed. Most of this running dialogue/monologue is mediated through tape recordings, phone conversations, letters, and diaries. The author further complicates the narrative with "rearrangements of time, multiple perspectives on a single action, and the deliberate blurring of causal and narrative connections," noted *New Republic* reviewer Richard Gilman. But the novel's real theme is language and the elusiveness of meaning in communication. The broader Mexican society is also satirized in this "brilliant celebration of the comedy of life," remarked Stephen Geller in the *New York Times Book Review. Gazapo* became a best-seller in Mexico and has been translated into English.

Language is the explicit subject of Sáinz's novel *Obsesivos días circulares* ("Obsessive Circular Days"). The narrator-protagonist Terencio works as a caretaker at a private religious school for girls that is later revealed as a brothel owned by an underworld figure. An introverted and suspicious intellectual, Terencio seeks refuge from this brutal and chaotic world in sexual and linguistic fantasies, but ultimately his words betray him. Though judged an interesting literary experiment, *Obsesivos días circulares* was faulted for its pretentious tone and overly complex structure. But Sáinz scored another big success with his third novel, *The Princess of the Iron Palace*. The narrator and "princess" of the title is a young, married middle-class woman who recalls her youth working after school as a sales clerk at the Iron Palace, a huge Mexico City department store. Self-centered and materialistic, the princess tells her story in a running monologue of "entertaining non sequiturs, inspired malapropisms, . . . and inventive expletives," remarked Suzanne Ruta in the *Voice Literary Supplement*. The sharp-tongued narrator sheds comic light on the transgressions of Mexico's ruling elite as she nostalgically remembers her youthful nights on the town. A best-seller in Mexico, the translated novel was also well received in the United States.

BIOGRAPHICAL/CRITICAL SOURCES:

BOOKS

Sáinz, Gustavo, *Gustavo Sáinz,* Empresas, 1966.

PERIODICALS

New Republic, August 17, 1968.
New York Times Book Review, July 21, 1968.
Times Literary Supplement, November 6, 1970.
Voice Literary Supplement, September, 1987.
World Literature Today, summer, 1983.

* * *

SALAS, Floyd (Francis) 1931-

PERSONAL: Born January 24, 1931, in Walsenburg, Colo.; son of Edward (a restaurant owner) and Anita (a housewife; maiden name, Sanchez) Salas; married Velva Daryl Harris (a nursery school owner), January, 1948 (divorced, 1970); married Virginia Ann Staley, June 25, 1979 (divorced, 1981); children: Gregory Francis. *Education:* Attended California College of Arts and Crafts, 1950-54, Oakland Junior College, 1955-56, and University of California, Berkeley, 1956-57; San Francisco State College (now University), B.A., 1963, M.A., 1965. *Politics:* Democrat. *Religion:* "Agnostic-Theist."

ADDRESSES: Home and office—1206 Delaware St., Berkeley, Calif. 94702. *Agent*—Linda Allen, 1949 Green St. No. 5, San Francisco, Calif. 94123.

CAREER: San Francisco State University, San Francisco, Calif., lecturer in English, 1966-67, state coordinator of Poetry in the Schools, 1973-76; writer, 1967-75; Peralta College for Non-Traditional Studies, Berkeley, Calif., instructor in creative writing, 1975-76; University of California, Berkeley, assistant boxing coach, 1975—, lecturer in English, 1977-78; writer, 1978-80; Foothill College, Los Altos, Calif., lecturer in creative writing, 1979—; Sonoma State University, Rohnert Park, Calif, instructor in English, 1984—. Teacher of creative writing at correctional camp for youth, Folsom State Prison, San Quentin Prison, and private workshop classes.

AWARDS, HONORS: Rockefeller Foundation scholar at El Centro Mexicano de Escritores, 1958; Joseph Henry Jackson Award from the San Francisco Foundation, 1964, for *Tattoo the Wicked Cross;* Eugene F. Saxton fellowship, 1965; fellowship from National Endowment for the Arts, 1978; Bay Area writing project fellowship, 1984.

WRITINGS:

Tattoo the Wicked Cross (novel), Grove, 1967.
What Now My Love (novella), Grove, 1969.
Lay My Body on the Line (novel), Y'bird Press, 1978.

EDITOR AND CONTRIBUTOR

I Write What I Want, San Francisco State University, 1974.
Word Hustlers, Word Hustlers Press, 1976.
To Build a Fire, Mark Ross Publishers, 1977.
Stories and Poems from Close to Home, Ortalda & Associates, 1986.

OTHER

Work represented in anthologies, including *The San Francisco Bark* and *Calafia.* Contributor of poems, articles, and reviews to periodicals, including *Writer, Transfer,* and *Hyperion.*

WORK IN PROGRESS: Fandango and *La Favorita,* historical novels; *State of Emergency,* a political novel; *Wooman,* a novel; and *Brothers Keepers.*

SIDELIGHTS: Floyd Salas writes: "Boxing and writing have been intertwined throughout my life. I went to the University of California on a boxing scholarship, the very first one offered there. I found that fighting and writing complemented each other. Both require the same basic traits of character: dedication, durability, and courage, as well as the need to be spiritually pure and humble if you want to do well. I teach boxing the same way I teach writing. Both are very simple, composed of only three technical elements each. In boxing, the elements are the jab, the cross, and the hook. All punches are one of these three. In writing, the elements are description, narration, and dialogue. All writing is one or another, or a combination of them."

Salas described the experiences that guided him toward a writing career. "In 1946, when I was in juvenile hall for a street fight, I wrote a song about a midnight rambler, a young kid's version of being a 'cool cat.' In summer school that year, a play I wrote was produced, though I wasn't identified as the playwright. Then I didn't write again until I was eighteen and was in the county jail for knocking out a cop. There I wrote Valentine's Day verses for the other prisoners. When I was nineteen and my older brother, Eddy, committed suicide, the poems came again. Though they were corny and sentimental, they had emotional power. I began to think of being a writer, but I went to art college first. I did well, but I found myself writing poems instead of drawing pictures in my free time. I transferred to an academic college to get on the boxing team, get a scholarship, and become a writer. At the age of twenty-three I got in trouble again and didn't pursue my goal until the next year, when I entered Oakland Junior College and transferred to the University of California at Berkeley. I quit Cal to write, and in 1957 I wrote my first short stories. They won me a Rockefeller Foundation writing scholarship. When I came back from Mexico, I worked to get back on my financial feet and started studying with Walter Van Tilburg Clark at San Francisco State. In the fall of 1961, I started working on my first novel, *Tattoo the Wicked Cross,* and I finished it along with a master's degree program four years later. When the novel was published in 1967, I became a writer.

"*Tattoo the Wicked Cross* was not an autobiographical novel. I heard the primary story about the rape of a little kid in Preston Reform School. The boy then put lye in the food of his attackers and caused them much misery. That sparked my interest, and I went to the library to do some research on poisons. I put myself in the shoes of a young boy and, using my own experience in a juvenile hall at age fifteen and at a country jail farm at age twenty as reference material, I created the story of Aaron D'Aragon.

"I wrote *What Now My Love* because I had a story to tell about smoking pot. I had been an early martyr for pot, and it cost me my wife and son. I learned that one cop, Harry Anslinger, was put out of a job by the legalization of alcohol. He went around the country during the 1930s, campaigning for the outlawing of drugs, including marijuana, and got himself named head of the federal narcotics bureau for life. I wanted to tell that story, but I also saw the other side. The youth of the country were a bunch of consumers who lived off the largess of their parents, but dealt in dope on the black market, practicing the same values but with a different commodity.

"I did shake things up with *Lay My Body on the Line*. Some old-time and very successful radicals quit being nice to me after they read that book. I wrote about a true democrat, who fought fascism on all sides, including the campus left. I still believe that a democracy, no matter what the economic system, communist or capitalist, is better than a dictatorship. I believe that some politicians really do mean well, but that none of them can be trusted and that all of them should be subject to scrutiny by the voters. There should be no dictatorship of any kind, communist or otherwise. This belief was the motivating factor behind my own behavior in the years of demonstrations and my reason for writing the book."

BIOGRAPHICAL/CRITICAL SOURCES:

PERIODICALS

New York Times Book Review, September 17, 1967.
Time, September 8, 1967.

* * *

SALAZAR BONDY, Sebastián   1924-1965

PERSONAL: Born 1924 in Lima, Peru; died 1965.

CAREER: Playwright, poet, essayist, critic, and story writer. Lived for a time in Buenos Aires, Argentina, where he wrote for the newspaper *La Nación.*

WRITINGS:

(With Jorge Eduardo Eielson and Javier Sologuren) *La poesía contemporánea del Perú,* Editorial Cultura Antártica (Lima), 1946.
Máscara del que duerme: Dibujos de Luis Seoane, Botella al Mar (Buenos Aires), 1949.
(With César Miró) *Ollantay,* Ediciones de "Mar del Sur" (Lima), 1953.
No hay isla feliz: Drama en tres actos (also see below), Ediciones Club de Teatro, (Lima), 1954.
Algo que quiere morir: Drama en tres actos (also see below), Editorial Talfa (Buenos Aires), 1956.
(Editor with Alejandro Romualdo) *Antología general de la poesía peruana,* Librería Internacional del Perú (Lima), 1957.
Pobre gente de París, J. Mejía Baca (Lima), 1958.
Seis juguetes, Editorial Nuevos Rumbos, 1958.
Arte milenario del Perú: Láminas y textos, Ministerio de Educación Pública (Lima), 1958.
Cuentos infántiles peruanos, Editorial Nuevos Rumbos (Lima), 1958.
Confidencía en alta voz: Poemas, Ediciones Vida y Palabra (Lima), 1960.
Del hueso tallado al arte abstracto: Introducción al arte, Ediciones Peruanas Simiente, 1960.

Vida de Ximena, Ediciones de la Escuela Nacional de Bellas Artes (Lima), 1960.
El señor gallinazo vuelve a Lima, Ediciones de la Pelota de Trapo (Lima), 1961.
Teatro: Rodil, No hay isla feliz, Algo que quiere morir, [and] *Flora Tristán,* Editorial Losada (Buenos Aires), 1961.
Cuba, nuestra revolución, Ediciones de la Patria Libre (Lima), 1962.
(With V. Roel Pineda and J. Matos Mar) *La Encrucijada del Perú,* Arca (Montevideo), 1963.
Conducta sentimental, Editorial Celza (Bogota), 1963.
La cerámica peruana prehispánica, Universidad Nacional Autónoma de México, 1964.
(Editor) Garcilaso de la Vega, el Inca, *Comentarios reales de los Incas,* Editorial Universitaria de Buenos Aires, 1964, 3rd edition, 1971.
Dios en el cafetín, Populibros Peruanos (Lima), 1964.
El fabricante de deudas, Ediciones Nuevo Mundo (Lima), 1964.
Lima: Su moneda y su ceca, Novagrafica (Lima), 1964.
Lima, la horrible, Populibros Peruanos, 1964.
(Editor) *Poesía quechua,* Universidad Nacional Autónoma de México, 1964.
Poemas, 1960-1965, F. Moncloa (Lima), 1966.
El tacto de la araña: Sombras como cosas sólidas, poemas, 1960-1965,
Sebastián Salazar por él mismo, F. Moncloa, 1966.
Comedias y juguetes, F. Moncloa, 1967.
Piezas dramáticas, F. Moncloa, 1967.
Poemas, F. Moncloa, 1967.
Alférez Arce, teniente Arce, capitán Arce, Casa de la Cultura del Peru (Lima), 1969.
El espejo no hace milagros, Servicio de Publicaciones, Teatro Universitario, U.N.M. de San Marcos, 1970.
El trapecio de la vida, Servicio de Publicaciones, Teatro Universitario, U.N.M. de San Marcos, 1971.
Sombras como cosas sólidas y otros poemas, edited by Luis Losyza, Editorial Libres de Sinera, 1974.
Todo esto es mi país, Fondo de Cultura Económica, 1987.

SIDELIGHTS: Known primarily for his plays, Sebastián Salazar Bondy was also renowned for his controversial *Lima, la horrible,* in which Peru's capital city was depicted as a town of poverty and ugly shanties. Mario Benedetti, writing in *Letras del continente mestizo,* called *Lima, la horrible* "one of those books destined to shake the tree of the continent vigorously." Mario Vargas Llosa, writing in *Alcor,* described *Lima, la horrible* as "a book whose subject, style, and purpose renew a genre in Peru and show its writer to be a splendid essayist." Salazar Bondy's plays often concerned historical events and characters. *Rodil,* the story of a military siege in the 1820's, was described by José Miguel Oviedo of *RPC* as "outstanding for the care and theatrical economy of its structure." Writing in *Behind Spanish American Footlights,* Willis Knapp Jones claimed that Salazar Bondy wrote in a "beautiful literary language such as Arthur Miller might have employed."

BIOGRAPHICAL/CRITICAL SOURCES:

BOOKS

Benedetti, Mario, *Letras del continente mestizo,* 2nd edition, Editorial Arca, 1970.
Jones, Willis Knapp, *Behind Spanish American Footlights,* University of Texas Press, 1966.

PERIODICALS

Alcor, March-April, 1964.

RPC, Number 7/8, 1966.

* * *

SALINAS, Luis Omar 1937-

PERSONAL: Born June 27, 1937, in Robstown, Tex.; son of Rosendo and Olivia (Treviño) Salinas. *Education:* Attended Fresno State University, 1967-72.

ADDRESSES: Home—2009 Ninth St., Sanger, Calif. 93652.

CAREER: Poet, editor, and interpreter.

AWARDS, HONORS: California English Teachers citation, 1973; Stanley Kunitz Poetry Prize, 1980, for *Afternoon of the Unreal;* Earl Lyon Award, 1980; General Electric Foundation Award, 1983.

WRITINGS:

Crazy Gypsy: Poems, Origenes Publications, 1970.
(Editor with Lillian Faderman) *From the Barrio: A Chicano Anthology,* Canfield Press, 1973.
(With others) *Entrance: Four Chicano Poets; Leonard Adame, Luis Omar Salinas, Gary Soto, Ernesto Trejo* (anthology), Greenfield Review Press, 1975.
I Go Dreaming Serenades (poetry), Mango, 1979.
Afternoon of the Unreal (poetry), Abramás Publications, 1980.
Prelude to Darkness (poetry), Mango, 1981.
Darkness Under the Trees: Walking Behind the Spanish (poetry), Chicano Studies Library Publications, University of California, 1982.
The Sadness of Days: Selected and New Poems, Arte Público, 1987.

Editor of *Backwash* at Fresno State University, 1969-70. Poems have been anthologized in *Speaking for Ourselves: American Ethnic Writing,* edited by Lillian Faderman, Scott Foresman & Co., 1969; *Mexican-American Authors,* edited by Amérigo Paredes and Raymund Paredes, Houghton, 1972; *We Are Chicanos,* edited by Philip D. Ortego, Washington Square Press, 1973; *Time to Greeze! Incantations From the Third World,* edited by Janice Mirikitani and others, Glide Publications, 1974; *Settling America: The Ethnic Expression of Fourteen Contemporary Poets,* edited by David Khekdian, Macmillan, 1974; *Voices of Aztlán: Chicano Literature of Today,* edited by Dorothy E. Harth and Lewis M. Baldwin, New American Library, 1974; and *Festival de Flor y Canto: An Anthology of Chicano Literature,* edited by Alurista and others, University of Southern California Press, 1976. Contributor to periodicals, including *San Francisco Chronicle, Transpacific, Partisan, Bronze, Es Tiempo,* and *Revista Chicano-Riqueña.*

WORK IN PROGRESS: Saving Grace, a book of poems.

SIDELIGHTS: Born in Texas, poet Luis Omar Salinas spent a few early years in Mexico, but from the age of nine he lived with an aunt and uncle in California. While supporting himself with a variety of jobs, Salinas attended college in California and became involved in the literary community at Fresno State University. He is best known for his surrealistic vision, which he defines in *Chicano Literature* as "the strange fullness of the unreal." In Salinas's view, dreamlike and fantastical imagery can better convey reality and suffering as it is experienced by people than can a conventional "realistic" approach. The author's work often addresses such problems as poverty, prejudice, and the alienation that Mexican-Americans undergo in American society. In *Chicano Literature* he summarized his poetic aspirations as "somehow to come to terms with the tragic and through the tragic gain a vision which transcends this world in some way." Through his unusual observations, imagery, and metaphors, Salinas reveals common aspects of reality which have been overlooked because they are accepted as normal. "For Salinas the common or 'normal' dulls our senses and deadens our response to the tyranny of the mechanical habits of daily living. By creating 'the fullness of the unreal,' he defamiliarizes the world for us and then forces us to confront the 'true' nature of the society that surrounds us," according to *Chicano Literature.*

BIOGRAPHICAL/CRITICAL SOURCES:

BOOKS

Martínez, Julio A. and Francisco A. Lomelí, editors, *Chicano Literature: A Reference Guide,* Greenwood Press, 1985.

* * *

SAMORA, Julian 1920-

PERSONAL: Born March 1, 1920, in Pagosa Springs, Colo. *Education:* Adams State College, B.A., 1942; Colorado State University, M.S., 1947; postgraduate study at University of Wisconsin, 1948-49; Washington University, Ph.D., 1952.

ADDRESSES: Office—P.O. Box 534, University of Notre Dame, Notre Dame, Ind. 46556.

CAREER: High school teacher in Walsenburg, Colo., 1942-43; Adams State College, Alamosa, Colo., instructor, 1944-45; University of Colorado, School of Medicine, Denver, assistant professor of preventive medicine and public health, 1955-57; Michigan State University, East Lansing, assistant professor of sociology and anthropology, 1957-59; University of Notre Dame, Notre Dame, Ind., professor of sociology, 1959—, professor emeritus, 1985—, head of department, 1963-66. Visiting professor at University of New Mexico, 1954, Michigan State University, 1955, Universidad Nacional de Colombia, 1963, University of California, Los Angeles, 1964, and University of Texas, 1971. Past or present commissioner of President's Commission on Rural Poverty, National Upward Bound, President's Commission on Income Maintenance Programs, Colorado Anti-Discrimination Commission, and Indiana Civil Rights Commission. Has done field work in the United States, Colombia, and the U.S.-Mexico border area. Consultant to U.S. Commission on Civil Rights, U.S. Public Health Service, National Endowment for the Humanities, Ford Foundation, and other public and private groups.

AWARDS, HONORS: Whitney Foundation fellow, 1951-52; fellow of the American Sociological Association, 1978; La Raza Award, 1979; National Endowment for the Humanities scholar, 1979; honorary alumni award from Colorado State University, 1981; Emily M. Schlossberger Award from University of Notre Dame Press, 1981; scholar of National Association of Chicano Scholars, 1983; Special Presidential Award from University of Notre Dame, 1985; certificate of achievement from Adams State College, 1985; medal of honor from National Hispanic University, 1985; award from Midwest Latino Council of Higher Education, 1985.

WRITINGS:

(Contributor) Benjamin Paul, editor, *Health, Culture, and Community,* Russell Sage, 1955.
(Contributor) James K. Skipper, Jr. and Robert C. Leonard, editors, *Social Interaction and Patient Care,* Lippincott, 1965.
La Raza: Forgotten Americans, University of Notre Dame Press, 1966.

(Contributor) W. Richard Scott and Edmund H. Volkart, editors, *Medical Care: Readings in the Sociology of Medical Institutions,* Wiley, 1966.

(With Richard A. Lamanna) *Mexican Americans in a Midwest Metropolis: A Study of East Chicago,* Graduate School of Business Administration, University of California, Los Angeles, 1967.

(With E. Galarza and H. Gallegos) *Mexican-Americans in the Southwest,* McNally & Loftin, 1969.

Los Mojados: The Wetback Story, University of Notre Dame Press, 1971.

(With P. V. Simon) *A History of the Mexican American People,* University of Notre Dame Press, 1977.

Gunpowder Justice: A Reassessment of the Texas Rangers, University of Notre Dame Press, 1979.

Contributor of numerous articles to sociology journals.

* * *

SANCHEZ, Florencio 1875-1910

PERSONAL: Born in 1875 in Uruguay; died in 1910.

CAREER: Journalist, political activist, playwright, and writer.

WRITINGS:

PLAYS

La gringa (four-act comedy), [Uruguay], 1904, reprinted, introduction and notes by Jay Thomas Lister and Ruth Richardson, Knopf, 1927, reprinted, Huemul (Buenos Aires), 1970, translation by A. Coester published as "The Foreign Girl" in *Plays of the Southern Americas,* Books for Libraries Press (Freeport, N.Y.), 1971.

Barranca abajo (three-act drama), [Uruguay], 1905, reprinted, Prometeo, 1981.

POSTHUMOUS PUBLICATIONS

Los muertos (three-act drama), Argentores (Buenos Aires), 1935, reprinted, La Pampa (Buenos Aires), 1961.

M'hijo el dotor (three-act drama), prologue by Fermín Estrella Gutiérrez, Kapelusz (Buenos Aires), 1953, reprinted, Juventud (La Paz, Argentina), 1981.

En familia (three-act comedy), La Pampa, 1961, reprinted, Colihue, 1981.

Also author of articles, letters, and short prose works; other plays include *Canillita, Nuestros hijos, El caudillaje criminal en Sud América, Los curdas, Mano santa, Los derechos de la salud, Un buen negocio, La pobre gente, El pasado, El desalojo, La tigre, Moneda falsa, Marta Gruni* (farce), and *Cartas de un flojo.*

COLLECTIONS

El teatro del uruguayo Florencio Sánchez, Cervantes (Barcelona), 1926.

Teatro de Florencio Sánchez, Sopena Argentina, 1939.

Teatro completo de Florencio Sánchez, compiled by Dardo Cúneo, Claridad (Buenos Aires), 1941.

Teatro completo, prologue by Vicente Martínez Cuitiño, "El Ateneo," 1951.

Representative Plays of Florencio Sánchez, translated by Willis Knapp Jones, Pan American Union (Washington), 1961.

Obras completas, compiled with introduction by Jorge Lafforgue, Schapire (Buenos Aires), 1968.

Works also published in multititle volumes and in other collections; works represented in anthologies, including *Teatro uruguayo contemporáneo,* Aguilar (Madrid), 1960.

BIOGRAPHICAL/CRITICAL SOURCES:

BOOKS

Rela, Walter, *Florencio Sánchez, persona y teatro,* Ciencias, 1981.

* * *

SANCHEZ (y SANCHEZ), George I(sidore) 1906-1972

PERSONAL: Given names sometimes spelled Jorge Isidoro; born October 4, 1906, in Albuquerque (one source says Barela), N.M.; died April 5, 1972, in Austin, Tex.; son of Telesfor and Juliana (Sánchez) Sánchez; married Virginia Romero, June 15, 1925 (divorced, 1947); married Luisa G. Guerroro, August 30, 1947; children: George Eugene, Juliana Consuelo. *Education:* University of New Mexico, A.B., 1930; University of Texas, M.S., 1931; University of California, Ed.D., 1934.

CAREER: Teacher, principal, and supervisor in schools of rural New Mexico, 1923-30; New Mexico State Department of Education, Santa Fe, director of division of information and statistics, 1930-35; Julius Rosenwald Fund, Chicago, Ill., research associate, 1935-37; Government of Venezuela, Caracas, asesor técnico general for Ministerio de Educación and director of Instituto Pedagógico Nacional, 1937-38; University of New Mexico, Albuquerque, research associate and associate professor of education, 1938-40; University of Texas, Austin, professor of Latin American education, 1940-72, chairman of department of history and philosophy of education, 1951-59, director of Center for International Education, beginning 1963. Visiting lecturer at University of Southern California, Colorado State College of Education, and University of Mexico. Conducted education surveys of Navajo for U.S. Office of Indian Affairs, 1946, in Venezuela for U.S. Office of Education, 1961, and in Peru for U.S. Agency for International Development, 1962; member of Citizens Committee on a New Frontier Policy in the Americas, 1960, and of advisory council of Peace Corps, 1961; consultant to numerous government agencies. Member of board of Travis Junior College.

MEMBER: League of United Latin American Citizens (president, 1941-42), National Education Association, Progressive Education Association, Southwest Council on the Education of Spanish-Speaking People (president, 1945-72), New Mexico Education Association (president), Sociedad Mexicana de Geografía y Estadística, Sociedad Nacional Argentina de Estudios Históricos, Phi Delta Kappa, Phi Kappa Phi, Sigma Delta Pi.

AWARDS, HONORS: Grant from Carnegie Corporation for study of the people of rural New Mexico, 1938-39; grant from Carnegie Endowment for study of education in Mexico, 1941-42.

WRITINGS:

Mexico: A Revolution by Education, foreword by Rafael Ramírez, Viking, 1936, reprinted, Greenwood Press, 1971.

The Equalization of Educational Opportunity: Some Issues and Problems, University of New Mexico Press, 1939.

Forgotten People: A Study of New Mexicans, University of New Mexico Press, 1940, reprinted, Calvin Horn, 1967.

The Development of Higher Education in Mexico, King's Crown Press (New York), 1944, reprinted, Greenwood Press, 1970.

The People: A Study of the Navajos, foreword by William Zimmerman, Jr., U.S. Indian Service, 1948.

(With Howard Putnam) *Materials Relating to the Education of Spanish-Speaking People in the United States: An Annotated Bibliography,* Institute of Latin American Studies, University of Texas, 1959.

Arithmetic in Maya, [Austin, Tex.], 1961.

The Development of Education in Venezuela, U.S. Department
of Health, Education, and Welfare, Office of Education,
1963.

Mexico, Ginn, 1966.

Editor of *Inter-American Education: Occasional Papers,* for University of Texas Press, beginning 1946. Contributor to periodicals, including *Curriculum Journal, Journal of Applied Psychology,* and *Journal of Social Psychology.* Editorial consultant to
The Nation's Schools, beginning 1944.

SIDELIGHTS: George I. Sánchez was a lifelong advocate for
Hispanic Americans of the southwestern United States. After
using a Carnegie grant to study the inhabitants of rural New
Mexico during the late 1930s, Sánchez was inspired to write his
1940 book, *Forgotten People.* The book focuses on the descendants of New Mexico's early Spanish-speaking settlers, depicting
their struggles to earn a living and to preserve their culture after
the area was annexed by the United States during the mid-
nineteenth century. Reviewing a reprint of the work for *Nation*
in 1968, Philip Darraugh Ortego wrote: "*Forgotten People* is as
relevant today as it was in 1940. It is one of the great books in
the literature of the Southwest." Sánchez, who showed an interest in the education of Spanish-speaking people throughout his
career, spent the last years of his life campaigning to make bilingual education available to Hispanics in Texas.

BIOGRAPHICAL/CRITICAL SOURCES:

BOOKS

Humanidad: Essays in Honor of George I. Sánchez, Chicano
Studies Center Publications, University of California, Los
Angeles, 1977.

PERIODICALS

Nation, April 8, 1968.

* * *

SANCHEZ, Luis Rafael 1936-

PERSONAL: Born in 1936 in Humacao, Puerto Rico.

ADDRESSES: Office—Department of Literature, University of
Puerto Rico at Río Piedras, Ponce de Leon Ave., Río Piedras,
P.R. 00931.

CAREER: Dramatist, novelist, short story writer, and poet. Professor of literature at University of Puerto Rico, Río Piedras,
P.R.

WRITINGS:

PLAYS

Los ángeles se han fatigado [and] *Farsa del amor compradito*
(first half of title means "The Angels Have Grown Tired"),
Ediciones Lugar (San Juan), 1960 (also see below).

. . . O casi el alma: Auto da fé en tres actos (title means "Almost
the Soul: Auto da fé in Three Acts"; first produced in San
Juan at Teatro Tapia, April 23, 1964), Ediciones Rumbos
(Barcelona), 1966, published as *Casi el alma: Auto da fé en
tres actos,* Editorial Cultural (Río Piedras, P.R.), 1974.

La pasión según Antígona Pérez (two-act; first produced in San
Juan at the eleventh theater festival of the Institute of
Puerto Rican Culture, May 30, 1968; produced as "The
Passion of Antígona Pérez" in New York at Cathedral
Church of St. John the Divine, 1972), Ediciones Lugar
(Hato Rey, P.R.), 1968.

La hiel nuestra de cada día (title means "Our Everyday Bile"),
Editorial Cultural, 1976 (also see below).

Teatro de Luis Rafael Sánchez (title means "Plays of Luis Rafael
Sánchez"; contains *Los ángeles se han fatigado, Farsa del
amor compradito,* and *La hiel nuestra de cada día*), Editorial Antillana, 1976.

Quintuples (title means "Quintuplets"; two-act; first produced in
San Juan at the Centro de Bellas Artes de Puerto Rico, October 3, 1984), Ediciones del Norte, 1985.

Also author of "La Espera" (title means "The Wait"), 1959.

OTHER

En cuerpo de camisa: Cuentos (short stories), Ediciones Lugar,
1966, fourth augmented edition, Editorial Cultural, 1984.

La guaracha del Macho Camacho (novel), Ediciones de la Flor
(Buenos Aires), 1976, translation by Gregory Rabassa published as *Macho Camacho's Beat,* Pantheon, 1980.

Fabulación e ideología en la cuentística de Emilio S. Belavel (nonfiction), Instituto de Cultura Puertorriqueña (San Juan),
1979.

(Contributor) Rose S. Minc, editor, *Literature and Popular Culture in the Hispanic World: A Symposium,* Ediciones Hispanoamericanas, 1982.

La importancia de llamarse Daniel Santos, Ediciones del Norte,
1988.

SIDELIGHTS: Luis Rafael Sánchez is one of Puerto Rico's outstanding literary figures. His plays and short stories have earned
him a reputation throughout the Spanish-speaking world, and
his translated first novel, *Macho Camacho's Beat,* was a major
critical success in the United States. Sánchez's work is distinguished by what critics consider strikingly original structural innovations and an adept manipulation of contemporary Spanish
idioms. His themes range from the cultural distortions in mod-
ern-day Puerto Rico to existential tragicomedy and the nature
of the work of the imagination.

Sánchez has worked most frequently as a dramatist, his plays
staged regularly on his native island. "Casi el alma: Auto de fé
en tres actos" ("Almost the Soul: Auto da fé in Three Acts"),
first produced at San Juan's Teatro Tapia in 1964, is a comic existential fable about two marginal characters who start a religion
called "Dios, Sociedad Anónima," or "God, Inc." The work explores the paradox of creating faith out of a lack of faith. "La
pasión según Antígona Pérez" ("The Passion of Antígona
Pérez"), staged originally at the Institute of Puerto Rican Culture theater festival in 1968 and later taken on tour in English
translation by the Puerto Rican Traveling Theater, centers on
the theme of Latin American dictatorship. A more recent play,
"Quintuples" ("Quintuplets"), functions at once as a family
vaudeville act, a suspense comedy parody, and a philosophical
meditation on the meaning of acting and dramatic creation. The
play is written as a tour de force for two actors, who alternate
playing the five Morrison siblings and their father, El Gran Semental, or "The Great Stud," in six solo scenes.

Sánchez is best known in the United States for his novel *Macho
Camacho's Beat,* the English translation of *La guaracha del
Macho Camacho.* Set in San Juan in the mid-1970s, the novel offers a savagely sardonic look at contemporary Puerto Rican culture and society, refracted in four related characters: Vicente Re-
inosa, a venal local politician and faithful servant of U.S. business interests; his dim-witted son Benny, who (literally) loves his
Ferrari sports car; Vicente's bored, frigid, moneyed wife Graciela; and his unnamed, lower-class mulatto mistress. The author
eschews traditional plot and narrative for fragmented vignettes
that flit from character to character to the fatuous leitmotif of
guaracha singer Macho Camacho's radio hit, "Life Is a Phenom-

enal Thing." Sánchez unsparingly depicts the societal distortions wrought by Spanish colonialism and American neocolonialism in Puerto Rico, critics noted, but his anger is enriched with humor and an underlying affection for the island's frolicsome spirit. "This novel, which functions brilliantly on linguistic, structural, and socio-political levels, is defined by an extravagant and mordant sense of the comic," Gilbert Sorrentino remarked in the *Washington Post Book World*. "Like all excellent comic writing, the laughter is generated by language, not situation."

Indeed, critics observed, Sánchez's rhyming wordplay, shifting narrative voices, and subtle ear for the idioms of popular culture give the novel much of its thematic power. "Sánchez's linguistic resources are multiplex, and he uses them with profligate genius: the book is short, but densely written and its language occurs in clusters of verbal energy," noted Sorrentino. "Out of it all he has made a novel that totally exploits its materials and that operates as do all true works of literary art: it exists only in terms of its medium, its ocean of words. Devoid of cant and sentimentality, it is a literary event." *Nation* reviewer Robert Houston credited translator Gregory Rabassa with a "heroic job of re-creating" Sánchez's effervescent prose in English. The critic declared that Sánchez's "fine diversity, his rhyming jingles and outrageous alliteration, even his puns have found their way naturally and fluently into English."

BIOGRAPHICAL/CRITICAL SOURCES:

BOOKS

Contemporary Literary Criticism, Volume 23, Gale, 1983.

PERIODICALS

Nation, May 23, 1981.
New York Review of Books, October 22, 1981.
New York Times Book Review, January 18, 1981.
Washington Post Book World, February 8, 1981.

* * *

SANCHEZ, Oscar Arias
See ARIAS SANCHEZ, Oscar

* * *

SANCHEZ, Ricardo 1941-

PERSONAL: Born March 29, 1941, in El Paso, Tex.; son of Pedro Lucero (a dealer in scrap metals) and Adelina (Gallegos) Sánchez; married Maria Teresa Silva, November 28, 1964; children: Rikard-Sergei, Libertad-Yvonne, Pedro-Cuauhtémoc (deceased), Jacinto-Temilotzín. *Education:* Took extension courses from Alvin Junior College, 1965-69; Union Graduate School, Ph.D., 1975. *Politics:* "AnarchoHumanist." *Religion:* "Indigenist-non-sectarian."

CAREER: Incarcerated in California state prisons, c. early 1960s, and Texas Department of Corrections in Huntsville, Tex., 1965-69; Vista community worker, El Paso, Tex., 1969; research director of Project MACHOS, Inc., 1969; *Richmond Afro-American Newspaper,* Richmond, Va., correspondent, 1969; University of Massachusetts, School of Education, Amherst, staff writer, research assistant, and instructor, 1970; Colorado Migrant Council, Denver, director of Itinerant Migrant Health Project, 1970-71; University of Texas, El Paso, consultant, writer, and lecturer for Chicano Affairs Program and Teacher Corps & TTT Program, 1971-72; New Mexico State University, Las Cruces, community staff consultant and lecturer for Social

Welfare Teaching Center, 1972-73; El Paso Community College, El Paso, professor of poetry, literature, and critical theory, 1975, National Endowment for the Arts poet in residence, 1975-76; University of Wisconsin, Milwaukee, visiting professor and lecturer for Spanish-Speaking Outreach Institute, 1977; University of Utah, Salt Lake City, assistant professor of humanities and Chicano studies, 1977-80; deputy director of Project SER, 1980-81; Noel Theraputic, Austin, Tex., associate director, 1981-82; Brown Schools, Austin, psychiatric trainer, 1982; Poets of Tejas Reading Series, San Antonio, Tex., founder and manager, 1982—; Paperbacks y mas, San Antonio, owner and manager, 1983—; Poetry Tejas International, San Antonio, director, 1983—. Free lance writer, poet, and consultant; developer of television programs and cassette recordings on Chicano culture and literature; lecturer and participant in symposia, colloquia, and seminars throughout the United States.

Training consultant, writer, and lecturer for American Program Bureau, Boston, Mass., 1970-72, and La Academia de la Nueva Raza, Dixon, N.M., 1971-72; co-founder and counseling supervisor of Trinity-Opportunities Industrialization Center, El Paso, 1972. Board member of Southwest Poets' Conference, 1970—, Father Rahm Health Clinic, El Paso, 1971-73, Trinity Chicano Coalition, El Paso, 1971-73, Texas Council on Alcoholism, El Paso, 1972-73, and La Luz Mexican American Cultural Center of the El Paso diocese, 1974-76. Chairman of Project TREND, El Paso, 1972-73; co-founder and associate of Chicano Barrio Associates (CHIBAS), El Paso, 1972—; founder and board member of Chicano Light and Power, Inc., El Paso, 1974—. National Endowment for the Arts literary panel member, 1979-82; member of Texas Commission for the Arts, 1982-85; trustee of San Antonio Library System, 1985-87.

MEMBER: International P.E.N., Poets and Writers, Inc. (New York City).

AWARDS, HONORS: Frederick Douglass fellowship in journalism, 1969; Ford Foundation graduate fellow, Union Graduate School, 1973-75; outstanding professor award from the Chicano Student Association, University of Utah, 1979.

WRITINGS:

Canto y grito mi liberación/The Liberation of a Chicano Mind, Mictla, 1971, Doubleday-Anchor, 1973.
(Editor) *Los cuatro* (title means "The Four"), Barrio Press, 1971.
Obras (title means "Works"), Quetzal-Vihio Press, 1971.
Mano a mano (title means "Hand to Hand"), Conference of Unity & Action, 1971.
Hechizospells, Chicano Studies Center, University of California, 1976.
Milhuas blues y gritos norteños (title means "Milwaukee Blues and Northern Cries"), Spanish-Speaking Outreach Institute, University of Wisconsin, 1980.
Brown Bear Honey Madness: Alaskan Cruising Poems, Slough Press, 1982.
Amsterdam cantos y poemas pistos (title means "Amsterdam Songs and Drinking Poems"), Place of Herons, 1983.
Selected Poems, Arte Público Press, 1985.

Also author of *Perdido: A Barrio Story,* 1985, unpublished manuscripts, including "In and Out," "Mexi-Coloured Moods," "With Love & Protest," and "Florimoquiando," and screenplay *Entelequía.* Work represented in several anthologies, including *Points of Departure,* edited by Ernece B. Kelly, Wiley, 1972; *We Are Chicanos,* edited by Philip D. Ortego, Washington Square Press, 1973; *Festival de flor y canto,* University of Southern California Press, 1976; and *Canto al Pueblo: An Anthology of Experiences,* edited by Leonard Carillo and others, Penca Books, 1978.

Contributor to *Publishers Weekly, De Colores, El Diario, Greenfield Review* and numerous other magazines, reviews, newspapers, and journals. Co-founder and editor of Mictla Publications, 1970-75; special issues editor, *De Colores: Journal of Emerging Raza Philosophies,* 1975; arts columnist for *Express-News,* San Antonio, 1985-86.

SIDELIGHTS: A trenchant critic of the rascist, conformist, and materialistic aspects of contemporary American society, author Ricardo Sánchez believes Chicano literature must participate in the political emancipation of the Chicano people by heightening awareness of their identity and distinctive culture and traditions. "I feel that the survival of our *raza* [race] is indeed important," the author told John David Bruce-Novoa in *Chicano Authors: Inquiry by Interview,* "thus I sense that only a politicizing poetics can be of value." Sánchez regularly flays his literary colleagues for what he perceives as their accommodationism, lack of critical rigor, and "moral and social cowardice" before the bitter realities of Chicano *barrio* life. The author is particularly acerbic about a romanticizing strain of *indigenismo* (indigenism) in Chicano literature, which he bluntly described in the *Chicano Authors* interview as a perpetuating source of "quasimystical idiocies."

Sánchez's own literary works reflect a life shaped by the rough urban *barrio,* including childhood years spent in a poor El Paso slum, stints in prison in Texas and California, and community organizing work in Chicano neighborhoods in several ern cities. The author co-founded Mictla Publications to publish his first book, *Canto y grito mi liberación/The Liberation of a Chicano Mind,* in 1971. Sánchez's pungent descriptions of *barrio* life are written in a distinctive stream-of-consciousness style that mixes free verse and prose in English, Spanish, and various Chicano *barrio* and prison slangs. According to Sánchez in *Chicano Authors,* this language "is created out of linguistic fusion, not from a demarcated/fragmentary chaos, but . . . out of synthesis." A deep anger over the Chicano's social lot suffuses the book, but critics have also remarked on the exuberant spirit of creative vigor generated by the author's original word combinations and juxtapositions.

Sánchez's preference for verbal spontaneity and loose aural textures over more formal stylistic structures is also evident in *Hechizospells,* a major collection of poems, essays, and other writings published in 1976. The overriding theme is again the plight of the Chicano endeavoring to build a coherent identity out of his dual roots in the Spanish-Mexican and North American cultures. True to his iconoclastic form, Sánchez lambastes social scientists, politicians, educators, prison officials and myriad other "dehumanizing" agents in both the contemporary Anglo and Chicano societies. Although his language is occasionally "direct" and "incisive," most of Sánchez's writing "is impressionistic and visceral, filled with phantasmagoric images and deeply personal symbolism," remarked critic Charles M. Tatum in *World Literature Today.* Dubbing *Hechizospells* "a literary happening," Tatum added, "Sánchez's panoply of images, shocking statements, feints, attacks and glimpses of personal anguish are sometimes self-indulgent but never dull."

Sánchez told *HW:* "I write in order to liberate myself from past inculcations and to enjoin myself with all who want to create a more sanguine society. As a Chicano I realize the privation that those who are different must suffer. Writing becomes the vehicle for self expression and the means toward one's humanization. My writings are trilingual, i.e., Spanish, English, or an admix-

ture of both—flowing in and out of the linguistic worlds I am able to inhabit simultaneously—creating thus a new world view that contains both. In quest of humanizing liberation do I write, in order to distill from the sordidness of societal oppressiveness a view of beingness which sings and shouts out love, dignity, and the peacefulness of freedom."

AVOCATIONAL INTERESTS: Chess, art, dance, dramatics, readings in history, philosophy, folklore, political theory.

BIOGRAPHICAL/CRITICAL SOURCES:

BOOKS

Bruce-Novoa, John David, *Chicano Authors: Inquiry by Interview,* University of Texas Press, 1980.

PERIODICALS

Hispano, January 24, 1977, May 9, 1977.
Revista Chicano-Riqueña, December, 1977.
Tiempo, December 27, 1976.
World Literature Today, summer, 1977.

* * *

SANCHEZ, Thomas 1944-

PERSONAL: Born February 26, 1944, in Oakland, Calif.; son of Thomas and Geraldine (Brown) Sanchez; married Stephanie Spielberger (a landscape painter); children: Dante (daughter). *Education:* San Francisco State College (now University), B.A., 1966, M.A., 1967.

ADDRESSES: Home—Key West, Fla.; and Los Angeles, Calif. *Agent*—Jett Rink Associates, Box 1493, Venice, Calif. 90291.

CAREER: Writer. Active in human rights organizations such as Congress for Racial Equality (CORE) and the United Farm Workers during the 1960s; covered 1973 takeover at Wounded Knee for Pacifica Radio. Author and host of a five-part ABC-TV special on the California Hispanic community. Lecturer at San Francisco State University, University of California, Pennsylvania State University, and other organizations. Awards judge, National Endowment for the Arts.

MEMBER: Southwestern Humanities Council (member of board of directors), California Council for the Humanities in Public Policy (member of board of directors).

AWARDS, HONORS: National Endowment for the Arts fellowship in fiction; Guggenheim fellowship.

WRITINGS:

Rabbit Boss (novel), Knopf, 1973, reprinted, Vintage, 1989.
(Contributor) *Four Visions of America: Henry Miller, Thomas Sanchez, Erica Jong, Kay Boyle,* Capra, 1977.
Zoot-Suit Murders (novel), Dutton, 1978.
Native Notes from the Land of Earthquake and Fire (nonfiction), Sandpiper Press, 1979.
(With Lawrence C. Powell) *Angels Burning; "Ocian" in View,* Capra, 1987.
Mile Zero (novel), Knopf, 1989.

Contributor to anthologies; contributor of articles to *Esquire, Los Angeles Times, San Francisco Chronicle,* and other periodicals. Member of editorial board, *Minority Voices: An Inter-Disciplinary Journal of Literature and the Arts;* contributing editor, *Santa Barbara Magazine.*

SIDELIGHTS: Thomas Sanchez's historical novel *Rabbit Boss* traces four generations of a small tribe of Indians, the Washo, who lived in an area around the California-Nevada border. The novel opens with an encounter between Gayabuc, a descendant of the tribe's powerful elder, the Rabbit Boss, and the ill-fated Donner party who, lost in the Sierras in winter, were forced into cannibalism. The first of his people to see white men, Gayabuc is repelled by their cannibalism and warns the rest of his tribe, beginning the Washo legend that all white men are cannibals. This theme of white cannibalism continues throughout the novel, as H. L. Van Brunt comments in the *Christian Science Monitor:* "Cannibalism at the Donner Pass is becoming the symbol of greedy dreams turned to madness by an indifferent wilderness. To an Indian the image of the white man as cannibal must be irresistible. There are scenes as powerful as the opening one throughout this novel, as well as sharply focused character studies." Calling *Rabbit Boss* "a rare and wonderful book," *Washington Post Book World* contributor Patrick Bernuth likewise observes that the author "has managed to weave this country [the Sierras] and its ancient people deep into his first novel. It is a remarkable achievement," the critic continues. "[Sanchez] has vividly brought the life the Indian's ironic vision of the white man as a savage, as a waster, earth-tourist and thief."

Van Brunt, who finds the novel "abundant and imaginative" in its descriptions, nevertheless faults it as "overlong and diffuse. Long 'mystical' passages throughout the book impede a willing reader's progress." *New York Times Book Review* contributor Gordon Burnside, however, believes that these elaborate sections make the novel "powerful": "As Sanchez tells it, the safely familiar exaggeration of American frontier humor turns itself inside-out and reappears as the secret language of demons." "Re-creating frontier life with authority and immediacy," Patrick Fanning states in *Library Journal,* Sanchez's work is "illuminated by the author's personal, searing vision . . . [and is] impressive as literature, history, and sociology." A *National Observer* critic similarly asserts that "*Rabbit Boss* deserves to become an American classic. [It is] a great novel, spanning a century in the life and death of an Indian tribe, told with epic perspective and infinite compassion." As a *Times Literary Supplement* reviewer concludes, "*Rabbit Boss* is beautiful, poetic, powerful. Thomas Sanchez has a dominating talent."

Zoot-Suit Murders, Sanchez's second novel, is a mystery set against the riots which took place in Los Angeles in the early 1940s, when the Chicano community was terrorized by truckloads of sailors. Mexican-American women and children were brutalized and their "zoot-suited" men were hunted, beaten, stripped, and shaved. Sanchez's story involves the murder of two FBI agents and its possible connections to the barrio and to fascist and communist groups. John Thomas Stovall writes in the *Chicago Tribune:* "By juxtaposing fiction and fact, Sanchez has created a vivid tale of political intrigue and romance. Sanchez, a master of pictorial detail, accurately describes the energies and squalor of the barrio to reveal one of the novel's recurrent themes: the vulnerability of its inhabitants, a condition fueled by racial prejudice and exploited by almost every character in *Zoot-Suit Murders.*" This novel, maintains a *Publishers Weekly* reviewer, "surpasses a simple mystery story," especially in its "unexpected and shocking climax." As Stovall explains, in *Zoot-Suit Murders* Sanchez "has created a powerful fiction based upon fact—not just upon historical fact, but upon subtler truths about human nature."

"There are a handful of writers who dare to wrestle larger-than-life themes, pursue extremes and transcend the normal limitations of prose to reach for a personal vision of The Great American Novel," *Playboy* critic Digby Diehl observes. "Thomas Pynchon, Norman Mailer and Robert Stone come to mind. With *Mile Zero,* Thomas Sanchez joins them." The author spent ten years preparing the novel, during which time he lost his home and his previous novels went out of print. Nevertheless, his effort has been worthwhile, note critics like *New York Times Book Review* contributor Erica Abeel: "[Sanchez' previous work], it is now clear, was only a warm-up for the dazzling achievement of 'Mile Zero.' Mr. Sanchez' new novel is marked by the same commanding sense of place, the same mix of politics and poetry. But," the critic continues, *Mile Zero* "is more shapely, leaner and free of 'Rabbit Boss's' diffuseness and *longueurs.* Its brilliantly contrived plot uncoils with the suspense of a thriller. Nothing is gratuitous," Abeel relates; "characters and actions are linked in a hidden web, sometimes with devastating irony. And it is funny, a comic masterpiece crackling with back-handed wit and laugh-out-loud humor."

Taking place on Key West, Florida—"Mile Zero" of U.S. Highway 1—the novel follows a series of varied characters whose lives have intertwined: St. Cloud, a former antiwar activist drowning his self-doubt in alcohol; Lila, a complex young Southern woman who becomes focus of St. Cloud's passion; and Justo Tamarindo, a Cuban-American police detective confronted with a series of bizarre crimes on the island. Although Justo's pursuit of Zobop, the mysterious figure who leaves strange messages at the crime scenes, "forms the main action of the novel," states Alan Cheuse in Chicago *Tribune Books,* along the way "Sanchez manages to create the little world of Key West, with its natives, the so-called 'conchs,' its drifters and tourists and illegals and everyone in between." Allen H. Peacock concurs with this assessment, asserting in the *Detroit News* that *Mile Zero* "succeeds more often than not as fiction and magnificently as a spooky, troubling paean to the furtive and flagrant microcosm of America that is Key West in the '80s. . . . *Mile Zero* is above all a novel about Key West itself—its history, colors, smells, tropical allure and deadly menace."

Some critics, however, find the author's detours into the history of Key West and its inhabitants distracting. *Los Angeles Times Book Review* contributor Alejandro Morales, for instance, although he thinks the book is "an accomplished novel" that is "rich in the cultural and literary intertextuality of Steinbeck and Cervantes, Joyce and Shakespeare," writes that "Sanchez falters: He has created truly interesting characters but placed them in a meandering story. Their stories are individualized," the critic elaborates, "rather than united in a clear and concise plot." Ron Hansen likewise remarks in the *Washington Post Book World* that "word drunkenness gets in the way in some passages here, and from first to last Sanchez gives free rein to a kind of flamboyant and torrid writing." Nevertheless, the critic admits that "the immense power and passion of *Mile Zero* owes a great deal to just that willingness to risk foolishness and excess on behalf of his chilling vision of a grotesque American future."

"Sanchez's range is broad—from the lyrical wash of language that opens the novel to the jangly-nerved sequences in which 'Zobop' speaks," comments Cheuse. The result, adds the critic, is "prose that's as agile and pulsating as the blend of American blues and Caribbean rhythms that comes from the region." Abeel similarly praises the author for the variety of his writing: "Sanchez avoids the predictable. He describes his own stylistic practice in St. Cloud's professed liking for 'sentences that slipped off one another with strikingly misguided purpose.' The book's ending," Abeel continues, "is itself a marvel or ambiguity—tragic, funny and hopeful all at once. 'Mile Zero' is a novel of uncommon richness and resonance." As Diehl concludes, *Mile Zero* "is a rare and exhilarating experience, a brilliant wide-angle metaphorical treatise on modern American life."

MEDIA ADAPTATIONS: A film documentary on Sanchez and the writing of *Rabbit Boss* was produced by the University of California.

BIOGRAPHICAL/CRITICAL SOURCES:

BOOKS

Bestsellers 90, Issue 1, Gale, 1990.

PERIODICALS

Chicago Tribune, December 10, 1978.
Christian Science Monitor, July 18, 1973.
Detroit News, November 5, 1989.
Library Journal, May 1, 1973.
Los Angeles Times, October 18, 1989.
Los Angeles Times Book Review, September 17, 1989.
National Observer, June 16, 1973.
New York Times Book Review, March 10, 1974, October 1, 1989.
People, October 16, 1989.
Playboy, September, 1989.
Publishers Weekly, April 2, 1973, September 4, 1978, August 4, 1989.
Time, July 30, 1973.
Times Literary Supplement, March 1, 1974.
Tribune Books (Chicago), September 24, 1989.
Washington Post Book World, June 3, 1973, July 29, 1973, October 8, 1989.

*   *   *

SANCHEZ-KORROL, Virginia

PERSONAL: Born in New York, N.Y.; daughter of Antonio Sanchez-Feliciano (a laborer) and Elisa (a housewife; maiden name, Santiago) Baeza; married Charles R. Korrol (a physician); children: Pamela, Lauren. *Education:* State University of New York at Stony Brook, Ph.D.

ADDRESSES: Office—Department of Puerto Rican Studies, Brooklyn College of the City University of New York, Bedford and Ave. H, Brooklyn, N.Y. 11210.

CAREER: Brooklyn College of the City University of New York, Brooklyn, N.Y., associate professor and chairman of department of Puerto Rican Studies. Consultant to New York State Department of Education; member of Huntington, Long Island Quincentenary Commission.

MEMBER: American Historical Association, American Studies Association (chairman of international committee), Latin American Studies Association.

AWARDS, HONORS: Ford Foundation fellowship, 1987.

WRITINGS:

From Colonia to Community: The History of Puerto Ricans in New York City, 1917-1948, Greenwood Press, 1983.
(Co-author) *The Puerto Rican Struggle: Essays on Survival in the United States,* Waterfront Press, 1984.
(Co-author) *Restoring Women to History: Women in the Histories of Asia, Africa, Latin American and the Caribbean and the Middle East,* Organization of American Historians, 1988.

Author of numerous essays and book reviews on Latino topics.

WORK IN PROGRESS: History of Puerto Rican Women Teachers in United States; Integrated History of Latinos in United States.

SANCHEZ-SCOTT, Milcha

ADDRESSES: Home—2080 Mount St., Los Angeles, Calif. 90068.

CAREER: Playwright.

WRITINGS:

PLAYS

Dog Lady; and, The Cuban Swimmer: Two One-Act Plays (both produced in New York City, May, 1984), Theatre Communications Group, 1984.
Roosters (first produced at the Los Angeles Theater Center), published in *On New Ground: Contemporary Hispanic American Plays,* Theatre Communications Group, 1987.
"Stone Wedding," first produced at the Los Angeles Theater Center, December, 1988.

Also author of "Carmen" (adapted from Georges Bizet's opera of the same title), first produced at the Los Angeles Theater Center, and unpublished and unproduced play, "Latina."

BIOGRAPHICAL/CRITICAL SOURCES:

PERIODICALS

New York Times, May 10, 1984.

*   *   *

SANTA CRUZ (GAMARRA), Nicomedes 1925-

PERSONAL: Born in 1925 in Peru.

CAREER: Poet.

WRITINGS:

Décimas, Juan Mejía Baca (Lima, Peru), 1960, 2nd complete edition, Librería Studium, 1966.
Cumanana: Décimas de pie forzado y poemas, Juan Mejía Baca, 1964.
Canto a mi Perú, Librería Studium, 1966.
Ritmos negros del Perú, Losada (Buenos Aires), 1971, revised and enlarged edition, 1973.
Décimas y poemas: Antología, Campodónico, 1971.
La décima en el Perú, Instituto de Estudios Peruanos, 1982.

Contributor of poems and articles to *El Comercio* and *Estampa.*

SIDELIGHTS: Poetry by Afro-Peruvian Nicomedes Santa Cruz celebrates the black experience in Latin America and articulates his concerns about the need for integration in Peru, South Africa, and throughout the world. Popular with audiences, he is known for skillful readings of his rhythmic poetry in which he affirms that poetry is a spoken art. Firmly identified with his black heritage, he is the first Peruvian to address in long poems the problems of black Africans. Though his primary subject is the black experience, he is not limited to an ethnic vision; he promotes universal brotherhood and human rights for people of all colors.

MEDIA ADAPTATIONS: Many poems by Santa Cruz have been popularized as songs.

BIOGRAPHICAL/CRITICAL SOURCES:

BOOKS

Cuché, Denys, *Poder blanco y resistencia negra en el Perú,* Instituto Nacional de Cultura, 1975.
Hildebrandt, Martha, *Peruanismos,* Moncloa-Campodónico, 1969.

Jackson, Richard L., *The Black Image in Latin American Literature,* University of New Mexico Press, 1976.
Salas, Teresa C., *Asedios a la poesía de Nicomedes Santa Cruz,* Editora Andina (Quito, Ecuador), 1982.

PERIODICALS

Cuadernos Americanos, Number 5, 1981.
El Comercio, Dominical Semanario, October 1, 1961, May 24, 1964.
Estampa, May 24, 1964, September 24, 1967.
Expreso, April 6, 1964, June 4, 1964.
Jornal de Letras, Number 169, 1963.
Phylon, March, 1982.
Siempre, Number 1103, 1974.

*   *   *

SARDUY, Severo 1937-

PERSONAL: Born February 25, 1937, in Camagüey, Cuba; son of Severo and Mercedes Sarduy. *Education:* Attended L'Ecole du Louvre.

ADDRESSES: Home—2 rue Lakanal, 92330 Secaux, Paris, France. *Office*—27 rue Jacob, Paris VI, France. *Agent*—Carmen Balcells, Diagonal 580, Barcelona 21, Spain.

CAREER: Novelist, poet, essayist, literary critic. Adviser to French publishing house Seuil.

MEMBER: Société des Gens de Lettres (France).

AWARDS, HONORS: Prix Médicis étranger, 1972, for *Cobra;* Guggenheim fellowship, 1975; Prix Italia; Prix Paul Gilson.

WRITINGS:

Gestos (novel; title means "Gestures"), Seix Barral, 1963.
De donde son los cantantes (novella), Mortiz, 1967, translation by Suzanne Jill Levine published in *Triple Cross* as "From Cuba With a Song," Dutton, 1972.
Escrito sobre un cuerpo: Ensayos de crítica (essays; title means "Written on a Body"), Sudamericana, 1969.
Flamenco, Manus Presse, 1969.
(Contributor) H. M. Erhardt, *Mood Indigo,* Manus Presse, 1970.
Cobra (novel), Sudamericana, 1972, translation by Levine, Dutton, 1975.
Overdose (poetry), Palmas, Inventarios Provisionales, 1972.
Big Bang (poetry), Fata Morgana, 1973.
Barroco (essays; title means "Baroque"), Sudamericana, 1974.
Maitreya, Seix Barral, 1977, 2nd edition, 1981.
La doublure, Flammarion, 1981.
La simulación (essays and lectures), Monte Avila Editores (Caracas, Venezuela), 1982.
(With Annemieke van de Pas) *Micro-opera de Benet Rossell* (criticism), Ambit, 1984.
Colibrí (novel), Argos (Barcelona, Spain), 1984.
For Voice, translation by Philip Barnard, Latin American Literary Review Press, 1985.
(With others) *Antonio Saura, figura y fondo* (criticism), Edicions del Mall, 1987.
Un testigo fugaz y disfrazado (poems), Edicions del Mall, 1987.
El Cristo de la rue Jacob (prose), Edicions del Mall, 1987.

Also author of *Sobre la playa* (title means "On the Beach"), 1971, *La caida* (title means "The Fall"), 1974, *Relato,* 1974, and *Los matadores de hormigas* (title means "The Ant Killers"), 1976. Contributor to periodicals, including *Tel Quel.*

WORK IN PROGRESS: Cocuyo, a novel.

SIDELIGHTS: Cuban-born Severo Sarduy is known for experimental, linguistically complex fiction, which includes such novels as *Gestos* ("Gestures") and *Cobra* and the novella *De donde son los cantantes.* He studied medicine, art, and literature in his native land until 1960, when he received a government grant to study art history in Europe and left the country, eventually settling permanently in Paris, France. There Sarduy has also become respected for his work in literary theory and linguistics; his essays and criticism concern subjects and issues explored by such French scholars as semiotician Roland Barthes and deconstructionist literary critic Jacques Derrida, as well as others associated with the French literary journal *Tel Quel.* Some of Sarduy's most important theoretical ideas are found in the essay collections *Escrito sobre un cuerpo* and *Barroco.*

A French literary influence—most notably that of the *nouveau roman* and authors such as Alain Robbe-Grillet—is apparent in Sarduy's fiction. His novels contain fragmented plots, little psychological characterization, and an abundance of surface imagery that depicts the human being as an object among other objects. Perhaps most importantly, as critics point out, Sarduy's writing places a heavy emphasis on language as it both creates and changes reality, and as it evidences the author's preoccupation with the multiple meanings of words. According to Jerome Charyn in his *New York Times Book Review* critique of *Cobra,* for example, "Language is everything in Sarduy's book." In addition, critics consistently note the pervasive theme of transformation in Sarduy's work. Everything from character to cosmos, *New York Review of Books* contributor Michael Wood notes, is conditioned by language and the continuous, endless transformations in the universe: "Men become women and women become dwarfs; people die and do not die; Paris becomes Amsterdam, which in turn becomes Nepal."

Review 74 contributor Roberto González Echevarría views Sarduy's first two works—the 1963 *Gestos* and the 1967 *De donde son los cantantes*—as "rehearsals" for the well-received *Cobra,* which appeared in 1972. In *Gestos,* for example, the influence of the *nouveau roman* reveals itself in Sarduy's attention to description, as it does in the later novel. "An objective, unfastened, disinterested language dances before the eyes of the reader," the critic remarks, "except that almost all the objects described in [*Gestos*] are pictures. In other words, the novel does not produce an immediate reality but gives instead detailed descriptions of canvases by well-known painters and projects the action of the story upon them." At the bidding of words, reality again undergoes a series of metamorphoses in *De donde son los cantantes,* which was translated in 1972 as "From Cuba With a Song." In the book, *New York Times Book Review* critic E. Rodríguez Monegal reports, "the moth-eaten image of Christ which two acolytes carry to Havana (they are also transvestites) gradually rots away in keeping with the metamorphosis of the Cuban landscape and the Spanish language. When they reach the tropical capital they find subways, kirsch factories, snow."

In his third novel, Sarduy concentrates most heavily on the theme of transformation. "*Cobra* is a book of changes," Wood comments, "and its title indicates not its meaning but the kind of activity it is engaged in." The book's narrative presents a hero-heroine named Cobra who begins life as a female wax doll, then undergoes a sex-change operation in a mysterious Tangier abortion clinic, joins a motorcycle gang in Amsterdam that mutilates and destroys her/him in a kinky religious ceremony, and becomes, finally, an embodiment of the Hindu god of creation and destruction, Shiva. However, the real protagonist of the book, Wood suggests, may be the word *cobra* in all its possible references. At various times in the novel, *cobra* is the name of a snake, a motorcycle gang, a singer, a group of artists, and a form of the Spanish verb *cobrar*. "The references define the word cobra as a sort of crazy semantic crossroads, a linguistic point where unlikely meanings intersect, and it is the intersection that counts rather than the meanings themselves," Wood observes. *Review 74* contributor Robert Adams concurs, noting that the snake-like shedding of personae and meaning "positively forbids us to read [*Cobra*] in depth. . . . The book is primarily a stream of images, glittering, exotic, trite and disgusting, cosmic and squalid, grotesque and funny, strung on a set of generative puns."

Cobra was admired by such critics as Helene Cixous, who writes in another *Review 74* article that "*Cobra* is in a class of its own, unrelated to any 'serious' genre, whether encoded or codable, to any type except the one whose new genius it invents: a bizarre hybrid, a composite of snake, writings, rhythms, of a flight of luminous traces and a series of infinitesimal sparkling instants." A *New Yorker* critic similarly remarks: "What is impressive is the rich vocabulary, the freewheeling imagination, and the utter cockiness. When, in a footnote, the author addresses us as 'moronic reader,' he has a certain charm." And while Adams receives "a deep sense of astral chill" from the novel, Wood concludes that "*Cobra* remains a remarkable book, a nervous flighty homage to the life of language."

BIOGRAPHICAL/CRITICAL SOURCES:

BOOKS

Contemporary Literary Criticism, Volume 6, Gale, 1976.
Gazarian Gautier, Marie-Lise, *Interviews With Latin American Writers,* Dalkey Archive Press, 1989.
González Echevarría, Roberto, *La ruta de Severo Sarduy,* Ediciones del Norte, 1987.

PERIODICALS

Nation, June 11, 1973.
New Yorker, January 27, 1975.
New York Review of Books, March 20, 1975.
New York Times Book Review, December 24, 1972, March 9, 1975.
Review 74, winter, 1974.

*   *   *

SAURA (ATARES), Carlos 1932-

PERSONAL: Born January 4, 1932, in Huesca, Aragón, Spain; son of Antonio Saura Pacheco (an attorney and civil servant) and Fermina Atarés Torrente; married Adele Medrano (marriage ended); married wife, Mercedes; children: (first marriage) Carlos, Antonio; (with Geraldine Chaplin) Shane. *Education:* Attended journalism school in Madrid, 1952; graduated from Instituto de Investigaciones y Experiencias Cinematográficas (Madrid), 1957.

CAREER: Filmmaker. Free-lance photographer, 1950-53; Instituto de Investigaciones y Experiencias Cinematográficas (renamed Escuela Oficial de Cinematografía), Madrid, Spain, professor of direction, 1957-64. Director of films, including "Bodas de sangre" (released in U.S. as "Blood Wedding"), 1981. Codirector of stage productions of "Bodas de sangre," "Carmen," and "El amor brujo," during 1980s. Member of Bertrand Russell tribunal on Latin American political torture, during 1970s.

AWARDS, HONORS: Awards for best direction from Berlin Film Festival, 1966, for "La caza," and 1968, for "Peppermint frappé"; Jury Prize from Cannes Film Festival, 1974, for "La prima Angélica"; Special Jury Grand Prize from Cannes Film Festival, 1976, for "Cría cuervos"; named film figure of 1977 by jury of Luis Buñuel Cinema Prize (Spain); named Director of the Year by *International Film Guide,* 1978; nominated for Academy Award (Oscar) for best foreign language film from Academy of Motion Picture Arts and Sciences, 1979, for "Mamá cumple cien años," and c. 1984, for "Carmen"; Golden Bear award from Berlin Film Festival, 1981, for "De prisa, de prisa"; prize for artistic contribution from Cannes Film Festival, 1983, for "Carmen"; Special Jury Prize from Montreal Film Festival, 1986, for "Bodas de sangre," "Carmen," and "El amor brujo."

WRITINGS:

SCREENPLAYS; AND DIRECTOR; FULL-LENGTH FEATURES, EXCEPT AS NOTED

"La tarde del domingo" (short subject; title means "Sunday Afternoon"; based on a story by Fernando Guillermo de Castro), [Spain], 1957.
(With José Ayllón) "Cuenca" (short documentary), Estudios Moro, 1958.
(With Mario Camus and Daniel Sueiro) "Los golfos" (title means "The Hooligans"; first shown at Cannes Film Festival, 1960), Films 59, 1962.
(With Camus) "Llanto por un bandido" (title means "Lament for a Bandit"), Agata Films/Atlantic Cinematografica/Méditerranée Cinéma, 1964.
(With Angelino Fons) "La caza" (title means "The Hunt"), Querejeta, 1966.
(With Rafael Azcona and Fons) "Peppermint frappé," Querejeta, 1967.
(With Fons) "Stress es tres, tres" (title means "Stress Is Three, Three"), Querejeta, 1968.
(With Azcona and Geraldine Chaplin) "La madriguera" (title means "The Honeycomb"), Querejeta, 1969.
(With Azcona) "El jardín de las delicias" (title means "The Garden of Delights"), Querejeta, 1970.
(With Azcona) "Ana y los lobos" (title means "Ana and the Wolves"; Querejeta, 1973), published in *L'Avant Scáne,* November, 1974.
(With Azcona) *La prima Angélica* (released in U.S. as "Cousin Angelica"; Querejeta, 1974), Querejeta, 1976.
Cría cuervos (title means "Raise Ravens"; released in U.S. as "Cria!"; Querejeta, 1976), Querejeta, 1975.
"Elisa, vida mía" (title means "Elisa, My Life"), Querejeta, 1977.
"Los ojos vendados" (title means "Blindfolded Eyes"), Querejeta, 1978.
"Mamá cumple cien años" (title means "Mama Turns One Hundred"), Querejeta, 1979.
"De prisa, de prisa" (title means "Hurry, Hurry"), Querejeta/Moliere, 1981.
"Dulces horas" (released in U.S. as "Sweet Hours"), New Yorker Films, 1982.
(With Jean Claude Carriere) "Antonieta" (based on the novel by Andres Henestrosa), Gaumont/Conacine/Nuevo Cine, 1982.
(With Antonio Gades) "Carmen" (based on the novella by Prosper Mérimée and the opera by Georges Bizet), Orion Classics, 1983.
(With Fernando Fernán Gómez) "Los zancos" (title means "The Stilts"), Piedra, 1984.
(With Gades) "El amor brujo" (title means "Love, the Magician"; based on the ballet by Manuel de Falla), Orion Classics, 1986.
"El Dorado," Iberoamericana de TV/Chrysalide Films/Canal Plus/FR 3 Films, 1988.

Contributor to periodicals.

SIDELIGHTS: "Carlos Saura is a great film maker who has not [always] gotten his due," wrote Michael Wilmington of the *Los Angeles Times.* A screenwriter and director whose films reflect the culture of his native Spain, Saura is most widely known for "Carmen," a 1983 dance film that ranked among the highest-grossing movies in his country's history and garnered an Academy Award nomination. Since the 1950s he has directed more than twenty other films, which range, Wilmington noted, "from brutal realism . . . stinging social satire . . . and fierce compassion . . . to a near-mystical exploration of the bonds of consciousness, the union of present and past." Saura has won several prizes at the Cannes and Berlin film festivals, and admirers have likened him to two prestigious directors who are among his favorites: Luis Buñuel, a Spanish expatriate who used surrealism to criticize society, and Ingmar Bergman, who probed his characters' hidden psychological torments. Even Saura's detractors, who have complained that his intricate scenarios were difficult to understand, often praised his mastery of film technique and his readiness to assert a distinctive artistic vision. He developed such independence while enduring the long dictatorship of General Francisco Franco, whose strong censorship policies condemned most Spanish films to mediocrity. "For many years during that lonely era," said Spanish journalist Rosa Montero in *Horizon,* Saura was "our only 'different' director."

As a small child in the 1930s Saura witnessed the Spanish Civil War, during which the rebellious Franco and his ultraconservative allies seized power by overthrowing a democratically elected government. The war acquainted Saura with bombings, hunger, and death, as well as with political divisiveness that extended to his own family. "I was really an exile," he recalled in Virginia Higginbotham's *Spanish Film Under Franco.* "I never understood why . . . the good were the bad and the bad were the good." In his late teens Saura traveled Spain as a free-lance photographer, and his work, which often featured dancers and music festivals, was displayed in such venues as the Royal Photography Society of Madrid. By 1952 he enrolled in Madrid's government film school. There he shared the growing interest in neorealism, an Italian movement that tried to depict the daily lives of ordinary people through the use of on-location filming and nonprofessional actors. Saura used a hand-held camera for his graduation film, "La tarde del domingo" ("Sunday Afternoon"), which showed housemaids in a dance hall on their day off; his first feature-length film as a professional, "Los golfos" ("The Hooligans"), was the first Spanish film to be shot wholly on location.

"The Hooligans" shows a group of boys who try to escape poverty by training one of their number as a bullfighter; the gang commits thefts and robberies to fund their endeavor. The film violated Spain's rigid censorship codes, which enforced a view of the country as a pious, family-oriented nation lacking in social problems. Decades later, Saura told Peter Besas in *Behind the Spanish Lens* that "The Hooligans" caused the toughest, most demoralizing censorship battle of his career. The novice filmmaker's script was rejected four times by the censors, who then cut the finished work severely and prevented its domestic release for two years. "We saw no way out. We were unknown," Saura recalled. "I was convinced I'd never make another film." Subsequently Saura tried to accommodate himself to the norms of Spanish filmmaking by working on the big-budget costume drama "Llanto por un bandido" ("Lament for a Bandit"), which he hoped to inject with meaningful comments on Spanish life. But the film's high cost subjected it to strong control from producers, who altered the work greatly; the finished product was so far from Saura's original intent that he considered the experi-

ence a personal defeat. Not long after the film was released in 1963, Saura lost his position as a professor at the government film school—"mostly," reported Richard Schickel in *Harper's,* "because of his general pessimism, which ran counter to the regime's insistent optimism."

To reclaim artistic control over his work, Saura resolved to make films that needed only a small group of actors and a small budget. He formed an alliance with producer Elías Querejeta, who was willing to endure the financial and legal struggles required to foster creative filmmaking. Together, Saura told the *New York Times,* the two men became "one force, one fighting body." The team's first film, described by Wilmington as "brutal realism," was "La caza" ("The Hunt"). As Saura told Besas, he made the film at a point in his life "when I was overcome by the pressures within Spain, when I felt I was going to burst." "The Hunt" spotlights three middle-aged veterans who fought for Franco during the civil war. Two of the men are unhappy failures; the third is a strong-willed business success. When they reunite after several years for a rabbit hunt, they appear tense, unfriendly, and fascinated by killing, and by the movie's end they have killed each other. The film brought Saura international renown, including an award for best direction from the Berlin Film Festival and the praise of prominent American reviewers. " 'The Hunt' is the toughest Spanish picture I have ever seen, and the most amazingly revealing," wrote Bosley Crowther of the *New York Times. New Yorker*'s Brendan Gill said the picture was "as . . . flawless as I would dare ask any picture to be."

The background of the three main characters led many observers to call the film a political allegory about the civil war, and Saura began to acquire a reputation as a "political filmmaker." Saura, however, resists such a narrow view of his work. "I have always been interested more in the individual than in society," he declared in *Film Quarterly.* "For me," he noted, "a labor dispute is no more political than the difficulties two people face to go on living together." Commentators such as *Nation*'s Robert Hatch have suggested that for Saura, Franco's conservative regime merely systematized a repression of the individual that was endemic to Spanish society. As Saura suggested in the *New York Times,* much of his work discusses "personal suffocation," which could originate in "Spanish religion, education, [or] family life."

To air such controversial concerns without interference from the censor, Spanish filmmakers such as Saura increasingly forsook realism in favor of a more indirect style, replete with symbolism and fantasy, freely mixing present and past, reality and imagination. "I wonder whether with this continued containment," Saura told the *New York Times* in 1971, "we are perhaps inventing a new language—of silences, symbols." Such "imaginative potential," Saura suggested in *Film Quarterly,* is a distinctive trait of Hispanic culture—one that artists used in other times of repression. As Higginbotham observed, a likely role model for Saura and his peers was Luis Buñuel, who was in his thirties at the time of the Spanish civil war and left his country for self-imposed exile. Buñuel's films generally avoid straightforward political statements, using irony and imagery to challenge the pretensions of the established social order. "Viridiana," for instance, questions simple religious truths by showing the fate of a naive young woman who admits beggars to her home out of Christian charity. The vagrants stage a raucous banquet, which Buñuel presents as an ugly parody of Christ's Last Supper, and then they violently assault their benefactress. Buñuel shot the 1961 film in Spain, his first work there since the 1930s; the small group of filmmakers that arranged his return included Saura, who proudly numbers himself among Buñuel's earliest Spanish fans.

Buñuel soon left Spain, but he remained good friends with Saura and praised the younger man's work in "The Hunt." When Saura added fantasy to his work in the late 1960s, he conceived his first such film—"Peppermint frappé"—as a tribute to Buñuel. The movie centers on a quiet small-town doctor named Julián. The unmarried and sexually repressed Julián has odd obsessions about women, the result, a *Variety* reviewer surmised, of "an overly severe sexual and religious upbringing." Julián dreams of an ideal woman and believes he has found her in the person of his brother's sophisticated new wife. The wife, played by Saura's onetime companion Geraldine Chaplin, responds derisively when Julián professes his love. She also mocks his repeated claims that he has seen her at a religious folk festival, where participants beat drums until their hands become bloody and scarred. The rejected Julián eventually arranges the newly-weds' deaths by poisoning their glasses of peppermint frappé, and as the film ends he maintains his fantasies by focusing them on his nurse—also played by Geraldine Chaplin. "This is a careful, complete film," concluded the *Variety* reviewer, "very Spanish in its theme and treatment yet expressive of a deeper, social problem common to many places." "Peppermint frappé," the reviewer declared, "marks the artistic maturity of [its] young director."

Saura quickly created two further films resembling "Peppermint frappé"—"Stress es tres, tres" and "La madriguera"—that focused tightly on obsessive personal relationships among a few affluent adults. Then he widened the range of his fantasy-laden style, creating what many observers consider his most successful works. "El jardín de las delicias" ("The Garden of Delights") centers on Antonio, a brain-damaged businessman who cannot recall the number of his huge Swiss bank account. Greedy relatives attempt to revive his memory by forcing him to re-enact early childhood traumas, ranging from his father's brutal discipline to the chaos of the civil war. Since the relations are bad actors and Antonio can scarcely talk, the re-enactments become a pageant of Spanish life that is, in Hatch's words, "ghoulishly bizarre." The relatives finally recreate the auto accident that injured Antonio, and in its bloody aftermath they join him in the family garden, moving dazedly in their wheelchairs. Praising Saura's "unfaltering eye for human evil," *Time*'s Mark Goodman called the director "a worthy protégé" of Buñuel. Many commentators have called the work a veiled political comment on Spain: Antonio and his clan, some surmised, could represent the ruling classes of the aging Franco's regime. But *Life*'s Richard Schickel declared that one need not find a "hidden message" in the film "to be held in fascination by a well-acted study in psychological violence that tears at our consciousness with clever, velvet claws."

Censors banned the completed "Garden of Delights" for many months, releasing it only after Querejeta showed a smuggled copy at the New York Film Festival to great acclaim. Saura, once more frustrated with his homeland, responded with a deliberately provocative movie—"Ana y los lobos" ("Ana and the Wolves"). One of the only films that Saura admits was politically motivated, it spotlights a chambermaid who works for an aging matriarch and her three mentally unbalanced sons. One son is a religious fanatic, one a sexual psychopath, and one a militarist, and as Saura remarked in the *New York Times,* "They represent for me the three monsters of Spain . . . perversions of religiosity, repressed sexuality and the authoritarian spirit." Spanish authorities banned filming of the work, requiring Saura to submit a rewritten script; he complied, then shot the film from the original anyway.

Saura's next works downplayed satire in favor of compassion. In two acclaimed films from the mid-1970s—"La prima Angélica" ("Cousin Angelica") and "Cría cuervos" ("Raise Ravens"; released in the United States as "Cria!")—he portrayed the pain of childhood and suggested how such pain could linger into maturity. "Childhood is not always the time of joy that people talk about," Saura said in the *Los Angeles Times*. "Often, it's a time of sadness. Children don't really know where they stand, and adults create enormous barriers." In "Cousin Angelica" mild-mannered businessman Luis Cano returns to the town where he spent part of his boyhood during the civil war. He is flooded with memories that include a wartime bombing, a childish romance with his cousin Angélica, and the beating he received from Angélica's father after the two youngsters tried to run away together. The film's flashbacks do not show Luis as a boy, but as a naive, helpless adult—a device reviewers praised for portraying how completely the adult Luis is haunted by his past. "To say Saura employs flashbacks would not at all convey the effect," wrote Hatch, "which is to persuade the viewer that past and present are a single web." "The mechanics of the mind are very complicated," observed Saura in *Film Quarterly.* "What we call reality may be everyday life, dreams, memories, obsessions. . . . I try to find a luminous window or open door to this kind of reality." Vincent Canby of the *New York Times* called the film "extraordinarily compelling" and "a voyage into the past quite unlike any other I've ever seen in a movie."

"Cria" spotlights a little girl named Ana who views the ugly truths of adult life with stoic calm. She is at the deathbeds of both her parents: her mother, sensitive and withdrawn, succumbs painfully to cancer; then her father, a blatant philanderer, dies in a tryst with his mistress. Left under the care of an aunt she dislikes, Ana remains alienated and preoccupied with death. As in "Cousin Angelica," Saura uses ambiguous stylistic devices to suggest the state of Ana's mind. When the orphaned Ana is lonely, her dead mother mysteriously arrives to comfort her. Ana's mother looks exactly like Ana will as an adult, for actress Geraldine Chaplin appears in both roles. The young Ana possesses a box of what she thinks is poison, and reviewers were unable to agree whether she had used it to kill her father. "Saura is not telling a story in the common sense," wrote Hatch. "He is evoking the trance-like state of a child cruelly misused on the assumption that a barrier protects the young from adult predicaments." "The film is more meditative and delicate than . . . 'Cousin Angelica,' " wrote *New Yorker*'s Penelope Gilliatt, "and it is just as rare."

By the time "Cria" was released in 1976, the aging Franco was dead; Spain quickly became a democracy and film censorship nearly disappeared. As Saura had anticipated in the 1960s, the new freedom brought about a change in the nature of his films. Still creating roughly one picture a year, he explored a wide variety of styles. "Elisa, vida mía" ("Elisa, My Life") and "Los ojos vendados" ("Blindfolded Eyes") are psychological dramas with multiple layers of illusion and reality: in the former, a loner confronts the daughter he deserted long ago; in the latter, an actress and a director find that the play they are presenting about political torture has echoes in their own lives. "Mamá cumple cien años" ("Mama Turns One Hundred"), which is a sequel to "Ana and the Wolves," and "Dulces horas" ("Sweet Hours"), about a man's infatuation for his mother, both approach their subject matter with a surprisingly light and comic tone. "Antonieta" and "El Dorado" are international coproductions that are extensively concerned with Latin American history; "De prisa, de prisa" ("Hurry, Hurry"), by contrast, spotlights Madrid juvenile delinquents in a contemporary drama similar to "The Hooligans." Some observers were disappointed with the nature of Saura's new work. "Since Franco's death, Mr. Saura's films have become less and less forceful," wrote Canby in 1981. He likened the result to "cinematic exercises." "Repression," surmised Tom Allen of the *Village Voice,* "added an urgency and subtextual sting to [Saura's] films." But Saura was unapologetic. "When Franco died, Spain changed," he told the *New York Times.* "There is complete freedom, so I am free, too. I feel freer to do things that are more personal."

The most popular of Saura's projects during the 1980s were his three dance films: "Bodas de sangre" ("Blood Wedding"), "Carmen," and "El amor brujo" ("Love, the Magician"). Each is based on a performance by the dance company of Antonio Gades, a dancer and choreographer whose work melds Spanish flamenco dancing and ballet. The dance performances tell dramatic stories based on well-known works about Spain, but the films were praised less for their scripts than for capturing the excitement of dance itself. Several reviewers called Saura a skilled "choreographer" of camera work; Wilmington lauded the "almost seamless collaboration" between Saura and Gades. Saura was inspired to do the films after seeing the Gades company in rehearsal. "It's great to watch the physical force, the process, the raw *effort* [of dancers as they practice]," he said in the *New York Times,* and accordingly, both "Blood Wedding" and "Carmen" feature rehearsals rather than performances before an audience. All three films show Saura's familiar mixture of illusion and reality: "Blood Wedding" begins as a low-key backstage documentary, then focuses on dramatic dancing; "Carmen" shows a backstage romance that parallels the love-and-jealousy plot of its flamenco ballet; "Love, the Magician" shows a ballet filled with magic and superstition, but the dancers perform on an obvious stage set. While some observers suggested that the three movies were minor works in light of Saura's potential, others seemed to agree with Wilmington, who praised the films as "hymn[s] to both passion and artifice." "Watching ['Carmen']," wrote Mark Le Fanu in *Films and Filming,* "is to sense that an artist can have no duty more urgent, more noble, than to pass on, by intelligent interpretation, the living traditions of his country."

Though Saura's future work might take many different forms, it seems likely to continue such devotion to Spanish subject matter. Even at the height of his difficulties with censorship, Saura refused to leave his country, which he considered a source of his artistic inspiration. As an aspiring director in the 1960s, he pondered the effect of exile on Luis Buñuel. "Abroad [Buñuel] has had always to contend with people who do not understand the Spanish mind," Saura observed in *Harper's.* "Great as his films are they would have been still greater if he could have stayed in Spain."

AVOCATIONAL INTERESTS: Photography.

BIOGRAPHICAL/CRITICAL SOURCES:

BOOKS

Besas, Peter, *Behind the Spanish Lens: Spanish Cinema Under Fascism and Democracy,* Arden Press, 1985.
Contemporary Literary Criticism, Volume 20, Gale, 1982.
Cowie, Peter, editor, *The International Film Guide,* A. S. Barnes/Tantivy Press, *1978,* 1977, *1979,* 1978.
Fiddian, Robin W. and Peter W. Evans, *Challenges to Authority: Fiction and Film in Contemporary Spain,* Tamesis Books, 1988.
Higginbotham, Virginia, *Spanish Film Under Franco,* University of Texas Press, 1987.
Hopewell, John, *Out of the Past: Spanish Cinema After Franco,* British Film Institute, 1986.
Schwartz, Ronald, *Spanish Film Directors (1950-1985): 21 Profiles,* Scarecrow Press, 1986.

PERIODICALS

Cineaste, Number 3, 1981.
Film Comment, July-August, 1980.
Film Journal, October, 1961.
Film Quarterly, summer, 1971, spring, 1979.
Films and Filming, December, 1961, January, 1976, March, 1982, January, 1984, September, 1986, January, 1987.
Films in Review, June-July, 1967, October, 1977, November, 1981, February, 1984.
Harper's, September, 1967.
Horizon, January-February, 1983.
Hudson Review, summer, 1978.
Journal of the University Film and Video Association, Number 3, 1983.
Life, May 19, 1967, March 19, 1971.
Los Angeles Times, May 6, 1973, August 18, 1978, January 19, 1983, December 21, 1983, July 26, 1986, December 25, 1986.
Monthly Film Bulletin, October, 1961, March, 1973, November, 1975, September, 1978, February, 1984, January, 1987.
Nation, May 15, 1967, March 8, 1971, June 4, 1977.
New Republic, April 3, 1971, May 28, 1977, December 5, 1983.
Newsweek, March 1, 1971, November 9, 1981.
New York, February 15, 1971, May 23, 1977, June 20, 1977.
New Yorker, April 29, 1967, March 13, 1971, May 23, 1977, June 6, 1977, November 1, 1982.
New York Times, September 20, 1966, April 25, 1967, November 26, 1967, September 19, 1970, February 12, 1971, October 27, 1971, November 23, 1972, May 13, 1977, May 19, 1977, January 11, 1980, October 25, 1981, November 8, 1981, November 15, 1981, October 22, 1982, November 7, 1982, March 11, 1983, October 20, 1983, October 30, 1983, December 15, 1985, December 23, 1986, January 2, 1987, January 11, 1987.
Quarterly Review of Film Studies, spring, 1983.
Saturday Review, February 27, 1971, July 23, 1977, November-December, 1983.
Sight and Sound, spring, 1974, autumn, 1974, autumn, 1978, autumn, 1986.
Thousand Eyes, October, 1976.
Time, September, 28, 1970, June 6, 1977.
Variety, May 25, 1960, September 6, 1967, September 18, 1968, July 16, 1969, September 16, 1970, May 23, 1973, May 8, 1974, July 24, 1974, February 4, 1976, May 11, 1977, May 31, 1978, October 3, 1979, October 1, 1980, March 4, 1981, April 29, 1981, March 3, 1982, November 10, 1982, May 18, 1983, August 15, 1984, April 2, 1986, May 11, 1988.
Village Voice, February 18, 1971, June 20, 1977, January 21, 1980, October 28, 1981, November 2, 1982, October 25, 1983, January 17, 1984, December 30, 1986.

—Sketch by Thomas Kozikowski

* * *

SCHON, Isabel 1940-

PERSONAL: Born January 19, 1940, in Mexico City, Mexico; immigrated to United States, 1972, naturalized citizen, 1982; daughter of Oswald (an attorney) and Anita (Gritzewsky) Schon; married R. R. Chalquest (a professor); children: Vera.

Education: Attended Universidad Nacional Autónoma de México, 1967-70; Mankato State College (now University), B.S. (cum laude), 1971; Michigan State University, M.A., 1972; University of Colorado, Ph.D., 1974.

ADDRESSES: Home—2017 East Meadow Dr., Tempe, Ariz. 85282. *Office*—Department of Reading, Education, and Library Science, College of Education, Arizona State University, Tempe, Ariz. 85287.

CAREER: American School Foundation, Mexico City, Mexico, founding director of Educational Media Center, 1958-72; Arizona State University, Tempe, assistant professor, 1974-79, associate professor, 1979-82, professor of library science, 1983—. Administrative assistant at Kettering Foundation's Materials Dissemination Center, 1966; visiting professor at American schools in Guayaquil and Quito, Ecuador, 1971, and University of the Americas, Mexico, 1972. Member of education committee of Arizona-Mexico Commission, 1979; member of Arizona Online Users Group, 1981—. Conducts workshops; designs library media centers; guest on radio programs; consultant to British Library and libraries at University of Budapest and at Sorbonne, University of Paris.

MEMBER: American Library Association, Reforma: National Association of Spanish Speaking Librarians, American Association of School Librarians, Arizona State Library Association.

AWARDS, HONORS: Grants from U.S. Office of Education, 1978-79, Arizona State Department of Education, 1979-80, 1980-81, and American Library Association, 1982-83; Herbert W. Putnam Honor Award from American Library Association, 1979, for research on the effects of books on Hispanic students; Grolier Foundation Award from the American Library Association, 1986; Women's National Book Award from the Women's National Book Association, 1987.

WRITINGS:

Los medios educativos en la individualización del aprendizaje (title means "Educational Media and Individualized Learning"), American School Foundation, 1970.
Mexico and Its Literature for Children and Adolescents, Center for Latin American Studies, Arizona State University, 1977.
(Author of foreword) Anita R. Peterson, *Library Service to the Spanish-Speaking,* Inglewood Public Library, 1977.
(Contributor) Arnulfo D. Trejo, editor, *Library and Information Services for the Spanish-Speaking,* Unviersity of Arizona, 1978.
A Bicultural Heritage: Themes for the Exploration of Mexican and Mexican-American Culture through Books for Children and Adolescents, Scarecrow, 1978.
Books in Spanish for Children and Young Adults: An Annotated Guide, Scarecrow, 1978, Series 2, 1983, Series 3, 1985, Series 4, 1987, Series 5, 1989.
A Hispanic Heritage: A Guide to Juvenile Books about Hispanic People and Cultures, Scarecrow, 1980, Series 2, 1985, Series 3, 1988.
(Contributor) J. W. Noll, editor, *Taking Sides: Clashing Views on Controversial Educational Issues,* 2nd edition, Dushkin, 1983.
(Contributor) David W. Foster, editor, *The Hispanic United States,* American Library Association, 1983.
Dona Blanca and Other Hispanic Nursery Rhymes and Games, Denison, 1983.
(Contributor) *Spanish-Language Books for Public Libraries,* American Library Association, 1986.

Basic Collection of Children's Books in Spanish, Scarecrow, 1986.
Books in Spanish for Children and Young Adults, Series 5, Scarecrow, 1989.

Author of bilingual (English and Spanish) filmstrip and teaching guide series on Mexican history, art, and culture, for American School Foundation. Contributor of about sixty articles and reviews to education and library journals, including *Children's Books International* and *English Journal.*

WORK IN PROGRESS: Researching the effects of special school library programs on students' library use and attitudes.

SIDELIGHTS: Isabel Schon commented: "I have always been fascinated by books. Reading has been a source of joy, comfort, and learning all my life. Hence, I was most surprised when I came to the United States to see the lack of understanding that so many of my colleagues and friends had about Hispanic peoples and cultures. Moreover, there were very few guides available that described and evaluated books in Spanish for young readers. So I combined my interests and started writing guides for adults to select books for and about Hispanic children and adolescents.

"I strongly believe that we should do our best to introduce children to the joys of reading at an early age so that they will ultimately become critical readers and critical thinkers."

* * *

SCORZA, Manuel 1928-1983

PERSONAL: Born 1928 in Lima, Peru; died November 27, 1983, in a plane crash in Madrid, Spain. *Education:* Attended University of Lima.

CAREER: Spent time in Peruvian prison and was exiled from country; founder and secretary-general of Movimiento Comunal del Perú.

AWARDS, HONORS: Received Premio Nacional de Literatura.

WRITINGS:

(Editor) *Satíricos y costumbristas: Autores de la colonia, emancipación y república,* Patronato del Libro Peruano (Lima), 1957.
(Editor) *Segunda serie de autores peruanos,* Patronato del Libro Peruano, 1957.
(Editor) *Poesía contemporánea del Perú,* Casa de la Cultura del Perú (Lima), 1963.

POEMS

Los adioses, Festivales del Libro (Lima), 1959.
Las imprecaciones, Festivales del Libro, 1960.
Desengaños del mago, Festivales del Libro, 1961.
Réquiem para un gentilhombre, Santiago Velarde (Lima), 1962.
Poesía amorosa, Populibros Peruanos, c. 1963.
El vals de los reptiles, Universidad Nacional Autónoma de México, 1970.
Poesía incompleta, Dirección General de Publicaciones, Universidad Nacional Autónoma de México, 1976.
Poesía, Municipalidad de Lima Metropolitana, Secretaria de Educación y Cultura, 1986.

"LA GUERRA SILENCIOSA" SERIES; NOVELS

Redoble por rancas, Editorial Planeta (Barcelona), 1970, translation by Edith Grossman published as *Drums for Rancas,* Harper, 1977.
Historia de Garabombo, el invisible, Editorial Planeta, 1972, published as *Garabombo, el invisible,* Monte Avila (Barcelona), 1978.

El jinete insomne, Monte Avila, 1978.

Cantar de Agapito Robles, Monte Avila, 1978.

La tumba del relámpago, Siglo Veintiuno Editores (Mexico), 1979.

La danza inmóvil, Plaza & Janés, 1983.

SIDELIGHTS: Because of his involvement in a peasant uprising in his native Peru, Manuel Scorza was imprisoned for a time and finally exiled from his homeland. From the early 1960s until the time of his death in 1983 Scorza lived in Paris. His "La guerra silenciosa" series ("The Silent War") was inspired by the peasant revolt. Mixing actual history with fantasy, the novels depict the struggle between the Creoles and the Indians of Peru. Scorza's books have been translated into more than twenty languages.

BIOGRAPHICAL/CRITICAL SOURCES:

BOOKS

Myers, Doris, editor, *Lives on the Line: The Testimony of Contemporary Latin American Authors,* University of California Press, 1988.

OBITUARIES:

PERIODICALS

Review, Number 32, January-March, 1984.

*   *   *

SELTZER, Chester E.   1915-1971
(Amado [Jesús] Muro)

PERSONAL: Born 1915 in Cleveland, Ohio; died of a heart attack, October 3, 1971, in El Paso, Tex.; son of Louis B. Seltzer (a newspaper editor); married Amada Muro, 1946; children: Charles, Robert. *Education:* Attended University of Virginia, 1933, and Kenyon College, 1935.

CAREER: Short story writer under the pseudonym Amado Muro; journalist for several newspapers, beginning 1940, including the *Miami Herald, San Antonio Express, El Paso Herald-Post,* and *San Diego Union.*

AWARDS, HONORS. Best American Short Stories included the author's work in its list of "Distinctive Short Stories" in 1970, 1972, and 1973.

WRITINGS:

The Collected Stories of Amado Muro, Thorp Springs Press, 1979.

Also author of short stories "Cecilia Rosas," "Hobo Jungle," "Hungry Men," "Mala Torres," "María Tepache," "My Aunt Dominga," "My Grandfather's Brave Songs," "Night Train to Fort Worth," "Street of the Crazy Women," "Sunday in Little Chihuahua," and "Two Skid Row Wretches." Contributor of articles and editorials to newspapers.

SIDELIGHTS: Chester E. Seltzer wrote short fiction under the pseudonym Amado Muro, which he derived from his wife's name, Amada Muro. Several of his stories describe hobo characters based on men he encountered in his travels. Seltzer roamed throughout the U.S. Southwest and Mexico, hitching rides on freight trains, eating at charitable missions, seeking work, and becoming thoroughly familiar with the struggles of poor people. Most of his published fiction, however, focuses on the people of Parral, Chihuahua, Mexico, and the fictional El Paso barrio, "Little Chihuahua." Though not Hispanic himself, Seltzer had great affection for Chicanos and, according to a contributor in

Chicano Literature, was able to capture the essence of their culture: "The main threads of Chicano culture—the values, customs, beliefs, and language of the people—run consistently and accurately throughout his *barrio* stories, more so than in the work of any other American writer who chose to depict Mexicans and their culture." The author began to write under the name Muro in the 1950s and as such he was long thought a Chicano writer. After Seltzer's death, however, essayist Elroy Bode uncovered his background and wrote a short biography of the author.

Seltzer was born into an eminent family in Cleveland, Ohio. His father, Louis B. Seltzer, was editor of the *Cleveland Press* and his grandfather, Charles Alden Seltzer, wrote popular Western adventure stories. The *Chicano Literature* contributor suggests that Seltzer adopted the pseudonym Amado Muro partly to avoid recognition of the family name. He majored in journalism at the University of Virginia in 1933, and in 1935 he studied creative writing at Kenyon College where he became acquainted with poets Randall Jarrell and Robert Lowell.

Soon after beginning his journalism career in 1940, Seltzer was imprisoned as a conscientious objector for refusing to fight in World War II. "Politically he was living in the 60's long before the 60's arrived," remarked *New York Times Book Review* contributor Larry McMurtry. Upon release from prison Seltzer married and began a family in El Paso, Texas. He resumed writing, working for various papers throughout the West and supporting his family from a distance. On more than one occasion Seltzer suffered for his pacifism; the *San Diego Union* fired him in 1950 for his antiwar stance, and during the war in Vietnam a newspaper removed him from its editorial page because he sided with peace demonstrators. During the course of his career, he expressed his convictions not only in editorials against war, but also against the Ku Klux Klan, poverty, and the exploitation of farm workers.

According to McMurtry, *The Collected Stories of Amado Muro* "pay[s] tribute to the humor, generosity and spirit of the poor Mexicans Seltzer admired and to the graceful language they speak." The critic added that the author's best stories are those featuring street scenes and conversations of the townspeople. The *Chicano Literature* contributor concurred: "The power of the stories lies in Seltzer's vivid descriptions and in his use of the 'oral tradition,' letting the characters speak for themselves."

BIOGRAPHICAL/CRITICAL SOURCES:

BOOKS

Martínez, Julio A., and Francisco A. Lomelí, editors, *Chicano Literature: A Reference Guide,* Greenwood Press, 1985.

PERIODICALS

Arizona Quarterly, autumn, 1978.
Nation, April 6, 1974.
New York Times Book Review, May 30, 1982.
Texas Observer, March 30, 1973.
Western American Literature, number 10, 1975.

*   *   *

SENDER, Ramón (José)   1902-1982

PERSONAL: Born February 3, 1902, in Chalamera de Cinca, Spain; immigrated to United States, 1942, naturalized citizen, 1946; died of emphysema, January 15, 1982, in San Diego, Calif.; son of José (a farmer) and Andrea (Garces) Sender; married Amparo Barayón, January 7, 1934 (died October 11, 1936); married

Elizabeth de Altube, 1937 (divorced); married Florence Hall, August 12, 1943 (divorced September 3, 1963); children: (first marriage) Ramón, Andrea; (second marriage) Emmanuel. *Education:* Instituto de Segunda Enseñanza de Teruel, Bachillerato, 1917; University of Madrid, Licenciado en filosofía y letras, 1924.

ADDRESSES: Home—San Diego, Calif. *Agent*—American Literary Agency, 11 Riverside Dr., New York, N.Y. 10023.

CAREER: El Sol, Madrid, Spain, editor and literary critic, 1924-30; free-lance writer in Madrid, 1930-36, and in Mexico, 1939-41; Amherst College, Amherst, Mass., professor of Spanish literature, 1943; Metro-Goldwyn-Mayer, Inc., New York, N.Y., translator and adapter, 1943-45; University of Denver, Denver, Colo., professor of Spanish literature, 1946; University of New Mexico, Albuquerque, professor of Spanish literature, 1947-63; University of Southern California, Los Angeles, professor of Spanish literature, until 1973. Visiting professor of Spanish at Ohio State University, 1950, University of California, Los Angeles, 1962, and University of Southern California, 1965. *Military service:* Served as reserve officer on Spanish infantry mission to Morocco, 1923-24; received Medal of Morocco and Military Cross of Merit. Spanish Republican Army, 1936-39; became major on general staff.

MEMBER: Hispanic Society of America, Spanish Confederated Societies (New York; honorary member), Ateneo (Spain; member of governing board and secretary of Ibero-American section), National Council on Culture (Spain), Alliance of Intellectuals for the Defense of Democracy (Spain), Phi Sigma Iota, Alpha Mu Gamma.

AWARDS, HONORS: National Prize for Literature (Spain), 1935, for *Mister Witt en el cantón;* Guggenheim fellow, 1942-43; Premio de la Literatura, 1966; D.Litt., University of New Mexico, 1968, and University of Southern California; Planeta Prize (Spain), 1969, for *En la vida de Ignacio Morel;* nominated for Nobel Prize for Literature, 1979.

WRITINGS:

El problema religioso en Méjico (nonfiction), preface by Ramón del Valle-Inclán, Imprenta Argis (Madrid), 1928.

Imán (novel), Editorial Cenit (Madrid), 1930, reprinted, Ediciones Destino (Barcelona), 1976, translation by James Cleugh published as *Earmarked for Hell,* Wishart, 1934, published as *Pro Patria,* Houghton, 1935.

Teresa de Jesús, Editorial Zeus (Madrid), 1931.

El verbo se hizo sexo (nonfiction), Sociedad Anónima Editorial (Madrid), 1931.

Siete domingos rojos (novel), Colección Balagué (Barcelona), 1932, revised edition, Editorial Proyección (Barcelona), 1973, translation by Sir Peter Chalmers Mitchell published as *Seven Red Sundays,* Liveright, 1936, reprinted, Collier, 1961.

La noche de las cien cabezas (novel), Imprenta de J. Pueyo (Madrid), 1934.

Viaje a la aldea del crimen (nonfiction), Imprenta de J. Pueyo, 1934.

Mister Witt en el cantón (novel), Espasa-Calpe (Madrid), 1936, reprinted, Alianza Editorial (Madrid), 1976, translation by Mitchell published as *Mr. Witt Among the Rebels,* Faber, 1937, Houghton, 1938.

Counter-attack in Spain (nonfiction), translated from the original Spanish manuscript by Mitchell, Houghton, 1937 (published in England as *The War in Spain: A Personal Narrative,* Faber, 1937).

Proverbio de la muerte (novel), Ediciones Quetzal (Mexico), 1939, revised edition published as *La esfera,* Aguilar (Madrid), 1969, translation by F. Giovanelli published as *The Sphere,* Hellman, Williams (New York), 1949.

El lugar del hombre (novel), Ediciones Quetzal, 1939, reprinted, Ediciones Destino, 1960, translation by Oliver La Farge published as *A Man's Place,* Duell, 1940, revised Spanish edition published as *El lugar de un hombre,* Ediciones CNT (Mexico), 1958, reprinted, Ediciones Destino, 1976.

Hernán Cortés (nonfiction), Ediciones Quetzal, 1940.

Mexicayotl (nonfiction), Ediciones Quetzal, 1940.

O. P.: Orden público (novel), Publicaciones Panamericanas (Mexico), 1941.

Epitalamio del Prieto Trinidad (novel), Ediciones Quetzal, 1942, reprinted, Ediciones Destino, 1973, translation by Eleanor Clark published as *Dark Wedding,* Doubleday, 1943.

Crónica del alba, Editorial Nuevo Mundo (Mexico), 1942, translation by Willard R. Trask published as *Chronicle of Dawn* (also see below), Doubleday, 1944, annotated Spanish edition, edited and introduced by Florence Hall, Crofts, 1946.

El rey y la reina (novel), Editorial Jackson, 1949, reprinted, Ediciones Destino, 1972, translation by Mary Low published as *The King and the Queen,* Vanguard, 1948.

El verdugo afable (novel), Nascimento (Santiago, Chile), 1952, translation by Hall published as *The Affable Hangman,* J. Cape, 1954, Las Américas Publishing Co., 1963.

Mosén Millán (novel), [Mexico], 1953, Heath, 1964, published as *Réquiem por un campesino español/Requiem for a Spanish Peasant* (parallel English and Spanish texts), translated by Elinor Randall, Las Américas Publishing Co., 1960, Spanish text reprinted, Ediciones Destino, 1976.

Hipogrifo violento (novel), [Mexico], 1954, translation by F. W. Sender published as *Violent Griffin* in *Before Noon: A Novel in Three Parts* (also see below), University of New Mexico Press, 1957.

Ariadna (novel), [Mexico], 1955, published as *Los cinco libros de Ariadna,* Ediciones Ibérica (New York), 1957, reprinted, Ediciones Destino, 1977.

Unamuno, Valle-Inclán, Baroja y Santayana (critical essays), Ediciones de Andrea (Mexico), 1955.

Before Noon: A Novel in Three Parts (contains *Chronicle of Dawn, Violent Griffin,* and *The Villa Julieta* [translation by F. W. Sender from original Spanish manuscript of *La Quinta Julieta*]), University of New Mexico Press, 1957.

El diantre: Tragicomedia para el cine según un cuento de Andreiev, Ediciones de Andrea, 1958.

Los laureles de Anselmo (novel), Ediciones Atenea (Mexico), 1958.

Emen hetan (novel), Libro Mex (Mexico), 1958.

El mancebo y los héroes (novel), Ediciones Atenea, 1960.

Las imágenes migratorias (poems), Ediciones Atenea, 1960.

La llave (novel; also see below), Editorial Alfa (Montevideo, Uruguay), 1960.

(With Valle-Inclán) *Memorias del marqués de Bradomín,* Las Américas Publishing Co., 1961.

Examen de ingenios: Los noventayochos (critical essays), Las Américas Publishing Co., 1961.

Novelas ejemplares de Cíbola, Las Américas Publishing Co., 1961, translation by Hall and others published as *Tales of Cíbola,* 1964.

La tesis de Nancy (novel), Ediciones Atenea, 1962.

La luna de los perros, Las Américas Publishing Co., 1962.

Los tontos de la concepción (nonfiction), Editorial Coronado (Sandoval, New Mexico), 1963.

Carolus Rex (historical novel), Editores Mexicanos Unidos (Mexico), 1963.

Jubileo en el zócalo: Retablo commemorativo, edited by Hall, Appleton, 1964.

La aventura equinoccial de Lope de Aguirre, antiepopeya (novel), Las Américas Publishing Co., 1964.

Cabrerizas altas, Editores Mexicanos Unidos, 1965.

El bandido adolescente, Ediciones Destino (Barcelona), 1965.

Valle-Inclán y la dificultad de la tragedia (nonfiction), Editorial Gredos (Madrid), 1965.

El sosia y los delegados (nonfiction), B. Costa-Amic (Mexico), 1965.

Tres novelas teresianas (fiction), Ediciones Destino, 1967.

Las Gallinas de Cervantes y otras narraciones parabólicas (nonfiction), Editores Mexicanos Unidos, 1967.

Ensayos sobre el infringimiento cristiano, Editores Mexicanos Unidos, 1967.

La llave y otras narraciones (fiction), Editorial Magisterio Español (Madrid), 1967.

Las criaturas saturnianas, Ediciones Destino, 1968.

Don Juan en la mancebía: Drama litúrgico en cuatro actos, Editores Mexicanos Unidos, 1968.

El extraño Señor Photynos y otras novelas (fiction), Ayma (Barcelona), 1968.

Novelas de otro jueves, Aguilar, 1969.

Comedia del Diantre y otras dos, Ediciones Destino, 1969.

En la vida de Ignacio Morel (novel), Editorial Planeta (Barcelona), 1969.

Nocturno de los 14 (novel), Iberama Publishing Co. (New York), 1969.

Tres ejemplos de amor y una teoría (nonfiction), Alianza Editorial, 1969.

Ensayos del otro mundo, Ediciones Destino, 1970.

Relatos fronterizos, Editores Mexicanos Unidos, 1970.

Tánit (novel), Editorial Planeta, 1970.

Zu, el ángel anfibio (novel), Editorial Planeta, 1970.

La antesala, Ediciones Destino, 1971.

El fugitivo, Editorial Planeta, 1972.

Páginas escogidas, edited and introduced by Marcelino C. Peñuelas, Editorial Gredos (Madrid), 1972.

Donde crece la marihuana: Drama en cuatro actos, Escelicer (Madrid), 1973.

Túpac Amaru, Ediciones Destino, 1973.

Una virgen llama a tu puerta, Ediciones Destino, 1973.

Libro armilar de poesía y memorias bisiestas, Aguilar, 1974.

La mesa de las tres moiras (novel), Editorial Planeta, 1974.

Nancy, doctora en gitanería, Editorial Magisterio Español, 1974.

Nancy y el bato loco, Editorial Magisterio Español, 1974.

Las tres sorores, Ediciones Destino, 1974.

Cronus y la señora con rabo, AKAL (Madrid), 1974.

El futuro comenzó ayer: Lecturas mosaicas, CVS Ediciones (Madrid), 1975.

La efemérides (novel), Sedmay Ediciones (Madrid), 1976.

Arlene y la gaya ciencia, Ediciones Destino, 1976.

El pez de oro, Ediciones Destino, 1976.

Obra completa, Ediciones Destino, 1976.

El Alarido de Yaurí, Ediciones Destino, 1977.

Gloria y vejamen de Nancy, Editorial Magisterio Español, 1977.

El Mechudo y la Llorona, Ediciones Destino, 1977.

Adela y yo, Ediciones Destino, 1978.

El superviviente, Ediciones Destino, 1978.

(Editor) *Cinco poetas disidentes escrito en Cuba,* Transaction, 1978.

Solanar y lucernario aragonés, Heraldo de Aragón (Saragossa, Spain), 1978.

La mirada inmóvil, Editorial Argos Vergara, 1979.

Also author of novel *La Quinta Julieta* (also see above), B. Costa-Amic, and of one-act plays "The House of Lot," "The Secret," and "The Photograph"; author of introduction to *Reflejos de España* by A. Monros, Federación Social de Montreal. Contributor to magazines and literary periodicals.

WORK IN PROGRESS: Poetry; works in philosophy and history.

SIDELIGHTS: Though Ramón Sender was forced to spend more than half his life in countries other than his native Spain, he was nevertheless regarded as one of that nation's most distinguished novelists. Sender's path to exile began during his years at the University of Madrid, where his political activities on behalf of various reformist causes angered school authorities and ultimately led to his expulsion and even to a brief period of imprisonment. Sender did, however, manage to earn a degree, and in 1924 he went to work as an editor and literary critic for the liberal publication *El Sol.* Six years later he severed his official ties with *El Sol* and became a free-lance writer contributing to many different newspapers and journals and publishing novels, essays, and plays.

When civil war broke out in Spain in the summer of 1936 Sender was among the first to join the army of the Republic in its fight against the forces of Generalissimo Francisco Franco. But the young writer's military career was brief; Sender left Spain in 1937, not long after learning that his wife and brother had been executed by the Fascists for sympathizing with the republican cause. In an attempt to garner support for the beleaguered government, Sender then set out on a speaking tour of Europe and the United States as a representative of the Republic. The victory of Franco's troops in 1939, however, meant that Sender faced the prospect of permanent exile. After traveling and writing in Mexico for several years, he settled in the United States, spending most of the remaining forty years of his life in the Southwest and writing (in Spanish) about the world he had left behind in 1937.

Critics have tended to divide Sender's best-known works of fiction into two categories that correspond to these two major periods in his life. In the first category are novels Sender wrote *before* leaving Spain, such as *Imán* and *Siete domingos rojos;* in the second category are novels he wrote *after* leaving Spain, including *La esfera* and *Crónica del alba* and its sequels, a series many believe is his greatest achievement. For the most part, noted John Devlin in his book *Spanish Anticlericalism: A Study in Modern Alienation,* "the earlier group evokes the fights, illusions and hardships of [Sender's] fellow Spaniards before and during the Republic. [The] latter works reveal a continual philosophic evolution and search for values in the twentieth century world of turmoil."

Imán, Sender's first novel, is one of those works concerned with the political and social atmosphere of pre-civil war Spain. A fictionalized account of events the author witnessed during the Spanish military's attempt to suppress a revolt among the Moors in Morocco in the early 1920s, *Imán* reflects on the uselessness of the campaign and the brutal sacrifices expected of the lower classes in the name of patriotism and economic gain. Commenting on the English translation of *Imán* which was published in the United States as *Pro Patria,* Charles C. King remarks in his critical study, *Ramón J. Sender,* that this particular novel is significant not only because it is Sender's first, "but also because in style and human content it accurately foreshadows [his] prolific . . . novelistic production of the next four decades." Viance, the army private who serves as the principal narrator of the story, is, according to King, "both an individual soldier and a symbol of the Spanish underprivileged masses. . . . There is a parallel between the treatment meted out to Viance by his officers and the treatment of the Spanish lower classes by the upper classes through the centuries. . . . In the end Viance breaks national boundaries, becoming a universal symbol of the common man as victim of injustice and man's inhumanity to man." In addition, wrote the critic, *Pro Patria* resembles subsequent Sender novels in that it displays "a direct, sober, verbal style, an impersonal distancing of the author from the work, the same grim—sometimes gruesome—humor . . . , the same interweaving of objective and subjective realities to create the novel's own private world, the harshest of visual detail alongside lyrical and metaphysical fantasy, the flight into delirium and dreams which sometimes cast a surrealistic spell over the action, and the ever-present probing of ultimate reality, mystery."

In a review written at the time of the book's publication in 1935, a *Times Literary Supplement* critic remarked that it is appropriate to regard *Pro Patria* "less as a work of fiction than as an impressive piece of journalism contributing an unpublished page to the detailed history of the present." But as Paul Allen observed in *Books,* Sender was not entirely successful at blending the two genres. Observed the critic: "All this is not for the squeamish certainly. Nor for the strong. For it seems hardly possible that any one can have stomach or nerves strong enough to read it unmoved. Nor can one take refuge in doubt. Señor Sender was on the scene. . . . But so intense was his desire to cram into the book all the searing things he had felt and seen he forgot he was writing a novel."

The *Christian Century*'s Raymond Kresensky also noted that *Pro Patria* lacks many of the qualities of a good novel. "There is no romance, no sentiment, and very little humaneness [in this book]," he began. "Not once is it lightened by even a glimmer of humor. Those with weak stomachs will not be able to read through the three hundred pages of ghastly experiences."

Though Otis Ferguson of the *New Republic* agreed that "as a novel [*Pro Patria*] is confusing and incomplete, half this, half that," he went on to state that it is nevertheless "more valuable, in what it has to tell us of things we could not imagine, than any five-foot shelf of Life and Death in Recent Leading Fiction." V. S. Pritchett expressed a similar view, declaring in the *New Statesman and Nation* that "*Pro Patria* has dignity but no great distinction, and the attempt to create a symbolical Spanish soldier type is not very successful. . . . [Yet] it would be a pity if, after our glut of war books, this intelligent and sensitive Spanish document were put aside."

A few reviewers were somewhat more generous in their praise of Sender's first novel. Commented a *Saturday Review of Literature* critic: "[*Pro Patria*] is as full of humanity as it is of terror. It is like so many current war stories, a narrative of futility. . . . If it makes the reader shudder, [it] also inevitably makes him think." William Plomer of the *Spectator* noted that "only a man of rare imaginative power and literary skill, a man both honest and brilliant, could have produced this record of a prolonged and complicated nightmare. Senor Sender makes it clear that he had no need to invent anything. . . . Private Viance has as great a significance as any character in recent fiction."

Unlike those reviewers who did not like the author's documentary approach, the *Nation*'s Florence Codman was pleased to see that Sender disclaimed all "literary and aesthetic prejudices" before beginning *Pro Patria.* "The agreeable thing about this book," Codman stated, "is its total lack of pretenses—sentimental, egotistic, social, or artistic. In fact, I recall no recent

examples of war fiction in which there is so little attitude and so generous a permission to let bare incidents, within their context, speak for themselves. It is Sender's compliment to his subject to have realized that no inflation could make it more ghastly or render his hero more pitiable or more dignified."

Sender's second novel, *Siete domingos rojos,* continued the examination of politics and society in pre-civil war Spain, this time from the point of view of a group of communists, anarchists, and trade unionists who stage an unsuccessful general strike in Madrid. Though this book also struck many critics at the time of its publication as more documentary than literary in style, it nevertheless demonstrated the author's growing preoccupation with experimental philosophies and different ways of perceiving reality. Discussing the English translation, *Seven Red Sundays,* Sherman H. Eoff suggested in *The Modern Spanish Novel* that Sender's interest in "the mysterious 'presence' that lurks behind commonplace existence" and in "the notion that the heart of human reality is concealed in a nonrational and phantomlike quality" foreshadowed the French existentialists in some ways. Explained Eoff: "Bolder—and less organized—than the French in his expression of ideas, and less dedicated to novelistic technique as a goal in itself, [Sender] evinces a lusty primitivism whose existentialist affinity is an aspect rather than a systematic trend of thought." King observed in his book that "Sender uses external or ordinary reality in *Seven Red Sundays* as a solid base of operations, as a kind of trampoline from which to launch his leaps to 'higher' realities. The chapter in which the moon becomes a character is an example of unrestrained imagination which clearly violates the usual norms for a 'realistic' work. . . . [Thus,] the 'realism' of *Seven Red Sundays* is a strange fusion of ordinary reality with other 'realities,' imaginative 'realities' that sometimes add an intellectual dimension, at others a lyrical or metaphysical overtone."

Perhaps the most philosophical of Sender's many works is *La esfera,* the first novel he wrote after leaving Spain. The English translation, *The Sphere,* is described by King as "an ambitious attempt to fuse into an artistic unity the realistic, the lyrical-metaphysical, the fantastic, and the symbolic." *The Sphere* follows a Spanish refugee on a transatlantic voyage that is marred by several murders, a mutiny, and a shipwreck. In this complex story, Sender explored a variety of universal opposites—life and death, love and hate—and tried to synthesize them into higher unities or "spheres" that incorporated elements of the purely rational and conventional "everyday" world as well as the chaotic and fragmented world of the subconscious and the unconscious. According to King, "The dramatic tension of *The Sphere,* as it is in all of Sender's fiction, is . . . between [these] two worlds. . . . Sender seeks ever to write in the twilight zone where [they] merge."

One of the more unusual, yet significant, "opposites" the author discussed in *The Sphere* was "man" and "person." As Sender himself explained in a passage from the novel, a man is (in a somewhat mystical sense) "the source of all truth, of each universal and innate truth," and "an integral part of *the infinite intellect of God.*" A "person," on the other hand, is the individualized "mask" that begins to develop soon after birth and continues to grow and change throughout life—in essence, the sum of those qualities that makes one man different from another. In Sender's view, this process of individualization isolates a man from his fellow man and gradually takes him farther and farther away from his instinctive nature.

In his essay on *The Sphere,* King pointed to this man-person antithesis as the source of Sender's major philosophical convictions. It was, for instance, the basis for his belief in the "natural unity of all created objects" and his "deep faith in the value of man *simply because he is man*"; it also led him ultimately to deny the existence of death. (According to Sender, man, the "eternal substance," is immortal; what "dies" is the person, "that growing individualization of the human being.")

Sender demonstrated his preoccupation with these and other thought-provoking concepts in many of his subsequent works of fiction, including *El lugar del hombre, Epitalamio del prieto Trinidad, El rey y la reina,* and *El verdugo afable.* For the most part, critics found these books bewildering yet fascinating in their symbolic complexity and blend of reality and fantasy. One particular group of post-exile novels, however, did not exhibit quite the same abstruseness. Known by the general title of the first work in this particular series, *Chronicle of Dawn,* these novels depict early twentieth-century Spain in a tenderly nostalgic light, primarily through the eyes of a republican refugee, Pepe Garces, as he lies dying in a French prison camp during the final months of the civil war. Though Sender's series is, as Bertram Wolfe observed in *New York Herald Tribune Books,* first and foremost "a remarkably beautiful tale of romantic and heroic childhood which will take its place alongside the very best in its genre," it is also, declared the *New York Times*'s Marjorie Farber, a war story unlike any other in its portrayal of "what happens to the good men, and to all men, in the course of the fight."

Nearly all the critics who were familiar with the English translations of three novels in the series—*Chronicle of Dawn, Violent Griffin,* and *The Villa Julieta*—were charmed as well as saddened by the author's simple narrative of youth. In his *Nation* review, for example, Paul Blackburn called *Before Noon* "one of the sweetest-tempered books I have read in a long time. In fact, I can recall no book of prose at all with which to set it. I thought that only poetry could be this warm. This does not seem to be so much a result of Mr. Sender's style (an enviable clarity in itself), as of his attitude toward his character, Pepe Garces. I don't think Pepe can avoid being mostly Ramón Sender, ages ten to twelve. I do not know what Mr. Sender thinks of himself as man, but he adores that boy! I am grateful; you will be too. . . . The fabric of the book will catch you up, both in its gross take and in its delicacies, so that you will read, impatient for the next development."

Isaac Rosenfeld of the *New Republic* found that the technique of beginning the story in the present and then returning to the past creates "an idyllic effect. . . . But it is the tone in which remembered experience is set down and the purpose these scenes serve which give *Chronicle of Dawn* its quality of delight." The critic was also impressed by "the renewed ease" with which the author handled symbolism in the book. Remarked Rosenfeld: "[In previous novels Sender's] symbolism appeared to be getting out of hand, even at times symbolizing nothing so much as itself in an iconography run riot, religious in its overtones but wary of the reality to which it owed some final commitment. *Chronicle of Dawn* is to my mind a very welcome reconstruction of the symbol."

Farber applauded Sender for at last writing "an astonishingly true and moving" book which examines "the total truth of our tragedy"—in short, "the whole monstrous discrepancy between human potential and the inhuman, mechanized result: the love perverted or corrupted, the courage exploited, the nobility thrown away." She was also pleased to note Sender's "tone of respect" and "unusual honesty and clarity" in recording "the physical details and the passionate emotions of childhood," explaining that "Sender's humor contains none of the underlying

contempt of [novelist Booth] Tarkington's attitude toward Penrod; nor does he ever allow nostalgia to falsify his memories into the pastel prettiness of [William] Saroyan. Pepe may be young, but he is a human being—a young man in the most dignified literal sense."

Unlike Farber, however, *Nation* critic Diana Trilling did not find Sender's portrait of Pepe particularly dignified. "For all Mr. Sender's good prose," she stated, "[*Chronicle of Dawn*] was marred for me by the fatal coyness with which Mr. Sender reproduces the mind of a ten-year-old." Others, too, had some less-than-flattering observations to make about the book. As Edwin Honig commented in the *Saturday Review:* "Despite the delicacy and charm of its details, the novel is somber and bare, and at times appears too far removed from the sources of feeling it exploits. . . . After the first true heat and *vraisemblance* are struck in *Chronicle of Dawn,* the novel seems to jerk along without developing characters or situations beyond the passing events themselves." In his *Commonweal* review, Paule Berault described *Chronicle of Dawn* as a childhood memory "with all the weaknesses and the charm of this form" and expressed his disappointment with Sender's all-too-brief mention of that "drama [the Spanish civil war] which was the forerunner of that which spread all over the world." As far as Berault was concerned, Sender's sober yet powerful explanation of how and why the dying Pepe came to tell his story "far surpasses the rest of the book."

At least two critics believed that Sender did not err in downplaying the political and social realities of the 1930s in his novel. *Saturday Review*'s Ralph Bates, for example, speculated that the author, "driven out of his own land with memories too horrible for contemplation," probably felt "compelled to reorder his thinking [and thus] deliberately returned to that [time when] the spirit was whole and hard and pure." Continued the critic: "Sender must go back, as [Pepe] must do, not in order to comfort the heart with dreams of a Golden Epoch, but in order to collect and concentrate himself, to pare off the impurities, particularly the uncleanness of the political world of compromise and ungodly tolerance . . . This return to childhood is a kind of voluntary seclusion, a monasticism of the spirit that is far more rigorous than the imprisonments which have been made to serve the same purpose by other writers. . . . That is the significance of this simple, astonishing book. That is why it is so singularly pure, for against its one banal memory there are set within it scores of startling and altogether beautiful things."

Rosenfeld agreed that Sender's "reconstruction of [Pepe's] childhood is . . . not an escape from political responsibility, nor even a simple flight from hopelessness. It is, rather, a justification of the hopeless. . . . Only through the reconstruction of the times and experiences in which the ideal had meaning—the childhood of hope—can one examine, with the most unsparing honesty, the significance of the ideal, and know, without delusion, precisely what was lost when 'all was lost.' "

Sender's lifelong desire to determine "precisely what was lost when 'all was lost' " did not, however, leave him bitter or pessimistic. It is true, noted critic John Devlin, that as "a novelist with philosophical inclinations" Sender did continually seek out the "explanations behind reality—not only the reality of Spain of his day, but of human existence, as well." Nevertheless, concluded Devlin, "an examination of [his] first novel reveals, under literary symbols, that he discovered in the worst of situations and people a small light shining in the midst of the surrounding darkness of chaos and cruelty. This note is [Sender's] saving grace; it pervades and becomes the touchstone of all his major works."

BIOGRAPHICAL/CRITICAL SOURCES:

BOOKS

Contemporary Literary Criticism, Volume 8, Gale, 1978.
Devlin, John, Spanish Anticlericalism: A Study in Modern Alienation, Las Américas Publishing Co., 1966.
Eoff, Sherman H., The Modern Spanish Novel, New York University Press, 1961.
King, Charles C., Ramón J. Sender, Twayne, 1974.
Sender, Ramón, Chronicle of Dawn, annotated Spanish edition, edited and introduced by Florence Hall, Crofts, 1946.

PERIODICALS

Books, October 6, 1935, October 11, 1936.
Christian Century, November 6, 1935.
Christian Science Monitor, May 12, 1937, May 24, 1949.
Commonweal, May 26, 1944.
Manchester Guardian, May 1, 1936, April 23, 1937.
Nation, October 2, 1935, October 24, 1936, November 2, 1940, April 24, 1943, March 18, 1944, April 19, 1958.
New Republic, October 16, 1935, October 14, 1936, February 3, 1941, April 5, 1943, April 24, 1944, May 31, 1948, November 30, 1963.
New Statesman and Nation, September 8, 1934, January 16, 1937, April 10, 1937.
New Yorker, April 19, 1958.
New York Herald Tribune Weekly Book Review, March 28, 1943, March 12, 1944, May 16, 1948.
New York Times, September 22, 1935, October 18, 1936, January 30, 1938, November 3, 1940, March 28, 1943, February 20, 1944, June 27, 1948, May 1, 1949, January 19, 1958.
San Francisco Chronicle, June 19, 1949, February 16, 1958.
Saturday Review of Literature, October 19, 1935, September 26, 1936, January 29, 1938, December 21, 1940, May 15, 1943, April 15, 1944, June 4, 1949, April 12, 1958, September 7, 1963.
Spectator, September 14, 1935, April 16, 1937.
Times Literary Supplement, October 25, 1934, May 2, 1936, April 17, 1937.
Washington Post Book World, September 29, 1963.

OBITUARIES:

PERIODICALS

AB Bookman's Weekly, February 22, 1982.
Chicago Tribune, January 19, 1982.
Times (London), January 19, 1982.

*   *   *

SENDER BARAYON, Ramón 1934-

PERSONAL: Born October 29, 1934, in Madrid, Spain; immigrated to United States, 1939, naturalized citizen, 1947; son of Ramón J. Sender (a writer) and Amparo Barayón (a pianist); married Judith Levy (a teacher and counselor), February 14, 1982; children: Xaverie, Jonathan, Andres, Sol Ray. Education: San Francisco Conservatory of Music, B.Mus. (magna cum laude), 1962; Mills College, M.A., 1966.

ADDRESSES: Home— San Francisco, Calif. Office— P.O. Box 460141, San Francisco, Calif. 94146-0141. Agent—Howard Sandum, 144 East 84th St., New York, N.Y. 10028.

CAREER: San Francisco Tape Music Center, San Francisco, Calif., co-founder and co-director, 1962-65; free-lance editor, writer, and composer, 1966—. Host of writers conference at Whole Earth Electronic Link (The Well), Sausalito, Calif., 1986—. Board member of Good Sound Foundation.

MEMBER: Authors Guild.

AWARDS, HONORS: National Endowment for the Arts fellow, 1983.

WRITINGS:

(With Alicia Bay Laurel) Being of the Sun (nonfiction), Harper, 1973.
The Morning Star Scrapbook, Friends of Morning Star, 1976.
Zero Weather (novel), Family Publishing, 1980.
A Death in Zamora (nonfiction), University of New Mexico Press, 1989.

Contributor to periodicals, including Signal, Modern Utopian, and Co-Evolution Quarterly. Contributing editor of Whole Earth Catalog/Review, 1986—.

WORK IN PROGRESS: Native to Your Heart, "a nonfiction account of my experiences in a Christian sect as a twenty-three year old," publication expected in 1991.

SIDELIGHTS: In 1939, the year revolutionary leader Francisco Franco seized control of Spain, Ramón Sender Barayón fled to the United States with his younger sister and their father, renowned novelist Ramón J. Sender. Perhaps because the children were so young, Sender did not tell them of their mother's violent death three years before, and in later he years he kept silent about the subject. His son, however, remained curious, and after his father's death in 1982 Sender Barayón began to investigate his mother's history. Sender Barayón's 1989 book A Death in Zamora reveals that his mother, Amparo Barayón, had been executed in 1936 in her hometown of Zamora while her husband was fighting with a militia in Spain's civil war. After being betrayed to a fascist group by her brother-in-law and denied absolution by her priest (she had lived with Sender before marrying him in a civil—not Catholic—ceremony), Barayón was taken to a cemetery in Zamora where she was shot by a rejected lover, who belonged to the fascist organization. Barayón was "a lovely, independent woman, who lived with passion, who was devoted to her children and who had married a famous revolutionary writer," summarized William Herrick in the New York Times Book Review. "For all that she was murdered." Despite calling A Death in Zamora occasionally "confusing," Herrick deemed Sender Barayón's account "a very moving document."

Sender Barayón wrote: "Although I trained as a composer, I have concentrated on literature for the past ten years. I flatter myself by saying I am the most prolific, underpublished author in northern California. I enjoy most writing in the 'future fantasy' genre, but currently I am working on a series of autobiographical memoirs dealing with varied aspects of what seems—at least to others—to have been an adventuresome existence. I write these memoirs to put personal ghosts to rest, in the belief that if I speak from the heart I can touch what is universally shared by all humankind: a yearning for freedom, justice, and peace.

"My advice to aspiring writers is this: Develop the 'three-by-five card habit.' Always have a stack of index cards in your pocket or on a bedside table."

BIOGRAPHICAL/CRITICAL SOURCES:

PERIODICALS

New York Times Book Review, June 18, 1989.

SERNA, Ramón Gómez de la
See GOMEZ de la SERNA, Ramón

* * *

SETIEN, Miguel Delibes
See DELIBES SETIEN, Miguel

* * *

SILVA, Beverly 1935-

PERSONAL: Born May 12, 1935, in Los Angeles, Calif.; daughter of Cecilio (a businessman) and Marian (a homemaker; maiden name, Langstaff) Cruz; married Juvencio Garcia (a landscape contractor), November 19, 1982; children: Geof Silva, Carla Silva, Madelyn Silva-Baker, Joy Silva. *Education:* San Jose State University, M.A., 1976. *Politics:* Liberal Democrat. *Religion:* None.

ADDRESSES: Home—2155 Lanai Ave. #53, San Jose, Calif. 95122.

CAREER: Writer; part-time instructor of English at community colleges and teacher of English as a second language for school districts.

WRITINGS:

The Second St. Poems, Bilingual Review/Press, 1983.
(Co-editor) *Nosotras: Latina Literature Today,* Bilingual Review/Press, 1985.
The Cat and Other Stories, Bilingual Review/Press, 1986.

Contributor of poetry to numerous literary journals.

WORK IN PROGRESS: The Story of a Bricklayer, a novel "based on memories of my grandfather"; *The Guadalupe Flows,* a novel based on life in downtown San Jose in a Mexican barrio in the late 1970s.

SIDELIGHTS: Beverly Silva told *HW:* "My circumstances are well described in Tillie Olsen's *Silences.* The high cost of living keeps me away from my writing. All my work has been done without support and in spare moments of my life. Also—as a minority woman, getting published has been difficult."

* * *

SKARMETA, Antonio 1940-

PERSONAL: Born November 7, 1940, in Antofagasta, Chile; son of Antonio and Magdalena (Vranicic) Skármeta; married Cecilia Boisier (a painter), 1964 (divorced); children: Beltrán, Gabriel. *Education:* Attended University of Chile; received M.A. from Columbia University.

ADDRESSES: Home—Goethestrasse 37, 1000 Berlin 12, West Berlin, West Germany. *Agent*—Carmen Balcells, Diagonal 580, Barcelona 08021, Spain.

CAREER: University of Chile, Santiago, professor of contemporary Latin American literature, in the early 1970s; Film and Television Academy, West Berlin, West Germany, professor of screenwriting, 1978-81; freelance writer and filmmaker, 1981—. Worked as a journalist and book translator in Chile; visiting professor at colleges and universities in Europe and the United States; film director in West Germany.

MEMBER: International P.E.N. (West Germany).

AWARDS, HONORS: Premio Casa de las Américas from the government of Cuba, 1969, for short story collection *Desnudo en*

el tejado; first prizes from the Biarritz, France, and Huelva, Spain, film festivals, both 1983, for film "Ardiente paciencia"; Guggenheim fellowship, 1986.

WRITINGS:

SHORT STORIES

El entusiasmo (title means "Enthusiasm"), ZigZag, 1967.
Desnudo en el tejado (title means "Nude on the Housetop"), Sudamericana (Buenos Aires), 1969.
Tiro libre, Siglo Veintiuno (Buenos Aires), 1973.
No pasó nada y otros relatos (title means "Nothing Happened and Other Stories"), Pehuén, 1985.

NOVELS

El ciclista del San Cristóbal (title means "The Cyclist of San Cristobal"), Quimantu, 1973.
Soñé que la nieve ardía, Planeta (Barcelona), 1975, translation by Malcolm Coad published as *I Dreamt the Snow Was Burning,* Readers International, 1985.
Novios y solitarios, Losada (Buenos Aires), 1975.
Chileno!, translated from the Spanish by Hortense Carpentier, Morrow, 1979.
La insurrección (also see below), Ediciones del Norte (Hanover, N.H.), 1982, translation by Paula Sharp published as *The Insurrection,* Ediciones del Norte, 1983.
Ardiente paciencia (also see below), Ediciones del Norte, 1985, translation by Katherine Silver published as *Burning Patience,* Pantheon, 1987.

OTHER

(Translator with Cecilia Boisier) Elizabeth Bowen, *La casa en París,* ZigZag, 1969.
(Contributor) Rodrigo Quijada, editor, *Crónicas de Chile,* J. Alvarez (Buenos Aires), 1973.
(Editor) *Joven narrativa después del golpe: Antología* (title means "Young Chilean Narrative After the Coup: An Anthology"), The American Hispanist, 1976.

Also author of the screenplays "Es herrscht Ruhe im Land," "La insurrección," and "Ardiente paciencia." Author of radio plays and song lyrics. Work represented in anthologies, including *Tres cuentistas: René Marqués, Antonio Skármeta, Luis Britto Garcia,* Casa de las Américas, 1979. Contributor of articles and essays to newspapers, magazines, and literary journals.

SIDELIGHTS: Antonio Skármeta is a leading figure of the so-called "postboom generation" of Latin American novelists, whose writings reflect the political and social disturbance in the region during the past two decades. A Chilean who fled into exile in Europe when a bloody military coup toppled socialist President Salvador Allende in 1973, Skármeta is best known as a novelist, but he has also written short stories, screenplays, and literary criticism. Skármeta's fiction reflects "the crisis, the conflict and the search for identity" experienced by a whole generation of young South American intellectuals driven from their native lands by the repressive governments of the 1970s, critic Malva E. Filer observed in *World Literature Today.* Thematically, the author himself has noted, his work and that of his generation is rooted in concrete everydayness and shows greater interest in building a bond of shared experience with the reader than in exploring the mythic and transcendental questions that animate the writings of such "boom" figures as Julio Cortázar and Gabriel García Márquez.

Skármeta told *HW* that his second novel, *Soñé que la nieve ardía* (translated as *I Dreamt the Snow Was Burning*) "is an attempt to capture the mood of Chilean youngsters in the early seventies under Allende's socialist government." *Chileno!,* which was published in English in 1979, draws on the author's personal experience as an exile in West Berlin to tell the story of a sixteen-year-old Chilean boy living as a political refugee in the West German city. The political setting for *La insurrección* (*The Insurrection*) is the Sandinista-led popular rebellion against the Anastasio Somoza dictatorship in the city of León, Nicaragua, in 1978. Using straight narrative as well as letters, poems, and other literary devices to tell the story, *La insurrección* traces the revolution's course through the personal lives of a humble local family. Fast-paced and cinematic in its vivid imagery, the story was made into a prizewinning film written by Skármeta and directed by Peter Lilienthal.

The author returns to a Chilean setting in *Ardiente paciencia,* translated as *Burning Patience,* his most popular novel among English readers. Skármeta described his book to *HW* as a chronicle of "the warm but volatile friendship between Chile's great poet Pablo Neruda and a young postman who uses Neruda's poetry to seduce the girl he loves." The novel also reflects on the nature of language and poetry, yielding comically flowery conversations between Neruda and his young apprentice. "The whole book, in fact," *Village Voice* critic Enrique Fernandez observed, "is written in a mock epic tone, bursting with hyperbole, that is both a parody of and homage to Neruda's poetry." *Burning Patience* "is a witty and imaginative meditation on the relationship between literature and reality, and a wry, affectionate depiction of youthful passion," added Jonathan Yardley in the *Washington Post.* Skármeta later penned the screenplay for a film version of *Burning Patience* that won first prize at two European film festivals.

BIOGRAPHICAL/CRITICAL SOURCES:

BOOKS

Meyer, Doris, editor, *Lives On the Line: The Testimony of Contemporary Latin American Authors,* University of California Press, 1988.
Silva Cáceres, Raúl, *Del cuerpo a las palabras: La narrativa de Antonio Skármeta,* Literatura Americana Reunida (Madrid), 1983.

PERIODICALS

Hispania, September, 1986.
Los Angeles Times Book Review, May 3, 1987.
New York Times Book Review, May 3, 1987.
Times Literary Supplement, April 15, 1988.
Village Voice, July 28, 1987.
Washington Post, April 15, 1987.
World Literature Today, summer, 1983, summer, 1984, summer, 1986.

* * *

SMITH, Rolando (R.) Hinojosa
See HINOJOSA(-SMITH), Rolando (R.)

* * *

SOLORZANO, Carlos 1922-

PERSONAL: Born May 1, 1922, in Guatemala, Mexico; married Beatrice Caso, September 3, 1946; children: one son, two daughters. *Education:* National University of Mexico, B.A., 1939, M.A., 1944, Ph.D., 1946.

ADDRESSES: Home—Condor 199, Col. Alpes Tlacopac, Mexico 01010 DF, Mexico.

CAREER: Playwright, novelist, and essayist. National University of Mexico, artistic director of the university theatre, 1952-62, professor, 1960-85, professor emeritus, 1985—. Director of National Theatre, 1977-82. Visiting lecturer at numerous universities in Mexico and abroad.

MEMBER: International P.E.N., Hispanic Society of America (corresponding member), Playwrights and Composers Society, Spanish Royal Academy of Language (corresponding member), Latin American Community of Writers Society.

WRITINGS:

Del sentimiento de lo plástico en la obra de Unamuno, [Mexico], 1944.
El hechicero: Tragedia en tres actos, Cuadernos Americanos, 1955.
Las manos de Dios, B. Costa-Amic, 1957, reprinted, Center for Curriculum Development, 1971, translation by W. Keith Leonard and Marlo T. Soria published as *The Hands of God,* Hiram College, 1968.
Tres actos, El Unicornio, 1959.
Teatro latinoamericano del siglo, Nueva Visión, 1961.
Teatro guatemalteco contemporáneo, Aguilar, 1964.
El teatro hispanoamericano contemporáneo, Fondo de Cultura Económica, 1964, reprinted, 1981.
(Compiler) *Teatro breve hispano-americano contemporáneo,* Aguilar, 1970.
Las celdas, J. Mortiz, 1971.
(Compiler) *Los fantoches,* Odyssey Press, 1971.
(Compiler and author of introduction) *El teatro actual latinoamericano,* De Andrea, 1972.
Testimonios teatrales de México, Universidad Nacional Autónoma de México, 1973.
Los falsos demonios, J. Mortiz, 1973.
Teatro breve, J. Mortiz, 1977.

Work has been included in numerous anthologies including *Uno, dos, tres: Tres dramas mexicanos en un acto,* edited by Jeanine Gaucher-Shultz and Alfredo O. Morales, Odyssey Press, 1971, and *Teatro centroamericano contemporáneo,* del Pulgarcito, 1977. Contributor to journals and magazines.

SIDELIGHTS: Carlos Solórzano's works have been translated into English, French, Russian, Italian, Hungarian, Polish, and German.

* * *

SOSA, Roberto 1930-

PERSONAL: Born in 1930 in Yoro, Honduras.

CAREER: Poet. Professor, University of Honduras; director, University of Honduras Press. Juror in literary competitions, including Miró (Panama) 1976, Casa de las Américas (Cuba), 1979, and Rubén Darío (Nicaragua), 1980.

MEMBER: Honduran Academy of Language, Honduran Journalists' Union (president).

AWARDS, HONORS: Juan Ramón Molinas Award (Honduras), 1967, for *Mar interior;* Adonais Award (Spain), 1968, for *Los pobres;* Casa de las Américas Award, 1971, for *Un mundo para todos dividido;* a primary school in Tegucigalpa, Honduras, formerly named for John F. Kennedy, was renamed in Sosa's honor, as was a street in Sosa's birthplace of Yoro, Honduras.

WRITINGS:

Muros (title means "Walls"), [Tegucigalpa, Honduras], 1966.

Mar interior (title means "The Sea Inside"), Escuela Superior del Profesorado Francisco Morazán (Tegucigalpa), 1967.

(Editor and author of notes and prologue with Oscar Acosta) *Antología de la nueva poesía hondureña* (poetry anthology), Editorial Ulúa (Tegucigalpa), 1967.

(Editor and author of notes with Acosta) *Antología del cuento hondureño* (story anthology), prologue by Arturo Quesada, Departamento de Extensión Universitaria (Tegucigalpa), 1968.

Breve estudio sobre la poesía y su creación (title means "A Brief Study of Poetry and Its Creation"), Escuela Superior del Profesorado Francisco Morazán, 1969.

Los pobres (also see below; poems; title means "The Poor"), Ediciones Rialp (Madrid), 1969, reprinted, Editorial Guaymuras (Tegucigalpa), 1983.

Un mundo para todos dividido (also see below; poems; title means "A World for All Divided"), Casa de las Américas (Havana), 1971.

Prosa armada, Editorial Guaymuras, 1981.

The Difficult Days (includes poems, in English and the original Spanish, from *Un mundo para todos dividido* and *Los pobres;* also includes interviews with Sosa from *Plural* and *Alcaraván*), translated by Jim Lindsey, Princeton University Press, 1983.

Poems by Roberto Sosa: Bilingual Edition, translated and introduced by Edward V. Coughlin, Spanish Literature Publications, 1984.

Secreto militar (poems), Editorial Guaymuras, 1985.

13 poemas (bilingual edition in Spanish and German), Ediciones Hormiga Roja, 1987.

Hasta el sol de hoy: Antología poética (poems), Instituto de Cooperación Iberoamericana, Ediciones Cultura Hispánica, 1987.

Also author of *Caligrams,* 1959. Editor, *Presente.* In addition to English and German, Sosa's poetry has been translated into French and Russian.

SIDELIGHTS: A noted Honduran writer and cultural leader whose work has at times been banned by the Honduran government, Roberto Sosa is the author of poems which, comments Carolyn Forché in the dustjacket for *The Difficult Days,* "are lyric testimonies of political terror and personal grief, often mysteriously fused." In an interview for *Alcaraván,* translated and reprinted in *The Difficult Days,* Sosa remarks how the death of his father was an important turning point in his writing career: "It brought me to a complete revision of my method of poetic composition. It helped me better identify myself with the social marginality from which I come. It allowed me to write poetry whose central proposition is that to be valid."

Sosa also comments on how his poem "My Father" became a foundation of his work: "It let me fashion other poems at that same level of quality. After a few years, you begin to see what you really have written, and you never stop feeling the terror that what you've made might be worth nothing. It's the terror of every artist . . . that he might not have contributed to the dignification of man, which is one of the tasks of art. If not, why write? It's possible, I think, that a poem or a story could help civilize those who govern; that's why we need governors who read."

BIOGRAPHICAL/CRITICAL SOURCES:

BOOKS

Sosa, Roberto, *The Difficult Days,* translated by Jim Lindsey, Princeton University Press, 1983.

PERIODICALS

Alcaraván, July, 1981.
Choice, April, 1984.
Hispania, March, 1986.
Plural, May, 1982.
Publishers Weekly, August 12, 1983.

*   *   *

SOTO, Gary 1952-

PERSONAL: Born April 12, 1952, in Fresno, Calif.; son of Manuel and Angie (Trevino) Soto; married Carolyn Oda, 1975; children: Mariko. *Education:* California State University, Fresno, B.A. (magna cum laude), 1974; University of California, Irvine, M.F.A., 1976.

ADDRESSES: Home—1020 Santa Fe, Albany, Calif. 94108. *Office*—Department of English-Chicano Studies, University of California, Berkeley, Calif. 94720.

CAREER: University of California, Berkeley, associate professor, 1985—.

MEMBER: Coordinating Council of Literary Magazines (member of board).

AWARDS, HONORS: Academy of American Poets Prize, 1975; award from *Nation,* 1975, for "The Discovery"; United States Award from International Poetry Forum, 1976, for *The Elements of San Joaquin;* Bess Hokin Prize from *Poetry,* 1978; Guggenheim fellowship, 1980; creative writing fellowship from National Education Association, 1982; Levinson Award from *Poetry,* 1984; American Book Award from Before Columbus Foundation, 1985, for *Living up the Street.*

WRITINGS:

The Elements of San Joaquin (poems), University of Pittsburgh Press, 1977.

The Tale of Sunlight (poems), University of Pittsburgh Press, 1978.

Father Is a Pillow Tied to a Broom (poems), Slow Loris Press, 1980.

Where Sparrows Work Hard (poems), University of Pittsburgh Press, 1981.

Black Hair (poems), University of Pittsburgh Press, 1985.

Living up the Street: Narrative Recollections (prose memoirs), Strawberry Hill Press, 1985.

Small Faces (prose memoirs), Arte Público, 1986.

The Cat's Meow, Strawberry Hill Press, 1987.

(Editor) Luis O. Salinas, *The Sadness of Days* (poems), Arte Público, 1987.

Lesser Evils: Ten Quartets (essays), Arte Público, 1988.

(Editor) *California Childhood: Recollections and Stories of the Golden State,* Creative Arts Book Company, 1988.

Contributor of poetry to periodicals, including *Antaeus, Nation, New Republic, North American Review, Poetry,* and *Revista Chicano-Riqueña.* Contributor of articles to *Bloomsbury Review, Image, MELUS, Parnassus,* and *San Francisco Review of Books.*

WORK IN PROGRESS: Where We Left Off, poems.

SIDELIGHTS: Gary Soto is an American poet and prose writer influenced by his working-class Mexican-American background. Born in Fresno, California, in the center of the agricultural San Joaquin Valley, he worked as a migrant laborer during his childhood. In his writing, as Raymund Paredes noted in the *Rocky Mountain Review,* "Soto establishes his acute sense of ethnicity and, simultaneously, his belief that certain emotions, values, and experiences transcend ethnic boundaries and allegiances." Many critics have echoed the assessment of Patricia De La Fuente in *Revista Chicano-Riqueña* that Soto displays an "exceptionally high level of linguistic sophistication."

In his first volume of poetry, *The Elements of San Joaquin,* Soto offers a grim portrait of the lives of Mexican Americans. His poems depict the violence of urban life, the exhausting labor of rural life, and the futility of trying to recapture the innocence of childhood. In the book *Chicano Poetry* Juan Bruce-Novoa repeatedly likened Soto's poetic vision to T. S. Eliot's bleak portrait of the modern world, *The Waste Land.* Soto uses windswept dust as a dominant image, and he also introduces such elements as rapes, unflushed toilets, a drowned baby, and, as Bruce-Novoa quotes him, "men/ Whose arms/ Were bracelets/ Of burns." Soto's skill with the figurative language of poetry has been noted by reviewers throughout his career, and in *Western American Literature* Jerry Bradley praised the metaphors in *San Joaquin* as "evocative, enlightening, and haunting." Though unsettled by the negativism of the collection, Bruce-Novoa felt the work "convinces because of its well-wrought structure, the craft, the coherence of its totality." Moreover, he thought, because it brings such a vivid portrait of poverty to the reading public, *San Joaquin* is "a social as well as a literary achievement."

Soto's social concerns and aspects of his poetic style have led several critics to compare him to poet Philip Levine, who taught Soto at the Fresno campus of California State University. Levine's poetry focuses on the degraded lives of American working people, and, as Vicki Armour-Hileman noted in *Denver Quarterly,* its plain language and short, run-on lines are similar to Soto's work. When Soto spoke to *Contemporary Authors,* he acknowledged Levine's influence but stressed his familiarity with other poets too.

Many critics have also observed that Soto's writing transcends social commentary. Bruce-Novoa said that one reason why the author's work has "great significance within Chicano literature" is because it represents "a definite shift toward a more personal, less politically motivated poetry." As Alan Williamson suggested in *Poetry,* Soto avoids either idealizing the poor for their oppression or encouraging their violent defiance. Instead, he focuses on the human suffering that poverty engenders. When Peter Cooley reviewed Soto's second volume of poetry, *The Tale of Sunlight,* in *Parnassus,* he praised the author's ability to temper the bleakness of *San Joaquin* with "imaginative expansiveness." The poems in *Sunlight,* many of which focus on a child named Molina or on the owner of a Hispanic bar, display both the frustrations of poverty and what Williamson called "a vein of consolatory fantasy which passes beyond escapism into a pure imaginative generosity toward life." Williamson cited as an example "the poem in which an uncle's gray hair is seen as a visitation of magical butterflies."

When Soto discusses American racial tensions in the prose collections *Living up the Street* and *Small Faces,* he uses vignettes drawn from his own childhood. One vignette shows the anger the author felt upon realizing that his brown-skinned brother would never be considered an attractive child by conventional American standards. Another shows Soto's surprise at discovering that, contrary to his family's advice to marry a Mexican, he was falling in love with a woman of Japanese ancestry. In these deliberately small-scale recollections, as Paredes noted, "it is a measure of Soto's skill that he so effectively invigorates and sharpens our understanding of the commonplace."

In *Black Hair,* Soto focuses on his friends and family. He portrays fondly the times he shared with his buddies as an adolescent and the more recent moments he has spent with his young daughter. Some critics, such as David Wojahn in *Poetry,* felt that Soto was thus moving away from his strengths as a writer. While acknowledging that "by limiting his responses to a naive aplomb, Soto enables himself to write with a freshness that is at times arresting," Wojahn considered the work "a disappointment." He praised *San Joaquin* and *Tale of Sunlight* as "thematically urgent . . . and ambitious in their scope" and said that "compared to them, *Black Hair* is a distinctly minor achievement." Others, such as Ellen Lesser in *Voice Literary Supplement,* were charmed by Soto's poetic tone, "the quality of the voice, the immediate, human presence that breathes through the lines." Lesser contended that Soto's celebration of innocence and sentiment is shaded with a knowledge of "the larger, often threatening world." In the *Christian Science Monitor,* Tom D'Evelyn hailed Soto's ability to go beyond the circumstances of his own life and write of "something higher," concluding, "Somehow Gary Soto has become not an important Chicano poet but an important American poet. More power to him."

BIOGRAPHICAL/CRITICAL SOURCES:

BOOKS

Bruce-Novoa, Juan, *Chicano Poetry: A Response to Chaos,* University of Texas Press, 1982.
Contemporary Literary Criticism, Volume 32, Gale, 1985.
Dictionary of Literary Biography, Volume 82: *Chicano Writers, First Series,* Gale, 1989.
Martínez, Julio A. and Francisco A. Lomelí, editors, *Chicano Literature: A Reference Guide,* Greenwood Press, 1985.

PERIODICALS

American Book Review, July-August, 1982.
Christian Science Monitor, March 6, 1985.
Denver Quarterly, summer, 1982.
Parnassus, fall-winter, 1979.
Poetry, March, 1980, June, 1985.
Revista Chicano-Riqueña, summer, 1983.
Rocky Mountain Review, Volume 41, numbers 1-2, 1987.
San Francisco Review of Books, summer, 1986.
Voice Literary Supplement, September, 1985.
Western American Literature, spring, 1979.

—Sketch by Thomas Kozikowski

*   *   *

SOTO, Pedro Juan   1928-

PERSONAL: Born July 11, 1928, in Catano, Puerto Rico.

ADDRESSES: Office—University of Puerto Rico, Río Piedras, P.R. 00931.

CAREER: Employed by Publications Department, Puerto Rico Division of Education, 1955-66; employed by Associated Press, Puerto Rico Bureau, 1966-67; professor, University of Puerto Rico, Río Piedras, 1969-88. Journalist, educator, literary critic, dramatist, author. *Military service:* Served in United States Army.

MEMBER: PEN (past president of Puerto Rico chapter).

AWARDS, HONORS: Awards for short stories, "Garabatos," 1953, and "Los inocentes," 1954; award from Puerto Rico Atheneum, 1956, for play "El huésped"; award from Casa de las Américas, 1982, for *Un oscuro pueblo sonriente.*

WRITINGS:

"El huésped" (play; also see below), first produced by the experimental theater of Puerto Rico Atheneum, 1955; produced in Mexico for World Olympics, 1968; produced on television by NBC-TV as "The Guest," 1974.

Spiks (short stories), Los Presentes, 1956, translation from Spanish and introduction by Victoria Ortiz published as Spiks: Stories, Monthly Review Press, 1973.

Usmaíl, Club del Libro de Puerto Rico, 1959, reprinted, Editorial Cultural (Río Piedras), 1980.

Ardiente suelo, fría estación (novel), Editorial Veracruzana (Mexico), 1961, reprinted, Editorial Cultural, 1988, translation by Helen Lane published as Hot Land, Cold Season, Dell, 1973.

(With Nina Kaiden and Andrew Vladimir) Puerto Rico: The New Life/La Nueva Vida (bilingual anthology), Renaissance Press, 1966.

El francotirador (novel), Mortiz, 1969.

A solas con Pedro Juan Soto (self-interview), Ediciones Puerto (Río Piedras), 1973.

El huésped, las máscaras y otros disfraces (play and narrative), Ediciones Puerto, 1973.

Un decir (short stories), Ediciones Huracán (Río Piedras), 1976.

Un oscuro pueblo sonriente (novel), Casa de las Américas (Cuba), 1982, reprinted, Editorial Cultural, 1984.

En busca de J. I. de Diego Pandró (essays and interviews), Editorial Universitaria (Río Piedras), 1990.

Also author of Los perros anónimos, 1950, "Garabatos" (short story), 1953, "Los inocentes" (play), 1954, "Las máscaras" (three-act play), 1958, and Temporada de duendes, 1970. Contributor to periodicals, including Visión, El Diario de Nueva York, and Revista del Instituto de Cultura Puertorriqueña.

*   *   *

SOTO, Shirlene A(nn) 1947-

PERSONAL: Born January 22, 1947, in San Luis Obispo, Calif. Education: San Francisco State University, B.A., 1969; University of New Mexico, M.A., 1971, Ph.D., 1977.

ADDRESSES: Office—Department of History, California Polytechnic State University, San Luis Obispo, Calif. 93407.

CAREER: Assistant professor of history at California Polytechnic State University, San Luis Obispo.

MEMBER: American Studies Association, Latin American Studies Association, Mesa Chicana Graduate Student Association, Phi Alpha Theta.

AWARDS, HONORS: Ford Foundation fellow, 1970.

WRITINGS:

The Mexican Woman: A Study of Her Participation in the Revolution, 1910-1940, R & E Research Associates, 1979.

The Emergence of the Modern Mexican Woman, 1910-1940: Her Participation in the Revolution and Her Struggle for Equality, Arden Press, 1989.

Contributor to professional journals.

*   *   *

SOUZA, Raymond D(ale) 1936-

PERSONAL: Born March 11, 1936, in Attleboro, Mass.; son of Joseph B. (a worker in a jewel factory) and Linda (Pimental) Souza; married Martha Heckmaster (a teacher of Spanish), December 23, 1966; children: Richard, Robert. Education: Attended University of Massachusetts, 1954-56; Drury College, B.A. (magna cum laude), 1958; University of Missouri, M.A., 1960, Ph.D., 1964.

ADDRESSES: Home—1732 West 21st St. Ter., Lawrence, Kan. 66044. Office—Department of Spanish and Portuguese, University of Kansas, Lawrence, Kan. 66046.

CAREER: High School teacher of Spanish in Salem, Mo., 1958-59; Kent State University, Kent, Ohio, instructor in Spanish, 1961-62; University of Kansas, Lawrence, assistant professor, 1963-68, associate professor, 1968-73, professor of Spanish, 1973—, chairman of Department of Spanish and Portuguese, 1968-74, chairman of summer school in Guadalajara, Mexico. Exxon Intra-University Visiting Professor of Linguistics and Philosophy, 1981-82.

MEMBER: Instituto International de Literatura Iberoamericana, Association of North American Columbanists (president, 1987-89), Modern Language Association of America, American Association of Teachers of Spanish and Portuguese, American Numismatic Association, Kansas Foreign Language Association.

AWARDS, HONORS: Ford Foundation research grants, 1966 and 1968; American Philosophical Society grant, 1968; Tinker Foundation research grant, summer, 1982.

WRITINGS:

Major Cuban Novelists: Innovation and Tradition, University of Missouri Press, 1976.

(Contributor) Juan Valencia and Edward Coughlin, editors, Homanje a Octavio Paz, Editorial Universitaria Potosina, 1976.

(Contributor) Raymond L. Williams, editor, Aproximaciones a Gustavo Alvarez Gardeazabal, Plaza y Janés (Bogota), 1977.

(Contributor) Gaston F. Fernández, editor, La narrativa de Carlos Alberto Montaner, Planeta/Universidad (Madrid), 1978.

(Contributor) Justo C. Ulloa, editor, José Lezama Limas: Textos Críticos, Universal (Miami), 1979.

(Contributor) Mechtild Strausfeld, editor, Aspekte von José Lezama Limas "Paradiso," Suhrkamp Verlag, 1979.

Lino Novas Calvo, Twayne, 1981.

The Poetic Fiction of José Lezama Lima, University of Missouri Press, 1983.

(Contributor) Williams, editor, Ensayos de literatura columbiana, Plaza y Janés, 1985.

(Contributor) Daniel Maratos and Marnesba D. Hill, editors, Escritores de la diáspora cubana/Cuban Exile Writers: A Bibliographical Handbook, Scarecrow, 1986.

La historia en la novela hispanoamericana moderna, Tercer Mundo Editores (Bogota), 1988.

Contributor of about forty articles and twenty reviews to language and Spanish studies journals.

WORK IN PROGRESS: A book on Guillermo Cabrera Infante.

SIDELIGHTS: Raymond D. Souza told CA: "My research and publications deal with Spanish-American literature, and I am particularly interested in prose fiction and poetry as well as literary theory. I became involved in writing about Spanish-American literature because the subject interests me and I enjoy communicating my findings to others. I have never been able to separate teaching from research because I find that a dynamic relationship exists between these two activities. Discoveries and knowledge gained in research inevitably find expression in class, and new ideas uncovered while teaching have resulted in exciting research."

Souza's *Major Cuban Novelists: Innovation and Tradition* "is indeed a highly useful introduction and important contribution to the study of the Cuban novel," according to Jorge A. Marban in the *International Fiction Review.* Marban notes that in this survey of the Cuban novel from the mid-1800s to 1969, the author "strives at clarity, conciseness, and meaningful simplicity when discussing complex and difficult matters." Critics also value Souza's studies of Lino Novas Calvo and José Lezama Lima. "There are few critics who know Novas Calvo the man and Novas Calvo the writer as well as Professor Souza; the fruit of that intimate knowledge is this highly recommended Twayne book [*Lino Novas Calvo*]," writes Myron I. Lichtblau in *Hispania.*

Of *The Poetic Fiction of José Lezama Lima,* contributor David William Foster comments in *International Fiction Review,* "[it] is an excellent example of a critical approach to a complex work of fiction that falls into neither the sort of reductionist interpretation—plot summaries and thematic paraphrasings—that are often the lot of contemporary narratives nor into the deconstructionist 'paratextualizing' that are often intriguing intellectual constructs but leave one with a (sinful) nostalgia for the text under scrutiny. As a consequence, Souza has made a valuable contribution to the criticism on *Paradiso* that will satisfy the demands of both major critics of Lezama Lima's work and the non-specialist reader." Furthermore, notes Ramón Magrans in the *Kentucky Romance Quarterly,* Souza "has proven the author's conviction that order and unity do exist in this world although they are not always apparent in our time-bound universe." Magrans calls this reading of Lezama Lima's works "a major accomplishment."

AVOCATIONAL INTERESTS: Numismatics, sailing.

BIOGRAPHICAL/CRITICAL SOURCES:

PERIODICALS

Hispania, December, 1982.
International Fiction Review, Number 4, 1977, Volume 12, number 2, 1985.
Kentucky Romance Quarterly, Volume 32, number 4, 1985.
World Literature Today, summer, 1977.

*   *   *

SPOTA (SAAVEDRA), Luis 1925-1985

PERSONAL: Born July 13, 1925, in Mexico City, Mexico; died of pancreatic cancer, January 20, 1985, in Mexico City, Mexico.

CAREER: Journalist and writer. Television news commentator.

AWARDS, HONORS: City of Mexico prizes for *Más cornadas da el hambre,* 1950, *Las grandes aguas,* 1951, and *Vagabunda;* National Literature Prize for the play *El area de los sometidos.*

WRITINGS:

De la noche al día (stories), Tollocan, c. 1945.
El coronel fué echado al mar (novel; title means "The Colonel Was Tossed to the Sea"), [Mexico], 1947.
Más cornadas da el hambre (novel), [Mexico], c. 1948, 2nd edition, D. F. Porrúa, 1959, translation by Barnaby Conrad published as *The Wounds of Hunger,* Houghton, 1957.
Murieron a mitad del río (novel; title means "They Died in the Middle of the River"), [Mexico], 1948, 4th edition, Costa-Amic, 1973.

Vagabunda (novel), [Mexico], 1950, 2nd edition, D. F. Porrúa, 1959.
La estrella vacía (novel; title means "The Empty Star"), Librería de M. Porrúa, 1950.
Casi el paraíso (novel), Fondo de Cultura Económica, 1956, revised edition, Diana, 1970, translation by Ray Morrison and Renate Morrison published as *Almost Paradise,* Doubleday, 1963.
Las horas violentas (novel; title means "The Violent Hours"), 1958, 2nd edition, Libro Mex, 1959, reprinted, Costa-Amic, 1981.
La sangre enemiga (novel), Fondo de Cultura Económica, 1959, revised edition, Grijalbo (Mexico), 1981, translation by Robert Molloy published as *The Enemy Blood,* Doubleday, 1961.
El tiempo de la ira (novel), Fondo de Cultura Económica, 1960, reprinted, Grijalbo (Mexico), 1981, translation by Robert Molloy published as *The Time of Wrath,* Doubleday, 1962.
El area de los sometidos (play; title means "The Area of the Vanquished"), Costa-Amic, 1962.
La pequeña edad (novel; title means "The Tender Age"), Fondo de Cultura Económica, 1964.
La carcajada del gato (novel; title means "The Cat's Laugh"), Mortiz, 1964, reprinted, Grijalbo (Barcelona), 1977.
Los sueños del insomnio (novel; title means "The Dreams of Insomnia"), Mortiz, 1966, reprinted, Grijalbo (Barcelona), 1977.
Lo de antes (novel; title means "What Went Before"), Diana, 1968, reprinted, Grijalbo (Mexico), 1981.
Las cajas (novel), Mortiz, 1973.
El viaje, Mortiz, 1973.
Palabras mayores (novel), Grijalbo (Barcelona), 1975, revised, 1981.
Retrato hablado (novel), Grijalbo (Barcelona), 1975.
Sobre la marcha, Grijalbo (Barcelona), 1976.
El rostro del sueño, Grijalbo (Mexico), 1979.
Mitad oscura, Grijalbo (Mexico), 1982.
Paraíso 25, Grijalbo (Mexico), 1983.

Also author of *Las grandes aguas, La plaza,* and *El primer día,* all novels. Author of essays, plays, and biographies. Contributor to *Hoy, Excélsior, Novedades, Política,* and *Espejo.*

SIDELIGHTS: Luis Spota was one of Mexico's most popular and prolific novelists. Though his works sometimes met with mixed reviews, he won the City of Mexico Prize, one of the country's highest literary honors, three times, and his novels are well read in his country. The author was born into wealth, but his family lost its fortune in 1934, and Spota left school to support himself with a variety of jobs, including brief stints as a bullfighter, seaman, waiter, and encyclopedia salesman. He eventually obtained work as an office boy at a weekly magazine in Mexico and thus began his journalism career. Spota worked for several Mexican newspapers, developing the brash, sometimes sensational journalistic style that would also characterize his novels.

Many of Spota's early novels are autobiographical, incorporating knowledge gained from his various occupations. The 1947 *El coronel fué echado al mar* ("The Colonel Was Tossed to the Sea") drew on his experiences aboard a steamer. In the novel an American ship is carrying wounded soldiers, but hiding this fact from the enemy. Several patients die, but no "burials" occur. After each death a great abundance of meat is served and the crew begins to suspect they are eating the dead. A nurse clears up the mystery, explaining that the bodies require storage in the refrigerators for preservation until autopsies can be performed.

The grotesque humor of the story became a trademark of later novels. Though Walter M. Langford, writing in *Mexican Novel Comes of Age*, did not consider *El coronel fué echado al mar* one of Spota's best novels, he asserted that "two characteristics that are to become basic to his style are readily visible in this work: a true capacity for creating dialogue that is natural to the characters and the circumstances, and an equal talent for narration that holds the reader's attention from start to finish."

Spota's familiarity with the bullring served him in the novel *Más cornadas da el hambre*, later translated as *The Wounds of Hunger*. The story tells of man driven to become a bullfighter because, as the bullfighters say, "the wounds of hunger wound worse" than gorings by the bulls. Praised for its unromantic, brutal depiction not only of bullfighting but of poverty, the novel received the City of Mexico Prize in 1950. Spota, who described himself as "left" politically, continued to focus on social concerns in other novels. His 1948 novel, *Murieron a mitad del río* ("They Died in the Middle of the River"), for instance, describes the lives of Mexicans who illegally immigrate to the United States and suffer exploitation as laborers, while the 1958 *Las horas violentas* ("The Violent Hours") focuses on the control over Mexican labor unions, depicting twelve hours of a strike in a canning factory before an outbreak of violence.

Spota's highly acclaimed and popular 1956 novel, *Casi el paraíso*, translated as *Almost Paradise*, satirizes Mexico's upper class, "lay[ing] bare the sham, hypocrisy, and false values of many among the highest echelon of Mexican society," wrote Langford. The protagonist—a self-styled Italian playboy/prince—almost achieves paradise by marrying into a wealthy Mexican family, but his plans fail when his true origins come to light.

With the publication in 1960 of *El tiempo de la ira*, translated as *The Time of Wrath*, Spota turned to the subject of dictatorship, a familiar theme in Latin American literature. Beginning with César Darío's plans to overthrow the government, the novel traces the fictional leader's rise to power until his assassination by an aide. Langford named *El tiempo de la ira* among the most outstanding novels on the topic, praising the detailed characterization of Dario as a leader concerned about his country's welfare, but ruthless in protecting his own power.

La carcajada del gato, published in 1964, also met with critical approval. Recalling *Casi el paraíso* with its dark, pessimistic tone, *La carcajada del gato* concerns a demented father who imprisons his family at home, forbidding any contact with the outside world in an effort to fashion a new version of humanity. This results in such sordid developments as incest—and eventually—the family's plot to murder the father.

While some reviewers have objected to the violence and cynicism that pervades much of Spota's writings, they have praised his reforming satiric voice evident in other works. Spota's direct, bold prose, together with quick-paced narrative and imaginative plots, makes for arresting and suspenseful fiction.

BIOGRAPHICAL/CRITICAL SOURCES:

BOOKS

Langford, Walter M., *The Mexican Novel Comes of Age*, University of Notre Dame Press, 1971.
Spota, Luis, *The Wounds of Hunger*, Houghton, 1957.

OBITUARIES:

PERIODICALS

Chicago Tribune, January 23, 1985.

STORNI, Alfonsina 1892-1938
(Tao Lao)

PERSONAL: Born May 29 (some sources say May 22), 1892, in Sala Capriasca, Switzerland; immigrated to Argentina, 1896, naturalized citizen, 1920; committed suicide by drowning, October 25, 1938, in Mar del Plata, Argentina; daughter of Alfonso (a beer manufacturer) and Paula (Martignoni) Storni; children: Alejandro Alfonso. *Education:* Received teacher's diploma, 1910.

CAREER: Writer. Elementary school teacher in Rosario, Argentina, 1911; held series of odd jobs in Buenos Aires, Argentina, 1911-13; Freixas Brothers (import firm), Buenos Aires, market researcher, beginning in 1914; teacher at various schools in Argentina, 1917-26; drama teacher at children's theater, 1921. Public lecturer.

AWARDS, HONORS: Premio Anual del Consejo Nacional de Mujeres, 1917; First Municipal Prize and Second National Prize, both 1920, both for *Languidez*.

WRITINGS:

POETRY

La inquietud del rosal (title means "The Disquietude of the Rosebush"), prologue by Juan Julián Lastra, La Facultad, 1916.
El dulce daño (title means "Sweet Pain"), Sociedad Cooperativa, 1918.
Irremediablemente (title means "Irremediably"), Sociedad Cooperativa, 1919.
Languidez (title means "Languor"), Sociedad Cooperativa, 1920.
Poesías, Cervantes (Barcelona), 1923.
Ocre, Babel, 1925.
Poemas de amor (title means "Love Poems"), Nosotros, 1926.
Mundo de siete pozos (title means "World of Seven Wells"), Tor, 1934.
Mascarilla y trébol (title means "Mask and Clover"), El Ateneo, 1938.
Antología poética (anthology compiled by Storni), Espasa-Calpe Argentina, 1938, reprinted, Losada, 1973.
Los mejores versos de Alfonsina Storni, Nuestra América, 1958.
Poesías de Alfonsina Storni, preface by son, Alejandro Alfonso Storni, Universitaria de Buenos Aires, 1961.
Antología poética, selected by Alfredo Veirave, Centro Editor de América Latina, 1968.
Alfonsina Storni, Argentina's Feminist Poet: The Poetry in Spanish With English Translations, edited by Florence Williams Talamantes, San Marcos Press, 1975.
Tres poetistas: Juana de Ibarbourou, Gabriela Mistral, Alfonsina Storni, selected by Luisa Amada Solis, Editores Mexicanos Unidos, 1985.
Selected Poems, translated by Dorothy Scott Loos, Amana Books, 1986.

Contributor to periodicals.

OTHER

El amo del mundo (three-act play; title means "The Master of the World"; first produced in Buenos Aires at the Cervantes Theater, March 10, 1927), published in periodical *Bambalinas*, 1927.
Cimbelina en 1900 y pico (play based on Shakespeare's *Cymbeline*; title means "Cymbeline in 1900 or So"), published in

Dos farsas pirotécnicas, Cooperativa Editorial Buenos Aires, 1932 (also see below).

Polixena y la cocinerita (one-act play; title means "Polixena and the Little Cook"), published in *Dos farsas pirotécnicas,* Cooperativa Editorial Buenos Aires, 1932 (also see below).

Dos farsas pirotécnicas (plays; title means "Two Pyrotechnical Farces"; contains "Cimbelina en 1900 y pico" and "Polixena y la cocinerita"), Cooperativa Editorial Buenos Aires, 1932.

Teatro infantil (title means "Plays for Children"), Ramón J. Roggero y Cía, 1950, reprinted with illustrations by Julia Díaz, Librería Huemul, 1973.

Cinco cartas y Una golondrina (title means "Five Letters and 'A Swallow' "), Instituto Amigos del Libro Argentino, 1959.

Obras escogidas (selected works), Sociedad Editora Latino Americana, 1984.

Also author of short story "Catalina," and of unpublished and unproduced plays "La técnica de Mister Dougall," 1927, and "La sirvienta moderna," "La sirvienta mecánica," and "Los cazadores de fieras" (for children). Contributor of stories and nearly one hundred articles, sometimes under the pseudonym Tao Lao, to periodicals, including *Nosotros, La Nota, Atlántida,* and *La Nación.*

COLLECTED WORKS

Obras completas, six volumes, Meridión, 1957.

Obra poética completa (collected poetry), Meridión, 1961.

Obras completas, eight volumes, Sociedad Editora Latino Americana, 1964.

Omnibus editions include *Alfonsina Storni: Antología,* introduction and selection by María de Villarino, Ediciones Culturales Argentinas, 1961, and *Alfonsina Storni: Edición commemorativa con ocasión de cumplirse el vigésimo quinto aniversario de su muerte,* annotated by Carlos A. Andreola, Nobis, 1963.

SIDELIGHTS: Alfonsina Storni was one of the first feminist writers to emerge in Argentina in the early part of the twentieth century. The first woman in her country to join a literary group, she wrote in a variety of genres, including fiction, drama, and nonfiction. Storni is best remembered, however, for a body of poetry that expresses her passionate internal conflicts and desires as well as her opposition to the injustices of her male-dominated culture. While her early poetry was known for its emotionally charged lyricism, her final two collections—*Mundo de siete pozos* and *Mascarilla y trébol*—were lauded for their tighter form and more abstract imagery and are now generally regarded as her most innovative works. Storni's poetry, which enjoys wide popularity in Argentina, was collected and released in English in 1975.

Storni was born in the Italian region of Switzerland during her parents' visit to their native land. Her parents had settled in San Juan, Argentina, where her father and his brothers owned and operated a beer factory; the family returned to South America when Storni was four years old. Their arrival back in Argentina, however, marked the beginning of Storni's childhood difficulties: by 1900 the brewery had failed, resulting in the loss of the family's social position and precipitating her father's descent into depression and alcoholism. In an attempt to regain a steady income, her father opened a small cafe in the nearby town of Rosario. The venture was largely unsuccessful, however, and by the time Storni was twelve in 1904, she was forced to help meet family expenses by taking in sewing and waiting on tables at the cafe. Two years later, the restaurant too had failed, and the fourteen-year-old Storni had become, as a factory worker, her family's main source of financial support. Critics have suggested that Storni's early responsibilities influenced the development of the feminist ideas in her work.

In 1907, after her father's death and her mother's subsequent re-marriage, Storni became interested in the theater. No longer burdened with having to help support her family, she joined a traveling acting company, and she spent the following year on tour with the group. Storni decided, however, through bouts of depression and homesickness, that she was unsuited for the pressures and traveling of stage life. She gave up acting, but her interest in the theater remained throughout her literary career.

Although working during childhood had greatly disrupted her education, Storni left the tour determined to become a teacher. She was accepted at a teachers' training school despite a failing grade on her entrance exam, and she completed her courses successfully while working as a chorus girl on the weekends. In 1911 Storni returned to teach in Rosario, where she fell deeply in love with a married man of high standing in the community. When their illicit affair resulted in her pregnancy, Storni decided that their relationship could no longer continue and opted to leave Rosario rather than endure the disapproval and gossip of the townspeople. She moved instead to Buenos Aires, where she held menial jobs until her son Alejandro was born in April, 1912.

While supporting herself and her small child in a low-paying position as a market research analyst, Storni began her literary career, publishing her first short story in 1914 and her first book of poems, *La inquietud del rosal* ("The Disquietude of the Rose Bush") in 1916. The verses in this volume express the emotional pain Storni experienced at the end of her love affair. Although not well received by critics, who considered them self-indulgent and melodramatic, the poems' lyricism was nevertheless thought to evidence Storni's potential as a writer. Later in her career, Storni herself renounced *La inquietud del rosal* in an interview quoted in Sonia Jones's *Alfonsina Storni:* "My first book . . . today frankly embarrasses me. I would love to be able to destroy every single copy of that book until there was not a single trace of it left."

In 1918, Storni produced her second collection of poetry, *El dulce daño* ("Sweet Pain"). Like *La inquietud del rosal, El dulce daño* concerns the pain and longings of disappointed love, but Storni's confessional poems of suffering were judged by critics to be somewhat balanced by others in the volume that express the author's spirituality and her desire for passionate, ideal love. They saw, too, in her prosaic images from everyday life and in her use of repetition as a poetic device, an increasing stylistic maturity. More importantly, Storni's second collection of verse marked her emergence as Argentina's first feminist poet. Drawing on her experiences of hardship, independence, and motherhood, many of *El dulce daño*'s poems project outrage against the injustices of her provincial, male-dominated culture, express scorn for women who accepted roles of passivity, and candidly explore aspects of female sexuality.

La inquietud del rosal and *El dulce daño* established Storni as a new voice in Argentinean culture. Shortly after the former book's publication, she became the first woman in the country to join a literary circle, from which she obtained critical comment and encouragement. At this time she also began writing articles and essays on women's rights, urging the government to grant women the vote and anticipating a time when women would enjoy the same privileges as Argentinean men. Storni's unconventional views, however, along with her status as an unmarried mother, sometimes resulted in critical censure of her work. Irritated at her frank, often resentful attacks on female stereotypes and on those who propagate them, some of her contemporary critics attributed her feminist ideas to personal dissatisfaction and dismissed her arguments for parity between the sexes as the merely the complaints of an unhappy woman.

The years 1919 and 1920 were eventful for Storni. She enjoyed growing recognition for her poetry and prose, and she traveled with her son throughout Argentina, teaching, and giving lectures on the work of other South American female poets, including Uruguay's Delmira Agustini and Juana de Ibarbourou. At this time she joined "Anaconda," a literary group led by the Uruguayan novelist Horacio Quiroga and the Argentinean author Leopoldo Lugones, both of whom became Storni's lifelong friends. Also in 1919, Storni published *Una golondrina,* a novella concerned with the psychological aspects of male-female relationships.

1919 and 1920 also saw the publication of more poetry: *Irremediablemente* ("Irremediably") and *Languidez* ("Languor"). These primarily autobiographical works are often regarded as the second and third parts of a progression, begun with *El dulce daño,* through which Storni attempts to reconcile her resentment of chauvinistic attitudes with her desire for romantic love. The verses in *El dulce daño* explore pain and transcendence, those in *Irremediablemente* focus on disillusionment, and many poems in the subsequent *Languidez* share the theme of renunciation of physical passion for other types of love, such as that existing between siblings, between mother and child, and between the individual and his fellow man. *Languidez* earned Storni two of Argentina's most prestigious literary awards in 1920.

As her literary occupations increased, though, Storni began to experience episodes of nervous exhaustion and depression which would recur intermittently for the rest of her life. Upon the advice of her doctor, Storni took the first of several vacations in the town of Cordova. After recuperating, she accepted a job teaching drama at a children's theater, where she produced and wrote children's plays throughout the early 1920s. Storni's works for children are collected in the volume *Teatro infantil.*

In 1925, Storni published *Ocre,* her fifth book of poetry. In contrast to the emotional, self-absorbed tone that had pervaded her previous works and from which Storni had begun to turn away in *Languidez, Ocre* was noted for its more serene, detached poetic voice as well as for its irony. As Jones noted, "In the early collections the poet was the protagonist of the various dramas that unfolded. But in this volume, something entirely new has happened: [Storni] has stepped outside herself . . . and has become the rather analytical observer of her own life. She now views herself from a distance, with perspective that [places] herself in a larger framework." Storni returned the next year to the subjective, however, with the collection *Poemas de amor* ("Love Poems"), which consists of sixty-seven short proselike pieces—again concerned with the sentimental aspects of love. Jones related that Storni regarded *Poemas de amor* as her one of her favorite collections, but critics, for the most part, ignored it.

After publishing *Poemas de amor* Storni vowed to concentrate on stage writing, believing the theater a better forum than poetry for expressing her feminist ideas. She completed her first drama for adults, *El amo del mundo* ("The Master of the World"), in 1927. The three-act play concerns Márgara, an attractive, educated, intelligent woman, and Claudio, an older suitor who, after to proposing to Márgara, withdraws his offer when she confesses she has borne an illegitimate son. He marries instead the shallow and dishonest Zarcillo, a younger woman whose chastity is a pretense. Critics thought the play a technical and artistic failure, and it closed after only a three-day run. According to Jones,

however, *El amo del mundo* contains many of Storni's most pointedly feminist themes.

By the late 1920s, Storni had become a well-known author in her country, maintaining associations with several literary circles and giving public lectures. She continued to write plays, completing *Cimbelina en 1900 y pico* ("Cymbeline in 1900 or So"), a farce based on Shakespeare's *Cymbeline,* and the one-act *Polixena y la cocinerita* ("Polixena and the Little Cook"). Despite her productivity, however, her depressions recurred, and she suffered a nervous breakdown in 1928. She regained her mental stability after another trip to Cordova, and in 1930 she embarked on a European tour, spending several months in Spain promoting the work of Latin American artists and writers.

After a second trip to Europe in 1934, Storni published *Mundo de siete pozos* ("World of Seven Wells"). In her sixth poetical work, Storni made a nearly total break from the subjective lyricism and inner conflict that characterizes most of her previous poetry. Centering instead on the external world, the free verse and traditional sonnets in *Mundo de siete pozos* display Storni's increased attention to imagery. Several critics considered Storni's new cerebral, ironic tone as an indication of a growing despair and preoccupation with death. Citing the volume's proliferation of sea imagery, for example, Sidonia Carmen Rosenbaum noted in her *Modern Women Poets of Spanish America—The Precursors* that "never a poetess of joy and laughter, [Storni] sinks still deeper into the bitter waters of sadness and hopelessness. . . . If in other books she spoke of the sea, it seemed to be in a somewhat causal manner. Not so here where the sea and the thought of finding peace in its icy, turbulent depths, become almost an obsession."

In 1935 Storni was diagnosed with breast cancer. She underwent a radical mastectomy, but her health did not improve. During the last three years of her life Storni battled illness and depression, and suffered grief at the losses of her friends Quiroga and Lugones—both of whom committed suicide. *Mascarilla y trébol* ("Mask and Clover"), Storni's last book of verse, was published in 1938. The author called the poems in this volume "antisonnets," because they retain the traditional sonnet's metrical structure but do not rhyme. According to Jones, many readers who admired Storni's emotionalism were disappointed in this collection's display of abstraction, fantasy, and extended metaphor, but modern critics have come to regard *Mascarilla y trébol* as her most mature and innovative work. Moreover, Jones felt that the book evidenced the end of Storni's spiritual turmoil. "The most original aspect of this volume is found in her quiet triumph over the heretofore incessant demands of her active and frustrating life," the critic commented. "All her mental efforts to negate her physical and sentimental needs met with failure, until she accepted her impending death and so saw life in an entirely new perspective. There is no inner conflict, no tension, no sign of struggle, . . . only a sorrowful understanding . . . devoid of her former anger and rebelliousness."

In October, 1938, fearing that her cancer had spread to her lungs, Storni committed suicide by drowning herself in the ocean near the village of Mar del Plata, Argentina. Assessing Storni's significance in modern literature, Rachel Phillips concluded in her *Alfonsina Storni: From Poetess to Poet:* "She is interesting precisely by reason of the inner pressures which forced out of her the poetry of her last volumes, that is, by reason of her growth as a human being, and her resultant growth as a poet. Interesting enough, in fact, to be able to survive . . . a promotion from the upper ranks of women poets, into the place which is properly hers as a maker, as a poet in the true sense of the word."

BIOGRAPHICAL/CRITICAL SOURCES:

BOOKS

Jones, Sonia, *Alfonsina Storni,* Twayne, 1979.

Phillips, Rachel, *Alfonsina Storni: From Poetess to Poet,* Tamesis Books, 1975.

Rosenbaum, Sidonia Carmen, *Modern Women Poets of Spanish America—The Precursors: Delmira Agustini, Gabriel Mistral, Alfonsina Storni, Juana de Ibarbourou,* Hispanic Institute in the United States, 1945.

Twentieth-Century Literary Criticism, Volume 5, Gale, 1981.

PERIODICALS

World Literature Today, spring, 1987.

—*Sketch by Emily J. McMurray*

*   *   *

SUAREZ, Virgil   1962-

PERSONAL: Born in 1962 in Cuba; immigrated to United States, c. 1970.

CAREER: Writer.

WRITINGS:

Latin Jazz (novel), Morrow, 1989.

SIDELIGHTS: At the age of eight Virgil Suarez emigrated with his family from Cuba to the United States. Suarez's first novel, *Latin Jazz,* chronicles the experiences of a family that leaves Cuba to settle in Los Angeles after Fidel Castro comes to power. The novel also depicts one family member's incarceration in a Cuban prison and his eventual release to the United States, as well as problems faced by the immigrants' children in America.

BIOGRAPHICAL/CRITICAL SOURCES:

PERIODICALS

Vista, May 21, 1989.

SUAREZ LYNCH, B.
See BIOY CASARES, Adolfo and BORGES, Jorge Luis

*   *   *

SUCRE, Guillermo   1933-

PERSONAL: Born in Venezuela in 1933. *Education:* Attended schools in Chile, Mexico, and France.

CAREER: Director of *Imagen;* critic and poet. Former professor of Spanish at University of Pittsburgh; former staff member of literary journals *Zona Franca* and *Mundo Nuevo.* Affiliated with "Sardio," a Venezuelan literary group.

WRITINGS:

(Editor) *Las mejores poesías venezolanas* (anthology), Organización Continental de los Festivales del Libro, División Venezolana, 1958.

Mientras suceden los días (poetry), Cordillera, 1961.

Borges, el poeta, Universidad Nacional Autónoma de México, 1967, corrected and enlarged edition, Monte Avila, 1974.

La mirada (poetry), Tiempo Nuevo, 1970.

La máscara, la transparencia: Ensayos sobre poesía hispanoamericana (essays), Monte Avila, 1975.

En el verano cada palabra respira el verano (poetry), Alfa Argentina (Buenos Aires), 1976.

(Translator with Julieta Sucre) William Carlos Williams, *La primavera y todo,* Monte Avila, 1980.

(Editor and author of prologue) *Viejos y nuevos mundos,* Biblioteca Ayacucho, 1983.

Contributor of critical essays to books and periodicals.

BIOGRAPHICAL/CRITICAL SOURCES:

PERIODICALS

Times Literary Supplement, August 27, 1971.

*   *   *

SURIA, Violeta López
See LOPEZ SURIA, Violeta

T

TAFOLLA, (Mary) Carmen 1951-

PERSONAL: Born July 29, 1951, in San Antonio, Tex.; married Ernest Bernal. *Education:* Austin College, B.A., 1972, M.A., 1973; University of Texas at Austin, Ph.D., 1981.

ADDRESSES: Office—Department of Women's Studies, California State University, Fresno, Calif. 93710.

CAREER: Texas Lutheran College, Seguin, Tex., director of Mexican American Studies Center, 1973-76, 1978-79; California State University, Fresno, associate professor of women's studies, 1984—. Member of board of directors of Sherman Tutorial and Educational Program, 1972-73, and Mexican-American Information and Services Center, Seguin, 1975; member of Coalition of Minority Professionals at ALC Universities and Mexican American Coalition for Higher Education.

MEMBER: Modern Language Association of America, National Association for Bilingual Education, American Association of Teachers of Spanish and Portuguese, Texas Association for Chicanos in Higher Education, Texas Association for Bilingual Education, Sigma Delta Pi.

AWARDS, HONORS: Chicano Poetry Prize, University of California, Irvine, 1987, for unpublished manuscript "Sonnets to Human Beings."

WRITINGS:

(With Cecilio García-Camarillo and Reyes Cárdenas) *Get Your Tortillas Together* (poems), Rifan, 1976.
(Contributor) *The Spanish Speaking Church in the United States,* Our Sunday Visitor, 1976.
Curandera (poetry), M & A Editions, 1983.
(Contributor) Daydí-Tolson, editor, *Five Poets of Aztlán,* Bilingual/Editorial Bilingüe, 1985.
To Split a Human: Mitos, machos, y la mujer chicana (prose), Mexican American Cultural Center (San Antonio), 1985.

Work represented in anthologies, including *Chicano Literature Anthology,* Mexican American Cultural Center (San Antonio), and *Floricanto II: An Anthology of Chicano Literature,* University of Texas Press. Contributor to periodicals, including *Southern Exposure, Revista Chicano-Riqueña, Maize,* and *Caracol.*

WORK IN PROGRESS: A novel, *The Land of the Locos.*

SIDELIGHTS: Carmen Tafolla's "most characteristic and powerful poems," according to Yolanda Broyles González in the *Dictionary of Literary Biography,* "are those in which she brings barrio personalities to life using their own voices. . . . Tafolla shows a rare sensitivity toward the registers of barrio speech of persons from various age groups and walks of life."

BIOGRAPHICAL/CRITICAL SOURCES:

BOOKS

Dictionary of Literary Biography, Volume 82: *Chicano Writers,* Gale, 1989.

* * *

TAIBO, Paco Ignacio II 1949-

PERSONAL: Born January 11, 1949, in Gijón, Spain; son of Paco Ignacio and Maricarmen Taibo; married Paloma Saiz, 1971; children: Marina. *Religion:* None.

ADDRESSES: Home—Benjamin Hill 242-4, Colonia Condesa, Mexico D.F., Mexico.

CAREER: Writer; free-lance journalist, 1972—. Director, Etiqueta Negra and Biblioteca Policiaca; professor, Universidad Autónoma de México, Mexico City, 1984-89.

MEMBER: International Association of Crime Writers (president), PEN, Mystery Writers of America.

AWARDS, HONORS: Premio Grijalbo Novela, 1982; Cafe Gijón, 1986; Premio Nacional Historia, INAH, 1986; Premio Francisco Javier Clavijero for best book of history, 1987, for *Los Bolshevikis;* Premio Hammett for best crime fiction novel in Spanish, 1987, for *La vida misma;* Premio Novela Latinoamericana, 1989.

WRITINGS:

CRIME FICTION

Días de combate (title means "Battle Lines"), Grijalbo (Mexico), 1976.
Cosa fácil, Grijalbo, 1977, translation by William I. Neuman published as *An Easy Thing,* Viking, 1990.
No habrá final feliz (title means "No Happy Ending"), Láser, 1981.
Algunas nubes (title means "Some Clouds"), Leega, 1985.

Sombra de la sombra, Planeta, 1986, translation published as *The Shadow's Shadow,* Viking, 1991.

La vida misma (title means "The Real Thing"), Planeta, 1987.

(Contributor) *Raymond Chandler's Phillip Marlowe,* Knopf, 1988.

Sintiendo que el campo de batalla . . . (title means "Feeling That the Battlefield . . ."), Júcar, 1989.

Amorosos fantasmas (title means "Loving Phantoms"), Promexa, 1990.

Cuatro manos/Four Hands, Ediciones B, Grupo Z, 1990.

Sueños de frontera (title means "Frontier Dreams"), Promexa, 1990.

HISTORY

La huelga de los sombrereros (title means "The Hatmakers' War"), CEHSMO, 1980.

Asturias 1934, Júcar, 1980, 3rd edition edited by Silverio Cañada, Gijón, 1984.

(With Jorge Fernández) *El primer primero de mayo en México* (title means "Mexico's First May Day"), Asociación Mundial Centros de Estudios Históricos sobre Movimiento Obrero, 1981.

La gran huelga del verano del 20 en Monterrey (title means "The Great Strike of the Summer of 1920 in Monterrey"), Oidmo, 1981.

(Editor with Sealtiel Alatriste Lozano) *México, historia de un pueblo* (multi-volume history comic book), Nueva Imagen, (and author) Volume 9: *La pata de palo de Santa Ana,* 1981, (and author with Jorge Fernández Tomás) Volume 10: *La sangre derramada* (title means "Spilled Blood"), 1981, (and author) Volume 20: *Los hombres de Aguaprieta* (title means "The Men of Aguaprieta"), 1982.

(With Rogelio Vizcaíno) *El socialismo en un solo puerto,* Extemporáneos, 1983, 2nd edition published in *La cultura en México,* Siempre, 1988, 3rd corrected and enlarged edition published as *Las dos muertes de Juan Escudero* (title means "The Two Deaths of Juan Escudero"), Mortiz, 1989.

(Compiler and author of prologue) José C. Valadés, *El socialismo libertario mexicano* (title means "Libertarian Socialism in Mexico"), Universidad Autónoma de Sinaloa, 1984.

Iraupuato mi amor, Información Obrera/Macehual/Leega, 1984.

(With Vizcaíno) *Memoria roja* (title means "Red Memory"), Leega/Júcar, 1984.

(Co-author) *Octubre 1934, cincuenta años para la reflexión* (title means "October 1934, Fifty Years of Reflection"), Siglo Veintiuno, 1985.

(With Luis Hernández) *Danzón en Bellas Artes,* Información Obrera, 1985.

Los Bolshevikis, Mortiz, 1987.

Ataca Oaxaca, Leega, 1987.

Pascual décimo round (title means "Pascual, Tenth Round"), Universidad Autónoma de Sinaloa, 1988.

Arcángeles (title means "Archangels"), Alianza, 1988.

Santa Clara, la batalla del Che (title means "Santa Clara, Che's Battle"), Planeta, 1989.

OTHER

Nacimiento de la memoria (anthology; title means "The Birth of Memory"), ENAH, 1971.

Heroes convocados (novel), Grijalbo, 1982, translation published as *Calling All Heroes,* Plover Press, 1990.

Doña Eustolia blandió el cuchillo cebollero y otras historias (short stories), Universidad Autónoma de Sinaloa, 1984.

Pistolero y otros reportajes (anthology and notes on writings of Mario Gil), Universidad Autónoma de Sinaloa, 1985.

Reportaje (anthology), Universidad Autónoma de Sinaloa, 1985.

(Author of prologue and notes) *Bajando la frontera* (anthology), Leega/Júcar, 1985.

De paso (novel; title means "En Route"), Leega, 1986.

El regreso de la verdadera araña y otras historias que pasaron en algunas fábricas (title means "The Return of the Real Spider and Other Stories"), Mortiz, 1988.

Fantasmas nuestros de cada día (essay), Marco Polo, 1988.

Also author of *Regreso* (novel), 1989.

WORK IN PROGRESS: A translation of *Cuatro manos/Four Hands* by Viking; a translation of *De paso* by Plover Press.

SIDELIGHTS: Author of several books, including histories and mystery novels, Paco Ignacio Taibo II is known for his "witty, literate" writing, such as that which characterizes *Cosa fácil,* a mystery published in English translation as *An Easy Thing.* A *Publishers Weekly* reviewer calls this work, which concerns Mexican private eye Hector Belascoarán Shayne's attempts to solve three different puzzles, a "first-rate detective novel," and notes that "in complexity of social setting, ingenious plotting and philosophical depth, Taibo ranks with the best."

MEDIA ADAPTATIONS: *Días de combate* and *Cosa fácil* were both made into films in 1982; *Algunas nubes* was filmed in 1989; *Amorosos fantasmas* was adapted for television by Producciones Alton, 1989.

BIOGRAPHICAL/CRITICAL SOURCES:

Publishers Weekly, November 10, 1989.

* * *

TAO LAO
See STORNI, Alfonsina

* * *

THOMAS, Piri 1928-

PERSONAL: Name originally John Peter Thomas; informally changed name as a youth; born September 30, 1928, in New York, N.Y.; son of John (a laborer) and Delores (Mantanez) Thomas; married Daniela Calo, April 20, 1958; children: Ricardo, San-dee. *Education:* Attended New York City public schools.

CAREER: Writer, c. 1952—. Imprisoned for attempted armed robbery, 1950-56; volunteer worker in prison and drug rehabilitation programs in New York, N.Y., 1956—; Center for Urban Education, New York City, staff associate, beginning in 1967. Vice-president of Third World Cinema Productions; trustee of Community Film Workshop Council and of American Film Institute.

MEMBER: Authors Guild.

AWARDS, HONORS: Louis M. Rabinowitz Foundation grant, 1962; Lever Brothers community service award, 1967.

WRITINGS:

Down These Mean Streets (autobiography), Knopf, 1967.

"The Golden Streets" (two-act play), first produced in New York City at Riverside Park by Puerto Rican Traveling Theatre, September 9, 1970.

Saviour, Saviour, Hold My Hand (autobiography), Doubleday, 1972.

Seven Long Times (autobiography), Praeger, 1974.
(Author of introduction) Lefty Barretto, *Nobody's Hero: A Puerto Rican Story,* New American Library, 1977.
Stories From El Barrio (young adult), Knopf, 1978.

SIDELIGHTS: Piri Thomas is an author best known for his three autobiographies: *Down These Mean Streets; Savior, Savior, Hold My Hand;* and *Seven Long Times.* In his writing, which he began while in prison during the 1950s, Thomas addresses the stereotypes he feels society placed on his Puerto Rican and black heritage. He told Christopher Lehmann-Haupt in a 1967 interview in the *New York Times Book Review* why he decided to write in prison: "I said, 'Man, where am I at? I got a mind; let's see if I can use it,' so I jumped into books. Cause, like, dig it, you pull time, you got a lot of time. . . . I got to the point where I said, 'Man, I'm gonna try to do some prose writing.' " Thomas completed his first book in four years while still in prison, but a few years after his 1956 release the manuscript was accidentally destroyed. "It was my only copy," he related to Lehmann-Haupt, "and I started to feel myself cough up some tears, man. But then I said, 'Heeeeeey! You ain't no punk kid. You did it once, you do it twice.' " After several more years of writing, Thomas finished *Down These Mean Streets.*

Upon the 1967 publication of this first autobiography, *New York Times Book Review* contributor Daniel Stern wrote: "The book's literary qualities are primitive. Yet it has an undeniable power that I think comes from the fact that it is a report from the guts and heart of a submerged population group, itself submerged in the guts and hearts of our cities. It claims our attention and emotional response because of the honesty and pain of a life led in outlaw, fringe status, where the dream is always to escape."

Thomas wrote *Down These Mean Streets* in his Spanish Harlem dialect mixed with a style of language he picked up in prison. Most critics admired his ability to do this while retaining a highly personal contact with the many readers unfamiliar with this speech. "It is something of a linguistic event," said Stern. "Gutter language, Spanish imagery and personal poetics (sometimes forced, but often richly successful) mingle into a kind of individual statement that has very much its own sound." Through these "rough-hewn words shines a new voice," agreed James Nelson Goodsell, writing for the *Christian Science Monitor,* "one which may well add significant chapters to ethnic literature in the United States." Other critics liked the honest attitude in which the book was done, conspicuously lacking sociological judgments. Nelson Aldrich, for instance, averred in *Book Week* that the book "demands to be read as literature, not as raw data for social research. Thomas knows himself; his recollection of his youth is completely honest, and his writing—though occasionally flawed by self-conscious barbaric yawps—is wonderfully powerful. His achievement is to have so thoroughly taken the measure of his individuality that he adds significantly to our sense of the richness and shame of being an American."

Of Thomas's second autobiography, *Saviour, Saviour, Hold My Hand,* Larry Garvin wrote in his *Crisis* review, "The telling of this story and its stylistic execution mark a shift in style for Piri. We no longer have the gut experience flung at us for what it's worth. Piri begins to place it within his own developing framework. If the result is tentative and seemingly incomplete at times, it is nevertheless compelling; if it doesn't stand on its own (though by and large, I think it does), it sits well as a transitional work between *Down These Mean Streets* and *Seven Long Times.* For in *Saviour,* Piri has taken one step back from his experience; and that one step has provided a developing objectivity which comes to its fruition in *Seven Long Times.*" Garvin felt the chro-

nological narrative used for *Down These Mean Streets* works well because of its speed and intensity of delivery, "but, it breaks down considerably in *Saviour,*" he added, "which sometimes lacks a consistency of style. The chapters often read like a quest for subject matter; Piri picking his way through the middle years of his life, looking for a viable hook on which to hang his creative expression." *Seven Long Times,* Thomas's third autobiographical work, was critically better received than *Saviour,* but *Down These Mean Streets* remained the most widely praised of the three. "With the publication of these three books," concluded Garvin, "Piri Thomas has established himself as a writer deserving to be heard."

BIOGRAPHICAL/CRITICAL SOURCES:

PERIODICALS

Best Sellers, June 1, 1967.
Book Week, May 21, 1967.
Christian Science Monitor, June 15, 1967.
Crisis, June-July, 1975.
Life, June 9, 1967.
Nation, September 25, 1967.
Newsweek, May 29, 1967.
New York Times Book Review, May 21, 1967, September 17, 1972, March 4, 1979.
Saturday Review, August 5, 1967, September 30, 1972.
Times Literary Supplement, June 11, 1970.

*   *   *

TIMERMAN, Jacobo 1923-

PERSONAL: Born January 6, 1923, in Bar, Ukraine, U.S.S.R.; immigrated to Argentina, 1928, became citizen, citizenship revoked, 1979, later restored; immigrated to Israel, 1979, became citizen; son of Natan and Eva (a clothing vendor; maiden name, Berman) Timerman; married Risha Mindlin (a pianist), May 20, 1950; children: Daniel, Hector, Javier. *Education:* Attended National University of La Plata.

CAREER: Free-lance writer for literary magazines, Buenos Aires, Argentina, beginning in 1947; reporter for *La Razón* (newspaper), Buenos Aires; broadcast journalist in Buenos Aires; publisher of *Primera Plana* (weekly newsmagazine), Buenos Aires; *Confirmado* (weekly newsmagazine), Buenos Aires, publisher, beginning in 1969; *La Opinión* (newspaper), Buenos Aires, publisher, 1971-77; publisher at Timerman Editores (book publishing company), Buenos Aires; columnist for *Ma'ariv* (newspaper), Tel Aviv, Israel.

AWARDS, HONORS: David Ben-Gurion Award from the United Jewish Appeal, 1979; Hubert H. Humphrey Freedom Prize from the Anti-Defamation League of B'nai B'rith, 1979; Golden Pen of Freedom from the International Federation of Newspaper Publishers, 1980; *Prisoner Without a Name, Cell Without a Number* was selected one of the twenty best books of 1981 by *Saturday Review; Los Angeles Times* book prize for current interest, 1981, and Kenneth B. Smilen/Present Tense Literary Award for biography and autobiography, both for *Prisoner Without a Name;* Maria Moors Cabot Prize for contributions to inter-American understanding; Arthur Morse Award from Aspen Institute.

WRITINGS:

NONFICTION

Prisoner Without a Name, Cell Without a Number, translated by Toby Talbot from original Spanish manuscript "Preso sin nombre, celda sin número," Knopf, 1981.

The Longest War: Israel in Lebanon, translated by Miguel Acoca, Knopf, 1982.
Chile: Death in the South, translated by Robert Cox, Knopf, 1987.

Contributor to newspapers and magazines, including *New York Times Magazine, New Yorker,* and *Davar* (Israel).

WORK IN PROGRESS: A book on Cuba.

SIDELIGHTS: In the early morning of April 15, 1977, Jacobo Timerman, publisher of an influential daily newspaper that had criticized human rights violations by the Argentine military government, was kidnapped from his Buenos Aires apartment by twenty armed men acting on orders of high army officers. He was subsequently held without charges in prison, sometimes in secret, and subjected to brutal torture despite court orders for his release. Discharged from prison, he spent another thirty months under house arrest. After intense pressure from the U.S. Government under President Jimmy Carter and from international human rights groups, Timerman was finally freed in September, 1979; he was also, however, stripped of his Argentine citizenship and summarily expelled to Israel. He recounted his ordeal in *Prisoner Without a Name, Cell Without a Number,* which won accolades as an acute description of the psychological condition produced by arbitrary imprisonment and torture and as a searing indictment of antidemocratic trends in Argentine society.

During the period of profound social instability that Argentina experienced in the early 1970s, Timerman recalls in *Prisoner Without a Name,* both government authorities and political extremists made repeated attempts to silence his newspaper. In the six years he published the daily *La Opinión,* an equal number of presidents, both military and civilian, sought to govern the country while leftist urban guerrillas battled rightist death squads and members of the armed services violated human rights with impunity. According to *Prisoner Without a Name,* several of these governments sought to censor *La Opinión*'s criticism of economic mismanagement and political repression by withholding state advertising revenue and blocking distribution of some newspaper issues. At the same time, Timerman reports, factions from both the political right and left threatened him with death, and his home and office were bombed because of his newspaper's opposition to political extremes. *La Opinión* also took controversial positions on international issues, strongly supporting Israel while condemning human rights abuses by the military regime in Chile and the Soviet Union's treatment of political dissidents.

In February, 1976, seeing no solution for Argentina's ills under the administration of President Isabel Perón, Timerman printed an article in *La Opinión* urging the country's military leaders to move against the civilian government to restore public order and end the spiral of political violence. "The revolt against the Perón presidency found its principal proponent in *La Opinión,*" Timerman acknowledges in his book, "for we insisted on the need to fill the vacuum in which the country dwelt."

The Argentine armed forces overthrew Perón in a March coup and almost immediately began massive roundups of citizens deemed subversive, which included, according to the author, all opponents or potential opponents of military rule. In his book, Timerman observes how "military leaders hastily organized their personal domains, each one becoming a warlord in the zone under his control, whereupon the chaotic, anarchistic, irrational terrorism of the Left and of Fascist death squads gave way to intrinsic, systemized, rationally planned terrorism." As detentions and kidnappings of Argentinians mounted, Timerman and *La Opinión* passed from initial support of the junta to increasing

criticism of the government's human rights record. The newspaper regularly published the names and circumstances of "disappeared" persons, urging the authorities to account for their whereabouts and end illegal imprisonments. Of all the Argentine press, Timerman states that only *La Opinión* and the English-language *Buenos Aires Herald* were bold enough to demand the government's accountability for rights violations.

The consequence, Timerman writes, was his own kidnapping on orders from a far-right sector of the military. In *Prisoner Without a Name,* the author describes his confinement in clandestine prisons, interrogation, and torture at the hands of police and military officials he regards as Nazi-like in their anti-Semitic views and sadistic behavior. Unable to bring a legal case against him, Timerman's captors sought to force him to confess to links with a group of leftist guerrillas and to participation in a supposed Zionist plot to seize the Argentine region of Patagonia as a second Jewish homeland. The author endured solitary confinement, a mock execution, electric shocks to his genitals, and regular beatings; Timerman charges that he received extra punishment as a Jew. According to the author, his psychological survival depended upon a difficult process of divesting himself of all hope and interest in the outside world to reach a condition of absolute passivity, while at the same time avoiding a relationship of dependency with his torturers.

Timerman credits his eventual release into house arrest and final safe passage out of the country in large measure to persistent appeals to the Argentine Government on his behalf by the Carter administration's human rights office and by the Vatican. On the other hand, he is sharply critical in his book of what he sees as a failure by the Argentine Jewish community's leadership to speak out forcefully in his own case and on behalf of the estimated fifteen hundred other Jews who have disappeared in the years of military rule in Argentina. On a U.S. tour to promote *Prisoner Without a Name* after its 1981 publication, Timerman also voiced strong criticism of the Reagan administration's policy of tolerating human rights violations by right-wing nations, such as Argentina, allied to the United States.

Reviewing *Prisoner Without a Name, Cell Without a Number* in the London *Times,* Anthony Holden opined, "Timerman's testimony should prove a lasting work of prison literature." Referring to the author's description of the techniques he discovered to preserve his emotional and psychological strength under torture, the critic termed the book "something of a manual for those who may one day have to attempt to survive such an ordeal." *New York Times Book Review* critic Anthony Lewis remarked, "Timerman writes with passion, but a passion controlled almost to the point of detachment. The effect is devastating." Lewis concluded, "He gives an unforgettable picture of . . . state terrorism."

After settling with his family in Israel, where he authored *Prisoner Without a Name,* Timerman also resumed his career as a journalist. When Israel invaded Lebanon in 1982, he wrote *The Longest War: Israel in Lebanon* to argue that the invasion was militarily unjustified and politically damaging to Israel. In his book, Timerman calls the Lebanese conflict Israel's first aggressive war and the first undertaken without defined security objectives. He takes the view that Israeli Prime Minister Menachem Begin and Defense Minister Ariel Sharon fought the war more to strengthen Israel's geopolitical position vis-a-vis its Arab neighbors than for the declared purpose of removing a Palestinian threat to Israel's northern border. Timerman also accuses Begin and Sharon of harboring a deluded belief that Israel's conflict with the Palestinians can be solved by military means alone.

In fact, the author argues, the Israeli-Palestinian dispute is "a conflict over equal rights" requiring political compromise on both sides, and "Israel will have peace only when it can accept living together with a Palestinian state in the same region."

In his London *Times* review of *The Longest War,* Edward Mortimer observed that the author "mercilessly demolishes a number of crucial Israeli myths. Timerman is not taken in by the 'welcome' of the Lebanese to the Israeli invader" and he does not accept that the horrors of the invasion will force acceptance of a political solution. While questioning Timerman's interpretation of Israeli objectives in the war, *New York Times* critic Christopher Lehmann-Haupt credited *The Longest War* with "a powerful argument that the policy of the Begin Government toward the Palestinians has been tantamount to carrying on a blood feud, with the only instrument of justice being acts of revenge."

According to *Los Angeles Times* reporter Kenneth Freed, Timerman's strong opposition to the Lebanese invasion brought him considerable unpopularity in Israel and he subsequently moved to New York. In January, 1984, after the democratic civilian government of Raúl Alfonsín had taken office in Argentina, Timerman returned to Buenos Aires to seek justice against his torturers and the restitution of his newspaper and property. "For an Argentinian, to go back now, is to see his country in a kind of Camelot," Timerman told the *New York Times*'s E. J. Dionne, Jr., shortly before his departure. "After three, four generations of dictatorship, Argentinians are very strongly for democracy. I am amazed, I am impressed and I can't believe it." In Argentina, Timerman filed a civil suit against former Buenos Aires Chief of Police Ramón J. Camps and former President General Jorge Rafael Videla, whom the Alfonsín government also brought to trial on criminal charges for human rights violations. Timerman also met personally with President Alfonsín, who promised to restore his Argentine citizenship and help him win compensation for his newspaper.

Though conditions had improved in Argentina, political oppression continued to plague the neighboring country of Chile. In 1987 Timerman published *Chile: Death in the South,* a book describing life under the military regime of Chile's President General Augusto Pinochet. *New York Times* contributor Lehmann-Haupt called the book "a wrenching portrait of the South American country's suffering. . . . It tells of the torture, rape and murder inflicted on the citizenry as a matter of state policy." The book documents the people's efforts to thwart government-sponsored kidnapping attempts; and the testimony from victims of such crimes supports Timerman's likening of militarist abductors to Nazis.

According to *Washington Post Book World*'s Patrick Breslin, Timerman questions "how Chile, with its proud democratic tradition, its dynamic and urbane people, could succumb for so long [fourteen years] to a dictator who seems a caricature of the Latin American strongman." Timerman blames the political parties and Chilean people for not coming to an agreement about how to combat the abuses of the Pinochet government and suggests that they are avoiding full knowledge of their predicament. Stressing that the people of Chile are deluding themselves in hoping that a dramatic overthrow and return to pre-Pinochet Chile is possible, Timerman argues that "until they . . . accept that the Chile of nostalgia has been utterly vanquished, they will not be able to bring a new Chile out of Pinochet's valley of death," wrote Breslin. As in his other books, Timerman takes a nonviolent position, advocating a gradual transition to democracy within the framework of the current government, rather than a "glorious" coup. While *Los Angeles Times Book Review* contributor Richard Eder declared that "Timerman's style is extreme," the critic added that "his message, on the other hand, is of a moderation, even a benignity, that startles in its contrast. . . . Timerman's prescriptions for a solution are low-keyed, and dramatic only in their avoidance of drama." Timerman advises that the people of Chile need to "find a road to democracy within an antidemocratic context," reported *New York Times* contributor Lehmann-Haupt, and that "the future they must fight for has nothing to do with giving up one's life to recover the past." Breslin was skeptical about some of Timerman's claims, but he characterized Timerman as a prophet who rails against a country's mistakes out of love and concern for its welfare.

BIOGRAPHICAL/CRITICAL SOURCES:

BOOKS

Timerman, Jacobo, *Prisoner Without a Name, Cell Without a Number,* Knopf, 1981.

PERIODICALS

American Poetry Review, November/December, 1981.
Detroit News, June 14, 1981.
Los Angeles Times, January 8, 1984.
Los Angeles Times Book Review, December 20, 1987.
New York Times, September 20, 1979, September 30, 1979, May 7, 1981, December 3, 1982, December 31, 1983, March 11, 1984, November 14, 1987, December 17, 1987.
New York Times Book Review, May 10, 1981, January 10, 1988.
Publishers Weekly, May 29, 1981.
Times (London), July 30, 1981, December 2, 1982.
Tribune Books, December 13, 1987.
Washington Post, September 20, 1979.
Washington Post Book World, January 31, 1988.

* * *

TIO (y NAZARIO de FIGUEROA), Aurelio   1907-

PERSONAL: Born March 3, 1907, in San Germán, P.R.

ADDRESSES: c/o University of Puerto Rico Press, P.O. Box 23322, UPR Station, Río Piedras, P.R. 00931-3322.

CAREER: Engineer and historian. Engineer with the Puerto Rican Department of Public Works. Has served on advisory commission on Historical Monuments, Institute of Puerto Rican Culture.

MEMBER: Puerto Rican Institute of Engineers, Puerto Rican Academy of History, Society of Puerto Rican Authors, Puerto Rico Academy of Arts and Sciences, Costa Rican Academy of Genealogical Sciences.

WRITINGS:

Fundación de San Germán y su significación en el desarrollo político, económico, social y cultural de Puerto Rico, Biblioteca de Autores Puertorriqueños (San Juan), 1956.
(Editor) *Nuevas fuentes para la historia de Puerto Rico: Documentos inéditos o poco conocidos cuyos originales se encuentran en el Archivo General de Indias en la ciudad de Seville, España,* Ediciones de la Universidad Interamericana de Puerto Rico (San Germán), 1961.
Dr. Diego Alvarez Chanca: Estudio biográfico, Instituto de Cultura Puertorriqueña, Universidad Interamericana de Puerto Rico (San Juan), 1966.
Lengua e historia, University of Puerto Rico Press, 1983.

TORRES, José Acosta 1925-

PERSONAL: Born December 13, 1925, in Martindale, Tex.; married Patricia Resch (an art teacher), August 15, 1970; children: Gregory, Maruca, Angela. *Education:* Southwest Texas State College (now University), B.S., 1950, M.Ed., 1952; Universidad Interamericana, Ph.D., 1965; further study at Spanish Language Institute (National Defense Education Act), Our Lady of the Lake College, San Antonio, 1963, and at University of Texas at Austin, 1967, 1968. *Religion:* Roman Catholic.

CAREER: Elementary school teacher, 1950-58, assistant principal, 1958-60, high school acting assistant principal, 1960-62, coordinator of foreign language department, 1962-65, all in San Antonio, Tex.; San Antonio College, San Antonio, Tex., instructor, 1965-68, assistant professor of Spanish, 1968-70; Southwest Educational Development Laboratory, Austin, Tex., curriculum development specialist, 1970-72; U.S. Office of Education, project coordinator in Crystal City, Tex., 1972-73; St. Edward's University, Austin, Tex., assistant professor of education, beginning 1973; Texas A&I University, in Kingsville, Kingsville, Tex., formerly assistant professor in migrant and bilingual education. Coordinator of foreign language department, Fort Sam Houston, 1965-66; consultant to HemisFair '68, to Good Samaritan Center education project, 1969, and to *Compton's Encyclopedia* and *Encyclopedia Britannica;* vice-president of Intercontinental Translations; initiator and director of community classes in arts and crafts for disadvantaged children and of citizenship classes for Mexican-American adults. *Military service:* U.S. Army, 1944-45; received Purple Heart.

MEMBER: American Association of Teachers of Spanish and Portuguese, Texans for the Educational Advancement of Mexican-Americans, Kappa Pi (past president), Phi Delta Kappa.

AWARDS, HONORS: Certificate of Commendation from Spanish Government, 1963, for article on Junipero Serra; certificate of commendation from New Braunfels (Tex.) Kiwanis Club, 1969, for services benefiting youth of the community; Literary Award from Spanish Government, 1969, for HemisFair '68 essay.

WRITINGS:

Ortografía comparativa, Southwest Educational Development Laboratory (Austin, Tex.), 1972.
Composición creativa, Southwest Educational Development Laboratory, 1972.
Spanish/English Bilingualism, Southwest Educational Development Laboratory, 1972.
Spanish/English Publications, Southwest Educational Development Laboratory, 1972.
Cachito mío (short stories; title means "My Little One"), Quinto Sol Publications, 1974.
Chicanito Sixty-Nine, Quinto Sol Publications, 1975.

Alamo Messenger (newspaper) columnist, 1955-58, Spanish language editor, 1962-64; *La Voz,* (newspaper), columnist, 1955-58, editor, 1958-62; editor and cofounder, *Hispanavoz* (newspaper), 1964-66. Contributor of about 300 articles, in Spanish and in English, to various publications, including *Texas Outlook* and *El Grito.*

* * *

TORRES BODET, Jaime 1902-1974

PERSONAL: Born April 17, 1902, in Mexico City, Mexico; committed suicide by gunshot, May 13, 1974, at his home in Mexico City; son of Alejandro Torres Girbent (a theatrical producer and businessman) and Emilia Bodet de Torres; married Josefina Juárez, March, 1929. *Education:* Studied law at University of Mexico, 1918-1920.

ADDRESSES: Home—Mexico City, Mexico.

CAREER: Diplomat, statesman, writer, orator, and educator. National Preparatory School, Mexico City, Mexico, secretary and teacher of literature, 1921-22; Mexican Ministry of Education, Mexico City, head of libraries department, 1922-24; University of Mexico, Mexico City, professor of French literature, 1924-28; Mexican legation, Madrid, Spain, third secretary, 1929-31; Mexican embassy, Paris, France, second secretary, 1931-32; Mexican embassy, The Hague, Netherlands, acting charge d'affaires, 1932-34; Mexican embassy, Buenos Aires, Argentina, acting charge d'affaires, 1934-35; Mexican embassy, Paris, first secretary, 1935-36; Ministry of Foreign Affairs, Mexico, head of diplomatic department, 1936-37; Mexican embassy, Brussels, Belgium, charge d'affaires, 1937-40; Mexican Under-Secretary for Foreign Affairs, 1940-43; Mexican Minister of Education, 1943-46; Mexican Minister of Foreign Affairs, 1946-48; United Nations Educational, Scientific, and Cultural Organization (UNESCO), Paris, director-general, 1948-52; Mexican ambassador to France, 1954-58; second term as Mexican Minister of Education, 1958-64. Head of Mexican delegation to Ninth International Conference of American States (Bogota), 1948, which drafted the Charter of the Organization of American States; represented Mexico at Conference of Education and Economic and Social Development in Latin America, 1962.

MEMBER: International PEN.

AWARDS, HONORS: Gold medal, Pan American League; gold medal, French Legion of Honor; National Prize for Literature (Mexico), 1966; doctor honoris causa, University of New Mexico and University of Southern California; decorations from Order of the Glittering Stars (China), Order of the Cedar (Lebanon), Order of Polonia Restituta (Poland), Order of the Polar Star (Sweden), Order of Leopold and Order of the Crown (both Belgium), Order of Merit Carlos Manuel de Céspedes (Cuba), Order of Juan Pablo Duarte and Order of Christophe Colomb (both Dominican Republic), Order of Vasco Núñez de Balboa (Panama), Order of Morazán (Honduras), Knight Commander of Order of Quetzal (Guatemala), Order of the Liberator (Venezuela), Order of the Sun (Peru), Great Officer of Order of the Andean Condor (Bolivia), Order of "Al Mérito" (Ecuador), Order of Boyaca (Colombia), Order of Merit (Chile), Great Cross of the Order of San Martín the Liberator (Argentina).

WRITINGS:

POEMS

Fervor (title means "Fervor"), introduction by E. González Martínez, Ballescá (Mexico), 1918, reprinted, [Mexico], 1968.
Canciones (title means "Songs"), Cultura (Mexico), 1922.
El corazón delirante (title means "The Impassioned Heart"), introduction by Arturo Torres Rioseco, Porrúa (Mexico), 1922.
La casa (title means "The House"), Herrero (Mexico), 1923.
Los días (title means "The Days"), Herrero, 1923.
Nuevas canciones (title means "New Songs"), Calleja (Madrid), 1923.
Poemas (title means "Poems"), Herrero, 1924.
Biombo (title means "Folding Screen"), Herrero, 1925.
Poesías (anthology), Espasa-Calpe (Madrid), 1926.
Destierro (title means "Exile"), Espasa-Calpe (Madrid), 1930.
Cripta (title means "Crypt"), R. Loera y Chávez (Mexico), 1937.

Sonetos (title means "Sonnets"), Gráfica Panamericana (Mexico), 1949.

Selección de poemas, selected by Xavier Villaurrutia, Nueva Voz (Mexico), 1950.

Fronteras (title means "Frontiers"), Fondo de Cultura Económica (Mexico), 1954.

Poesías escogidas (selections from previous works), Espasa-Calpe (Buenos Aires), 1954.

Sin tregua (title means "No Truce"), Fondo de Cultura Económica, 1957.

Trébol de cuatro hojas (title means "Four-Leaf Clover"), privately printed (Paris), 1958, Universidad Veracruzana, 1960.

Poemes (French translations of Torres Bodet's poems), Gallimard (Paris), 1960.

Selected Poems of Jaime Torres Bodet (text in English and Spanish), edited and translated by Sonja Karsen, Indiana University Press, 1964.

Poesía de Jaime Torres Bodet, Finisterre (Mexico), 1965.

Versos y prosas, introduction by Karsen, Ediciones Iberoamericanas (Madrid), 1966.

Obra poética (collected poems, 1916-66), introduction by Rafael Solona, two volumes, Porrúa, 1967.

Viente poemas, Ediciones Sierra Madre (Monterrey, Mexico), 1971.

FICTION

Margarita de niebla (novel; title means "Margaret's Fog"), Cultura, 1927.

La educación sentimental (novel; title means "The Sentimental Education"), Espasa-Calpe (Madrid), 1929.

Proserpina rescatada (novel; title means "Proserpina Rescued"), Espasa-Calpe (Madrid), 1931.

Estrella de día (novel; title means "Movie Star"), Espasa-Calpe (Madrid), 1933.

Primero de enero (novel; title means "First of January"), Ediciones Literatura (Madrid), 1935.

Sombras (novel; title means "Shades"), Cultura, 1937.

Nacimiento de Venus y otros relatos (stories; title means "Birth of Venus and Other Stories"), Nueva Cultura (Mexico), 1941.

CRITICISM

Perspectiva de la literatura mexicana actual 1915-1928 (title means "View of Present-Day Mexican Literature 1915-1928"), Contemporáneos, 1928.

Contemporáneos: Notas de crítica (essays; title means "Contemporaries: Notes on Literary Criticism"), Herrero, 1928.

Tres inventores de realidad: Stendhal, Dostoyevski, Pérez Galdós (essays; title means "Three Inventors of Reality: Stendhal, Dostoyevski, Pérez Galdós"), Imprenta Universitaria (Mexico), 1955.

Balzac, Fondo de Cultura Económica, 1959.

Maestros venecianos (essays on painters; title means "Venetian Masters"), Porrúa, 1961.

León Tolstoi: Su vida y su obra (title means "Leo Tolstoy: His Life and Work"), Porrúa, 1965.

Rubén Darío: Abismo y cima (title means "Rubén Darío: Fame and Tragedy"), Universidad Nacional Autónoma de México/Fondo de Cultura Económica, 1966.

Tiempo y memoria en la obra de Proust (title means "Time and Memory in Proust's Work"), Porrúa, 1967.

SPEECHES

Educación mexicana: Discursos, entrevistas, mensajes (main title means "Mexican Education"), Secretaría de Educación Pública (Mexico), 1944.

La escuela mexicana: Exposición de la doctrina educativa, Secretaría de Educación Pública, 1944.

Educación y concordia internacional: Discursos y mensajes (1941-1947) (main title means "Education and International Concord"), El Colegio de México, 1948.

Teachers Hold the Key to UNESCO's Objectives, Naldrett Press, 1949.

Doce mensajes educativos (title means "12 Educational Messages"), Secretaría de Educación Pública, 1960.

Doce mensajes cívicos (title means "Twelve Civic Messages"), Secretaría de Educación Pública, 1961.

La voz de México en Bogotá y Los Angeles (title means "The Voice of Mexico in Bogotá and Los Angeles"), Secretaría de Educación Pública, 1963.

Patria y cultura, Secretaría de Educación Pública, 1964.

Discursos (1941-1964), Porrúa, 1964.

A number of speeches by Torres Bodet have been published individually.

OTHER

(Translator from the French and author of introductory essay) Andre Gide, *Los límites del arte y algunas reflexiones de moral y de literatura,* Cultura, 1920.

(Editor and author of prologue) José Martí, *Nuestra América,* Secretaría de Educación Pública, 1945.

Tiempo de arena (also see below; autobiography; title means "Time of Sand"), Fondo de Cultura Económica, 1955.

Obras escogidas (selected works; contains poems, essays, speeches, and reprint of *Tiempo de arena*), Fondo de Cultura Económica, 1961.

Liberar el alsa de América con la luz de la educación, [Mexico], 1962.

(Editor and author of introduction) Rubén Darío, *Antología de Rubén Darío* (anthology), Universidad Nacional Autónoma de México/Fondo de Cultura Económica, 1967.

Memorias (memoirs), Porrúa, Volume 1: *Años contra el tiempo,* 1969, Volume 2: *La victoria sin alas,* 1970, Volume 3: *El desierto internacional,* 1971, Volume 4: *La tierra prometida,* 1972.

Equinoccio, Porrúa, 1974.

Founder of literary reviews, including *La Falange,* with Ortiz de Montellano, 1922, and *Contemporáneos,* 1928.

WORK IN PROGRESS: Another volume of his autobiography, left unfinished at the time of his death.

SIDELIGHTS: "Quintessentially the intellectual-in-politics," according to *Time,* Mexico's Jaime Torres Bodet was both an accomplished statesman and writer. According to Sonja Karsen in her book *Jaime Torres Bodet,* he "achieved the unusual distinction of successfully combining the qualities of the man of action with the sensitivity of the man of letters." During his long career in government, Torres Bodet was famous as an advocate of literacy and education. As Mexico's Minister of Education in the 1940s, he developed a campaign entitled "Each One Teach One," which in two years increased the literate population in Mexico by more than one million people. Later, as director-general of the United Nations Educational, Scientific, and Cultural Organization (UNESCO), he advocated that world peace and liberty hinged upon people being educated, especially upon their being able to read. From his post at UNESCO, he led the development of specialized educational materials for individual countries, until he resigned in 1952 when his budget was cut by over $2.5 million. Torres Bodet also worked many years in the Mexican diplomatic service and in the late 1940s was Mexican Minister of Foreign Affairs. He represented his country at numerous international conferences, and in 1948 led the Mexican delegation which helped formulate the Charter of the Organization of American States.

As a writer, Torres Bodet authored over twenty books of poetry, six novels, a volume of short stories, and numerous critical studies, ranging from studies of Balzac, Tolstoy, and Rubén Darío, to European painting. He was a leading member of the group called "The Contemporáneos," which sparked a revival of Mexican lyric poetry in the 1920s and 1930s. He was also known for his novels and essays; some scholars, such as Antonio Castro Leal, have ranked his prose among the finest of Mexican writers. Karsen states that his novels, like those of other "Contemporáneos" writers who produced fiction, were influenced by innovations of European writers of the period such as Kafka, Joyce, and Proust. Like Proust, Torres Bodet especially held the importance of memory to the writer. According to Karsen, poetry and prose represented to him "different ways of approximation and expression of the same poetic substance, from which he trie[d] to lift the opaque veil which hides the secret of life." The main themes of his poetry, also at work in his fiction, include "the haunting . . . search for his own identity and the attempt to establish an identity with his fellow men, . . . one of utter loneliness, of nothingness, of being and not being, . . . [and] a constant preoccupation with the evanescence of time which finally leads us to the theme of death." In his prose, Torres Bodet was "less interested in the nature of the activities to be observed, than in observing all activities in a special way," creating thereby, according to Karsen, "a sensibility hitherto unknown in Mexical letters."

Torres Bodet's contributions as a writer were officially recognized in 1966 when President Díaz Ordaz bestowed him with the Mexican National Prize for Literature. From 1969 to 1972, Torres Bodet published four volumes of an autobiography, *Memorias,* which recounted his years as a statesman within Mexican and world politics. In 1974, he committed suicide at his home in Mexico City. The *New York Times* reported that Torres Bodet, suffering from prostate cancer, wrote in a final note: "I prefer to call on death myself at the right time."

BIOGRAPHICAL/CRITICAL SOURCES:

BOOKS

Carballo, Emmanuel, *Jaime Torres Bodet,* Empresas Editoriales (Mexico), 1968.
Cowart, Billy F., *La obra educativa de Torres Bodet en lo nacional y lo internacional,* El Colegio de México, 1966.
Forster, Merlin H., *Los Contemporáneos 1920-1932,* Ediciones De Andrea, 1964.
Jaime Torres Bodet en quince semblanzas, Ediciones Oasis (Mexico), 1965.
Jarnés, Benjamín, *Ariel disperso,* Stylo (Mexico), 1946.
Karsen, Sonja, *A Poet in a Changing World,* Skidmore College, 1963.
Karsen, Sonja, *Jaime Torres Bodet,* Twayne, 1971.
Kneller, George F., *The Education of the Mexican Nation,* Columbia University Press, 1951.
Laves, Walter L. C., and Charles A. Thomson, *UNESCO: Purpose, Progress, Prospects,* Indiana University Press, 1957.

PERIODICALS

Américas, March, 1949, August, 1969.
Antioch Review, winter, 1968-69.
Books Abroad, spring, 1967, autumn, 1970.
Christian Science Monitor, September 14, 1946.
Nature, December 4, 1948.

OBITUARIES:

PERIODICALS

New York Times, May 14, 1974.
Time, May 27, 1974.

* * *

TREJO, Arnulfo D(uenes) 1922-

PERSONAL: Born August 15, 1922, in Villa Vicente Guerrero, Durango, Mexico; son of Nicolas F. and Petra (Duenes) Trejo; married Phyllis Bowen, May 21, 1954 (divorced); married Annette Foster Loken, July 1, 1967; children: (first marriage) Rachel, Rebecca, Ruth; stepdaughter: Linda Loken. *Education:* University of Arizona, B.A., 1949; University of the Americas, M.A. (Spanish language and literature), 1951; Kent State University, M.A. (library science), 1953; National University of Mexico, Litt.D. (with honors), 1959.

ADDRESSES: Home—1515 E. First St., Tucson, Ariz. 85719. *Office*—Graduate School of Library Science, College of Education, University of Arizona, Tucson, Ariz. 85721.

CAREER: National University of Mexico, Mexico City, assistant librarian, 1954-55; University of California at Los Angeles, reference librarian, 1955-59; California State University, Long Beach, assistant librarian, 1959-63; University of California at Los Angeles, assistant professor, 1965-66, associate professor of library science, 1966-68; University of Arizona, Tucson, associate professor of library science and English, 1970-75, professor of library science, 1975—. Library director of ESAN (graduate school of business administration), Lima, Peru, 1963-65; American Library Association consultant to United States Agency for International Development (USAID), Caracas, Venezuela, 1968-70. Member of board of directors, Tucson Public Library, 1967-68, and City of Tucson Historical Committee, 1972; president of El Tiradito Foundation, 1972-73. *Military service:* U.S. Army, Infantry, 1943-45; served in South Pacific theater; became sergeant; received Philippine Liberation Ribbon, Purple Heart with oak leaf cluster, and Bronze Star Medal.

MEMBER: American Library Association (council member, 1974—), REFORMA (National Organization of Spanish-Speaking Librarians in the United States; president, 1971-74), American Association of University Professors, Seminar on the Acquisition of Latin American Library Materials, Phi Delta Kappa, Beta Phi Mu, Phi Kappa Phi, Sigma Delta Pi.

AWARDS, HONORS: Simón Bolívar Award, Colegio de Biblioteconomos, Venezuela, 1970; El Tiradito Awards, El Tiradito Foundation, 1973 and 1975; annual award from League of Mexican-American Women, 1973; Rosenzweig Award, Arizona State Library Association, 1976; Distinguished Alumni Award, Kent State University School of Library Science.

WRITINGS:

Bibliografía comentada sobre administración de negocios (title means "Annotated Bibliography on Business Administration"), Addison-Wesley, 1967, 2nd edition published as

Bibliografía comentada sobre administración de negocios y disciplinas conexas, 1967.

Diccionario etimológico del léxico de la delincuencia (title means "Etymological Dictionary of the Language of the Underworld"), UTEHA, 1969.

(Editor) *Directory of Spanish-Speaking/Spanish Surnamed Librarians in the United States,* Bureau of School Services, College of Education, University of Arizona, 1973, revised edition published as *Quien es Quien: A Who's Who of Hispanic-Heritage Librarians in the United States,* Bureau of School Services, College of Education, University of Arizona, 1986.

Bibliografía Chicana: A Guide to Information Services, Gale, 1975.

(Editor and contributor) *Proceedings of the April 28-29, 1978, Seminario on Library and Information Services for the Spanish-Speaking: A Contribution to the Arizona Pre-White House Conference,* Graduate Library Institute for Spanish-Speaking Americans (Tucson, Arizona), 1978.

(Editor and contributor) *The Chicanos: As We See Ourselves* (essays by fourteen Chicano scholars), University of Arizona Press, 1979.

Contributor to *American Library, Arizona Highways, Folklore Americas, Wilson Library Bulletin,* and other magazines.

SIDELIGHTS: Arnulfo D. Trejo's reference works on Chicano librarians and scholars are recommended as important contributions to a field previously described only by Anglo observers.

* * *

TRIANA, José 1932(?)-

PERSONAL: Born in 1932 (some sources say 1931 or 1933) in Camagüey (some sources say Bayamo), Cuba; immigrated to France, 1980. *Education:* Studied in Santiago, Cuba.

ADDRESSES: Home—Paris, France.

CAREER: Writer. Worked in Madrid, Spain, during 1950s; worked for Editorial Nacional (Cuban government publishing house), during 1960s; performed conscript labor as a political punishment; worked in Paris, France, beginning in 1980s. Visiting professor at Dartmouth, 1981.

AWARDS, HONORS: Prize for drama from Casa de las Américas, 1965, Gallo de La Habana Award for best play from Sixth Latin American Theater Festival (Havana, Cuba), 1966, and award from Colombian Theater Festival, all for *La noche de los asesinos.*

WRITINGS:

El mayor general hablará de teogonía (one-act play; title means "The Major General Will Speak of Theogony"; first produced in 1960), published with *El Parque de la Fraternidad* (also see below).

Medea en el espejo (play; title means "Medea in the Mirror"; first produced in 1960), published with *El Parque de la Fraternidad* (also see below).

El Parque de la Fraternidad (one-act play; title means "Brotherhood Park"; first produced in 1962), Cuban Union of Writers and Artists, 1962.

"La casa ardiendo" (play; title means "The Burning House"), first produced in 1962.

"La visita del angel" (play; title means "The Angel's Visit"), first produced in 1963.

La muerte del ñeque (three-act play; title means "The Death of the Villain"; first produced in 1963), Revolución (Havana), 1964.

La noche de los asesinos (two-act play; title means "The Night of the Assassins"; first produced in Havana, Cuba, at Sixth Latin American Theater Festival, 1966; produced on the West End at Aldwych Theatre, 1967), Casa de las Américas (Havana), 1965, translation by Pablo Armando Fernandez and Michael Kustow published as "The Criminals" in *The Modern Stage in Latin America: Six Plays,* edited by George Woodyard, Dutton, 1971.

(Editor and author of introduction) *La generación del 98: Unamuno, Valle-Inclán, Baroja, Machado, Azorín,* Editora del Consejo Nacional de Cultura, Editorial Nacional (Havana), 1965.

(Editor and author of introduction) Jean Giraudoux, *Teatro,* Editora del Consejo Nacional de Cultura, 1965.

(Editor and author of introduction) *Teatro español actual,* Instituto del Libro (Havana), 1970.

Worlds Apart (play), produced in London, England, at Pit Theatre, 1987.

Ceremonial de guerra, Persona, 1989.

SIDELIGHTS: "José Triana," wrote Frank Dauster in *Dramatists in Revolt,* "is one of a brilliant group of young dramatists who made the Cuban theater of the 1960s one of the most vital in the Spanish-speaking world." Triana's career prospered during the early years of the Cuban Revolution, when Fidel Castro's Marxist government, which took power in 1959, encouraged a wide variety of literary activity as part of its effort to change the nature of Cuban society. While some writers carefully aligned their works with Marxist political doctrines, Triana and many of his peers felt free to make bold personal statements about the world around them. "It is not my purpose to write political pamphlets," he said in 1964, according to Dauster, "but to look, to dig, to dig into ourselves, into our defects, the sense of evil, of cruelty." The author gave an international appeal to his dramas of Cuban life by borrowing from a wide range of theatrical traditions, ranging from the ancient Greek interest in mythology to the modern concern for emotionally gripping ritual.

Triana shared with Cuba's Marxist leaders an underlying skepticism about the traditional structure of Cuban society. In particular, as George McMurray observed in *Spanish American Writing Since 1941,* he was "sharply critical of stagnant and decayed institutions such as the church and the family." But while Marxist politicians tended to see the Revolution as the successful culmination of a broad-based movement toward reform, playwright Triana seemed more pessimistic, writing about isolated individuals making ill-considered and unsuccessful efforts at revolt. The resulting works, reviewers have observed, often resemble those of Europe's "theater of the absurd," a movement among dramatists during the years after World War II that placed characters in bizarre and nightmarish situations in order to demonstrate the futility of human existence.

Triana wrote his first major play, *El mayor general hablará de teogonía* ("The Major General Will Speak of Theogony"), while residing in Spain during the late 1950s. A harsh commentary on the nature of religious faith, the work centers on a lower-class Cuban family that has accepted the charity of a landlord known as the Major General. Each member of the family—husband, wife, and the wife's sister—is plagued by a sense of moral failure; each expects the Major General to play a strong role in their lives. As the play unfolds, the characters seem unaware that many of their words and actions parody verses of the Bible and Catholic religious ritual. While the wife prepares for a visit from the General, she speaks of him as a figure of great generosity; the husband and his sister-in-law, by contrast, expect the General to judge them harshly for the consequences of their illicit love affair years before and decide to kill him when he arrives. By this point the Major General seems emblematic of an all-powerful God, perhaps destined to undergo a violent challenge like the crucified Christ. But the General's arrival frustrates such expectations: the entire family kneels before him, squelching the murder attempt before it has begun; the General, far from displaying his power, treats his lodgers with disinterest and boredom. "Triana's attack is directed not at God but at his worshippers, who are stupid, weak, and vacillating," wrote Dauster. "If, by some extraordinary accident, they were to destroy the Major General, they would inevitably find or fabricate another."

With the success of Castro's revolution, Triana returned to Cuba and quickly became prominent in the country's new theater community. His plays were produced for the first time—not only *El mayor general* but a series of grim works set among Cuba's pre-revolutionary working classes. "Our normal life, until almost the other day, was the past social structure in which we lived and moved," he said, according to Dauster. "It is just that we judge that social structure." In *El Parque de la Fraternidad* ("Brotherhood Park") three stock characters of traditional Cuban theater—an Afro-Cuban woman, an old man, and a young man—meet in the ironically named park of the title, where they exchange empty remarks and fail to communicate meaningfully with each other. *Medea en el espejo* ("Medea in the Mirror"), one of Triana's most admired works, retells an ancient Greek myth in the setting of a Cuban tenement. The play charts the growing madness of María, a woman who has been abandoned by her lover Julián for an opportune marriage. As the action unfolds María gazes obsessively into her mirror, speaks in an affectedly poetic language that contrasts sharply with her sordid surroundings, and finally murders the children she had by the faithless Julián. *La muerte del ñeque* ("The Death of the Villain") evokes the apparatus of Greek tragedy, as a proud and foolish criminal boss meets his doom, slain by three other criminals whose dice-playing makes them resemble the mythological forces of fate and chance.

Triana returned to the stark absurdism of *El mayor general* for a play that observers consider his finest work, *La noche de los asesinos* ("The Criminals"). The action takes place in the shoddy basement of a Cuban home, where three adolescent children engage in an evening of impassioned and frightening role-playing. They enact the murder of their parents and the subsequent court trial, playing all participants in the story, including the parents and the police. At the end of the play, the adolescents trade parts and prepare to begin their ritual again. As many reviewers have noted, Triana refuses to side with either parents or children in "The Criminals." The parents may be oppressive, but they have also been dehumanized by years of personal disappointments; the children may be oppressed, but they are also cruel and irrational. "No one is innocent," observed Lawrence H. Klibbe in *Books Abroad;* "the recriminations of parents . . . and the children have some mutual validity." The author's conclusion, Klibbe surmised, is that "human beings create much of their own agony." "The Criminals" became one of the most widely known Hispanic plays of the 1960s. Winner of a highly prestigious award from Casa de las Américas, a Cuban government publishing house, the work was rapidly translated into several languages

and produced around the world. It was performed both in Paris and in London, where it opened on the West End and was the first Latin American play to be staged by a professional English company.

Meanwhile, as Triana's career began to flourish, a fierce debate raged in Cuba about the political duty of writers. As Terry L. Palls suggested in *Latin American Literary Review,* absurdist playwrights, with their broad statements about the pain of the human condition, failed to meet the need of Cuba's rulers for revolutionary propaganda. "Since these absurd plays did not reflect any collectively recognizable aspect of the Revolution," Palls wrote, "they were criticized by the hard line revolutionaries in Cuba and their authors were pressured to write more politically relevant works." Because "The Criminals" was "an allegory of authoritarianism," according to *New Statesman*'s Victoria Radin, Triana eventually saw his works banned and was conscripted into manual labor.

In 1980, when Castro suddenly allowed thousands of discontented Cubans to leave the country, Triana went into exile and settled in Paris. There he completed the play *Worlds Apart,* which he had begun in Cuba. "It is in some ways a bitter work," wrote Radin, "but the author's disgust is directed primarily at what he sees as the insane code of sexual honour that dishonours and deforms both men and women, but especially women." The principal characters—and victims—include Alicia, a sexually frigid woman who is nonetheless dying of a venereal disease she received from her husband, and Victoria, who passively accepts an arranged marriage and then stages a futile, passionate revolt by having an extramarital affair. Radin praised the play, which she said "display[s] a . . . sense of the appalling ties that bind families together and those individual disappointments and egotisms that render them alien and cruel."

"Originally an advocate of Castro's revolution," Radin reported, Triana "still calls himself a socialist."

BIOGRAPHICAL/CRITICAL SOURCES:

BOOKS

Lyday, Leon F. and George W. Woodyard, editors, *Dramatists in Revolt: The New Latin American Theater,* University of Texas Press, 1976.
McMurray, George R., *Spanish American Writing Since 1941: A Critical Survey,* Ungar, 1987.
Woodyard, George, editor, *The Modern Stage in Latin America: Six Plays,* Dutton, 1971.

PERIODICALS

Books Abroad, winter, 1967.
Latin American Literary Review, Volume 4, number 7, 1975.
Latin American Theatre Review, fall, 1976, fall, 1977, spring, 1980.
Modern Drama, September, 1966, March, 1973.
New Statesman, May 15, 1987.

—*Sketch by Thomas Kozikowski*

*   *   *

TRISTAN
See GOMEZ de la SERNA, Ramón

U

ULIBARRI, Sabine R(eyes)   1919-

PERSONAL: Born September 21, 1919, in Santa Fe, N.M.; married Connie Limón, 1942; one child. *Education:* University of New Mexico, B.A., 1947, M.A., 1949; University of California, Los Angeles, Ph.D., 1959.

ADDRESSES: Office—Department of Modern and Classical Languages, University of New Mexico, Albuquerque, N.M. 87131.

CAREER. Writer and educator. Teacher in Río Arriba County, N.M., schools, 1938-40; El Rito Normal School, El Rito, N.M., teacher, 1940-42; University of New Mexico, Albuquerque, associate professor, 1947-68, professor of Spanish, 1968—, chairman of modern and classical languages department, 1971-80. Consultant, D.C. Heath-Louis de Rochemont project for teaching Spanish on television, 1962; directed National Defense Education Act (NDEA) Language Institute, Quito, Ecuador, 1963-64; director of University of New Mexico Andean Study Center, Quito, 1968. *Military service:* U.S. Air Force, 1942-45; flew thirty-five combat missions as a gunner; received Distinguished Flying Cross and Air Medal four times.

MEMBER: Modern Language Association of America, American Association of Teachers of Spanish and Portuguese (vice president, 1968; president, 1969), Rocky Mountain Modern Language Association.

AWARDS, HONORS: Named distinguished citizen of Quito, Ecuador, 1964; member of Academia Norteamericana de la Lengua Española, 1978; Governor's Award for Excellence in Literature, 1988; Distinguished Alumni Award and Regents' Medal of Merit, University of New Mexico, 1989; Hispanic Heritage Award, 1989.

WRITINGS:

Spanish for the First Grade, Department of Modern and Classical Languages and College of Education, University of New Mexico, 1957.

El mundo poético de Juan Ramón; estudio estilístico de la lengua poética y de los símbolos. Edhigar (Madrid, Spain), 1962.

Fun Learning Elementary Spanish, [Albuquerque], Volume I, 1963, Volume II, 1965.

Tierra Amarilla: Cuentos de Núevo México, Casa de Cultura (Quito, Ecuador), 1964, English translation by Thelma Campbell Nason, with illustrations by Kercheville, published as *Tierra Amarilla: Stories of New Mexico,* University of New Mexico Press, 1971.

Al cielo se sube a pie (poetry), Alfaguara (Madrid), 1966.

Amor y Ecuador (poetry), Jose Porrua Turanzas (Madrid), 1966.

(Compiler, editor, translator, author of introduction, and contributor) *La fragua sin fuego/No Fire for the Forge* (stories and poems; parallel text in English and Spanish), translation by Flora V. Orozco and others, San Marcos Press (Cerrillos, N.M.), 1971.

El alma de la raza, University of New Mexico Minority Group Cultural Awareness Center, 1971.

Mi abuela fumaba puros y otros cuentos de Tierra Amarilla/My Grandma Smoked Cigars and Other Stories of Tierra Amarilla (parallel text in English and Spanish), illustrations by Dennis Martínez, Quinto Sol Publications (Berkeley), 1977.

Primeros encuentros/First Encounters (parallel text in English and Spanish), Editorial Bilingüe/Bilingual Press (Ypsilanti, Mich.), 1982.

El gobernador Glu Glu, Editorial Bilingüe/Bilingual Press, 1988.

El Cóndor, and Other Stories (parallel text in English and Spanish), Arte Publico Press (Houston, Tex.), 1989.

SIDELIGHTS: Author and scholar Sabine R. Ulibarrí is an important figure in Chicano literature, notes Charles M. Tatum in his essay in *Chicano Literature: A Reference Guide.* "His poetry is filled with color, finely rendered images, and language carefully selected and appropriate to the content," says Tatum, adding that Ulibarrí's prose is "a kind of intrahistory, a chronicling and recording of the values, sentiments, relationships, and texture of the daily lives of his friends and family." Ulibarrí has documented his native New Mexico in several collections of short stories. In *My Grandma Smoked Cigars and Other Stories of Tierra Amarilla,* for instance, "Ulibarrí presents a tapestry of childhood memories of life among the hardy and proud *hispanos* of Tierra Amarilla," writes Tatum in *World Literature Today.* Drawing upon local legends, traditions, and superstitions for these stories, Ulibarrí "combines them with vivid details from his childhood to create a rich mixture of fact and fiction." As Tatum remarks in *Chicano Literature,* "Ulibarrí believes that . . . historians do not understand at a deep level the Hispanic heritage that predates by hundreds of years the arrival of the Anglo soldier and businessman in the mid-nineteenth century. He recognizes that the Hispanic world that he knew as a child is fast disappearing under the attack of the aggressive Anglo culture."

BIOGRAPHICAL/CRITICAL SOURCES:

BOOKS

Lomelí, Francisco A. and Donald W. Urioste, *Chicano Perspectives in Literature: A Critical and Annotated Bibliography,* Pajarito Publications (Albuquerque), 1976.

Martinez, Julio A. and Francisco A. Lomelí, editors, *Chicano Literature: A Reference Guide,* Greenwood Press, 1985.

Meier, Matt S., *Mexican American Biographies: A Historical Dictionary, 1836-1987,* Greenwood Press, 1988.

PERIODICALS

English Journal, November, 1982.
Southwestern American Literature, spring, 1972.
World Literature Today, summer, 1978.

*   *   *

UMPIERRE (HERRERA), Luz María   1947-
(Luzma)

PERSONAL: Born October 15, 1947, in Santurce, P.R.; daughter of Eduardo (an executive with the motor vehicle department of Puerto Rico) and Providencia (a telephone operator for Chase Manhattan Bank; maiden name, Herrera) Umpierre. *Education:* Universidad del Sagrado Corazón, B.A., 1970; Bryn Mawr College, M.A., 1976, Ph.D., 1978; postdoctoral studies at University of Kansas, 1981-82.

ADDRESSES: Home—1225 College St., Apt. B-206, Bowling Green, Ky. 42101. *Office*—Modern Language and Intercultural Studies, Western Kentucky University, Bowling Green, Ky. 42101.

CAREER: Academia María Reina, Río Piedras, P.R., instructor in Spanish and head of Spanish department, 1971-74; Haverford College, Haverford, Pa., instructor in Spanish, 1975-76; Rutgers, the State University of New Jersey, New Brunswick, N.J., assistant professor, 1978-84, associate professor, department of Spanish and Portuguese, 1984-89; Western Kentucky University, Bowling Green, professor and chair, Modern Languages and Intercultural Studies, 1989—. Director of Spanish House, Bryn Mawr College, 1974-77. Visiting lecturer, Immaculata College, 1978—. Guest writer at several colleges and universities in the United States; lecturer and/or chair at numerous Latin American and women's literature conferences in the United States. Conducts poetry readings. Consultant to National Endowment for the Humanities. Secretary for New Jersey Voters for Civil Liberties. Speaker at March on Washington for Gay and Lesbian Rights; has made guest appearances on radio programs.

MEMBER: Modern Language Association (Ethnic Studies representative, Delegate Assembly, 1985-87), American Association of Teachers of Spanish and Portuguese, Feministas Unidas, National Organization of Women, Phi Sigma Iota.

AWARDS, HONORS: First prize for essay, Chase Manhattan Bank, 1976; first prize for poetry, International Publications, 1977; National Research Council/Ford Foundation fellowship, 1981-82; grants from Rutgers University, 1981, 1985, and 1986.

WRITINGS:

Una puertorriqueña en Penna, Masters (San Juan), 1979.
En el país de las maravillas, Third Woman Press (Indiana University), 1982.
Nuevas aproximaciones críticas a la literatura puertorriqueña contemporánea, Cultural (Puerto Rico), 1983.
Ideología y novela en Puerto Rico, Playor (Spain), 1983.

. . . Y otras desgracias / And Other Misfortunes . . ., Third Woman Press, 1985.
The Margarita Poems, Third Woman Press, 1987.
(Contributor) Elizabeth and Timothy Rogers, editors, *In Retrospect: Essays on Latin American Literature,* Spanish Literature Publications, 1987.

Poems represented in anthologies. Translator, with Nancy Gray Díaz, of Rosario Ferré's "Opprobium." Contributor to *Bibliographical Dictionary of Hispanic Literature in the United States* and *Encyclopedia of World Literature—20th Century.* Contributor of articles and reviews to numerous journals and other periodicals in the United States and Latin America, including *Revista Chicano-Riqueña, Gay Studies Newsletter, Plural, Latin American Theatre Review, Hispanic Journal, Revista de Estudios Hispánicos, Sojourner, Hispania, Third Woman,* and *Bilingual Review-Revista Bilingüe;* contributor of poems to journals and newspapers, including *El Mundo.* Associate editor, Third Woman Press, 1982—; reader and consultant, *Latin American Theater Review,* 1983—, *Revista Chicano-Riqueña,* 1984—, and *National Women Studies Association Journal,* 1987.

WORK IN PROGRESS: A book of essays on lesbian and gay writing; a book of poems on "women that have had an impact on me but who have died"; research on gay and lesbian literature.

SIDELIGHTS: Luz María Umpierre told *HW:* "Most of my writings rise from my condition as a Lesbian and Puerto Rican woman in the United States. My poetry books deal with the alienation I have felt in the U.S.A. I also want the literature of my country, Puerto Rico, to be better known and to this effect I have devoted many of my research pieces to it. I am also interested in women writers and have made a serious commitment to myself since 1982 to write mostly on women."

BIOGRAPHICAL/CRITICAL SOURCES:

BOOKS

Marting, Diane, editor, *Women Writers of Spanish America,* Greenwood Press, 1987.

OTHER

"Puerto Rican Writers in the U.S.A." (film), produced by Zydnia Nazario, 1988.

*   *   *

UNAMUNO (y JUGO), Miguel de   1864-1936

PERSONAL: Born September 29, 1864, in Bilbao, Spain; died December 31, 1936, in Salamanca, Spain; married Concepción Lizárraga Ecénarro, 1891; children: ten. *Education:* Attended Colegio de San Nicolás and Instituto Vizacaíno, Bilbao, Spain; University of Madrid, Ph.D., 1884.

CAREER: Educator, poet, novelist, and playwright. University of Salamanca, Salamanca, Spain, professor of Greek, 1891-1924, 1930-34, and rector, 1901-1914, 1934-36; exiled to Canary Islands, 1924, and lived and wrote in France, 1924-30; placed under house arrest for criticism of Franco government, 1936. Cortes (Spanish parliament) deputy from Salamanca; president, Council for Public Education. Taylor lecturer, Oxford University.

AWARDS, HONORS: Cross of the Order of Alfonso XII, 1905; honorary doctorate, University of Grenoble, 1934.

WRITINGS:

FICTION

Paz en la guerra, F. Fe, 1897, translation by Allen Lacy and Martin Nozick with Anthony Kerrigan published as *Peace in War* (Volume 1 of "Selected Works"), edited by Kerrigan, Princeton University Press, 1983.
Amor y pedogogía, 1902, Espasa-Calpe, 1934.
El espejo de la muerte (also see below), 1913, Compañía Iberoamericana de Publicaciones, 1930.
Niebla, 1914, Renacimiento, 1928, translation by Warner Fite published as *Mist,* Knopf, 1928.
Abel Sánchez: Una historia de pasión, Renacimiento, 1917, translation published as *Abel Sanchez,* edited by Angel del Río and Amelia de del Río, Holt, 1947.
Tres novelas ejemplares y un prólogo, Espasa-Calpe, 1920, translation by Angel Flores published as *Three Exemplary Novels and a Prologue,* A. & C. Boni, 1930.
La tía Tula (also see below), Renacimiento, 1921.
San Manuel Bueno, mártir, y tres historias más (also see below), Espasa-Calpe, 1933, translation by Francisco de Segovia and Jean Pérez published in bilingual edition as *San Manuel Bueno, mártir,* Harrap, 1957.
Cuentos (stories), edited by Eleanor Krane Paucker, Minotauro, 1961.
Ver con los ojos y otros relatos novelescos (stories), Espasa-Calpe, 1973.
San Manuel Bueno, mártir [and] *La novela de don Sandalio, jugador de ajedrez* (title means "The Novel of Don Sandalio, Chessplayer"; also see below), edited with introduction and notes by C. A. Longhurst, Manchester University Press, 1984.

Also author of *Tulio Montalban y Julio Macedo,* 1920.

PLAYS

El otro, misterio en tres jornadas y un epílogo (title means "The Other"; also see below), Espasa-Calpe, 1932.
El hermano Juan; o, El mundo es teatro, Espasa-Calpe, 1934.
La esfinge (also see below), 1934, Alfil, 1960.
Soledad (also see below), Espasa-Calpe, 1957.
El pasado que vuelve, edited by Manuel García Blanco, Alfil, 1960.

Also author of *La venda* (also see below), *La princesa,* [and] *Doña Lambra,* 1913, *Fedra* (also see below), 1924, *Sombras de sueño,* 1931, *Raquel encadenada* (also see below), 1933, *La difunta,* 1959, and *Medea* (also see below).

POETRY

Poesías, J. Rojas, 1907.
Rosario de sonetos líricos, Imprenta Española, 1911.
El Cristo de Velázquez, Calpe, 1920, translation by Eleanor L. Turnbull published as *The Christ of Velazquez,* Johns Hopkins Press, 1951.
Teresa, Renacimiento, 1923.
De Fuerteventura a París (verse and prose), Excélsior, 1925.
Poems, translation by Turnbull, Johns Hopkins Press, 1952.
Cancionero: Diario poético, edited by Federico de Onís, Losada, 1953.
Cincuenta poesías inéditas (previously unpublished work), edited by García Blanco, Papeles de Son Armadans, 1958.
Poemas de los pueblos de España, selected by García Blanco, Anaya, 1961.
Poesías escogidas, selected by Guillermo de Torre, Losada, 1965.

The Last Poems of Miguel de Unamuno, translation by Edita Mas-López, Fairleigh Dickinson University Press, 1974.

Also author of *Rimas de dentro,* 1923.

ESSAYS

En torno al casticismo, F. Fe, 1902.
Vida de Don Quijote y Sancho, F. Fe, 1905, translation by Homer P. Earle published as *The Life of Don Quixote and Sancho,* Knopf, 1927.
Mi religión y otros ensayos breves, 1910, Espasa-Calpe, 1942, translation by Stuart Gross published as *Perplexities and Paradoxes,* Philosophical Library, 1945.
Soliloquios y conversaciones, 1911, Espasa-Calpe, 1942.
Del sentimiento trágico de la vida en los hombres y en los pueblos, 1913, Renacimiento, 1928, translation by J. E. Crawford Flitch published as *The Tragic Sense of Life in Men and in Peoples,* Macmillan, 1926.
La agonía del cristianismo, 1925, Renacimiento, 1931, translation by Pierre Loving published as *The Agony of Christianity,* Payson & Clark, 1928, translation by Kurt F. Reinhardt published as *The Agony of Christianity,* Ungar, 1960.
Essays and Soliloquies, translation and introduction by Flitch, Knopf, 1925.
Cómo se hace una novela (title means "How to Make a Novel"; also see below), Alba, 1927.
Dos artículos y dos discursos, Historia Nueva, 1930.
Algunas consideraciones sobre la literatura hispano-americana, Espasa-Calpe, 1947.
Visiones y comentarios, Espasa-Calpe, 1949.
España y los españoles (also see below), edited with notes by García Blanco, Aguado, 1955.
Inquietudes y meditaciones, prologue and notes by García Blanco, Aguado, 1957.
La vida literaria, Espasa-Calpe, 1967.
El gaucho Martín Fierro, Américalee, 1967.

Also author of *Tres ensayos,* 1900, and *El porvenir de España,* with Angel Ganivet, 1912 (also see below).

JOURNALISTIC PIECES

Pensamiento político, edited by Elías Díaz, Tecnos, 1965.
Desde el mirador de la guerra, edited by Louis Urrutia, Centre de Recherches Hispaniques (Paris), 1970.
Discursos y artículos, Escelicer, 1971.
En torno a las artes: Del teatro, el cine, las bellas artes, la política y las letras, Espasa-Calpe, 1976.
Escritos socialistas: Artículos inéditos sobre el socialismo, 1894-1922, edited by Pedro Ribas, Ayuso, 1976.
Artículos olvidados sobre España y la primera guerra mundial, edited by Christopher Cobb, Támesis, 1976.
Crónica política española (1915-1923), edited by Vicente González Martín, Almar, 1977.
República española y España republicana, edited by González Martín, Almar, 1979.
Unamuno: Artículos y discursos sobre Canarias, edited by Francisco Navarro Artiles, Cabildo Insular de Fuerteventura, 1980.
Ensueño de una patria: Periodismo republicano, 1931-36 (political), Pre-Textos, 1984.

LETTERS

(With Juan Maragall) *Epistolario,* Edimar, 1951, revised edition, Distribuidora Catalonia, 1976.
(With Juan Zorrilla de San Martín) *Correspondencia,* [Montevideo], 1955.

Trece cartas inéditas de Miguel de Unamuno a Alberto Nin Frías, La Mandrágora, 1962.

Cartas inéditas, compiled by Sergio Fernández Larraín, Zig-Zag, 1965.

(With Alonso Quesada) *Epistolario,* edited by Lázaro Santana, Museo Canario, 1970.

Cartas 1903-1933, compiled by Carmen de Zulueta, Aguilar, 1972.

Unamuno "agitador de espíritus" y Giner: Correspondencia inédita, edited by D. Gómez Molleda, Narcea, 1976.

(With Leopoldo Gutiérrez Abascal and Juan de la Encina) *Cartas íntimas: Epistolario entre Miguel de Unamuno y los hermanos Gutiérrez Abascal,* edited with notes by Javier González de Durana, Equzki, 1986.

(With José Ortega y Gasset) *Epistolario completo Ortega-Unamuno,* edited by Laureano Robles Carcedo with Antonio Ramos Gascón, El Arquero, 1987.

AUTOBIOGRAPHY

Recuerdos de niñez y de mocedad, V. Suárez, 1908, selected and edited by William Atkinson, Longmans, Green, 1929.

En el destierro (recuerdos y esperanzas), selected and annotated by García Blanco, Pegaso, 1957.

Mi vida y otros recuerdos personales, complied by García Blanco, Losada, 1959.

Diario íntimo (also see below), edited by P. Félix García, Escelicer, 1970.

De mi vida, Espasa-Calpe, 1979.

OMNIBUS VOLUMES IN ENGLISH

Abel Sanchez and Other Stories, translated by Kerrigan, Regnery, 1956.

Our Lord Don Quixote and Sancho with Related Essays (Volume 3 of "Selected Works"), translated and edited by Kerrigan, Princeton University Press, 1967.

The Tragic Sense of Life in Men and Nations (Volume 4 of "Selected Works"), translated and edited by Kerrigan, Princeton University Press, 1972.

The Agony of Christianity and Essays on Faith (Volume 5 of "Selected Works"), translated and edited by Kerrigan, Princeton University Press, 1974.

Novela/Nivola (Volume 6 of "Selected Works"; includes *How to Make a Novel*), translated and edited by Kerrigan, Princeton University Press, 1976.

Ficciones: Four Stories and a Play (Volume 7 of "Selected Works"; includes *The Other, Tía Tula,* and *The Novel of Don Sandalio, Chessplayer*), translated and edited by Kerrigan, Princeton University Press, 1976.

The Private World: Selections from the Diario Intimo and Selected Letters (Volume 2 of "Selected Works"), translated by Kerrigan, Lacy, and Nozick, edited by Kerrigan, Princeton University Press, 1984.

ANTHOLOGIES AND OMNIBUS VOLUMES IN SPANISH

Ensayos (essays), seven volumes, Fortanet, 1916-18, revised edition, two volumes, Aguilar, 1942.

Ensayos y sentencias de Unamuno, edited with introduction and notes by Wilfred A. Beardsley, Macmillan, 1932.

Prosa diversa, selected by J. L. Gili, Oxford University Press, 1939.

Antología poética (poetry), edited by Luis Felipe Vivanco, Escorial, 1942.

Antología poética (poetry), edited by José María de Cossio, Espasa-Calpe, 1946.

Obras selectas (selected works), Pléyade, 1946.

De esto y de aquello, edited by García Blanco, Sudamericana, 1950.

Obras completas (collected works), Aguado, 1950-51.

Teatro: Fedra. Soledad. Raquel encadenada. Medea. (plays), edited by García Blanco, Juventud, 1954.

Obras completas (collected works), ten volumes, edited by García Blanco, Aguado, 1958-61.

Teatro completo, edited by García Blanco, Aguilar, 1959.

Antología, edited by Luis Gonzalez Seara, Doncel, 1960.

Antología, Fondo de Cultura Económica, 1964.

El espejo de la muerte, y otros relatos novelescos, Juventud, 1965.

Cancionero: Antología (poetry), selected by Ramos Gascón, Taurus, 1966.

Unamuno: Sus mejores páginas, edited by Philip Metzidakis, Prentice-Hall, 1966.

Obras completas, Las Américas, Volume 1: *Paisajes y ensayos,* Volume 2: *Novelas,* Volume 3: *Nuevos ensayos,* Volume 4: *La raza y la lengua,* Volume 5: *Teatro completo y monodiálogos,* Volume 6: *Poesía,* Volume 7: *Meditaciones y ensayos espirituales,* 1966-69.

La agonía del cristianismo, Mi religión, y otros ensayos (collected essays), Las Américas, 1967.

Tres nivolas de Unamuno (novels), edited by Demetrios Basdekis, Prentice-Hall, 1971.

El porvenir de España y los españoles (contains *El porvenir de España* and *España y los españoles*), Espasa-Calpe, 1972.

Novela (novels), edited by Eugenio de Bustos Tovar, Noguer, 1976.

Antología poética (poetry), edited by José Maria Valverde, Alianza, 1977.

Antología poética (poetry), edited by Mercedes Santos Moray, Editorial Arte y Literatura, 1979.

Jubilación de don Miguel de Unamuno: Cuaderno de la Magdalena y otros papeles (papers), Librería Estudio, 1980.

Unamuno múltiple: Antología, edited by Amelia de del Río, University of Puerto Rico, 1981.

La esfinge; La venda; Fedra (plays), edited by José Paulino, Castalia, 1987.

Poesía completa, Alianza, 1987—.

Works also published in multiple editions.

OTHER

Paisajes (travel), 1902, Aguado, 1950.

De mi país (travel), F. Fe, 1903.

Por tierras de Portugal y de España (travel), V. Prieto, 1911.

Contra esto y aquello, Renacimiento, 1912.

(Editor) *Simón Bolívar, libertador de la América del Sur, por los más grandes escritores americanos,* Renacimiento, 1914, reprinted with prologue by Manuel Trujillo as *Bolívar,* Biblioteca Ayacucho, 1983.

Andanzas y visiones españolas (travel), Renacimiento, 1922.

Romancero del destierro, Alba, 1928.

La ciudad de Henoc: Comentario 1933, Séneca, 1941.

Cuenca ibérica (lenguaje y paisaje), Séneca, 1943.

El caballero de la triste figura, Espasa-Calpe, 1944.

Almas de jóvenes, Espasa-Calpe, 1944.

La dignidad humana, Espasa-Calpe, 1944.

Paisajes del alma, Revista de Occidente, 1944.

La enormidad de España, Séneca, 1945.

Madrid, Aguado, 1950.

Mi Salamanca, selected by Mario Grande Ramos, Escuelas Gráficas de la Santa Casa de Misericordia, 1950.

(With Rubén Darío) *Don José Lázaro, 1862-1947,* edited by Antonio R. Rodríguez Moñino, Castalia, 1951.

Viejos y jóvenes, Espasa-Calpe, 1956.

Autodiálogos, Aguilar, 1959.

Escritos de toros, Unión de Bibliofilos Taurinos, 1964.

Mi bochito, selected by García Blanco, Librería Arturo, 1965.

La raza vasca y el vascuence: En torno a la lengua española, Espasa-Calpe, 1968.

(Translator) Arthur Schopenhauer, *Sobre la voluntad en la naturaleza,* Alianza, 1970.

Solitaña (bilingual edition), edited by Pablo Bilbao and Emilia Doyaga, Washington Irving, 1970.

Libros y autores españoles contemporáneos, Espasa-Calpe, 1972.

Monodiálogos, Espasa-Calpe, 1972.

Gramática y glosario del Poema del Cid, edited by Barbara D. Huntley and Pilar Liria, Espasa-Calpe, 1977.

La muerte de Ramírez y las olvidadas memorias del general Anacleto Medina, A. Peña Lillo, 1980.

Also translator of *Etica de las prisiones, Exceso de legislación, De las leyes en general,* by Herbert Spencer, three volumes, 1895, *His-toria de la económica política,* by J. K. Ingram, c. 1895, and *Historia de las literaturas castellana y portuguesa,* by Ferdinand J. Wolf, two volumes, 1895-96.

SIDELIGHTS: "At his death in 1936," Arthur A. Cohen claimed in the *New York Times Book Review,* "Miguel de Unamuno was the most influential thinker in Spain, more renowned than his younger contemporary [José] Ortega y Gasset and regarded by his own aficionados as the greatest stylist in the Spanish language since Cervantes." Author of fiction, drama, poetry, philosophical essays, and a variety of nonfiction, Unamuno "dug deeper into the national spirit than any of his contemporaries, a generation whose collective project was the exploration of Spanishness," Enrique Fernández proposed in the *Voice Literary Supplement.* "Quixote incarnate, he lived out his nationality to its logical philosophical conclusions. . . . The soul-searching of the first Spanish moderns, who would be called the generation of 1898, found its fullest expression in Unamuno. In poems, plays, novels, and essays," the critic continued, Unamuno questioned "Spanishness, modernity, science, politics, philosophy, faith, God, everything."

The foremost questions for Unamuno were often existential, exploring issues of death, mortality, and faith. "Written all over [Unamuno] are the passions and yearnings of a sincere religious searcher," Paul Ilie commented in *Unamuno: An Existential View of Self and Society.* "[He] is, at the same time, clouded by the doubts and anguish of a rational mind too sophisticated for the simple faith of ordinary men." These religious doubts led to several turbulent spiritual crises, from which Unamuno "developed the dominant convictions of his later life," as Howard T. Young described in *The Victorious Expression: A Study of Four Contemporary Spanish Poets:* "to struggle for the sake of struggle, to believe in the need to believe, even if he himself could not believe. His paradoxes symbolize a lasting insecurity." Indeed, as Frances Wyers noted in *Miguel de Unamuno: The Contrary Self,* Unamuno's work was marked by paradox, "a persistent contrariness, an almost desperate need to set up oppositions and then collapse them into a single entity, to take sides and then switch, to deny and then deny the denial or to assert that what was denied was really affirmed. . . . Unamuno's paradoxes are the result of an unexamined, almost frantic, effort to tie together opposing aspirations."

In searching for resolutions to his doubts, Unamuno brought a profound passion to his writing, an intensity which informs all his work. "On whatever page we open one of his writings we find an identical atmosphere, a permanent and invariable note, forced into use with equal passion . . . throughout all of his volumes and all of his life," Julián Marías stated in his study *Miguel de Unamuno.* This repetition of atmosphere and theme reflected the author's foremost concern: "Man in his entirety, man who goes from his birth to his death, with his flesh, his life, his personality, and above all his desire never to die completely," as Marías defined it. "It is living, suffering man who interests Unamuno, not the abstraction humanity," A. Dobson said in a *Modern Languages* essay. "What makes man authentically human is his fear of death, and for Unamuno, the preservation of the individual's personality is his supreme task."

"The evolution of [Unamuno's] thought was marked by three books or great essays, more professions of faith than philosophical treatises:" *The Life of Don Quixote and Sancho, The Tragic Sense of Life in Men and Peoples,* and *The Agony of Christianity,* as Arturo and Ilsa Barea catalogued in their book *Unamuno.* In these works, Unamuno fought what *Nation* contributor Mark Van Doren referred to as "the windmills of despair," an emotion inspired by his knowledge of his own mortality. Nevertheless, the critic added, "Unamuno fights because he knows there is not a chance in the world to win. He has tasted the glory of absurdity. He has decided to hope what he cannot believe. He has discovered grounds for faith in the very fact that there are no grounds." Thus it was this "continuous struggle with death," according to Cohen, that for Unamuno "makes [life] worth living. . . . Any means by which a man subverts the kingdom of death is a triumph for life and, in Unamuno's clever logic, for eternity."

This conflict between faith and reason, between "the truth thought and the truth felt," Salvador de Madariaga remarked in *The Genius of Spain,* became the primary focus of Unamuno's meditations. "It is because *The Tragic Sense of Life* is the most direct expression of [Unamuno's conflict] that this book is his masterpiece." In this essay, Angel and Amelia de del Río recounted in the introduction to *Abel Sanchez,* "Unamuno analyzes what he calls the tragic essence of modern civilization, resulting from the longing for knowledge which, guided by reason, has destroyed man's faith in God and in immortality, a faith necessary for his emotional life. Hence, modern humanity, incapable of solving the problem, is forced to struggle in uncertainty, and at the same time to strive after truth, a struggle and agony inherently tragic." In a style that would characterize all Unamuno's essays, the Bareas asserted, *The Tragic Sense of Life* "was not meant as an orderly philosophical treatise on the human condition, but as one man's record of his thoughts on life and death, confessed before his fellow-mortals with all the passionate sincerity of which that man was capable." The work "is the greatest of the many monologues Unamuno wrote," the critics continued. "Every bit of reasoning in it springs from his intimate spiritual needs; nothing is 'objective.' This is as he meant it to be, and he argues at the very beginning of the book that this subjectivity is the only truthful approach possible." The result, as Van Doren described it, was "modern Catholicism's richest, most passionate, most brilliant statement of the grounds that exist for faith in immortality, now that reason and science have done their worst."

In *The Life of Don Quixote and Sancho* Unamuno brought a new approach to the literary essay. As Demetrios Basdekis summarized in his *Miguel de Unamuno,* "it is literary criticism which is not quite a critical essay; it is a novelizing of a particular novel and a theory of the novel in general; it is creative prose which is not quite prose fiction, although it sometimes borders on this." In arguing that the character of Don Quixote surpassed his creator—that Cervantes was unaware of his own work's implications—Unamuno "set forth the essential premise of all his intellectual criticism: madness is reality, and historical objectivity is madness," Cohen stated. Thus, "the chivalric vocation and undertakings of Don Quixote, continuously pragmatized by his sympathetic squire [Sancho Panza], are treated by Unamuno as the ultimate pilgrimage." "Don Quixote became in the eyes of Unamuno a prophet, a divinely inspired figure preaching the doctrine of quixotism, which is the doctrine of immortality through mundane glory, salvation through high-minded battle against the mean reality of the world," Young postulated. "Turning Cervantine irony into the tragic irony of life, Unamuno exalted Don Quixote as a stirring figure struggling against human fate." "Unamuno's *The Life of Don Quixote and Sancho*," concluded Basdekis, "is a major theoretical doctrine; in turn it is a huge step toward his 'novel of extreme situations' entitled *Mist*."

"As a novelist, Unamuno was often ahead of his time, especially in his denial of the usual boundaries between life and art," Allen Lacy maintained in a *Nation* article. Novels such as *Mist, Abel Sánchez,* and *San Manuel Bueno, mártir,* are "very fresh even in the 1960s," said Lacy, "especially for [their] improvisatory technique. His sense of the novel as a vehicle of serious play, as a comic metaphysic, has strong affinities to the best work of Jorge Luis Borges and John Barth." Proposing a new form which he called a "nívola," Unamuno attempted a spontaneous creation that would give its characters their own existence. "With the guiding principle of the nonreality of the material world in view, the *nívolas* eliminate all externals, particularly settings and character descriptions," in order to focus on individual personalities, L. Livingstone noted in *Hispania*. "The destruction of form in the *nívola* . . . gives it an other-worldliness, a timelessness and freedom from spatial dimensions, that reproduce the author's hunger for immortality."

As José Ferrater Mora explained in *Unamuno: A Philosophy of Tragedy*, the author "emphasized that the characters he depicted—or more exactly, in whose innards he poked about—were truly intimate because of what they revealed of themselves. With the 'soul of their soul' laid bare, Unamuno held, they were indistinguishable from truly existing beings." This theory is exemplified in several works, especially the last chapter of *Mist*, in which, Carlos Blanco Aguinaga related in *Modern Language Notes*, "the conventions of Fiction, and therefore of existence, are broken." Wanting to discuss the possibility of suicide, the protagonist Augusto Pérez travels to Salamanca to speak to Unamuno, whom he knows as a learned philosopher—only to learn that he is a fictional character subject to the whims of his creator and thus unable to commit suicide. Augusto returns to his home and soon dies after a strangely compulsive bout of overeating, leaving the reader to wonder whether Unamuno or Augusto willed the death. *Mist* "abounds in ingenious conceptions and paradoxes," the del Ríos observed, resting "on an idea that is eminently paradoxical, as Unamuno's ideas regularly are."

Despite his success as an essayist and novelist, Unamuno "maintained that he would be best remembered by his poetry," the Bareas reported. "His rough-tongued poems with their blend of fervour and contemplation brought indeed a new note into Spanish lyrical poetry at the turn of the century, but their poetic form was never strong enough to absorb the sentiments and thoughts that inspired them." As Young outlined, Unamuno believed that "ideas—and, consequently, feelings, for in Unamuno the two could never be separated—take precedence over all other considerations. What the poet says is more important than how he says

it; meter, rhyme, and pattern are secondary to content and emotion."

As a result, much of Unamuno's poetry tended to be prosaic and "inelegant," as Young termed it; thus, it is a "pleasant surprise" to discover "the Miltonic flow of *The Christ of Velazquez,* and the subdued sadness of his later sonnets." The former work, a book-length poem, "is Unamuno's major accomplishment in poetry," Basdekis remarked, a "blank verse hymn . . . liberally sprinkled with paraphrase and quotations from the Old and New Testaments." Inspired by seventeenth-century Spanish painter Diego Velázquez's masterpiece depicting Christ's crucifixion, Unamuno's poem reflects his usual focus by "sing[ing] in resounding tones of the Incarnation, Death, and Resurrection of Jesus, and derives from these beliefs his hope of escaping total death," Martin Nozick suggested in his study *Miguel de Unamuno*. "Free of the mesh of doctrine and philosophy, he is carried away by pure love, by a fundamental devotion to Gospel whose meanings he deepens, embroiders, and personalizes." Despite the length of the poem, Madariaga stated, it "easily maintains [a] lofty level throughout, and if he had written nothing else Unamuno would still remain as having given to Spanish letters the noblest and most sustained lyrical flight in the language. It abounds in passages of ample beauty, and often strikes a note of primitive strength in the true Old Testament style." *The Christ of Velazquez,* concluded Nozick, is "a major work of unflagging vitality and resonances, a Cantata to the Son of God on the Cross, made up of wave upon wave of Whitmanesque rhythms, or what Unamuno himself called 'a sort of rhythmoid, dense prose.' "

The intense emotions Unamuno brought to *The Christ of Velazquez* and his other works have led critics to observe a poetic sense in all his writing. "For Unamuno, a poem or novel (and he holds that a novel is but a poem) is the outpouring of a man's passion, the overflow of the heart which cannot help itself and lets go," Madariaga proposed. The Bareas similarly commented that "Unamuno's true poetic creation was the personality he projected into all his work; his 'agony,' his ceaseless struggle with himself and the universe, was the core of every one of his novels and stories, poems and essays." "His style, rather than the clear, orderly style of a philosopher, is always that of a poet, impassioned, full of images, sometimes difficult because of the abundance of allusions, paradoxes, digressions, parentheses, exclamations, and ingenious plays upon words and ideas," the del Ríos wrote. Ferrater Mora similarly declared that in analyzing Unamuno's work, "it must always be kept in mind that a poetic *élan* breathes within it, that the written word is meant to be only a shadow of the creative voice. . . . Unamuno wanted to dissolve all 'genres,' all classifications, to fuse all 'genres' together in the deathless fountain of poetry. For Unamuno the only 'literary form' was the poem, and the numerous, perhaps infinite, forms that the poem adopts."

The author's poetic emphasis and concern with human mortality have led many critics to characterize his work as distinctively Spanish. Calling Unamuno "the greatest literary figure of Spain [of his time]," Madariaga asserted that the author "is head and shoulders above [his contemporaries] in the highness of his purpose and in the earnestness and loyalty with which, Quixote-like, he has served all through his life. . . . Unamuno, by the cross which he has chosen to bear, incarnates the spirit of modern Spain," the critic continued. "His eternal conflict between faith and reason, between life and thought, between spirit and intellect, between heaven and civilization, is the conflict of Spain herself." Cohen likewise noted a unique Spanish temperament in the author's work; "the principal debate, the argument that undergirds all of Unamuno's life and thought and gives to it a power most peculiarly Spanish and most thoroughly universal . . . is Unamuno's contest with death." The critic elaborated, stating that "Spain, a culture which has stylized violence, is overwhelmed with death and committed to resurrection."

"In the last analysis, it is useless to attempt to define the subject matter, the ideas, and the substance of Unamuno's writing," the del Ríos suggested, "because his combined work, his life, and his personality, have for root and impulse a dynamic or dialectical contraction whose import Unamuno formulated again and again." The critics added that Unamuno's "metaphysical concepts of desperation, anguish, and agony . . . are, for him, the essence of the Spanish spirit, composed of dissonances, with its perpetual conflict between the ideal and reality, between heaven and earth, between its Sancho Panza-like sense of the immediate and its quixotic yearning for immortality." "[It was] for Unamuno, a figure who transcends the notion of generations and who speaks, at one and the same time, as both modern and universal man, to synthesize and spell out in his poetry, essays and, especially, in his 'nivolas' the dilemma of the individual 'of flesh and bones,' as he was found of saying, alienated both psychologically and metaphysically in the twentieth century," J. F. Tull contended in the *Humanities Association Bulletin.* "Though he ravaged all genres," Fernández remarked, "Unamuno is hard to classify as a writer—if he even *is* a writer." His fiction and poetry, "though powerful, is more philosophical than lyrical," the critic continued, and his philosophical writings "are emotional and personal" rather than logical or theoretical. "Too writerly to be a philosopher, too philosophical to be an artist," Fernández concluded, "Unamuno is, as he deserves to be, a category unto himself."

MEDIA ADAPTATIONS. Julio de Hoyos adapted one of the novellas from *Tres novelas ejemplares. Nada menos que todo un hombre,* into a drama titled "Todo un hombre."

BIOGRAPHICAL/CRITICAL SOURCES:

BOOKS

Barea, Arturo and Ilsa Barea, *Unamuno,* translated by I. Barea, Bowes & Bowes, 1952.

Basdekis, Demetrios, *Unamuno and Spanish Literature,* University of California Press, 1967.

Basdekis, Demetrios, *Miguel de Unamuno,* Columbia University Press, 1969.

Bleiberg, Hermán and E. Inman Fox, editors, *Spanish Thought and Letters in the Twentieth Century: Miguel de Unamuno: 1864-1964,* Vanderbilt University Press, 1966.

Ferrater Mora, José, *Unamuno: A Philosophy of Tragedy,* translated by Philip Silver, University of California Press, 1962.

Ilie, Paul, *Unamuno: An Existential View of Self and Society,* University of Wisconsin Press, 1967.

Lacy, Allen, *Miguel de Unamuno: The Rhetoric of Existence,* Mouton & Co., 1967.

López, Julio, *Unamuno,* Júcar, 1985.

Madariaga, Salvador de, *The Genius of Spain, and Other Essays on Spanish Contemporary Literature,* Oxford University Press, 1923.

Marías, Julián, *Miguel de Unamuno,* translated by Frances M. Lopez-Morillas, Harvard University Press, 1966.

Nozick, Martin, *Miguel de Unamuno,* Twayne, 1971.

Rubia Barcia, José, and M. A. Zeitlin, editors, *Unamuno: Creator and Creation,* University of California Press, 1967.

Rudd, Margaret Thomas, *The Lone Heretic: A Biography of Miguel de Unamuno y Jugo,* University of Texas Press, 1963.

Twentieth-Century Literary Criticism, Gale, Volume 2, 1979, Volume 9, 1983.

Unamuno, Miguel de, *Abel Sanchez,* edited by Angel del Río and Amelia de del Río, Holt, 1947.

Wyers, Frances, *Miguel de Unamuno: The Contrary Self,* Támesis, 1976.

Young, Howard T., *The Victorious Expression: A Study of Four Contemporary Spanish Poets,* University of Wisconsin Press, 1964.

PERIODICALS

Hispania, December, 1941.

Humanities Association Bulletin, winter, 1970.

Modern Language Notes, Volume 79, number 2, 1964.

Modern Languages, June, 1973.

Nation, May 17, 1922, June 24, 1968.

New York Times Book Review, December 16, 1973.

Voice Literary Supplement, May, 1987.

—*Sketch by Diane Telgen*

* * *

UNGER, David 1950-

PERSONAL: Born November 6, 1950, in Guatemala City, Guatemala; immigrated to United States; son of Luis (a restaurant worker) and Fortuna (a secretary; maiden name, Yarhi) Unger; married Esti Dunow (an artist), May 15, 1977; children: Mia, Zoe. *Education:* Attended Boston University, 1968-71; University of Massachusetts, B.A., 1973; Columbia University, M.F.A., 1975.

ADDRESSES: Home—209 West 86th St., No. 801, New York, N.Y. 10024. *Office*—Division of Humanities, NAC 6293, City College of New York, New York, N.Y. 10031. *Agent*—Susan Bergholz, 340 West 72nd St., New York, N.Y. 10023.

CAREER: Columbia University, Translation Center, New York City, publicist for Latin American Writer Exchange Program, 1978-79; high school English teacher at Walden School, 1979-82; Teachers and Writers Collaborative, New York City, writer in residence at various schools, 1983-87; co-director, Latin American Book Fair, 1983—; Latin American Writers Institute, New York City, co-director, 1987—. Adjunct faculty, College of New Rochelle, School of New Resources, 1978-87; guest translator, Columbia University, 1979—; instructor in Spanish and Portuguese Department, University of Massachusetts, summers, 1984-85; teacher of graduate seminar, New York University, 1988.

AWARDS, HONORS: Pushcart Prize Citation, 1978; translation grants from Translation Center, 1978, and New York State Council on the Arts, 1981 and 1983; Spanish Government Tourist Board Award for *Spain: An Insight Guide,* 1989.

WRITINGS:

(Translator with Jonathan Cohen and John Felstiner) Enrique Lihn, *The Dark Room and Other Poems,* New Directions, 1978.

(Contributor of translations) *A Longing for the Light,* Harper, 1979.

(Contributor) *Echad: An Anthology of Latin American Jewish Writers,* Micah Publications, 1980.

(Translator with Lewis Hyde) Vicente Aleixandre, *World Alone,* Penmaen Press, 1981.

(Translator with the author) Isaac Goldemberg, *Just Passing Through,* Point of Contact/Ediciones del Norte, 1981.

(Editor and co-translator) Nicanor Parra, *Antipoems: New and Selected,* New Directions, 1985.

(Contributor) *Anthology of Contemporary Latin American Literature,* Fairleigh Dickinson University Press, 1986.

Neither Caterpillar nor Butterfly (poetry), Es Que Somos Muy Pobres Press (New York), 1986.

(Contributor) *Spain: An Insight Guide,* APA Productions, 1987.

Contributor of poetry, articles, translations, and reviews to periodicals, including *New York Times Book Review.*

WORK IN PROGRESS: No Way of Life, a novel scheduled for completion in December, 1990.

SIDELIGHTS: David Unger told *HW:* "Critics have pointed out the dual nature of my writing: Latin American in subject matter/content, and North American in style and structure. The fact that I came to the United States at a young age and write in English may have much to do with this. Still, I would say that my literary preference runs toward Latin American poetry: the work of Peruvian César Vallejo and Chileans Pablo Neruda and Nicanor Parra."

* * *

URISTA, Alberto H. 1947-
(Alurista)

PERSONAL: Born August 8, 1947, in Mexico City, Mexico; immigrated to the United States, 1961; son of Balthazar and Ruth (Heredia) Urista; married Irene Mercado, August 8, 1969 (divorced, 1976); married Xelina Rojas, June 16, 1977; children: (first marriage) Tizoc, Maoxiim; (second marriage) Zamna, Zahi. *Education:* San Diego State University, B.A., 1970, M.A., 1978; University of California, San Diego, Ph.D. (Spanish literature), 1983.

ADDRESSES: Office—Department of Foreign Languages, California Polytechnic State University, San Luis Obispo, Calif. 93407.

CAREER: Friendly Center, Orange, Calif., counsellor, 1963-67; San Diego Children's Home, San Diego, Calif., psychiatric childcare worker, 1967-68; San Diego State University, San Diego, lecturer in Chicano studies, 1968-74, 1976-83, executive director of Chicano Studies Center, 1971-73; University of Texas at Austin, lecturer in Chicano studies, 1974-76; Colorado College, Colorado Springs, assistant professor, beginning 1983; currently a staff member of the foreign language department, California State Polytechnic College, San Luis Obispo. Instructor in psychology, Southwestern Junior College, 1973-74; distinguished visiting lecturer, University of Nebraska, 1979; has lectured and given poetry recitals at numerous colleges and universities and on radio and television programs. San Diego State University, co-founder of MECHA (Movimiento Estudiantil Chicano de Aztlán), 1967, of Chicano studies department, 1968, and of Chicano Studies Center, 1969; co-founder, Centro Cultural de la Raza, 1971. Coordinator and instructor, Volunteers in Service to America (VISTA), San Diego, summer, 1970; teacher corps instructor, San Diego, 1971-72. Member of board of directors and president, Intercultural Council of the Arts, 1978—; member of board of directors, Community Video, 1979—; member of board of directors and executive committee, Combined Arts and Educational Council of San Diego County, 1980. Organizer of Festival Floricanto, an annual literary event.

MEMBER: International Academy of Poets, National Association of Chicano Studies, Association of Mexican-American Educators, Movimiento Estudiantil Chicano de Aztlán, Toltecas en Aztlán.

AWARDS, HONORS: Ford Foundation fellowship, 1976; California Art Council creative writing award, 1978; McArthur Chair of Spanish, McArthur Foundation, 1984.

WRITINGS:

ALL UNDER PSEUDONYM ALURISTA

Floricanto en Aztlán (poems; title means "Flower-song in Aztlán"), Chicano Studies Center, University of California, Los Angeles, 1971, 2nd edition, 1976.

Nationchild Plumaroja, 1969-1972 (poems; title means "Nationchild Redfeather"), Centro Cultural de la Raza, 1972.

Colección Tula y Tonán: Textos generativos (juvenile), nine volumes, Centro Cultural de la Raza, 1973.

Timespace Huracán: Poems, 1972-1975, Pajarito Publications, 1976.

A'nque/Alurista: Acuarelas hechas por Delilah Merriman-Montoya (poems; title means "Even Though/Alurista: Watercolors Done by Delilah Merriman-Montoya"), Maize, 1979.

Spik in Glyph? (poems), Arte Público Press, 1981.

Return: Poems Collected and New, Bilingual Press/Editorial Bilingüe, 1982.

Tremble Purple: Seven Poems, Getting Together, 1986.

EDITOR

(And contributor) *El Ombligo en Aztlán: An Anthology of Chicano Student Poetry,* Chicano Studies Center, San Diego State University, 1971.

Alex Kiraca, *Space Flute and Barrio Paths,* Chicano Studies Center, San Diego State University, 1972.

Gloriamalia Flores, *And Her Children Lived,* Centro Cultural de la Raza, 1974.

Juanfelipe Herrera, *Rebozos of Love,* Centro Cultural de la Raza, 1974.

Lin Romero, *Happy Songs and Bleeding Hearts,* Centro Cultural de la Raza, 1974.

Ricardo Teall, *No Flights Out Tonight,* Pajarito Publications, 1975.

Carmen Tafolla, Cecilio García-Camarillo, and Reyes Cárdenas, *Get Your Tortillas Together,* Caracol Publications, 1976.

(And contributor) *Festival Flor y Canto I: An Anthology of Chicano Literature,* University of Southern California Press, 1976.

(And contributor) *Festival Flor y Canto II: An Anthology of Chicano Literature,* Center for Mexican-American Studies, University of Texas at Austin, 1979.

Herberto Espinoza, *Viendo morir a Teresa y otros relatos,* Maize, 1983.

(With wife, Xelina Rojas-Urista) L. J. Griep-Ruiz, *Daily in All the Small,* Maize, 1984.

(With Rojas-Urista) Gary D. Keller, *Tales of El Huitlacoche,* Maize, 1984.

(With Rojas-Urista) Ricardo Cobián, *Para todos los panes no están todos presentes,* Maize, 1985.

(With Rojas-Urista) *Southwest Tales: A Contemporary Collection,* Maize, 1986.

CONTRIBUTOR

Octavio Ignacio Romano-V. and Herminio Ríos C., editors, *El Espejo,* Quinto Sol, 1969.

Castaneda-Shular, Tomás Ybarra-Frausto, and Joseph Sommers, editors, *Literatura Chicana: Texto y Contexto,* Prentice-Hall, 1972.

Stan Steiner and Luis Váldez, editors, *Aztlán: An Anthology of Mexican-American Literature,* Vintage, 1972.

Walter Lowenfals, editor, *From the Belly of the Shark,* Vintage, 1973.

Romano-V. and Rios C., editors, *Chicano Drama,* El Grito Books, 1974.

Lewis M. Baldwin and Dorothy Harth, editors, *Voices of Aztlán: Chicano Literature of Today,* Mentor Books, 1974.

Cárdenas, editor, *Chicano Voices,* Houghton, 1975.

Roberto Garza, editor, *Contemporary Chicano Theater,* University of Notre Dame Press, 1975.

Syquia Mirikitani and others, editors, *Time to Greez,* Glide Urban Center Publications, 1975.

Ishmael Reed, editor, *Calafia: The Calfornia Poetry,* Y'Bird Books, 1979.

OTHER

Author of play, "Dawn," published in the periodical *Grito,* 1974. Contributor to numerous periodicals, including *La Raza, Revista Chicano-Riqueña, El Gallo, Aztlán* and *Hispamerica.* Co-editor and founder, *Maize.*

SIDELIGHTS: Alberto H. Urista, who is best known by his pen name, Alurista, is "considered by many to be the poet laureate of Chicano letters," according to *Dictionary of Literary Biography* contributor Judith Ginsberg. Since his writings were first published in the late 1960s, Alurista has made a number of significant contributions toward making Chicano poetry a vital part of contemporary literature. He is "one of the first to succeed in the creation of interlingual texts," writes Ginsberg, who also adds that "Alurista was perhaps the first to establish the concept of Aztlán at the level of literature and formal ideology as a cultural, political, geographical, and mythical symbol of the aspirations of the Chicano people." Alurista asserts and promotes the value of his people not only through his literature, but also as a teacher and active member of organizations that champion ethnic awareness. He is a co-founder of the Chicano Student Movement of Aztlán (MECHA), the founder and co-editor with his wife Xelina of the Chicano literary magazine *Maize,* the co-founder of the Chicano studies department at San Diego State University, and the chief organizer of the annual literary event, Festival Floricanto. Both as a writer and as an activist, Alurista has accomplished much for Chicanos in the United States.

An immigrant from Mexico, Alurista arrived in San Diego, Calif., during the 1960s when Chicano activism was beginning to reach its peak. The young Alurista was particularly inspired at the time by the farmworkers' strike led by César Chávez. "It was the farmworkers who brought Chicanos to the forefront of national consciousness," the poet tells Tomás Ybarra-Frausto in *Modern Chicano Writers: A Collection of Critical Essays.* "As I watched the pilgrimage from Delano, I said to myself, that man Chávez is either a fool, a fanatic or a truly wise man. And very soon his genius was apparent." In *Chicano Authors: Inquiry by Interview* Alurista relates to Juan Bruce-Novoa in both Spanish and English (the Spanish has been translated and italicized) that after seeing Chávez, "I made my decision about using my writing skills, my *literature, as a means of communication.* I'm convinced that my *poetry reflects,* or at least I try deliberately to reflect the experience of our people."

Conversant with all the world's major religions and interested in existential philosophy, Alurista is extremely well-read. He can speak fluent Spanish and English (as well as their Chicano and Black dialects), and is familiar with Mayan and the Náhuatl language of the Aztecs. But despite his thorough education, Alurista complains to Bruce-Novoa: "Formal education has attempted, if you will, to hinder my education. Schooling is where you are trained to follow directions, and as a poet, as a writer, as a creative person that is the last thing I wanted."

In keeping with this independent attitude, the poet refused his first editor's request that he write in only one language. An important part of Chicano literature, contends Alurista, is the vitality and diversity of its language use. By employing various forms of Spanish, English, and ancient Amerindian languages in their writing, Alurista attests to Bruce-Novoa that Chicano writers like himself show "our versatility and multidimensional view of the world. That makes us stronger, a broadly based, more universal people. And as writers, that puts us in a completely different category in the history of world literature."

Alurista's first poetry collection, *Floricanto en Aztlán,* ("Flowersong in Aztlán"), is also his best-known and most influential work. The concept of Aztlán that is central to the book refers to the Náhuatl myth of a lost paradise—once the homeland of the Aztecs—located in what is now the southwestern part of the United States. Thus, *Floricanto en Aztlán* extols the virtues of pre-Columbian society as well as that of their Chicano descendants in an effort by the author to exhort "his fellow Chicanos to struggle for their freedom, their values, and their culture," explains Ginsberg. Alurista considers the United States to be an imperialistic power and advocates a nonviolent cultural revolution against Anglo-Saxon domination. This philosophy is further developed in the poet's second collection, *Nationchild Plumaroja, 1969-1972* ("Nationchild Redfeather, 1969-1972"), which is also considered to be an important work. Like its predecessor, *Nationchild Plumaroja* combines a bilingual style with references to ancient Indian culture in a collection of one hundred poems that emphasize the importance of the Chicano identity.

With Alurista's next three collections, *Timespace Huracán: Poems, 1972-1975, A'nque/Alurista,* and *Spik in Glyph?,* the poet began to experiment more with poetic form. Still using references to Mayan and Aztec culture, *Timespace Huracán* is written entirely in Spanish instead of the author's customary bilingual idiom, while *A'nque/Alurista* and *Spik in Glyph?* emphasize a highly "esoteric" style, according to Ginsberg. In *Timespace Huracán* Alurista also introduces the term "time-space" for the first time in his poetry. Explaining this word to Bruce-Novoa, the poet comments that there are three types of time-space: historical time-space, "which is the collective time-space, one that describes reality as accorded by a consensus of people," a personal time-space "that is very individual, psychological," and a mythological time-space "that unifies the personal and historical time-spaces." Alurista tries to express all three time-spaces in his poetry in order to present a unified picture of reality. This is an essential point in his work, for the poet strongly believes that "given the power to describe reality, we can construct a more human reality beginning with a more human description."

Although his poems have been widely praised by many reviewers, some critics have found fault with what they feel is the poet's romanticization of pre-Columbian history. Even the author of the introduction to Alurista's *Return: Poems Collected and New,* Gary D. Keller, admits that the author "is vulnerable to not representing the past as critically as he has engaged the present." Several critics also believe that Alurista's more recent poetry is not as powerful as his earlier efforts, though this does not detract from his importance. For example, Cordelia Candelaria, author of *Chicano Poetry: A Critical Introduction,* observes: "The fact that the poet has remained a respected figure among Chicano writers despite the dropping off in quality of . . . [his] later volumes reconfirms the greatness of his earlier work." Ginsberg similarly attests that "verbal pyrotechnics . . . threatened to diminish the power of his expression," but she is encouraged by the new poems in *Return: Poems Collected and New.* These new efforts, says Ginsberg, "suggest a reengagement with more accessible language and human themes and a movement away from the often brittle and obscure wordplay of *A'nque/Alurista* and *Spik in Glyph?*"

Even though a number of critics consider Alurista's later works to be less significant and influential than *Floricanto en Aztlán* and *Nationchild Plumaroja,* the ground-breaking impact of these first two collections has been more than enough to establish Alurista's reputation as a major Chicano author. He remains "the best known and most prolific Chicano poet," declares Luis Leal and Pepe Baron in *Three American Literatures.* Predicting the present importance and future potential for Chicano writers, Alurista tells Bruce-Novoa that these authors should create *"a revolution within the literature as much as the literature itself should awaken the desire for liberty in the people. . . . [We] have an opportunity here, and we would be fools to throw it away. That opportunity is to continue to work and work very hard. Write with desire. This cultivation is going to reap a good crop. The historical time-space in which we live is going to focus on this terrenal belly-button of consciousness between Hispanic America and Anglo-Saxon North America. Amerindia is going to bloom. That's inevitable."*

Some of Alurista's manuscripts are kept at the Nettie Lee Benson Collection, Latin American Collection, University of Texas at Austin.

BIOGRAPHICAL/CRITICAL SOURCES:

BOOKS

Actas del XVI Congreso del Instituto Internacional de Literatura Iberoamericana, Michigan State University, 1975.
Alurista, *Return: Poems Collected and New,* Bilingual Press/Editorial Bilingüe, 1982.
Baker, Houston A., Jr., *Three American Literatures,* Modern Language Association, 1982.
Bruce-Novoa, Juan, *Chicano Authors: Inquiry by Interview,* translation by Isabel Barraza, University of Texas Press, 1980.
Bruce-Novoa, Juan, *Chicano Poetry: A Response to Chaos,* University of Texas Press, 1982.
Candelaria, Cordelia, *Chicano Poetry: A Critical Introduction,* Greenwood Press, 1986.
Dictionary of Literary Biography, Volume 82: *Chicano Writers,* Gale, 1989.
Jiménez, Francisco, *The Identification and Analysis of Chicano Literature,* Bilingual Press/Editorial Bilingüe, 1979.
Lomelí, Francisco A., and Donald W. Urioste, *Chicano Perspectives in Literature: A Critical and Annotated Bibliography,* Pajarito Publications, 1976.
Maldonado, Jesus, *Poesía Chicana: Alurista, el Mero Chingón,* Centro de Estudios Chicanos (Seattle), 1971.
Ybarra-Frausto, Tomás, and Joseph Sommers, editors, *Modern Chicano Writers: A Collection of Critical Essays,* Prentice-Hall, 1979.

PERIODICALS

Bilingual Review/Revista Bilingüe, January-August, 1978.
De Colores, Volume 3, number 4, 1977.
Palabra, spring, 1981.
Revista Chicano-Riqueña, winter, 1976.
Xalman, spring, 1977.

—*Sketch by Kevin S. Hile*

* * *

USIGLI, Rodolfo 1905-1979

PERSONAL: Born November 17, 1905, in Mexico City, Mexico; died June 18, 1979, in Mexico City, Mexico; son of Alberto and Carlota (Wainer) Usigli. *Education:* Attended Escuela Popular Nocturna de Música y Declamación, beginning in 1923, and Yale University, 1935-36.

CAREER: Dramatist and author. National University of Mexico, Mexico City, teacher of history and technique of the theater, 1931 and beginning in late 1940s, founder of drama school, 1937; Ministry of Public Education, Mexico City, director of Teatro Radiofónico, 1933; Teatro de Orientación (alternative theater), Mexico City, director and translator of plays, beginning in 1938; Presidency of the Republic, Mexico City, chief of press office, 1938; chief of theater section of department of fine arts, 1938-39; Teatro de Media Noche (alternative theater), Mexico City, founder and director, 1940; worked in Mexican diplomatic service as cultural attache in Paris, France, 1944-46, as minister plenipotentiary in Beirut, Lebanon, 1957-60, and as ambassador in Oslo, Norway, 1960-72.

MEMBER: Amigos del Teatro Mexicano.

AWARDS, HONORS: Rockefeller Fellowship for drama study at Yale University, 1935-36; award from Latin American Drama Contest, 1965, for *Corona de luz;* National Prize for Literature from Mexico, 1972.

WRITINGS:

PLAYS

El apóstol: Comedia (three-act; title means "The Apostle"), first published serially in *Resumen,* January 13-February 3, 1931.
Estado de secreto: Comedia (three-act; title means "State of Secrecy"), first produced in Guadalajara, Mexico, at Teatro Degollado, 1936.
Medio tono: Comedia (three-act; title means "Halftone"; first produced in Mexico City at Palacio de Bellas Artes, November 13, 1937), Dialéctica (Mexico City), 1938, translation by Edna Lue Furness published as *The Great Middle Class* in *Poet Lore,* summer, 1968.
Sueño de día (radio drama; title means "Day Dream"; first produced for Teatro Radiofónico [Mexico City], April 14, 1939), published in *América,* February 10, 1949.
La mujer no hace milagros: Comedia de malas maneras (three-act; title means "Women Don't Work Miracles"; first produced in Mexico City at Teatro Ideal, October, 1939), Departamento de Divulgación de la Secretaría de Educación Pública (Mexico City), 1949.
La crítica de "La mujer no hace milagros": Comedieta (one-act), published in *Letras de México,* January 15, 1940.
Vacaciones: Comedieta (one-act; first produced in Mexico City at Teatro Rex, March 23, 1940), published in *América,* June, 1948.
La familia cena en casa: Comedia (three-act; title means "The Family Dines at Home"; first produced in Mexico City at Teatro Ideal, December 19, 1942), Unión Nacional de Autores, 1942.

El gesticulador: Pieza para demagogos (three-act; title means "The Gesticulator [or 'The Impostor']: Play for Demagogues"; first produced in Mexico City at Palacio de Bellas Artes, May 17, 1947), published serially in *El Hijo Pródigo,* May-July, 1943, Letras de México, 1944.

Corona de sombra: Pieza antihistórica (three-act; first produced in Mexico City at Teatro Arbeu, April 11, 1947), published in *Cuadernos Americanos,* November-December, 1943, Cuadernos Americanos, 1947, translation by William F. Stirling published as *Crown of Shadows: An Antihistorical Play,* Wingate, 1946.

Otra primavera (three-act; first produced in Mexico City at Teatro Virginia Fábregas, August, 1945), Sociedad General de Autores de México, 1947, translation by Wayne Wolfe published as *Another Springtime,* Samuel French, 1961.

La última puerta: Farsa impolítica, first published in *Hoy,* March-April, 1948.

El niño y la niebla (three-act; title means "The Child and the Fog"; first produced in Mexico City at Teatro del Caracol, April 6, 1951), published in *México en la Cultura,* June-July, 1950, Nuevo Mundo, 1951.

Noche de estío: Comedia (three-act), first produced in Mexico City at Teatro Ideal, July 6, 1950.

Los fugitivos (three-act; first produced in Mexico City at Teatro Arbeu, July 22, 1950), published in *México en la Cultura,* 1951.

La función de despedida: Comedia (three-act; first produced in Mexico City at Teatro Ideal, April 10, 1953), published in *México en la Cultura,* February, 1951, Alvaro Arauz, 1952.

Aguas estancadas (three-act; title means "Stagnant Waters"; first produced in Mexico City at Teatro Colón, January 18, 1952), published in *México en la Cultura,* April-May, 1952.

Jano es una muchacha (three-act; title means "Janus Is a Girl"; first produced in Mexico City at Teatro Colón, June 20, 1952), Nuevo Mundo, 1952.

Un día de éstos. . . . : Farsa impolítica (three-act; first produced in Mexico City at Teatro Esperanza Iris, January 8, 1954), Stylo, 1957, translation by Thomas Bledsoe published as *One of These Days . . .* in *Two Plays: "Crown of Light," "One of These Days . . . ,"* introductions by Willis Knapp Jones, J. Cary Davis, and Usigli, Southern Illinois University Press, 1971.

Vacaciones II: Comedieta (one-act), published in *México en la Cultura,* February 5, 1956.

Mientras amemos: Estudio en intensidad dramática (three-act; title means "While We Love"; first produced in 1956), [Mexico], c. 1956.

La exposición: Comedia divertimiento (three-act), published in *Cuadernos Americanos,* May-June, 1959, Cuadernos Americanos, 1960.

Corona de fuego: Primer esquema para una tragedia antihistórica americana (title means "Crown of Fire"), first produced in Mexico City at Teatro Xola, September 15, 1961.

Corona de luz: Comedia antihistórica (three-act; first produced in Mexico City at Teatro Hidalgo, January 5, 1969), Fondo de Cultura Económica, 1965, translation by Thomas Bledsoe published as *Crown of Light* in *Two Plays: "Crown of Light," "One of These Days . . . "* (also see above).

Tres comedietas (one-act plays; includes "Un navío cargado de . . . : Comedia marítima" [title means "A Ship Loaded With . . . "], "El testamento y el viudo: Comedia involuntaria," and "El encuentro: Comedieta"), Finisterre, 1966.

Carta de amor: Monólogo heterodoxo, published in *Revista de la Universidad de México,* June, 1968.

El gran circo del mundo (three-act), published serially in *Cuadernos Americanos,* January-April, 1969.

Los viejos: Duólogo imprevisto (one-act; title means "The Old People"), Finisterre, 1971.

¡Buenos días, señor Presidente! Moralidad en dos actos y un interludio según "La vida es sueño" (two-act; title means "Good Morning, Mr. President"), J. Mortiz, 1972.

Plays represented in anthologies, including *Antología de obras en un acto,* Collección Teatro Mexicano, 1960.

COLLECTIONS

Teatro completo (title means "Complete Theater"), Fondo de Cultura Económica, Volume 1 (includes the previously unpublished works *4 chemins 4* [written in French], *Falso drama: Comedieta, El presidente y el ideal: Comedia,* and *Alcestes: Moraleja*), 1963, Volume 2 (includes the previously unpublished works *Dios, Batidillo, y la mujer: Farsa americana, Las madres y los hijos, La diadema: Comedia moral,* and *Corona de fuego*), 1966, Volume 3 (includes *El caso Flores* and collected prologues and epilogues to plays), 1979.

Corona de sombra [and] *Corona de fuego* [and] *Corona de luz,* Porrúa, 1982.

El gesticulador y otras obras de teatro, Secretaría de Educación Pública, Cultura SEP (Mexico City), 1983.

El gesticulador [and] *La mujer no hace milagros,* Mexicanos Unidos, 1985.

TRANSLATOR

Babette Deutsch, *Walt Whitman, constructor para América,* Séneca, 1942.

Georges Schehadé, *Historia de Vasco,* Universitaria, 1959.

Also translator of articles and poems for periodicals, and of plays for performance at Teatro de Orientación, including S. N. Behrman's "Biography."

OTHER

México en el teatro (history and criticism of Mexican drama), Mundial, 1932, translation with an introduction by Wilder P. Scott published as *Mexico in the Theater,* Romance Monographs, 1976.

Caminos del teatro en México (history and criticism of Mexican drama), Secretaría de Relaciones Exteriores, 1933.

Conversación desesperada (poems), Nandino, 1938.

(Author of introduction) Josephina Niggli, editor, *Mexican Folk Plays,* University of North Carolina Press, 1938.

Itinerario del autor dramático, y otros ensayos (drama criticism), Casa de España en México, 1940.

Ensayo de un crimen (novel; title means "Rehearsal for a Crime"), América, 1944, Siglos, 1980.

(Contributor) *Proceedings of the Conference on Latin American Fine Arts,* University of Texas Press, 1952.

(With Mauricio Magdaleno) *Homenaje a Alfredo Gómez de la Vega,* Seminario de Cultura Mexicana, 1959.

Antonio Ruiz et l'art dangereux de la peinture (nonfiction), [Beirut, Lebanon], 1960.

Juan Ruiz de Alarcón en el tiempo, Secretaría de Educación Pública, Subsecretaría de Asuntos Culturales, 1967.

Obliteración, Usigli, 1973.

Conversaciones y encuentros: Bernard Shaw, Lenormand, Jean Cocteau, Clifford Odets, André Breton, Elmer Rice, Paul Muni, B. Traven, T. S. Eliot, Novaro, 1974.

Imagen y prisma de México; Presencia de Juárez en el teatro universal: Una paradoja, Casa de la Cultura Ecuatoriana (Quito, Ecuador), 1976.

(Contributor) Esperanza Zambrano, *La vida plena* (anthology), National University of Mexico, 1983.

Contributor of articles and reviews to periodicals, including *América, Armas y Letras, Cuadernos Americanos, Excélsior, El Hijo Pródigo, Hispania, Hoy, Imagen, Letras de México, El Martes, México en la Cultura, El Nacional, Noticias Gráficas, Novedades, Panoramas, Ruta, Theatre Arts,* and *El Universal Ilustrado.*

SIDELIGHTS: "Rodolfo Usigli," wrote a reviewer for *Books Abroad* in 1953, "has a confidence in his destiny that is almost Napoleonic." Usigli, who became known as one of Latin America's leading dramatists, was born in Mexico in 1905 at a time when that country lacked all but the rudiments of professional theater. Convinced that theater was vital to Mexican society, Usigli toiled as a critic, producer, director, and teacher of drama, as well as the author of more than three dozen plays. "More than any other figure," observed Frank Dauster in *Inter-American Review of Bibliography,* Usigli became "a symbol of the labor, devotion and stubborn insistence on quality which have marked the small group responsible for the formation of an important drama movement in Mexico." In 1972 he received his country's National Prize for Literature.

Though born and raised in Mexico, Usigli was the son of Italian and Polish immigrants, and he later surmised that his non-Mexican ancestry may have enabled him to view his fellow citizens from a more detached perspective. The family struggled financially after the death of Usigli's father, but Usigli's assertive bearing with his classmates led them to dub him "Visconde" ("Viscount"). Since Mexico had no drama school, the young Usigli taught himself about plays by reading several each day; "by the age of twenty," observed Willis Knapp Jones in *Two Plays,* the author "had become a respected theatre critic." Within a few years he had written *México en el teatro* (*Mexico in the Theater*), one of the first efforts to survey all of Mexican drama from the coming of the Spanish in the 1500s until modern times. The book marked Usigli's emergence as a major commentator on the nature and goals of theater in Mexico, a role the author continued to relish in subsequent books on the theater, in journalistic articles, and in lengthy prefaces and epilogues to his plays.

As a rising critic and dramatist Usigli repeatedly stressed theater's fundamental role as a means of communicating ideas among members of a society. The stage, he declares in *Mexico in the Theater,* "has been everywhere a tribunal for criticism and an institution of learning." Whether in France with Molière, in Russia with Nikolai Gogol and Anton Chekhov, or England with George Bernard Shaw, "it has been the forerunner of the great political, social and intellectual transformations." Usigli thus seems to have felt a duty to exhort his fellow Mexicans on the best ways for theater to realize its social purpose, and his readiness to dispute with other theater critics became legendary. In concert with other aspiring dramatists of his generation such as Xavier Villaurrutia, he castigated the state of Mexican theater in the early twentieth century. Centuries ago, he observed, Mexicans had looked to theater as a source of religious truth, whether Aztec or Christian. But by the early 1900s, Mexican theater had become an empty spectacle in which performers flaunted their declamation, plays were shallow and formulaic, and reviewers lacked the informed judgment to foster higher standards. Usigli, who advocated serious training for playwrights and actors alike, accepted a grant in 1935 to study drama at Yale University and then made an ill-fated effort to establish a drama school at the National University of Mexico. He applauded when his peers es-

tablished small alternative theater groups in the 1930s, and he joined one such troupe, the Teatro de Orientación, as a director and translator in 1938. When he tried to establish his own Teatro de Media Noche in 1940, however, established theater critics repaid his earlier jibes by helping to drive the project into bankruptcy. Eventually Usigli decided that alternative theater was becoming too elitist, and he added it to the many other subjects of attack in his articles.

For Usigli, the ideal Mexican dramatist would have a high intellectual purpose while retaining a broad appeal among the general public. One of Usigli's notable accomplishments, observers suggest, was to survey European culture for ideas about drama, then use his knowledge to write distinctively Mexican plays that were both insightful and popular. Believing that any conscientious playwright should present audiences with a frank portrayal of their society, he adopted as role models some of Europe's most respected social critics. He studied Molière, whose comedies expose human foibles; Henrik Ibsen, who wrote well-crafted psychological dramas that often involve social issues; and especially Shaw, whose plays contain lively intellectual debates among characters with sharply contrasting points of view. Most any Usigli play decries or satirizes pretension and hypocrisy, ranging from 1942's *La familia cena en casa* ("The Family Dines at Home"), about snobbishness in the upper classes, to 1959's *La exposición* ("The Exposition"), about behind-the-scenes bickering at an art exhibition.

Some of Usigli's social criticism seems frankly designed to jolt his audience with its irreverence, as the playwright himself suggested in the introduction to *Two Plays.* Usigli called his many political satires "impolitic" plays because, he wrote, he refused to spare any political viewpoint. Moreover, he continued, "The Spanish adjective not only means rash or imprudent but is also the equivalent of impolite, and I have always upheld the theory that drama, and the theatre at large, . . . is an art in shirt-sleeves." Some of Usigli's most shocking—and most popular—plays seem to be inspired by the scandals of his predecessors. Ibsen, for instance, stunned nineteenth-century Europe with his play *Ghosts,* in which a widow's refusal to admit that her husband exposed her to syphilis returns to haunt her when her son turns out to be infected and insane. In the mid-1930s Usigli wrote a comparable play called *El niño y la niebla* ("The Child and the Fog"), in which a woman's many lies to her husband, including her denial that insanity runs in her family, are embodied in her mentally disturbed son. Eventually, when she tries to trick her son into killing his father, the overwhelmed young man commits suicide instead. For more than a decade Mexican producers refused to stage the play because of its subject matter, but when it finally premiered in 1951 it broke box-office records. Usigli rapidly matched this success with *Jano es una muchacha* ("Janus is a Girl"), a play which—like Shaw's *Mrs. Warren's Profession*—contrasts the sexual frankness of prostitutes with the hypocrisy of seemingly respectable people. The main character, Víctor, is sexually inhibited at home but passionate when he visits the local brothel; eventually he is shocked to realize that his daughter has followed his example, living as a prim schoolgirl by day and a prostitute by night. The play has "a perilous theme," Gordon Ragle observed in *Hispania,* "yet the ugly has a 'rightness' which does not offend as the author contrasts and plumbs the 'realities' of the two worlds, the brothel and the home." In a prologue to the play, Ragle noted, Usigli "observes trenchantly that only by destroying sexual hypocrisy can we determine to what point prostitution is an essential part of society."

Given the limitations of Mexican theater at the time Usigli began his career, he recognized that playwrights of his generation would have made a major advance simply by developing an audience for realistic plays about the problems of daily life. But for the long term, Usigli harbored far greater ambitions for drama. As Solomon Tilles suggested in *Latin American Theatre Review*, Usigli felt that drama had a spiritual mission comparable to that of religion, capable of bringing society "to an awareness of a greater reality." Just as moral law is one of the "higher realities" conveyed by religion, theater could be used to give citizens a sense of their identity and purpose as a nation. A historian, Usigli observed in *Mexico in the Theater*, can only convey the facts when writing about his country, but a playwright can—and should—try to understand what historical events say about the nature of a country. The resulting plays would show the audience what Usigli called "anti-historical myths": "myths" in the positive sense that they are stories about the basic beliefs of a people; "anti-historical" because they go beyond the historian's concern with mere facts. Tilles suggested that Usigli's goal could be compared to that of the ancient Greek tragedians, who used dramas about the downfall of great and powerful people to confront their audiences with deep truths about the nature of human existence.

Usigli's first, and one of his best, efforts at such high national drama was written in the late 1930s and titled *El gesticulador: Pieza para demagogos* ("The Gesticulator [or 'The Impostor']: Play for Demagogues"). The play is based on Usigli's premise that hypocrisy and fraud, which he attacked in many plays throughout his life, are major traits of Mexican culture. "The Mexican's capacity for gesticulation is infinite," wrote Usigli in an epilogue to the play; according to Ragle, Usigli's use of "gesticulation" comes from the Spanish word "gesto," connoting a false face or a mask. Gesticulation, the playwright continued, "is always opposed to reality" and comprises the Mexican's way "of saving himself from it and of avoiding and fleeing the truth." *El gesticulador* centers on César Rubio, a failed Mexican historian who is disdained by his own family for clinging to an illusion of worldly success. When a naive historian from the United States asks Rubio if he is actually a long-missing Mexican political hero with the same name, Rubio cannot resist a few moments of stolen glory and replies that he is. The American spreads word that General César Rubio, hero of the Mexican people, has reappeared, and Rubio is willingly swept along by a wave of adulation and popularity. While Rubio's son remains angry and disappointed with his father, the daughter is so eager to believe in heroes that she decides her father is now telling the truth. So far the play seems basically a stinging political satire, and theater producers, dismayed by Usigli's portrait of Mexican hero-worship, refused for years to stage the work. But by the play's final act, which transcends the invective of satire, Rubio is redeemed as a man by living up to the role he has assumed. He revives the missing general's political career, which had been associated with goals of the Mexican Revolution such as social equality and economic opportunity. Eventually he accepts assassination at the hands of a political rival rather than drop his role and return to his petty and meaningless past. Living a lie has enabled Rubio to embrace a higher truth—the political ideals of his fellow citizens. After *El gesticulador* finally premiered in 1947, it won critical acclaim both in Mexico and around the world.

Usigli went on to conceive a trilogy of plays—*Corona de fuego* ("Crown of Fire"), *Corona de luz* (*Crown of Light*), and *Corona de sombra* (*Crown of Shadows*)—about the deeper significance of major events in Mexican history. He traced his inspiration to the German philosopher Georg Hegel, who believed that history comprised distinct eras, each a step in the development of the human race. The first play in the cycle, *Corona de fuego,* shows the conquest of Aztec Mexico by the Spanish in the 1500s. In *Modern Language Journal,* Wilder P. Scott observed that the work is "frequently grouped among the [author's] weaker plays," despite the fact that Usigli prepared for it by writing the rest of the trilogy beforehand. Scott suggested that *Corona de fuego* is marred by the decision of the playwright, who generally wrote in contemporary prose, to use verse and archaic language. Much more popular with reviewers was the second play of the cycle, *Crown of Light,* which shows the beginnings of a unified Mexican culture as Mexico's Indians accept the Christianity of their Spanish conquerors. Usigli clearly did not want the play to praise Spanish imperialism: Act I, set in Spain, shows the Spanish Emperor Charles V cynically ordering Catholic prelates to win the Indians' allegiance by faking a miracle. In Act II the Emperor's command is foiled by Bishop Juan Zumárraga, a leader of the church in Mexico, who believes that religious faith should spring from rational choice and so refuses to convert the Indians by resorting to lies. The impasse is resolved in Act III, when masses of Indians convert in response to a miracle that is apparently free of Spanish intrigue: Indians attest that the Virgin Mary has appeared to them as an Indian woman, known to later history as the Virgin of Guadalupe. The conversion results from a symbolic compromise, in which Indians accept Christianity because Christianity seems to have accepted their dignity as human beings. "Here, as elsewhere," wrote Isabel Magaña Schevill in *Hispania,* "Usigli has created a play of impeccable taste and powerful, dramatic impact."

The most widely known play of the cycle is probably *Crown of Shadows,* which helped to make Usigli a playwright of international renown after he wrote and staged it during the 1940s. Last play of the cycle in historical terms, it shows the rise of Mexico's sense of national identity as the country rejected a French-imposed government during the mid-nineteenth century. As with several other works of Mexican literature, the play takes a surprisingly conciliatory tone towards its main characters, European aristocrats Maximilian and Carlota, who were installed by French troops as emperor and empress of Mexico. In Usigli's interpretation of history, according to Peter R. Beardsell in *Latin American Theatre Review,* the ill-fated pair are redeemed by the extent of their suffering and by the insights that they gain.

Crown of Shadows begins in 1927 in the sickroom of former empress Carlota, who resided in Europe and retreated into madness after her husband was executed by a Mexican firing squad in 1867. She is visited by a Mexican historian who encourages her to relive in her mind the turbulent years of her reign. By dividing the stage in half between the nineteenth century and the twentieth, Usigli alternately shows the audience Carlota's memories and her latter-day reactions to them. As Carlota recalls, the newly proclaimed emperor Maximilian gained increasing respect for his adopted country and decided he would rather fight for the honor of ruling Mexico than return to the safety of Europe. When he lost he faced the firing squad with great dignity. "The execution," wrote Beardsell, "should be seen as a kind of sacrificial death" that enabled the Mexican people to assert their nationhood. Prompted by the historian, the elderly Carlota acknowledges that she was wrong to usurp the self-determination of Mexico; in a spirit of what Beardsell calls "poetic justice," Usigli then allows Carlota to die with a sane and tranquil mind. Her sixty years of madness, the reviewer explained, are such a clear warning of "the folly of excessive personal ambition . . . that the dramatist can even afford to reward rather than punish her." In *Inter-American Review of Bibliography,* Frank Dauster hailed *Crown of Shadows* as "one of the finest plays ever written in Spanish America." Usigli garnered yet higher praise when, as a novice diplomat in Europe during the mid-1940s, he presented an English translation of the work to the elderly George Bernard Shaw. Shaw found the play superior to anything he had written at the same stage in his career, and he responded to Usigli: "Mexico may kill you with hunger, but it can never deny your genius."

In the long run Mexico gave Usigli both recognition and financial reward. He was unable to support himself as a playwright, but he rose to ambassador in his country's diplomatic corps and served until retirement in 1972. He lived to see nearly all his plays performed or published, though in some cases he had waited for decades. By the 1960s, Dauster observed, Usigli had "emerge[d] as a sort of elder statesman of Mexican drama." His once-controversial work, however, was seen as outmoded by many younger dramatists, who abjured realistic depictions of society in favor of more abstract and experimental plays. Faced with such a trend, according to Wilder P. Scott in *Romance Notes,* Usigli defiantly labeled himself a "conservative dramatic theorist" and clung to his belief that "the essential material of the theater must be human passions and ideas." In succeeding decades, as playwrights increasingly returned to social themes in their works, Usigli's instincts seemed to be vindicated. Younger writers who have studied under Usigli include Emilio Carbadillo, praised for his ability to blend fantasy and reality in his plays, and novelist Carlos Fuentes, whose best-known effort as a playwright—*Todo los gatos son pardos (All Cats Are Grey)*—is a Usiglian drama about the meaning of the Spanish conquest of Mexico. When Usigli died in 1979, he was hailed by Mexican journalists as the creator of modern Mexican theater.

MEDIA ADAPTATIONS: "Medio tono" was adapted for a film starring Dolores del Río; "El niño y la niebla" and "Otra primavera" were adapted for film; *Ensayo de un crimen* was adapted by Luis Buñuel and Eduardo Ugarte Pages for a film of the same title, [Mexico], 1962 (released in U.S. as "The Criminal Life of Archibald de la Cruz").

BIOGRAPHICAL/CRITICAL SOURCES:

BOOKS

Jones, Willis Knapp, *Behind Spanish American Footlights,* University of Texas Press, 1966.
Usigli, Rodolfo, *Two Plays: "Crown of Light," "One of These Days . . . ,"* translation by Thomas Bledsoe, introductions by Willis Knapp Jones, J. Cary Davis, and Usigli, Southern Illinois University Press, 1971.
Usigli, Rodolfo, *Mexico in the Theater,* translation with an introduction by Wilder P. Scott, Romance Monographs, 1976.

PERIODICALS

Books Abroad, January, 1933, April, 1942, July, 1944, winter, 1950, spring, 1953, summer, 1961, summer, 1964.
Hispania, December, 1954, March, 1955, May, 1963, December, 1964, May, 1968, September, 1968, September, 1973.
Inter-American Review of Bibliography, October-December, 1964.
Latin American Theatre Review, spring, 1970, spring, 1971, fall, 1972, fall, 1976, fall, 1977.
Modern Language Journal, December, 1973.
Romance Notes, spring, 1970.
Texas Quarterly, spring, 1959.
Theatre Arts, January, 1935, August, 1938, May, 1941, May, 1953.

OBITUARIES:

PERIODICALS

Hispania, May, 1980.

—*Sketch by Thomas Kozikowski*

*   *   *

USLAR PIETRI, Arturo   1906-

PERSONAL: Born May 16, 1906, in Caracas, Venezuela; married Isabel Braun, 1939; children: two sons. *Education:* Received degree in social sciences from Central University of Caracas and doctorate in political science from Central University of Venezuela.

ADDRESSES: Home—Avenida Los Pinos 49, La Florida, Caracas, Venezuela.

CAREER: Venezuelan Government, served as senator in national congress, presidential candidate, 1963, served as Minister of Education and Minister of Foreign Affairs, represented Venezuela abroad in various diplomatic posts, including cultural attaché at embassy in Paris; instructor in literature at Central University of Venezuela, Caracas; instructor at Columbia University; member of Academy of Social and Political Sciences.

WRITINGS:

Barrabas, y otros relatos (stories), [Caracas, Venezuela], 1928, published as *Barrabas y otros cuentos,* Bruguera (Barcelona, Spain), 1978, reprinted under original title, 1983.
Las lanzas coloradas (historical novel), originally published in 1930, reprinted, Alianza (Madrid, Spain), 1983, translation by Harriet de Onís published as *The Red Lances,* introduction by Federico de Onís, Knopf, 1963.
Red (stories), illustrations by Fabbiani, Elite (Caracas), 1936.
(Editor with Julián Padrón) *Antología del cuento moderno venezolano (1895-1935)* (stories), two volumes, Escuela Técnica Industrial, Taller de Artes Gráficas (Caracas), 1940.
Apuntes sobre los principales aspectos venezolanos del programa de estudios de economía política de la Facultad de Derecho de la Universidad Central de Venezuela, [Caracas], 1941.
Sumario de economía venezolana para alivio de estudiantes (nonfiction), Centro de estudiantes de derecho (Caracas), 1945, 2nd edition, revised with Hernán Avendaño Monzón, D. F. Maza Zavala, and Bernardo Ferrán, Fundación Eugenio Mendoza (Caracas), 1958.
Las visiones del camino (travel), [Caracas], 1946.
El camino de El Dorado (novel; title means "The Way to El Dorado"), Losada (Buenos Aires, Argentina), 1947.
Letras y hombres de Venezuela (essays), Fondo de Cultura Económica (Mexico), 1948, reprinted, Mediterráneo (Madrid), 1974.
Treinta hombres y sus sombras (stories; title means "Thirty Men and Their Shadows"), [Buenos Aires], 1949, reprinted, Losada, 1974.
De una a otra Venezuela, Mesa Redonda (Caracas), 1950, reprinted, Monte Avila (Caracas), 1980.
Las nubes (essays), Ediciones del Ministerio de Educación, Dirección de Cultura y Bellas Artes (Caracas), 1951.
Apuntes para retratos, [Caracas], 1952.
Arístides Rojas, 1826-1894, Fundación Eugenio Mendoza, 1953.
Tierra venezolana (travel), illustrations by Alfredo Boulton, EDIME (Caracas), 1953, reprinted, Mediterráneo, 1974.
Obras selectas (selected works), Edime (Madrid), 1953, reprinted, 1977.

Tiempo de contar (selected stories), J. López Elias (Caracas), 1954.

Breve historia de la novela hispanoamericana, EDIME, 1954, reprinted, Mediterráneo, 1974.

El otoño en Europa (travel), photographs by Boulton, Mesa Redonda, 1954.

El petróleo en Venezuela: Discurso de incorporación, Academia de Ciencias Políticas y Sociales (Caracas), 1955.

Pizarrón, EDIME, 1955.

Valores humanos: Charlas por televisión (biography), EDIME, second series, 1956, third series, 1958.

Teatro: El día de Antero Albán. La Tebaida. El Dios invisible. La fuga de Miranda (plays), EDIME, 1958.

Materiales para la construcción de Venezuela, Orinoco (Caracas), 1959.

(Editor) *Sumario de la civilización occidental,* EDIME, 1959.

(Editor) *Lecturas para jóvenes venezolanos,* 4th edition, EDIME, 1959.

Chúo Gil y las tejedoras: Drama en un preludio y siete tiempos (play), [Caracas], 1960, reprinted, Monte Avila, 1983.

La ciudad de nadie. El otoño en Europa. Un turista en el Cercano Oriente (essays), Losada, 1960.

El laberinto de fortuna: Un retrato en la geografía (novel), Losada, 1962. *Del hacer y deshacer de Venezuela* (essays), [Caracas], 1962.

Estación de máscaras (novel; sequel to *El laberinto de fortuna: Un retrato en la geografía*), Losada, 1964.

La palabra compartida: Discursos en el Parlamento, 1959-1963, Pensamiento Vivo (Caracas), 1964.

Valores humanos: Biografías y evocaciones (biography), four volumes, EDIME, 1964.

Hacia el humanismo democrático, Frente Nacional Democrático (Caracas), 1965.

Pasos y pasajeros (stories), Taurus (Madrid), 1966.

Petróleo de vida o muerte, [Caracas], 1966.

Oraciones para despertar, Comité de Obras Culturales (Caracas), 1967.

La lluvia y otros cuentos (stories), Zig-Zag (Santiago), 1968.

Las vacas gordas y las vacas flacas, Ediciones del Concejo Municipal del Distrito Federal (Caracas), 1968.

Catorce cuentos venezolanos (stories), Ediciones de la Revista de Occidente (Madrid), 1969.

En busca del Nuevo Mundo, Fondo de Cultura Económica, 1969.

Treinta cuentos: Antología (stories), Monte Avila, 1969.

Veinticinco ensayos: Antología (essays), Monte Avila, 1969.

Vista desde un punto (essays), Monte Avila, 1971.

La vuelta al mundo en diez trancos, Tiempo Nuevo (Caracas), 1971.

Bolivariana (essays), Horizonte (Caracas), 1972.

Manoa (poems), Arte (Caracas), 1972.

Moscas, árboles y hombres (stories), Planeta (Barcelona), 1973.

La otra América (essays), Alianza, 1974.

Del estado, la economía, la universidad y los ranchos: Cuatro textos ocasionales, [Caracas], 1974.

(With Pedro Emilio Coll and Ramón Díaz Sánchez) *Tres cuentos venezolanos* (stories), Ediciones Culturales INCE (Caracas), 1974.

El globo de colores, Monte Avila, 1975.

Viva voz, Italgráfica (Caracas), 1975.

Oficio de difuntos (novel), Seix Barral (Barcelona), 1976.

El prójimo y otros cuentos (stories), Bruguera, 1978.

Fantasmas de dos mundos (essays), Seix Barral, 1979.

Escritura (in French and Spanish), illustrations by Jesús Rafael Soto, Macanao (Caracas), 1979.

"Las lanzas coloradas" y cuentos selectos (stories), Biblioteca Ayacucho (Caracas), 1979.

Los libros de Miranda, La Casa de Bello (Caracas), 1979.

Los ganadores (stories), Seix Barral, 1980.

Educar para Venezuela, Gráficas Reunidas (Madrid), 1981.

La isla de Róbinson (novel), Seix Barral, 1981.

Cuéntame a Venezuela, Lisbona (Caracas), 1981.

Fachas, fechas y fichas, Ateneo de Caracas, 1982.

Bolívar hoy, Monte Avila, 1983.

Venezuela en el petróleo, Urbina & Fuentes (Caracas), 1984.

(With others) *Venezuela en seis ensayos* (essays), Monte Avila, 1985.

Godos, insurgentes y visionarios (essays), Seix Barral, 1986.

Medio milenio de Venezuela, Departamento de Relacione Públicas de Lagoven (Caracas), 1986.

33 cuentos (title means "33 Stories"), edited by Efrain Subero, illustrations by Antonio Lazo, Petróleos de Venezuela, 1986.

El hombre que voy siendo, Monte Avila, 1986.

Also author of monographs.

SIDELIGHTS: Both a writer and a statesman, Arturo Uslar Pietri achieved recognition in Latin American literature primarily for his poetic fiction and his essays. The vividness of his writing, with "arresting similes and metaphors," won praise from critics such as *Saturday Review* contributor Donald A. Yates, and he has been called a master of the short story. One of the first writers to apply the term "magic realism" to Latin American fiction that juxtaposes reality and wondrous events, Uslar Pietri used the technique in his own writing, which often focuses on Venezuela. His best writing has come to be regarded as classic South American literature.

Uslar Pietri won particular acclaim for *Las lanzas coloradas,* translated as *The Red Lances* in 1963, which was his first novel. Set during Venezuela's struggle for independence from Spain in the early 1800s, the book depicts several minor characters "irrevocably involved in what [Uslar Pietri] deemed the moment of emergence of the national character," described Yates. One character sides with the republicans, who wish to break away from Spanish rule, another joins the royalists, on the other side of what amounts to a civil war. "All the characters," noted Herbert L. Matthews in the *New York Times Book Review,* "are killed, as they would have been in real life." Uslar Pietri's realism in the novel includes descriptions of the brutalities committed by war leaders and what Matthews called an "evil, brooding atmosphere" hanging over everything. Violent, bloody, the book nonetheless seemed to Matthews "a poetic evocation" of the difficult birth of a country. Assessing *The Red Lances* in 1963 upon its publication in English, Matthews declared that "it remains today as fresh and vivid as it was in 1930."

BIOGRAPHICAL/CRITICAL SOURCES:

BOOKS

Alcántara, Tomás Polanco, editor, *El valor humano de Arturo Uslar Pietri: Homenaje de la Academia Nacional de la Historia a su numerario Dr. Arturo Uslar Pietri,* La Academia (Caracas), 1984.

Arturo Uslar Pietri: Homenaje en sus 80 años, Universidad Santa Maria (Caracas), 1986.

Foster, David William and Virginia Ramos Foster, *Modern Latin American Literature,* Ungar, 1975.

Galicias, René Molina, editor, *El amparo a Rondalera* (trial proceedings in the case of the Asociación Civil Experimental

Rondalera versus Arturo Uslar Pietri), Ediciones Síntesis Juridica (Caracas), 1984.

Miliani, Domingo, *Uslar Pietri, renovador del cuento venezolano,* Monte Avila, 1969.

Peña, Alfredo, *Conversaciones con Uslar Pietri,* Ateneo de Caracas, 1978.

Vivas, José Luis, *La cuentística de Arturo Uslar Pietri,* Universidad Central de Venezuela (Caracas), 1963.

PERIODICALS

New York Times Book Review, October 20, 1963.
Saturday Review, October 12, 1963.
World Literature Today, winter, 1978, winter, 1980.

V-W

VALCARCEL, Emilio Díaz
See DIAZ VALCARCEL, Emilio

* * *

VALDEZ, Luis (Miguel) 1940-

PERSONAL: Born June 26, 1940, in Delano, California; son of Francisco (a farm worker) and Armida Valdez; married wife, Lupe, August 23, 1969; children: Anahuac, Kinan, Lakin. *Education:* San Jose State University, B.A., 1964.

ADDRESSES: Home—53 Franklin St., San Juan Bautista, Calif. 95045. *Office*—P.O. Box 1240, San Juan Bautista, Calif. 95045. *Agent*—Joan Scott, Writers & Artists Agency, 11726 San Vicente Blvd., Suite 300, Los Angeles, Calif. 90049.

CAREER: Actor, director, and writer. Founder and artistic director of El Teatro Campesino, 1965—. Member of San Francisco Mime Troupe, 1964; union organizer for United Farm Workers Organizing Committee in Delano, Calif., 1965-66; lecturer in Chicano history and theatre arts at University of California, Berkeley, 1970-71; lecturer at University of California, Santa Cruz, 1971 and 1977; member of California Arts Council, 1976-81, National Endowment for the Arts Congressional Committee for the State of the Arts, 1978, and board of directors of Theatre Communications Group, 1978-79.

MEMBER: Directors Guild of America, Writers Guild of America, Society of Stage Directors and Choreographers.

AWARDS, HONORS: Prize from playwriting contest, c. 1961, for "The Theft"; Obie Award from *Village Voice,* 1968, for "demonstrating the politics of survival"; awards from Los Angeles Drama Critics, 1969 and 1972, for work with El Teatro Campesino; special Emmy Award for directing from KNBC-TV, 1973; award from Los Angeles Drama Critics Circle, 1978, for play "Zoot Suit"; grant from Rockefeller Foundation, 1978; nomination for Golden Globe for best musical film, 1981, for "Zoot Suit"; award for best musical from San Francisco Bay Critics Circle, 1983, for "Corridos!"; honorary doctorates from Columbia College, San Jose State University, and California Institute of the Arts; also shared other awards for work with El Teatro Campesino.

WRITINGS:

PLAYS

The Shrunken Head of Pancho Villa (first produced in San Jose at San Jose State College, 1964), El Centro Campesino Cultural, 1967.
(And director) "Los vendidos" (one-act; title means "The Sellouts"), first produced in 1967.
"Vietnam Campesino" (one-act), first produced in 1969.
"Soldado Razo" (one-act), first produced in 1969, produced with "The Dark Root of a Scream" (also see below) in New York City in 1985.
Actos (one-act works; first produced in 1969-70), Cucaracha Press, 1971.
(And director) "Bernabé" (one-act), first produced in 1970, published in *Contemporary Chicano Theatre,* edited by Roberto J. Garza, University of Notre Dame Press, 1975.
(And director) "La virgin del Tepeyac" (musical), first produced in San Juan Bautista, Calif., 1971.
"The Dark Root of a Scream" (one-act), first produced in 1971, produced with "Soldado Razo" (also see above) in New York City at Public/Martinson Hall, August, 1985, published in *From the Barrio: A Chicano Anthology,* edited by Lillian Falderman and Luis Omar Salinas, Canfield Press, 1973.
(And director) "La carpa de los Rasquachis," produced in New York City at Chelsea Westside, October, 1974.
(And director) "El fin del mundo" (title means "The End of the World"), first produced in 1976.
(And director) "Zoot Suit," produced in Los Angeles at Mark Taper Forum, April, 1978, produced in New York City at Winter Garden, March, 1979 (also see below).
(And director) "Bandito: The American Melodrama of Tiburcio Vasquez," first produced in 1980.
(And director) "I Don't Have to Show You No Stinking Badges," produced in Los Angeles at the Theatre Center, February, 1986.

Also author of "The Theft" (one-act), 1961. Work represented in anthologies.

SCREENPLAYS

(And director) "I Am Joaquin," El Centro Campesino Cultural, 1969.

(And director) "Zoot Suit" (adapted from his own play), Universal, 1982.

(And director) "La Bamba," Columbia, 1987.

OTHER

(Editor with Stan Steiner) *Aztlan: An Anthology of Mexican American Literature,* Knopf, 1972.

Pensamiento Serpentino: A Chicano Approach to the Theatre of Reality, Cucaracha Press, 1973.

Also writer and director of television productions, including "Corridos! Tales of Passion and Revolution," PBS-TV. Contributor to periodicals, including *Arte Nuevo, Latin American Theatre Review, Performing Arts,* and *Ramparts.*

SIDELIGHTS: Luis Valdez is a distinguished figure in both the stage and film worlds. He began his writing career with "The Theft," a one-act work completed in 1961, and followed that with "The Shrunken Head of Pancho Villa," a full-length production staged in 1964 when he was still a student at San Jose State College. During the mid-1960s, after graduating from college, Valdez worked with a mime troupe, then joined the United Farm Workers, a labor union comprised of migrants. With union members, Valdez staged improvisations designed to address and express problems and issues pertinent to the rank and file. As an outgrowth of these endeavors, Valdez formed El Teatro Campesino, a theatre company that would present his works throughout the United States in the ensuing decades.

During the rest of the 1960s El Teatro Campesino enjoyed steadily increasing prominence in the theatre world. In 1967 the company toured the United States in a production that included both dramatic and musical works, and in 1969 it performed at an international festival in France. By that time, however, the company had broken from the United Farm Workers and established itself as a blue-collar performing group. Among the works that El Teatro Campesino presented during these years was Valdez's early play "The Shrunken Head of Pancho Villa."

In 1970 the company performed Valdez's "Bernabé," which details a simpleton's intellectual development as he realizes a greater tie to his Chicano heritage. Valdez continued exploring the Chicano experience in works such as "Vietnam Campesino," "Soldado Razo," and "The Dark Root of a Scream," each of which addressed aspects of Chicano involvement in the Vietnam War. "Soldado Razo" and "The Dark Root of a Scream" were eventually presented together in New York City, whereupon *New York Times* reviewer D. J. R. Bruckner acknowledged El Teatro Campesino as a company devoted to political and social issues. Bruckner was particularly impressed with "Soldado Razo," which he described as "a simple, brief and very effective piece of political theater." In addition, Bruckner observed that the play's finale, concerning a young soldier's death and his family's subsequent grief, was "profoundly . . . moving."

By the mid-1970s, Valdez and El Teatro Campesino enjoyed substantial popularity in the United States and Europe. Among the company's most successful productions from this period was Valdez's "La carpa de los Rasquachis," a gripping depiction—with music—of a Mexican farmworker's hard life in America. Another work, "El fin del mundo," illuminated the Chicano urban experience. Valdez's most popular work from the 1970s, however, is probably "Zoot Suit," his entertaining account of an actual murder trial that occurred in Los Angeles in the early 1940s. In this play, Valdez offers a jarringly offbeat account—replete with music and dance numbers—of several young Chicanos doomed to life imprisonment for murder despite a disturbing lack of evidence.

Valdez wrote and directed a film version of "Zoot Suit" in 1982, but the adaptation fared poorly with such influential critics as the *New York Times*'s Vincent Canby, who called it "a mess." More appreciative was *Washington Post* writer Richard Harrington, who lamented the film's notoriety. Noting that the work was made within two weeks and for only three million dollars, Harrington conceded that "its limitations are apparent," but he nonetheless hailed it as "a powerful film."

After completing the "Zoot Suit" film, Valdez resumed stage work with El Teatro Campesino. Among the company's most celebrated Valdez productions from the 1980s is "I Don't Have to Show You No Stinking Badges," about a middle-class Chicano family and their uneasy assimilation into the American mainstream. The parents are actors specializing in demeaning bit parts such as migrant workers, gardeners, and servants. Their son is a disillusioned law student who resents his parents for making social and artistic compromises. Having returned home after abruptly leaving school, the son becomes increasingly disturbed, and he eventually threatens to kill both his parents and himself.

"I Don't Have to Show You No Stinking Badges" proved extremely popular upon production beginning in 1986. *Newsweek*'s Gerald C. Lubenow hailed the work as evidence that "Valdez has come triumphantly into his own," and reported that the play "has been cheered in Los Angeles and San Diego." For Lubenow, the work was "as much a story of generational conflict as of assimilation." *Los Angeles Times* reviewer Sylvie Drake expressed a mixed appraisal, finding the work "muddled" but added that Valdez was nonetheless an entertaining artist. "His inventiveness is tickling every minute," Drake wrote. "He comes up with more than a few zingers." A more wholeheartedly generous review was supplied by John R. Petrovksky, who wrote in *Hispania* that the play "takes on many themes and manages to treat them all with humor and yet, by the end, depth."

After reaping the rewards of "Badges," Valdez returned to film in 1987 with "La Bamba," which recounts the brief career of Chicano pop musician Ritchie Valens, who enjoyed significant popularity in the late 1950s before perishing in the same airplane crash that killed fellow performers Buddy Holly and the Big Bopper. With "La Bamba" Valdez proved himself a proficient, engaging filmmaker. Among the critics impressed with Valdez's work was the *Washington Post*'s Hal Hinson, who acknowledged the film's "energetic . . . spirit" and its "infectious freshness." Another *Post* writer, Richard Harrington, was at least as enthusiastic, praising "La Bamba" as a "poignant and passionate portrayal" of the ill-fated Valens. Janet Maslin, in her review for the *New York Times,* commended "La Bamba" more for its "warmth" and its "strong feeling for Valens's Chicano roots," while Desson Howe found it "a glorious, drug-free shot in the arm for romantics."

With successes on both the stage and in film, Valdez has established himself as a key figure in the world of performance arts. And though he seems preoccupied with Chicano concerns, critics have noted that his best works transcend ethnic considerations of race or nationality. As *Newsweek*'s Lubenow noted, "He has succeeded by shaping the experience of Chicanos into drama that speaks to all Americans."

BIOGRAPHICAL/CRITICAL SOURCES:

BOOKS

Huerta, Jorge A., *Chicano Theatre: Themes and Forms,* Bilingual Press, 1982.

Meier, Matt S., *Mexican American Biographies: A Historical Dictionary*, Greenwood Press, 1988.

PERIODICALS

American Film, July-August, 1987.
Caracol, April, 1967.
Chicago Tribune, January 25, 1982, July 24, 1987.
Drama Review, December, 1974.
Educational Theatre Journal, March, 1974.
Globe and Mail (Toronto), July 25, 1987.
Hispania, September, 1986.
Los Angeles Times, August 18, 1978, February 7, 1986, July 24, 1987.
Newsweek, May 4, 1987.
New York Review of Books, August 31, 1972.
New York Times, May 4, 1978, March 26, 1979, January 22, 1982, August 10, 1985, July 24, 1987.
Performance, fall, 1973.
Theatre Quarterly, March-May, 1975.
Time, August 17, 1987.
Tulane Drama Review, summer, 1967.
Vista, July 23, 1989.
Washington Post, July 24, 1987, July 27, 1987.

—*Sketch by Les Stone*

* * *

VALENZUELA, Luisa 1938-

PERSONAL: Born November 26, 1938, in Buenos Aires, Argentina; came to the United States, 1979; daughter of Pablo Francisco Valenzuela (a physician) and Luisa Mercedes Levinson (a writer); married, 1958 (divorced); children: Anna-Lisa. *Education:* University of Buenos Aires, B.A.

ADDRESSES: Home—La Pampa 1202 (SD), 1428 Buenos Aires, Argentina. *Office*—New York Institute for the Humanities, 26 Washington Place, New York, N.Y. 10003.

CAREER: La Nación, Buenos Aires, Argentina, editor of Sunday supplement, 1961-72; free-lance writer for magazines and newspapers in Buenos Aires, 1972-78; Columbia University, New York City, writer-in-residence, 1979-80; New York University, New York City, visiting professor, 1985-90. Fellow of New York Institute for the Humanities.

AWARDS, HONORS: Awards from Fondo Nacional de las Artes, 1966 and 1973, and Instituto Nacional de Cinematografía, 1973, for script based on *Hay que sonreír;* Fulbright fellowship, Iowa International Writers' Program, 1969; Guggenheim fellowship, 1983.

MEMBER: PEN, Fund for Free Expression (member of Freedom to Write Committee).

WRITINGS:

Hay que sonreír (novel; also see below), Américalee, 1966.
Los heréticos (short stories; also see below), Paidós, 1967.
El gato eficaz (novel; portions have appeared in periodicals in English translation under title "Cat-O-Nine-Deaths"), J. Mortiz, 1972.
Aquí pasan cosas raras (short stories; also see below), Ediciones de la Flor, 1975.
Clara: Thirteen Short Stories and a Novel (translations by Hortense Carpentier and J. Jorge Castello; contains translations of *Hay que sonreír*, published as "Clara," and stories from *Los heréticos*), Harcourt, 1976.

Como en la guerra (novel; also see below), Sudamericana, 1977, translation by Helen Lane published as *He Who Searches*, Dalkey Archive Press, 1987.
Strange Things Happen Here: Twenty-Six Short Stories and a Novel (translations by Lane; contains "He Who Searches" and translation of *Aquí pasan cosas raras*), Harcourt, 1979.
Libro que no muerde (title means "Book That Doesn't Bite"; includes stories from *Aquí pasan cosas raras* and *Los heréticos*), Universidad Nacional Autónoma de México, 1980.
Cambio de armas (short stories), Ediciones del Norte, 1982, translation by Deborah Bonner published as *Other Weapons*, Ediciones del Norte/Persea Books, 1986.
Cola de lagartija, Bruguera, 1983, translation by Gregory Rabassa published as *The Lizard's Tail*, Farrar, Straus, 1983.
Donde viven las águilas (short stories), Celtia, 1983, translation published as *Up Among the Eagles*, North Point Press, 1988.
Open Door (short stories), translation by Carpentier and others, North Point Press, 1989.

Also author of script for film adaptation of *Hay que sonreír* and a play, "National Reality from the Bed," 1990. Contributor to *La Nación* and *Crisis;* contributor to U.S. periodicals, including *Vogue* and *Village Voice*.

WORK IN PROGRESS: Novela negro con argentinos, for Plaza y Janés (Spain) and Ediciones del Norte (United States), translation by Asa Zatz to be published as *Black Novel with Argentines*, Simon & Schuster.

SIDELIGHTS: "Luisa Valenzuela's writing belongs to that class of contemporary works Umberto Eco has called 'open works,' " Patricia Rubio observes in *Salmagundi*. "In them the harmonious representation of reality, supported by logic and syllogism, is replaced by a more ample and complex vision in which the laws of causality cease to operate in a linear fashion. The ordered *Weltanschauung* of the standard realist narrative . . . disintegrates in the face of desire, cruelty, the instinctual, the magical, the fantastic, the sickly." Noting the magical and the fantastic elements in the Argentine novelist and short story writer's work, critics often describe her fiction—with its mixture of the fantastic and the real—as belonging to that popular Latin American school of writing called magic realism. Not content with this characterization, Valenzuela is quoted by *Time* magazine's R. Z. Sheppard as saying, "Magical realism was a beautiful resting place, but the thing is to go forward." She has forged into new fictive territory: her work is much more bizarre, erotic and violent than that of magic realism's best-known proponents, such as Gabriel García Márquez and Julio Cortázar. As one of the few Latin American women writers to achieve wide-spread recognition in the United States, Valenzuela also distinguishes herself from other contemporary Latin American writers by bringing a decidedly feminist slant to the male-dominated world of Hispanic literature.

As Rubio points out, Valenzuela's work—with the exception of *Hay que sonreír*, her first novel (published in English translation as "Clara"), and *The Heretics*, her first collection of short stories—is highly experimental. Constantly shifting points of view, extensive use of metaphors, and word-play have become her trademark. In her fiction the form of the work as well as the words used to write it are equal candidates for renewal. *Hispania* contributors Dorothy S. Mull and Elsa B. de Angulo observe that Valenzuela's linguistic experimentations include "efforts to distort language, to 'break open' individual words to examine how they function, to expose their hidden facets as a watchmaker might probe and polish the jewels in a timepiece." In the *Voice Literary Supplement* Brett Harvey notes, "Valenzuela plays with words, turns them inside out, weaves them into sensuous webs. She uses them as weapons, talismans to ward off danger and name the unnameable."

An effort to name the unnameable seems to be a strong motivating force behind Valenzuela's fiction, in this case the unnameable being the surreal reality of Argentine politics. Emily Hicks finds politics such an important facet of Valenzuela's novella, *He Who Searches,* that the critic writes in a *Review of Contemporary Fiction* essay, "The reader of this text will not be able to understand it without considering the current political situation in Argentina." Valenzuela has herself admitted the political content of her work. For example, in an interview with Evelyn Picon Garfield in *Review of Contemporary Fiction,* Valenzuela notes that the reason she wrote her most popular novel, *The Lizard's Tail,* was for "only one purpose: to try to understand." Valenzuela explains that it is almost impossible for her to comprehend how the Argentine people allowed themselves to become victims of the harsh military regimes that dominated their country for such a long time. In a similar conversation with Barbara Case in a *Ms.* interview, Valenzuela reveals that the magic found in her work is paradoxically the result of the reality the writer discovered in her native land. "Everything is so weird now and it becomes more and more strange," Valenzuela explains. "We thought we had this very civilized, integrated, cosmopolitan country, and suddenly we realized we were dealing with magic. It's been discovered that a minister in Isabel Perón's cabinet was in real life a witch doctor and had books published on witchcraft. Argentinians were caught in a trap of believing ourselves to be European while ignoring all our Latin American reality."

The Lizard's Tail, has been described as a roman a clef based on the life of the cabinet minister Valenzuela mentions in her interview with Case. José López Rega, Perón's Minister of Social Welfare, appears in the novel as the Sorcerer, a man who has three testicles. He refers to this third testicle as his sister "Estrella" and dreams of having a child with her. "Of course this character," Case observes, "renounces women since he already has one built in—his own 'trinity of the crotch.' But in this unique parody of Latin machismo, his third testicle, Estrella, exists in the Sorcerer to restrain him. When he gets too feisty, Estrella contracts with pain and leaves him doubled up on the floor." Through the use of first-person monologues—described as the Sorcerer's novel or diary—and additional first- and third-person narrations, Valenzuela tells the story of the Sorcerer's rise to power, his fall, his plans to return to power, and his death. Other characters include the Sorcerer's mother (whom he boils and drinks), the Generalissimo, the Dead Woman Eva, and Valenzuela herself.

The work seems to contain everything that readers have come to expect in Valenzuela's fiction: magic, power, political commentary, circular time, female/male conflicts and violence. However, some critics believe Valenzuela tries to cover too much in the work. *New York Times Book Review* contributor Allen Josephs states, "Her attempt at virtuosity tends to undermine the novel. In order to convince the reader of the Sorcerer's madness and narcissistic depravity, she resorts to surrealism, hyperbole and self-indulgent prose. The parody becomes increasingly self-conscious as the novel proceeds." Reviewer Herbert Gold also criticizes the novel, writing in the *Los Angeles Times Book Review,* "She is trying for intelligence and trying for magic; but the novelist here points to herself too much. . . . She broods about making magic too much to be able to make the magic. She wants to be wild; that's not the same as wildness."

Other critics praise the novel, seeing it as an important work of Latin American fiction. In *Review of Contemporary Fiction* Marie-Lise Gazarian Gautier calls *The Lizard's Tail* "one of the most fascinating novels written in recent years by a Latin American." Harvey refers to it as "a gorgeously surreal allegory of Argentine politics." In her *Review* essay on the work, critic and translator Edith Grossman finds the novel "remarkable" and notes that in it "Valenzuela reaffirms the powerful significance of language and the value of the artful word as legitimate modes of understanding the dark enigmas of brutality and violence."

Valenzuela's criticism of Argentine politics is often coupled with her equally harsh look at the fate of women in such a society. In her *World Literature Today* essay on the writer, Sharon Magnarelli finds Valenzuela "always subtly political and/or feminist." Magnarelli detects a link between Valenzuela's word-play and her portrayal of women in her fiction, believing that the Argentine's "work is clearly an attempt to free language and women from the shackles of society." Valenzuela's novel, *Hay que sonreír,* deals with Clara, a young woman who comes to Buenos Aires from the provinces and turns to prostitution in order to support herself. In the novel one sees the beginnings of Valenzuela's characteristic experimentation with form: the story is told through first and third person narrations alternating between past and present tenses. The book also contains a clear statement of the writer's feminist concerns. "One of the main themes of the text," Magnarelli notes, "is unquestionably contemporary woman's plight with the social expectations that she will be passive, silent, industrious (but only in areas of minor import), possessed by a male (be he father, husband, or pimp) and that she will continue to smile (*hay que sonreír* ['one has to smile' in English]) in spite of the exploitation or violence perpetrated against her."

Critics also comment on the female protagonists of the stories in Valenzuela's collection, *Other Weapons,* five narratives dealing with male/female relationships. While many Argentine writers have focused attention on the larger social and economic ramifications of their country's continually violent political situation, Valenzuela, as both *Voice Literary Supplement* contributor Brett Harvey and *Review* contributor Mary Lusky Friedman comment, reveals how the stress of living in a repressive society undermines interpersonal ties between individuals in that society. "*Other Weapons* is a book that testifies to the difficulty of forging, in politically distressed times, sustaining personal relationships," Friedman observes. "The failures of intimacy that Valenzuela depicts are the quieter casualties of Argentina's recent crisis." In Valenzuela's work, as Valerie Gladstone points out in the *New York Times Book Review,* "Political absurdity is matched only by the absurdity of human relations."

BIOGRAPHICAL/CRITICAL SOURCES:

BOOKS

Contemporary Literary Criticism, Volume 31, 1985.

PERIODICALS

Hispania, May, 1986.
Los Angeles Times Book Review, September 11, 1983.
Ms., October, 1983.
New York Times Book Review, October 2, 1983, October 30, 1988.
Review, January-May, 1984, July-December, 1985.
Review of Contemporary Fiction, fall, 1986.
Salmagundi, spring-summer, 1989.
Time, March 7, 1983.
Voice Literary Supplement, December, 1985.

World Literature Today, winter, 1984.

—*Sketch by Marian Gonsior*

* * *

VALLEJO, Antonio Buero
  See BUERO VALLEJO, Antonio

* * *

VALLEJO, César (Abraham) 1892-1938

PERSONAL: Born March 16, 1892, in Santiago de Chuco, Peru; died April 15, 1938, of a chronic illness variously reported as tuberculosis, acute intestinal infection, and malaria; married Georgette Phillipart. *Education:* Trujillo University, 1910-11, 1913-17, B.A. in literature, 1915, and law degree; studied medicine at University of San Marcos in Lima, 1911.

CAREER: Poet and free lance writer. Worked in his father's notary office, in mine offices, as a tutor, and in an estate accounts office; teacher, Centro Escolar du Verones and Colegio Nacional de San Juan, 1913-17; lived in Lima, Peru, 1917-23; teacher, Colegio Barrós, 1918-19, and another school, 1920; involved in political riot, Santiago de Chuco, Peru, and imprisoned, 1920-21; teacher, Colegio Guadalupe, 1921-23; lived in Europe after 1923; secretary, Iberoamerican press agency, 1925. Worked as journalist and helped publish *Nuestra España* in Spain during the Spanish Civil War, 1936-38.

AWARDS, HONORS: National short story contest winner, c. 1921.

WRITINGS:

POETRY

Los heraldos negros (title means "The Black Messengers", also see below), includes "Canciones de hogar" (also see below), [Lima], 1918, Perú Nuevo, 1959, published as *Los heraldos negros, 1918,* Losada (Buenos Aires), 1961.
Trilce, Talleres Tipografía de la Penitenciaría (Lima, Peru), 1922, 2nd edition with introduction by José Bergamín, Cía Iberoamericana de Publicaciones (Madrid), 1931, reprinted, Losada, 1961, published with essays by Antenor Orrego and Bergamín, Fondo de Cultura Popular, 1962, translation by David Smith published as *Trilce,* Grossman (New York), 1973.
Poemas humanos (also see below), Presses Modernes (Paris), 1939, Perú Nuevo, 1959, translation by Clayton Eshleman published as *Poemas Humanos: Human Poems,* Grove Press, 1969.
España, aparta de mí este cáliz (also see below), with introductory essay "Profecía de América" (title means "Prophecy of America"), Séneca (Mexico), 1940, Perú Nuevo, 1960, Dirección de Cultura Ministerio de Educación (Havana, Cuba), 1961, Editorial Fundamentos (Madrid), 1984, translation by Alvaro Cardoña-Hine published as *Spain, Let This Cup Pass from Me,* Red Hill, 1972, translation by Eshleman and José Rubia Barcia published as *Spain, Take This Cup from Me,* Grove Press, 1974.
Antología de César Vallejo, compiled by Xavier Abril, Editorial Claridad, 1942.
Antología, compiled by Edmundo Cornejo U., Hora del Hombre, 1948.
Poesías completas (1918-1938), compiled by César Míro, Losada, 1949.
Los mejores versos de César Vallejo, [Buenos Aires], c. 1956.
La vida, y quince poemas: Antología poética, compiled by José Escobar and Eugenio Martínez Pastor, Baladre, 1958.

Poemas, compiled with notes by Ramiro de Casabellas, Perrot (Buenos Aires), 1958.
Poemas escogidos, compiled with prologue by Gustavo Valcárcel, Editora Latinoamericana, 1958.
Poemas humanos (1923-1938) [and] *España, aparta de mí este cáliz (1937-1938),* Losada, 1961, Laia, 1985.
Poesías completas, Volume 1: *Los heraldos negros,* Volume 2: *Trilce,* Volume 3: *España, aparta de mí este cáliz,* Volume 4: *Poemas humanos,* Perú Nuevo, 1961.
César Vallejo: Sus mejores obras, (includes *Los heraldos negros, Trilce, Rusia en 1931,* and *Reflexiones al pie del Kremlin*), Ediciones Perú, 1962.
Twenty Poems (bilingual edition), selection and translations by Robert Bly, James Wright, and John Knoepfle, with essay by Wright, Sixties Press, 1962.
Antología poética, with introduction by Valcárcel, Impresiones Nacional de Cuba, 1962.
Los heraldos negros y Trilce, Ediciones Perú, 1962.
Poesías completas, with prologue by Roberto Fernández Retaman, Casa de las Américas (Havana), 1965.
Antología, edited with notes by Julio Ortega, Editorial Universitaria, 1966.
César Vallejo, edited by wife, Georgette de Vallejo, P. Seghers (Paris), 1967.
Seven Poems, translation by Eshleman, R. Morris, 1967.
Obra poética completa, with manuscript facsimiles, edited by G. de Vallejo, (includes *Los heraldos negros* and *Poemas humanos;* also see below), F. Moncloa, 1968, later edition edited by Enrique Ballón Aguierre, Biblioteca Ayacucho (Caracas), 1979, original Spanish edition reprinted, Ediciones Norte, 1983.
Obras completas (three volumes), Mosca Azul (Lima), Volume 1: *Contra el secreto profesional,* 1968, Volume 2: *El arte y la revolución,* 1968, Volume 3: *Obra poética completa,* with revised biographical essay by G. de Vallejo, 1974.
Poemas-Kavitaem (bilingual edition in Spanish and Hindi), translation and preface by Premlata Verma, [Delhi, India], 1969.
César Vallejo: An Anthology of His Poetry, edited with an introduction and notes by James Higgins, Pergamon Press, 1970.
Un hombre pasa, translation by Michael Smith, New Writers' Press, 1970.
Ten Versions from Trilce, translations by Charles Tomlinson and Henry Gifford, San Marcos Press, 1970.
Neruda and Vallejo: Selected Poems, translation by Bly, Wright, and Knoepfle, edited by Bly, Beacon Press, 1971.
Poesías completas de César Vallejo, J. Pablos Editor (Mexico), 1971.
Selected Poems, edited by Gordon Brotherston and Ed Dorn, Penguin, 1976.
César Vallejo: The Complete Posthumous Poetry, translation by Eshleman and Barcia, University of California Press, 1978.
Perfil de César Vallejo: Vida y obra antología poética, edited by Juan Larrea and others, Gráfica San Andrés, 1978.
Poesía completa, Premiá Editora (Mexico), 1981.
Canciónes de hogar: Songs of Home, translation by Richard Schaaf and Kathleen Ross, Ziesing Bros., 1981.
Selected Poems of César Vallejo, translation by H. R. Hays, Sachem, 1981.
Obra poética completa: César Vallejo, with introduction by Américo Ferrari, Alianza, 1982.
Palms and Guitar, translation by J. C. R. Green, Aquila/Phaethon Press, 1982.
Así es la vida, tal como es la vida, edited with introduction by Juan Antonio Massone, Editorial Nascimento, 1982.

Poemas humanos; España, aparta de mí este cáliz, Laia (Barcelona), 1985.

Selected Poetry, edited by Higgins, F. Cairns, 1987.

Poemas en prosa; Poemas humanos, España, aparta de mí este cáliz, Cátedra, 1988.

Poesía completa, Ediciones Consejo de Integración Cultura Latinoamericana, 1988.

Works also collected in *Poesía completa,* edited by Larrea, 1978. Contributor to literary magazines in Peru and Europe.

FICTION

Escalas melografiadas (short stories; also see below), Talleres Tipografía de la Penitenciaría (Lima, Peru), 1923.

Fabla salvaje (novella; also see below), [Lima], 1923, Editorial Labor, 1965.

El tungsteno: La novela proletaria (also see below), Editorial Cenit (Madrid), 1931, first Peruvian edition published as *Tungsteno,* Ediciones de Cuadernos Trimestrales de Poesía, 1958, translation by Robert Mezey with preface by Kevin O'Connor published as *Tungsten: A Novel,* Syracuse University Press, 1988.

Novelas: Tungsteno, Fabla salvaje, Escalas melografiadas, Hora del Hombre, 1948.

Tungsteno y Paco Yunque (also see below), J. Mejía Baca & P. L. Villanueva, 1957.

Novelas y cuentos completos, F. Moncloa (Lima), 1967, 2nd edition, Moncloa-Campodonico, 1970.

Paco Yunque, [Lima], 1969, first Honduran edition with illustrations by Pablo Picasso, Editorial Girándula (Honduras), 1981.

OTHER

Rusia en 1931; Reflexiones al pie del Kremlin (also see below), Ediciones Ulises (Madrid), 1931, published in two volumes, Perú Nuevo, 1959.

El romanticismo en la poesía castellana, Juan Mejía Baca & P. L. Villanueva, 1954.

Artículos olvidados, compiled with prologue by Luis Alberto Sánchez, Asociación Peruana por la Libertad de la Cultura, 1960.

Rusia ante el segundo plan quinquenal, Gráfica Labor, 1965.

Literatura y arte, Ediciones del Mediodía (Buenos Aires), 1966.

Battles in Spain, translation by Eshleman and Barcia, Black Sparrow Press, 1978.

Desde Europa, edited by Jorge Puccinelli, Instituto Raúl Porras Barranchea (Lima), 1969, Ediciones Fuente de Cultura Peruana, 1987.

Cartas a Pablo Abril, Rodolfo Alonso (Buenos Aires), 1971.

Teatro completo, two volumes, La Católica, 1979.

Epistolario general (letters), Pre-Textos, 1982.

Autopsy on Surrealism, translation by Schaaf, edited by James Scully, Curbstone, 1982.

The Mayakovsky Case ("El caso Maiakovski," a critical essay), translation by Schaaf, edited by Scully, Curbstone, 1982.

Crónicas (prose works; in several volumes), Volume 1, Universidad Nacional Autónoma de México, Dirección General de Publicaciones, 1984.

La cultura peruana: Crónicas (collected essays), selection by Aguirre, Mosca Azul, 1987.

Also author of "Lockout," a play. Translator of *L'Elévation,* by Henri Barbusse, 1931. Works represented in *Espadaña,* published in León, Spain, 1944-51, and in *Aula Vallejo,* a serial publication of Instituto del Nuevo Mundo, Universidad Nacional de Córdoba, 1961—. Contributor of articles to *Mundial, El Comercio, Variedades,* and to newspapers in Spain and France. Cofounder and contributor, *Favorables-Paris-Poemas.*

SIDELIGHTS: Peruvian expatriate César Vallejo was a major poet who was among the first Latin American writers to produce a body of work having a strong voice known for its authenticity and originality. Deeply rooted in his mixed European and Peruvian Indian heritage, his poetry expressed universal themes related to the human condition. Sometimes called a surrealist poet, "Vallejo created a wrenching poetic language for Spanish that radically altered the shape of its imagery and the nature of its rhythms. No facile trend setter, Vallejo forged a new discourse in order to express his own visceral compassion for human suffering," Edith Grossman writes in the *Los Angeles Times Book Review.* "A constant feature of his poetry is a compassionate awareness of and a guilt-ridden sense of responsibility for the suffering of others," observes James Higgins in *The Poet in Peru: Alienation and the Quest for a Super-Reality.* His compassion was informed by his own painful experience as an inmate in a Trujillo prison, as an expatriate political activist, and as a witness of the holocaust of the Spanish Civil War. He also endured poverty and a chronic illness of which he died in 1938. Grossman relates, "He saw the world in piercing flashes of outrage and anguish, terror and pity. . . . A passionate, tragic poet, he mourned our loss of moral innocence and despaired of the injustice that moves the world."

Vallejo was born in Santiago de Chuco, a small village in the northern Andes mountains. Raised Catholic and encouraged to become a priest, he discovered that he could not keep the requirement of celibacy. His family relationships remained secure and close. For a time, he was a clerk in his father's notary office. His mother's friendship, in particular, was a sustaining force in his life until her death in 1923 (some sources say 1918). The comfort of his rural life set for Vallejo a standard against which all later experiences seemed needlessly sadistic.

Early poems in his first collection *Los heraldos negros* ("The Black Messengers") relate Vallejo's bewilderment when struck with the harshness of city life in Trujillo and Lima, where he studied medicine, literature, and law. While a student he encountered a number of crushing disillusionments. Introduced to the ideas of Marx, Darwin, and Rationalist philosophers, Vallejo felt that the faith in which he was raised was no longer viable. Together with other intellectuals, he became actively interested in his pre-Columbian heritage and was anguished to learn of the suffering of Indians in his country. When the parents of his lover broke off their relationship for reasons he did not understand, he attempted suicide. Higgins summarizes that "the unthinkable [was] commonplace" in the city. Vallejo's "arrival in Lima therefore, marks his initiation into a seemingly absurd and senseless world whose meaning escapes him," he reasons. Unable to replace the caring family he had lost, Vallejo felt alienated in the city. Alienation and the apparent senselessness of his suffering became his recurrent themes.

Poems in *Los heraldos negros,* like most Latin American poetry of that time, follow the conventions of European literature known as the *modernista* movement. The *modernistas,* D. P. Gallagher explains in *Modern Latin American Literature,* highlighted their language's capacity for melody; breaking a taboo, Vallejo added erotic lyrics to the descriptions of beautiful landscape common to this style. *Modernista* poets Leopoldo Lugones and Julio Herrera y Reissig influenced the young Vallejo significantly. "They were both masters of the violently suprising image, and their poetry is free of the jaded air of fatigued mimicry that many *modernista* poems had come to display," Gallagher comments. By the end of *Los heraldos negros* in the "Canciones de hogar" ("Songs of Home") section, Vallejo had given voice to concerns which would remain his major themes: he lamented his status as an orphan unprepared for the brutality of life in a world where God himself seemed troubled by limitations, impotence, and death. In addition, the urgency of personal statement and original idiom in these poems show that Vallejo had outgrown his dependence on traditional literary models. Thus he presented a mature original voice having more social relevance and literary importance than his *modernista* mentors, Gallagher adds.

After a number of years in Trujillo and Lima, in 1920 Vallejo returned to his birthplace where he became involved in a political melee during which the town's general store burned down. He was accused of instigating the conflict and jailed for three months. Added to the death of his mother, the isolation and savagery of conditions there effected him deeply. "The subject of a number of poems, that experience reinforced his belief in the world's arbitrary cruelty and his sense of inadequacy in the face of it," Higgins writes in *A History of Peruvian Literature*. Accordingly, poems written in prison (collected in *Trilce*) are markedly different from the idyllic poems of *Los heraldos negros*.

Trilce is more difficult, more intense, and more original than Vallejo's first volume. Pared of all ornamental language, these poems convey the poet's personal urgency as he cries out against the apparent meaninglessness of his suffering. *Trilce* introduces the wrenched syntax that allows Vallejo to get beyond the constraints of received linguistic conventions to a language that is true to his experience. Writing in *A History of Peruvian Literature*, Higgins catalogues the elements of Vallejo's diction: "Vallejo confounds the reader's expectations by his daring exploitation of the line pause, which often leaves articles, conjunctions and even particles of words dangling at the end of a line, by his frequent resort to harsh sounds to break the rhythm, by employing alliterations so awkward as to be tongue-twisters. He distorts syntactic structures, changes the grammatical function of words, plays with spelling. His poetic vocabulary is frequently unfamiliar and 'unliterary', he creates new words of his own, he often conflates two words into one, he tampers with clichés to give them new meaning, he plays on the multiple meaning of words and on the similarity of sound between words. He repeatedly makes use of oxymoron and paradox and, above all, catachresis, defamiliarising objects by attributing to them qualities not normally associated with them."

Vallejo's wrenched syntax is not a mere literary performance; it is the means necessary "to discover the man that has been hitherto hidden behind its decorative facades. The discovery is not a pleasant one, and the noise in the poems make it consequently aggressive and not beautiful," Gallagher observes. Out of Vallejo's self-discovery comes an "unprecedented, raw language" that declares Vallejo's humanness despite his confinement to make a statement "about the human problems of which Vallejo is a microcosm," Gallagher adds. *New York Review of Books* contributor Michael Wood explains, "With Vallejo it is an instrument—the only possible instrument, it seems—for the confrontation of complexity, of the self caught up in the world and the world mirrored in the self. It is an answer, let us say, to the simultaneous need for a poetry that would put heart into an agonizing Spain and for a poetry that will not take wishes for truths." Gallagher suggests that Vallejo was "perhaps the first Latin American writer to have realized that it is precisely in the discovery of a language where literature must find itself in a continent where for centuries the written word was notorious more for what it concealed than for what it revealed, where 'beautiful' writing,

sheer sonorous wordiness was a mere holding operation against the fact that you did not dare really say anything at all."

The facade separating Vallejo from the truth about himself—and all men—was one of many boundaries he strove to break through by means of writing. This is most evident in *Trilce* where the poet recognizes the physical fact of his imprisonment as an archetype of the human struggle against all imposed limits. For example, for Vallejo, the Spanish Civil War points to the existence of man's greater struggle, an "a priori" or predetermined conflict between an individual and his desires for transcendence, as he phrased it in *Poemas humanos*. "More than a political event," states Gallagher, to Vallejo the war was yet another facet of entropy, "that dismemberment of unity which we have seen him observing even in his own body."

Vallejo saw that beyond the obvious constraints of government, society, and culture, man is incarcerated by time, space, and his biological limitations. Repeatedly the later poems complain of "the frustration of the poet's spiritual aspirations by the limitations of the flesh," relates Higgins in *The Poet in Peru*. The poet's transcendent hopes seemed to be precluded by an inescapable biological determinism, Jean Franco notes in *César Vallejo: The Dialectics of Poetry and Silence*. "While his spirit holds up to him a vision of a higher life, his experience of hunger and illness brings home to him the extent to which his existence is lived on an elemental level, through that frail, decaying body of his which constantly demands satisfaction of its appetites and repeatedly breaks down under the effects of illness and age," Higgins elaborates in *The Poet in Peru*. He adds, "Much more serious, the poet-doctor insinuates, is the malaise brought on by reasoning which, by destroying illusions and laying bare the vanity of things, insidiously undermines his spiritual health. Since man is unable to find any meaning to life, he has no real existence and lives only through the anguished sense of futility which is slowly destroying him and which has become contagious in an age when all human values seem to have failed." Though it becomes more subtle in later books, the theme of man versus his limits continues throughout Vallejo's work.

In 1923, Vallejo moved to Europe. Until 1930, when he was expelled from France for his unorthodox politics, he lived in Paris where he wrote articles about the need to get beyond the phoniness of much contemporary poetry. Literary posturing sustained by simple mimicry of the style currently in vogue may disguise a poet's lack of talent but will not render a vital contribution to life or art, he maintained in *Literatura y arte*. The harshness of his standards is perhaps forgivable in that he applied them relentlessly to his own work, Gallagher comments. By achieving authenticity in innovative language, Vallejo influenced many younger poets to embrace nontraditional techniques.

In the 1920s and '30s Vallejo became more engaged in politics. His three visits to the Soviet Union—the first in 1928—aided the formulation of his political views. He wrote a number of didactic works that are effective due to their sincere passion, Gallagher notes. These include *Rusia en 1931* and *Reflexiones al pie del Kremlin*, first published in Spain and not printed in Peru until almost thirty years later. Also in this category is the novel *El tungsteno* ("Tungsten"), which condemns an American company for exploiting its Peruvian workers to get the element it needed to make weapons. Political statements emerge in his other works as well, but they do not dominate. Vallejo was an ambivalent Marxist, at most. Gallagher reports, "Vallejo regards Communism, in *Poemas humanos* and 'España, aparta de mí este cáliz,' as . . . just the vague sighting of a way out from a world that nevertheless remains as hermetically frontier-bound as that of *Trilce.* " Higgins finds evidence in *Poemas humanos* that Vallejo sometimes admired the single-mindedness of those who could submit themselves to "the cause," but again found it impossible to subject himself without question to Marxist or communist ideals. He moved to Spain during its war years to work as a journalist and lend support to his friends in defense of the Spanish Republic. At the same time, Vallejo admired the brotherhood achieved among the activists who gave their lives to serve what they believed was the improvement of life for the poor.

After he died in 1938, his widow Georgette de Vallejo selected poems for publication in *Poemas humanos.* Gallagher maintains that the style of this volume is best described as "eccentric," in two senses of the word. *Poemas humanos* was written in a highly personal idiom. Vallejo expressed the suffering of people in general, for instance, in the terms of his own specific experience in a violently contorted language. Secondly, Vallejo's word choice was often "ex-centric" or off center to parallel the ambiguous nature of contemporary experience. In Vallejo's poems, things and events do not function as symbols; they signify no apparent cause, no omen behind the objects and events of daily life. At the same time the poems are haunted by the dread that meaning does exist, but man cannot grasp it. If man's "a priori" contest is "beyond reckoning," as Vallejo wrote in *Poemas humanos,* it must also lay somewhat beyond words. Vallejo's unique diction is a natural extension of his personal crisis.

Though he won little critical acclaim before his death, Vallejo came "to be recognized as an artist of world stature, the greatest poet not only of Peru but of all Spanish America," Higgins sums up in *The History of Peruvian Literature.* Gallagher concludes, "There is no poet in Latin America like Vallejo, . . . who has bequeathed so consistently personal an idiom, and no poet so strictly rigorous with himself. It is a curiously subtle, menacing world that he has left us in his mature works." Vallejo will be remembered for discovering a unique poetic language that approximates what he perceived as the frustration inherent in the human condition and the chaos of the world. Franco comments that for Vallejo, using that language was a vital exercise of freedom: "Vallejo knew that with every automatic word and gesture man contributes to his own damnation and imprisonment. His great achievement as a poet is to have interrupted that easy-flowing current of words which is both a solace and the mark of our despair, to have made each poem an act of consciousness which involves the recognition of difficulty and pain." Therefore, Vallejo is seen as the spiritual godfather of many innovations in poetic technique. *New York Times Book Review* contributor Alexander Coleman observes that Vallejo, "the standard for authenticity and intensity" in Hispanic literature, opened the way for future poets by leaving to them "a language swept clean, now bright and angular, ready for the man in the street."

BIOGRAPHICAL/CRITICAL SOURCES:

BOOKS

Abril, Xavier, *César Vallejo a la teoría poética,* Taurus (Madrid), 1962.

Abril, Xavier, *Exégesis trílcica,* Labor, 1980.

Aguierre, Enrique Ballón, *Vallejo como paradigma: Un caso especial de escritura,* Instituto de Cultura, 1974.

Asturrizaga, Juan Espejo, *César Vallejo: Itinerario del hombre, 1892-1923,* Librería-Editorial Juan Mejía Baca, 1965.

Chávez, Iván Rodríguez, *La ortografía poética de Vallejo,* Compañía de Impresiones y Publicidad, 1974.

Coyné, Andre, *César Vallejo y su obra poética,* Letras Peruanas, 1957.

Daydí-Tolson, Santiago, *The Post-Civil War Spanish Social Poets,* Twayne, 1983.

de Vallejo, Georgette, in Vallejo, César, *Obra poética completa,* F. Moncloa, 1968.

de Vallejo, Georgette, *Vallejo: Allá ellos, allá ellos, allá ellos!,* Zalvac, 1980.

Escobar, Alberto, *Como leer a Vallejo,* P. L. Villanueva, 1973.

Ferrari, Américo, *El universo poético de César Vallejo,* Monte Avila (Caracas), 1972.

Flores, Angel, editor, *Aproximaciones a Vallejo,* two volumes, Las Américas (New York), 1971.

Flores, Angel, editor, *César Vallejo, Síntesis biográfica, bibliografía y índice de poemas,* Premiá Editora, 1982.

Franco, Jean, *César Vallejo: The Dialectics of Poetry and Silence,* Cambridge University Press, 1976.

Fuentes, Victor, *El cántico material y espiritual de César Vallejo,* Anthropos Editorial del Hombre, 1981.

Gallagher, D. P., *Modern Latin American Literature,* Oxford University Press, 1973.

García, Francisco Martínez, *César Vallejo; acercamiento al hombre y al poeta,* Colegio Universitario de León, 1976.

Higgins, James, *Visión del hombre y de la vida en las últimas obras poéticas de César Vallejo,* Siglo Veintiuno, 1970.

Higgins, James, *The Poet in Peru: Alienation and the Quest for a Super-Reality,* F. Cairns, 1982.

Higgins, James, *A History of Peruvian Literature,* F. Cairns, 1987.

Larrea, Juan, *César Vallejo; o, Hispanoamérica en la cruz de su razón,* Universidad de Córdoba, 1958.

Larrea, Juan, *César Vallejo: Héroe y mártir indo-hispano,* Biblioteca Nacional (Montevideo), 1973.

Larrea, Juan, *César Vallejo y el surrealismo,* A. Corazón (Madrid), 1976.

Larrea, Juan, *Al amor de Vallejo,* Pre-Textos, 1980.

Larrea, Juan, and others, *Perfil de César Vallejo,* Gráfica San Andrés, 1978.

Mariátegui, José Carlos, in *Siete ensayos de la realidad peruana,* 9th edition, Biblioteca Amauta (Lima), 1964.

Merino, Antonio, and Julio Vélez, editors, *España en César Vallejo,* Editorial Fundamentos, 1984.

More, Ernesto, *Vallejo en la encrucijada del drama peruano,* Librería y Distribuidores Bendezú (Lima), 1968.

Neale-Silva, Eduardo, *César Vallejo en su fase trílcica,* University of Wisconsin Press, 1975.

Ortega, Julio, editor, *César Vallejo,* Taurus (Madrid), 1974.

Ortega, Julio, *La teoría poética de César Vallejo,* DelSol Editores, 1986.

Osuna, Yolanda, *Vallejo, el poema, la idea,* Universidad Central de Venezuela, 1979.

Paoli, Roberto, *Poesie di César Vallejo,* Lecrici, 1964.

Paoli, Roberto, *Mapas anatómicos de César Vallejo,* D'Anna, 1981.

Twentieth Century Literary Criticism, Volume 3, Gale, 1980.

Vallejo, César, *Poemas humanos,* 1939, Nuevo Perú, 1959, translation by Clayton Eshleman published as *Poemas humanos: Human Poems,* Grove Press, 1969.

Vallejo, César, *Literatura y arte,* Ediciones del Mediodía (Buenos Aires), 1966.

Vega, José Luis, *César Vallejo en "Trilce,"* Universidad de Puerto Rico, 1983.

Yurkievich, Saúl, in *Fundadores de la nueva poesía latinoamericana,* Barral (Barcelona), 1971.

Zilio, Giovanni Meo, *Stile e poesia in César Vallejo,* Liviana (Padua, Italy), 1960.

PERIODICALS

Amaru, Number 13, October, 1970.
Aula Vallejo, Number 1, 1961, Number 2/4, 1963, Number 5/7, 1967, Number 8/10, 1971, Number 11/13, 1974.
Courier, June, 1988.
Cuadernos Americanos, Volume 14, number 91, January, 1957.
Fiction International, summer, 1986.
Hispamerica, Volume 2, April 6, 1974.
Hispania, September, 1987.
Hispanic Review, Volume 50, number 3, 1982.
Hudson Review, winter, 1979.
Los Angeles Times Book Review, January 1, 1989.
Nation, October 28, 1968.
New York Review of Books, December 21, 1978.
New York Times Book Review, March 23, 1969, June 8, 1969, February 26, 1989, May 7, 1972.
Poetry, June, 1969, January, 1981.
Revista Iberoamericana Volume 34, number 71 (special Vallejo issue), April, 1970.
Times Literary Supplement, September 25, 1969, January 18, 1980, June 14, 1989.
Tri-Quarterly, fall, 1968.
Village Voice, March 21, 1989.
Virginia Quarterly Review, winter, 1980.
Visión del Perú, Number 4, 1969.
Western Humanities Review, winter, 1969.
West Indian Review, July, 1939.

—Sketch by Marilyn K. Basel

* * *

VARDERI, Alejandro 1960-

PERSONAL: Born January 17, 1960, in Caracas, Venezuela; son of Ramón (a jeweler) and Juana (a homemaker; maiden name, Tobías) Varderi. *Education:* Attended Universidad Católica Andrés Bello, 1977-80; Universidad Central de Venezuela, B.A., 1984; University of Illinois, M.F.A., 1987; New York University, Ph.D. candidate.

ADDRESSES: Home—New York, N.Y. *Office*—Spanish Department, New York University, 10 University Place, New York, N.Y. 10003.

CAREER: Writer, literary and art critic, editor. Accounting assistant, 1978-79; director of finances, AIESEC Venezuela, 1978-80; assistant in projects and bonds department, La Metropolitana Insurance Company, 1979-80; printing coordinator, State Foundation for the Arts (Fundarte), 1984-85; editorial assistant, 1988-89, and reader in Spanish, French, and Portuguese literature, 1988-90, Pantheon Books.

AWARDS, HONORS: Center for Latin American Studies "Rómulo Gallegos" fellowship, 1978; National Short Story Contest (Venezuela), second prize, 1979, and first prize, 1980; National Contest of Fiction (Venezuela), first prize, 1981; recipient of various university grants and awards, 1987-90.

WRITINGS:

Cuerpo plural (stories), La Gaveta (Caracas), 1978.
Ritos cívicos (novel), La Gaveta, 1980.
Ettedgui: Arte-información para la comunidad, Oxígeno (Caracas), 1985.
Estado e industria editorial (economic study), Fundarte (Caracas), 1986.
Nuevos narradores del Distrito Federal (anthology), Fundarte, 1986.

Anotaciones sobre el amor y el deseo (essays), Academia Nacional de la Historia, 1986.
Para repetir una mujer (novel), Salvat (Barcelona), 1987.

Also author of unpublished works *Amantes irreverentes* and *Mujer de pájaro.* Contributor of more than one hundred articles to periodicals in the United States, Venezuela, and Spain, including the *Miami Herald.* Founding associate editor, *La Gaveta Ilustrada,* 1976-81, *Imagen,* 1984-85, *Criticarte,* 1984-85, *Oxígeno,* 1985-87, *Línea Plural,* 1986-88, and *Enclave,* 1990.

WORK IN PROGRESS: A novel "recreating a century (1892-1992) in the life of a Catalan family living between Catalonia and South America"; a book of essays on Spanish women writers; a Spanish translation of "an American gay novel dealing with *pre* and *post* AIDS sexuality in New York City"; a book about postmodernism in cinema and literature.

SIDELIGHTS: Alejandro Varderi, who speaks Spanish, Catalan, English, French, Portuguese, and Italian, told *HW* that the novel he is working on "combines my personal experience and my family's background in a world of fictional characters. As a child born in Venezuela from Catalan parents I have always been fascinated by the singularities of both cultures: Catalans are very responsible, hard workers, and usually hold their feelings, whereas Venezuelans are the opposite. In this novel I am trying to make both realities merge within a postmodern cultural frame."

* * *

VARGAS LLOSA, (Jorge) Mario (Pedro) 1936-

PERSONAL: Born March 28, 1936, in Arequipa, Peru; son of Ernesto Vargas Maldonaldo and Dora Llosa Ureta; married Julia Urquidi, 1955 (divorced); married Patricia Llosa, 1965; children: (second marriage) Gonzalo, Alvaro, Morgana. *Education:* Attended University of San Marcos; University of Madrid, Ph.D., 1959. *Politics:* Member of Fredemo, a center-right political party which is part of the Liberty Movement coalition.

CAREER: Writer. Journalist with *La Industria,* Piura, Peru, and with La Radio Panamericana and *La Crónica,* both in Lima, Peru, during 1960s; worked in Paris, France, as a journalist with Agence France-Presse, as a broadcaster with the radio-television network URTF, and as a language teacher; University of London, Queen Mary College and Kings College, London, England, faculty member, 1966-68; University of Washington, Seattle, writer in residence, 1968; University of Puerto Rico, Río Piedras, visiting professor, 1969; *Libre,* Paris, co-founder, 1971; Columbia University, New York, N.Y., Edward Laroque Tinker Visiting Professor, 1975; former fellow, Woodrow Wilson Center, Washington, D.C.; former host of Peruvian television program "The Tower of Babel"; Peruvian presidential candidate, Liberty Movement, 1990.

AWARDS, HONORS: Premio Leopoldo Alas, 1959, for *Los jefes;* Barral Prix Biblioteca Breve, 1962, for *La ciudad y los perros;* Premio de la Crítica Española, 1963, for *La ciudad y los perros,* and 1967, for *La casa verde;* Premio Nacional de la Novela, 1967, for *La casa verde;* Ritz Paris Hemingway Award, 1985, for *The War of the End of the World;* Premio Internacional Literatura Romulo Gallegos, for *La casa verde.*

WRITINGS:

Los jefes (story collection; title means "The Leaders"), Editorial Roca, 1959.

Los cachorros (novella), Editorial Lumen, 1967, translation by Ronald Christ and Gregory Kolovakos published, with six short stories, as *The Cubs and Other Stories,* Harper, 1979.

La novela, Fundación de Cultura Universitaria, 1968.

Lletra de batalla per "Tirant lo Blanc," Edicions 62, 1969.

Antología mínima de M. Vargas Llosa, Editorial Tiempo Contemporáneo, 1969.

(With Julio Cortázar and Oscar Collazos) *La literatura en la revolución y la revolución en la literatura,* Siglo Vientiuno Editores, 1970.

Día domingo, Ediciones Amadis, 1971.

García Márquez: Historia de un deicidio, Seix Barral, 1971.

La historia secreta de una novela, Tusquets, 1971.

Obras escogidas, Aguilar, 1973.

La orgia perpetua: Flaubert y "Madame Bovary," Seix Barral, 1975, translation by Helen Lane published as *The Perpetual Orgy: Flaubert and Madame Bovary,* Farrar, Straus, 1986.

Art, Authenticity and Latin American Culture, Wilson Center (Washington, D.C.), 1981.

La señorita de Tacna, Seix Barral, 1982, first produced under title "Señorita from Tacna" in New York at INTAR Hispanic American Arts Center, 1983; produced under title "The Young Lady from Tacna" in Los Angeles at the Bilingual Foundation of the Arts, May, 1985.

Kathie y el hipopótamo: Comedia en dos actos, Seix Barral, 1983, translation by Kerry McKenny and Anthony Oliver-Smith produced as "Kathie and the Hippopotamus" in Edinburgh, Scotland, at the Traverse Theatre, August, 1986.

La cultura de la libertad, la libertad de la cultura, Fundación Eduardo Frei, 1985.

La chunga, Seix Barral, 1986, translation by Joanne Pottlitzer first produced in New York at INTAR Hispanic American Arts Center, February 9, 1986.

Elogio de la madrastra, Tusquets (Barcelona), 1988.

Also author of play "La Huida" (title means "The Escape"), produced in Piura, Peru; contributor to *The Eye of the Heart,* 1973.

NOVELS

La ciudad y los perros, Seix Bartal, 1963, translation by Lysander Kemp published as *The Time of the Hero,* Grove, 1966.

La casa verde, Seix Barral, 1966, translation by Gregory Rabassa published as *The Green House,* Harper, 1968.

Conversación en la catedral, Seix Barral, 1969, translation by Rabassa published as *Conversation in the Cathedral,* Harper, 1975.

Pantaleón y las visitadoras, Seix Barral, 1973, translation by Christ and Kolovakos published as *Captain Pantoja and the Special Service,* Harper, 1978.

Aunt Julia and the Scriptwriter, Farrar, Straus, 1982 (published in the original Spanish as *La tía Julia y el escribidor,* 1977).

The War of the End of the World, translation by Lane, Farrar, Straus, 1984 (published in the original Spanish as *Guerra*).

Historia de Mayta, Seix Barral, 1985, translation by Alfred MacAdam published as *The Real Life of Alejandro Mayta,* Farrar, Straus, 1986.

Who Killed Palomino Molero?, translation by MacAdam, Farrar, Straus, 1987 (published in the original Spanish as *¿Quién mató a Palomino Molero?*).

El hablador, Seix Barral, 1988, translation by Lane published as *The Storyteller,* Farrar, Straus, 1989.

SIDELIGHTS: Peruvian writer Mario Vargas Llosa often draws from his personal experiences to write of the injustices and corruption of contemporary Latin America. At one time an admirer of communist Cuba, since the early 1970s Vargas Llosa has been opposed to tyrannies of both the political left and right. He now advocates democracy, a free market, and individual liberty, and he cautions against extreme or violent political action, instead calling for peaceful democratic reforms. In 1989 he was chosen to be the presidential candidate of Fredemo, a political coalition in Peru; he later withdrew from the race. Through his novels—marked by complex structures and an innovative merging of dialogue and description in an attempt to recreate the actual feeling of life—Vargas Llosa has established himself as one of the most important of contemporary writers in the Spanish language. His novels, a London *Times* writer comments, "are among the finest coming out of Latin America."

As a young man, Vargas Llosa spent two years at the Leoncio Prado Military Academy. Sent there by his father, who had discovered that his son wrote poetry and was therefore fearful for the boy's masculinity, Vargas Llosa found the school, with its "restrictions, the military discipline and the brutal, bullying atmosphere, unbearable," he writes in the *New York Times Magazine.* His years at the school inspired his first novel, *The Time of the Hero* (first published in Spanish as *La ciudad y los perros*). The book is, R. Z. Sheppard states in *Time,* "a brutal slab of naturalism about life and violent death." The novel's success was ensured when the school's officials objected to Vargas Llosa's portrayal of their institution. "One thousand copies were ceremoniously burned in the patio of the school and several generals attacked it bitterly. One of them said that the book was the work of a 'degenerate mind,' and another, who was more imaginative, claimed that I had undoubtedly been paid by Ecuador to undermine the prestige of the Peruvian Army," Vargas Llosa recalls in his *New York Times Magazine* article.

In the award-winning *The Green House* (*La casa verde* in the Spanish edition), Vargas Llosa draws upon another period from his childhood for inspiration. For several years his family lived in the Peruvian jungle town of Piura, and his memories of the gaudy local brothel, known to everyone as the Green House, form the basis of his novel. The book's several stories are interwoven in a nonlinear narrative revolving around the brothel and the family that owns it, the military that runs the town, a dealer in stolen rubber in the nearby jungle, and a prostitute who was raised in a convent. "Scenes overlap, different times and places overrun each other . . . echoes precede voices, and disembodied consciences dissolve almost before they can be identified," Luis Harss and Barbara Dohmann write in *Into the Mainstream: Conversations with Latin-American Writers.* Gregory Rabassa, writing in *World Literature Today,* notes that the novel's title "is the connective theme that links the primitive world of the jungle to the primal lusts of 'civilization' which are enclosed by the green walls of the whorehouse." Rabassa sees, too, that Vargas Llosa's narrative style "has not reduced time to a device of measurement or location, a practical tool, but has conjoined it with space, so that the characters carry their space with them too . . . inseparable from their time." Harss and Dohmann find that *The Green House* "is probably the most accomplished work of fiction ever to come out of Latin America. It has sweep, beauty, imaginative scope, and a sustained eruptive power that carries the reader from first page to last like a fish in a bloodstream."

With *Conversation in the Cathedral* (first published in Spanish as *Conversación en la catedral*), Vargas Llosa widened his scope. Whereas in previous novels he had sought to recreate the repression and corruption of a particular place, in *Conversation in the Cathedral* he attempts to provide a panoramic view of his native country. As John M. Kirk states in *International Fiction Review,* this novel "presents a wider, more encompassing view of Peruvian society. [Vargas Llosa's] gaze extends further afield in a determined effort to incorporate as many representative regions of Peru as possible." Set during the dictatorship of Manuel Udria in the late 1940s and 1950s, the society depicted in the novel "is one of corruption in virtually all the shapes and spheres you can imagine," Wolfgang A. Luchting writes in the *Review of the Center for Inter-American Relations.* Penny Leroux, in a review of the book for *Nation,* calls it "one of the most scathing denunciations ever written on the corruption and immorality of Latin America's ruling classes."

The nonlinear writing of *Conversation in the Cathedral* is seen by several critics to be the culmination of Vargas Llosa's narrative experimentation. Writing in the *Review of the Center for Inter-American Relations,* Ronald Christ calls the novel "a masterpiece of montage" and "a massive assault on simultaneity." Christ argues that Vargas Llosa links fragments of prose together to achieve a montage effect that "promotes a linking of actions and words, speech and description, image and image, point of view and point of view." Kirk explains that in *Conversation in the Cathedral,* Vargas Llosa is "attempting the ambitious and obviously impossible plan of conveying to the reader all aspects of the reality of [Peruvian] society, of writing the 'total' novel." By interweaving five different narratives, Vargas Llosa forces the reader to study the text closely, making the reader an "accomplice of the writer [which] undoubtedly helps the reader to a more profound understanding of the work." Kirk concludes that *Conversation in the Cathedral* is "both a perfect showcase for all the structural techniques and thematic obsessions found in [Vargas Llosa's] other work, as well as being the true culmination of his personal anguish for Peru."

Speaking of these early novels in *Modern Latin American Literature,* D. P. Gallagher argues that one intention of their complex nonlinear structures is to "re-enact the complexity of the situations described in them." By juxtaposing unrelated elements, cutting off dialogue at critical moments, and breaking the narration, Vargas Llosa suggests the disparate geological conditions of Peru, recreates the difficulties involved in living in that country, and re-enacts "the very nature of conversation and of communication in general, particularly in a society devoted to the concealment of truth and to the flaunting of deceptive images," Gallagher believes. Ronald de Feo points out in the *New Republic* that these early novels all explore "with a near-savage seriousness and single-mindedness themes of social and political corruption." But in *Captain Pantoja and the Special Service* (*Pantaleón y las visitadoras* in its Spanish edition), "a new unexpected element entered Vargas Llosa's work: an unrestrained sense of humor," de Feo reports.

A farcical novel involving a military officer's assignment to provide prostitutes for troops in the Peruvian jungle, *Captain Pantoja and the Special Service* is "told through an artful combination of dry military dispatches, juicy personal letters, verbose radio rhetoric, and lurid sensationalist news reports," Gene Bell-Villada writes in *Commonweal.* Vargas Llosa also mixes conversations from different places and times, as he has in previous novels. And like these earlier works, *Captain Pantoja and the Special Service* "sniffs out corruption in high places, but it also presents something of a break, Vargas Llosa here shedding his high seriousness and adopting a humorous ribald tone," Bell-Villada concludes. The novel's satirical attack is aimed not at the military, a *Times Literary Supplement* reviewer writes, but at "any institution which channels instincts into a socially acceptable ritual. The humor of the narrative derives less from this serious underlying motive, however, than from the various linguistic codes into which people channel the darker forces."

The humorous tone of *Captain Pantoja and the Special Service* is also found in *Aunt Julia and the Scriptwriter* (*La tía Julia y el escribidor* in the original Spanish edition). The novel concerns two characters based on people in Vargas Llosa's own life: his first wife, Julia, who was his aunt by marriage, and a writer of radio soap opera who Vargas Llosa names Pedro Camacho in the novel. The 18-year-old narrator, Mario, has a love affair with the 32-year-old Julia. Their story is interrupted in alternate chapters by Camacho's wildly complicated soap opera scripts. As Camacho goes mad, his daily scripts for ten different soap operas become more and more entangled, with characters from one serial appearing in others and all of his plots converging into a single unlikely story. The scripts display "fissures through which are revealed secret obsessions, aversions and perversions that allow us to view his soap operas as the story of his disturbed mind," Jose Miguel Oviedo writes in *World Literature Today.* "The result," explains Nicholas Shakespeare in the *Times Literary Supplement,* "is that Camacho ends up in an asylum, while Mario concludes his real-life soap opera by running off to marry Aunt Julia."

Although *Aunt Julia and the Scriptwriter* is as humorous as the previous novel, *Captain Pantoja and the Special Service,* "it has a thematic richness and density the other book lacked," de Feo believes. This richness is found in the novel's exploration of the writer's life and of the relationship between a creative work and its inspiration. In the contrasting of soap opera plots with the real-life romance of Mario and Julia, the novel raises questions about the distinctions between fiction and fact. In a review for *New York,* Carolyn Clay calls *Aunt Julia and the Scriptwriter* "a treatise on the art of writing, on the relationship of stimuli to imagination." It is, de Feo observes, "a multilayered, high-spirited, and in the end terribly affecting text about the interplay of fiction and reality, the transformation of life into art, and life seen and sometimes even lived as fiction."

In *The War of the End of the World,* Vargas Llosa for the first time sets his story outside of his native Peru. He turns instead to Brazil of the 19th century and bases his story on an apocalyptic religious movement which gained momentum towards the end of the century. Convinced that the year 1900 marked the end of the world, these zealots, led by a man named the Counselor, set up the community of Canudos. Because of the Counselor's continued denunciations of the Brazilian government, which he called the "antichrist" for its legal separation of church and state, the national government sent in troops to break up this religious community. The first military assault was repulsed, as were the second and third, but the fourth expedition involved a force of some 4,000 soldiers. They laid waste to the entire area and killed nearly 40,000 people.

Vargas Llosa tells Wendy Smith in *Publishers Weekly* that he was drawn to write of this bloody episode because he felt the fanaticism of both sides in this conflict was exemplary of present-day Latin America. "Fanaticism is the root of violence in Latin America," he explains. In the Brazilian war, he believes, is a microcosm of Latin America. "Canudos presents a limited situation in which you can see clearly. Everything is there: a society in which on the one hand people are living a very old-fashioned life and have an archaic way of thinking, and on the other hand progressives want to impose modernism on society with guns. This creates a total lack of communication, of dialogue, and when there is no communication, war or repression or upheaval comes immediately," he tells Smith. In an article for the *Washington Post,* Vargas Llosa explains to Curt Suplee that "in the history of the Canudos war you could really see something that has been happening in Latin American history over the 19th and

20th centuries—the total lack of communication between two sections of a society which kill each other fighting *ghosts,* no? Fighting fictional enemies who are invented out of fanaticism. This kind of reciprocal incapacity of understanding is probably the main problem we have to overcome in Latin America."

Not only is *The War of the End of the World* set in the 19th century, but its length and approach are also of that time. A writer for the London *Times* calls it "a massive novel in the l9th century tradition: massive in content, in its ambitions, in its technical achievement." Gordon Brotherston of the *Times Literary Supplement* describes the book as being "on the grand scale of the nineteenth century," while Salman Rushdie of *New Republic* similarly defines the novel as "a modern tragedy on the grand scale." Richard Locke of the *Washington Post Book World* believes that *The War of the End of the World* "overshadows the majority of novels published here in the past few years. Indeed, it makes most recent American fiction seem very small, very private, very gray, and very timid."

Vargas Llosa's political perspective in *The War of the End of the World* shows a marked change from his earlier works. He does not attack a corrupt society in this novel. Instead he treats both sides in the Canudos war ironically. The novel ends with a character from either side locked in a fight to the death. As Rushdie observes, "this image would seem to crystallize Vargas Llosa's political vision." This condemnation of both sides in the Canudos conflict reflects Vargas Llosa's view of the contemporary Latin American scene, where rightist dictatorships often battle communist guerrillas. Suplee describes Vargas Llosa as "a humanist who reviles with equal vigor tyrannies of the right or left (is there really a difference, he asks, between 'good tortures and bad tortures'?)."

Although his political views have changed during the course of his career, taking him from a leftist supporter of communist Cuba to a strong advocate of democracy, Vargas Llosa's abhorrence of dictatorship, violence, and corruption has remained constant. And he sees Latin American intellectuals as part of a continuing cycle of "repression, chaos, and subversion," he tells Philip Bennett in the *Washington Post.* Many of these intellectuals, Vargas Llosa explains further, "are seduced by rigidly dogmatic stands. Although they are not accustomed to pick up a rifle or throw bombs from their studies, they foment and defend the violence." Speaking of the ongoing conflict in Peru between the military government and a Maoist guerrilla movement, Vargas Llosa clarifies to Suplee that "the struggle between the guerrillas and the armed forces is really a settling of accounts between privileged sectors of society, and the peasant masses are used cynically and brutally by those who say they want to 'liberate' them."

Vargas Llosa believes that a Latin American writer is obligated to speak out on political matters. "If you're a writer in a country like Peru," he tells Suplee, "you're a privileged person because you know how to read and write, you have an audience, you are respected. It is a moral obligation of a writer in Latin America to be involved in civic activities." This belief led Vargas Llosa in 1987 to speak out when the Peruvian government proposed to nationalize the country's banks. His protest quickly led to a mass movement in opposition to the plan, and the government was forced to back down. Vargas Llosa's supporters went on to create Fredemo, a political party calling for democracy, a free market, and individual liberty. Together with two other political parties, Fredemo established a coalition group called the Liberty Movement. In June of 1989, Vargas Llosa was chosen to be the coalition's presidential candidate for Peru's 1990 elections. Visit-

ing small rural towns, the urban strongholds of his Marxist opponents, and the jungle villages of the country's Indians, Vargas Llosa campaigned on what he believes is Peru's foremost problem: "We have to defend democracy against the military and against the extreme Left." Opinion polls in late summer of 1988 showed him to be the leading contender for the presidency, with a 44 to 19 percent lead over his nearest opponent.

"A major figure in contemporary Latin American letters," as Locke explains, and "the man whom many describe as the national conscience of his native Peru," as George de Lama writes in the *Chicago Tribune,* Vargas Llosa is usually ranked with Jorge Luis Borges, Gabriel García Márquez, and other writers of what has been called the Latin American "Boom" of the 1960s. His body of work set in his native Peru, Suzanne Jill Levine writes in the *New York Times Book Review,* is "one of the largest narrative efforts in contemporary Latin American letters. . . . [He] has begun a complete inventory of the political, social, economic and cultural reality of Peru. . . . Very deliberately, Vargas Llosa has chosen to be his country's conscience." But Vargas Llosa warns that a writer's role is limited. "Even great writers can be totally blind on political matters and can put their prestige and their imagination and fantasy at the service of a policy, which, if it materialized, would be destruction of what they do . . . ," Sheppard quotes Vargas Llosa as telling a PEN conference. "To be in the situation of Poland is no better than to be in the situation of Chile. I feel perplexed by these questions. I want to fight for societies where perplexity is still permitted."

MEDIA ADAPTATIONS: "The Cubs" was filmed in 1971; *Captain Pantoja and the Special Service* was filmed in 1976 (Vargas Llosa directed the film, which was banned in Peru); *Aunt Julia and the Scriptwriter* was adapted as a television series in Peru and as a screenplay written by William Boyd and directed by Jon Amiel in 1989.

AVOCATIONAL INTERESTS: Tennis, gymnastics, waterskiing, movies.

BIOGRAPHICAL/CRITICAL SOURCES:

BOOKS

Contemporary Literary Criticism, Gale, Volume 3, 1975, Volume 6, 1976, Volume 9, 1978, Volume 10, 1979, Volume 15, 1980, Volume 31, 1985, Volume 42, 1987.
Feal, Rosemary Geisdorfer, *Novel Lives: The Fictional Autobiographies of Guillermo Cabrera Infante and Mario Vargas Llosa,* University of North Carolina Press, 1986.
Gallagher, D. P., *Modern Latin American Literature,* Oxford University Press, 1973.
Harss, Luis, and Barbara Dohmann, *Into the Mainstream: Conversations with Latin-American Writers,* Harper, 1967.
Rossmann, Charles, and Alan Warren Friedman, editors, *Mario Vargas Llosa: A Collection of Critical Essays,* University of Texas Press, 1978.
Williams, Raymond Leslie, *Mario Vargas Llosa,* Ungar, 1986.

PERIODICALS

Bookletter, April 28, 1975.
Bulletin of Bibliography, December, 1986.
Chicago Tribune, January 3, 1989, June 23, 1989, August 3, 1989.
Chicago Tribune Book World, October 7, 1979, January 12, 1986.
Commonweal, June 8, 1979.
Hispania, March, 1976.
Hudson Review, winter, 1976.

International Fiction Review, January, 1977.
Los Angeles Times, May 20, 1985, December 18, 1988.
Los Angeles Times Book Review, February 2, 1986.
Nation, November 22, 1975.
National Review, December 10, 1982.
New Leader, March 17, 1975, November 15, 1982.
New Republic, August 16-23, 1982, October 8, 1984.
Newsweek, February 10, 1986.
New York, August 23, 1982.
New York Review of Books, March 20, 1975, January 24, 1980.
New York Times, March 30, 1985, January 8, 1986, February 9, 1986, February 12, 1986, September 10, 1989.
New York Times Book Review, March 23, 1975, April 9, 1978, September 23, 1979, August 1, 1982, December 2, 1984, February 2, 1986, October 29, 1989.
New York Times Magazine, November 20, 1983.
Partisan Review, Volume 46, number 4, 1979.
Publishers Weekly, October 5, 1984.
Review of the Center for Inter-American Relations, spring, 1975.
Saturday Review, January 11, 1975.
Spectator, May 14, 1983.
Time, February 17, 1975, August 9, 1982, January 27, 1986, March 10, 1986, September 7, 1987.
Times (London), May 13, 1985, August 5, 1986.
Times Literary Supplement, October 12, 1973, May 20, 1983, March 8, 1985, May 17, 1985, July 1, 1988.
Tribune Books (Chicago), October 29, 1989.
Washington Post, August 29, 1983, October 1, 1984, March 26, 1989.
Washington Post Book World, August 26, 1984, February 9, 1986.
World Literature Today, winter, 1978, spring, 1978.

*   *   *

VASQUEZ, Richard 1928-

PERSONAL: Born June 11, 1928, in Southgate, Calif.

ADDRESSES: Home—3345 Marengo, Altadena, Calif. 91001.

CAREER: Owner of construction company, beginning in 1945; cab driver, until 1959; *Santa Monica Independent,* Santa Monica, Calif., reporter, 1959-60; *San Gabriel Valley Daily Tribune,* San Gabriel, Calif., reporter, 1960-65; historian for book publisher, and account executive for Wilshire Boulevard Public Relations firm, 1965-70; *Los Angeles Times,* Los Angeles, Calif., feature writer, beginning 1970; free-lance writer. *Military service:* U.S. Navy, 1945.

AWARDS, HONORS: Sigma Delta Chi award, 1964, for article on the city government of Irvingdale, Calif.

WRITINGS:

Chicano (novel), Doubleday, 1970.
The Giant Killer (novel), Manor Books, 1978.
Another Land (novel), Avon Books, 1982.
Is There a Dinosaur in This House? (for children), Vantage, 1985.

Contributor of articles and poems to *La Raza, Revista Chicano-Riqueña,* and *Los Angeles Times.*

WORK IN PROGRESS: A fourth novel, entitled *And They Shouted Viva.*

SIDELIGHTS: Journalist Richard Vásquez is known for writing *Chicano,* a best-selling novel frequently used in high school and college courses. Vásquez has also written poems, articles, and other novels, but his literary reputation is primarily based on

Chicano. Published in 1970, the epic novel spans four generations of the Sandoval family in their quest to establish themselves in America. The story opens with Héctor Sandoval leading his family out of Mexico during the revolution of 1910, a period of social unrest brought on by widespread dissatisfaction with Mexican President Porfirio Díaz, whose policies broadened the gap between the rich and the poor. The Sandovals find that living in America does not bring them the happiness and financial security they seek; instead, American life gradually destroys them. Héctor becomes an alcoholic when he cannot find work, his daughters turn to prostitution after being raped, and his wife moves back to Mexico to marry an old lover after Héctor dies. Subsequent generations of Mexican-American Sandovals meet with similar misfortune. Those who find contentment, albeit fleeting, are the few who can forget their Mexican heritage and adapt to the materialistic ways of American life. *Chicano* received mixed reviews: American critics generally found the novel engrossing, but several Chicano reviewers faulted the book's use of cliches and stereotypical characters. Despite its detractors, *Chicano* remains a popular classroom text, and for this reason Vásquez is considered an important contributor to Chicano literature.

BIOGRAPHICAL/CRITICAL SOURCES:

BOOKS

Chicano Literature: A Reference Guide, Greenwood Press, 1985.

PERIODICALS

Aztlán, fall, 1970.
El Grito, spring, 1970.
La Luz, May, 1977.
New York Times Book Review, March 22, 1970.
Southwestern American Literature, May, 1971.
West Coast Review of Books, July, 1980.

*   *   *

VAZQUEZ AMARAL, José 1913-1987

PERSONAL: Born April 1, 1913, in Los Reyes, Jalisco, Mexico; died of a heart condition, February 24, 1987, in Summit, N.J.; married Mary Helen Madiraca; children: Pedro, Lydia Watson, Marta Alicia López, Maria Elena, Jacinta Rosa Amaral. *Education:* Escuela Nacional de Preparatoria, Ph.B. and B.Litt., 1935; Universidad Nacional Autónoma de México, Licenciar en Derecho, 1941.

ADDRESSES: Home—Warren, N.J. *Office*—Department of Romance Languages, Rutgers, The State University, New Brunswick, N.J. 08903.

CAREER: National University of Mexico, Ciudad Universitaria, professor of English, 1935-42; visiting professor of Latin American literature at Tulane University, New Orleans, La., 1942-43, and Swarthmore College, Swarthmore, Pa., 1943-47; Rutgers, The State University, New Brunswick, N.J., began as associate professor and Latin America specialist, became professor of romance languages, 1947-87, head of Spanish and Portuguese department, 1947-82. Former lawyer, Hill-de la Sierra, Prado, Mex. Atlantic seaboard representative, Mexico Minister of Education.

MEMBER: International Institute of Iberoamerican Literature (secretary, 1943).

AWARDS, HONORS: Thornton Niven Wilder Prize from Translation Center of Columbia University, 1987; Distinguished

Service Medal of the President of Mexico; National Prize for Linguistics and Literature (Mexico).

WRITINGS:

Los Gringos, Costa Amic, 1969.
The Contemporary Latin American Narrative, Las Américas, 1970.
(Translator) *The Cantos of Ezra Pound,* Joaquín Mortiz, 1975.

Also translator of *Walt Whitman* and *Biography of Mexico.*

OBITUARIES:

PERIODICALS

New York Times, February 26, 1987.

*   *   *

VELEZ-IBANEZ, Carlos G(uillermo) 1936-

PERSONAL: Born October 27, 1936, in Nogales, Ariz.; son of Adalberto Garcia (a mechanic) and Luz (a homemaker; maiden name, Ibanez) de Velez; married Maria Teresa Marques (a psychologist), June 28, 1974; children: (from previous marriage) Carlos, Lucy, Miguel, Carmelita; (from marriage to Marques) Mariel. *Education:* University of Arizona, B.A., 1961, M.A. (English), 1968; University of California, San Diego, M.A. (anthropology), 1972, Ph.D., 1975.

ADDRESSES: Home—5141 North Amapola Circle, Tucson, Ariz. 85745. *Office*—Department of Anthropology, University of Arizona, Tucson, Ariz. 85721.

CAREER: High school teacher in Coolidge, Ariz., 1961-63, and Tucson, Ariz., 1964-68; San Diego Junior College (now State University), San Diego, Calif., assistant professor of Mexican-American studies, 1968-71, chairman of department, director of Community Education Project, and chairman of Bilingual Systems Task Force, all 1969-71; University of Washington, Seattle, lecturer in anthropology, 1974; University of Southern California, Los Angeles, visiting assistant professor of anthropology, 1975-76; University of California, Los Angeles, assistant professor, 1976-82, associate professor, 1982, adjunct associate professor of anthropology, 1982—; University of Arizona, Tucson, associate professor, 1982-83, professor of anthropology, 1983—, director of Bureau of Applied Research in Anthropology, 1982—, associate dean of faculty of social and behavioral sciences, 1984-86. Visiting associate at Smithsonian Institute, 1986—. Associate director of Bilingual Institute at Washington State University, summer, 1974; member of Smithsonian Folklife Advisory Council, 1985; conducted field research in the southwest United States and Mexico; consultant to Human Resources Corp., East Los Angeles Center for Law and Justice, and Southwest Education Laboratory. *Military service:* U.S. Marine Corps, 1957-59.

MEMBER: CIBOLA Anthropology Association (member of executive committee, 1981-84; president, 1985—), American Anthropological Association (fellow; member of executive committee, 1985), Society for Applied Anthropology (fellow), American Ethnological Society, Mexican American Educators Association, Southwestern Anthropological Society, Phi Delta Kappa.

AWARDS, HONORS: Ford Foundation fellow, 1972-73, 1973-74, and 1974-75; National Science Foundation fellow, 1973-74 and 1974-75; Distinguished Phillips Visitor at Haverford College, 1981; Rockefeller Foundation fellow, 1981-82; fellow of the Center for the Advanced Study of Behavioral Sciences, 1987.

WRITINGS:

Bonds of Mutual Trust: The Cultural Systems of Rotating Credit Associations Among Urban Mexicans and Chicanos, Rutgers University Press, 1983.
Rituals of Marginality: Politics, Process, and Culture Change in Central Urban Mexico, 1969-1974, University of California Press, 1983.

CONTRIBUTOR

Barbara Myerhoff and Andre Simic, editors, *Life's Career—Aging: Cultural Variations on Growing Old,* Sage Publications, 1978.
Arnulfo Trejo, editor, *Chicanos As We See Ourselves,* University of Arizona Press, 1979.
Margarita Melville, editor, *Twice a Minority,* Mosby, 1980.
Magdalena Mora and Adelaida del Castillo, editors, *Mexican Women in the United States: Struggles Past and Present,* Chicano Research Center, University of California, Los Angeles, 1980.
Ray Valle and William A. Vega, editors, *Hispanic Natural Supports: Health Promotion Perspectives,* Department of Mental Health, Sacramento, Calif., 1980.
M. R. Miranda and R. A. Ruiz, editors, *Chicano Aging and Mental Health,* U.S. Department of Health and Human Services, 1981.

Also contributor to *Mexico-U.S. Relations: A Reader,* edited by Mauricio Mazon, Chicano Research Center, University of California, Los Angeles.

OTHER

Co-editor of monograph series, Chicano Research Center, University of California, Los Angeles, 1976—. Contributor of articles and reviews to journals in the social sciences and to newspapers. Associate editor of *Human Organization: Journal of the Society for Applied Anthropology,* 1980—, and *American Ethnologist,* 1984—; contributing editor of *Aztlan: International Journal of Chicano Studies Research,* 1981-85; member of editorial board of *Sociology and Social Research,* 1975-76.

WORK IN PROGRESS: Corporate Continuities in Hispanic Households in the U.S. Borderlands.

SIDELIGHTS: Carlos G. Velez-Ibanez told *HW:* "My basic motivation for writing and research is to discover myself in the process. Self is a socially activated invention, the many facets of which are mostly hidden in dimensions either suppressed or made obscure by the expectations of others.

"My research has carried me to the Middle East, Africa, the subcontinent of India, Latin America, and Asia. We are much more alike than we are different; the clothes of culture fool us all."

BIOGRAPHICAL/CRITICAL SOURCES:

BOOKS

Blauner, Robert, *Racism in America,* Harper, 1972.
Mora, Magdalena and Adelaida del Castillo, *Mexican Women in the United States: Struggles Past and Present,* Chicano Research Center, University of California, Los Angeles, 1980.
Vigil, J. D., *From Indians to Chicanos: A Sociocultural History,* Mosby, 1980.

PERIODICALS

American Anthropologist, March, 1980, September, 1980, September, 1984.

Contemporary Psychology, December, 1978.
Contemporary Sociology, July, 1979.

* * *

VELOZ MAGGIOLO, Marcio E. 1936-

PERSONAL: Born August 13, 1936, in the Dominican Republic.

CAREER: Universidad Autónoma de Santo Domingo, Ciudad Universitaria, Santo Domingo, Dominican Republic, director, Sección de Antropología; editor, *Revista Dominicana de Arqueología y Antropología.*

WRITINGS:

El sol y las cosas, Arquero, 1957.
El buen ladrón, Arquero, 1960, 2nd edition published as *Judas: El buen ladrón,* Librería Dominicana, 1962.
Intus, Arquero, 1962.
El prófugo, Ediciones Brigadas Dominicanas, 1962.
Creonte: Drama en un acto, Arquero, 1963.
La vida no tiene nombre (also see below), [Santo Domingo], 1965.
Los ángeles de hueso (also see below), Editora Arte y Cine, 1967.
Arqueología prehistórica de Santo Domingo, McGraw, 1972.
Cultura, teatro y relatos en Santo Domingo, UCMM, 1972.
El precerámico de Santo Domingo, Editora Cultural Dominicana, 1973.
Las poblaciones aborígenes de la Isla Española, Museo del Hombre Dominicano, 1973.
Apuntes sobre prehistoria de Santo Domingo, [Santo Domingo], 1974.
(With Plinio Pina and Manuel García Arévalo) *Esquema para una revisión de nomenclaturas arqueológicas del poblamiento precerámico en las Antillas,* Ediciones Fundación García-Arévalo, 1974.
(With Pina and Elpidio Ortega) *El Caimito, un antigua complejo ceramista de las Antillas Mayores,* Ediciones Fundación García-Arévalo, 1974.
De abril en adelante, Ediciones de Taller, 1975.
(With others) *Cayo Cofresí, un sitio precerámico de Puerto Rico,* Ediciones de Taller, 1975.
Medioambiente y adaptación humana en la prehistoria de Santo Domingo, Ediciones de Taller, 1976.
(With others) *Arqueología de Yuma, República Dominicana,* Ediciones de Taller, 1976.
(With others) *Arqueología de Punta de Garza,* Universidad Central del Este, 1977.
(With others) *Arqueología de Cueva de Berna,* Universidad Central del Este, 1977.
(Contributor) *Indigenous Art and Economy of Santo Domingo,* Editiones Cohoba, 1977.
Sobre cultura dominicana y otras culturas, Editora Alfa y Omega, 1977.
De donde vinó la gente, Editora Alfa y Omega, 1978.
(With Fernando Luna Calderón and Renato O. Rímoli) *Investigaciones arqueológicas en la Provincia de Pedernales, República Dominicana,* Universidad Central del Este, 1979.
Novelas cortas (contains *La vida no tiene nombre, Nosotros los suicidas,* and *Los ángeles de hueso*), Editora Alfa y Omega, 1980.
Vida y cultura en la prehistoria de Santo Domingo, Universidad Central del Este, 1980.
Los modos de vida mellacoides y sus posibles orígenes, Museo del Hombre Dominicano, 1981.
La biografía difusa de Sombra Castañeda, Monte Avila Editores, 1981.

La fértil agonía del amor, Ediciones de Taller, 1982.
La palabra reunida (selected poems), Universidad Central del Este, 1982.
Apearse de la máscara, Biblioteca Nacional, 1986.
Arqueología y patrón de vida en el poblado circular de Juan Pedro, República Dominicana, Museo del Hombre Dominicano, 1986.

SIDELIGHTS: A respected anthropologist at the Universidad Autónoma de Santo Domingo, Marcio E. Veloz Maggiolo has also written novels of Dominican history. *De abril en adelante,* a novel about the Dominican revolutionary turmoil of 1965, employs, for the first time in Dominican literature, *nouveau roman* techniques to tell its story.

* * *

VERBITSKY, Bernardo 1907-

PERSONAL: Born 1907, in Buenos Aires, Argentina.

WRITINGS:

Es difícil empezar a vivir, Editorial Losada, 1941.
Calles de tango, Editorial Vorágine, 1953, published as *Una cita con la vida,* Editorial Platina, 1958.
La esquina, Editorial Sudamericana, 1953.
Un noviazgo, Editorial Goyanarte, 1956.
Villa Miseria también es América, G. Kraft, 1957.
Megatón, Editorial Platina, 1959, 2nd edition, M. Gleizer, 1962.
El teatro de Arthur Miller, Siglo Veinte, 1959.
Vacaciones, Instituto Amigos del Libro Argentino, 1959.
La tierra es azul, Losada, 1961.
Hamlet y Don Quijote, Editorial Jumcana, 1964.
Un hombre de papel, Editorial J. Alvarez, 1966.
La neurosis monta su espectáculo, Paidós, 1969.
Una pequeña familia, Centro Editor de América Latina, 1969.
Cuatro historias de Buenos Aires, Editorial Raynela, 1970.
Café de los angelitos, Corregidor, 1972.
Etiquetas a los hombros, Editorial Planeta, 1972.
Enamorado de Joan Baez, Editorial Planeta, 1975.
Literatura y conciencia nacional, Editorial Paidós, 1975.
Octubre maduro, Macondo Ediciones, 1976.
Hermana y sombra, Editorial Planta, 1977.
A pesar de todo, Monte Avila Editores, 1978.

SIDELIGHTS: Bernardo Verbitsky's novels of social realism often focus on such themes as Jewish life in modern South America, the problems of the lower classes, and life in the slums of Buenos Aires. His concern for the poor and his depiction of those forces denying the individual freedom the poor desire make his work powerful and persuasive.

* * *

VERDU, Matilde
See CELA, Camilo José

* * *

VIANA, Javier de 1868-1926

PERSONAL: Born in 1868 in Montevideo, Uruguay; died in 1926.

CAREER: Writer, rancher, politician, revolutionary, and medical student.

WRITINGS:

Campo, A. Barreiro y Ramos, 1896, 3rd edition, C. García, 1921.

Gaucha, A. Barreiro y Ramos, 1899.
Yuyos (cuentos camperos), O. M. Bertani, 1912.
Macachines, O. M. Bertani, 1913.
Gurí, y otras novelas, Editorial-América, 1916.
Paisanas (costumbres del campo), C. García, 1920.
Leña seca; cuentos camperos, C. García, 1920.
Con divisa blanca, V. Matera, 1921.
Del campo y de la ciudad (cuentos), C. García, 1921.
Potros, toros y aperiases (novelas gauchas), C. García, 1922.
La biblia gaucha, C. García, 1925.
Tardes del fogón, C. García, 1925.
Pago de deuda; Campo amarillo y otros escritos, C. García, 1934.
Abrojos, C. García, 1936.
Cardo azul, G. F. Prado Amor, 1939.
Sobre el recado, C. García, 1941.
Crónicas de la revolución del Quebracho, C. García, 1943.
Javier de Viana, Ministerio de Instrucción Pública y Previsión Social, 1962.
Selección de cuentos, Ministerio de Instrucción Pública y Previsión Social, 1965.
Javier de Viana: Sus mejores cuentos cortos, Ediciones de la Banda Oriental, 1968.
Antología de cuentos inéditos: Javier de Viana, Editorial Sandino, 1973.
La tapera del cuervo y otros cuentos, Ediciones de la Banda Oriental, 1979.
Alzando el poncho, Arta, 1983.

Also author of plays "La Nena," 1905, "La dotora," 1907, and "Pial de volcao," 1914.

SIDELIGHTS: Best known for his realistic stories of hard-living gauchos, the cowboys of South America, Javier de Viana wrote from firsthand experience. He worked as a gaucho before beginning his writing career. Viana is credited with writing honest portraits of the cattlemen and successfully debunking earlier romantic notions of them.

BIOGRAPHICAL/CRITICAL SOURCES:

BOOKS

Garganigo, John F., *Javier de Viana,* Twayne, 1972.

*   *   *

VILARIÑO, Idea   1920-

PERSONAL: Born August 18, 1920, in Montevideo, Uruguay; daughter of Leandro Vilariño (a poet) and Josefina Romani.

ADDRESSES: Home—Presidente Battle 2592, Apartado Postal 11600, Montevideo, Uruguay.

CAREER: Teacher of literature at a preparatory school, 1952-55; teacher at Instituto "Alfredo Vázquez Acevedo," 1955-73. Co-founder and co-director of literary review, *Número,* 1949-55.

AWARDS, HONORS: "Rodo" literary prize from Intendencia Municipal de Montevideo, 1987.

WRITINGS:

POETRY

La suplicante (title means "The Supplicant"), self-published, [Montevideo], 1945.
Cielo, cielo (title means "Sky, Sky"), self-published, [Montevideo], 1947.
Paraíso perdido (1945-1948) (title means "Paradise Lost . . ."), Número (Montevideo), 1949.

Por aire sucio (title means "Through Dirty Air"), Número, 1950.
Nocturnos (title means "Nocturnes"), Número, 1955, reprinted, Schapire (Buenos Aires), 1976.
Poemas de amor (title means "Love Poems"), [Montevideo], 1957, 2nd edition, Alfa (Montevideo), 1962.
Pobre mundo (title means "Poor World"), Banda Oriental (Montevideo), 1966.
Treinta poemas (title means "Thirty Poems"), Tauro, 1967.
Poesía, 1941-1967 (title means "Poetry . . ."), Arca (Montevideo), 1970.
Segunda antología (title means "Second Anthology"), Calicanto (Montevideo), 1980.
No, Calicanto, 1980.

Contributor of poems in English translation to *The Borzoi Anthology of Latin American Literature,* Volume 2: *The Twentieth-Century—From Borges and Paz to Guimaraes Rosa and Donoso,* edited by Emir Rodríguez Monegal with the assistance of Thomas Colchie, Knopf, 1986.

OTHER

Julio Herrera y Reissig: Seis años de poesía (title means "Julio Herrera y Reissig: Six Years of Poetry"; monograph), Número, 1950, reprinted, Técnica, c. 1974, published as *Julio Herrera y Reissig: Poemas comentados* (title means "Julio Herrera y Reissig: Annotated Poems"), 1978.
Grupos simétricos en poesía (title means "Symmetrical Groups in Poetry"), Universidad de la República (Montevideo), 1958.
Las letras de tango: La forma, temas y motivos (title means "Tango Lyrics: Form, Themes and Motifs"), Schapire, 1965.
(Editor) Juan Parra del Riego, *Nocturnos y otros poemas* (title means "Nocturnes and Other Poems"), Siete Poetas Hispanoamericanos (Montevideo), 1965.
(Compiler) *Antología de la violencia* (title means "Anthology of Violence"), Schapire, 1972.
Los salmos (title means "The Psalms"), Casa de Estudiantes (Montevideo), 1974, 2nd edition, 1977.
La literatura bíblica: El Antiguo Testamento (title means "Biblical Literature: The Old Testament"), Técnica, 1976.
(Translator) W. H. Hudson, *La tierra púrpura; Allá lejos y hace tiempo,* Ayacucho (Caracas), 1980.
Introducción a literatura bíblica, Técnica (Montevideo), 1981.
(Editor) *Tangos: Antología* (title means "Tangos: Anthology"), Centro Editor de América Latina (Buenos Aires), 1981.
El tango, CEDAL, 1981.
(Editor and author of prologue) *El tango cantado* (title means "The Sung Tango"), Calicanto, 1981.
Conocimiento de Darío (title means "Understanding Darío"), Arca, 1988.
La masa sonora del poema: Sus organizaciones vocálicas. Indagaciones en algunos poemas de Rubén Darío, Arca, 1989.
La sudicia luce del Giorno (anthology), Spanish and Italian texts, Urbino, 1989.

Also author of *Grupos simétricos en la poesía de Antonio Machado,* 1951, *Pius Servien y los ritmos,* 1952, and *La rima en Herrera y Reissig,* 1955. Also translator of works by William Shakespeare. Contributor to periodicals, including *Clinamen, Asir, Hiperión, Marcha,* and *Puente.*

SIDELIGHTS: In his *Spanish-American Literature: A History* Enrique Anderson Imbert describes Uruguay's Idea Vilariño as the most representative poet of the generation that surfaced in that country immediately after World War II. Like the other members of the group, Vilariño focuses on death and hopelessness in her poetry. "The appearance of Idea's first book, *La supli-*

cante, in 1945," note Emir Rodríguez Monegal and Thomas Colchie in *The Borzoi Anthology of Latin American Literature,* "was an extraordinary event in Uruguayan poetry, not only because of the freshness in rhythm and language that her work represented . . ., but also because of the desolate, sincere, pathetic vision of the world that, in well-minted verses, the new and implacable voice transmitted." Rodríguez Monegal and Colchie also observe that Vilariño has written "some of the most devastating love poems written in Spanish today" and place her work in the tradition of erotic poetry developed in Latin America by Uruguayan poet Delmira Agustini and the Nobel prize-winning Chilean poet Gabriela Mistral.

BIOGRAPHICAL/CRITICAL SOURCES:

BOOKS

Anderson Imbert, Enrique, *Spanish-American Literature: A History,* Volume 2: *1910-1963,* 2nd edition revised and updated by Elaine Malley, Wayne State University Press, 1969.
Diccionario de literatura uruguaya, Arca-Credisol, 1987.
Rodríguez Monegal, Emir, with the assistance of Thomas Colchie, editors, *The Borzoi Anthology of Latin American Literature,* Volume 2: *The Twentieth Century—From Borges and Paz to Guimaraes Rosa and Donoso,* Knopf, 1986.

* * *

VILLANUEVA, Alma Luz 1944-

PERSONAL: Born October 4, 1944, in Lompoc, Calif.; children: Antoinette, Ed, Marc Goulet, Jules Villanueva-Castaño. *Education:* Norwich University, Vermont College, M.F.A., 1984. *Religion:* "Native Person of the Earth."

ADDRESSES: Home—Santa Cruz, Calif. *Office*—c/o Bilingual Review/Press, Hispanic Research Center, Arizona State University, Tempe, Ariz. 85287-2702.

CAREER: Writer.

MEMBER: Amnesty International, Greenpeace, Save the Children.

AWARDS, HONORS: First prize in poetry, Third Chicano Literary Prize, University of California, Irvine, 1977, for "Poems"; American Book Award, 1989, for *The Ultraviolet Sky.*

WRITINGS:

Bloodroot (poetry), Place of Herons Press (Austin, Tex.), 1977.
(Contributor) *Third Chicano Literary Prize, 1976-1977* (contains prize-winning "Poems"), Department of Spanish and Portuguese, University of California, Irvine, 1977.
Mother, May I? (also see below; poetry), Motheroot Publications (Pittsburgh, Pa.), 1978.
Life Span (poetry), Place of Herons Press, 1984.
La Chingada (poetry), Bilingual Review/Press, 1985.
The Ultraviolet Sky (novel), Bilingual Review/Press, 1988.
Naked Ladies (novel), Bilingual Review/Press, in press.
Planet (poetry), Bilingual Review/Press, in press.

CONTRIBUTOR TO ANTHOLOGIES

Jennifer McDowell, editor, *Contemporary Women Poets,* Merlin Press, 1977.
David Kherdian, editor, *I Sing a Song to Myself,* Morrow, 1978.
Joseph Bruchac, editor, *The Next World,* Crossing Press, 1978.
Hispanics in the United States, Bilingual Review/Press, Volume 1, 1980, Volume 2, 1982.
Stanford's Women Writing Poetry in America, Stanford University Press, 1982.

Women Poets of the World, Macmillan, 1983.
Marta Ester Sánchez, *Contemporary Chicana Poetry: A Critical Approach to an Emerging Literature* (contains *Mother, May I?* and excerpts from *Bloodroot*), University of California Press, 1985.
Alcatraz, Alcatraz Editions, 1985.
Nosotras, Bilingual Review/Press, 1986.
Erlanger Studien: Contemporary Chicano Poetry, [Berlin, West Germany], 1986.
The World's Best Poetry, Volume 4, Roth Publishing, 1987.
Tongues and Prophesies, University of Georgia Press, 1988.
Unsealed Lips, Capra Press, 1988.
She Rises Like the Sun, Crossing Press, 1989.
Quarry West, University of California, Santa Cruz, 1989.
Contemporary Chicana Poetry, University of South Carolina Press, 1989.

OTHER

Also author of a book of poems entitled *Shakti;* author of several children's stories; contributor of poems to high school text books. Contributor of poetry and short stories to periodicals, including *Somos* and *American Poetry Review.* Contributing editor, *American Poetry Review,* 1985.

WORK IN PROGRESS: A collection of short stories entitled *La Llorona/Weeping Woman.*

SIDELIGHTS: "Alma [Luz] Villanueva's poetry stands out for its universal quality and its tone of undaunted exploration of a wide variety of themes," notes Charles Tatum in *Chicano Literature: A Critical History.* Among her range of topics, Villanueva often expresses the search for female and personal identity within the masculine, Chicano, and technological confines of culture. Tatum comments on a strength of Villanueva's work: "While her poems make basic statements about her family, her womanhood, her Chicanismo, she is never prosaic but instead is able to elevate her self-perceptions and observations of others to eloquent poetic statements."

Villanueva told *CA:* "Recently, a woman wrote to me and told me she chose *Mother, May I?* (a book of poetry) to write her masters thesis. In closing, she told me this: 'Finally, I can say to you what *Mother, May I?* has meant to me. Reading those very personal words, I felt as though you had grasped the essence of your life—your very soul—and wrung it out upon the page to share with me. Thank you, thank you for doing that.' When I wrote *Mother, May I?* I never imagined that I'd receive a letter like hers. Which makes me acknowledge the paradox, the mystery of writing: that when we touch the most personal, the most hidden within ourselves, we touch the other, the outer, the universal. To the 'beginning writer': Writing takes all your courage—to stand by your work and see it through to publication—courage and luck (and discipline, discipline, discipline). But, imagine, someone understanding what you meant to say . . . someone saying thank you."

MEDIA ADAPTATIONS: Recordings of Villanueva can be found on *Like the Free Spirit of Birds,* a tape cassette available from New Radio and Performing Arts (New York City), "Women's Spirituality," a videotape produced for "Poetry Archives Series" of the Poetry Center, available from San Francisco State University, and "Hispanic Poets Read," a taped reading with Juan Felipe Herrera produced for "Poetry Archives Series."

BIOGRAPHICAL/CRITICAL SOURCES:

BOOKS

Sánchez, Marta Ester, *Contemporary Chicana Poetry: A Critical
    Approach to an Emerging Literature,* University of Califor-
    nia Press, 1985.
Tatum, Charles, *Chicano Literature: A Critical History,* Twayne,
    1982.

PERIODICALS

Bilingual Review, May-August, 1980.
Carta Abierta, June, 1978.
Revista Chicano-Riqueña, fall, 1978.

* * *

VILLANUEVA, Tino 1941-

PERSONAL: Born December 11, 1941, in San Marcos, Tex.; son
of Lino B. and Leonor (Rios) Villanueva. *Education:* Southwest
Texas State University, B.A., 1969; State University of New
York at Buffalo, M.A., 1971.

ADDRESSES: Home—89 Massachusetts Ave., Suite 270, Boston, Mass. 02115.

CAREER: State University of New York at Buffalo, instructor
in Spanish, 1969-71; Boston University, Boston, Mass., lecturer
in Spanish, 1971-76; Wellesley College, Wellesley, Mass., instructor in Spanish, 1974—. Announcer and program director
for "La Hora Hispana," broadcast for the Spanish-speaking
community by Harvard University radio station WHRB. *Military service:* U.S. Army, 1964-66.

MEMBER: American Association of Teachers of Spanish and
Portuguese,

AWARDS, HONORS: Ford Foundation Fellowship, 1978-79.

WRITINGS:

(Contributor) O. Romano and H. Ríos, editors, *El espejo/The
    Mirror: Selected Chicano Literature,* Quinto Sol Publica-
    tions, 1972.
Hay otra voz Poems (title means "There Is Another Voice
    Poems"), Mensaje, 1972, 3rd edition, 1979.
(With others) *Literatura chicana: texto y contexto* (title means
    "Chicano Literature: Text and Context"), Prentice-Hall,
    1973.
(Contributor) Philip D. Ortego, editor, *We Are Chicanos: An An-
    thology of Mexican-American Literature,* Washington
    Square Press, 1974.
Chicanos: Antología de ensayos y literatura (title means "Chi-
    canos: Anthology of Essays and Literature"), Fondo de
    Cultura Económica, 1979.
Shaking Off the Dark, Arte Público Press, 1984.

Also author of *Poesía de oposición entre 1955-1963 en Gabriel
Celaya, Angel González y J. M. Caballero Bonald,* 1981. Contrib-
utor of poetry to *San Antonio Express/News, Persona, El Grito,
Entre Nosotros, Caribbean Review, Hispamerica: Revista de Li-
teratura, Revista Chicano-Riqueña, Poema Convidado,* and
Texas Quarterly. Contributor of essays to *Cuadernos Hi-
spanoamericanos, Papeles de Son Armadans,* and *Journal of
Spanish Studies: Twentieth Century.*

SIDELIGHTS: Tino Villanueva began receiving recognition as
a poet with the publication of *Hay otra voz Poems* ("There Is Another Voice Poems") in 1972. Also author of short stories and
criticism, he has been described as a deliberate craftsman. His

poems combine social realism and poetic imagery and show the
influences of the late American poet Dylan Thomas as well as
other contemporary voices. His poems often build upon a single
key word whose meaning might at first seem simple but whose
connotations lend greater complexity and irony to the work.
Much of his poetry revolves around images of "time, death, and
silence," according to Juan Bruce-Novoa in *Chicano Authors: Inquiry by Interview;* Villanueva's "central preoccupation is the
disappearance of living beings (or a culture) without having really lived at all, or at least without having left us a record of the
passage."

In the context of Chicano literature, Villanueva is neither a strident advocate of social rebellion nor a harsh cynic railing against
injustice. Rather, he emerges as a gentle, reasonable voice urging
his people to strengthen themselves through education and self-
awareness. His 1984 *Shaking Off the Dark,* for instance, carries
a "sophisticated tone of ethnicity," remarked *World Literature
Today* contributor Antonio Olliz Boyd. The collection of poems,
some of which are in Spanish, others in English, constitute "an
unusual approach to poetic biculturalism," Boyd noted, adding
that such an "integration constitutes, perhaps, part of the growth
that Villanueva indicates is the social maturation essential for the
correction of social injustices."

BIOGRAPHICAL/CRITICAL SOURCES:

BOOKS

Bruce-Novoa, Juan, *Chicano Authors: Inquiry by Interview,* Uni-
    versity of Texas Press, 1980.

PERIODICALS

World Literature Today, winter, 1982, spring, 1985.

* * *

VILLARREAL, José Antonio 1924-

PERSONAL: Born July 30, 1924, in Los Angeles, Calif.; natural-
ized Mexican citizen, 1973; son of José Heladio (a Mexican revo-
lutionary) and Felícitas (Ramírez) Villarreal; married Barbara
Gentles (an administrative assistant), May 14, 1953; children:
Ian, Kelly Villarreal deFarcy, Caleb. *Education:* University of
California, Berkeley, B.A., 1950, graduate study, 1958. *Politics:*
Liberal. *Religion:* None.

ADDRESSES: Home—1116 South Eighth Ave., Edinburg, Tex.
78539.

CAREER: Lockheed Aircraft Corp., Palo Alto, Calif., consultant, senior technical editor, proposal writer, and speech writer
in Palo Alto, Sunnyvale, and Redlands, 1960-68; Ball Brothers
Research Corp., Boulder, Colo., supervisor of technical publications and public relations, 1968-71; University of Colorado,
Boulder, assistant professor of English, 1971-72; University of
Texas at El Paso, assistant professor of English literature and
writer in residence, 1972-73; *Now in Mexico,* Mexico City, editor
in chief of weekly periodical for travel agents, 1973-74;
XHRA-FM Radio, Guadalajara, Mexico, translator and newscaster, 1974-75; University of Santa Clara, Santa Clara, Calif.,
writer in residence and professor of English and creative writing,
1975-76; Texas A & I University, Laredo, professor of literature
of the Southwest, 1976; free-lance writer in Zacatecas, Mexico,
1976-77; University of the Americas, Mexico City, professor of
literature and composition, 1977-78; American School Foundation, Mexico City, professor of English, 1977-82; Universidad
Autónoma de México, Mexico City, professor of English at
School of Chemistry, 1978-79; Pan American University, Edin-

burg, Tex., instructor in English, 1982-84; California State University, Los Angeles, professor of literature, 1985, professor of composition and advanced writing, 1985-86; writer. Teacher of English as a second language at Centro de Estudios Universitarios, San Angel, Mexico, summer, 1977; Regents Lecturer and professor at University of California, Riverside, 1978; counselor at juvenile correctional institutions; consultant, public speaker, and broadcaster on radio and television. *Military service:* U.S. Navy, 1942-46.

WRITINGS:

Pocho (novel), Doubleday, 1959.
The Fifth Horseman: A Novel of the Mexican Revolution, Doubleday, 1974, 2nd edition, Bilingual Press, 1984.
Clemente Chacón (novel), Bilingual Press, 1984.

Contributor of stories, poems, and articles to magazines and newspapers, including *Los Angeles Times, San Francisco Review, Pegasus, Holiday, West,* and *Empire.*

WORK IN PROGRESS: The Houyhnhnms, a novel, publication expected in 1990; *Cuentos de mi raza,* a collection of short stories.

SIDELIGHTS: Because little had been written of the Mexican-American experience before José Antonio Villarreal published his first novel in 1959, *Pocho* "is notable not only for its own intrinsic virtues, but as a first voice from a people new in our midst who up to now have been almost silent," John Bright states in *Nation.* The story of Richard Rubio, a young second-generation Mexican-American growing up in California during the 1930s, *Pocho* illustrates "the pressures [that] Richard experiences as a result of being caught between two cultures, generations, and societies," describes Tomás Vallejos in a *Dictionary of Literary Biography* essay. These tensions also affect Richard's family, as his mother rebels against his father's traditional machismo; eventually the entire family breaks up, with Richard leaving to enter the military. Despite this sociological angle, Villarreal's novel "is more than the story of cultural conflict," adds Vallejos. "It is also a bildungsroman, a novel about self-discovery and maturation" that has led several critics to compare it to James Joyce's *Portrait of the Artist as a Young Man.*

William Hogan concurs with this assessment of the novel's literary value; writing in the *San Francisco Chronicle,* he notes that "always, 'Pocho' is the story of Richard Rubio's youth, and awakening. While the language is often rough," the critic continues, "the story is essentially a tender and moving one. Villarreal fights no cause here. He is concerned only with a boy. He portrays him with depth and with a narrative grace and honesty rare these days in a first novel." Other critics, however, believe that Richard's maturity and introspective nature strain credulity. "Richard is not an altogether convincing character, especially in his boyhood philosophical musings," comments Charles M. Tatum in *Chicano Literature;* "he has an intellectual maturity that is well beyond his years." In contrast, Bright feels that it is Richard's "very unusualness [that] becomes the novel's virtue, heightens its sense of reality, and removes it from the picaresque." Despite its faults, "*Pocho* remains the unmatched novel of 'identity crisis,' " asserts Roberto Cantú in *Chicano Literature: A Reference Guide,* a novel that "represents the conflicts and dilemmas of a Mexican family residing in the United States."

While not as widely reviewed as *Pocho,* Villarreal's subsequent novels have explored varying aspects of the Chicano experience while also demonstrating literary virtues. In *The Fifth Horseman* Villarreal builds a background for *Pocho* by relating the events leading up to the Mexican Revolution of 1910, a conflict that led many Mexicans, such as Richard Rubio's parents, to escape to the United States. Taking place on a wealthy hacienda, "the narrative is centered on the figure of its protagonist, Heraclio Inés, who is a 'different,' daring, and rebellious *peón* of predetermined mission," as Cantú summarizes. Heraclio, who has joined Pancho Villa's army, eventually becomes disenchanted with the war and leaves Mexico, hoping to return someday and help rebuild his country. While Cantú finds Heraclio's exploits predictable, he admits that they are "full of wonder and entertainment," and concludes that "one could say that [*The Fifth Horseman*] is his most ambitious [book]."

Similarly, *Clemente Chacón,* which follows a young Mexican who becomes a successful businessman in the United States, is "more complex than his other books," remarks Vallejos; ". . .certainly it is artistically his most sophisticated work," containing some of "the most memorable [characters] Villarreal has created." Villarreal's work has "opened new possibilities in Chicano fiction," Juan Bruce-Novoa writes in *Chicano Authors: Inquiry by Interview.* Although the author prefers to classify his work broadly as "American" rather than narrowly as "Chicano," the critic concludes that, nevertheless, "it would be difficult to understand Chicano literature without taking into account the work of José Antonio Villarreal."

Villarreal told *CA:* "Although I write novels, I consider myself a storyteller. This is because my introduction to literature at an early age was in the oral tradition. In those days my people were migrants, following crops throughout California, living almost always in tents outdoors—for me, a most bucolic life which I loved. The only diversion for the men after twelve hours of labor in the fields or orchards was to sit around a campfire after supper and tell stories of their homelands, different parts of Mexico. As I recall, I was usually the only child who listened.

"At the time I knew only Spanish. It was not until my second year at school that I began to write and converse in English, and by the fifth grade, although I read and wrote in Spanish and spoke Spanish exclusively within our home, the idiom had become my second language. By then I knew that I wished to be a writer and attempted to write vignettes about my people. When I was perhaps thirteen years old, I realized that the non-Mexican population in my country did not know about us, did not know we existed, had no idea that we would be a part of the mainstream of America and contribute to what I believe is true, the melting pot. I resolved then that I would write about my people. I wished that the American public would know of us. I believed, and still do, that I could best accomplish this through fiction.

"With the advent of the civil rights struggle, *Pocho* was discovered by Mexican-American activists, who now called themselves Chicanos. *Pocho* had been out of print for a number of years. It was acclaimed by the Chicano movement as a precursor to what was now being called Chicano literature. I approved of the movement and later, as an educator, I was disillusioned by some methods used in the struggle for equality. I experienced heavy criticism because my work did not emphasize the hatred, racism, and discrimination Mexican-Americans suffered. On the other hand, the movement used hatred and racism and taught it to young students in the classroom as tools to fight oppression. It was impossible for me to teach either prejudice.

"It came to pass that criticism of *Pocho* began to appear—very little of which dealt in literary assessment—in Chicano journals. For the most part, I was attacked for my posture. I knew that my work contributed to the advancement of my people. I have always written of what I know, what I have seen or experienced.

I have always had a reverence for literature as a vehicle for truth, honesty, and fidelity. My work must reflect those values. For the above reasons, although I am still called a Chicano writer, I repudiate that classification. I am an American writer. My work falls into a sub-genre of American literature."

BIOGRAPHICAL/CRITICAL SOURCES:

BOOKS

Baker, Houston A., Jr., editor, *Three American Literatures,* Modern Language Association of America, 1982.

Bruce-Novoa, Juan, *Chicano Authors: Inquiry by Interview,* University of Texas Press, 1980.

Dictionary of Literary Biography, Volume 82: *Chicano Writers, First Series,* Gale, 1989.

Jiménez, Francisco, editor, *The Identification and Analysis of Chicano Literature,* Bilingual Press, 1979.

Kanellos, Nicolas, editor, *Understanding the Chicano Experience Through Literature,* University of Houston, 1981.

Martínez, Julio A. and Francisco A. Lomelí, editors, *Chicano Literature: A Reference Guide,* Greenwood Press, 1985.

Tatum, Charles M., *Chicano Literature,* Twayne, 1982.

Vento, Arnold C., José Flores Peregrino Alurista, and others, editors, *Portraits of the Chicano Artist as a Young Man: The Making of the "Author" in Three Chicano Novels,* Pajarito Publishers, 1979.

PERIODICALS

Bilingual Review, spring, 1976.
Denver Quarterly, fall, 1981.
Explorations in Ethnic Studies, July, 1981.
Hispania, December, 1985.
MELUS, summer, 1978, fall, 1979, winter, 1981.
Minority Voices, fall, 1977.
Nation, January 9, 1960.
Phantasm, Volume IV, number 6, 1979.
Publishers Weekly, November 16, 1970, December 17, 1973.
San Francisco Chronicle, October 9, 1959.

*   *   *

VILLASEÑOR, Edmund
  See VILLASEÑOR, Víctor E(dmundo)

*   *   *

VILLASEÑOR, Víctor
  See VILLASEÑOR, Víctor E(dmundo)

*   *   *

VILLASEÑOR, Víctor E(dmundo) 1940-
  (Edmund Villaseñor, Víctor Villaseñor)

PERSONAL: Born May 11, 1940, in Carlsbad, Calif.; son of Salvadore (in business) and Lupe (Gómez) Villaseñor; married Barbara Bloch, December 29, 1974; children: David Cuauhtemoc. *Education:* Attended University of San Diego and Santa Clara University.

ADDRESSES: Home—1302 Stewart St., Oceanside, Calif. 92054.

CAREER: Construction worker in California, 1965-70; writer, 1970—. *Military service:* U.S. Army.

WRITINGS:

(Under name Edmund Villaseñor) *Macho!* (novel), Bantam, 1973.

(Under name Víctor Villaseñor) *Jury: The People vs. Juan Corona* (nonfiction), Little, Brown, 1977.

Rio Grande, Putnam, 1989.

Contributor to *Aztlan.*

SIDELIGHTS: Chicano author Víctor E. Villaseñor has attained recognition well beyond the small and somewhat insular Chicano literary community. Villaseñor's first novel, *Macho!,* benefited from being published at the height of a powerful migrant farmworkers' organizing campaign in California in 1973. The novel recounts a year in the life of Roberto García, a young Tarascan Indian from the state of Michoacán, Mexico, who migrates illegally to California in 1963 to work in the fields. Villaseñor describes García's intense culture shock in abandoning his isolated, tradition-bound village for the rich but lonely and frightening land of the north. The victim of exploitation and discrimination in the United States, García finally decides to go back to his village and resume working his family's small farm. But he returns a changed man who can no longer accept without question the traditional Mexican social code, particularly the *machista* demand that he take blood vengeance against the villager who murdered his father. Thus, García's adventure reflects the Chicano's transcultural experience—the melding of features from both the Spanish-Mexican and North American societies.

Villaseñor's second book, *Jury: The People vs. Juan Corona,* is a nonfiction account of the trial of Juan Corona, a California labor contractor who was convicted in 1973 of murdering twenty-five derelicts and drifters. After covering the trial as a journalist, Villaseñor decided to write a book focusing on the jury's agonizing struggle to reach a fair verdict in one of the worst mass murder cases in U.S. history. By exhaustively interviewing all of the jurors over a period of months, Villaseñor was able to reconstruct the details of eight days of emotionally charged deliberations that led the jury from an original majority favoring acquittal to a unanimous verdict of guilty.

Villaseñor's examination of the highly complicated and controversial case offers provocative insights into the workings of the American jury system. The author questions the system, quoting a Corona juror agonizing over whether a man's life should rest in the hands of twelve ordinary people seemingly ill-equipped by education or training to sort out a tangled skein of law and evidence. Based on the Corona trial, Villaseñor determines that the system does indeed work: in the crucible of unrestricted deliberations, a jury will rise to the solemn challenge of judging and render its verdict with integrity and good faith. In light of the Corona jury members' obvious human frailties, Villaseñor nevertheless concludes in *Jury,* "In becoming close to all the jurors and their families, I regained a respect and admiration for my fellow man."

Villaseñor told *HW:* "I was born in the barrio of Carlsbad, California, and raised on a ranch four miles away in Oceanside. Both my parents are from Mexico, and I grew up in a house where there were no books. When I started school, I spoke more Spanish than English. I was a D student and every year of school made me feel more stupid and confused—many of these feelings had to do with being Chicano. In my junior year of high school, I told my parents I had to quit school or I would go crazy. Finally, they allowed me to quit. I was eighteen years old. I felt free, I felt wonderful, but I didn't know what to do with my freedom.

"I worked on the ranch, I worked in the fields—I was making money and it felt great. But then that fall when the other kids went back to school and the illegal workers went back to Mexico,

I didn't know what to do with my life. An older cousin got me into college on a temporary basis if I finished high school. It was the University of San Diego and it was just getting started and was not yet accredited. On this campus I found out that books were not punishment, and if I couldn't remember dates I wasn't necessarily stupid. I flunked English of course (because I only had the reading ability of a fifth grader) and every other course except for philosophy and theology.

"The shock of my life came that year when a teacher told me I was very bright. But still I felt like I was going crazy. I was beginning to realize that I was ashamed of being Mexican. So I boxed. I fought with such a rage of confusion that I was undefeated.

"The following summer for the first time in my life I began to drink and discover my sexuality and feel wonderful and yet terrible from guilt. My parents sent me to Mexico where I fell in with some hip people. I was introduced to Mexican art, Mexican history, and I read my first book, Homer's *Iliad,* as well as *Tender Is the Night* by F. Scott Fitzgerald, and *The Little Prince.* I began having all night talks with an older woman. I felt good about myself. I wanted to stay in Mexico and never return to the United States where I felt ashamed of being Mexican. But my parents came for me and after weeks of arguments I agreed to go back home for awhile.

"I found myself feeling like a bombshell—ready to explode, prepared to kill anyone who made me feel ashamed. I was reading a copy of James Joyce's *Portrait of the Artist as a Young Man,* given to me by the woman in Mexico, when it hit me: I would write. Instead of killing or bashing people's brains out, I would change their minds. I would write good books that reach out and touch people and I would influence the world. I got a dictionary and a high school English grammar book and I built a desk and I began to read books eight months out of the year. I'd go to bookstores and buy ten books at a time, read them, dissect them, and then reassemble them. Then for four months of the year I'd support myself in construction.

"Then I began to write. I wrote for ten years, completing nine novels and sixty-five short stories and receiving more than 260 rejections before I sold my first book, *Macho!* Then, while I waited for *Macho!* to be published, I read about Juan Corona being arrested for twenty-five murders. Immediately I thought, Another Mexican being arrested. Hell, no man could kill twenty-five people. He must be innocent. So I talked to my publisher and he told me to look into it and write a short letter about what kind of book I thought I could write. They commissioned me to do the book. I spent the next three years investigating and writing about the Corona case."

BIOGRAPHICAL/CRITICAL SOURCES:

BOOKS

Villaseñor, Víctor, *Jury: The People vs. Juan Corona,* Little, Brown, 1977.

PERIODICALS

Christian Science Monitor, October 13, 1977.
English Journal, January, 1974.
Examiner and Chronicle (San Francisco), November 6, 1973.
New York Times Book Review, May 1, 1977.

* * *

VILLAURRUTIA, Xavier   1903-1950

PERSONAL: Born in 1903, in Mexico City, Mexico; died in 1950. *Education:* Studied drama at Yale University, 1935-36.

CAREER: Poet and dramatist; associated, with José Gorostiza, with the arts magazine *Contemporáneos,* 1928-31.

AWARDS, HONORS: Rockefeller Foundation grant, 1935.

WRITINGS:

POETRY

Reflejos, Editorial "Cvltvra," 1926.
Nocturnos (also see below) Fábula, 1933.
Nostalgia de la muerte (includes *Nocturnos, Nocturno de los ángeles, Nocturno mar,* and *Nocturno rosa*), Ediciones del Sur, 1938, 2nd edition, Ediciones Mictlan, 1946.
(Contributor) *Laurel, antología de la poesía moderna en lengua española,* Editorial Seneca, 1941.
Décima muerte y otros poemas no coleccionados, Nueva Voz, 1941.
Canto a la primavera y otros poemas, Editorial Stylo, 1948.

Also contributor to *Ocho poetas* (includes *Primeros poemas*), 1923.

PLAYS

¡En qué piensas! (also see below), Letras de México, 1938, published as *¿En qué piensas? Misterio en un acto,* Center for Curriculum Development (Philadelphia), 1971.
Sea usted breve: Farsa en un acto (also see below), E. Nandino, 1940.
La hiedra: Pieza en tres actos, Editorial "Cvltvra," 1941.
La mujer legítima: Pieza en tres actos, R. Loera y Chávez, 1943.
Autos profanos (five sketches; includes "Parece mentira," ".En que piensas!," "Ha llegado el momento," "Sea usted breve," and "El ausente"), Ediciones Letras de México, 1943.
Invitación a la muerte: Drama en tres actos (first produced at Teatro del Palacio de Bellas Artes, July 27, 1947), Ediciones Letras de México, 1944.
El yerro candente, Ediciones Letras de México, 1945.
El pobre Barba Azul: Comedia en tres actos, Sociedad General de Autores de México, 1947.
La tragedia de las equivocaciones, Gráficos Guanajuato, 1950.
El solterón: Obra en un acto, [Mexico], 1954.
(Contributor) *Teatro mexicano contemporáneo* (includes "Parece mentira," ".En que piensas!," and "Sea usted breve,"), Aguilar, 1959, 3rd edition, 1968.

Also author of "Juego peligroso."

OTHER

Textos y pretextos: Literatura—drama—pintura, La Casa de España en México, 1940.
Poesía y teatro completos, Fondo de Cultura Económica, 1953.
Obras: Poesía, teatro, prosas varias, crítica, Fondo de Cultura Económica, 1953, 2nd edition, 1966.
Cartas de Villaurrutia a Novo, 1935-1936, Instituto Nacional de Bellas Artes, Departamento de Literatura, 1966.
Crítica cinematográfica (film criticism), compiled by Miguel Capistrán, Dirección General de Difusion Cultural, Universidad Nacional Autónoma de México, 1970.
(Compiler and author of prologue) Ramón López Velarde, *El león y la virgen* (poetry), 2nd edition, Universidad Nacional Autónoma de México, 1971.

* * *

VIÑAS, D.
See VIÑAS, David

VIÑAS, David 1929(?)-
(D. Viñas; Raquel Weinbaum, a pseudonym)

PERSONAL: Born July 28, 1929 (one source says 1927), in Buenos Aires, Argentina; son of Ismael Pedro and Esther (Porter) Viñas. *Education:* Arts degree from National University of Buenos Aires; received doctorate autonoma in Madrid, Spain.

ADDRESSES: Córdoba 1646, Buenos Aires, Argentina. *Agent—* Jorge Timossi, Havana, Cuba.

CAREER: Literary critic for *Contorno,* Argentina, c. 1950s; professor and writer. Affiliated with Plural de México, 1981, and El Periodista, Buenos Aires, 1984.

MEMBER: P.E.N., Argentian Society of Writers, Playwrights of Argentina.

AWARDS, HONORS: Gerchunoff prize, 1955, for *Cayó sobre su rostro;* awards from Editorial G. Kraft, 1957, for *Un dios cotidiano,* from Editorial Losada, c. 1959, for *Los dueños de la tierra,* from Casa de las Américas, 1967, for *Los hombres de a caballo,* and from Argentina National Theatre, 1973.

WRITINGS:

NOVELS

Cayó sobre su rostro (title means "He Fell on His Face"), Ediciones Doble P (Buenos Aires), 1955.

Los años despiadados (title means "Pitiless Years"), Editorial Letras Universitarias (Buenos Aires), 1956.

Un dios cotidiano (title means "An Everyday God"), Editorial G. Kraft (Buenos Aires), 1957, reprinted, Centro Editor de América Latina (Buenos Aires), 1981.

Los dueños de la tierra (title means "The Lords of the Land"), Editorial Losada (Buenos Aires), 1959, reprinted, Folios (Mexico), 1982.

Dar la cara, Editorial Jamcana (Buenos Aires), 1962.

Los hombres de a caballo (title means "The Men on Horseback"), Casa de las Américas (Havana, Cuba), 1967.

Cosas concretas, Editorial Tiempo Contemporáneo (Buenos Aires), 1969.

Jauría, Granica (Buenos Aires), 1974.

Cuerpo a cuerpo, Siglo Veintiuno Editores (Mexico), 1979.

OTHER

Las malas costumbres (short stories), Editorial Jamcana, 1963.

(Author of introduction and notes) Florencio Sánchez, *M'hijo el dotor,* Huemul (Buenos Aires), 1964.

Literatura argentina y realidad política (essays), J. Alvarez (Buenos Aires), 1964, revised edition, Ediciones Siglo Veinte (Buenos Aires), Volume 1: *De Sarmiento a Cortázar,* 1971, 2nd edition, 1974, Volume 2: *Apogeo de la oligarquía,* c. 1975 (also see below), Volume 3: *La crisis de la ciudad liberal,* 1973 (also see below).

Laferrère: Del apogeo de la oligarquía a la crisis de la ciudad liberal (essays), Universidad Nacional del Litoral (Rosario, Argentina), 1965 (also see above).

En la semana trágica, J. Alvarez, 1966.

Argentina: Ejército y oligarquía (essays), [Havana], 1967.

De los montoneros a los anarquistas (essays), C. Pérez (Buenos Aires), 1971.

Lisandro (play), Editorial Merlin (Buenos Aires), 1971 (also see below).

Grotesco, inmigración y fracaso: Armando Discépolo (essays), Corregidor (Buenos Aires), 1973.

Dorrego, Maniobras, [and] *Túpac Amarú* (plays), Ediciones Cepe (Buenos Aires), c. 1974 (also see below).

(With others) *La Putería,* edited by Roberto Ruiz Rojas, Latina (Bogota, Columbia), 1977.

(With Marta Eguía) *Louis Pasteur* (biography), Editorial Hernando (Madrid), 1977.

Qué es el fascismo en Latinoamérica (essays), Enlace (Barcelona, Spain), 1977.

México y Cortés (essays), Editorial Hernando, c. 1978.

Ultramar, Edascal (Madrid), c. 1980.

(Under name D. Viñas; with I. Viñas, J. J. Sebreli, and others) *Contorno: Selección,* edited with a prologue by Carlos Mangone and Jorge Warley, Centro Editor de América Latina, c. 1981.

Contrapunto político en América Latina: Siglo XX (essays), Instituto de Capacitación Política (Mexico), 1982.

Indios, ejército y frontera (essays), Siglo Veintiuno Editores, 1982.

Anarquistas en América Latina (essays), Editorial Katún (Mexico), 1983.

(With others) *Más allá boom: Literatura y mercado* (essays), Folios, 1984.

Dorrego [and] *Túpac-Amarú* (plays), Editorial Galerna (Buenos Aires), c. 1985 (also see above).

Lisandro [and] *Maniobras* (plays), Editorial Galerna, c. 1985 (also see above).

Author of television scripts and of film scenarios for "The Chief" and "The Candidate." Contributor, sometimes under the pseudonym Raquel Weinbaum, to periodicals, including *Les Temps Modernes, El País, Settimana, Autrement, Centro,* and *Reunión.*

SIDELIGHTS: David Viñas is an award-winning Argentine writer whose novels and essays reflect the political and social turmoil of his country. Political instability has been part of most of Argentina's history, but it has been especially pronounced during Viñas's lifetime. Living through several revolutions and military coups d'etat strongly influenced him to become an outspoken Marxist. Often viewed as an angry critic, Viñas connects his personality traits to his environment: "My worst fault is in not being sincere enough, because there was no room for sincerity in the military and religious world where I was brought up. Struggling against it, I sometimes get violent, and as I don't like that I try to avoid people," Viñas was quoted by Héctor Grossi in an *Américas* article excerpted in *Modern Latin American Literature.* As a literary critic Viñas vents some of his anger in essays that analyze Argentine literature, politics, and history. These works frequently attack Argentina's oligarchy and argue that political and economic control should belong to all the people, not just to the elite.

Viñas's novels explore many of the same themes he addresses in his essays. As a social realist, he follows the Soviet school of writers who use fictional versions of real events to show how the world is moving towards socialism. His novels, consequently, typically center on historical incidents or periods. *Los hombres de a caballo,* for example, details the history of Argentina's military and focuses on its 1964 campaign in Peru, revealing the military to be no longer for but against the people. Published in 1967 and considered to be one of his best novels, *Los hombres de a caballo* won a prize from its publisher, Casa de las Américas. "It was well deserved," wrote Evelio Echevarría in a *Books Abroad* review contained in *Modern Latin American Literature.* The critic added that the book "displays a massive structure in which frequent monologues, flashbacks, conversation pieces, and narratives are well interwoven and directed toward their end." Critics have suggested that this novel and other works by Viñas speak for a generation of Argentineans who are ready for political and social reform.

BIOGRAPHICAL/CRITICAL SOURCES:

BOOKS

Foster, David William and Virginia Ramos Foster, editors, *Modern Latin American Literature,* Ungar, 1975.

PERIODICALS

Américas, January, 1960.
Books Abroad, spring, 1968.

* * *

VITIER, Cintio
   See VITIER (y BOLAÑOS), Cynthio

* * *

VITIER (y BOLAÑOS), Cynthio 1921-
   (Cintio Vitier)

PERSONAL: Born in 1921 in Havana, Cuba.

CAREER: Poet, critic, anthologist. Biblioteca Nacional José Martí (Cuban National Library), Havana, Cuba, formerly director at the Sala Martiana, currently a researcher.

WRITINGS:

UNDER NAME CINTIO VITIER

(Editor) *Cincuenta años de poesía cubana (1902-1952): Ordenación, antología y notas,* Dirección de Cultura del Ministerio de Educación (Havana), 1952.
Lo cubano en la poesía, Universidad Central de Las Villas (Santa Clara, Cuba), 1958.
Escrito y cantato, 1954-1959, [Havana], 1959.
(Compiler) *Las mejores poesías cubanas,* Organización Continentals de los Festivales del Libro (Havana), 1959.
(Editor) *Los grandes románticos cubanos: Antología* (poetry anthology), Organización Continental de los Festivales del Libro, 1960.
(Editor) Silverte de Balboa Troya y Quesada, *Espejo de paciencia,* Comisión Nacional Cubana de la Unesco, 1962.
(Editor) *Los poetas románticos cubanos: Antología,* Consejo Nacional de Cultura (Havana), 1962.
(With Fina García Marruz) *Estudios críticos,* Biblioteca Nacional José Martí, 1964.
Los versos de Martí: Tres conferencias de Cintio Vitier, Universidad de La Habana, 1968.
(With García Marruz) *Temas martianos,* Biblioteca Nacional José Martí, 1969, 2nd edition, Huracán (Río Piedras, P.R.), 1981.
Poetas cubanos del siglo diecinueve: Semblanzas, Unión (Havana), 1969.
(Contributor) Iván A. Schulman, *La influencia de Martí en la prosa madura de Darío,* [Havana], c. 1969.
Crítica sucesiva, Unión de Escritores y Artistas (Havana), 1971.
(Translator and author of prologue) Arthur Rimbaud, *Iluminaciones* (translation of *Les Illuminations*), Visor (Madrid), 1972.
(Editor and author of introduction) *José Martí: Antología di testi e antología critica,* Edizioni di Ideologie (Rome), 1974.
Ese sol del mundo para una historia de la eticidad cubana, Siglo Veintiuno (Mexico), 1975.
De peña pobre: Memoria y novela, Siglo Veintiuno, 1978.
(Author of prologue, notes, and chronology) José Martí, *Obra literaria,* Biblioteca Ayacucho (Caracas, Venezuela), 1978.

(Editor and author of introduction) Ernesto Cardenal, *Poesía,* Casa de las Américas (Havana), 1979.
La fecha al pie, Unión de Escritores y Artistas de Cuba, 1981.
(Compiler and author of prologue and notes) Juan Ramón Jiménez, *Juan Ramón Jiménez en Cuba,* Arte y Literatura (Havana), 1981.
(Editor and author of introduction) Samuel Feijóo, *Poesía,* Letras Cubanas, 1984.
Los papales de Jacinto Finalé, Letras Cubanas, 1984.
(Editor and author of introduction) Feijóo, *Prosa,* Letras Cubanas, 1985.
Rejando la leña está (novella), Letras Cubanas, 1986.

Also editor of anthology *Diez poetas cubanos, 1937-1947,* 1948, and author and editor of *La crítica literaria y estética en el siglo diecinueve cubano,* Biblioteca Nacional José Martí.

POEMS; UNDER NAME CINTIO VITIER

Poemas (1937-1938), [Havana], 1938.
Experiencia de la poesía, notas, [Havana], 1944.
De mi provincia: Poemas, Orígenes (Havana) 1945.
Sustancia, [Havana], 1950.
Vísperas, 1938-1953, Orígenes, 1953.
Canto llano, 1954-1955, Orígenes, 1956.
La luz del imposible, [Havana], 1957.
Poética, [Havana], 1961.
Testimonios, 1953-1968, Unión de Escritores y Artistas de Cuba, 1968.
Antología poética, Letras Cubanas, 1981.
(With García Marruz) *Viaje a Nicaragua,* Letras Cubanas, 1987.

Also author of *Extrañeza de estar,* 1943.

OTHER

Contributor to literary magazine, *Orígenes.*

SIDELIGHTS: Cynthio Vitier is one of the most important Cuban literary critics and anthologists of the twentieth century. A poet himself, Vitier's early work composed before the Cuban Revolution was abstract and cryptic. After the revolution ended in 1959, however, the author switched to a more realistic style. The first poems of this second phase in Vitier's work were bombastic and generally regarded as unremarkable; but by the mid-1960s he was able to compose poems, such as those contained in *Testimonios, 1953-1968,* that have been highly praised.

* * *

WEINBAUM, Raquel
   See VIÑAS, David

* * *

WOLFF, Egon 1926-

PERSONAL: Born in 1926 in Chile.

CAREER: Chemical engineer; author; playwright, 1958—.

WRITINGS:

Niñamadre (three-act play), Instituto Chileno-Norteamericano de Cultura (Santiago, Chile), 1966.
Los invasores (two-act play), Ercilla (Santiago, Chile), 1970.
Paper Flowers: A Play in Six Scenes, translated from the Spanish by Margaret Sayers Peden, University of Missouri Press, 1971.
El signo de caín (includes the play "Discípulos del miedo"), Ediciones Valores Literarios (Santiago, Chile), 1971.

(With Frieda Wolff) *Judeus no Brasil Imperial: Uma pesquisa nos documentos e no noticiário carioca da época* (nonfiction), Centro de Estudos Judaicos (Sao Paulo), 1975.

Teatro, Nascimento, 1978.

(With Frieda Wolff) *A odisséia dos judeus de Recife* (nonfiction), Centro de Estudos Judaicos, 1979.

Sepulturas de israelitas, Universidade de Sao Paulo, 1976.

Sepulturas de israelitas—II: Uma pesquisa em mais de trinta cemitérios nao israelitas, (nonfiction), Cemitério Comunal Israelita (Rio de Janeiro), 1983.

Participaçao e contribuiçao de judeus ao desenvolvimento do Brasil (nonfiction), [Rio de Janeiro], 1985.

(With Frieda Wolff) *Campos: Ascensao e declinio de uma coletividade* [Rio de Janeiro], 1986.

Pareja de trapo: La balsa de la Medusa, Universitaria (Santiago, Chile), 1988.

Depoimentos, [Rio de Janeiro], 1988.

Also author of the plays "Mansión de lechuzas," "Discípulos del miedo," and "Alamos en la azotea." Editor, with Frieda Wolff, of *Dicionário biográfico,* 1986—. Work represented in anthologies, including *Tres obras de teatro,* Casa de las Américas, 1970; *Three Contemporary Latin-American Plays,* edited by Ruth S. Lamb, Xerox College Pub., 1971; and *Teatro chileno contemporáneo,* Bello, 1982.

Y

YAÑEZ, Agustín   1904-1980

PERSONAL: Born May 4, 1904, in Guadalajara, Mexico; died January 17, 1980, in Mexico City, Mexico; son of Elpidio Yáñez and María Santos Delgadillo; married Olivia Ramírez Ramos; children: four daughters, two sons. *Education:* Attended University of Guadalajara and National University of Mexico; received degrees in law and philosophy.

CAREER: Teacher in Mexico, beginning in 1923; held numerous university and educational positions, including professor of literary theory, beginning in 1942, at National University of Mexico, and professor at the Universidad Femenina, 1946-50; held numerous positions in the Mexican Government, including undersecretary to the president, 1962-64, secretary for public education, 1964-70, and governor of the state of Jalisco. Writer.

MEMBER: Seminario de Cultura Mexicana de la Lengua, Academia Mexicana de la Lengua.

AWARDS, HONORS: Named to Mexican National College by the Republic of Mexico, 1952.

WRITINGS:

IN ENGLISH TRANSLATION

Al filo del agua (novel), illustrations by Julio Prieto, Porrúa, 1947, reprinted with prologue by Antonio Castro Leal, 1967, translation by Ethel Brinton published as *The Edge of the Storm,* University of Texas Press, 1963.
Las tierras flacas (novel), Joaquín Mortiz, 1962, translation by Brinton published as *The Lean Lands,* University of Texas Press, 1968.

IN SPANISH

(Editor and author of introduction and notes) *Crónicas de la conquista de México,* Universidad Nacional Autónoma, 1939.
Flor de juegos antiguos, Universidad de Guadalajara, 1941.
(Editor and contributor) *Mitos indígenas,* Universidad Nacional Autónoma, 1942.
Archipiélago de mujeres, Universidad Nacional Autónoma, 1943.
Melibea, Isolda y Aldo en tierras cálidas, Espasa-Calpe Argentina (Buenos Aires), 1946.
(Editor) Justo Sierra, *Periodismo político,* Universidad Nacional Autónoma, 1948, reprinted, 1977.

Poesías y estudio general sobre Don Justo Sierra, su vida, sus ideas y su obra, Universidad Nacional Autónoma, 1948, reprinted, 1977.
Fray Bartolomé de las Casas, el conquistador conquistado, Ediciones Xochitl, 1949.
(Editor) Bartolomé de las Casas, *Doctrina,* Universidad Nacional Autónoma, 1951.
(Contributor) Antonio Gómez Robledo, *Filosofía y lenguaje,* Imprenta Universitaria, 1956.
Discursos por Jalisco (essays), Porrúa, 1958.
La creación (novel; title means "The Creation"), Fondo de Cultura Económica, 1959.
Ojerosa y pintada, la vida en la ciudad de México (novel; title means "The Hollow-Eyed and Painted"), Librio Mex, 1960.
La tierra pródiga (novel; title means "The Lush Land"), Fondo de Cultura Económica, 1960.
(Editor and contributor) *El pensador mexicano,* Universidad Nacional Autónoma, 1963.
Proyección universal de México: Crónica del viaje realizado por el Presidente de México Adolfo López Mateos, a India, Japón, Indonesia y Filipinas, 1962, [Mexico], 1963.
Los sentidos al aire (stories), illustrations by Francisco Moreno Capdevila, Instituto Nacional de Bellas Artes, 1964.
Tres cuentos (title means "Three Stories"), Joaquín Mortiz, 1964.
(With others) *Oaxaca,* [Mexico], 1965.
Discursos al servicio de la educación pública, 1964-65 (essays and lectures), Secretaría de Educación Pública, 1966.
(Editor with Catalina Sierra), Francisco Indalecio Madero, *Epistolario (1910),* Ediciones de la Secretaría de Hacienda, 1966.
Obras escogidas (selected works), prologue by José Luis Martínez, Aguilar, 1968.
Agustín Yáñez, edited by Alfonso Rangel Guerra, Empresas Editoriales, 1969.
Las vueltas del tiempo, Joaquín Mortiz, 1973.
(Editor) Justo Sierra, *Discursos,* Universidad Nacional Autónoma, 1977.
(Editor) Justo Sierra, *La educación nacional: Artículos, actuaciones y documentos,* Universidad Nacional Autónoma, 1977.
(Editor) Justo Sierra, *Ensayos y textos elementales de historia,* Universidad Nacional Autónoma, 1977.

Contributor of numerous articles on literature, history, philosophy, psychology, politics, and economics to scholarly journals and periodicals.

Editor of book series, including *Textos de Literatura Mexicana, Bibliotheca Scriptorum Graecorum et Romanorum Mexicana,* and *Ediciones Comemorativas del IV Centenario de la Universidad.* Editor of periodicals *Bandera de Provincias,* 1929-30, and *Occidente,* 1944-45.

SIDELIGHTS: Agustín Yáñez is widely regarded as one of Mexico's first modernist novelists. He is best known for *Al filo del agua* (*The Edge of the Storm*) and *Las tierras flacas* (*The Lean Lands*)—novels that portray from a psychological perspective the social and cultural changes brought about in his country after the Mexican Revolution. Using such techniques as dream sequences, flashbacks, and interior monologues, which he is said to have learned from his studies of European and American letters, Yáñez is considered to have begun the modernist trend in Mexican fiction. Critics have compared his work to that of French authors Honoré de Balzac and Marcel Proust, as well as to that of Carlos Fuentes, another acclaimed Mexican writer.

Published in 1947, *Al filo del agua* was Yáñez's first novel. The work, translated in 1963 as *The Edge of the Storm,* depicts a small Mexican village just before and immediately after the outbreak of the Revolution. Contrasting the traditions of the predominantly mestizo population with the tyranny of the village Catholic church and local government, the work blends culturally accurate details with narrations of the inner lives of its characters. *The Edge of the Storm* is regarded as a landmark in Mexican literature, heralding the introduction of the psychological novel to Latin American fiction.

Yáñez is also known to English speaking readers as the author of *Las tierras flacas,* a novel acclaimed for its sensitive portrayal of provincial culture. Translated as *The Lean Lands,* it is the story of the demise of Epifanio Trujillo, a small-town boss who simultaneously dominates the village peasants and refuses to cooperate with the progressive new Mexican government. Opposing Trujillo is his illegitimate son, Jacob Gallo, who must fight not only his father, but also the superstitious and ignorant villagers when he attempts to bring modernized farming methods to the area. The novel ends pessimistically, with many of the major characters dying violent deaths and Gallo assuming his father's place as the corrupt village master.

In addition to his literary reputation, Yáñez was an esteemed educator and public servant, holding numerous government and academic positions. In 1952, he was awarded the highest honor given in Mexico: he was named to the prestigious National College, a sixteen-member board of the country's most respected scholars.

BIOGRAPHICAL/CRITICAL SOURCES:

PERIODICALS

Saturday Review, June 21, 1969.

*   *   *

YGLESIAS, José 1919-

PERSONAL: Born November 29, 1919, in Tampa, Fla.; son of José and Georgia (Milian) Yglesias; married Helen Bassine (a novelist), August 19, 1950; children: Rafael; stepchildren: Lewis Cole, Tamar Lear. *Education:* Attended Black Mountain College, 1946. *Politics:* "Should like to overthrow capitalism." *Religion:* "What?"

ADDRESSES: Home—North Brooklin, Maine 04661.

CAREER: Writer of nonfiction, novels, and short stories. Held jobs as dishwasher, stock clerk, assembly line worker, and typist-correspondent, 1937-42; *Daily Worker,* New York, N.Y., film critic, 1948-50; assistant to vice-president, Merck, Sharp & Dohme International (pharmaceutical concern), 1953-63. Regents Lecturer at University of California, Santa Barbara, winter, 1973. Occasional reader for publishing companies. *Military service:* U.S. Navy, 1942-45; received Naval Citation of Merit.

MEMBER: PEN.

AWARDS, HONORS: Guggenheim fellowship, 1970, 1976; National Endowment for the Humanities award, 1974.

WRITINGS:

A Wake in Ybor City (novel), Holt, 1963, reprinted, Arno, 1980.
The Goodbye Land (excerpts first published in *New Yorker*), Pantheon, 1967.
In the Fist of the Revolution: Life in a Cuban Country Town, Pantheon, 1968.
An Orderly Life (novel), Pantheon, 1968.
Down There, World Publishing, 1970.
The Truth about Them (novel), World Publishing, 1971.
Double, Double (novel), Viking, 1974.
The Kill Price (novel), Bobbs-Merrill, 1976.
The Franco Years, Bobbs-Merrill, 1977.
Home Again (novel), Arbor House, 1987.
Tristan and the Hispanics (novel), Simon & Schuster, 1989.

TRANSLATOR

Juan Goytisolo, *Island of Women,* Knopf, 1962.
Goytisolo, *Sands of Torremolinos,* Knopf, 1962.
Xavier Domingo, *Villa Milo,* Braziller, 1962.
Goytisolo, *The Party's Over,* Grove, 1966.

OTHER

Contributor of reviews, stories, and articles to *New Yorker, New York Times Magazine, Holiday, Esquire, Nation, New Republic, Venture, New York Review of Books, Massachusetts Review, New York Times Book Review, Book Week,* and other publications.

SIDELIGHTS: A bilingual American of Cuban and Spanish descent, José Yglesias traveled to Galicia, Spain, in 1964 to trace the details of his father's birth and death there and, as a result, wrote *The Goodbye Land.* Accompanied by his wife, Helen, and their then eleven-year-old son, Rafael, Yglesias vividly reacts to the trip as he meets his relatives, visits the land of his father, and experiences life in this quaint, mountainside village. "This book is about the son's journey to the village where his father's last years were spent," wrote a reviewer for the *Times Literary Supplement.* "It has its own quiet suspense and the discovery of facts; more important, it has the very delicately registered sense of self-discovery. . . . The result is as true a picture as one can hope to get of a by-way of modern European history as reflected in the experience of one family."

Written, according to Gerald Brenan of the *New York Review of Books,* in "a deceptively simple style, [it] takes one right into the mysteries of Galician life, as an account by a complete foreigner could never do. . . . The picture it presents of the primitive peasant mind—its warmth and kindness, its reserve and suspicion, its strong family feeling, its obsession about land and money—is the best I have read anywhere." And Clancy Sigal noted in the *New York Times Book Review* that "Yglesias has written a moving and polished book. . . . I was . . . won by his gentleness and control. It is not often that one finds a 'travel book' so affecting, generous and tender."

In most of his books written since *The Goodbye Land,* critics have noted that while avoiding sociological analysis and political moralizing, Yglesias's accounts of life in Cuba and Latin America seek to explore the essence of individual lives, emphasizing personal statements in order to reach the "underlying realities of the revolutionary experience." Yglesias's *In the Fist of the Revolution: Life in a Cuban Country Town* captures many of the emotions of a number of people as they embraced the optimism the Cuban Revolution triggered. *In the Fist of the Revolution* was written from material collected in 1967 during Yglesias's three-month stay in the town of Mayarí, Cuba. In Mayarí, as well as throughout Cuba, this feeling of hope and renewal seemed to prevail despite the presence of many problems such as government disorganization, food shortages, and the disruption of manufacturing.

Norman Gall remarked in the *New York Times Book Review:* "The dearth of information on the quality of these developments makes José Yglesias's modest book . . . the kind of social reporting on the Cuban Revolution that has long been missing. Mr. Yglesias is an honest and experienced reporter who, though sympathetic, refuses to be drugged by revolutionary rhetoric. He focuses carefully on the character of life in [*In the Fist of the Revolution*] and on the essential quality of the Cuban people that has remained nicely intact through the convulsions of the past decade." In conclusion, Juan de Onis wrote in *New Leader:* "The Cuban Revolution is a strongly emotional experience, and Yglesias does not shield himself from it behind false objectivity. . . . [He] has a writer's ear for dialogue. He speaks fluent, colloquial Spanish, to the point that many of the Cubans with whom he talked remarked, 'you are more like one of us', . . . Out of their individual stories emerges a sort of collective memory of the pre-revolutionary past, which is full of contradictions, and a picture of the present which does not hide the tensions and psychological contortions of a turbulent period of transition."

Yglesias's narrative study, *Down There,* is written similarly from the personal viewpoints of people in Brazil, Cuba, Chile, and Peru. Yglesias conducted interviews with a number of young revolutionaries and presented their thoughts and philosophies of what life is like for them in these select countries. *Down There* is often cited as being valuable particularly for its disregard of the "official line" on Latin America and for making available to North Americans a more balanced view of these societies. In a review published in the *New Yorker,* a critic remarked: "Yglesias writes not as a spokesman but as a translator or interpreter, so that North Americans can appreciate the sentiments of revolutionary South Americans, who regard Che Guevara as a hemispheric hero and Cuba as the world's best hope, and who believe that the United States is to blame for everything that is—and has been—wrong with their countries." "The ideas and impressions relate deviate from the 'official line,' but they are significant for understanding current Latin America," explained E. S. Johnson in the *Library Journal.*

Yglesias returned to Spain in 1975 and 1976 and was in Spain when the Spanish dictator Francisco Franco died. This experience was the catalyst for *The Franco Years,* a book profiling a number of Yglesias's Spanish acquaintances—detailing their existence during Franco's rule and the effect of his Fascist regime on the lives of the Spanish people. *The Franco Years* is, according to John Leonard in the *New York Times,* "a modest and extremely interesting series of interviews, filtered through a sympathetic intelligence, with Spaniards of various ages, professions and political persuasions who managed to survive Franco's dreary rule." In a *Saturday Review* article on *The Franco Years* Robert Stephen Spitz wrote that "like the sculptor who whittles a graceful swan from a block of ice, José Yglesias has unearthed the spirit of a nation long buried under the shroud of political tyranny. . . . The author spent a great deal of time among dedicated poets, loving infidels, political aspirants, and mine workers whose advanced stages of silicosis forced them to replace toil with courage. This is a powerful work about survivors who found strength in their oppression."

However, Jane Kramer did not find the book entirely satisfactory. She commented in the *New York Times Book Review:* "This is a good book. . . . Yglesias is a fine novelist, and I almost wish that he had tried a novel here, that he had taken a novelist's license with this research of so many years and shaped it into a more expressive narrative than these sketches offer. His discretion as a journalist seems to go against him. . . . He reaches for drama and then abandons it to some absolute standard of fair-mindedness that, in the end, flattens what he tries to say instead of underlining it. He is obviously a man of decency and compassion—he has many gifts—but he cannot turn understatement onto its cutting edge, and this book, so deliberately, so decently understated, is often bland where it should be powerful."

Leonard was much more accepting of *The Franco Years:* "Mr. Yglesias genuinely likes people. . . . He follows them around—poets, farmers, folklorists, showmen, technocrats, macho waiters, pretty boys of the Madrid homosexual circuit, an old anti-Semite who never leaves home—and he listens. Whether they are going to jail, as most of them have, or starting new political parties, as many of them do, they are allowed their dignity. . . . And always, in a way that I suppose is unintentional and whose manner is impossible to convey, Mr. Yglesias himself comes across as a nice guy. We like him, as much for what he restrains himself from saying—his personal views on property, on rhetoric, on heroism—as for his enthusiasm for the people he meets. He is a kind skeptic."

Yglesias's interest in chronicling the lives and contemporary history of Hispanic people extends also to his novels set in the United States. Yglesias's novels such as *The Truth about Them, The Kill Price, Home Again,* and *Tristan and the Hispanics* deal with the adjustment of working-class Cuban emigre families to American life and seem to reflect Yglesias's intent as a writer. "[I] should like in my work," he told *CA,* "to bring into clear view the moral views and approach to experience of workers, something which seems to me missing from most fiction; [I] should like as well, to do this in the lucid, unpretentious manner of E. M. Forster."

Many reviewers believe that Yglesias is quite successful in his desire to clearly present his subjects and honestly reflect the uniqueness of the emotions, dreams, and disappointments found in people of Hispanic heritage living in America. For example, *The Truth about Them* tells the generational story of a Cuban-American family planting roots in Florida. Yglesias follows the narrator, Pini, as he traces his grandmother's arrival in the United States from Cuba as a young woman to the present witnessing her children and their children as they emerge into America's middle-class. The reader meets the various characters that make up Pini's family as the essence of their lives grow and change over the years and generations.

In his review of *The Truth about Them,* Thomas R. Edwards commented in the *New York Review of Books:* "Yglesias's perspective on America has considerable freshness. These are not the conventional poor people of social protest novels, though they knew poverty well enough in hard times and felt the confused and inept discriminations. . . . As Cubans the family has an identity that for a time remained indifferent to the pressures of their new land. Success, not suffering, dissolves this identity as the third generation begins to prosper, as third generations somehow tend to do." "Blood is thicker than dogma in this book," remarked Martin Levin in the *New York Times Book Review.* Of *The Truth about Them* Levin wrote: "It glows with a respect for human dignity. It delights in the *brio* of a closeknit clan who are broke but not poor. It celebrates those ethnic distinctions that add salt to civilization."

Yglesias continues his study of individual behavior, awareness, and reaction in his next three novels: *The Kill Price, Home Again,* and *Tristan and the Hispanics. The Kill Price* views the relationship between a free-lance journalist of Hispanic descent, Jack Moreno, and his best friend, Wolf, a novelist who is Jewish. The book is set in New York City on a hot, steamy, summer night as Moreno reminiscences while keeping vigil with his dying friend. Various acquaintances arrive on the scene casting additional dimensions to the men's life stories. A *Publishers Weekly* reviewer believed *The Kill Price* is "a splendidly written, sometimes deeply probing story of individuals whose concerns specifice into something approaching universals."

Anatole Broyard felt an aversion for Wolf, the dying protagonist of *The Kill Price.* The critic commented in the *New York Times:* "I was glad to see him die. I was tired of his not very witty pontifications, his unimaginative male chauvinism, his egomania, his sexual braggadocio, and his unkindness." But, recognizing Yglesias's craft, he added: "Mr. Yglesias is an old hand at fiction and he writes well—almost too well for me to believe that the negative impact Wolf had on me was an accident. Perhaps the author wanted to correct the sentimental notion that dying ennobles a man, that powerlessness purifies."

Another study in self-awareness and rediscovery is *Home Again,* Yglesias's story of an aging Cuban-American novelist's return to his home and family in Florida and, as Brunet explained in the *Los Angeles Times Book Review,* his "reacquaintance with his Cuban relatives and heritage and the rediscovery of his powers as a writer." Clay Reynolds wrote in the *New York Times Book Review* that *Home Again* is "built on the promising theme of a

frustrated older man's attempt to come to terms with his ethnic background and political commitments. . . . Mr. Yglesias' prose is relaxed and trendy, with sparse dialogue and economical description."

In *Tristan and the Hispanics,* young New Yorker and Yale student Tristan Granados is sent by his family to Tampa, Florida, to arrange for the funeral of his grandfather. Antonio Granados was a once respected leftist novelist who had little contact with Tristan. Tristan is unprepared for the cultural shock he feels when he first meets his grandfather's extended family and assortment of colorful friends who live in a warm, loving emigré Cuban community. However, after several days Tristan discovers the richness of his heritage and begins to look at life and people differently. A reviewer for *Library Journal* noted that *Tristan and the Hispanics* is "a frequently funny and refreshingly down-to-earth novel."

AVOCATIONAL INTERESTS: Vegetable gardening.

BIOGRAPHICAL/CRITICAL SOURCES:

PERIODICALS

Library Journal, October 15, 1970, March 15, 1989.
Los Angeles Times Book Review, September 27, 1987.
New Leader, June 3, 1968.
New Republic, July 20, 1968.
New Yorker, October 17, 1970.
New York Review of Books, March 25, 1971, March 9, 1972.
New York Times, May 28, 1976, October 18, 1977.
New York Times Book Review, July 16, 1967, July 14, 1968, July 25, 1976, October 30, 1977, November 1, 1987.
Publishers Weekly, March 29, 1976, August 22, 1977, January 6, 1989.
Saturday Review, June 8, 1968, November 12, 1977.
Times Literary Supplement, February 22, 1968.

—*Sketch by Margaret Mazurkiewicz*

*   *   *

YUNKEL, Ramar
See MARTIN (MONTES), José L(uis)

Z

ZAMORA, Bernice (B. Ortiz) 1938-

PERSONAL: Born January 20, 1938, in Aguilar, Colo.; father was a coal miner, farmer, and automobile painter; mother worked for an optical company (maiden name, Valdez); marriage to husband named Zamora ended, 1974; children: Rhonda and Katherine. *Education:* University of Southern Colorado, B.A.; Colorado State University, M.A., 1972; Stanford University, Ph.D., 1986; attended Marquette University, 1973.

CAREER: Poet. Instructor of Chicano studies, University of California, Berkeley.

MEMBER: Modern Language Association, Bay Area Chicano Poets/Chicano Writers' Union, Ancient Mystical Order Rosae Crucis.

WRITINGS:

(With José Antonio Burciaga) *Restless Serpents* (poems), Diseños Literarios (Menlo Park, Calif.), 1976.
(Editor with José Armas) *Flor y Canto IV and V: An Anthology of Chicano Literature,* Pajarito, 1980.

Contributor to anthologies, including *Calafia: The California Poetry,* edited by Ishmael Reed, 1979, and *Chicanos: Antología histórica y literaria,* 1980. Contributor to *Caracol, De Colores, Mango, Atisbos,* and *Revista Chicano-Riqueña.* Editor, *De Colores,* 1979; guest editor, *El Fuego de Aztlán.*

SIDELIGHTS: "Bernice Zamora's considerable reputation as a poet rests largely on one book, *Restless Serpents,*" writes Nancy Vogeley in *Dictionary of Literary Biography.* "Zamora's poetry in *Restless Serpents* explores such topics as Chicano cultural traditions, the experience of women in that culture, language, and the power of poetry." The clarification of relationships is an important element of Zamora's writing, including the reinterpretation of sexual relationships. "The primary determinant of Zamora's poems in *Restless Serpents* is sex," writes Marta Ester Sánchez in *Contemporary Chicana Poetry: A Critical Approach to an Emerging Literature.* Sánchez continues, stating that *Restless Serpents* "represent[s] attempts to redefine sexual relationships between men and women as well as relationships between a text and its literary source." Sánchez emphasizes that "if there is a fundamental loyalty marking Zamora's poetic consciousness, it is to her female voice, to her identity as a woman."

Zamora does not see herself as a traditional feminist, however. She told Juan Bruce-Novoa for *Chicano Authors: Inquiry by Interview:* "It would be a mistake . . . to call [Chicana writers] feminist writers. To be a purely feminist writer is to ignore the issue of race—racial discrimination, division, and deprivation—these are entirely overlooked by the feminists." She continued, "besides, our relationship with our men is far different than that of the feminist with her man. These are the affinities we share with Blacks as I have discussed them with those Black writers I know." And Vogeley recounts that "although Zamora admits a feminist message in her poetry, she says her primary anger is directed against oppression in all forms."

Zamora sees Chicanos as connected with other non-white races, especially in their literature: "An oral tradition is one important affinity we share with Native Americans and Blacks; another is our penchant for integrating our religious and spiritual symbols with our arts; and most important is our similar experience of resistance to cultural suppression," she told Bruce-Novoa. She continued: "The common ground we have with Blacks is, of course, our respective oral traditions and our heavy reliance on internal rhythms for expression. We may write in English, but we rarely write in iambic pentameter." Zamora also told Bruce-Novoa that "the rhythmic expressions in poetry, the humor and poignancy . . . the experimentation and extension of our oral tradition in the novel," are among the strengths of Chicano writing. She believes that its weaknesses "lie in our critical writings. We have yet to learn to separate the cultural qualities from the societal and academic ones in order to restructure a balanced approach."

BIOGRAPHICAL/CRITICAL SOURCES:

BOOKS

Bruce-Novoa, Juan, *Chicano Artists: Inquiry by Interview,* University of Texas Press, 1980.
Bruce-Novoa, Juan, *Chicano Poetry: A Response to Chaos,* University of Texas Press, 1982.
Dictionary of Literary Biography, Volume 82: *Chicano Writers: First Series,* Gale, 1989.
Sánchez, Marta Ester, *Contemporary Chicana Poetry: A Critical Approach to an Emerging Literature,* University of California Press, 1985.
Sommers, Joseph and Tomás Ybarra-Frausto, *Modern Chicano Writers: A Collection of Critical Essays,* Prentice-Hall, 1979.

ZAPATA OLIVELLA, Manuel 1920-

PERSONAL: Born March 17, 1920, in Lorica, Colombia; son of Anthonio and Edelmira (Olivella) Zapata; married Rosa Bosch, December 23, 1962; children: Harlem, Edelma. *Education:* University of Cartagena, Colombia, B.A., 1937, graduate study, 1938; National University, Bogotá, Colombia, M.D., 1948.

ADDRESSES: Home—Calle 23A, No. 19-68, Bogotá, Colombia.

CAREER: Physician, psychiatrist, and author. Intern at clinic of Dr. Alfonso Ortiz Tirado, Mexico City, Mexico, 1944, Hospital Floresta, Mexico, 1945, and Psychiatric Hospital for Women, Bogotá, Colombia, 1948; general practitioner of medicine in El Cesar, Colombia, 1948-52, Córdoba, Colombia, 1953-55, Atlántico, Colombia, 1955, Bolívar, Colombia, 1959-60, and Bogotá, 1960 and 1967-68; birth clinic of Dr. Lamaze, Paris, France, assistant in psychoprophylaxis, 1958. Visiting professor at numerous universities, including Howard University, University of Kansas, and University of Toronto. Co-founder and artistic director of Colombian Folkloric Dances, 1958; chief of National Ministry of Education's division of popular culture, 1966; organizer of First Congress of Colombian Culture and of First Colombian Dramaturgists cycle of play reading, both 1966; founder, publisher, and director of literary periodical *Letras Nacionales.* General secretary of Second National Folklorists Congress, Ibagué, Colombia, 1965; second general secretary of Latinoamerican Writers Congress, Mexico City, 1967; judge for First National University Folkloric Group Exhibition, Colombia, 1968; Director, producer, and script writer of Colombian radio and television programs.

AWARDS, HONORS: First National Play Theater Prize from *Spiral;* First National Novel Prize from Colombian Language Academy; Second National Novel Prize from Colombian Language Academy.

WRITINGS:

Hotel de vagabundos (play), Espiral (Bogotá, Colombia), 1955.
Cuentos de muerte y libertad, [Bogotá], 1961.
He visto la noche (travel book), Imprenta Nacional de Cuba (San Rafael, Argentina), 1962, published as *He visto la noche: Las raíces de la furia negra,* Bedout (Medellín, Colombia), 1969.
Corral de negros (novel), Casa de las Américas (Havana, Cuba), 1963, published as *Chambacú: Corral de negros,* Bedout, 1967.
Detrás del rostro (novel), Aguilar (Madrid), c. 1963.
En Chimá nace un santo, Seix Barral (Barcelona), c. 1963.
Tierra mojada (novel), Bullón (Madrid), 1964.
¿Quién dió el fusil a Oswald? y otros cuentos (short stories), Revista Colombiana (Bogotá), 1967.
Tradición oral y conducta en Córdoba: Estudio investigativo elaborado para la División de Desarrollo Social Campesino del INCORA (essay collection), Publicación de INCORA (Bogotá), 1972.
"Caronte liberado" (play), published in *Teatro,* Instituto Colombiano de Cultura (Bogotá), 1972.
El hombre colombiano: Con un resumen en inglés al final (essay collection), Canal Ramírez-Antares (Bogotá), c. 1974.
El folclor en los puertos colombianos (essay collection), Puertos de Colombia (Bogotá), 1977.
Chango, el gran putas, Oveja Negra (Bogotá), c. 1983.
Etnografía colombiana (essay collection), ICFES (Bogotá), 1984.
El fusilamiento del diablo, Plaza y Janés (Bogotá), 1986.

Nuestra voz: Aportes del habla popular latinoamericana al idioma español (essay collection), Ecoe (Bogotá), 1987.

Also author of *Pasión vagabunda,* 1948, *China Six A.M.,* 1962, and *La calle diez,* 1962, and of the plays "Pasos del Indio," 1963, "Las tres monedas de oro," 1966, and "El retorno de Caín."

SIDELIGHTS: Manuel Zapata Olivella is a well-known Latin American black author who has written short stories, plays, and novels along with essay collections on sociology, history, and music. A physician and psychiatrist involved in several Colombian cultural programs, Zapata Olivella writes works that seek to free blacks and other races from all forms of repression. One of his best-known novels, *Corral de negros,* reflects many of the author's persistent concerns and features an often-jailed political activist who is killed while trying to advance civil rights in his community.

BIOGRAPHICAL/CRITICAL SOURCES:

BOOKS

Jackson, Richard L., *The Black Image in Latin American Literature,* University of New Mexico Press, 1976.

*   *   *

ZAVALA, Iris M(ilagros) 1936-

PERSONAL: Born December 27, 1936, in Ponce, Puerto Rico; daughter of Romualdo and Maria M. (Zapata) Zavala. *Education:* University of Puerto Rico, B.A., 1957; University of Salamanca, M.A., 1961, Ph.D. (summa cum laude), 1962. *Politics:* None. *Religion:* None.

ADDRESSES: Home—Keizersgracht 71, 1015 CE Amsterdam, Netherlands. *Office*—Rijksuniversiteit te Utrecht, Faculteit der Letteren, Kromme Nieuwegracht 29, 3512 HD Utrecht, Netherlands.

CAREER: University of Puerto Rico, Río Piedras, assistant professor of Spanish literature, 1962-64; Hunter College of the City University of New York, New York City, assistant professor of Hispanic literature, 1968-69; State University of New York at Stony Brook, associate professor, 1969-71, professor of Hispanic and comparative literature, 1971-83, joint professor of comparative literature, 1976-83, director of graduate studies, 1970-72 and 1975-1981, chair, 1973-74; Rijksuniversiteit Utrecht, Utrecht, Netherlands, chair of Hispanic literatures, 1983—, chair and director of Spanish Institute, 1984—. Visiting lecturer, Queens College, 1966; visiting professor, University of Puerto Rico, 1978 and 1981, and Universitá della Calabria, 1985; visiting scholar, El Colegio de México, 1979. Consultant, Casa de España (Utrecht), 1984—. Has conducted more than 90 lectures throughout Europe, the United States, and Latin America. Consultant to universities and organizations. Member, National Committee, 46th International Congress of Americanists, 1985-86.

MEMBER: Modern Language Association of America (Spanish 5, member of executive committee, 1972-73, chairman, 1974-75; member of commission on minority groups, 1973-74), American Association of Teachers of Spanish and Portuguese (member of committee on bilingual education, 1971-72), Society for Spanish and Portuguese Historical Studies (member of executive council, 1968-72).

AWARDS, HONORS: Grant, University of Puerto Rico, 1963; grant, Instituto de Cultura Puertorriqueña, 1964; research fellow, El Colegio de México, 1964; research fellow, Organization of American States, 1964-65; award from American Philosophical Society, 1966; Guggenheim fellow, 1966-67; grant, Social Science Research Council, 1972; award from American Council of Learned Societies/Social Science Research Council, 1972-73; Premio de Literatura Puertorriqueña (National Literary Prize, Puerto Rico), 1964, 1965, and 1972; grants, State University of New York at Stony Brook, 1969 and 1970; Premio del Instituto de Literatura (New York and Puerto Rico), 1978; Finalista Premio Herralde (novela), 1983; Condecoration from King Juan Carlos of Spain, Encomienda, Lazo de Dama de la Orden de Mérito Civil, 1988, for contributions made to Spanish culture.

WRITINGS:

Unamuno y su teatro de conciencia (title means "Unamuno and His Philosophical Theatre"), Acta Salmanticensia, University of Salamanca (Salamanca, Mexico), 1963.

Barro doliente (poems; title means "Repenting Clay"), La Isla de los Ratones (Santander), 1965.

La angustia y el hombre: Ensayos de literatura española (main title means "Literature of Anguish in the 19th Century"), Universidad Veracruzana (Mexico), 1965.

(Editor with Clara E. Lida) *La Revolución de 1868: Historia, pensamiento, literatura* (title means "Revolution of 1868: History, Thought, and Literature"), Las Américas, 1970.

Masones, comuneros y carbonarios, Siglo Veintiuno (Madrid), 1970.

Ideología y política en la novela española del siglo XIX (title means "Ideology and Politics in the 19th Century Spanish Novel"), Anaya (Madrid), 1971.

Poemas prescindibles (title means "Dispensable Poems"), Anti-Ediciones Villa Miseria, 1972.

Románticos y socialistas: Prensa española del XIX, Siglo Veintiuno, 1972.

(Editor with Rafael Rodríguez; also author of introduction) *Libertad y crítica en el ensayo puertorriqueño,* Puerto, 1973, revised edition translated as *The Intellectual Roots of Independence: An Anthology of Puerto Rican Political Essays,* Monthly Review Press, 1979.

Escritura desatada (poetry), Puerto, 1974.

Fin de siglo: Modernismo, 98 y bohemia, Cuadernos para el Diálogo (Madrid), 1974.

(Editor) Alejandra Sawa, *Iluminaciones en la sombra.* [Madrid], 1977, 2nd edition, Alhambra (Madrid), 1986.

Clandestinidad y libertinaje erudito en los albores del siglo XVIII, Ariel (Barcelona), 1978.

(With Carlos Blanco Aguinaga and Julio Rodríguez Puértolas) *Historia social de la literatura española (en lengua castellana),* three volumes, Castalia (Madrid), 1978-79, 2nd edition, 1983.

El texto en la historia, Nuestra Cultura (Madrid), 1981.

Kiliagonía (novela), Premiá Editora, 1982, translation by Susan Pensak published as *Chiliagony,* Third Woman Press, Indiana University, 1984.

Historia y crítica de la literatura española, Volume 5: *Romanticismo y realismo,* Crítica (Barcelona), 1982.

Que nadie muera sin amar el mar (poetry), Visor (Madrid), 1983.

(Editor with Myriam Díaz-Diocaretz) *Women, Feminist Identity, and Society in the 1980's: Selected Papers,* Benjamins (Amsterdam), 1985.

(Editor with Teun A. van Dijk and Díaz-Diocaretz) *Approaches to Discourse, Poetics, and Psychiatry,* Benjamins, 1987.

Nocturna mas no funesta (novela), Montesinos (Barcelona), 1987.

Lecturas y lectores del discurso narrativo dieciochesco, Rodopi (Amsterdam), 1987.

(With others) *Estelas, laberintos, nuevas sendas: Unamuno, Valle-Inclán, García Lorca, la Guerra Civil,* Anthropos (Barcelona), 1988.

Romanticismo y costumbrismo, Espasa Calpe (Madrid), 1989.

Rubén Darío bajo el signo del cisne, University of Puerto Rico, 1989.

(Editor) *El modernismo y otros ensayos de Rubén Darío,* Alianza (Madrid), 1989.

Modernidad, carnaval político, esperpento: Valle Inclán, Orígenes (Madrid), 1989.

Unamuno y el pensamiento dialógico, Anthropos, 1990.

Teorías de la modernidad, Tuero (Madrid), 1990.

Estudios sobre Bajtin y su círculo, Espasa Calpe, 1990.

Contributor of over 80 articles to publications throughout Europe, the United States, and Latin America. Editor of books series, including "Critical Theory: Interdisciplinary Approaches to Language, Discourse and Ideology," Benjamins, 1984—, "Teoría Literaria: Texto y Teoría," Rodopi, 1986—, and a series for Alianza Editorial/Alianza Teoría, 1989—. Member of editorial or advisory boards to journals in the United States, Latin America, and Europe.

WORK IN PROGRESS: El libro de Apolonia o de las islas (novel); *La concupiscencia de los ojos: Historia apócrifa del bolero* (creative essay); *The Great Narrative: Hispanic Modernism and the Social Imaginary,* for Indiana University Press.

SIDELIGHTS: Iris M. Zavala told *CA:* "I continue to maintain my adolescent goals: that scholarship and creation are the same creative process and that I will try to merge them. Therefore, the reader (if any) will find that my books of poetry and my novella make wide use of history, philosophy, art, literature and foreign languages. Many friends have helped me in writing my books, most are dead and illustrious: Dante, Cervantes, Erasmus, Goethe, Marx. Their peculiar erudition will save me, I hope, from lamentable blunders. Indefatigable research in archives and libraries has given me whatever understanding I have of memories, expectations and disappointments.

"Since in the capitalist age a human being must dutifully put on layers of makeup and dress, Ms. Zavala is a professor of Hispanic and comparative literature, a literary critic and a poet. I earnestly hope that I have been able to slip out of each new fashion, reappraising to my readers the nature of literature, bedfellow of truth."

BIOGRAPHICAL/CRITICAL SOURCES:

PERIODICALS

Choice, January, 1981.

* * *

ZURITA (CANESSA), Raúl 1951-

PERSONAL: Born January, 1951, in Santiago, Chile. *Education:* University of Federico Santa María, Valparaíso, 1973.

ADDRESSES: Home—Santiago, Chile. *Office*—c/o Editorial Universitaria SA(r), María Luisa Santander 0447, Casilla 10220, Santiago, Chile.

CAREER: Poet.

WRITINGS:

Purgatorio, 1970-1977, Universitaria (Santiago, Chile), 1979, translation by Jeremy Jacobson published under same title in Spanish and English edition, Latin American Lit., c. 1985.

Anteparaíso (poetry), Asociados (Santiago), c. 1982, translation by Jack Schmitt published as *Anteparadise: A Bilingual Edition,* University of California Press, c. 1986.

Canto a su amor desaparecido, Universitaria, c. 1985.

El amor de Chile (poetry), photographs by Renato Srepel, Montt Palumbo (Santiago), 1987.

SIDELIGHTS: Chilean poet Raúl Zurita's works reflect his experience of the American-supported military coup in Chile in 1973. Thousands were killed or exiled during the coup, and the country's first freely elected Marxist president, Salvador Allende, committed suicide—according to military records— shortly after the takeover. *Los Angeles Times Book Review* contributor W. S. Merwin praised Zurita's courage in pursuing his artistic vision after living through "the grotesque reign of terror that followed the coup." Commenting on the nature of the poems contained in *Anteparadise,* Merwin remarked, "Zurita's poems come off the page as though they were a series of paintings on another plane, oddly silent, disturbing, grotesque, beautiful, as things seen."

BIOGRAPHICAL/CRITICAL SOURCES:

PERIODICALS

Los Angeles Times Book Review, December 7, 1986.

Nationality Index

This index lists all Hispanic writers alphabetically under their country of origin and/or citizenship.

ARGENTINA
Alvarez Murena, Héctor Alberto
Anderson Imbert, Enrique
Arlt, Roberto
Banchs, Enrique J.
Benedetto, Antonio di
   See di Benedetto, Antonio
Bioy Casares, Adolfo
Borges, Jorge Luis
Bullrich, Silvina
Casares, Adolfo Bioy
   See Bioy Casares, Adolfo
Cortázar, Julio
Costantini, Humberto
Denevi, Marco
di Benedetto, Antonio
Dragún, Osvaldo
Fernández Moreno, Baldomero
Fernández Moreno, César
Gálvez, Manuel
Gambaro, Griselda
Gelman, Juan
Gerchunoff, Alberto
Gil-Montero, Martha
Girondo, Oliverio
Girri, Alberto
Guevara, Ché
   See Guevara, Ernesto
Guevara, Ernesto
Guido, Beatriz
Güiraldes, Ricardo
Jaimes Freyre, Ricardo
Juarroz, Roberto
Lugones, Leopoldo
Lynch, Benito
Mallea, Eduardo
Marechal, Leopoldo
Martínez, Tomás Eloy
Molina, Enrique
Moyano, Daniel
Mujica Láinez, Manuel
Murena, H. A.
   See Alvarez Murena, Héctor
Niosi, Jorge
Ocampo, Silvina
Ocampo, Victoria
Orozco, Olga
Payró, Roberto J.
Puig, Manuel
Sábato, Ernesto

Sáenz, Dalmiro A.
Storni, Alfonsina
Timerman, Jacobo
Valenzuela, Luisa
Verbitsky, Bernardo
Viñas, David

BOLIVIA
Jaimes Freyre, Ricardo
Prada Oropeza, Renato

BRAZIL
Castro, Américo

CHILE
Allende, Isabel
Barrios, Eduardo
Bombal, María Luisa
Donoso, José
Dorfman, Ariel
Godoy Alcayaga, Lucila
Hahn, Oscar
Huidobro, Vincente
   See Huidobro Fernández,
     Vincente García
Huidobro Fernández,
   Vicente García
Lihn, Enrique
Mistral, Gabriela
   See Godoy Alcayaga, Lucila
Neruda, Pablo
Parra, Nicanor
Prado, Pedro
Rojas, Manuel
Skármeta, Antonio
Wolff, Egon
Zurita, Raúl

COLOMBIA
Arciniegas, Germán
Artel, Jorge
Buenaventura, Enrique
Caballero Calderón, Eduardo
García Márquez, Gabriel
Márquez, Gabriel García
   See García Márquez, Gabriel
Orjuela, Héctor H.
Pizarro, Agueda
Reyes, Carlos José
Rivera, José Eustasio
Zapata Olivella, Manuel

COSTA RICA
Arias Sánchez, Oscar
Bruce-Novoa, Juan D.
Dobles, Fabián
Duncan, Quince
Sánchez, Oscar Arias
   See Arias Sánchez, Oscar

CUBA
Arenas, Reinaldo
Armand, Octavio Rafael
Arozarena, Marcelino
Arrufat, Antón B.
Cabrera, Lydia
Cabrera Infante, G.
Cardoso, Onelio Jorge
Carpentier, Alejo
Catalá, Rafael
Cuza Malé, Belkis
Díaz-Alejandro, Carlos F.
Fernández, Roberto G.
Fernández Retamar, Roberto
Fornes, Maria Irene
Gracia, Jorge J. E.
Guillén, Nicolás
Infante, G. Cabrera
   See Cabrera Infante, G.
Lezama Lima, José
Machado, Eduardo
Martínez, Julio A.
Morales Carrión, Arturo
Padilla, Heberto
Pau-Llosa, Ricardo
Piñera, Virgilio
Sarduy, Severo
Suarez, Virgil
Triana, José
Vitier, Cynthio

DOMINICAN REPUBLIC
Bosch, Juan
Gómez Rosa, Alexis
Veloz Maggiolo, Marcio E.

ECUADOR
Adoum, Jorge Enrique
Aguilera Malta, Demetrio
Carrera Andrade, Jorge
Estupiñán Bass, Nelson
Icaza, Jorge
Ortiz, Adalberto

Rodríguez O., Jaime E.
Ruiz, Ramon Eduardo

EL SALVADOR
Argueta, Manlio
Beneke, Walter

GUATAMALA
Arévalo Martínez, Rafael
Asturias, Miguel Angel
Cardoza y Aragón, Luis
Monterroso, Augusto
Unger, David

HONDURAS
Sosa, Roberto

MEXICO
Alurista
    See Urista, Alberto H.
Aridjis, Homero
Arreola, Juan José
Avendaño, Fausto
Azuela, Arturo
Azuela, Mariano
Benítez, Fernando
Bodet, Jaime Torres
    See Torres Bodet, Jaime
Bornstein-Somoza, Miriam
Buendía, Manuel
    See Girón, Manuel Buendía
        Téllez
Campa, Arthur L.
Campobello, Nellie
Carballido, Emilio
Castellanos, Rosario
Chumacero, Alí
Corpi, Lucha
Díaz Mirón, Salvador
Fuentes, Carlos
Galarza, Ernesto
García Ponce, Juan
Garro, Elena
Girón, Manuel Buendía Téllez
González, José Luis
González-Crussi, F.
González Martínez, Enrique
Gorostiza, Celestino
Gorostiza, José
Guzmán, Martín Luis
Ibargüengoitia, Jorge
Jiménez, Francisco
Leal, Luis
Leon-Portilla, Miguel
López Portillo, José
López y Fuentes, Gregorio
Montes de Oca, Marco Antonio
Muniz, Angelina
Mutis, Alvaro
Nervo, Amado
Novo, Salvador
Pacheco, José Emilio
Padilla, Raymond V.

Paz, Octavio
Pellicer, Carlos
Pérez-Gómez, Alberto
Poniatowska, Elena
Portillo, José López
    See López Portillo, José
Quinn, Anthony
Reyes, Alfonso
Romero, José Rubén
Rosario Green, María del
Rulfo, Juan
Sabines, Jaime
Sainz, Gustavo
Schon, Isabel
Solórzano, Carlos
Spota, Luis
Taibo, Paco Ignacio II
Torres Bodet, Jaime
Trejo, Arnulfo D.
Urista, Alberto H.
Usigli, Rodolfo
Vázquez Amaral, José
Villaurrutia, Xavier
Yáñez, Agustín

NICARAGUA
Aguila, Pancho
Alegría, Claribel
Cabezas, Omar
Cardenal, Ernesto
Cruz, Arturo, Jr.
Cuadra, Pablo Antonio
Darío, Rubén

PANAMA
Blades, Rubén
Casaccia Bibolini, G.
Quintero, José

PARAGUAY
Bastos, Augusto Roa
    See Roa Bastos, Augusto
Roa Bastos, Augusto
Rodríguez-Alcalá, Hugo

PERU
Alegría, Ciro
Arguedas, José María
Belli, Carlos Germán
Chocano, José Santos
Cisneros, Antonio
Goldemberg, Isaac
González Prada, Manuel
Gutiérrez Merino, Gustavo
Héraud, Javier
Llosa, Mario Vargas
    See Vargas Llosa, Mario
Moro, César
Salazar Bondy, Sebastián
Santa Cruz, Nicomedes
Scorza, Manuel
Vallejo, César
Vargas Llosa, Mario

PUERTO RICO
Alegría, Ricardo E.
Balseiro, José Agustín
Colón, Jesus
Colorado, Antonio J.
Cruz, Victor Hernández
Cruz Monclova, Lidio
Dávila, Virgilio
Díaz Valcárcel, Emilio
Enamurado Cuesta, José
Fernández Méndez, Eugenio
Ferré, Rosario
Figueroa, Loida
Figueroa, Pablo
Flores, Angel
Gallego, Laura
Géigel Polanco, Vincente
Hernández Aquino, Luis
Hostos, Adolfo de
Hostos, Eugenio María de
Laguerre, Enrique A.
Lizardi, Joseph
Lloréns, Washington
López Suria, Violeta
Maldonado-Denis, Manuel
Marqués, René
Martín, José L.
Marzán, Julio
Matos Paoli, Francisco
Meléndez, Concha
Morales, Angel Luis
Morales, Jorge Luis
Muñoz Marín, Luis
Pagan Ferrer, Gloria M.
Palés Matos, Luis
Palma, Marigloria
    See Pagan Ferrer, Gloria M.
Pasarell, Emilio J.
Pérez Marchand, Monelisa L.
Pietri, Pedro
Piñero, Miguel
Ramírez de Arellano, Raphael W.
Ribera Chevremont, Evaristo
Rosa-Nieves, Cesáreo
Sánchez, Luis Rafael
Soto, Pedro Juan
Tío, Aurelio
Umpierre, Luz María
Zavala, Iris M.

SPAIN
Alas, Leopoldo
Aleixandre, Vicente
Alonso, Dámaso
Alvarez, Alejandro Rodríguez
Azorín
    See Martínez Ruiz, José
Benavente, Jacinto
Blasco Ibáñez, Vicente
Buero Vallejo, Antonio
Buñuel, Luis

Casona, Alejandro
  See Alvarez, Alejandro
    Rodríguez
Cela, Camilo José
Cernuda, Luis
Clarín
  See Alas, Leopoldo
Delibes Setien, Miguel
Díaz Plaja, Guillermo
Diego, Gerardo
Echegaray, José
Florit, Eugenio
Fusi, Juan Pablo
Galdós, Benito Pérez
  See Pérez Galdós, Benito
García Lorca, Federico
Gasset, José Ortega y
  See Ortega y Gasset, José
Gómez de la Serna, Ramón
Goytisolo, Juan
Guillén, Jorge
Jiménez, Juan Ramón
Lorca, Federico García
  See García Lorca, Federico
Madariaga, Salvador de
Martín, Luis
Martínez Ruiz, José
Menéndez Pidal, Ramón
Novás Calvo, Lino
Ortega y Gasset, José
Pérez Galdós, Benito
Saura, Carlos
Sender, Ramón
Setien, Miguel Delibes
  See Delibes Setien, Miguel
Unamuno, Miguel de
Vallejo, Antonio Buero
  See Buero Vallejo, Antonio

UNITED STATES

Acosta, Oscar Zeta
Acuña, Rodolfo F.
Adame, Leonard
Agosín, Marjorie
Aguilar Melantzon, Ricardo
Alegría, Fernando
Alvarez, Lynne
Anaya, Rudolfo A.
Apodaca, Rudy S.
Arias, Ron
Avalle-Arce, Juan Bautista de
Babín, María Teresa
Baca, Jimmy Santiago
Baez, Joan
Barayón, Ramón Sender
  See Sender Barayón, Ramón
Barrio, Raymond
Bernal, Vincente J.
Brito, Aristeo
Bruce-Novoa, Juan D.
Burciaga, José Antonio

Candelaria, Cordelia Chávez
Candelaria, Nash
Cardenas, Reyes
Cardozo-Freeman, Inez
Castaneda, Carlos
Castillo, Ana
Cervantes, Lorna Dee
Chacón, Eusebio
Chávez, Denise
Chávez, Fray Angélico
  See Chávez, Manuel
Chávez, John R.
Chávez, Manuel
Cisneros, Sandra
Cofer, Judith Ortiz
Cruz, Gilbert R.
De León, Nephtalí
Delgado, Abelardo B.
Durán, Roberto
Elizondo, Sergio D.
Espinosa, Aurelio M.
Espinosa, Aurelio M., Jr.
Ferrater-Mora, José
Fornes, Maria Irene
Gallardo, Edward
Gamarra, Eduardo
Gamboa, Harry Jr.
García, Lionel G.
García, Richard A.
García, Sam
García Rocha, Rina
Garza, Roberto J.
Gómez-Quiñones, Juan
Gómez Rosa, Alexis
Gonzáles, Sylvia Alicia
González T., César A.
Hahn, Oscar
Herrera, Juan Felipe
Herrera-Sobek, María
Hijuelos, Oscar
Hinojosa, Rolando
Hoyos, Angela De
Huerta, Jorge A.
Islas, Arturo
Kanellos, Nicolás
Keller, Gary D.
López, Diana
Manguel, Alberto
Martín, Luis
Martínez, Max
Medina, Robert C.
Mellizo, Carlos
Méndez M., Miguel
Meyer, Doris
Mohr, Nicholasa
Montoya, José
Mora, Pat
Moraga, Cherríe
Morales, Alejandro
Morton, Carlos

Muro, Amado
  See Seltzer, Chester E.
Nava, Gregory
Nava, Julian
Niggli, Josefina
Novoa, Juan Bruce
  See Bruce-Novoa, Juan D.
Ortego y Gasca, Philip D.
Otero, Miguel Antonio
Pacheco, Henrícus Luis
Paredes, Américo
Portillo Trambley, Estela
Quintana, Leroy V.
Quirarte, Jacinto
Rabassa, Gregory
Ramirez, Susan E.
Ramírez de Arellano, Diana
Rechy, John
Ríos, Isabella
  See López, Diana
Rivera, Geraldo
Rivera, Tomás
Robles, Mireya
Rodriguez, Richard
Rojas, Arnold R.
Rojas, Guillermo
Romano, Octavio I.
Romero, Orlando
Rosales, Francisco A.
Sagel, Jim
Salas, Floyd
Salinas, Luis Omar
Samora, Julian
Sanchez, George I.
Sánchez, Ricardo
Sanchez, Thomas
Sanchez-Korrol, Virginia
Sanchez-Scott, Milcha
Seltzer, Chester E.
Sender Barayón, Ramón
Silva, Beverly
Soto, Gary
Soto, Shirlene A.
Souza, Raymond D.
Tafolla, Carmen
Thomas, Piri
Torres, José Acosta
Ulibarrí, Sabine R.
Valdez, Luis
Vásquez, Richard
Velez-Ibanez, Carlos G.
Villanueva, Alma Luz
Villanueva, Tino
Villarreal, José Antonio
Villaseñor, Víctor E.
Yglesias, José
Zamora, Bernice

URUGUAY

Agustini, Delmira
Amorim, Enrique

Barrios, Pilar E.
Benedetti, Mario
Galeano, Eduardo
Herrera y Reissig, Julio
Ibarbourou, Juana de
Martínez Moreno, Carlos
Onetti, Juan Carlos
Peri Rossi, Cristina

Quiroga, Horacio
Rein, Mercedes
Reyles, Carlos
Rodríguez Monegal, Emir
Sánchez, Florencio
Urista, Alberto H.
Viana, Javier de
Vilariño, Idea

VENEZUELA
Blanco Fombona, Rufino
Caballero, Manuel
Díaz, Jorge
Gallegos, Rómulo
Sucre, Guillermo
Uslar Pietri, Arturo
Varderi, Alejandro